Mastering Windows Server 2025

Fifth Edition

Accelerate your journey from IT Pro to System Administrator using the world's most powerful server platform

Jordan Krause

Mastering Windows Server 2025

Fifth Edition

Portfolio Director: Kartikey Pandey
Relationship Lead: Reshma Raman
Project Manager: Sonam Pandey
Content Engineer: Sayali Pingale
Technical Editor: Simran Ali
Copy Editor: Safis Editing
Indexer: Pratik Shirodkar
Proofreader: Sayali Pingale
Production Designer: Aparna Bhagat
Growth Lead: Shreyans Singh

First published: October 2016
Second edition: March 2019
Third edition: July 2021
Fourth edition: May 2023
Fifth edition: October 2025

Production reference: 2250925

Published by Packt Publishing Ltd.
Grosvenor House
11 St Paul's Square
Birmingham
B3 1RB, UK.

ISBN 978-1-83702-991-4

www.packtpub.com

Contributors

About the author

Jordan Krause is an IT professional with more than 25 years of experience and has received 10 Microsoft MVP awards for his work with Microsoft server and networking technologies. One of the world's first experts on Microsoft DirectAccess, his authorship journey began with a book about Microsoft remote access technologies and has evolved into a dozen books on more extensive topics such as Windows Server, security, Group Policy, and even cookbooks (not the food kind). Jordan lives in beautiful West Michigan (USA) and manages a team of IT engineers spread across the country.

About the reviewer

Premnath Sambasivam is a seasoned IT professional with over 12 years of experience in the industry. He is a passionate Microsoft enthusiast and currently works for a leading US-based global retail company as a senior cloud engineer. He specializes in designing and implementing solutions using Microsoft technologies, including Microsoft Azure, Active Directory, and Microsoft **System Center Configuration Manager (SCCM)**. He reviewed the books *Mastering Windows Server 2019* and *Mastering Windows Security and Hardening*, which is also published by Packt Publishing.

Table of Contents

Chapter 14: Containers 591

Chapter 15: Hyper-V   615

Preface

Working in IT is so very interesting. It is complicated, problematic, complex, rewarding, and even dramatic some days. There are so many facets to working with technology; many people focus on one area and build a lifelong career out of it, never encroaching on other aspects of IT. You can specialize in custom computer builds, deployments, printers, networks, security, and the list goes on and on. When talking about IT within a business environment, there is almost always one common thread woven throughout the options: Windows Server. Servers of any flavor are designed to serve up information to your users and computers, and while Microsoft does not hold the entire market on servers, a career in IT guarantees you will interface with Windows Server at some point. During my career, I have had the privilege of working in many hundreds of business environments, and without exception, they have all been standing on top of Windows Server infrastructure. Some of these "datacenters" have looked like a coffee cart shoved in the corner of a utility closet, some have been enormous buildings littered with facial recognition cameras and argon gas tubes. Perhaps my favorite server discovery was the one we found hanging in a rack inside a single-stall bathroom. Right there on the wall! What is so fascinating about Windows Server is that it is universal to all these environments. Some businesses have small and simple needs when providing data to users, while others require rows and rows of server racks to get the job done across hundreds of thousands of people. In both scenarios, the Windows Server operating system running on those servers is the same.

Windows Server 2025 is Microsoft's latest and greatest way of serving up information. It stores files, validates identities, connects your remote workforce, routes network traffic, and protects your business in the process. This is starting to sound like an infomercial, but it's all true. I genuinely don't know where we would be without Windows Server underpinning so much of the computing world.

New versions of Windows Server always come with updates and enhancements. Sometimes they are subtle tweaks to already-great features and capabilities. Sometimes these updates are "in your face," such as the new graphical interface brought to us by Windows Server 2025, finally bringing the refreshed Windows 11 look and feel into the server world. We are here to dive into what's new and fresh, but also to build a foundational baseline for working with Windows Server in general. So much of this knowledge carries from one version to the next. Change is constant, but the theories and ideologies that underpin system administration will carry you to success when stepping into any Windows-centric environment. The information provided in these pages seeks to build that baseline, enabling anyone familiar with computers to start working with servers, while at the same time, providing seasoned professionals with updated information to get the most out of Windows Server 2025.

Many businesses today employ a hybrid approach to serving up data. They continue to host physical server hardware inside an office or datacenter, and have also dipped their toes into cloud hosting. Almost always, both on-premises and cloud hosting platforms are running instances of Windows Server, so no matter your perspective on cloud journeys, knowing and understanding Windows Server is a key component to successful systems administration. The advent of cloud-based computing has not released us from the responsibility of understanding server administration; indeed, it has arguably made server administration more complex.

A lot of fresh IT engineers are coming into the workforce prepared with some knowledge of SaaS resource administration, such as Microsoft 365 and SharePoint, and this is wonderful! One of my primary motivations in writing this book is to provide a resource for new and growing admins to be successful in their careers. You may have learned through school or certification exams how to begin working in these new cloud platforms, but perhaps lack the foundational knowledge of the Microsoft technology that underpins a lot of Azure: Windows Servers. So many of the roles that exist inside Windows Server are foreign to engineers, but this is critical information to know as you continue your IT career journey and grow into more advanced positions. To pinpoint just one example, I often ask questions during interviews about DNS. It is entirely surprising to me how often answers to these questions come up short. DNS has been one of the staple roles in any Windows Server environment for as far back as I can remember, but until you have worked with it and gone through some of the learning hardships firsthand, it seems this is a common area that is somehow missed during standard IT learning.

I use DNS as an example because it's true, but also because it is very meme-worthy. "It's always DNS." You may have heard some of your tenured administrators say these words, but until you experience it for yourself, you may not quite appreciate their significance. The answer to so many questions lies within this one little role; incorrect configuration of DNS can cause multitudes of problems. I found the following graphic on the internet and take no credit for it, but also find it completely true, and hilarious.

Figure 1: It's always DNS

Technical books are supposed to be a little mundane; that is why they are called technical books. It's the nature of the industry, I suppose. I tried to resist this stereotype wherever possible; you may even find a dad joke or two scattered throughout these pages. I genuinely hope that you find this book to be a helpful resource and that the information learned here can be directly applied to your work in information technology.

Who this book is for

Anyone interested in Windows Server 2025 or in learning more in general about a Microsoft-centric datacenter will benefit from this book. An important deciding factor when choosing which content was appropriate for such a volume was making sure that anyone who had a baseline in working with computers could pick this up and start making use of it within their own networks.

If you are already proficient in Microsoft infrastructure technologies and have worked with prior versions of Windows Server, then there are some focused topics on the aspects and parts that are brand-new and only available in Server 2025. On the other hand, if you are currently in a desktop support role, or if you are coming fresh into the IT workforce, care was taken in the pages of this book to ensure that you will receive a rounded understanding, not only of what is brand-new in Server 2025, but also what core capabilities it includes as carryovers from previous versions of the operating system, which are still crucial information to have at hand when working in a Microsoft-driven datacenter.

What this book covers

Chapter 1, Getting Started with Windows Server 2025, gives us an introduction to the latest Server operating system and an overview of the new technologies and capabilities that it can provide. We will also spend a little bit of time exploring the updated interface for those who may not be comfortable with it yet.

Chapter 2, Installation and Management, dives right into the very first thing we will have to do when working with Server 2025: install it! While this seems like a simple task, there are several versioning and licensing variables that need to be understood before you proceed with your own installation. From there, we will start to expand upon Microsoft's centralized management mentality, exploring ways we can manage and interact with our servers without ever having to log in to them.

Chapter 3, Active Directory, leads us into the most core and essential role that exists in a Windows Server environment. AD is the central repository for many different types of data inside most corporate infrastructures, and without understanding the tools that exist to interface with this directory, you will not be able to do much work with those fancy new servers.

Chapter 4, DNS and DHCP, segues into two other important roles that exist in almost every network. DNS and DHCP are both necessary technologies and concepts to understand for any IT administrator, and both happen to be roles that can be serviced from Windows Server 2025. We'll dig into both.

Chapter 5, Group Policy, showcases a fantastic policy engine that can be used inside any Active Directory environment to create a centralized management location for your users and workstations. Whether you are interested in setting up password policies, configuring security lockdowns on your systems, automatically mapping network drives, or even distributing software, Group Policy is a powerful tool that is often underutilized.

Chapter 6, File Management, is all about storing and securing one of your company's most valuable assets: data. Windows Server 2025 is so much more than a general file server. We'll talk about automated drive mappings via GPO and Intune, FTP, DFS-R, and even mapped network drives that connect over the internet, without VPN, via the new SMB over QUIC protocol!

Chapter 7, Certificates, jumps into one of the pieces of Windows Server that has existed for many years, and yet most server administrators that I meet are unfamiliar with it. We'll take a closer look at certificates as they become more and more commonly required for new technologies that we roll out. By the end of this chapter, you should be able to spin up your own PKI and start issuing certificates for free!

Chapter 8, Networking with Windows Server 2025, begins with a baseline navigation of IPv4 and an introduction to that big, scary IPv6, and continues from there into building a toolbox of items that are baked into Windows Server 2025 and can be used in your daily networking tasks. We will also discuss the parts and pieces that make up software-defined networking.

Chapter 9, Remote Access, looks at the different remote access technologies that are built into Windows Server 2025. Follow along as we explore the capabilities and recent changes in VPN, DirectAccess, Web Application Proxy, and Always On VPN.

Chapter 10, Hardening and Security, gives some insight into security and encryption functions that are built into Windows Server 2025. Security is the primary focus of CIOs everywhere, so we'll explore what protection mechanisms are available to us out of the box. We'll even get our hands dirty with the recently refreshed Windows **Local Administrator Password Solution (LAPS)**.

Chapter 11, Server Core, throws us into the shrinking world of headless servers. Server Core has flown under the radar for many years, but is critical to understand as we bring our infrastructures into a more security-conscious mindset. We'll make sure you have the information necessary to make your environment more secure and more efficient, all while lowering the amount of space and resources that are consumed by those servers. We'll also find an answer to the question, "Whatever happened to Nano Server?".

Chapter 12, PowerShell, gets us into the newer, bluer (or black or yellow or purple, or whatever color you desire!) command-line interface so that we can become comfortable using it and also learn why it is so much more powerful than Command Prompt. PowerShell is quickly becoming an indispensable tool for administering servers, especially in cases where you are adopting a centralized management and administration mindset. We will also take a look at the latest Microsoft command-line interface, Windows Terminal, natively included in Windows Server 2025 but requiring some work to get it into other versions of the server operating system.

Chapter 13, Redundancy in Windows Server 2025, looks at the platforms in this recent operating system that provide powerful data and computing redundancy. Follow along as we discuss network load balancing, failover clustering, Storage Spaces Direct, and build our own instance of Storage Replica.

Chapter 14, Containers, incorporates the terms *open source* and *Linux* into a Microsoft book! Application containers are quickly becoming the new standard for hosting modern, scalable applications. Learn how to begin writing your DevOps story using tools such as Windows Server containers, Hyper-V containers, Docker, and Kubernetes.

Chapter 15, Hyper-V, covers a topic that every server administrator should be very familiar with. Organizations have been moving their servers over to virtual machines en masse for many years. We'll use this chapter to make sure you understand how that hypervisor works and give you the resources required to build and manage one if and when you have the need.

Chapter 16, Remote Desktop Services, showcases an enormous functionality set built into Windows Server 2025; indeed, the administration of RDS servers is a skill set unto its own. Providing users with virtual desktop sessions on a farm (collection) of Windows servers can literally change your entire ideology about how users access their information.

Chapter 17, Troubleshooting, provides information about tools and software included with Windows Server that can be used to troubleshoot common problems. We expect Server 2025 to be Microsoft's most stable and reliable server operating system to date, yet as you all know, nothing is perfect, and issues are bound to present themselves. Here, we discover tools such as Resource Manager, Performance Monitor, and System Insights that help to keep our servers tuned and running well.

To get the most out of this book

Each technology that we discuss within the pages of this book is included in, or relates directly to, Windows Server 2025. If you can get your hands on a piece of server hardware and the Server 2025 installer files, you will be equipped to follow along and try these things out for yourself. We will talk about and reference some enterprise-class technologies that come with stiffer infrastructure requirements to make them work fully, and so you may have to put the actual testing of those items on hold until you are working in a more comprehensive test lab or environment, but the concepts are all still included in this book.

We will also discuss some items that are not included in Server 2025 itself, but that are used to extend its capabilities and features. Some of these items help tie us into an Azure cloud environment, and some are provided by third parties, such as using Docker and Kubernetes on your Server 2025 to interact with application containers. Ultimately, you do not need to use these tools to manage your new Windows Server 2025 environment, but they do facilitate some pretty cool things that I think you will want to explore.

As I have done with my own test lab used throughout the pages of this book, if you have one server or high-powered computer available and download the Windows Server 2025 installer, you can easily enable the ability to create many virtual machines and different instances of Server 2025. In this case, you may want to skip ahead to certain sections of *Chapter 2* and *Chapter 15*, so that you are equipped to install a host operating system and configure Hyper-V upon it, then loop back to the beginning of the book so you have the same platform available as I did when building out these pages and the servers I used to populate them. With a simple test lab environment, you will be able to follow along with every piece of technology we build together in this book.

Download the color images

We also provide a PDF file that has color images of the screenshots/diagrams used in this book.

You can download it here: https://packt.link/gbp/9781837029914

Conventions used

There are a number of text conventions used throughout this book.

`CodeInText`: Indicates code words in text, database table names, folder names, filenames, file extensions, pathnames, dummy URLs, user input, and X/Twitter handles. For example: "Inside DNS, I am going to create an alias record that redirects `intranet` to `WEB1`."

Any command-line input or output is written as follows:

```
Uninstall-WindowsFeature -Name Windows-Defender
```

Bold: Indicates a new term, an important word, or words that you see on the screen. For instance, words in menus or dialog boxes appear in the text like this. For example: "Simply find the appropriate OU for his account to reside within, right-click on the OU, and navigate to **New | User**."

> Warnings or important notes appear like this.

> Tips and tricks appear like this.

Get in touch

Feedback from our readers is always welcome.

General feedback: If you have questions about any aspect of this book or have any general feedback, please email us at `customercare@packt.com` and mention the book's title in the subject of your message.

Errata: Although we have taken every care to ensure the accuracy of our content, mistakes do happen. If you have found a mistake in this book, we would be grateful if you could report this to us. Please visit `http://www.packt.com/submit-errata`, click **Submit Errata**, and fill in the form.

Piracy: If you come across any illegal copies of our works in any form on the internet, we would be grateful if you would provide us with the location address or website name. Please contact us at `copyright@packt.com` with a link to the material.

If you are interested in becoming an author: If there is a topic that you have expertise in and you are interested in either writing or contributing to a book, please visit `http://authors.packt.com/`.

Your Book Comes with Exclusive Perks - Here's How to Unlock Them

Unlock this book's exclusive benefits now

UNLOCK NOW

Scan this QR code or go to `https://packtpub.com/unlock`, then search this book by name. Ensure it's the correct edition.

Note: Keep your purchase invoice ready before you start.

Enhanced reading experience with our Next-gen Reader:

- **Multi-device progress sync:** Learn from any device with seamless progress sync.
- **Highlighting and notetaking:** Turn your reading into lasting knowledge.
- **Bookmarking:** Revisit your most important learnings anytime.
- **Dark mode:** Focus with minimal eye strain by switching to dark or sepia mode.

Learn smarter using our AI assistant (Beta):

- **Summarize it:** Summarize key sections or an entire chapter.
- **AI code explainers:** In the next-gen Packt Reader, click the **Explain** button above each code block for AI-powered code explanations.

> **Note:** The AI assistant is part of next-gen Packt Reader and is still in beta.

Learn anytime, anywhere:

- Access your content offline with DRM-free PDF and ePub versions—compatible with your favorite e-readers.

Unlock Your Book's Exclusive Benefits

Your copy of this book comes with the following exclusive benefits:

- ☁ Next-gen Packt Reader
- ✦ AI assistant (beta)
- 🖥 DRM-free PDF/ePub downloads

Use the following guide to unlock them if you haven't already. The process takes just a few minutes and needs to be done only once.

How to unlock these benefits in three easy steps

Step 1

Keep your purchase invoice for this book ready, as you'll need it in *Step 3*. If you received a physical invoice, scan it on your phone and have it ready as either a PDF, JPG, or PNG.

For more help on finding your invoice, visit `https://www.packtpub.com/unlock-benefits/help`.

> **Note:** Did you buy this book directly from Packt? You don't need an invoice. After completing Step 2, you can jump straight to your exclusive content.

Step 2

Scan this QR code or go to `https://packtpub.com/unlock`.

On the page that opens (which will look similar to *Figure 2* if you're on desktop), search for this book by name. Make sure you select the correct edition.

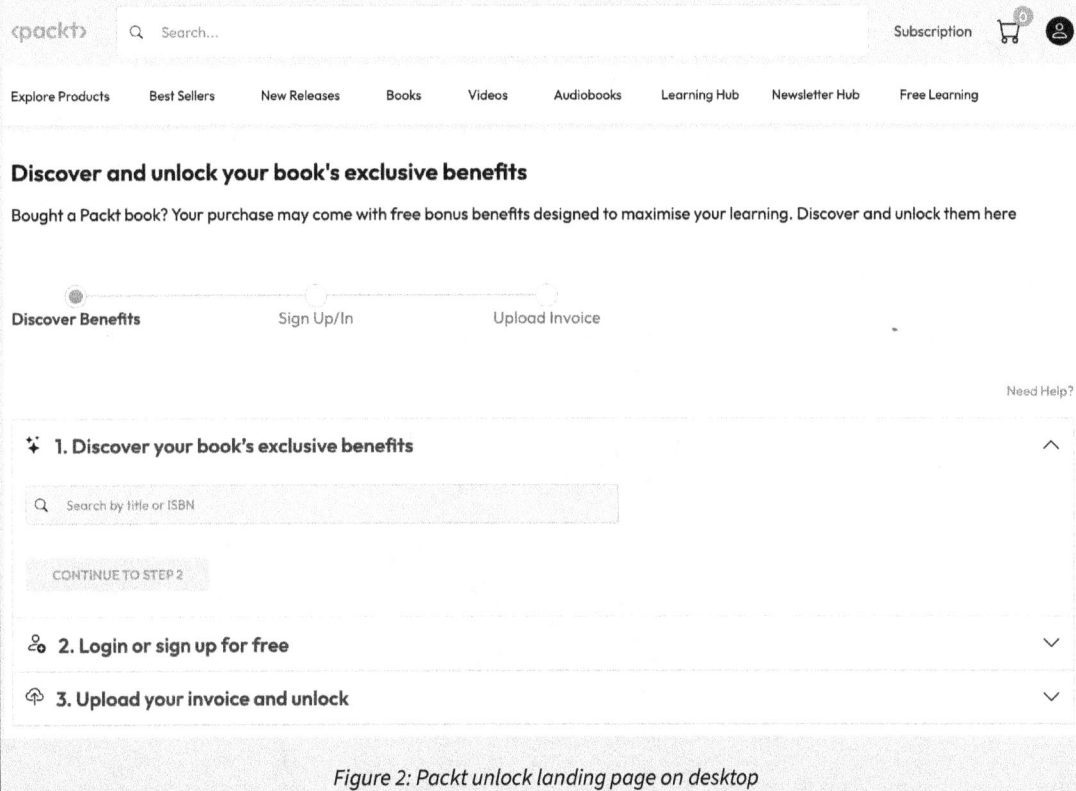

<packt>	Q Search...						Subscription	🛒⁰	👤

Explore Products   Best Sellers   New Releases   Books   Videos   Audiobooks   Learning Hub   Newsletter Hub   Free Learning

Discover and unlock your book's exclusive benefits

Bought a Packt book? Your purchase may come with free bonus benefits designed to maximise your learning. Discover and unlock them here

Discover Benefits   Sign Up/In   Upload Invoice

Need Help?

✦ **1. Discover your book's exclusive benefits**   ∧

  Q Search by title or ISBN

  CONTINUE TO STEP 2

⚲ **2. Login or sign up for free**   ∨

☁ **3. Upload your invoice and unlock**   ∨

Figure 2: Packt unlock landing page on desktop

Step 3

Sign in to your Packt account or create a new one for free. Once you're logged in, upload your invoice. It can be in PDF, PNG, or JPG format and must be no larger than 10 MB. Follow the rest of the instructions on the screen to complete the process.

Need help?

If you get stuck and need help, visit `https://www.packtpub.com/unlock-benefits/help` for a detailed FAQ on how to find your invoices and more. The following QR code will take you to the help page directly:

Note: If you are still facing issues, reach out to `customercare@packt.com`.

Share your thoughts

Once you've read *Mastering Windows Server 2025, Fifth Edition*, we'd love to hear your thoughts! Scan the QR code below to go straight to the Amazon review page for this book and share your feedback.

https://packt.link/r/1837029911

Your review is important to us and the tech community and will help us make sure we're delivering excellent quality content.

1

Getting Started with Windows Server 2025

Driving around the interface of Windows Server is usually comfortable territory for anybody who regularly works on a Windows computer. This is because, historically, Windows Server operating systems have utilized the same code base for a graphical interface as their workstation counterparts. Additionally, in most cases throughout Windows rollout history, it has been true that any release of a major version of Windows Server follows closely on the heels of a Windows workstation version increase, and familiarity with your desktop equates to automatic ease of navigation on the new server. In fact, let's take a minute and walk through that history for anybody here who is not on the gray-hair side of IT (me) and may not have this historical context.

Many years ago, Microsoft adjusted its operating system release ideology so that the latest Windows Server operating system maintained a similar graphical structure, and very similar release date, to whatever the latest and greatest Windows client operating system was going to have. This has been the trend for some time now, with Server 2008 R2 closely reflecting Windows 7, Server 2012 feeling a lot like Windows 8 (unfortunately), and many of the same usability features that came with the Windows 8.1 update also included with Server 2012 R2. This, of course, carried over to Server 2016 as well—giving it the same look and feel as if you were logged into a Windows 10 workstation.

At the time of Server 2016's release, we were already familiar and comfortable with the Windows 10 interface, and it felt quite natural to jump right into Server 2016 and start giving it a test drive. Windows Server 2019 diverged from this standard path a little bit by maintaining a look and feel that was very similar to its predecessor, Windows Server 2016. Why did Windows Server 2019 not come with a fancy new graphical interface to match the new version of the Windows client operating system? Because Microsoft changed the game with Windows 10. Now, instead of releasing new versions of Windows (11, 12, 13, and so on), we were, for the time being, simply sticking with Windows 10 and giving it sub-version numbers, indicative of the dates when each operating system version was released. For example, Windows 10 version 1703 was released around March 2017. Windows 10 version 1709 was released in September 2017.

Then came 1803 and 1809—although 1809 was delayed a little and didn't release until somewhere closer to November, which wasn't the original plan. Follow that up with 1903 and 1909, and you start to see a pattern emerging. Then we moved into the year 2020, and suddenly our spring release of Windows 10 was called 2004. Hmm… 2004 sounds fine when you pronounce it "twenty-oh-four", indicating the year 2020 and the month of April, but when seeing 2004 on paper, most folks started calling it "two-thousand-four," which sounds quite old and outdated, don't you think? I can't say for sure, but perhaps this is part of the reason that the next release version of Windows 10 went by the name 20H2. This nomenclature seems to have stuck around, and we are continuing the trend with bi-annual client OS releases that reflect this pattern. All in all, you can see that Microsoft's current plan is to continue releasing a new feature release version of the Windows operating system every 6 months or so.

However, expecting IT departments to lift and shift all of their servers just for the purposes of moving to an OS that is 6 months newer is crazy; sometimes it takes longer than that simply to plan a migration, let alone execute it.

Anyway, I'm getting ahead of myself a little, as we will discuss the versioning of Windows Server later in this chapter, in our *Windows Server versions and licensing* section. The point here is that Windows Server 2019 looks and feels like the latest version of the Windows client operating system that was released at about the same time—that OS being Windows 10 1809.

Now, forget everything I ever told you, as we cue the caveat of Windows Server 2022. When this last major server version hit shelves, it was *after* Windows 11 was out in the wild, yet Server 2022 stuck with the more traditional Windows 10 graphical interface. At the time, I thought this to be a good idea, and indeed, I maintain that, given some discomforts with Windows 11 at the time, this seems to have been a good move, whether it was intentional or a side effect of the updated GUI not being quite ready to ride on a server. Whatever the true reason, Microsoft essentially left the GUI alone when releasing Windows Server 2022. It is genuinely difficult to tell, graphically, whether you are working on 2019 or 2022 without checking **System Properties**.

So, what about Windows Server 2025? I just finished creating an instance of this brand-new operating system, it booted successfully, and I'm staring this in the face.

Figure 1.1: The Server 2025 lock screen

I'm sure you saw where this was going. We now have the Windows 11 graphical interface! At this point in the Windows 11 journey, you should be quite comfortable with using it. Indeed, as I type these words, we are facing the fact that Windows 10 goes end-of-life in less than one year. We will see much more of this updated interface as we work through the entire book, but for the purpose of this chapter, I want to discuss more of the conceptual enhancements and benefits brought to us through Windows Server 2025.

Before we get started talking about the features of Windows Server, it is important to establish a baseline for usability and familiarity with the operating system itself before diving deeper into the technologies running under the hood.

Let's spend a few minutes exploring the new graphical interface and options that are available for finding your way around this latest release of Windows Server, as we cover the following topics:

- The purpose of Windows Server
- Your head in the clouds
- Windows Server versions and licensing
- Overview of new and updated features

- Features deprecated in Server 2025
- Navigating the interface
- Windows settings
- Task Manager
- Task View

Let's get started!

The purpose of Windows Server

What is a server? Is that a silly question? I don't think so. It's a good question to ponder, especially now that the definition of servers and server workloads changes on a regular basis. The answer to this question for Windows clients is simpler. A Windows client machine is a requester, consumer, and contributor of data.

Data is life for many businesses. Where is this data kept? From where is this data being pushed and pulled? What enables the mechanisms and applications running on the client operating systems to interface with this data? What secures these users and their data? The answers to these questions reveal the purpose of servers in general. Servers house, protect, and serve up data to be consumed by clients.

Everything revolves around data in business today. Our email, documents, databases, customer lists—everything that we need to do business—is data. That data is critical to us. Servers are what we use to build the fabric upon which we trust our data to reside.

We traditionally think about servers using a client-server interface mentality. A user opens a program on their client computer, this program reaches out to a server in order to retrieve something, and the server responds as needed. This idea can be correctly applied to almost every transaction you may have with a server. When your domain-joined computer needs to authenticate you as a user, it reaches out to Active Directory on the server to validate your credentials and receive an authentication token. When you need to contact a resource by name, your computer asks a DNS server how to get there. If you need to open a file, you ask the file server to send it your way.

Servers are designed to be the brains of our operation, and often by doing so transparently. In recent years, large strides have been taken to ensure resources are always available and accessible in ways that don't require training or a large effort on the part of our employees. It used to be true that the general user population knew the name of your server and how to contact it because that was required for them to be able to get the information they needed.

If their mapped drives disappeared, it wasn't uncommon that everyone would know how to throw \\server\share into **File Explorer** to get there via plan B.

It also used to be the case that your average business only ran one single server, enabling plan B above to be true. Today, our server landscape is vastly different, with even small businesses running a virtualization host that typically contains a dozen or more virtual servers, and much effort is made so that your workforce doesn't know or care anything about that server infrastructure; they simply expect to have access to their data, 100% of the time.

In most organizations, many different servers are needed to provide your workforce with the capabilities they require. Each service inside Windows Server is provided as, or as part of, a **role**. When you talk about needing new servers or configuring a new server for any particular task, what you are really referring to is the individual role or roles that are going to be configured on that server to get the work done. A server without any roles installed is useless, though, depending on the chassis, could make an excellent paperweight. A 3U SAN device could weigh upward of 100 pounds and keep your desk orderly even in the middle of a hurricane!

If you think of roles as the meat and potatoes of a server, then the next bit we will discuss is sort of like adding salt and pepper. Beyond the overhead roles you will install and configure on your servers, Windows also contains many **features** that can be installed, which sometimes stand alone but, more often, complement specific roles in the operating system. Features may add functionality to the base operating system, as is the case with **Telnet Client**. Or, a feature may be added to a server in order to enhance an existing role, such as adding the **Network Load Balancing** feature to an already equipped remote access or IIS server. The combination of roles and features inside Windows Server is what equips that piece of metal to do work.

This book will, quite obviously, focus on a Microsoft-centric infrastructure. In these environments, the Windows Server operating system is king and is prevalent across all facets of technology. There are alternatives to Windows Server and different products that can provide some of the same functions for an organization, but it is quite rare to find a business environment anywhere that is running without some semblance of a Microsoft infrastructure.

Windows Server contains an incredible amount of technology, all wrapped up in one small installation disk. With Windows Server 2025, Microsoft has us thinking out of the box about what it means to be a server in the first place, and it comes with some exciting new capabilities, which we will spend time covering in these pages. Things such as PowerShell, containers, **Windows Admin Center**, software-defined storage, and software-defined networking are changing the way that we manage and size our computing environments; these are exciting times to be or to become a server administrator!

Your head in the clouds

The cloud. You've probably heard of it. In fact, you have likely heard it in many different contexts, some of which don't make any sense at all. That is the power of a buzzword in the technical world; it often ends up misused and spoken of inappropriately. Those things aside, the idea of cloud infrastructure is an incredibly powerful one that anybody working in IT needs to understand.

A cloud fabric is one that revolves around virtual resources—**virtual machines (VMs)**, virtual disks, and even virtual networks. Being "plugged into" the cloud typically enables things such as the ability to spin up new servers on a whim, or even the ability for particular services themselves to increase or decrease their needed resources automatically, based on utilization.

Think of a simple e-commerce website where a consumer can go to order goods. Perhaps 75% of the year, the company can operate this website on a single web server with limited resources, resulting in a fairly low cost of service. But the other 25% of the year, maybe around the holiday seasons, utilization ramps way up, requiring much more computing power. Prior to cloud mentality, this would mean that the company would need to size its environment to fit the maximum requirements all the time, in case it was ever needed. They would be paying for more servers and much more computing power than was needed for much of the year. With a cloud fabric, which gives the website the ability to increase or decrease the number of servers it has at its disposal as needed, the total cost of such a website or service can be drastically decreased. This is a major driving factor of the cloud in business today.

Public cloud

Most of the time, when your neighbor Suzzi Knowitall talks to you about the cloud, she is simply talking about the internet. Well, more accurately, she is talking about some service that she uses, which she connects to by using the internet. For example, Office 365, Google Drive, OneDrive, and Dropbox—these are all public cloud resources, as they store your data *in the cloud*. In reality, your data is just sitting on servers that you access via the internet, but you can't see those servers, and you don't have to administer and maintain those servers, which is why it feels like magic and is then referred to as the cloud.

To IT departments, the term *cloud* more often means one of the big three cloud hosting providers. Since this is a Microsoft-driven book, and since I truly feel this way anyway, Microsoft Azure is top-notch in this category. Azure itself is another topic for another book (or many other books), but it is a centralized cloud computing architecture that can host your data, your services, or even your entire network of servers.

Moving your datacenter to Azure enables you to stop worrying or caring about server hardware, replacing hard drives, and much more. Rather than purchasing servers, unboxing them, racking them, installing Windows on them, and then setting up the roles you want configured, you simply click a few buttons to spin up new virtual servers that can be resized at any time for growth. You then pay ongoing op-ex costs for these servers—monthly or annual fees for running systems in the cloud—rather than the big upfront cap-ex costs for server hardware.

Other cloud providers with similar capabilities are numerous, but the big three are Azure, Amazon (AWS), and Google. As far as enterprise is concerned, Azure simply takes the cake and eats it too. I'm not sure that the others will ever be able to catch up with all of the changes and updates that Microsoft constantly makes to the Azure infrastructure.

Private cloud

While most people working in the IT sector these days have a pretty good understanding of what it means to be part of a cloud service, and many are indeed doing so today, a term that is being pushed into enterprises everywhere and is still often misunderstood is **private cloud**. At first, I took this to be a silly marketing ploy, a gross misuse of the term "cloud" to try and appeal to those hooked by buzzwords. Boy, was I wrong. In the early days of private clouds, the technology wasn't quite ready to stand up to what was being advertised.

Today, however, that story has changed. It is now entirely possible to take the same fabric that is running up in the true public cloud and install it right inside your datacenter. This enables you to provide your company with cloud benefits such as the ability to spin resources up and down, run everything virtualized, and implement all of the neat tips and tricks of cloud environments, with all of the serving power and data storage remaining locally owned and secured by you. Trusting cloud storage companies to keep data safe and secure is absolutely one of the biggest blockers to implementation on the true public cloud, but by installing your own private cloud, you get the best of both worlds—stretchable compute environments with the security of knowing you still control and own all of your data.

This is not a book about clouds, public or private. I mention this to give a baseline for some of the items we will discuss in later chapters, and also to get your mouth watering a little bit to dig in and do a little reading yourself on cloud technology. You will find that Windows Server 2025 interacts in many ways with the cloud, and you will notice that so many of the underlying systems available in Server 2025 are similar to, if not the same as, those becoming available in Microsoft Azure.

In these pages, we will not focus on the capabilities of Azure, but rather a more traditional sense of Windows Server as would be utilized on-premises. With the big push toward cloud technologies, it's easy to get caught with blinders on and think that everything and everyone is quickly running to the cloud for all of their technology needs, but it simply isn't true. Most companies will have the need for many on-premise servers for many years to come; in fact, many may never put full trust in the cloud and will forever maintain their own datacenters. These datacenters will have local servers, which will require server administrators to manage them. That's where you come in.

Windows Server versions and licensing

Anyone who has worked with the design or installation of Windows Server in recent years is probably wondering which direction we are taking in this book. You see, there are different capability editions, different technical versions, plus different licensing models of Windows Server. Let's take a few minutes to cover those differences to give you a well-rounded knowledge of the different options, and so that we can define which portions we plan to discuss over the course of this book.

Standard versus Datacenter

When installing the Windows Server 2025 operating system onto a piece of hardware, as you will experience in *Chapter 2, Installation and Management*, you will encounter two different choices of server capability:

- The first is Server 2025 **Standard**, which is the default option and one that includes most of your traditional Windows Server roles. While I cannot give you firm details on pricing because that could potentially be different for every company, depending on your agreements with Microsoft, Standard is the cheaper option and is most commonly used for installations of Windows Server 2025.

- **Datacenter**, on the other hand, is the luxury model. There are some roles and features within Windows Server 2025 that only work with the Datacenter version of the operating system, and they are not available in Standard. If ever you are looking for a new piece of Microsoft technology to serve a purpose in your environment, make sure to check the requirements to find out whether you will have to build a Datacenter server. Keep in mind that Datacenter can cost significantly more money than Standard, so you generally only use it in places where it is actually required. For example, if you are interested in hosting a **Storage Spaces Direct (S2D)** environment, you will be required to run the Server 2025 Datacenter edition on those servers.

One of the biggest differences between Standard and Datacenter that even small businesses may need to consider is the number of **Virtual Machines (VMs)** that they can legally host. Out-of-the-box Server 2025 Standard can only run two VMs at any given time, which is a pretty limiting factor if you are looking to build out a Hyper-V server. Datacenter allows you to run an unlimited number of VMs, which makes it a no-brainer when building your virtualization host servers. For running Hyper-V, the Datacenter edition is often the way to go.

There is more information on this topic that makes the previous paragraph complicated. Both Server 2025 Standard and Server 2025 Datacenter have the technical ability to run many VMs. Whether or not you are allowed to do so comes down to licensing. We will discuss more on this topic when we talk about Windows Server licensing structures later in this chapter.

Running a container infrastructure will also impact your decision-making on Windows Server licensing. While your host container server can run an unlimited number of traditional containers, whether that host server is Windows Server Standard or Datacenter, if you want to move into the enhanced world of Hyper-V-isolated containers, similar restrictions apply. A container host server running Windows Server Standard is limited to running two Hyper-V containers, but bumping up your host to Windows Server Datacenter will bring you back into the unlimited category. An easy way to remember this is that each Hyper-V container is essentially its own VM, and so the limit of two applies in the Standard OS, whether talking about regular VMs or Hyper-V container VMs. Again, remember that this is a licensing limitation, not a technical one.

Windows Server 2025 Essentials

Some of you may remember the **Small Business Server (SBS)** editions of Windows Server, which were sort of an all-in-one variant of the Windows Server operating system, intended to be the one and only server inside a small business environment. While SBS fell by the wayside many years ago, Microsoft has offered an **Essentials** edition of each Windows Server release since that time, to fill the small business gap. If your organization has fewer than 25 users and fewer than 50 devices, and if you do not intend to grow beyond that point, purchasing and installing Windows Server 2025 Essentials can be a coupon clipper to getting your data infrastructure up and running in a cost-friendly way. Keep in mind that it comes with limitations, and as soon as you want to grow your business to more than 25 users, you'll have to bite the bullet, purchase Server Standard, and migrate over to it.

Windows Server 2025 Datacenter: Azure Edition

Hold up, what is this thing? The Windows Server 2022 rollout introduced us to this brand-new thing, a special version of Windows Server that obviously has some tie-ins to Azure. But what does this mean for you? Whether or not you will ever touch the new Azure Edition depends on what kinds of things you are doing in the Azure world. If you host virtual machines in Azure, you now have the option of selecting your new VM to run this special Azure Edition, and it then enables some cool new features that are unique to this edition. What is most interesting to me about the latest 2025 release of Azure Edition is that some of the capabilities that you could only find through 2022 Azure Edition have now been ported over into the normal Server 2025 Datacenter. For example, in 2022, you could only do hot-patching and SMB over QUIC if you deployed 2022 Azure Edition. This is no longer the case, and both of those functions exist in normal Server 2025 Datacenter. However, new feature sets were added to 2025 Azure Edition that do not (yet) exist in normal 2025 Datacenter, so you see how this trend continues.

The big catch with Azure Edition is just that—it can only run in an Azure environment. So if you have Azure cloud-hosted VMs, you can now get those VMs to run Azure Edition. Without making this too complicated, since we are talking mostly about on-premise resources in this book, there is one other special scenario where you might be able to run Windows Server 2025 Azure Edition from within the physical walls of your building. That is for those of you running something called **Azure Local** (formerly known as **Azure Stack HCI**). The scope of this book does not include Azure Local, but the easiest way to think about it is the point where rubber meets the road for a private cloud, which we already discussed. It is possible to build your own implementation of Azure, right inside your own datacenter, using Azure Local. If you are running a private cloud such as this, you will then be able to run VMs within that environment that use Windows Server 2025 Datacenter: Azure Edition.

Three different user interfaces

Now let's discuss the different footprints and user interfaces that you can run on your Windows Server 2025 machines. There are two variants of Windows Server that can be used, and we will also fill in some history about a third option that used to exist and is still often a complication in this topic. Choosing the correct interface depends on what capabilities and security you are looking for.

Desktop Experience

This is the most common choice among Windows Servers everywhere. Whether you are building Windows Server 2025 Standard or Datacenter, you have a choice of running Windows Server with or without a graphical user interface. The point-and-click interface with a traditional look and feel is called **Desktop Experience**. This allows things such as RDPing into your servers, having a traditional desktop, and being able to use the graphical Server Manager right from your logged-in server, and all in all, it is the best way to go if you are new to server administration.

If you are familiar with navigating around inside Windows 11, then you should be able to at least make your way around Windows Server 2025 running Desktop Experience. This is the version of Windows Server 2025 that we will focus on for the majority of this book, and almost all of the screenshots will be taken from within a Desktop Experience environment.

Server Core

As you will see when we install Windows Server 2025 together, the default option for installation is *not* Desktop Experience. What this means is that choosing the default install path would instead place a headless version of Windows Server onto your machine, most commonly referred to as Server Core.

The nature of being headless makes Server Core faster and more efficient than the Desktop version, which makes sense because it doesn't have to run all of that extra code and consume all of those extra resources for launching and displaying a huge graphical interface.

Almost anything that you want to do within Windows Server is possible to do on either Server Core or Desktop Experience, the main differences being the interface and security. To be able to use Server Core, you definitely have to be comfortable with a command-line interface (namely PowerShell), and you also have to consider remote server management to be a reliable way of interacting with your servers. We will talk much more about Server Core in *Chapter 11, Server Core*.

The largest benefit that Server Core brings to the table, other than performance, is security. Most malware that attempts to attack Windows Servers is reliant upon items that exist inside the GUI of Desktop Experience. Since those things aren't even running inside Server Core—alas, you couldn't get to a *desktop* even if you wanted to—attacks against Server Core machines are far, far less successful.

Nano Server — now only for containers

A third platform for Windows Server 2025 does exist, known as **Nano Server**. This is a tiny version of Windows Server, headless like Server Core but running an even smaller footprint. The last time I booted up Nano Server, it consumed less than 500 MB of data for the complete operating system, which is incredible.

Nano Server was a hot topic surrounding the release of Server 2016, because at that time, Microsoft was pressing forward with plans to include a whole bunch of roles inside Nano Server so that we could start replacing some of our bloated, oversized everyday servers with Nano. It used to be the case that you could use the Windows Server installation media (I suppose you could still make it happen with Server 2016 installation media) to spin out a VHDX file that allowed you to boot into Nano Server and check it out, but that mentality of *Nano Server as an actual server* has since gone by the wayside.

As of Windows Server version 1803 (we'll discuss what *Server 1803* means in the next section of this chapter), Nano Server is married to the use of containers. In fact, the only way to spin up a Nano Server is to download it as a **container base OS image**, and then boot that image on an existing container host server. We will discuss both in more detail in *Chapter 14, Containers*. If you know what containers and modern applications are, and are interested in using them, then you will benefit from learning all there is to know about Nano Server. If you are not in a position to work with containers, you will probably never run into Nano Server in your environment.

Licensing models — what happened to SAC?

Up until the release of Windows Server 2022, you had a decision to make on which licensing model and release cadence you wanted to follow. Microsoft releases some versions of Windows Server, the ones you are likely familiar with, on a 2–3 year basis, and other versions on a biannual cadence. Can you imagine new versions of Windows Server shipping twice a year? I would imagine that to be a very difficult thing to keep up with for both manufacturer and consumer, and as of August 2022, that reality seems to have sunk in as we experienced the demise of this super-aggressive release cadence. Let's discuss the ways that Windows Server versions roll out and what changed in 2022.

Long-Term Servicing Channel (LTSC)

Some of you probably think that LTSC is a typo, as in previous years, this model was called **Long-Term Servicing Branch (LTSB)**. While you can go with either, and people will generally know what you are talking about, LTSC is now the proper term.

Windows Server 2025 is an LTSC release. Essentially, LTSC releases are what we have always thought of as our traditional Windows Server operating system releases. Server 2008, Server 2008 R2, Server 2012, Server 2012 R2, Server 2016, Server 2019, Server 2022, and now Server 2025 are all LTSC releases. It is Microsoft's expectation that LTSC versions of Windows Server will continue to be released every 2–3 years, and will include both headless as well as full graphical interface flavors of the operating system.

LTSC versions of Windows Server have always been the most common; indeed, many IT administrators have never even heard of the alternative **Semi-Annual Channel (SAC)** releases. Anytime that you are building a server with the intention of utilizing Desktop Experience for a fully graphical interface, your only option is LTSC anyway. It has always made the most sense for any servers running with the purpose of a domain controller, certificate server, file server, and so on to run within the context of LTSC.

With LTSC versions of Windows Server, you continue to get the same support we are used to seeing from Microsoft operating systems: five years of mainstream support followed by five years of available extended support.

Throughout this book, we will work and gain experience with Windows Server 2025—the LTSC release, which is now the only release.

Semi-Annual Channel (SAC) (now retired)

While this is now mostly irrelevant, it is still good to understand the history of SAC, and indeed, you may well encounter SAC releases of Windows Server in your IT escapades. The first thing you will notice when stumbling upon an SAC release of Windows Server is the strange naming convention for operating system versions. Rather than calling it *Server 2019*, you were really running Windows Server 1803, 1809, 1903, 1909, and so on. It followed the same mentality and release cadence that Windows 10 did. What that implies is that these new versions of Windows Server SAC were released at much shorter intervals than LTSC. The SAC channel received two major releases every year—generally in the spring and the fall. Because of this fast release cadence, support for SAC versions of Windows Server lasted for a short 18 months. If you use SAC, you had better get used to always jumping on the latest version shortly after it releases.

If swapping out your server operating systems twice a year sounds daunting, you're not alone. Thankfully, Microsoft recognizes this and realizes that the general server administrator population is not going to use this model for their regular, everyday servers. Rather, SAC versions of Windows Server were only ever going to be used to run containers and containerized applications. In this new world of flexible application hosting, where applications are being written in ways that the infrastructure resources behind those applications can be spun up or spun down as needed, containers are a very important piece of that DevOps puzzle. If you host or build these kinds of applications, you will almost certainly be using containers—now or in the future. When you find yourself in the position of researching and figuring out containers, you may then stumble on information and documentation that leads you to those older SAC server releases.

It is important to note that SAC versions of Windows Server only came in the Server Core flavor—you'll find no graphical desktop interface here!

While Microsoft has officially retired SAC licensing and operating systems as of August 2022, customers heavily into containerization may still find some similar benefits by moving to Azure Local (formerly Azure Stack HCI).

License purchase and packs

When defining differences between the Standard and Datacenter versions of Windows Server 2025, we referenced the fact that "out-of-the-box" Server 2025 Standard allows for the running of two VMs, but that it wasn't a technical limitation and that more VMs were possible. This idea segues into a bit of a confusing topic—the way that Windows Server is licensed. When you purchase "a Windows Server 2025 Standard License," you are purchasing the rights to install Server 2025 Standard onto one physical piece of hardware, and to run two VMs on top of that host operating system. In effect, you can run three instances of Windows Server 2025 Standard. As soon as you make your move to spin up a third VM, you are required to repurchase the same amount of licensing all over again. Doing so actually gives you the ability to then run a total of four VMs. So if you only need three, well... too bad; you pay for four. Effectively, you repurchase your Windows Server 2025 Standard licensing for every two additional VMs that you need to run.

In addition to considering the number of VMs, the amount of licensing you purchase in the first place depends on the size of your hardware. More specifically, it depends on the processors you have installed.

Core packs (physical server licensing)

Here is where things get a little dicey. You must license each physical server based on the number of processor cores that exist inside it. Most physical servers contain one or two CPUs. The number of cores that those CPUs contain could be vastly different. What you are required to license is the number of cores.

Hyperthreading doesn't count. If you have one CPU with one core and it can do hyperthreading (logical cores), this counts as one core. If you have dual CPUs, each with 8 cores, now we're talking about 16 cores in total. This is the number to license.

There is some confusing history about why these are called **core packs** instead of simply core licenses, but since you can never purchase a single core license (why would you, since CPU cores always come in even numbers), you will always be purchasing packs of licensing, core packs.

Except... (this is the moment when you realize why large companies employ full-time staff just to deal with licensing)... there are also some rules of minimum license purchase. You cannot cover a server with four core packs, because Microsoft says you can't. Here are the rules of a minimum license purchase:

- Any physical server requires a minimum of 16 cores to be licensed.

- Even if your server has fewer than 16 cores, you must adhere to the prior rule and license for at least 16 cores.

- Every physical CPU requires at least 8 cores to be licensed, whether or not that CPU has 8 cores. But again, even if your server has only 1 CPU with 8 cores, you must still license the server for 16 cores based on the server-level minimum.

Wow, that is a lot of rules. Ultimately, many physical servers in smaller businesses will fall into the category of requiring a minimum of 16 cores to be licensed. That's easy math, and in fact, when faced with purchasing Windows Server licensing, you will find that most places offer a 16-CPU core pack, which perfectly fits that need. When you grow your hardware to contain more than 16 CPU cores, you pull out the calculator and start purchasing additional core packs.

vCore licensing (virtual server licensing)

Most on-premise servers that I encounter continue to be licensed by physical CPU cores, but introduced to us in late 2022 was the idea of per-VM licensing, instead of physical server licensing. vCore licensing is what it sounds like, licensing for Windows Server based on the number of vCPU cores you are running, instead of physical CPU cores. There are also a couple of minimums to keep in mind with vCore licensing:

- Each VM must be licensed for at least 8 virtual cores. If you have a smaller VM that uses fewer than 8 cores, you'll still have to pay for 8.

- Each customer requires a minimum of 16 virtual cores.

You may be tempted to start looking into vCores and running numbers to find out whether this new licensing model is cheaper for your environment, but there is one large caveat to keep in mind. Per-VM licensing was created for a specific purpose, primarily if you have a reason to run a small number of VMs on a large host, where physical licensing costs don't make sense. This can sometimes be the case in cloud or hybrid-cloud scenarios, where you are using or renting host space from another entity. One requirement for vCore licensing that will be a determining factor for many businesses as to whether it can be used is that vCore licenses are only available to customers with active Software Assurance or subscription licenses.

At what point do I turn to Datacenter?

The Server 2025 Standard licensing strategy is scalable up to a certain point. Technically, you could forever increase the licensing that you purchase and the VMs that you run with that licensing, but wait a minute—didn't we say that Server 2025 Datacenter permits you to run unlimited VMs? Indeed we did. While Server 2025 Datacenter costs a lot more than Server 2025 Standard, if you are facing a requirement to run many virtual machines, it may be more cost-effective to simply purchase Datacenter and not have to deal with all of the intricacies of Standard licensing.

The breaking point is usually around 12 VMs. If you run 12 or fewer VMs on a single server, you will likely save some money by running the numbers on Standard licensing, but it depends on what physical CPUs you have. If you need to run more than 12 VMs, it is most likely true that purchasing a single (16-core) Datacenter license will be your cheaper option.

Client Access Licenses (CALs)

So far, all we have talked about is Windows Server licensing, just for the server side. Microsoft also requires businesses to purchase and own CALs, to cover any user who needs to connect to resources on that server. This one is more straightforward to calculate—add up the numbers of users that you are going to point to resources on your server, and make sure you purchase that many (or more) CALs. Oftentimes, when you purchase Windows Server licensing, you will find options that combine server and CAL licensing, such as "Server 2025 16 core licenses + 25 CALs."

If you have ever purchased CALs before, there is a decent chance you have been building a new server or implementing a **Remote Desktop Services (RDS)** environment. We will discuss RDS much more in an upcoming chapter on the topic, but RDS CALs are one type of CAL that you may find yourself purchasing, even on top of your normal Windows Server CALs. Out of the box, any Windows Server allows two user accounts to RDP into it at the same time, but no more. When implementing an RDS server, you often want many more people to be able to connect at the same time. The purchase and installation of RDS CALs is necessary for that to work properly.

Pay-as-you-go licensing

Whoa, what is this?? With the advent of Windows Server 2025, Microsoft has released a brand new way to pay for your Server 2025 instances, without needing to purchase cap-ex style perpetual licenses or core packs whatsoever. Enter pay-as-you-go licensing. Key to success with this new venture, the servers you are deploying must be tapped into Azure Arc (more on that later in this book). Assuming that you have Arc-enabled your servers, you can now license them through your Azure subscription, the cost as of this writing being $33.58 USD per CPU core, per month. As with most things in Azure, you only pay for what you need.

Overview of new and updated features

The newest version of the Windows Server operating system is always an evolution of its predecessor. There are certainly pieces of technology contained inside that are brand-new, but there are even more places where existing technologies have been updated to include new features and functionality. In the case of Windows Server 2025, there are even some functions and features that are specifically called out by Microsoft as being deprecated and leaving us for good. As is often the case with Microsoft operating system releases, there are many intricate and under-the-hood changes, but not all of them are going to impact the way that you work on servers. For a full list of changes, you can simply visit Microsoft's Learn documentation, search "What's new in Server 2025?", and get a play-by-play. Re-creating a cut and paste list here would be insulting to you as a reader and able-bodied IT person, so for the purposes of this chapter, I have selected new and updated feature sets that genuinely interest me as I believe these will also be the most interesting changes to you, in the businesses that you support. Let's spend a few minutes providing an overview of some (truly interesting) changes that exist in Windows Server 2025.

CPU compatibility

For anyone who has worked with Windows Server for a long time, you likely hold it in your mind as tightly bound with Intel Xeon processors. Historically, I have found it quite rare to experience a production physical server that is running anything other than Xeon CPUs. This mindset may suddenly shift with Windows Server 2025, as Microsoft now supports a range of both Intel and AMD processors to run its latest operating system.

Updated in-place upgrades

If you've been following Microsoft's progression of Windows Server through the years, and have helped to bring environments from 2016 -> 2019 -> 2022, you probably realize already that the in-place upgrade option has been significantly enhanced and improved over these years. Upgrading servers used to be a real challenge, and it was often easier to simply create a brand new server and transition your roles and data to it. I would say that starting with Server 2019, the option to in-place upgrade really stabilized and has continued to improve in the years since. Why are we talking about it in the "What's new?" section? Because you can now in-place upgrade a server right from inside Windows Update settings! This is common knowledge in the Win10 -> Win11 world, but unprecedented for Windows Server. Shortly, we will spend some time installing Windows and upgrading a previous Windows Server to 2025, and we'll also test out this new capability to allow that server to self-install Server 2025 by simply clicking some buttons inside the Windows Update settings. This is the same mechanism that Windows workstations have used to implement in-place feature updates for years. While the new Windows Update single-button mechanism for upgrading is only available on very recent servers, Microsoft has also expanded in-place upgrade capabilities when using the Windows Server 2025 installation media. As long as you have that ISO or DVD from which you can launch into an installer, you can perform what is known as **N-4 versioning**. That is, you can in-place upgrade 4 versions at a time! What this means in plain text is that you can pop Windows Server 2025 installation media into Windows Server 2012 R2 (or anything newer), and it will in-place upgrade all the way to Windows Server 2025. Holy moly, that is impressive.

Hotpatching

Windows Server hotpatching is an idea that came to light during the Server 2022 release, but only pertained to servers running the special Windows Server 2022 Azure Edition SKU. I recently attended a Microsoft presentation where it was made known, at no surprise to anyone, that hotpatching was by far the #1 requested update for Windows Server 2025's release.

Now integrated into Windows Server 2025, with no reliance on the special Azure Edition version, hotpatching enables your servers to continue patching their regular monthly patch cycle, *without rebooting*! Microsoft releases and installs these monthly security patches in a new way that puts the updated code into place in real time, no longer requiring a restart of those services or the operating system to bring them to life. Then, once per quarter, Microsoft releases a more traditional round of updates that do require a restart, but seriously, if we could get away with restarting servers once per quarter rather than once per month, think about all of the increased uptime percentages and decreased headaches with planning out maintenance windows.

One very important thing to remember with hotpatching: even though this capability is now built into any version of Windows Server 2025, it can only be employed if your server(s) are tapped into Azure Arc, as this is the mechanism through which hotpatching is administered and managed.

The Windows 11 experience is here!

It was a surprise to many when Windows Server 2022 hit shelves still running a Windows 10 graphical interface, as Windows 11 was already in the wild. Whatever rough edges existed at the time have now been polished, and Windows Server 2025 looks and feels like Windows 11. At this point, Win11 should be familiar territory for anyone who regularly works in IT or with computers at all. It will be nice to fall back into standards when bouncing between workstations and servers in Microsoft-centric infrastructures. Bringing the Windows 11 experience to Server 2025 also brings related toolsets, such as the current **Windows Terminal** and the updated **Task Manager**, both of which we will explore within this book.

Azure Edition

We already discussed Windows Server 2025 Datacenter: Azure Edition, but it is still worth calling out that this Azure-specific version still exists and is updated in 2025. Previously, hotpatching and SMB-over-QUIC were two of the primary differentiators between a classic Server 2022 and the Azure Edition, and it is worth noting again that Microsoft is really listening to its audience, as they have now pulled these two great technologies into every version of Windows Server 2025, making them more accessible to the masses.

Bluetooth

In Windows Server 2025, we now have Bluetooth, because...why not? I'm not sure how often this will be utilized, but you can now tap Bluetooth keyboards, mice, headphones, and so on directly to your servers. Maybe this will be particularly useful for developers who might be running Server 2025 on their local workstations as they build out new software (for those not familiar with containers, anyway).

Wireless networking

Similar to my feelings about Bluetooth, when I first saw this, I almost laughed out loud. Are people really going to wirelessly connect Windows Servers? I do have to admit that wireless connectivity has improved dramatically over the past 10 years, and if you're interested in wirelessly connecting your server, the **Wireless LAN Service** feature is now installed by default. Microsoft doesn't really expect this to be a common need, though, and so the service is configured to manually start by default. You will need to intentionally start the service in order to use wireless on your new server.

Microsoft accounts

Most reading this have probably added Entra accounts, Microsoft accounts, or Microsoft work/school accounts to various Windows 10 or Windows 11 computers through the **Settings** -> **Accounts** tool. This same capability to make the operating system integrally aware of a Microsoft account now exists in Windows Server 2025 as well.

Credential Guard

Credential Guard has been around as a technology for a while, but is now enabled by default in Windows Server 2025, as long as your system meets hardware and licensing requirements. This is a technology that greatly improves security surrounding NTLM passwords, Kerberos tickets, and the credentials that get stored in Windows by applications. You've probably heard about pass-the-hash and pass-the-ticket attacks, and Credential Guard helps to block those types of attacks from happening.

Azure Local

Formerly called Azure Stack HCI, Azure Local is essentially a mechanism to utilize Windows Server 2025 to build your own private cloud. This enables you to employ Azure-specific capabilities, capacities, and protections within your physical building.

Windows Admin Center (WAC)

WAC originally came to us around the same time as Windows Server 2019, and really built some steam with the release of Server 2022. With 2025's release, WAC is even more tightly integrated with Microsoft's cloud services, now being tied into Azure Arc. This enables you to manage your Windows Server instances from inside the Azure Arc portal, whether your servers are on-prem or cloud-based!

To be clear, you can still run Windows Admin Center on a local server and allow it to manage your servers, without using Azure Arc at all. In fact, we will be deploying this free tool together later in this book.

Active Directory improvements

There is so much talk about Azure, it can feel like the classic Windows Server is dying. My perception is quite the opposite; the truth in many cloud migration cases is that we are still running regular ole Windows Server instances—they just happen to live in the cloud on Microsoft's hardware instead of our own. It may seem surprising that Microsoft has pumped a bunch of improvements into something as classic as Active Directory, but ultimately, AD is timeless and will still be around for decades to come. There is quite a list of under-the-hood improvements that have been made to **Active Directory Domain Services (AD DS)** with the release of Windows Server 2025, most of which you probably wouldn't care too much about. One stand-out is a major improvement to the JET database that underpins AD, which has been using 8k-sized page files since the year 1999. These pages have now been increased to 32k, a 4x increase, which removes AD object limitations that have always existed in the past. Additionally, default machine account passwords have increased security by using randomly generated computer account passwords, and AD DS can now utilize **Non-Uniform Memory Access (NUMA)** to take advantage of CPUs in all processor groups, where previously it could only use a single group.

Active Directory also gains some major security improvements, now utilizing current algorithms and encryption methods. For example, LDAP now supports TLS1.3 and Kerberos can run AES SHA256/384.

Delegated Managed Service Accounts (dMSA)

Service accounts in Active Directory have always been a necessary and important tool, but they can be used for evil just as quickly as for good. New with Windows Server 2025, dMSAs link the authentication of these accounts directly to a device's identity in AD, which prevents attackers from harvesting credentials through a compromised account.

Dynamic Tracing (DTrace)

DTrace is not a brand-new toolset, but previously required installation in Windows. With Windows Server 2025, DTrace is now included out of the box, accessed via your favorite command line. This utility allows for monitoring and debugging of real-time system performance, and can even script actions to be taken based on monitored probes. We will take a closer look at DTrace in our last chapter, *Troubleshooting*.

Windows Local Administrator Password Solution (LAPS)

LAPS has been around for a long time, but is historically underutilized. Fresh attention has been given to this technology, which is a centralized management tool used to control local administrator passwords on all of your domain-joined machines. With LAPS, it is possible for every workstation to always have a unique local administrator password, which will keep attackers guessing for a very long time. New LAPS policies allow you to specify things such as the length of passwords and using word phrases instead of random characters for easier readability. There is a new AD attribute as well, called `msLAPS-CurrentPasswordVersion`, that helps to solve issues caused by reimaging or rolling back workstations, where in the past that action could cause the local administrator password to be out of sync between the workstation and AD, and AD would never update itself to store the correct password. Now it can. We'll take a look at LAPS as we implement it together later, in our chapter on security.

ReFS improvements

The **Resilient File System**, better known as **ReFS**, has some under-the-hood improvements in Server 2025 that should automatically cause you to experience things such as faster file copies and reduced storage space. Work has been done to optimize ReFS's deduplication and compression capabilities. These updates will improve daily interaction with files, as well as enhancing the capabilities of Dev Drive by enabling block cloning.

Compress to...

I can't tell you how many times I have installed third-party tools such as 7-Zip recently, because the built-in Windows Zip function seems to be a little flaky in recent versions of the Windows operating system. Never fear, I think we have a resolution to this issue beginning in Server 2025. In fact, right-clicking on a file now gives you a new **Compress to...** option, which allows you to easily compress files out to ZIP, 7-Zip or TAR files with a single click.

SMB over QUIC

Okay, I am very excited about this one! With the release of Windows Server 2022, we learned about this cool new SMB protocol that securely enables SMB traffic (file shares) to natively map directly over the internet using TLS1.3 without needing any kind of VPN connection. This enables mapped network drives to file servers to work directly, but still securely, over the internet. That is incredible! The downside to using SMB over QUIC was that it required you to utilize a special edition of the operating system, Windows Server 2022 Azure Edition. *This is no longer a requirement!* SMB over QUIC is now built natively into Windows Server 2025 Standard or Datacenter. We will take a closer look at this new file access protocol in *Chapter 6, File Management*.

OpenSSH

In previous versions of Windows Server, you were required to install a tool manually to use OpenSSH. It is now built into Windows Server 2025, indicating Microsoft expects this to be more widely used moving forward. They have also added a new local group to Windows called **OpenSSH Users** for easy control over who can or cannot access your devices using OpenSSH.

Windows VPN hardening

Routing and Remote Access Service (RRAS) has been serving up Windows Server-based VPN connectivity for many, many years. Throughout that time, there have been a couple of VPN protocols that have always been enabled options, but those protocols are now considered to be unsafe, compromised, and all-around bad ideas. Namely, I'm talking about PPTP and L2TP, which you will now find disabled by default in Windows Server 2025. They can still be enabled if needed, but Microsoft rightly expects you to now be making use of SSTP or IKEv2 for all Windows-based VPN connectivity.

Azure Arc

While this is not inherently a technology about Windows Server, Azure Arc is a cloud-based server management platform that could certainly interact with all instances of Server 2025 (and more), allowing you to centrally manage even on-prem servers from Azure. Tapping local servers into Azure Arc is as simple as running through a quick wizard in the operating system or by using PowerShell. As Microsoft continues to add new Azure-like features to on-prem versions of Windows Server, we should expect that plugging those servers into Azure Arc will become a routine and necessary action to enable those new functions.

AI-ready

As I was researching interoperability between Windows Server 2025 and AI, I was sick to my stomach to find that many of the articles written about AI are, indeed, written by AI itself. It is still fairly obvious to the human brain at this point. In fact, I found entire websites that seem to have been created by AI. These websites are full of buzzwords and popular phrases, but in the end, they lack any real content. While there are clearly some people tying Server 2025 and AI together in what they are writing, and certainly AI-written articles have decided to self-promote AI (cue end-of-the-world scenarios), this seems to be the reality of where Server 2025 meets AI.

Server 2025 includes some improvements that help this latest operating system to be better ready to service AI workloads, as companies move further and further into this space. **GPU partitioning**, in particular, allows companies to divide GPUs across multiple applications and services, increasing system performance in a way that is particularly helpful for AI workloads. For example, a single physical GPU can be split among multiple VMs.

Also, NVMe storage boost allows for up to 60% faster IOPS compared to Server 2022, which will significantly enhance data retrieval and processing, integral for large data transactions commonly associated with the AI world.

Feedback Hub

How many times have you seen or experienced something on a Windows machine and thought, "I wish I could report this to Microsoft, but would anybody actually look at it?" We now have a mechanism to do exactly that. Feedback or problems can be reported to Microsoft directly from the Windows Server 2025 interface via Feedback Hub. You can even include screen recordings!

Hyper-converged infrastructure (Azure Local)

I already mentioned Azure Local, formerly known as Azure Stack HCI, in the list of new features Microsoft is offering. If the term **Hyper-Converged Infrastructure (HCI)** is new to you, a little backstory may prove beneficial here.

When you see the term HCI, it is important to understand that we are not talking about a specific technology that exists within your server environment. Rather, HCI is a culmination of a number of different technologies that can work together and be managed together, all for the purpose of creating the mentality of a **Software-Defined Datacenter (SDDC** as it is sometimes referred to).

Specifically, HCI in the Microsoft world is most often referred to as the combination of Hyper-V and **Storage Spaces Direct (S2D)** on the same cluster of servers. Clustering these services together enables some big speed and reliability benefits over hosting these roles separately and on their own systems. It also creates a tech stack that begins to resemble the way that Azure runs, but within your own physical server infrastructure.

Another component that is part of, or related to, an SDDC is **Software-Defined Networking (SDN)**. Similar to how compute virtualization platforms (such as Hyper-V) completely changed the landscape of what server computing looked like 15 or more years ago, we are now finding ourselves capable of lifting the network layer away from physical hardware and shifting the design and administration of our networks to be virtual and managed by the Windows Server platform.

Where the idea of HCI really takes a leap, as it relates directly to the Windows Server 2025 release, is through integration with Azure Local. Now that we can run private clouds within our datacenter walls, Microsoft has provided us with true cloud capabilities through the use of Windows Server 2025 Datacenter: Azure Edition within that Azure Local environment.

Features deprecated in Server 2025

We expect each new operating system release to include new and updated features, but don't generally think too much about what might be old enough to be removed completely when a new version is released. The removal of old, unnecessary, and insecure code can only be a healthy update for Windows Server. Removing these components in Server 2025 does not mean that Microsoft will not continue to support them on existing servers, but they have no plans to continue developing these technologies in the future. Let's look at some deprecations for Server 2025.

SAC releases

As we have already discussed, the SAC releases of Windows Server will no longer be built and released. The future of on-premise Windows Server is through the standard LTSC release channel.

Guarded fabric and shielded VMs

Technically, these were already deprecated with Server 2022, but it's a big enough announcement that we should mention it again. Guarded fabric and shielded VMs were big news in Server 2016, and Microsoft will continue to support customers who use guarded hypervisor fabrics and shielded VMs, but there are no plans for future development of this technology.

IIS6 Management Console and SMTP server

The trusty, rusty, 20-year-old IIS console has been removed, in lieu of the newer IIS management console that has already existed for years. You would think that everyone should already be using the newer console, and this would not have a large impact, but I am continually surprised to find at least a couple of customers every year who are still using IIS6 to relay SMTP mail. Yikes, get away from that thing today!

Wordpad

No real surprise here, I can't say that I have watched anybody launch Wordpad in more than 10 years. With alternatives such as Word or even Notepad, which has been recently enhanced, this old text editor is now six feet under.

NTLMv1

Hopefully, you won't notice this change, but this old authentication method has now been removed, and Microsoft hopes you have everything moved over to Kerberos. While NTLMv1 specifically is the only one fully removed in Server 2025, any other flavor of NTLM is also on its way out the door and will no longer be developed by Microsoft. In other words, don't rely on NTLMv2, as that will also be removed during a future release.

PowerShell 2.0

This engine is now removed. PowerShell 5.0 or higher has been the standard for many years at this point—applications that rely on 2.0 are due for an upgrade!

TLS 1.0 and 1.1

While not fully removed, these old protocols are disabled by default. Any applications still relying on either of these versions of TLS have gray hair at this point and should be upgraded or replaced.

Windows Internal Database (WID)

This one came as a surprise to me! Microsoft has utilized its internal database for many functions over the years. WID is still fully in Windows Server 2025 as it is still utilized by many roles, such as ADFS, IPAM, Remote Desktop, and WSUS. The big news here is that Microsoft is no longer going to develop anything new in WID, and it may be removed in a future release. They are making recommendations that companies who utilize these services start sliding them over to the free (or paid) version of SQL.

Windows Server Update Services (WSUS)

This is another component that still exists in Windows Server 2025 today, but Microsoft has announced no plans to actively develop it in the future. With operating system updates now being steered by new tech such as hotpatching and the update process being managed by Azure Arc or other tools, Microsoft's own server-side update mechanism is becoming yesterday's news. Please don't misunderstand: you can still use WSUS today and can even build a brand new WSUS environment right now in 2025, but this news from Microsoft means you should begin researching alternatives within the next few years.

Navigating the interface

Let's jump in the wayback machine for a minute and walk through some graphical interface history. Microsoft Windows users have always known and loved their computers, and a large part of the reason Windows became such a standard in the business world is that the global workforce is familiar with navigating a Windows world. This familiarity has paid unimaginable dividends for Microsoft over the years, but there have been a couple of bumps in the road. Unfortunately, Microsoft turned a lot of people off with the introduction of Windows 8 and Server 2012, not because functionality or reliability was lacking, but because the interface was so vastly different from what it had been before. It was almost like running two separate operating systems at the same time. You had the normal desktop experience, in which all of us spent 99.9% of our time, but then there were also those few moments where you found yourself needing to visit the full-page **Start** menu. More likely, you stumbled into it without wanting to. However you ended up there, inside that full-screen, tablet-like interface, for the remaining 0.01% of your Server 2012 experience, you were left confused, disturbed, and wishing you were back in the traditional desktop. I am, of course, speaking purely from experience here. There may be variations in your personal percentages of time spent, but based on conversations I was involved in at the time, I am not alone in these views, and I haven't even mentioned the magical, self-appearing **Charms bar**. Some bad memories are better left in the recesses of the brain.

The major update of Windows 8.1 and Server 2012 R2 came with the welcome relief from these symptoms. There was an actual **Start** button in the corner again, and you could choose to boot primarily into the normal desktop mode. However, should you ever have the need to click on that **Start** button, you would find yourself right back on the full-page **Start** screen, which I still found almost all server admins trying their best to avoid at all costs.

Well, it turns out that Microsoft does listen to the people and brought some much-needed relief in Windows 10 and Windows Server 2016, and they have not deviated in such a major way since. Whether working on Windows Server 2016, 2019, or 2022, you will experience comfort and stability in the flavor of a Windows 10 look and feel, which finally wiped away the full-screen **Start** menu and brought balance back to the universe.

Then came Windows 11...

Certainly updated, but not nearly as egregiously as the Windows 8 release, Windows 11 is much more rounded and polished while still maintaining Windows-centric roots. As far as the current server graphical interface goes, Windows Server 2025 receives the same facelift, taking on the interface of Windows 11 workstations. If you are comfortable navigating inside Windows 11, you are already well suited to Windows Server 2025.

For anyone new to working within Windows or just looking for some tips and tricks to get them rolling, this section is for you.

The updated Start menu

All throughout Windows 10 sub-version releases, there were small ongoing changes to the **Start** menu. Backpedaling from Windows 8, we rediscovered a real **Start** button that launches a real **Start** menu— one that doesn't take over the entire desktop. To be honest, personally, I almost never open the **Start** menu at all, other than to search for an application or feature that I want. We will cover more on that very soon.

Now that we have moved into the Windows 11 interface, **Start** menu interoperability is relatively the same as Windows 10, though, as I'm sure you noticed during your first interaction with Windows 11, the **Start** button and **Taskbar** icons have moved into the middle of your screen. Why? Nobody has been able to tell me a sure answer to that, but it takes some getting used to.

Other than the arguably annoying slide of the **Start** button to the middle of the taskbar, the new **Start** menu is quite useful. Click on that button, and a few nice things stand out:

- Viewing of all applications installed on the server is possible by clicking the **All apps** button, but we are creatures of habit, and many times, when the **Start** button is pressed, we are re-visiting an application or task that we have done a hundred times before. Pinning commonly used items to the top of your **Start** menu can save time and clicks during your daily work.

- Clicking that **All apps** button lists all applications installed on the server, in alphabetical order. This is very useful for launching an application or for doing a quick check to find out whether a particular app or feature is installed on your server.

- The bottom of the **Start** menu includes a couple of buttons for quick access to account or system items. Easily and more clearly accessible here than in previous versions is the ability to shut down, restart, or log out of a server.

- **Search**, the text bar on top of the **Start** menu, is by far its most useful decoration, as you can simply click the **Start** button on your keyboard and immediately begin typing the name of any application, setting, or document that you want to launch.

You can see all of these functions in *Figure 1.2*:

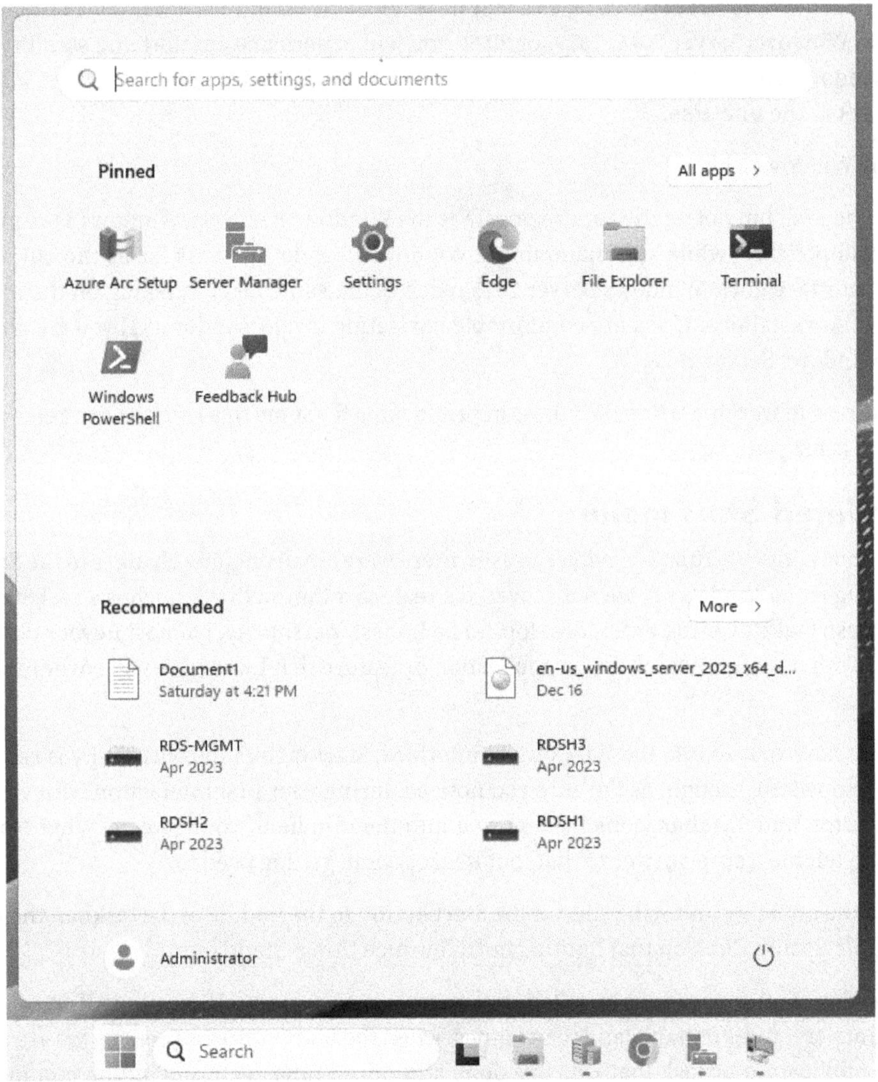

Figure 1.2: The new Start menu

Now that is a breath of fresh air. A simple but useful **Start** menu, and more importantly, one that loads quickly over remote connections such as RDP or Hyper-V consoles.

The Quick Admin Tasks menu

As nice as it is to have a functional **Start** menu, as a server administrator, I still very rarely find myself needing to access the traditional menu for my day-to-day functions. This is because many items that I need to access are quickly available to me inside the **Quick Admin Tasks** menu, which opens by simply right-clicking on the **Start** button. This menu has been available to us since the release of Windows 8, but many IT professionals still make little use of this functionality.

This menu has become an important part of my interaction with Windows Server operating systems, and hopefully, it will be for you as well. Right-clicking on the **Start** button shows us immediate quick links to do things such as open **Event Viewer**, view **System properties**, check **Device Manager**, and even shut down or restart the server.

The two most common functions that I call for in this context menu are the **Run** function and using it to quickly launch a **Terminal** prompt. Even better is the ability from this menu to open either a regular user context Terminal prompt or an elevated/administrative Terminal prompt. Using this menu properly saves many mouse clicks and shortens troubleshooting time:

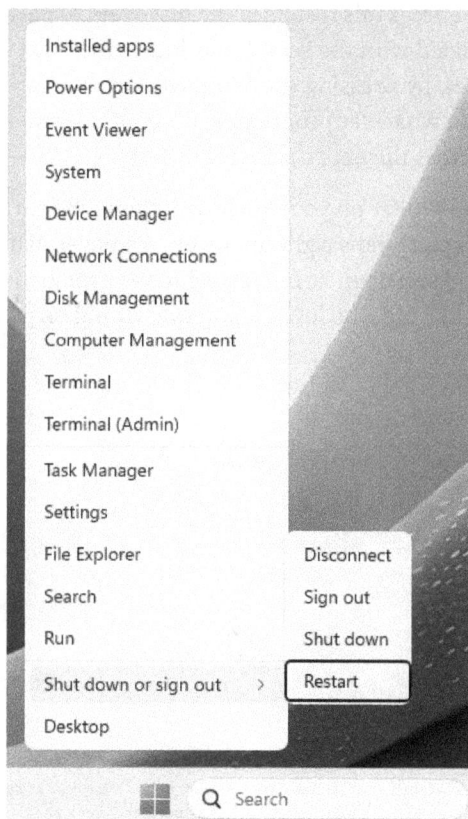

Figure 1.3: The Quick Admin Tasks menu

Alternatively, this menu can be invoked using the *WinKey* + *X* keyboard shortcut! In fact, accessing this menu via keyboard shortcuts has become popular enough that many people have begun referring to this admin menu as the "WinKey+X menu," though that is not technically accurate.

Using the Search function

While the **Quick Admin Tasks** menu hidden behind the **Start** button is useful for calling common administrative tasks, using the **Search** function inside the **Start** menu is a powerful tool for interfacing with literally anything on Windows Server. Depending on who installed applications and roles on your servers, you may or may not have shortcuts available to launch them inside the **Start** menu. You also may or may not have desktop shortcuts or links to open these programs from the taskbar. I find that it is often difficult to find specific settings that you are trying to tweak, by point-and-clicking your way through the interface. **Control Panel** is slowly being replaced by the newer **Settings** menu in newer versions of Windows, and sometimes this results in the discovery of particular settings being difficult. All of these troubles are alleviated with the search bar inside the **Start** menu. By simply clicking on the **Start** button or, even easier, by pressing the Windows key (*WinKey*) on your keyboard, you can simply start typing the name of whatever program, setting, or document you want to open, and you will see search results from across the entire server.

As a most basic example, press *WinKey* on your keyboard, then type notepad, and press the *Enter* key. You will see that good old Notepad opens right up for us. We never had to navigate anywhere in the Programs folder in order to find and open it. In fact, we never even had to touch the mouse, which is music to the ears of someone like me who loves doing everything he possibly can via the keyboard:

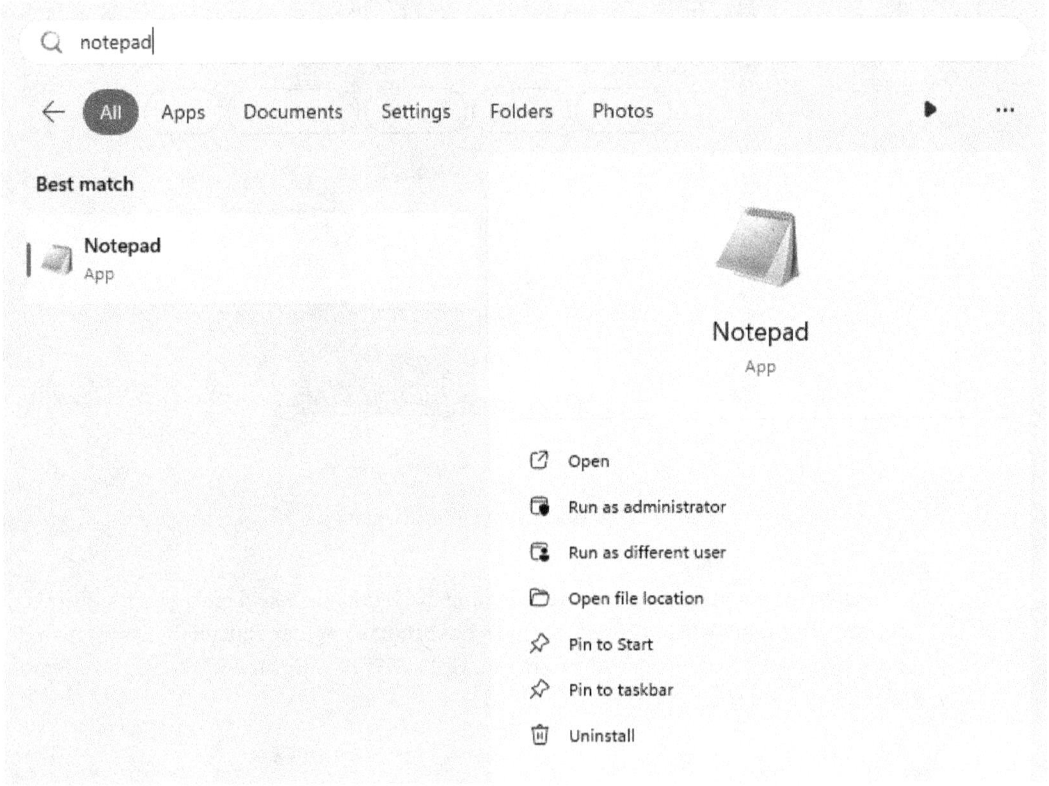

Figure 1.4: Windows Search

An even better example is to pick something that would be buried deep inside **Settings** or **Control Panel**. How about changing the speed of your mouse? A traditional server admin might open **Control Panel** (if they can find it), probably navigate to the **Hardware** or **Appearance and Personalization** sections, because nothing else looks obviously correct, and still not find what they were looking for. After poking around for a few more minutes, they would start to think that Microsoft forgot to add this setting altogether. But alas, these mouse power settings are simply buried somewhere else, and to be honest, I don't think Microsoft really expects admins to manually seek things out at this point. We will discuss the new **Settings** screen momentarily, from which many common settings are being re-grouped into new homes, but ultimately, for the purposes of this example, you are currently stuck at the point where you cannot find the setting you want to change. What's the quick solution? Press your *WinKey* to open the **Start** menu, and type mouse speed. You'll see in the list of available options showing in the search menu one called **Change the mouse pointer display or speed**. Click on that and you will have found the setting you were looking for all along:

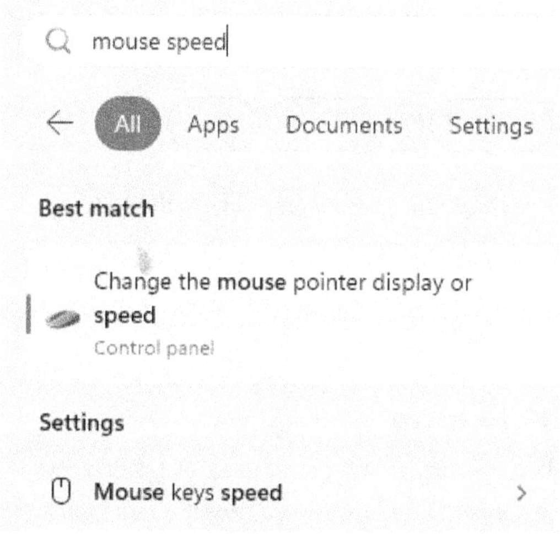

Q   mouse speed|

←   All   Apps   Documents   Settings

Best match

Change the **mouse** pointer display or
speed
Control panel

Settings

Mouse keys **speed**   >

Figure 1.5: Searching for settings

Any other applications, settings, or even documents on your server that are related to "mouse speed" will also be displayed in your search results. I don't know of a more powerful way to open applications or settings on Windows Server 2025 than using the search bar inside the **Start** menu. Give it a try today!

Pinning programs to the taskbar or Start menu

While Windows Server 2025 provides great searching capabilities so that launching hard-to-find applications is very easy, sometimes it's easier to have quick shortcuts for commonly used items available with a single click down in the traditional taskbar. Alternatively, pin them directly to your **Start** menu for easy access in the future. Whether you have sought out a particular application by browsing manually through the **Start** menu or have used the **Search** function to pull up the program that you want, you can simply right-click on the program and choose **Pin to taskbar** to stick a permanent shortcut to that application in the taskbar at the bottom of your screen. Once you have done this, during future logins to your session on the server, your favorite and most-used applications will be waiting for you with a single click.

As you can see in *Figure 1.6*, you also have the ability to pin programs to the **Start** menu, which of course is another useful place from which to launch them regularly:

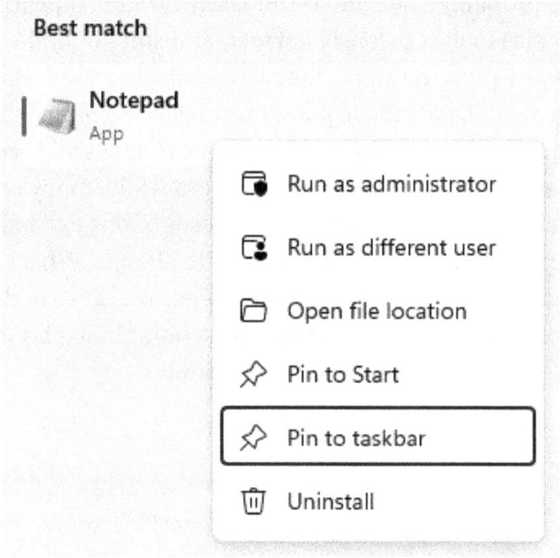

Figure 1.6: Pinning programs to the taskbar

Many readers will already be very familiar with the process of pinning programs to the taskbar, so let's take it one step further to portray an additional function you may not be aware is available to you when you have applications pinned.

The power of right-clicking

We are all familiar with right-clicking in any given area of a Windows operating system in order to use some more advanced functions. Small context menus displayed upon a right-click have existed since the two-button mouse rolled off the assembly line.

We often right-click in order to copy text, copy documents, paste these, or get into a deeper set of properties for a particular file or folder. Many day-to-day tasks are accomplished with that mouse button. What I want to take a minute to point out is that software makers, Microsoft and otherwise, have been adding even more right-click functionality into application launchers themselves, which makes it even more advantageous to have them close at hand, such as inside the taskbar.

The amount of functionality provided to you when right-clicking on an application in the taskbar differs, depending on the application itself. For example, if I were to right-click on Command Prompt, I have options to either open **Command Prompt** or **Unpin from taskbar**. Very simple stuff. If I right-click again on the smaller menu option for **Command Prompt**, I have the ability to perform the same functions, but I could also get further into **Properties** or **Run as administrator**. So, I get a little more enhanced functionality the deeper I go:

Figure 1.7: Right-click to find Run as administrator

With other programs, you may find even more results. And the more you utilize your servers, the more data and options you will start to see in these right-click context menus. Two great examples are **Notepad** and **Remote Desktop Client**. On my server, I have worked on a few text configuration files, and I have used my server to jump into other servers to perform some remote tasks. I have done this using the Remote Desktop client. Now, when I right-click on **Notepad** as listed in my taskbar, I have quick links to the most recent documents that I have worked on:

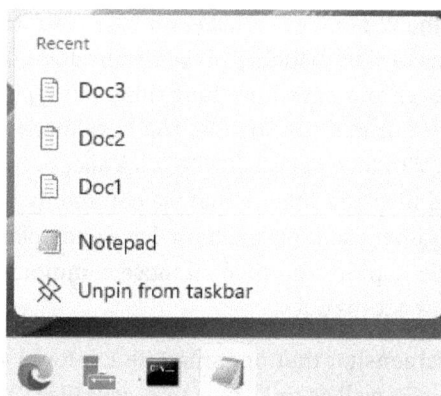

Figure 1.8: Right-clicking reveals recent documents

When right-clicking on my RDP icon, I now have quick links listed right here for the recent servers that I have connected to. I don't know about you, but I RDP into a lot of different servers on a daily basis. Having a link for the Remote Desktop client in the taskbar, automatically keeping track of the most recent servers I have visited, definitely saves me time and mouse clicks as I work through my daily tasks:

Figure 1.9: Recent RDP connections

These right-click functions have existed for a couple of operating system versions now, so it's not new technology, but it is being expanded upon regularly as new versions of applications are released. It is also a functionality that I don't witness many server administrators utilizing, but perhaps they should start doing so in order to work more efficiently, which is why we are discussing it here.

Something that is enhanced in the Windows 11 and Server 2025 platforms that is also very useful on a day-to-day basis is the **Quick access** view, which is presented by default when you open **File Explorer**. We all know and use **File Explorer** and have for a long time, but typically, when you want to get to a particular place on a hard drive or to a specific file, you have many mouse clicks to go through in order to reach your destination. Windows Server 2025's **Quick access** view immediately shows us both recently and frequently opened files and folders that we commonly access from the server. We, as admins, often have to visit the same places on the hard drive and open the same files time and time again. Wouldn't it be great if **File Explorer** lumped all those common locations and file links in one place? That is exactly what **Quick access** does.

You can see in the following screenshot that opening **File Explorer** gives you quick links to open both frequently accessed folders as well as links to your recent files. A feature like this can be a real time-saver, and regularly making use of these little bits and pieces available to you, in order to increase your efficiency, demonstrates to colleagues and those around you that you have a real familiarity and comfort level with this latest round of operating systems:

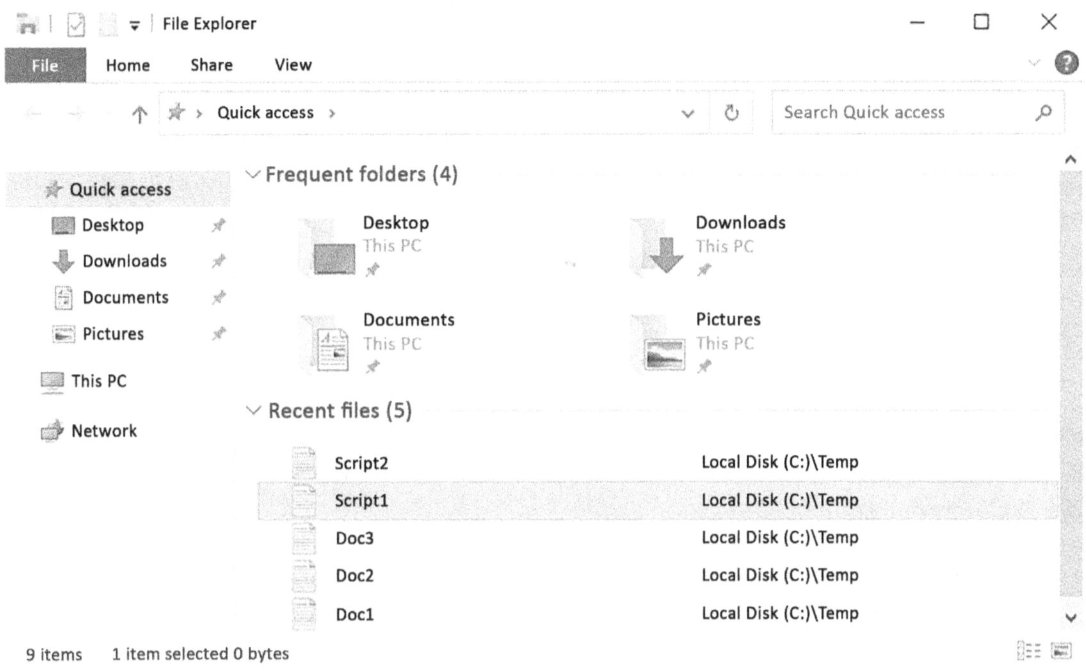

Figure 1.10: Quick access

You'll also notice the small pushpin icons next to some of those **Quick access** locations. You can easily right-click on any folder location via **File Explorer** and choose **Pin to Quick access**, adding it to your **Quick access** menu, and Windows will maintain that pinned location right here inside the **Quick access** section until you choose to unpin it.

> Yet another way that you can use right-clicking to your advantage is when you want to launch **Terminal** or **PowerShell** in a particular directory on a filesystem. Opening PowerShell in a standard method will land your PowerShell window directly in C:\Users\ (username). Depending on what you need to do with PowerShell, you might spend many keystrokes navigating your way to the correct directory on your server from which you need to run a script or make some changes. Alternatively, if you are already inside **File Explorer,** you can hold down your *Shift* key and then right-click on any directory and choose the **Open in Terminal** option or **Open PowerShell window here.** This will immediately launch a new instance of Terminal or PowerShell, with your current directory being the folder you right-clicked on!

App snapping

Some of you may be familiar with add-ins to Windows called **PowerTools**, one of which allows you to easily carve out segments of your screen for different applications. When running multiple windows or applications onscreen at the same time, **PowerTools** allows an easy way to "snap" applications to a certain size or section of the screen, without any manual click-and-drag resizing of windows. Microsoft has baked some of this capability directly into Windows 11, and now that we are running the Win11 interface inside Windows Server 2025, application snapping is natively included in this newest server operating system as well. To be clear, **PowerTools** still offers other cool functions, but app snapping that we are discussing here is now a native capability and will work out of the box in Server 2025.

App snapping is quite intuitive, and you won't need a lot of instruction to make use of it, but it's good to know that there are three different ways you can call it to action:

- Drag a window to the top-center of your screen and hold it there
- Hover your mouse over the top of any window's maximize button
- Use *WinKey + Z*

Invoking any of the preceding three procedures will display a nice little bar, which provides you with tons of different options about where and how you would like to position this window. Take a look at the following screenshot, where I have hovered my mouse over the top of the maximize button in a **File Explorer** window.

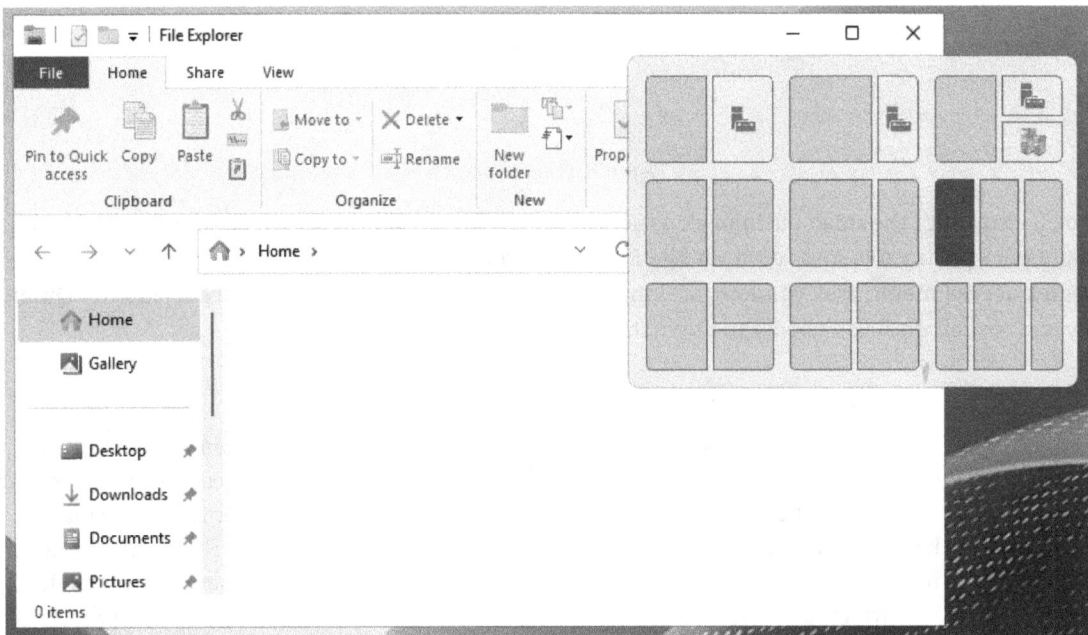

Figure 1.11: App snapping in action

As you can see, simply selecting one of the available screen zones will immediately snap this **File Explorer** window into that size and shape. My mouse is currently hovering over the option you see in blue, which would place **File Explorer** in the far-left, third section of my screen. When selecting a zone that includes other gray-colored zones, Windows will snap your application into that position, and then immediately ask you what application you would like to place in the other remaining open sections of the screen. I use this functionality all the time when repositioning windows on my workstation—why not on servers?

App snapping is fairly intuitive. As you can see in *Figure 1.11*, the top three options for **File Explorer** positioning have automatically given me options that will auto-position the other apps I currently have open on this server. Those apps are **Server Manager** and the **Hyper-V Manager** console, which are easily identifiable by their icons. Selecting one of those top options will immediately place **File Explorer** on the left, with the other applications displayed alongside it toward the right. In *Figure 1.12*, you can see that I selected the upper-right option, which laid **File Explorer** alongside both of the other open applications.

Figure 1.12: After snapping

🔍**Quick tip:** Need to see a high-resolution version of this image? Open this book in the next-gen Packt Reader or view it in the PDF/ePub copy.

📖**The next-gen Packt Reader** is included for free with the purchase of this book. Scan the QR code OR go to `https://packtpub.com/unlock`, then use the search bar to find this book by name. Double-check the edition shown to make sure you get the right one.

One more tip related to this topic: If you know me at all, you know that I touch the mouse as little as possible, trying my best to live in a keyboard-only world. Your open applications and windows can also be snapped around your screen(s) with zero mouse interaction at all, by employing the following hotkeys:

- *WinKey + Left Arrow*: Snap the active window to the left half of your current screen
- *WinKey + Right Arrow*: Snap the active window to the right half of your current screen
- *WinKey + Up Arrow*: Maximize the current window
- *WinKey + Down Arrow*: Minimize the current window
- *WinKey + M*: Minimize all open windows, which is pretty useful

When using multiple monitors, use these hotkeys:

- *WinKey + Shift + Left*: Move the current window to the next monitor on your left
- *WinKey + Shift + Right*: Move the current window to the next monitor on your right

That may seem like a lot of keyboard functions to keep in the human memory banks, but they will become muscle memory in no time. Trust me, the time savings are worth it!

Windows Settings

If you work in IT and have used Windows 10 on a client machine for any period of time, it's a sure bet that you have already worked within the newer **Settings** interface. **Settings** in Windows Server 2025 is just what the name implies, an interface from which you configure various settings within the operating system.

What can sometimes be difficult or confusing about the existence of **Settings** is that we also have a different landing platform for settings contained inside Windows that has been around for a zillion years. It's called **Control Panel**.

The **Settings** menu inside Windows isn't a brand-new idea, but it looks and feels quite new when compared to **Control Panel**. Windows Server 2012 and 2012 R2 had a quasi-presence of this newer **Settings** screen that, as far as I know, went largely unused by systems administrators. I believe that to be the effect of poor execution, as the **Settings** menu in 2012 was accessed and hidden behind the **Charms** bar, which most folks have decided was a terrible idea. We will not spend too much time on technology of the past, but the **Charms** bar in Server 2012 is a little bit like an AMC Pacer in the car world. You may have never even heard of it, or you may be old enough to have had the unfortunate experience of owning one yourself, and it is now irrevocably part of your own story. The **Charms** bar was a menu that presented itself when you swiped your finger in from the right edge of the screen. What's that, you ask? Servers don't usually have touchscreens? I'm right there with you—not any that I have ever worked on, anyway. So, the **Charms** bar was also presented when you hovered the mouse up near the top right of the screen. It was quite difficult to access, yet it seemed to always appear whenever you didn't want it to, such as when you were trying to click on something on the right side of the screen, and instead you clicked on something inside the **Charms** bar that suddenly popped out of nowhere.

I am only giving you this background information in order to segue into this next idea. Much of the user interface in Windows 10+, and therefore Windows Server 2016+, can be considered a small step backward from the realm of finger swipes and touchscreens. Windows 8 and Server 2012 were so focused on big app buttons and finger swipes that a lot of people got lost in the shuffle. It was so different from what we had ever seen before and difficult to use at an administrative level. Because of feedback received from that release, the graphical interface and user controls, including both the **Start** menu and the **Settings** menu in Windows Server 2025, are sort of smack-dab in the middle between Server 2008 and Server 2012. This backward step was the right one to take, and I have heard nothing but praise so far for the newer user interfaces.

So, getting back to the **Settings** menu, if you click on your **Start** button, then click on that little gear labeled **Settings**, you will see this new interface:

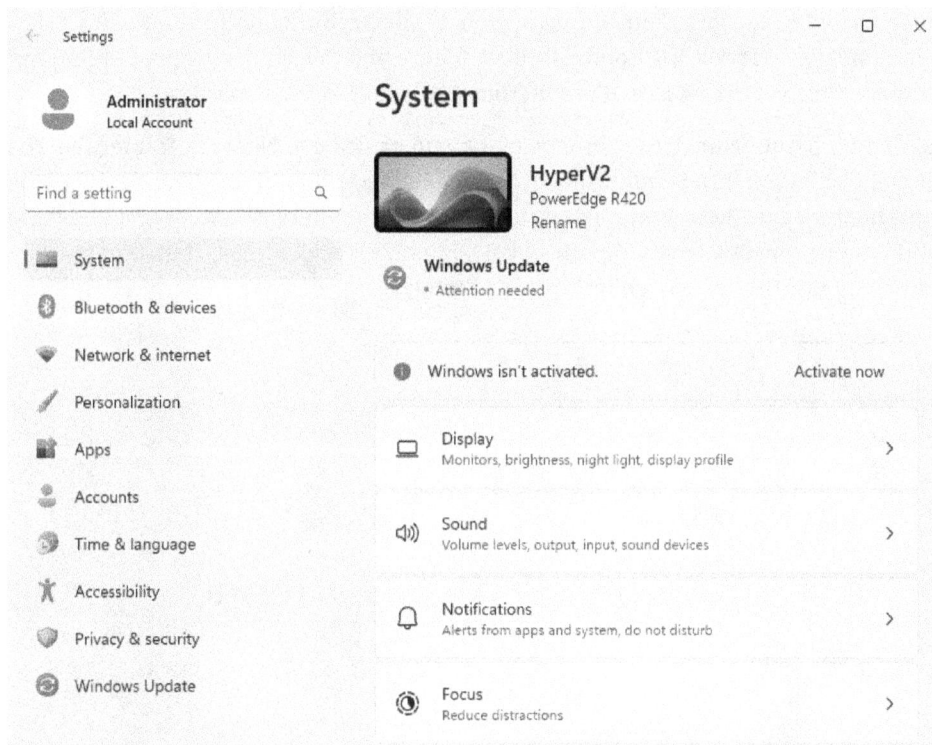

Figure 1.13: Windows Settings

There are many settings and pieces of the operating system that you can configure in this new **Settings** menu. Some settings in Windows now only exist in this interface, but many can still be accessed either here or through the traditional **Control Panel**. The goal seems to be a shift toward all configurations being done through the new menu in future releases, but, for now, we can still administer most setting changes through our traditional methods if we so choose. I mentioned Windows Update earlier, and that is a good example to look over. Historically, we would configure our Windows Update settings via **Control Panel**, but they have now been completely migrated over to the new **Settings** menu in Windows Server 2025. Search **Control Panel** for Windows Update, and the only result is that you can view currently installed updates. But, if you search the new **Settings** menu for Windows Update, you'll find it right away.

Remember, you can always use the Windows search feature to look for any setting! Hit your *WinKey* and type Windows Update, and you'll be given quick links that take you straight into the appropriate **Settings** menus.

For the moment, you will have to use a combination of **Control Panel** and the **Settings** menu to do your work. This gets confusing occasionally. With each new release of the Windows operating system, Microsoft moves more and more functions directly into **Settings**, lessening the requirements on **Control Panel**. As an example, even in Windows Server 2022, if you wanted to change a NIC's IP address, you would always need to visit one of the older configuration screens. You could view NIC settings inside the **Settings** console, but clicking the button to edit the IP address of a network card would then launch the older **Network Connections** screen. While **Network Connections** still exists and you can certainly still use it to edit NIC configurations, for the first time in the history of Windows Server, you can now change your IP address directly from inside the **Settings** interface!

Go ahead and try it out. Launch the **Settings** menu and navigate to **Network & internet**. Then click **Ethernet** in the right column. Scrolling down a little bit, you will find your **IP assignment** displayed, alongside a button called **Edit**. Previously, selecting the option here to edit an IP address would immediately launch a separate window to the old-style **Control Panel** screens, but as of today, we have the ability to edit our IP address right here inside **Settings**!

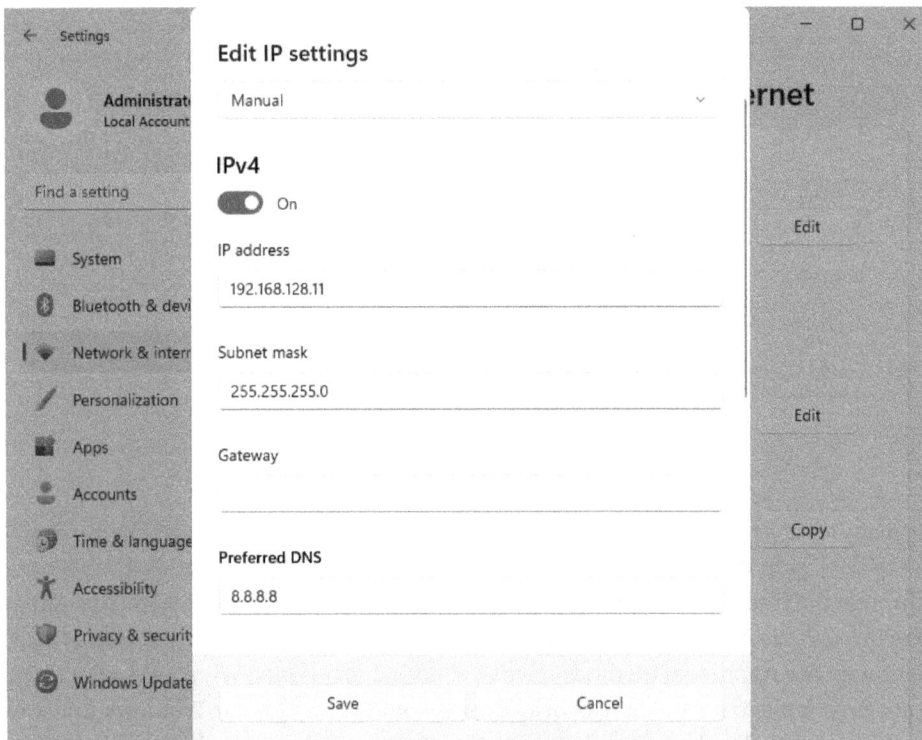

Figure 1.14: Editing IP address inside Settings

While Microsoft continues to move Windows configuration items into the **Settings** console, don't be surprised if you still run across some items that take you back to those classic **Control Panel** screens. They still exist, even if they are starting to collect dust on the shelf.

Two ways to do the same thing

Potentially confusing as well, until you get used to navigating around in here, is that you can sometimes accomplish the same task in either **Control Panel** or the **Settings** menu, but the process that you take in each interface can have a vastly different look and feel. Let's take a look at that firsthand by trying to create a new user account on our server, once via **Control Panel**, and again via **Settings**.

Creating a new user through Control Panel

You are probably familiar with this. Open **Control Panel** and click on **User Accounts**. Then, click on the **User Accounts** heading. Now, click on the **Manage another account** link. Inside this screen is the **Add a user account** option. Click on that and you get the dialog box where you enter a username and password for your new user:

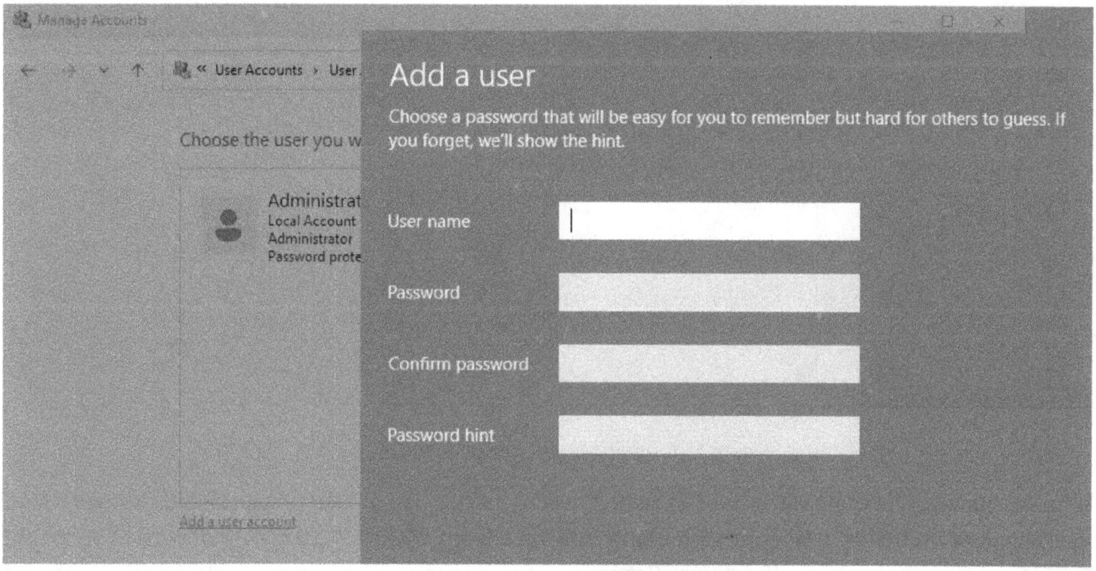

Figure 1.15: Adding a user account via Control Panel

Creating a new user through the Settings menu

Let's take this newer **Settings** interface for a test drive. Open the **Settings** menu and click on **Accounts**. Now, click on **Other users** in the right column. There is an **Add account** button here; go ahead and click on that:

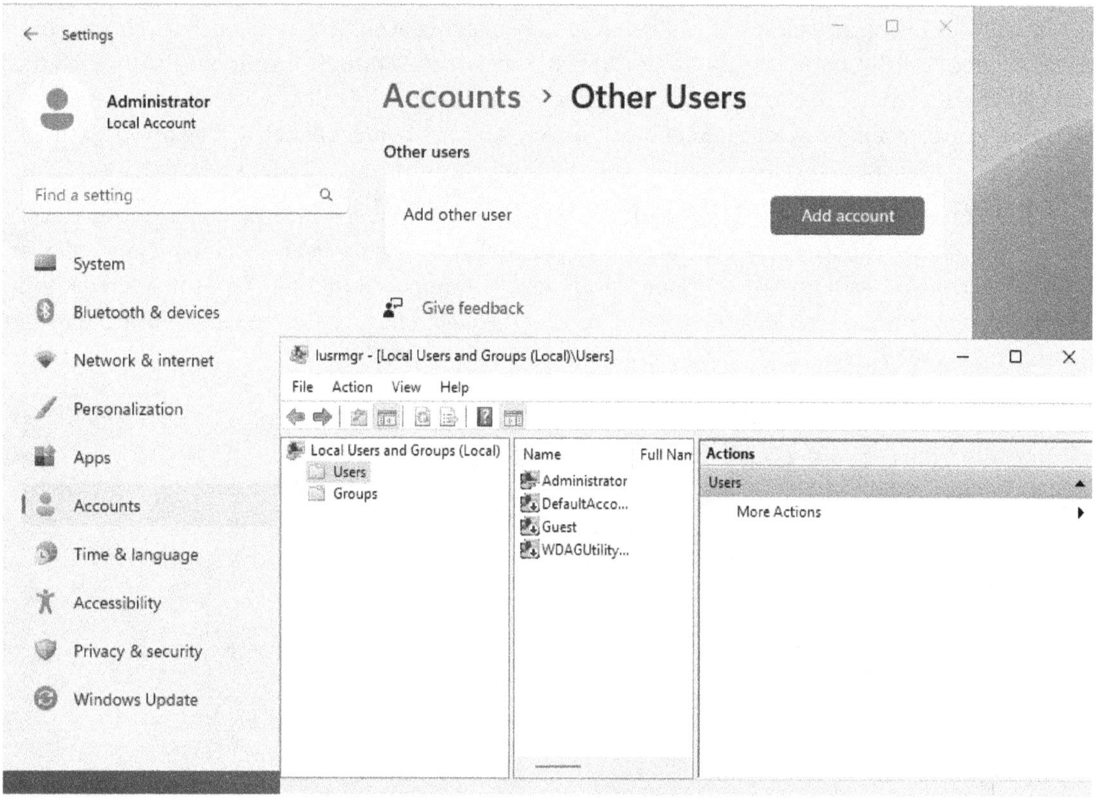

Figure 1.16: Adding a user account via Settings

What in the world is that? Not what I expected, unfortunately. To my surprise, the old **Control Panel** user account launches a nice, fresh-looking interface from which I can create new user accounts. Accessing user accounts via the newer **Settings** console launches me into the old **Local Users and Groups** manager. Technically, from here, I could go ahead and create new user accounts, but it seems like there is some sort of a disconnect here. You would naturally think that the new **Settings** would initiate the newer, nicer screen to add new user accounts, but we found the opposite to be true.

We walked through this simple example of attempting to perform the same function through two different interfaces to showcase that there are some items that can, and must, be performed within the new **Settings** menu context, but there are many functions within Windows that still need to be accomplished through our traditional interfaces. While **Control Panel** continues to exist, and probably will for a very long time, you should start navigating your way around the **Settings** menu and figure out what is available inside, so that you can start to shape your ideas for the best combination of both worlds in order to manage your servers effectively.

Just one last thing to point out as we start getting comfortable with the way that the new **Settings** menu looks: many of the settings that we configure in our servers are on/off types of settings. By that I mean we are setting something to either one option or another. Historically, these kinds of configurations were handled by either drop-down menus or radio buttons. That is normal; that is expected; that is Windows. Now, you will start to see little swipe bars, or sliders, that allow you to switch settings on or off, like a light switch. Anyone who has used the settings interface of any smartphone knows exactly what I am talking about. This user interface behavior has now made its way into the full Windows operating systems and is probably here to stay. Just to give you an idea of what it looks like in the context of the new **Settings** menu, here is a screenshot of the current **Windows Update** -> **Advanced options** settings page.

This is a good example of those on/off slider buttons:

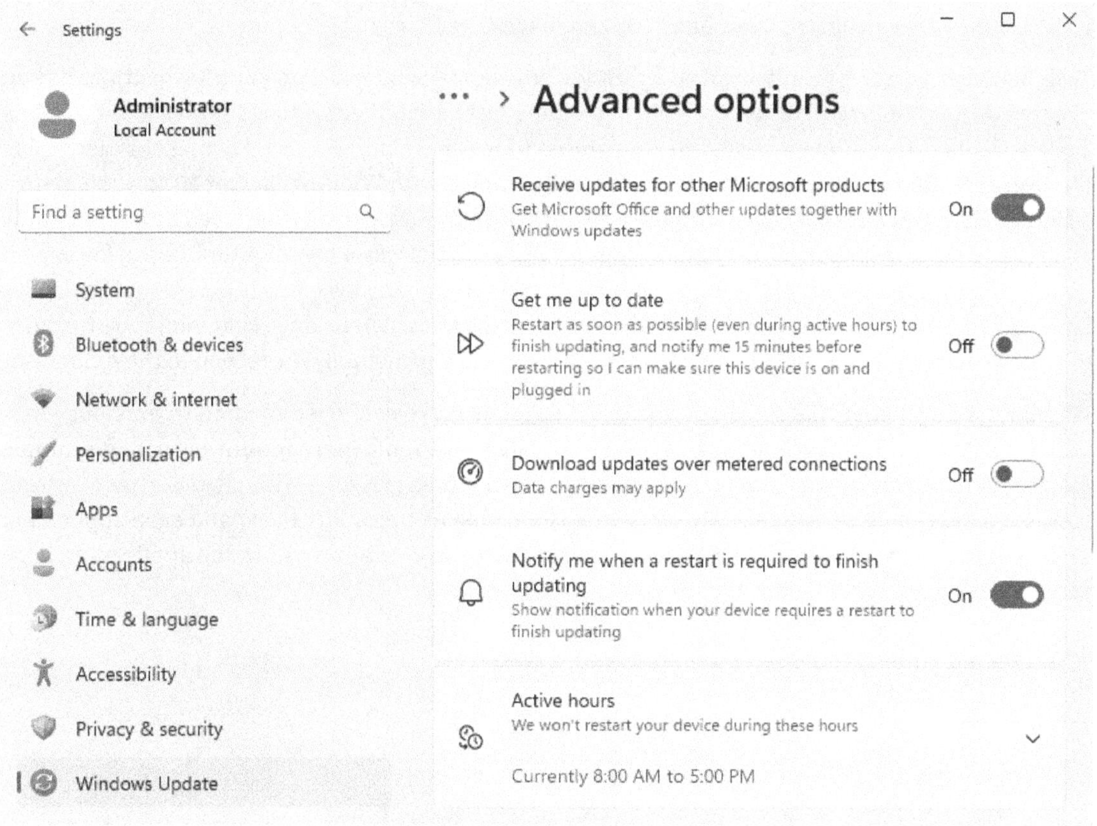

Figure 1.17: Windows Update | Advanced options

Let's explore the **Task Manager** tool next.

Task Manager

Task Manager is a tool that has existed in all Windows operating systems since the first days of the graphical interface, but it has evolved quite a bit over the years. This tool is essential for troubleshooting problems happening inside Windows, and for terminating applications or processes that seem to be "stuck." One of the goals of Windows Server 2025 is to be even more useful and reliable than any previous version of Windows Server has been. So, it only makes sense that we finally remove **Task Manager** altogether, since it simply won't be needed anymore, right?

I'm kidding, of course! While Server 2025 will hopefully prove itself to indeed be the most stable and least needy operating system we have ever seen from Microsoft, **Task Manager** still exists and will still be needed by server administrators everywhere. If you haven't taken a close look at **Task Manager** in a while, it has changed significantly over the past few releases. Now that we have adopted the Windows 11 GUI, along with it comes a brand-new **Task Manager**.

Task Manager is still typically invoked by either hitting *Ctrl + Alt + Del* on your keyboard and then clicking on **Task Manager**, or by right-clicking on the taskbar and then choosing **Task Manager**. You can also launch **Task Manager** with the key combination *Ctrl + Shift + Esc* or by typing `taskmgr` inside the **Run** or **Search** dialog boxes. If you have already worked with Windows Server 2022, you'll notice a change right away. Previously, a miniature version of **Task Manager** was displayed by default—only a simple list of applications that were currently running. This was a useful interface for forcing an application to close that may be hung up, but not for much else, and my guess is that 99% of **Task Manager** launches were immediately followed by a click on the **More details** link. That miniature instance of **Task Manager** is gone, and launching **Task Manager** via any method will get you to the full toolset.

We immediately notice that the displayed information is more user-friendly than in previous years, with both **Apps** and **Background processes** being categorized in a more intuitive way and multiple instances of the same application being condensed down for easy viewing. This gives a faster overhead view of what is going on with our system, while still giving us the ability to expand each application or process to see what individual components or windows are running within the application, such as in *Figure 1.18*:

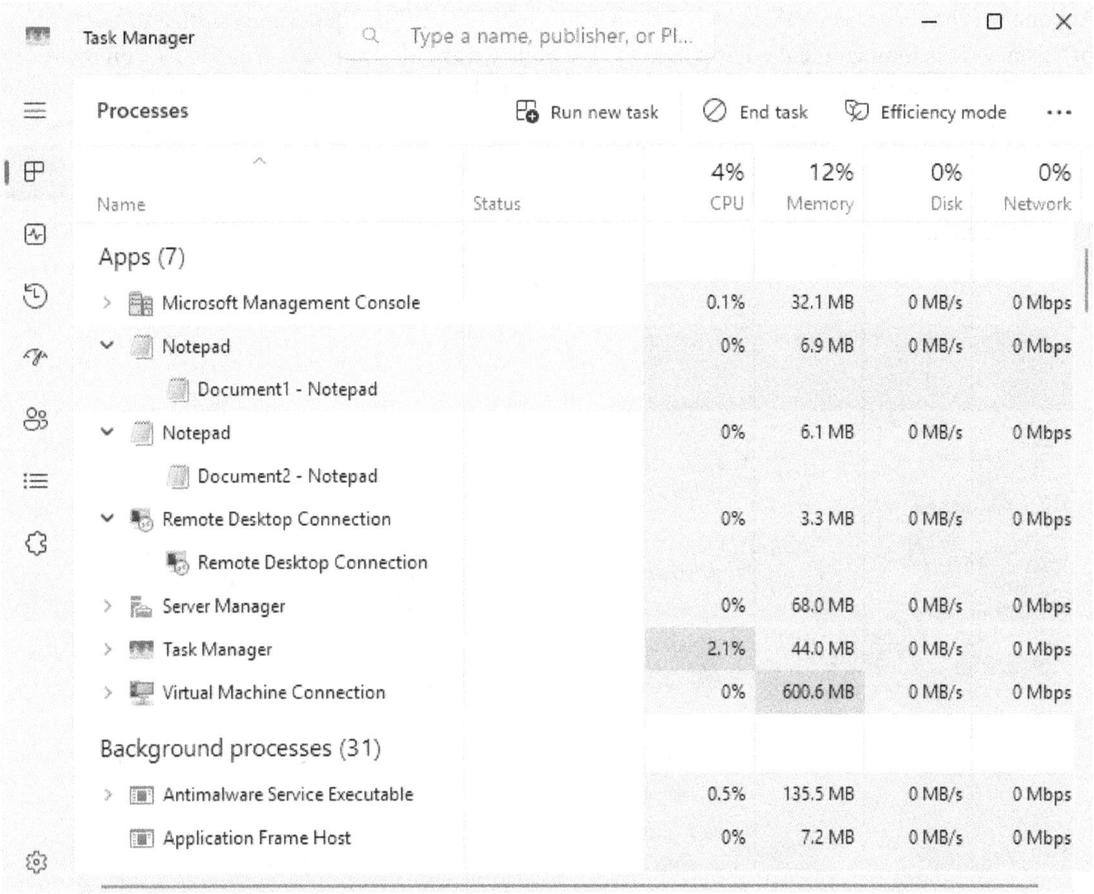

Figure 1.18: Task Manager: Processes

> One of the greatest additions to this new **Task Manager** is the search bar on top! Never before has it been so easy to quickly narrow in on a problematic application or process, or to seek out specific information for your troubleshooting.

Make sure to check out the other sections available inside **Task Manager** as well, listed on the left-hand side. **Users** will show us a list of currently logged-in users and the amount of hardware resources that their user sessions are consuming. This is a nice way to identify on a Remote Desktop Session Host server, for example, an individual who might be causing a slowdown on the server. The **Details** tab is a little bit more of a traditional view of the **Processes** tab, splitting up much of the same information but in the older style that we were used to seeing in versions of the operating system long ago. Then, the **Services** tab is pretty self-explanatory; it shows you the Windows services currently installed on the server, their statuses, and offers the ability to start or stop these services as needed, without having to open the **Services** console separately. **Startup apps** is a quick way to see what applications are configured to start when the operating system starts, and you can easily enable or disable that from happening per application.

Anyone who has been using Windows 11 for a while may already have experience with another section of this new **Task Manager**, called **App history**. Previously, **Task Manager** was only focused on real-time data. While certainly useful for live troubleshooting and the fixing of problems that are happening right now, historical data is always part of troubleshooting methodology. We now have some historical data right here inside **Task Manager**! This instance of Windows Server 2025 that I am using has not been running for very long, and so the **App history** screen is quite boring at the moment. However, if I open the same window on my Windows 11 workstation that I have been using for a while, we'll see a good representation of the useful information this tool is going to present.

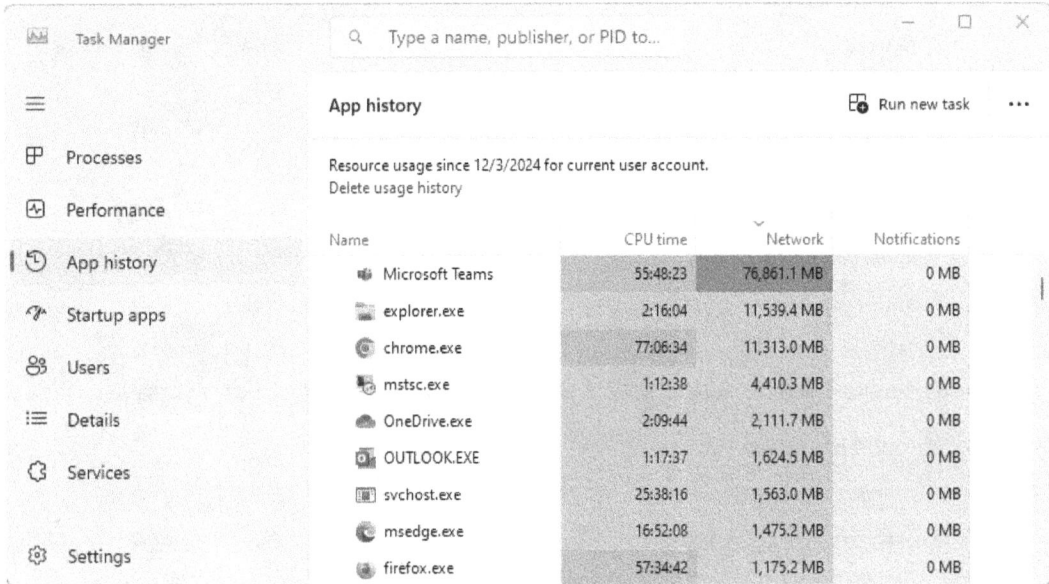

Figure 1.19: Task Manager: App history

The section of **Task Manager** that I skipped over so that I could mention it more specifically next is the **Performance** tab. This is a pretty powerful one. Inside, you can quickly monitor CPU, memory, and Ethernet utilization. As you can see in the following screenshot, I haven't done a very good job of planning resources on this particular virtual machine, as my CPU is hardly being touched but I am almost out of system memory:

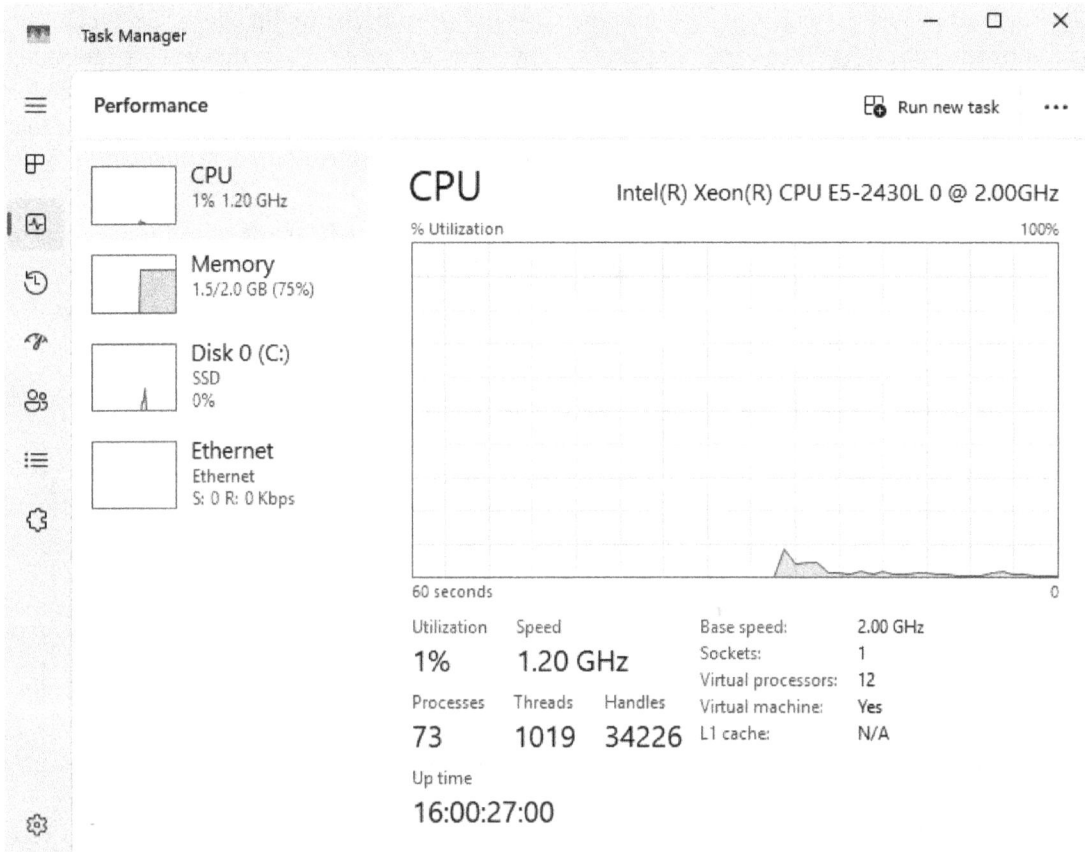

Figure 1.20: Task Manager: Performance

Another useful piece of information available inside this screen is server uptime, and I visit **Task Manager** often for exactly this reason. Discovering the amount of time that a server has been running without a restart can be critical when troubleshooting an issue, and I watch admins time and time again calculating system uptime based on log timestamps. Using **Task Manager** is a much easier way to find that information!

If you are interested in viewing more in-depth data about server performance, there is another application in Windows called **Resource Monitor**. In fact, two other technologies provided inside Windows Server 2025 are useful for monitoring system status, particularly for hardware performance: **Resource Monitor** and **Performance Monitor**. Open up these tools and start testing them out, as they can provide both troubleshooting information and essential baseline data when you spin up a new server. This baseline can then be compared against future testing data so that you can monitor how new applications or services installed on a particular server have affected their resource consumption. We will discuss these additional monitoring tools in *Chapter 17, Troubleshooting*.

Moving back to **Task Manager,** there is just one other little neat trick I would like to test. Still inside the **Performance** tab, go ahead and right-click on any particular piece of data that you are interested in. I will right-click on the **CPU** information near the left side of the window. This opens up a dialog box with a few options, of which I am going to click on **Summary view**. This condenses the data that was previously taking up about half of my screen real estate into a tiny little window, which I can move to the corner of my screen. This is a nice way to always keep hardware utilization data on the screen as you navigate through and work on your server, so that you can watch for any spikes or increases in resource consumption when making changes to the system:

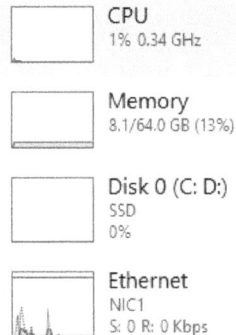

CPU
1% 0.34 GHz

Memory
8.1/64.0 GB (13%)

Disk 0 (C: D:)
SSD
0%

Ethernet
NIC1
S: 0 R: 0 Kbps

Figure 1.21: Task Manager: Summary Resources

Now let's check out an often-underutilized function called **Task View**!

Task View

Task View is a sweet feature that first appeared in Windows 10 and Windows Server 2016 and continues to carry over into Server 2025. It is a similar idea to that of holding down the *Alt* key and then pressing *Tab* in order to cycle through the applications that you currently have running. For anyone who has never tried that, go ahead and hold down those two keys on your keyboard right now. Depending on what version of Windows you are running, your screen might look slightly different from this, but in effect, it's the same information. You can see all of the programs you currently have open, and you can cycle through them from left to right using additional presses of the *Tab* button. Alternatively, use *Alt* + *Shift* + *Tab* in order to cycle through them in reverse order. When you have many windows open, it is perhaps easier to simply use the mouse to jump to any specific window:

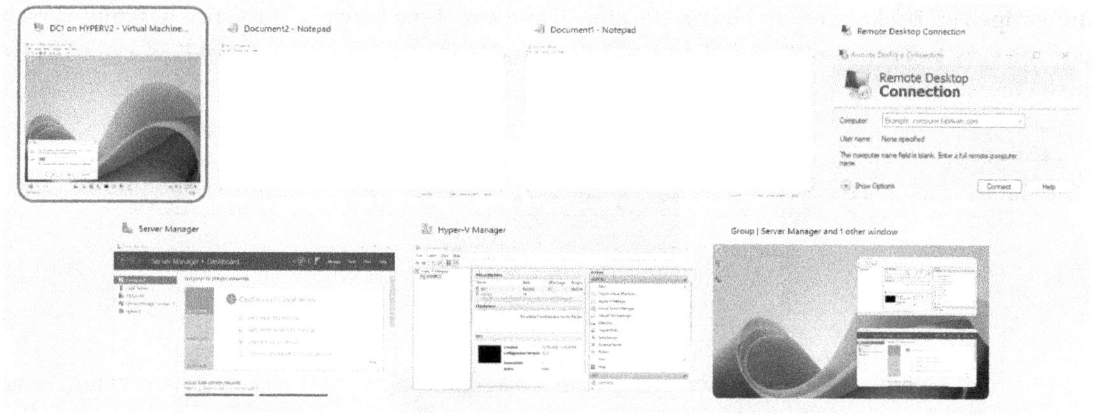

Figure 1.22: Alt + Tab to shuffle between open windows

Task View is quite a bit more powerful than this, because it adds the capability of managing multiple full desktops' worth of windows and applications. For example, if you were working on two different projects on the same server, and each project required you to have many different windows open at the same time, you would start to burn a lot of time switching back and forth between all of your different apps and windows in order to find what you were looking for. Using **Task View**, you could leave all of your open windows for the first project on your first desktop, and open all of the windows dealing with the second project on a second desktop. Then, with two clicks, you could easily switch back and forth between the different desktops, using the **Task View** button. By default, **Task View** is the little button down in the taskbar, immediately to the right of the search bar. Go ahead and click on it now—it looks like this:

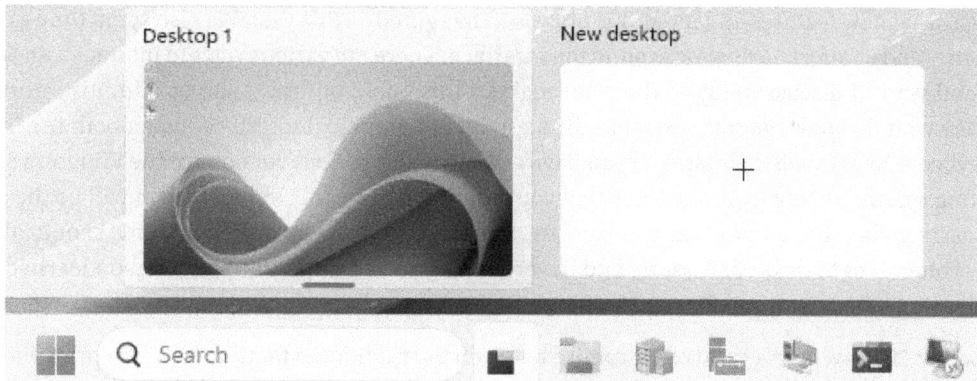

Figure 1.23: The Task View button

You'll now see a listing of your currently open windows; this looks very similar to the *Alt + Tab* functionality we looked at earlier. The primary difference is the option called out in *Figure 1.23*, which gives you the option to create a new desktop. Go ahead and click on that, and you will now discover that clicks on the **Task View** button show that you are running two separate desktops, **Desktop 1** and **Desktop 2**. Flip back and forth between the two desktops, and you will find that you can run completely separate applications between the two desktop views. In *Figure 1.24*, you can tell that I have different things open on **Desktop 1** than I do on **Desktop 2,** and switching between these two desktops is very fast and easy. You can even drag and drop existing windows between different desktops, right on this **Task View** screen:

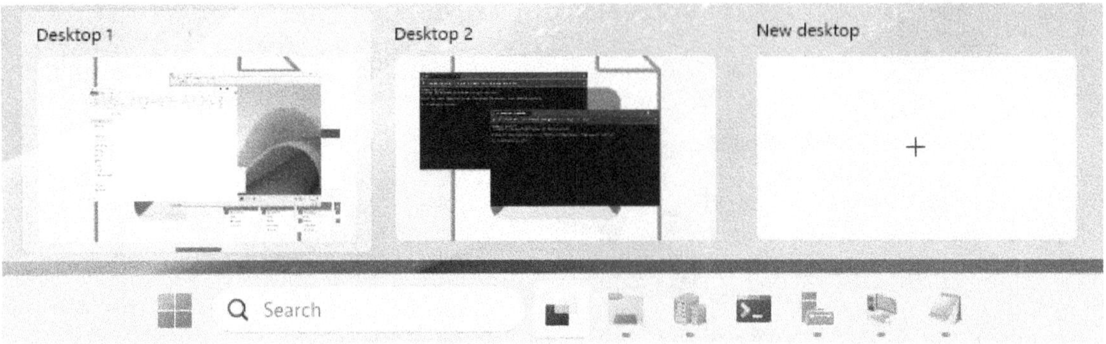

Figure 1.24: Navigating multiple desktops

Task View is a great way to stay organized and efficient by utilizing multiple desktops on the same server. I suppose it is kind of like running dual monitors, or three, four, or more, all from a single physical monitor screen.

If you want to avoid having to click on the icon for **Task View**, pressing *WinKey + Tab* on your keyboard does the same thing!

Summary

This first chapter on Windows Server 2025 was an exploration of what it means to be a server and to discover what new features and functions Microsoft has gifted us this year. We also spent time gaining familiarity and comfort navigating around the interface. There are various ways to interact with Server 2025, and we will discuss many of them throughout this book, but most server administrators will interface with this new operating system through the full graphical interface, using both the mouse and keyboard to perform their tasks. If you have worked with previous versions of the Windows Server operating system, then a lot of the tools that you will use to drive this new platform will be the same, or at least similar, to the ones that you have used in the past. New operating systems should always be an evolution of their predecessors, and never entirely new. I think this was a lesson learned with the release of Windows 8 and Server 2012.

With Server 2025, we find a great compromise between the traditional familiarity of the prior versions of Windows and the new benefits that come with rounded edges and touch-friendly screens, which will be used more and more often as we move toward the future of Windows-based devices. In the next chapter, we'll start putting rubber to the road as we install and begin managing Windows Server 2025.

Questions

Put your knowledge to the test with the following questions. If you need a hand (or just want to double-check), you'll find all the answers in the *Appendix* section of the book.

1. In Windows Server 2025, how can you launch an elevated Terminal prompt with two mouse clicks?
2. What is the keyboard combination to open the **Quick Admin Tasks** menu?
3. What is the name of Microsoft's cloud service offering?
4. Which Windows Server release model has disappeared with the advent of Windows Server 2022?
5. How many virtual machines can run on top of a Windows Server 2025 Standard host, with default licensing?
6. What installation option for Windows Server 2025 does not have a graphical user interface?
7. Which is the correct verbiage for the latest release of Windows Server 2025, **Long-Term Servicing Branch (LTSB)** or **Long-Term Servicing Channel (LTSC)**?
8. What is the correct tool from which to change configurations on Windows Server 2025, **Windows Settings** or **Control Panel**?
9. What key combination can be used to launch **Task View** without touching your mouse?

2

Installation and Management

Reading about all of the great things that Windows Server 2025 brings into your life is helpful, but I realize that some of you are sitting back thinking, *That's great to read about, but how do I really get started playing around with this for myself?* Reading about technology is never as good as experiencing it for yourself, and most people learn best when they are working hands-on with their research subject. One of the biggest goals of this book is to make sure we enable you to *use* the product. Rattling off facts about new features and efficiency is fine and dandy, but ultimately worthless if you aren't able to make it work in real life. So, let's make this chunk of raw server metal do some work for us.

In this chapter, we will be covering the following:

- Technical requirements
- Installing Windows Server 2025
- Installing roles and features
- Centralized management and monitoring
- Windows Admin Center
- Azure Arc
- Quick server rollouts with Sysprep
- In-place upgrading to Windows Server 2025

Technical requirements

When planning for the build of a new server, many of the decisions that you need to make are licensing-type decisions. What roles do you intend to install on this server? Do they require a special edition? Can the more common Server 2025 Standard edition handle it, or do we need the Datacenter edition for our purposes? Is Server Core going to be beneficial from a security perspective, or do we need the full Desktop Experience? In these days of Hyper-V servers having the ability to spin up virtual machines on a whim, we often proceed without much consideration of the hardware of a server, but there are certainly still instances where physical equipment will be responsible for hosting the Windows Server 2025 operating system.

In these cases, you need to be aware of the requirements for this new platform, so let us take a minute to list those specifics. This information is available in longer form on the Microsoft Learn website if you need to double-check any specifics, but here are your summarized minimum system requirements (`https://learn.microsoft.com/en-us/windows-server/get-started/hardware-requirements?tabs=cpu&pivots=windows-server-2025`):

- **CPU**: 1.4 GHz 64-bit that supports a number of things—NX, DEP, CMPXCHG16b, LAHF/SAHF, PrefetchW, and SLAT.

- **RAM**: 512 MB ECC memory minimum for Server Core, or a recommended 4 GB minimum for a server running Desktop Experience. Microsoft officially lists it as 2 GB minimum, 4 GB recommended; however, I can tell you that it is possible to install and run Desktop Experience with far fewer than 2 GB (such as inside a test lab), but the performance of that server will suffer. Interestingly, the Server 2025 installer will not even work unless your **virtual machine** (VM) server has at least 800 MB of RAM, so you'll need to start there. Following **operating system** (OS) installation, you could back it down lower if needed.

- **Disk**: Server 2025 requires a **PCI Express (PCIe)** storage adapter. ATA/PATA/IDE are not allowed for boot drives. The minimum storage space requirement is 32 GB, but Desktop Experience consumes about 4 GB more space than Server Core, so take that into consideration.

Keep in mind, these are the *bare minimum* specs that your server is going to require. Any real server in a production environment will need far more memory and disk space, and there is no magic number for what you will need. It depends on what workload you are going to expect out of your server.

One example of hardware that is not specifically *required* but is almost certainly going to be in place for 99% of servers being built is a TPM 2.0 chip. These hardware chips have been around for many years now and enable functionality such as BitLocker. You don't necessarily need to run BitLocker on your server, but these chips are now considered commonplace, and you really should never buy a workstation or server that does not have a TPM 2.0.

In fact, there is some cool news about just how far you can go with assigning resources in this new version. Windows Server 2022 supported 48 TB of memory and 2,048 logical CPU cores, which was really impressive. Compared with Windows Server 2025, these numbers are small potatoes. Windows Server 2025 now boasts support for 4 PB of RAM (yes, you read that right, petabytes!!!), and an *unlimited* number of CPU cores. Administrators with an actual need to run more than 48 TB of memory in a single server are probably using it as a big-time hypervisor or as part of their Azure local infrastructure, but can you imagine a SQL server with petabytes of memory? It is a common thing for SQL servers to chew up however much RAM you throw at the server, causing us to impose limits within SQL itself about how much memory it can grab. Perhaps with a PB at its disposal, SQL would actually leave some unallocated for the OS. Nah, probably not...

Installing Windows Server 2025

In general, the installation process for Microsoft OSs has improved dramatically over the past 20 years. I assume that a lot of you, as IT professionals, are also the de facto *neighborhood computer guru*, constantly asked by friends and family to fix or rebuild their computers. If you're anything like me, this means you are still occasionally rebuilding operating systems such as Windows 7, maybe even XP. Looking at the bright blue setup screens and finding a keyboard with the *F8* key are imperative to this process. To spend two hours simply installing the base OS and bringing it up to the highest service pack level is pretty normal. Compared to that timeline, installing a modern OS such as Windows Server 2025 is almost unbelievably fast and simple.

It is very likely that many of you have completed this process numerous times already, and if that is the case, feel free to skip ahead a couple of pages. But for anyone new to the Microsoft world, or new to IT in general, I'd like to take just a couple of quick pages to make sure you have a baseline to get started with. Without earning your **Installing an OS 101** badge on your tool belt, that shiny server will make for an interesting piece of wall art.

Burning that ISO

The first thing you must do is acquire some installation media. The simplest and most straightforward way to implement a single new server is to download an .ISO file from Microsoft, burn that .ISO file to a DVD (don't worry, we will cover USB media next), and slide that DVD in to be used for installation. If you are testing out Server 2025 for personal reasons and do not own any licensing for it, open a search engine such as **Bing** and search for something like `Download Windows Server 2025 Evaluation`. Make sure to click the link that is an actual `Microsoft.com` entity, and you will find options for either evaluating Windows Server 2025 inside Azure, or downloading an .ISO file and saving it onto the hard drive of your computer.

If you do happen to own licensing for Server 2025, or if for any reason you have a Microsoft Visual Studio license, then there is an even better way to acquire your installation media. Simply log in to your **Visual Studio** portal and use the **Downloads** section to search for Windows Server 2025. In the past, Microsoft software portals were quite confusing and difficult to find what you were looking for. The Visual Studio portal has been recently updated and is by far the most user-friendly interface for grabbing software and license keys that I have ever seen from Microsoft.

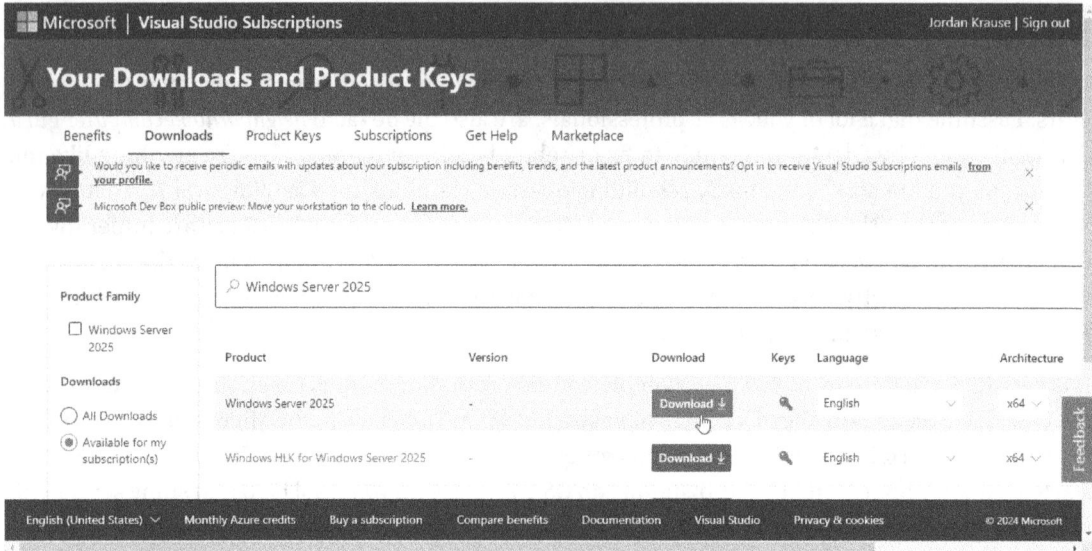

Figure 2.1: Downloading the installer with Visual Studio

In the past, the trickiest part of getting an .ISO file to be a workable DVD was the need to download some kind of third-party tool in order to burn it to a disk while making it bootable. If you are running an older client OS on your computer, this may still be the case for you. I have watched many who are new to this process take the .ISO file, drag it over to their disk drive, and start burning the disk. This creates a DVD with the .ISO file sitting on it, but that .ISO file is still packaged up and not bootable in any way, so the disk would be worthless to your new piece of server hardware. Luckily, the newer versions of the Windows client operating systems have built-in functions for dealing with .ISO files, which makes the correct burning process very simple.

Once you have your .ISO file for the Windows Server 2025 installation downloaded onto your computer, insert a fresh DVD into your disk drive and browse to the new file. Simply right-click on the .ISO file, and then choose your menu option for **Burn disc image.** This launches a simple wizard that will extract and burn your new .ISO file the correct way onto the DVD, making it a bootable installation media for your new server, as shown in *Figure 2.2*:

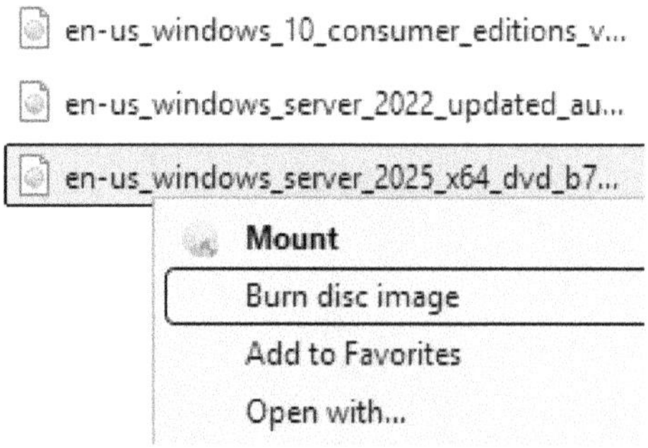

Figure 2.2: Burning your .ISO file onto a DVD

It is probable that when you attempt to download Windows Server 2025 and use this Windows Disc Image Burner utility with a DVD that you grabbed off your stack of standard blank DVDs, you will receive the following error message: **The disc image file is too large and will not fit on the recordable disc.**

This should come as no surprise because our operating system installer files have been getting larger and larger over the years. We have now reached the critical tipping point where the standard Server 2025 ISO installer is larger than a standard 4.7 GB DVD. To burn this ISO onto a DVD, you will need to hit the store and find some dual-layer disks that can handle more data.

Creating a bootable USB stick with software

DVDs can be cumbersome and annoying, and now they are also too small for our purposes. Therefore, when installing newer, larger operating systems, it is becoming commonplace to prep a USB stick to use for the installation of the operating system rather than relying on a DVD.

To do this, all you need is a Windows computer, a USB stick that is at least 8 GB, and access to the internet. You will need to download the same ISO that we discussed earlier, as that contains all of the installation files for Server 2025. Then, you will also need to download and install some kind of bootable USB creation tool.

There are various free ones available (**Rufus** is pretty popular), but the one straight from Microsoft is called the **Windows 7 USB/DVD Download Tool**. Why does it still to this day have this crazy name that includes the words *Windows 7* right in it? Don't ask me.

Regardless of the old name, it works well and is a quick, easy, and free way to prep your bootable USB sticks for fresh operating system installations. I should point out that this tool has nothing to do with Windows 7. It will take any .ISO file and turn it into a bootable USB stick. That ISO can be a Windows 10 or Server 2022 ISO file, and it still works just fine. You can also install and run the Windows 7 USB/DVD Download Tool on a Windows 10 or 11 workstation without any trouble.

Once the USB/DVD Download Tool is installed, launch the application and simply walk through the four-step wizard.

This process will erase and format your USB stick. Make sure nothing important is stored there!

You will need to identify the ISO that you want the tool to grab information from, then choose your USB stick from a drop-down list. After that, simply click the **Begin copying** button, and this tool will turn your USB stick into a bootable stick capable of installing the entire Windows Server 2025 OS, as shown in *Figure 2.3*:

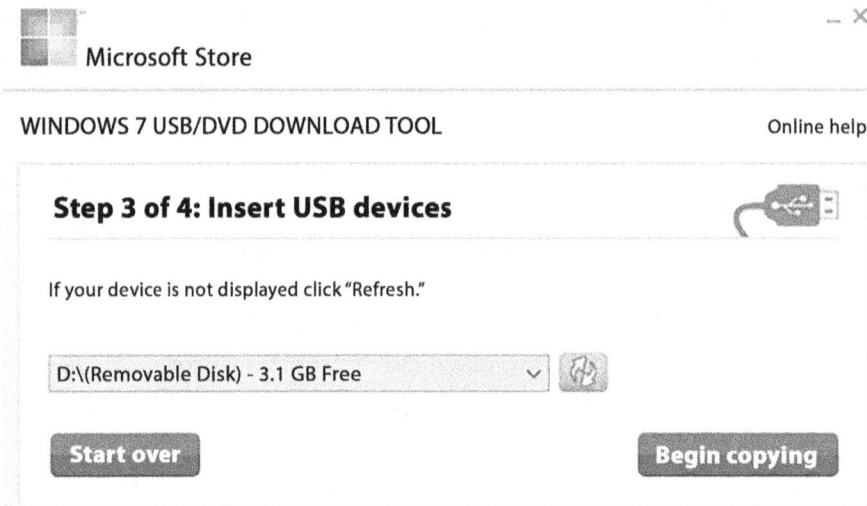

Figure 2.3: Creating a bootable USB stick

Creating a bootable USB stick with PowerShell

Alternatively, there is another option to create a bootable USB drive that doesn't involve software at all. I tend to prefer the Windows 7 Download Tool because it is very fast, and I already have it installed on my computer. If you aren't interested in more software on your computer, Microsoft has provided a PowerShell script that serves the same purpose. Here are the steps you would take to perform this task:

1. Download *and mount* the ISO. It is important that you right-click on the ISO and choose the option to "mount" it, which opens that ISO to see all files inside, and assigns this file a drive letter on your system. Take note of this drive letter, so that it can be specified when you run this script.

2. Plug in your USB stick and also take note of the drive letter that Windows assigns to this stick; you'll need to specify it in a minute.

3. Launch PowerShell and paste in the following script. This script is directly from Microsoft; I make no claims on its creation. When run, this script will ask you to specify the drive letter being used by your USB drive, and then ask for the drive letter being used by the mounted ISO file. Once specified, the script will format this USB stick to be empty and bootable, and then copy all contents from the ISO:

    Select the USB drive letter:

    ```
    $usbDriveLetter = Read-Host "Enter USB drive letter (Ex: E)"
    ```

    Format the USB drive:

    ```
    Format-Volume -DriveLetter $usbDriveLetter -FileSystem NTFS
    -NewFileSystemLabel "WinServerUSB" -Confirm:$false | Out-Null
    ```

Select the ISO file mount point:

```
$isoMountPointDriveLetter = Read-Host "Enter ISO mount point drive letter
(Ex: F)"
```

Copy the ISO files to the USB drive:

```
$source = "$($isoMountPointDriveLetter):" $destination =
"$($usbDriveLetter):" robocopy $source $destination /COPYALL /Z /E /SEC
/R:3 /W:3
```

Make the USB drive bootable:

```
$usbDriveNumber = (Get-WmiObject -Class Win32_DiskDrive | Where-Object
{$_.InterfaceType -eq "USB" -and $_.DeviceID -like "*$usbDriveLetter"}).
Index bootsect /nt60 $usbDriveLetter | Out-Null
```

Receive a task completion notification:

```
Write-Host "Copy operation complete" Start-Sleep -Seconds 2
```

♀ **Quick tip:** Enhance your coding experience with the **AI Code Explainer** and **Quick Copy** features. Open this book in the next-gen Packt Reader. Click the **Copy** button

(1) to quickly copy code into your coding environment, or click the **Explain** button

(2) to get the AI assistant to explain a block of code to you.

```
                                                    Copy      Explain
function calculate(a, b) {
    return {sum: a + b};                             1          2
};
```

📖 **The next-gen Packt Reader** is included for free with the purchase of this book. Scan the QR code OR visit https://packtpub.com/unlock, then use the search bar to find this book by name. Double-check the edition shown to make sure you get the right one.

Your USB drive is now prepped and ready.

Running the installer

Now, go ahead and plug your newly created DVD or bootable USB into the new server hardware. Boot to it, and you will finally see the installation wizard for Windows Server 2025. Now, there really are not that many options for you to choose from within these wizards, so we won't spend a lot of time here. For the most part, you are simply clicking on the **Next** button to progress through the screens, but there are a few specific places where you will need to make decisions along the way.

After choosing your language and keyboard settings, the next screen is something we have never seen previously in a Windows Server installer. Repair of server operating systems has always been a little cumbersome, requiring you to boot into **Recovery Mode** and seek out troubleshooting functions. Microsoft has now built a **Repair my PC** option directly into the installer process! While we have no reason to select that option here because we are installing a fresh server and the top option is clearly right for us today, I love this adjustment of the setup wizards. Those who have been through Windows Server setup before will also notice that this installation wizard makes more common sense than in years past.

On this initial screen, you simply define that you intend to install Windows Server. That makes sense and is very straightforward. In previous versions of Windows Server installation, the screen asked whether you were planning to upgrade your server or install via **Custom settings**. That older screen was always confusing to new admins and didn't carry a lot of common sense. I am excited to see this change!

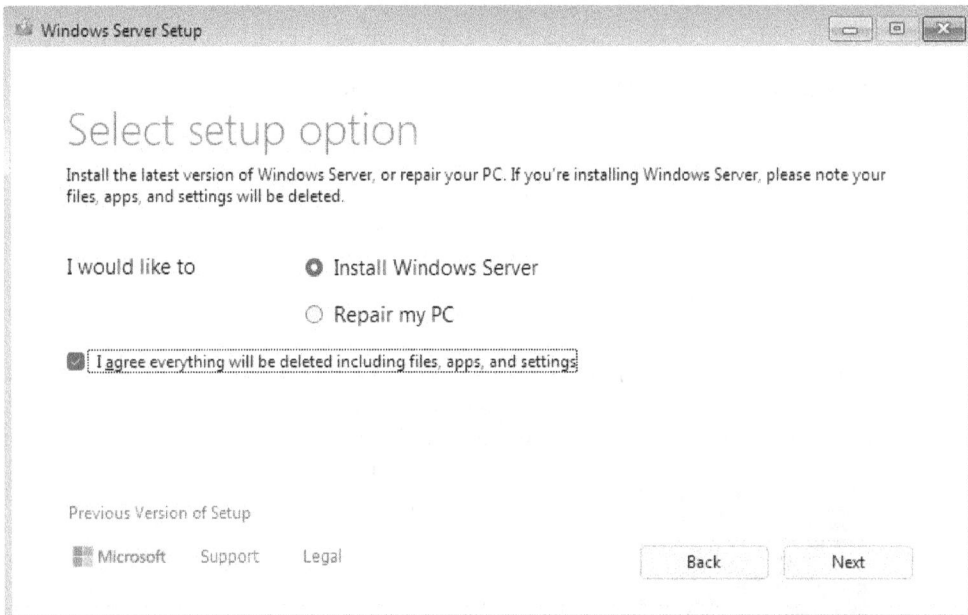

Figure 2.4: Installing Windows Server 2025

You may have also noticed the small link near the bottom of *Figure 2.4*, **Previous Version of Setup.** I cannot think of a technical reason why Microsoft is maintaining both versions of the installer here inside setup, so perhaps this option is simply for those who prefer the older installer and are not quite ready for the change to the updated interface. No matter the reason, if you prefer to look at the older installation wizard screens that were our home base for installing the OS from Server 2016 through Server 2022, simply click on that little link, and you will instead find yourself looking at that old familiar hue of dark blue.

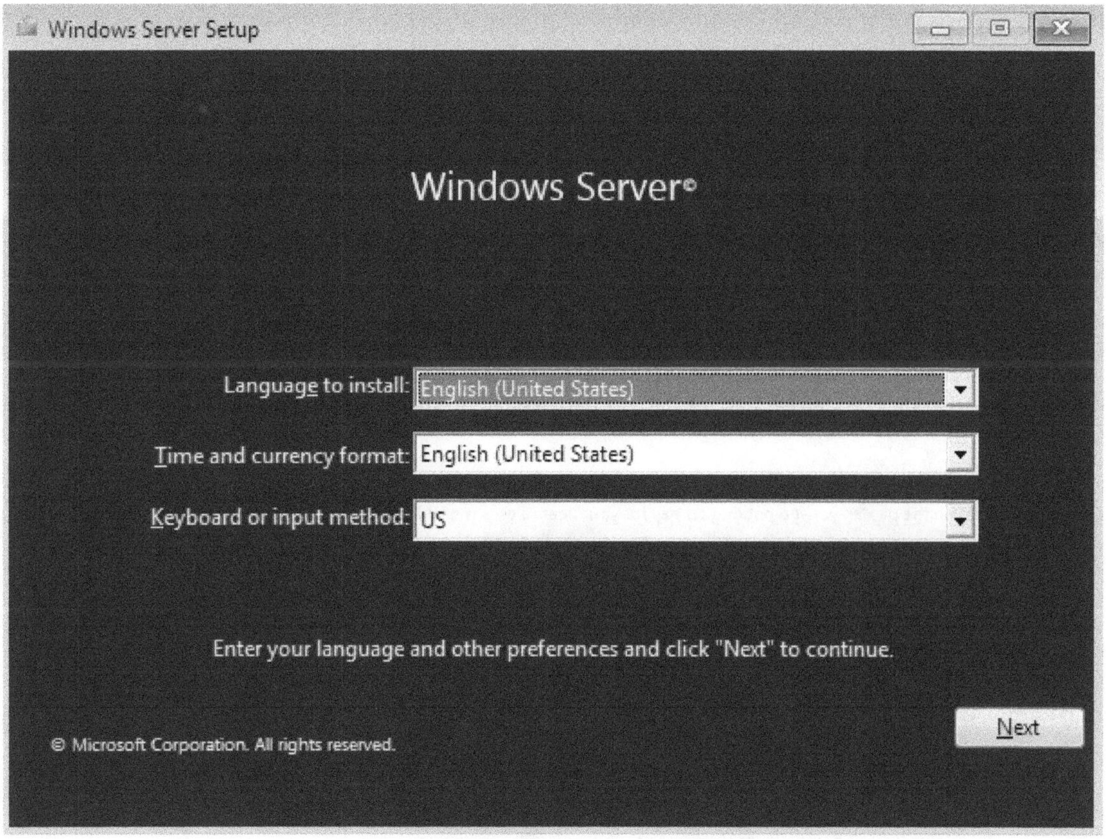

Figure 2.5: Previous version of setup

Moving forward with the updated installation process, check the box shown in *Figure 2.4* to acknowledge that your existing files, apps, and settings will be deleted (we are installing on a fresh drive, so nothing exists), and then we find ourselves facing another updated screen with a brand-new option. The ability to utilize a product key to license your new server is nothing new, but the **Pay-as-you-go** option is very unexpected! We talked about this new option in *Chapter 1*; rather than purchasing one-time perpetual licensing for your server operating system, you now have the ability to tie this new server into an Azure subscription, and (just as you would do for servers running inside Azure) pay for only what you use on this new server. This is quite a novel idea for on-prem server infrastructure!

If you are building out a test lab or have not yet purchased your Server 2025 licensing, simply click the link near the bottom (**I don't have a product key**), and you will progress to the next screen without specifying any information for licensing. This will place Windows Server 2025 into a fully working mode, but not legally activated, and you will always have a watermark displayed in the lower-right part of your screen until you do license this new instance of Windows.

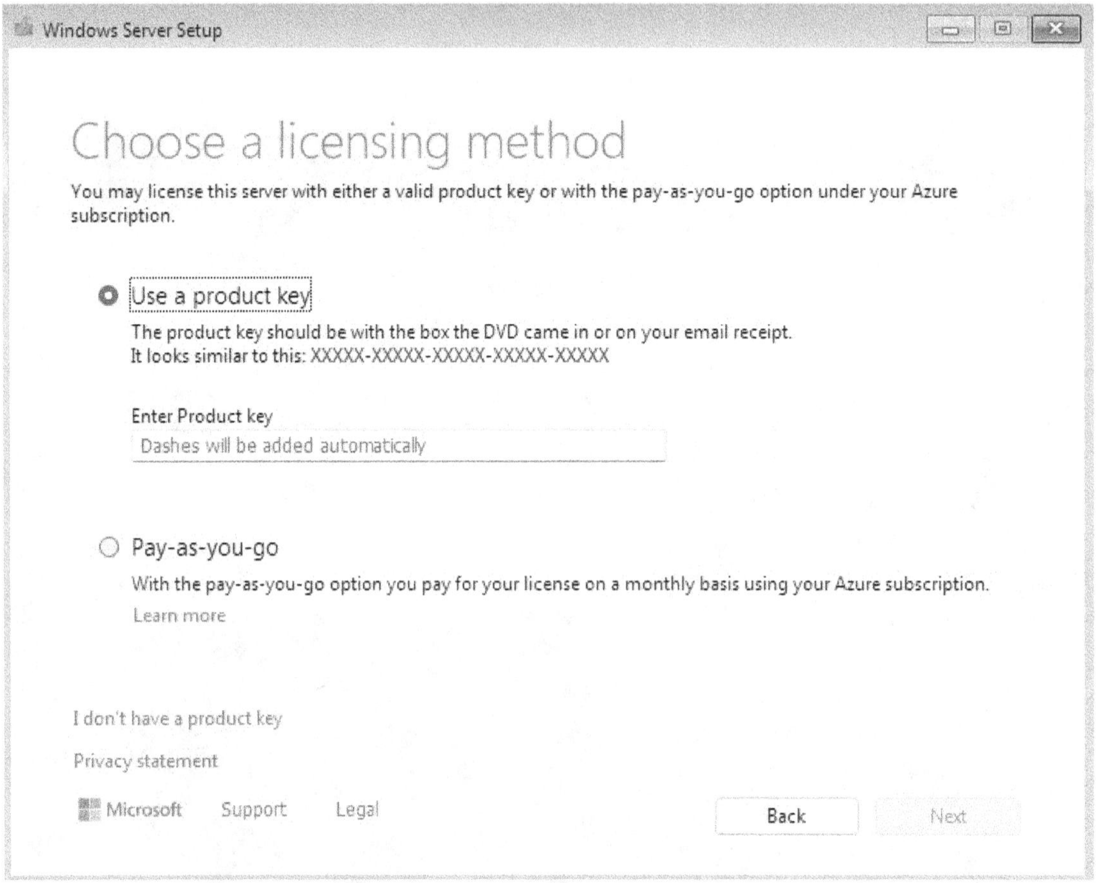

Windows Server Setup

Choose a licensing method

You may license this server with either a valid product key or with the pay-as-you-go option under your Azure subscription.

- ⊙ Use a product key
  The product key should be with the box the DVD came in or on your email receipt.
  It looks similar to this: XXXXX-XXXXX-XXXXX-XXXXX-XXXXX

  Enter Product key
  Dashes will be added automatically

- ○ Pay-as-you-go
  With the pay-as-you-go option you pay for your license on a monthly basis using your Azure subscription.
  Learn more

I don't have a product key

Privacy statement

Microsoft   Support   Legal   Back   Next

Figure 2.6: Licensing your new server

Our next screen is interesting and one where you will want to pay close attention. You will find four different installation options for Windows Server 2025. There are what seem to be the "regular" installers for Windows Server 2025 Standard or Datacenter, and then other options that include the words (**Desktop Experience**) for each. Typically, in the Microsoft installer world, clicking on **Next** through every option gives you the most typical and common installation path for whatever it is that you are installing. *Not so with this wizard.* If you simply glide by this screen by clicking on **Next**, you will find yourself with an installation of **Server Core** in the end.

We will talk more about Server Core in *Chapter 11*, but for now, I will just say that if you are expecting to have a server that looks and feels like what we talked about in *Chapter 1, Getting Started with Windows Server 2025*, this default option is not going to be the one that gets you there. This "Desktop Experience" that the wizard is talking about is the full Windows Server graphical interface, which you are more than likely expecting to see once we are done with our installation. So, for the purposes of our installation here, where we want to interact with the server using full color and a mouse, go ahead and choose an option that includes **Desktop Experience** before clicking on the **Next** button, as shown in *Figure 2.7*:

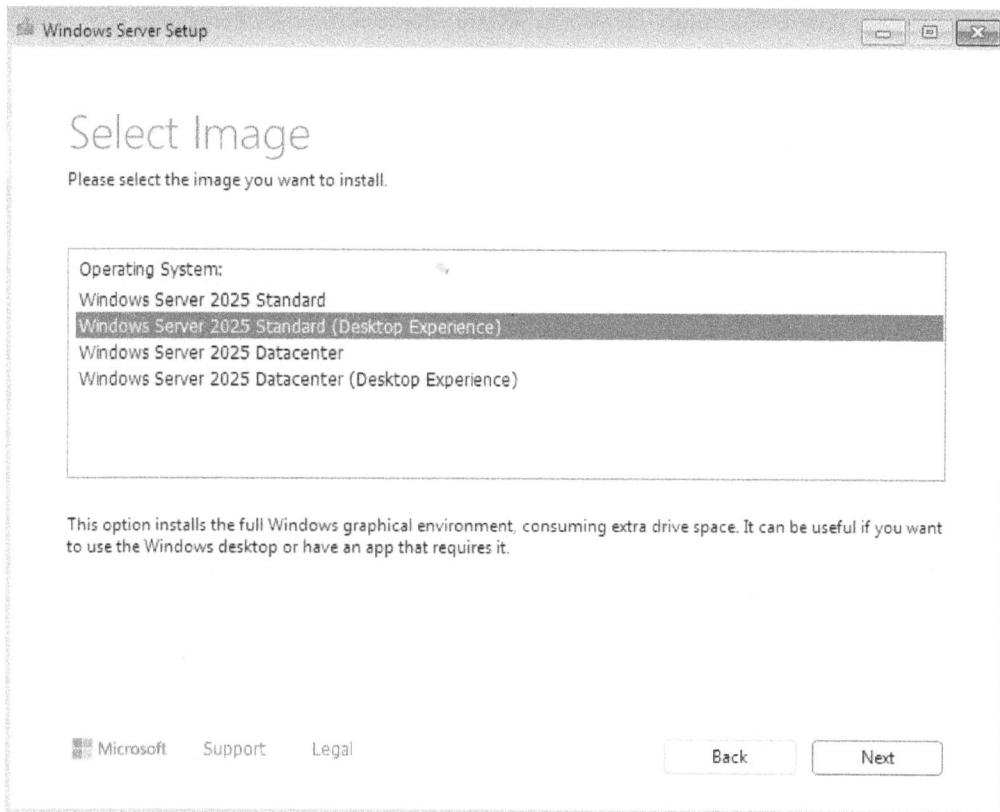

Figure 2.7: Windows Server 2025 installation options

In some previous versions of Windows Server, we had the ability to migrate back and forth from a full Desktop Experience to Server Core, even after the operating system was installed. This does not work in Windows Server 2025! The ability to transition between the two modes disappeared years ago, so it is even more important that you plan your servers properly from the beginning.

After agreeing to licensing terms, we now need to decide *where* we want to install our new copy of Windows Server 2025. In many cases, you will simply click on **Next** here because your server will have just a single hard disk drive, or maybe a single RAID array of disks, and, in either case, you will see a single pool of free space onto which you can install the OS. If you have multiple hard drives installed on your server and they have not been tied together in any way yet, then you will have multiple choices of where to install Windows Server.

I have a single hard disk attached to my virtual server, which has never been used, so I can simply click on **Next** to continue. Note here that if your drives had existing or old data on them, you would have the opportunity, with some built-in disk management tools, to format the disk or delete individual partitions. If you are using some specialized disks that take specific drivers, there is also a **Load driver** button, which you can use to inject these special drivers into the installation wizard in order to view and use these kinds of disks.

Also, it is important to note on this screen that while there is a **Create Partition** button, you do *not* have to do this in order to continue. Many new admins assume that you must manually create the partition so Windows knows where to install its files. On the contrary, if you have unallocated space selected, as I do in *Figure 2.8*, and then simply click **Next**, the installer will take care of creating the necessary partitions for you:

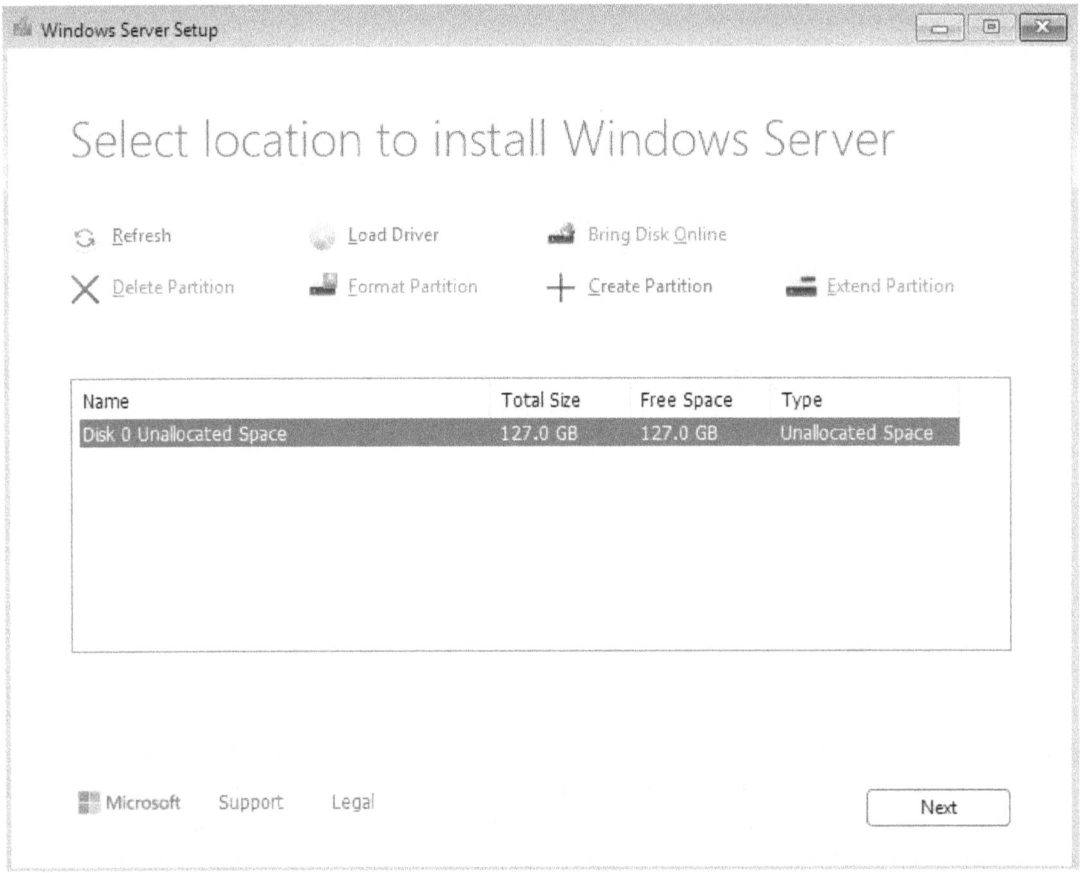

Figure 2.8: Windows installation destination

Now, review your summary screen of installation options, and click that final **Install** button.

That's it! You will see the server installer start going to town, copying files, installing features, and getting everything ready on the hard drive. This part of the installer runs on its own for a few minutes, and the next time you need to interact with the server, it will be within the graphical interface where you get to define the administrator password. Once you have specified a password, you will find yourself on the Windows desktop. Now you are *really* ready to start making use of your new Windows Server 2025.

Installing roles and features

Installing the OS gets your foot in the door, so to speak, using your server as a server. However, you can't actually do anything useful with your server at this point. On a client desktop system, the base OS is generally all that is needed to start working and consuming data. The server's job is to serve up that data in the first place, and until you tell the server what its purpose is in life, there really isn't anything useful happening in that base OS. This is where we need to utilize **roles** and **features**.

Windows Server 2025 contains many different options for roles. A role is just what the name implies: the installation of a particular role onto a server defines that server's role in the network. In other words, a role gives a server some purpose in life. A feature, on the other hand, is more of a subset of functions that you can install onto a server. Features can complement roles or stand on their own. There are pieces of technology available in Windows Server 2025 that are not installed or turned on by default because these features wouldn't be used in all circumstances. Everything in the later chapters of this book revolves around the functionality provided by roles and features. They are the bread and butter of a Windows server, and, without their installation, your servers make good paperweights, but not much else.

As we will not take the time in each chapter to cover the installation of every particular role or feature that will be used within the chapter, let's take some time right now to cover the most common paths that admins can take in order to get these roles and features installed on their own servers.

Installing a role using the wizard

Without a doubt, the most common place that roles and features get installed is right inside the graphical wizards available as soon as your OS has been installed. By default, a tool called **Server Manager** launches automatically every time you log in to Windows Server 2025. We will take a closer look at Server Manager itself later in this chapter, but for our purposes here, we will simply use it as a launching platform to get to our wizard, which will guide us through the installation of our first role on this new server we are putting together.

Since you have just logged in to this new server, you should be staring at the **Server Manager** dashboard. Right in the middle of the dashboard, you will see some links available to click on, a quick-start list of action items numbered one through five. If you haven't already done so, put into place any local server configuration that you may need on this machine through the first link, which is called **Configure this local server**.

Items that you will likely want in place are things such as a permanent hostname for the server, IP addressing, and, if you are joining this server to an existing domain (we will discuss domains in *Chapter 3, Active Directory*), you typically handle that process prior to implementing any new roles on the server. But, in our case, we are more specifically interested in the role of installation itself, so we will assume that you have already configured these little bits and pieces to have your server identified and routing on your network.

Go ahead and click on step 2, **Add roles and features**. Another way you can launch the same wizard is by clicking on the **Manage** menu from the top bar inside **Server Manager** and then choosing **Add Roles and Features** from the drop-down list. Selecting either link will bring you into our wizard for installation of the roles, as shown in *Figure 2.9*:

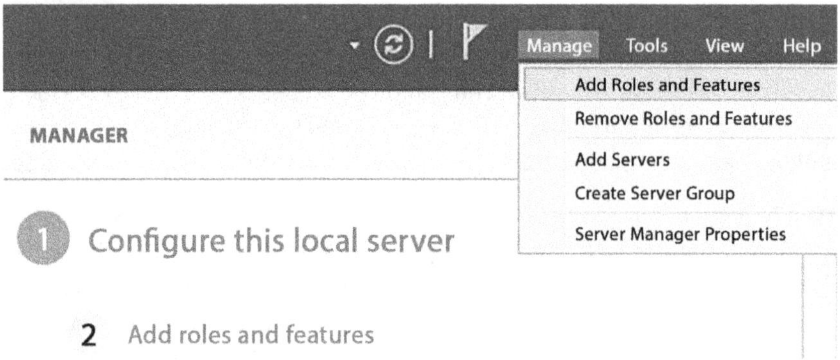

Figure 2.9: Adding roles

You are first taken to a summary screen about installing roles. Go ahead and click **Next** to bypass this screen. Now, we get into our first option, which is an interesting one. We are first asked whether we want to continue with a **role-based** or **feature-based installation**, which is exactly what we have been talking about doing. But the second option here, **Remote Desktop Services installation**, is important to note. Most of us consider the **Remote Desktop Services** (RDS) components of Windows Server to be just another role that we can choose when setting up our server, similar to the installation of any other role. While that is basically true, it is important to note that RDS is so functionally different from the other kinds of roles that the entry path into the installation of any of the RDS components invokes its own wizard by choosing the second option here. So, if you ever find yourself looking for the option to install RDS, and you have glossed over this screen because you are so used to clicking **Next** through it, like I am, remember that you need to head back there to tell the wizard that you want to deal with an RDS component, and the remainder of the screens will adjust accordingly. We will explore RDS more thoroughly in a later chapter of this book.

At the moment, I am working on building out a new test lab full of Windows Server 2025 boxes, and I am still in need of a **domain controller** (DC) to manage Active Directory in my environment. Before installing Active Directory on a server, it is critical that I have a few prerequisites in place, so I have already accomplished those items on my new server. The items that I need to have in place prior to the AD DS role installation are as follows:

- **Static IP:** Assign a static IP address to this server; it is important that a DC maintains a constant IP on the network.
- **DNS:** Define a DNS server on the NIC. If you are building a lab or the beginning of a network, this new DC may well become your first DNS server, in which case, defining 127.0.0.1 as your first DNS server is acceptable.
- **Hostname:** Make sure to give this server a good name. Once you turn a server into a DC, it is unsupported and will cause you grief if you ever try to rename that server.

I have already accomplished these items on my server, so I will continue through my role installation wizard here by leaving the option set to **Role-based or feature-based installation** and clicking on **Next**, as shown in *Figure 2.10*:

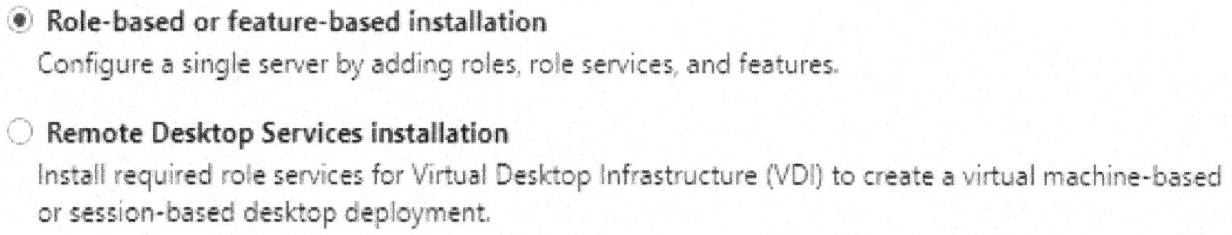

◉ **Role-based or feature-based installation**
   Configure a single server by adding roles, role services, and features.

○ **Remote Desktop Services installation**
   Install required role services for Virtual Desktop Infrastructure (VDI) to create a virtual machine-based or session-based desktop deployment.

Figure 2.10: Selecting Role-based or feature-based installation for most roles

Our **Server Selection** screen is a very powerful one. If you've been through this process before, you have likely glossed over this screen, simply clicking on the **Next** button to progress through it. But essentially, what this screen is doing is asking you where you would like to install this new role or feature. By default, each server will only have itself listed on this screen, so clicking on **Next** to continue is more than likely what you will be doing. However, there are a couple of neat options here.

First, if your Server Manager is aware of other servers in your network and has been configured to monitor them, you will have the option here to install a role or feature remotely onto one of the other servers. We will dig a little deeper into this capability shortly. Another feature on this page, which I haven't seen many people utilize, is the ability to specify that you want to install a role or feature onto a virtual hard disk. Many of us work almost exclusively with virtual servers in this day and age, and you don't even need your virtual server to be running in order to install a role or feature to it! As long as you have access to the VHDX file (the hard disk file) from where you are running Server Manager, you can select a **virtual hard disk** from this screen, which allows you to inject the new role or feature directly into that hard drive. But, as is the case 99% of the time that you will wander through this screen, we are logged directly into the server where we intend to install the role, and so we simply click on **Next**.

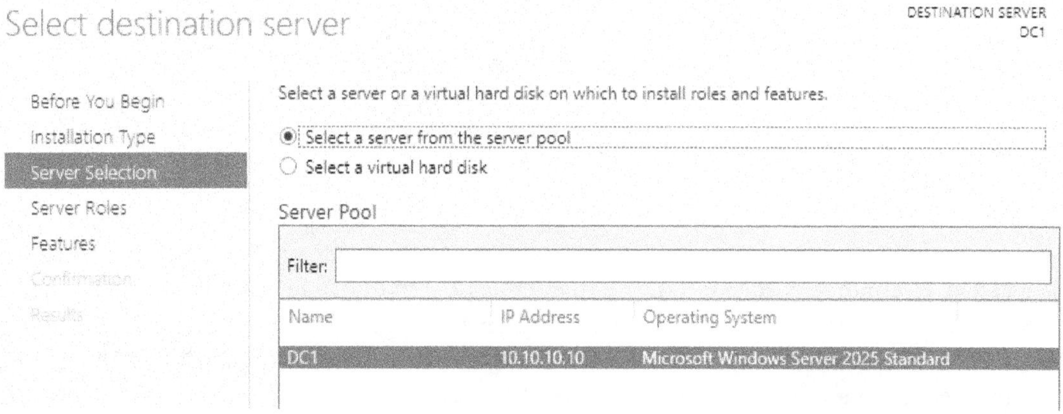

Select destination server   DESTINATION SERVER
                                                                                      DC1

Before You Begin	Select a server or a virtual hard disk on which to install roles and features.
Installation Type	◉ Select a server from the server pool
Server Selection	○ Select a virtual hard disk
Server Roles	Server Pool
Features	Filter:
Confirmation	
Results	Name IP Address Operating System
	DC1 10.10.10.10 Microsoft Windows Server 2025 Standard

Figure 2.11: Selecting the destination server

Next, we have our list of roles that are available to be installed. Clicking on each role will give you a short description of the purpose of that role if you have any questions; we will also talk more about the core infrastructural roles throughout our next few chapters to give you even more information about what the roles do. All we need to do here to install a role onto our new server is check the box and click **Next**. Since this is going to be a domain controller, I will choose the **Active Directory Domain Services** role, and I will multipurpose this server to also be a **DNS server** and a **DHCP server**. With these roles, there is no need to rerun through this wizard three separate times to install all of these roles; I can simply check them all here and let the wizard run the installers together. Whoops, when I clicked on my first checkbox, I got a pop-up message that the **Active Directory Domain Services (AD DS)** role requires some additional features in order to work properly. This is normal behavior, and you will notice that many of the roles that you install will require additional components or features to be installed. All you need to do is click on the **Add Features** button, and it will automatically add these extra pieces for you during the installation process. An example of this is shown in *Figure 2.12*:

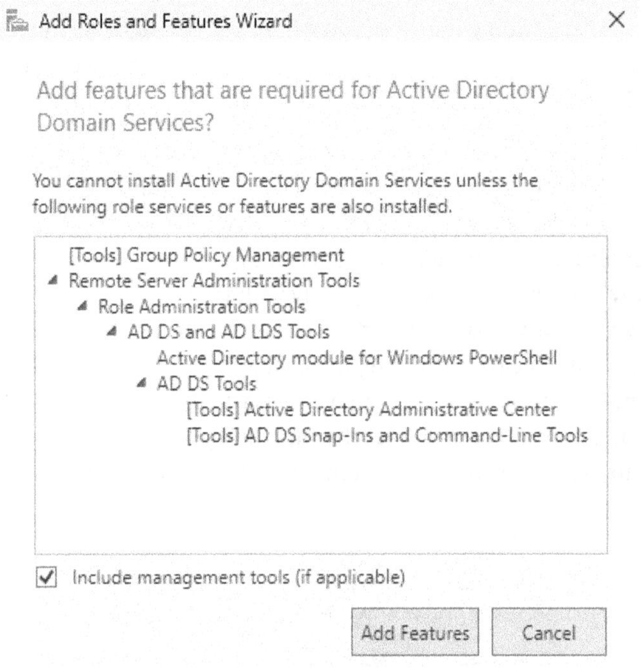

Add Roles and Features Wizard ✕

Add features that are required for Active Directory
Domain Services?

You cannot install Active Directory Domain Services unless the
following role services or features are also installed.

[Tools] Group Policy Management
⊿ Remote Server Administration Tools
   ⊿ Role Administration Tools
      ⊿ AD DS and AD LDS Tools
         Active Directory module for Windows PowerShell
      ⊿ AD DS Tools
         [Tools] Active Directory Administrative Center
         [Tools] AD DS Snap-Ins and Command-Line Tools

☑ Include management tools (if applicable)

Add Features   Cancel

Figure 2.12: Additional features

Now that we have all three of our roles checked, it's time to click on **Next**. And, just to make it clear to all of you, I was not *required* to install all of these roles at the same time; they are not all dependent on each other. It is very common to see these roles all installed onto the same server, but I could split them up onto their own servers if I so desired. In a larger environment, you may have AD DS and DNS installed together, but you might choose to put the DHCP role onto its own server, and that is just fine.

I am configuring this server to support a small lab environment, so for me, it makes sense to put these core infrastructure services together in the same box, as shown in *Figure 2.13*:

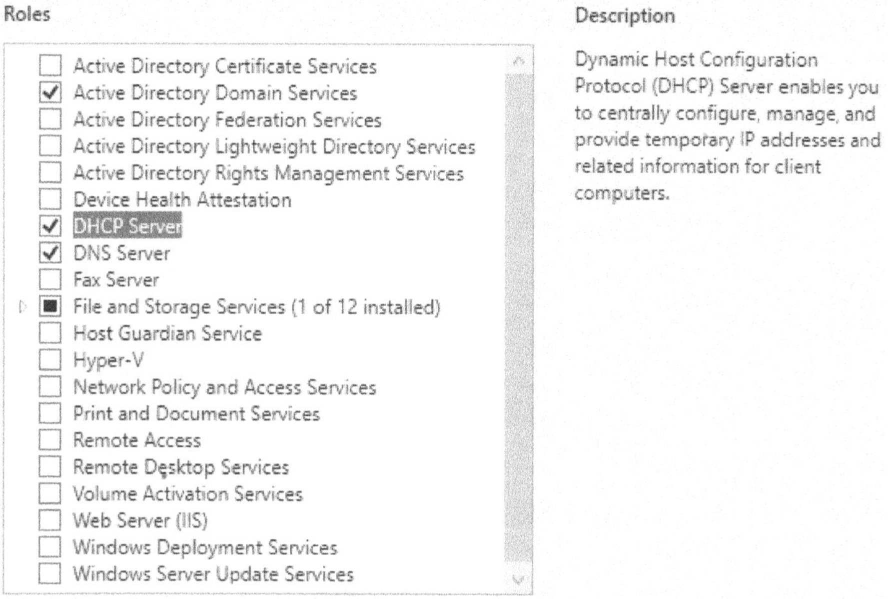

Roles

| | Description |

- [ ] Active Directory Certificate Services
- [✓] Active Directory Domain Services
- [ ] Active Directory Federation Services
- [ ] Active Directory Lightweight Directory Services
- [ ] Active Directory Rights Management Services
- [ ] Device Health Attestation
- [✓] DHCP Server
- [✓] DNS Server
- [ ] Fax Server
- [■] File and Storage Services (1 of 12 installed)
- [ ] Host Guardian Service
- [ ] Hyper-V
- [ ] Network Policy and Access Services
- [ ] Print and Document Services
- [ ] Remote Access
- [ ] Remote Desktop Services
- [ ] Volume Activation Services
- [ ] Web Server (IIS)
- [ ] Windows Deployment Services
- [ ] Windows Server Update Services

Description

Dynamic Host Configuration Protocol (DHCP) Server enables you to centrally configure, manage, and provide temporary IP addresses and related information for client computers.

Figure 2.13: Role selection

After clicking **Next**, we have now landed on the page where we can install additional features to Windows Server 2025. In some cases, you may have a need to install only a particular feature, not a role at all, and in these cases, you would have bypassed the **Server Roles** screen altogether and gone immediately to the **Features** installation screen. Similar to the role installation screen, go ahead and check off any features that you would like to install, and click on **Next** again. For our new domain controller, we do not currently require any additional features to be specifically added, so I will simply finish the wizard, which starts the installation of our new roles.

After the installation process has been completed, you may or may not be prompted to restart the server, depending on which roles or features you installed and whether they require a restart. Once you have landed back inside Server Manager, you will notice that you are now being prompted near the top with a yellow exclamation mark, as seen in *Figure 2.14*. Clicking here displays messages about further configurations that may be required in order to complete the setup of your new roles and finalize their use on the server.

The roles for AD DS, DNS, and DHCP are now successfully installed, but there is some additional configuration that is required for those roles to do their work. For example, to finish turning my server into a domain controller, I need to run through a "promotion" process to define my domain or to specify an existing domain that I want to join. We will work through this together in *Chapter 3*. There are also some loose ends that we need to tie up before putting DHCP into action. *Figure 2.14* shows these remaining tasks, with quick links that can be used to click into them and complete the role installation processes:

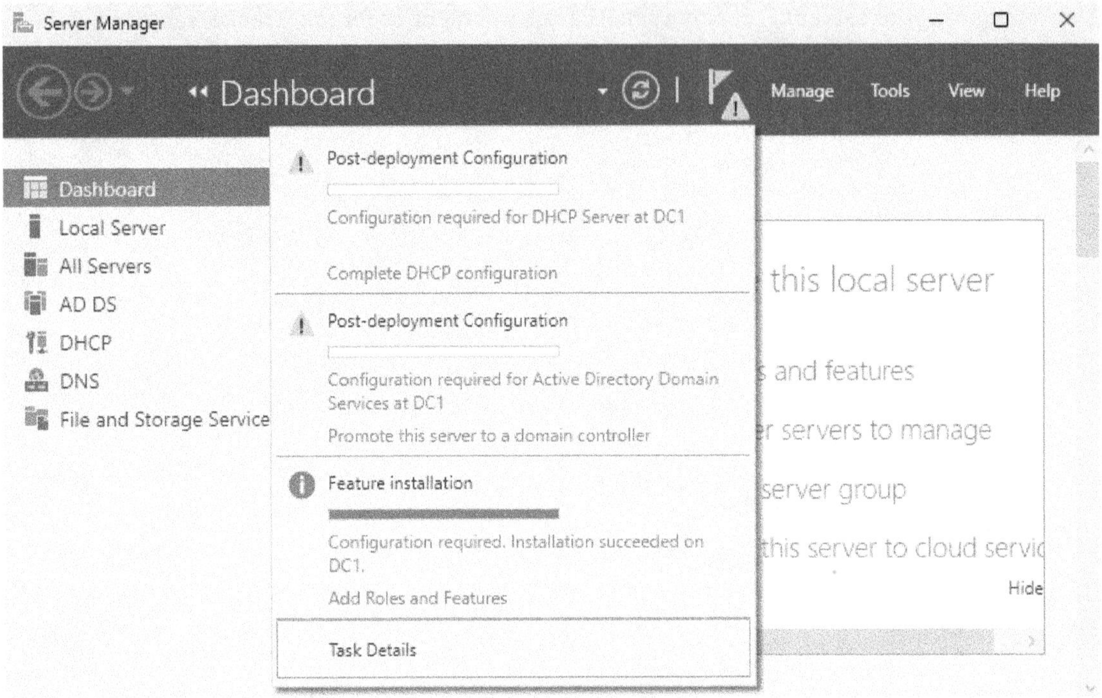

Figure 2.14: Post-deployment Configuration

Installing a feature using PowerShell

Now that you have seen the graphical wizards for installing roles and features, you could certainly always use them to put these components into place on your servers. But Microsoft has put much effort into creating a Windows Server environment where almost anything within the OS can be manipulated using PowerShell, and the addition of roles and features is included in those capabilities. Let's look at the appropriate commands we can use to manipulate roles and features on our server directly from a PowerShell prompt. We will view the available list of roles and features, and we will also issue a command to install a quick feature onto our server.

Open an elevated prompt that is capable of running PowerShell, most easily accomplished via the **Quick Admin** tasks menu, accessed by right-clicking on the **Start** button and choosing to launch an admin session of **Terminal**. Then, use the following command to view all of the available roles and features that we can install on our server. It will also show you which ones are currently installed:

```
Get-WindowsFeature
```

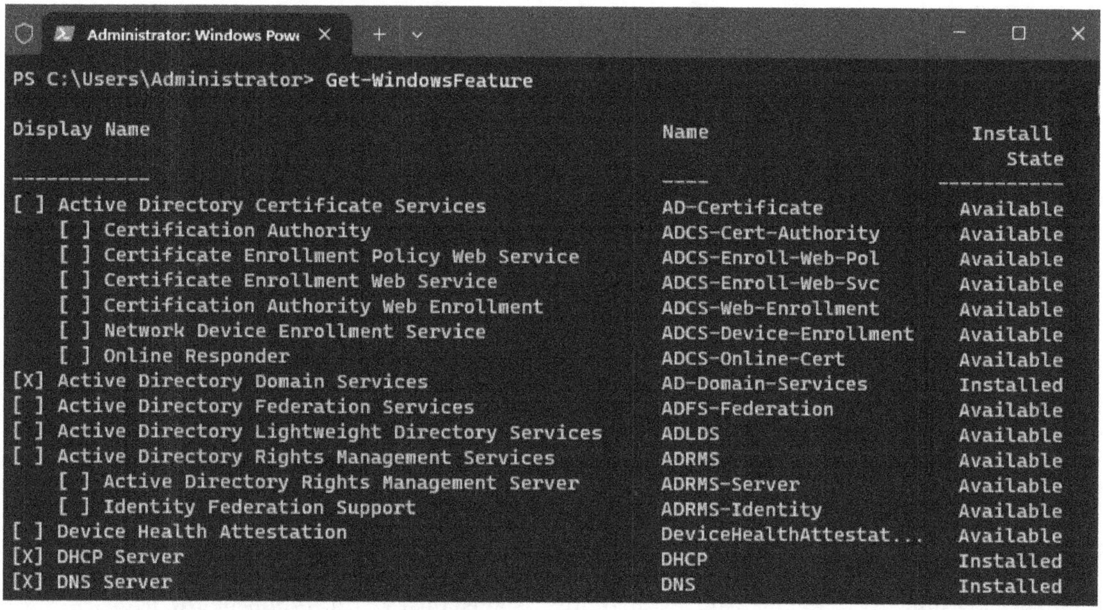

Figure 2.15: A list of all the roles and features available and installed

What I would like to do on this server is install the **Telnet Client** feature. I use Telnet Client regularly for testing network connections, so it is helpful to have it on this machine. Unfortunately, my Terminal window currently has pages and pages of different roles and features in it, and I'm not sure what the exact name of the Telnet Client feature is in order to install it. So, let's run Get-WindowsFeature again, but this time let's use some additional syntax in the command to pare down the amount of information being displayed. I want to see only the features that begin with the letters TEL, as shown in the following examples:

```
Get-WindowsFeature -Name TEL*
```

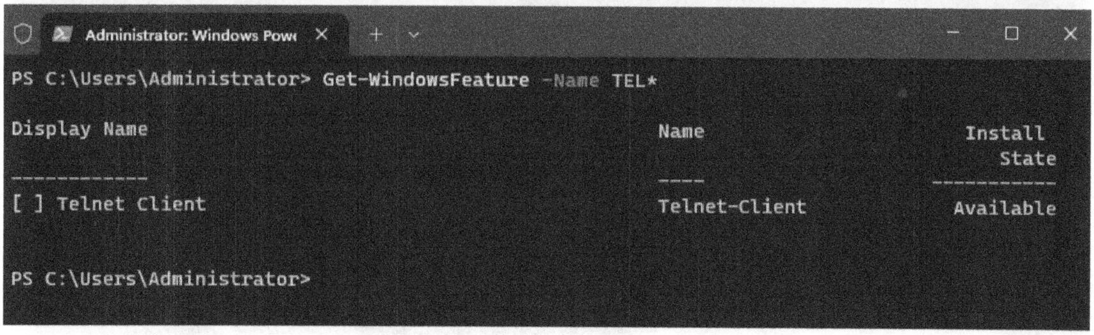

Figure 2.16: A list of features beginning with the letters TEL

There it is! Okay, so now that I know the correct name of the feature, let's run the command to install it, as shown in the following example:

```
Add-WindowsFeature Telnet-Client
```

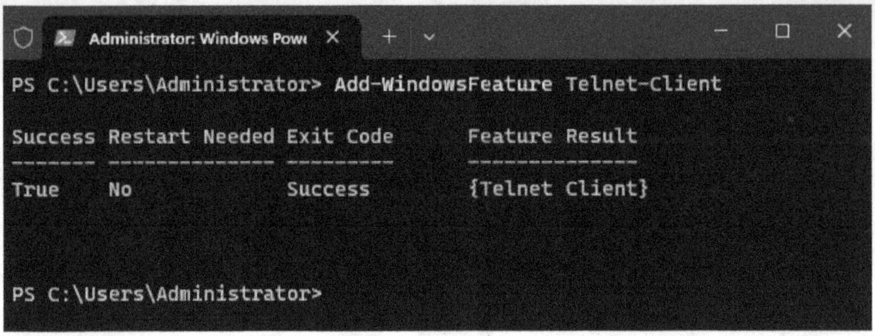

Figure 2.17: Installing Telnet Client via PowerShell

One last thing to show you here—there is also a way to manipulate the Get-WindowsFeature cmdlet to quickly show only the roles and features currently installed on a server. Typing Get-WindowsFeature | Where Installed presents us with a list of the currently installed components. If I run that on my domain controller, you can see all the parts and pieces of my roles for AD DS, DNS, and DHCP, as well as my newly installed Telnet Client feature, as shown in *Figure 2.18*:

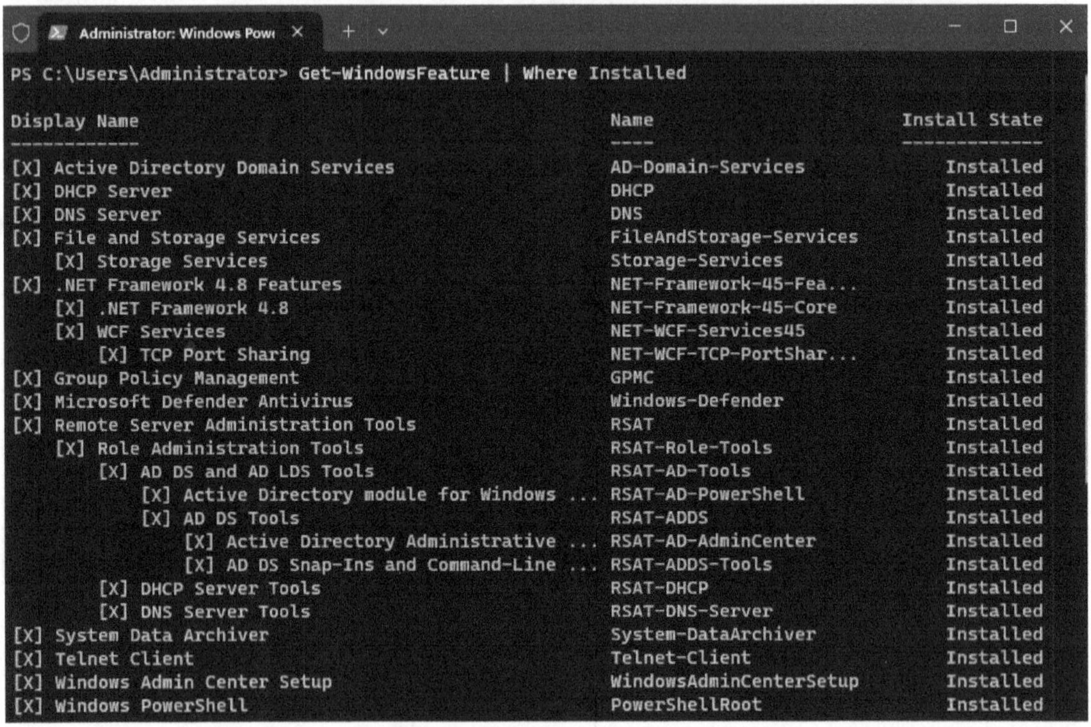

Figure 2.18: A list of currently installed roles and features

Centralized management and monitoring

Whether you are installing new roles, running backups and maintenance programs, or troubleshooting and repairing a server, it is common sense that the first thing you would do is log directly into the server that you need to work on. Long ago, this meant walking up to the server and logging on with the keyboard and mouse that were plugged directly into that hardware. Then, quite a number of years ago, this became cumbersome, and technology advanced to the point where we had the **Remote Desktop Protocol (RDP)** available to us. We quickly transitioned over to logging in to our servers remotely using RDP. Even though it's been around for many years, RDP is still an incredibly powerful and secure protocol, giving us the ability to quickly connect to servers from the comfort of our desks. And, as long as you have proper network topology and routing in place, you can work on a server halfway around the world just as quickly as one sitting in the cubicle next to you. In fact, I recently read that mining rights were being granted in outer space. Talk about a co-location for your data center! Maybe someday, we will use RDP to connect to servers in outer space. I bet Elon has some ideas about that. While there are many tools available for remotely managing your server infrastructure, RDP is the platform of choice for 99% of us out there.

Why talk about RDP? Because you probably all use it daily, and I needed to let you know that Windows Server 2025 includes some tools that make it much less necessary for our day-to-day workflow. The idea of centralized management in the server world has grown through the last few Windows Server OS rollouts. Most of us have so many servers running that checking in with them all daily would consume way too much time. We need some tools that we can utilize to make our management, monitoring, and even configuration processes more efficient in order to free up time for more important projects.

Follow along as we discuss the toolsets Microsoft has built natively into Windows Server 2025 to be able to manage and monitor servers from the comfort of your desk. You may notice the lack of Azure Arc in this section, which is by design, as I plan to take a firsthand look at Azure Arc and join a server to it in a later section of this chapter.

Server Manager

If you have worked on Windows Server recently, you are familiar with the idea that, upon logging in to any of your servers, you are always presented with a large window opening on top of the desktop. This auto-launching program is **Server Manager**. As the name implies, it's here to help you manage your server. However, in my experience, the majority of server administrators do not utilize Server Manager. Instead, they close it as fast as they can and curse it under their breath because it's been popping up and annoying them during every server login for the past 10 years.

Stop doing that! It's here to help, I promise. *Figure 2.19* shows the default view of **Server Manager** on my new domain controller:

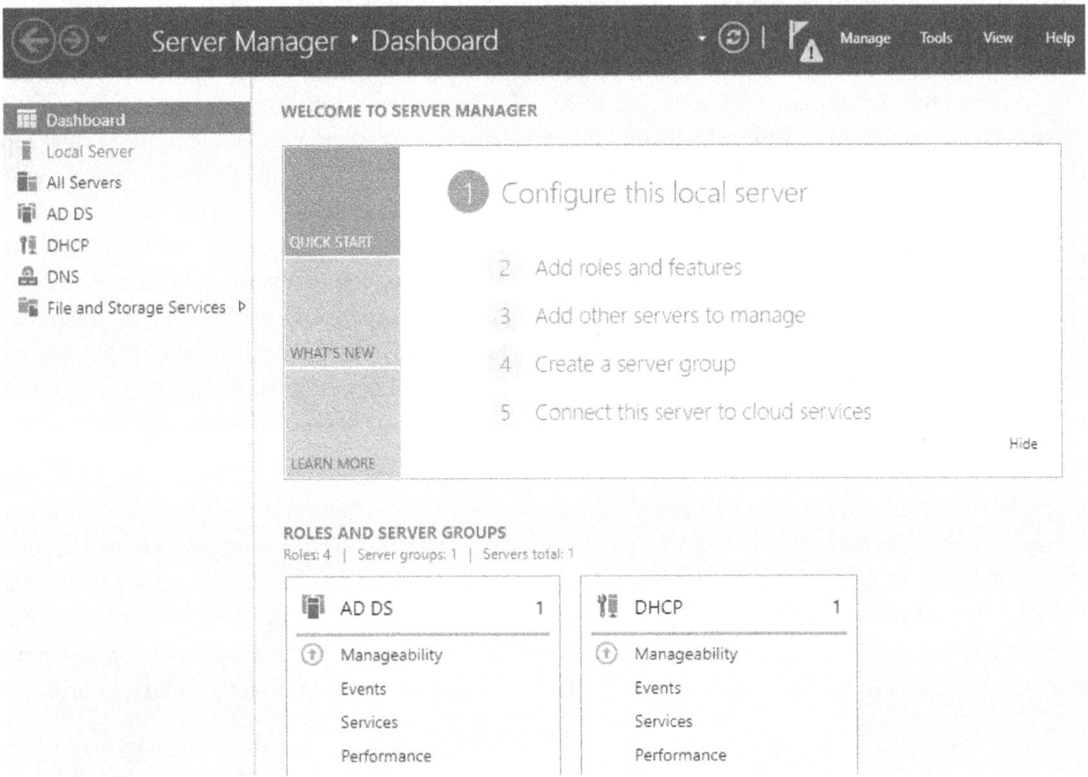

Figure 2.19: Server Manager on my domain controller

What I like about this opening automatically is that it gives me a quick look at what is currently installed on the server. Looking at the column on the left side shows you the list of roles installed and available for management. Clicking on each of these roles brings you to some more particular configuration and options for the role itself. I often find myself hopping back and forth between many different servers while working on a project, and leaving Server Manager open gives me a quick way of double-checking that I am working on the correct server.

The **ROLES AND SERVER GROUPS** section at the bottom is also very interesting. You might not be able to see the colors in the figure if you are reading a printed copy of this book, but this gives you a very quick view of whether or not the services running on this server are functioning properly. Right now, both my **AD DS** and **DHCP** functions are running normally, so I have a nice green bar running through them. But, if anything was amiss with either of these roles, it would be flagged bright red, and I could click on any of the links listed under those role headings in order to track down what the trouble is.

Up near the top-right corner, you can see a few menus, the most useful of which, to me, is the **Tools** menu. Click on that, and you will see a list of all the available **administrative tools** to launch on this server. Yes, this is essentially the same Administrative Tools folder that long ago existed as an actual folder inside the **Start** menu, now stored more conveniently here inside Server Manager. Server Manager is possibly the easiest way to access this myriad of tools, all from a single location:

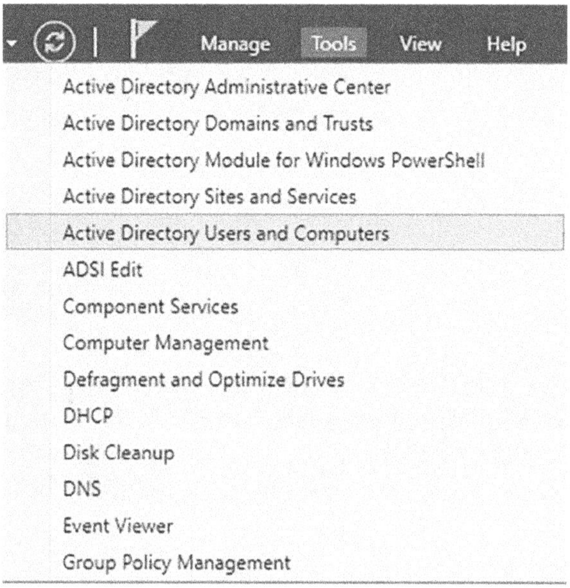

Figure 2.20: The Tools menu in Server Manager

So far, the functions inside Server Manager that we have discussed are available on any installation of Windows Server 2025, whether it is standalone or part of a domain. Everything we have done only deals with the local server that we are logged in to. Now, let's explore what options are available to us in Server Manager for the centralization of management across multiple servers. The new mentality of managing many servers from a single server is often referred to as *managing from a single pane of glass*. We will use Server Manager on one of our servers in the network to make connections to additional servers, and after doing that, we should have much more information inside Server Manager that we can use to keep tabs on all of those servers.

Front and center inside the **Server Manager** console is the section entitled **WELCOME TO SERVER MANAGER**. Under that, we have a series of steps or links that can be clicked on. The first one lets you configure settings that are specific only to this local server. We already did some work with the second step when we added a new role to our server. Now, we will test out the third step: **Add other servers to manage**.

By the way, this same function can also be called by clicking on the **Manage** menu at the top and then choosing **Add Servers**, as shown in *Figure 2.21*:

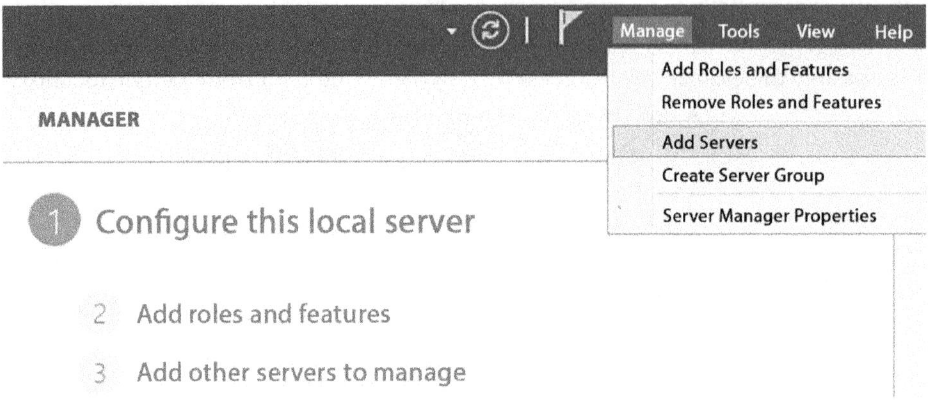

Figure 2.21: Adding servers to Server Manager

Most of you will be working within a domain environment where the servers are all domain-joined, which makes this next part really easy. Simply click on the **Find Now** button, and the machines available within your network will be displayed. From here, you can choose the servers that you want to manage and move them over to the **Selected** column on the right, as shown in *Figure 2.22*:

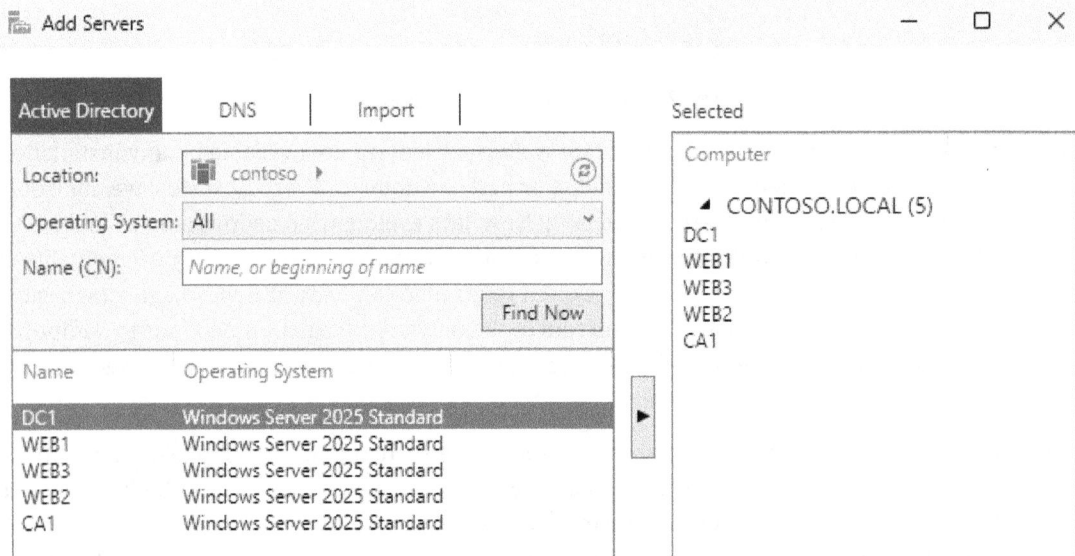

Figure 2.22: Selecting the servers you want to manage

After clicking **OK**, you will see that Server Manager has transformed before your very eyes, to give you more information about all of these servers and the roles that are installed on them. Now, when you log in to this single server, you immediately see critical maintenance information about all of the systems that you have chosen to add here. You could even use one dedicated server to handle the management of your whole arsenal of servers. For example, I am currently logged in to a brand-new server called CA1. I do not have any roles installed on this server, so, by default, Server Manager looks pretty basic. As soon as I add other servers (my domain controllers) to be managed, my Server Manager on the CA1 server now contains all of the details about CA1 and my domain controllers, so I can view all facets of my infrastructure from this single pane. As you can see in *Figure 2.23*, I even have flags here indicating that some services are not running properly within my infrastructure:

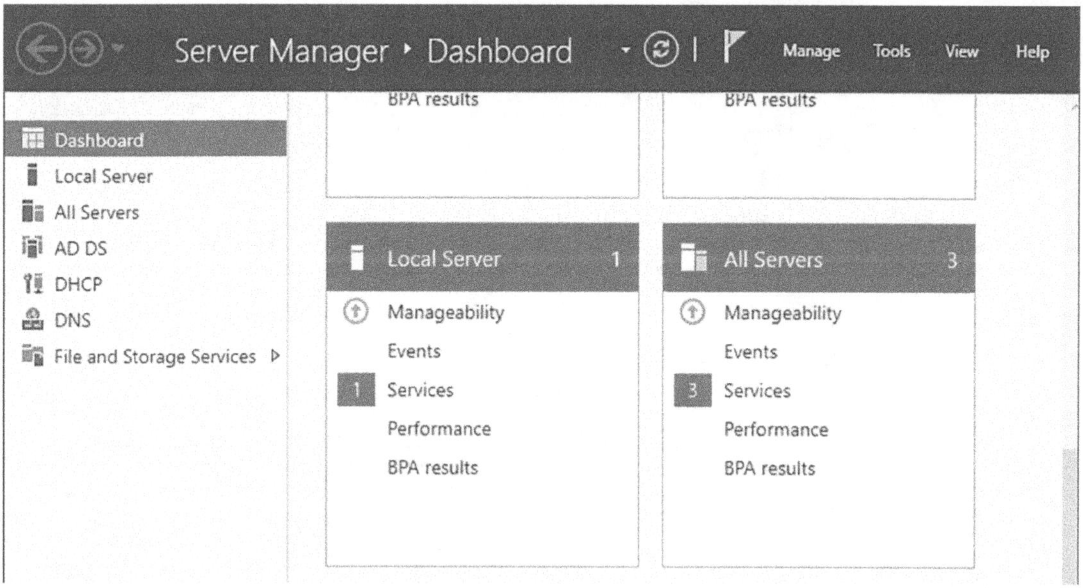

Figure 2.23: Remote management via Server Manager

Clicking on the **All Servers** link or on one of the specific roles gives you even more comprehensive information collected from these remote servers. Adding multiple servers to Server Manager is not only useful for monitoring but also for future configurations. Do you remember a few pages ago when we added a new role using the wizard? That process has suddenly evolved on this particular server to become more comprehensive since we have now tapped this server into our other servers in the network.

If I now choose to add a new role from inside Server Manager that is aware of multiple servers in the network, when I get to the screen asking me where I want to install that role, I see that I can choose to install a new role or feature onto one of my other servers, even though I am not working from the console of those servers, as shown in *Figure 2.24*:

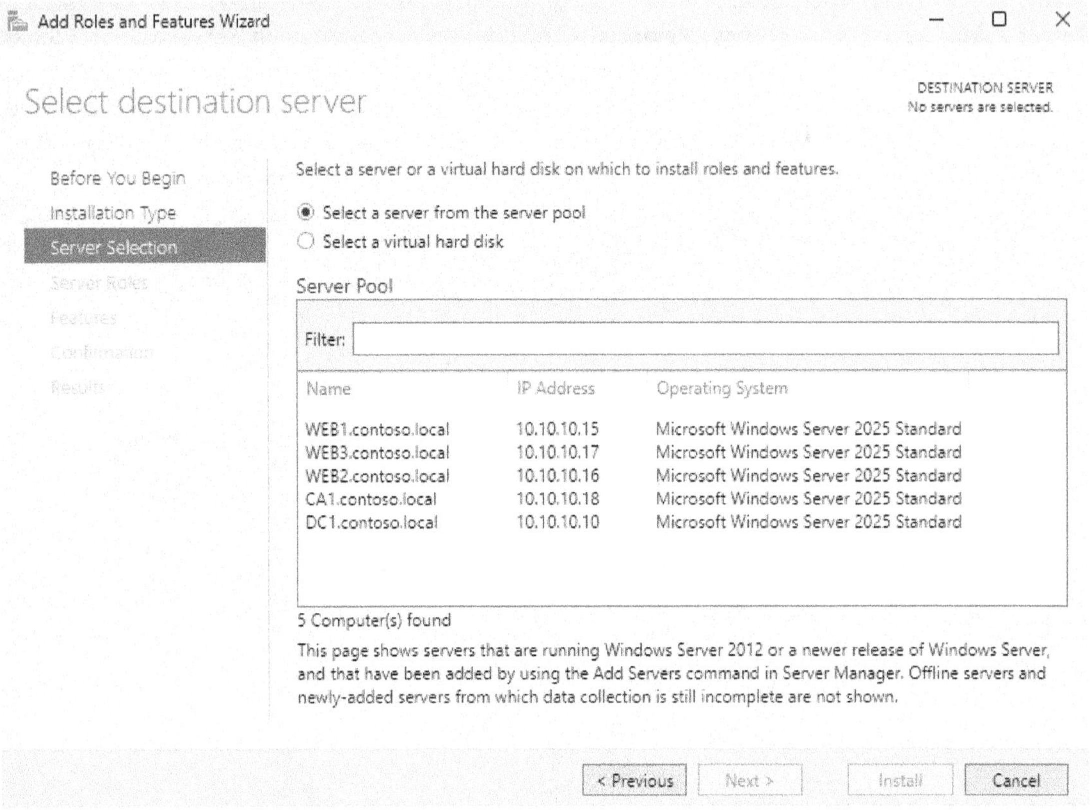

Figure 2.24: Selecting a server for remote installation of a new role or feature

If I wanted to install the web server role onto WEB1, a new server that I am prepping to be a web server, I would *not* have to log in to the WEB1 server. Right here, from Server Manager running on CA1, I could run through the **Add Roles** wizard, define WEB1 as the server that I want to manipulate, and install the role directly from here.

Remote Server Administration Tools

Using Server Manager on a single server to manage and monitor all of your servers is pretty handy, but what if we could take one more step out of that process? What if I told you that you didn't have to log in to *any* of your servers, but could perform all of these tasks from the computer sitting on your desk?

This is possible by installing a toolset from Microsoft called the **Remote Server Administration Tools (RSAT)**. I have a regular Windows 11 client computer online and running in our network, also domain-joined. I am now going to add an optional feature to this Windows 11 computer to give it the RSAT toolset.

Open **Settings** on the client computer and type the word optional into the search bar. One of the options presented will be **Optional features**. Go ahead and click that. Once inside **Optional features**, click the **View features** button. This will open a list of many optional features to choose from, including a lot of language options, but if you scroll down in the list, you will eventually come to a number of different entries that start with **RSAT:** (or you can simply search for RSAT). If there were only a select number of the tools that you wanted to use from this Windows 11 client, you could be selective here and only install the admin consoles that you actually needed, as you can see in *Figure 2.25*:

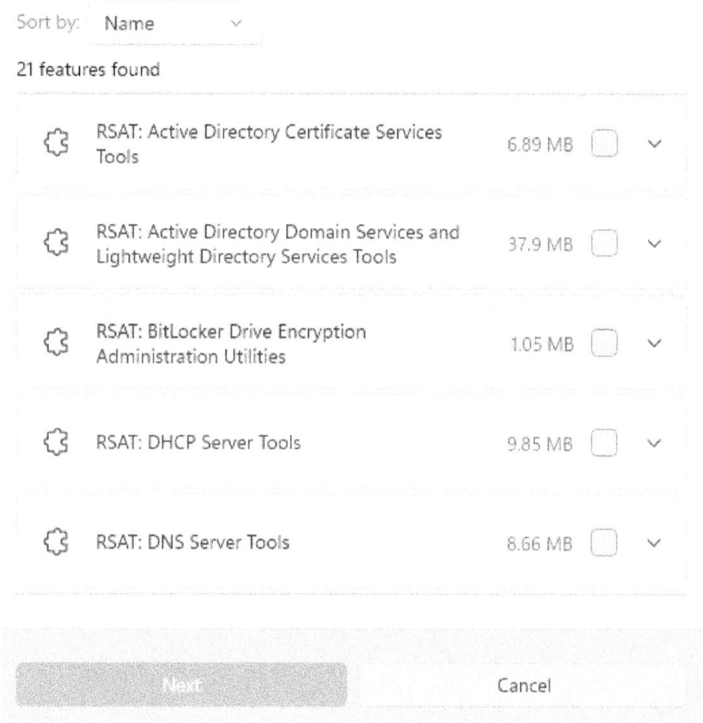

Figure 2.25: Installing RSAT features on Windows 11

RSAT is also available for Windows 10 if you are still running that on your workstation. However, if your version of Windows 10 is older than 1809, you won't find these options on your **Settings** screen. Instead, you can download and install the whole RSAT package from the following link: https://www.microsoft.com/en-us/download/details.aspx?id=45520.

After walking through the process to get these tools on my Windows 11 client computer, I can't seem to find any program that is called *Remote Server Administration Tool*. That would be correct. Even though the names of these features we are installing all begin with *RSAT*, the components that are getting installed onto your system are the actual Windows Server system tools.

If you peruse your **Start** menu, you will now find options for both Server Manager, just like on a server, along with a folder full of Windows tools! This makes sense, except that if you don't realize the name discrepancy, it can take you a few minutes to figure out why you cannot find what you just installed.

So, go ahead and launch Server Manager by finding it in the **Start** menu, by using the search bar, or even by saying *Hey, Cortana, open Server Manager*. Sorry, I couldn't resist. But whatever your method, open up Server Manager on your desktop computer, and you will see that it looks and feels just like Server Manager in Windows Server 2025. And, in the same way that you work with and manipulate it within the server operating system, you can take the same steps here in order to add your servers for remote management.

In *Figure 2.26*, you can see that I have walked through the **Add other servers to manage** step and selected some of the servers that are within my test network. I now have access, right here from my Windows 11 client computer, to manage and monitor all of the servers in my lab without even having to log in to them:

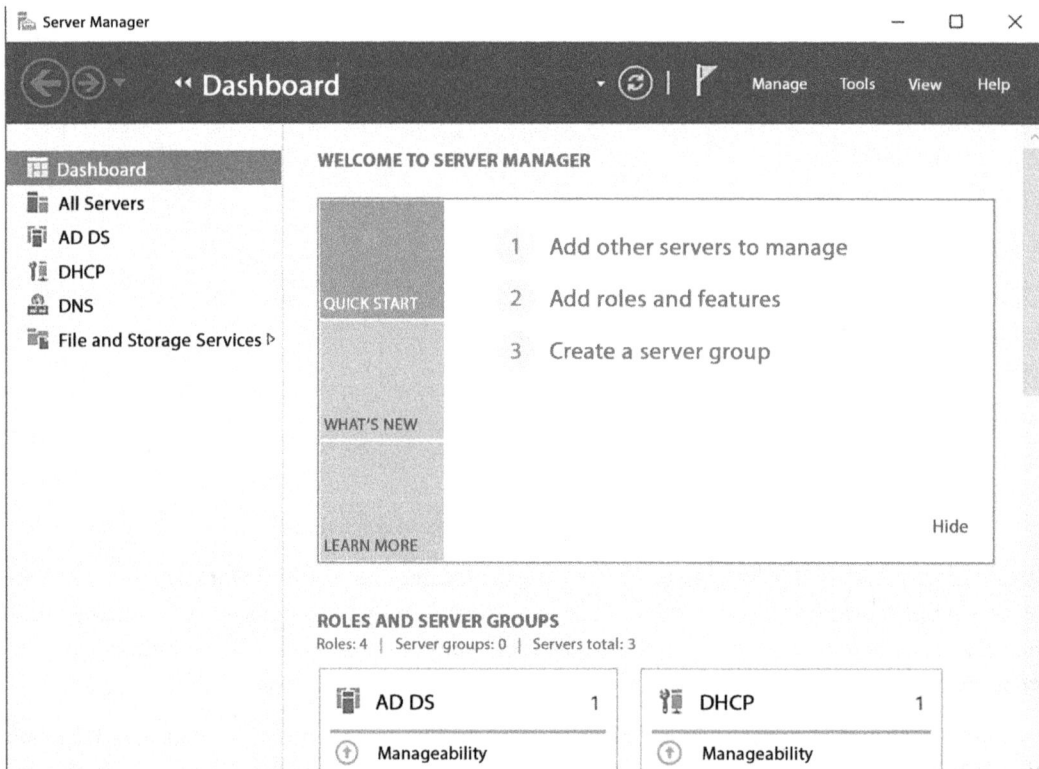

Figure 2.26: Centralized management via Server Manager

Does this mean RDP is dead?

With these new and improved ways to manage the underlying components of your servers without having to log in to them directly, does this mean that our age-old friend RDP is going away? Certainly not! We will still have the need to access our servers directly sometimes, even if we go all-in with using the newer management tools. And I expect that many administrators out there will continue using RDP and full desktop-based access for all management and monitoring of their servers simply because that is what they are more comfortable with, even if newer, more efficient ways now exist to accomplish the same tasks.

Remote Desktop Connection Manager

Since most of us do still utilize RDP occasionally (or often) when bouncing around between our servers, let's take a quick look at a tool that can at least make this task more manageable and centralized. I won't spend a lot of time looking over individual features or capabilities of this tool since it is a client-side tool and not something that is specific to Windows Server 2025. You can use this to handle RDP connections for any and all of your servers or even all of the client computers in your network. **Remote Desktop Connection Manager (RDCM)** is an incredibly useful platform for storing all of the different RDP connections that you make within your environment. You can save connections so that you don't have to spend time trying to remember server names, sort servers into categories, and even store credentials so that you don't have to type passwords when connecting to servers. Though a disclaimer should come with that one: your security folks may not be happy if you choose to employ the password-storing feature.

RDCM has led a tumultuous life. It was available as a direct download from Microsoft for years and through many versions, until a vulnerability was identified in the software, causing Microsoft to shut it down and stop offering it to us. Thankfully, the Sysinternals team at Microsoft grabbed it, fixed it up, and resurrected it for continued use.

You can download RDCM from the following link: `https://learn.microsoft.com/en-us/sysinternals/downloads/rdcman`. Once downloaded and extracted, this tool is a standalone executable that can be run on almost any Windows OS. The beauty of so many Sysinternals tools is that they are self-explanatory. To make use of RDCM, all you need to do is launch it, create a new group (saved as an RDG file), and start adding servers to it.

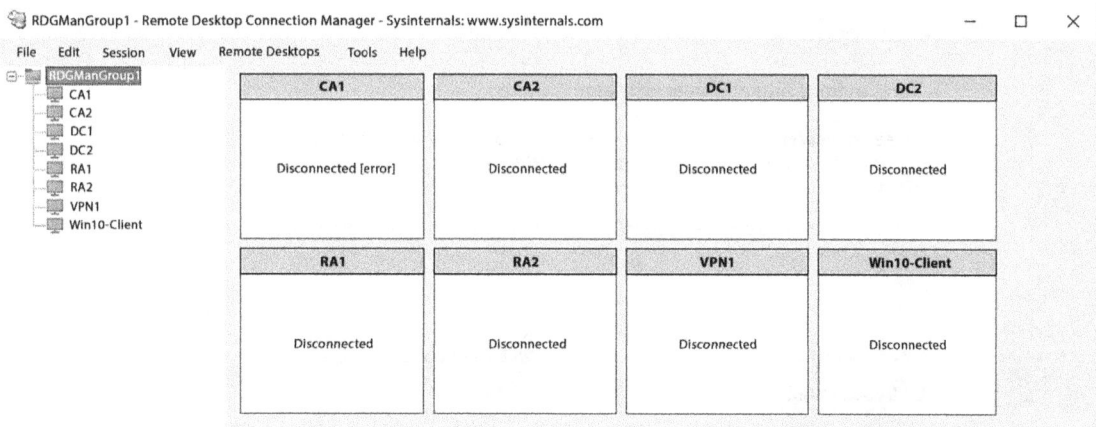

Figure 2.27: The RDCM tool

After saving your server RDP connections into RDCM, this tool provides you with a centralized and fast way to RDP into any of the servers that you administer. No need to remember their names or IP addresses from this point forward!

Windows Admin Center

Now, forget everything I just told you about remote server management and focus on this instead. I'm kidding... sort of. All of the tools we have already discussed are still stable, relevant, and great ways to interact with and manage Windows Server. However, there are a couple of newer offerings from Microsoft that tackle the idea of centralized server management in a whole new way. The first of these is the **Windows Admin Center (WAC)**.

WAC is a server and client management platform that is designed to help you administer your machines in a more efficient manner. This is a browser-based tool, meaning that, once installed, you access WAC from a web browser, which is great. No need to install a management tool or application onto your workstation—simply sit down and tap into it with a URL.

WAC can manage your servers (all the way back to Server 2008 R2) and your server clusters, and even has some special functionality for managing hyper-converged infrastructure clusters. You have the ability to manage servers hosted on-premises as well as inside Azure, and you can even manage client machines in the Windows 10 and 11 flavors.

What's the cost of such an amazing, powerful tool? FREE!

WAC even has support for third-party vendors creating extensions for the WAC interface, so this tool is going to continue growing. If you have followed along with the test lab configuration in the book so far, you will recognize the words "Windows Admin Center" from a pop-up window that displays itself every time Server Manager is opened. Microsoft wants administrators to know about WAC so badly that they are reminding you that you should start using it every time you log in to a Server 2025 box, as shown in *Figure 2.28*:

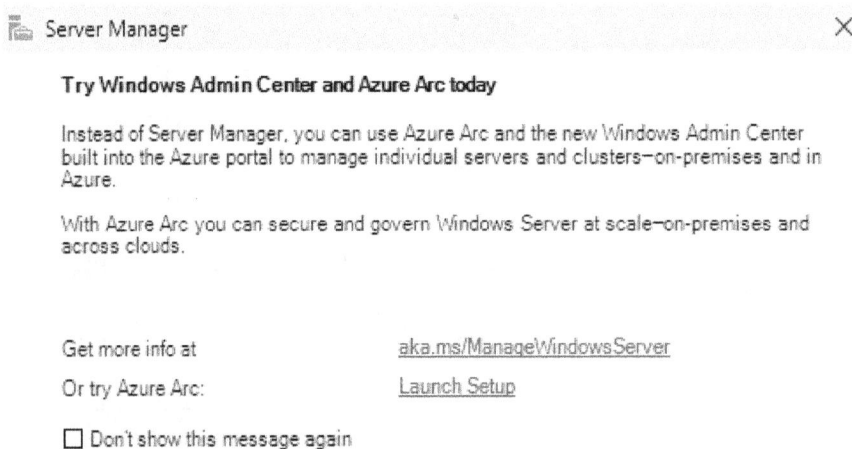

Figure 2.28: Even Server Manager recommends using WAC

Installing WAC

Enough talk, let's try it out! First, we need to choose a location to install the components of WAC. True, I did say that one of the benefits was that we didn't need to install a client software component, but what I meant was that once WAC is implemented, then tapping into it is as easy as opening up a browser. That website needs to be installed and running somewhere, right? While you could throw the whole WAC system onto a Windows 10 client, let's take the approach that will be more commonly utilized in the field and install it onto a server in our network. I have a system running called WEB3 that is not yet hosting any roles or websites; it's just an empty server at this point. Sounds like a good place to install the WAC components. Let's work through that together.

Download WAC here: https://aka.ms/WACDownload.

Once downloaded, run the installer on the host machine. There are either a few simple decisions or many technical decisions you need to make for this installer, depending on whether you choose **Express setup** or **Custom setup**. For the environment I am building, I am going to run through **Express setup** and accept the default port, certificate, and authentication settings. This will provide me with a website instance of WAC that I can log in to from any other system on my network, using a self-signed SSL certificate. In a production environment, you would want to install a real SSL certificate to be used by this website and better protect it, but my lab is not even connected to the internet, so I am safe continuing forward, allowing the wizard to generate a self-signed certificate for this website.

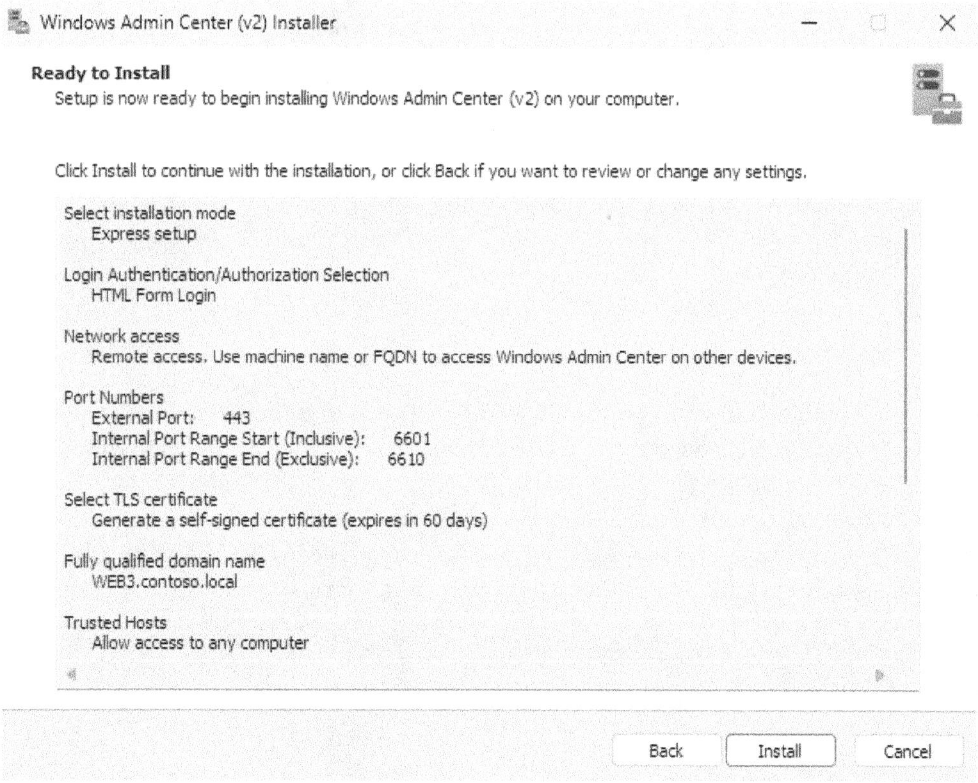

Figure 2.29: Installing WAC

The rest of the options in **Express setup** are very self-explanatory. Click through them to finish installing WAC, and once finished, you will now be hosting the WAC website on this server. For my installation, the new web address is `https://WEB3.contoso.local`.

Launching WAC

Now for the fun part, try logging in! To tap into WAC, you simply open a supported browser from any machine in your network and browse to the WAC URL. Once again, mine is `https://WEB3.contoso.local`. Microsoft recommends using Edge, but it also works with Chrome. I am logged in to my Windows 10 workstation and will simply open the Edge browser and try to hit my new site, as shown in *Figure 2.30*:

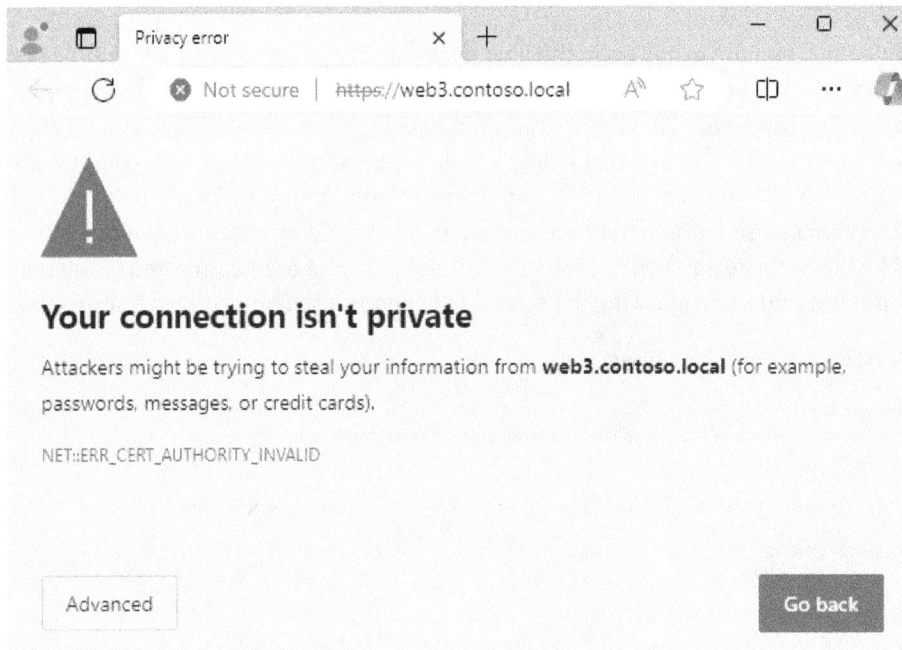

Figure 2.30: Opening a WAC URL in Microsoft Edge

As you can see, I am dealing with a certificate warning. This is to be expected because I am using a self-signed certificate, which, once again, is a bad idea. I only justify it because I'm running in a test lab. If you want to remove the certificate warning, make sure to skip ahead to *Chapter 7, Certificates*, where we will cover all the necessary information to make that possible. Since I am expecting this within my lab and am okay with the risk for our purposes today, I can click the **Advanced** button and then click the **Continue to web3.contoso.local** link to proceed. I am now presented with a login prompt:

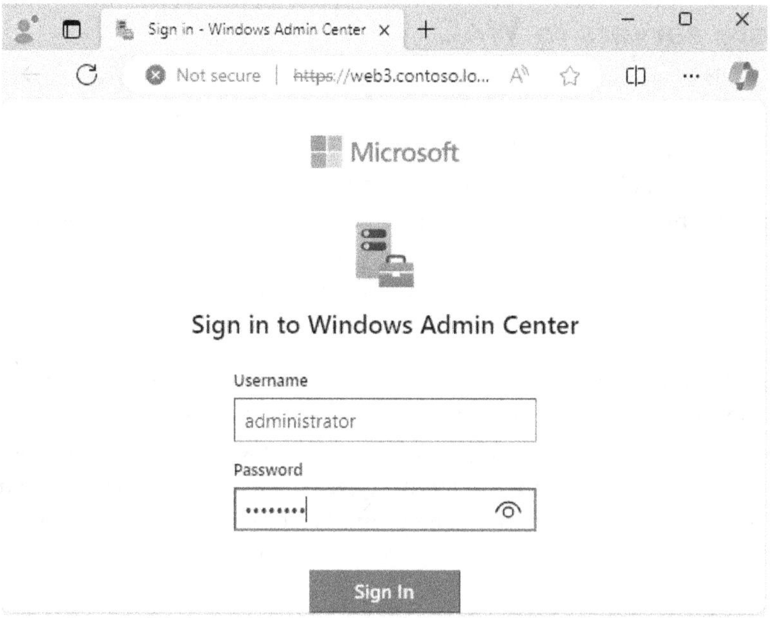

Figure 2.31: Sign in to use WAC

Even though I am logged in to a Windows 10 computer that is domain-joined, and I am logged in with domain credentials, the WAC website does not automatically try to inject those credentials for its own use but rather pauses to ask who you are. If I simply input my domain credentials here, I am now presented with the WAC interface, as shown in *Figure 2.32*:

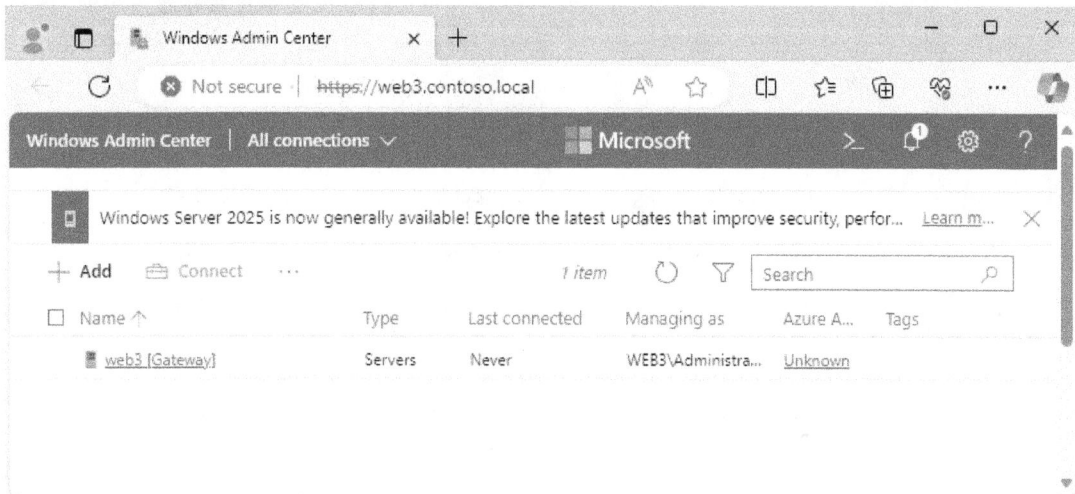

Figure 2.32: WAC interface

Adding more servers to WAC

Logging in to WAC is great, but not very useful until you add a bunch of machines that you want to manage. To do that, simply click the **+ Add** button that is shown onscreen. You will be presented with choices to add a new server, a new PC, a Windows Server cluster, or even an Azure VM. Make your selection and input the required information. I don't have any clusters in my test lab, not yet anyway, so I am going to add connections to the standard servers that I have been running in the environment. If I select the option to add a Windows Server, I can type out the individual server names, import a list of server names, or even select the **Search Active Directory** option. I'll go ahead and try that search function to test how well this works.

I have already set up a number of different servers in my lab and joined them to my domain (we'll talk more about domains in the next chapter), but how do I make WAC search for them here? When I click **Search Active Directory**, I still get a field asking me to type in a server name, but there is a note about wildcards being allowed. Aha! If you simply type an asterisk (*) into the search field and click the **Search** button, WAC polls your domain and presents a full list of machines that can be added to the console:

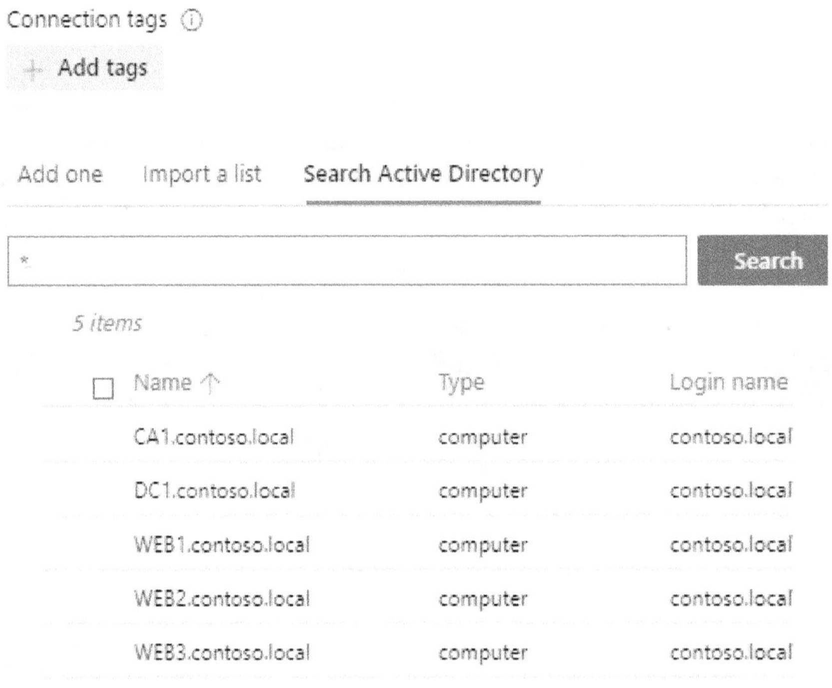

Connection tags ⓘ

╶╴ Add tags

Add one   Import a list   Search Active Directory

| * | | **Search** |

5 items

☐	Name ↑	Type	Login name
	CA1.contoso.local	computer	contoso.local
	DC1.contoso.local	computer	contoso.local
	WEB1.contoso.local	computer	contoso.local
	WEB2.contoso.local	computer	contoso.local
	WEB3.contoso.local	computer	contoso.local

*Figure 2.33: Search using **

Now, simply select the checkboxes next to each server that you would like to administer via WAC and click the + **Add** button. You can see in *Figure 2.34* that WAC now contains information about all of the servers in my environment:

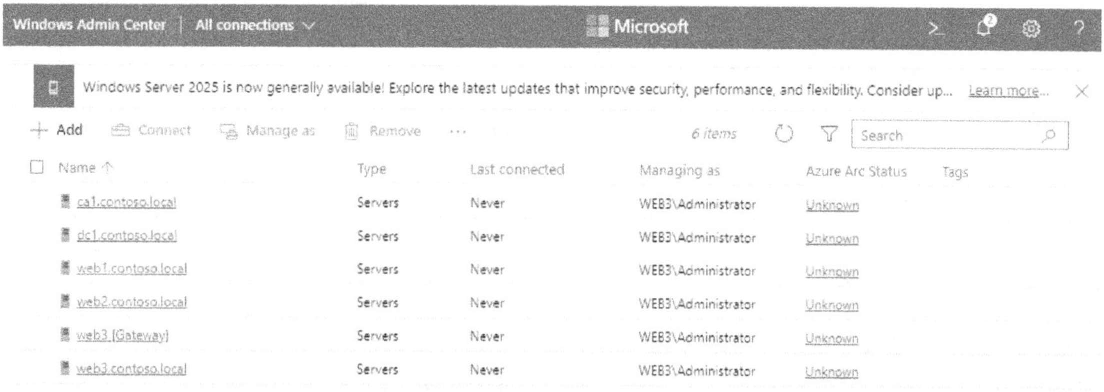

Figure 2.34: Servers successfully imported into WAC

Managing a server with WAC

Beginning the management of a server from within WAC is as simple as clicking on the server name. As you can see in *Figure 2.35*, I have selected my DC1 server, as it is currently the only machine with some real roles installed and running:

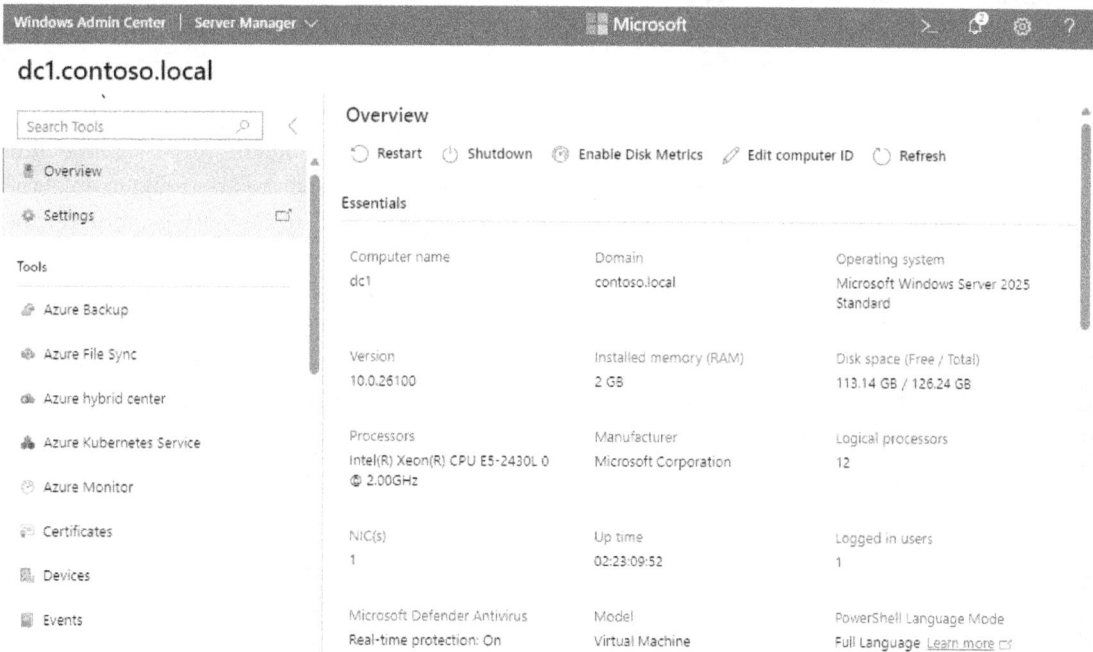

Figure 2.35: DC1 server information

From this interface, I can manage many different aspects of my DC1 server's operating system. There are power control functions, and the ability to run backups on my server, and I can even view and install certificates from here! You can monitor the performance of the server, view its event logs, manipulate the local Windows Firewall, and launch a remote PowerShell connection to the server. The goal with WAC is for it to be your one-stop shop for remotely managing your servers, and I would say it is well on its way to accomplishing that goal.

I don't yet have any Server Core instances running in my lab, but rest assured that WAC can be used to manage Server Core instances just as well as servers running Desktop Experience. This makes WAC even more potent and intriguing to server administrators. When we get to *Chapter 11, Server Core*, we'll make sure to wrap back to this idea and in some way manipulate a Server Core instance through this WAC console.

Changes are as easy as pie

Monitoring information about your servers from a single place such as WAC is great and powerful, but the coolest part about WAC is that you have some serious capabilities to manipulate your servers as well, straight from this web interface.

This is yet another place where you can add roles or features to your servers, create scheduled tasks, start or stop services, or even do things such as edit the registry and add Windows Firewall rules. Let's make a quick change to our DC1 server to prove this. All of my VMs are inside a test lab that is running within Hyper-V, and so interaction with my servers to this point has been directly from Hyper-V console sessions. It is basically as if I am walking up to these servers and logging in to them from the console every single time I need to interact with them. At this point, RDP has never been enabled on DC1, but I wonder whether there is a way to enable that easily right from inside WAC?

Within the menus along the left side of WAC, you may notice one called **Remote Desktop**. This sounds like it might be our starting point, but this function is actually a tool for launching an RDP connection from WAC directly into the server. While this is also very cool, it's not what we are trying to do at the moment. Instead, you'll want to visit **Settings** up near the top left, and inside **Settings**, look for the submenu called **Remote Desktop**. This is our location to make changes to the way that remote desktop is configured on DC1. Immediately after clicking into this section of settings, you can see options for whether or not to allow remote desktop connections to this computer, and currently, this is disabled. These are the same options that you would face if you were to log directly into the DC1 server and manipulate remote desktop connectivity settings. You can see in *Figure 2.36* that I have now selected the **Allow remote connections to this computer** option —previously, this was not enabled:

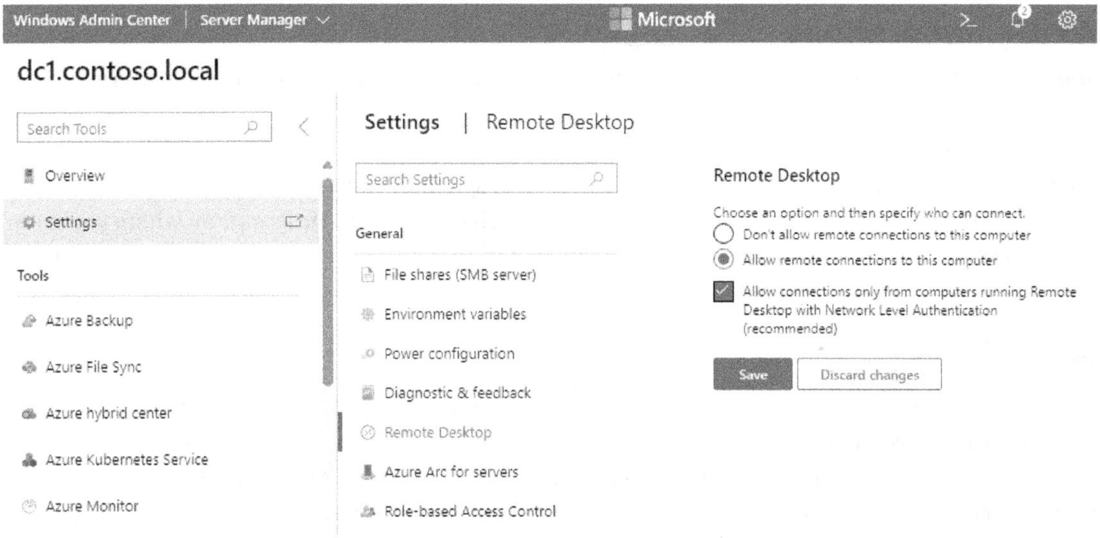

Figure 2.36: Enabling remote desktop connectivity to DC1

Simply changing the setting here and clicking the **Save** button causes WAC to reach out to DC1 and enable this remote desktop setting, after which I can immediately connect to it using RDP from my Windows 11 computer. I never needed to log in to DC1 to enable remote logins to DC1!

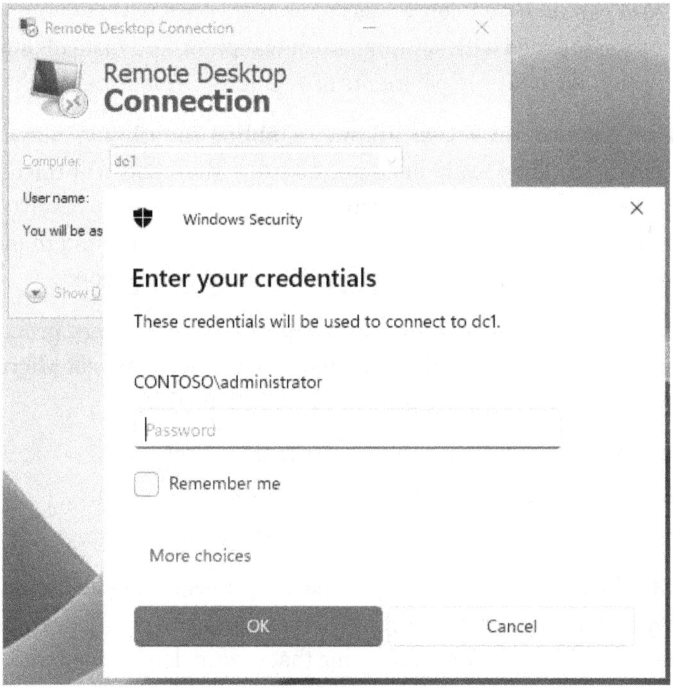

Figure 2.37: RDP is now enabled

Azure integrations

You'll notice inside WAC that there are numerous tools related to Azure. If you have an Azure environment or are thinking about getting started with one, your on-premises WAC can be used to administer both on-premises servers as well as Azure servers. WAC can also be used to bind your on-premises environment together with your Azure environment through things such as **Azure File Sync** and **Azure Backup.** These tools can be a powerful way of creating a hybrid cloud configuration, where you maintain servers in both environments, and can also be used to help ease a transition from a traditional datacenter into a cloud-only mentality.

Azure Arc

Another place you may have noticed the word "Azure," even in some of our screenshots of WAC, are references to Azure Arc that are showing up all over the place. As we already discussed a little bit in *Chapter 1*, Azure Arc is another centralized administration pane that can be used to manage Azure servers, of course, but also on-premise servers and infrastructure. Azure Arc is accessed through your company's Azure portal, and not all companies are yet tapped into Azure, so you may or may not have access to look inside this toolset.

While this book is not inherently about Azure technologies, a couple of great reasons you may want to enable Azure Arc in your environment and begin tying your servers into it are pay-as-you-go licensing and hotpatching. We also discussed both of these in *Chapter 1*, but as a quick refresher, new instances of Windows Server 2025 can now be licensed based on usage, via pay-as-you-go licensing. This can remove your capex costs associated with spinning up new servers, and instead, plug those new servers into an Azure subscription for monthly payments of Windows Server licensing.

Hotpatching is a game changer for server uptime, enabling monthly Windows patches to install themselves *without rebooting.* Then, only once per quarter, Microsoft will release a "normal" patch sequence that will restart your server. Moving from monthly to quarterly restarts of servers will save time, headaches, and money. What is the requirement to be able to use and manipulate hotpatching settings on your new servers? Having them plugged into Azure Arc, of course!

Let's join one of my servers to Azure Arc so you can experience the current process of doing so. I say "current" process because this is still a little bit clunkier than what I expect Microsoft will land on in the finality, but as I write these words, the process is essentially this:

1. Log in to Azure Arc and define the new server to be joined.
2. Azure creates a PowerShell script, which you can then download.
3. Run the script on your server, and it is now tapped into Azure Arc.

The reason I think Microsoft will update this process is that every new instance of Windows Server 2025 now has a systray tool running by default called **Azure Arc**, and right-clicking on that systray icon displays a **Launch Azure Arc setup** option. Launching that wizard does indeed walk through some steps to check prerequisites, check network connectivity, and attempt to install **Azure Connected Machine agent** onto the new server, but no matter how many times I tried or from how many different new servers, the wizard fails every time to download the components that it needs. So, my hope is that in the future, this wizard will be an even simpler way to connect servers to Azure Arc, on an ad-hoc basis.

To be able to successfully pull a server into Azure Arc, your Azure environment must first meet and be prepped with some prerequisites, which can be found here: `https://learn.microsoft.com/en-us/azure/azure-arc/servers/learn/quick-enable-hybrid-vm#prerequisites`.

Adding a server to Azure Arc

Log in to your Azure portal (`portal.azure.com`) and search for `Azure Arc`. Once here, navigate to **Azure Arc resources** > **Machines** and click the **Add/Create** button. This will present you with a handful of options about what type of addition you are trying to accomplish. The first option here is typically the place to go when wanting to add a single server into Azure Arc for testing: **Add a single server**. Under that category, you are going to click on **Generate script**.

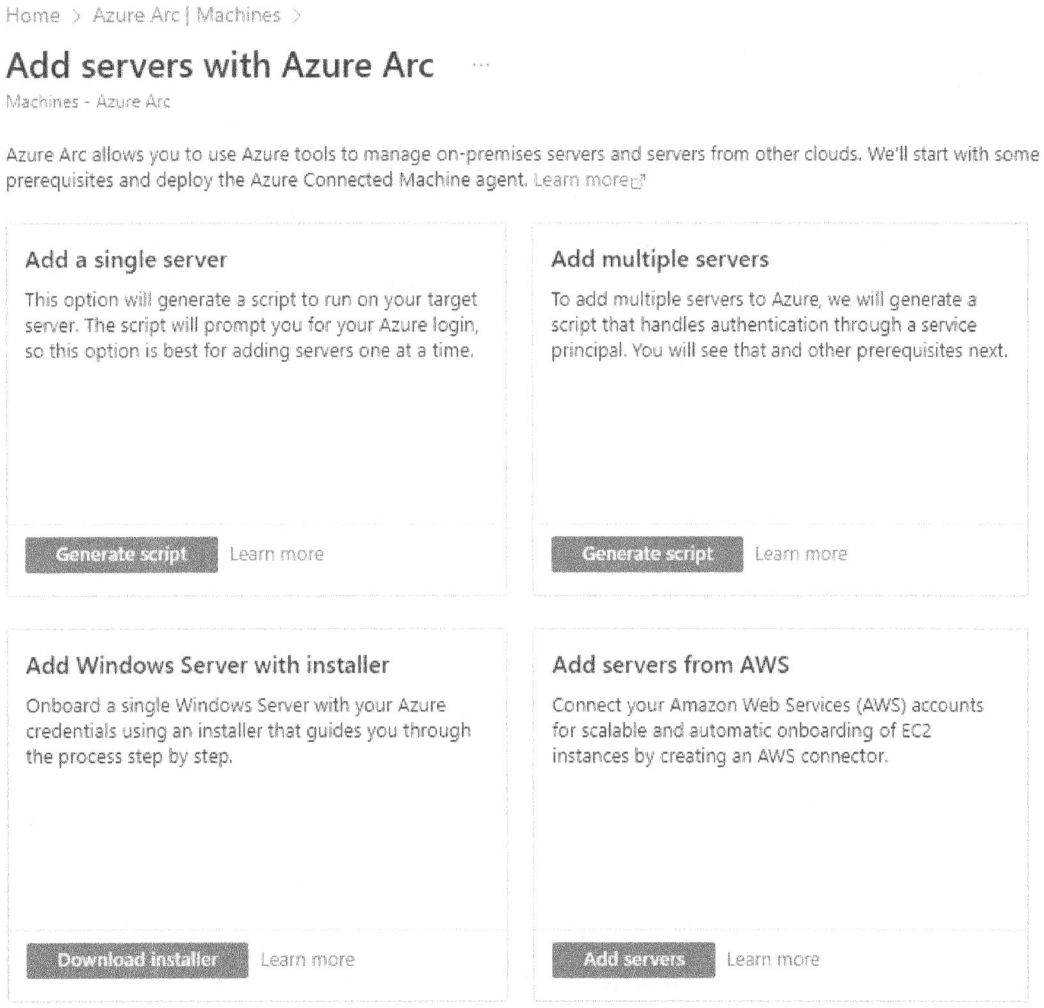

Home > Azure Arc | Machines >

Add servers with Azure Arc ...
Machines - Azure Arc

Azure Arc allows you to use Azure tools to manage on-premises servers and servers from other clouds. We'll start with some prerequisites and deploy the Azure Connected Machine agent. Learn more

---

Add a single server

This option will generate a script to run on your target server. The script will prompt you for your Azure login, so this option is best for adding servers one at a time.

[Generate script] Learn more

Add multiple servers

To add multiple servers to Azure, we will generate a script that handles authentication through a service principal. You will see that and other prerequisites next.

[Generate script] Learn more

Add Windows Server with installer

Onboard a single Windows Server with your Azure credentials using an installer that guides you through the process step by step.

[Download installer] Learn more

Add servers from AWS

Connect your Amazon Web Services (AWS) accounts for scalable and automatic onboarding of EC2 instances by creating an AWS connector.

[Add servers] Learn more

Figure 2.38: Adding a server to Azure Arc

Creation of this installation script is quite straightforward; simply choose which subscription, resource group, and region this server will be joined to. At the bottom of the wizard, you will have to define your connectivity method. Unless you have special networking configured between your on-prem and Azure environments, where you could select one of the more secure options, you most likely will go with **Public endpoint** here. This sounds a little scary, but it just means that your on-prem server will reach into Azure with its information using the internet. That traffic is still encrypted and secured, and sent over port 443.

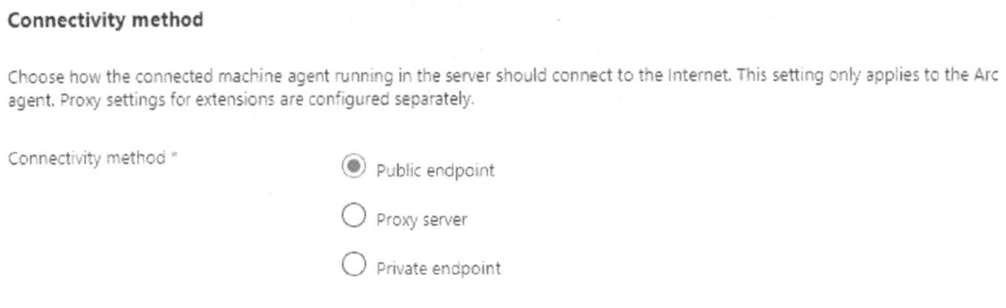

Connectivity method

Choose how the connected machine agent running in the server should connect to the Internet. This setting only applies to the Arc agent. Proxy settings for extensions are configured separately.

Connectivity method *

⦿ Public endpoint

◯ Proxy server

◯ Private endpoint

Figure 2.39: How will your server connect to Azure Arc?

Next, you find options to tag your server. This applies Azure tags to this object that is about to be created inside Azure, for the same reasons that you would tag anything inside Azure. Following this quick screen, we are finally ready to select **Download and run script**.

Add a server with Azure Arc   ···   ✕

Basics   Tags   Download and run script

1. Download or copy the following script

```
1    $global:scriptPath = $myinvocation.mycommand.definition
2
3    function Restart-AsAdmin {
4        $pwshCommand = "powershell"
5        if ($PSVersionTable.PSVersion.Major -ge 6) {
6            $pwshCommand = "pwsh"
7        }
8
9        try {
10           Write-Host "This script requires administrator permissions to install the Azure Connected Machine
             Agent. Attempting to restart script with elevated permissions..."
11           $arguments = "-NoExit -Command `"& '$scriptPath'`""
12           Start-Process $pwshCommand -Verb runAs -ArgumentList $arguments
13           exit 0
14       } catch {
15           throw "Failed to elevate permissions. Please run this script as Administrator."
16       }
17   }
18
19   try {
20       if (-not ([Security.Principal.WindowsPrincipal] [Security.Principal.WindowsIdentity]::GetCurrent()).
         IsInRole([Security.Principal.WindowsBuiltInRole]::Administrator)) {
21           if ([System.Environment]::UserInteractive) {
22               Restart-AsAdmin
```

Figure 2.40: Download or copy this script, and run it on your server

The only thing left to do is copy or download that script and run it! Launch PowerShell ISE on the server to be joined (be careful not to run the x86 version), run this script, and with most things in the Azure world, you will want to then let this sit and bake for 10 minutes or so. Shortly, your on-premises server will be listed inside the Azure Arc portal, ready for you to manage it from here!

If you refer back to *Figure 2.38*, there is a secondary installation option for Azure Arc that doesn't involve a script at all. By clicking the **Download installer** button under **Add Windows Server with installer**, you can add servers into Azure Arc through a more traditional method, instead of running a script.

Quick server rollouts with Sysprep

At the beginning of this chapter, we walked through the process of installing the Windows Server 2025 OS onto your new server. Whether this was a physical piece of hardware or a virtual machine that we were working with, the installation process was essentially the same. Plugging in the DVD or USB stick, booting to it, and letting the installer run its course is an easy enough thing to do, but what if you need to build out 10 new servers instead of just 1? This process would soon start to get tedious, and it would seem like you were wasting a lot of time having to do the exact same thing over and over again. You would be correct—this does waste a lot of time, and there is an easier and faster way to roll out new servers as long as you are building them all from a relatively similar hardware platform. If you are building out your servers as virtual machines, which is so often the case these days, then this process works great and can save you quite a bit of time on new server builds.

Now, before I go too far down this road of describing the Sysprep process, I will also note that there are more involved technologies available within the Windows infrastructure that allow automated OS and server rollouts, which can make the new server rollout process even easier than what I am describing here. The problem with some of the automated technologies is that the infrastructure required to make them work properly is more advanced than many folks will have access to if they are just learning the ropes with Windows Server. In other words, having a fully automated server rollout mechanism isn't very feasible for small environments or test labs, which is where a lot of us live while we are learning about these new technologies.

So, anyway, we will not focus on an automated approach to server rollouts, but rather we will do a few minutes of extra work on our very first server, which then results in saving numerous minutes of setup work on every server that we build afterward. The core of this process is the **Sysprep** tool, which is baked into all versions of Windows, so you can take this same process on any current Windows machine, whether it be a client or a server.

Sysprep is a tool that prepares your system for duplication. Its official name is the **Microsoft System Preparation Tool**, and to sum up what it does in one line, Sysprep allows you to create a master *image* of your server that you can reuse as many times as you want in order to roll out additional servers. A key benefit to using Sysprep is that you can put customized settings onto your master server and install things such as Windows Updates prior to Sysprep, and all of these settings and patches will then exist inside your master image.

Using Sysprep saves you time by not having to walk through the OS installation process, but it saves you even more time by not having to wait for Windows Update to roll all of the current patches down onto every new system that you create.

Now, some of you might be wondering why Sysprep is even necessary. If you wanted to clone your master server, you could simply use a hard disk imaging tool, or if you were dealing with virtual machines, you could simply copy and paste the VHDX file itself in order to make a copy of your new server, right? The answer is yes, but the *big problem* is that the new image or hard drive that you just created would be an exact replica of the original one. The hostname would be the same, and, more importantly, some core identification information inside Windows, such as the operating system's **security identifier** (**SID**) number, would be *exactly the same*. If you were to power on both the original master server and a new server based on this exact replica, you would cause conflicts and collisions on the network as these two servers fought for their right to be the only server with that unique name and SID. This problem exacerbates itself in domain environments, where it is even more important that each system within your network has a unique SID/GUID—its identifier within Active Directory. If you create exact copies of servers and bring them both online, let's just say neither one is going to be happy about it, which, in turn, will make you very unhappy about how your servers are behaving. If you do this inside a production environment, you can wreak havoc on your network. I know from personal experience what it looks like to help someone recover their domain after a DC's hard drive was simply copied, pasted, and turned on as a second server. It's the definition of a bad day.

Sysprep fixes all of these inherent problems with the system duplication process by randomizing the unique identifiers in the OS. To prepare ourselves to roll out many servers using a master image we create with Sysprep, here is a quick-reference summary of the steps we will take:

1. Install Windows Server 2025 onto a new server.
2. Configure customizations and updates on your new server.
3. Run Sysprep to prepare and shut down your master server (make sure it does not restart).
4. Create your master image of the drive (copy it).
5. Build new servers using copies of the master image.

Now, let's cover these steps in a little more detail.

Installing Windows Server 2025 onto a new server

First, just like you have already done, we need to prepare our first server by getting the Windows Server 2025 OS installed. Refrain from installing any full roles onto the server because, depending on the role and its unique configuration, the Sysprep process that we run shortly could cause problems for individual role configurations. Install the OS and make sure device drivers are all squared away, and you're ready for the next step.

Configuring customizations and updates on your new server

Next, you want to configure customizations and install OS updates on your new server. Each setting or installation that you can do now that is universal to your batch of servers will save you from having to take that step on new servers in the future. This portion may be slightly confusing because I just told you a minute ago not to install roles onto the master server. This is because a role installation makes numerous changes to the OS, and some of the roles that you can install lock themselves down to a particular hostname running on the system. If you were to do something like that to a master server, that role would more than likely break when brought up on a new server. Customizations that you can put into place on the master server are things such as plugging in files and folders that you might want on all of your servers, such as an `Admin Tools` folder or something like that. You could also start or stop services that you may or may not want running on each of your servers and change settings in the registry if that is part of your normal server prep or hardening process. Whatever changes or customizations you put into place, it's not a bad idea to run a full slew of tests against the first new server that you build from this master image, just to make sure all of your changes made it through the Sysprep process.

Now is also the time to let Windows Update install and to put any patches on this new server that you want to have installed on all of your new servers in the future. There is nothing more frustrating than installing a new OS in five minutes, only to have to sit around and wait four hours for all the current updates and patches to be installed before you can use the new server. By including these updates and patches in the master image, you save all of that download and installation time for each new server that you spin up.

> Continue to save yourself time and effort by creating a new master image every few months. This way, the newest patches are always included in your master image, and it continues to save you more and more time throughout the life of Windows Server 2025.

Running Sysprep to prepare and shut down your master server

Now that our master server is prepped how we want, it is time to run the Sysprep tool itself. To do that, open an administrative **Terminal** or **Command Prompt** window and browse to `C:\Windows\System32\Sysprep`. Now, you can make use of the `sysprep.exe` utility inside that folder to launch Sysprep itself.

As with many executables that you run from Command Prompt, there are a variety of optional switches that you can tag onto the end of your command to make it do specific tasks. From your **Command Prompt** window, if you simply run the `sysprep.exe` command, you will see a graphical interface for Sysprep, where you can choose between the available options, as shown in *Figure 2.41*:

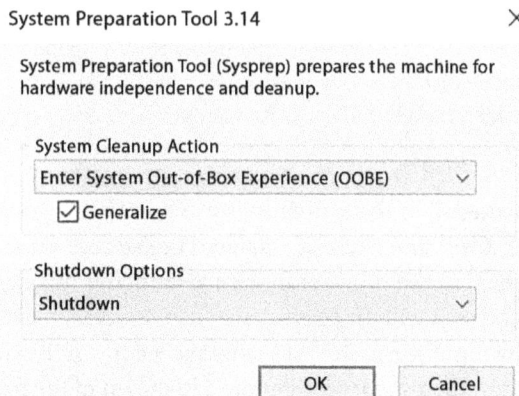

Figure 2.41: Sysprep options

Since I always use the same set of options for Sysprep, I find it easier to simply include all of my optional switches right from the command-line input, therefore bypassing the graphical screen altogether. Here is some information on the different switches that are available to use with `sysprep.exe`:

- `/quiet`: This tells Sysprep to run without status messages on the screen.
- `/generalize`: This specifies that Sysprep is to remove all of the unique system information (SID) from the Windows installation, making the final image usable on multiple machines in your network because each new one spun up from the image will get a new, unique SID.
- `/audit`: This restarts the machine into a special audit mode, where you have the option of adding additional drivers into Windows before the final image gets taken.
- `/oobe`: This tells the machine to launch the mini-setup wizard when Windows next boots.
- `/reboot`: This restarts when Sysprep is finished.
- `/shutdown`: This shuts down the system (not a restart) when Sysprep is finished. This is an important one and is one that I typically use.
- `/quit`: This closes Sysprep after it finishes.
- `/unattend`: There is a special answer file that you can create, which, when specified, will be used in conjunction with the Sysprep process to further configure your new servers as they come online. For example, you can specify in this answer file that a particular installer or batch file is to be launched upon the first Windows boot following Sysprep. This can be useful for any kind of cleanup task that you might want to perform, for example, if you had a batch file on your system that you used to flush out the log files following the first boot of new servers.

The two options that are most important for our purpose of wanting to create a master image file that we can use for quick server rollouts in the future are the `/generalize` switch and the `/shutdown` switch.

The `/generalize` switch is very important because it replaces all of the unique identification information, the SID info, in the new copies of Windows that come online. This allows your new servers to co-exist on the network with your original server and with other new servers that you bring online. The `/shutdown` switch is also very important because we want this master server to become sysprepped and then immediately shut down so that we can create our master image from it.

> Make sure that your server does NOT boot into Windows again until after you have created your master image or taken your master copy of the VHDX file. The first time Windows boots, it will inject the new SID information, and you want that only to happen on new servers that you have created based on your new image.

So, rather than simply throwing all of the switches at you and letting you decide, let's take a look at the ones that I typically use. I will make use of `/generalize` so that I make my new servers unique, and I also like to use `/oobe` so that the mini-setup wizard launches during the first boot of Windows on any of my new systems. Then, I will, of course, also use `/shutdown` because I need this server to be offline immediately following Sysprep so that I can take a copy of the hard drive to be used as my master image. So, my fully groomed `sysprep` command is shown in the following code:

```
sysprep.exe /generalize /oobe /shutdown
```

After launching this command, you will see Sysprep moving through some processes within Windows, and after a couple of minutes, your server will shut itself down, as shown in *Figure 2.42*:

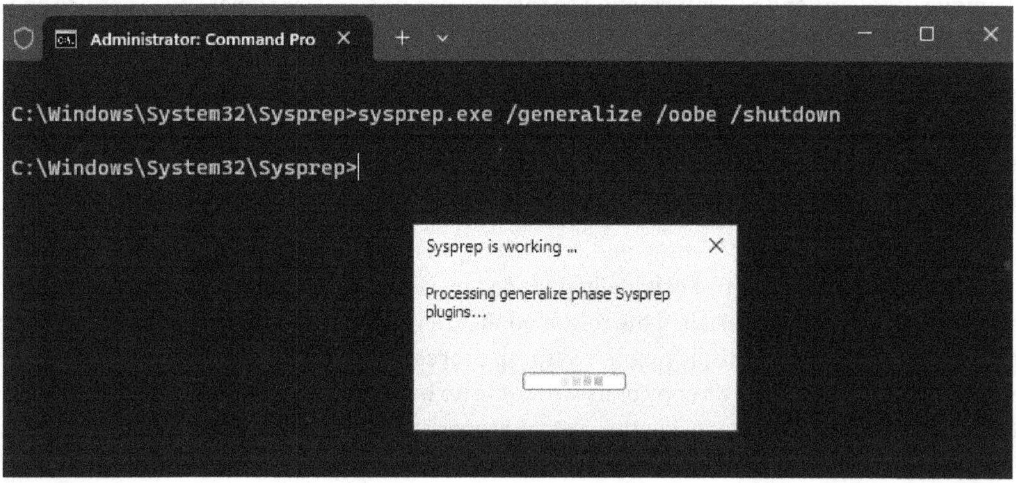

Figure 2.42: Sysprep and shutting down

You are now ready to create your master image from this hard disk.

Creating your master image of the drive

Our master server is now shut down, and we are ready to create our master image from this server. If it is a physical server, you can use any hard disk imaging utility to create an image file from the drive. An imaging utility, such as one from the company Acronis, will create a single file from your drive. This file contains an image of the entire disk that you can use to restore onto fresh hard drives in new servers in the future. On the other hand, most of you are probably dealing with virtual servers most often in your day-to-day work lives, and prepping new servers in the virtual world is even easier.

Once our master server has been sysprepped and shut down, you simply create a copy of the VHDX file. Log in to your Hyper-V server, copy and paste the hard disk file, and you're done! This new file can be renamed WS2025_Master_withUpdates.VHDX, or whatever you would like it to be named, to help you keep track of the current status of this image file. Save this image file or a copy of the VHDX file somewhere safe on your network, where you will be able to quickly grab copies of it whenever you need to spin up a new Windows Server 2025. Remember, you do *not* want to boot this actual VHDX file, as that would then remove its sysprepped-ness (yes, I realize that is not a real word). Instead, never boot this master image, but instead, create copies of it whenever building new servers.

Building new servers using copies of the master image

Now, we get to the easy part. When you want to create new servers in the future, you simply copy and paste your master file into a new location for the new server, rename the drive file to something appropriate for the server you are creating, and boot your new virtual machine from it. Here is where you see the real benefit from the time that Sysprep saves, as you can now spin up many new servers all at the same time by doing a quick copy and paste of the master image file and booting all of your new servers from these new files. No need to install Windows or pull out that dusty installation DVD!

As the new servers turn on for the first time and boot into Windows, they will run through the out-of-box experience, mini-setup wizard. Also, in the background, the OS gives itself a new, random, and unique hostname and SID information so that you can be sure you do not have conflicts on your network with these new servers.

New servers created from a sysprepped image file always receive a new hostname when they boot. This often confuses admins who might have named their master server something such as MASTER. After booting your new servers, you can expect to see randomized names on your new servers, and you will have to rename them according to their new duties in life.

For example, before running Sysprep and creating my master image, the server that I was working on was named DC2 because I had originally intended to use it as a domain controller in my network. However, because I had not installed the role or configured anything domain-related on it, this server was a perfect candidate for displaying the Sysprep process, and so I used it in our text today. I sysprepped it, shut it down, made a copy of its VHDX file (to be my master image file), and then I started DC2 back up. You can now see inside the system properties that I am back to having a randomized hostname, and so if I still want to use this server as DC2, I will have to rename it again now that it has finished booting through the mini setup, as shown in *Figure 2.43*:

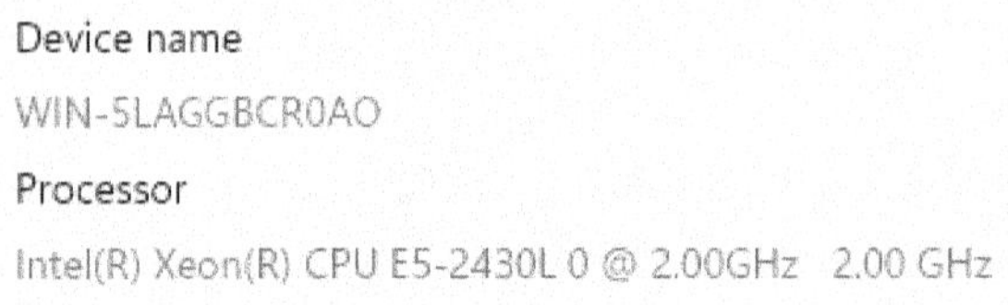

Device name

WIN-5LAGGBCR0AO

Processor

Intel(R) Xeon(R) CPU E5-2430L 0 @ 2.00GHz   2.00 GHz

Figure 2.43: Randomized hostname following Sysprep

Hopefully, this process will provide helpful information that can save you time when building new servers in your own environments. Get out there and give it a try the next time you have a new server to build! You can further benefit from the Sysprep tool by keeping many different master image files. Perhaps you have a handful of different kinds of servers that you prep regularly—there is nothing stopping you from creating several different master servers and creating multiple master images from these servers.

In-place upgrading to Windows Server 2025

Before wrapping up this chapter, let's enter into this taboo topic. As technology consumers, we are very much used to the idea of in-place upgrades. In fact, we expect them to work flawlessly, and we whine and complain when they don't. iPhone operating systems, Android version updates, Windows feature pack installations, and even something like a Windows 7 to Windows 10 upgrade are all expected to work seamlessly after a couple of simple pushes of a button. Those of us who have worked in Windows Server administration for more than a few years do NOT have this same mindset about server upgrades. For so many years, it was normal that in-place Windows Server upgrades were almost guaranteed to tank your server, causing it to be useless in the end. Due to this, server upgrades almost always meant replacing the server rather than upgrading it. You would leave the production server running, spin up a new one in parallel, configure all of the roles and specs needed on that server, then plan an after-hours migration of data and apps to the new server so that, the next morning, hopefully, everything was up and working on the new server. Then, you shut the old server down. This is normal. This is Windows Server upgrades. This is the life of a sysadmin.

Things have changed...

Starting with in-place upgrades from Server 2012R2 to Server 2016, it was suddenly possible to be successful with an in-place Windows Server upgrade. Not all the time, but sometimes. Since it was still sporadic, it was not commonly attempted, and we continued to stick to old methods of replacing servers. Then, Server 2019 came out, and in-place upgrades from 2016 to 2019 were actually quite stable, and you could even get away with upgrading 2012R2 straight to 2019, but again, this only worked *some* of the time.

Windows Server 2022 and 2025 continue that trend of improvement. Windows Server OS in-place upgrades are stable and introduce us to a much more efficient way to upgrade servers than the old rip-and-replace methods. Let's take a minute and prove this. On my Hyper-V host, where I run test labs, I have numerous Server 2025 VMs, but I still have many Server 2022 and even 2019 VMs sitting offline from previous projects.

I just finished joining one of those to my new lab network, and I will now attempt an in-place upgrade from Server 2019 directly to Server 2025.

Before we get into this, let's expand the idea of multi-version jumps. With the introduction of Windows Server 2025, Microsoft now supports what is sometimes known as N-4 updates. In other words, the ability to jump **four** full Windows Server versions, all at once. In other, other words, this means that Microsoft supports in-place upgrades directly from Windows Server 2012R2 up to Windows Server 2025. This is quite amazing when you think about it. At this point, nobody in the world *should* be running Server 2012R2, but don't try to hide it from me. I know you still do.

Downloading and running the installer

Running the installer is pretty much all you need to do. We already downloaded the .ISO installer file earlier in this chapter, in the *Installing Windows Server 2025* section. Copy this file to the older Server 2019, and double-click on the file to mount it. If you're using a virtual machine, all you need to do is visit the VM's settings and attach the .ISO file to the VM, and it now appears as if the Server 2025 installation DVD is connected to this server. Double-click on that virtual disk, and the Windows Server 2025 installation wizard will launch.

Figure 2.44: Starting an in-place upgrade to Windows Server 2025

The upgrade wizards are essentially the same as when we accomplished a fresh Windows Server 2025 installation earlier in this chapter. Walk through those wizards, choosing your licensing options and which version of Server 2025 you want to put into place, and you'll be on your way to an upgraded server! One extra decision for the upgrade versus installing fresh is that you get to decide whether you want to keep files, settings, and apps or not. I don't know why you would ever want to ditch your settings and apps when upgrading a production server to a new OS, but the option exists regardless.

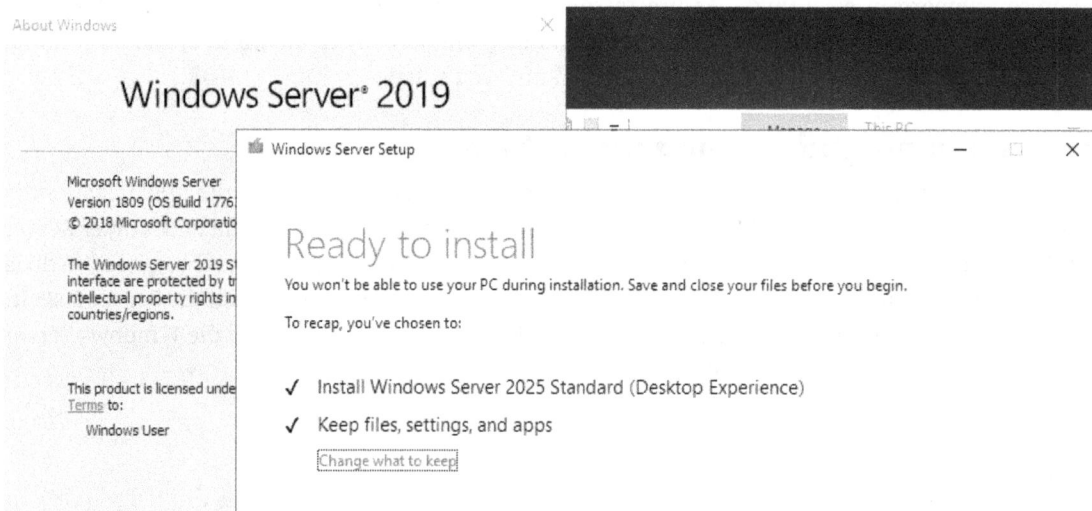

Figure 2.45: In-place upgrade from 2019 to 2025

That's it! Once those options have been decided upon, the installation process kicks off, and after a little bit of time and a few automated restarts of the server, you should find yourself back at a login screen of the same server with the same roles and files present, but now running the Windows Server 2025 operating system.

Upgrading from Settings

Wait a minute, there is one more option for the in-place upgrade methodology! You may have already noticed this option on some of your existing servers and wondered what in the world was going on. It is normal to expect a Windows 11 upgrade button when visiting the Windows Update settings inside a Windows 10 computer, but to have the same OS upgrade method available in the server world is kind of mind-blowing. Microsoft has now introduced the ability for the internal Windows Update engine to be able to self-upgrade Windows Server 2022 to Windows Server 2025.

While not yet existing on all servers out in the wild, visiting **Settings** > **Windows Update** may provide you with a new option to launch the Windows Server 2025 upgrade process right from here, without needing to first acquire installation media, as shown in *Figure 2.46*:

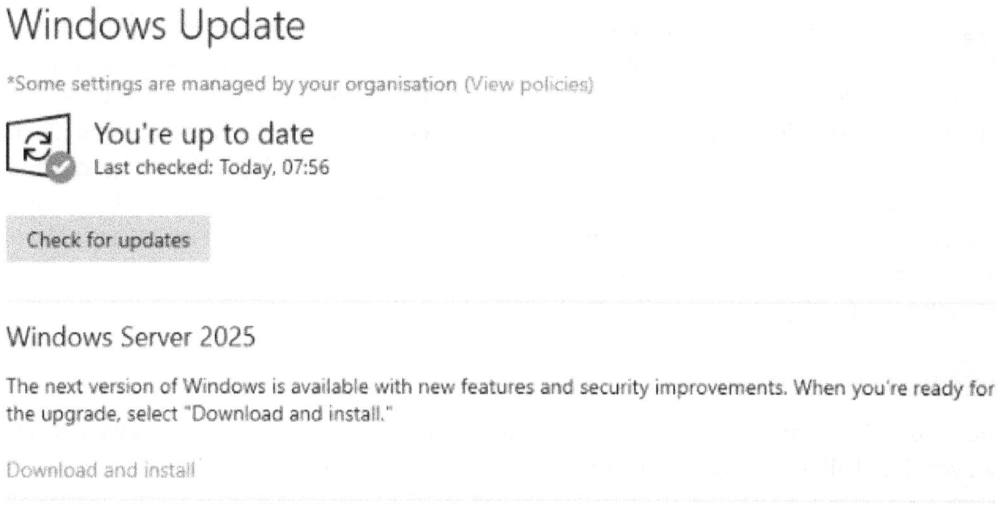

Windows Update

*Some settings are managed by your organisation (View policies)

You're up to date
Last checked: Today, 07:56

Check for updates

Windows Server 2025

The next version of Windows is available with new features and security improvements. When you're ready for the upgrade, select "Download and install."

Download and install

Figure 2.46: In-place 2025 upgrade from Windows Settings???

Two special notes about this new capability. First, Microsoft says it will never allow the Server 2025 upgrade process to run all on its own. This new option is currently creating some fear among sysadmins that they may have servers self-update and cause issues. Again, per Microsoft's own words, it will always wait for you to click this button and choose to upgrade.

Second, if you are in-place upgrading multiple versions, such as N-4, bringing a server from 2012R2 to 2025 directly, this will always require using the Windows Server 2025 installation media and running the installer manually.

Summary

Anyone interested in being a Windows Server administrator needs to be comfortable with installing and managing servers, and covering those topics establishes an important baseline for moving forward. It is quite common in today's IT world for new OS releases to be thoroughly tested by companies before deploying them, both because server hardware resources are so easily available to us through virtualization technologies and because most business systems are now being designed for 100% uptime. This kind of reliability requires very thorough testing of any platform changes, and to accomplish such testing of the Windows Server 2025 OS in your environment, you will burn quite a bit of time spinning through the basic installation processes numerous times. I hope that you can put the suggestions provided in this chapter to good use in saving you precious extra minutes when dealing with these tasks in your Windows Server world.

Years ago, quite a bit of effort was regularly put into figuring out which roles and services could co-exist because the number of servers available to us was limited. With the virtualization and cloud paradigm shift, many companies have a virtually unlimited number of servers that can be running, and this means we are running much larger quantities of servers to perform the same jobs and functions. The management and administration of these servers then becomes an IT burden, and adopting the centralized administration tools and ideas available   within Windows Server 2025 will also save you considerable time and effort in your daily workload. In the next chapter, we will start to dive into some of the most commonly used roles and tools in a Windows Server environment and the core infrastructure technologies surrounding Active Directory.

Questions

Put your knowledge to the test with the following questions. If you need a hand (or just want to double-check), you'll find all the answers in the *Appendix* section of the book.

1. What is the name of the web-based, centralized server management tool from Microsoft (fun fact, this toolset was originally known as **Project Honolulu**)?
2. True or False? Windows Server 2025 needs to be installed on rack-mount server hardware.
3. True or False? By choosing the default installation option for Windows Server 2025, you will end up with a user interface that looks quite like Windows 11.
4. What is the PowerShell cmdlet that displays currently installed roles and features in Windows Server 2025?
5. True or False? Server Manager can be used to manage many different servers at the same time.
6. What is the name of the toolset that can be installed on a Windows 11 computer in order to run Server Manager on that client workstation?
7. Which built-in tool is used to prepare the Windows operating systems for imaging or replication?
8. What is the oldest version of Windows Server that can be in-place upgraded to Windows Server 2025?

3

Active Directory

Working on computers and working in IT can be two very different things. Throughout my career, I have interviewed hundreds of people seeking to land an IT role. When talking to any engineer who already has some experience working within a corporate IT environment, the topic of Active Directory is old hat. They are familiar with what it is, what it does, and with at least some of the toolsets provided to manipulate it. Hiring for entry-level engineering positions takes an entirely different twist, as these interviews often include people who have worked with computers for years, and are very good at it, but who literally have no idea what Active Directory is or does. If your experience with computers is building them, repairing them, and working within the operating system, you probably have had zero reasons to understand this technology called Active Directory, even though it is the one central thing that underpins almost every corporate network across the globe.

Each of you reading this book will have a different acquired skillset and level of experience with the Windows Server environment. As I mentioned previously, building a server and working through the installation of the operating system is great progress and a very important first step for doing real work in your environment. But until you know and understand the purposes behind the main roles available in Windows Server 2025, the only thing your new server does is consume electricity.

A server is intended to serve data. The kind of data that it serves and to what purpose depends entirely on what roles you determine the server must... well... *serve*. Appropriately, you must install roles within Windows Server 2025 to make it *do* something. We already know how to get roles installed on our server, but we have not talked about any of the purposes behind these roles. Over the next few chapters, we will start looking into what I commonly refer to as the *core infrastructural roles* available within Windows Server. This involves discussing the role's general purpose, as well as working through specific tasks that pertain to those roles. These are the things you will be responsible for doing in your daily tasks as a server administrator.

We begin with the single most important role in all of the on-premises Microsoft world, **Active Directory (AD)**. AD, as it is commonly referred to, is a directory service that serves as a kind of database, storing and centralizing various types of information about your organization. User accounts, computer accounts, certificates, policies, DNS, and even file replication are all things that you can find hooked into AD.

As we look over the parts and pieces of AD, it will become clearer what information is stored within and why it is so important. If you are new to IT and do not yet have a good grasp of AD, make sure to learn this technology! AD is the hinge upon which almost everything in a Windows Server world revolves. Is it possible to utilize Windows servers without them being connected and joined to Active Directory? Yes. Is it likely you will ever find this scenario at play in the real world? No.

During many Windows Server operating system releases, the number of new or improved features inside Active Directory is low. Windows Server 2025 bulks that trend, and we have already mentioned the Active Directory improvements in *Chapter 1*. If you glazed over that section because you were, at the time, unfamiliar with AD's purpose and thought it didn't pertain to you, you are welcome to re-read those updates. Ultimately, while many protocols and security features used by Active Directory were improved for this 2025 release, these changes are largely "under the hood." In other words, we don't have a bunch of new buttons and screens to interact with due to these changes, but everything that you do inside Active Directory is enhanced simply by using Windows Server 2025 to run it, as opposed to any older version of the Windows Server operating system. In this chapter, we will learn about the following:

- What is a domain controller?
- Creating your first domain
- Multiple domain controllers for redundancy
- Active Directory Users and Computers
- Active Directory Domains and Trusts
- Active Directory Sites and Services
- Active Directory Administrative Center
- Read-only domain controllers
- FSMO roles
- Demoting an old domain controller
- Intro to Group Policy
- Microsoft Entra ID

What is a domain controller?

If we are going to discuss the core infrastructure services that you need to piece together your Micro-soft-driven network, there is no better place to start than with the domain controller. A **domain controller**, commonly referred to as a **DC**, is simply a server that hosts AD. It is a central point of contact, a central "hub" so to speak, that is accessed prior to almost any communication that takes place between a client and server in your network. Perhaps the easiest way to describe it is as a storage container for all *identification* that happens on the network. Usernames, passwords, computer accounts, groups of computers, servers, groups and collections of servers, security policies, file replication services, and many more things are stored within and managed by DCs. If you are not planning to have a DC be one of the first servers in your Microsoft-centric network, you might as well not even start building that network. DCs are essential to the way that our computers and devices communicate with each other and with the server infrastructure inside our companies.

Active Directory Domain Services

If you've stopped reading at this point to go install the *Domain Controller* role onto your server, welcome back! There is no role called *Domain Controller*. The role that provides all these capabilities is called **Active Directory Domain Services, or AD DS**. This is the role that you need to install on a server. By installing that role, you will have turned your server into a DC. The purpose of running a DC, really, is to create a directory, or database, of objects in your network. This database is known as **Active Directory**, and is a platform inside which you build a hierarchical structure to store objects, such as usernames, passwords, and computer accounts. You might be thinking, *Didn't we just say these same words in a slightly different way?* and you're not wrong. AD is important, and I want to make sure you understand it. A career in IT guarantees that you will, in some way, interface with AD in your work.

Most of the time, when you hear anyone talking about *Active Directory*, it is likely that what they really mean is a single **domain** within the directory. There is a whole hierarchy within an AD schema, comprising forests, trees, domains, and organizational units. We will discuss each of these organizational levels of AD as we navigate through the tools that you will be utilizing to interact with AD further along in this chapter.

Once you have created a domain in which you can store accounts, objects, and devices, you can then create user accounts and passwords for your employees to utilize for authentication. You can then also join your other servers and computers to this domain so that they can accept and benefit from those user credentials. Creating and joining a domain is the secret sauce that allows you to walk from computer to computer within your company and log in to each of them with your own username and password, even when you have never logged in to that computer before. Even more powerful is the fact that it enables directory-capable applications to authenticate directly against AD when they need authentication information. For example, when I, as a domain user, log in to my computer at work with my username and password, the Windows operating system running on my computer reaches out to a DC server and verifies that my password is correct.

Once it confirms that I really am who I say I am, AD issues an authentication token back to my computer, and I can log in to Windows. Then, once I am on my desktop, I am able to launch applications. For example, I might open **File Explorer** and navigate to one of my drive letters to open a document that is housed on my file server. The file server is only going to allow certain people or groups to have access to this file. How does the file server understand who I am? How does it ascertain my user identity? Did I need to re-enter my username and password to be able to open this file? No. And the reason I do not have to re-authenticate myself over and over again as I open more applications is that these servers are all part of the same domain, and have the same universal understanding of that authentication token AD gave me during login. My user account and these machines I am interacting with are all part of the same domain.

When this is true, and it is for most business networks, my authentication token can be shared among many programs. So, once I log in to the computer itself, my applications can launch and open, and pass my credentials through to the application server, without any further input from me as a user. It would be quite a frustrating experience indeed if we required our users to enter passwords all day, every day, as they opened the programs that they need in order to do their work.

AD itself is a broad enough topic to warrant its own book, and indeed, there have been many written on the topic. Now that we have a basic understanding of what it is and why it's critical to have in our Windows Server environment, let's get our hands dirty using some of the tools that get installed on your DC during the AD DS role installation process.

Creating your first domain

I must admit that I have cheated a little bit and have already been working from within a domain for the purpose of taking screenshots for the book up to this point. My test lab already has a DC1 server up and running, and on it, I have configured a domain called contoso.local. However, saying "domains are important" and not showing you how to create one would not be helpful to you, and so we are going to build a brand-new domain now, on a brand-new server.

You probably recognize **Contoso** if you've ever read over Microsoft tutorials or example configuration documentation, because it is one of several fake business names Microsoft often uses in documentation or for the purpose of showing example scenarios. I am using it here as well, but you could name your domain anything you want to. For setting up our second domain, I am going to pull another company name from the Microsoft hat, **Fabrikam.**

One of the first things that needs to be decided before you can build a domain is the name of the domain. We don't want to discuss DNS in depth here because there's another whole chapter for that, but everyone uses DNS every day, whether they realize it or not. Every time you type any website name—microsoft.com, google.com, bing.com, and so on—you are inputting a name, which DNS is then going to turn into an IP address. You also know that the ending of website names can take on many forms. The most common is .com, but you may visit websites that also end with .org, .biz, .info, .tech, .edu, .mil, and many more.

Let's take microsoft.com as an example. If you simply visit microsoft.com, you'll see the main website for the company. If you visit learn.microsoft.com, you will land on their documentation and learning platform page. Visiting portal.microsoft.com takes you to a Microsoft 365 sign-in page, and if you have a Microsoft 365 account, you can sign in here and perform many functions. The different addresses you are typing into the web browser are taking you to vastly different web pages and systems, yet the domain names being called for in the browser all end with the same microsoft.com. This means that microsoft.com is the primary domain name for all of these things, also known as a **domain suffix** or a top-level domain.

Why am I running down this rabbit hole? Because this is important information to understand when you decide on your internal domain name. Just like a domain suffix on the internet, when you build your internal domain and then later join computers and servers to that domain, each of those devices is going to have a true, full name of `computername.domainname.something`. In my current domain, `contoso.local`, a full server name that exists right now is `DC1.contoso.local`.

Most internal domains that I have encountered in the world end with `.local`. Is it possible to name your internal domain something that ends in one of these internet-based suffixes, such as `Contoso.com`? Yes! You can name your internal domain whatever you want, and in fact, if you have plans to host email in Office 365, using an internal domain that matches your public domain name used for email carries some advantages. Some of you may be thinking at this point, "I already own `contoso.com` (insert your own business website name here), so wouldn't it be less confusing overall if I also name my internal domain the same thing? `contoso.com`?" The answer is yes and no. For certain scenarios that involve cloud resources, like Office 365 and Azure, yes, using a `.com` internal domain can make a more seamless transition to the cloud. However, prior to these cloud technologies, it was always Microsoft's recommendation to end your internal domain with `.local`. We will talk more about why this is the case in *Chapter 4, DNS and DHCP*, when we discuss something called **split-brain DNS**.

Prep your domain controller

Okay, I have decided to use `fabrikam.local` as my internal domain name. Now, how do I make that a reality? We only need one server to build a domain: the server that you want to be your DC. I have a new Windows Server 2025 VM running and plugged into a network, but so far, I have not configured anything at all on the server. There are three simple things that need to happen on any server that you plan to turn into a DC:

1. **Set a static IP address:** Head into your NIC properties and define a static IP address for this server. Even if you already have a DHCP server running in your network to hand out IP addresses, you do not want DC servers to ever change IPs. It is possible to do so, but quite challenging. So, best practice dictates that whatever IP address you define for your DC, plan on that being its IP address forever.

2. **Set a good hostname:** Similar to IP addressing on a DC, it is not recommended to ever change the name of a DC server. In fact, this is quite a bit more complicated than IP addressing, and you should definitely plan that whatever name you give your server today will forever be its name on your network until the day you decommission this server entirely.

3. **Set the DNS server address:** Head back into your NIC properties and configure the DNS server address that your DC is looking for to be itself. What? Itself? It's not a DNS server! Not yet, but other than rare circumstances, almost every DC will also become a DNS server. DNS integrates with AD, and there is a lot of benefit to hosting these services together, so most Microsoft environments you encounter will have AD DS and DNS installed together on DC servers. Generally, when setting up your first DC, you will always start by pointing the NIC's DNS settings to the server's own IP address.

You can see in *Figure 3.1* that I have now named my new server FAB-DC1, configured a static IP, and pointed DNS to itself:

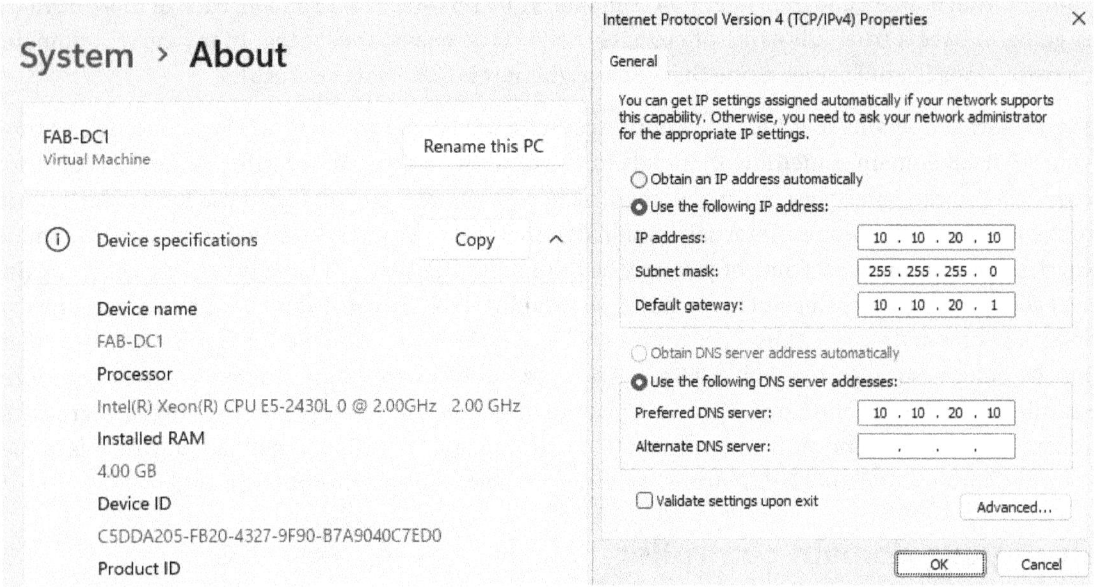

Figure 3.1: Prepping a server to become a DC

Install the AD DS role

Now that the server is prepped to be a DC, we can install the role! Since you are already familiar with the process of adding roles to servers, we won't step through the whole thing again. Simply utilize **Server Manager** or **PowerShell** to install the following components on your new server:

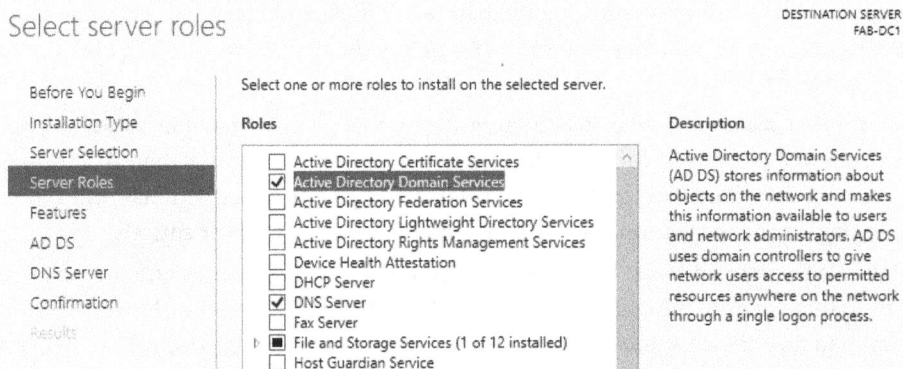

Figure 3.2: Installing AD DS and DNS Server roles

As mentioned, I am going to install **AD DS** for Active Directory and **DNS Server** so that this DC can also serve as a true DNS server for our new business. As you progress through the role installation wizard, you will encounter some informational text that is useful to read over, but there should be no further options that you need to select in order to get both of these roles installed on your server.

Configure the domain

Following the installation of the roles, you will notice a yellow exclamation mark near the top of Server Manager. Clicking on that icon, you can see text indicating that some configuration is required for the AD DS role:

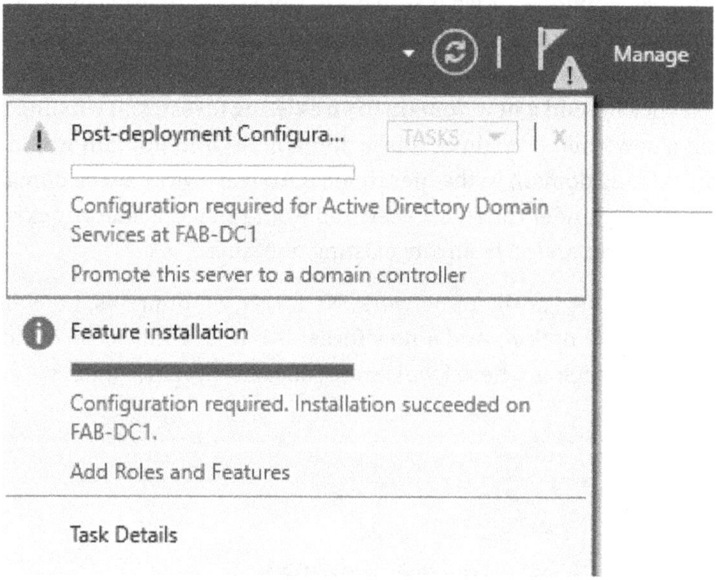

Figure 3.3: Additional configuration is required for the AD DS role

Click on the link that says **Promote this server to a domain controller**. This link will invoke the configuration wizard that is going to walk us through turning the server into a true DC.

Trees, forests, and... domains?

Wait a minute, the first screen we encounter in this promotion wizard, where we need to make a decision, is talking about shrubbery. I enjoy gardening, but what in the world are we talking about here?? You already know that a domain is like a database, containing information about many kinds of objects, but primarily user accounts and computer accounts that are part of that domain. What we have not really discussed yet is that a domain is not the top tier of its existence; rather, a *domain resides within a forest*. These are the two technical terms you will run across when working within AD (**domain** and **forest**), and references to a **tree** are more metaphorical, related to the layout of a forest with domains underneath the forest, with possible child domains listed beneath the domains. The whole schema, when mapped out on paper, may resemble the many branches of a tree; thus, we have the term *tree*.

A forest is the top tier in AD, and you could potentially have many different domains inside the same forest. Why would you want to do that? Most companies don't, and most of the time, you will find that any given company has exactly one internal domain, residing within one forest, and that's it.

One reason you may find multiple domains inside the same forest would be if the company had different divisions or business units that needed their authentication and systems to be separated from each other. In a single domain, remember that, often, any domain user can authenticate and log in to any domain computer, and perhaps you wanted to ensure that nobody in *Division A* was able to log in to computers that were owned by *Division B*. Creating multiple domains would be one way to accomplish that scenario.

As you walk through the domain configuration wizard that we have just launched on our new server, you will see many different options for what kind of DC this server may become. You may be adding a DC to an existing domain, adding a new domain to an existing forest, or creating a new forest altogether. Selecting each of these options in the wizard will present you with different sub-options related to that selection. If you click on **Add a new domain to an existing forest**, you will find that you then have options for creating a new child domain or a tree domain. A **child domain** would be a new domain that exists under an existing domain in the hierarchical AD tree, while a **tree domain** would be a new domain that resides directly under the forest itself and would sit alongside any existing domains, still under the same forest but separated from any existing domains.

Today, we have nothing in this Fabrikam network. No forest, no domains, no child domains. So we are going to choose the third option, **Add a new forest**. All that needs to be decided on this screen is the root domain name, which is where I will enter `fabrikam.local`, which we decided on earlier:

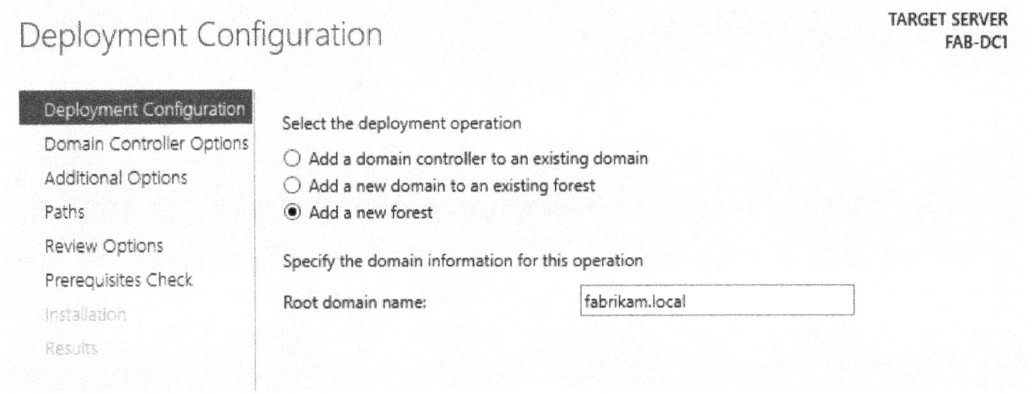

Figure 3.4: Creating a new forest

The remaining screens in this configuration wizard contain a number of options, but not many of them need to be populated if you are unsure of the answers. Especially if you are building out a test lab, the default options are generally sufficient. We'll do a quick summary here of each screen to point out options and what they mean.

Domain controller options

Now that you understand that there are at least two tiers to every AD, at minimum one forest and one domain, it is important to understand that each of those things has its own **functional level**. Forest and domain functional levels are classified by different versions of the Windows Server operating system releases. The Windows Server 2016 functional level has more features and accessories baked into it than Server 2012 R2 does, for example, and on and on. Something interesting to note is that Windows Server 2019 and 2022 did not introduce their own functional levels, which was a strange thing in the world of Windows Server releases. As you work through this wizard, you'll discover a large gap in the list of available levels. Windows Server 2025 is the default, of course, but the next newest option in the drop-down list lands on Windows Server 2016.

Why does the wizard even ask? Wouldn't it make sense that you would always want to select the newest from this list? In almost all cases, the answer is yes. One reason you may need to select an older functional level for either your forest or domain is if some technology you are planning to implement, or some version of device you plan to join to that domain, requires an older functional level version. This brings to light another valid scenario that might require a company to build a secondary domain under an existing forest: if a technology that you wanted to implement for the business carried some specific requirements that locked you into a certain version of functional level, but your primary production domain could not meet those requirements for whatever reason.

For our purposes today, we simply leave both forest and domain functional levels selected on the default Windows Server 2025.

On this screen of the wizard, you also have options to choose whether or not this DC will also be a DNS server (usually yes), whether it will be a **Global Catalog (GC)** server (also usually yes), or a read-only domain controller, which we will discuss later in this chapter.

The third option, and the only one that absolutely requires your attention, is to define a **Directory Services Restore Mode (DSRM)** password. I sincerely hope that you never have to enter AD recovery mode in order to restore information or your directory, but if you do, this password is going to be very important to that process:

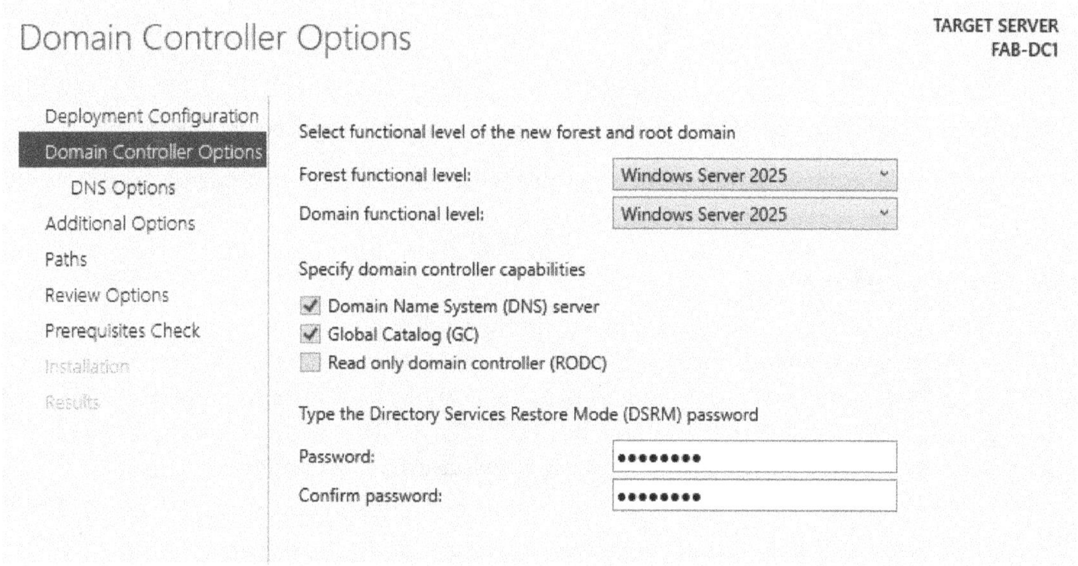

Figure 3.5: Domain Controller Options

DNS Options

If you were creating a new DC/DNS server that was going to live inside an existing tree, and particularly if your new server is going to play a child role, then you typically want to ensure that the parent's DNS zones have a delegation for this new DNS server you are creating, to ensure that names in your domain can be successfully resolved in the parent domain as well. The creation of that DNS delegation is the only option on this screen, and in cases where we are creating a brand-new forest and domain, there is no existing authoritative parent zone, so there is an expected warning message on-screen:

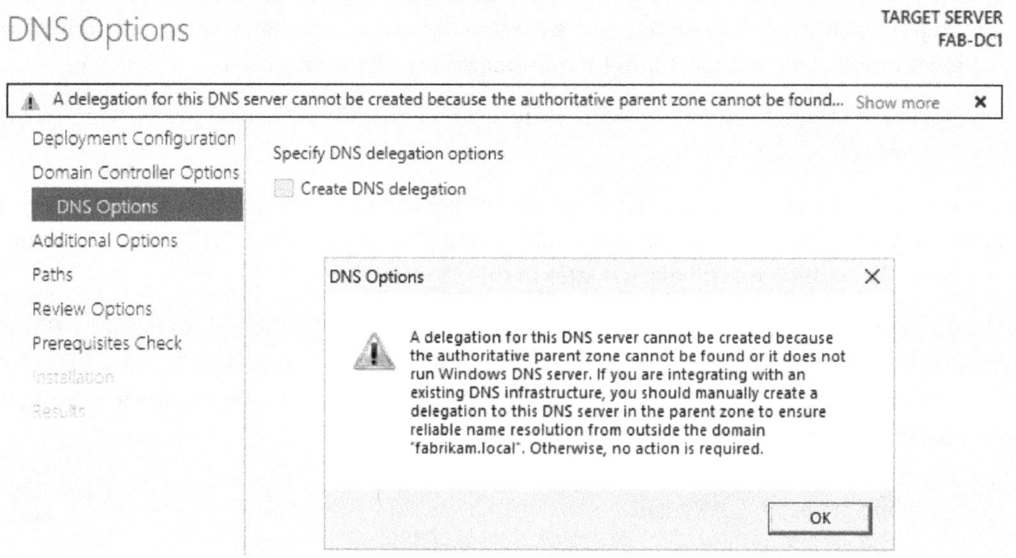

DNS Options   TARGET SERVER
                                                                                     FAB-DC1

⚠ A delegation for this DNS server cannot be created because the authoritative parent zone cannot be found... Show more ✕

Deployment Configuration   Specify DNS delegation options
Domain Controller Options   ☐ Create DNS delegation
DNS Options
Additional Options
Paths   DNS Options   ✕
Review Options
Prerequisites Check   ⚠ A delegation for this DNS server cannot be created because
Installation   the authoritative parent zone cannot be found or it does not
Results   run Windows DNS server. If you are integrating with an
                                            existing DNS infrastructure, you should manually create a
                                            delegation to this DNS server in the parent zone to ensure
                                            reliable name resolution from outside the domain
                                            'fabrikam.local'. Otherwise, no action is required.

                                                                                    OK

Figure 3.6: Expected warning message regarding no authoritative parent zone

Since we are building a new forest, there is nothing we need to do with this warning message, and we simply click **Next** to proceed.

Additional options

The NetBIOS domain name should self-populate in the wizard and will be the first portion of your domain name. In my example, it has inserted the word FABRIKAM into this field. Many people seem to think that NetBIOS is obsolete, but it is still used by applications to pass traffic around in some cases, so the options for configuring it here are still important. You don't need to do anything on this screen other than to ensure a NetBIOS name populates in the wizard and then continue.

Paths

AD stores quite a bit of very important information on your DC server. If desired, here, you can specify paths for storing this data if you want it to reside in a special location, such as on a dedicated hard drive. The default options are all within the C:\Windows folder, which is generally where everyone leaves it.

Review options, prerequisites check, and installation

That's it! You have now populated all the available options, and you are presented with a screen that allows you to review the selections you have made. Once satisfied that everything looks good on this screen, the wizard will run through a prerequisites check on your server to ensure it is ready to become a domain controller. This is the point where, if you forgot to assign a static IP or to set a DNS server in the NIC properties, the wizard will fail the prerequisites check and flag you with some warnings. In fact, you will likely see at least one or two warnings even if you have done everything perfectly: one regarding that DNS delegation that we already talked about, and another warning about cryptography algorithms. This is normal behavior for configuring a brand new forest/domain on Windows Server 2025.

Assuming you have everything in order, the wizard will continue on to installation, at the end of which your server will reboot, and it is now officially a DC for your network.

During the first login to your server, which is now a DC, you will notice at the login screen that you are now signing in with a domain account, no longer a local account on this server. DCs don't actually have local user accounts anymore; if you were using the built-in administrator account to sign in to your server before, as I was, that account and password have now been converted into *the* domain administrator account. This account can now be used to log in to any computer or server that is later joined to your domain and will automatically receive administrative rights on that device. Make sure you're using a good domain administrator password, and don't share it with anybody! To further strengthen security around these ultra-important passwords, consider storing them inside a trackable password vault. There are various available options, but using a password vault enables you to store your passwords in a secure location, accessible only to those who actually need them (your IT staff), and will allow you to track and audit which of your employees has accessed these passwords.

Multiple domain controllers for redundancy

Now that we have configured our first DC, we should jump in and start setting up objects inside AD, right? Not yet! I'm being a little dramatic here; of course, you can jump ahead and start using the tools that interface with AD, which we will discuss immediately following this section of our chapter. There are many businesses that have run or are still running a single DC successfully, without ever considering redundancy for this critically important role in your environment. If you think I'm being dense and that nobody in their right mind would ever run a production server environment today with a single DC, I'll have you know that I literally encountered such an environment only yesterday. What was the issue that I was tasked with investigating? Wouldn't you know it, a problem on the DC…

Is it possible to run a business with one DC? Yes, until something happens to it. Those of us on the side of common sense understand that this scenario is literally *begging* for disaster. Whenever setting up a real environment and not just monkeying around in a test lab, it is going to be super critical that you establish redundancy for your domain.

Adding a second DC is even easier than spinning up the first one. Simply take the same steps that you did last time, with one exception to the way that the NIC is configured:

1. Spin up a new server.
2. Set a static IP.
3. Configure a good permanent hostname.
4. Deviation from before: Instead of configuring your NIC's DNS server settings to point at the new server itself, point your primary DNS to the existing DC's IP address.

Now, when you add the AD DS and DNS server roles and walk through the same configuration wizard that we just witnessed a few minutes ago, this time, you are going to choose the **Add a domain controller to an existing domain** option. Then, all you have to do is select or type the name of the domain and provide administrative credentials for that domain:

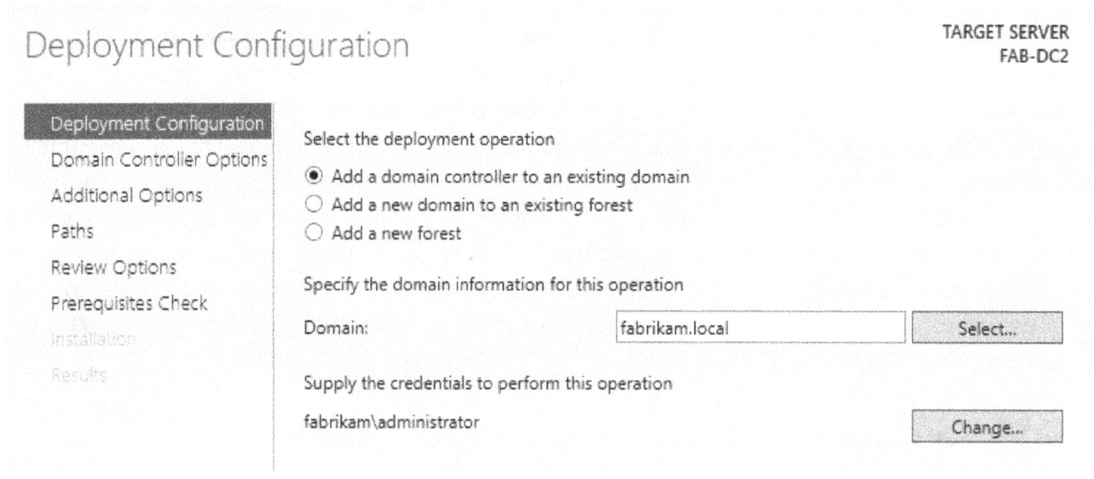

Deployment Configuration

TARGET SERVER
FAB-DC2

Deployment Configuration
Domain Controller Options
Additional Options
Paths
Review Options
Prerequisites Check
Installation
Results

Select the deployment operation

- ◉ Add a domain controller to an existing domain
- ○ Add a new domain to an existing forest
- ○ Add a new forest

Specify the domain information for this operation

Domain: fabrikam.local   Select...

Supply the credentials to perform this operation

fabrikam\administrator   Change...

Figure 3.7: Adding a new DC to an existing domain

The rest of the wizard is pretty straightforward, but you'll notice that you have a new drop-down menu on the **Domain Controller Options** screen that allows you to select a site name. If you had multiple AD sites, you would select here which site this new DC is being installed into. We will discuss more about Active Directory Sites and Services in a later section of this chapter. You will also notice that you have to once again create a password for **Directory Services Restore Mode**. This password is configured per DC, so it could potentially be different for each of your DC servers.

If you remember everything we have done so far, you will realize that right now, both of our DC servers are pointing to FAB-DC1 as their primary DNS server, as defined inside the NIC properties. As long as each DC can contact a DNS server, your domain is going to function properly, but now that we have two DCs (which are also DNS servers) created for the purpose of redundancy, your overall solution will be made even better if you ensure that both DCs are aware of each other from a DNS perspective.

There are two different ways to go about this, both are considered to be good practice:

- Configure each DC to have a primary DNS server address of itself, and the secondary DNS server address to be the other DC. This causes DNS lookups on those servers to happen slightly faster, but has the potential drawback that you might have to wait for AD replication to happen between the two servers before newly created DNS records are available on both servers.

- Configure both (or all) of your DCs to use a single DNS server as the primary DNS server on your network, with themselves as the secondary DNS server. If all of your DCs are looking to a centralized DNS server, then any updates or additions you make to that DNS server are immediately available on all DCs. However, if that central DNS server goes offline, it will cause all other DCs some grief and delays as they take a second to realize that they now need to fail over to themselves for name resolution.

Whoops, I said there were two ways to do this, and generally, you'll find that either of the preceding options is the way that DNS is configured in most environments. But there is a third possibility here that is sort of a mix between the two. You could configure each DC's NIC settings so that the primary DNS server is any different DNS server in your environment, and then make the secondary DNS server point back at itself. This causes DNS lookups to always happen across the network, which generates more traffic than the other options, but also ensures that each DC can stand on its own accord if the other one fails. In this third scenario, if there were two DCs in the network, you are basically just pointing them at each other while using themselves as a backup.

I can't tell you what is best for your own environment, but what I do most of the time is configure each DC to declare itself as the primary DNS server, and just remember that whenever I create new DNS records, it might take a few minutes for them to replicate between the DCs. One additional advantage to going with the first option, where each DC points at itself primarily, is that it simplifies troubleshooting, especially in situations where you may have multiple DCs spread across different network segments or geographical regions.

> When you configure a DC to point itself to itself for primary DNS, it is generally recommended to utilize the localhost IP address `127.0.0.1`, rather than the DC's actual IPv4 address.

One more important note on the topic of populating DNS server information into the NIC properties of your DC servers. **Never configure DCs to point at public DNS servers.** Plugging `8.8.8.8` or something similar into a NIC's DNS settings is a common thing to do for internet-connected **home computers**. Not for servers. Do not carry this mentality into your business. Your DCs must register special records within AD, and pointing a DC's NIC at a public DNS server will cause that process to fail.

I have actually had to clean up this mess, caused by that exact scenario—a company was having some internet connectivity troubles, and as part of troubleshooting, an IT person decided to replace the actual DNS server information inside the NIC properties of every server in the network with `8.8.8.8`. Let's just say that didn't work out very well...

Active Directory Users and Computers

There is not a single tool that is used to manage all facets of AD. Since it is such an expansive technology, our configuration of the directory is spread across a number of different management consoles. Let's look at each of them and at some of the most common tasks that you will be performing inside these tools. Any of these management consoles can be launched from any of your DC servers, and just as we saw in a previous chapter, the easiest way to launch these consoles is right from the **Tools** menu in the upper-right corner of **Server Manager**.

We'll start with the tool that is alphabetically last in the list of our AD tools, because this is by far the one that the everyday server administrator will use most often. **Active Directory Users and Computers** is the console from which all of the user accounts and computer accounts are created and managed. Open it up, and you will see the name of your domain listed in the left-hand column. Expand your domain name, and you will see several folders listed here. If you are opening this on an existing DC in a well-grown network, you may have pages and pages of folders listed here. If this is a new environment, there are only a handful. The most important pieces to point out here are **Computers** and **Users**. As common sense would dictate, these are the default containers in which new computer accounts and user accounts that join the domain will be located.

While this window looks quite a bit like **File Explorer** with a tree of folders, these *folders* really aren't folders at all. Most of the manila-colored folder icons that you see here are known as **organizational units (OUs)**. I say *most of* because there are a few containers that exist out of the box that are legitimate storage containers for holding objects, but they are not officially called OUs. The ones we pointed out earlier, **Users** and **Computers**, are actually these generic storage containers and are not traditional OUs. However, any new folders that you create for yourself inside AD are going to be OUs. The difference is depicted in the manila folder icon. You can see in the upcoming screenshots that some of the manila folders have an extra little graphic on top of the folder itself. Only those folders that have the extra little yellow thing are real OUs.

OUs are the structural containers that we use inside AD in order to organize our objects and keep them all in useful places. Just like with folders on a file server, you can create your own hierarchy of organizational units here, in order to sort and manipulate the location inside AD of all your domain-joined network objects and devices. In the following screenshot, you can see that instead of having just plain Users and Computers folders, I have created some new OUs, including sub-OUs (more officially known as **nested OUs**), so that as I grow my environment, I will have a more structured and organized directory:

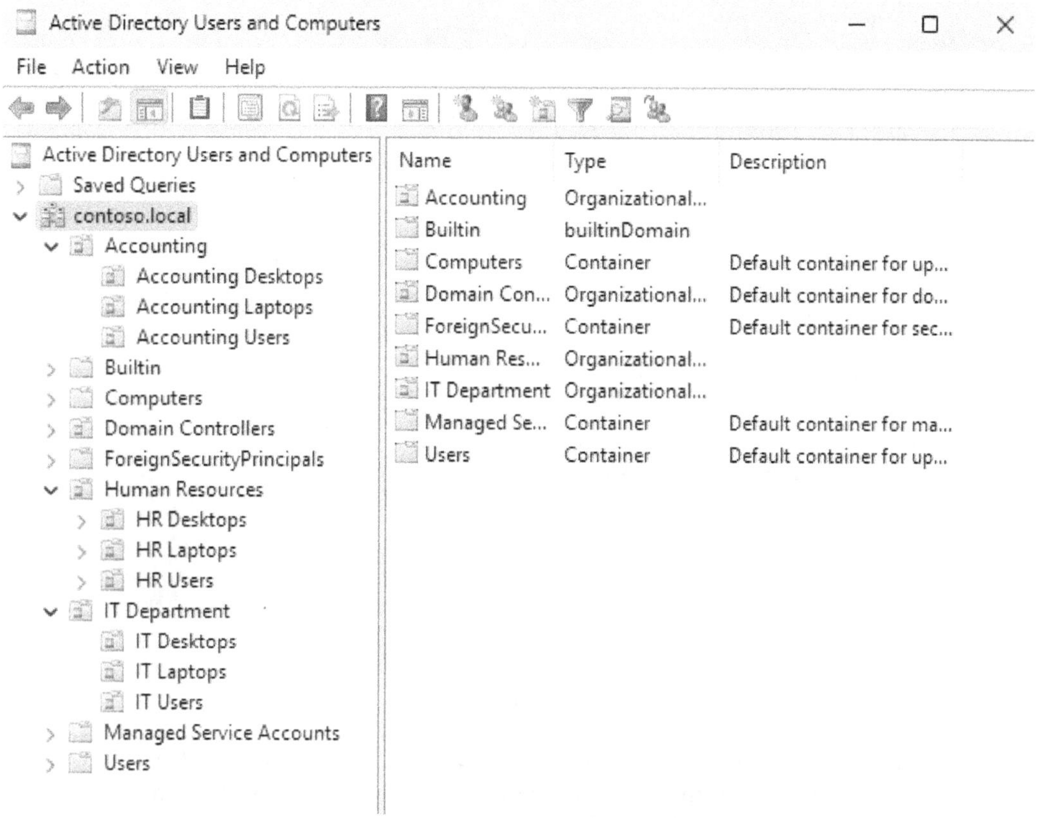

Figure 3.8: AD structure

User accounts

Now that we have some OUs ready to contain our objects, let's create a new user. Say we have a new server administrator coming on board, Joe Admin, and we need to get him an AD login so that he can start his job. Simply find the appropriate OU for his account to reside within, right-click on the OU, and navigate to **New | User**. We are then presented with an information-gathering screen about all the things that AD needs in order to create this new account. Most of the information here is self-explanatory, but if you are new to AD, the one field I will point out is **User logon name**. Whatever information is put in this field is the user's official **username** on the network. Whenever they log in to a computer or server, this is the name they will input as their login.

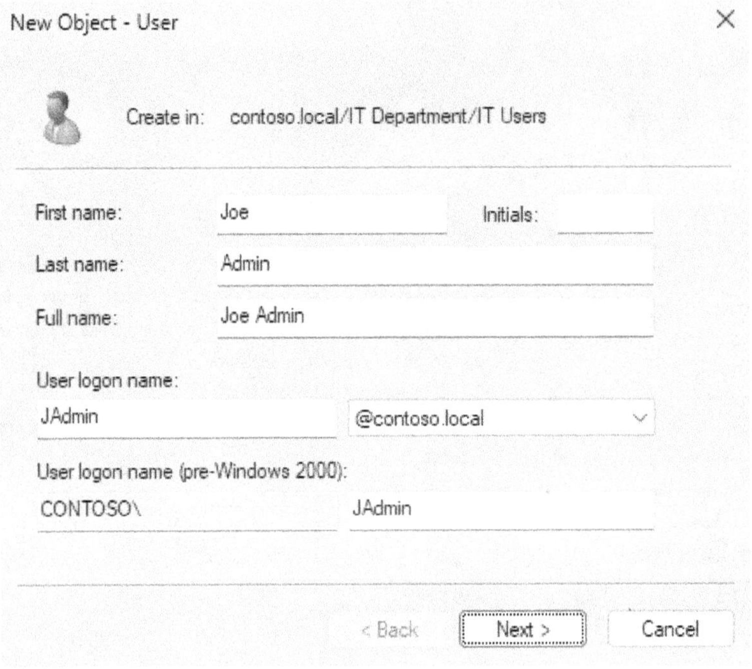

New Object - User   ✕

       Create in: contoso.local/IT Department/IT Users

First name: Joe   Initials:

Last name: Admin

Full name: Joe Admin

User logon name:
JAdmin   @contoso.local   ⌄

User logon name (pre-Windows 2000):
CONTOSO\   JAdmin

                    < Back   Next >   Cancel

Figure 3.9: Creating a new AD user

When finished, our new admin can utilize the new username and password to log in to computers and servers on the network, within the security boundaries we have established on those machines, of course. But that is another topic for another chapter.

Security groups

Another useful unit of organization inside AD is **security groups**. We can do quite a bit to distinguish between different types and kinds of users and computer accounts using OUs, but what about when we need a little cross-contamination in this structure? Perhaps we have an employee who handles some HR and some accounting responsibilities. File and folder permissions on our file servers are typically managed by individualized or group-based access to read and write into particular folders. Susie from HR needs to have access to the payroll folder, but Jim from HR does not

Both Susie and Jim reside inside the same OU, so at that level, they will have the same permissions and capabilities, but we clearly need a different way to distinguish between them so that only Susie gets access to payroll information. By creating security groups inside AD, we grant ourselves the ability to add and remove specific user accounts, computer accounts, or even other groups so that we can granularly define access to our resources. You create new groups in the same way that you create user accounts, by choosing the OU where you want the new group to reside, and then right-clicking on that OU and navigating to **New | Group**. Once your group has been created, right-click on it and head into **Properties.** You can then click on the **Members** tab; this is where you add in all the users that you want to be a part of this new group:

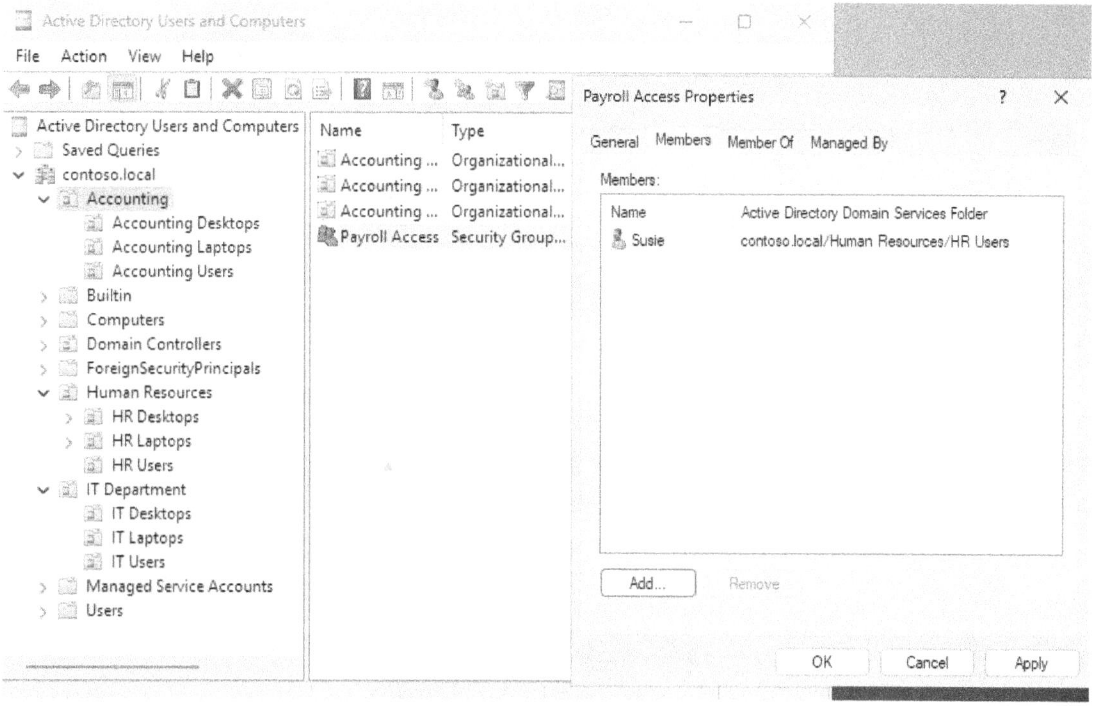

Figure 3.10: Creating a new group

Prestaging computer accounts

It is very common to utilize Active Directory Users and Computers for creating new user accounts because, without the manual creation of a user account, that new person is going to be completely unable to log in to your network. It is far less common, however, to think about opening this tool when joining new computers to your domain. This is because most domains are configured so that new computers are allowed to join the domain by actions performed on the computer itself, without any work being done inside AD beforehand. In other words, as long as someone knows a username and password that has administrative rights within the domain, they can sit down at any computer connected to the network and walk through the domain-join process on that local computer. In fact, in many domains, you don't even need administrative rights to join a machine to a domain.

By taking a few steps on the computer, you can easily join it to the domain, and AD will create a new computer object for it automatically. These autogenerating computer objects place themselves inside the default **Computers** container, so in many networks, if you click on that `Computers` folder, you will see a number of different machines listed, and they might even be a mix of both desktop computers and servers that were recently joined to the domain and haven't been moved to an appropriate, more specific OU yet. In my growing lab environment, I recently joined several machines to the domain. I did this without ever opening **Active Directory Users and Computers**, and you can see that my new computer objects are still sitting inside that default **Computers** container:

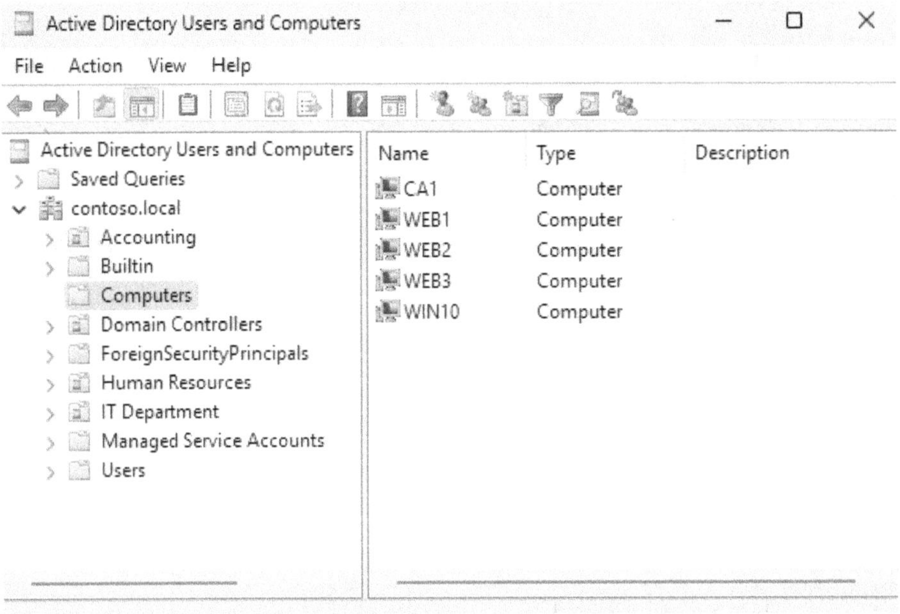

Figure 3.11: AD's default Computers container

You may even notice that my Fabrikam servers do not show up in this list. Great observation! My primary server base for this test lab is all focused around Contoso.local. I established Fabrikam.local as a completely separate domain for some later purposes, but those two domain environments are not tied together in any way, and are unaware of each other for now.

Allowing new computer accounts to place themselves inside the default **Computers** container is generally not a big problem for client systems, but if you allow servers to be autogenerated in that folder, it can cause you huge issues. Many companies have security policies in place across the network, and these policies are often created in a way that they will be automatically applied to any computer account residing in one of the generalized OUs. Using security policies can be a great way to lock down parts of client machines that the user doesn't need to access or utilize, but if you inadvertently cause these **lockdown** policies to apply to your new servers as soon as they join the domain, you can effectively break the server before you even start configuring it. Trust me, I've done it. And unfortunately, your new server objects that get added to AD will be identified and categorized the same as any client workstation that is added to the domain. You cannot specify a different default container for servers simply because they are a server and not a regular workstation.

So, what can be done to alleviate this potential problem? The answer is to **prestage** the domain accounts for your new servers. You can even prestage *all* new computer accounts as a matter of principle, but I typically only see that requirement in large enterprises. Prestaging a computer account is very much like creating a new user account. Prior to joining the computer to the domain, you create the object for it inside AD. By accomplishing the creation of the object before the domain-join process, you get to choose which OU the computer will reside in when it joins the domain. You can then ensure that this is an OU that will or will not receive the security settings and policies that you intend to have in place on this new computer or server. I highly recommend prestaging all computer accounts in AD for any new servers that you bring online. If you make it a practice, even if it's not absolutely required all the time, you will create a good habit that may someday save you from having to rebuild a server that you broke simply by joining it to your domain.

Prestaging a computer object is extremely fast and simple; let's do one together. In the future, I plan to build a Windows Server that hosts the *Remote Access* role to connect my roaming users to the network from their homes, coffee shops, and so on. Some components in the *Remote Access* role are finicky when it comes to network security policies, and so I would rather ensure that my new RA1 server will not receive a whole bunch of lockdown settings as soon as I join it to the domain. I have created an OU called Remote Access Servers, and I will now prestage a computer object inside that OU for my RA1 server.

Right-click on the Remote Access Servers OU and choose **New** | **Computer**. Then, simply populate the **Computer name** field with the name of your server. Even though I have not built this server yet, I plan to name it RA1, so I simply type that into the field:

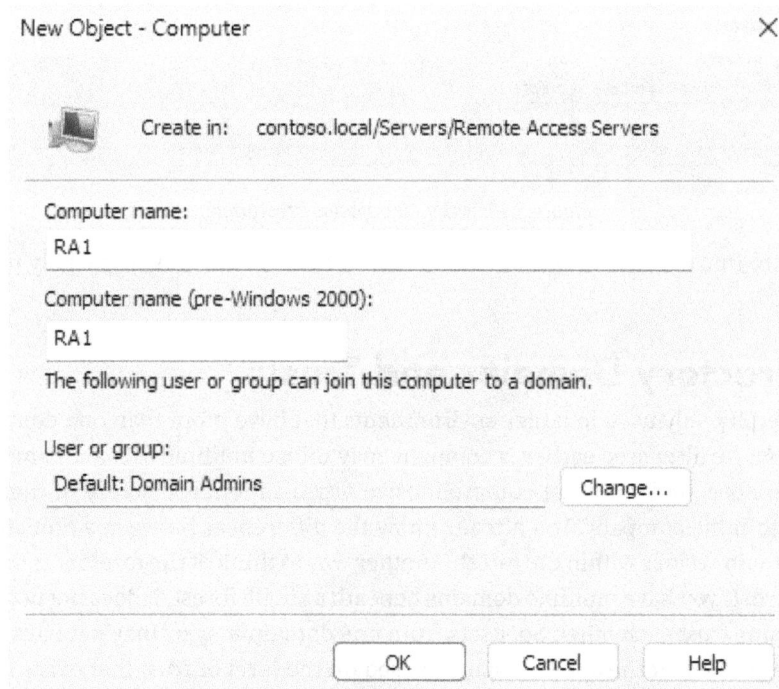

New Object - Computer   ✕

Create in: contoso.local/Servers/Remote Access Servers

Computer name:

RA1

Computer name (pre-Windows 2000):

RA1

The following user or group can join this computer to a domain.

User or group:

Default: Domain Admins   Change...

OK   Cancel   Help

Figure 3.12: Prestaging a computer in the domain

That's it! With a couple of simple mouse clicks and typing in one server name, I have now prestaged (pre-created) my computer object for the RA1 server. If you look closely at the previous screenshot, you will notice that you could also adjust which users or groups are allowed to join this particular computer to the domain. If you plan to build a new server and want to make sure that you are the only person allowed to join it to the domain, this field is easily updated to accommodate that requirement.

Once I actually get around to building that server, and I go ahead and walk through the steps of joining it to my domain, AD will realize that the name of my new server matches an object already in AD, and will associate my new server with this prestaged RA1 object instead of creating a brand new object inside the generic **Computers** container:

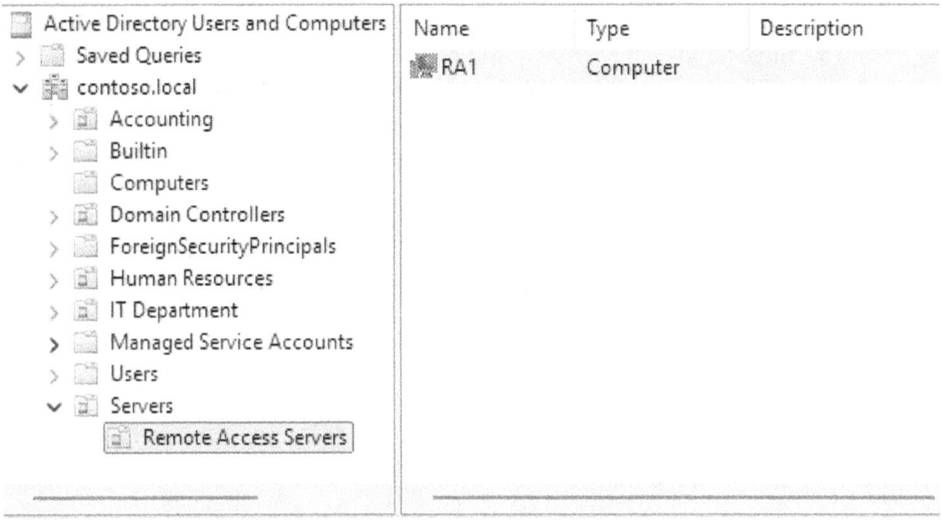

Figure 3.13: RA1's AD object is prestaged

Now, let's venture into another important component of the AD toolbox, especially useful in larger environments...

Active Directory Domains and Trusts

This tool is generally only used in larger environments that have more than one domain within the same network. As we discussed earlier, a company may utilize multiple domain names to segregate resources or services, or for a more comprehensive organizational structure of their servers and namespaces within the company. You already know the differences between a domain and a forest and how the domain resides within the forest. Another way to think of the forest is as the boundary of your AD structure. If you have multiple domains beneath a single forest, it does not necessarily mean that those domains trust each other. So, users from one domain may or may not have permission to access resources on one of the other domains, based on the level of trust that exists between those domains. When you have a domain and are adding child domains under it, there are trusts placed automatically between those domains, but if you need to merge some domains together in a way other than the default permissions, **Active Directory Domains and Trusts** is the management tool you use to establish and modify those trust relationships.

Growing organizations often find themselves in a position where they need to regularly manage domain trusts as a result of business acquisitions. If Contoso acquires Fabrikam, and both companies have fully functional domain environments, it is often advantageous to work through an extended migration process to bring the Fabrikam employees over to Contoso's AD, rather than suffer all the loss associated with simply turning off Fabrikam's network. So, for a certain period of time, you would want to run both domains simultaneously and could establish a trust relationship between those domains in order to make that possible.

Building a trust

Earlier, I mentioned that I already had DCs and a whole test lab network built for contoso.local, and in this chapter, we established a new fabrikam.local domain. These domains are not associated with each other in any way; they are completely separate forests. As such, a user account in one domain would absolutely not be able to log in to any machine that is joined to the other domain.

Let's change that. We are going to use Active Directory Domains and Trusts to establish a two-way trust relationship between these domains, which will enable exactly that scenario – users from contoso.local will be able to log in to computers joined to fabrikam.local, and vice versa. It is possible to establish either one-way or two-way trusts. Most commonly in the wild, I see two-way trusts because they enable more information to flow between the two domains, and in the case of an acquisition, that is most often what we are looking to accomplish. If there was a need for this trust to only flow in one direction, such as allowing contoso.local accounts to log in to fabrikam.local machines but not allow Fabrikam employees to sign in to Contoso equipment, that would be possible with a one-way trust.

There are three components to building a successful trust relationship:

- Network connectivity
- Conditional DNS forwarding
- Configuring the trust

Let's go over them briefly.

Network connectivity

The first one is common sense; those domains need to be able to talk to each other! If you have acquired a company and their servers are in a different physical location, you will likely need to build out some form of site-to-site VPN connectivity between the two physical sites and establish routing so that the DCs can communicate with one another.

In my test lab, I have Contoso and Fabrikam servers IP-addressed into separate subnets, but they are all part of one test lab network, so they can already communicate with each other at a TCP/IP level.

Make sure that you can get packets back and forth between the DCs, in both directions, before proceeding with the remaining steps of the trust build.

Conditional DNS forwarding

We haven't done anything in the DNS management console to this point, but it is installed on all of our DCs. The next chapter is going to cover many more items related to the management of DNS itself, but for now, we will need to utilize DNS management and make a change inside each domain. Currently, if I were to log in to a Contoso workstation and ping `fabrikam.local`, or if I signed in to a Fabrikam computer and tried `ping contoso.local`, either of these functions would fail completely, because the two domains have no idea that those DNS namespaces are supposed to resolve to DNS servers in those domains.

To bring name resolution full circle between the two domains, I need to set up conditional forwarding inside each domain.

I log in to DC1, one of my DCs for `contoso.local`, and launch the **DNS Manager** tool from Server Manager's **Tools** menu. Once inside, beneath my server name, there is a folder called `Conditional Forwarders`. If I right-click on that folder, I can then select the option to create a new conditional forwarder:

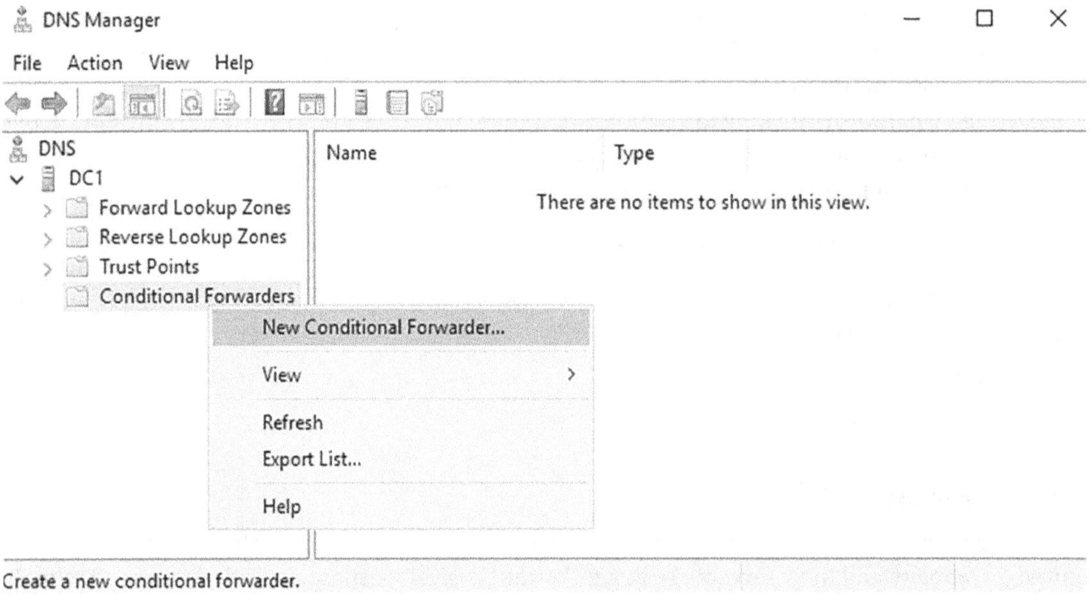

Figure 3.14: Creating a new conditional forwarder

Next, enter the remote domain name that you are trying to contact into the **DNS Domain** field. Then, populate the IP addresses of the DNS servers within that other domain. The screen should be able to take your IP address and query the remote server to discover the server FQDN of that server. I also generally select the **Store this conditional forwarder in Active Directory** checkbox, so that all of my AD-enabled DNS servers can perform this forwarding. Here are the selections I have made within my contoso.local DNS server, which then tells it how to reach out and talk to fabrikam.local:

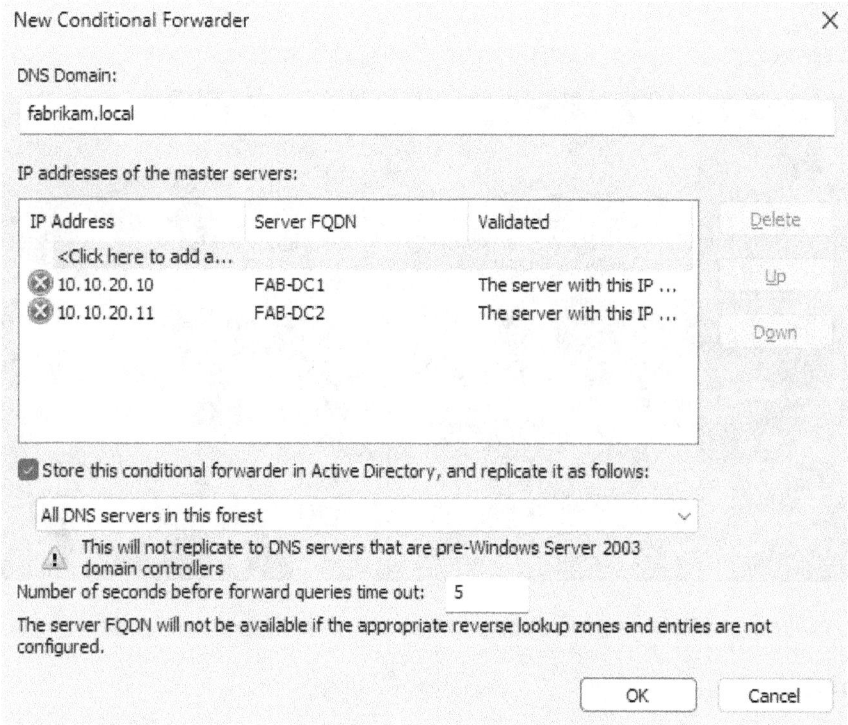

Figure 3.15: Configuring the conditional forwarder

You should now see the new conditional forwarder populate inside DNS Manager, and if you pull up Terminal and try to ping the remote domain, fabrikam.local in my case, you can see that name resolution for that remote domain is now successful, where it would have failed prior to our conditional forwarder being created:

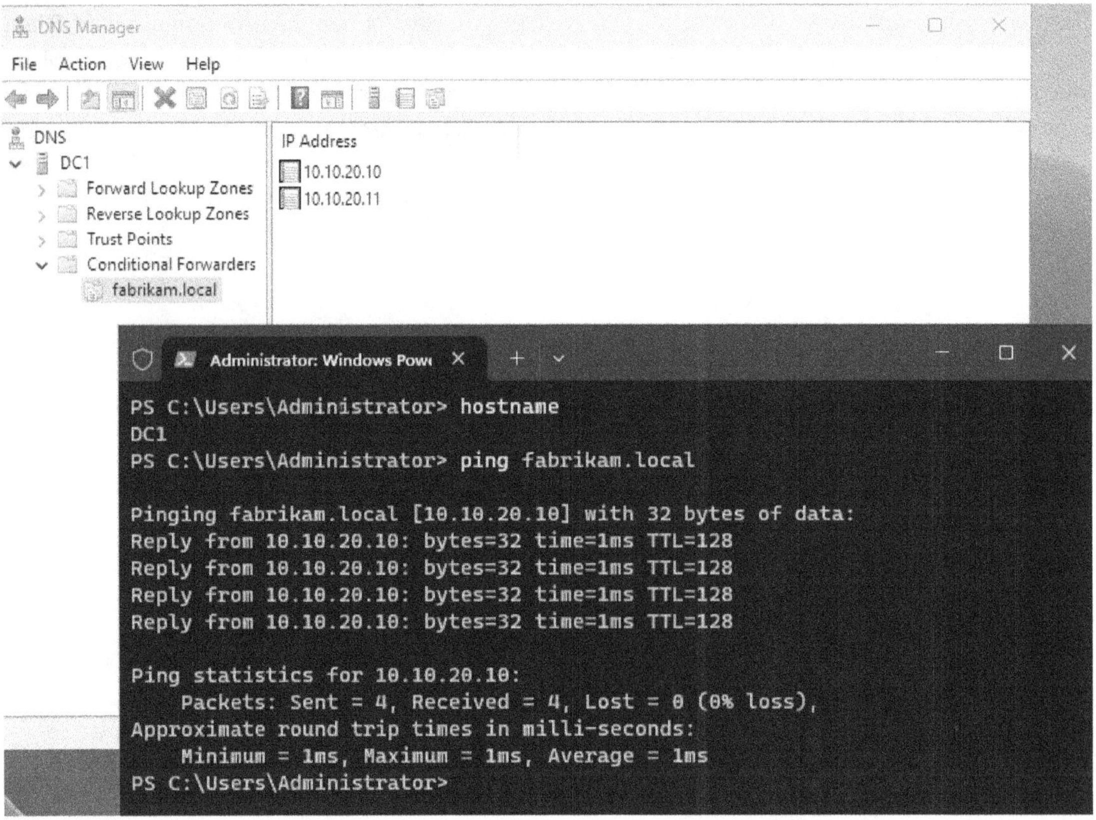

Figure 3.16: Successfully pinging fabrikam.local from a contoso.local server

Do it again!

We have now created a conditional forwarder from contoso.local toward fabrikam.local, but remember that we want to establish a two-way trust, and so we must now configure the same type of forwarder inside the fabrikam.local domain, pointing back at contoso.local's DCs. Follow the same steps as previously to create the second conditional forwarder. Once we complete that step, name resolution is successfully working cross-domain, and we are now ready to configure the trust.

Configuring the trust

VPN or other forms of connectivity between the two domains: Check.

Conditional forwarding set up between the two domains: Check.

Time to create a trust!

Log in to one of your DCs (I am going to use DC1.contoso.local) and launch **Active Directory Domains and Trusts**. Once inside, you should see the name of your domain listed in the left window pane. Right-click on the name of your domain and select **Properties**. Inside **Properties** for your domain, you will see the second tab is called **Trusts**. Go ahead and choose this tab, and at the bottom, there is a button to create a new trust (**New Trust...**). You can see this screen and button in *Figure 3.17*.

There are a few options for naming your trust, but when creating a trust between two forests, as we are today, you want to specify the full DNS name of the remote forest to which you are connecting. In my example, I am creating this trust from inside the contoso.local domain, so I am going to specify fabrikam.local on this screen, as seen here:

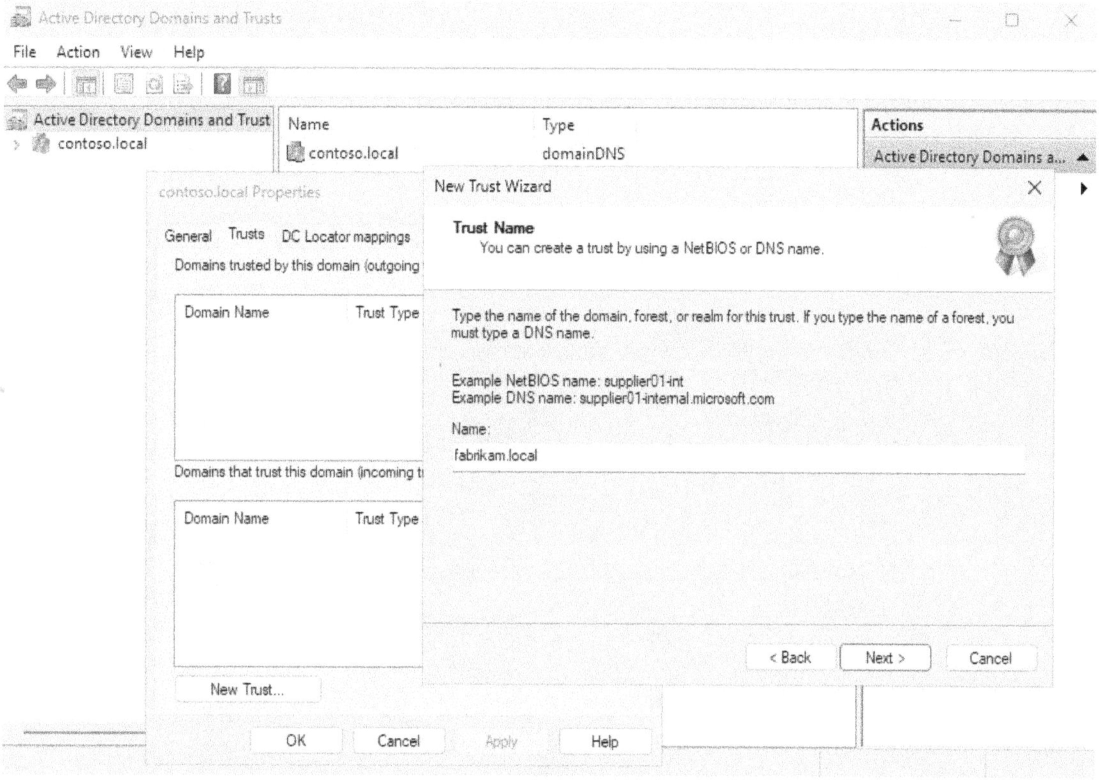

Figure 3.17: Creating a new trust

Now, you will encounter a few screens that present various options about how this new trust is to be established. You can create a trust based on domains or forests (**External trust** or **Forest trust**), you can create this as a two-way trust or a one-way trust in either direction, and you can decide to allow authentication to happen forest-wide or to be more selective. There are good descriptions of what each of these options means right inside the wizard interface as you progress, but what I am interested in establishing today is a total **two-way transitive trust** between contoso.local and fabrikam.local, so I am selecting the following options:

- **Forest trust**
- **Two-way**
- **This domain only**
- **Forest-wide authentication**

A trust password – you can specify anything you want as the trust password; the important part is that you remember it because you will have to enter the same trust password again when you move over to your second forest or domain, and walk through these steps again to create the other side of the trust.

Figure 3.18 summarizes the selected settings:

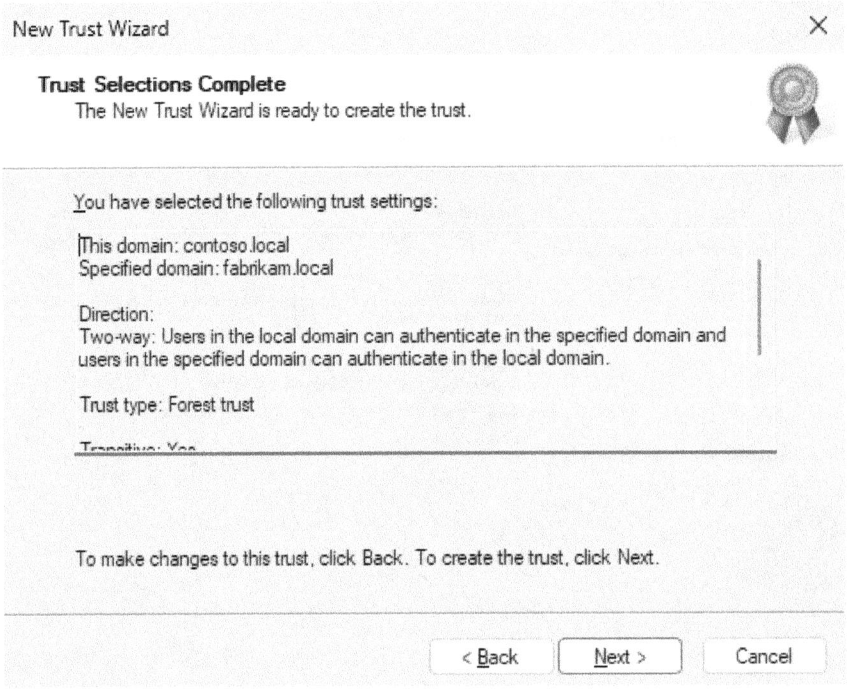

New Trust Wizard   ×

Trust Selections Complete
The New Trust Wizard is ready to create the trust.

You have selected the following trust settings:

This domain: contoso.local
Specified domain: fabrikam.local

Direction:
Two-way: Users in the local domain can authenticate in the specified domain and users in the specified domain can authenticate in the local domain.

Trust type: Forest trust

Transitive: Yes

To make changes to this trust, click Back. To create the trust, click Next.

< Back   Next >   Cancel

Figure 3.18: Summary of trust settings

The last step of the wizard is whether or not you want to confirm the outgoing trust. Since at this point we have only created one side of the trust, remember we still need to visit `fabrikam.local`'s DC and set up the other side of the trust; at this point, we do not want to confirm the outgoing trust because the trust setup is not yet complete.

Now that one side of the trust is established in `contoso.local`, log in to a DC in `fabrikam.local` and walk through the same setup process. You may have noticed earlier that I had an option when establishing my Contoso side of the trust to create the trust for both this domain and the specified domain. The idea behind this option is that you can create both ends of the trust all at once, via the same wizard and from only one DC, but my experience is that this function doesn't work very well. Therefore, I always take the approach of establishing each side of the trust one at a time, from within each domain. Once complete, you now have an established two-way transitive trust between your two forests:

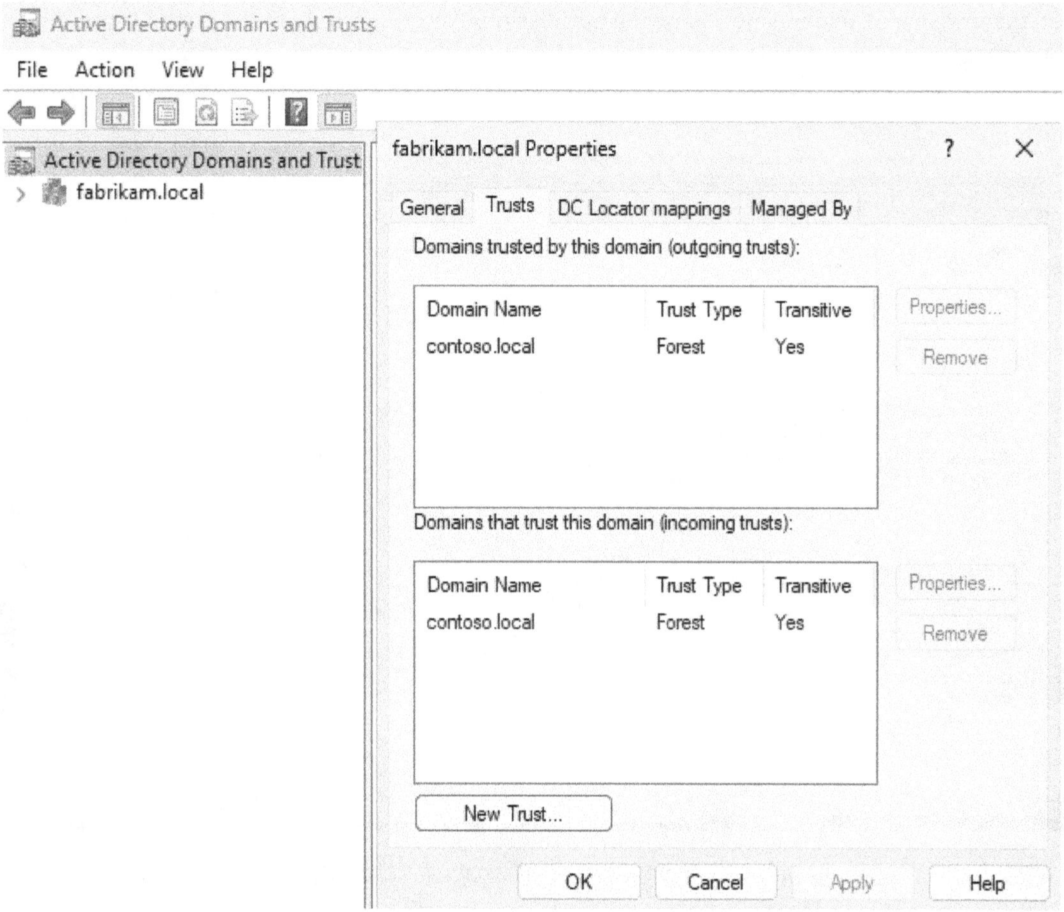

Figure 3.19: Two-way trust completed

Test it out!

We have a trust. Great! Now, what can we do with it? Remember that trusts are all about allowing cross-authentication to happen between domains. You should now be able to hop onto a computer in either domain and log in to it with a user account from the other domain (assuming there is nothing in your network that is restricting logins such as this). Another quick and easy test is to try setting up a file share, which is a very common thing to share back and forth across multiple domains. Set up a folder on any server in one domain and share it as you would with any folder. Now, visit the **Security** tab to set some NTFS permissions on this folder.

When you click the **Add...** button to include more permissions on this screen, it, of course, defaults to the domain that this server is joined to. However, if you click on the **Locations...** button, you now have the ability, **only because the trust exists,** to specify your remote domain as the location you are searching, and you are then able to add user accounts or groups to your folder share permissions from that remote domain, granting those users access to your shared folder. You can see in *Figure*

3.20 that my `Share1` folder is now allowing permissions for groups in both the `CONTOSO` domain and the `FABRIKAM` domain:

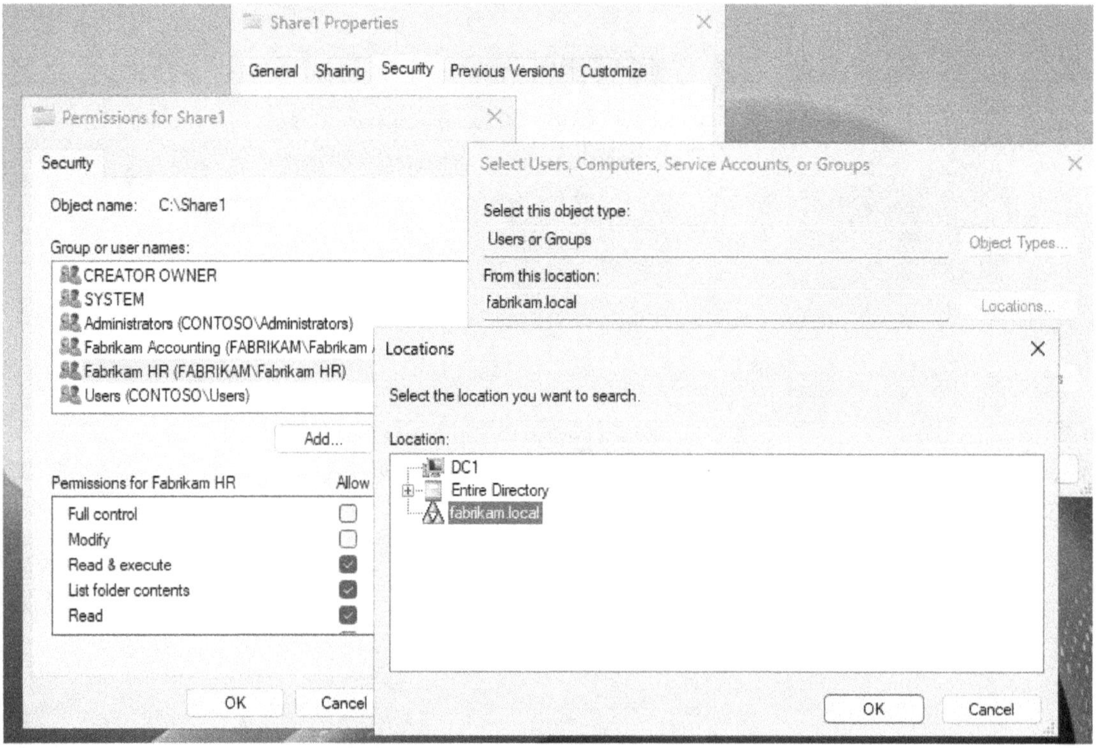

Figure 3.20: Share1 folder permissions reflect both domains

Active Directory Sites and Services

Sites and Services is another tool that is generally only employed by companies with larger AD infrastructures. As is the case with any server, if having one DC is good, then having two DCs is even better. As your company grows larger, so does your AD infrastructure. Before you know it, you will be looking into setting up servers in a second location, then a third, and so on. In a domain-centric network, having DC servers in each significant site is a general practice, and you could soon be looking at dozens of DC servers running in your network.

Turning on new DCs and joining them to your existing domain so that they start servicing users and computers is pretty easy. The harder part is keeping all of the traffic organized and flowing where you want it to. If you have a primary data center where the majority of your servers are located, you probably have multiple DCs onsite in that data center. In fact, to make your AD highly available, it is essential that you have at least two DCs. But let's pretend you then build a new office that is quite large, where it makes sense to install a local DC server in that office so that the computers in that office aren't reaching over the **wide area network (WAN)** to authenticate all the time. If you were to spin up a server in the new office and turn it into a DC for your network, it would immediately start working. The problem is that the client computers aren't always smart enough to know which DC they need to talk to. You may now have computers in the remote office that are still authenticating back to the main data center's DCs. Even worse, you probably also have computers in the main office that are now reaching over the WAN to authenticate with the new DC that is in the remote office, even though there are DCs right on the local network with them!

This is the situation in which Active Directory Sites and Services become essential. In here, you build out your different physical sites and assign the DCs to these sites. Domain-joined users and computers within this network follow the rules that you have put into place via Sites and Services, so that they are always talking to and authenticating from their local DC servers. This saves time, as the connections are faster and more efficient, and it also saves unnecessary bandwidth and data consumption on the WAN, which often saves you dollars.

The next page gives us a look at Active Directory Sites and Services. As you can see, there are multiple sites listed here, and they correspond to network subnet information. This is the way that Active Directory Sites and Services tracks which site is which. When a client computer comes online, it obviously knows what subnet it is part of, based on the IP address it is using. Active Directory Sites and Services then knows, based on that IP address, which site the client now resides in.

That site identification then helps AD steer authentication requests to the proper DCs, and also helps things such as Group Policy (which we will talk about shortly) to be able to process site-specific information. There is a good chance you will have to make use of this tool someday if you are part of a growing organization. Adding new objects into Active Directory Sites and Services is about as easy as it gets. Configure all of your sites by simply right-clicking on the Sites folder and then choosing **New Site**. You can name your sites anything you like.

Once all sites are placed inside Active Directory Sites and Services, you add your subnets in a similar fashion, by right-clicking on the Subnets folder and choosing **New Subnet**. When you create a new subnet, you plug in the identifying network information about that subnet, and the bottom of the screen allows you to select which site the subnet resides within. You can see that process in *Figure 3.21*, as well as a look into my sample Active Directory Sites and Services, which is now populated with multiple sites and multiple subnets:

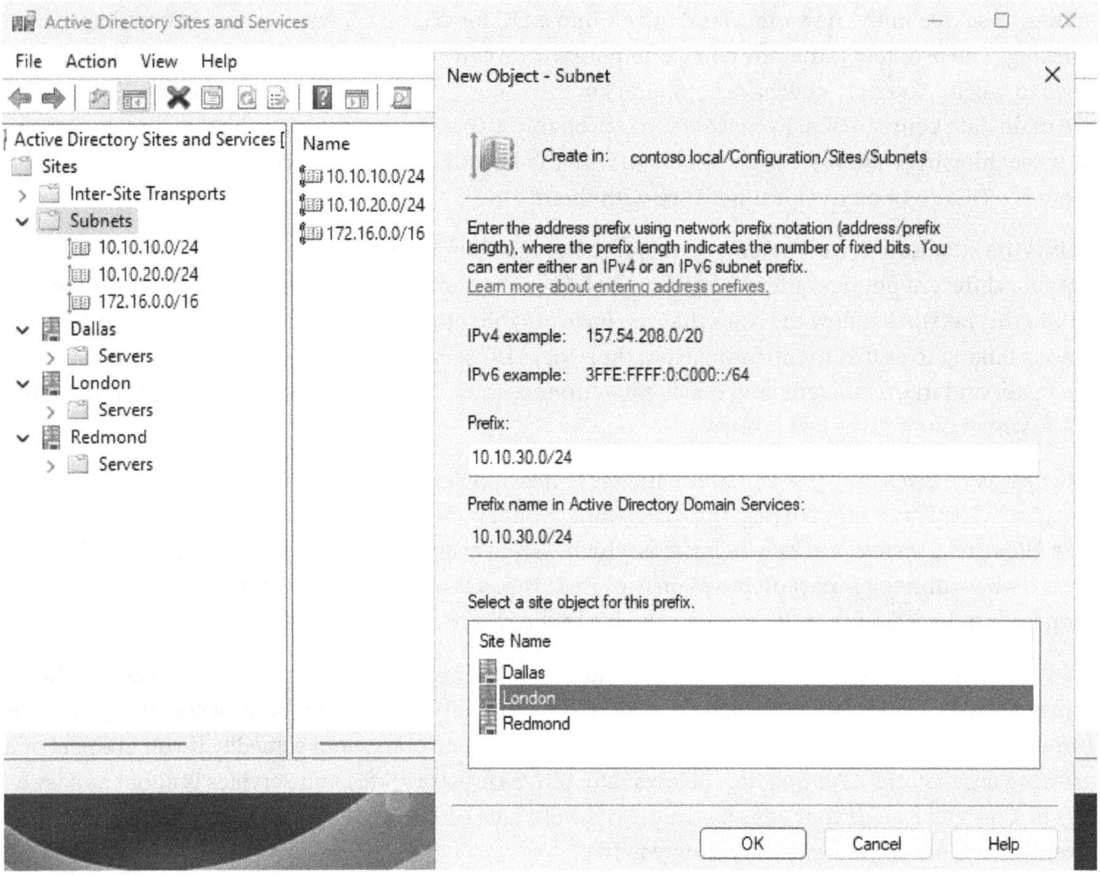

Figure 3.21: Defining subnets in Active Directory Sites and Services

Active Directory Administrative Center

While it is critical to understand and be familiar with the tools we have looked at so far that help us manage AD, you can tell that their aesthetics are a bit dated. The **Active Directory Administrative Center** (**ADAC**), on the other hand, has a much more streamlined interface that looks and feels like the newer Server Manager that we are all used to working with every day. Many of the functions available within the ADAC accomplish the same things that we can do through Active Directory Users and Computers, Domains and Trusts, and Sites and Services, but it pulls these functions into a more structured interface that brings some of the most utilized functions up to the surface and makes them easier to run.

One great example is right on the landing page of ADAC. A common help desk task in any network is the resetting of passwords for user accounts. Whether the user forgot their password, changed it recently and mistyped it, or you are resetting a password during some other sort of troubleshooting, resetting a password for a user account typically involves numerous mouse clicks inside Active Directory Users and Computers to get the job done. Now, there is a quick link called **RESET PASSWORD**, shown right there on the main page of the ADAC. Also useful is the **GLOBAL SEARCH** feature right next to it, where you can type anything into the **Search** field, and it will scour your entire directory for results relating to your search. This is another common task in AD that previously required multiple clicks to accomplish:

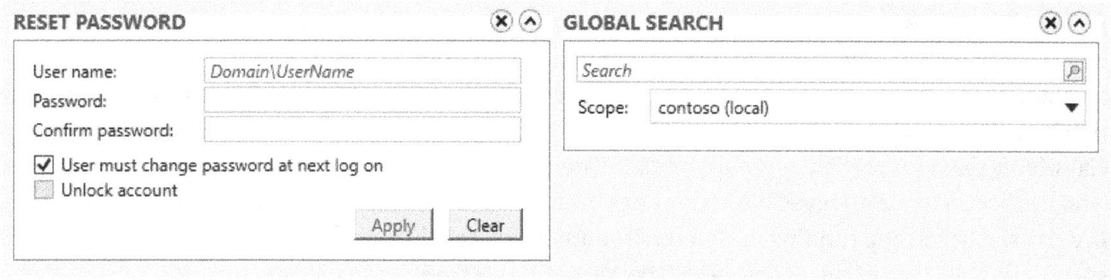

Figure 3.22: Useful tools inside ADAC

If you click on the name of your domain in the left navigational tree, you will dive a little deeper into the capabilities of ADAC. As you can see, the information listed here is being pulled from AD and looks like the same information you would see in Active Directory Users and Computers. That is correct, except instead of having to right-click for every function, such as new user creations or searches, you now have some quick **tasks** available on the right that can quickly launch you into accomplishing these functions. Also interesting are the links for raising the forest or domain functional level on this screen.

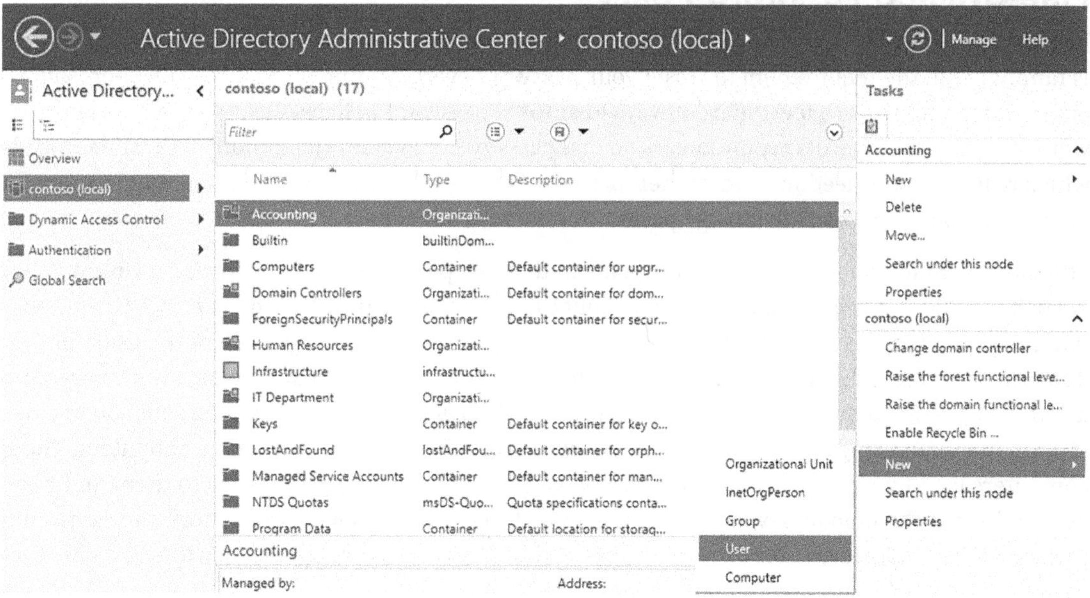

Figure 3.23: ADAC user interface

In order to raise a functional level from inside our classic tools, I watch most admins accomplish this by launching Active Directory Domains and Trusts. So, one of the big benefits of the newer ADAC tool is that it gives you a centralized management window from which you can accomplish tasks that would normally have taken multiple windows and management consoles.

Dynamic Access Control

In addition to teaching old dogs new tricks, ADAC also brings some functionality to the table that is not available anywhere in the classic tools. If you once again take a look at the tree to the left, you will see that the next section in the list is **Dynamic Access Control** (DAC). This is a technology that is all about the security and governance of your files and the company data that you need to hold onto tightly, making sure it doesn't fall into the wrong hands. DAC gives you the ability to tag files, thereby classifying them for particular groups or uses. Then, you can create access control policies that define who has access to these tagged files. Another powerful feature of DAC is reporting functionality. Once DAC is established and running in your environment, you can do reporting and forensics on your files, such as finding a list of the people who have recently accessed a classified document.

DAC can also be used to modify users' permissions based on what kind of device they are currently using. If our user Susie logs in with her company desktop on the network, she should have access to those sensitive HR files. On the other hand, if she brings her personal laptop into the office and connects it to the network, we might not want to allow access to these same files, even when providing her domain user credentials, simply because we do not control the security on that laptop. These kinds of distinctions can be made using DAC policies.

Fine-Grained Password Policy

Just about anyone who has ever had to use a Windows computer as part of employment at a business is familiar with the requirement to "reset your password every x number of days." In a Microsoft AD environment, there are a few different ways to enforce password policies that require a certain password length, set complexity requirements on that password, and define maximum ages for passwords, which result in users needing to reset their passwords every so often. It is a common requirement for companies to require users to change passwords every 30 days or so.

The most common and certainly easiest place to define a password policy is by using Group Policy. We will cover this in more detail as we talk about the default domain policy in *Chapter 5, Group Policy*, but that policy is going to apply one set of password requirements settings to *all* of the users in your domain, bar none. What if your needs are slightly more complex? For example, maybe you require a complex password that needs to be changed every 30 days for all your office staff, but you manage IT for a manufacturing company that also has some shared computers out on the shop floor. These computers log in with domain accounts so that you can effectively push policies to them and grant permissions at the domain level, but you don't need these shop floor logins to have the same complexity on their passwords, nor do you care about those passwords changing since they are only ever used inside the network.

Enter the **Fine-Grained Password Policy**. Such a policy meets those expanded needs to a "T" by allowing you to configure differing password policies for different groups of people inside AD. We are actually going to build a fine-grained password policy in *Chapter 10, Hardening and Security*, so we'll have to wait on the details until then. The reason I mention it here is that the creation of a fine-grained password policy requires the use of ADAC, so we will be working within this newer console to create the policy.

Active Directory Recycle Bin

Speaking of technologies that are configured from inside ADAC, and in this case, one that can save you a lot of heartburn, let's discuss the **AD Recycle Bin**. As the name implies, this is a container into which objects that are deleted from AD move before they are permanently deleted. Anyone who has worked on a help desk knows about user termination tickets, those often-mundane tasks that need to be accomplished on a regular basis. In many cases, those former employee user accounts are deleted from AD to keep things clean. However, many of you who have worked on a help desk for a considerable amount of time also know that companies tend to hire the same people back, sometimes within mere days of their departure. Depending on the infrastructure of the business you are supporting, perhaps recreating the user account from scratch is no big deal, but it is becoming more and more problematic with things such as Entra Directory synchronization and immutable IDs. In these cases, boy, would it be nice if we had an "oops" button we could click to bring the formerly deleted user account back to life.

Enter the AD Recycle Bin. That is exactly the capability provided by this tool. The only trouble? It's not enabled by default. Let's go ahead and enable it together and test it out.

Open ADAC and click on the name of your domain in the left-hand list. Then, glance over at the right side of your screen, and sitting right there is an **Enable Recycle Bin...** button.

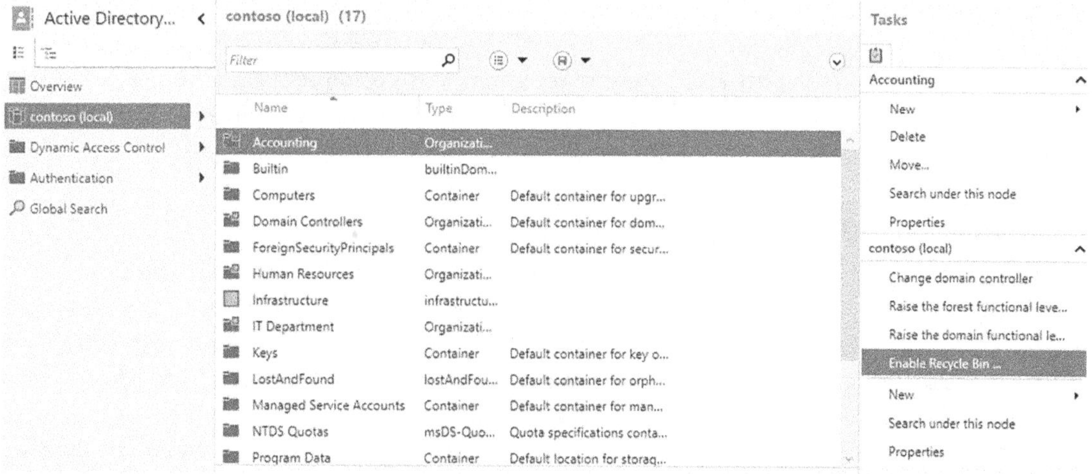

Figure 3.24: Enabling the AD Recycle Bin

Click this task, and you are presented with a simple selection. You should encounter a dialog box that states, **Are you sure you want to perform this action? Once Recycle Bin has been enabled, it cannot be disabled.** Seems pretty straightforward; if you are ready to make this move in your environment, go ahead and click on the **OK** button. When you do this, AD is updated to reflect the change, and it may take a few minutes for this to activate on all your DC servers. After letting it sit and bake for a while, close and relaunch your ADAC window, and click on the name of your domain again. If you look closely, you will now find a new folder listed in the middle pane called `Deleted Objects`.

This did not exist before you enabled the AD Recycle Bin. My `Deleted Objects` folder is currently empty, but I will go ahead and delete our test account for Susie, and then check inside. After deleting Susie's account and then double-clicking on that folder called `Deleted Objects`, I can easily find my deleted account for Susie, and from here, simply right-click on it and choose **Restore**.

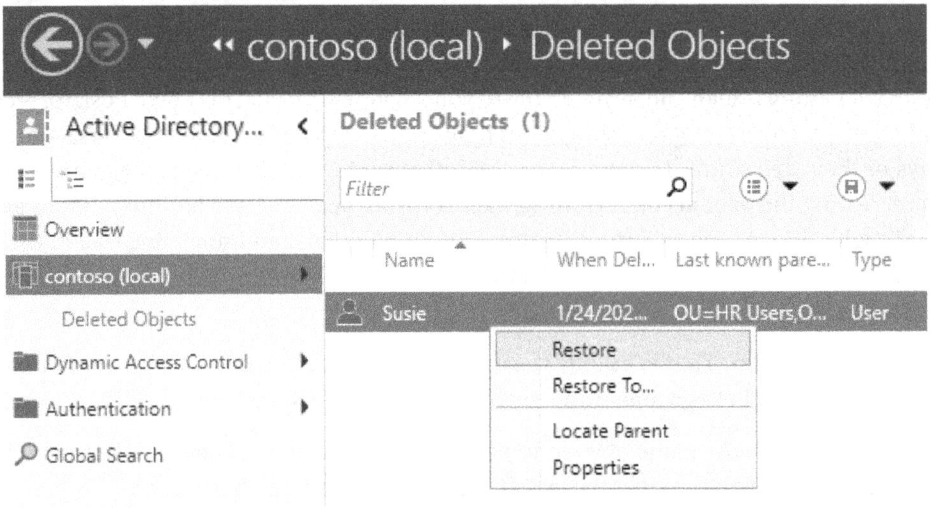

Figure 3.25: Restoring a user account from AD Recycle Bin

By taking this simple action, my user account for Susie is restored directly into the same `HR Users` OU that she was part of before, with preexisting user account configuration intact. This is so much faster than recreating a new account and trying to make sure it has all of the original configuration!

Read-only domain controllers

The first DC you set up in your network will be a fully writable one, able to accept data from the domain-joined users and computers working within your network. In fact, most DCs in your network will likely be fully functional and writable. However, it's worth taking a quick minute to point out a limited-scope DC that can be installed called a **read-only domain controller (RODC)**. Just like the name implies, an RODC can only have its directory data read from it. Writes that might try to be accomplished in the domain from a user's computer, such as a password change or new user account creation, are impossible with an RODC. Instead, RODCs receive their directory data from other, more traditional DCs and then utilize that data to verify authentication requests from users and computers. Where would a limited-access DC like this be beneficial? Many companies are installing them in smaller branch offices or less secure sites so that the local computers onsite in those smaller offices have quick and easy access to read from and authenticate to the domain without the potential security risk of an unauthorized user gaining access to the physical server and manipulating the entire domain in bad ways. Another valid use case for an RODC is within a DMZ, a protected network where you would typically never dream of installing a full DC because a DMZ network is all about access restriction and keeping internal network information safe.

Configuration of a RODC is not a totally disparate process, consisting of yet another role or feature, but simply a different option to select when running through the standard installation process of the AD DS role, which we have already worked with a number of times throughout this chapter. In fact, let's set one up right now. I just created a new VM in my environment (RODC1) and have given it an IP address and hostname. After installing the AD DS role, as I have done with other DCs in my environment already, I am now going to run the configuration wizard that helps me promote this server to be a DC.

Since I am adding another DC to an existing domain, the first selection is pretty straightforward. It is when we come to the **Domain Controller Options** screen that we make a deviation from the way we have run through this wizard in the past. You see that little checkbox that says **Read only domain controller (RODC)**? Go ahead and check that box:

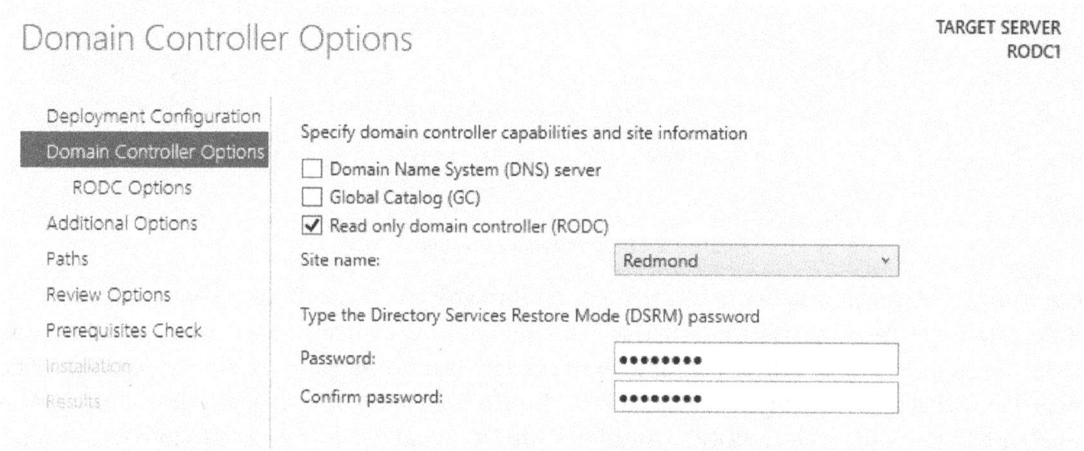

Figure 3.26: Defining a new DC as an RODC

After clicking **Next** on this screen, you are now presented with new options that we have never seen before, on a screen titled **RODC Options**. Most interestingly here is the field where we can define which user accounts, or groups of user accounts, are allowed or denied permission to replicate their passwords to RODCs. There are predefined objects in these fields. Take note of two AD groups called **Allowed RODC Password Replication Group** and **Denied RODC Password Replication Group**. Are these brand-new groups that are going to be added to AD when I finish this wizard? No! While there is a good chance you have never taken notice of these groups before, they already exist inside AD, but are simply unused if you never roll out an RODC in your environment:

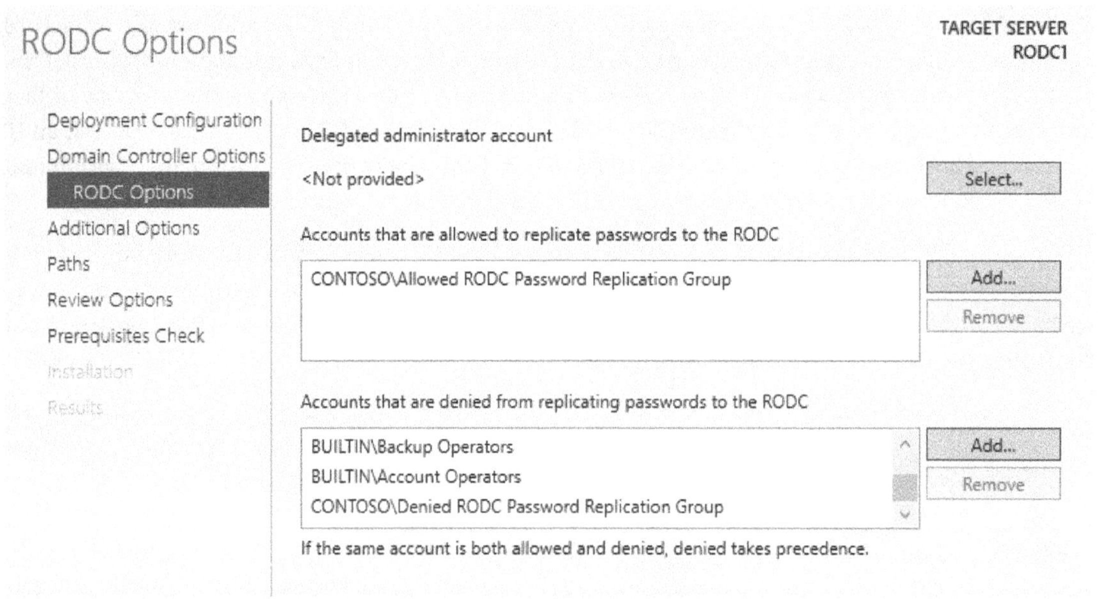

RODC Options

Deployment Configuration
Domain Controller Options
RODC Options
Additional Options
Paths
Review Options
Prerequisites Check
Installation
Results

Delegated administrator account

<Not provided>   [Select...]

Accounts that are allowed to replicate passwords to the RODC

| CONTOSO\Allowed RODC Password Replication Group | [Add...] |
| | [Remove] |

Accounts that are denied from replicating passwords to the RODC

BUILTIN\Backup Operators	[Add...]
BUILTIN\Account Operators	[Remove]
CONTOSO\Denied RODC Password Replication Group	

If the same account is both allowed and denied, denied takes precedence.

Figure 3.27: Built-in groups related to RODC

The choice is yours on whether to utilize these built-in groups or specify your own groups that are either allowed to replicate passwords to this RODC or denied from being able to do so. RODCs are all about keeping security as tight as possible, so you generally don't want any passwords getting cached on an RODC that won't actually be needed for that local office's authentication. Physical security is yet another advantage of using an RODC instead of a full DC. What if someone breaks into your branch office and steals the physical server? If bad people were to get their hands on a full DC, all usernames and passwords in your domain would be stored on that hard drive. With an RODC, only the accounts that have been allowed to cache are contained on the stolen server.

Each RODC has its own definition of allowances and denials. By default, every RODC that you add into your domain will follow through these same wizard steps, and if you leave all the default options in place, then all RODCs in your environment will treat those built-in allowed and denied RODC groups as their definitions, meaning that all RODCs in your environment will be caching the same passwords because they all pay attention to the same groups. However, each RODC maintains its own set of users and groups that are allowed or denied caching. This **RODC Options** screen can be configured differently for every RODC that you establish.

What if you want to make changes to these definitions in the future? Easy enough, you simply need to know where to look for this information to be able to change it. The list of accounts that are allowed or denied caching is generally called the **password replication policy** (PRP) for each RODC. To find an RODC's PRP, simply open up Active Directory Users and Computers and find the object for your RODC, right-click on that Computer object, and visit **Properties**. Inside the properties of your RODC, navigate to the tab called **Password Replication Policy**. Here, you can view and manipulate the password caching policy for each RODC individually:

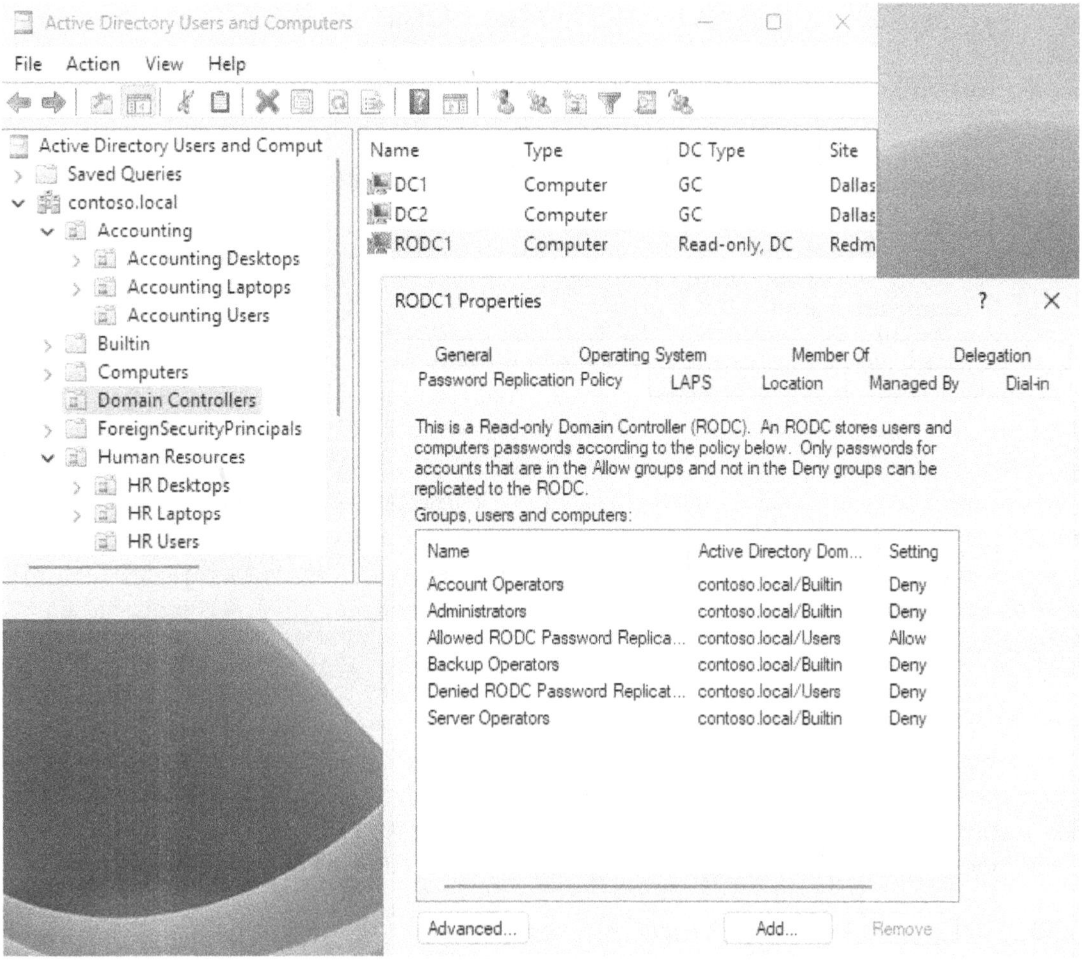

Figure 3.28: Password Replication Policy settings

Denials always win! In the Microsoft world, a permission denial always takes priority over a permission allowance. The same is true for RODC caching. If a user account is a member of groups that fall inside both the *allow RODC caching* and *deny RODC caching* categories, it will be denied caching for that account.

FSMO roles

AD is like a database, a potentially huge database, synced across a potentially huge number of different DC servers in your environment. In an environment with lots of DCs spread across numerous sites, the potential for change-based conflict is huge. What if DC1 in Redmond receives a change and needs to sync it around the entire domain, and at the same time, DC22 in London receives instructions to sync a change that conflicts with the change of DC1? What now? Who wins? In the early days of AD, there was one single master DC server, known as the **primary domain controller** (PDC), that was responsible for making all changes like this. Technically, the PDC role no longer exists, but some of the same protections are still in place under the hood using **Flexible Single Master Operation** (FSMO) roles. Every instance of AD has FSMO roles and FSMO role holders. In a lot of cases, the same DC holds all five of the FSMO roles, but they could technically be managed by different DC servers. Here are the five FSMO roles:

- Schema master
- Domain naming master
- RID master
- PDC emulator
- Infrastructure master

We aren't going to discuss each of these in depth for the purposes of our chapter, because the typical IT admin doesn't need to know that level of detail. What you do need to understand, however, is that they exist, and that at least one of your DCs is hosting these roles. This knowledge becomes critically important if you remove or replace a DC that was hosting one of these roles, or that server dies, and you now have chaos inside your directory. Thankfully, it is quite easy to find out what server or servers are hosting these roles, and also now easy to transfer the FSMO roles to a different DC in your environment, should the need arise. The key things to remember are that you have FSMO roles, they are extremely important to the workability and health of AD, and that if their server disappears, you need to move them to another server asap.

Viewing current FSMO role holders

To find FSMO role holders via a graphical interface, you're going to have to check three different administrative tools. This is because some FSMO roles are forest-wide, and some are domain-wide. Therefore, it is possible to have many more than five FSMO roles within a forest, and their technical homes are inside different admin consoles. Let's first list where you could find this information via the GUI.

RID, PDC, and Infrastructure master

Open **Active Directory Users and Computers**, right-click on the name of your domain, and click **Operations Masters....** The three tabs here will indicate which DC is hosting the corresponding roles.

Schema master

Right-click the **Start** button and click **Run**. Then, type `regsvr32 schmmgmt.dll` and click **OK**. This process enables something called **Active Directory Schema** to be available from inside the MMC console, which you can then open by following the next steps.

Right-click the **Start** button, click **Run**, type `MMC`, and click **OK**. Now, navigate to **File** > **Add/Remove Snap-in...** and add the Active Directory Schema to your MMC console. Once added, right-click **Active Directory Schema** and look inside **Operations Master** to find the schema master server.

Domain naming master

Open **Active Directory Domains and Trusts**, right-click on the words **Active Directory Domains and Trusts**, and click on **Operations Master...** to view the domain naming master server.

View them all in one place

While the graphical interfaces are good to know about and useful for finding individual FSMO role holders, most of the time, you would rather just see them all listed together, right? Thankfully, we have some very old tools still hanging around, even in Windows Server 2025, that can do exactly this.

Open an administrative terminal on one of your DC servers, and simply run the following command: `netdom query fsmo`.

This single command lists all five FSMO roles and their current master servers, as seen in the following screenshot:

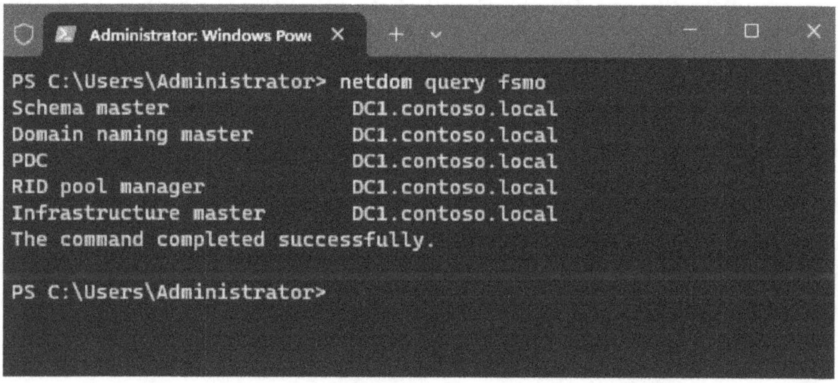

```
PS C:\Users\Administrator> netdom query fsmo
Schema master                    DC1.contoso.local
Domain naming master             DC1.contoso.local
PDC                              DC1.contoso.local
RID pool manager                 DC1.contoso.local
Infrastructure master            DC1.contoso.local
The command completed successfully.

PS C:\Users\Administrator>
```

Figure 3.29: Viewing FSMO role holders via terminal

FSMO role visibility through PowerShell

And, of course, we can also see these through PowerShell, though surprisingly, it requires two separate commands to do so. Given this, I prefer good old `netdom` via Command Prompt or Terminal if I am manually looking for FSMO role ownership information, but there are certainly use cases where pulling this information from PowerShell would be beneficial for scripting or other purposes, so here are the commands to find the same information using PowerShell:

- Find domain-level FSMO roles:

```
Get-ADDomain | select InfrastructureMaster, PDCEmulator, RIDMaster
```

- Find forest-level FSMO roles:

```
Get-ADForest | select DomainNamingMaster, SchemaMaster
```

Transferring FSMO roles

Now for the fun part, transferring these FSMO roles to new servers. Pulling the trigger on changes like this can be very intimidating if you haven't done it before. I mean, you're yanking a significant underpinning of AD and moving it to a new place. What could go wrong? No reason to fret, moving these roles around is quite easy, and you'll be surprised to find that it happens almost immediately after you click the button or press the *Enter* key. If you are moving FSMO roles one at a time, each of the graphical interface methods for viewing the master also includes a **Change** button that can be used to quickly and easily shift individual FSMO roles from one server to another. The key to doing this is that you must connect to the domain using the *new destination* server to whom you are planning to transfer your role.

As you have seen, all FSMO roles in my test lab are held by DC1, which makes sense because it was my first DC. I now want to move only the PDC role to my DC2 server. To accomplish this transfer of power, I log in to my newer DC2. Remember, there are three different places you may need to visit to move FSMO roles, depending on which roles you are working with, but for the PDC role, I need to perform the following: **Active Directory Users and Computers** > right-click the domain name > **Operations Masters** > **PDC** > **Change**. Uh oh, when I clicked that **Change** button, I was presented with the following error. What gives?

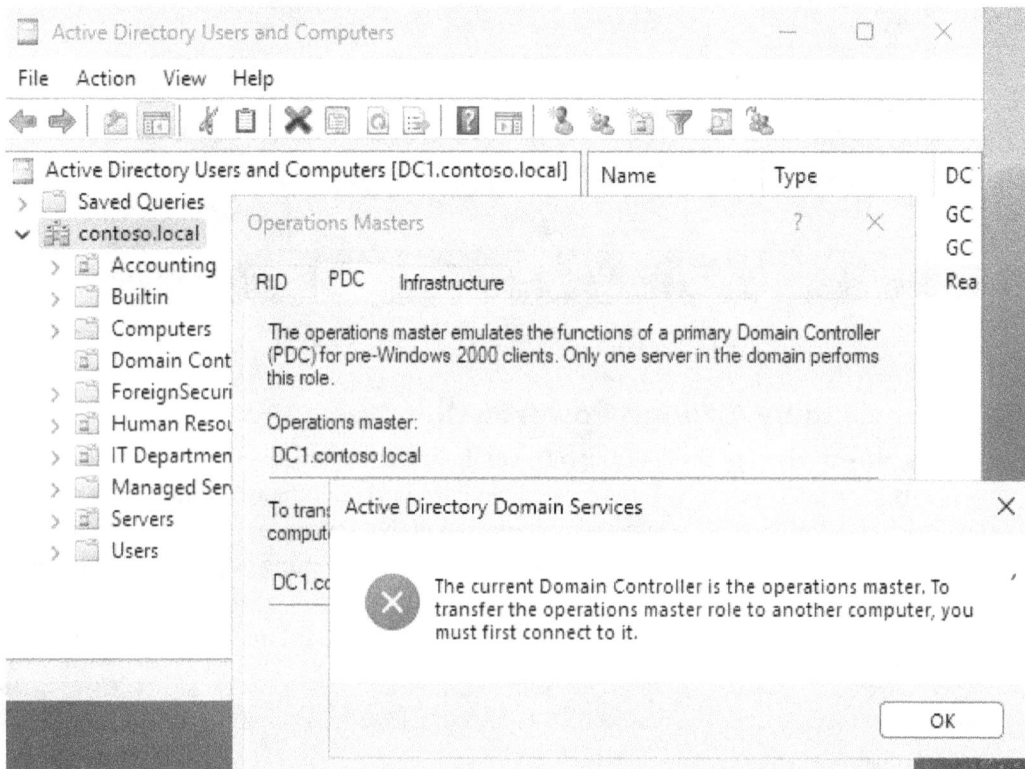

Figure 3.30: Attempting to transfer the PDC role

If you look closely at the previous screenshot, you'll notice that **DC1** is displayed in a couple of different places, primarily near the top of my **Active Directory Users and Computers** window. I told you that I would need to log in to my DC2 server to change this role, and simply wanted to prove that this process will not work if you are logged in to the DC that already holds the FSMO role. If I right-click on **Active Directory Users and Computers** [DC1.contoso.local] and choose the **Change Domain Controller...** option, I will be able to connect to the domain through DC2 instead. Once I accomplish that, I can now successfully migrate the PDC role to DC2. Alternatively, I could log out of DC1 completely and log in to DC2 instead, ensuring that DC2 is indeed the server listed inside my **Active Directory Users and Computers** window, as in *Figure 3.31*, and you'll find that transferring this PDC FSMO role is now a simple matter of clicking that **Change** button.

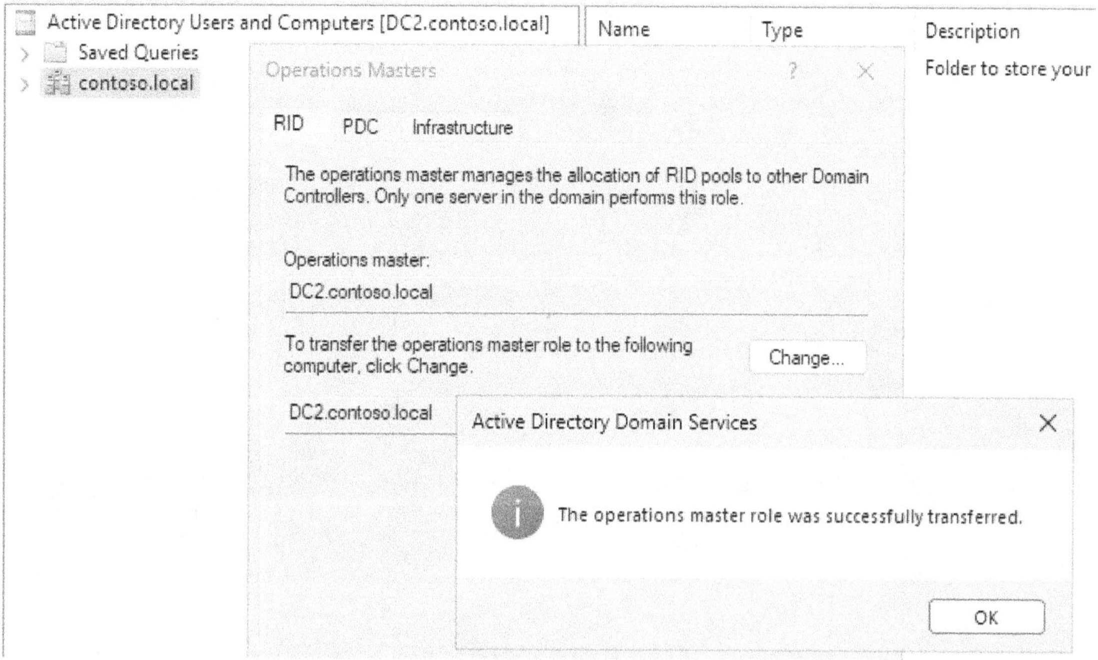

Figure 3.31: The PDC role has been moved to DC2

Transferring FSMO roles via PowerShell

As with everything inside Windows Server, if you can accomplish it via a graphical interface, you can almost certainly find a way to do the same thing with PowerShell. While viewing FSMO role ownership was slightly easier via an old Command Prompt command, transferring the roles between DCs is definitely easiest to accomplish by using PowerShell. To transfer roles, simply log in to the server to which you are going to transfer the roles and run as few or as many commands as you need. There is a separate command to run for each FSMO role, and by running all five, we have now quickly and smoothly transferred all FSMO roles onto my DC2 server.

Pro tip: You can even move multiple roles at the same time, by following any one of the following commands and simply comma-separating the different roles to transfer, as you can see in *Figure 3.32*:

- Transfer `RIDMaster`:

```
Move-ADDirectoryServerOperationMasterRole -Identity "DC2" RIDMaster
```

- Transfer `PDCEmulator`:

```
Move-ADDirectoryServerOperationMasterRole -Identity "DC2" PDCEmulator
```

- Transfer `InfrastructureMaster`:

```
Move-ADDirectoryServerOperationMasterRole -Identity "DC2"
InfrastructureMaster
```

- Transfer `SchemaMaster`:

```
Move-ADDirectoryServerOperationMasterRole -Identity "DC2" SchemaMaster
```

- Transfer `DomainNamingMaster`:

```
Move-ADDirectoryServerOperationMasterRole -Identity "DC2"
DomainNamingMaster
```

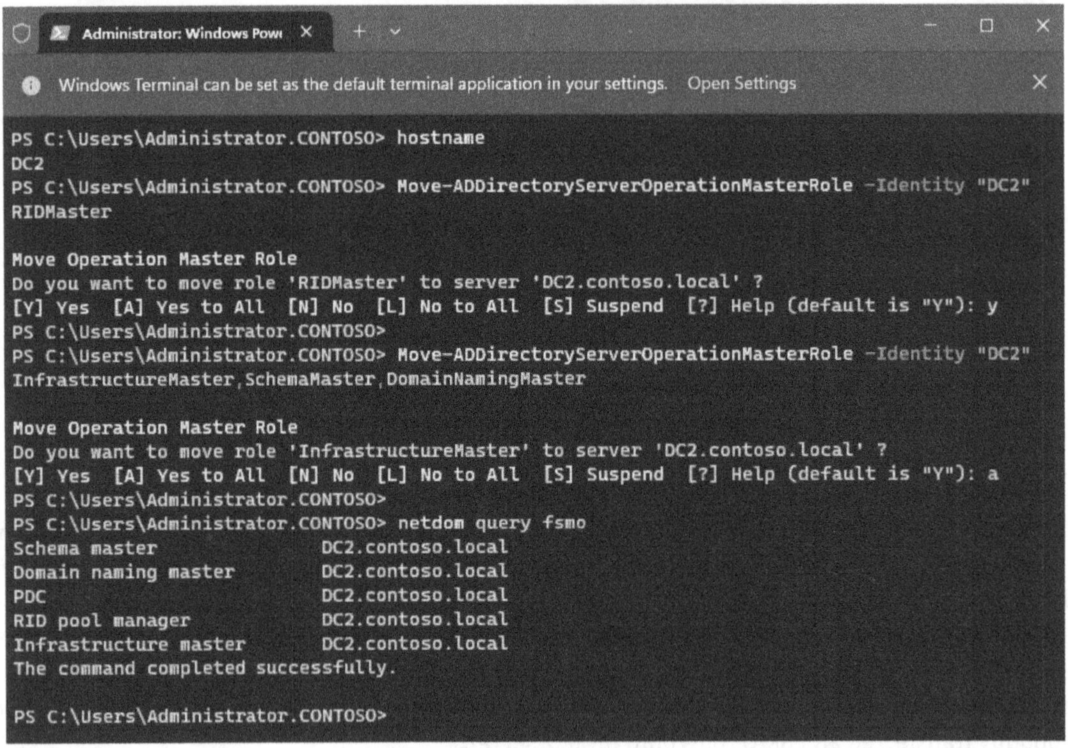
Administrator: Windows Powe
Windows Terminal can be set as the default terminal application in your settings. Open Settings
PS C:\Users\Administrator.CONTOSO> hostname
DC2
PS C:\Users\Administrator.CONTOSO> Move-ADDirectoryServerOperationMasterRole -Identity "DC2"
RIDMaster
Move Operation Master Role
Do you want to move role 'RIDMaster' to server 'DC2.contoso.local' ?
[Y] Yes [A] Yes to All [N] No [L] No to All [S] Suspend [?] Help (default is "Y"): y
PS C:\Users\Administrator.CONTOSO>
PS C:\Users\Administrator.CONTOSO> Move-ADDirectoryServerOperationMasterRole -Identity "DC2"
InfrastructureMaster,SchemaMaster,DomainNamingMaster
Move Operation Master Role
Do you want to move role 'InfrastructureMaster' to server 'DC2.contoso.local' ?
[Y] Yes [A] Yes to All [N] No [L] No to All [S] Suspend [?] Help (default is "Y"): a
PS C:\Users\Administrator.CONTOSO>
PS C:\Users\Administrator.CONTOSO> netdom query fsmo
Schema master DC2.contoso.local
Domain naming master DC2.contoso.local
PDC DC2.contoso.local
RID pool manager DC2.contoso.local
Infrastructure master DC2.contoso.local
The command completed successfully.
PS C:\Users\Administrator.CONTOSO>

Figure 3.32: All FSMO roles have been transferred to DC2

Demoting an old domain controller

Creating new servers and turning them into DCs is technically known as **promoting** those servers to become DCs. This process is fairly straightforward and easy to accomplish in a fresh environment without any history of changes or issues, such as inside a test lab. Now, let's cover one of the messier things that you may encounter as a server administrator: removing an old DC server. The process of removing a DC from your environment is known as **demoting**. Demoting a DC can be straightforward if the old server is online, or it can be a little convoluted if the old server has died, and you are now trying to remove all traces of it from the domain without being able to take the standard removal steps.

Demoting while the old server is still online

If you are removing an old DC and it is still online, the process is fairly painless. Log in to that server, and accomplish the following steps:

1. Open **Server Manager**.
2. Click **Manage** followed by **Remove Roles and Features**.
3. Make sure your old server is selected.
4. Uncheck **Active Directory Domain Services**.
5. If this server is also a DNS server, it is easiest if you remove the DNS Server role *before* accomplishing the AD DS removal.
6. You will receive a **Validation Results** pop-up screen. On this screen, click the **Demote this domain controller** link.

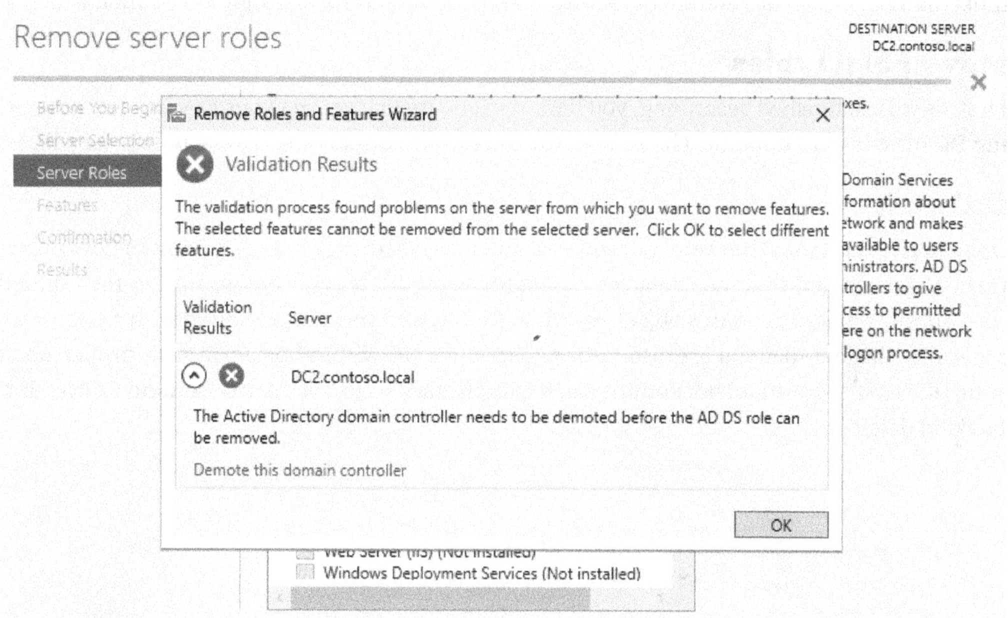

Figure 3.33: Demoting a DC via Server Manager

You will also be asked whether you want to force the removal of this DC—it is generally recommended NOT to check this box unless you are removing the very last DC from your domain.

A few more **Next** boxes and specifying a new local administrator password (remember, this server will no longer be a DC, so the wizard will be creating a new local administrator account), and you're off to the races. The server is demoted and removed from AD, and when it finishes restarting, there will be a plain Windows Server sitting on your network.

Cleaning up Active Directory Sites and Services

The DC demotion process via Server Manager cleans up almost everything, but if you open **Active Directory Sites and Services**, you will still find a reference to the old DC name, listed under the Servers folder under whichever site that server resided. Simply right-click on the old server name and delete it, and you're all set.

Demoting when the old server is gone

Here is a scenario that most tenured AD administrators have encountered at least once. The reason we have redundant DCs is in case one of them dies, right? Well...what happens when *that* happens?

Running to Server Manager and attempting to clean up or remove the old DC will get you nowhere. Without being able to contact the server that is now offline, Server Manager is not going to know what to do to remove that server from all of the places it is plugged and referenced inside AD. Instead, you must manually clean up references to the old server, which is surprisingly easier than you might think.

Move FSMO roles

First, as we just finished describing, you'll want to ensure that you get your FSMO roles moved to a working DC in your environment. Thankfully, the old server does not need to be online for this to happen.

Delete it

Open **Active Directory Users and Computers**, and navigate to the OU called **Domain Controllers**. Inside this OU, you should find the Computer object for every DC in your environment, including the dead one. Simply right-click on this object and click **Delete**, and you are presented with a warning message regarding the fact that you are attempting to delete a DC without performing a proper demotion. If your DC is really gone and not coming back, simply check the **Delete this Domain Controller anyway** box and delete it.

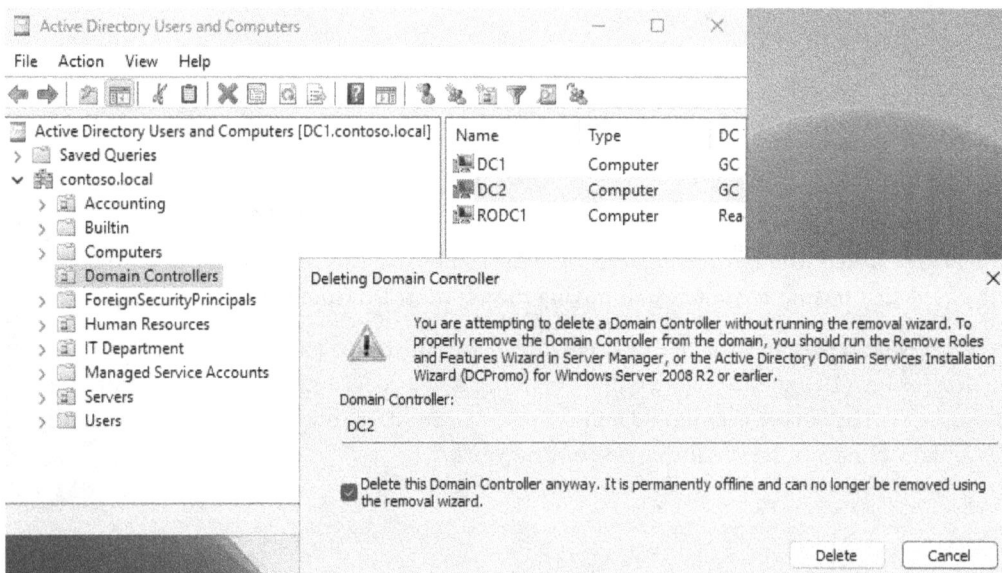

Figure 3.34: Manually removing a DC from AD

Clean up Sites and Services and DNS

Following either removal method, make sure to visit **Active Directory Sites and Services** to clean up any traces or pointers that still reference the old DC (DC2 in my case). In addition to Sites and Services, when you forcibly remove a DC from AD, it often leaves behind traces of the old DC inside DNS. We have not talked in depth about DNS at this point, but if you open the **DNS Manager** console and expand the available folders, looking inside each one, you will almost certainly find traces of the former DC.

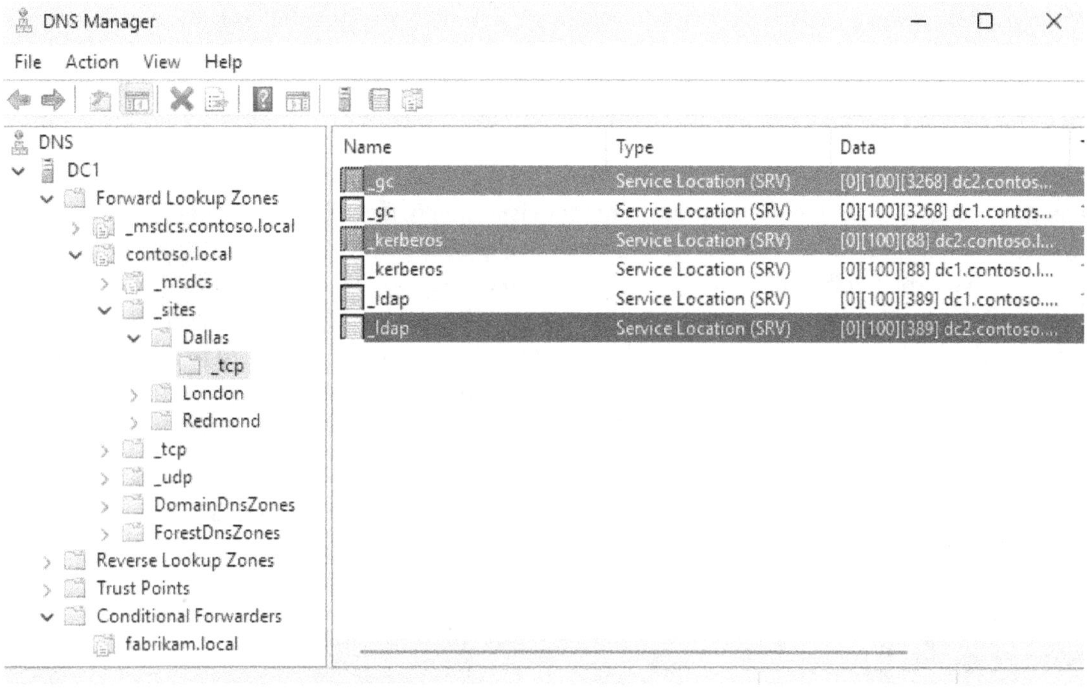

Figure 3.35: Cleaning up DNS following a manual DC deletion

These records are no longer needed and could cause problems or delays in DNS, so they should all be removed.

Intro to Group Policy

In a network that is based upon Windows Server and AD, it is almost always the case that the primary set of client computers is also based upon the Microsoft Windows operating systems, and that these machines are all domain-joined. Setting everything up this way not only makes sense from an organizational perspective inside AD but also allows centralized authentication across devices and applications, as we have already talked about. I know that a couple of the examples I gave earlier in the book went something like, *What about when a company has a security policy in place that...* or *Make sure your servers don't get those existing security policies because....* So, what are these magical **security policies** anyway, and how do I set one up?

This is the power of Group Policy. It enables you to create **Group Policy Objects (GPOs)** that contain settings and configurations that you want to apply to either computers or users in your AD domain. Once you have created and built out a GPO with a variety of settings, you then have the option to steer that GPO in whatever direction you choose. If you have a policy that you want to apply to all desktop systems, you can point it at the appropriate OU or security group in AD that houses all of your domain-joined desktop computers. Or maybe you created a GPO that only applies to your Windows 10 computers in a particular site; you can filter it appropriately so that only those systems receive the policy. And the real magic is that the issuance of these settings happens automatically, simply by those computers being joined to your domain. You don't have to touch the client systems at all in order to push settings to them via a GPO. You can tweak or lock down almost anything within the Windows operating system by using Group Policy.

Once again, I'm looking at the list of available roles on my Windows Server 2025, and I am just not seeing one called **Group Policy**. Correct again: there isn't one! In fact, if you have been following along with the lab setup in this book, you already have Group Policy fully functional in your network. Everything that Group Policy needs to work is part of AD DS. So, if you have a DC in your network, then you also have Group Policy on that same server, because all of the information Group Policy uses is stored inside the directory. Since the installation of the AD DS role is all we need to use Group Policy, and we have already done that on our DC, we are already prepared to start using Group Policy to send policies and preferences to our computers and users within the domain.

But wait! Group Policy is a large enough topic that it really needs its own chapter, which is exactly what I have decided to do. If you're interested in centralizing administration and policy with this fascinating tool, which you should be, continue reading, as we will dive deeper into all things GPO in *Chapter 5, Group Policy*.

Microsoft Entra ID

I've said it before and I will probably say it again: this book's primary focus is Windows Server capabilities *inside* your network. Even so, many of these concepts and tools will carry directly over to your cloud journey inside Azure, as a lot of cloud administration work is still really Windows Server administration work, but with your Windows Servers running inside Azure.

The topic of Active Directory in the cloud is... cloudy.

Active Directory is all about authentication and identification. It is the source of truth for who your user accounts are, and what computer accounts are owned by your business. As many companies prepare or are moving into the cloud, we, of course, seek similar functionality in a cloud resource. From Microsoft's cloud toolset, what is our answer to authentication and identification? **Microsoft Entra**.

The reason I called Microsoft Entra *cloudy* is not only to be punny, but because this topic can be confusing if you haven't heard about it before. There are actually three different ways that you can authenticate and identify computers and users inside Microsoft's cloud, and I thought it would be a helpful addition to this chapter to describe each of them.

Entra ID

The first step into Microsoft cloud authentication for most companies is Entra ID. This is the SaaS-based identity engine that underpins Microsoft 365. If you are using Microsoft 365 for email hosting, or even if you are simply using Microsoft 365 applications on your computers and utilize M365 user accounts to log in to those apps, all of those user accounts are stored, maintained, and administered inside Microsoft Entra ID. Management of accounts and objects inside Entra ID happens most often through a web browser, by simply logging in to your Microsoft admin portal and navigating from there.

Active Directory on an Azure VM

Another completely separate way to manage authentication inside Microsoft Azure is to create a virtual server in Azure and promote it to be a DC, exactly as we have done within this chapter. For many companies, Azure is really treated like a large Hyper-V server, granting you the ability to host an unlimited number of VMs. Moving your resources into Azure may involve a combination of full Azure servers as well as SaaS services such as Entra ID, but the point of this section is to make sure you know that you can absolutely run a traditional DC server inside Azure. In fact, most customers that I work with who are interested in putting any server resources in Azure begin this journey with a single DC in Azure. Spinning up a DC here and creating a site-to-site link between Azure and your local data center opens a world of possibilities. You are essentially just extending your domain into your private Azure space, and in AD's eyes, Azure is simply another site, just like Dallas, London, or Redmond in our examples today. Once your existing domain is extended into Azure, you can also now quite easily slide your existing servers into Azure, where they can happily run while you take steps to power down and recycle that old physical server hardware.

Microsoft Entra Domain Services

The most confusing iteration of cloud-based AD is something called Microsoft Entra Domain Services, which was formerly known as **Azure Active Directory Domain Services**, or **AADDS** for short. It's not often that we come across five-letter acronyms, so I suppose it's no surprise that something with such a significant name would require significant learning to make use of it.

Entra Domain Services is different from Entra ID because it is a more classic AD environment. When running Entra Domain Services, you can take Azure VMs and join them to this instance of AD, just like you would with on-premises servers joining on-premises AD. The big difference with Entra Domain Services compared to our previous scenario of AD on an Azure VM is that Entra Domain Services has no server attached to it. You do not have to pay for the compute resources in Azure to run a Windows Server instance that happens to be a DC. Instead, AD is offered up as a sort of PaaS, where you can tap into AD and make use of its authentication mechanisms, even NTLM and Kerberos, without having to log in to or maintain an actual server. As you can see, this often creates confusion for those tasked with building it, but in the end, it can be quite beneficial in that you don't have to maintain a server, and Entra Domain Services even integrates with Entra ID, which creates a more uniform authentication experience across your cloud infrastructure.

Entra Connect

All these Azure/Entra-based authentication methods sound great, but if I already have servers in my data center and now want to slowly open the valve to begin creating cloud resources and migrating some of my workloads into that cloud, does that mean I need to maintain two separate authentication methods during this hybrid period? Not at all!

Almost every company that goes through cloud migration begins by creating a hybrid environment, where resources exist both in-cloud and on-premises. Indeed, some companies plan to remain in hybrid mode indefinitely. In any hybrid scenario, which you will almost certainly encounter during your time working in IT, a tool called **Entra Connect** is the magic glue that holds these things together. Entra Connect is a piece of software that is installed on one of your local servers, most usually on a DC, but not necessarily so. Once installed, a simple configuration wizard walks through the process of defining what this tool needs to accomplish. Its purpose is to take information that exists inside your local AD and sync that data upward into Entra ID. Most notably, it syncs user accounts, their accompanying passwords, and various attributes of the AD object. This means that users will have the same identity (username and password) for their M365 and Azure resources as they do for their normal workstations in the office. The same password for local network drives on a file server will work for M365 email, and anytime their password changes in AD, it will sync automatically to Entra.

Entra Connect is also an important piece to the puzzle for some information that you may want to sync back downstream, in the opposite direction. Passwords are the prime example. A common help desk ticket is helping someone reset their password, but these tickets are always high alert because they come with a sense of urgency (the user cannot work until you help them). However, you need certain guarantees from the user that they really are who they say they are, or you may be helping a malicious actor gain entry to this account. In the Microsoft 365 world, there is a web service called **Self-Service Password Reset**, where you can simply steer users to the website, and they are able to self-reset their M365 password from this interface, using a combination of variables they need to answer, most notably the MFA that is on their own device. This makes help desk involvement in password resets very easy and safe, and leaves the power of password change in the user's own hands. But... in a hybrid scenario, where your AD passwords are the source of truth and sync into Entra, you are now attempting to take a backward approach to changing that password. Not to fear, this scenario, the backward syncing of passwords from Entra to AD, is another thing that Entra Connect helps with.

Entra Connect was formerly known as Azure AD Connect, and a lot of documentation still references "AD Connect" or "AAD Connect." This is good to know in case you are searching for something and unable to find it listed under *Entra Connect*.

Summary

Anyone who has been around Windows Server before knows that AD is nothing new and certainly not a breathtakingly hot topic that is specific to the release of Windows Server 2025. AD has been the authentication underpinning of any Microsoft-centric environment for a very long time and will continue to be far into the future for anyone who hosts an on-premises data center. As we have just finished discussing, AD is no longer relevant only inside your physical walls, but also flows throughout the Azure world. Knowing about and understanding AD is entirely critical for the mastery of Windows

Server 2025, because without this knowledge, your career in server administration won't even get off the ground.

Some hints were dropped in this chapter about another core infrastructure technology that almost always runs alongside AD on all of your DC servers: DNS. To effectively manage a Microsoft infrastructure, in my opinion, there are three in-the-box server technologies that any admin must be able to work with fluently: AD, DNS, and DHCP. Follow along to *Chapter 4, DNS and DHCP*, in which we will cover the latter.

Questions

Put your knowledge to the test with the following questions. If you need a hand (or just want to double-check), you'll find all the answers in the *Appendix* section of the book.

1. Inside Active Directory, a container (folder) that holds computer and user accounts is called a(n)...

2. What is the term for creating a computer account inside AD prior to that computer being joined to your domain?

3. Which management tool is used to specify that certain physical locations in your network are bound to particular IP subnets?

4. What is the name of a special DC that cannot accept new information, only synchronize from an existing DC?

5. What tool is needed to create a fine-grained password policy?

6. What must be configured inside DNS prior to establishing a forest trust?

7. What is the command-line command that shows you all FSMO role holders at once?

8. True or False? It is faster to manually remove a DC from the domain than it is to follow the Server Manager role removal wizard.

9. What identity and authentication service underpins Microsoft 365?

4

DNS and DHCP

Without a doubt, I consider **Active Directory Domain Services (AD DS)** to be the most common and central role inside any Microsoft-centric network, with **DNS** and **DHCP** sliding in at #2 and #3 in order of importance. I am yet to meet an admin who has chosen to deploy a new domain without deploying DNS at the same time, and every network has a need for DHCP, whether or not that service is provided by a Windows server. Either of these roles *could* be served by something other than a traditional server. There are other companies and even dedicated appliances that exist to provide DNS within a corporate network, which have some advantages and some disadvantages. Regarding DHCP, there are plenty of options for providing that service outside of the Windows world, as most firewalls and even switches are capable of also being DHCP "servers" in a network. Indeed, if you are sitting at home reading this text, it is most likely that your computer is connected to a DHCP server built into your home router. Although the preceding sentences are true, the majority of internal DNS and DHCP services for *businesses* around the world are provided by Windows servers, and these two roles are very commonly located alongside AD DS on at least some of the **domain controller (DC)** servers in any given network.

In this chapter, we will cover both DNS and DHCP provided by Windows Server 2025, getting to know their purposes and walking through some common terminology and tasks related to these roles. In this chapter, we will be covering the following:

- The purpose of DNS
- Types of DNS records
- Split-brain DNS
- Types of DNS zones
- DNS-over-HTTPS
- IP addressing with DHCP
- Creating a DHCP scope
- DHCP reservations
- DHCP failover
- IPAM

The purpose of DNS

Domain Name System (DNS) is similar to Active Directory in that it is a structured database that is often stored on DC servers and distributed automatically around your network to other DC/DNS servers. Where an AD database contains information about your domain objects, DNS is responsible for storing and resolving all of the *names* on your network. What do I mean by names? Whenever a user or computer tries to contact any resource by calling for a name, DNS is the platform responsible for turning that name into something else in order to get the traffic to the correct destination. You see, the way that traffic gets from the client to the server is via networking, and typically via the TCP/IP stack, using an IP address to get to its destination.

When I open an application on my computer to access some data that resides on a server, I could configure the application so that it communicates directly to my server by using the server's IP address on the network. If an application on my computer needed to communicate with a server called APP01, and that server was using an IP address of 10.10.10.15 on the network, I could plug 10.10.10.15 into my application configuration, and it would open successfully. If I set up hundreds of different computers this way, all pointing to IP addresses, it would work fine for a while. But the day will come when, for whatever reason, that IP address might need to change. Or perhaps I add a second server to share the load and handle my increased user traffic. What to do now? Revisit every client computer and update the IP address being used? Point half of the computers at one server and half at the other? Certainly not.

This is one of the reasons that DNS is critical to the way that we design and manage our infrastructures. By using DNS, we can employ names instead of IP addresses. With DNS, my application can be configured to talk to APP01 or whatever my server name is, and if I need to change the IP address later, I simply change it inside the DNS console to the updated IP address, and immediately, all of my client computers will start resolving the APP01 name to the new IP address. Or I can even use a more generic name, such as intranet, and have it resolve across multiple different servers. We will discuss more about that shortly.

Any time a computer makes a call to a server, service, or website, it is using DNS to resolve that name to a more useful piece of information to make the network connection happen successfully. The same is true both inside and outside of corporate networks. On my personal laptop right now, if I open **Edge** and browse to https://www.bing.com/, my internet provider's DNS server is resolving bing.com to an IP address on the internet, which is the address that my laptop communicates with, and so that page opens successfully. When we are working inside our own corporate networks, we don't want to rely on or trust a public provider with our internal server name information, and so we build our own DNS servers inside the network. Since DNS records inside a domain network are almost always resolving names to objects that reside inside Active Directory, it makes sense that DNS and AD DS would be tightly integrated. That rings true in the majority of Microsoft networks, where it is a very common practice to install both the AD DS role plus the DNS role on your DC servers. If you remember back to our previous chapter, that is exactly what we did when we built DC1 and DC2.

Types of DNS records

Having installed our DNS role on a server in the network, we can start using it to create **DNS records**, which resolve names to their corresponding IP addresses, or other pieces of information needed in order to route our traffic around the network.

Assuming that you are working in a domain network, you may be pleasantly surprised to discover that a number of records already exist inside DNS, even though you haven't created any of them. When you are running Active Directory and DNS together, the domain-join process that you take with your computers and servers self-registers a DNS record during that process, which means creating a DNS record for each new server or computer is not something that you need to remember to accomplish.

I have not yet created any DNS records in my new lab environment, not purposefully anyway, and yet when I open the **DNS Manager** console from inside the **Tools** menu of **Server Manager**, I see numerous records already existing. When I joined each of these machines to the domain, it automatically registered these records for me so that the new servers and workstations were immediately resolvable within our domain:

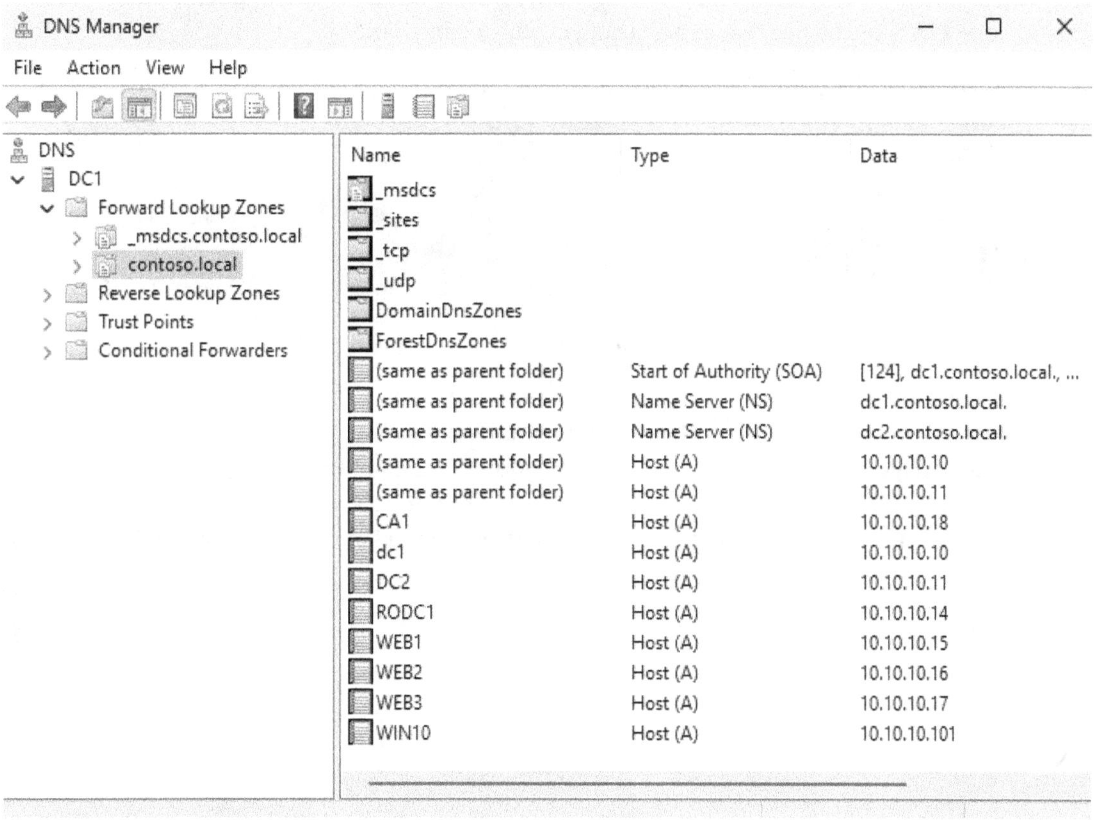

Figure 4.1: DNS Manager

Host record (A or AAAA)

The first kind of DNS record we are looking at is the most common type that you will work with. A **host record** is the one that resolves a particular name to a particular IP address. It's pretty simple, and for most of the devices on your network, this will be the only kind of record that exists for them inside DNS. There are two different classes of host records that you should be aware of, even though you will likely only be using one of them for at least a few more years. The two different kinds of host records are called an **A record** and an **AAAA record**, which is pronounced **quad A**.

The difference between the two? A records are for **IPv4** addresses and will be used in most companies for years to come. AAAA records serve the exact same purpose (resolving a name to an IP address) but are only for **IPv6** addresses, and will only be useful if you use IPv6 in your network.

In *Figure 4.1*, you can see some Host (A) records that were self-created when those machines joined our domain. I also have another server running on my network that has not yet been domain-joined, and so it has not self-registered into DNS. This server is called RA1; you may remember that we already pre-staged an AD object for this server, but since it is not yet joined to the domain, it has not self-registered a DNS record. If I log in to any other system on my network at this moment, I fail to contact my RA1 server by name, since that name is not yet plugged into DNS:

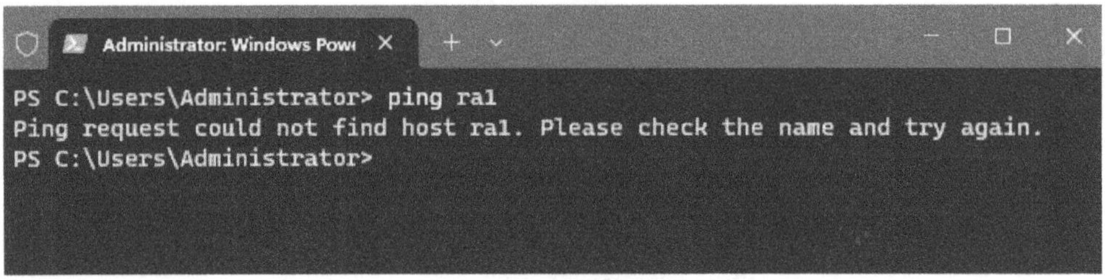

```
PS C:\Users\Administrator> ping ra1
Ping request could not find host ra1. Please check the name and try again.
PS C:\Users\Administrator>
```

Figure 4.2: RA1 server does not resolve

For now, I am going to choose not to join this server to the domain, so that we can manually create a DNS record for it and make sure that I am able to resolve the name properly after doing that. Back inside DNS Manager on your DNS server, right-click on the name of your domain listed under the Forward Lookup Zones folder, and then choose **New Host (A or AAAA)...**. Inside the screen to create a new host record, simply enter the name of your server and the IP address that is configured on its network interface:

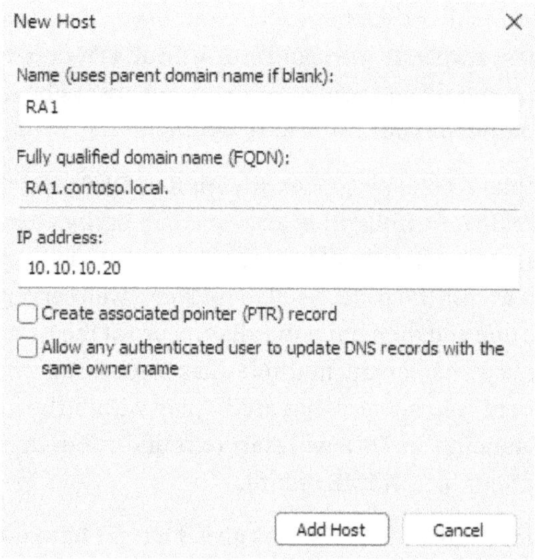

Figure 4.3: Adding a new host record

Now that we have created this new host record, we should immediately be able to start resolving this name inside our domain network. Moving back to the client machine from which I was trying to ping RA1 earlier, I'll try the same command again, and this time, it resolves and replies successfully, even though RA1 is not yet joined to our domain. If I had instead worked through the process of joining RA1 to the domain, I never would have needed to manually create this A record, but I wanted to show you the process:

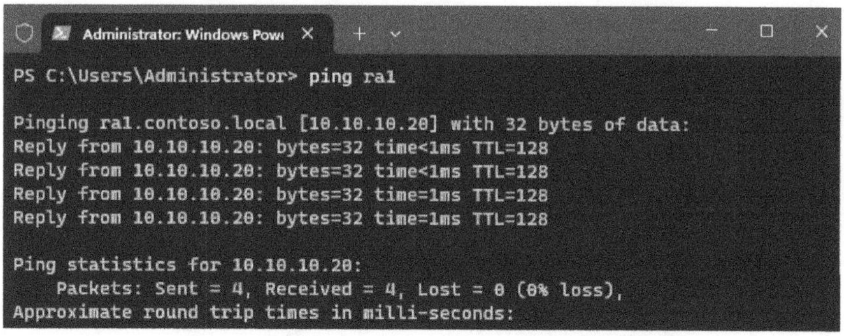

Figure 4.4: Successfully pinging RA1

Alias record – CNAME

Another useful type of DNS record is **CNAME** (canonical name), which, more commonly these days, is called an **alias record**. This is a record that takes a name and points it at another name. You can almost think of a CNAME as a nickname. It sounds a little silly at first glance because, in the end, you are still going to have to resolve your final name to an IP address by using a host record in order to get the traffic where it needs to go, but the purposes of an alias record can be vast. A good example to portray the usefulness of an alias record is when you are running a web server that is serving up websites within your network. Rather than force all of your users to remember a URL such as `http://web1.contoso.local` to access a website, we could create an alias record called `intranet` and point it at `WEB1`. This way, the more generalized `intranet` record can always be utilized by client computers, which is a much friendlier name for your users to remember.

In addition to creating a happier user experience with this new DNS record, you have at the same time created additional administrative flexibility because you can easily change the server components that are running beneath that record, without having to adjust any settings on the client machines or retrain employees on how to access the page. Need to replace a web server? No problem, just prep the new server alongside the old one and then point the alias record at the new server. Need to add another web server? That's easy too, as we can create multiple alias records, all with the same `intranet` name, and point them at the different web servers that are in play within the environment. This creates a very simple form of load balancing, as DNS will start to round-robin the traffic among the different web servers, based on that `intranet` CNAME record.

In fact, rather than continue to talk about this, let's give it a try. I have a website running on exactly that URL in my environment, but currently I can only access it by typing in `http://web1.contoso.local`. Inside DNS, I am going to create an alias record that redirects `intranet` to `WEB1`:

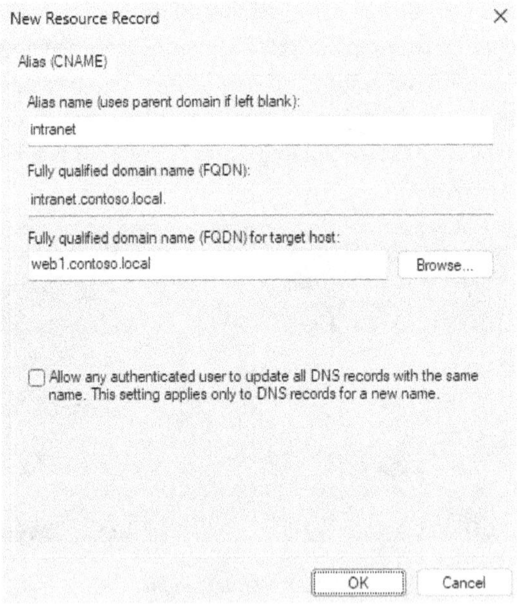

New Resource Record   ✕

Alias (CNAME)

Alias name (uses parent domain if left blank):

intranet

Fully qualified domain name (FQDN):

intranet.contoso.local.

Fully qualified domain name (FQDN) for target host:

web1.contoso.local   Browse...

☐ Allow any authenticated user to update all DNS records with the same
   name. This setting applies only to DNS records for a new name.

OK   Cancel

Figure 4.5: Creating a new alias record

Now, when I ping `intranet`, you can see that it resolves to my `WEB1` server. And when accessing the web page, I can simply type the word `intranet` into my address bar inside a web browser to launch my page. The website itself is not aware of the name change being made, so I didn't have to make any modifications to the website, only within DNS:

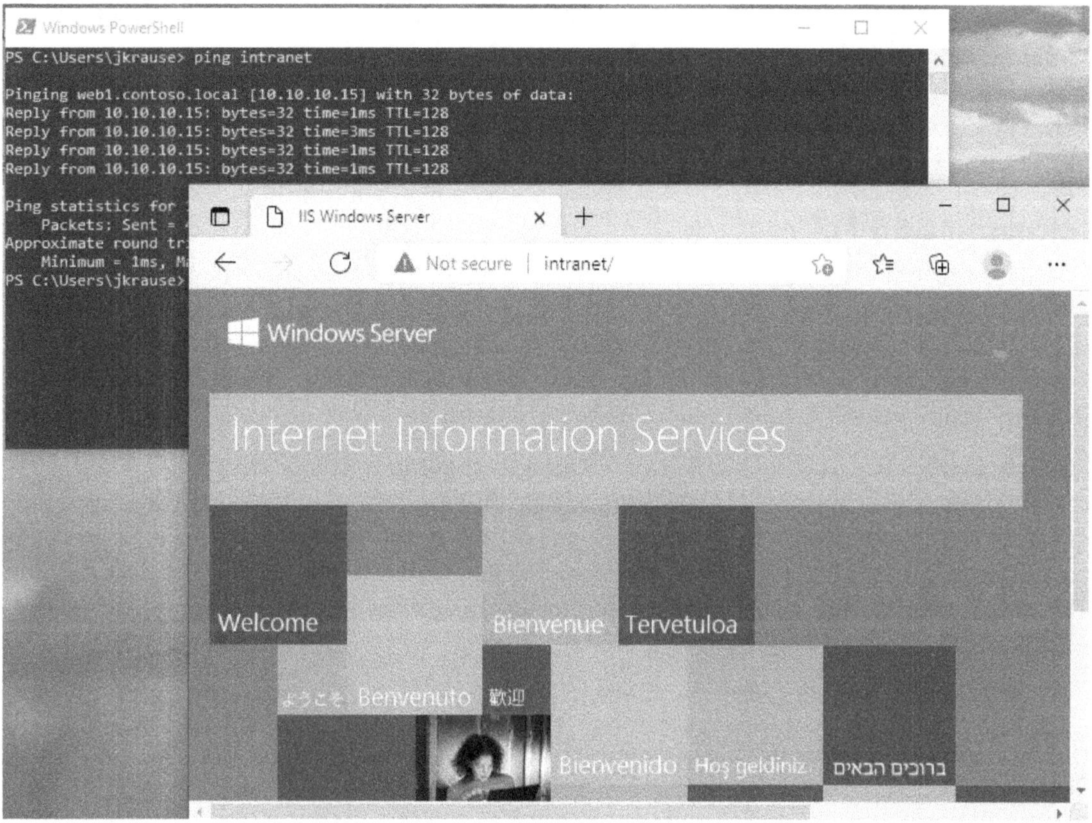

Figure 4.6: Visiting WEB1's site using the new intranet alias

Mail exchanger record

A third type of DNS record is called a **mail exchanger** (**MX**) record. In your everyday duties, you will not have to encounter or configure MX records nearly as often as A or CNAME records, but they are important to understand nonetheless. An MX record is all about email services and delivery. Whatever domain name follows the @ symbol in your email address, the DNS servers that are handling that domain name must contain an MX record telling the domain where to point for its mail services. MX records are most commonly used within public DNS for name resolution happening over the internet. For companies hosting their own email on local Exchange servers, your public DNS servers will contain an MX record that steers email to your Exchange environment. For companies hosting their email in a cloud service such as Office 365, your public DNS records would need to contain an MX record that directs email traffic toward the cloud provider that is hosting your mailboxes.

Whenever an email is sent outbound, the internet needs to determine how to deliver that email. Public internet DNS is checked for whichever domain the email is destined for, and the MX record contained within that DNS configuration defines where the email is sent. If you don't have an MX record, or if it disappears for some reason, you will receive zero emails to your domain. This is important to understand for email delivery troubleshooting purposes. How would an MX record possibly disappear? Usually, during website changes. When a business decides to migrate to a new website, it is typically the website developer making those changes. As part of those changes, they need access to DNS to be able to point your company website name at whatever new IP address is being used to host the website, and if the wrong options are selected during migration, your MX record could become null in the process. If you encounter any email delivery problems following changes in DNS, it is most likely that something is wrong with your MX record.

Microsoft 365 MX records

Now that so many businesses host their email in Microsoft's Office 365 platform, let's take a firsthand look at an MX record that points to this system. Even though millions of mailboxes across thousands of companies now host their email in the same Microsoft 365, every company will have a unique MX record associated with its M365 environment. Finding your specific MX record criteria is pretty simple (but very critical to get it correct); you just need to know where to look.

Log in to your Microsoft 365 admin portal, and navigate to **Settings** > **Domains**. Here, you will see all of the domain names that you have configured inside the portal. Click on the name of the domain in question, and then click on **DNS records**. Here, you will see all DNS records that need to be present in your company's public DNS provider that are required for Microsoft 365 services to work successfully. The most important for email delivery is the MX record, listed right on top, but all three of the records under the **Microsoft Exchange** heading are very important:

```
0 contoso-com.mail.protection.outlook.com
```

Once you ensure this MX record is successfully created in your domain's public DNS records, the internet now knows that any email destined for an address ending in @contoso.com needs to be delivered to Microsoft 365 hosting services, and Microsoft takes it and delivers it to your appropriate company and mailbox from there.

TXT record

TXT is simply short for **text** record. TXT records are used within DNS for various purposes, and they can contain just about any kind of information. Sometimes, TXT records are placed for actual human reading of some type of info, but more likely, you will be asked to create a TXT record at some point as a form of validation.

For example, most websites are protected by SSL certificates, and the process of purchasing an SSL certificate is straightforward. However, you certainly wouldn't want any yahoo with a laptop and internet access to be able to purchase a certificate that can protect a website name that ends in a domain name that your business owns, right? So, **certification authorities (CAs)** (the places where you purchase SSL certificates) will require some sort of validation process before allowing you to purchase a certificate for your domain name.

Sometimes that validation process is simply allowing the CA to send an email to an address associated with that domain name where you can then manually validate by clicking on a link in that email, or sometimes you will be asked to create a TXT record with a very exact set of characters in your public DNS records. The implication and validation, of course, is that if you really do own that domain name, you will have access to receive email or to create DNS records within that domain. When the CA sees your newly created TXT record that contains the data they asked you to input, they know you really do own that domain, and they will then issue your new certificate. An attacker trying to spoof your website and acquire an SSL certificate maliciously would not have such access to your domain's DNS settings.

SPF record

There are a few special kinds of TXT records, a common one being **Sender Policy Framework (SPF)** records. This record pertains to the delivery of emails, but while an MX record identifies which servers email should flow *toward*, an SPF record identifies which locations email is coming *from*. SPF records are part of spam and spoofing calculations, used to identify the locations on the internet from which email from your domain is expected to be flowing. Let's take a look at a couple of example SPF records, which will help you to understand how they are formatted, and also assist in describing why they are necessary:

```
v=spf1 [IP address 1] [IP address 2] [include:<domain>] -<enforcement rule>
```

The preceding is standard formatting for an SPF TXT record. For simple email systems where all email flows from one public IP address on the internet, or from one hosted email system, your record will be nice and short. A great example is email coming from Microsoft 365. Everyone who hosts email in M365 should have an SPF record with (at minimum) the following information inside:

```
v=spf1 include:spf.protection.outlook.com -all
```

SPF record information is used by receiving email servers to validate the mail coming inbound. That mail server will receive the email, discover which domain it came from, and reach back out over the internet to that domain's DNS servers to check for the existence of an SPF record. If it doesn't find such a record, your email has a much higher chance of being flagged as spam. If it does find an SPF record, the mail server then checks the entries in that record, which identifies the safe places that we expect mail to be flowing from, and confirms that the email did, in fact, originate from one of those places. In our preceding Microsoft 365 SPF record, we included the domain spf.protection.outlook.com. All email that flows from Office 365 servers will match this origination, so this simple record is the only thing needed to be in place for safe delivery of email from your Microsoft 365 tenant.

> You may have noticed that I keep interchanging Microsoft 365, Office 365, and M365. These are all commonly used nomenclatures to refer to the same thing: email that is hosted on Microsoft's servers.

Now, pretend that your SPF record is already in place and working with your hosted email, but that you set up an on-premise SMTP relay server so that your copiers on the network have the ability to scan to email. This is a common request by businesses, and something that I find in the wild on a very regular basis. The nature of your SMTP server doesn't really matter; there are various ways to accomplish that. What you'll usually find, though, is that when you send an email from your copier, that email may start getting flagged as spam. Sometimes it lands in the recipient's junk mail folder, and sometimes it is captured and not delivered to them at all. Why is this? If you have an on-site SMTP relay where the email is coming from, remember the copier just hands the email over to the SMTP relay, and that relay is the person who is shuttling the email over the internet.

That relayed email is not coming from `spf.protection.outlook.com`, but rather email sent from your on-premise SMTP server is coming from your ISP's outbound public IP address. Your SPF record needs to be adjusted to include this additional safe sender, so that recipients of your email will know that emails coming from your physical building are legit. Let's build out an SPF record that includes a single IP address:

```
v=spf1 ip4:8.8.8.8 include:spf.protection.outlook.com -all
```

That's it! By simply updating your SPF record to include the public IP address that the copier scans are coming from, your recipient email servers will better trust that incoming mail.

I'm obviously using `8.8.8.8` as an example in the preceding text; don't plug this into your own SPF records! You will want to identify your actual outbound IP address and use that information instead.

It is also easy to add multiple IP addresses, for example, if your business owns multiple buildings, each with their own ISP connections, and wants email traffic to be able to flow from devices (such as copiers) in each location:

```
v=spf1 ip4:8.8.8.8 ip4:4.4.2.2 include:spf.protection.outlook.com -all
```

The -all enforcement rule

What is that `-all` part at the end of an SPF record, anyway? I'm glad you asked! The declaration at the end of an SPF is telling the receiving mail server how strictly it should enforce these SPF rules. There are three different ways that you could configure that enforcement rule:

- `-all`: This is generally the way you always want to set up SPF records. `-all` means "hard fail." It sets the SPF rules as firm, so recipient mail servers will follow these rules.

- `~all`: Use this alternative if you are unsure that you have all IP addresses listed in your SPF record for a soft fail scenario. I would only use this as a temporary measure, and honestly, I don't know that I have ever encountered an SPF record in a production environment that is configured as such.

- `?all`: The last option here is neutral. Use it only for testing SPF records, as it will not help mail delivery until you later change it over to `-all`.

DKIM signatures

Another increasingly common type of DNS "record" related to email delivery is **DomainKeys Identified Mail (DKIM)**. In the distant past, no special DNS records were required on the internet to be able to deliver email successfully, because stupid spammers and attackers weren't yet holed up in their basements with nothing better to do. Once these things started becoming prevalent, SPF became commonplace to combat it and prove identity for real email delivery. Email attacks continue to escalate, and now it's the norm to establish both SPF and DKIM in public DNS to further prove the reliable identity of your real email.

DKIM is not actually its own "type" of DNS record, but a series of tools that work together to help verify the authenticity of email. Once you work toward enabling DKIM in your environment, you will find that the DNS records created in your public DNS are actually CNAME records, which we already discussed.

Since Microsoft 365 is so popular, let's log in to the M365 administrative portal and discover what exactly is needed to enable DKIM in our environment. Log in to portal.office.com and navigate to the following, or simply search for DKIM in the Search field of the **Admin** portal:

Admin | Security | Policies & Rules | Threat Policies | Email authentication settings | DKIM

You know what? Just go ahead and visit the admin center and then search for DKIM. Microsoft changes the placement of things in the **Security** portal so often, it is most likely that it will be changed again before this book is in print. Oh, Microsoft.

Hopefully, you are now looking at a heading that says **DomainKeys Identified Mail (DKIM)** and a listing of all domains that are plugged into your 365 environment. You will see a status next to each domain, and a simple **Disabled/Enabled** toggle switch. Flipping this switch to **Enabled** is all you must do on the M365 side to enable DKIM on your email domain, but if you try it, you'll receive a rather nasty-looking error on-screen:

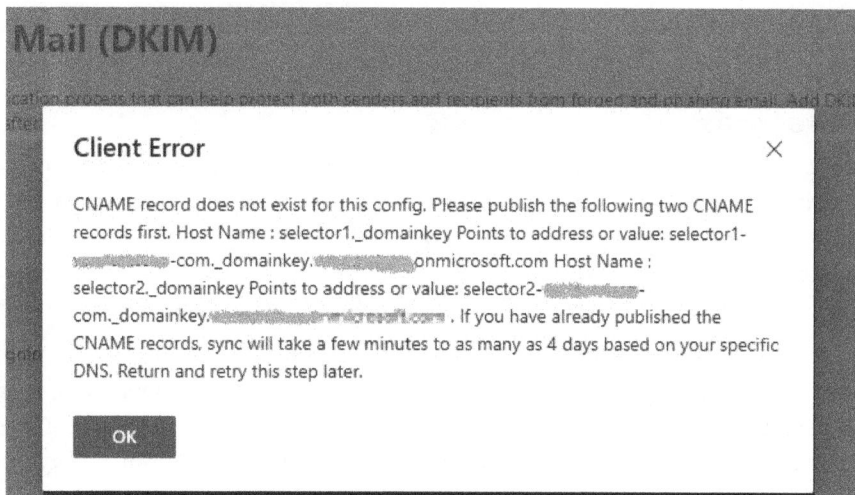

Figure 4.7: Read closely to find your needed CNAME records

If you read over the messy text very carefully, you will find that this **Client Error** screen is telling you exactly what you need to create inside your public DNS in order to have the proper CNAME records that DKIM is looking for. Using this information, which I, of course, obfuscated in my earlier screenshot, head over to your public DNS provider and add the specified CNAME records. After waiting for those DNS records to become live on the internet, which could take a few minutes or a few days depending on your DHS hoster, you will now be able to revisit the DKIM screen inside M365's **Security** portal, and successfully flip the toggle to enable DKIM on that email domain. That's it!

Name server (NS) record

Here is another type of DNS record that you don't have to deal with on a day-to-day basis, but you should still know what it's there for. An NS record is an identifier within a DNS zone that tells it which **name servers** (your DNS servers) to use as the authorities for that zone. If you look at the NS records listed in your internal DNS right now, you will recognize that it is calling out the names of your DNS servers on the network. When you add a new DC/DNS server to your domain, a new NS record for this server will be automatically added to your DNS zone:

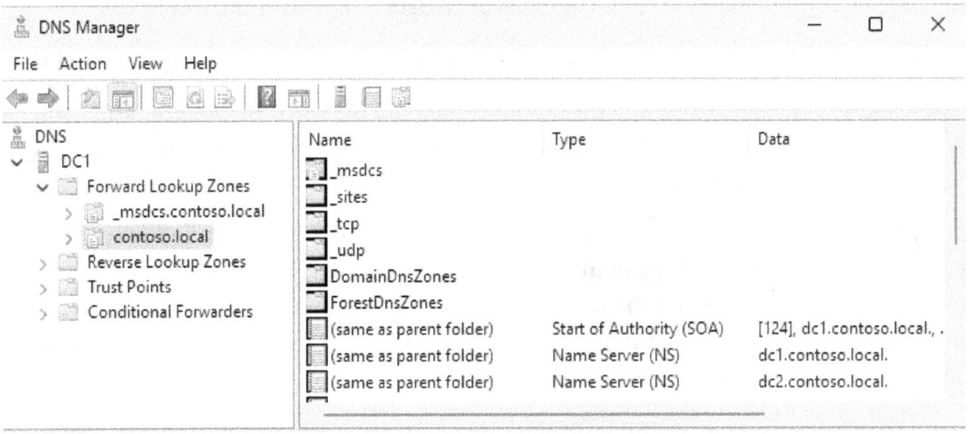

Figure 4.8: Viewing NS records in your zone

Public NS records

NS records are critical to understanding when working with public/internet DNS records. I can't tell you how many times I have assisted admins who were trying to create new DNS records for their zone and struggling because it seemed like no matter what they plugged into the DNS settings, their new records would never show up and work on the internet. After a quick look, we discovered that their NS record for the domain was pointing at a different DNS server or service altogether, which they didn't even realize was part of their company's DNS equation. Here's an example scenario that helps explain.

You inherit an already established infrastructure as you take over server administration for a company. The previous admin has all passwords documented; things are looking good so far. The director of marketing for the company has their own company credit card, and comes to you on day two to let you know that rather than navigate the proper IT purchasing channels, they just signed up for *XYZ* marketing service, which is going to help send out blasts of emails. This marketing company requires things called CNAME records to be created in your public DNS so that your email and their systems can work together. Now, it's up to you to put those CNAME records into place.

No big deal, right? You reference the password document and find a record labeled **DNS** that has login credentials for **GoDaddy**. Sounds like the jackpot, and makes sense, as GoDaddy is a pretty common platform on the internet for managing DNS zones. You log in to GoDaddy, edit the DNS zone for your domain, and add your new CNAME records. The CNAME records aren't resolving yet, but you know that DNS propagation takes a while to roll around the internet, so you inform Mr. Marketing that his new service should be up and running within 24 hours. You're a hero!

Except... 24 hours roll around, and it's still not working. Mr. M is starting to push back, and you're realizing that that quarterly bonus may not be so sure a bet. Unfortunately, you have forgotten one critical piece of the puzzle. Even though you have a GoDaddy account *and* it is labeled **DNS**, *and* you were able to create new DNS records within that account, it is entirely possible that the registrar for your domain is actually pointing NS records at a different DNS service entirely! A useful tool in this scenario is the DNS Lookup tool from MXToolbox.com.

A quick search for that on the internet will find you the current link. You simply type your domain name into the DNS Lookup tool, and it will spit back at you which NSs are in place, and which service is hosting your DNS records on the internet.

Following the previous procedure, you discover that the NS records for your domain are, in fact, pointing to Network Solutions, not GoDaddy at all! As it turns out, your IT predecessor wasn't entirely sure how to do a domain transfer, and they got it part-way there but never finished the process, so while you have GoDaddy available and your domain is even listed inside the GoDaddy console, when any computer on the internet tries to look up DNS info for your domain, the NS records are telling that computer to head toward Network Solutions for the domain's DNS servers, not GoDaddy at all. You now have two choices. You can either log in to Network Solutions and add your CNAME records there, and they will work because Network Solutions is currently the service that is doing DNS resolution for your domain, or you can finish that migration and update your NS records so that they point at GoDaddy's DNS servers instead of Network Solutions.

In summary, this is the flow that happens with a DNS lookup:

1. Client/server makes a call for DNS.
2. NS records identify which DNS servers are authoritative for the domain you are calling for.
3. DNS lookups are steered to those servers.
4. DNS resolution happens.

ipconfig /flushdns

Just one final note to finish this section. I have been saying things like *Now, when I do this…* or *Immediately following this change…* and if you are creating some of your own records, you may have noticed that it sometimes takes a while for your client computers to recognize these new DNS records. That is normal behavior, and the time it takes before your change rolls around to the whole network will depend entirely on how large your network is and how Active Directory replication is configured. When you create a new DNS record on one DC, your new record needs to replicate itself to all of the other DCs in your network. This process alone can take upward of a couple of hours if AD is not configured for faster replication. Typically, it only takes a few minutes. And then, once the new record exists on all of your DC servers, your clients may still take a little bit of time to utilize the new record, because client computers in a domain network hold onto a cache of DNS data. This way, they don't have to reach out to the DNS server for every single name resolution request. They can more quickly refer to their local cache in order to see what the information was from the last time they checked in with the DNS server. If you are trying to immediately test out a new DNS record that you just created and it's not working, you may want to try to run the `ci` command on your client computer. This forces the client to dump its locally cached copies of DNS resolver records and go grab new information from the DNS server. After flushing your cache, the new record should resolve properly.

Split-brain DNS

In all of our lab configurations, screenshots, and examples, you will notice that the domains we create on the internal network always end with `.local`. This is purposeful and is generally considered best practice. Public DNS zones, as you well know, can end in a myriad of ways.

Websites or services that live on the internet may end with .com, .org, .edu, .biz, .info, .tech, .construction—the list goes on and on. These are known as top-level domains, and the creative use of such DNS suffixes should remain on the internet and away from our internal DNS zones.

Now, many of you may already work in corporate environments where your internal DNS is configured as something other than .local, and so you already realize that internal domains can certainly be configured as one of these other suffixes. For example, Microsoft.com is obviously one of the public domains that Microsoft owns, and they could very well also have used Microsoft.com as an internal DNS zone. In fact, it could even be their primary domain name inside Active Directory right now, and this wouldn't *necessarily* cause any problems, but it certainly increases the *potential* for problems, or at least creates a more complex DNS environment in general.

Whenever a company configures its internal DNS to match its external DNS, this is commonly referred to as **split-brain DNS**. Years ago, there were articles published on the internet by Microsoft warning administrators against doing this, as it caused confusion and problems with some Microsoft roles and technologies that companies would try to deploy in their environments. As time went on, many people either didn't know or simply ignored this recommendation, and so the world is now awash with networks where split-brain DNS exists. Many of these environments are so populated and complex that they will never be changed at this point, and so Microsoft and the world had no choice but to adapt. Thankfully, in today's world, most roles or services that you deploy are written in a way that they accommodate for possible split-brain DNS out of the box, but some still require special considerations.

One example is Microsoft DirectAccess, which we will cover in *Chapter 9, Remote Access*. When deploying DirectAccess, there is a critical piece of client-side technology called the **Name Resolution Policy Table** that must be populated based on your internal DNS architecture. For companies using a .local domain internally, this configuration is a piece of cake, and no special considerations are needed. For anyone with split-brain DNS, this sometimes turns into a convoluted mess, and for anyone not well versed in the intricacies of DirectAccess, simply having split-brain DNS in your environment could very well mean that you are never able to get DirectAccess working in your environment. It's possible, but more challenging.

At first glance, you would think that administration would be made easier if internal DNS zones matched public DNS zones, but this simply isn't true. The opposite, in fact, is what you will find. Whenever you publish any external service, you will then have to make special considerations with your internal DNS to make that service work as intended from inside the network, because internal DNS zones will typically trump external ones. Split-brain DNS ends up being more work on a daily basis.

Over the past few years, I have seen a couple of Microsoft documents related to Office 365 that recommend administrators who are setting up new internal domains to do so by intentionally using split-brain DNS, configuring their internal DNS zones to match their public DNS. For example, they might recommend that if your public domain is contoso.com, your internal domain should also be set up for contoso.com instead of contoso.local. After reading over these articles, and based on my own experiences, I don't agree. Setting up split-brain DNS makes *some* aspects of Office 365 administration and integration easier, but if you step back and look at the whole IT picture, it's still more complicated overall. Configuring your on-premises internal DNS to be split-brain creates extra complexities with Entra Domain Services rollouts as well.

As the saying goes, you can lead a horse to water but can't make it drink. You have now been informed that utilizing the same DNS zone inside your network as what you use on the internet could cause you some headaches. What you decide to do with this information in the future, well, that's up to you...

Types of DNS zones

You are now familiar with creating different types of DNS records, but that information is only going to enable you to create new records inside of an already existing DNS zone. At present, in our test lab, we have only one DNS zone available to us, contoso.local, which was created automatically when we built the contoso.local domain. As of right now, computers that are using one of my contoso.local DCs as their DNS server are only able to look up DNS records that I have plugged into my DNS zone.

With the DNS server provided by Windows Server 2025, you can certainly build out many different DNS zones to increase name resolution capabilities in your network. There are plenty of different reasons why you might want to create additional DNS zones, and you should understand what types of zones are available to implement. Let's take a minute and discuss the different types of zones available to us.

Active Directory integrated zones

This is not a zone type, per se, but rather an option that can be selected when you create some types of DNS zones. When creating that new zone, you will find a checkbox that states **Store the zone in Active Directory**. When selected, this means that the new zone you are creating is going to be stored inside Active Directory, rather than being standalone on the DNS server from which you are creating the zone. Being stored inside AD means that this new zone is capable of being replicated automatically to all DC servers in your domain, which means that your DNS zone is highly available and more quickly accessible across your entire network. In general, if the type of zone you are creating allows storage inside Active Directory, do it.

After opening up the **DNS Manager** tool on your DC, you'll notice that any current DNS zones are listed beneath folders titled Forward Lookup Zones and Reverse Lookup Zones. What's the difference?

Forward lookup zones

Zones configured inside forward lookup zones are your traditional DNS zones. Their purpose is to take an incoming DNS request, such as from a client computer, and turn that DNS name request into an IP address that is handed back to the client computer. Forward lookup zones are almost always where DNS administrators will be working.

Reverse lookup zones

If "reverse" is the opposite of "forward," then the same must be true within a DNS context. Reverse lookup zones are responsible for mapping IP addresses backward into names. You may not even realize that these happen in your environment, but you can easily test them out anytime. You likely all know how to use the ping command, which relies on DNS to turn a name into an IP address. That, of course, is being handled by a forward lookup zone, as we see here:

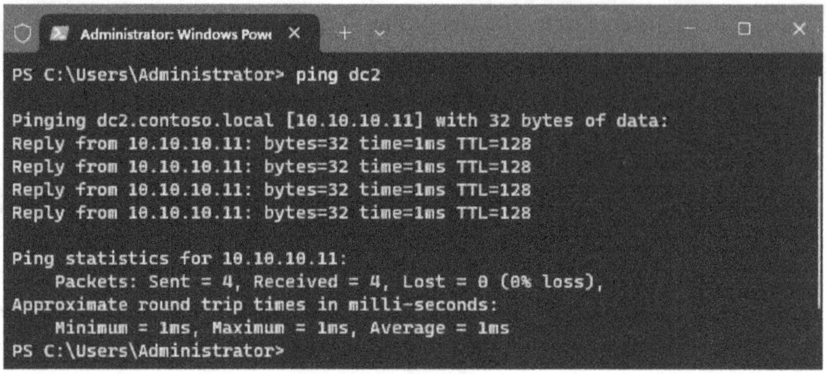

Figure 4.9: Resolving a name to an IP address

Did you know you can also use the ping command to perform the opposite? What if you want to query DNS to find out what hostname the 10.10.10.11 IP address maps back to?

```
ping -a 10.10.10.11
```

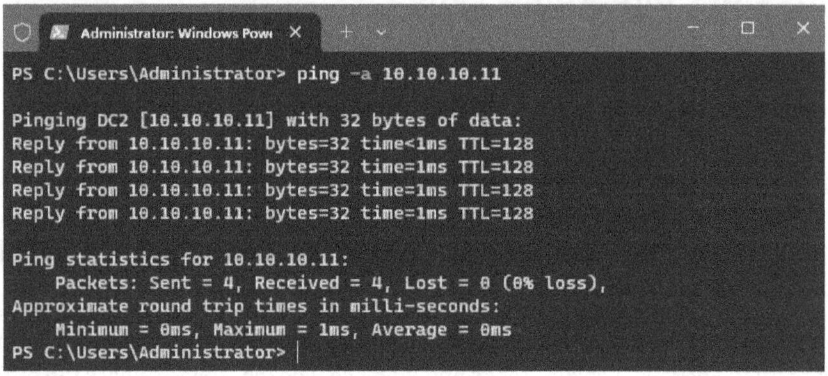

Figure 4.10: Querying DNS to find a hostname from an IP address

This reverse lookup, converting IP addresses back to names, has shown us that the IP address 10.10.10.11 has a reverse **pointer (PTR)** record mapping back to our DC2 server. This type of lookup is handled by a reverse lookup zone inside DNS. Reverse lookup zone creation is handled in the same way as forward lookup zone creation is handled, and we will work through creating a new DNS zone in just a few minutes. What is important to understand is that reverse zones are not automatically generated; you will need to intentionally create a reverse lookup zone if you have a reason for this functionality to exist in your environment.

Now that we understand the difference between forward and reverse lookup zones, right-clicking on **Forward Lookup Zones** and selecting **New Zone...** lands us with three choices on which type of zone we would like to create:

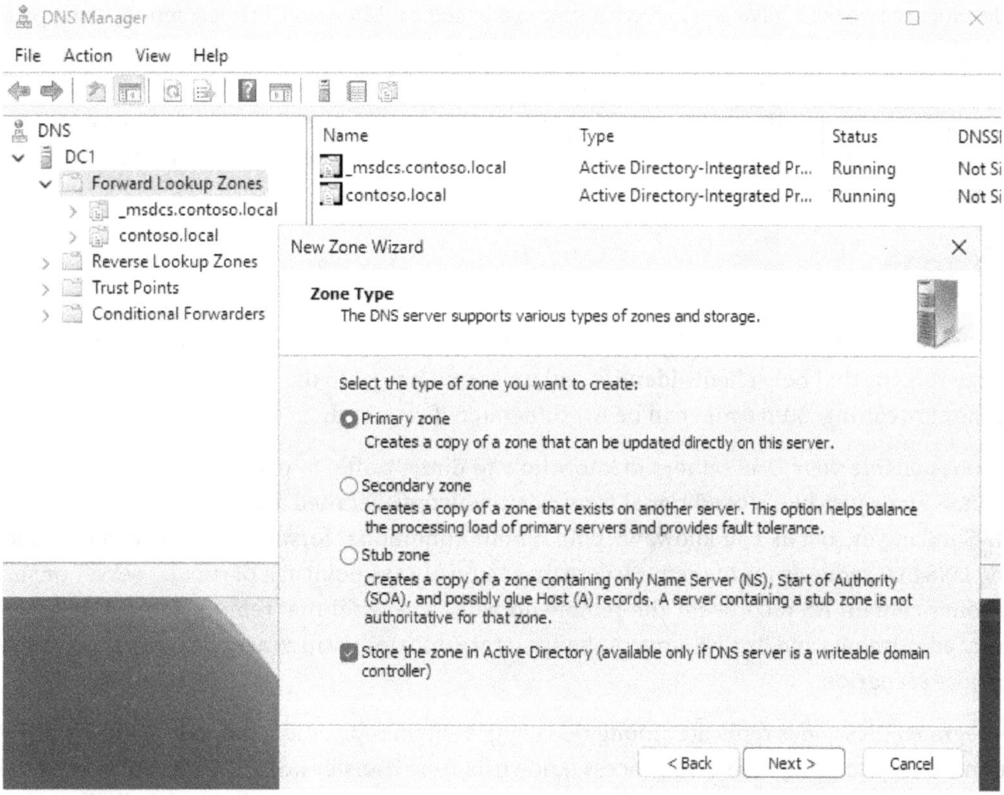

Figure 4.11: DNS zone types

Primary zone

The majority of DNS zones within internal networks are primary zones. This indicates that it is the "parent," so to speak. The master copy of any particular DNS zone is going to be the primary zone for that domain. When changes and updates are made to DNS records, it always happens within the primary zone. We will create a new primary zone together in just a few minutes. You can choose for primary zones to be stored in Active Directory, or not.

Secondary zone

Based on their names, it would seem secondary zones might be less important than primary zones, and that is generally true. A secondary zone is simply a read-only copy of a primary zone. Because it is read-only, no updates can be made within a secondary zone; it is always syncing from the primary zone. Secondary zones can be used to spread the DNS computing power among multiple servers, taking the load off the primary zones, but it is important to know that secondary zones are not Active Directory-integrated. When you try selecting the option to create a new secondary zone, you will notice that the AD checkbox grays out.

Inside most networks I have worked with that are based on Microsoft infrastructure, your primary zones all get set up to be Active Directory-integrated, which means they are syncing around to all of your DC-based DNS servers anyway. In this case, secondary zones are less likely to be needed. If you deviate from that mentality and create DNS servers that are not also DCs (which you can absolutely do), then you may want to take care that you understand the use cases of secondary zones, because it is more likely in this scenario that you would utilize them.

Stub zone

The third selection on your **New Zone Wizard** screen is **Stub zone**. Like secondary zones, stub zones are copies of primary zones but only contain certain pieces of information. Namely, stub zones contain resource records that help clients identify and more quickly get to the full DNS servers for whatever zone they are calling. Stub zones can be AD-integrated if required.

Stub zones enable your DNS servers to know how to direct traffic to resolve records inside another domain. Sounds just like a conditional forwarder, which we learned about in the previous chapter, right? Similar, yes, but as you know, we pointed our conditional forwarder at a specific IP address, telling DNS that requests for the remote domain should always point at a particular server or servers. Stub zones contain NS records for the remote domain, so even if that remote domain makes some internal adjustments and its DNS servers change or are updated, stub zones can more accurately deal with those scenarios.

AD-integrated DNS zones replicate among DCs using domain replication, but non-AD-integrated DNS zones have to sync using their own process, known as **zone transfers**. Stub zones can be used to help make the zone transfer process more efficient and create faster name resolution for client computers.

Creating a new forward lookup zone

We will finish out this section with a quick walk-through on creating a new DNS zone. The process is straightforward, but there are a few options to consider along the way. In most cases, when creating new DNS zones, you will be doing so in order to enable internal client computers to resolve names for a new internal namespace (.local, for example), so that you can utilize that internal naming scheme for accessing servers and resources inside the network.

For our example, let's create a new primary zone just like we would for any internal namespace, but we are going to configure the DNS zone with a name that conflicts with a well-known internet namespace. This walk-through will not only portray the options available as we configure a DNS zone but also give a glimpse into what kind of challenges can present in a split-brain DNS scenario. It also portrays the fact that when clients are inside the network, their internal DNS servers have priority over internet DNS servers.

Inside **DNS Manager**, right-click on Forward Lookup Zones and select **New Zone…**. Now, select the options to create a new primary zone, and I am going to choose to store mine in Active Directory. Refer to *Figure 4.11* if you need a reference point on these options.

We now encounter a screen titled **Active Directory Zone Replication Scope**. This screen and options only present themselves when the **Store inside AD** option is checked; otherwise, the wizard would have bypassed this screen. Here you have options for how extensively you would like this new DNS zone to replicate among your DCs. You can replicate to all DCs inside the domain, or even the whole forest.

Next, name the zone. The name that you provide for the zone here is the namespace for which the zone is going to contain records. The possibilities here are endless. I could even type in Jordan.local as my DNS zone, or Jordan.com. This is actually a legitimate website that wraps over to Nike.com, which I suppose is fair because Michael Jordan is a little bit more popular than I am.

Now, I typed Jordan.com just to be silly, but it will portray exactly what I was going to show you, so let's stick with it. This is possibly the weirdest thing I've ever done inside **DNS Manager**.

To prove what is happening here, first, from a client computer in my network, I have pulled up a web browser and verified that I can successfully get to Jordan.com. If I ping that name, you can see that it resolves to a public IP address, which is expected. This is the public, internet-routable IP address of the web server upon which Jordan.com is hosted:

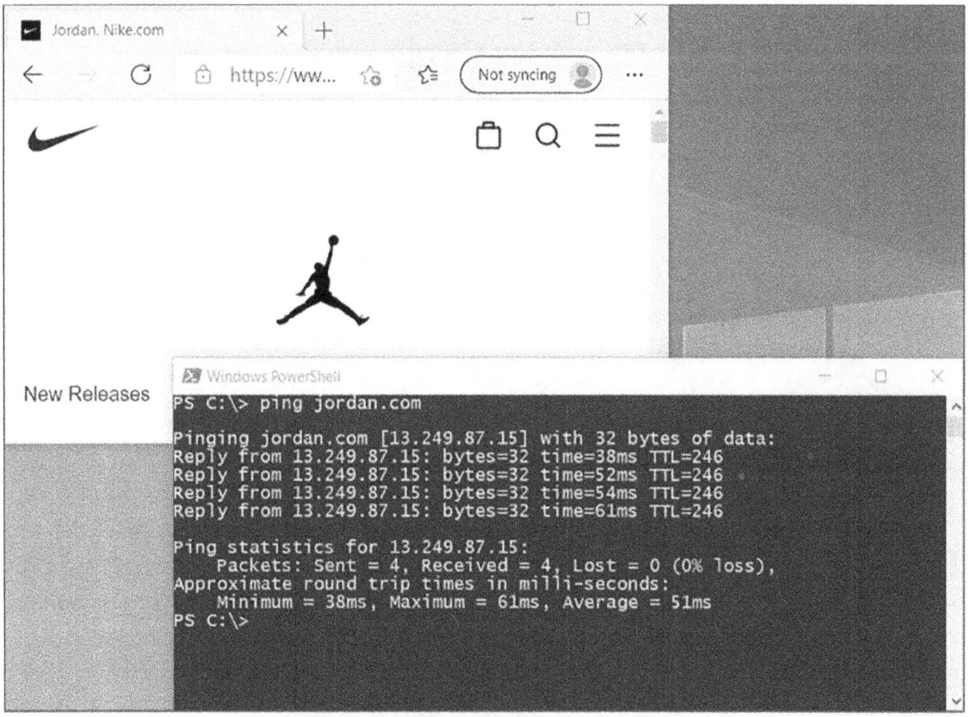

Figure 4.12: Resolving a public DNS zone

This is completely normal behavior, right? Type in a website URL, which is a DNS name; DNS resolves it to the IP address that hosts the website, and your browser takes you there. Next, finish the creation of our new Jordan.com internal DNS zone on our internal DNS server.

Walking through the zone creation wizard, I have typed in a zone name of Jordan.com, and the next screen that I must answer is regarding **Dynamic Update**. Server administrators always have the ability to manually create DNS records inside DNS zones, but if you have hundreds of client computers in your environment, do you really want the creation of DNS records to be a full-time job? Thankfully, there is no need to do this, as client computers that are joined to your domain will automatically attempt to register their own hostname and IP address with DNS servers whenever they connect to the network. This process is known as a dynamic update, and the settings on this screen show you options regarding these updates. You can allow or disallow dynamic updates for each zone and set some requirements around how secure the updating process needs to be. In most domain environments, configuring the top option is what you will do, only allowing secure updates in your zone. If you have legacy equipment or non-Microsoft products abundant in your network, you may need to select the second option to allow both secure and nonsecure updates:

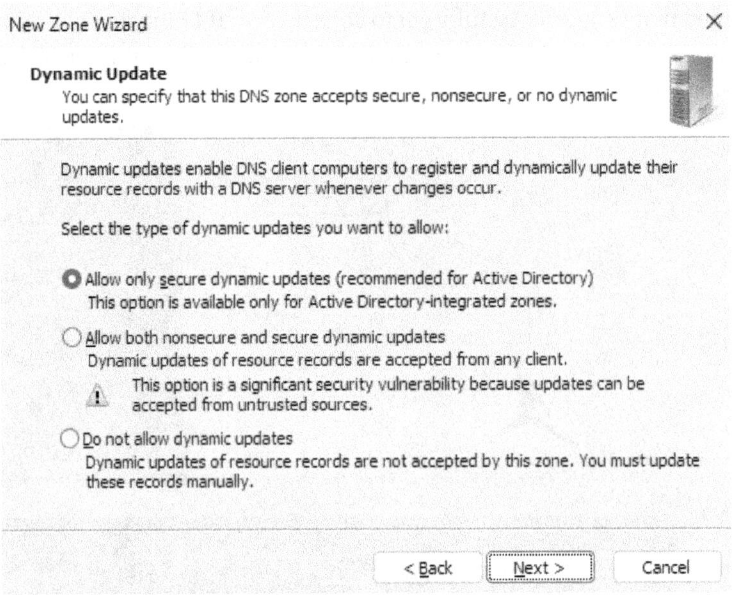

Figure 4.13: Security options for DNS dynamic updates

That's it! The final screen of the wizard is simply a settings review, and after clicking **Finish**, your new DNS zone is immediately available and working to resolve names in the new Jordan.com namespace, for any client computers that are using this server as their DNS server. As you can see in *Figure 4.14*, the Jordan.com zone is now listed in **DNS Manager**, and I went ahead and created a couple of A records so that any requests for Jordan.com or www.Jordan.com return an IP address of 10.10.10.23 (see what I did there? Number 23?):

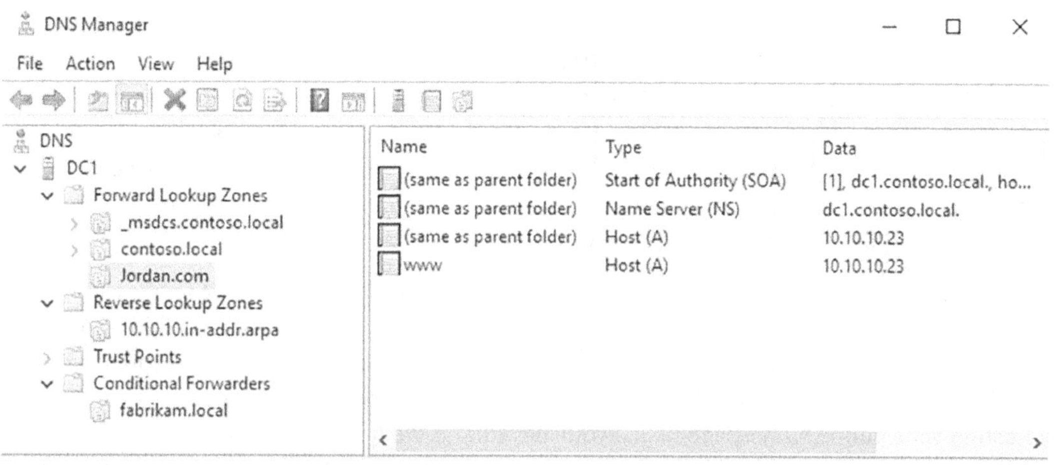

Figure 4.14: Creating an internal Jordan.com DNS zone

Now that our new zone is created inside the network, what has changed? Let's move back to that client computer in my test network, and try both browsing and pinging Jordan.com again:

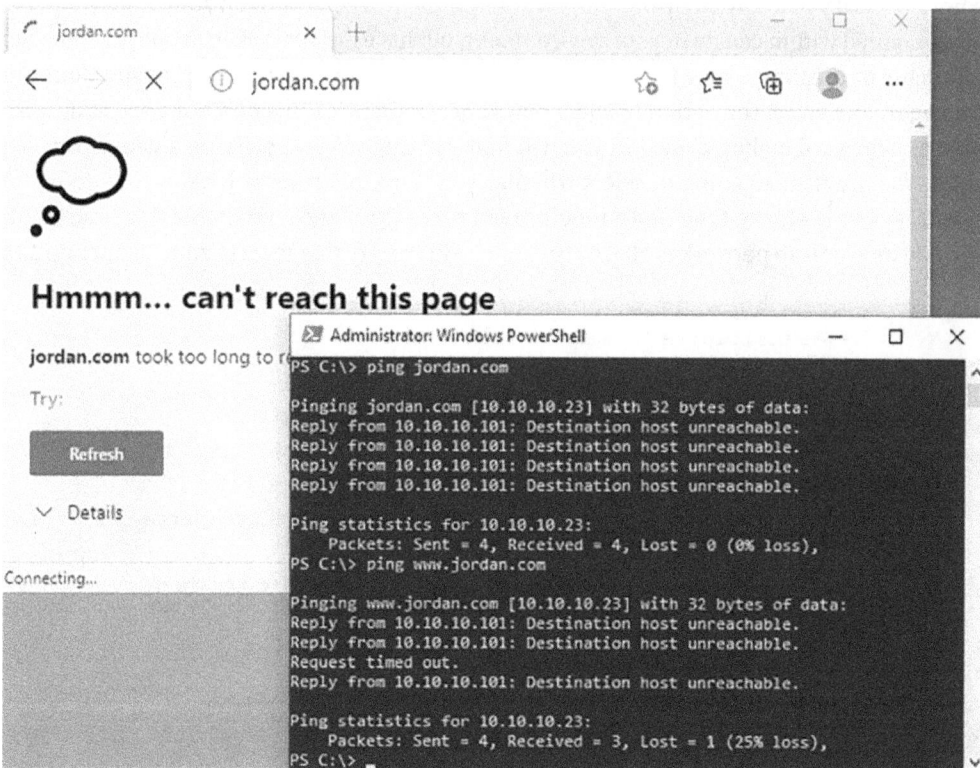

Figure 4.15: Pinging Jordan.com again

Prior to creating this new zone, my client request for Jordan.com was simply forwarded to public internet DNS servers, because my internal DNS servers did not have any of their own definitions for what to do with Jordan.com lookups. After creating an internal DNS zone for Jordan.com, we have now interrupted access to the website, because our own DNS server now has its own ruleset for what to do with these name requests! If I were to build out my own website on a web server and give that server an IP address of 10.10.10.23, my client computer would have successfully loaded my custom website when typing Jordan.com into their browser.

This example serves two purposes. First, to walk through the creation of a new DNS zone to review the options available, and to show how easy it is. Second, to make sure you understand that your internal corporate DNS servers have priority over public internet DNS servers. This means you need to take care when creating DNS zones and when deciding whether or not you want to pursue split-brain DNS by hosting your public namespace inside your network as well, because your internal DNS servers are going to be the primary resolvers for those zones. Split-brain DNS requires more attention and maintenance on a regular basis.

Creating a new reverse lookup zone

While not necessary in many environments, we talked about reverse lookup zones and what the PTR records contained within can do in your environment, but have not yet looked at one together. Similar to the process of creating a new forward lookup zone, right-click on **Reverse Lookup Zones** inside **DNS Manager**, and select the option to add a new zone. Options for this new zone are almost exactly the same as a forward lookup zone, but you will find that instead of specifying a namespace for this new zone, you are instead going to select whether you want this reverse lookup zone to be for the purpose of IPv4 or IPv6, and then find a requirement to specify a network ID that this zone is going to manage. My internal lab network is 10.10.10.x, so I will specify this reverse zone to operate as such:

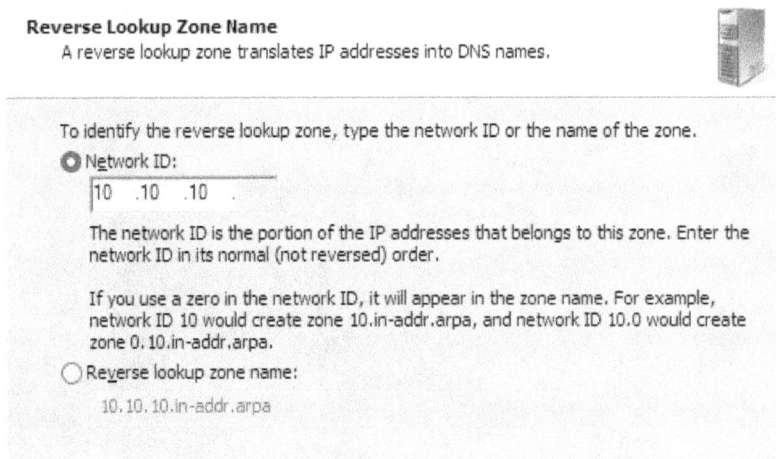

Figure 4.16: Creating a reverse lookup zone

If you enable this zone for secure dynamic updates, and if you have both DNS and DHCP running on servers in this environment, then from this point forward, when you join new computers or servers to the domain, they will automatically create both forward zone Host (A) records in DNS, as well as PTR records inside this new reverse zone. Reverse lookup zones are, therefore, usually hands-off. For our purposes today, I also wanted to show you what it looks like to manually create a new record inside our new reverse lookup zone. Right-click on the new zone and select the option to create a new PTR.

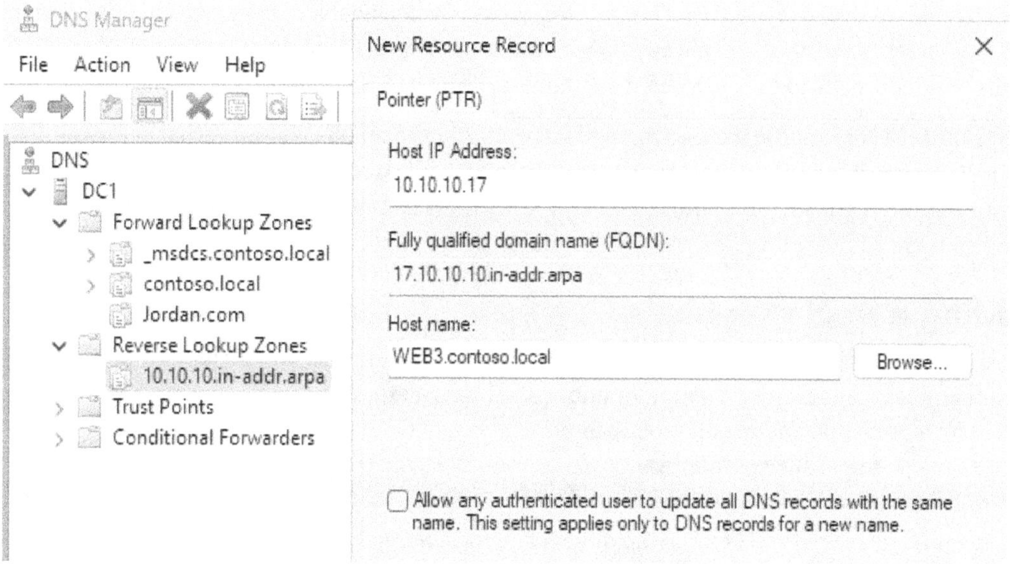

Figure 4.17: Creating a PTR record inside our reverse lookup zone

Simply enter the IP address and hostname of the server or computer that this PTR record points to, very similar to creating new Host records inside a forward lookup zone. Once your PTR records are populated, you can reverse-lookup machines in the environment all day long!

DNS-over-HTTPS

Hold your horses! For any of you who already know what DNS-over-HTTPS is, you may have jumped to the conclusion that seeing these words here in this book means that you can now host DoH within Windows Server DNS, but unfortunately, we are not there quite yet. We are discussing DNS-over-HTTPS here because it is a relevant technology, it is the future of DNS, and Microsoft has made the statement that DNS-over-HTTPS support is coming to Windows DNS Server in the future.

I wish that future were today, but alas… or should I say "doh"?

DoH (yes, this acronym makes me LOL) is becoming more and more important as we see increased sophistication in attacks on our network traffic. You are almost certainly already familiar with the concept of HTTPS and would never dream of visiting a sensitive location on the internet without seeing that familiar nomenclature in your browser's address bar. HTTPS means that all traffic flowing back and forth between your computer and a website is encrypted, but you now know that your computer doesn't even understand *how* to get to myfavoritebankingsite.com without first reaching out to ask the internet's DNS servers, *How do I get to this name?* The process of DNS doing its job and looking up a name and then submitting it back to your computer is *not* encrypted. So attackers may not gain access to your financials, thank goodness, but they could certainly find out what bank you use because the fact that you are visiting myfavoritebankingsite.com (this is not real, by the way), Google, Bing, Microsoft, or any other site that you frequent... well, those website names are information that would be interesting to an attacker and would not be very difficult for them to capture.

Enter the idea of DNS-over-HTTPS. DoH fills the gap, and when enabled, it means that even your initial DNS lookups are encrypted, as well as your web traffic afterward, of course. To successfully make use of DoH, you simply need to enable a client computer to point its DNS traffic at a DoH-enabled DNS server.

Currently, DoH is primarily focused on internet traffic, not so much on our internal networks. For any client computer that is connected to the internet, all you need to do is edit the IP address properties of your network card and point the DNS server definition at a DoH-capable endpoint. Some of the big-name companies providing DoH services available to the public internet are Google and Cloudflare.

Finding a DoH provider

Microsoft does recognize that DNS is heading this direction, and already includes a very useful PowerShell cmdlet that spits out a listing of public DoH providers. To find one, simply open PowerShell or Windows Terminal and run the following:

```
Get-DNSClientDohServerAddress
```

Once again, I just love that "Doh" is the official language here:

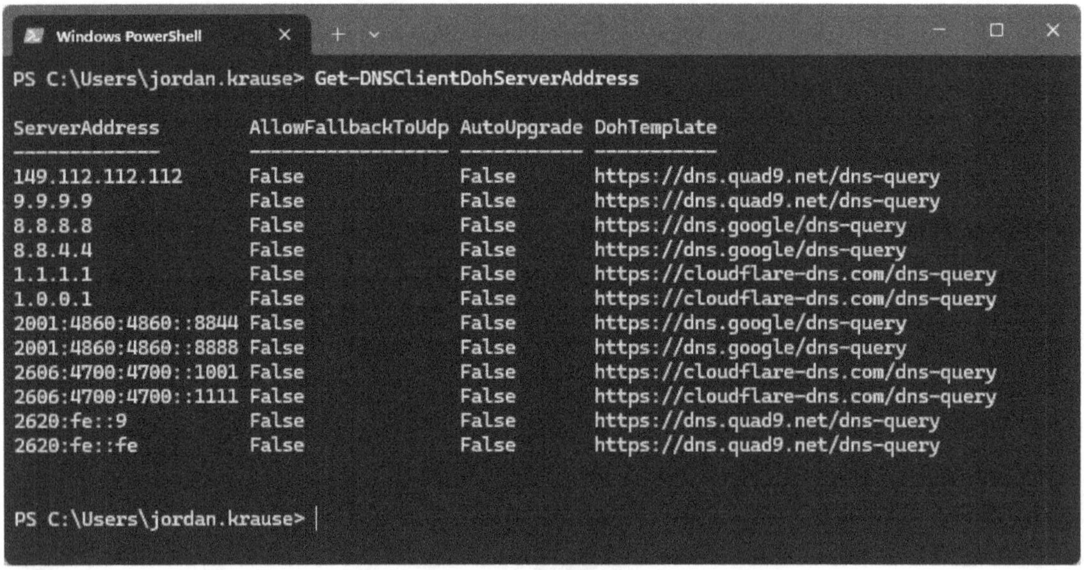

```
PS C:\Users\jordan.krause> Get-DNSClientDohServerAddress

ServerAddress            AllowFallbackToUdp AutoUpgrade DohTemplate
-------------            ------------------ ----------- -----------
149.112.112.112          False              False       https://dns.quad9.net/dns-query
9.9.9.9                  False              False       https://dns.quad9.net/dns-query
8.8.8.8                  False              False       https://dns.google/dns-query
8.8.4.4                  False              False       https://dns.google/dns-query
1.1.1.1                  False              False       https://cloudflare-dns.com/dns-query
1.0.0.1                  False              False       https://cloudflare-dns.com/dns-query
2001:4860:4860::8844     False              False       https://dns.google/dns-query
2001:4860:4860::8888     False              False       https://dns.google/dns-query
2606:4700:4700::1001     False              False       https://cloudflare-dns.com/dns-query
2606:4700:4700::1111     False              False       https://cloudflare-dns.com/dns-query
2620:fe::9               False              False       https://dns.quad9.net/dns-query
2620:fe::fe              False              False       https://dns.quad9.net/dns-query

PS C:\Users\jordan.krause>
```

Figure 4.18: Seeking out DNS-over-HTTPS servers on the internet

You are now equipped with IP addresses, from the ServerAddress column, that can be used to steer a workstation to a public DoH service.

Enabling DoH on a workstation

This part is easy for anyone already familiar with editing NIC properties. Simply open your TCP/IPv4 properties, find an appropriate DNS-over-HTTPS option in the drop-down menus, and point your DNS server address at one of the DoH servers on the internet:

Start | Settings | Network & internet | Ethernet

From this screen, find your network card and click **Edit** from the **DNS server assignment** section.

Click that drop-down menu, and change your DNS settings from **Automatic** to **Manual**. Then, click the toggle to enable IPv4.

You will now find the expected option to define your own DNS server, with another drop-down menu to select whether or not you want to use DNS over HTTPS. Specifying one of the IP addresses of a public DoH provider is the most important component here. In our previous screenshot, you may have noticed the DohTemplate information. This information is automatically pulled into your NIC configuration if you select to use automatic template settings, or you can choose to manually enter this information. With a workstation on the public internet, it is easiest to simply allow automatic configuration to happen, but in the future, once we have options to implement DoH on an internal DNS server, we may find ourselves making use of more manual configurations of these settings.

The last option to select on this screen is whether or not you want to allow **Fallback to plaintext**. This is fairly self-explanatory; if the DoH services are not behaving properly or if you try to visit a website that it cannot look up securely for some reason, your computer will fall back on traditional (non-encrypted) DNS lookups to get the job done. If you leave this slider set to **Off**, as I have done in my upcoming screenshot, you are going all-in on DoH, and if it has any trouble with name resolution, you simply won't get to your website.

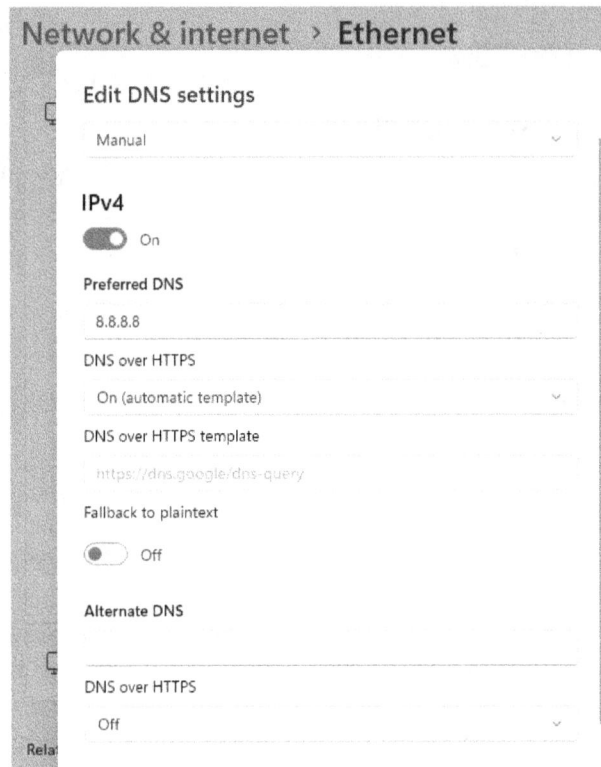

Figure 4.19: Using Google's public DoH service

Now, the astute among you have realized that DoH is a great idea, and that your DNS lookups are now hidden from the majority of the internet, but that you are still handing this listing of website lookups over to your DoH provider. Yes, you are exactly right. Without DoH being enabled, a company such as Google already knows what websites you search for and visit if you search for them via `Google.com`. But if you point your computer to Google's DoH presence for secure DNS-over-HTTPS lookups, you are increasing the security of your internet browsing, but you are also now telling Google every website that you visit from your computer.

Sidenote: Please do not walk around and configure all of your business computers to make use of a public service DNS-over-HTTPS provider! I wanted to walk through this example today to help you understand what DoH is and how to enable it. Inside your corporate domain environment, you will want your domain-joined workstations to continue throwing DNS requests against your internal, corporate DNS servers. If you suddenly usurp that and point all workstations at the public DNS, you will absolutely cause problems for your users whenever they attempt to access company-owned resources, such as internal servers. To bind internal name resolution together with DNS-over-HTTPS, we would need....

DNS-over-HTTPS on Windows DNS server

I really wish I could outline for you exactly how you can turn your Windows DNS server into a Windows DNS server that is enabled for DNS-over-HTTPS, but it simply isn't possible as of this writing. Microsoft is working on it, and once released, I expect this will quickly become a commonplace security enhancement that most businesses (any that have good IT admins such as yourself) will implement.

IP addressing with DHCP

IP addresses on your network are sort of like home addresses on your street. When you want to send a package to someone, you write their address on the front of the package and set it in the mailbox. In the same way, when your computer wants to send data to a server or another device on a network, each of those devices has an IP address that is used for the delivery of those packets. We know that DNS is responsible for telling the machines which name resolves to which IP address, but how do those IP addresses get put into place on the servers and computers in the first place?

Static addressing is simply the process of configuring IP addresses on your system manually, using your own hands as the configuration tool to plug all of your IP address information into the NIC settings on that device. While this is a quick and easy way to get network traffic flowing between a few endpoints, by giving them each a static IP address, it is not scalable. We often statically address our servers as a way of making sure that those IP addresses are not subject to change, but what about on the client and device side? Even in a small company with 10 employees, each person may have a desktop and a laptop; there are likely going to be printers on the network also needing IP addresses, and you may have a wireless network where employees or even guests can connect phones and other devices in order to gain internet access. Are you going to assign IP addresses by hand to all these devices? Certainly not.

Our answer to this problem is the **Dynamic Host Configuration Protocol (DHCP)**. This is a protocol that is designed to solve our exact problem by providing the ability for machines and devices to be plugged into your network and automatically obtain IP addressing information. Almost any user on any device in the entire world uses DHCP every day without even realizing it. When you connect your laptop or smartphone to a Wi-Fi router to gain internet access, a DHCP server gives you the ability to route traffic on that Wi-Fi network by assigning you IP addressing information. Often, in the case of public Wi-Fi or a simple home internet setup, your DHCP "server" is a service running on the wireless router itself. DHCP servers come in many flavors and on many types of equipment. Most firewalls are also capable of being DHCP servers for any or all of the subnets they manage. In our businesses where Windows Server rules the data center, our DHCP services are most often hosted on one or more Windows servers across the network.

Creating a DHCP scope

So far in the new Windows Server 2025 lab environment I have been building, I have been statically assigning IP addresses to all of the servers that are being built. This is starting to get old and is hard to keep track of. When the first DC was configured, I installed the DHCP role onto it, but haven't told it to start doing anything yet. What does a DHCP server need to start handing out IP addresses? It needs to know what IP addresses, subnet mask, default gateway, and DNS server addresses are within your network so that it can package that up and start handing the information out to the computers that request it. This package of information inside the DHCP server is called a **DHCP scope**. Once we define our scope, the DHCP server will start handing out IP addresses from that scope to our new servers and computers that do not already have static addresses defined.

Once again, we need to launch a management tool on our Windows Server 2025, and once again, the easiest way to launch that is by using the **Tools** menu inside **Server Manager**. On the server where the DHCP role is installed, go ahead and launch the **DHCP** console. Inside, you will see the name of your server where the DHCP server is running. Expand that, and you have options for both **IPv4** and **IPv6**. Yes, this means that you can use this DHCP server to hand out both IPv4 addresses as well as IPv6 addresses for those of you who are testing out IPv6, or have plans to in the future. For now, we are sticking with good old IPv4, and so I can right-click on **IPv4** and choose to create a new scope. This launches a **New Scope Wizard** window that walks you through the few pieces of information that the DHCP server needs in order to create a scope that is ready to start handing out IP addresses inside your network. I am setting my new scope to hand out IP addresses from `10.10.10.110` through `10.10.10.170`:

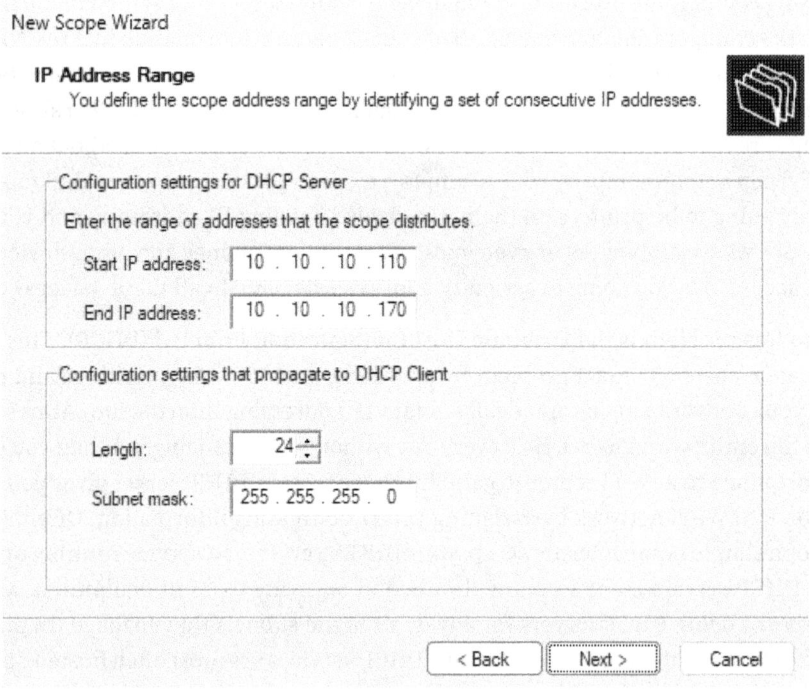

Figure 4.20: Creating a new DHCP scope

During this DHCP scope setup wizard, you will encounter a few additional options. Most have self-explanatory text on the screens, but let's take a moment to review the options you will uncover:

- **Subnet mask** and **Length**: Define the size of the subnet that you are asking DHCP to assign IP addresses within. If this is unfamiliar territory, make sure to visit *Chapter 8* at some point in your journey through this book.

- **Exclusions:** If there are any IP addresses within your defined scope that you would like DHCP to refrain from handing out, specify them here. An example of this would be an IP address for a server that is already statically assigned, and falls within the DHCP range that you declared earlier. DHCP will not know about any static IP addresses on your network, and so DHCP could still hand out that address and create a conflict on the network if you don't specify static addresses as exclusions. I can't tell you how many times I have watched IT admins do the "ping test" to find an available IP address, without even thinking about DHCP scopes. What if I were looking for an available IP address to place a new printer, and I did a simple `ping 10.10.10.151`. If no other devices had yet grabbed `10.10.10.151` from DHCP, this address would be free, and I would go ahead and assign it to my printer. Then tomorrow, a new computer joins wirelessly and DHCP could easily hand it `10.10.10.151`, because it has no way of knowing that you inserted your printer's static IP right in the middle of its DHCP scope. Anytime you are assigning an IP address to any device for any reason, make sure to keep DHCP in mind.

- **Lease Duration:** When a computer or device grabs an IP address from a DHCP server, that address is always "leased" out to the computer, and only for a specific amount of time. When this time expires, the client or device will reach back to DHCP to get another IP address. Perhaps the same one will be issued, perhaps a different IP address. **Lease Duration** is where you define the amount of time DHCP clients can retain their IP addresses before asking for a new one.

- **Configure DHCP Options:** There are many additional options that you can include with a DHCP-issued IP address. This is the place where you would define what information a client receives in addition to their IP address. You can declare your network's default gateway, the DNS servers present within your network, and even specify special options such as provisioning information for VoIP phones. The two most common pieces of information to define here are **Default Gateway (router)** and **DNS Servers**. By doing so, any time DHCP hands out an IP address to a workstation, it also gives that workstation the correct DNS servers and default gateway, which are both critical pieces of information for proper routing of traffic on your network.

The last option you encounter is whether you want to activate your scope now. Typically, yes, you would want to do this. Activating the scope means that the DHCP server is now ready to issue IP addresses based on this scope to any computer that asks for one. However, there is one important thing we have not accomplished yet, as this is the first time we have touched this new DHCP role on our DC1 server.

Authorizing the DHCP server

If the DHCP server you are working with has never been authorized within the network, you must do so before it can perform any work. To do this, from inside the **DHCP** management console, simply right-click on the name of your server and then select the **Authorize** option.

Figure 4.21: Authorizing a DHCP server

As soon as your DHCP server is authorized and your scope is activated, it is immediately active, and any computer in your network whose NIC is configured to grab an address automatically from a DHCP server will start doing so against this new DHCP server. You can witness proper authorization of a DHCP server by watching those red arrows in *Figure 4.21* change into green checkmarks, the little icons on the IPv4 and IPv6 headings. Green checkmarks indicate a successfully authorized DHCP server.

Now that our new scope has been created, you can expand the scope inside the **DHCP** console and see some additional information about this scope. By clicking on the Address Leases folder, you can see all the DHCP addresses that have been handed out by this DHCP server.

As you can see in *Figure 4.22*, I have a Windows 10 client computer on the network that does not have a static address, and so it has grabbed a DHCP address from my DHCP server. It has been given the first IP address that I defined in my scope, 10.10.10.110. The next machine that reaches in to grab an IP address from this DHCP server will receive 10.10.10.111, and so on from there:

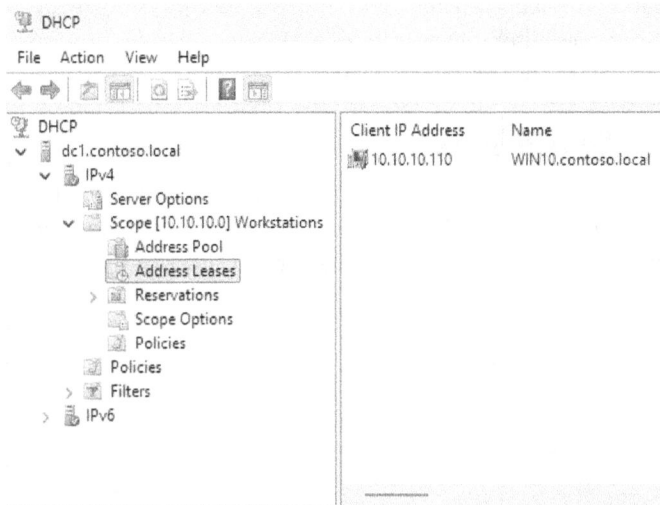

Figure 4.22: IP addresses assigned by DHCP

Scope options

DHCP scopes can be configured to hand out a very small set of information, as we have configured so far, or when needed, DHCP is capable of handing out a lot more. When a client reaches into DHCP to grab information, we are currently handing out an IP address and subnet mask, because these two pieces of information are critical to making traffic flow on our networks. Most networks, however, are going to require at least a couple of additional pieces of information to be given to DHCP clients for those devices to really be usable in a traditional corporate network. We very briefly discussed additional scope options that can be passed to client machines during IP address assignment. Now, let's take a look at how to get back into those options from within an existing DHCP scope and tweak them to our liking.

Listed under the new scope we just created, you will see a folder titled Scope Options. Right-click on Scope Options, and then select **Configure Options....**

Here, you will find many, many different checkboxes, all of which are available DHCP scope options. By selecting a checkbox and populating the necessary information for that particular scope option, you are then configuring this DHCP scope to give not only simple IP address and subnet mask information to all clients reaching in but additional information as well. Two very common ones are **003 Router** and **006 DNS Servers.** The **003 Router** designation is essentially your default gateway setting on the client NIC. Almost all networks will have a default gateway, typically a firewall or a router, and by selecting this option, you can define the default gateway address to be assigned to your DHCP clients.

In *Figure 4.23*, you can see that I have selected **006 DNS Servers** and configured the IP addresses of the DNS servers in my lab. Now, when my client computers pull IP addresses via DHCP, their NICs will also be automatically configured with these two DNS server addresses, which will cause them to be able to resolve DNS names in my environment:

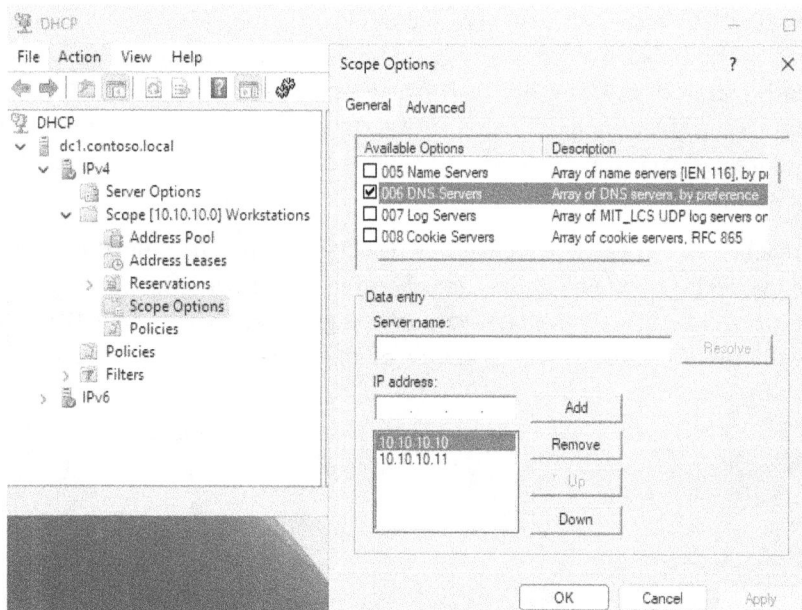

Figure 4.23: Using DHCP options

Another useful DHCP scope option is option 66. If you have a VoIP phone system and want to set up some automatic provisioning of your physical phones, it is easy to create a DHCP scope just for the phones and use option 66 to point at your phone system's provisioning link. When phones grab an IP address from the DHCP server, they will be automatically provisioned in the phone system as well!

DHCP reservations

Assigning IP addresses from a large pool is great, but these address leases are subject to expiry and change. This means that a computer that has 10.10.10.110 today might receive 10.10.10.125 tomorrow. Typically, this is fine from a desktop computer perspective, as they don't generally care what IP address they have. Client computers are usually reaching outward on the network, and other devices are rarely trying to find and contact them. What if you have a more permanent fixture in your network, such as a Windows server, but you don't want to have to deal with statically addressing this server? Another great example of such a device is a printer that is connected to your network. Some printers don't even have an interface from which you could assign a static IP address, and once your printer gets a DHCP address, you typically want that address to remain the same throughout the printer's life, because you'll be configuring computers to send their print jobs to that IP address. This is where **DHCP reservations** come into play. A reservation is the act of taking a single IP address within your DHCP scope and reserving it to a particular device. This device will receive the same IP address every time it connects through the DHCP server, and this particular IP address will not be handed out to any other device on your network. By using reservations inside DHCP, you can allow the DHCP server to handle the assigning of IP addresses even to your permanent servers, so that you do not have to manually configure the NICs of those servers, yet still maintain permanent IP addresses on those machines.

As a quick aside, while I am using it as an example today, I want to make sure it is clear that I am not recommending that you allow DHCP to manage IP addressing of Windows servers in your production network. Even with DHCP reservations in play, you would be putting a lot of unnecessary reliance on the DHCP server. With all of your servers being IP-addressed by DHCP, if that DHCP server goes offline or has some kind of issue, it could mean that *all* of your servers go offline, because they cannot figure out what IP address they are supposed to use. If DHCP goes down in an environment where servers have static IP addresses, you will certainly have client-side problems until you get things fixed, but your other servers will remain running and connected the entire time.

You can see the folder called Reservations in the **DHCP** console. Currently, there is nothing listed here, but by right-clicking on Reservations and choosing **New Reservation...**, we will create one for ourselves. Let's work once again with that WEB1 server. Right now, I have a static IP address assigned to WEB1, but I will instead create a reservation for it on the IP address 10.10.10.150:

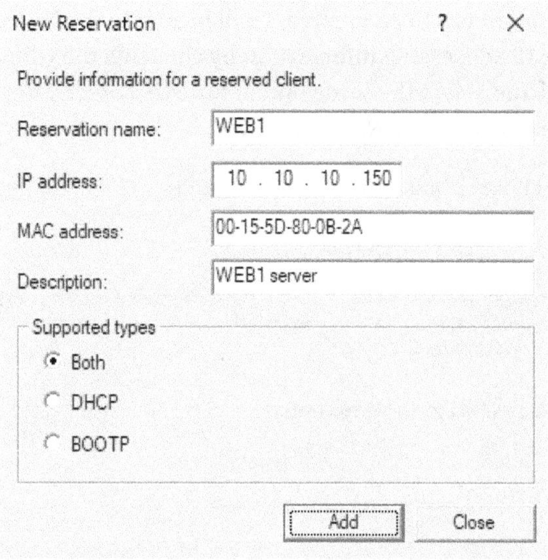

Figure 4.24: Setting up a reservation

Whoa, whoa, whoa... back the train up. Most of the information on this screen makes sense—a quick description of the server name and the IP address itself—but how did I come up with that MAC address? A **MAC address** is a network card's physical address on the network. When your networking equipment tries to send information to a certain IP address, or, in this case, when the DHCP server needs to hand a certain IP address to a particular NIC on a server, it needs a physical identifier for that network card. So, this MAC address is something that is unique to the NIC on my WEB1 server. Every network card on your network has a unique MAC address. By logging in to my WEB1 server, I can run ipconfig / all and see the MAC address listed for my NIC right in that output, that goofy-looking combination of letters and numbers shown as Physical Address. That is where I got this information. This is how DHCP decides when to invoke reservations. If a network interface asks DHCP for an IP address, and that device's MAC address is listed here in the reservation list, then the DHCP server will hand the reserved address back to the device every time, rather than one from the general pool:

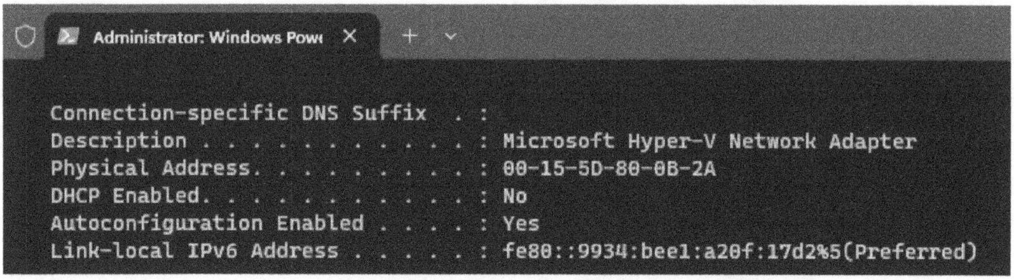

Figure 4.25: Finding the MAC address with ipconfig /all

Now that our DHCP reservation has been created, I will head into the NIC settings on my WEB1 server and get rid of all the static IP addressing information by choosing the **Obtain an IP address automatically** option. I'll go ahead and select the same option for DNS servers, to prove that DHCP is able to hand me both an IP address as well as DNS server info:

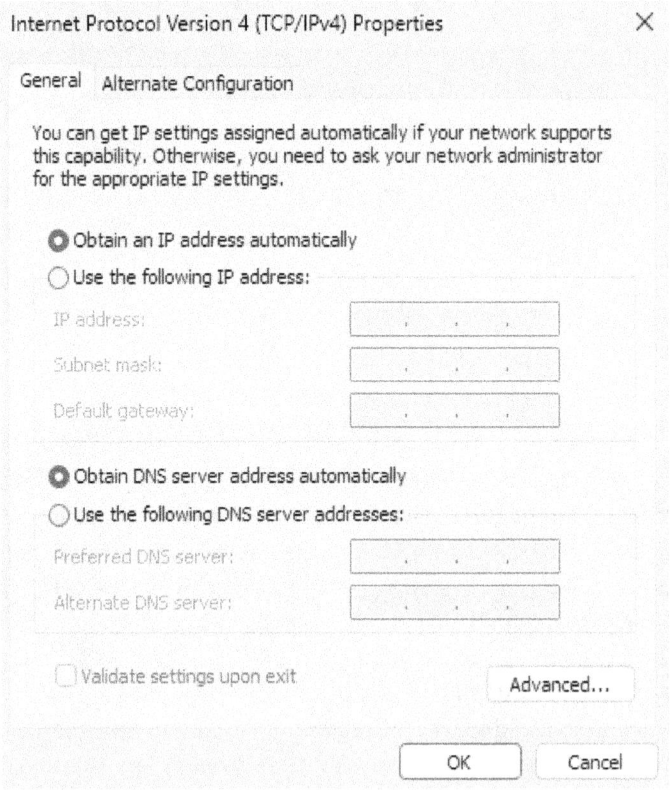

Figure 4.26: Removing the static IP address information

After doing that, WEB1 will reach over to the DHCP server and ask for an address, and you can see that I have now been assigned the reserved address of 10.10.10.150:

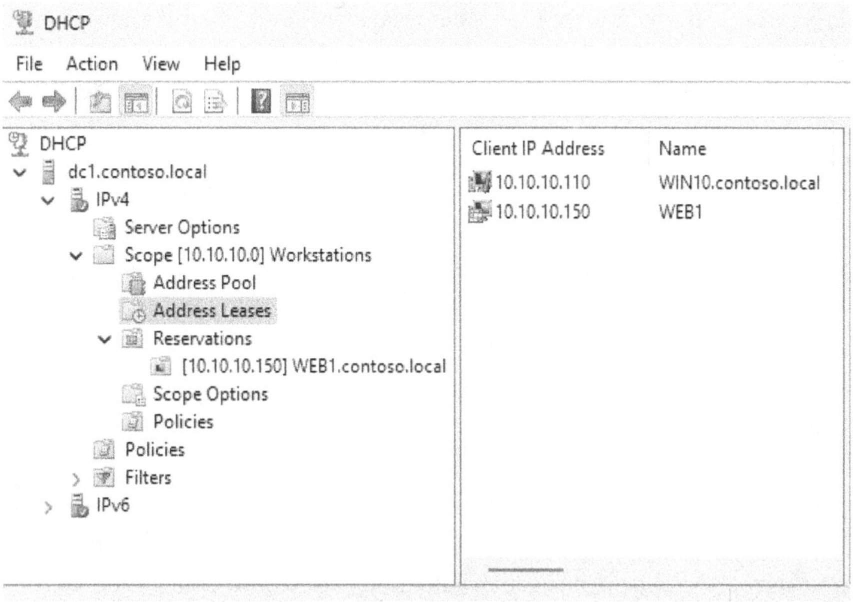

Figure 4.27: Reserving 10.10.10.150 for WEB1

This will always be the IP address of the WEB1 server from this point forward, unless I change my DHCP reservation or somehow change the MAC address of WEB1. This could possibly happen if I were to install a new NIC into WEB1.

You can also create DHCP reservations for objects other than Windows devices in your network. Since all you need is the MAC address of the device (and every device with a network adapter has a MAC address), it is easy to create reservations for devices such as print servers, copy machines, security alarm systems, cameras, wireless access points, and more.

DHCP failover

There is some truth to the phrase "never too much of a good thing" in the Windows server world. When building a production infrastructure, you want to implement redundancy everywhere that you can. With DHCP servers, you want to take great care when doing so. As we already discussed, DHCP "servers" come in many flavors. Maybe a Windows server, maybe a firewall, maybe a wireless access point, maybe even a Raspberry Pi that an employee has been tinkering with at home and suddenly decided it would be a good idea to bring it into the office and connect it to one of your RJ45 jacks under their desk. These devices are all capable of being DHCP servers and handing out IP addresses. You will quickly discover that any device looking for an IP address, which is likely every single client computer on your network, will simply grab an IP address from whichever DHCP server it can communicate with first. Your DHCP environment must be carefully crafted, and the introduction of any DHCP server into that environment that is unplanned or unexpected is referred to as a **rogue DHCP server**. These are bad news, and you need to seek them out and destroy them. Or maybe just find and disable them, but that sounds far less dramatic and fun.

This scenario plays out in the wild all the time, where a sudden introduction of a new piece of technology wreaks havoc on your IP addressing. I saw it just a few weeks ago, where a phone vendor installed a new phone system, and the entire network went sideways. This happened because the phone system was configured out of the box to run a DHCP server, so that VoIP phones can use the phone system to find an appropriate IP address for communication. What the phone vendor failed to realize was that almost every network in the world already has DHCP running, and if their phone system suddenly starts giving IP addresses of its own choosing to any device that asks, those devices are going to be unable to communicate with anything in their normal networks. Or possibly worse, if your intentional DHCP and this rogue DHCP are both handing out IP addresses within the same scope, for example, 192.168.1.x, you will be awash in IP addressing conflicts across your network.

Okay, enough doom and gloom. The moral of that example is to make sure you keep a close eye on what DHCP servers are running. Make sure they are intentional, and second-guess any device that a vendor wants to plug into your network. This is always good advice for a myriad of reasons. Moving back to the topic of good and planned redundancy...

Just like the creation of multiple DC servers creates good redundancy for Active Directory, the DHCP servers in your network can be tied together into a failover pair to create their own form of high availability. While it is true that the DHCP server role often happens to co-exist alongside the AD DS and DNS roles, this is not a requirement. You already know that it is easy to store DNS zones right inside Active Directory, so there is automatic replication of zone information, but this mentality is not true of DHCP scopes.

DHCP is a useful tool inside domain environments or outside domain environments. As such, it is not as tightly integrated a role as DNS. So when we create DHCP failover, we need to take a more manual approach, and whether or not the DHCP role happens to be hosted on top of a DC makes no difference.

Two DHCP servers

In a DHCP server failover environment, two DHCP servers can be configured and pointed at each other, and they will then replicate DHCP lease information between themselves, always keeping this information up to date. That way, if one DHCP server goes offline, the other can pick up the slack and continue issuing IPs and renewing the leases of those IPs.

I said "two" DHCP servers, and this is an important point of clarification. With Windows Server DHCP failover, you can only connect two DHCP servers together. No more. It is also important to note, as we progress into the world of IPv6, that DHCP failover is only intended for use with IPv4 scopes. The failover of DHCP servers would be unnecessary in the IPv6 world anyhow, as most IPv6 implementations are stateless, and the only information that DHCP needs to give to IPv6 clients are the options, which could simply be configured on multiple DHCP servers, and the clients care not from which server they pull that option information.

Hot standby mode

There are two different modes of operation that can be employed by DHCP failover: **hot standby mode** or **load-sharing mode**. Hot standby, as the name indicates, is more of a primary/failover mentality. One DHCP server is primary and is always responsible for an IPv4 scope, unless it becomes unavailable.

In that case, the failover DHCP server takes over until the primary can be restored.

Hot standby mode is useful for branch offices that are connected back to the primary network via a WAN of some sort. The local branch offices could have their own local DHCP server that handles DHCP primarily, but if that DHCP server were to go offline, DHCP requests would reach over the WAN link and grab a lease from the standby DHCP server sitting in your main site. In this kind of deployment, you could easily configure a single DHCP server in the main site to be the hot standby for multiple branch offices, as it is easy to configure multiple scopes on a DHCP server.

Load-sharing mode

Alternatively, indeed much more common, is load-sharing mode. This is the default mode of operation for DHCP failover. In load-sharing mode, two DHCP servers are configured with the same scope of information, and then both serve incoming clients. In doing so, they share the load between servers, both responding and also replicating information between themselves, so both are always aware of which IP addresses have been handed out to clients.

In load-sharing mode, you want both DHCP servers to be located in the same physical site. They need to have very fast communication between them to keep the replication data straight. I have seen DHCP failover configured across sites before, and can tell you definitively that it causes IP conflicts and similar issues. Keep them in the same site.

Configuring DHCP failover

Now we know about DHCP failover, how do we set it up? You already know that I have DC1 and DC2 in my test lab environment. Both servers are already DCs and DNS servers, though those facts have no bearing on DHCP configuration. These could be DCs, or simply domain-joined servers, or even non-domain-joined servers, and DHCP would have all of the same options for failover. Since I already have these two servers available to me, I am going to use them to create a DHCP scope that is replicated between both. This is an important point to clarify: DHCP failover is configured on a per-scope basis. You don't necessarily tie DC1 and DC2 together, but rather inside the DHCP scope properties, you establish failover between DC1 and DC2 for a particular scope (or scopes). This implies, then, that you have the ability to create DHCP scopes that are running in failover mode, and additionally create DHCP scopes on those same servers that are not doing any form of failover.

> Make sure the clocks are in sync! If your DHCP servers are domain-joined, their clocks should always be kept in sync automatically by Active Directory. If your DHCP servers are not domain-joined, you will want to ensure that the system clocks on both servers are using the same time source to always retain continuity.

DC1 already has the DHCP role installed, and we created a scope on it together, so that my Win10 client computer could grab a DHCP address and communicate with the rest of my network. DC2, however, does not yet have the DHCP role installed, so the first step is to go ahead and add that role.

Whenever creating new DHCP servers in a network, the role must be installed, of course, but there is a second critical piece of the puzzle to enable them to be recognized as DHCP servers. It is fairly obvious, but after installing the DHCP role onto a server, Server Manager will prompt you to complete the DHCP configuration. This pulls up a small wizard with basically just one step to accomplish—authorize your new DHCP server. This mini-wizard can be called via Server Manager immediately following role installation, or if you missed the prompt there and opened up right into the DHCP management tool, you can alternatively authorize a DHCP server by right-clicking on the server name inside the DHCP management tool, and then selecting **Authorize**. One way is not better than the other; the point is that each of your DHCP servers must be authorized before it can do anything.

OK, we now have two authorized DHCP servers in our environment, and a scope is already present on DC1. This scope is servicing clients already, handing out IP addresses in our network. Creating a failover for this scope is quite easy. Open up DHCP management on DC1, and navigate to find your IPv4 scope. Right-click on the scope itself, and select **Configure Failover...**:

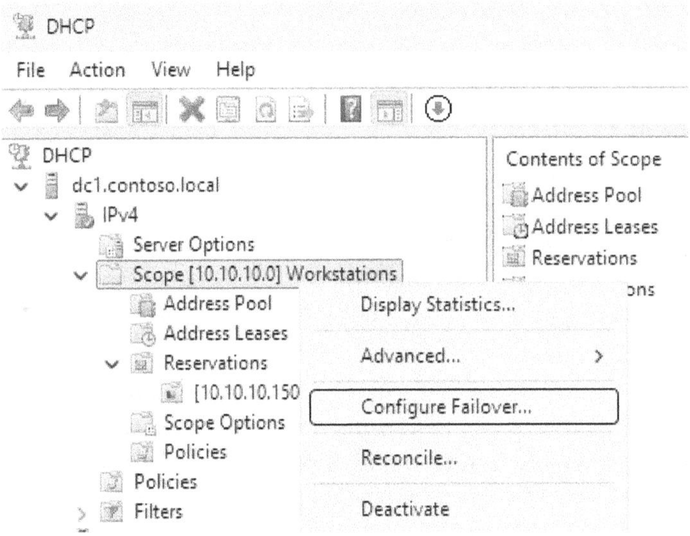

Figure 4.28: Configuring DHCP failover

Next, select which scopes you want to configure in failover. As I mentioned before, DHCP failover configuration is individual per DHCP scope. If your DHCP server has multiple scopes already established, you can select to configure failover on any or all of them. Then, on the second screen, we need to define the failover DHCP server. You can type out the name of the server on this screen, but what I like to do is click that **Add Server** button, which then displays any servers in your environment that are recognized as authorized DHCP servers. By using the button and then selecting the second DHCP server from the list, it gives you one more validation that you have properly authorized the second server (DC2, in my case) in your network. You can see this in *Figure 4.29*:

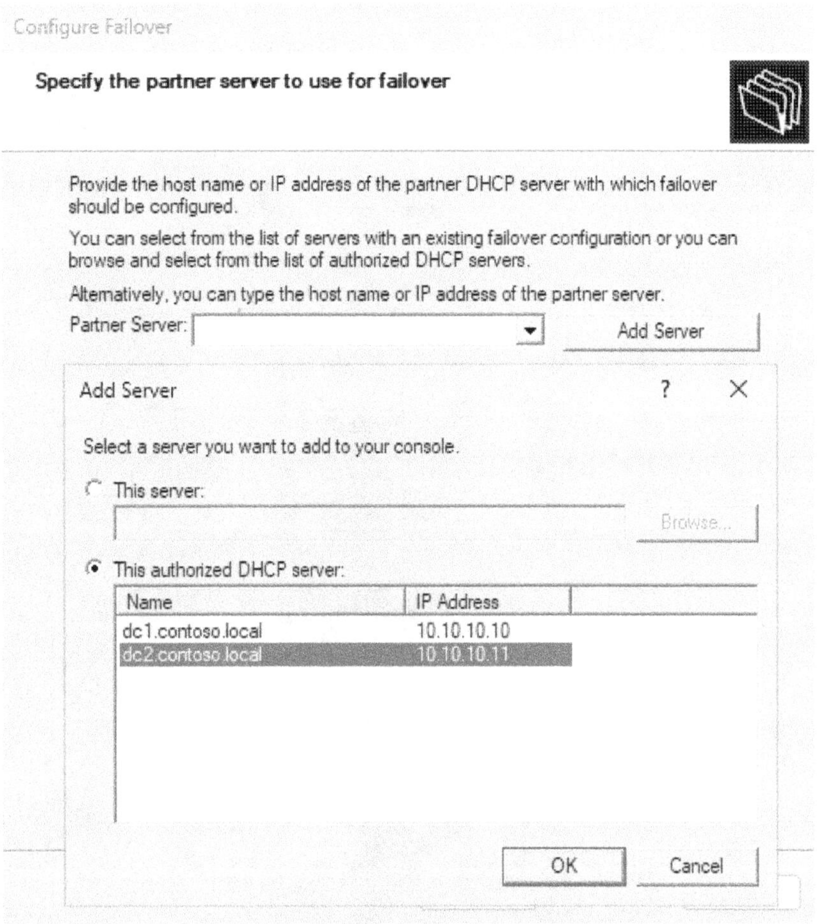

Configure Failover

Specify the partner server to use for failover

Provide the host name or IP address of the partner DHCP server with which failover should be configured.

You can select from the list of servers with an existing failover configuration or you can browse and select from the list of authorized DHCP servers.

Alternatively, you can type the host name or IP address of the partner server.

Partner Server: [▼]   Add Server

Add Server   ?   ✕

Select a server you want to add to your console.

○ This server:

[   ]   Browse...

◉ This authorized DHCP server:

Name	IP Address	
dc1.contoso.local	10.10.10.10	
dc2.contoso.local	10.10.10.11	

OK   Cancel

Figure 4.29: Selecting DC2 for DHCP failover

On the following screen of this wizard, we define all of the relationship parameters between the two DHCP servers. As you can see in our next screenshot, this is the screen where you define simple things that don't have too much impact, such as **Relationship Name** and creating a **Shared Secret** value that the two DHCP servers will use to interact with each other, but this screen is also where you create the definition of which type of failover is happening for this scope. We have already talked about **Load balance** mode and **Hot standby** mode, and here is where you would additionally define, in **Load balance** mode, what weights to assign the two servers for establishing that load balancing.

Unless you have a particular reason to deviate, the default settings are generally what you want. Make sure that **Maximum Client Lead Time** remains configured at one hour or more. You may bump that number down smaller for testing failover in your network, but in a production environment, one hour is the general recommendation:

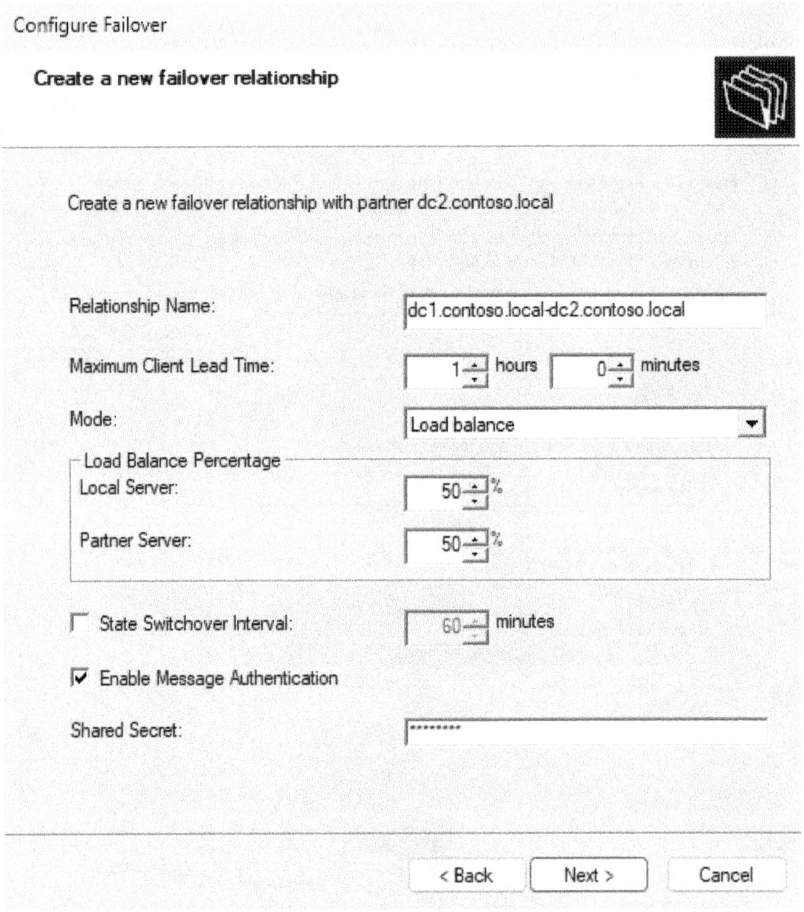

Configure Failover

Create a new failover relationship

Create a new failover relationship with partner dc2.contoso.local

Relationship Name:	dc1.contoso.local-dc2.contoso.local
Maximum Client Lead Time:	1 hours 0 minutes
Mode:	Load balance

Load Balance Percentage

Local Server: 50 %

Partner Server: 50 %

☐ State Switchover Interval: 60 minutes

☑ Enable Message Authentication

Shared Secret: ********

< Back   Next >   Cancel

Figure 4.30: Configuring failover relationship settings

That's it! Click **Next** a couple more times, and your DHCP failover configuration will be pushed out to the second DHCP server. Now, if one of these servers were to go offline or have some kind of issue, DHCP clients coming in fresh or whose DHCP leases are expiring will be able to acquire a lease from either DHCP server.

Now that DHCP failover has been established, you would sort of expect something inside the DHCP management console to have changed to visually indicate to us that there is failover configured on the scope, but that is not really the case. Everything in here looks exactly the same as before the failover creation. I point this out to let you know that during future visits to this console, or if you are a new admin to an existing infrastructure and want to quickly identify whether or not DHCP failover is established in your environment, you can find this information by right-clicking on each scope. In the menu list that is displayed with that right-click, you will now find a **Deconfigure Failover** option, which implies that failover is currently configured for this scope. Additionally, if you head into the properties of that scope, you will find a **Failover** tab that displays all pertinent information about DHCP failover:

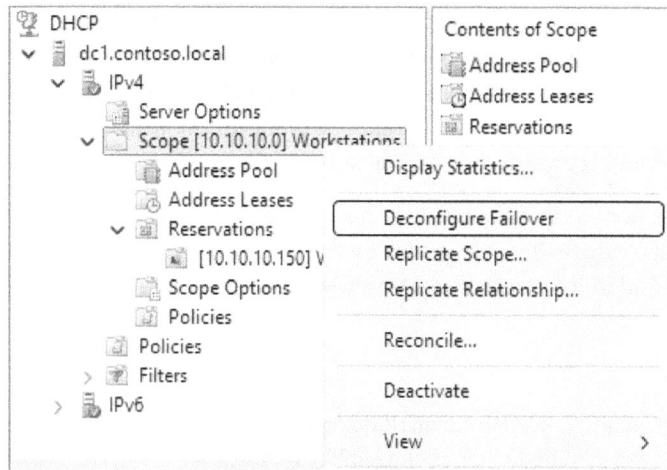

Figure 4.31: Deconfiguring failover

One last verification, let's log in to DC2 and see what the DHCP management console looks like now! Remember that previously, the only thing I had done on DC2 was to install the DHCP role and to authorize this server. I have never even opened the DHCP management console on this second server. If I do so now, you can see that my 10.10.10.0 scope has been replicated over to this server, including the current address lease information!

Figure 4.32: The 10.10.10.0 scope is now replicated to DC2

IPAM

The **IP Address Management (IPAM)** feature built into Windows Server 2025 is overlooked by many server administrators because it is a feature and not a full-blown role inside Windows. IPAM is a technology that allows centralized monitoring and management of DHCP and DNS in your environment.

If all of your infrastructure is sitting inside one building, it is easy enough to simply use the DNS and DHCP management tools from any server or workstation in your network and have full control over both of those technologies. But how about larger and enterprise-class networks that span many locations, each with its own sets of DNS and DHCP servers? IPAM is useful for gathering up all those differing namespaces and scopes and providing access to them from one interface.

Let's install the IPAM feature in my lab so you have an idea of where to start, should you choose to explore or employ this feature. Begin by choosing a server upon which you want to install IPAM, and simply walk through **Add Roles and Features Wizard** to add the feature called **IP Address Management (IPAM) Server**.

> It is not recommended to install IPAM onto a DC or onto a DHCP server, as that will hinder its ability to acquire information from these systems.

Now that the feature is installed, launching Server Manager will display a new section in the left window pane called **IPAM**. Go ahead and click on **IPAM**, and you are presented with a series of six tasks that need to be accomplished in order to use IPAM:

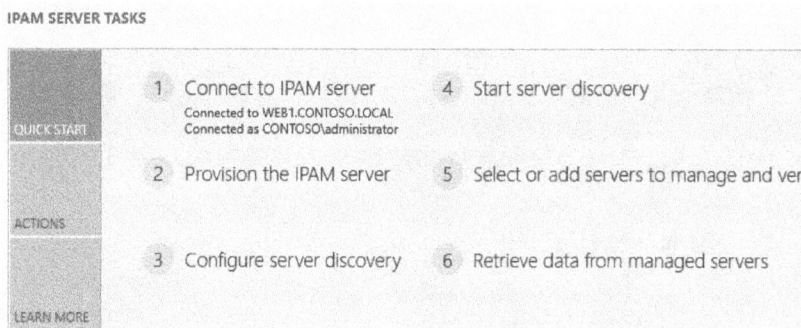

IPAM SERVER TASKS

QUICK START

ACTIONS

LEARN MORE

1	Connect to IPAM server	4	Start server discovery
	Connected to WEB1.CONTOSO.LOCAL		
	Connected as CONTOSO\administrator		
2	Provision the IPAM server	5	Select or add servers to manage and veri
3	Configure server discovery	6	Retrieve data from managed servers

Figure 4.33: IPAM server tasks

The first step is already finished; we are connected to the IPAM server. In my lab, I installed IPAM on my WEB1 server, but not for any particular reason. You could dedicate a server to this task or install the feature onto an existing server.

Moving on to *step 2*, **Provision the IPAM server**, you will have a chance to read over some good descriptive text about how IPAM plans to interact with your servers. You have the option of manually configuring each server (who's going to do that?), but clearly, the way Microsoft expects most of us to centrally roll this out is through the use of Group Policy. We will discuss Group Policy in the next chapter of this book, but for the purpose of setting up IPAM, we can pretty much just flow through these configuration wizards, selecting the default settings, and understand that, under the hood, this console is establishing GPOs for us, which will then be pushed down to the servers in our network to configure them for reporting into IPAM.

The only selections that need to be made inside *step 2* are which database for IPAM to utilize and which provisioning method should be used to send IPAM settings out to your servers. For the database, if you have a SQL server, you may certainly use it to store IPAM information, but the default selection is **Windows Internal Database (WID)**, which is a built-in database platform used by many of the Windows Server roles and features. We will utilize WID for this new IPAM server, and as we already mentioned, the rolling out of IPAM settings to other servers in your environment is easily accomplished via Group Policy.

As a sidenote on WID itself, it has recently been added to Microsoft's "no longer developing" list. This means that WID is still 100% a valid technology inside Windows Server 2025, and they even declare that it is used by roles such as ADFS, ADRMS, IPAM, RD Broker, and WSUS. However, at some point in the future, WID will likely be removed from Windows Server, and at that point in time, if you were facing the decision to install something such as IPAM, you would either need to choose a then-older platform (such as Server 2025) to run it, or change gears on database selection. Rather than using the internal WID, you could, instead, install the free version of SQL to serve this need. On the screen where you select **Group Policy Based** as the provisioning method, you will also need to define a GPO name prefix. When this console reaches into Active Directory and creates the GPOs needed for IPAM to work, it will define names for the GPOs and those names cannot be altered, but what Microsoft allows here is for you to assign a prefix to those GPO names, so that when you later look inside the Group Policy management tool, all of the GPO configurations related to IPAM will be listed together, all having the same prefix that you define on this screen:

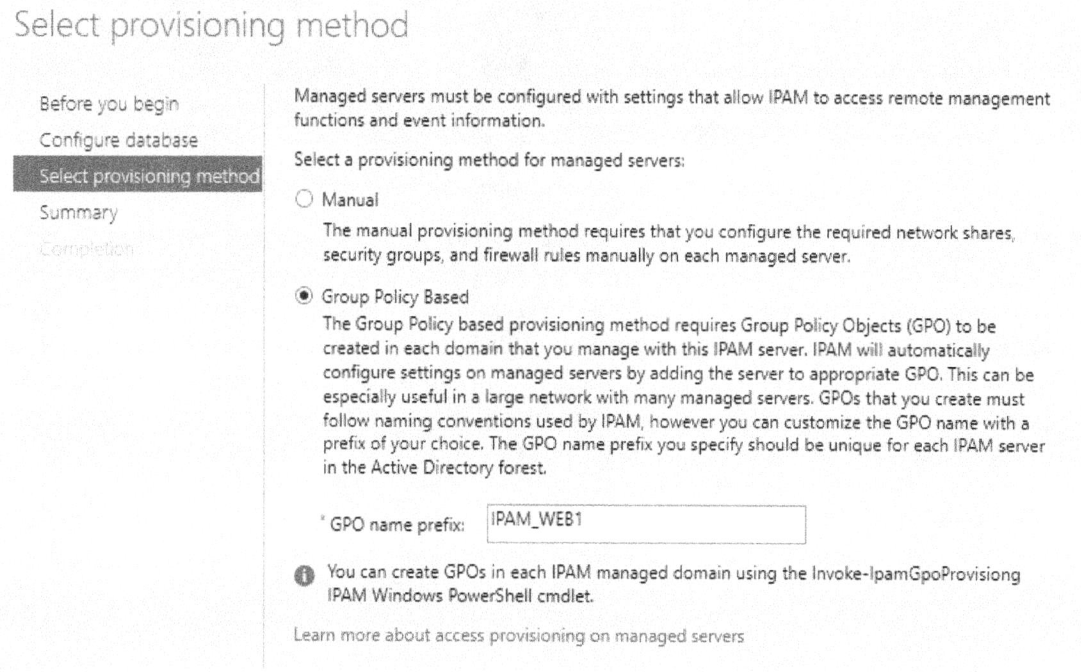

Select provisioning method

Before you begin

Configure database

Select provisioning method

Summary

Completion

Managed servers must be configured with settings that allow IPAM to access remote management functions and event information.

Select a provisioning method for managed servers:

○ Manual

The manual provisioning method requires that you configure the required network shares, security groups, and firewall rules manually on each managed server.

◉ Group Policy Based

The Group Policy based provisioning method requires Group Policy Objects (GPO) to be created in each domain that you manage with this IPAM server. IPAM will automatically configure settings on managed servers by adding the server to appropriate GPO. This can be especially useful in a large network with many managed servers. GPOs that you create must follow naming conventions used by IPAM, however you can customize the GPO name with a prefix of your choice. The GPO name prefix you specify should be unique for each IPAM server in the Active Directory forest.

* GPO name prefix: | IPAM_WEB1 |

ⓘ You can create GPOs in each IPAM managed domain using the Invoke-IpamGpoProvisiong IPAM Windows PowerShell cmdlet.

Learn more about access provisioning on managed servers

Figure 4.34: Using GPOs to implement IPAM

You'll notice a little informational text in *Figure 4.34* as well as on the summary screen when you finish *step 2*, regarding a PowerShell cmdlet called `Invoke-IpamGpoProvisioning`. Common sense would tell us that after *step 2* in the IPAM implementation, you would move on to *step 3*, right? Actually, not in this case. Configuring server discovery (*step 3*) is a step that we need to take soon, but at this point, the IPAM console is waiting for those GPOs to be created so that they can be used and referenced during the rest of the setup process.

Pause on your work inside the IPAM steps, and open an administrative PowerShell or Terminal prompt, making sure that you are logged in to your server with a domain admin account. Then, simply run `Invoke-IpamGpoProvisioning`. This will ask you to key in the name of your domain, as well as that `GPOPrefixName` you specified during the wizard; be sure to type it in exactly the same!

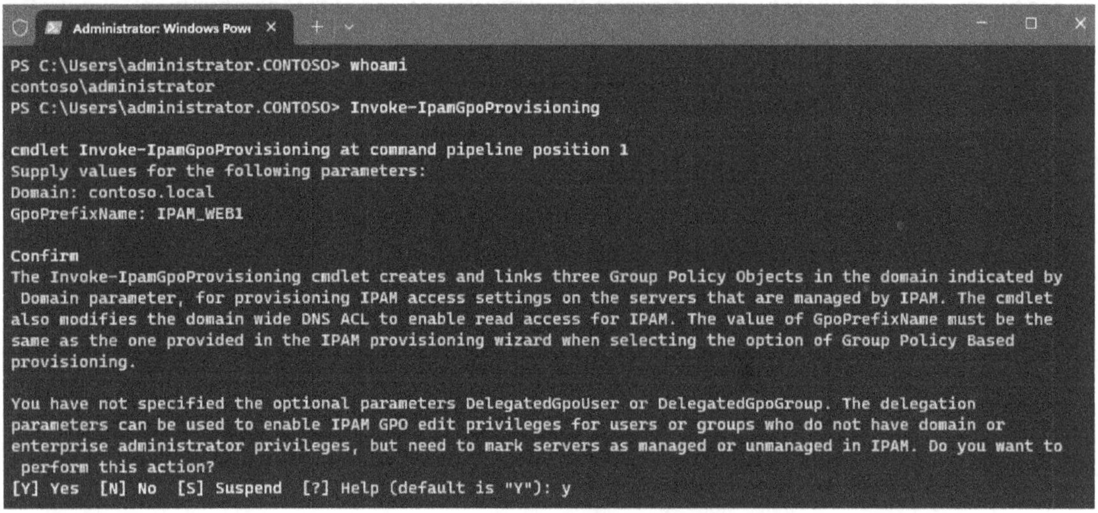

```
Administrator: Windows Powe    ×    +   ∨                                                        −    □    ×

PS C:\Users\administrator.CONTOSO> whoami
contoso\administrator
PS C:\Users\administrator.CONTOSO> Invoke-IpamGpoProvisioning

cmdlet Invoke-IpamGpoProvisioning at command pipeline position 1
Supply values for the following parameters:
Domain: contoso.local
GpoPrefixName: IPAM_WEB1

Confirm
The Invoke-IpamGpoProvisioning cmdlet creates and links three Group Policy Objects in the domain indicated by
 Domain parameter, for provisioning IPAM access settings on the servers that are managed by IPAM. The cmdlet
also modifies the domain wide DNS ACL to enable read access for IPAM. The value of GpoPrefixName must be the
same as the one provided in the IPAM provisioning wizard when selecting the option of Group Policy Based
provisioning.

You have not specified the optional parameters DelegatedGpoUser or DelegatedGpoGroup. The delegation
parameters can be used to enable IPAM GPO edit privileges for users or groups who do not have domain or
enterprise administrator privileges, but need to mark servers as managed or unmanaged in IPAM. Do you want to
 perform this action?
[Y] Yes  [N] No  [S] Suspend  [?] Help (default is "Y"): y
```

Figure 4.35: Running Invoke-IpamGpoProvisioning

You will be required to enter Y and press *Enter* three times to finish this command. In reading the warning text that is being displayed, the same text three times in a row, this is asking you for confirmation, simply because when these three GPOs are being created, their security filtering settings are being modified away from the default GPO security filtering behavior. We will explain GPO security filtering soon, but for IPAM's purposes, simply type Y and continue through these prompts. Now that `Invoke-IpamGpoProvisioning` has done its work, if we sneak a quick peek into the **Group Policy Management** console, you can see that there are three new GPOs that did not exist a minute ago:

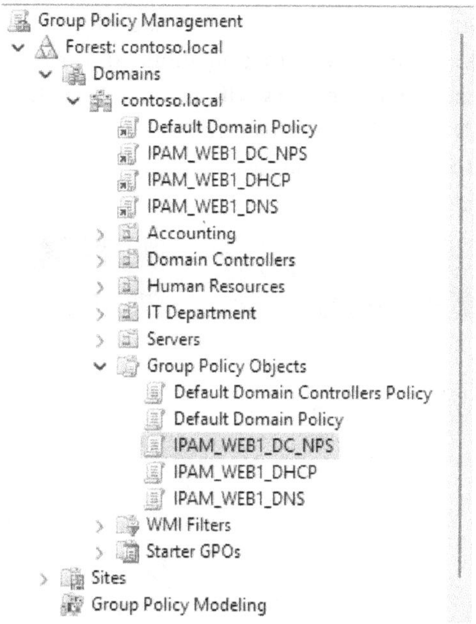

Figure 4.36: Invoke-IpamGpoProvisioning has created three new GPOs

Now, back inside the IPAM configuration on WEB1, we will go ahead and click on *step 3*, **Configure server discovery**. Inside, use the **Get forests** and **Add** buttons to query your domain for infrastructure services that can be monitored by IPAM. Your domain should be listed, with checkboxes selected on the components that the wizard was able to discover about your domain. In my case, I have discovered all three—**Domain controller, DHCP server**, and **DNS server**. I will leave all three checked so that IPAM can pull data about these roles and click **OK**:

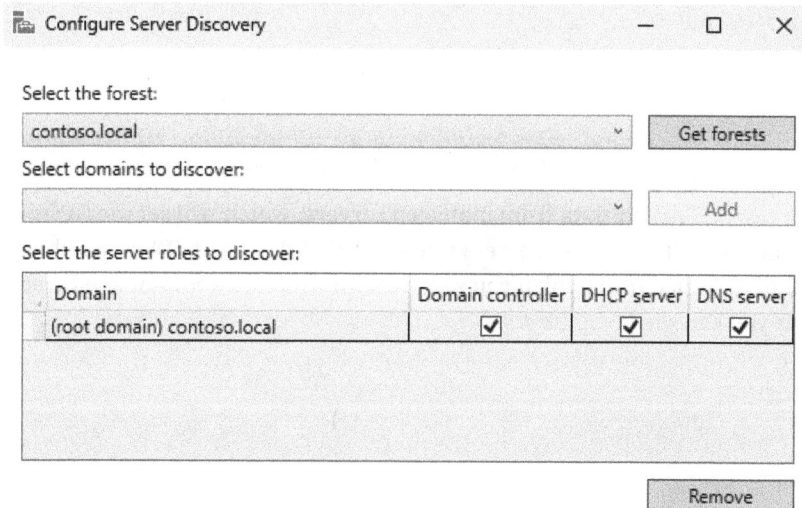

Figure 4.37: Configuring server discovery

Move on to *step 4*, **Start server discovery**. This launches a scheduled task in the background that is reaching out and discovering additional information about your infrastructure. Once finished, click on *step 5*, **Select or add servers to manage and verify IPAM access**. Here, you should see the servers listed that are hosting your AD DS, DNS, and DHCP roles. Right-click on each server that you want to manage, and then select **Edit Server...**. Inside this screen, for each server, change the server's **Manageability status** field to **Managed**:

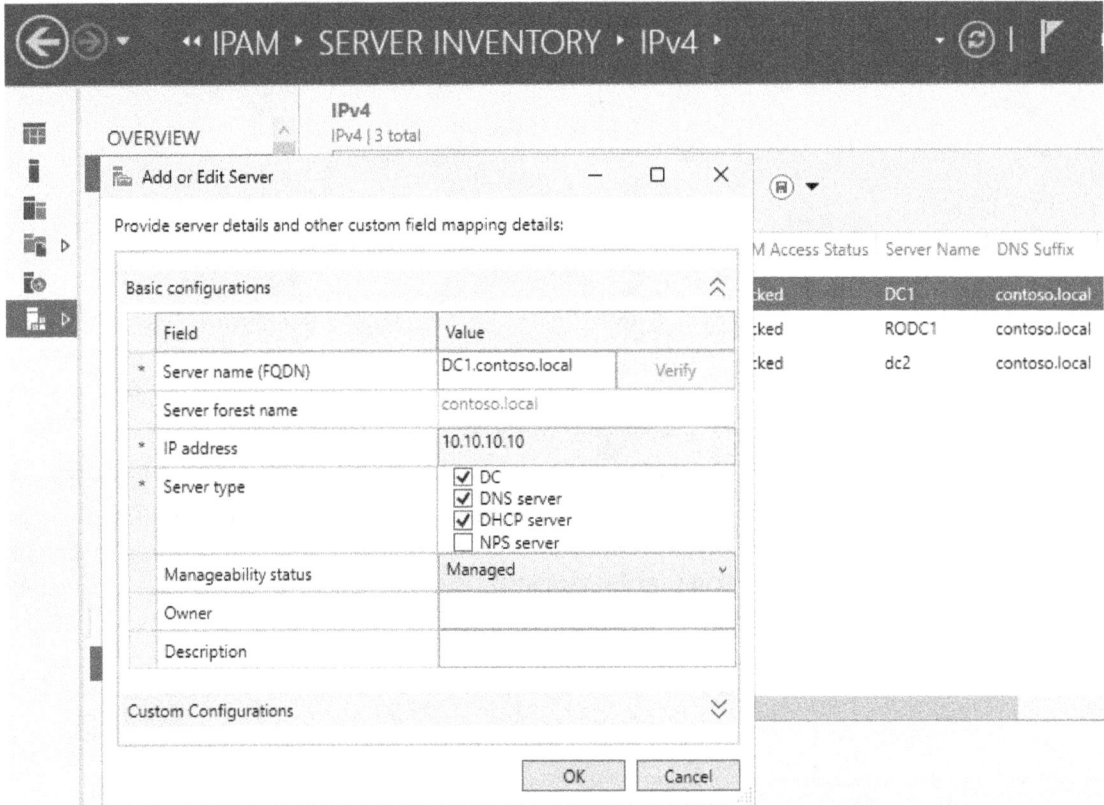

Figure 4.38: Setting IPAM to manage these servers

Finally, click on *step 6*, **Retrieve data from managed servers**, which will set the GPOs into action and start pulling information from those servers into the IPAM database. When finished, you will now have a centralized interface from which you can view information about Active Directory, DNS, and DHCP scopes, as you can see in *Figure 4.39*:

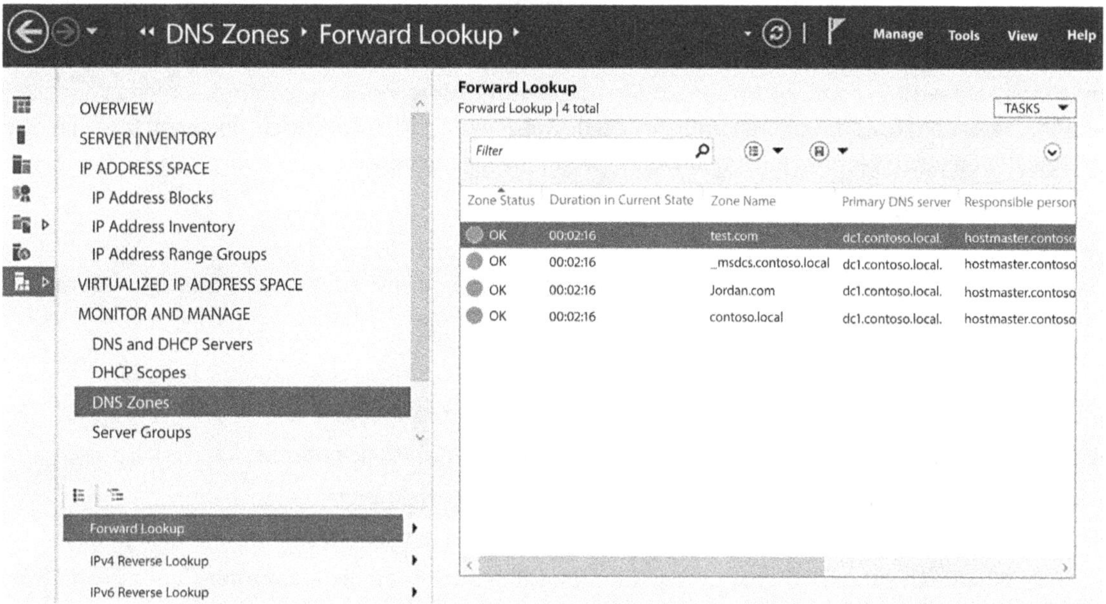

Figure 4.39: IPAM's centralized interface

Management of DHCP from within IPAM is particularly useful, as classic administration of DHCP from within its own management console can get pretty messy in an environment with many different DHCP scopes. IPAM provides an interface from which you can quickly and easily see information about all scopes together, and even run some fun PowerShell cmdlets to quickly gather data that would have otherwise taken manual poking and prodding to discover in the past:

- `Find-IpamFreeSubnet`
- `Add-IpamSubnet`
- `Find-IpamFreeRange` (this one is nice because it helps you quickly discover a range of available IP addresses)
- `Add-IpamRange`

Summary

The Microsoft core stack of infrastructure technologies generally consists of Active Directory, DNS, and DHCP, and often, you will find all three of these housed on the same servers. Understanding these technologies and knowing how to utilize their associated toolsets is an essential part of any server administrator's life. A Microsoft-centric network running Windows servers almost guarantees that this network is built upon Active Directory and DNS. As a manager in an IT company, I will tell you with certainty that having a grasp on these concepts and tools will greatly improve your chances of landing that sysadmin role you've been seeking.

I hope these last two chapters have been beneficial to your overall understanding of the ways companies make use of Windows Server technology and have given you something to help prepare for IT life in a business setting. Next, we turn to another baked-in component of any Active Directory-focused environment, but one that is often underutilized. Group Policy is an amazingly powerful tool that can be used to enhance security and create automation inside any domain.

Questions

Put your knowledge to the test with the following questions. If you need a hand (or just want to double-check), you'll find all the answers in the *Appendix* section of the book.

1. Which kind of DNS record directs email flow?
2. Which type of DNS record resolves a name to an IPv6 address?
3. Which DNS zone type resolves IP addresses backward into hostnames?
4. Which DHCP option is often used for VoIP phone provisioning?
5. Which mode of DHCP failover is often used between branch offices and a primary site?
6. What is the standard recommendation and default setting for **Maximum Client Lead Time** when configuring load-balanced DHCP failover?
7. Which Windows Server roles can IPAM tap into?
8. What does the ingenious acronym "DoH" stand for?

Join us on Discord

For discussions around the book and to connect with your peers, join us on Discord at https://packt.link/discordcloud or scan the QR code below:

5

Group Policy

If you find yourself reading this book from front to back, indeed a good and not at all weird way to read a book, you already have a general idea of what Group Policy is and does (because we talked about it in *Chapter 3, Active Directory*). However, I've been around IT folks long enough to know that reading a book from cover to cover is rare, and attention spans rarely accommodate such a quest. Therefore, any of you hitting up this chapter in a random fashion because the words "Group Policy" drew your attention or you have a specific need that you are hoping to be answered in this chapter, fear not! Let's again summarize the great and glorious power of Group Policy.

It's easy to understand the general use of the word "policy," meaning some kind of ruleset, structure, or standard to which you need something to adhere. In our case, we're talking about Microsoft Windows-based computers (and servers). Applying policies to computers, such as security policies, application policies, or printer policies, sounds like a great idea. If applying policies to a computer is great, applying policies to a group of computers must be even better, hence the term "Group Policy." In a nutshell, Group Policy is a centralized way to issue policies to groups of users or computers inside your domain network. "Domain" is a key word here, as Group Policy can only identify and manipulate users or computers if they are part of your Active Directory domain. Here's a quick list of the topics we plan to cover together:

- Group Policy Objects
- Building a GPO (a few, actually!)
- Scoping a GPO
- Computer settings and user settings
- Policy versus preference
- Default Domain Policy
- Administrative templates
- The Central Store

Group Policy Objects

The overlying technology we are talking about here is called Group Policy, and an individual instance of Group Policy is known as a **Group Policy Object**, commonly referred to as a **GPO**.

A GPO is a single package that contains one or many policy settings and applies to a domain computer, a domain user, or sometimes many computers and users, all at the same time.

GPOs are stored inside Active Directory and are replicated among your domain controller servers. Every time a domain user logs into a domain-joined computer that is connected to your network, the computer reaches out to Active Directory and asks, "Hey, got any GPO settings for me?" Then, a whole slew of activity commences as a domain controller hands over all of the GPO settings that it contains that apply to the computer and/or user logging in. This is a key piece of information. GPOs are scoped upon creation, giving you the power to define to whom each policy is applied—extremely powerful stuff. These policy settings then plug themselves into place on your computer, forcing certain things to happen (or not happen) at the discretion of your IT department. You can lock down settings, force settings into place, or even configure default settings while still allowing users to override them. You can throw certain settings at some computers and completely opposite settings at others. You could even apply conflicting GPOs to the same computers and sit back and watch them fight to see who comes out as the winner in the end. If you don't understand how Group Policy works, it is very easy to cause huge problems in your network, as it is very, very easy to apply settings to *every* machine in the domain. A single GPO has the potential to bring your entire network to its knees if misused.

So... *that's* reassuring, right? Trust me, while Group Policy comes with a warning label and *"with great power comes great responsibility"* and all that, you will want to use GPOs more than you are now after seeing all that they can do.

Group Policy background refresh cycle

I mentioned that Group Policy processes through its list of rules and settings on your domain-joined computers every time a user logs in, and that is true. What is also true is that Group Policy reprocesses itself at intervals throughout the day, even while the user remains logged in. By default, and almost nobody changes it, something called a background refresh happens every 90 minutes. This means that implementing new GPOs during the day generally works fine because those settings will roll into place even without users needing to log off or restart their computers. There are exceptions to this, though, as some GPO settings are unable to process as background cycles and can only take effect during the login process. Some examples of such GPOs are a login script (which can only run during logon or logoff of a computer) or even something such as a mapped network drive. Some GPOs will only push themselves into place during the user login process.

Many times, I find myself testing GPO settings as I make changes to them, and it would make for a very inefficient workday if I had to wait 90 minutes or restart my test computer after every little tweak or change to a GPO. Thankfully, we have a quick and easy command-line tool that can be used to force Group Policy to reach out and do its thing, any time of any day!

```
gpupdate /force
```

Running this command in Command Prompt or PowerShell on a domain-joined client computer will cause it to immediately reach out and grab updated GPO settings. Keep in mind, your computer does need to be able to contact a domain controller for Group Policy to process, so this isn't going to work if your work laptop is sitting in your house and not connected via VPN.

But for any computers in the office or in some way connected to your corporate network, you can run gpupdate all the live-long day and continually roll new policies and changes into place.

Building a GPO

There's nothing quite as satisfying as jumping in and getting your hands dirty, so let's get down to business and build a new GPO. Don't worry, we will be careful not to apply this GPO to anything yet and save that for the next section. As with most Microsoft technologies, there is a special management console in Windows Server, solely for the purpose of interacting with Group Policy, appropriately named the **Group Policy Management Console (GPMC)**. Logging into any of your domain controller servers, you can launch the GPMC from in **Administrative Tools**, in the **Tools** menu of Server Manager, or by launching GPMC.MSC from **Start | Run**, Command Prompt, Terminal, or PowerShell:

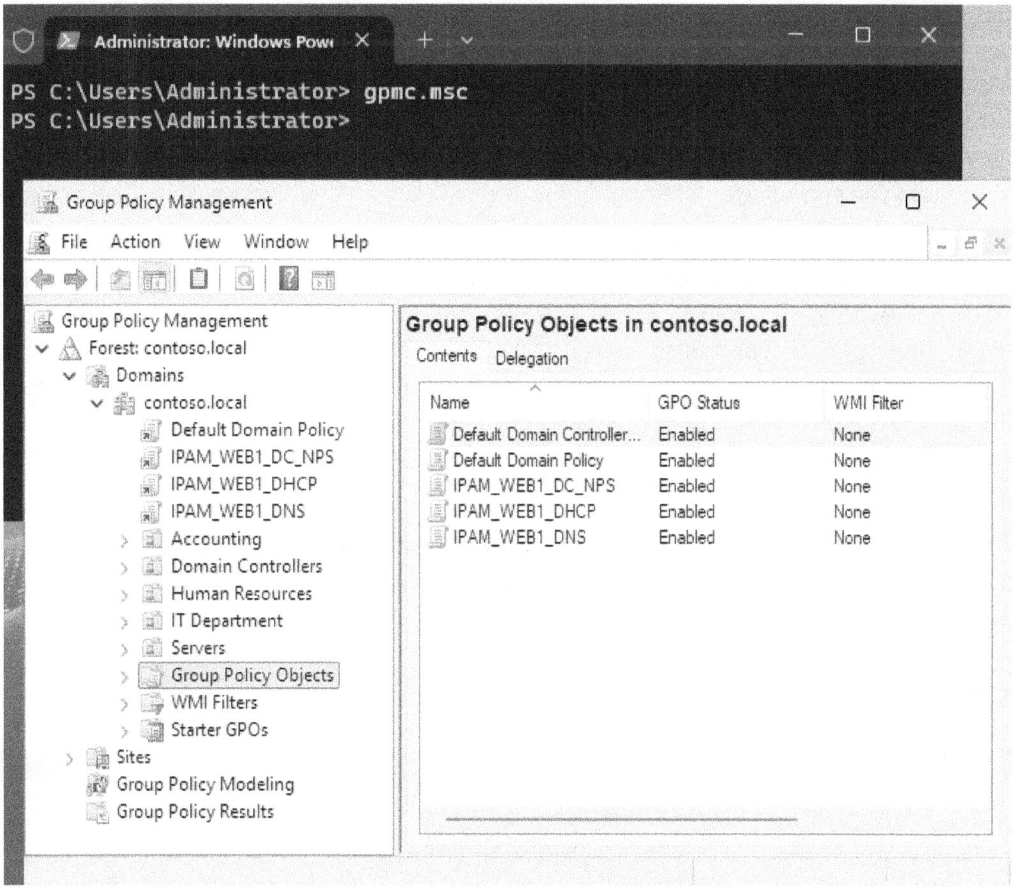

Figure 5.1: GPMC

You'll notice in *Figure 5.1* that there are already some GPOs listed here. They are a combination of default GPOs that always exist when you install Active Directory (we'll talk about the Default Domain Policy a little later in this chapter) and the IPAM GPOs that the IPAM configuration process put into place for us in *Chapter 4, DNS and DHCP*. To create a new GPO in a way that does not yet apply to any workstations or users, right-click on the `Group Policy Objects` folder and select **New**. Create a name for your new GPO, click **OK**, and you have created a Group Policy Object! So far, your new GPO is void of any settings or configurations, and it does not apply to anything or anybody, so it is precisely pointless. We will soon change that...

Adding trusted sites

I named my first GPO *Trusted Sites* because I am going to use this new GPO to cause some URLs to be recognized as trusted sites in Windows on my Windows 10 and 11 computers. Anyone who recognizes the term "Trusted Sites" might wonder whether, in the year 2025, I am actually going to travel the road of pushing configurations into Internet Explorer properties. Yes, indeed! Even though Internet Explorer itself is effectively dead and has been replaced by Edge for web browsing purposes, IE was so tightly integrated into Windows code that there are still many occasions where manipulation of IE settings changes behavior or enables certain functions within Windows itself. Only a couple of weeks ago, I helped an engineer create a GPO exactly like this because a customer's line-of-business application would not work properly unless a handful of URLs were plugged into **Internet Explorer Trusted Site** settings, even though that company does *not* use Internet Explorer. Sometimes these applications might be trying to run JavaScript or ActiveX controls or something like that, which would be one reason you may find yourself continuing to visit IE security settings on your client computers.

When tasked with a change that needs to take place on all of your users' computers, you *could* remain reactive and print off an instructions page for the helpdesk on how to do this on each computer, and ask them to spend the time doing it manually for every user who calls in because they cannot access the application. Or, you could get smart and proactive, and create a GPO that makes these changes for you automatically on every workstation to save yourself from dealing with all of those phone calls. This is just one tiny example of the power that Group Policy possesses, but it's a good example because it is useful, and it is a setting that is buried way down in the GPO settings, so you can get a feel for just how deep these capabilities go.

Right-click on the new GPO and choose **Edit...** Now navigate to **Computer Configuration | Policies | Administrative Templates | Windows Components | Internet Explorer | Internet Control Panel | Security Page**. See, I told you it was buried in there!

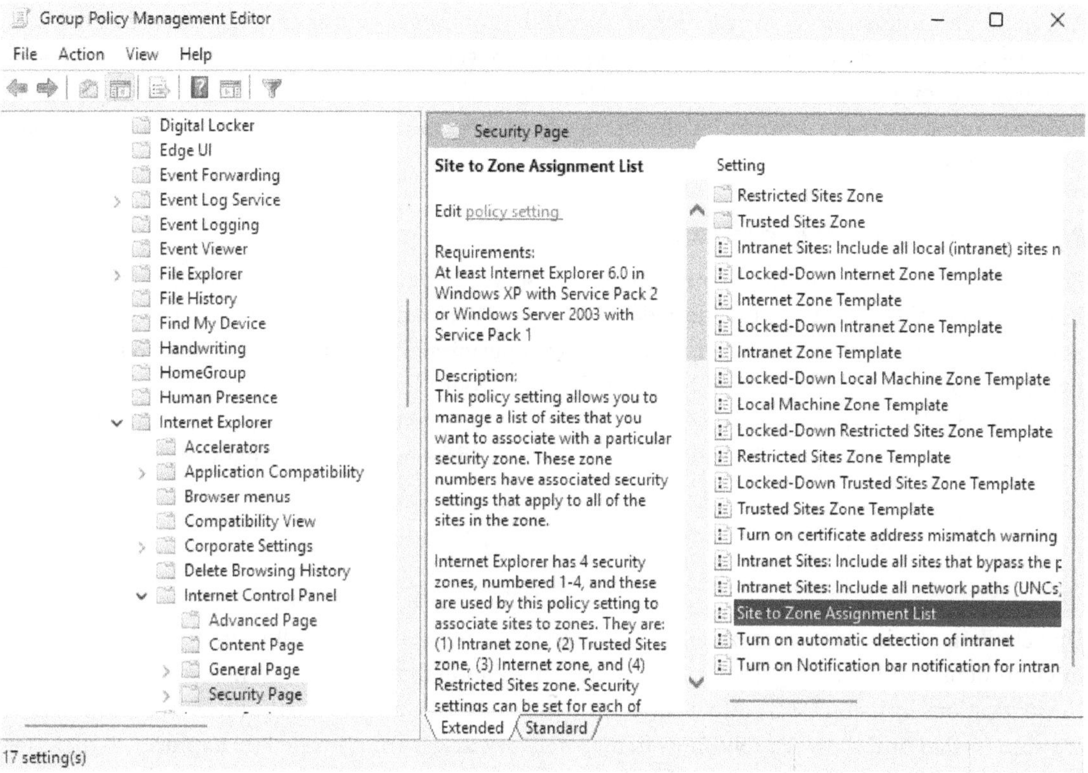

Figure 5.2: Creating a GPO to manage trusted websites

Now, double-click on **Site to Zone Assignment List** and set it to **Enabled**. This allows you to click on the **Show...** button, within which you can enter websites and give them zone assignments. Each GPO setting has a nice descriptive text to accompany it, telling you exactly what that particular setting is for and what the options mean. As you can see in the text for this one, in order to set my websites to be trusted sites, I need to give them a zone assignment value of **2**. And, just for fun, I also added a site that I do not want to be accessible to my users and gave it a zone value of **4** so that `badsite.contoso.com` is a member of the restricted sites zone on all of my desktop computers.

Here is my completed list:

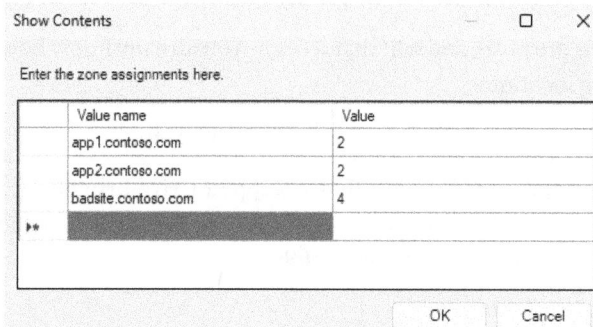

Figure 5.3: Assigning websites to different zones

Are we done? Almost. As soon as I click on the **OK** button, these settings are now stored in my GPO and are ready to be deployed. As you know, we have not yet done any work to assign this new GPO to any users or computers, so for now, the GPO is populated with these settings but still doing nothing. Before we push out these settings, let's build out a few more common GPOs to make sure our examples here are well-rounded.

Mapping network drives

File servers are some of the most common types of servers that exist because all companies across all industries need to create and maintain documentation to run their businesses. This is not a chapter about how to build a file server, set up shares, restrict permissions, or utilize a **Distributed File System (DFS)** to improve the overall flexibility and resiliency of your file server infrastructure, although these are all good things to learn and we will do exactly that in *Chapter 6, File Management*. Until we get to that chapter, I have created a few really simple shared folders in my test lab that we will make use of:

- \\DC1\HR
- \\DC2\Accounting
- \\WEB3\Installers

Our challenge today is to automate the mapping of these locations on all user workstations in my environment. I could put together a piece of documentation that shows users how to manually get to these locations by using UNC paths plugged into the address bar of File Explorer. Or maybe even take it a step further and show my folks how to map network drives from inside **File Explorer** so that they end up with drive letters assigned on their computers for ongoing access to these locations. Doing so would work, but it would put an administrative burden on my users and also lead to the possibility of users having differing drive letters. Grace might use her "R" drive letter to map to the accounting share, while Jackson may decide that "T" is his accounting drive letter of choice. If this were to happen, someday one user may send a sharing link to another that is based on their drive letter location, and that link would fail to open for the recipient. This and many more complications arise if you grant users the ability to map their own network drives.

Obviously, there is a better way to handle this situation. One of the very common chores we task a GPO with is the standardized creation of mapped network drives on client computers. Inside a new GPO, we can define UNC paths for shares and assign drive letters to them. We can then assign that GPO to users and computers, and drive letters will magically map when your users log in to their computers.

Create a new GPO for this purpose, and edit that GPO, as you already know how to do it. This time, we navigate to the following location:

User Configuration | Preferences | Windows Settings | Drive Maps.

Right-clicking on **Drive Maps** and choosing **New | Mapped Drive** brings you into the configuration section for a single mapped drive letter. You can see in the following screenshot that I am mapping a drive to \\DC1\HR, and assigning it a drive letter of H:

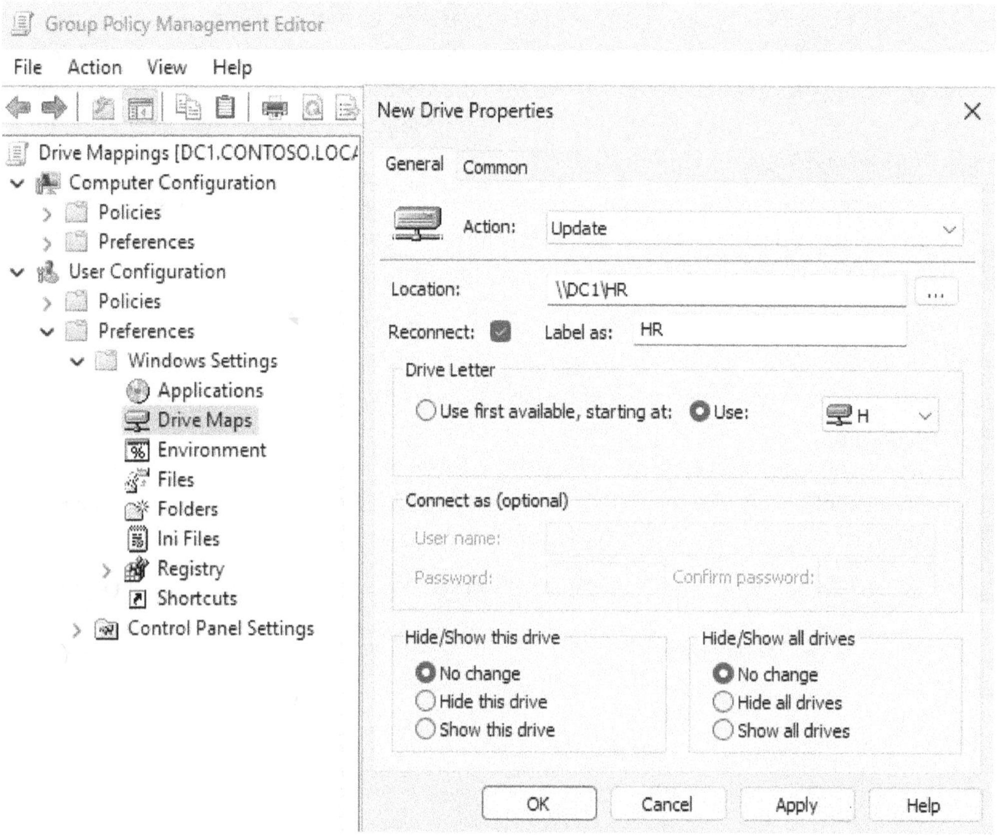

Figure 5.4: Mapping drives with Group Policy

You'll notice the **Action** drop-down menu has four different options: **Create**, **Replace**, **Update**, and **Delete**. This series of options is commonly referred to as CRUD, which is hilarious. What is no joke, however, is the important distinction between these options and that you absolutely must understand how they work if you are going to create successful GPOs.

Many GPO preference configurations contain this same CRUD drop-down selection. Here is a quick summary of each available option as it relates to our new drive-mapping policy:

- **Create:** Use this action to create the new mapped drive only if it does not already exist. If the H: drive is already in use on a workstation, this new mapping will then be ignored. In our example, if I were to configure this new drive mapping for **Create**, it would only take an action if the H: drive letter was currently open and available.

- **Replace:** Use this action to remove an existing setting and replace it with a new setting. In our case, it will update whatever mapped drive is using H: to \\DC1\HR. For drive mappings, the **Replace** option is redundant because the **Update** option effectively does the same. However, other GPO preferences that you push out, a connection to a new printer perhaps, could make more effective use of the **Replace** selection.

- **Update:** This is the default action for most preference settings and is generally the most useful. If the setting that we are configuring (H: drive) doesn't exist, **Update** will create it. Additionally, if the setting (H: drive) is already in place on the workstation, it will now be updated to reflect our new definition inside the GPO. Drive mapping policies almost always use the **Update** action to push new drive letters into place.

- **Delete:** This removes the specific setting from the client machine. If you are removing a network share and want to ensure that it is removed from all of the computers in your domain, this would be a useful action to ensure that happens.

Before clicking **OK** on this new drive mapping, go ahead and visit the **Common** tab. This tab and its five options are commonly shown on many preference settings that you plug into a GPO. Most of these are self-explanatory, though we will discuss item-level targeting more in just a few pages. For our drive-mapping GPO, I'd like to point out the **Run in logged-on user's security context** checkbox. This tells Group Policy to run whatever setting or preference the GPO is putting into place under the logged-in user's account. For mapped drives, this is particularly useful because you typically want users to interface with their mapped drives in their regular user context.

While it is not common to check this box for most GPO settings, for drive-mapping GPOs, I always do:

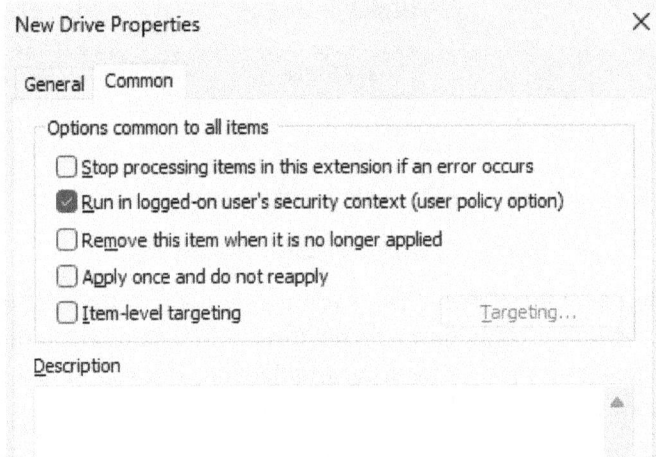

Figure 5.5: Map drives under the user's security context

Rinse and repeat for any additional drive letters that you want to include in your new GPO, and you are now well on your way to automating the mapping of all drive letters across your entire network! I set up drive letter mappings for each of my shared folders and also included a GPO setting to delete the Z: drive if it exists.

There has never been a Z: drive in my test lab, but here you can see what a drive deletion looks like inside the policy:

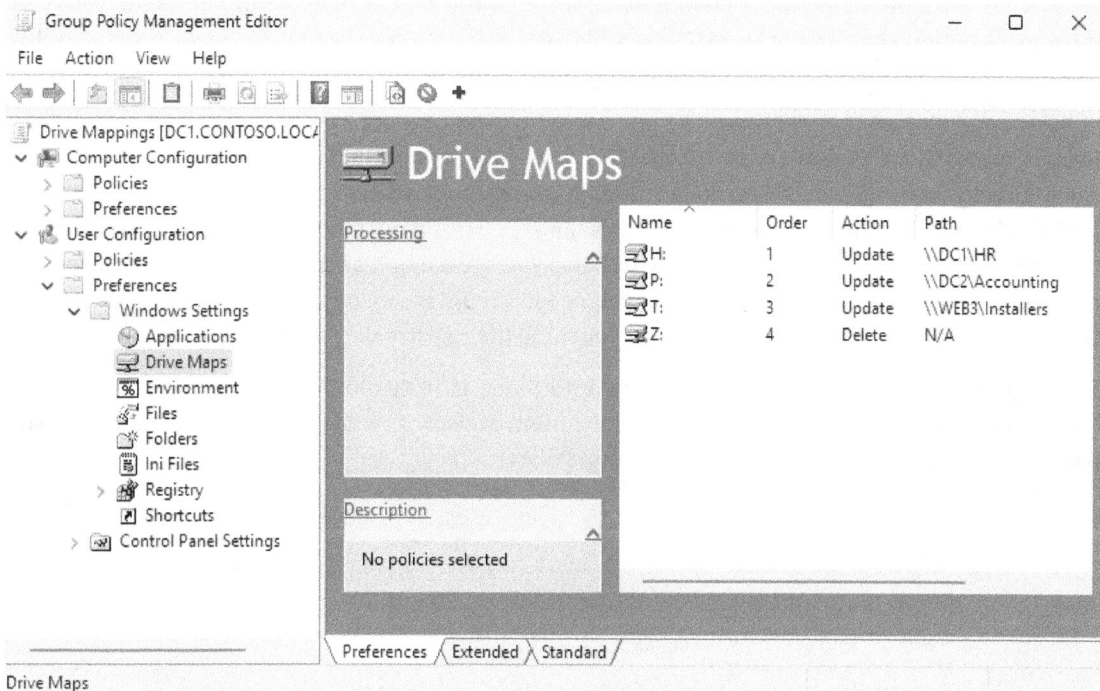

Figure 5.6: Mapped drives via GPO

Once again, this new GPO is now filled with settings but does not apply to any users yet. Never fear—once we finish creating a few more example GPOs, we will move on to scoping GPO settings, which is where we will push the new GPOs into action and verify that settings and mapped drives show up automatically on our client computers.

Installing registry keys

In much the same way that mapped network drives can be pushed to users via GPO, we can implement registry keys and values on computers automatically as well. This is spectacularly powerful because almost anything within a Windows environment can be manipulated by using registry keys. Create yet another new GPO and, this time, navigate to the following location:

User Configuration | Preferences | Windows Settings | Registry

Creating, replacing, updating, or deleting registry keys flows in very much the same fashion as it does for mapping network drives. The tricky bit is making sure that the options are specified properly, or they won't work, particularly the **Key Path** and **Value** information. For our example, I am going to push a registry value that prevents users from being able to change their desktop background image and specifies a custom desktop background of my own.

In my experience, the easiest way to ensure that a GPO-based registry setting is configured properly within the GPO is to manually edit the registry first, placing the new registry key and/or value that you are working with on the server or computer from which you are running the GPMC. When you click the ellipsis button shown in *Figure 5.7*, you will then be able to successfully navigate directly to this regkey and simply select it, instead of worrying about whether you are typing the syntax correctly to make the **Key Path** field happy.

Keep in mind, GPMC is similar to any other Windows Server administrative console, in that you can use it directly from a Domain Controller, from another server, or even from a Windows client workstation where you have installed the RSAT tools. Be very careful not to manually chop up the registry too much on a Domain Controller, simply because you are using it as the point from which you are editing GPOs. It is much smarter to set up the needed registry key on a client workstation and run GPMC from there, in which case you are not touching the registry on your Domain Controller at all.

The registry information that I am putting into place is `HKCU\SOFTWARE\Microsoft\Windows\CurrentVersion\Policies\System`. Inside the system registry key, the registry value name is **Wallpaper**. Here is my populated entry inside Group Policy:

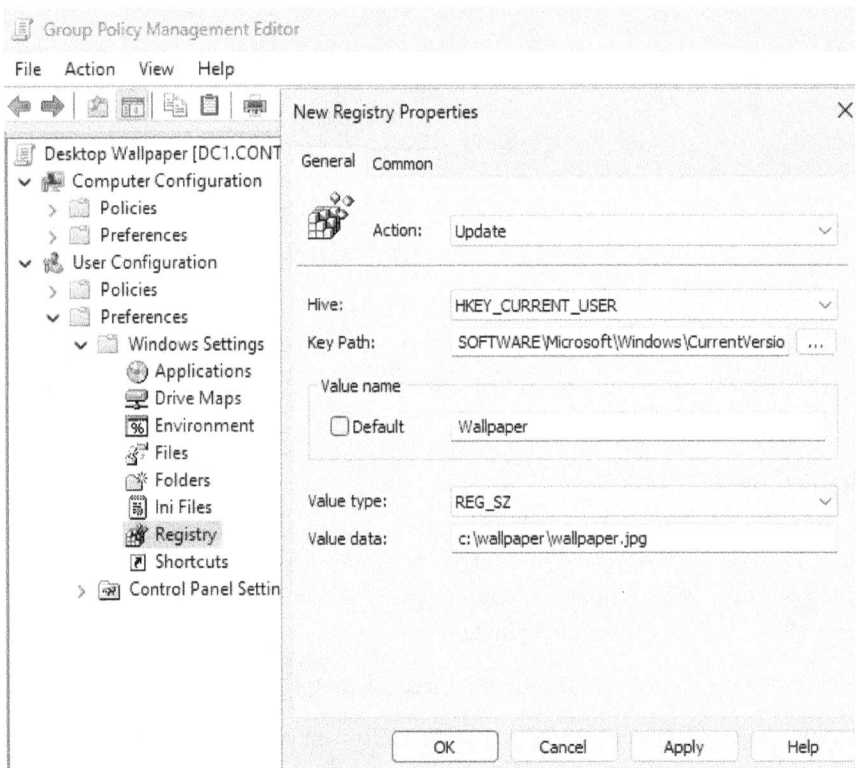

Figure 5.7: Adding registry keys via Group Policy

Because I have selected this registry value to be pushed as an **Update** action, every time that Group Policy processes on this computer, it is going to ensure that this registry key is present, thus continually preventing users from being able to adjust their desktop wallpaper.

I chose this example because it is straightforward and because, often in Group Policy, you will find that there are multiple ways to accomplish the same thing. Instead of using a registry value to lock down wallpaper settings, I could have alternatively created a GPO that utilized the following GPO setting, and it would have accomplished the same thing without having to touch registry settings:

User Configuration | Policies | Administrative Templates | Desktop | Desktop | Desktop Wallpaper

Preventing the shutdown of the system

It is very common to utilize GPOs to push security lockdown parameters to computers or servers. Many corporations use Remote Desktop Servers to provide virtual desktops for users to log in to. When users work in an RDS session, they navigate using the keyboard and mouse from their computers, but everything they work on or click on happens inside a multi-user server environment. If these users were to do something such as shutting down the server, even accidentally, that would have an enormously negative impact on other users of that server. The same type of logic could apply to common-use kiosk workstations, perhaps shared computers that are often accessed by a myriad of employees. There are many common lockdown restrictions for these types of environments, but one that I often find to be in place is a policy setting that prevents users from being able to shut down the computer they are logged in to.

Creating another GPO, or editing an existing one to implement this restriction alongside settings that already apply to your kiosk machines or RDS servers, or to whichever machines you want to apply this policy to, navigate to the following location:

Computer Configuration (or User Configuration) | Policies | Administrative Templates | Start Menu and Taskbar

Now, seek out the setting called **Remove and prevent access to the Shut Down, Restart, Sleep, and Hibernate commands**. Double-click this setting and flip it to **Enabled**.

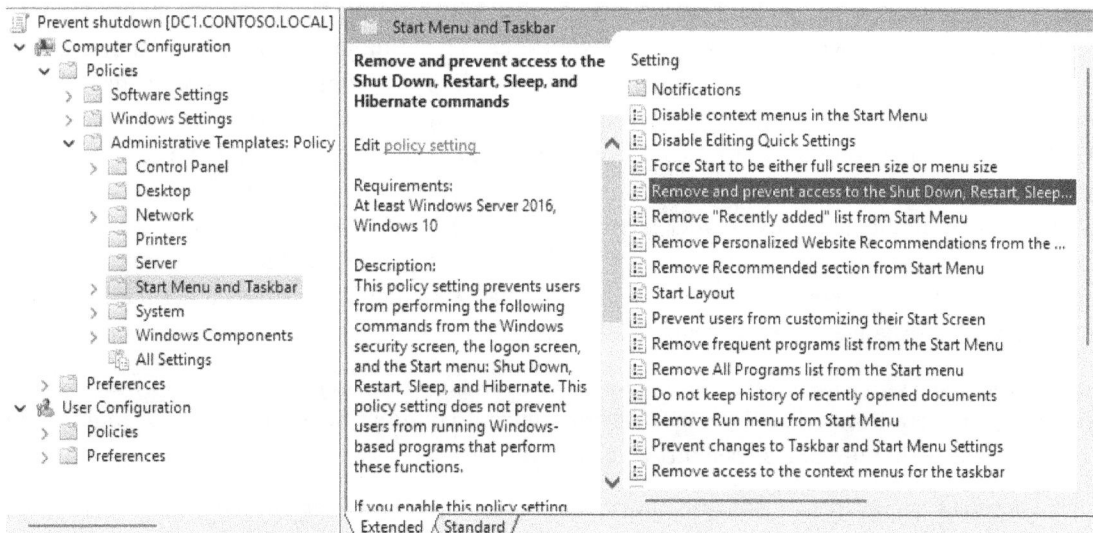

Figure 5.8: GPO to prevent shutdown or restart

Once enabled, this is a simple single-action policy restriction that will prevent select users from being able to shut down computers or servers within your domain environment. To which computers or users this policy applies has not yet been determined, as we still have not discussed how to properly scope a GPO. Never fear, that information is soon to come! Once this GPO is applied, if a user were to attempt to shut down a computer, they would no longer see the option to be able to do so. In fact, this policy is not only a graphical update to hide the button. Even if the user were IT-smart enough to attempt something such as pressing *Alt + F4* at the desktop or initiating a shutdown via Command Prompt, they would be prevented from doing so.

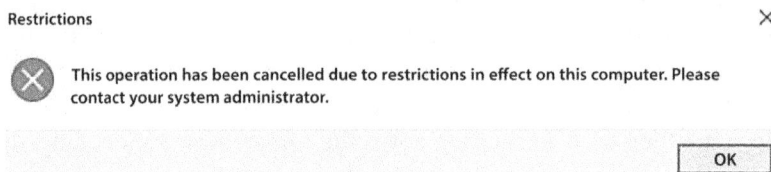

Figure 5.9: The user is prevented from shutting down the system

While this Group Policy setting is a great way to keep 99% of your users from accidentally or intentionally shutting down or restarting an RDS server, this setting is technically a "Start Menu and Taskbar" setting. What this is really doing is hiding away options for the user to interact with GUI tools for shutdown or restart functions; it does not *block* the shutdown commands. If an end user were savvy enough to launch Command Prompt or PowerShell and throw some commands around, they could still reboot an RDS server if they really wanted to. These types of users are a little outside the scope of my example here, but if you find yourself with problematic end users who are bent on doing things they shouldn't be doing, there are many more restrictive options available to push with local security or GPO-based policies.

Disabling removable USB drives

Have you ever heard of the *Dropped Drive Experiment*? Originally implemented by penetration testers, it is an extremely creative way of testing your workforce to find out how security-savvy they are. You may or may not know that plugging an unknown USB stick into your computer is risky business. There are many viruses and attacks that can be accomplished by simply convincing a user to plug an infected USB drive into their computer. The user doesn't even need to click on anything to be compromised; the act of plugging the USB stick into your computer is all it takes. The premise of the Dropped Drive Experiment is simply to load USB sticks with malicious software, drop one or more in a company parking lot, and see what happens. Chances are people are going to find these USB sticks and plug them into their computers to see what is on them. At that point, it is too late; the attacker already has control of your system and your information.

If ever you find a USB stick sitting on the ground, or even if a vendor hands you one as a fancy way of providing marketing materials about their business during a trade show, there is only one appropriate action to take with these USB sticks: throw them in the garbage.

Can you send an email to your staff and inform them of this risk? Sure. Can you ask them to never plug USB drives into their computers? Sure. Will they actually listen? I can almost guarantee they won't. Protection against this scenario is what our next example of a GPO setting is all about. Flip one simple switch inside a GPO that applies to all your domain computers, and you provide immediate protection to your business against this very real vulnerability:

Computer Configuration | Policies | Administrative Templates | System | Removable Storage Access | All removable storage classes: Deny all accesses

Enable this option, and you're good to go.

Adding a shortcut to the desktop

Let's walk through one more sample GPO before moving on to the next section. A fairly common ticket we see on support desks goes something like this: "Could you push out an icon to everybody's computer for such-and-such?" Now, some companies will have their own RMM toolsets from which you may be able to accomplish this task in a myriad of ways, but we are limited to a simple test lab with a couple of Windows Servers. Can we do this?

Computer Configuration or User Configuration | Preferences | Windows Settings | Shortcuts

Similar to the way that you craft a new network drive mapping, printer, or registry key, create a new shortcut here and define the necessary properties. You can see in *Figure 5.10* that my new icon is going to be a shortcut pointing to a URL, which will land my users on our company's intranet website. After configuring this GPO and scoping it to apply to all domain-joined computers in my network, this is now my guarantee that a link to our company's intranet site will exist on everybody's computers, even new computers that are deployed in the future!

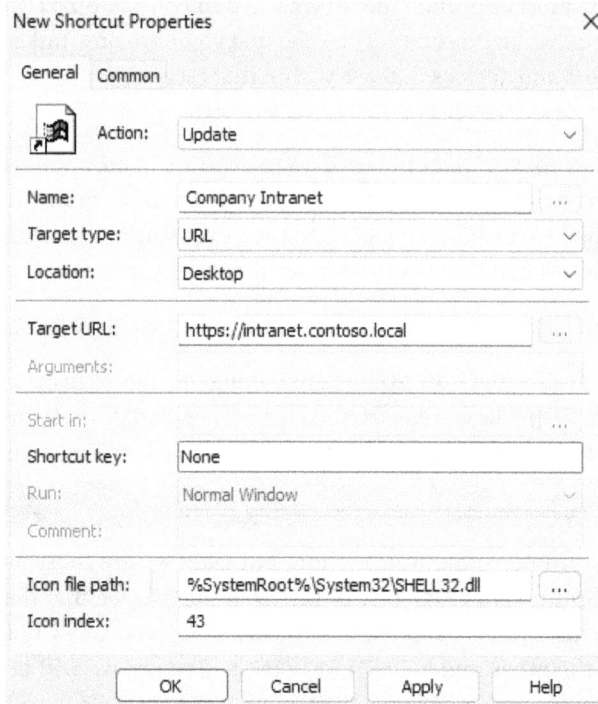

Figure 5.10: Pushing out a desktop shortcut to all computers

Today, we sent out a URL shortcut to everyone's desktop, but you could just as easily send out a shortcut pointing to an application executable and store that icon somewhere else, such as the **Quick Launch** toolbar or even inside the `All Users Startup` folder. The ability to centrally control shortcuts can be a powerful one.

Scoping a GPO

I briefly mentioned the ability to scope GPOs, which is the ability to determine what GPO settings need to apply to what computers or users in your environment. This is probably the single most important piece of the Group Policy puzzle to understand and lock into memory. You have already seen a few examples of plugging settings into GPOs, and information is abundant on the internet with useful and exact policy settings and how to put those into place. If there is some particular task you are trying to accomplish on a large scale, turn to search engines and look for that item while including the search word *GPO*, and you'll quickly find information about how to set up your new GPO to do that thing.

What those articles, Microsoft documents, and blog posts are *not* going to define for you is to what extent you push those settings into your network, and how to ensure your new GPO is not too far-reaching. That decision is yours alone. In this section, we will discuss the different options available within every GPO that allow you to pinpoint very specific details about who should or should not receive those GPO settings.

Links

A GPO link is arguably the most important tool in your Group Policy toolbox. Links simply take a GPO and bind it to a location in Active Directory. The GPO that you have now linked will start applying its contained settings to users and devices that are within that location.

We have created multiple GPOs inside Group Policy but have not yet applied them to anything. What this means is that we have not yet *linked* those GPOs to anything, and when we do, that is when they will be set loose and start doing their work. Before we link one of our new GPOs, let's take a look at which GPOs currently apply to my Windows 10 computer. That way, we can check again after creating our link to prove to ourselves that the new GPO is doing something.

Gpresult

So far, we haven't talked at all about how to check individual machines to discover what policies may or may not apply to them. Let's take a break from configuration and do that now. Logging into my Windows 10 client machine, I can open Command Prompt, PowerShell, or Terminal and run the following:

```
Gpresult /r
```

This spits out quite a bit of interesting information, but what we are most interested in here is the section called **Applied Group Policy Objects**. In fact, you may notice that there are two sections to this output and find two instances of **Applied Group Policy Objects**. One will be listed beneath **COMPUTER SETTINGS**, and the other under **USER SETTINGS**. Shortly, we will describe the differences between computer and user settings within a GPO, but for our example now, I want to point out that the output on my test client shows us that no GPOs are being applied at the **User Settings** level, as you can see in *Figure 5.11*:

```
Applied Group Policy Objects
-------------------------------
        N/A
```

Figure 5.11: No GPOs applied to the user

After becoming more familiar with Group Policy, you may often find yourself running Gpresult and wanting to narrow down the results to either computer or user settings. You can easily do this by adding a switch to your Gpresult command:

```
Gpresult /r /scope computer Gpresult /r /scope user
```

Continuing with the link

Back inside the GPMC, find the location to which you want to **link** your new GPO. I am going to link my **Drive Mappings** GPO and prove to you that all of my mapped network drives are created automatically during my next login to a workstation. The user account I am logging in with resides inside an OU called **Accounting Users**. Seeking out the **Accounting Users** OU, I right-click on it and choose the **Link an Existing GPO...** option. On the screen that follows, find your newly created GPO and select it. You have now linked the GPO to this specific OU, and this change immediately takes effect in your network. You can see in *Figure 5.12* that my GPO link is displayed under the **Accounting Users** OU:

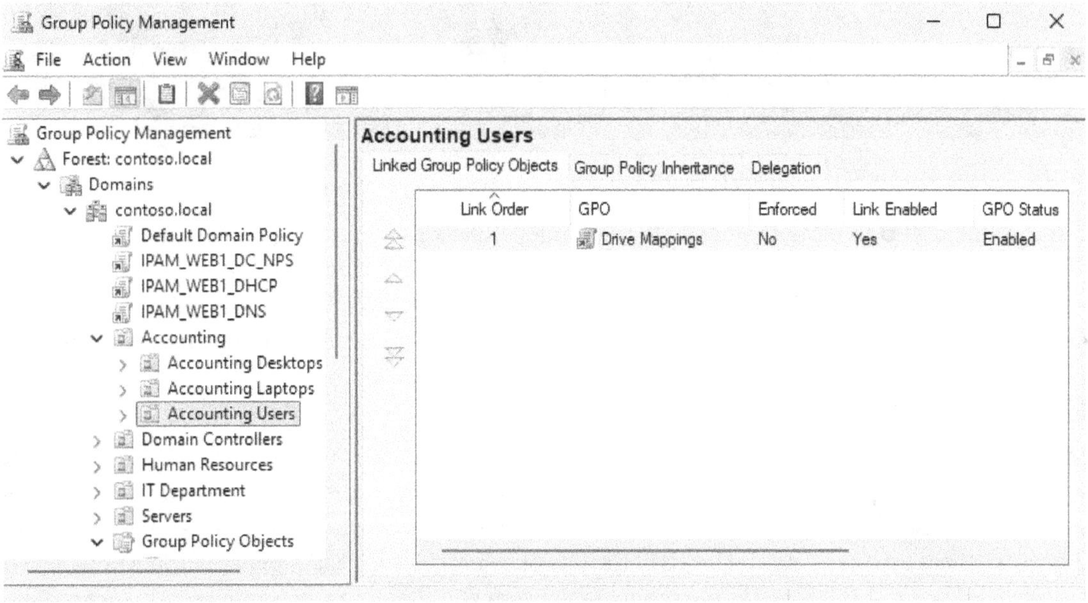

Figure 5.12: Linking a GPO to the Accounting Users OU

The next time users inside this OU log in to a domain-joined computer, their network drives should be mapped for them during the login process.

Logging in to my Windows 10 workstation, I now find that to be true, and running gpresult /r again proves that my GPO has successfully been applied!

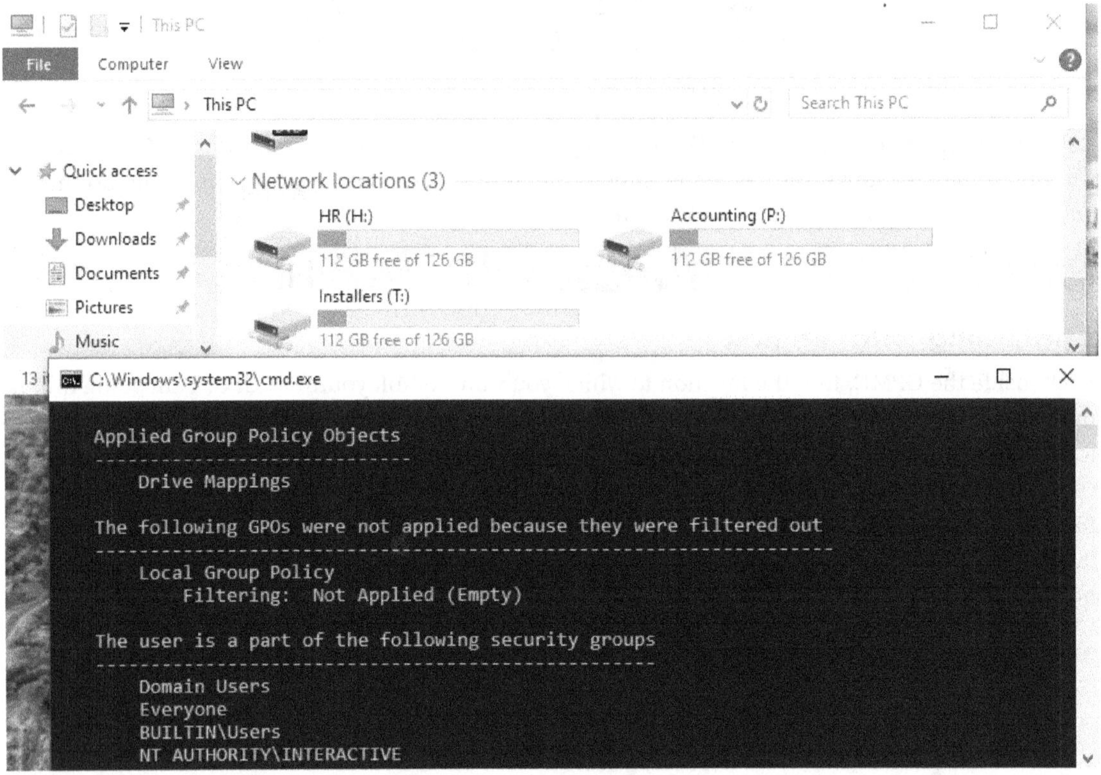

Figure 5.13: GPO has been successfully implemented

You can link a GPO to more than one OU. Just follow the same process again, this time choosing a different OU to make the link, and that GPO will now apply to both OUs that have active links. You can remove links by right-clicking on them and deleting them (don't worry, deleting a GPO link does not delete the GPO), or by clicking on the Group Policy Object itself to view and modify its link properties.

Group Policy processing order

In the GPO linking example that was just completed, we linked a GPO to a specific OU. You probably noticed in some of the screenshots that there are GPOs linked at different levels too, such as right at the root of my contoso.local domain. What's that all about? As it turns out, when logging in to a computer, there are four different levels of Group Policy processing that happen. The location of your links can make a big difference to the proper effect your GPO has on your computers and users. Let's discuss these four levels of GPO processing.

Local Policy

Assuming you have worked in IT for a little while, it is very likely that you have followed a blog post or forum that has led you to a modification via gpedit.msc. Running gpedit.msc on any Windows system brings you into **Local Group Policy Editor**. This is the set of policy objects and settings that exist on an individual machine. They can be manipulated manually via gpedit.msc or they can be manipulated and overwritten by GPOs.

The key point that I want to make is that when your Windows computer boots and logs in, the very first thing that happens is that settings inside **Local Group Policy Editor** are processed. Since Local Policy is first to apply, it means that any levels of Active Directory Group Policy, which we are about to discuss, will take priority over Local Policy. In other words, your computer may have Local Policy settings in place, but milliseconds later during the boot process, those local settings could be overwritten by AD policy settings.

Site-level policies

Remember back in *Chapter 3, Active Directory*, when we discussed Active Directory sites and services? They come into play here. If your environment is large enough to contain multiple sites, it is possible to link GPOs at an individual site level, thus enabling Group Policy to issue settings to computers or users based on which site they reside within.

Having GPOs linked to sites is quite a rare occurrence in my experience, but it is something to keep in the back of your mind when troubleshooting GPO applications. Computers and users will only receive site-level policies when they physically reside within those sites, based on the IP addressing scheme and subnets you defined inside AD sites and services. If a computer is handed GPO settings based on a site-level link, and these settings contradict what is in Local Group Policy, the site-level policies will override the Local Policy, and these will be the new settings as you continue the login process.

Domain-level policies

Some policies and settings are going to be things that you want to apply to all machines or users in an entire domain, and the appropriate place for those settings is domain-level GPOs. As we talk about all these different policy levels, it's important to point out that the GPOs themselves are not different. A GPO is a GPO. The level at which the GPO is *linked* is what we are discussing in relation to these hierarchical levels.

Links created at the root, or top level, of a domain inside Group Policy Management will, by default, attempt to apply to any user or computer that is part of the domain. There are many other factors that can filter domain-linked GPOs, but for the most part, if you link a GPO to the domain name, you had better be okay with the settings inside that GPO applying to potentially every workstation, every server, and every user. If you peek back a few pages at some of the screenshots from inside the GPMC, you will see that my IPAM GPOs are all linked directly to contoso.local. These are known as domain-level links.

Pretending that we are still flowing through a computer login process with these examples, domain-level policies apply after site-level policies. So, any settings that came down to you via site-level policies have now been added to, or potentially overridden by (if there was a conflict), our domain-level policies.

OU-level policies

We started our login journey with Local Group Policy settings, which were then added to or over-written by site-level GPOs, and those were then added on to again (or overwritten again in the case of conflicts) by domain-level GPOs. You can guess where this is heading. OU-level policies now apply on top of domain-level GPOs.

OUs, as you know, are containing folders for computer and user accounts that are joined to your domain. Most companies take advantage of using multiple OUs inside Active Directory to differentiate types of machines and users. Servers are separated from workstations, accounting users are different from HR users, and so on. Nesting OUs is a common practice as well. Just like creating folders inside of other folders by using File Explorer, you can use AD Users and Computers to create OUs inside other OUs. This is important to the organization of your domain objects, and it is also important to Group Policy.

Linking GPOs to particular OUs gives us flexibility in handing different settings to different groups of people or machines. When a GPO is linked to a single OU, only computers or users inside that OU, or downstream from it, will be affected by the GPO. You can even have multiple GPOs linked to the same OU.

Nested OUs provide an additional tier to this GPO workflow. Remember, the general rule is that Group Policy processes from the top down, so GPOs that are linked to a nested OU will most likely outweigh GPOs that are linked at a higher-level OU.

Security Filtering

Now that you have created a GPO and linked it to a particular OU, you have enough information to start using Group Policy in your environment. Using links to determine what machines or users get what policies is the most common method that I see admins use, but there are many circumstances where you might want to take filtering a step further. What if you had a new GPO and had it linked to an OU that contained all of your desktop computers, but then decided that some of those machines needed the policy and some did not? It would be a headache to have to split those machines up into two separate OUs just for the purpose of this policy that you are building. This is where **GPO Security Filtering** comes into play.

Security Filtering is the ability to filter a GPO down to particular Active Directory objects. On any given GPO in your directory, you can set filters so that the GPO only applies to particular users, particular computers, or even particular groups of users or computers. I find that using groups is especially useful.

For our **Drive Mappings** GPO, right now I have it linked to my **Accounting Users** OU, but what if I wanted to filter that GPO in a different way? Rather than limit the scope of this GPO to a single OU, I would prefer to make it a little bit further-reaching, and I'm going to link the GPO to my contoso.local domain. Yikes, doesn't that mean it's going to apply to everything? Yes, *unless* you utilize the **Security Filtering** section to define user accounts or groups of accounts to which it should apply.

> I always make my security filtering decisions before creating a link. Links are live as soon as you create them, so building Security Filtering first ensures proper distribution from the start.

Clicking on any GPO inside the GPMC will display information about that GPO, and the **Scope** tab displays any links that exist for this GPO, as well as security filtering information. All new GPOs will have **Authenticated Users** defined inside **Security Filtering**, which essentially means "all domain users *and* computers."

Remember that it means both! In the next screenshot, you can see my **Drive Mappings** GPO, which is linked to the **Accounting Users** OU. It has **Authenticated Users** listed for **Security Filtering**. If I were to simply remove the existing OU link and create a new domain-level link, this GPO would immediately start applying to all user accounts in my whole domain:

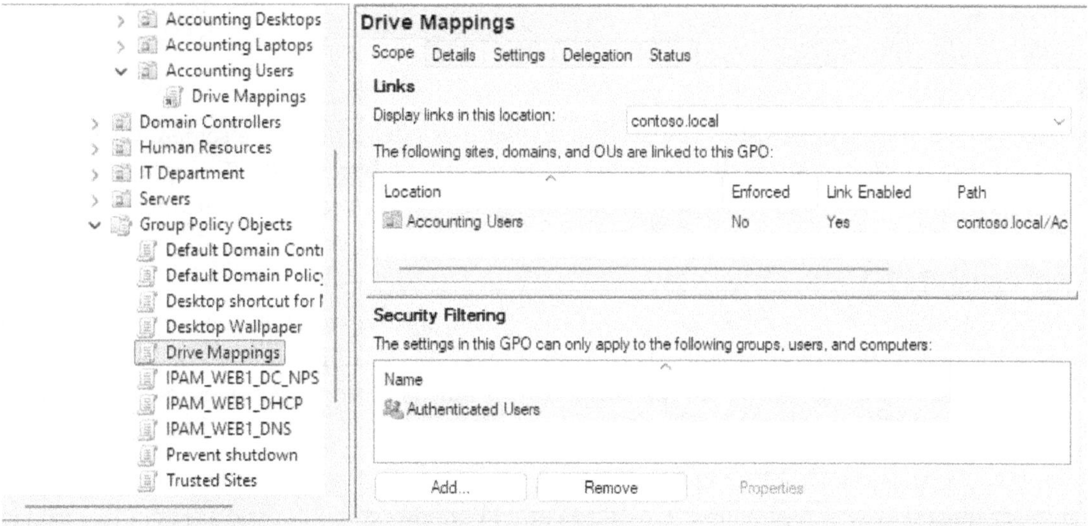

Figure 5.14: Security Filtering settings for GPOs

Instead of doing that, I will adjust my **Security Filtering** settings first. All accounting users are part of a security group called **Acct Group** (I'm so creative!). Adding **Acct Group** to **Security Filtering** for this GPO and **REMOVING Authenticated Users** means that now, no matter where I link this GPO, only members of the **Acct Group** group are going to receive the GPO settings. Now that I have added **Acct Group** to **Security Filtering**, I can safely link the GPO to the top level of my domain and remain confident that only members of **Acct Group** will receive my GPO settings:

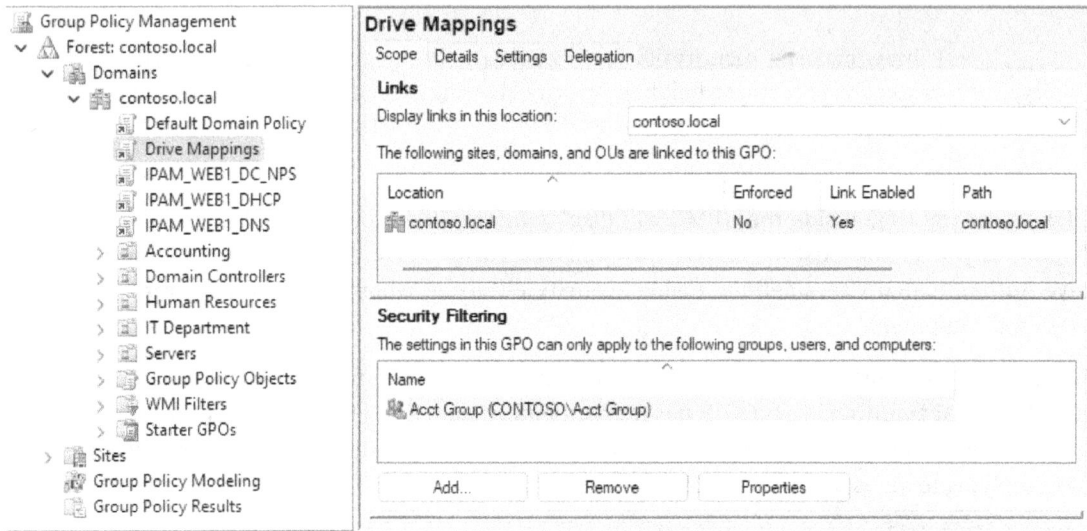

Figure 5.15: Filtering a GPO to Acct Group

Another cool feature that is just a click away is the **Settings** tab on this same screen. Click on that tab, and it will display all of the configurations currently set inside your GPO. This is very useful for checking over GPOs that someone else may have created to see what settings reside inside the policy.

WMI Filtering

Using a combination of well-designed links and security filtering to narrow the scope of your GPOs, you will likely be able to perfectly plan and apply policy settings 90% of the time. Our next few sub-headings reflect that remaining 10%, as we cover some of the advanced filtering techniques that are available to get even more granular when filtering GPOs.

WMI Filtering is a genius, although slightly confusing, tool to further define GPO application. WMI filters tap into the WMI information that exists on every Windows computer and use that WMI data to further filter GPO settings. WMI filters can be defined to look for operating system version numbers, types of CPU, quantities of RAM, the amount of available disk space, and sometimes even things such as BIOS firmware. Once a WMI filter is defined, you can then select that filter for each GPO, in the section titled **WMI Filtering**, which is immediately below **Security Filtering** inside the GPMC.

WMI filters enable you to do things such as "only install this huge piece of software if there is at least 5 GB of available disk space" or "only implement these firewall settings on machines running a Windows Server operating system." Another real-world example uses WMI Filtering to identify whether or not a machine is running mobile hardware, which allows your GPOs to apply only to laptops and tablets, and not desktop computers.

WMI Filtering draws information from other components inside the operating system, and therefore, causes Group Policy to take a little bit more time and CPU processing power to function. This can cause an increase in system resources on your endpoint computers and also slow logins, as that processing happens in the background.

Building WMI filters is getting in the weeds with Group Policy, and so for further instruction on that, I will point you toward the *Summary* section at the end of this chapter, where I will reference another publication dedicated entirely to Group Policy.

Item-level targeting

Links, **Security Filtering**, and **WMI Filtering** are fantastic ways to determine which GPOs apply to which computers and users. But what if you need to take it a step further? What if you have a single GPO that contains multiple settings, and you only want some of those settings to apply to certain users or computers, and other settings in the same policy to apply to different users and computers?

A prime example of this is a **Drive Mappings** GPO. It is common to place all network drives in a single GPO in the domain and call it *Mapped Drives* or something similar. It is also common that not all users should get all mapped network drives. What is the best way to handle that? For this scenario, you could break your GPO out into many smaller GPOs, creating a separate GPO for each drive letter and then determining with links and filters which users get which drive letters. But then you have a horde of GPOs to deal with.

Enter **Item-level targeting**. You may not remember, but earlier we glanced at a special **Common** tab that exists inside many GPO settings. One of the five settings inside the **Common** tab is **Item-level targeting**, and this is exactly the clarifying setting we need to make our **Drive Mappings** GPO dreams come true.

Referencing the same **Drive Mappings** GPO that I have worked with for many pages now, you know that this policy contains multiple drive letters. Currently, my **Acct Group** users receive all of those mapped drives. Let's pretend for a minute that I only want **Acct Group** to receive one of those drive letter mappings and not the others. Editing the GPO, I double-click on my P: drive mapping, and then visit the **Common** tab. Here, I check the box for **Item-level targeting** and click on the **Targeting...** button.

Inside **Targeting Editor**, choose **New Item** and you will find a large list of criteria that can be utilized for these additional targeting parameters:

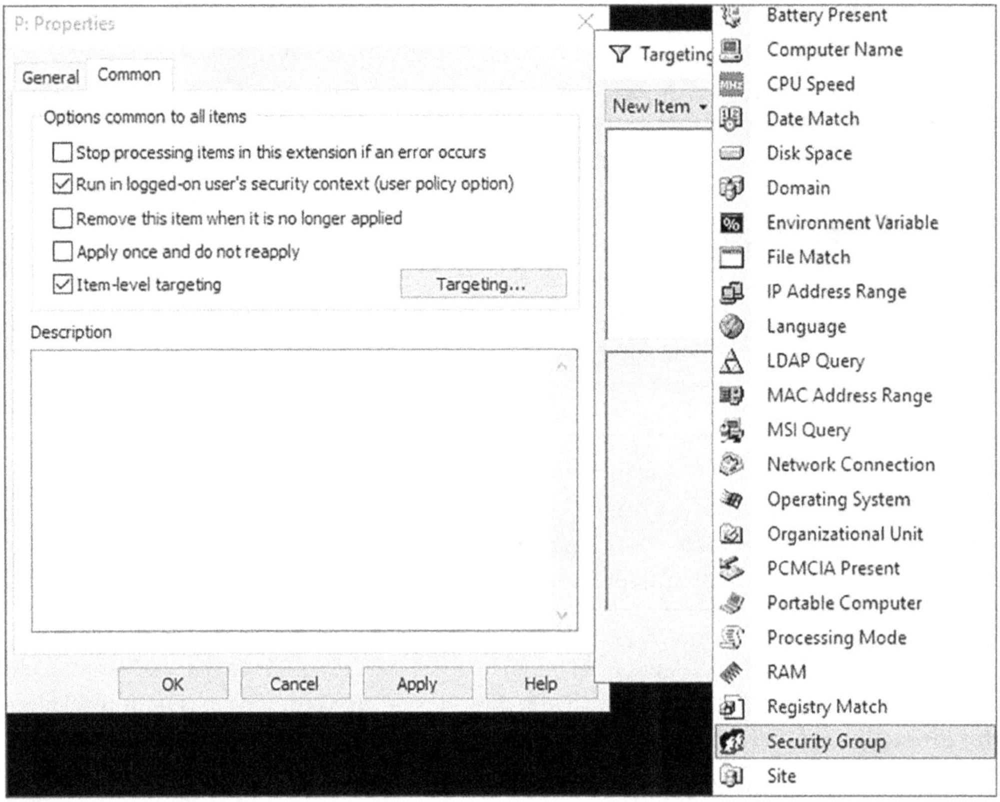

Figure 5.16: Adding a new security group in Targeting Editor

I want to instruct this GPO that the P: drive should only be mapped for users who are part of the **Acct Group** security group.

Choosing to add a new security group to my ILT, I can define **Acct Group** and you can see in *Figure 5.17* that my P: drive ILT settings have now been updated so that only if the user is a member of the CONTOSO\Acct Group security group will that user receive the P: drive mapping when they log in:

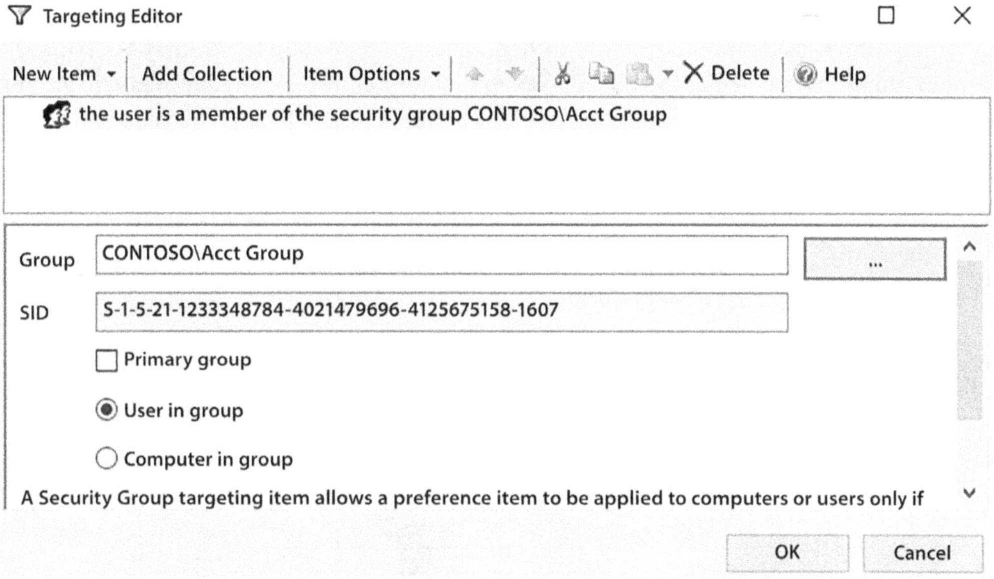

Figure 5.17: Applying the P: drive mapping to CONTOSO\Acct Group

Repeat this process with the rest of the drive letters in your GPO, and you now have a single GPO containing all drive letter mappings for your entire organization. You can link this GPO to the domain and leave it security-filtered for all authenticated users, as it is by default, and yet based on ILT, only drive letters that correspond to their appropriate groups will now be mapped for each user who logs in. ILT is the bomb! *Wow*, I can't believe I just typed that...

Delegation

Consider this scenario: the executive leadership at your company has asked you to lock down security restrictions on all computers in the domain. That sounds like a job for Group Policy! Except, since they are the leadership and don't want their own systems to hinder their ability to browse Instagram and configure desktop backgrounds of smiling kittens, they have required that these lockdown settings apply to everyone *except* members of the *Leadership* group in Active Directory.

We know plenty of ways to filter GPOs *to* certain users or groups, but how do we filter GPOs for everything *except* a certain user or group? For this, we visit GPMC, click on the GPO in question, and visit the tab called **Delegation**.

If your GPO has custom security filtering applied, you'll notice the names of those users or groups on the **Delegation** screen as well.

When configuring **Security Filtering**, what the GPMC is really doing is configuring delegation permissions on the GPO in the background. I have navigated to the **Delegation** tab of my **Drive Mappings** GPO, which is currently still security-filtered for **Acct Group**. Inside **Delegation**, clicking on the **Advanced...** button near the bottom left brings me into the nitty-gritty security details behind the delegation and permissions settings on this GPO.

In *Figure 5.18*, you can see that **Acct Group** currently has **Read** and **Apply group policy** permissions configured to **Allow**. This is what happened when I added **Acct Group** to **Security Filtering**. This is the set of permissions that makes the magic happen so that, whenever someone logs in to a computer in my domain, they are allowed to both read settings in this GPO and to apply settings from this GPO:

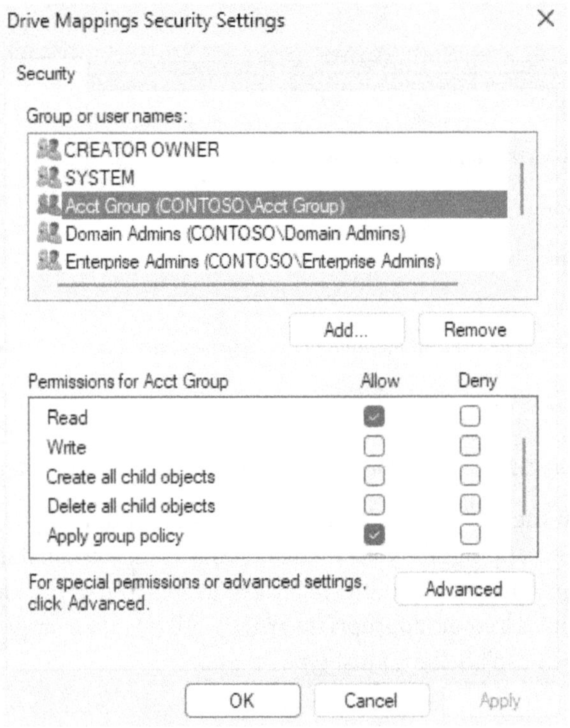

Figure 5.18: Acct Group has read and apply permissions

Circling back to the matter at hand, in the Microsoft world, a denial of permission always trumps a permission allowance. If you need to deny a particular user, computer, or group from receiving GPO settings from a particular GPO, you simply add them to the **Delegation** permissions and check the **Deny** box for **Apply group policy**. Even if they are allowed a Group Policy based on another permission entry in this list, they will now be denied this GPO applying to them. To make this crystal clear with another screenshot, here you can see that my **Leadership** group is now denied from applying the **Desktop Wallpaper** GPO.

When anybody logs in who is part of this **Leadership** group, they will *not* receive the wallpaper restrictions that are in place for the rest of my users:

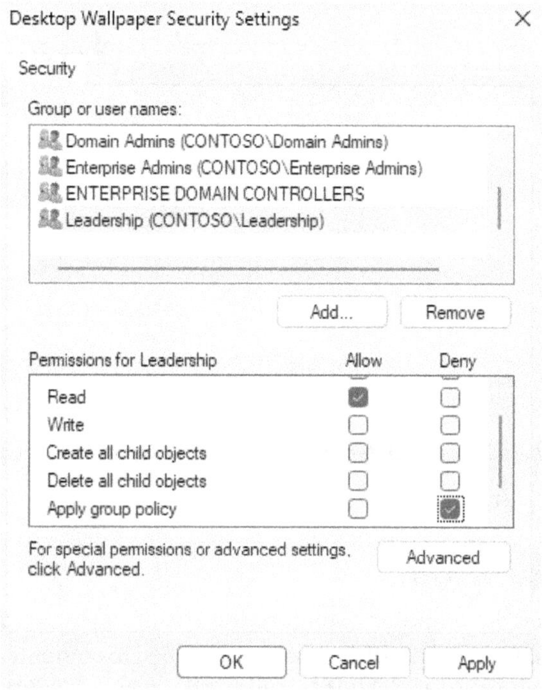

Figure 5.19: Denying a group from receiving this GPO

Use with caution! Creating GPO denials inside the **Delegation** tab works great, but it is very easy to forget or overlook these settings in the future. I have assisted admins numerous times with troubleshooting a GPO that did not seem to be applying properly, only to find out that a denied permission inside **Delegation** was causing all the grief.

Computer settings and user settings

After poking around inside GPOs for a few minutes, you are likely to notice that **Group Policy Management Editor** is split into two different sections. When drilling down inside a GPO to find the particular setting that you are about to roll into place, the first choice you need to make is whether you are working on a **Computer Configuration** or a **User Configuration**. Understanding the differences and always keeping these differences in mind is important not only for finding the setting you are searching for but also for ensuring that your new GPO is linked to the correct place and applies to the proper type of object.

You can see these two sections of any GPO in *Figure 5.20*:

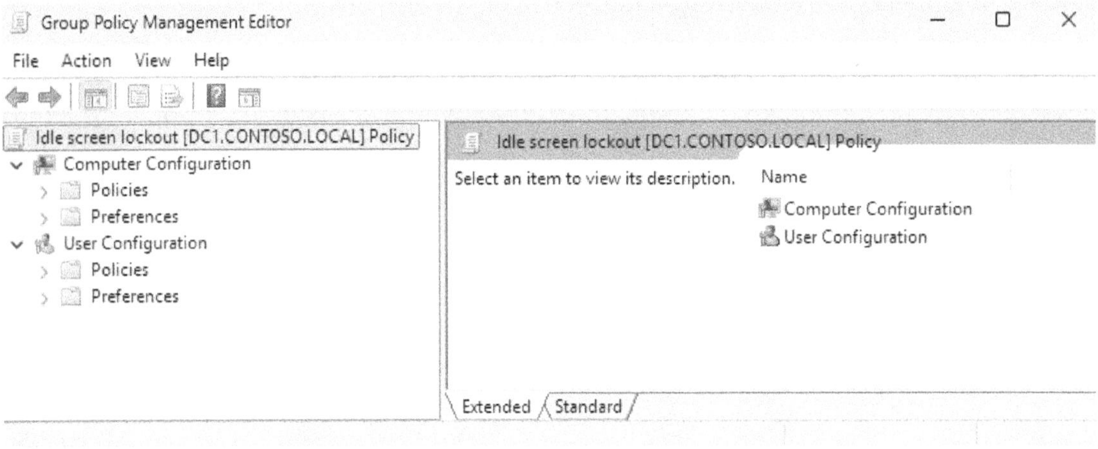

Figure 5.20: Computer Configuration and User Configuration

Let's briefly go over these options.

Computer Configuration

All GPO settings listed beneath **Computer Configuration** are, of course, settings that can apply to your domain-joined computers. Duh! Aren't all GPO settings applied to computers? No, they are not. Many GPO settings do apply to the computer object in Active Directory, and all these types of GPO settings fall beneath **Computer Configuration**. Some GPO settings are even things that you can configure at either a computer level or a user level. Other times, you might have similar options inside both **Computer Configuration** and **User Configuration** that accomplish the task in slightly different ways.

A good example is an idle screen lockout policy. It is a common requirement for companies to require computer screens to lock themselves after a certain number of minutes of inactivity. This way, if a user walks away from their computer and forgets to manually lock the screen, it will self-lock after, say, 15 minutes.

If you are tasked with creating such a policy, you need to decide whether you want this GPO to apply at the computer level or the user level. This will have to be decided by you, based on your normal user activity.

If you determine that the best method for locking the screen is to do so at the computer level, meaning that the screen will lock after 15 minutes no matter who is logged into that computer, then this is the specific configuration that you want to set inside your GPO:

Computer Configuration | Policies | Windows Settings | Security Settings | Local Policies | Security Options

Interactive logon: Machine inactivity limit = Enabled and specified to 900 seconds (15 minutes)

User Configuration

On the other hand, many other GPO settings apply not to the computer account at all, but rather to the domain user who is logging in to that computer. **User Configuration** settings follow the user account around and apply to whichever workstation the user logs in to. If you look back at our **Drive Mappings** GPO, you'll see that the network drive configurations that we created in that GPO all fall under **User Configuration**. This means that those drive mappings will attempt to map themselves anywhere that the user logs in. You cannot create mapped network drives as a native GPO setting from within **Computer Configuration**.

Revisiting our idle screen lockout example, what if you have decided that you want the idle screen to happen for a certain type of user, or perhaps even all users, and that the screen lock will happen for those users, no matter which computer they log in to? In this case, there is no specific "screen-lock" policy setting that you can configure inside **User Configuration**, but what is generally recommended is to get creative with screen saver settings, which are **User Configuration** settings. If you configure the following four GPO settings, you will effectively create the same behavior as the **Computer Config** machine inactivity limit timeout setting, but this policy will take effect based on user accounts rather than computer accounts:

User Configuration | Policies | Administrative Templates | Control Panel | Personalization Enable screen saver = Enabled

Force specific screen saver = Use this to define which screen saver you want to run Screen saver timeout = Enabled and set to 900 seconds

Password protect the screen saver = Enabled

Linking GPOs accordingly

As you seek out GPO configurations to put into place in your environment, sometimes you will find you have no choice between computer or user configuration, as some options will only exist in one location or the other. Other times, you will find that the settings you are putting into place could be configured from either place, and the decision of how to best set the GPO depends upon which level you want the GPO settings to apply.

This decision ties in directly with the location to which you are going to link this GPO! If your GPO contains **Computer Configuration** settings, those settings can only apply to computer objects and so that GPO would need to be linked to OUs that contain computer objects, or linked at the domain level, of course, which covers all OUs.

Vice versa is also true; if your new GPO contains only **User Configuration** settings, that GPO is only going to apply to user objects, and any links you create for that GPO should be links to OUs that contain the user objects to which you want the GPO to apply.

You may have already figured this out, but it is generally best practice to create GPOs as either computer-based GPOs or user-based GPOs. A single GPO can contain a lot of different settings, and if that GPO is linked at a high enough tier, it might indeed be able to apply both user and computer configuration settings all from within a single GPO. But this makes for a higher administrative burden on that single GPO, and it is typically considered best practice for any GPO to contain only **Computer Configuration** settings or **User Configuration** settings. Try not to mix the two.

Group Policy loopback processing

There is a special function inside GPOs that essentially blends computer and user configuration together, to be used in special cases: namely, if you have the requirement to push **User Configuration** settings to particular computers but want those computers to treat them as if they were **Computer Configuration** settings, applying the same policy settings to *any* user who was to log in to that computer.

Maybe Laura in HR has a certain set of policies on her everyday workstation, but also occasionally logs into a public kiosk workstation sitting in the lobby. You have a set of lockdown restrictions that are applied to that kiosk, but since it is domain-joined, normally, when Laura logs into the kiosk, Group Policy would treat it just like it was her own workstation and apply all of the same user-based GPO settings. If you create a **User Configuration** GPO that has loopback policy processing enabled and link the GPO to this kiosk workstation, it will now apply all of those special configurations to Laura, even though she does not receive these GPO settings on her regular computer. If Laura were to log in to this kiosk and have access to sensitive documents based on her standard login policies, you would probably want to stop that from happening when she logs in to this public access kiosk workstation, just as one example of where this might be useful. Another scenario where loopback processing is commonly used is when working with Remote Desktop servers and using GPOs to apply settings to all users who log into an RDSH.

For more detail on loopback processing, I will once again direct you to the *Summary* section at the end of this chapter, where I'll refer you to a great location for learning more on this topic.

Policy versus preference

There is an important distinction that every Group Policy administrator needs to understand about GPO settings. There are two different types of policy settings, and they behave very differently. Now that we understand the differences between **Computer Configuration** and **User Configuration**, the next tier you'll notice inside **Group Policy Management Editor** are sub-folders titled **Policies** and **Preferences**.

Policies

Managed policies, the items listed under the **Policies** section of both computer and user configurations, generally behave like true gentlemen. These are settings that you put into place and expect results, forcing the setting into place, and nothing the user tries to do can change them. When reversing course and removing a GPO from a system, they happily comply. What do I mean by that? When you plug some policy settings into a GPO and then link that GPO to a location, you expect those settings to be put into place on the machines or users to which you have filtered the GPO. And that indeed works for any GPO setting, whether policy or preference, managed or unmanaged. But what about when that GPO no longer applies to a user or machine? What if you delete the GPO link, or adjust security filtering on the GPO so that it no longer applies to a workstation? Do those settings continue to be applied, or are they actively removed?

The answer to that question depends on whether you are working with a policy or a preference. Policy items will actively remove themselves from a computer when a GPO no longer applies. This is true of most built-in configuration settings inside Group Policy. Technically, under the hood, what is really happening is that Group Policy monitors four special sections of the Windows Registry and reprocesses all of them during Group Policy refresh cycles. All GPO settings that affect these areas of the registry are capable of self-removal. Unmanaged policy settings, even some of those listed beneath the `Policies` folder, could potentially fail to remove their settings when a GPO is unlinked. It just depends on what setting you are talking about and what it is manipulating on the client machines to make the change.

Technically, there are managed policies and unmanaged policies – and both of these things are outside the scope of Group Policy preferences, which we will discuss next.

Preferences

Policies force things to happen, no matter what the user wants. Preferences, on the other hand, are often reversible by the user. Preferences are a good way to configure settings that will make life easier for the user, but you need to ultimately be OK with the fact that those changes and settings could be changed again manually by your users. Some GPO settings exist inside both policies and preferences, and this is your deciding factor—do you want to allow users to manipulate and change the configuration, or always force it into place?

Preferences are also sticky! While most policy settings will self-remove when a GPO stops applying to a computer, preferences do not. This is very important to understand when deleting GPOs or GPO links. Group Policy preferences do not live in those special sections of the registry that we talked about earlier, and so Windows does not actively rescan those settings to find out whether they should continue to apply. When a GPO puts a preference setting into place, even though the user could adjust that setting if they wanted to, removal of the GPO will *not* revert the computer to its original, default state. The GPO preference setting will hang around and continue to apply to the machine even after the GPO is long gone. To change a preference setting back to defaults, the user will either have to adjust it themselves, or you will need to push out a new GPO that accomplishes that reversal.

Default Domain Policy

Throughout this chapter, we have bounced in and out of the GPMC a number of times, and now that you know what a GPO looks like and how to identify GPO links, you have probably noticed a GPO linked to the root of the domain called **Default Domain Policy**. This GPO comes built in with Group Policy. Every environment has one unless an admin has taken steps to delete it, which I would not recommend.

The Default Domain Policy applies to every user and computer that is part of your domain directory. Since this GPO is completely enabled right off the bat and applies to everyone, it is commonplace for companies to edit this default policy to enforce global password policies or security rules that need to apply to everyone. In fact, many who are unfamiliar with Group Policy and uncomfortable with creating, linking, and filtering their own GPOs will just continually throw more and more settings in the Default Domain Policy. There are even many blog posts about creating GPO settings that instruct you to edit the Default Domain Policy.

All of these settings will apply successfully, of course—to *all* users on *all* machines, including servers in your network. Eventually, this mentality is going to come back and bite hard.

My general rule is to never touch the Default Domain Policy except for one reason—creating global password expiry and complexity requirements within your domain. In fact, in some cases, not even a password policy is appropriate for the Default Domain Policy. As an example, say you wanted to create a fine-grained password policy that comes with some additional bells and whistles, such as the ability to require different password criteria for some users compared to others. We will cover fine-grained password policies in *Chapter 10, Hardening and Security*, so for the time being, let's stick with the idea that we want to create one password policy and apply it to everyone. This seems like a good example to walk through, and remember, if you find yourself heading into the Default Domain Policy to do anything other than password management, you're probably doing it wrong. Just create your own GPO, for crying out loud!

With any GPO that you see in the management console, if you right-click on that GPO and then choose **Edit…** you will see a new window open, and this GPO editor contains all of the internals of that policy. This is where you handle any settings or configurations that you want to be a part of that particular GPO. So, go ahead and edit **Default Domain Policy** and then navigate to **Computer Configuration | Policies | Windows Settings | Security Settings | Account Policies | Password Policy:**

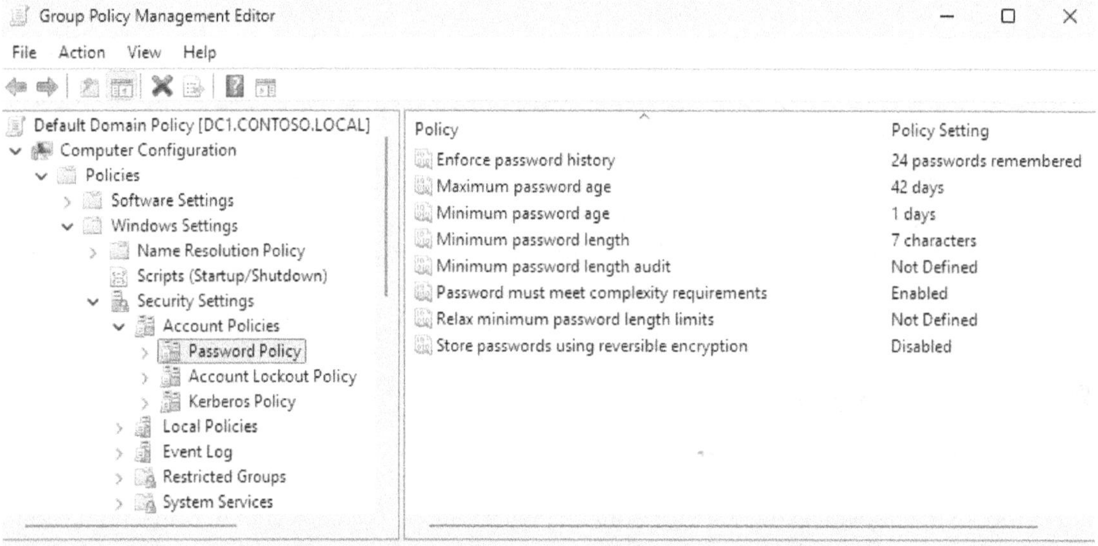

Figure 5.21: Password settings in Default Domain Policy

Here, you can see the list of settings that currently comprise **Password Policy** within your domain. These settings are out-of-the-box behavior for a brand new Windows Server environment, and are currently active in my environment, even though I took no intentional steps to enable them. Double-clicking on any of these settings allows you to modify them, and that change immediately starts to take effect on all of your domain-joined computers in the network. For example, you can see that the default minimum password length is set to 7 characters. Most companies have already worked through discussions about their written policy on the standard length of passwords in the network, and in order to set up your new directory infrastructure to accept your decision, you simply modify this field.

Changing the minimum password length to 14 characters here would immediately require the change to be made for all user accounts the next time they reset their passwords.

It's worth repeating: while the Default Domain Policy is a very quick and easy way to get some settings configured and pushed out to everyone, tread carefully when making changes to this default policy. Every time you make a setting change here, remember that it is going to affect everyone in your domain, including yourself. Many times, you will be creating policies that do not need to apply to everyone. In those cases, it is highly recommended that you stay away from the Default Domain Policy. Instead, set up a new GPO for accomplishing whatever task it is that you are trying to put into place.

Administrative Templates

Go ahead and edit a GPO, any GPO, so that you have **Group Policy Management Editor** open in front of you. Expand the **Policies** folder for either **Computer Configuration**, **User Configuration**, or both, and you will notice a folder inside each called **Administrative Templates**. Most of us generally think of **Administrative Templates** the same as any other GPO configuration setting—simply a collection of items with which you can manipulate users or computers, right? Sort of, but while **Software Settings** and **Windows Settings** are built into Group Policy and are basically the same for any domain environment, **Administrative Templates** is customizable.

Administrative Templates showcases the flexibility of Group Policy. Each setting within **Administrative Templates** is pulled from template files that reside on your domain controller servers. These template files are ADMX files. All of the information needed to display the setting inside **Group Policy Management Editor** is contained inside these ADMX files. This information includes the different selectable options, any drop-down boxes that need to be displayed, and what the description fields will say when an admin double-clicks on the policy setting.

Along with each ADMX file comes an accompanying ADML file. This is a language file that is used to define the language for the settings contained within the ADMX file.

Back in Windows XP (and earlier) days, these file types did not exist. Settings inside **Administrative Templates** were based on ADM files instead. Nobody should be running Windows XP anymore, except I know that some of you are, because I still touch Windows XP machines for some customers at least once a month. So I figured I would include that info as an FYI. Sidenote: get rid of your Windows XP computers!

Windows 7 and newer know how to work with ADMX/ADML files, so I'm going to assume that your environment is fully up to date. Hopefully that means you don't even have any unsupported Windows 7 or Windows 8 machines hanging around, but...

Implementing ADMX/ADML files

There are two reasons why you might find yourself monkeying around with ADMX files. The first is when moving to a newer version of Windows Server in your environment. Each release of the operating system—2012, 2012R2, 2016, 2019, 2022, 2025—comes with some new and updated Group Policy settings. When you install your first domain controller of a newer flavor in your environment, the installation will generally run through a process called ADPrep. This process prepares the Active Directory schema for the new operating system and also populates the new Group Policy settings. However, there are times when the first new release operating system you are introducing to the environment is not a domain controller. In this case, Group Policy won't be updated with new settings, but what if you wanted those new settings to be available within Group Policy anyway? Manually copying ADMX/ADML files into place could satisfy that need.

The second and most common reason to plug new ADMX/ADML files into place manually is when a software vendor, often Microsoft itself, releases custom ADMX files. These files, when installed in Active Directory, will provide new settings inside Group Policy that don't exist natively inside Windows Server. Let's try it right now!

Google Chrome (did I just say those words in a Microsoft book???) is one of the most popular web browsers on the planet. The centralized configuration of Chrome is something that many administrators struggle with. What may or may not be news to you is that Google has its own set of ADMX files! You can plug these files into Group Policy and utilize Google-defined settings directly from within the GPMC to push Chrome-related configurations out to your workforce.

First, we need to download these files. At the time of writing, this link will do the trick: `https://dl.google.com/dl/edgedl/chrome/policy/policy_templates.zip`.

If you are unable to use that link, simply perform a web search for `download chrome admx files` and you should be able to find it.

Copy these files to your domain controller and extract them so that you can find the ADMX and ADML files; they should be inside a folder called `windows`. The couple of ADMX files are located right there inside a subfolder called `admx`, and the ADML files will be grouped into folders by language. This matches what we will find inside Group Policy in just a minute. Now that you have the files in hand, go ahead and open the following folder on the domain controller:

```
%systemroot%\PolicyDefinitions
```

(On most servers, this will be `C:\Windows\PolicyDefinitions`.)

In *Figure 5.22*, you can see my Chrome files that have been downloaded, alongside the **PolicyDefinitions** folder. As you can also see, there are already numerous ADMX files inside **PolicyDefinitions**, as expected. These ADMX files are the reason that we have any settings currently inside Group Policy, under the **Administrative Templates** folders:

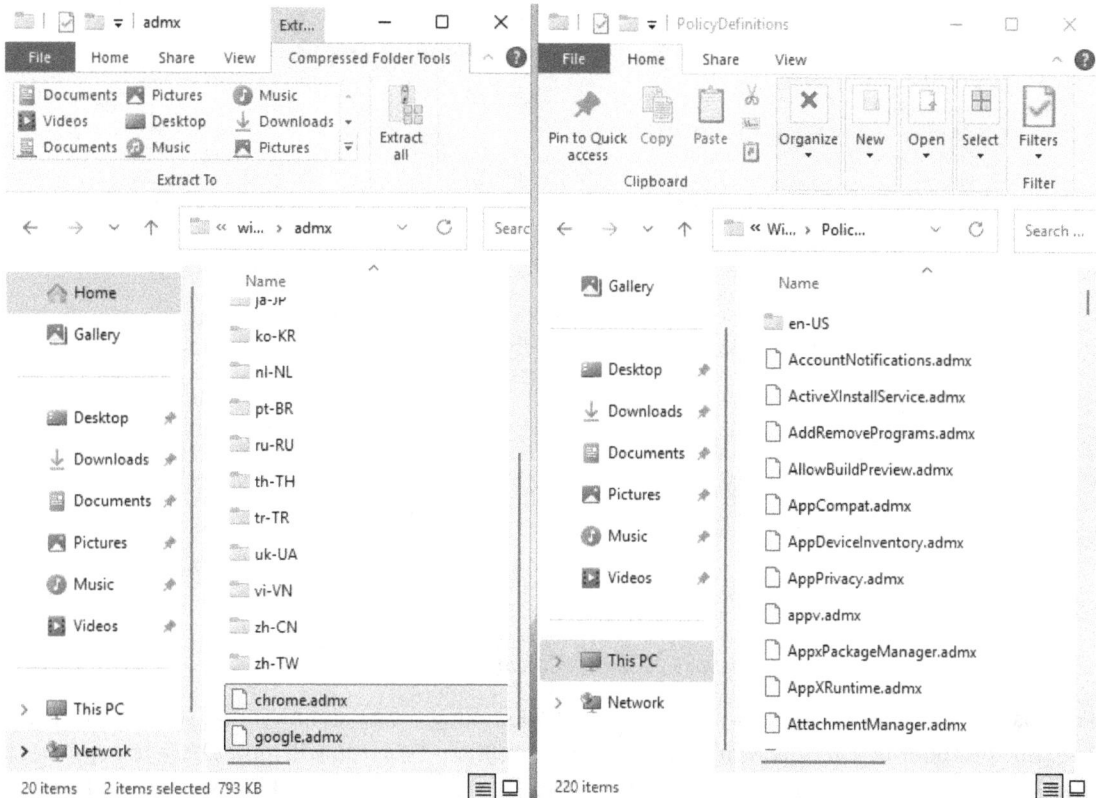

Figure 5.22: Copying new ADMX files to the domain controller

Simply copy your new Chrome ADMX files into **PolicyDefinitions**, and then copy the accompanying language ADML language file from its folder into the corresponding language folder inside **PolicyDefinitions**. That's it! As evidenced in my screenshot and the text you are reading, I am working within the context of US English, so I only need to copy the ADML files from within the en-US folder to the en-US folder that already exists inside PolicyDefinitions. There is no need to copy languages other than the one already existing on your server's hard drive. If you now close and reopen GPMC, take another look inside **Administrative Templates** to find some new Google Chrome settings!

There are tons of them in here, all from those two little ADMX files:

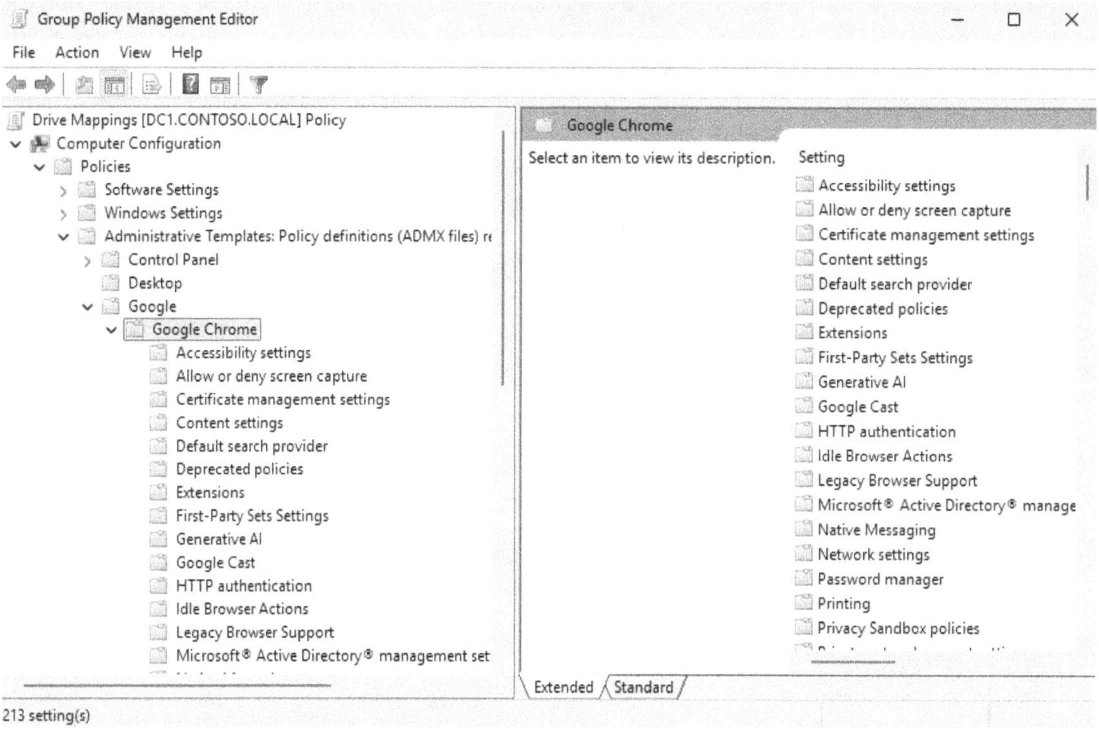

Figure 5.23: Google Chrome GPO settings

For this example, I am working with my test lab and making the assumption that you have a single domain controller in your environment. If you have multiple DCs, you will either have to copy these files into `%systemroot%\PolicyDefinitions` on each of your domain controller servers or continue reading the next section of this chapter to learn more about the Central Store.

The Central Store

When opening the GPMC and creating or editing a GPO, the settings available within your console session are settings pulled from ADMX/ADML files that are on the hard drive of the computer or server from which you are using the GPMC. When implementing new settings via ADMX files, it would be a huge chore to have to copy those new files into place on every one of your domain controllers, in addition to all of the client computers where you might have the RSAT tools installed. Thankfully, there is a solution to automate this for you!

The Central Store is something that can be enabled in Active Directory that allows the replication of ADMX/ADML files. Once you enable the Central Store, all of your Group Policy management machines, such as domain controllers, will look to the store as their repository for these template files.

Enabling the Central Store

All that it takes to enable the Central Store in Active Directory is the creation of two folders inside a special folder called **SYSVOL**. Once created, the GPMC will check this location on subsequent launches and pull in any new ADMX/ADML files that have been added. Log in to a domain controller server, and create the following new folder:

```
%systemroot%\SYSVOL\sysvol\contoso.local\Policies\PolicyDefinitions
```

Create an additional folder within your new **PolicyDefinitions** folder to contain language-specific ADML files. In my case, I need one for English, such as the following:

```
%systemroot%\SYSVOL\sysvol\contoso.local\Policies\PolicyDefinitions\en-US
```

Obviously, you'll want to replace contoso.local with your own internal domain name, and you're finished! As soon as you have created these two new folders, utilize this location from now on to copy in new ADMX and ADML files, and those new settings will show up from wherever you launch GPMC in the future.

Populating the Central Store

You probably didn't have an immediate reason to check inside one of your GPOs and find out what the **Administrative Templates** folder looks like now that we have enabled the Central Store, but let's go ahead and do that now. Open GPMC and edit any of your existing GPOs. Take a look inside one of the **Administrative Templates** folders, and it's empty! Yikes! You'll also notice that the name of the **Administrative Templates** folder has now changed to reflect the fact that it is looking to the Central Store for this information: **Administrative Templates: Policy definitions (ADMX files) retrieved from the central store.**

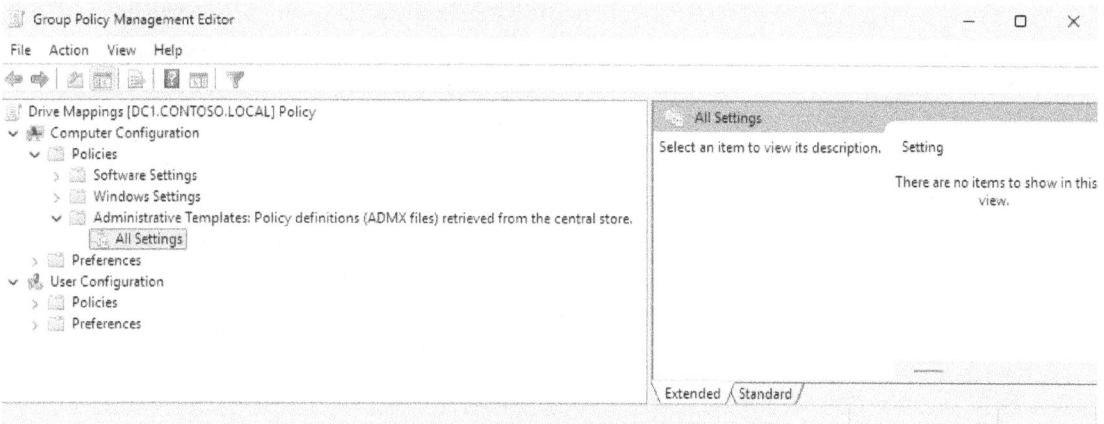

Figure 5.24: The Administrative Templates folder is empty!

Give us our settings back! Thankfully, they are still sitting on the hard drive of your domain controller, in the same location where we added the new Google settings just a few minutes ago. Perform the following file-copy jobs, and you should be back in business with all settings now stored inside the Central Store.

Copy `%systemroot%\PolicyDefinitions` to `%systemroot%\SYSVOL\sysvol\contoso.local\Policies\PolicyDefinitions`.

Copy `%systemroot%\PolicyDefinitions\en-US` to `%systemroot%\SYSVOL\sysvol\contoso.local\Policies\PolicyDefinitions\en-US` (adjust accordingly for whichever languages you need):

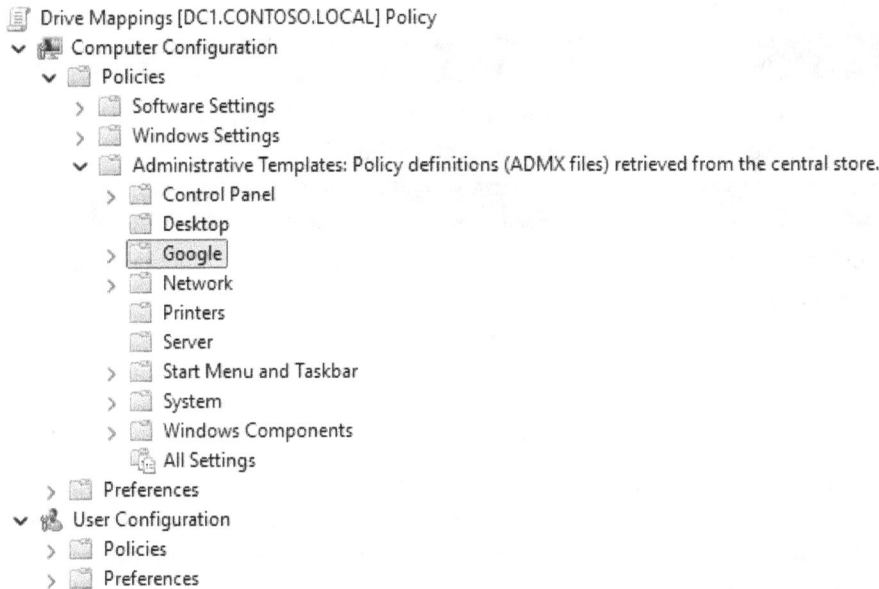

Figure 5.25: The Central Store is now populated with settings

As you can see, the **Administrative Templates** folder is still pulling from the Central Store, but following our file copies, the Central Store is now populated with ADMX files and settings to utilize inside a GPO. The Central Store is now available to all domain controllers in your environment, because **SYSVOL** is one of a few special folders that are automatically replicated among all Domain Controller servers in a domain, and what we have done today is simply make use of that replication.

Summary

Group Policy is an incredibly powerful tool to have at your disposal when working within a domain environment. Many pre-built configurations and settings exist, and as you have seen, some are being used whether you realize it or not, due to them being configured inside the Default Domain Policy. Because Group Policy even has the power to manipulate the registry on client machines, the sky is pretty much the limit on what you can manage on your client computers via GPOs.

Some of the most common ways I see Group Policy utilized are automatic drive mappings, printer installations, desktop personalizations, centralized security standards, and password management. Additionally, it can be used to push out RDS security policies, to lock down kiosk stations, to automatically install applications, and so much more. Group Policy is even commonly used to assist companies who are on cloud migration paths, through things such as centralized OneDrive administration.

As is the case with many topics in Windows Server, there is so much information related to Group Policy that it warrants a book of its own. Thankfully, I had the opportunity to do exactly that! If you are interested in discovering more about Group Policy and all of the ways that it can be used to secure your infrastructure, check out my title *Mastering Windows Group Policy* (`https://www.packtpub.com/en-us/product/mastering-windows-group-policy-9781789345438`).

Questions

Put your knowledge to the test with the following questions. If you need a hand (or just want to double-check), you'll find all the answers in the *Appendix* section of the book.

1. Are screensaver settings computer or user configuration?

2. Do domain-level or OU-level links process first?

3. What is the special GPO setting that forces user settings to apply to any user on a given computer?

4. What type of GPO filtering do you configure inside the GPO itself, such as with a mapped network drives policy?

5. True or False? It is possible for a user to override a Group Policy preference.

6. What is the default timer between Group Policy background refresh cycles?

7. What kind of GPO filtering could be utilized to assign settings only to laptop computers?

8. If you find a USB stick on the ground labeled "CEO financials," what should you do with it?

9. Bonus question: What is the name of Microsoft's cloud-based technology that provides some of the same functionality as Group Policy, but specifically for Entra-joined computers?

Unlock this book's exclusive benefits now

UNLOCK NOW

Scan this QR code or go to `https://packtpub.com/unlock`, then search for this book by name.

Note: Keep your purchase invoice ready before you start.

6

File Management

Everyone loves a good library, am I right? There's no sense of accomplishment quite like mastering the Dewey decimal system and inhaling layers of dust before discovering the content you seek. It's almost like being in an Indiana Jones movie, without the rolling boulder. While you may not share a passion for books in quite the same way as my homeschooling family, my attempt at a segue here is that every business I have ever worked with quickly builds up its own library-esque mountain of data. The way you have built your organizational structure for housing such digital volumes of data makes all the difference in whether or not this information is easily accessible to those who need it. In this chapter, I would like to take time to discuss another core narrative in the world of server administration—file management. While you may not be the person authoring all of this data and perhaps couldn't care less about the content, make no mistake that you are the party responsible for keeping it safe, secure, and accessible. Follow along as we dig into the following topics:

- Data is a company's lifeblood
- File shares
- Automated drive mappings
- File permissions
- Distributed File System (DFS)
- File Transfer Protocol (FTP)
- SMB over QUIC

Data is a company's lifeblood

A large portion of Microsoft's success tracks back to Office applications. Microsoft Word and Excel are so universally used, and have been for so long, that they have been common household names for much of my life. Even though many of us wish that it would simply go away at this point, email is integral to the way that we live and work. When email became popular and companies needed to decide on how to best house that information, they didn't have to turn their attention very far before realizing that Outlook was sitting right there, next to Word and Excel, waiting to be used. There are always naysayers about every globally adopted application, but the easy truth is that Word, Excel, and

Outlook are by far the most prevalent platforms with which the world creates documents, spreadsheets, and email communications. All these things are valuable data that you cannot simply leave to fate by allowing users to store it on their local computers.

Communication, processes, documentation, intellectual property, and papers of legalese. Words are powerful; words shape our entire existence. Why do I own my house? This piece of paper declares it. Why do I have a job? My employer and I signed these documents, stating the arrangement into existence. What stops someone from simply walking away with another person's property? The law, written into action and then upheld by people sharing this common ideology. This idea is fascinating, that words put down on paper can easily become legally binding, and thereby shape or reshape the world that we live in.

No matter what industry you are part of, you create words that matter. You create data that matters, and it would be harmful to your business to lose or have to re-create that data. This statement reminds me of a company that I recently worked with. This is a fairly small company that maintains, like so many in the manufacturing industry, very low standards for IT infrastructure. The amount of money spent on machinery and buildings in these places is usually quite high, and by all appearances, this is a business that prides itself on providing great products and understands what it takes to do that successfully, which is great! As with most modern CNC, lathe, and milling machinery, large and time-consuming CAD data accompanies every single project and part that is created by this company. Indeed, looking under the hood here exposed more than 8 TB of engineering files. The good news is that these files are, for the most part, spread out across only two separate network drive mappings, meaning that the ability for employees to find the data they are looking for was actually quite good. However, digging further into the server infrastructure supporting these files, we quickly found a house of cards. Everything, every single piece of that data, resides on a single physical server running Windows Server 2012R2 (hey, can't knock that it's been running successfully for more than a decade), with a single Veeam license that backs up the server to a USB drive once per day. Does that drive get swapped out and rotated off-site? No. Does it sync to the cloud somewhere? No. Was anybody even checking the backups? No...

Oh. My. Word. This is literally a disaster waiting to happen. The loss of this engineering data would cripple this business, very possibly to the point of no return. Now, this is not a chapter about backups, though we will discuss that later in the book. This is a chapter about data, and I hope the story illustrates how easy it is to take your data for granted, not understanding that, in many situations, it is quite literally the one thing that you cannot afford to mismanage. Let's dive in together to find out what file management opportunities exist inside Windows Server today.

File shares

The most common way for users at a company to open, save, and otherwise interact with company files is through traditional drive mappings. Anyone who has worked a helpdesk for any amount of time is very familiar with words such as "I can't get to my `K: drive`," "I seem to have lost connection to my `T: drive`," or "I'm working from home today and can't get to my `S: drive`." Offering up file shares on your file servers so that users can map drive letters to them is File Management 101, and an essential baseline to cover for anybody who touches file servers.

Once established, tapping a user's computer into a server-sourced file share can be accomplished in many ways, and we will look at some of those soon. Before you get to the point of mapping client computers, first, we need to create a file server and designate space to house those drive mappings. Where do we begin?

The role

As with any Windows Server purpose in life, there is an accompanying role in Windows to get the job done. It is possible to create folders and share those folders on any Windows computer in the world, whether officially a "file server" or not, and so file sharing is unique in that it does not *require* a role to be installed to be able to share files and folders. There is still an accompanying **File Server** role that can be installed, which provides additional tools and prioritizations inside Windows for your servers that are intentionally going to be file servers. Go ahead and install that role called **File Server**, and take note of how many sub-roles exist that are related to file and storage services, some of which we will utilize throughout this chapter.

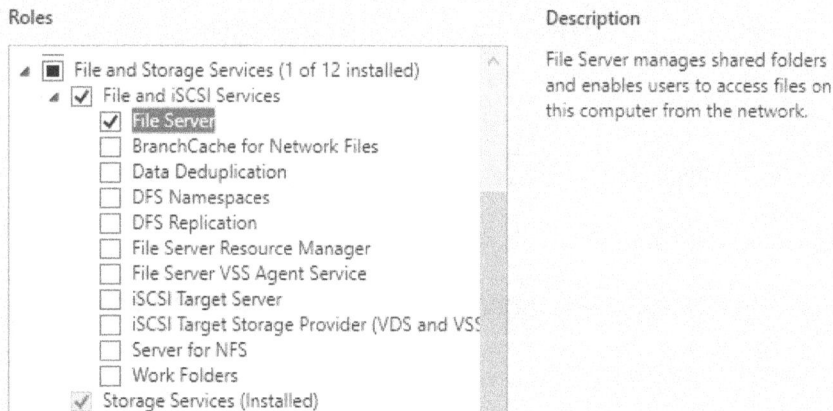

Figure 6.1: Installing the File Server role

Defining storage space

This may seem like a no-brainer, but your files need to be stored *somewhere*. This *somewhere* could be any folder location on your file server, but I mention it here because this is a very important step, and worthy of spending a few minutes thinking about. Is it possible to create a simple folder such as C:\Shares and start immediately sharing space from it? Sure. Is that very smart? Not in my opinion.

If possible—and in the world of VMs, it should be easily possible—plan for your file shares to sit on a volume that is separate from your operating system. Creating shares from the C: volume will inter-mix your user data with operating system data and create a lot of potential for problems later. What if your user documents cause the C: drive to run out of space? You could cause Windows to fall on itself, and the whole file server could stop working. What if a Windows Update needs to install itself on C:, because that is where Windows is running, and causes your file shares to be out of space? What if you somehow expand file share permissions too broadly, perhaps accidentally, and now users have the ability to browse around inside Windows system files on C:? There are so many reasons never to create file shares on C:, and instead install a separate hard disk, or at the very least a separate volume, for the purpose of keeping file shares.

On my FS01 server, which is a VM, I simply added a second virtual hard disk to this VM.

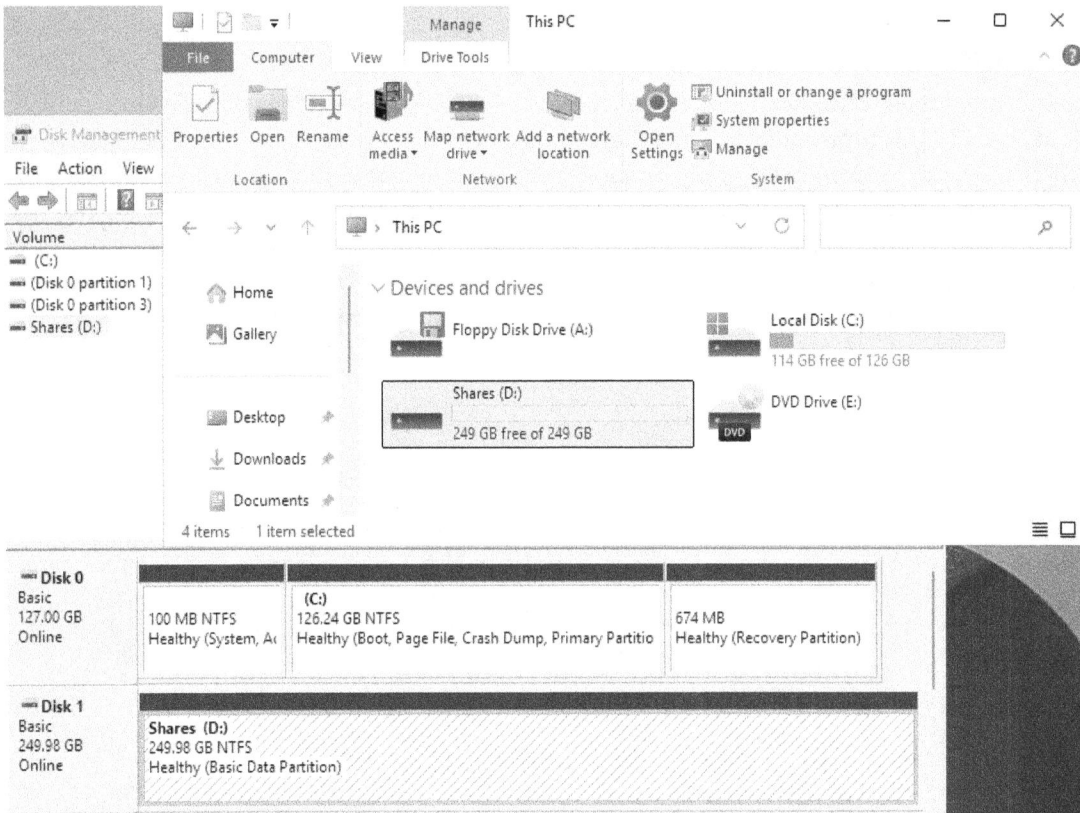

Figure 6.2: Creating a new disk for file sharing

This second disk is the D: drive on my server, and I am going to use it to store all the file shares for my business.

Planning carefully

As we flow through the configuration of my test lab, you will notice that I like to keep shared folders at a top-root level. I have created my D: volume to store folders that are going to be shared, and the folders that I plan to turn into shares are all going to sit directly inside the root of D:. It is absolutely possible to share folders from any location in Windows. For example, I could take the D:\Accounting\Payroll\ Documents\JobDescriptions folder and create a share that is simply called "Job Descriptions", and then share it with anybody who needs to see or contribute to our company's job posting information. I *could* do this, but it's risky business!

In the preceding scenario, it would be so, so easy to accidentally provide the wrong users with access to payroll information, because you are giving them permissions to access folders within the same file path. There are successful ways to create such a scenario, but it is never worth the risk. I have worked way too many tickets in my life where a customer has discovered that Sally has access to private CEO or HR files that she should definitely not have access to, only to find that somebody created a location for those "private" files in a place that would be almost impossible to keep safe and secure long-term.

Be very careful when planning your file shares, and don't allow a user's request to steamroll good planning. I find it a good rule to *never* create a file share in a subfolder location. If a new share is needed, put it directly in the root of the drive, alongside all of your other shares. This mentality will make your information more secure and much easier to administer long-term.

Creating shares

Call to action! Let's create some shares. I will be creating file shares on my FS01 server, upon which I have added a second virtual hard disk to use for the purpose of file shares and data storage, and I have installed the **File Server** role as we discussed. Since I have set myself up for success and have a brand new volume dedicated to file shares, I am going to plan from the very beginning for each share to have its own root folder inside my D: volume. It makes sense in my organization for each department to have a dedicated share where other departments do not have access, and also a general shared space where all groups and departments can swap content. I have created the following folders:

- `D:\Accounting`
- `D:\HR`
- `D:\IT`
- `D:\Marketing`
- `D:\Sales`
- `D:\Public`

Each of these folders will be individually shared so that only members of the corresponding department have access to them. The process for sharing each of these folders is simple. Right-click on the folder and navigate to **Properties**. Inside **Properties**, visit the **Sharing** tab. There are two buttons on this screen: either basic or advanced setup of your share. I recommend using **Advanced Sharing...** which provides the most options.

Inside **Advanced Sharing,** check the **Share this folder** box, and here you can adjust **Share name** if necessary. This is a good function to point out. Even though my physical folder is called `Accounting`, I could name my share something completely different, such as `Secret FBI Files`—just an example. Here is a screenshot encompassing all of the steps we have taken so far to create these folders and the process for sharing them.

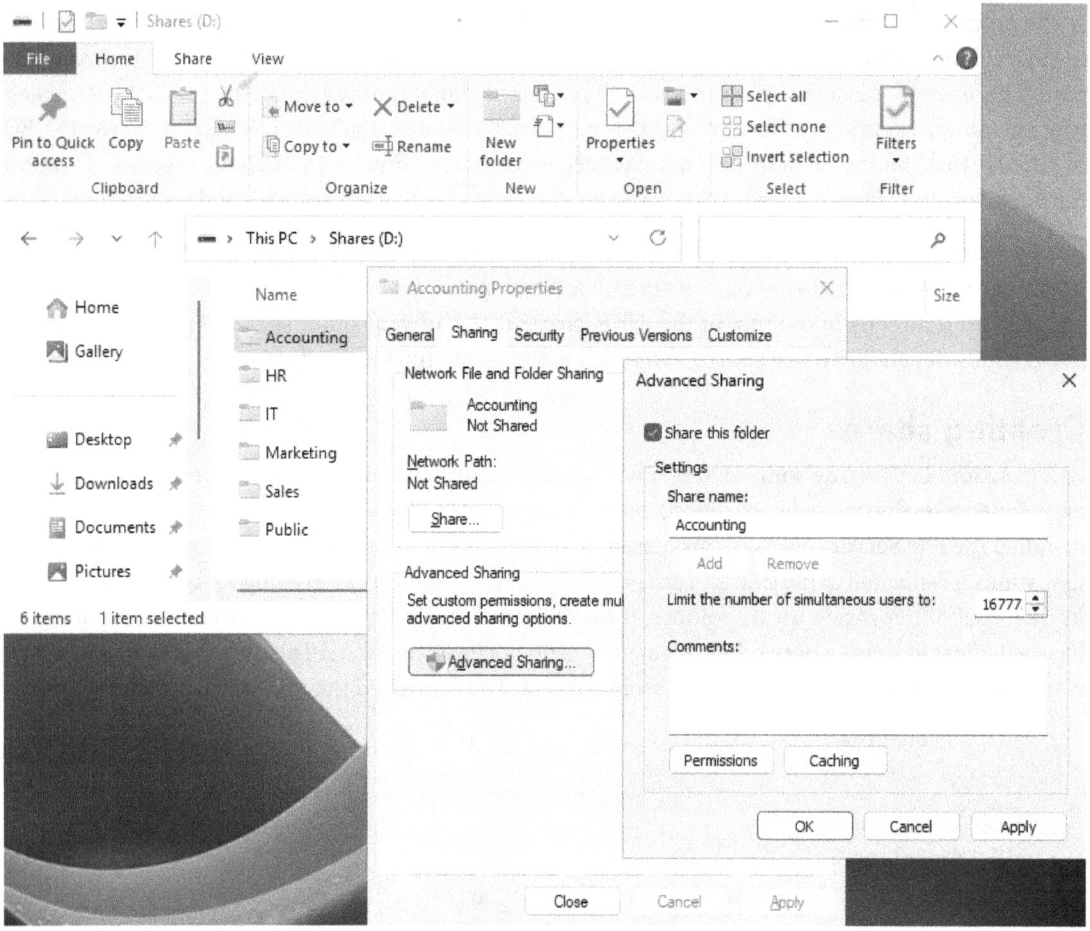

Figure 6.3: Creating a file share

Share permissions

We will talk more extensively about file permissions in an upcoming section of this chapter, but right here on our sharing screen, we also have a **Permissions** button. What's that all about? There are two tiers to permissions whenever accessing a Windows Server-based file share, and it is very important to understand that both exist and in which order they apply. When any user accesses any share, they will first be allowed or disallowed based on share permissions, which is the button we are currently looking at. Then, once they have passed the test to get into the share, they will again be allowed or disallowed based on security permissions.

It is general practice to keep share permissions broad and then create nitty-gritty permissions using the **Security** tab. "Broad" could mean a couple of different things. If you only expect users who have **Domain User** accounts to be accessing this file share, you could set up share permissions so that all members of Domain User have **Full Control** access. That is quite broad and may seem scary, but re-member that we will have the opportunity in a few minutes to make our permissions more granular at the **Security** tab level. Another common way to set up share permissions is to use the built-in group called **Everyone,** and give that group **Full Control** access. What is the difference between **Everyone** and **Domain** users? **Everyone** allows essentially anything through the door. This would include non-domain-joined computers or devices as well. This may come in handy if you have any machinery that needs access to files, such as a CNC machine on a shop floor, or a printer/scanner that may be trying to reach into the file share to store scanned documents.

Although it seems like a terrible idea from a security perspective, the most common way to set up file share permissions is to set **Everyone** to **Full Control,** then decide on the permissions you really want later, when we talk about file permissions. Here is an example of how I am going to configure all of my shares on FS01 at a sharing permission level.

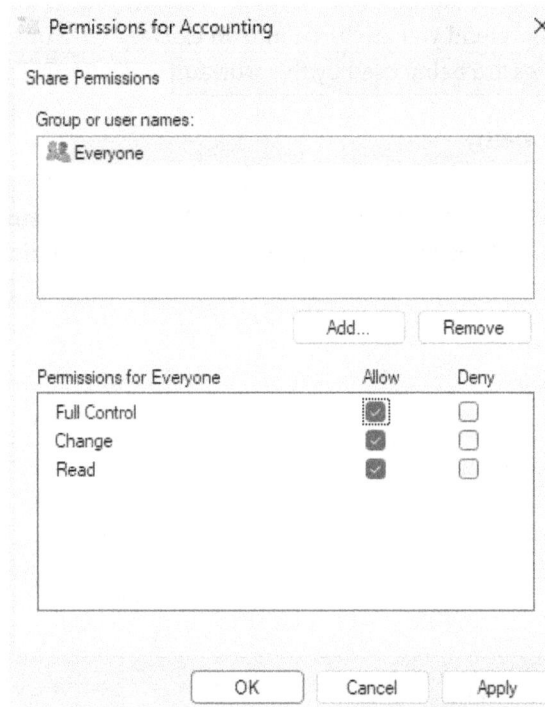

Figure 6.4: Common setup for share permissions

Even after reading this text, you may be tempted to narrow your share permissions only to provide access for those people who really need it. That is fine, but I can tell you from experience that it is unnecessary and creates a lot of troubleshooting headaches down the road. I have helped engineers numerous times to troubleshoot scenarios where certain users could not access certain files or folders on their file server. The engineer had racked their brain, mowing up and down through file permissions, and simply could not find any reason why access was being denied. Of course, you now know that they probably overlooked these share-level permissions completely. It's easy to forget that these permissions even exist, especially when working in an environment where your shares have been around and static for 10 years or more.

However you decide to set up permissions for your shares, keep these things in mind. My favorite way to handle them is to always go with **Everyone** = **Full Control** on the share level, and then granularize permissions inside the **Security** tab, to which we have a section dedicated in just a few pages.

Discovering shares

We have some folders stored in a strategic location on FS01, and each of them has been shared. Great! Now what? Before we get into creating permanent mappings to these shares from client computers, I wanted to point out a quick way to discover what shares are visible on any given server, without needing to know the names of those shares. The tasks we are about to walk through are tools that will come in handy hundreds or even thousands of times throughout your IT career, if you aren't already using them regularly. Let's pretend you are hired into an existing environment, and are now tasked with discovering what shares are being used by this workforce.

Computer Management

If you are already logged into the file server, discovering all file shares present on this system is easily accomplished by right-clicking on the **Start** button and launching **Computer Management**. Once inside, expand **System Tools** > **Shared Folders** > **Shares**. Here, you will quickly find any folder that is shared on this machine.

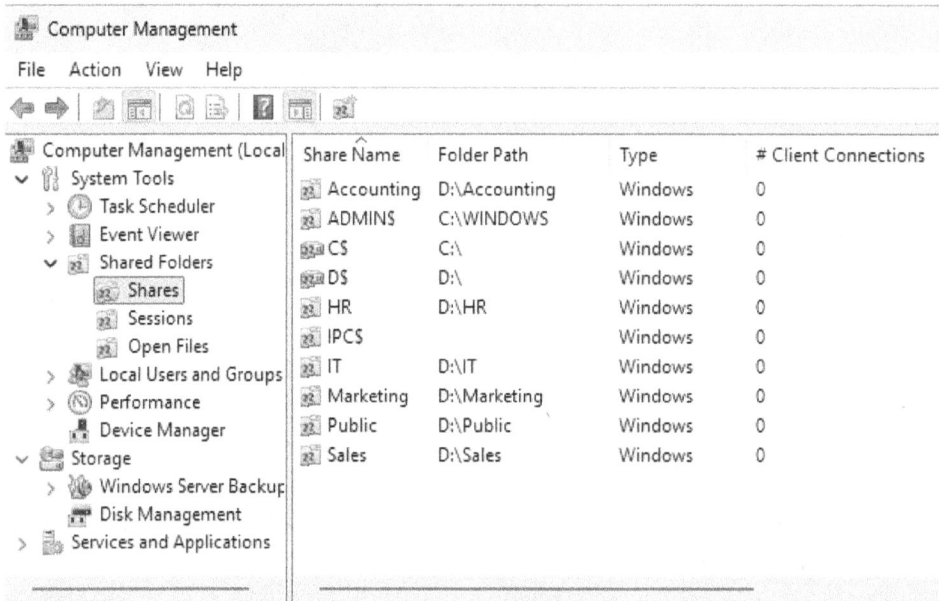

Figure 6.5: Using Computer Management to view active shares

You may notice one or more shares that end with **$**. These are still valid folders that are shared from this machine, but they are not visible via a public query of the server. Anytime you want to "share" a folder, but keep visibility of that share away from the general population, simply create the share name of your folder with a **$** at the end of the name.

In the next section, we will pull a public query of FS01 to find out what shares it is presenting to the outside world, and you will notice that my C$, D$, IPC$, and ADMIN$ shares are not visible. Yet, if I knew that insider information and mapped a connection directly to \\FS01\C$, it would work.

Backslash-Backslash (\\)

Now let's attempt to discover shares that exist on FS01, without even logging into that server. This can be a really useful task when exploring an environment for which you do not have unfettered access to log directly into servers, or just a quicker way to remind yourself of a share mapping without having to reference the server or documentation. From any machine within your network, simply open **File Explorer** and type \\SERVERNAME into the address bar. In my test lab, I am logged into my WIN10 computer and am navigating to \\FS01.

This action queries the FS01 server for any shares that it is presenting. In *Figure 6.6*, you'll notice all of the departmental shares that we created a few minutes ago, and there is even a printer being shared from here! I added that printer and shared it from FS01 for the purpose of showing this capability—whenever you are sitting in front of a workstation and want to map to something on a server, whether it be a file share or a printer, \\SERVERNAME is often the quickest way to find what you are looking for.

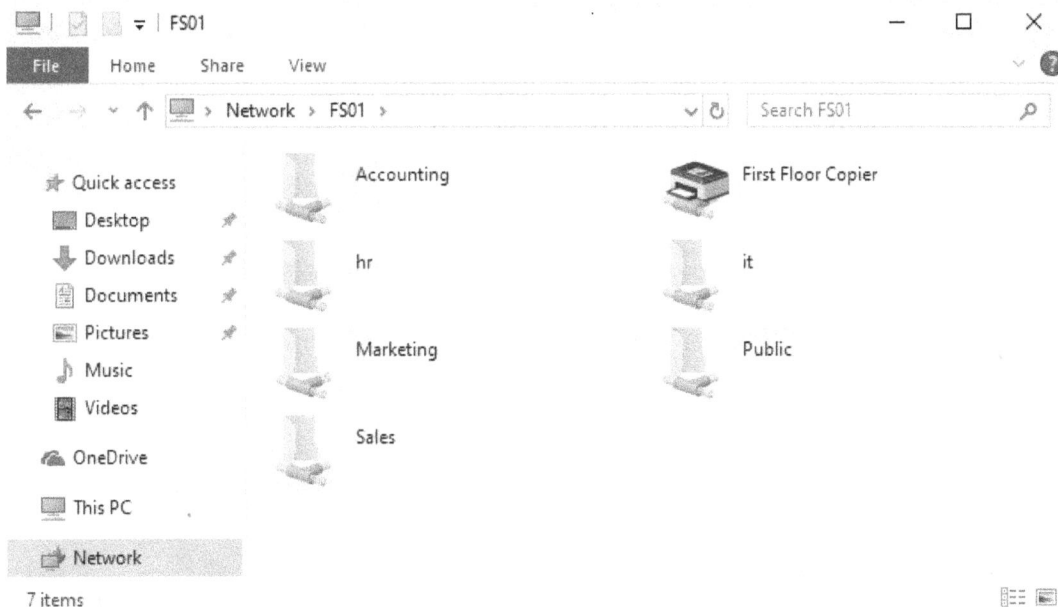

Figure 6.6: Querying FS01 for shared items

It would be entirely possible to train your users so that, each time they need to access information inside a file share, they open **File Explorer** and contact the server by name. However, that would become extremely annoying for users, and I'm sure you don't want to install a complaints box next to your office door. Instead, let's take this one step further and create a permanent drive mapping on this WIN10 workstation.

Mapping a drive

The term "mapping a drive" generally refers to selecting a folder that is shared from a server in your environment and creating a semi-permanent link to it through the use of a drive letter on the local workstation. By default, the "C: drive" is where all Windows operating system files are stored, and even end users generally understand this. If your computer has a CD/DVD drive, it oftentimes utilizes the D: drive designation on that computer. You may be wondering what happened to A: and B:. They used to be commonly utilized by these things called floppy drives, which I am certainly old enough to remember, but you may have never seen one.

Mapped network drives are the same idea, designating a specific drive letter as a semi-permanent link to a network location—usually a folder that is shared from a file server. I keep saying "semi-permanent" because it is entirely possible to disconnect drive letters and reconnect them to new places, which is fairly difficult to do with physical items such as C: and D:. Therefore, network drive mappings are usually higher in the alphabetical range, such as the K: drive, M: drive, S: drive...you get the picture.

We'll look at a couple of options for automating this drive mapping process in a few pages, but it is also important to know how to manually map a network drive when needed. One of the easiest ways is to query the file server just like we did a minute ago, by using \\FS01 in **File Explorer**. Once you see the network folder that you want to map to, simply right-click on that folder and select **Map network drive...**

A new window appears, with the folder destination already populated with the network location of the drive you right-clicked on. I am trying to map my \\FS01\Marketing location to my local M: drive, and all I need to do is right-click, choose to map the drive, select my M: drive letter from the drop-down list, and Bob's your uncle.

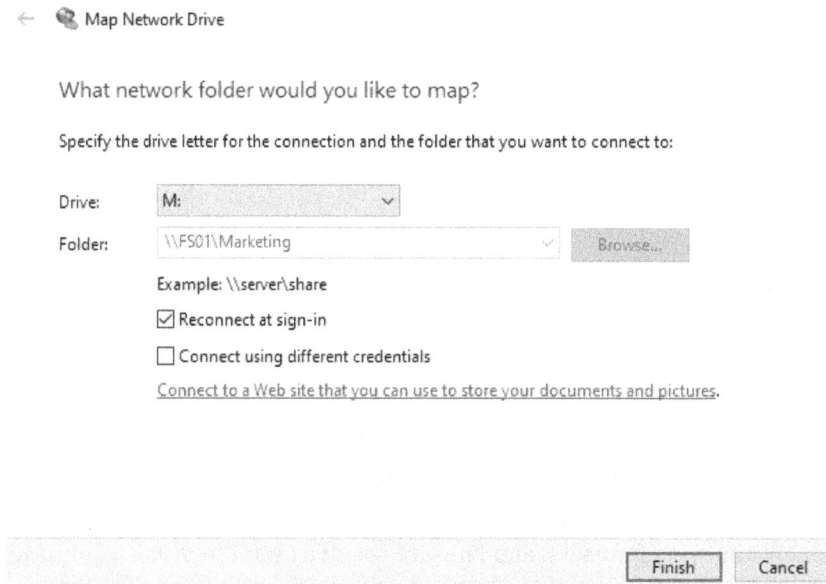

←   Map Network Drive

What network folder would you like to map?

Specify the drive letter for the connection and the folder that you want to connect to:

Drive: M:

Folder: \\FS01\Marketing   Browse...

Example: \\server\share

☑ Reconnect at sign-in

☐ Connect using different credentials

Connect to a Web site that you can use to store your documents and pictures.

Finish   Cancel

Figure 6.7: Manually mapping a drive letter

From this point forward, until I disconnect the drive letter or something happens inside Windows that disconnects it for me, every time that I open File Explorer, I will have an M: drive. Clicking on this M: drive connection will navigate me directly into the **Marketing** shared folder on my FS01 server.

Mapping via the command line

Anything accomplished via the graphical interface in the Microsoft Windows world is also accomplishable via the command line. Mapping network drives is something easily done from Windows Terminal, PowerShell, or good ole Command Prompt. Taking what you already know—that you must designate a drive letter to be mapped to a network location, open your favorite command-line interface and utilize the following context:

```
Net use S: \\FS01\Sales
```

The preceding command will immediately create a drive mapping of S: to the Sales share on FS01. However, and this is a big however, using the preceding command will mean that the next time you reboot this computer, the S: drive will disappear. If you refer back to *Figure 6.7*, you'll notice the **Reconnect at sign-in** checkbox. When mapping via the command line, we did not designate anything that specifies that we want to retain this drive letter on subsequent logins, so it assumes we do not want to do that. To correct this situation, because it is almost never the case that you want to map a network drive only for your current Windows session, simply add a /persistent switch to the end of your command, like this:

```
Net use S: \\FS01\Sales /persistent:yes
```

Now, each time you log back into this computer, your S: drive will be mapped to the Sales share. At any point, if you want to view your mapped drive letters right here in Command Prompt, net use will spit them out:

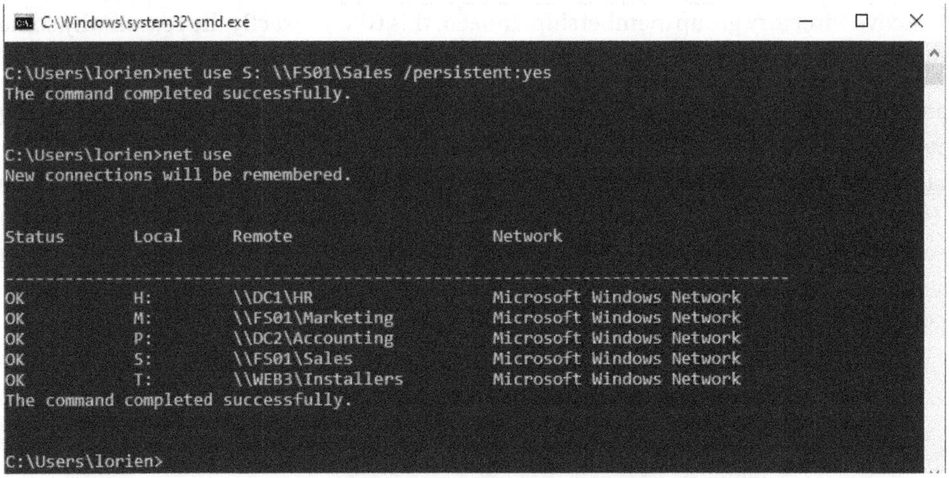

Figure 6.8: Using net use to create and view drive mappings

Backups, backups, backups

As already mentioned, we will talk more specifically about backup capabilities in Windows Server later, in *Chapter 17*. I mention it here because proper backups are of critical importance to any file server. Data is so valuable to all companies that protecting that data should be a top priority. Any IT department knows that the recovery of files or folders is a commonplace task. Sometimes users accidentally delete things, sometimes they nefariously delete things, sometimes they make mistakes while updating a file, and sometimes they unknowingly drag folders inside other folders. The list of reasons why you may have to turn to your backup system to recover files and folders from your file servers goes on and on.

Do not save money on backups. Get good ones, and make sure they back up once an hour during working hours. Sometimes you may want to push that further and back up file servers every 15 minutes. It all depends on your workers' habits and workflow.

Automated drive mappings

Knowing how to manually map network drives is essential information for working in IT, but unless your company consists of 10 people, you are certainly not going to walk around to every user at every computer anytime you want to make a drive mapping addition or adjustment. There are two primary technologies that exist in the Microsoft world for the purpose of automating this process. Let's take a look at both of them.

GPO drive mapping

This shouldn't come as a surprise if you have been reading through the book front to back. We already talked through the possibility of automating your drive map process in *Chapter 5*, when we worked together to create a Group Policy Object and configured settings inside that GPO to map network drives based on Active Directory group membership. Indeed, this GPO is exactly the reason why some of the drive letters shown in *Figure 6.8* exist.

Inside any traditional Active Directory domain environment, where servers and computers are joined to the domain and are regularly in contact with a Domain Controller server, establishing automated drive mappings via GPO is by far the most common approach to dealing with this topic. I don't want to rehash everything we talked about in *Chapter 5*, but there is granular ability inside GPOs to determine which employees get access to which drive letters, and to make sure those drive letters are automatically put into place every time those users log into their computers. If you missed that section, please turn back a few pages right now!

Intune drive mapping

More companies move resources into the cloud every day, and oftentimes, a business that has always used Microsoft technology inside its walls decides to continue using Microsoft technology outside of those walls. What this often means in practice is that M365 and Azure are entry points to cloud productivity, but almost never transitioning in one fell swoop. It would be pretty cavalier to spend a weekend throwing all company resources into the cloud and expecting users to deal with the differences and changes on Monday morning. So instead, most of these transitions take the approach of creating a hybrid environment for a while, where computers are hybrid-joined to both Active Directory and Entra.

I suppose that information is not necessarily here nor there when it comes to Intune capabilities. Whether your computers are "hybrid joined" or directly joined to Entra, Microsoft Intune has the ability to manipulate those computers. I mention this to reinforce the fact that this section about mapping network drives via Intune policy is only for companies that have moved far enough into the cloud space that their workstations are joined to Entra in some capacity. Using M365 for email is not enough; you must have already taken intentional steps to fully join machines to Entra so that they are "enrolled" inside Intune. The processes and licensing requirements for Entra-joining machines are outside the scope of this chapter, but I say this as a precursor that only some of you will have an environment that is capable of building an automatic drive mapping policy from inside Intune.

Assuming you do have Intune and your computers are already enrolled in it, your home for creating an automated drive mapping script is inside the Microsoft Admin portal, specifically inside the Microsoft Intune admin center (`intune.microsoft.com`). There are multiple different ways that you can use Intune to create drive mappings on your users' computers. The most classic is to ask Intune to run a PowerShell script on your computers, and that script handles the mapping of network drives. That is the approach we will take today, because the functionality is built into Intune without modifications. Alternatively, some people have created custom ADMX templates that can be uploaded into Intune that, once uploaded, create an even easier experience of defining network drive mappings inside an Intune configuration profile. This is an exciting topic, but our book is not really an Intune book, so as I mentioned, we will stick with the script method today, as it already exists inside any Intune environment:

Microsoft Intune admin center | Devices | Manage devices | Scripts and remediations | Platform scripts

Visiting this section of the Intune portal will bring you to the place where you can create or manage any number of scripts that you want to toss at your Intune-joined computers. As of right now, I have no such scripts, and so I simply click **Add > Windows 10 and later** to begin the process of crafting a new script that I will push to my Windows devices.

The options selectable in this wizard are self-explanatory, but after defining a name for my **Automatic Drive Mapping** policy, I am faced with a box asking me to upload a .PS1 script file. Uh oh, I don't have a script file...

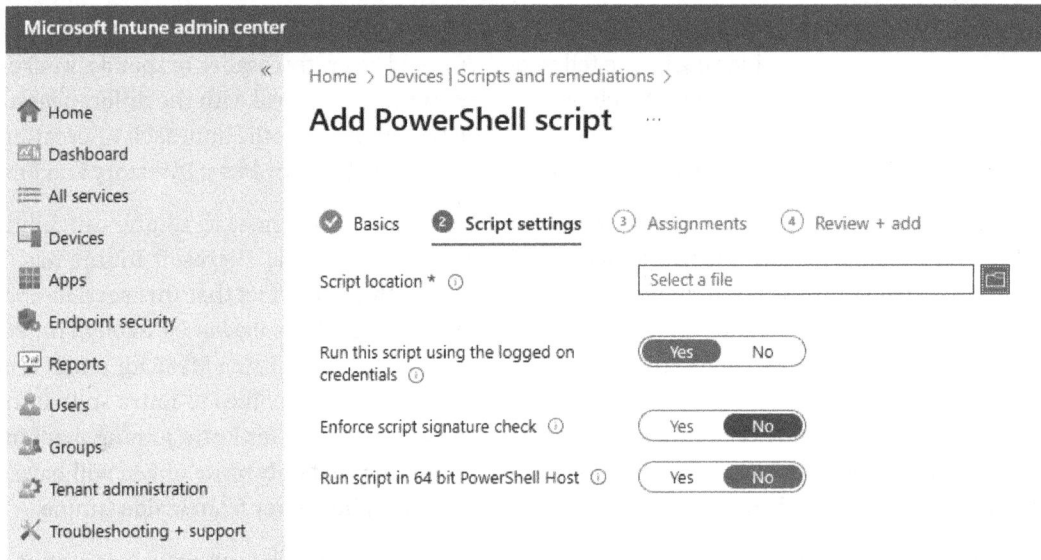

Figure 6.9: Creating an Intune policy that will run my non-existent script

Let's figure out how to remedy that.

Crafting the drive mapping script

I worked through this example backwards on purpose, because sometimes encountering issues causes us to remember better for next time. It will be helpful for you to generate your .PS1 PowerShell script before you try to add it to Intune. But, no harm done, we will go create the script now. Fortunately for us, Microsoft has a website hanging out there for anybody to use that allows you to simply enter your drive letters and drive mapping information, click a button, and it spits out a .PS1 script that you can bring right over to the Intune portal:

```
https://intunedrivemapping.azurewebsites.net/DriveMapping
```

Visit this site and select **Build from scratch**. Now simply use the **Edit**, **Delete**, and **Add entry** buttons as needed to inject all of the drive letters and mappings that you would like to accomplish via this PowerShell script. When finished, you should see a list of the automated drive mappings that you are asking this script to run, with a **Download PowerShell Script** button.

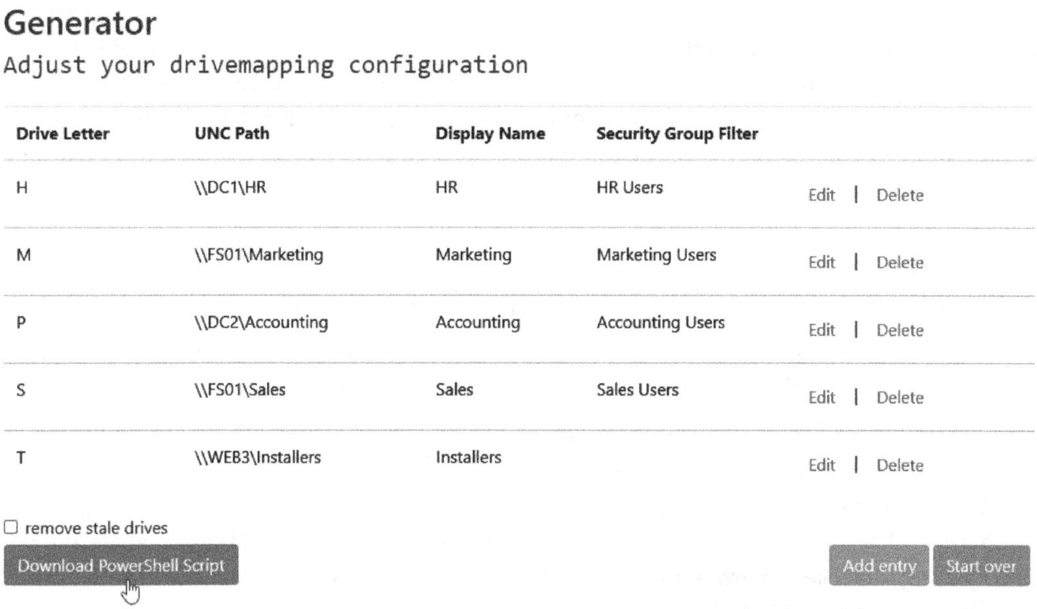

Generator
Adjust your drivemapping configuration

Drive Letter	UNC Path	Display Name	Security Group Filter		
H	\\DC1\HR	HR	HR Users	Edit	Delete
M	\\FS01\Marketing	Marketing	Marketing Users	Edit	Delete
P	\\DC2\Accounting	Accounting	Accounting Users	Edit	Delete
S	\\FS01\Sales	Sales	Sales Users	Edit	Delete
T	\\WEB3\Installers	Installers		Edit	Delete

☐ remove stale drives

Download PowerShell Script

Add entry   Start over

Figure 6.10: Crafting .PS1 using the Intune Drive Mapping Generator

Once downloaded, you simply upload this script into the Intune window and select what Entra group or groups you want it to apply to, and bingo—Intune will begin pushing this script down to your users. What this script does is create a scheduled task on each computer that attempts to run the script during user login. This is the activity that causes the script to map network drives automatically in the background, without the user having to do anything. Scripts are incredibly powerful and can be tweaked or manipulated in an unlimited number of ways. You could follow this same process to script any kind of change to your Windows computers. You could also tweak the .PS1 script before uploading to Intune to manipulate the scheduled task and cause it to run more often than only during user login, which is sometimes necessary if you have remote workers who rarely visit the office.

A special note about updating Intune drive mappings

Unfortunately, once you upload your drive mapping script to Intune, there is no way to edit that script from inside the admin center. Down the road, you may encounter the need to add a new drive mapping or edit an existing one, and you will visit the Intune portal only to find that you can see the name of the .PS1 script that is running but there is no way to edit or even to download that script to see what is going on within.

Instead, you'll need to create a new .PS1 script and upload the new copy into your Intune policy, replacing the old script with the new. This is easily done; the tricky bit is remembering what was inside the original script so that you can include that information in the new one. There are some secret-sauce ways of extracting this script from Intune but they're not for the faint of heart. Instead, take care to save a copy of your .PS1 script somewhere on your computer or on the network, so that you can easily come back and reference it again later.

File permissions

After a brief detour into the cloud, we are back on-prem and working with shares on the FS01 server. When creating these shares, we went into detail about share-level permissions and mentioned further file-level permissions, but have not yet taken a firsthand look at these.

Share permissions are processed first when any user attempts to access any shared folder or file. If you wanted to divvy up access in terms of who can get to what resources, you could do it at a share level, but it would be tricky and difficult to administer long-term. Instead, it is common practice to leave share-level permissions wide open (**Everyone = Full Control**) and handle your real file and folder access by using folder-level permissions. These permissions are accomplished inside the **Security** tab of any file or folder on a Windows file system.

File permissions inside the **Security** tab are sometimes referred to as **NTFS permissions**, but that is not technically accurate. You can define security permissions on files and folders, whether they are stored on a volume that has been formatted using FAT, FAT32, NTFS, or ReFS. I think the origin story behind calling them "NTFS permissions" is to help distinguish this level of permission from share-level permissions. But in keeping with proper definitions, we should call these file security permissions.

Logging back into FS01, I navigate to the D: drive where my shared folders are located, and I am going to play around with **Security** permissions for my **Accounting** folder. Share-level permissions are **Everyone = Full Control**, so there are no current restrictions on this folder other than what is inside the **Security** tab. Right-clicking on the **Accounting** folder and going into **Properties**, then the **Security** tab, I can quickly see the current definition for who has access to this folder. Right from this screen, I could also edit permissions and add or remove Active Directory users or groups of users, and selectively give them read-only access, modify access, or full control access. By default, administrators have access to this folder (which makes sense), and the general **Users** group also has some level of access. I don't like the idea of all users having access to my **Accounting** folder, so I have removed that designation and instead added an intentional group called **Acct Users**. As you can see in *Figure 6.11*, I have granted anybody who is a member of **Acct Users** group to have **Modify** permissions for data that sits inside the **Accounting** folder.

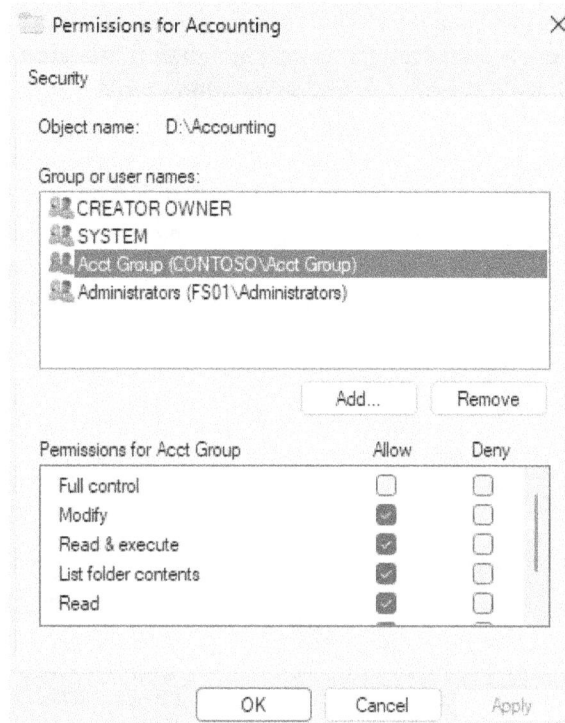

Figure 6.11: Adjusting file permissions for the Accounting folder

Let's define some of these permission options, in case you have any questions here:

- **Full control:** This gives truly full control of the folder. Users would have the ability to read, write, move, delete, or even come into these permission settings and make adjustments. Typically, the only entities you want to have **Full Control** permissions are IT administrator accounts.

- **Modify:** Selecting **Modify** automatically checks boxes for both read and write access.

- **Read & execute:** This allows users to read and open files and to execute application-type files. The key difference here is that if **Modify** is not also checked, users will be able to open files but not able to make changes within them.

- **List folder contents:** This allows users to navigate into this folder and to see what other subfolders or files are contained within. This one almost always accompanies **Read** permissions.

- **Read:** Pretty simple, this grants permission to read data from within this folder or file.

- **Write:** Similarly, the **Write** permission grants access for users to create new documents or folders.

- **Special permissions:** This can be lots of things. Rather than trying to tell you about them here, backtrack to the main **Security** tab for a folder and then click on the **Advanced** button. Inside **Advanced,** you will see a similar permission definition screen, but expanded with some new functions shown. Clicking on one of the permission principals, such as the **Acct Users** group, click the **Edit** button and you will find multiple tiers for crafting special and unique permissions. Some of the reasons you may create your own special permissions are if you want to set up permissions that only apply to one folder and for some reason do not apply to subfolders, or if you want to specifically allow users to be able to modify folder contents, but not to be able to delete anything inside those folders. Those and many more options are available within the advanced permissions screen for slicing and dicing up your file/folder permissions.

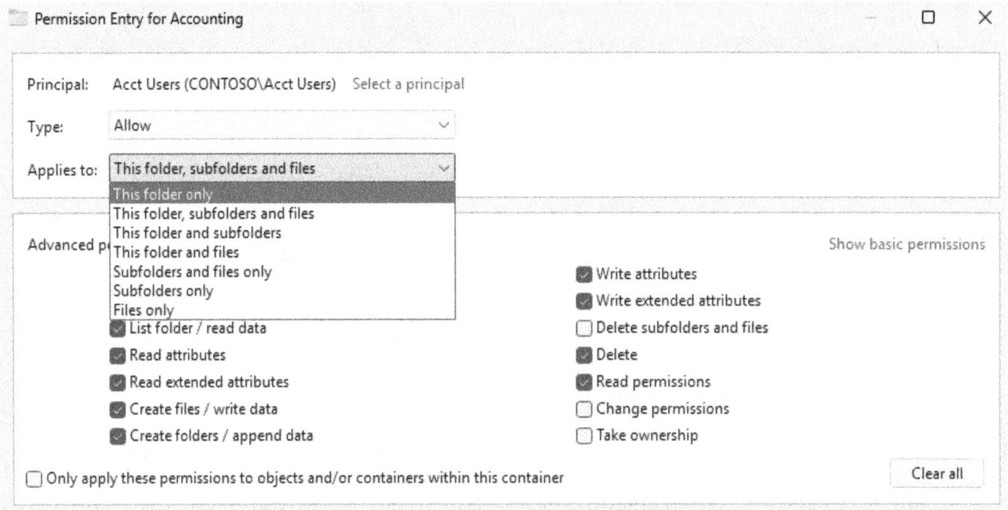

Figure 6.12: Advanced file and folder permissions

It would be almost impossible to discuss every permission scenario that you may encounter, but keep in mind that if you are tasked with a complex requirement for allowing or restricting access in a way that doesn't seem possible in the simpler permissions screens, the **Advanced** button opens a whole new world for file and folder permission options.

Use those groups!

When thinking through file and folder permissions, it's easy to get lost in a whirlwind of who needs access to view things, who needs access to modify things, and who doesn't need access at all...there are so many factors to consider. I find that making use of multiple standardized groups helps tremendously.

First, make sure your shared folders do not allow the generic **Users** directory to have access to them. If you do that, you may very well circumvent real permissions that you put into place on the same folder. Remove users and plan to utilize your own groups that are specific to the purpose. I find it extremely helpful to create an Active Directory group for users who need **Write/Modify** access to each share, and a separate group that grants read-only access to that same folder.

It is also very helpful to your future self to name these groups very specifically, so that you remember 5 years from now that these AD groups are for the purpose of file share permissions, and not other things. Here is an example, once again looking at my **Accounting** folder, of groups that I would set up in a production customer environment to serve this purpose.

Here are the group names:

- **Folder – Accounting – Read-Only**
- **Folder – Accounting – Read-Write**

After creating these groups, we of course add both of them into **Security** permissions for the **Accounting** folder, and set their permissions according to their names.

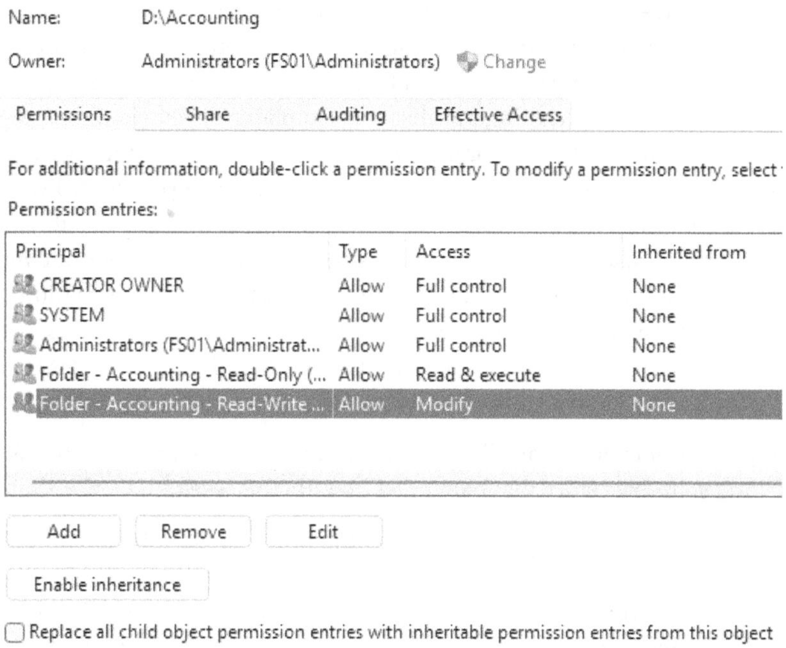

Name: D:\Accounting

Owner: Administrators (FS01\Administrators)   Change

Permissions	Share	Auditing	Effective Access

For additional information, double-click a permission entry. To modify a permission entry, select

Permission entries:

Principal	Type	Access	Inherited from
CREATOR OWNER	Allow	Full control	None
SYSTEM	Allow	Full control	None
Administrators (FS01\Administrat...	Allow	Full control	None
Folder - Accounting - Read-Only (...	Allow	Read & execute	None
Folder - Accounting - Read-Write ...	Allow	Modify	None

Add	Remove	Edit

Enable inheritance

☐ Replace all child object permission entries with inheritable permission entries from this object

Figure 6.13: Using groups to distinguish read-only versus read-write permissions

Using groups to build file and folder permissions is such a smart thing to do. If you *ever* find yourself adding an individual user account to file permissions, you are probably doing something wrong. Establishing good habits about folder permissions up front will save you so much thinking and headaches down the road. When groups are well defined, adding or removing users from folder permissions is as simple as adding or removing them from AD groups. There is literally no need to even log into the file server. You could, of course, utilize these same group names as specifications inside item-level targeting inside a drive mapping GPO, knocking out two birds with one stone.

Now let's discuss that little button and checkbox shown near the bottom of *Figure 6.13*. What is all this about inheritance and child object permissions?

To inherit or not to inherit...that is the question

By default, when you configure a root folder and create subfolders and files within, **Security** permissions from the parent root folder are inherited by all subfolders. Anything contained within that shared folder will have the same permissions, so you know that users who are in the group to grant them access to the folder also have permission to access all items stored within. Unfortunately, this is only the default behavior and it can be overruled. I am normally a big fan of flexibility in configuration, and so, from an ideological perspective, I think it is wonderful that you can "break inheritance" and cause certain subfolders to no longer pay attention to the permissions of their parent folder. In practice, however, I have only found this to be problematic.

In *Figure 6.13*, there is an **Enable inheritance** button. This implies that the folder whose permissions we are viewing is not currently inheriting access controls from its parent folder. That is because we are viewing permissions of a root folder, and I intentionally stopped it from inheriting permissions at the D: volume root, thus allowing all of my root folders to be individually managed for permissions. Alternatively, if any folder was inheriting permissions from above, you would instead see a **Disable inheritance** button listed here. Enabling or disabling inheritance is as simple as clicking that button, although treating this button like an easy button is bound to cause you grief. Every time that you enable or disable inheritance, the operating system has to rehash through all subfolders and files to set permissions accordingly, and in large file server structures with many tiers of data, there is a real possibility that it will run into some kind of problem. Making high-level permission changes to files and folders always comes with a little bit of risk in well-established environments, because a permission change literally rolls through every object one at a time, and if that process is interrupted, it will leave some of your files and folders with new permissions, and others with old permissions.

Let me prove to you why it is that I don't like moving away from standards and disabling inheritance on folders by telling you a true story that happened literally this week.

A company has a drive mapping for a public space, the folder is literally named Public, and share permissions are configured so that all domain users have access to read and write documents into it. Diving into this folder, there are many subfolders that people have added over the years, with one that stands out like a bright red thumb, a subfolder called **HR PRIVATE**. Yikes, that definitely sounds like a folder that you would *not* want to be sitting inside a public file space! Yet, there it is. At some point, the HR department decided they wanted to have a private space for their documents, and rather than requesting a new share and drive mapping, they self-created this **HR PRIVATE** folder and then asked IT to lock it down for them. This is easily done; all you need to do is click the **Disable inheritance** button and then configure your own specific file permissions on the **HR PRIVATE** folder. Bingo, that folder is now locked down! I recreated this scenario in my test lab, and you can see that even though **HR PRIVATE** exists inside a public folder space where everyone has access, individualized **Security** permissions exist on this one folder that only allow the **HR Users** group to have access to this folder. You can also see in the screenshot that inheritance has been disabled on **HR PRIVATE**, which is what allows this exception to the rules.

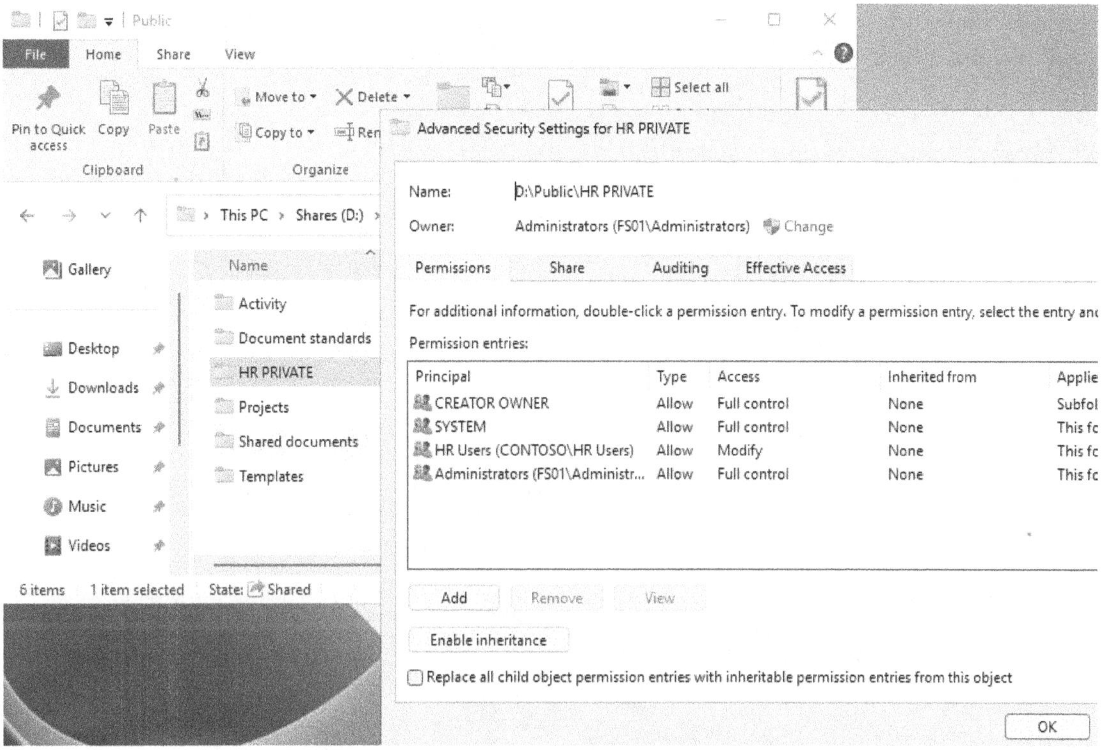

Figure 6.14: HR PRIVATE is currently locked down

Hopefully, you already recognize how dangerous this situation is, although as of right now, this folder is properly locked down and only users who are either administrators or members of the **HR Users** group will be able to access the **HR PRIVATE** folder in any way. As you can probably imagine, the issue that I was asked to help with was that non-HR users were able to access the **HR PRIVATE** folder, which was really, *really* bad. Rather than talk through my entire thought process about how this may have happened, let's take some actions in this lab to prove that it could easily happen to you.

Pretend that our file server is properly configured right now, as I just showed in *Figure 6.14*, so that **HR PRIVATE** sits among public folders, but is itself locked down. Nothing dangerous so far, except for this scenario involving unnecessary risk. Now, pretend that your IT staff receive a request that reads something like this: "Please ensure that members of the **Contractors** group do not have access to get to anything inside the public share."

Your new tier 1 engineer perks up, "I can take care of that!" Naturally, they log into the file server, find the root folder of the public share, and head inside **Security** permissions. Now, they may not be entirely familiar with all of the options in here, and certainly don't want to make any unnecessary changes, so they simply add the **Contractors** group into permissions with a specific **Deny** permission. So far, things are sounding okay, and then they notice that checkbox near the bottom of the permissions window: **Replace all child object permission entries with inheritable permission entries from this object.** Those words are a little strange, but the ticket request from our CEO did state that they wanted to block contractors from getting to *anything* inside the public share, and this checkbox sounds like it will accomplish exactly that. It's just a little checkbox, what harm could it cause?

Well, it caused exactly the issue that I discovered this week. After making that tiny change at the root level of public, re-visiting the **Security** tab of the **HR PRIVATE** folder now shows me that **HR PRIVATE** is configured to inherit permissions from above, and it is now denying access to the **Contractors** group (like every other folder is), but is now allowing read and modify access for **Domain Users** in our network.

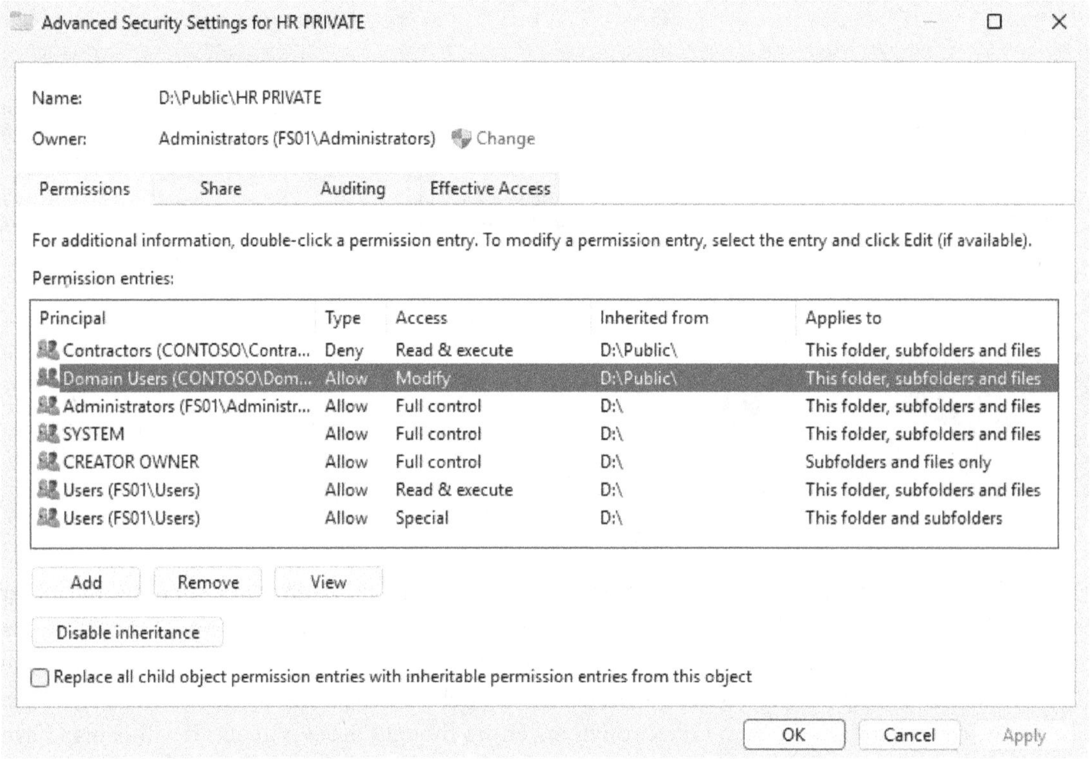

Figure 6.15: Permissions on HR PRIVATE have been overruled by a root-level change

You may be thinking, "I would never allow a green engineer to change permissions on the file server," and maybe that is true. But this scenario can be caused even by senior-level engineers. Maybe you attempted to change permissions on the **Public** folder, and as those permissions were working their way through all files and folders, the process was interrupted, and now some subfolders have your new permissions and some do not. You attempt to push those changes again, and continue to hit some kind of trouble. You may try checking that box to remediate the issue, or you may even turn to deeper command-line troubleshooting to try and combat these permission woes, but the whole time you are working from an understanding that the root folder being manipulated is called Public, and assume that all permissions inside Public should be the same. You may have no idea that, at some point, years in the past, the HR department unknowingly requested that those inherited permissions be circumvented. This situation can become even easier to step into if the differing, non-inherited folder is buried multiple layers deep. If you are adjusting permissions on D:\Public, would you really have any chance in the world of knowing that a folder such as D:\Public\Scans\MainOffice\HR was disabled from inheritance and should be considered "private"?

The moral of this story is not to beat up anybody who contributed to the situation, but rather, as a forewarning, to plan folder structures and permissions very carefully, and stick to the rules that you put into place. Maybe this means that you decide to never ever disable inheritance on folders—that is one way to keep things clean. If you do click that **Disable inheritance** button, just remember that you are setting yourself, or someone else, up for possible failure in the future.

Deny always wins

Most often, when thinking about file permissions, you will be taking the perspective of *granting* users access to areas of the file server. However, Microsoft's stance with pretty much everything is that a denial always trumps an allowance, and the same is true for file share permissions. Referring back to *Figure 6.15*, you can see that the **Contractors** group is now denied permission to the **HR PRIVATE** folder, and indeed that denial permission is actually configured at the root folder called **Public**. Any user account added to the **Contractors** group will be a member of both **Contractors** and **Domain Users**, but even though their rights as a domain user would normally allow them access to the **Public** share, membership of **Contractors** means that those users will be denied access to look inside the **Public** share at all.

Whenever adding a **Deny** permission to a folder, this is pretty clear by reading over the warning prompt that Microsoft displays when saving such a permission.

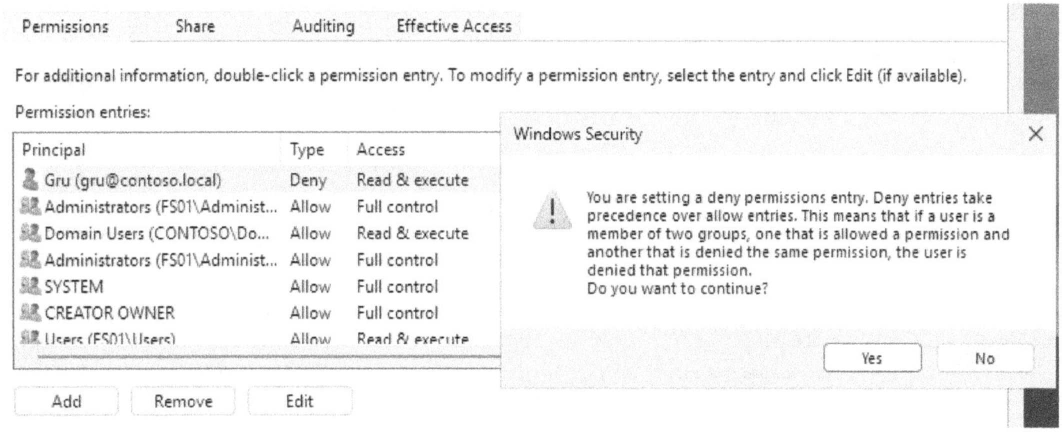

Figure 6.16: Let's keep Gru out of this folder

With all of the available tiers of permission, options to enable or disable inheritance for each folder, and denials taking priority over approvals, hopefully, you can now understand why thinking through your file shares and taking the time to plan carefully is time well spent.

Effective access

While we could probably talk all day about different file permission scenarios, let's end this section with just one more useful tool. When working within and modifying folder permissions, it is a common thing to ask yourself questions such as "I wonder if Susie can access this?" or "I hope this change really blocks Gru from accessing the HR folder—how can I confirm that?"

Thankfully, the **Advanced** screen within each folder's permissions has a tool called **Effective access**, which serves exactly this purpose.

Going back to the **HR PRIVATE** example, right-clicking on that folder and going into **Properties**, then the **Security** tab, and then clicking the **Advanced** button brings me to a screen we have visited before. What we have not yet done is click on the **Effective access** tab to see what it does. Click on **Effective access**, and then click on one of the relevant links to narrow your search down to either a specific user or group inside the domain. Once you have identified a user or group to test permissions against this folder, click the **View effective access** button, and you will immediately find results for what specific permissions that person or group does or does not have within this folder. Working through that example a couple of times, I can see that Susie (a member of the HR department) has access to read and modify inside this folder, but Gru (a contractor) does not. I am met with a series of green checkmarks or red x's, clearly indicating what level of access is available for each of those users.

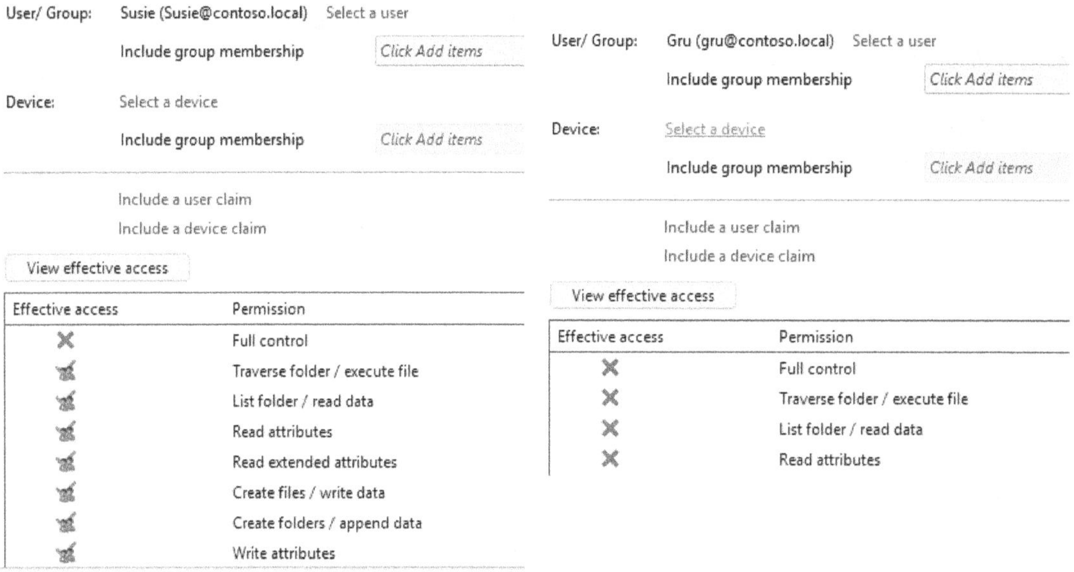

User/ Group:	Susie (Susie@contoso.local) Select a user	
	Include group membership	*Click Add items*
Device:	Select a device	
	Include group membership	*Click Add items*

Include a user claim
Include a device claim

[View effective access]

Effective access	Permission
✖	Full control
✔	Traverse folder / execute file
✔	List folder / read data
✔	Read attributes
✔	Read extended attributes
✔	Create files / write data
✔	Create folders / append data
✔	Write attributes

User/ Group:	Gru (gru@contoso.local) Select a user	
	Include group membership	*Click Add items*
Device:	Select a device	
	Include group membership	*Click Add items*

Include a user claim
Include a device claim

[View effective access]

Effective access	Permission
✖	Full control
✖	Traverse folder / execute file
✖	List folder / read data
✖	Read attributes

Figure 6.17: Effective access is a powerful tool for reviewing file permissions

Effective access is a great way to test recent changes and ensure they have taken effect, or to check on a particular user's level of access without needing to touch their computer or communicate with that user at all.

Distributed File System (DFS)

Proper configuration of a single file server is a great place to begin, but as your company grows, you are going to quickly outgrow the notion of one file server providing ownership over all documents. Creating another file server and manually sharing the load is easily done. You could slide some shares onto one server and other shares onto another. Thinking ahead to creating drive map policies for those drives, they begin to feel a little messy. With some file shares pointing at \\FS01 and some at \\FS02, even you may lose track of which server is providing which purpose, and your users certainly won't care to remember the differences.

Distributed File System (DFS) is a system that takes multiple servers that are running multiple shares and binds them all together under one common DNS name for access. These servers can all be sitting in one physical site or spread across multiple locations. Instead of accessing files by \\FS01 or \\FS02 and so on, users can get to any share they need by simply visiting \\contoso.local (just an example), and DFS takes care of the heavy lifting to determine which file server and share need to be passed along to the user's File Explorer window. There are two key components to the way that DFS works: **DFS Namespaces** and **DFS Replication**.

Thankfully, DFS is a technology that is built right into Windows Server! We are able to make use of these abilities without any further purchases or licensing; all it takes is time and knowledge. Let's build out a DFS environment together.

DFS namespaces

The core component of DFS, namespaces are the secret sauce that creates a centralized namespace for the purpose of accessing files across the network, even across multiple file servers located in multiple physical sites. A root namespace is established (most often reflecting the name of your internal domain), and that name can then be used for access to files. When accessing those files, users are unaware of where the files are stored. They might be opening files on FS01, FS02, DC1, and so on. The point is that they don't need to care; they simply access \\contoso.local and navigate from there, always knowing that the files they need are somewhere that appears to be centralized and is easy to remember.

Standalone versus domain-based namespaces

DFS configuration needs to be stored somewhere, of course. One or more servers are responsible for receiving requests from workstations and then deciding where those requests must navigate for successful connectivity. Let's say LAPTOP1 is asking for \\contoso.local\HR. Who is responsible for telling LAPTOP1 that the HR share is actually located on \\FS02\HR, and that is where they need to connect to? The DFS namespace, which is interactive on one or multiple servers, depending on your choice here.

Standalone DFS namespaces are independent, and I almost never find them in the wild. If you are somehow running a Windows environment *without* a domain, then I suppose this would be your ticket to entry for DFS. A standalone DFS is going to be hosted on a single server, which is a single point of failure, and I do not recommend you pursue this route.

Domain-based DFS namespaces are what everybody typically uses. Almost every business network is centered around an Active Directory network, and in such a network, enabling DFS in a domain-based fashion is a no-brainer, because your namespace information is stored in Active Directory itself, so that any domain controller can respond to those name lookup requests.

Establishing DFS namespaces

As with most technologies inside Windows Server, the beginning of life for any capability is the installation of a role. This is true for DFS. Log in to the server that you want to be your first DFS namespace server. Usually, this will be your file server, but it could also be a domain controller. I am going to add the **DFS Namespaces** role to FS01 (take note of the **DFS Replication** role that sits alongside **DFS Namespaces,** as we will make use of replication later in this chapter).

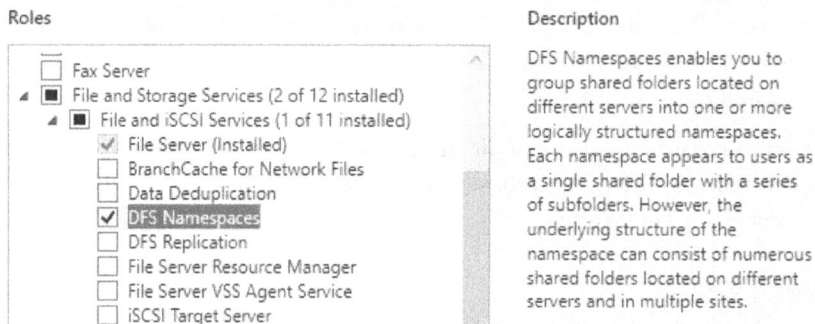

Figure 6.18: Installing the DFS Namespaces role

Once installed, you will find a new toolset inside your **Server Manager Tools** menu called **DFS Management**. This will be your home for configuring the DFS namespace and all shares and links that appear inside DFS. Clicking on **Namespaces** currently shows nothing, because we have not yet created a DFS namespace. Right-click on **Namespaces** and the **New Namespace...** option will get us kicked off.

First, define the server that will host this new DFS namespace. This is an important clarification to make. I installed the **DFS Namespaces** role on FS01, but I could have just as easily installed the role onto a different server while still wanting FS01 to host the namespace itself. In my simple test lab, and in most production networks I have worked within, we are going to use the same server for this purpose. The role is installed on FS01, and I am going to host the namespace on FS01.

Our next screen asks us to define **Namespace Name and Settings**. This is important, as this name will be visible and similar for every share that you add to the DFS. DFS namespaces, once created, are accessed by UNC paths such as the following (these are all separate examples):

- \\contoso.local\DFS
- \\contoso.local\Shares
- \\contoso.local\Files

When mapping network drives to DFS locations, whatever you specify as the namespace name will be reflected in the beginning portion of that mapping. Most often, you will use some automated method to map these drives, but in a surprising number of cases, your users will figure out how to manually navigate to your DFS location, because they see it all the time. This is the reason that I like going with something such as `Files` for the name, because it is very easy to remember if a user were to attempt to manually navigate to it.

Once a name has been defined, you will see the **Edit Settings...** button light up as available to click on. Go ahead and click on that. We won't make any changes here, but this screen tells you a little bit about how DFS works under the hood. Effectively, what DFS is doing is creating a share right here on the `FS01` server. That shared folder will be sitting in `C:\DFSRoots\Files`. At first glance, you may want to change that location because you are nervous that you don't want users to fill up the `C:` drive of this server. You can certainly change the location of this new DFS-specific share, but it's not generally necessary. This is because the new `C:\DFSRoots\Files` folder and share being created will only contain shortcuts to the actual file shares. Those file shares might exist on `FS01`, `FS02`, or any other server. We'll see that firsthand in just a minute. But it is important to understand that your DFS shared folder specified here will remain very small, as it only contains pointers to other locations.

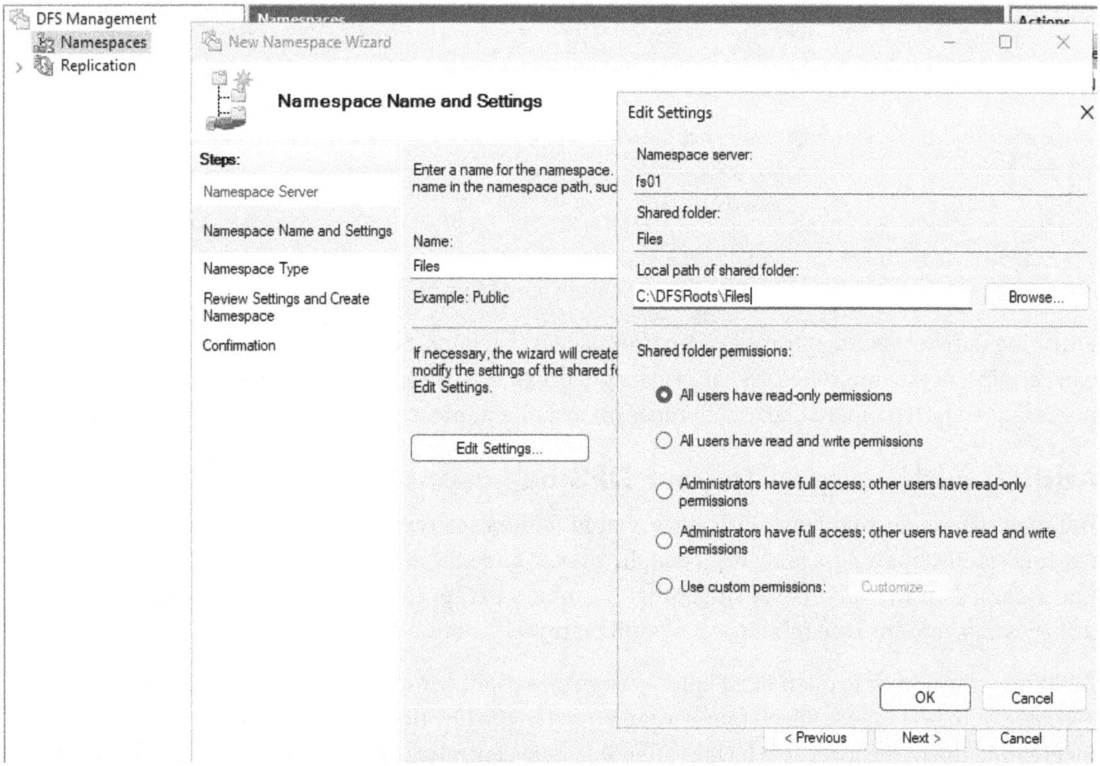

Figure 6.19: Creating our first DFS namespace

Next, we select whether this will be a domain-based or standalone namespace. We already discussed those differences, and 99% of the time, you'll want to stick with the default **Domain-based namespace**. Gotta love that **Enable Windows Server 2008 mode** checkbox left over from years ago. Clearly, DFS is a technology that has been around for a long time, and with the release of Server 2008 they made some enhancements to DFS that would have been optional at the time. Apparently, they are still optional, but why you would choose *not* to enable your domain-based DFS namespace to be capable of high availability is beyond me. Go ahead and leave that box checked. Also interesting in this screen is that you see a preview of what your exact namespace is going to look like on the network. I gave you a sneak peek into this already, but our new namespace is

`\\contoso.local\Files.`

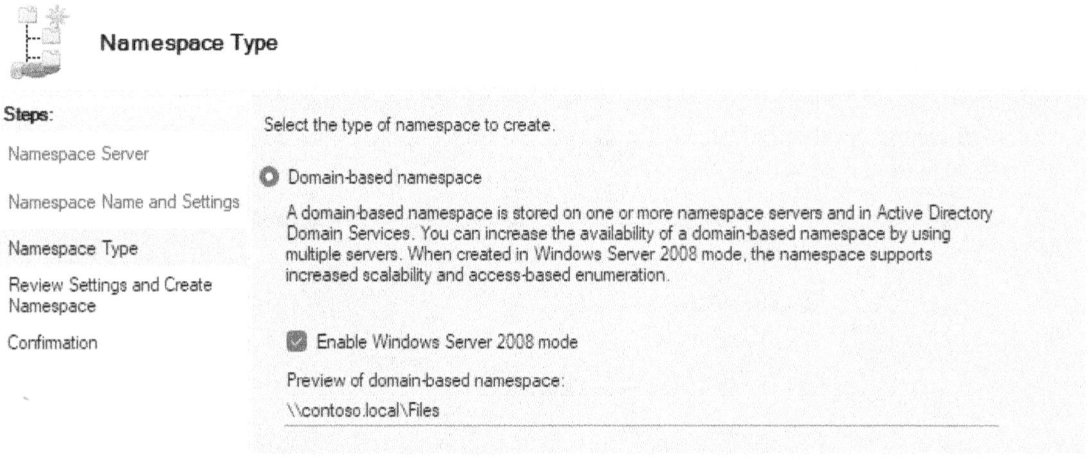

Figure 6.20: Defining our DFS namespace

Finishing out the wizard, our new DFS namespace is listed inside the **DFS Management** console. You can certainly create multiple DFS namespaces to break up access to certain types of files into separate namespaces, but in our test lab, I will focus on just one namespace and add my file shares to it.

Adding folder targets to your DFS namespace

You may remember that I currently have shared folders scattered all around my network. Some on `FS01`, certainly, but others on `FS02`, a couple on `DC1`, and still more on `DC2`. Wow, I just now realized that I named all my servers via single-digit numbers except for my file servers, where I added an unnecessary zero into the mix. Insert eyeroll (at myself) here.

Right now, if we were to open File Explorer from any client computer in this network and navigate to `\\contoso.local\Files`, File Explorer would open to the location, but it would be completely empty. By creating the namespace, we have crafted this new centralized share in our domain, but as of this moment, there are no shares linked into, or "targeted by," this namespace. Inside **DFS Management**, right-click on the name of your DFS namespace and select **New Folder…**. A simple screen emerges where we define **Name** and one or more folder targets. This is where we get some real action going. We are going to tell DFS about the files and folders that are shared on our network. As you can see in *Figure 6.21*, I have added numerous folders into my DFS namespace, all pointing at existing file/folder shares around my network. Some of these shares are on FS01, some on FS02, and some are even hosted from DC1 and DC2.

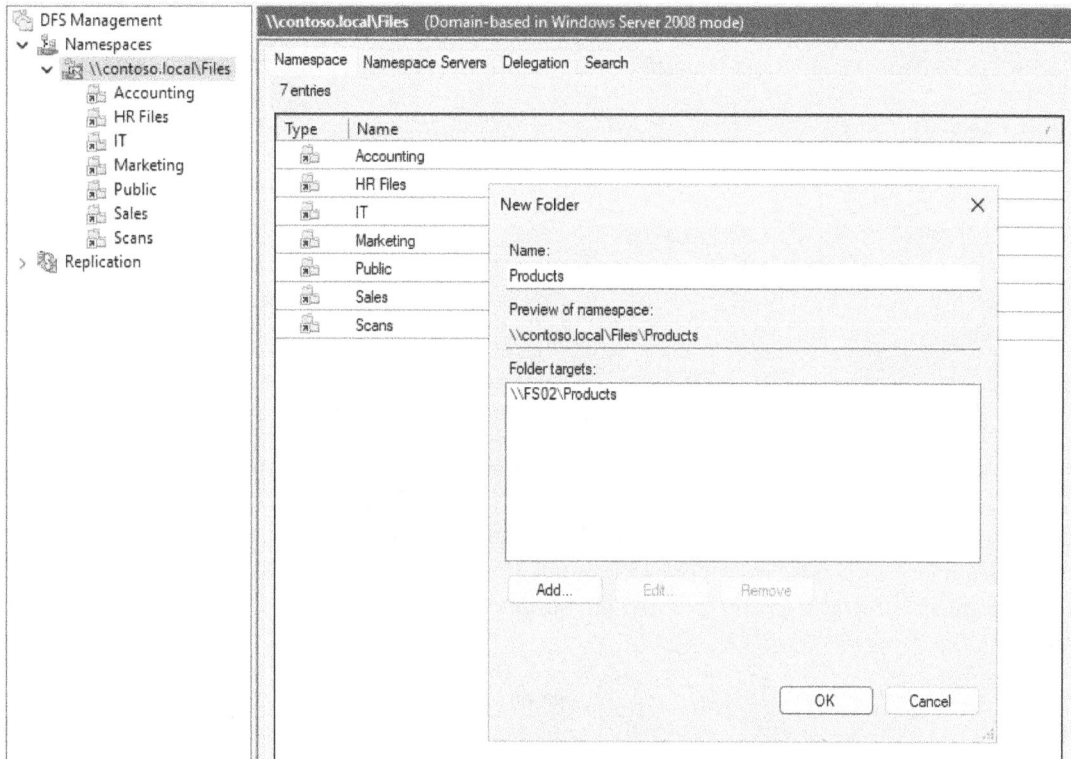

Figure 6.21: Adding folders (targets) to my DFS namespace

One special note about the **Name** field. Your shared folders are obviously shared with whatever name you chose for the share back when you created those shares. For example, HR. When adding pointers into the DFS for these shares, you do not have to call them by the same name. Even though my HR folder might be shared as such, I could choose to name this new folder inside the DFS HR Files as you can see in *Figure 6.21*, or anything else that I want to call it. The name you define here is the name that will be presented to users when they navigate the namespace.

Immediately after creating all these folder links inside my DFS namespace, I can take two actions to prove that this is really working, and to show you exactly what DFS usage looks like from a user perspective. First, on *FS01*, when I now open C:\DFSRoots\Files, I will see evidence of all the folder shortcuts I just added into the DFS. This is part of the magic behind the curtain of the DFS. When users hit up your namespace on their computers, they are really being steered to this special shared location, and from there bouncing to the actual shares located on other servers.

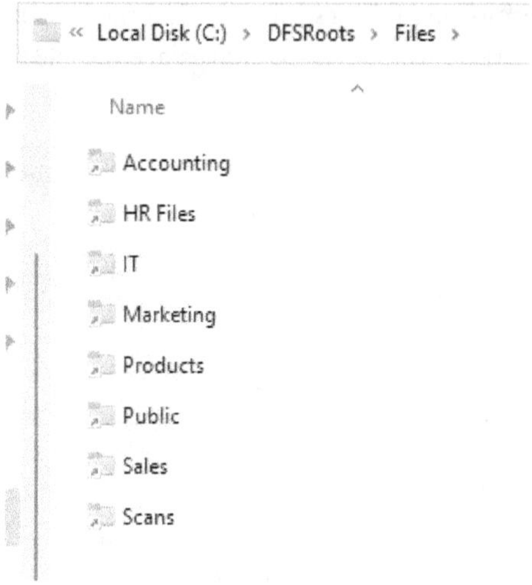

Figure 6.22: Folder shortcuts are stored inside the DFSRoots location

And for our final test to prove the DFS is working, open File Explorer on any workstation in the environment and navigate to \\contoso.local\Files. You should immediately see all of your shared folders together in one location, even though those shares are spread across four different servers in our environment. In the future, whenever you need to visit one of these shared folders, there is no need to remember what server it is stored on. Simply visit the DFS namespace and double-click on the folder from there!

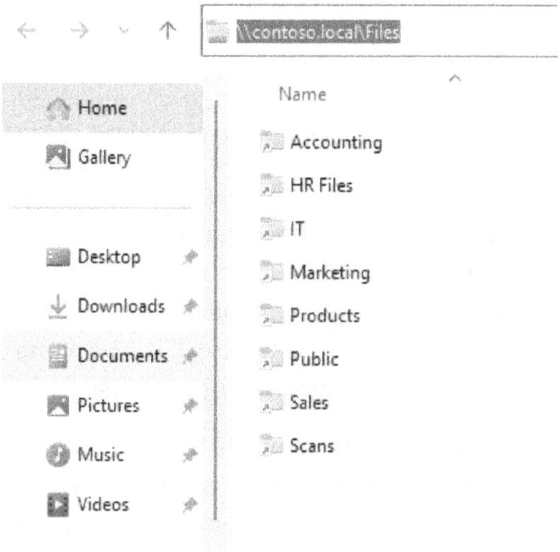

Figure 6.23: DFS presents all these shares in one place

Such is the power of DFS!

Re-mapping your network drives

This section is just a reminder of a common-sense task. Prior to running the DFS, you most likely had an extensive network drive mapping policy that was crafting many drive letters on users' computers. Once the DFS is implemented, you may be able to cut down drastically on that policy. If all your shared folders can live alongside each other inside one DFS namespace, you can now provide users with one single mapped drive, mapping of course directly to the DFS location. Or, even if you decide to break your file and folder mappings out into a couple of different DFS namespaces for privacy and security reasons, you have greatly reduced the number of network locations at play when dealing with network drive mappings. Be sure to revisit that policy and clean things up once the DFS is doing its work.

Another huge advantage of using the DFS when accessing files is that you have now obfuscated the actual file server names from users' eyeballs, and also from things such as mapped network drives. This creates a lot of flexibility for growth and maintenance down the road. If you ever need to move a folder share location from one server to another, you can do so silently in the background, and user drive mappings never even need to change, because you simply come into **DFS Management** and tell that shortcut to point at the new location. Or, maybe your file server is on its last legs and needs to be replaced with a new one. Build the new server, copy everything to it, and your cutover process will take about 3 seconds as you change those pointers inside DFS to steer them to the new server instead of the old one.

DFS replication (DFSR)

This technology is most commonly referred to as DFSR, but I have also seen it written out as DFS-R, DFS replication, or even DFS with replication. These all mean the same thing. In this section, we are going to enable the second component of DFS file management, which is the ability for servers not only to create shortcut pointers to folders on other servers but also to bind those shared folders together in a special way that replicates data between them. When DFSR is enabled, your file servers can keep files and folders synchronized all the time, even spanning across multiple sites. As a quick real-world example, I just helped someone configure DFSR for an "IT Tools" type of folder. This company has 6 or 7 different offices spread across multiple states, and each office has a local server. By configuring DFSR on one folder at each site, those folders all now stay in sync with each other. The addition of information or tools to one server automatically replicates to all six other sites. In most DFSR implementations, this happens via multi-master replication, or "full mesh" as Microsoft calls it, where an update to any node will be replicated to all other nodes.

DFSR is probably already running in your environment, without anyone knowing. Unless you are using very old infrastructure, Microsoft uses DFSR under the hood to replicate some information between domain controllers. For example, there is a special folder called SYSVOL that is very important to Active Directory, and when you do things such as creating GPOs, you of course want that policy information to remain consistent among domain controllers. For this information to be mirrored across your domain controllers, the SYSVOL folder is replicated among them all, using DFSR. I say "unless you are using old stuff" because DFSR does have a predecessor called **File Replication Service (FRS)** that used to accomplish the same function. The problems with FRS were numerous, most notably that it would simply delete information occasionally. As an example, if you were to be running Forest and

Domain functional levels of Server 2008 R2 but then introduce a Server 2012 domain controller to the mix, everything might run okay for a while. But you may someday perform a simple update to a GPO from your Server 2012 domain controller and find out the next day that your entire GPO was deleted. All settings inside it were simply...gone. FRS is troublesome, and newer domain controllers all run DFSR to keep themselves inline as a default.

Let's build DFSR together, and the screens we encounter will tell us a little bit more about how DFSR works as we move along.

Enabling DFSR

First, we need to provide shared folders on multiple servers. DFSR is going to take these shared folders and handle replication between them, but the creation of the folders, shares, and sharing permissions is all manual labor that must be accomplished first. Create shared folders on multiple servers—it can be two, three, or even ten servers, but just make sure that you set up sharing and file permissions exactly the same on these folders. You wouldn't want to confuse things by creating differing permissions on different shares, right? Now, even though permissions need to be the same among shared folders, it is interesting to note that the *names* of those shares do not have to be the same. I could set up two shared folders like this and tie them together in a replication group:

- `\\FS01\Accounting`
- `\\FS02\Accounting`

Or, I could add these three shared folders into a single replication group:

- `\\FS01\Accounting`
- `\\FS02\MoneyStuff`
- `\\DC1\Private`

The second set of example share names is much more confusing at a surface level, but remember that DFS namespaces are going to make these folders accessible via a nice, pretty name such as `\\contoso.local\Files\Accounting`. DFSR doesn't really care what share names it is binding together, but you want share and file *permissions* to be similar across them all. As your users travel among sites, you want them to maintain the ability to access this DFS folder from wherever they are, and no matter which server it is that they are tapping into.

Now that you have some folders shared on different servers, we want to make sure that the **DFS Replication** role is installed on each of those servers. You don't necessarily need the **DFS Namespaces** role installed, but I find it easiest to keep both of those roles installed on all servers where DFS is at play, so you probably want to go ahead and install both the **DFS Namespaces** and **DFS Replication** roles on each of your file servers where you plan to configure sync'd folders.

File servers joined to the domain—check

File shares created—check

DFS roles installed—check

Open the **DFS Management** console, and let's get down to business. I need to decide which shares on what servers need to be bound together in a replication group. Let's set up one replication group that spans two servers, and another group spanning three, just to show that this really works. I gave some examples earlier, but here are the real shares that I am going to bind together as replicated folders.

- Group 1:

    - `\\FS01\Accounting`
    - `\\FS02\Accounting`

- Group 2:

    - `\\FS01\HR`
    - `\\FS02\HR`
    - `\\DC1\HR`

(I do not generally recommend sharing user-facing files on a domain controller, but since this share already exists inside my test lab, let's run with it.)

Inside **DFS Management**, on one of the servers where you have the **DFS Management** tools installed, right-click on **Replication**, and create a new replication group. I am not going to screenshot every available option here, as that would really expand our page count without adding a whole lot of value, but we will certainly look at a few together, and we will talk through each step of the wizard as we progress.

Our first option is whether to establish a multipurpose replication group or a replication group for data collection. There is some good text on this screen defining differences between the two, but for DFS replication groups that users will be accessing on a regular basis, you typically want to choose **Multipurpose**.

Naming your replication group is usually simple. Most people name it by mirroring the share names that this group is going to be replicating. I will name Group 1 **Accounting**. Remember that I am creating two separate replication groups, but this means I will be navigating through this wizard two separate times to create the two groups. Group 2 will be called **HR**, eventually, but I didn't want to confuse you into thinking that I am somehow doing them both at once. For this first walk-through, I am only working on the **Accounting** replication group.

To add replication group members to this replication group, simply use the **Add...** button to add your servers where the shared folders are sitting. Inside my **Accounting** group, I am adding **FS01** and **FS02**.

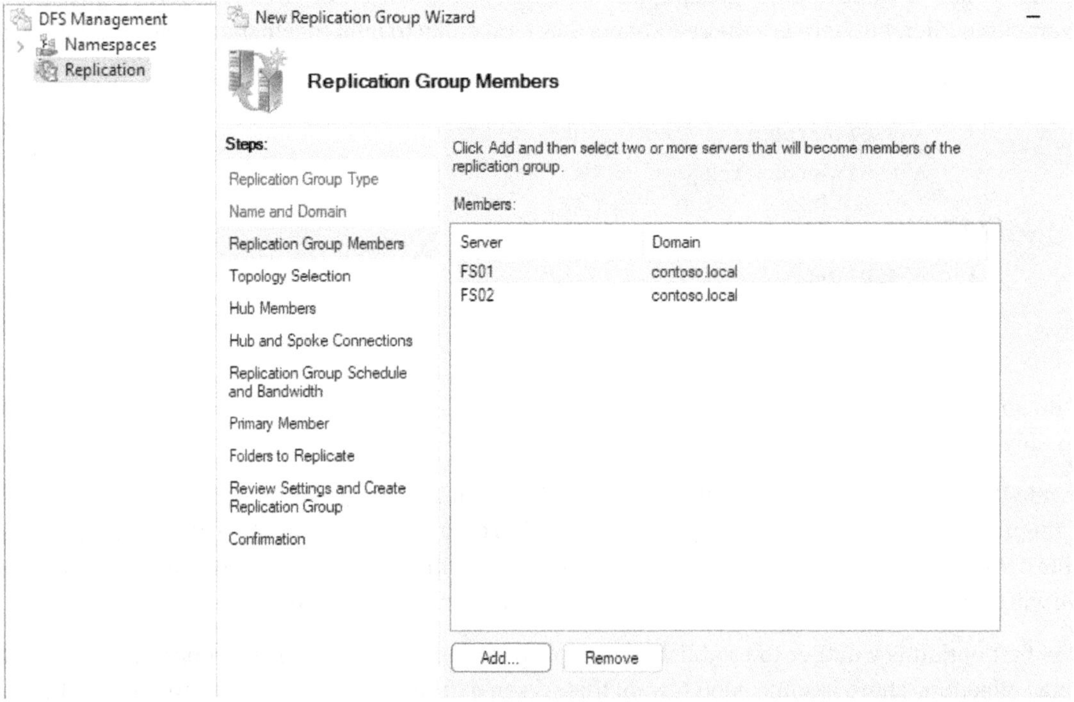

Figure 6.24: Walking through the wizard to create our first replication group

The **Topology Selection** screen offers some interesting selections. As you can see, in this first replication group, where I only have two file servers defined, my only options are **Full mesh** or **No topology**. It is most common across the DFS world for replication groups to be configured as **Full mesh**. This will tell all replication group members to keep their data in sync among themselves, but it is important to understand the limitation that **Full mesh** only works well if you have 10 or fewer members in the same group. **Hub and spoke** is currently grayed out, because I only added FS01 and FS02. For my second replication group, which I will create next, I am going to be adding three servers and so I could choose **Hub and spoke** if I wanted to. This topology is for environments with a lot of member servers, or for scenarios where you expect your data to only be updated on one server (the hub) and replicated outward to other member servers (the spokes).

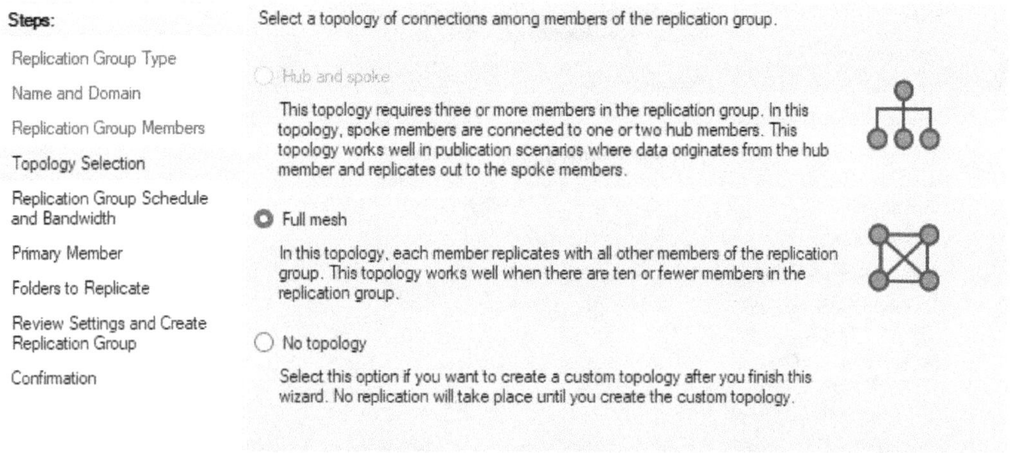

Steps:

Replication Group Type

Name and Domain

Replication Group Members

Topology Selection

Replication Group Schedule
and Bandwidth

Primary Member

Folders to Replicate

Review Settings and Create
Replication Group

Confirmation

Select a topology of connections among members of the replication group.

○ Hub and spoke

This topology requires three or more members in the replication group. In this
topology, spoke members are connected to one or two hub members. This
topology works well in publication scenarios where data originates from the hub
member and replicates out to the spoke members.

● Full mesh

In this topology, each member replicates with all other members of the replication
group. This topology works well when there are ten or fewer members in the
replication group.

○ No topology

Select this option if you want to create a custom topology after you finish this
wizard. No replication will take place until you create the custom topology.

Figure 6.25: Topology Selection choices for your DFS replication group

The **Replication Group Schedule and Bandwidth** page is self-explanatory, but a really cool function. Depending on your LAN/WAN capabilities, DFS could soak up a lot of bandwidth while users are trying to get their work accomplished. If you find that to be true in your environment (you probably won't with the massive internet connections we have today), you could visit this page and configure DFS to throttle the bandwidth it is allowed to use, and even set it to only replicate information during certain times of the day. This is a little bit risky if you expect users to update files on both or all of the servers in a replication group throughout the day; you may find yourself with many sync conflicts to deal with.

Primary Member reminds me of something I have not yet told you: when creating DFS replication groups, you will have to choose the *initial* source of truth for files. In my current example, I am using an Accounting folder that exists on two separate servers. If both of my Accounting folders already had documents and data inside, this screen would allow me to choose which one was the "right one." Whatever server I choose here will be authoritative during the initial data sync, so make sure you have the correct data on your primary server. Many times when we are setting up DFSR, we are taking an existing share and replicating it to a new share on a new server that is currently empty, which works out very well.

Under **Folders to Replicate**, go ahead and add the folder location that you want DFSR to start replicating. This screen displays an interesting component. So far, we have spoken about the Accounting folder in terms of shared folders, but when you select the Accounting folder here, you may notice that DFSR doesn't care about the fact that it's a shared folder. Rather, you select the physical path to this folder. In other words, `C:\Shares\Accounting` on my `FS01` server. This implies that DFSR doesn't require these folders to be shared at all. You would typically have the folders shared from both servers, so that users can tap into these folders (maybe with straight drive mappings, maybe through a DFS namespace), but there is no requirement for DFSR that the synchronized folders be shared. DFSR can be used to keep folders in sync across multiple servers, whether or not those folders are visible to users' eyeballs.

Steps:

Replication Group Type

Name and Domain

Replication Group Members

Topology Selection

Replication Group Schedule
and Bandwidth

Primary Member

Folders to Replicate

Local Path of Accounting on
Other Members

Review Settings and Create
Replication Group

Confirmation

To select a folder on the primary member that you want to replicate to other
members of the replication group, click Add.

Replicated folders:

Local Path	Replicated Folder Name	NTFS Permissions
C:\Shares\Accounting	Accounting	Use existing per...

[Add...]   Edit...   Remove

Figure 6.26: Defining the primary folder to be replicated by DFSR

After specifying FS01 as my primary replication server, the wizard correctly infers that the other side of this sync group is going to be FS02, and asks me to define what folder path I need to sync to on FS02. Use the **Local Path of Accounting on Other Members** screen to define the physical folder path on FS02.

That's it! You will now see a summary screen of the DFSR options being put into place, and then a warning that you may have to wait a little while before this replication takes effect. That is because we are using DFSR with Active Directory, and you need to wait for these changes to flow around your domain before FS01 and FS02 will start using the new replication group.

I walked through this wizard two separate times, creating one Accounting group and another HR group, as I mentioned near the beginning of this section. Back inside the main **DFS Management** screen, you can see both replication groups, now working in the background to keep my folders in sync with each other!

DFS Management
> Namespaces
∨ Replication
      Accounting
      HR

HR (contoso.local)

Memberships   Connections   Replicated Folders   Delegation

3 entries

State	Local Path	Membership Sta...	Member	Replicated Folder	Staging Quota
⊟ Replicated Folder: HR (3 items)					
	C:\HR	Enabled	DC1	HR	4.00 GB
	D:\HR	Enabled	FS01	HR	4.00 GB
	C:\Shares\HR	Enabled	FS02	HR	4.00 GB

Figure 6.27: We have now created two replication groups

After giving these new replication groups some time to sync up with each other, let's make sure this is really working.

Verifying it works

If your initial folder on the primary member had a bunch of data already inside it, the fact that DFSR is working might be really obvious. You should see that data sync'd to the specified folders on your other member servers. In my test lab, I didn't have much stored in those folders, so I am going to add some new folders and files into \\FS01\Accounting, and then add some other folders and files into \\FS02\Accounting. This would replicate common user behavior if I had users at two separate sites, each with one file server.

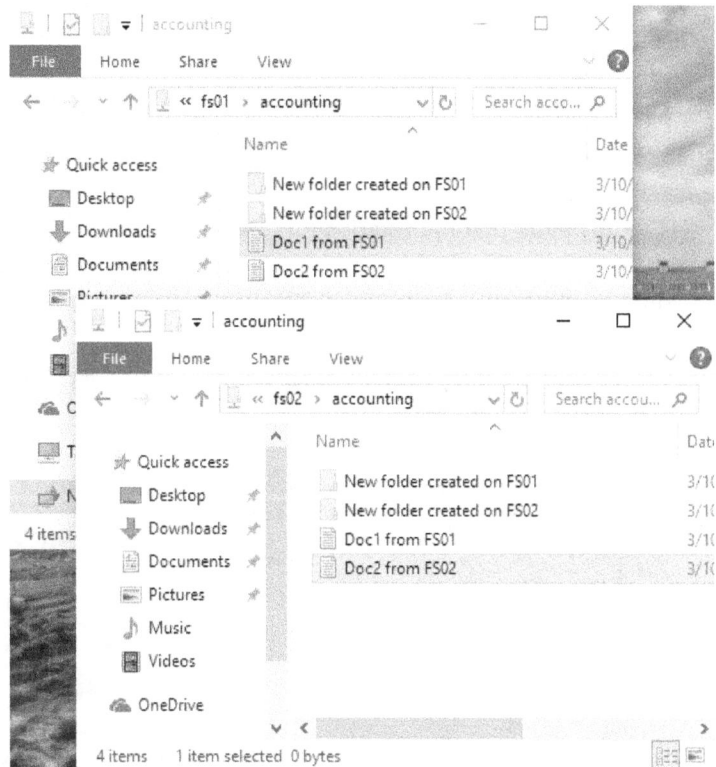

Figure 6.28: DFSR is working!

These files and folders are being immediately replicated between FS01 and FS02! One thing that is important to understand is that DFSR only replicates files once they are closed. If users are creating files and editing them for long periods of time, you may see delays in those file changes being sync'd to other servers. Once the user saves and closes the file, it will be spread around among the other servers in your DFSR group.

Filtering out certain files

DFSR is pretty awesome by default, but there are some more advanced things that can be done with it also. One of those is filtering out certain file types from being replicated. Why would you want to do that? Maybe you are utilizing a shared folder that is part of DFSR, and as an IT person, you are loading in some huge files. For example, an ISO to upgrade Windows Server. Perhaps DFSR will give you exactly what you want in copying a 6 GB file around to a bunch of file servers in your environment, or maybe you are working on a temporary project and you want to ensure that DFSR doesn't take these huge files and spend resources chugging them around the network when it really isn't necessary. Another example might be for TMP or BAK files, things that are not generally very important, and you may simply want to give DFSR some breathing room, to not worry about these files.

Back inside the **Replication** section of **DFS Management**, click on the replication group that you want to modify and then visit the tab called **Replicated Folders**. Inside this tab, you will see the list of folders that this group is syncing. Right-click on the folder you wish to modify, and head into **Properties**.

Here, you can see that BAK and TMP files are already being filtered out, even though I did not do that intentionally. All you need to do to exclude a file type—or, as you can see in *Figure 6.29*, even exclude an entire subfolder—is simply enter that information on this screen. In my example, I am going to be using a folder called Jordan_Temp for a while to finish a project that I am working on, and I plan to delete this folder when finished, so I don't want DFSR to spend any time trying to replicate the Jordan_Temp folder.

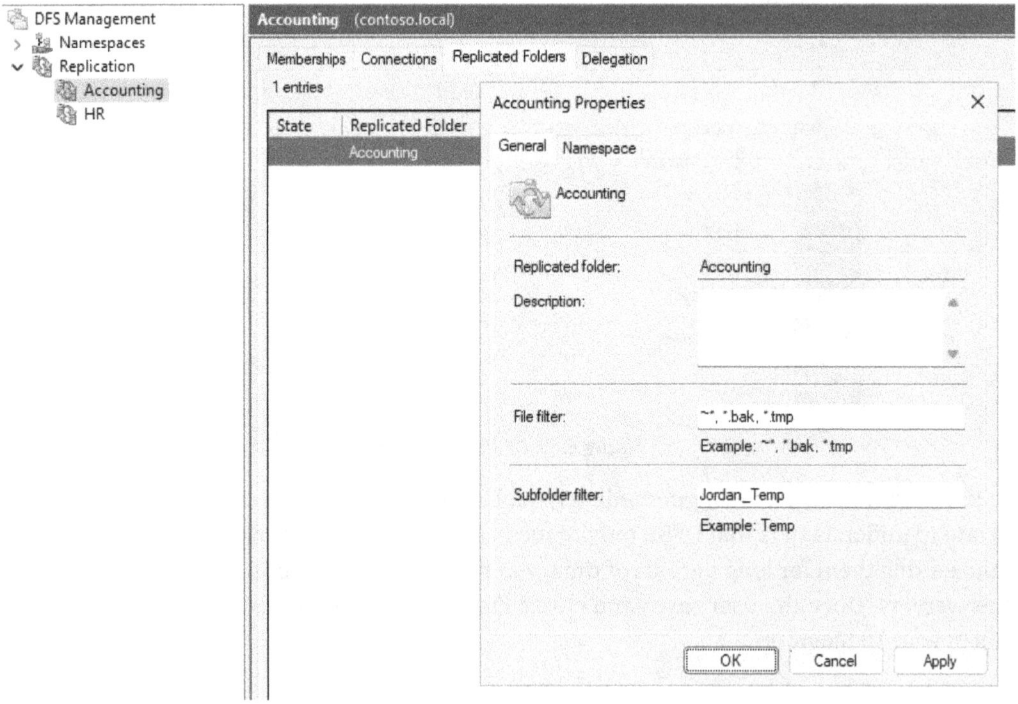

Figure 6.29: Excluding the Jordan_Temp folder from replication

File Transfer Protocol (FTP)

Most often, when discussing file access and protocols in the Windows world, we are talking about classic file sharing and access as has been described so far in this chapter. When a user accesses a regular network drive, this is generally making use of a protocol called **Server Message Block (SMB)** to browse, open, and save files on the network. SMB has gone through a few iterations over the years, and is certainly safer and more comprehensive than it has ever been, but today, you still would not allow SMB to flow natively over the internet because traffic is easily interceptable. We will talk shortly about a new way to use SMB that is actually safe for use over the internet, but this technology is quite new, and in most networks today, SMB is strictly for use within company walls, protected behind your firewalls.

File Transfer Protocol (FTP) is another protocol used to move files from one place to another, but using different methodology and toolsets. For most purposes, SMB beats FTP. SMB file shares are easy to create, easy to use, and allow for two-way traffic. You can copy something from a server and paste something back to that server at the same time. FTP is less functionally useful and quite a simple, straightforward file transfer mechanism, but it is valuable to understand what FTP is and how to use it, because there are some use cases where it will be necessary to forego SMB and look for something else. FTP is often that something else.

There are two use cases for FTP that I find to be common. The first is to provide a way for non-employees to be able to download or upload documents to your company. I say "non-employees" because your employees will likely have a company laptop with VPN access, and they can simply use their SMB-based network drives to access files and folders, no matter where they are. Non-employees, such as customers or vendors, will not and should not have such direct access to your network and file servers, but it's quite common that you need to share files with or retrieve files from one of these entities. Many times, these files are simply too large to be emailed, at which point you begin to explore solutions for moving files in and out of your network through the firewall. FTP can be used for exactly this purpose.

The second reason I see FTP being commonly utilized is primarily in the manufacturing industry, but I've even seen it used with some healthcare devices. Let's pretend that you have a really expensive piece of machinery, some kind of CNC. These can run to millions of dollars when new, so you've sourced a used one for only a few hundred thousand dollars. The trade-off here is that this machine was built in the year 2004. Now, that may seem really old, but in the world of high-dollar machines, it simply means that it has proven its worth and has probably been rebuilt/restored a few times over those years. It could still be an extremely useful tool for making parts and money—who cares if it's old? Well, you, as the IT person, should care because old=insecure, but you absolutely do not get a vote in decisions like this. Without even realizing it is coming, suddenly, this CNC is being installed on the shop floor. Whatever, it's a piece of machinery, what does it matter to me? Then you watch as they string a CAT6 cable over to said machine and plug it in. Hmm...I wonder what the purpose of that cable is? You've probably guessed by now: this CNC machine requires programming files to know how to run its jobs, and those files can be transferred to/from the machine via a network. It was a beautiful thing in 2004, plug-and-play and your Windows XP and Server 2003 machines could interact with this equipment all day long.

In some of these cases, the machinery doesn't know anything about SMB. In others, it may well be capable of receiving files via SMB, but only the early SMBv1, which has now been essentially outlawed by Microsoft due to how insecure it is. In either case, you face a real challenge because you are now tasked with figuring out a process that operators can follow to push programming files to this CNC. Enter FTP. I have seen a *lot* of these machines and faced this scenario dozens of times, and it is almost always true that the machine is capable of establishing an FTP connection with an FTP server. Is it clunkier than SMB? Sure. But when the only other option is that operators in the company physically carry their programming files back and forth to the machine via USB stick, FTP suddenly looks quite fancy.

FTP versus FTPS versus SFTP

FTP is not encrypted traffic, so it is risky to push standard FTP over the internet. There are two ways to enhance the security of FTP-like file transfers: FTPS and SFTP. Let's describe some key differences between them. If nothing else, this will help you to be able to quickly determine which one is at play when you step into an already-established environment.

FTP is for straightforward file transfers. These connections may be authenticated, but not encrypted. When setting up FTP or reviewing firewalls that host FTP connections, you'll find inbound port 21 being used, as well as a "passive" port range. FTP transmissions require large groups of ports to be dedicated to FTP, because every client that reaches the FTP server will begin on port 21, and then dynamically utilize one of many other ports to accomplish the file transfer.

FTPS is FTP with an added layer of TLS security. You may still find port 21 being used at the firewall level, but more likely it will be configured to use port 990. There will still be a passive port range identified on the firewall as well. You should really try to set up any FTP connection with this extra layer of security; running generalized FTP over the internet is quite risky in today's world.

SFTP is often confused with FTPS, but they are totally different. SFTP is still all about transferring files from one place to another, and in a secure fashion, but SFTP is not actually "FTP traffic" at all. Rather, SFTP is the SSH file transfer protocol and uses SSH to do its work. If you've worked with FTP servers before, you may even think right now that you can correctly identify FTP or FTPS by looking for either port 21 or 22 on the firewall, but if you find port 22 at play, you are actually looking at SFTP, an SSH-based protocol. It's not even real FTP!

Creating a Windows FTP server

To be honest, there are non-Microsoft FTP server solutions that are much more popular than the Windows Server FTP offering. These third-party options are more intuitive to set up and offer clearer security settings. One of the common FTP solutions to find in smaller companies is called FileZilla, primarily because it has a free option. This toolset does quite a great job of providing a really fast way to set up FTP connections between clients and servers by installing FileZilla on both ends of the equation.

This is a book about Windows Server 2025, so let's take a quick look at what it takes to build an FTP server using native functionality built into the operating system.

Installing the role

As with anything in Windows Server, there is a role built for the purpose, but this one isn't so easy to find. **FTP Server** is a component of **Web Server (IIS)**. On the primary screen, to select your new server role, you will need to check the box next to **Web Server**, and then click **Next** a couple of times to find yourself at the **Select role services** screen. Here, you will see a breakdown of all the different options and components of the **Web Server** role, and **FTP Server** is one of the selectable options here.

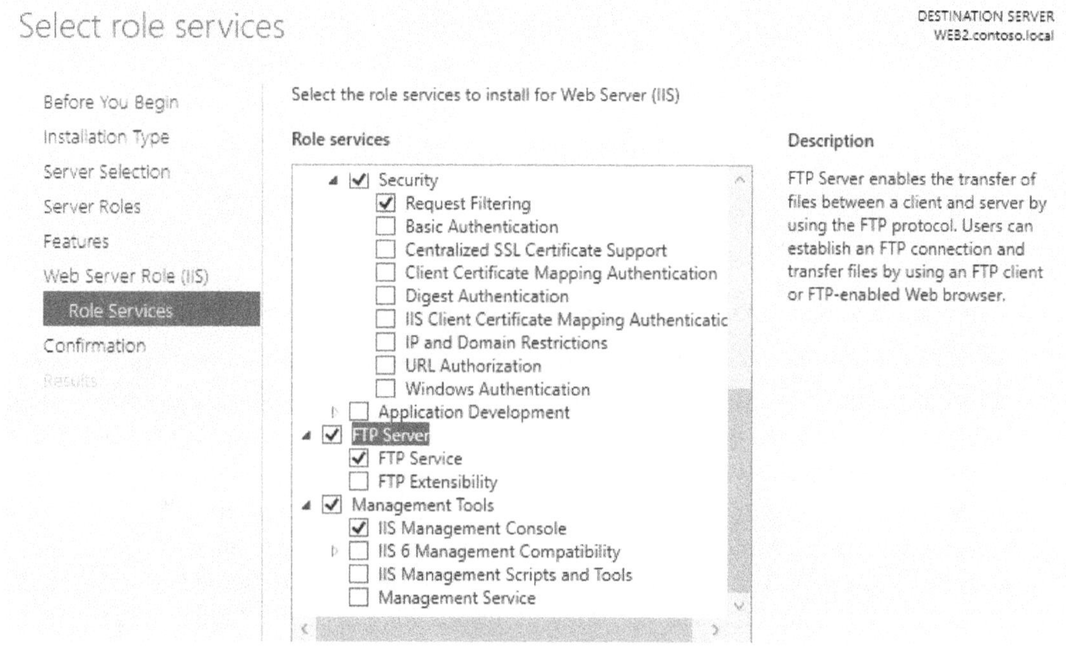

Figure 6.30: Finding and installing the FTP Server role

Configuring FTP services

Role now installed, you'll notice that **Server Manager** does not contain a tool that is named anything related to FTP. Rather, just like the role itself, you must utilize the web server tools to configure this server as an FTP server. Web services on Windows Server are served up by **Internet Information Services (IIS)**, and so this management console is the one used to create both websites as well as FTP listeners.

Launching IIS Manager, if you click on the name of your server in the left window tree, you will see many available icons for manipulating different aspects of FTP. As of right now, there is no FTP listener published on this server, but poking around in these buttons will help to shed light on the configurable options available to you.

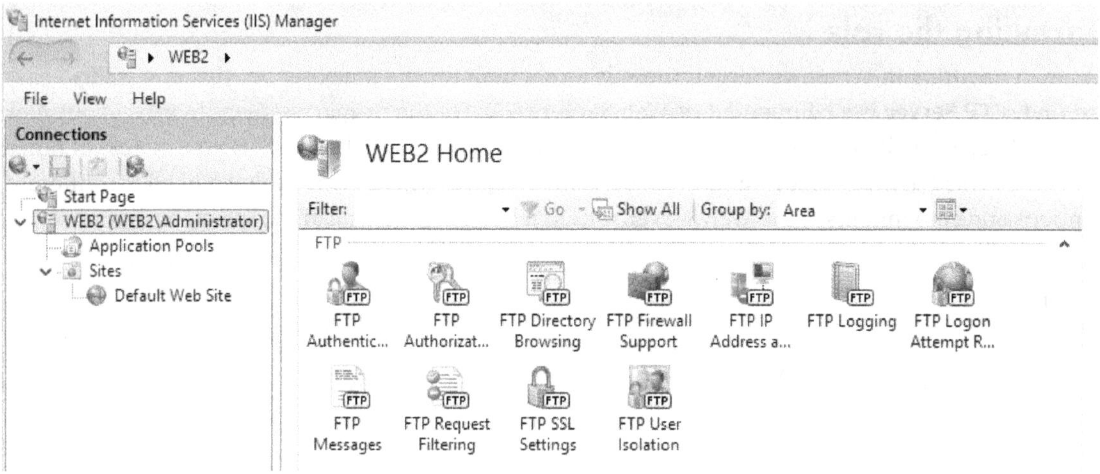

Figure 6.31: FTP configurable options inside IIS Manager

We are interested in a couple of specific ones and will discuss them further here:

- **FTP SSL Settings:** As previously discussed, secure flavors of FTP include TLS, which requires an SSL certificate. We will talk more about certificates in *Chapter 7*, but I want to point out this function because this is the applet you can visit to define the SSL certificate used by FTPS, or to swap out an expiring certificate with a fresh one annually.

- **FTP Firewall Support:** Here, you define which range of ports is to be used by FTP. You will also notice an **External IP Address of Firewall** field on this screen. Now, you certainly shouldn't plug this Windows FTP server directly into the internet. Rather, we assume that you are going to NAT traffic inbound through your firewall toward this FTP server. Configuring the public IP address that clients are going to utilize to contact your firewall on this screen allows for the FTP server to passively accept those connections, even though they are passing through a third party first (the firewall). After defining port information on this screen, IIS will reach into your **Windows Firewall with Advanced Security** ruleset and establish firewall rules locally on the server, allowing this traffic to be successful.

- **FTP Authorization Rules:** Use this section to specify what users are allowed to read or write via FTP. For my example today, I am specifying that anonymous users have both read and write permissions.

Once you are happy with your selections on this screen, our last step is to "publish" FTP from this server. In other words, we are going to tell the server to start listening for FTP client connections to come in via the FTP control port, typically port 21.

Still inside IIS Manager, right-click on the **Sites** folder and select the **Add FTP Site...** option.

Name your site, and select a physical path. This is a folder on the local server that will be used to store and present data to FTP clients. When a client connects to this FTP site to pull data, it will be data from within this folder. On the flip side, if an FTP client logs into FTP to upload a file, that new file will be dropped into the defined folder.

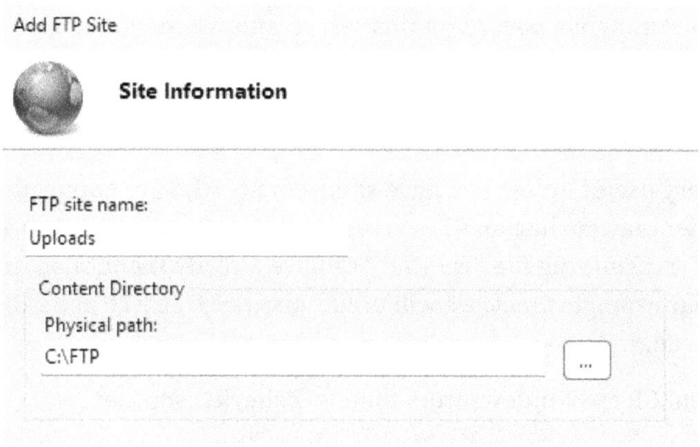

Add FTP Site

Site Information

FTP site name:

Uploads

Content Directory

Physical path:

C:\FTP

Figure 6.32: Establishing our first FTP site

If you'd like to run multiple FTP listeners on the same server, it is very possible, but you need to identify either a unique IP address for each one or a unique control port. On the **Binding** and **SSL** settings screen, you will find options for defining the IP address binding and port for your new FTP site. You will also find SSL certificate settings. Since I do not yet have any SSL certificates in my environment, I am going to set up this FTP site as **No SSL**, but obviously, a production environment that is exposed to the internet should be protected behind an SSL certificate and require SSL.

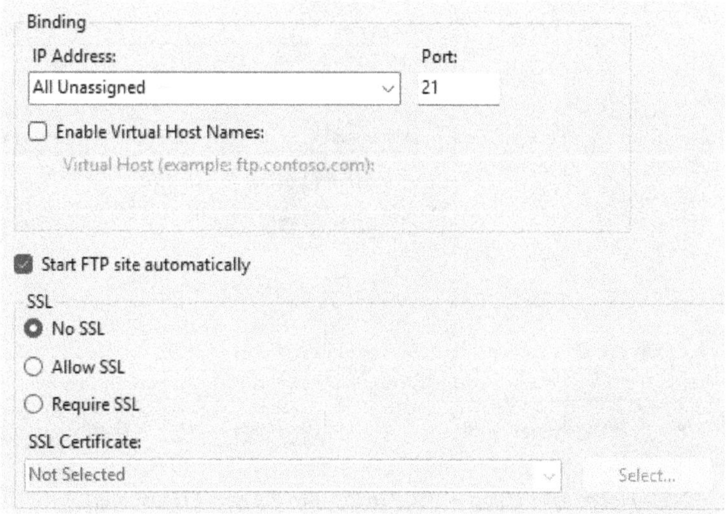

Binding

IP Address: Port:

All Unassigned   21

☐ Enable Virtual Host Names:

Virtual Host (example: ftp.contoso.com):

☑ Start FTP site automatically

SSL

⦿ No SSL

○ Allow SSL

○ Require SSL

SSL Certificate:

Not Selected   Select...

Figure 6.33: Configuring Binding and SSL settings for this site

The last setup screen for our FTP site is to identify authentication requirements for this new site. If you'd like any and all clients to tap into it, choose **Anonymous.** If you would like to restrict the FTP server to only be contactable by certain domain users or groups, choose the option for **Basic** authentication and select your user or groups as needed.

That's it! FTP is now listening via port 21 on this server, and we should be able to tap into it from an FTP client running on a workstation.

Testing file transfer via FTP

An FTP server isn't very useful unless you have some clients who are connecting to it! There are numerous ways that a client can tap into an FTP server, but most often it is through a software application specifically made for transmitting files via FTP. We have already mentioned one of those, a freebie called FileZilla. For our example today, we will utilize another free FTP app called **WinSCP**, which is quite popular in the wild.

You can download WinSCP for Windows from their website, `winscp.net`.

Once installed, launching WinSCP and connecting to your first FTP site is straightforward. Simply configure the name or IP address of the FTP server, the port it is running on, which protocol you want to use, and whether it requires encryption to make the connection. If you have a username/password required for login, go ahead and specify it here as well.

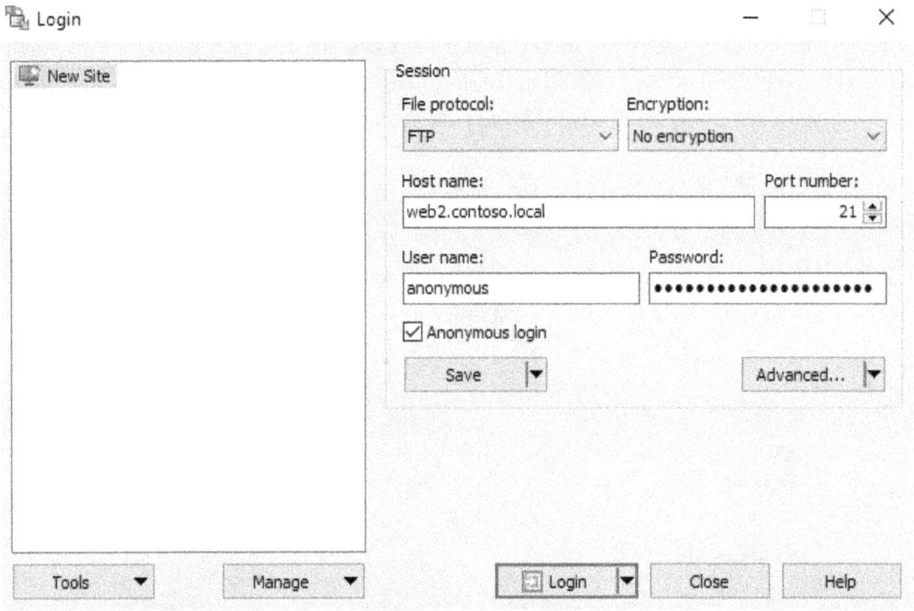

Figure 6.34: Using WinSCP to tap into the new FTP listener

When connected, WinSCP will show your local file system of the workstation in the left window pane, and the remote FTP server's folder structure on the right. You can see in *Figure 6.35* that there are already some files inside the FTP server that are easy to grab and download from here, or I can choose files from my local computer to "push" to the server, uploading them to the C:\FTP folder on that server.

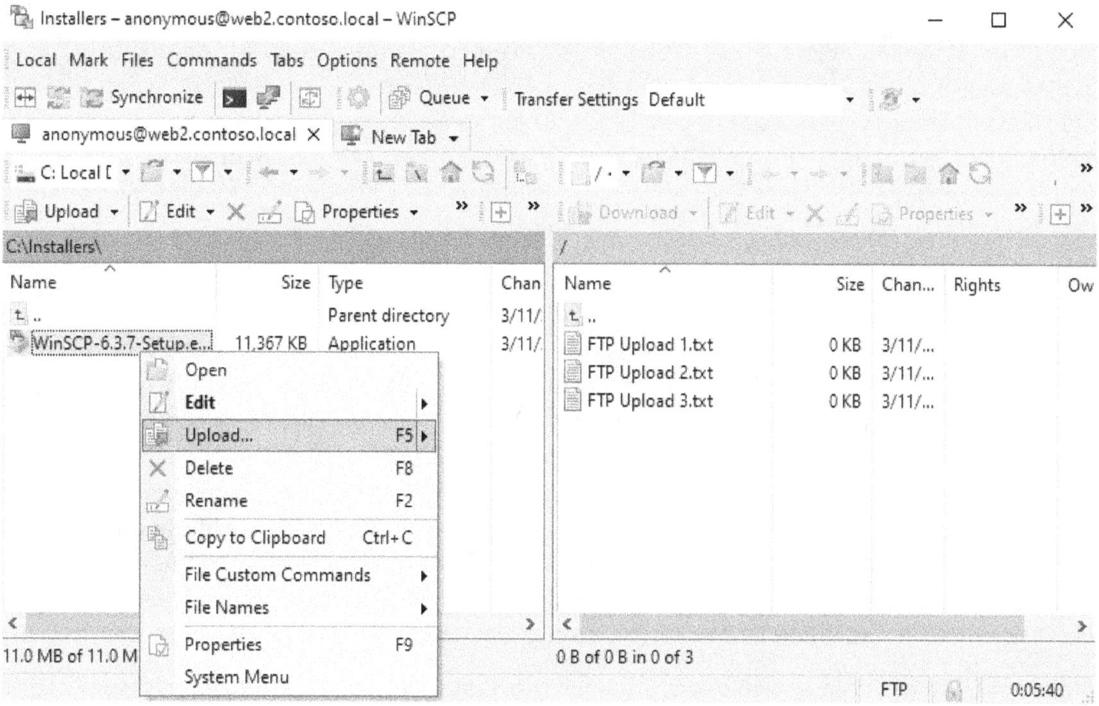

Figure 6.35: WinSCP is an easy way to download/upload files to an FTP server

Again, using FTP to transfer files around your internal network is not the greatest thing since sliced bread. There are much easier ways to do that, namely traditional drive mappings that use the SMB protocol. However, FTP has its place and is great information to keep in your back pocket. The next time you are struggling through getting files back and forth between a server and manufacturing equipment, Linux-based appliances, or even copy machines… remember that FTP could be your golden ticket!

SMB over QUIC

Numerous methods exist for users to access their documents. We have looked over a few together in this chapter, and there are others that we simply don't have time to discuss in depth. More and more of the general workforce is on the road or working from home, and many companies have turned to OneDrive, SharePoint, and even Azure Files to provide new and different ways for file access to happen without requiring a constant VPN connection back to the office.

Even though the preceding paragraph is true, there are so many companies still making use of classic Windows file servers, and entrance into something such as SharePoint is a heavy lift, because it greatly moves everybody's cheese. The user experience is vastly different. Classic file access via File Explorer and mapped network drives is still the preference of almost everybody working in an office, but this uses the SMB protocol, which is not inherently safe to publish over the internet. What if we could pull a magic lever and give all employees access to their files via mapped network drives inside File Explorer, but this access would work whether employees are inside *or even outside* of their office?

Hello, SMB over QUIC! As mentioned, there is no way that you, as a security-conscious administrator, would permit native SMB, which uses TCP port 445, to flow over the internet. What is the "QUIC" part of SMB over QUIC? Effectively, it means that these SMB connections are encrypted! Most firewalls will (and should) block TCP 445, so SMB over QUIC pushes itself through firewalls by utilizing port 443, similar to HTTPS traffic. SMB over QUIC technically uses UDP port 443, though in a lot of installations it makes use of both TCP 443 for something called KDC proxy and also UDP 443 to carry the workload. SMB over QUIC is encrypted via TLS 1.3, so it is quite secure and protected.

I mentioned the KDC proxy, and if you haven't heard of this before, it is an authentication component that underpins a few Microsoft technologies. KDC proxy is what causes the authentication magic to happen, where your SMB file connections can be successfully authenticated to a domain controller, even though that DC server is certainly not going to be exposed to the internet. If KDC proxy makes use of TCP 443, that does mean that the server you utilize for SMB over QUIC cannot be serving other web-facing purposes, such as hosting a website. You would certainly not want to combine these roles. Whatever server you use to host SMB over QUIC file access, let it be a file server and nothing else. One question that may pop into your mind as you think through what this could look like in your environment is can my SMB over QUIC server also be a "normal" file server? Yes! One of these servers can run regular file connections inside the network using TCP 445, while at the same time serving up files via SMB over QUIC using TCP/UCP 443 for those coming in from the internet, through your firewall.

SMB over QUIC has been available to us for a few years, but previously, you could only make use of this technology by deploying that special version of the operating system, Windows Server 2022 Datacenter: Azure Edition. The big news here is that with the release of Windows Server 2025, Microsoft has now enabled SMB over QUIC to work from *any* version of Server 2025!

Deployment via WAC

To make use of SMB over QUIC in your environment, you need to perform the following:

1. Build a file server running Windows Server 2025 or 2022 Datacenter: Azure Edition.

2. Identify a public DNS name to use for these connections, such as `files.contoso.com`, and install an SSL certificate on the file server that can validate and protect that name. Your SSL certificate must protect both this public name and the internal hostname of your server, so that SMB over QUIC can be successful whether users are inside or outside of the network. In our example, I have configured my SSL certificate to protect the following DNS names:

   - `Files.contoso.com`
   - `FS02.contoso.local`

3. Configure networking from the internet inbound to this server. Use your firewall to NAT traffic from a public IP address (where `files.contoso.com` resolves) to flow inbound to this new file server. You need to allow TCP and UDP port 443 to flow, and make sure you do *not* allow TCP 445! This would be a sure way to ask for bad things to happen in your network.

4. Configure the file server to be enabled and listening for SMB over QUIC requests. This part is fairly simple, but there is an inherent complication here, as of the time I am writing these words, because Microsoft has not yet updated **Windows Admin Center (WAC)** to be able to enable SMB over QUIC on Server 2025. I genuinely hope that by the time you are reading this, that stance has changed and you can now make use of WAC to deploy SMB over QUIC to your new Windows Server 2025 machines, but for the time being, these are the rules when configuring SMB over QUIC:

- **Windows Server 2022 Datacenter: Azure Edition = Installation via WAC or PowerShell**
- **Windows Server 2025 = Installation via PowerShell**

We will walk through configuration via both methods, in case one fits your needs better than the other. Inside WAC, it is very straightforward. We already have WAC running in this test lab; all I need to do is log into it, make sure it is configured to know about my new file server, and update one setting. I have already installed an SSL certificate on the FS02 server for `files.contoso.com`.

We are logged in to WAC and have navigated to the FS02 server. Here, we visit **Settings**, and the first screen that should be shown displays settings for **File shares (SMB server)**, but if yours does not default to this, navigate to these settings. There are a few interesting SMB-related settings on this page, but the section to configure SMB over QUIC is a simple button near the bottom.

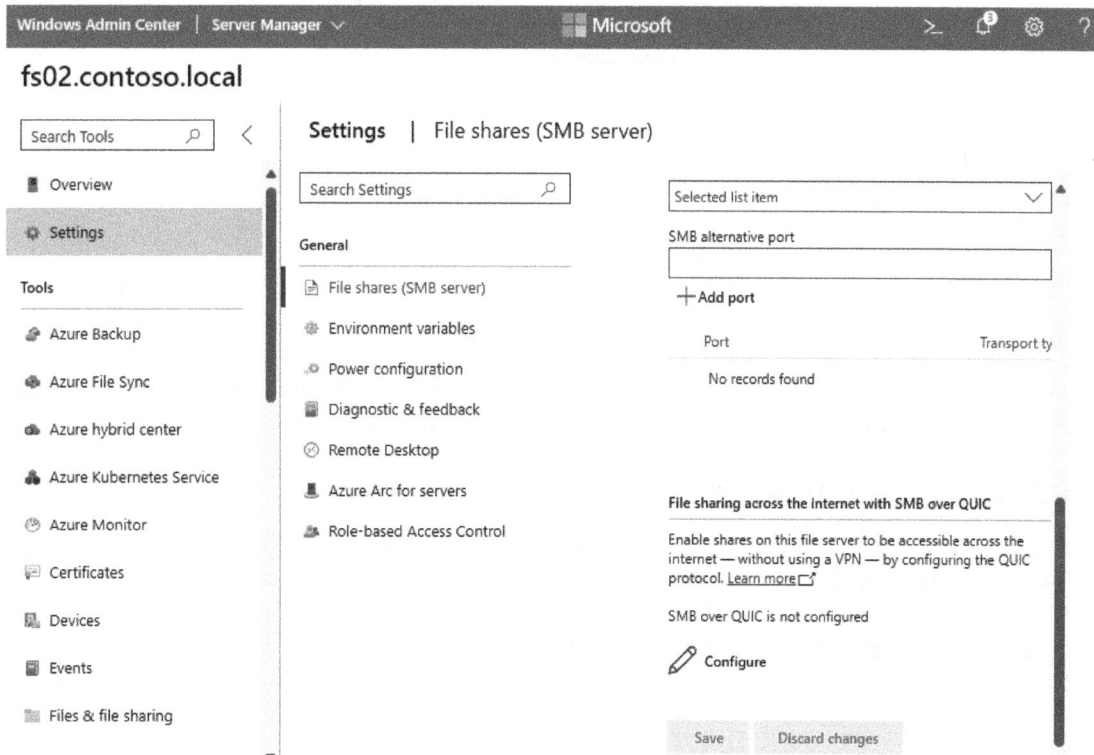

Figure 6.36: Configuring SMB over QUIC via Windows Admin Center

After clicking the **Configure** button, you will see all available options for configuring SMB over QUIC. With a few simple mouse clicks, we select the SSL certificate that needs to be used to protect this traffic, then choose the checkboxes for which DNS names clients will be contacting. The configuration wizard pulls these names from the SSL certificate, and it is **very important that your certificate, and therefore these checkboxes, reflect both the internal and external names**. In *Figure 6.37*, you can see both `files.contoso.com` and `fs02.contoso.local` DNS names are going to be part of this configuration.

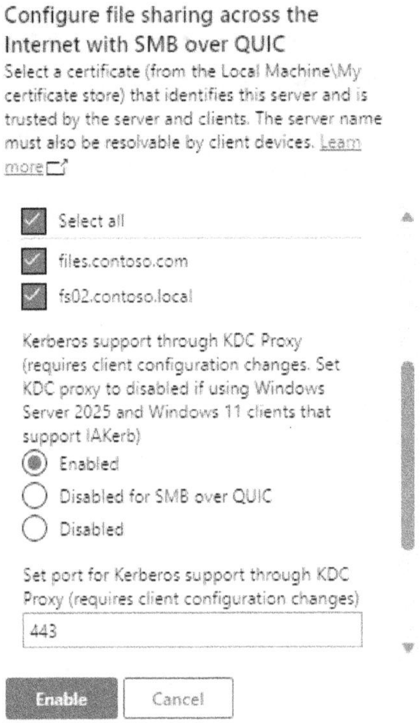

Figure 6.37: Configuring SMB over QUIC options

After those few selections, click the **Enable** button, and WAC will reach out to the file server to configure what is needed for SMB over QUIC to begin accepting connections!

Deployment via PowerShell

Once again, I really hope that Microsoft has permitted SMB over QUIC on Windows Server 2025 to be configured by WAC by the time you are reading these words, but just in case they haven't, or if you prefer PowerShell anyway, there is also a quick way to enable SMB over QUIC on Windows Server 2025 by using the CLI. Let's work through that together.

Once again, I am assuming that you already have your valid SSL certificate installed on this file server. Once you do, open PowerShell and work through the following cmdlets:

1. Show your installed certificate with this command:

```
Get-ChildItem -Path Cert:\LocalMachine\My
```

2. Plug your certificate into a variable that PowerShell can use moving forward. Obviously, you'll want to swap out files.contoso.com with your own DNS name:

```
$serverCert = Get-ChildItem -Path Cert:\LocalMachine\My | Where-Object
{$_.Subject -Match "files.contoso.com"}
```

3. Verify that it correctly pulled your certificate info into the variable:

```
$serverCert
```

4. Enable SMB over QUIC, telling it to make use of your certificate. You'll need to once again replace my DNS name with your own:

```
New-SmbServerCertificateMapping -Name files.contoso.com -ThumbPrint
$serverCert.Thumbprint -Storename My
```

```
PS C:\Users\administrator.CONTOSO> Get-ChildItem -Path Cert:\LocalMachine\My


    PSParentPath: Microsoft.PowerShell.Security\Certificate::LocalMachine\My

Thumbprint                                Subject
----------                                -------
8B03357263FAA852142F431B0E032FE1665AAD84  CN=files.contoso.com


PS C:\Users\administrator.CONTOSO> $serverCert = Get-ChildItem -Path Cert:\LocalMachine\My
 | Where-Object {$_.Subject -Match "files.contoso.com"}
PS C:\Users\administrator.CONTOSO> $serverCert


    PSParentPath: Microsoft.PowerShell.Security\Certificate::LocalMachine\My

Thumbprint                                Subject
----------                                -------
8B03357263FAA852142F431B0E032FE1665AAD84  CN=files.contoso.com


PS C:\Users\administrator.CONTOSO> New-SmbServerCertificateMapping -Name files.contoso.com
 -ThumbPrint $serverCert.Thumbprint -Storename My

Name             Subject                 Thumbprint                                DisplayNa
                                                                                   me
----             -------                 ----------                                ---------
files.contoso.com CN=files.contoso.com   8B03357263FAA852142F431B0E032FE1665AAD84  files....


PS C:\Users\administrator.CONTOSO>
```

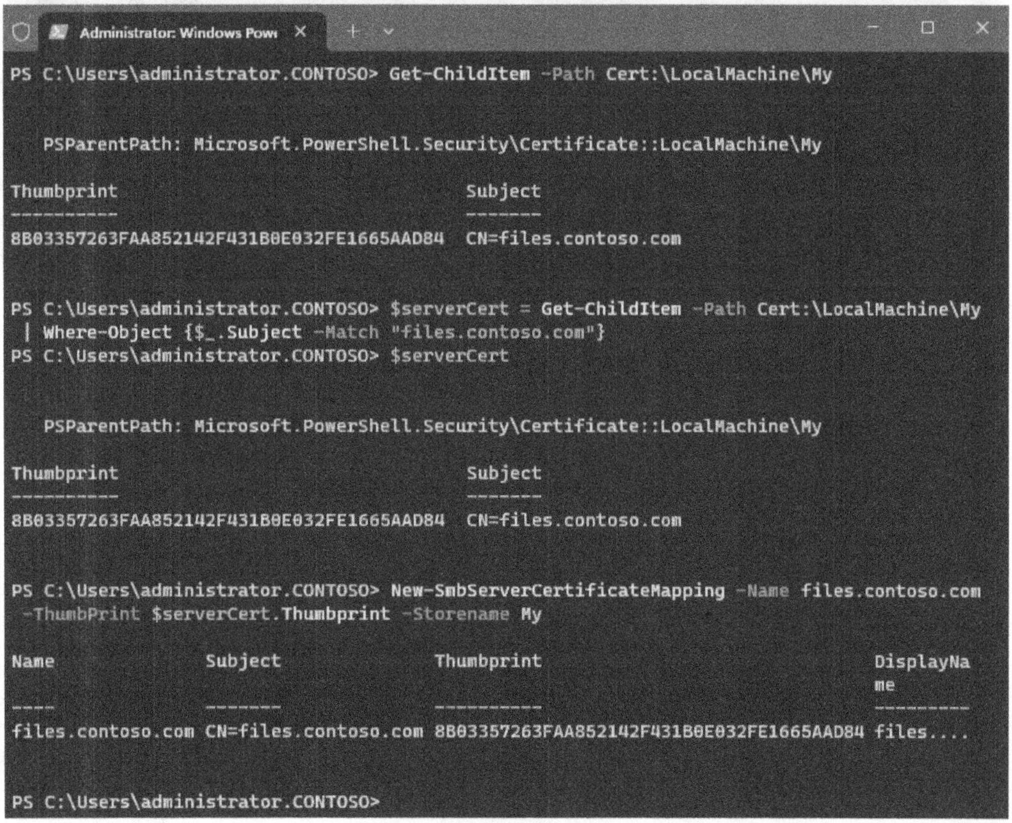

Figure 6.38: Configuring SMB over QUIC through PowerShell

That's it! I now have SMB over QUIC running on my FS01 server, courtesy of PowerShell. Earlier, I enabled SMB over QUIC on FS02 by configuring that server via WAC, and if I open Terminal on either of these servers and run netstat -ano, I can see in the output that both servers are listening on TCP 445, which is expected simply because both of these are file servers, but they are also now listening on TCP 443 and UDP 443, which are the ports used by SMB over QUIC.

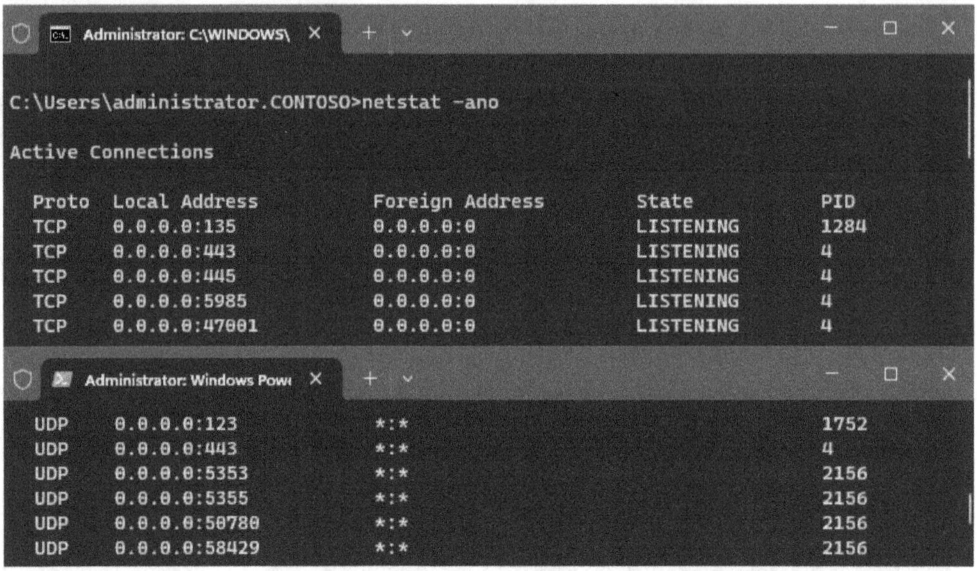

Figure 6.39: FS02 is now listening on TCP and UDP 443, ready for SMB over QUIC connections

I do want to add a note here that even though Microsoft's official stance is that you can only utilize PowerShell to configure SMB over QUIC on Windows Server 2025, inside my test lab, I just successfully utilized WAC to configure SMB over QUIC on FS02. You probably noticed that FS02 is running Windows Server 2025, so this is the exact scenario Microsoft calls out in their documentation that is currently not supported, and yet it worked just fine for me today. I'm not advocating that you work against Microsoft documentation, but it's entirely possible that their Microsoft Learn documentation simply needs some updating.

Testing it out!

I enabled SMB over QUIC on two different file servers, but only because I wanted to show the differences between WAC and PowerShell configuration methods. I would love to test and make sure this is really working from a client computer, and I will focus on the FS02 file server for this. One prerequisite is that I need the files.contoso.com name to resolve to the FS02 server, so I have, of course, configured the DNS to do this. In the real world, I would use my edge firewall to configure a NAT rule to push TCP 443 and UDP 443 to FS02 from a public IP address, and then I would configure my public DNS also to point files.contoso.com at this public IP address. The problem with that in my test lab is that I have built this lab specifically blocked away from the internet, and I cannot show you that exact scenario.

So, instead, I will use a local firewall rule on FS02 to block inbound TCP 445 traffic. If I block inbound TCP 445, this will break any ability for client workstations to access shared folders on this file server using normal, inside-the-network SMB, and force those clients to attempt access using SMB over QUIC instead. After creating this block rule inside **Windows Firewall with Advanced Security**, I have verified that I can no longer access my \\FS02\Scans folder, or any of the other folders shared from that server.

Figure 6.40: TCP 445 is blocked on FS02 and I can no longer access file shares

Except...if, instead of trying to access \\FS02\Scans from my client computer, I instead navigate File Explorer to \\files.contoso.com\Scans....Success! In a traditional environment with an inbound firewall and public IP addresses, I would be able to access file shares from the internet, outside of my building, even without building a VPN tunnel.

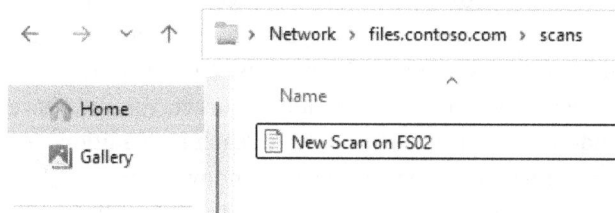

Figure 6.41: SMB over QUIC is working!

Although we have proven here that SMB over QUIC is working, by blocking TCP 445 and still being able to navigate files through `files.contoso.com`, your users are generally not going to remember that they need to open File Explorer, visit the address bar, and manually type in this destination. How can we translate these new file paths into traditional drive letter mappings? Let's explore that next.

Mapping SMB over QUIC network drives

"How do I map network drives using SMB over QUIC?" The short answer is that you do this exactly the same way you would map any network drive.

In current client workstation operating systems, the `net use` command attempts to connect using TCP 445, and if not available, fails over to UDP for SMB over QUIC. So, you can get away with regular old commands such as this:

```
Net use S: \\files.contoso.local\scans
```

(This tries TCP to see whether you're inside the network, then flips over to UDP.)

If you wanted to force a client to map their drive using SMB over QUIC and bypass TCP 445 altogether, you could tag your `Net use` command with the following bits:

```
Net use S: \\files.contoso.local\scans /TRANSPORT:QUIC
```

(This skips TCP and goes directly to UDP.)

Summary

Administration of your files can take on many forms. How does that saying go? This is data's world, we're just living in it. Sometimes we cannot control whether users make good decisions about how they work within files, but at least we can know that we have provided them with a safe, protected, and redundant mechanism for accessing those files. Automating your drive mappings can save a lot of time and effort. Making use of the DFS and especially adding onto that acronym by spinning up DFSR can make life easier for your workforce and create efficiencies for traveling users. While we as a population continue to become less and less patient with multiple steps to perform any task, Microsoft continues to innovate within the age-old topic of file access, by releasing a game-changer such as SMB over QUIC so that remote users can now access their files without having to connect to a clunky VPN.

One of the trickiest bits about working on this *Mastering* book series is deciding what content is appropriate to include. This largely depends on you, the audience, and what I have found over the years is that we have an extremely wide range of experience, backgrounds, and skillsets perusing these words. If you are someone who has followed along with previous editions of the book, released in the same cadence as Microsoft releases new versions of Windows Server, you may have realized that I like to include at least one brand-new, from-scratch chapter in each new edition. In this book, *Chapter 6* is the new chapter. Is file management a new idea as of Windows Server 2025? Absolutely not. Proper administration and safekeeping of company files is a core function of any server administrator. I simply bypassed this topic in previous editions. Following the release of *Mastering Windows Server 2022*, I received numerous feedback strands asking for information about file management, specifically about DFSR. I hope this chapter has filled in those gaps!

Questions

Put your knowledge to the test with the following questions. If you need a hand (or just want to double-check), you'll find all the answers in the *Appendix* section of the book.

1. For a shared folder, do permissions under the **Share** tab or the **Security** tab take priority?

2. When mapping network drives via GPO, are these settings stored in the **Computer Configuration** or **User Configuration** section of the policy?

3. As more companies move into cloud environments, how would you automate the mapping of network drives on your client computers, if those computers are joined to Entra and not part of a local domain?

4. If Tom has access to the entire HR directory today, what change could you make to block his access to the HR\Payroll subfolder?

5. What is the minimum number of member servers required to create a hub-and-spoke DFS Replication group?

6. When creating a DFS namespace, what kind of information is stored inside C:\DFSRoots (assuming you chose the default options when creating the namespace)?

7. Which free FTP client software did we utilize to connect to our FTP server?

8. When issuing the SSL certificate used by SMB over QUIC, which two DNS names must be included inside that certificate's DNS names?

9. What ports are used by SMB over QUIC when KDC proxy is enabled?

Join us on Discord

For discussions around the book and to connect with your peers, join us on Discord at https://packt.link/discordcloud or scan the QR code below:

7

Certificates

Gross, it says we need to use certificates to make this work!

Real-life quote from any admin after discovering their latest software purchase requires the use of certificates

If the preceding quote sounds familiar, or perhaps even a variant more colorful than this, you are not alone! But take heart, let's not scrap that new project just yet. For some reason, the use of certificates seems like a daunting task to many of us, even those who have worked in IT for many years. I think this is probably because there are many different options available on a certificate server, but there is not a lot of common sense or user-friendliness built into the management console for dealing with certificates. This, combined with a general lack of requirements for certificates on servers for so many years, means that even though this technology has existed for a long time, many server administrators have not had the opportunity to dig in and deploy certificates for themselves. I regularly deploy a couple of technologies that require the broad use of certificates in an organization, often needing to issue them to every workstation or user in the network, and I hear these kinds of concerns all the time. Issuing a certificate to a single business-critical webserver sounds daunting enough if you don't have any experience with the process, let alone issuing hundreds or thousands of certificates across the company.

Another common scenario is one where a company determines certificates to be in their best interests but lacks the on-staff resources to make it happen, and so hires a third party to implement certificates within the network. While this gets certificates rolling, it often leaves a knowledge gap that never gets filled, so you may have a certificate server up and running, but not be at all comfortable with modifying or utilizing it. Certificates expire, often after one year, and your newly purchased and installed certificates might carry you through the next 364 days, and suddenly stop working if you don't have the knowledge to manage them.

The broad term for a certificate environment is **public key infrastructure** (**PKI**). I call that out specifically because you will probably see PKI listed in documentation or requirements at some point if you haven't already. Your PKI is provided by servers in your network, and helping you understand how to configure those servers to issue certificates is the purpose of this chapter.

The servers that you determine to be your certificate servers are known as **certification authority** (**CA**) servers, and we will refer to them as CA servers throughout this book.

To get you started with using certificates in your network, here are the topics that we will cover in this chapter:

- Common certificate types
- Planning your PKI
- Creating a certificate template
- Issuing certificates
- Creating an auto-enrollment policy
- Obtaining a public authority SSL certificate
- Exporting and importing certificates
- OpenSSL for Linux webservers

Common certificate types

There are several different types of certificates that you may find a need to publish. As you will soon see, when you need a certificate that has a list of particular requirements, you can build a certificate template to match whatever specifications you like. So, in a sense, there aren't really certificate *types* at all, but just certificate templates that you scope to contain whatever pieces of information are needed for that certificate to do its job. While this holds true technically, it is generally easier to segment certificates into different groups, making them more distinguishable for the particular job that they are intended to perform.

User certificates

As the name implies, a user certificate is one used for purposes that are specific to the users holding those certificates. One driving force behind higher levels of certificate adoption in general is strengthening the network authentication process. Companies that are looking into stronger authentication in their environments often look at certificates as part of that authentication process. Smart cards are one of the mechanisms that can be used for this purpose, specifically, some sort of physical card to be plugged into a computer in order for the user to gain access to that computer.

Smart cards can also be stored virtually within a special place on modern machines, called the TPM. But that is a discussion for a different day. The reason we mention smart cards here is that, often, the core functionality of smart card authentication is provided by a user certificate that has been stored on that smart card. If you find yourself in the middle of a project to deploy smart cards or some form of physical key login, you will probably find yourself in need of a PKI.

Another popular strong authentication form is a **one-time password** (OTP), a function of multifactor authentication. These OTPs require the user to enter a randomly generated PIN in addition to their regular login credentials, and in some cases, when the user enters their PIN, they are issued a temporary user certificate to be used as part of their authentication chain.

Additional places where user certificates are commonly found include when companies employ file-encrypting technologies, such as **EFS** (short for **Encrypting File System**), or when building up **virtual private network** (VPN) systems to enable remote users to connect their laptops back to the corporate network. Many companies don't want to rely purely on a username and a password for VPN authentication, so issuing user certificates and requiring that they be present to build that VPN tunnel is commonplace.

Computer certificates

Often referred to as computer certificates or machine certificates, these are issued to computers to assist with the interaction between the network and the computer account itself. Technologies, such as SCCM, that interact with and manage the computer systems regardless of which users are logged in to those computers make use of computer certificates. These kinds of certificates are also used for encryption processing between systems on the network. For example, if you were interested in using IPsec to encrypt communications between clients and a highly secure file server, issuing computer or machine certificates to the endpoints within this communication chain would be essential to make that work properly. I often find myself issuing computer certificates to a business's machines to authenticate DirectAccess tunnels, a form of automated remote access. There are many different reasons and technologies you may be interested in that require the issuance of certificates to the client workstations in your environment.

SSL certificates

If you find yourself in the middle of the certificate road, where you haven't really managed a CA server but you have at one point issued and installed some kind of certificate, chances are that the certificate you worked with was an SSL certificate. This is by far the most common type of certificate used in today's technology infrastructure, and your company is more than likely using SSL certificates, even if you are not aware of them and do not have a single CA server running inside your network.

SSL certificates are most commonly used to secure website traffic. Any time you visit a website and see HTTPS in the address bar, your browser is using an encrypted packet stream to send information back and forth between your computer and the webserver that you are talking to. The webserver has an SSL certificate on it, and your browser has checked over that certificate before allowing you onto the web page, to make sure that the certificate is valid and that the website really is what it says it is. You see, if we did not use SSL certificates on websites, anyone could impersonate our site and gain access to the information being passed to the website.

Let's provide a quick example. Let's say one of your users is at a coffee shop, using public Wi-Fi. An attacker has figured out a way to manipulate DNS on that Wi-Fi network. Your user tries to visit `mail.contoso.com` to access the company's *Outlook Web Access* to check their email, but the attacker has hijacked that traffic, and the user is now accessing a website that looks like their company portal but is actually a website hosted by the attacker. Your employee types in their username and password, and *bingo*, the attacker now has that user's credentials and can use them to access your real network.

What prevents this from happening every day in the real world? **SSL certificates.** When you force your externally facing websites, such as that email login page, to be HTTPS sites, it requires the client browsers to check the SSL certificate that is presented with the website. That SSL certificate contains information that only you as a company have; it cannot be impersonated. This way, when users access your real login page, the browser checks the SSL certificate, finds it to be correct, and simply continues on its merry way. The users never even know they are being protected except for the little lock symbol up near their browser's address bar. On the other hand, if their traffic is being intercepted and redirected to a fake website, the SSL certificate check will fail (because the attacker would not have a valid SSL certificate for your company website name), and the user will be stopped in their tracks, at least to read through a certificate warning page before being able to proceed. At this point, the user should back off, realize that something is wrong, and contact IT staff to investigate the issue.

SSL certificates used by websites on the internet are almost never provided by your internal CA server but by a public CA. You have probably heard of many of them, such as Verisign, Entrust, DigiCert, and GoDaddy. Companies generally purchase SSL certificates from these public authorities because these authorities are trusted by default on new computers that users might purchase in the field. When you buy a new computer, even straight from a retail store, if you were to open up the local store of certificates that exist out of the box on that system, you would find a list of trusted root authorities. When you visit a website protected by an SSL certificate issued by one of these public authorities, that certificate, and therefore the website, is automatically trusted by this computer. The public CAs are publicly recognized entities, known for their capacity to securely issue SSL certificates.

When a company acquires an SSL certificate from one of these public authorities, there is an in-depth verification process that the authority goes through to make sure that the person requesting the certificate (you) is really someone working with the proper company and authorized to issue these certificates. This is the basis of security in using SSL certificates from a public CA. All new computers know by default to trust certificates that have been issued by these authorities, and you don't have to take any special actions to make your websites function on the internet. On the other hand, it is possible to issue SSL certificates from a CA server that you built yourself and have running inside your network, but it requires a couple of things that make it difficult, because your CA server is obviously not trusted by all computers everywhere, nor should it be. First, if you want to issue your own SSL certificate for use on a public website, you need to externalize at least part of your internal PKI, known as the **certificate revocation list (CRL)**, to the internet. Any time you take a component that is internal to your network and publicize it on the internet, you are introducing a security risk, so unless you absolutely have to do this, it is generally not recommended. The second reason it is difficult to utilize your own SSL certificates on public websites is that only your own company's domain-joined computers will know how to trust this SSL certificate. So, if a user brings their company laptop home and uses it to access their email login page, it will probably work fine. But if a user tries to access the same email login page from their home computer, which is not part of your domain or network, they will get a certificate warning message and have to take special steps in order to gain access to the website. What a pain for the users. You should never encourage users to accept risk and proceed through a certificate warning message—this is a recipe for disaster, even if the certificate they are clicking through is one issued by your own CA. It's a matter of principle never to accept that risk.

These issues can be alleviated by purchasing an SSL certificate from one of those public CAs, and so purchasing these kinds of certificates is the normal and recommended way to make use of SSL on your publicly facing websites. Websites that are completely inside the network are a different story, since they are not facing the internet and their security footprint is much smaller. You can use your internal CA server to issue SSL certificates to your internal websites, and not have to incur the cost associated with purchasing certificates for all of those websites.

There are a few different tiers of SSL certificates that you can purchase from a public CA, information for which is listed on the authority's own websites. Essentially, the idea is that the more you pay, the more secure your certificate is. These tiers are related to the way that the authority validates against the certificate requester, since that is really where security comes into play with SSL certificates. The authority is guaranteeing that when you access the page secured by their certificate, the certificate was issued to the real company that owns that web page.

Other than the validation tier, which you get to choose when purchasing a certificate, there is another option you have to decide on as well, and this one is much more important to the technical aspect of the way that certificates work. There are different naming conventions available to you when you purchase a certificate, and there is no best answer for which one to choose. Every situation that requires a certificate will be unique and will have to be evaluated individually to decide which naming scheme works best. Let's quickly cover three possibilities for an SSL certificate naming convention.

Single-name certificates

This is the cheapest and most common route to take when purchasing a certificate for an individual website or web service. A single-name certificate protects and contains information about a single DNS name. When you are setting up a new website at portal.contoso.com and you want this website to protect some traffic by using HTTPS, you would install an SSL certificate on the website. When you issue the request to your CA for this new certificate, you would input the specific name of portal.contoso.com into the **Common name** field of the request form. This single DNS name is the only name that can be protected and validated by this certificate.

Multi-domain or subject alternative name certificates

Multi-domain certificates, sometimes called **subject alternative name** (SAN) certificates, generally cost a little bit more than single-name certificates, because they have more capabilities. When you request a SAN certificate, you have the option of defining multiple DNS names that the certificate can protect. Once issued, the SAN certificate will contain a primary DNS name, which is typically the main name of the website, and further, inside the certificate properties, you will find listed the additional DNS names that you specified during your request. This single certificate can be installed on a webserver, or perhaps multiple servers, and used to validate traffic for any of the DNS names that are contained in the certificate. Now don't laugh, yes, I do realize that Lync is discontinued and even Skype for Business is leaving us, now that Teams has taken over the world, but an on-premises Lync server is a prime example of a technology that required the use of multi-domain certificates that protected numerous DNS names. Another example would be an on-premises Exchange server. Either of these technologies uses many different DNS names, but all names sit within the same DNS domain. Here is an example list of the names we might include in a single SAN certificate for the purposes of Lync:

- `lync.contoso.com` (the primary one)
- `lyncdiscover.contoso.com`
- `meet.contoso.com`
- `dialin.contoso.com`
- `admin.contoso.com`

These different websites/services used by Lync were then implemented across one or multiple servers, and you could utilize the same SAN certificate on all of those servers in order to validate traffic that is headed toward any of those DNS names.

It is possible to include multiple names in a SAN certificate that really have nothing to do with each other, and are used by completely different types of systems within your environment. For example, if you have an email portal, RD Gateway, and a VPN solution, you could certainly acquire one SAN certificate with the following names:

- `mail.contoso.com`
- `gateway.contoso.com`
- `vpn.contoso.com`

The preceding certificate would be a little weird and not a common thing to find in the real world. Instead, when facing the need to use a single certificate across multiple systems, it is much more common to purchase…

Wildcard certificates

Last but certainly not least is the wildcard certificate. This is the luxury model, the one that has the most capabilities, gives you the most flexibility, and at the same time offers the easiest path to implementation on many servers. The name on a wildcard certificate begins with an asterisk (*). This symbol means *any*, as in *anything preceding the DNS domain name* is covered by this certificate. If you own `contoso.com` and plan to stand up many public DNS records that will flow to many different websites and webservers, you could purchase a single wildcard certificate with the name `*.contoso.com`, and it may cover all of your certificate needs.

Typically, wildcards can be installed on as many webservers as you need, with no limit on the number of different DNS names that they can validate. I have run across an exception to this once, when a particular customer's agreement with their CA specified that they had to report and pay for each instance of their wildcard certificate that was in use. So, watch those agreements when you make them with your CA. Most of the time, a wildcard is meant to be a free-for-all within the company so that you can deploy many sites and services across many servers and utilize your wildcard certificate everywhere.

The downside of a wildcard certificate is that it costs more, significantly more. But if you have large certificate needs or big plans for growth, it will make your certificate administration much easier, faster, and more cost-effective in the long run.

Planning your PKI

Since we are revolving all of our discussion in this book around Windows Server 2025, this means that your internal CA server can and should be one provided by this latest and greatest of operating systems. As with most capabilities in Server 2025, the creation of a CA server in your network is as simple as installing a Windows role. When you go to add the role to a new server, it is the very first role in the list, **Active Directory Certificate Services (AD CS)**. When installing this role, you will be presented with a couple of important options, and you must understand the meaning behind them before you create a solid PKI environment.

> Your server's hostname and domain status cannot be changed after implementing the CA role. Make sure you have set your final hostname and joined this server to the domain (if applicable) prior to installing the AD CS role. You won't be able to change those settings later!

Role services

The first decision you need to make when installing the AD CS role is which role services you would like to install, as you can see in *Figure 7.1*:

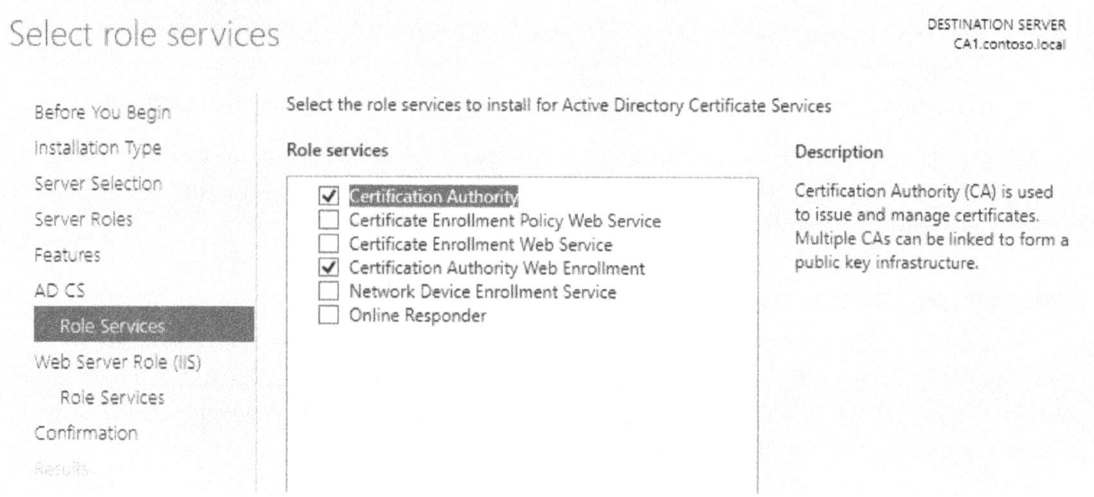

Figure 7.1: Installing the AD CS role

Clicking on each option will give you a description of its capabilities, so you can probably determine which pieces of the role you need by poking around on this screen. Here is a short summary of these options. Note that I am listing them out of order, because of the way that I typically see them configured in the field:

- **Certification Authority:** This is the primary certificate engine that needs to be installed for this server to officially become a CA.

- **Certification Authority Web Enrollment:** Often, this one gets installed as well, especially in environments that are small enough to be running a single CA server for the entire environment.

  The web enrollment portion will install **Internet Information Services (IIS)** (webserver) capabilities on this server and launch a small website that is used for the purpose of requesting certificates. We will discuss this further when we walk through issuing certificates from this web interface later in the chapter.

- **Certificate Enrollment Web Service** and **Certificate Enrollment Policy Web Service:** Most of the time, we are only concerned with issuing certificates to our company-owned, domain-joined systems. In those cases, these two selections are not necessary. If you plan to issue certificates to non-domain-joined computers from this CA server, you want to select these options.

- **Network Device Enrollment Service:** As the name implies, this piece of the CA role provides the capability to issue certificates to routers and other kinds of networking devices.

- **Online Responder:** This is a special function reserved for larger environments. Inside every certificate is a specification for a CRL. When a client computer utilizes a certificate, it reaches out and checks against this CRL to make sure that its certificate has not been revoked. The CRL is an important piece of the certificate security puzzle; in an environment with thousands of clients, your CRL may be very, very busy responding to all these requests. You can deploy additional CA servers that are running Online Responder to help ease that load.

For the purposes of our lab, and to cover the required capabilities of most small-to-medium businesses out there, I am going to select the two options shown in *Figure 7.1*: **Certification Authority** and **Certification Authority Web Enrollment**.

Enterprise versus standalone

Following the installation of your AD CS role, Server Manager will notify you that certificate services need some additional configuration, as is common with many role installations. When configuring your CA role for the first time, you will be presented with a big choice. Do you want this CA server to be an **enterprise CA** or a **standalone CA**?

Let's start with the enterprise CA. As the wizard will tell you, an enterprise CA server must be a member of your domain, and these certificate servers typically stay online so that they can issue certificates to computers and users who need them. Wait a minute! Why in the world would we want to turn a certificate server *off* anyway? We will discuss that in a minute, but if you intend to utilize this CA to issue certificates, it must obviously remain turned on. Most CA servers within a domain environment will be enterprise CAs. When creating an enterprise CA, your templates and some certificate-specific information can be stored within Active Directory, which makes integration between certificates and the domain tighter and more beneficial. If this is your first interaction with the CA role, I recommend you start with an enterprise CA because this better meets the needs of most organizations.

As you can correctly infer from the preceding text, this means that a standalone CA is less common to see in the wild. Standalone CAs can be members of the domain, or they can remain out of that part of the network and reside in a local workgroup. If you had a security requirement that dictated that your certificate server could not be domain-joined, that might be a reason why you would use a standalone CA. Another reason might be that Active Directory simply does not exist in the chosen environment.

In my eyes, it would be extremely rare to find a network where someone was trying to use Windows Server 2025 as their CA and, at the same time, was not running Active Directory Domain Services, but I'm sure there is a corner case somewhere that is doing exactly this. In that case, you would also need to choose standalone. A third example of when you would choose standalone is the event we alluded to already, where you might have a reason to turn off your server. When you employ this scenario, it is typically referred to as having an **offline root authority**. We haven't talked about root CAs yet, but we will in a minute. When you run an offline root, you create the top level of your PKI hierarchy as a standalone root CA, and then you build subordinate CAs underneath it. Your subordinate CAs are the ones doing the grunt work of issuing certificates, which means that the root can be safely shut down since it doesn't have any ongoing duties. Why would you want to do this? Well, most companies don't, but I have worked with some that have very high-level security policies, and this is why this topic might be relevant. If all of a company's CA servers are tied together as enterprise CAs with all of their information being stored inside Active Directory, a compromise to one of the subordinate issuing CAs could spell disaster for your entire PKI. It is possible that the only way to remediate an attack would be to wipe out the whole PKI environment, all of the CA servers, and build them up again. If you had to do this, it would mean not only rebuilding your servers but also reissuing brand-new copies of all your certificates to every user and device that has them.

On the other hand, if you were running a standalone root CA that was offline, it would not have been affected by the attack. In this case, you could tear down your affected subordinate certificate servers, but your core root server would have been safely hidden. You could then bring this root back online, rebuild new subordinates from it, and have an easier path to being 100% operational because your root keys that are stored within the CA would not have to be reissued, as they never would have been compromised in the attack.

As I said, I do not see this very often in the field, but it is a possibility. If you're thinking about moving forward with an offline root CA only because it seems like it's more secure, but you don't have a specific reason for doing so, I recommend you change gears and go ahead with an online enterprise root CA. While there are some security advantages to the offline root, most companies do not find those advantages to be worth the extra hassle that accompanies using an offline root CA. There are usability trade-offs when going down the offline route. If you find yourself wanting to set up a standalone CA that you are planning to take offline, but that is also domain-joined, now you're really asking for trouble. Such a server will quickly fall out of sync with the domain while it is offline, and down the road, when you find the need to turn that root CA back on, you have an enormous headache waiting for you.

In most cases, you'll want to select an enterprise CA and proceed from there.

Root versus subordinate (issuing)

This is the second biggest choice you need to make when building a new CA. Is your new server going to be a **root CA** or a **subordinate CA**? In some cases, even in a lot of Microsoft documentation, a subordinate CA is more often called an **issuing CA**.

Generally, in a multi-tiered PKI, the subordinate/issuing CAs are the ones that do the issuing of certificates to users and devices in your network.

The difference really is just a matter of what you want your CA hierarchy to look like. In a PKI tree, there is a single high-level certificate, self-signed by the root CA, that everything chains up to. A subordinate CA, on the other hand, is one that resides below a root CA in the tree, and it has been issued a certificate of its own from the root above it.

If your plans are to only run a single CA server, it must be a root. If you are creating a tiered approach to issuing certificates, the first CA in your environment needs to be a root, and you can slide subordinates underneath it. You are allowed to have multiple roots, and therefore multiple trees, within a network. So your particular PKI can be structured however you see fit. In smaller companies, it is very common to see only a single CA server, an enterprise root. For the sake of simplicity in administration, these customers are willing to take the risk that, if something happens to that server, it won't be that big of a deal to build a new one and reissue certificates.

For larger networks, it is more common to see a single root with a couple of subordinates below it. Typically, in this case, the root is only responsible for being the top dog and the holder of important keys, and the subordinate CAs are the ones doing the real work, issuing certificates to the clients.

Naming your CA server

At this point, now that you have installed the role, the hostname of the server itself is set in stone. You already knew this. But as you progress through the wizards to configure your CA for the first time, you will come across a screen called **Specify the name of the CA**. Huh? I thought we already did that when we set the hostname?

Nope, we do have our final hostname, and that server name is plugged into Active Directory as our server is joined to the domain, but the actual "CA name" is something else altogether. This is the name that will be identified inside the properties of every certificate that this CA issues. This is also a name that will be configured in various places inside Active Directory, since we are building an enterprise CA. The wizard identifies a possible name for you to use, which many administrators simply take and use. If you want to configure your own name, this is where you should do it.

Once you set the name here, this is the name of the CA forever:

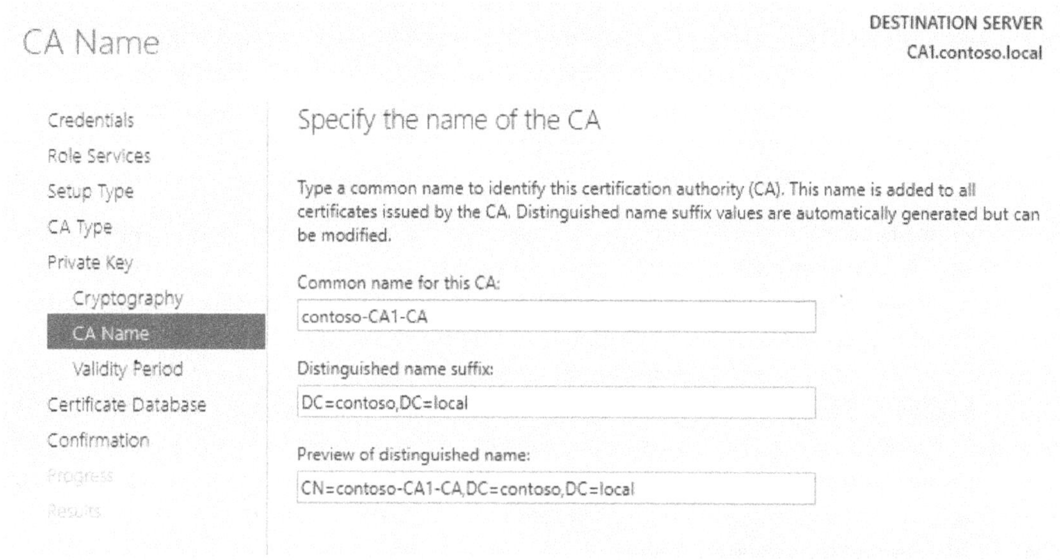

CA Name

Credentials
Role Services
Setup Type
CA Type
Private Key
  Cryptography
  CA Name
  Validity Period
Certificate Database
Confirmation
Progress
Results

Specify the name of the CA

Type a common name to identify this certification authority (CA). This name is added to all certificates issued by the CA. Distinguished name suffix values are automatically generated but can be modified.

Common name for this CA:

contoso-CA1-CA

Distinguished name suffix:

DC=contoso,DC=local

Preview of distinguished name:

CN=contoso-CA1-CA,DC=contoso,DC=local

Figure 7.2: Setting the name of the CA

Can I install the CA role onto a domain controller?

Since the role is officially called the **Active Directory Certificate Services** role, does that mean I should install this role onto one of my domain controller servers? No! Unfortunately, I have run across many small-to-medium businesses that have done exactly this, and luckily, they don't have too many problems. So technically, it does work. However, it is not a Microsoft-recommended installation path, and you should build your CAs on their own servers; try *not* to co-host them with *any* other roles whenever possible.

Creating a certificate template

Enough talk. It's time to get some work done. Now that our CA role has been installed, let's make it do something! The purpose of a certificate server is to issue certificates, right? So, shall we do that? Not so fast. When you issue a certificate from a CA server to a device or user, you are not choosing which *certificate* you want to deploy; rather, you are choosing which **certificate template** you want to utilize to deploy a certificate based on the settings configured inside that template. Certificate templates are sort of like recipes for cooking. On the CA server, you build out your templates and list all the particular ingredients (settings) that you want to incorporate into your final certificate.

Then, when the users or computers come to request a certificate from the CA server, they "bake" a certificate into their system by telling the CA which template recipe to follow when building that certificate. Relating certificates to food? Maybe that's a stretch, but it's 5:30 AM and I haven't eaten breakfast yet.

When you walk through the steps to configure your first CA server, it comes with some prebuilt certificate templates right in the console. In fact, one of those templates, called **Computer**, is typically preconfigured to the point where, if a client computer were to reach out and request a computer certificate from your new CA, it would be able to successfully issue one. However, where is the fun in using prebuilt templates and certificates? I would rather build my own template so that I can specify particular configurations and settings inside that template. This way, I know exactly what settings are contained within my certificates that will ultimately be issued to my computers in the network.

Once again, we need to launch the proper administrative console to do our work. Inside the **Tools** menu of **Server Manager**, click on **Certification Authority**. Once inside, you can expand the name of your CA and see some folders, including one at the bottom called `Certificate Templates`. If you click on this folder, you will see a list of the templates that are currently built into our CA server. Since we do not want to utilize one of these pre-existing templates, it is common sense that we would try to right-click here and create a new template, but this is actually not the correct place to build a new template. Understanding the reason why new certificate templates are not built directly from this screen must be above my pay grade because it seems silly that they aren't. Alas, in order to get to the proper screen for managing and modifying our templates, we need to right-click on the `Certificate Templates` folder and then choose **Manage**:

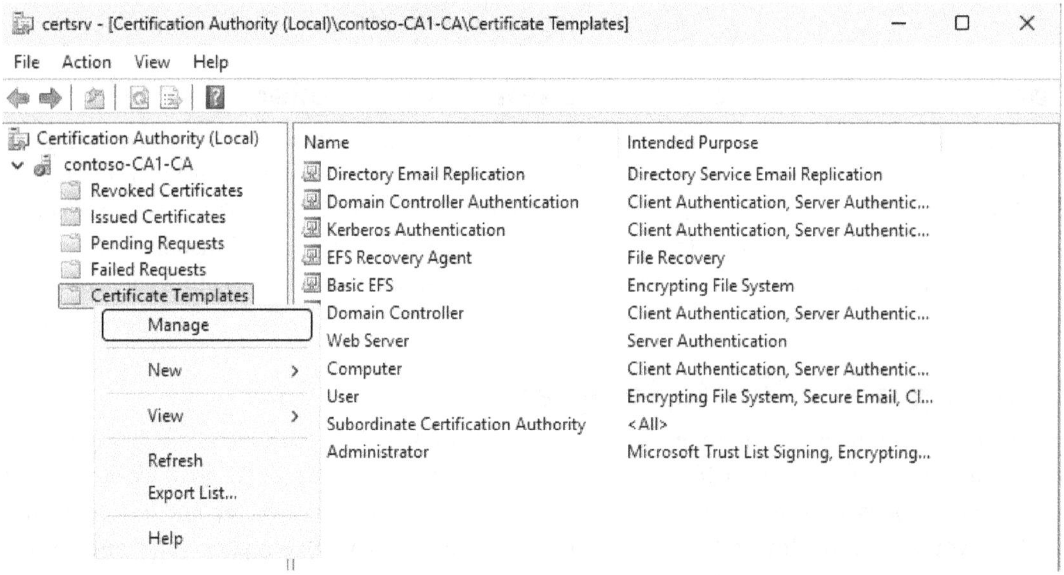

Figure 7.3: Managing certificate templates

Now, you see a much more comprehensive list of templates, including several that were not visible on the first screen. To build a new template, what we want to do is find a pre-existing template that functions similarly to the purpose that we want our new certificate template to serve.

Computer templates are becoming increasingly issued across many organizations due to more and more technologies requiring these certificates to exist. Yet, we don't want to utilize that baked-in template, which is simply called **Computer**, because we want our template to have a more specific name, and we want the flexibility to modify template settings. Perhaps we want the certificate's validity period to be longer than the default settings or some kind of similar specification. Right-click on the built-in **Computer** template and click on **Duplicate Template**. This opens the **Properties** screen for our new template, from which we first want to give our new template a unique name inside the **General** tab.

In an upcoming chapter, we will discuss DirectAccess, the remote access technology that will be used in our environment. A good implementation of DirectAccess includes machine certificates being issued to all mobile client workstations, so we will plan to make use of this new template for those purposes. The **General** tab is also the place where we get to define our validity period for this certificate, which we will set to **2 years:**

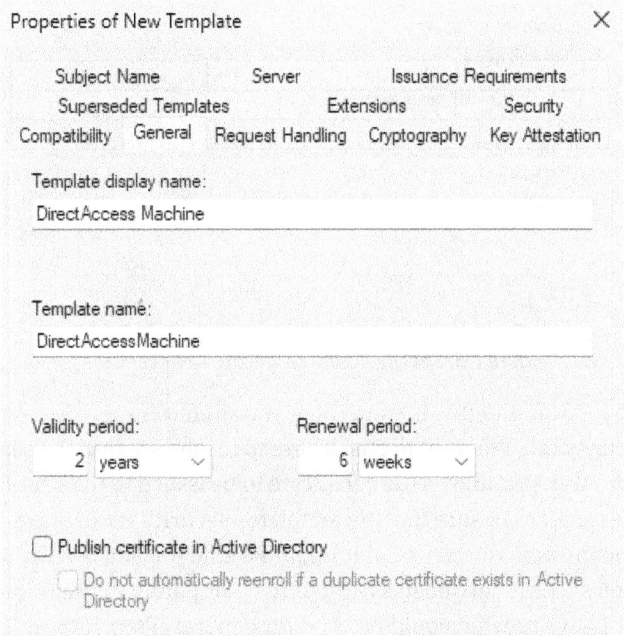

Figure 7.4: Crafting our certificate template

If the certificates that you want to issue require any additional setting changes, you can flip through the available tabs inside **Properties** and make the necessary adjustments. For our example, another setting I will change is inside the **Subject Name** tab.

I want my new certificates to have a subject name that matches the common name of the computer where it is being issued, so I have chosen **Common name** from the drop-down list:

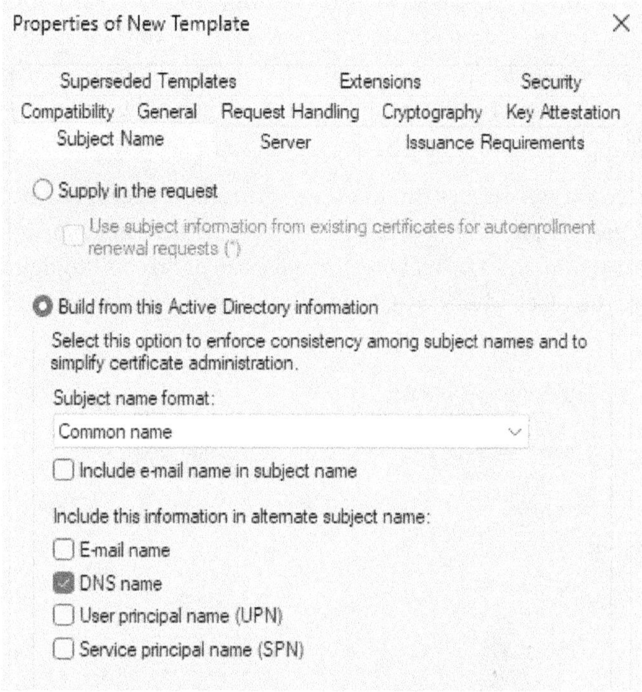

Figure 7.5: Specifying the certificate subject name

We have one more tab to visit, and this is something you should check for every certificate template that you build: the **Security** tab. We want to check here to make sure that the security permissions for this template are set in a way that allows the certificate to be issued to the users or computers that we desire, and at the same time, make sure that the template's security settings are not too loose, creating a situation where someone who doesn't need it might be able to get a certificate. For our example, I plan to issue these DirectAccess certificates to all of the computers in the domain, because the kind of machine certificate I have created could be used for general IPsec authentications as well, which I may someday configure.

So, I am just making sure that I have **Domain Computers** listed in the **Security** tab, and that they are set for **Read** and **Enroll** permissions, so that any computer that is joined to my domain will have the option of requesting a new certificate based on my new template:

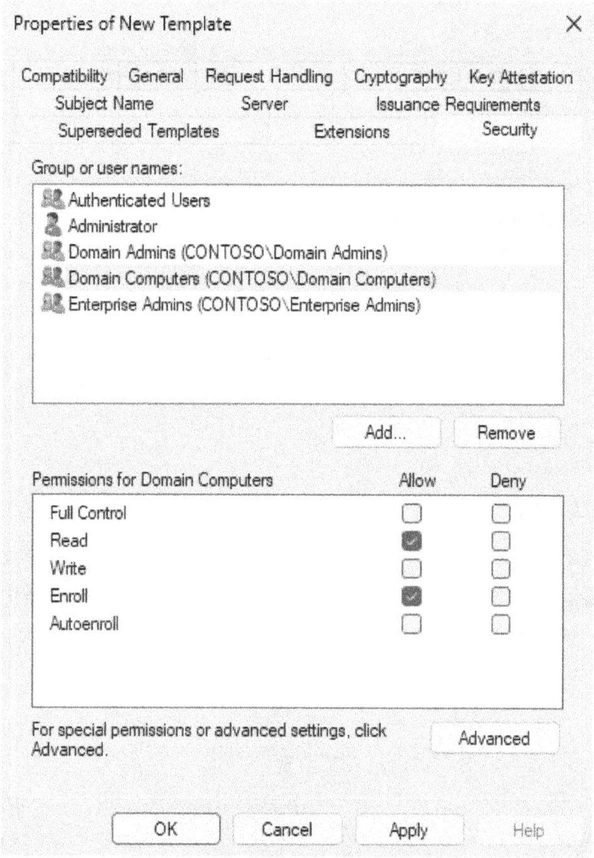

Figure 7.6: Certificate permissions

Since that is everything I need inside my new certificate, I simply click on **OK**, and my new certificate template is now included in the list of templates on my CA server.

Issuing certificates

Next comes the part that trips up a lot of people on their first attempt. We now have a brand-new template to issue, and we have verified that the permissions within that certificate template are appropriately configured so that any computer that is a member of our domain should be able to request one of these certificates, right? So our logical next step would be to jump onto a client computer and request a certificate, but there is one additional task that needs to be accomplished in order to make that possible.

Even though the new template has been **created,** it has not yet been **published.** So at the moment, the CA server will not offer our new template as an option to the clients, even though security permissions are configured for it to do so. The process to publish a certificate template is very quick—only a couple of mouse clicks—but unless you know about the need to do this, it can be a very frustrating experience because nothing in the interface gives you a hint about this requirement.

Publishing the template

If your **Certificate Templates** console is still open (the one where we were managing our templates), close it so you are back at the main CA management console. Remember how we noticed that the list of available certificate templates that shows up here is much shorter? This is because only these certificate templates are currently published and available to be issued. To add additional templates to the published list, including our new one, we simply right-click on the `Certificate Templates` folder and then navigate to **New | Certificate Template to Issue**:

Figure 7.7: Publishing our new template

Now, we are presented with a list of available templates that are not yet issued. All you need to do is choose your new template from the list and click on **OK**. The new template is now included in the list of "published" certificate templates, and we are ready to request one from a client computer:

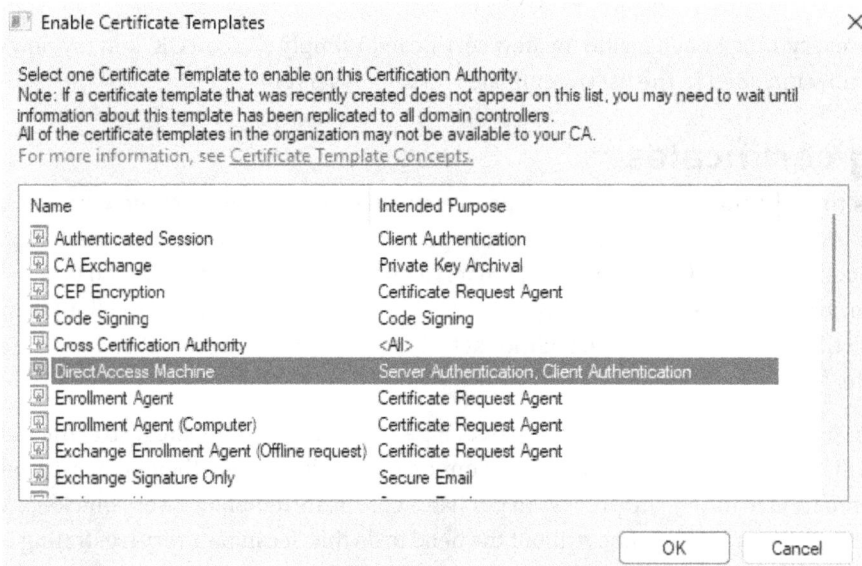

Figure 7.8: Selecting the new certificate template to issue

If you look through this list and do not see your newly created template, you may have to take an additional step. Sometimes, simply waiting will resolve this behavior, because occasionally the reason that the new template does not show up in the list is that you are waiting for your domain controllers to finish replicating. At other times, you will find that, even after waiting for a while, your new template is still not on this list. In that case, you probably just need to restart the CA service to force it to pull in the new template information. To restart the CA service, you right-click on the CA's name near the top of the **Certification Authority** management console and navigate to **All Tasks | Stop Service**. The stopping of that service typically only takes a second or two, and then you can immediately right-click on the CA name again, and this time navigate to **All Tasks | Start Service**, as seen in *Figure 7.9*.

Attempt to publish your new template again, and you should see it in the list:

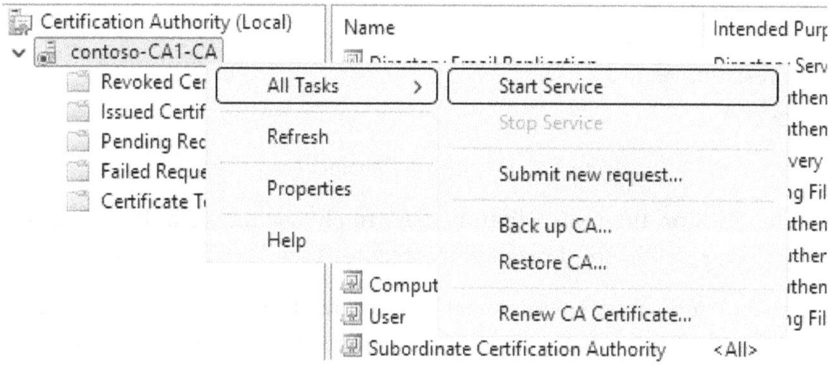

Figure 7.9: Restarting the CA service

Requesting a certificate from MMC

Our new certificate template has been created, and we have successfully published it within the CA console, thereby making it officially ready for issuing. It's time to test that out. Go ahead and log in to a regular client computer on your network. There are a couple of standard ways to request a new certificate on a client computer. The first is by using the good old MMC console. On your client computer, launch MMC and add the snap-in for **Certificates**. When you choose **Certificates** from the list of available snap-ins and click on the **Add** button, you are presented with some additional options for which certificate store you want to open. You get to choose between opening certificates for **My user account**, **Service account**, or **Computer account**. Since we are trying to issue a certificate that will be used by the computer itself, I will choose **Computer account** from this list, and click on **Finish**:

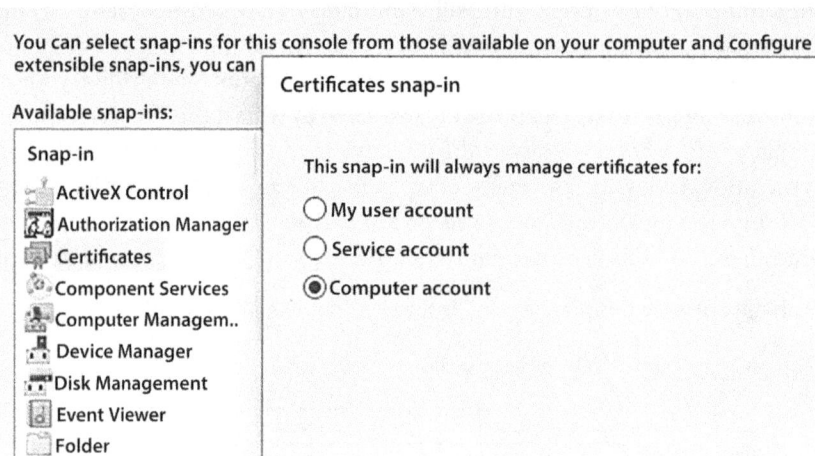

Add or Remove Snap-ins

You can select snap-ins for this console from those available on your computer and configure
extensible snap-ins, you can

Certificates snap-in

Available snap-ins:

Snap-in
ActiveX Control
Authorization Manager
Certificates
Component Services
Computer Managem..
Device Manager
Disk Management
Event Viewer
Folder

This snap-in will always manage certificates for:

○ My user account

○ Service account

◉ Computer account

Figure 7.10: Snapping in computer certificates

On the next page, click on the **Finish** button again to choose the default option, which is **Local computer**. This will snap in the local machine's computer-based certificate store inside MMC.

Alternatively, on any Windows version newer than Windows 8 and Windows Server 2012, there is an MSC shortcut for opening directly into the local computer's certificate store. Simply type CERTLM.MSC into a **Run** prompt, and MMC will automatically launch and create this snap-in for you.

When you are installing certificates onto a computer or server, this is generally the place you want to visit. Inside this certificate store, the specific location where we want to install our certificate is the Personal folder. This is true whether you are installing a machine certificate, as we are doing here, or installing an SSL certificate onto a webserver. The local computer's Personal certificate folder is the correct location for both kinds of certificates. If you click on Personal, you can see that we do not currently have anything listed there:

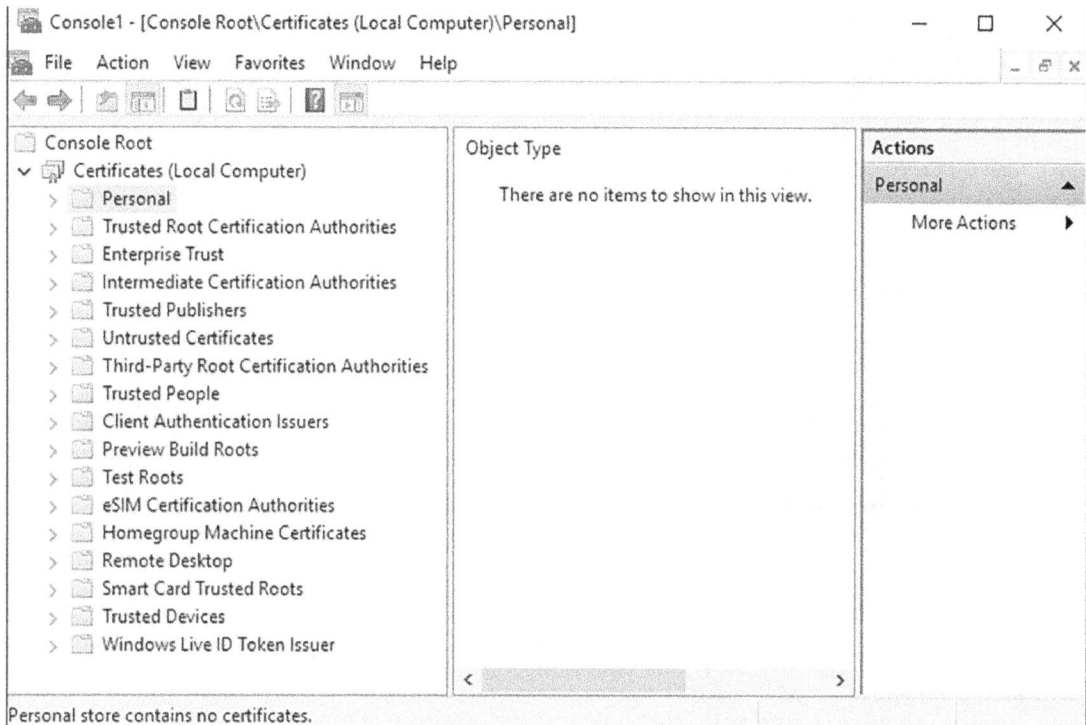

Figure 7.11: Personal is empty

To request a new certificate from our CA server, we simply right-click on the Personal folder and then navigate to **All Tasks | Request New Certificate....** Doing so opens a wizard; go ahead and click on the **Next** button once.

Now you encounter the screen shown in *Figure 7.12*, which looks like something needs to be done; however, in most cases, because we are requesting a certificate on one of our corporate, domain-joined machines, we actually do not need to do anything on the screen presented in the following screenshot.

Simply click **Next** again, and the wizard will query Active Directory to show all certificate templates that are available to be issued:

Figure 7.12: Click Next to query Active Directory

Next, the **Request Certificates** screen is shown, which is the list of templates that are available to use. This list is dynamic; it is based on what computer you are logged in to and what your user account permissions are. Remember when we set up the **Security** tab of our new certificate template? It is there that we defined who and what could pull down new certificates based on that template, and if I had defined a more particular group than domain computers, it is possible that my new **DirectAccess Machine** template would not be displayed in this list. However, since I did create that template to be issuable to any computer within our domain, I can see and select it here:

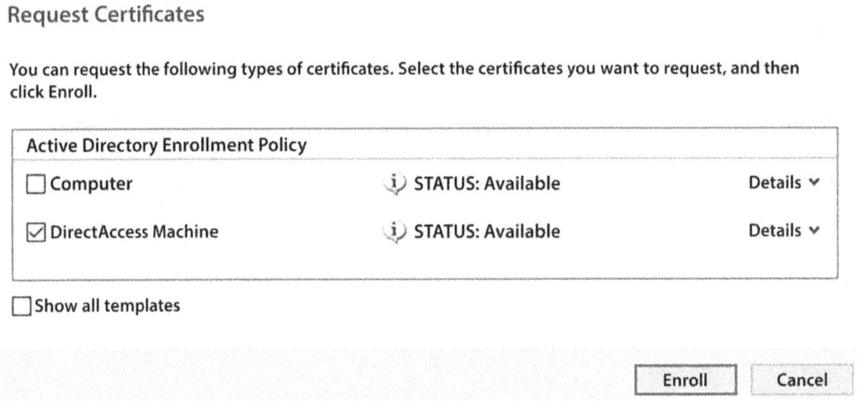

Request Certificates

You can request the following types of certificates. Select the certificates you want to request, and then click Enroll.

Active Directory Enrollment Policy		
☐ Computer	ⓘ STATUS: Available	Details ∨
☑ DirectAccess Machine	ⓘ STATUS: Available	Details ∨

☐ Show all templates

[Enroll]   [Cancel]

Figure 7.13: Certificate templates available for issuing

If you do not see your new template in the list, click on the **Show all templates** checkbox. This will give you a full list of all the templates on the CA server, and a description of each one with the reason that it is currently unavailable for issuing.

Put a checkmark next to any certificates that you want and click **Enroll**. Now, the console spins for a few seconds while the CA server processes your request and issues a new certificate that is specific to your computer and the criteria that we placed inside the certificate template. Once finished, you can see that your brand-new machine certificate is now inside Personal | Certificates in the MMC. If you double-click on the certificate, you can check over its properties to ensure that all of the settings you wanted to be pushed into this certificate exist:

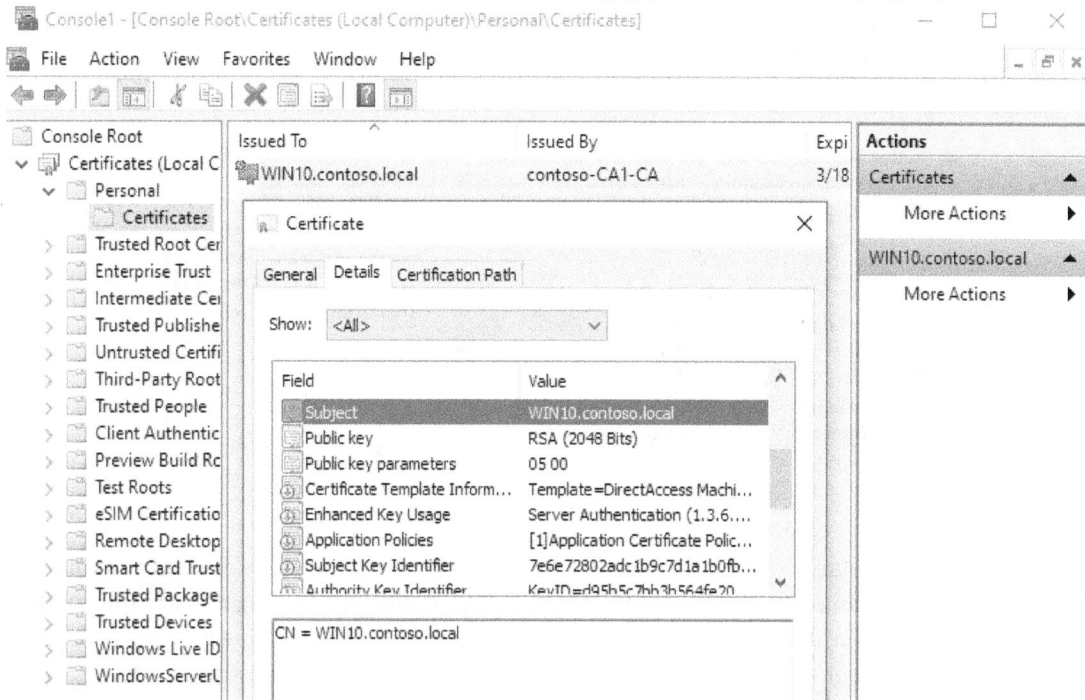

Figure 7.14: Certificate properties

Requesting a certificate from the web interface

I typically use the MMC for requesting certificates whenever possible, but in most cases, there is another platform from which you can request and issue certificates. I say *in most cases* because the existence of this option depends on how the CA server was built in the first place. When I installed my AD CS role, I made sure to choose the options for both **Certification Authority** and **Certification Authority Web Enrollment**.

This second option is important for our next section of text. Without the *web enrollment* piece of the role, we would not have a web interface running on our CA server, and this part would not be available to us.

If your CA server does not have **Certification Authority Web Enrollment** turned on, you can revisit the role installation page in **Server Manager** and add it to the existing role:

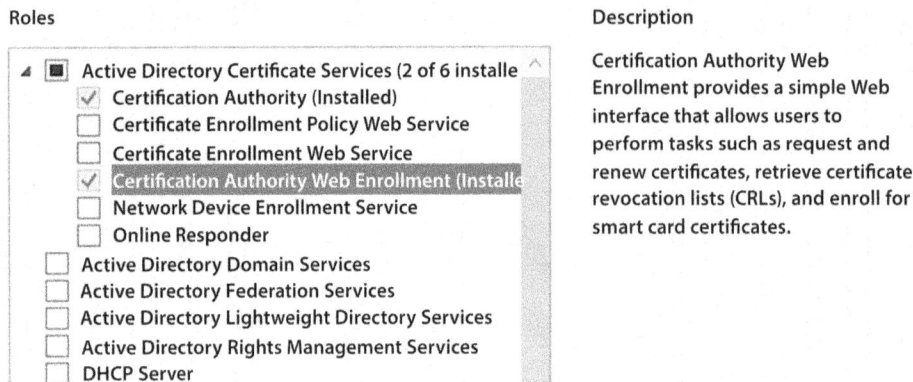

Roles   Description

▲ ■ Active Directory Certificate Services (2 of 6 installe   Certification Authority Web
    ☑ Certification Authority (Installed)   Enrollment provides a simple Web
    ☐ Certificate Enrollment Policy Web Service   interface that allows users to
    ☐ Certificate Enrollment Web Service   perform tasks such as request and
    ☑ Certification Authority Web Enrollment (Installe   renew certificates, retrieve certificate
    ☐ Network Device Enrollment Service   revocation lists (CRLs), and enroll for
    ☐ Online Responder   smart card certificates.
  ☐ Active Directory Domain Services
  ☐ Active Directory Federation Services
  ☐ Active Directory Lightweight Directory Services
  ☐ Active Directory Rights Management Services
  ☐ DHCP Server

Figure 7.15: Installing Certification Authority Web Enrollment

Once **Certification Authority Web Enrollment** is installed on your CA, there is a website running on that server that you can access via a browser from inside your network. Having this website is useful if you have the need for users to be able to issue their own certificates for some reason; it would be much easier to give them documentation or train them on the process of requesting a certificate from a website than to expect them to navigate MMC. Additionally, if you are trying to request certificates from computers that are not within the same network as the CA server, using MMC can be difficult. For example, if you have the need for a user at home to be able to request a new certificate, without a full VPN tunnel, MMC is more than likely not going to be able to connect to the CA server in order to pull down that certificate. But since we have this certificate enrollment website running, you could externally publish this website as you do with any other website in your network, using a reverse proxy or firewall to keep that traffic safe and present users with the ability to hit this site and request certificates from wherever they are.

To access this website, let's use our regular client computer again. This time, instead of opening MMC, I will simply launch **Edge**, or any other browser, and log in to the website running at https://<CASERVER>/ certsrv.

For my specific environment, that exact web address is `https://CA1/certsrv`:

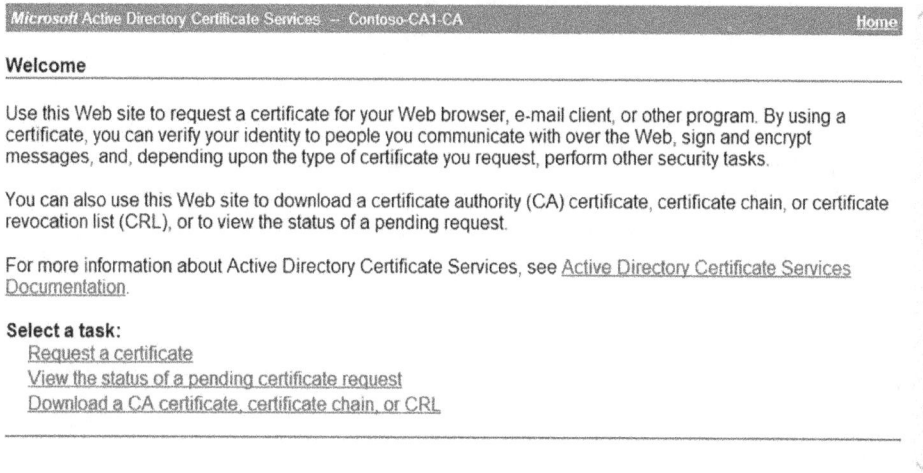

Figure 7.16: Viewing the CA web enrollment site

Our URL starts with HTTPS. This website must be configured to run on HTTPS instead of regular HTTP to allow the website to request certificates. It does not allow issuing certificates over HTTP because that information would be traveling in cleartext to the client. Enabling the website on the CA server for HTTPS ensures that the certificate issued will be encrypted while it travels. Depending on how your CA server was originally configured, it is possible that nobody has yet set up the `certsrv` website to run on HTTPS (port 443), and you may need to visit IIS Manager on your CA server to update the website binding before you can access it.

Clicking on the **Request a certificate** link brings you into a wizard in which you can request a new certificate from the CA server. When you ask users to navigate their own way through this web interface, it is typically for the purpose of a user-based certificate, since we have some pretty easy ways of automatically distributing computer-level certificates without any user interaction. We will discuss that in a moment. However, for this example, since we are asking our users to log in here and request a new user certificate, on the next page, we will choose the **User Certificate** link:

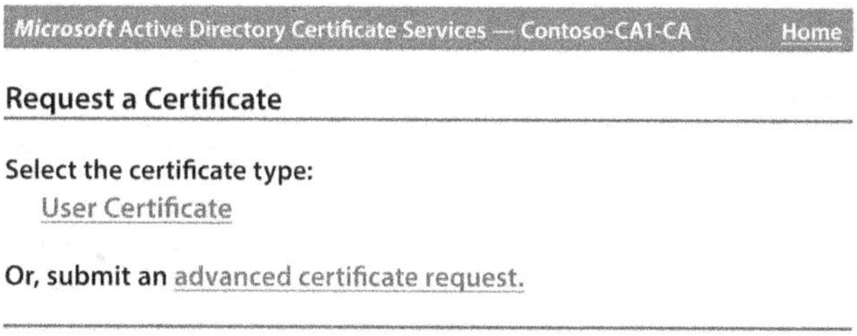

Figure 7.17: Selecting a certificate type

If you were not interested in a user certificate and wanted to use the web interface to request a machine certificate, a webserver certificate, or any other kind of certificate, you could instead choose the **advanced certificate request** link and follow the prompts to do so.

Next, click the **Submit** button, and once the certificate has been generated, you will see an **Install this certificate** link. Click on that link, and the new certificate that was just created for you will be installed on your computer. You can see in the following screenshot the response that the website gave me, indicating a successful installation, and you can also see I have opened the current user certificates inside MMC in order to see and validate that the certificate really exists:

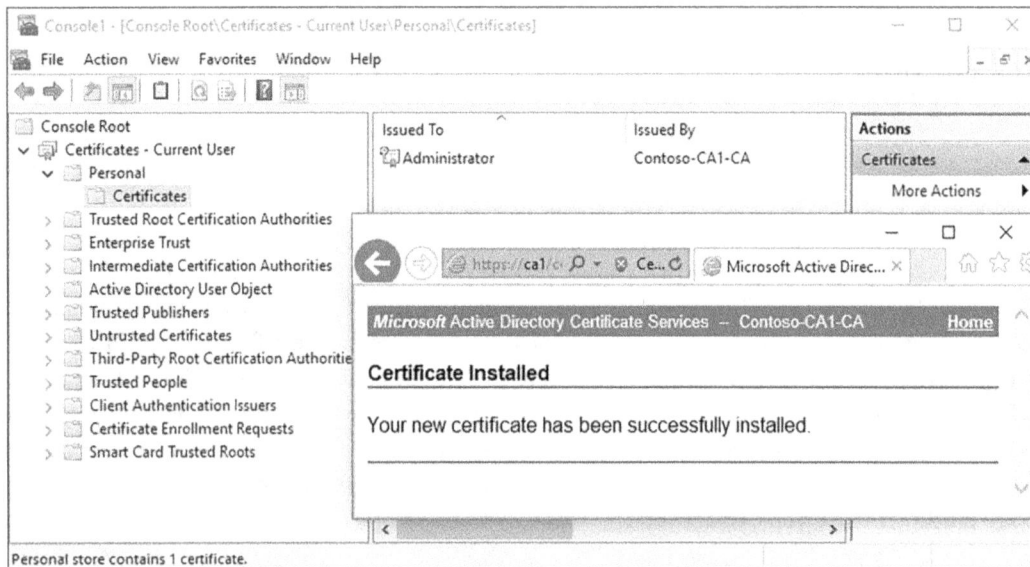

Figure 7.18: Certificate successfully installed

In this section, we have proven that our CA server is working; follow along with the next few pages as we take certificate issuance to the next level.

Creating an auto-enrollment policy

Our CA server is configured and running, and we can successfully issue certificates to the client machines. Great! Now, let's pretend we have a new project on our plates, and one of the requirements for this project is that all the computers in our network need to have a copy of this new machine certificate that we have created. Uh oh, that sounds like a lot of work. Even though the process for requesting one of these certificates is very quick—only a handful of seconds on each workstation—if you had to do that individually on a thousand machines, you'd be talking about a serious amount of time needing to be spent on this process. Furthermore, in many cases, the certificates that you issue will only be valid for one year. Does this mean we are facing an extreme amount of administrative work every single year to reissue these certificates as they expire? Certainly not!

Let's figure out how to utilize **Group Policy** to create a GPO that will auto-enroll our new certificates to all of the machines in the network, and, while we are there, also configure it so that when a certificate's expiration date comes up, the certificate will auto-renew at the appropriate intervals.

Let's pop into the **Certification Authority** management console on our CA server and look inside the Issued Certificates folder. I only want to look here for a minute to see how many certificates we have issued so far in our network. It looks like just a handful of them, so hopefully, once we are done configuring our policy, if we have done it correctly and it takes effect automatically, we should see more certificates starting to show up in this list:

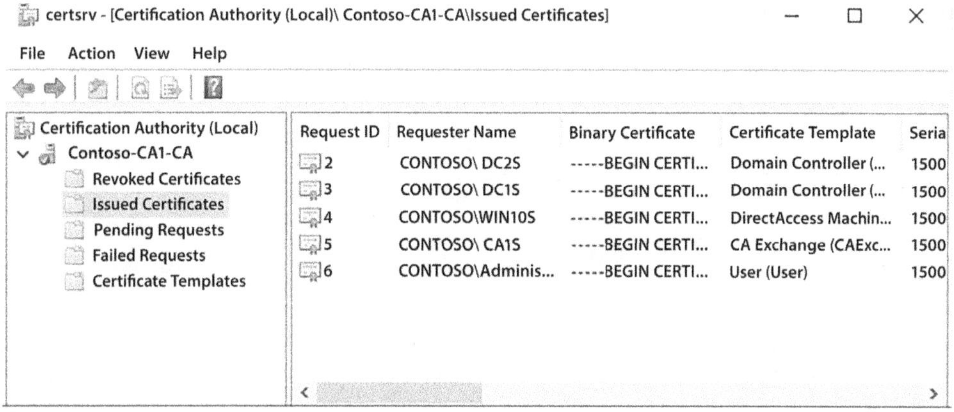

Figure 7.19: Certificates issued by our CA

Log in to a domain controller server, and then open up the **Group Policy Management** console. I have created a new GPO called **Enable Certificate Auto-enrollment**, and am now editing that GPO to find the settings I need to configure to make this GPO do its work:

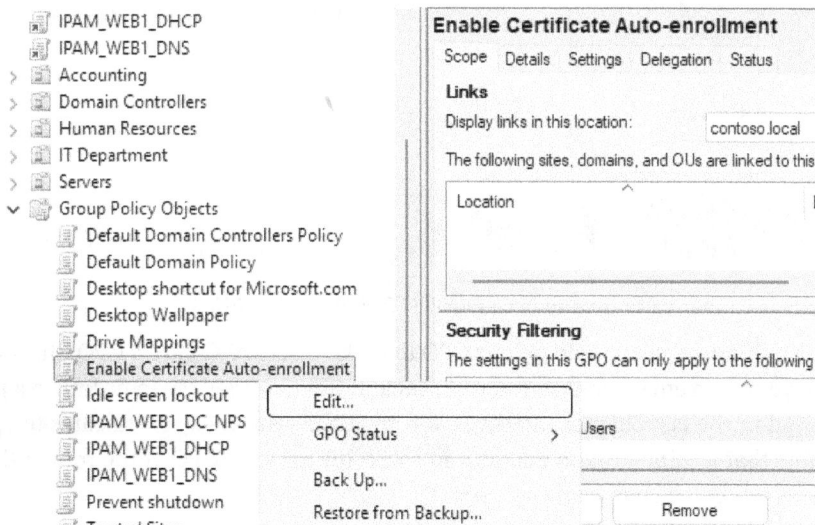

Figure 7.20: Editing the new Auto-enrollment GPO

The settings inside this GPO that we want to configure are located at **Computer Configuration | Policies | Windows Settings | Security Settings | Public Key Policies | Certificate Services Client - Auto-Enrollment**.

Double-click on this setting to view its properties. All we need to do is change the **Configuration Model** setting to **Enabled,** and make sure to check the box that says **Renew expired certificates, update pending certificates, and remove revoked certificates**. Also, check the box that says **Update certificates that use certificate templates.**

These settings will ensure that auto-renewal happens automatically when the certificates start running into their expiration dates over the next few years:

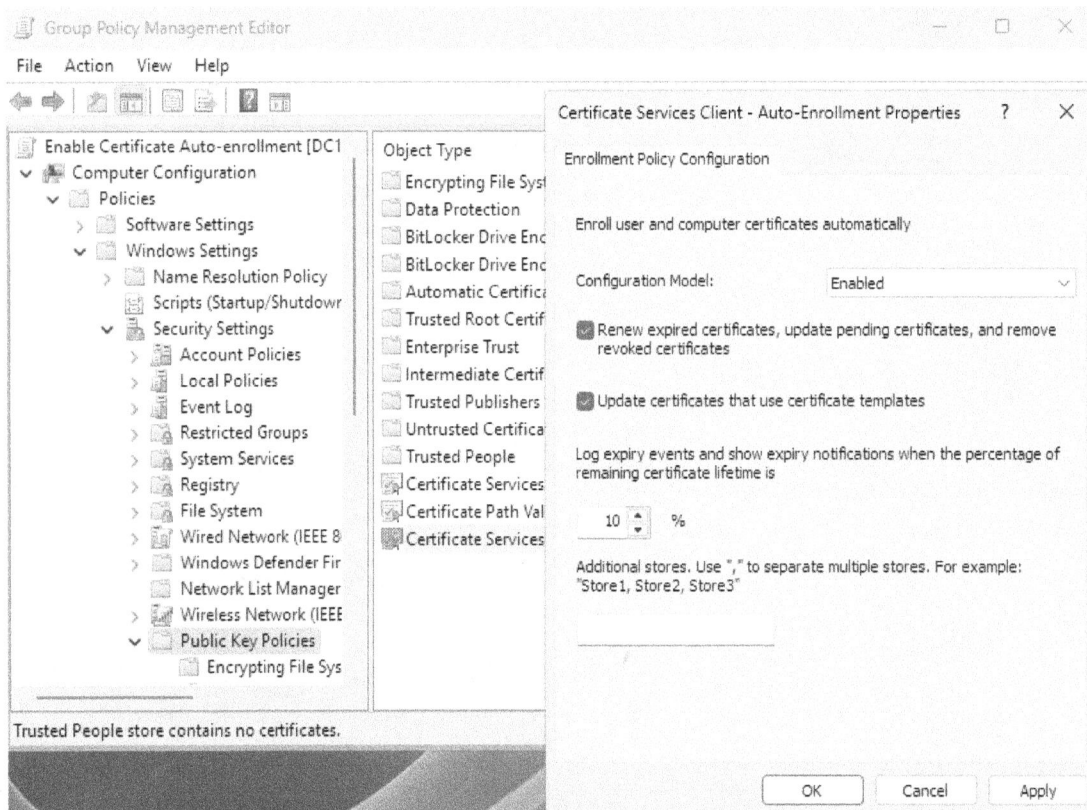

Figure 7.21: Enabling Auto-Enrollment

What is the last thing we need to do on our GPO to make it active? Create a GPO link so that it starts applying! For your own environment, you will probably create a more specific link to a particular OU, as we discussed in the last chapter; however, for my lab, I want these certificates to apply to every single machine that is joined to the domain, so I will link my new GPO at the root of the domain so that it applies to all of my clients and servers.

Now that the GPO is created and configured, and we have linked it to the domain, I would think that some new certificates would be issued, and there would be more names shown inside my Issued

`Certificates` folder inside my CA console. But there are not. Wait a minute, in our GPO, we didn't really specify anything particular to my DirectAccess machine certificate template, did we? Could that be the problem? No, there wasn't even an option for specifying which template I wanted to set up for auto-enrollment. So what gives?

When you enable auto-enrollment in Group Policy, you are simply flipping an on/off switch and turning it on for *every* certificate template. Now that we have a GPO that is configured to enable auto-enroll-ment and is linked to the domain, thus making it *live*, auto-enrollment has been enabled on every domain-joined computer for every certificate template that is published on our CA server.

Yet, none of them are issuing themselves to my computers. While I have successfully enabled certificate auto-enrollment in my environment, they are not being issued to computers because I need to adjust the security settings on my new **DirectAccess Machine** template. Currently, I have it configured so that all domain computers have **Enroll** permissions, but if you remember that **Security** tab within the certificate template's properties, there was an additional security identifier called **Autoenroll**. Every certificate template has the **Autoenroll** permission identifier, and it is not allowed by default. Now that the light switch has been flipped on for auto-enrollment in our domain, we need to enable the **Autoenroll** permission on any template that we want to start distributing itself. As soon as we enable that permission, these certificates will begin flowing around our network.

Head into the **Certificate Management** section of your CA server and open the **Properties** section of your new template, then make your way to the **Security** tab and allow **Autoenroll** permissions for the **Domain Computers** group.

This should tell the CA to start distributing these certificates accordingly:

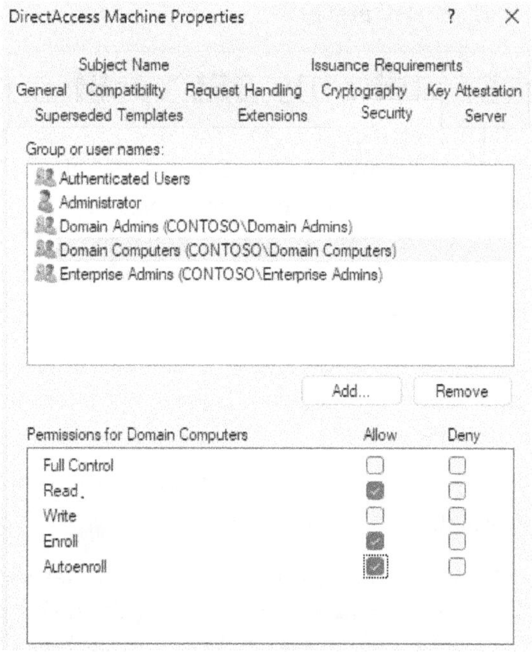

Figure 7.22: Template security for Autoenroll permissions

And sure enough, if I let my environment sit for a little while, giving Active Directory and Group Policy a chance to update on all my machines, I now see more certificates have been issued from my CA server:

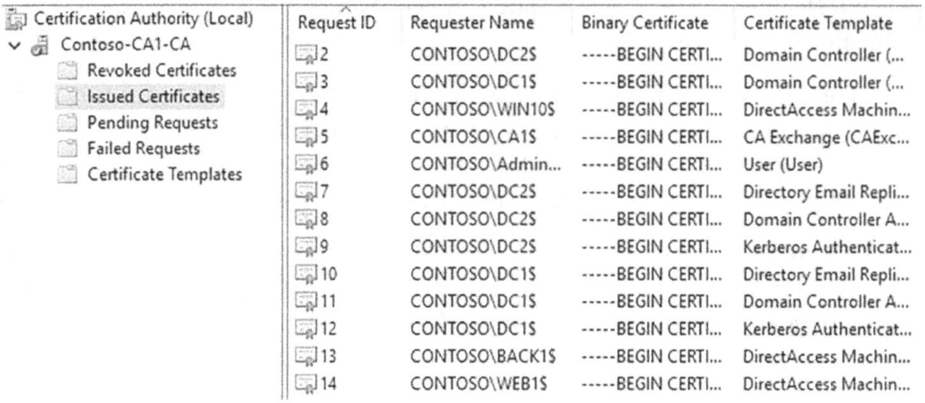

Certification Authority (Local)	Request ID	Requester Name	Binary Certificate	Certificate Template
∨ Contoso-CA1-CA	2	CONTOSO\DC2$	-----BEGIN CERTI...	Domain Controller (...
Revoked Certificates	3	CONTOSO\DC1$	-----BEGIN CERTI...	Domain Controller (...
Issued Certificates	4	CONTOSO\WIN10$	-----BEGIN CERTI...	DirectAccess Machin...
Pending Requests	5	CONTOSO\CA1$	-----BEGIN CERTI...	CA Exchange (CAExc...
Failed Requests	6	CONTOSO\Admin...	-----BEGIN CERTI...	User (User)
Certificate Templates	7	CONTOSO\DC2$	-----BEGIN CERTI...	Directory Email Repli...
	8	CONTOSO\DC2$	-----BEGIN CERTI...	Domain Controller A...
	9	CONTOSO\DC2$	-----BEGIN CERTI...	Kerberos Authenticat...
	10	CONTOSO\DC1$	-----BEGIN CERTI...	Directory Email Repli...
	11	CONTOSO\DC1$	-----BEGIN CERTI...	Domain Controller A...
	12	CONTOSO\DC1$	-----BEGIN CERTI...	Kerberos Authenticat...
	13	CONTOSO\BACK1$	-----BEGIN CERTI...	DirectAccess Machin...
	14	CONTOSO\WEB1$	-----BEGIN CERTI...	DirectAccess Machin...

Figure 7.23: Certificates are now being auto-enrolled

To automatically issue certificates from any template you create, simply publish the template and make sure to configure the appropriate auto-enroll permissions on that template. Once the auto-enrollment GPO is in place on those clients, they will reach out to your CA server and ask it for certificates from any template for which they have permission to receive a certificate. In the future, when that certificate is about to expire and the machine needs a new copy, the auto-enrollment policy will issue a new one prior to the expiration date, based on the timestamps you defined inside the GPO.

Certificate auto-enrollment can take what would normally be an enormous administrative burden and turn it into a completely automated process!

Obtaining a public authority SSL certificate

We are now comfortable grabbing certificates from our own CA server inside our own network, but what about handling those SSL certificates for our webservers that should be acquired from a public CA? For many of you, this will be the most common interaction that you have with certificates, and it's very important to understand this side of the coin as well. When you need to acquire an SSL certificate from your public authority of choice, there is a three-step process to do so: create a certificate request, submit the certificate request, and install the resulting certificate.

We are going to use my WEB1 server, on which I have a website running. Currently, the site is only capable of handling HTTP traffic, but when we turn it loose on the internet, we need to enable HTTPS to keep the information that is being submitted to the site encrypted.

To use HTTPS, we need to install an SSL certificate on the WEB1 server. This webserver is running the Microsoft web services platform, IIS.

The three-step process you take is the same if you are running a different webserver, such as Apache or NGINX, but the particular things that you have to do to accomplish these three steps will be different because Apache or any other webserver will have a different user interface from IIS. Since we are working on a Windows Server 2025 webserver, we are utilizing IIS 10.

Public/private key pair

Before we jump into performing those three steps, let's discuss why any of this even matters. You have probably heard of the term **private key**, but you may not quite understand what that means. When we send traffic across the internet from our client computers to an HTTPS website, we understand that the traffic is encrypted. This means that the packets are tied up in a nice little package before leaving our laptop so that nobody can see them while they travel, and are then unwrapped successfully when those packets reach the webserver. Our laptop uses a key to encrypt the traffic, and the server uses a key to decrypt that traffic, but how do they know what keys to use? There are two different encryption methodologies that can be used here:

- **Symmetric encryption:** The simpler method of encryption, symmetric, means that there is a single key, and both sides utilize it. Traffic is packaged up using a key, and the same key is used to unwrap that traffic when it reaches its destination. Since this single key is the all-powerful **Oz**, you wouldn't want it to get into the wrong hands, which means you will not be presenting it on the internet. Since you cannot safely share it on the internet, you would need some other way to manually get this key to both the client and the server. This obviously wouldn't work to give users copies of encryption keys whenever they visit your website. Therefore, symmetric encryption is not generally used for protecting internet website traffic. Rather, it is used more commonly in places where you control both sides of the communication stream, such as VPN traffic.

- **Asymmetric encryption:** This is our focus with HTTPS traffic. Asymmetric encryption utilizes two keys: a public key and a private key. The public key is included inside your SSL certificate, and so anyone on the internet can contact your website and get the public key. Your laptop then uses that public key to encrypt the traffic and sends it over to the webserver. Why is this secure if the public key is broadcast to the entire internet? Because the traffic can only be decrypted by using a corresponding private key, which is securely stored on your webserver. It is very important to maintain security over your private key and your webservers, ensuring that the key doesn't fall into anyone else's pocket.

Creating a certificate signing request

If you've already jumped ahead and acquired an SSL certificate from your public CA entity by logging in to their website, purchasing a certificate, and immediately downloading it, you've already missed the boat. For some reason, it is sometimes possible to download SSL certificates that cannot do anything; the reason they cannot do anything is that you haven't given that certificate any information about what private key to use on your server. An SSL certificate that is not aware of a corresponding private key is effectively useless.

When you install an SSL certificate onto a webserver, it is very important that the certificate knows about your private key. How do we make sure that happens? This is where the **certificate signing request (CSR)** comes into play. The first step in correctly acquiring an SSL certificate is to generate a CSR from your local webserver. When you create that file, the webserver platform creates the private key that is needed and hides it away on your server.

The CSR is then created in such a way that it knows exactly how to interact with that private key, and you then utilize the CSR when you log in to the CA's website to request the certificate.

The private key is not *inside* the CSR, and your CA vendor never knows what your private key is. This key is ultra-important and is only ever stored on your webserver, inside your organization.

To generate a CSR, open **IIS** from the **Tools** menu of Server Manager, and then click on the name of the webserver from the navigational tree on the left side of your screen. This will populate a number of different applets into the center of the console. The one we want to work with is called **Server Certificates**. Go ahead and double-click on that:

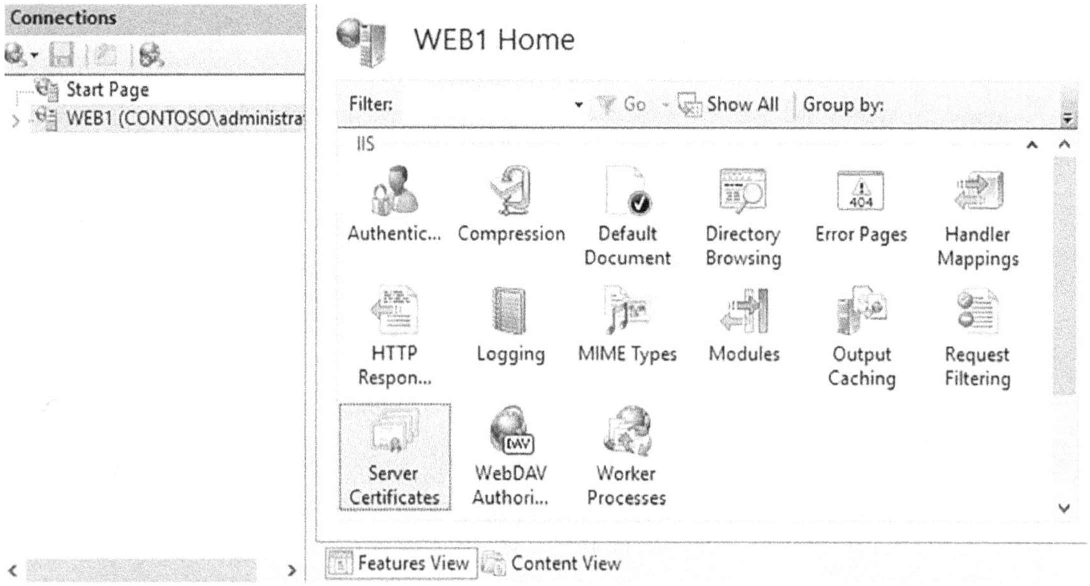

Figure 7.24: Viewing Server Certificates via IIS

Now, on the **Server Certificates** screen, you can see any existing certificates that reside on the server listed here. This is where we ultimately need to see our new SSL certificate so that we can utilize it inside our website properties when we are ready to turn on HTTPS. The first step to acquiring our new certificate is creating the certificate request to be used with our CA, and, if you look on the right side of your screen, you will see an **Actions** section, under which is listed **Create Certificate Request...**.

Go ahead and click on that action:

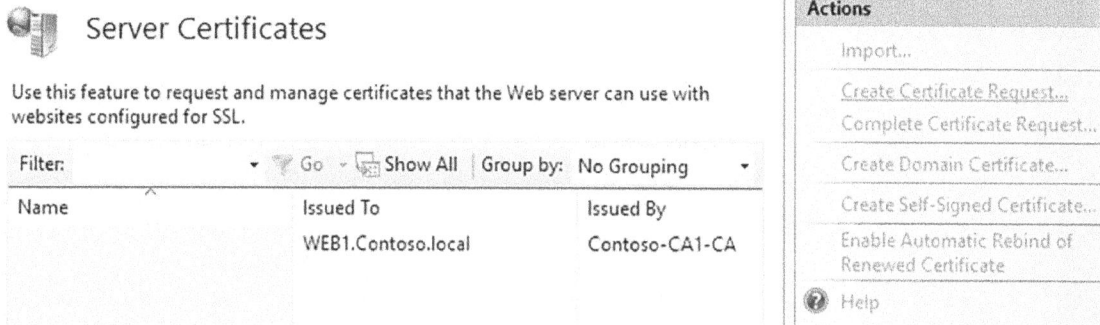

Figure 7.25: Creating a certificate request

In the resulting wizard, you need to populate the information that will be stored within your SSL certificate. The **Common name** field is the most important piece of information here. It needs to be the DNS name that this certificate is going to protect. So, basically, you enter the name of your website here, then continue with filling out the rest of your company-specific information. A couple of special notes here that often seem to trip up admins are that the **Organizational unit** value can be anything at all; I usually just enter the word Web. Also, make sure to spell out the name of your state; do not use an abbreviation:

Figure 7.26: Populating information for the certificate

On the **Cryptographic Service Provider Properties** page, you typically want to leave **Cryptographic service provider** set to its default, unless you have a specialized crypto card in your server and are planning to use it for handling encryption processing for this website. On an IIS server, you will almost always have **Microsoft RSA SChannel Cryptographic Provider** listed here. What you **do** want to change, however, is the **Bit length** value. The standard bit length for many years was **1024**, and that continues to be the default choice in Windows Server 2025. Please don't ask me why. The general industry for SSL encryption has decided that 1,024 is too weak, however, and the new standard is a minimum of

2,048 bits. When you head onto your CA's website to request a certificate, you will more than likely find that your request needs to have a minimum of 2,048 bits, possibly even 4,096. So, go ahead and change that drop-down setting to a minimum of **2048**:

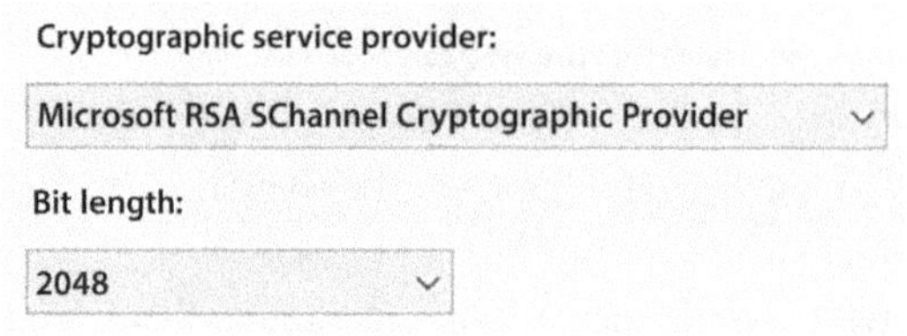

Cryptographic service provider:

| Microsoft RSA SChannel Cryptographic Provider | ∨ |

Bit length:

| 2048 | ∨ |

Figure 7.27: Setting the encryption bit length to 2048

The only thing left to do for our CSR is to give it a location and a filename. Saving this CSR as a text file is the normal way to go and serves our purposes well because all we need to do when we request our certificate is open the file and then copy and paste the contents. We have now created our CSR file, and we can utilize this file to request the certificate from our public CA.

Submitting the certificate request

Now, head over to the website for your public CA. Again, any of the companies that we mentioned earlier, such as **GoDaddy** or **Verisign**, are appropriate for this purpose. Each authority has its own look and feel for its web interface, so I cannot give you the exact steps that need to be taken for this process. Once you have an account and log in to the authority's site, you should be able to find an option for purchasing an SSL certificate. For some CAs, the purchasing process and the certificate acquisition process are two different things. For example, you may purchase and pay for your new SSL certificate and then discover that you must visit a different section of the interface to use the "certificate credit" you just purchased to create a certificate. On the other hand, some CAs walk you through the entire process from start to finish. In any case, once that certificate has been purchased, there will be a process for requesting and deploying that certificate.

Once you have found the interface used for generating the new certificate, you will generally be asked for four pieces of information:

1. **Validity period**: How long should this SSL certificate last? It used to be common that companies would purchase SSL certificates with one-year, two-year, or even three-year validity periods, meaning that the certificate was "good" for that amount of time. A few years ago, Apple flexed its muscles in this space and decided that the Safari web browser would only trust certificates that have a validity period of one year, more or less.

    Rather than push back, the industry said *"Sure, why not?"* and so moving forward, SSL certificates will only be valid for one year at a time. For clarity, you can still *purchase* an SSL certificate for multiple years at a time, which can sometimes get you a better deal on the cost per year, but even if you have purchased multiple years' worth of SSL certificate use, you will still need to replace the certificate *every year* with a fresh one from your certificate provider. We will talk more about this shortly, when we discuss rekeying certificates.

2. **Webserver platform:** What type of webserver are you running? The answer to this question impacts what type of file is available to download at the end of this process. When working with Windows Server, your answer will be **IIS**, but other possible options include **Apache**, **Tomcat**, **NGINX**, and many more Linux-based webserver selections.

3. **Domain ownership validation:** This one is interesting, and if you haven't been through this process before, you likely haven't thought about why it is necessary. What's to stop hacker Joe, sitting in an internet café halfway across the world, or a 12-year-old playing video games in their basement, or even your next-door neighbor from creating their own CA login and purchasing an SSL certificate that has *your* company name and website on it? The validation of domain ownership is a process to prove that you really own contoso.com (or whatever your domain is) so that only *you* are allowed to purchase valid SSL certificates that protect traffic for your domain name. The most common way to validate domain ownership is to select from a list of predefined email addresses inside the CA, after which the CA will send some flavor of validation email to that email address. For example, you might have a selection of email addresses such as the following:

   - admin@contoso.com
   - administrator@contoso.com
   - webmaster@contoso.com
   - hostmaster@contoso.com

   All you need to do is verify that you can receive an email to one of those email addresses, and by selecting this option, you will receive an email to that address that usually contains a link and a code. Simply copy the code and paste it into the link, and this is an easy way to validate domain ownership because, as the owner of that domain, only *you* would have access to those email addresses. A second form of ownership, if email doesn't pan out, is that the CA may give you a special DNS record that can be put into place in your domain's public DNS. You input the record, the CA sees that record show up on the internet, and they validate that you are the domain owner. This process takes much longer to accomplish than email verification, so it is rarely used.

4. **CSR:** The last (and most important) thing you will be asked to provide is the text from inside that CSR file we created a few minutes ago. There will be either an upload function or simply an input box, and all you need to do is copy/paste the entire contents of the CSR into that box.

If you open the text file we saved earlier, you will see a big lump of nonsense:

Figure 7.28: The text inside a CSR file

This mess of data contains information about your certificate request and is exactly what the CA needs in order to create your new SSL certificate so that it knows how to interact with your webserver's private key. Only the server that generated the CSR will be able to accept and properly utilize the SSL certificate that is based on this CSR.

Downloading and installing your certificate

Next, you sit back and wait. Depending on which authority you are using and on how often your company purchases certificates from this authority, your certificate might be available for download almost immediately, or it could take a few hours before that certificate shows up in the available downloads list. The reason for this is that some CAs utilize human approval for new certificates, and you are literally waiting for someone to take a look at the certificate request and your information to make sure you really work for the company and that you really own this domain name. Remember, the real benefit to a public SSL certificate is that the CA is guaranteeing that the user of this certificate is the real deal, so they want to make sure they aren't, for example, issuing a certificate for portal. contoso.com to someone in the Fabrikam organization by mistake.

Once you are able to download the certificate from the CA's website, go ahead and copy it over to the webserver from which we generated the CSR. It is critically important that you install this new certificate on the **same server**. If you were to install this new certificate on a different webserver, one that did not generate the CSR this certificate was built from, that certificate would import successfully, but would not be able to function. Once again, this is because the private key that the certificate is planning to interact with would not be present on a different server.

Back inside the IIS management console, we can now use the next action shown along the right side of *Figure 7.25*, called **Complete Certificate Request...**. This launches a short wizard in which you point at the newly downloaded certificate file, and the wizard then imports it into the server. Now that the certificate resides on the server, it is ready to be used by our website.

There is one additional item that I always check after installing or importing an SSL certificate. You can now see your new certificate listed inside IIS, and if you double-click on your new certificate, you will see the **Properties** page for the certificate. On the **General** tab of these properties, take a look near the bottom. Your certificate should display a little key icon and text that reads **You have a private key that corresponds to this certificate**. If you can see this message, your import was successful, and the new certificate file matched up with the CSR perfectly. The server and certificate now share that critical private key information, and the SSL certificate will be able to work properly to protect our website. If you do not see this message, something went wrong in the process of requesting and downloading your certificate. If you do not see the message here, you need to start over by generating a new CSR, because the certificate file that you got back must not have been keyed appropriately against that CSR, or something along those lines. Without the **You have a private key that corresponds to this certificate** text at the bottom of this screen, your certificate will *not* validate traffic properly. You can install it, you can tell a website to use it, everything will appear to be working inside IIS, but the website simply will not function until you fix that certificate.

Here is an example of what it should look like when working correctly:

Figure 7.29: This certificate properly matches up with a private key

Re-keying certificates

While poking around in your public CA's interface, you may have noticed a function or button to "re-key" a certificate. What does that mean? When you purchase a certificate, such as portal.contoso.com, from your CA, you are now able to use a CSR to craft a certificate based on that name. You then install that certificate onto your webserver, and it then protects traffic for your website, portal.contoso.com. Each year, you can repurchase the certificate, recreate a fresh CSR, and reinstall the certificate as if it were brand-new. But what if you need to reinstall this certificate in the middle of the year? Perhaps you paid for a certificate from January through January, but it is now July, and your webserver dies? You replace the server, reinstall your website, and realize that you need to get a new SSL certificate for this new server to protect traffic for the same portal.contoso.com website. Do you need to purchase another SSL certificate and take the hit for the cost of the six months that you didn't use? No, this is where rekeying a certificate can help you out. If you use your new webserver to generate a new CSR, you can then take that new CSR to your CA's website and find the certificate that you already purchased, and simply rekey the certificate against your new CSR. This process will invalidate the old copy of the certificate and will issue a new certificate based on the new CSR (based, of course, on the new server's private key), which you can then install on your new webserver. This way, you can continue to make use of that SSL certificate you purchased on a new server and finish out the year.

Another possible reason you might find yourself re-keying a certificate is when you have purchased multiple years' worth of an SSL certificate. If you purchased portal.contoso.com for three years, remember that you can only issue a certificate for one year at a time. So, every year, on or before that certificate's expiration date, you will need to revisit your CA and rekey your certificate to pull down a fresh copy, giving you protection for another year. You won't have to pay for this if you have already purchased the certificate for multiple years, but you will still need to perform the certificate rekey and replacement for your webserver to continue working properly.

Exporting and importing certificates

I often find myself needing to use the same SSL certificate on multiple servers. This might happen in the case where I have more than one IIS server serving up the same website, and I am using some form of load balancing to split the traffic between them. This need may also arise when working with any form of hardware load balancer, as you sometimes need to import certificates not only to the webservers themselves but also to the load balancer box. Another example is when using wildcard certificates; when you purchase a wildcard, you typically intend to install it on multiple servers.

Does this mean that you need to generate a new CSR from each server and request a new copy of the same certificate multiple times? Definitely not, and in fact, doing so could cause you other problems: remember that when a public CA rekeys a certificate—in other words, if you have already requested a certificate with a particular name and then come back again later to request another copy of the same certificate—that CA will most likely invalidate the first one as it issues the second copy. This is not always immediately apparent, as there is usually a timer set on the invalidation of the first certificate. If you revisit the CA's web interface and request a new copy of the same certificate using a new CSR for your second webserver, you might discover that everything works fine for a few days, but then suddenly the primary webserver stops validating traffic because its SSL certificate, the original copy, has expired.

When you need to reuse the same SSL certificate on multiple servers, you can simply export it from one and import it on the next. There is no need to contact the CA at all. This process is quite straightforward, and there are two common places where you can do it: inside either the MMC snap-in for certificates or from within IIS itself. It is important to note, though, that the process is slightly different depending on which avenue you take, and you must be especially aware of what is happening with the private key as you step through these wizards.

Exporting from MMC

Head back into your **Local Computer** certificate store in MMC and navigate to **Personal | Certificates** so that you can see your SSL certificate listed. Right-click on the certificate, and then navigate to **All Tasks | Export....** When you walk through this export wizard, the important part that I wanted to mention happens right away in the wizard steps. The first choice you have to make is whether to export the private key. Again, the private key is the secret sauce that allows the certificate to interact properly with the server on which it is installed. If you export without the private key, the exported certificate will not work on another server. So it is important here that, if you are exporting this certificate with the intention of installing it onto a second webserver and using it for validating SSL traffic, you select the top option, which says **Yes, export the private key:**

Export Private Key
You can choose to export the private key with the certificate.

Private keys are password protected. If you want to export the private key with the certificate, you must type a password on a later page.

Do you want to export the private key with the certificate?

◉ Yes, export the private key

○ No, do not export the private key

Figure 7.30: Exporting a certificate using MMC

As the wizard sufficiently warns you, when you choose to export a certificate that contains private key information, you are required to supply a password, which will be used to protect the exported PFX file. It is important to choose a good password. If you forget it, your exported file will be completely useless (which isn't terrible, because you can simply export it again). If you input a password that is very simple or easy to guess, anyone who gets their hands on this PFX file may be able to use your certificate and private key on their own webservers, which would not be good.

Exporting from IIS

Alternatively, an exported PFX file can be generated from inside the IIS console. Inside the **Server Certificates** applet for IIS, just right-click on the certificate and choose **Export....**

This launches a single-page wizard that simply asks you for a location and password:

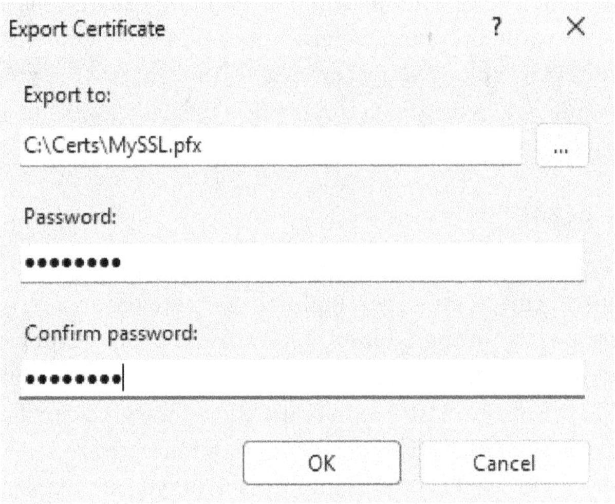

Figure 7.31: Exporting a certificate using IIS

We had many more options that we could have chosen or denied when we exported using MMC, so why is this so short? IIS makes assumptions for the rest of the settings to speed up the export process. When you are exporting an SSL certificate, it is almost a guarantee that you also intend to export the private key. Therefore, IIS simply makes that assumption and bypasses the rest of the choices. You are forced to enter a password because you don't have a choice about the private key; it will be included with the certificate export automatically. So, if you had some reason to export a certificate that did *not* contain the private key info, you could not utilize the IIS console for this task. You would need to open MMC and walk through the more extensive wizard found there.

Importing into a second server

Whichever direction you take to accomplish the export, once you have the fully fleshed PFX file available, importing into your second server is very easy. From within either console, MMC or IIS, you can right-click and choose the **Import** action. Walking through the steps, you simply choose the PFX file and then input the password that you used to protect the file. The certificate is then imported, and if you open **Properties**, you will see that the little key icon and the private key message are displayed properly at the bottom of the **Certificate Properties** screen. If you do not see the **You have a private key** message, you did something incorrectly during the export process, and you'll need to try it again.

Go ahead and try it yourself; find a server with an SSL certificate and test exporting that certificate with and without the private key. When you import into a new server, you will see that importing the certificate file without a private key does not lead to this message being displayed at the bottom of the properties page, but the exported file that does contain the private key results in the proper message being shown here. To take it a step further, try utilizing both certificates on a non-important website and see what happens. You will find that the certificate lacking the private key will fail to validate SSL traffic.

If you attempt to export an SSL certificate and the option to include the private key is grayed out, this means that when the original administrator installed this certificate on the webserver, they chose a special option that blocks the ability for the private key to be exported in the future. In this case, you will not be able to export the certificate with the private key.

OpenSSL for Linux webservers

This chapter should give you all the information needed to protect websites with public CA-based SSL certificates... as long as you are running a Windows webserver. While this is obviously a Microsoft-centric book, the majority of webservers out there are not running on Microsoft webserver platforms. Alas, you will likely run into just as many Linux-based webservers as you do instances of IIS, and it will be very helpful to your role as server administrator to be able to install certificates onto these webservers as well.

One significant difference between Windows and Linux webservers is the type of files used for certificates. IIS hides away the private key; you don't really deal with it at all. When downloading certificate files for IIS, those are usually CER or CRT files. A Linux webserver, however, expects something else. On most Linux webservers, the certificate file and the private key are each individual files that are quite visible right on the server. Both files generally have the PEM file extension.

Fortunately, the overall three-step process for acquiring and installing a certificate is exactly the same. Generate a CSR, use the CSR to get a certificate from your CA, and install the certificate on your webserver. Within those three steps are some significant differences between a Windows and a Linux platform. Let's discuss them.

Generate a CSR

Shortly, we will install a toolset called **OpenSSL** and use it for some certificate-related functions. There is a way within the OpenSSL tool to generate a private key file and a corresponding CSR file, but this is not the approach that I find to be the most user-friendly. Instead, when dealing with the requirement to install an SSL certificate onto a Linux-based webserver, I turn right back to the Windows world and generate my CSR from inside IIS. Wait a minute, what?? Didn't I just say that the processes in Windows and Linux are different? Yes, but bear with me for a minute. The CA doesn't care where the CSR file comes from, and so rather than use a CLI-based platform such as OpenSSL to monkey around with command syntax and eventually resort to Google to come up with the right commands, I simply create a CSR file exactly the same way that I would for a Windows Server, right inside IIS.

If you don't have a server with IIS installed, you can just as easily craft a CSR right from your Windows 10 or 11 computer. If you head into **Control Panel** and find the option to turn Windows features on or off, you will discover an option to install IIS. This installs the same IIS management interface to your Windows 10/11 computer as it would to a Windows Server. From within this IIS Management Console, you will have the same actions available to generate and complete certificate signing requests, right on your laptop. Once you have installed this feature, open IIS on your laptop and follow the exact process we outlined earlier, during our *Creating a certificate signing request* section.

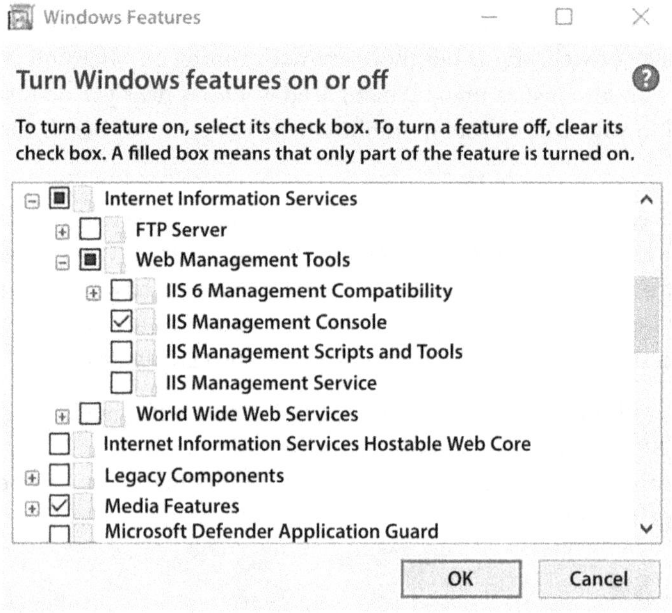

Figure 7.32: Installing IIS on Windows 10

Acquire the certificate

After using the IIS Management Console to generate a CSR file, follow the same series of steps that we previously discussed to submit your CSR to a CA, validate yourself as the owner of the domain, and download the resulting certificate file.

Install the certificate

Here is where we begin to steer the ship differently to deal with a Linux webserver. First of all, you need to install the certificate on the same IIS server (or workstation) from which you generated the CSR file. Once again, this is critically important so that your new certificate successfully pairs up with the private key that was created when you created your CSR. Once you have the new certificate installed and have validated that it looks good, you can now use the knowledge you have from a few pages ago and export this certificate (including the private key) to a PFX file.

Your newly created PFX file contains both the certificate and the private key. The only remaining step is to pump your PFX file through a couple of OpenSSL commands, which will then convert this PFX file into two separate PEM files, one containing the SSL certificate and another the private key. These two files are exactly what most Linux-based webservers are looking for when they ask you to provide an SSL certificate.

Here are the steps required to accomplish this last piece of the puzzle:

1. Download and install OpenSSL. The available version of this will change occasionally, so I cannot provide a static download link, but you can easily find it by searching the web. A specific version and filename that I know works for this purpose, because it is the one installed on my computer right now, is Win64OpenSSL-1_1_1n.exe.

2. Put your PFX file in a location that we will reference in our commands. For the sake of our example, I will assume your PFX file is named Export.pfx, and that it is sitting inside a folder called C:\Cert.

3. Open Command Prompt and navigate to the folder where OpenSSL is installed. For my version, this is the command to take me to that folder:

```
CD C:\Program Files\OpenSSL-Win64\bin
```

4. Run the following two commands:

```
openssl pkcs12 -in c:\cert\export.pfx -nokeys -out c:\cert\portal.
contoso.com-crt.pem -nodes

openssl pkcs12 -in c:\cert\export.pfx -nocerts -out c:\cert\portal.
```

(You will be asked to enter your PFX password after each of these commands.)

That's it! The preceding two commands will place two new files inside your C:\Cert folder. The first is your certificate, while the second is your private key. These two files will need to be either copied to a particular folder on your Linux webserver or uploaded into a graphical interface of whatever software you have running on that webserver, to specify the SSL certificate that is going to be used by the site.

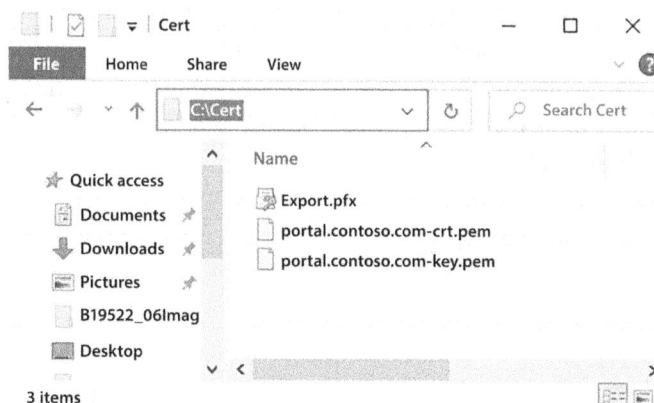

Figure 7.33: Converting a PFX into Linux-ready certificate files

These steps are kind of a weird combination of using Windows and Linux tools to get an SSL certificate into Apache, Tomcat, NGINX, or other similar webservers. I employ this method because I always have IIS at the ready by keeping its toolset installed on my Windows workstation, and this way, I can simply have those two OpenSSL commands stored away for quick access to convert certificate files when needed.

Linux chaining certificate

When installing SSL certificates on a Linux-based webserver, you may encounter one other requirement that doesn't exist in the Windows world: a **chain certificate**. Some Linux webservers will ask you to provide a PEM file for your certificate, a second PEM file containing your private key, and yet a third PEM file that is your chaining file. What in the world is a **chaining file**?

Whenever you download an SSL certificate from your public CA, your download will include multiple certificate files. Only one of those files is the real SSL certificate you are looking for; the other files are copies of the root and intermediate certificates, which are certificates provided by the CA to validate that your specific certificate was really crafted by them. These root/intermediate certs are the CA's own internet-based validation records.

On a Windows IIS webserver, you generally do nothing with these files, because the latest copies of all popular certification authority providers' root and intermediate certificates are always in place on a Windows server. If you do feel a need to manually install these subsidiary files when downloading your certificate, you simply double-click on them to install them into the appropriate `Trusted Root Certification Authorities` and `Intermediate Certification Authorities` folders inside `CERTLM.MSC`. This imports the certificates into those folders on an IIS server, and then when users tap into your SSL certificate to validate it, these root and intermediate certificates create a validation "chain" to the CA.

Some Linux-based webservers need a little more manual attention with their chaining files, and that is typically by way of crafting yourself a chaining certificate, or a chaining file, as some will call it. The process is fairly simple, but quite a mystery if you have never seen it before. This is what needs to happen:

1.   Copy your root and intermediate certificate files into a folder.
2.   Open each of these files using Notepad or any other text editor, and you will see a mess of numbers and letters, looking very much like our CSR file in *Figure 7.28*.
3.   Copy the contents of each of these files and paste them sequentially into a brand-new Notepad document. Place the root certificate on top, and then paste in one or more intermediate certificates immediately below the root inside the file. In the end, this Notepad will have two or three sets of gross-looking number/letter sequences.
4.   Save this new file as `Chain.pem` or whatever you want to name it.

5. Upload this new Chain.pem file into your Linux webserver application to use as the chaining certificate.

Figure 7.34: A newly created Chain.pem file

Linux webservers will not always ask you for a chaining file, but if they do, now you know what in the world that is. *Figure 7.34* shows us an example Chain.pem file that I just finished creating.

Summary

Humans tend to dislike what they don't understand. Certificates often get a bad rep, and I believe this is because most people see them as a headache to deal with. A box of complex mysteries. I see their point. Without knowing how to navigate through the various administrative consoles that deal with your certificate infrastructure, it would be difficult to make even the simplest certificate deployment successful. By walking through the most common certificate-related tasks that any server admin will eventually have to tackle within their own networks, I hope that you have now found some comfort and confidence to progress with those projects that might be currently sitting on hold, waiting for the certificate infrastructure to be built. SSL certificates are commonplace and important for any IT administrator to understand, but gaining control of a Windows internal CA, manipulating templates, issuing them to clients, and configuring auto-enrollment policies will really make your skill set stand out among the crowd.

Questions

Put your knowledge to the test with the following questions. If you need a hand (or just want to double-check), you'll find all the answers in the *Appendix* section of the book.

1. What is the name of the role inside Windows Server 2025 that allows you to issue certificates from your server?

2. What kind of CA server is typically installed first in a domain environment?

3. Should you install the CA role on a domain controller?

4. After creating a new certificate template, what next step needs to be taken before you can issue certificates to your computers or users from that new template?

5. What is the general name of the GPO setting that forces certificates to be issued without manual intervention by an administrator?

6. An SSL certificate will only be able to validate traffic properly if it shares key information with the webserver.

7. What is the primary piece of information that a public certification authority needs in order to issue you a new SSL certificate (hint: you generate this from your webserver)?

8. What kind of file contains both a certificate and a private key?

9. What is a command-line tool that can be used to manipulate certificates?

8

Networking with Windows Server 2025

This is a book about servers, specifically Windows Server. I often drop comments about servers making great paperweights if they don't have any roles installed; it is roles that give servers a purpose. Along those same lines, servers are quite useless if they are not connected to a solid network. The network is the platform that supports the company infrastructure; it makes up the channels that all devices inside the company use to communicate with each other.

Traditionally, there have been *server admins* and *network admins* in the IT industry, as separate roles, and in many places, that is still the case. An administrator who primarily works on servers does not generally have enough time in the day to also support the network infrastructure in an organization of any size, and the reverse is also true. Network administrators generally stick to their own equipment and management tools and aren't interested in diving too deeply into the Windows Server world. However, many of us work in smaller companies where many hats must be worn. Some days, the server admin and the network admin hats sit on top of each other, so we must understand at least the baseline of networking and the tools that we can use to troubleshoot connections that are not working. In addition, Windows Server 2025 includes components to build a newer type of networking mindset, one that many companies have not yet ventured into: network virtualization. There will always be some semblance of a physical network, using physical switches and routers to move packets around between different rooms and buildings. But now we are also incorporating the idea of **software-defined networking (SDN)** into our Windows servers, which gives us the capability to virtualize some of that configuration. Network traffic and routing can now be managed from within a server console, rather than command-line interfaces running directly on our routers and switches.

Hold the phone; I am getting ahead of myself. First, let's talk about some of the useful things inside Windows Server 2025 that do involve working with physical networks (or any networks) because these are going to be important for any administrator in today's networking world. Later, we will take a few moments to further explore this new idea of network virtualization.

The following are topics we plan to discuss in this chapter, areas where the lines between server administration and network administration begin to blur:

- IPv4 "need-to-know" information
- Introduction to IPv6
- Your networking toolbox
- The Windows routing table
- NIC teaming
- Software-defined networking

IPv4 "need-to-know" information

A general understanding of IPv4 networking is essential to do any type of work in the IT world, enough so that I have taken this topic for granted in previous editions of this book, always assuming that the reader already understood networking baselines. The more I work with engineers fresh in the industry, the more I realize that school and lab-based learning does not always stack up against the school of hard knocks, which accurately describes my journey into networking. This will not be a section where I talk in-depth about the TCP/IP protocol and things such as OSPF, BGP, or CRC error checking; rather, it is a simple country boy's description of networking components that are "need to know" so that you can successfully get your Windows servers talking to each other.

IP addresses

By far the most common network-based talking point among all IT people, IP addresses are unique identifiers on your network that allow any device to communicate with any other device. Think of IP addresses like house addresses. If you live at 123 Quincy Street and your brother lives at 456 Hawthorn Road, you have all the information needed to communicate with each other and to have "packets" delivered back and forth between your homes.

You already know that DNS turns names into IP addresses, so that you don't have to memorize hundreds or thousands of numbers that look like a hot mess until you have stared at them for so long that they suddenly make sense. Think back to when you first started working with computers, or think about just yesterday when you visited your in-laws for Sunday dinner and wowed everyone by running an `ipconfig` command while troubleshooting the wireless printer in the living room. IP addresses may seem simple to you now, but to most of the population, this is entirely like reading Greek. Don't feel bad if this is still unfamiliar territory.

DHCP, as we already discussed, often manages IP addressing within our networks. A DHCP server can be a tremendous help in keeping IP addressing straightened out, and for assigning addresses to devices on the network. To correctly build a DHCP server configuration, you must understand these basics of networking. In addition to DHCP, you will certainly have times, many times, where you are configuring static IP addresses on your devices. It is common practice not to rely on DHCP for IP addressing assignments to Windows servers, and instead exclude their addresses from DHCP altogether, in favor of configuring static IP addresses on each server. When a server has a static IP address, even if the DHCP server goes offline, that server will still be accessible and able to communicate with the network. Let's look at a screenshot of the IP address configuration screen inside Windows Server, so that we have something to reference throughout these talking points.

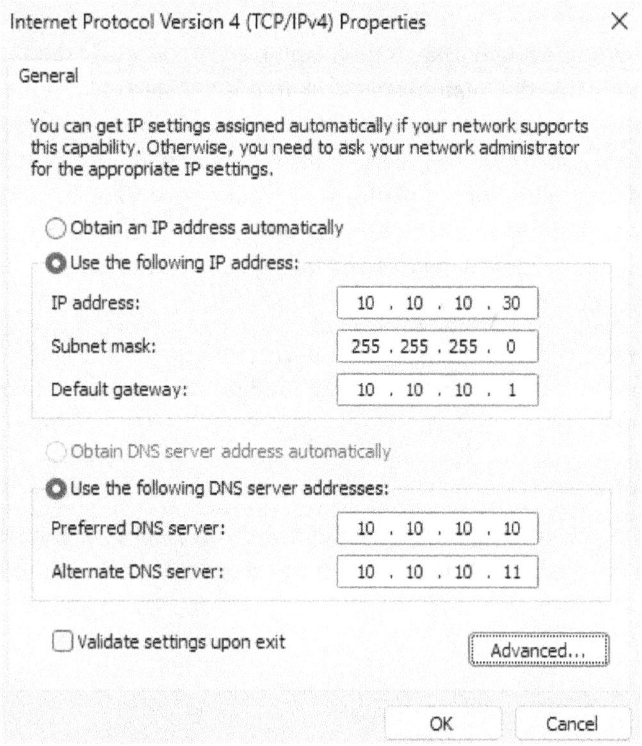

Figure 8.1: A typical IP addressing screen

Every device must have a unique IP address in your network. This is where DHCP becomes extremely helpful, but if you statically address your servers, you will want to maintain good documentation so that everybody knows which IP addresses are in use and which are still available. *Figure 8.1* depicts my FS01 server. Imagine I shut down this server for some maintenance, and while I'm working on it, another admin starts building a new server. If we don't keep good documentation about the fact that 10.10.10.30 is used by FS01, they may simply start pinging IP addresses within 10.10.10.x, find that the .30 IP address does not reply (because the server is shut down), and then configure 10.10.10.30 on their new server. This will work just fine for them, until I turn FS01 back on, at which time both of those servers are going to be in for a whirlwind of a ride as the networking equipment and other devices in the network struggle to figure out which instance of 10.10.10.30 is the real one. Mismanaged IP addresses and assigning duplicates can literally take down a network.

VPN overlap

One common place to encounter IP addressing overlaps is when helping users through VPN connection troubleshooting. Many businesses allow employees to bring a laptop home and create a VPN connection from their house into the corporate network, so that they can access company resources from home. If the user's home router assigns their laptop an IP address in the 192.168.1.x range, and there is also a network inside the business network that is 192.168.1.x, what happens? Things get messy is what happens, where sometimes that user may be able to access information over the VPN, sometimes not at all, and sometimes only certain servers and not others. These variables depend on the configuration and capabilities of the platform providing your VPN, but ultimately, the only way you will truly help that employee to have a normal, successful VPN connection is if you walk them through changing their entire home network to no longer run on 192.168.1.x, but something entirely different, perhaps 192.168.100.x or even 10.10.10.x.

So many home-class routers default to using 192.168.0.x or 192.168.1.x IP addresses that any network admin worth their salt should know to never configure a business network to utilize either of these IP addressing ranges.

Private addressing

Why is it that every time you read about internal networks in a book, or (hopefully) every time that you encounter one in the wild, the IP addresses always seem to look similar to these examples?

- 192.168.1.1
- 192.168.3.30
- 172.16.1.3
- 172.24.100.46
- 10.10.10.30
- 10.1.2.1

There are many, many combinations of numbers to create many unique IP addresses, but why do they always seem to begin with 192, 172, or 10 when dealing with IP addresses *inside* your network? This is because when IPv4 was invented, those engineers realized that standards were needed to create a safe separation between the public network (the internet) and the company's private networks. There are nowhere near enough public IPv4 addresses for every device that needs access to the internet to have a unique IP address directly on the internet, so a standard was created for sections of IP addressing that are deemed "private IP addressing space." In other words, you will never find the following IP addresses in use on the internet, and these addresses are always safe to utilize inside your private networks. In other words, any internal network that you ever create should be contained within the following:

- 192.168.0.0 through 192.168.255.255
- 172.16.0.0 through 172.31.255.255
- 10.0.0.0 through 10.255.255.255

If you ever hear someone talking about **RFC 1918**, this is exactly what is being discussed. The **Internet Engineering Task Force (IETF)** recognized this need for IP addressing space to be kept away from the public internet long ago, and RFC 1918 is the technical standard that was created to privatize these three groupings of IP addresses and make them be forever dedicated to only internal addressing. By making use of the preceding IP addressing options within our internal networks, we can create huge networking spaces to safely keep our devices separated from each other. And since none of these IP addresses will ever be used and routed over the public internet, every company can safely make use of the same sets of IP addresses without conflict occurring among different companies. This is the reason why so many home routers all run 192.168.1.x, and yet there are no conflicts on the internet because of it.

The reason I said "hopefully" you always find internal networks running only these private IP addresses is because it is entirely possible to utilize public IP addressing inside your network. I have come across networks such as these a few times in my career, and there is never a legitimate reason to have created the internal network that way. It was simply a network admin who wasn't quite sure what they were doing. You could certainly configure all your servers and computers inside your network to run something like 8.8.8.x, and they would be able to communicate with each other just fine. They would even be able to communicate with at least some of the internet, but anytime they tried to reach areas of the internet that make use of the "real" IP addresses (publicly owned IP addresses) within this range, communications would certainly fail, because your network routing rules and equipment would keep that traffic inside the network. Networks like these make for some very interesting stories!

Don't do it.

Subnet mask

Referring back to *Figure 8.1*, the next piece of information we must populate for a successful network connection is the subnet mask. In almost all home networks, you might find your IP address to be something like 192.168.1.100. This is your full IP address, but what isn't immediately obvious is that only the last portion (.100) is your individual workstation identifier on the network. The rest of that address (192.168.1) is known as a network address. In IPv4-land, the way that IP addressing works is that each of those four octets can contain a number from 0 through 255. You can define whether more of your IP addresses should be dedicated to network addressing, or to host/device addressing. There are three classes of IPv4 subnets, and each one has advantages/disadvantages because they allow either more separated networks within your environment, or more host addresses within each network. Let me break it down this way, by looking at a few different subnet mask options:

- Class A subnet = **255.0.0.0** = 128 different **networks**, each with 16,777,216 hosts
- Class B subnet = **255.255.0.0** = 16,384 **networks**, each with 65,536 hosts
- Class C subnet = **255.255.255.0** = 2,097,152 **networks**, each with 256 hosts

Any IPv4 subnet consists of 32 bits, four sections of 8 bits each. If you look closely at what numbers I put in **bold** above, you can see that in a Class A subnet, the first number is the network identifier, and the remainder of the address can be assigned to devices. In a Class B, half (16 bits) are a network identifier, and the latter half are for devices. In a Class C subnet, the most common, three-quarters of this address are assigned to be the network identification, and only the last part of this address can be used for device/host addressing.

So, in a Class C network that has a subnet mask of 255.255.255.0, there are 256 available addresses, but the first and last are always hands-off. For example, 192.168.1.0 is a subnet identification number that cannot be used by a device, and 192.168.1.255 is called a broadcast address, which also cannot be used by a device because it is inherently responsible for getting packets to their destination between two machines that are on the same subnet.

All these numbers make you dizzy after a while, and it's good to know that there is a shorthand way to discuss different subnet mask numbers. Instead of saying something such as 255.255.255.0, you can instead use the CIDR number /24. We often say things such as, "This is a slash-24 network," and in fact, some devices require you to specify the CIDR as a subnet mask identifier instead of the actual subnet mask number. Here are common CIDRs for the same subnet numbers we discussed earlier:

*   255.0.0.0 (/8)
*   255.255.0.0 (/16)
*   255.255.255.0 (/24)

There are many more CIDRs for other sizes of networks. As an example, let's say your internal network is 192.168.2.0/24 (meaning that you have 254 usable IP addresses, .1 through .254). What if your business grows and you run out of IP addresses? You could set up a second /24 network, such as 192.168.3.0/24. Each of these networks would be a separate /24, and the two networks would not know about each other at all. For devices on these two networks to communicate with each other, even if they were plugged into the same switch, you would need to introduce a Layer 3 router (gateway) into the mix, so that the router could then be aware of both individual networks and route traffic back and forth between them.

Or...you could move to a /23 network instead. When changing from /24 to /23, you are still running within a Class C subnet designation, but you double the number of host addresses. Adjusting to a /23 network means you would change your subnet mask to 255.255.254.0 on all of your devices, and once you do that, all of the IP addresses from 192.168.2.1 through 192.168.3.254 can know about and talk with each other, even without a router.

A subnet mask defines boundaries for routing. It tells your equipment what to expect by way of network packet flow. You can easily test these theories if you have access to two computers and a simple switch, or if you have a Hyper-V or VMware server where you can establish two VMs. Go ahead and set up an extremely simple network consisting of two devices connected together by a switch. Even with no firewall, router, or gateway to help them pass traffic from one network to another, you will find that if you set up IP addresses like this, the two computers will be able to communicate:

*   Computer 1 = 192.168.1.100/24 (255.255.255.0 subnet)
*   Computer 2 = 192.168.1.150/24 (255.255.255.0 subnet)

But if you change Computer 2 to be 192.168.2.150/24, the two computers are still physically connected to each other through the same switch, but they will no longer be able to communicate at all.

Then try changing from /24 to /16, like this:

*   Computer 1 = 192.168.1.100/16 (255.255.0.0 subnet)
*   Computer 2 = 192.168.128.150/16 (255.255.0.0 subnet)

Since we are now using a /16 subnet, that means the entire latter half of the IP address is dedicated to host addressing, and so even though 192.168.1.x and 192.168.128.x seem like they are very far apart, within a /16 network, these two sets of IP addresses (and everything in between) are all part of the *same network*. In this scenario, your two test computers would be able to talk to each other just fine.

Public subnetting

Our information so far all pertains to internal networks and private IP addressing, but the same math and mechanisms exist on the public internet. When purchasing internet service for a business, or even your home, a common question from the ISP is whether you want any static IP addresses to be part of your service. If you say yes, they will ask how many you need. The entire internet plays by the same IPv4 rules we have been discussing here, and so available and usable IPv4 addresses on the internet are limited. It is very common for companies to be given a very small set of usable IP addresses, maybe five or perhaps even one. The way that ISPs control the distribution of these tiny amounts of IP addresses is by dedicating even more of the IP address to be network identification, thereby causing less of the IP address to be usable for host addressing. When dealing with public IP addressing, it is common to see CIDRs and subnet masks such as the following:

- 255.255.255.252 (/30) = 2 usable IP addresses (1 for you to use)
- 255.255.255.248 (/29) = 6 usable IP addresses (5 for you to use)
- 255.255.255.240 (/28) = 14 usable IP addresses

...and so on.

If you ever need to remind yourself of these numbers, or figure out what subnet sizing is appropriate based on the number of IP addresses you require, you can turn to the internet and search "subnet calculator" to find numerous free online calculators to play around with subnetting information, or search "CIDR chart" to find images that can be printed to become a quick reference guide for subnet sizing.

Default gateway

While subnet masks can be a complex topic, your default gateway is quite simple. Inside any network interface's IP addressing information, you will find a field to define a gateway. Every computer or server has a built-in routing table that contains a list of rules and destinations for sending network traffic. If you are plugged into a network such as 192.168.1.0/24, when Windows attempts to contact any IP address that is within 192.168.1.x, it knows that the NIC is on-subnet (on-link) with those other IP addresses, and it simply throws the packets out of that NIC. If a server has two NICs, one on 192.168.1.0/24 and another on 10.10.0.0/16, once again, if any traffic needs to be sent to IP addresses within these networks, your server is smart enough, based on its own routing table, to get those packets where they need to go.

The routing table in Windows is built primarily based on what IP address and subnet mask are configured in your NICs. All Windows needs are those couple of pieces of information in order to build successful routing rules into those networks. It is also possible to manually manipulate a routing table and add custom rules, and indeed, we will do that later in this chapter, but what about when your computer or server needs to reach outbound and contact an IP address that is *not* listed in its routing table? Maybe you open a web browser and head to google.com, and DNS sends your request to 8.8.8.8 (I know this isn't accurate, but stick with me here)...how in the world does your computer know how to get to 8.8.8.8? The default gateway, that's how.

The default gateway is a "catch-all." Every time your machine needs to send network packets outbound to a location that is not listed in its local routing table, it will send those packets at whatever IP address is defined as your default gateway. This gateway is almost always a router or firewall of some kind. At home, it's probably your home wireless router. At work, it is likely a firewall or a switch that is acting as a Layer 3 routing mechanism on your network.

We will talk more about default gateways later, when we look more closely at the Windows routing table. But remember this—on any Windows computer, Windows Server, or really any networking device in the world, you should only ever have *one* default gateway on the entire system.

MAC addresses

Discussion of network traffic almost always lands on verbiage about IP addresses and subnets, which is accurate but not the full story. Every network card connected to your network has a unique identifier. Every computer NIC, every server, every printer, every PLC...the list goes on and on. You might be thinking, "Hey Jordan, we just finished talking about these identifiers—IP addresses!" You're not wrong, but you're also not comprehensively right.

IP addresses are configured on NICs and are every device's location on a network. However, when networking equipment such as firewalls, routers, and switches send traffic between sources and destinations, they are actually sending and tracking devices by information that is even further under the hood: MAC addresses. Every network card has a MAC address, which is a unique physical identifier on the network. IP addresses can be moved from one device to another, while MAC addresses are typically bound to the network card. On a Windows machine, you'll see some evidence later in this chapter that a NIC's MAC address is displayed when you look at an ipconfig command. For something like a label printer, the MAC address is usually printed on a sticker directly attached to the back of the printer. You may remember that we had to define a MAC address inside DHCP back in *Chapter 4*, so that DHCP could always hand the same IP address to the device with a specific MAC address.

Since we already discussed MAC addresses somewhat when discussing DHCP, and will work directly with them again later in this chapter, I won't expound upon this right now. But it is important to remember that IP addresses are not the end of the road when there is network traffic. DNS names are turned into IP addresses, IP addresses are turned into MAC addresses, and traffic then flows through your switches.

Introduction to IPv6

Welcome to the dark side! Unfortunately, that is how many people think of IPv6. While IPv6 is by no means a new thing, in my experience, it is still something that almost no one has deployed in their networks. While working with hundreds of different companies all over the world over the past few years, I have come across only two organizations that were running IPv6 over their entire production network, and one wasn't even truly native IPv6. Instead, they were using a tunneling technology, called ISATAP, over their whole network to make all of the servers and clients talk to each other using IPv6 packets, but these packets were still traversing an IPv4 physical network. Don't get me wrong; I found plenty of cases where companies were toying around with IPv6 and had some semblance of it configured in a sectioned-off piece of their networks, but using it for the entire production network? Most of us just aren't ready for such an enormous change. Why is it so difficult to put IPv6 into place? Because we have used IPv4 since basically the beginning of time, it's what we all know and understand, and there really isn't a great need to move to IPv6 inside our networks. Wait a minute; I thought there was some big scare about running out of IPv4 addresses? Yes, that is true for IP addresses on the public internet, but that has nothing to do with our internal networks. You see, even if we run out of public IPv4 addresses tomorrow, the internal networks of our companies are not going to be impacted. We can continue to run IPv4 inside the network for a long time to come, possibly forever and always, as long as we are comfortable using NAT technologies to translate the traffic down into IPv4 as it comes into our network from the internet. We have all used NAT in one form or another for almost as long as IPv4 has existed, so it is obviously something people are very comfortable with.

Let me be clear: I am not trying to convince you that sticking with IPv4 is the way of the future. I am just laying out the fact that, for most organizations over the next few years, this will simply be the truth. The reason I want to discuss IPv6 here is that, eventually, you will have to deal with it. And once you do, you'll actually get excited about it! There are some huge advantages that IPv6 has over IPv4, namely, the enormous number of IP addresses that can be contained within a single network. Network teams in companies around the world struggle every day with the need to build more and more IPv4 networks and tie them together. Think about it: there are many companies now with employee counts in excess of 10,000. Some have many, many times that number. In today's world, everyone needs almost constant access to their data. Data is the new currency. Most users now have at least two physical devices they utilize for work, sometimes more than that: a laptop and a tablet; a laptop and a smartphone; or a desktop, a laptop, a tablet, and a smartphone—you get the idea. In the IPv4 world, where you are dealing with comparatively small IP address ranges, you must get very creative with creating subnets in order to accommodate all of these physical devices. Each needs a unique IP address to communicate on the network.

The biggest advantage of IPv6 is that it resolves all these problems immediately and by default, by providing the capability to have a *huge* number of IP addresses within a single network. How many more addresses are we talking about? The following comparison data gives a little perspective:

- An IPv4 address is a 32-bit length address that looks like this: `192.168.1.5`
- An IPv6 address is a 128-bit length address that looks like this: `2001:AABB:CCDD:AB00:0123:4567:8901:ABCD`

As you can see, the IPv4 address is much shorter, which obviously means there are fewer possibilities for unique IP addresses. What you don't see is how much longer IPv6 addresses really are. These examples portray IPv4 and IPv6 addresses as we are used to seeing them, in their finished forms. Really, though, the IPv4 address is shown in decimal form, and IPv6 in hexadecimal. IPv6 addresses are shown and used via hex so that the addresses are compressed as much as possible. In reality, if you dig around under the hood, an IPv6 address in its native 128-bit form might look something like this (and indeed, this is how it looks inside the actual packet):

```
0001000001000001000011011001100000000000000000000010000000000000000
```

```
0001000000000000000000000000100000000000000000000000000000000000001
```

That's an impressive set of digits, but not something that is very usable or friendly to the human eye. So, rather than show the bits, what about an IPv6 address shown in decimal format in the same way that IPv4 addresses have always been shown? In that case, an IPv6 address might look something like this:

```
192.16.1.2.34.0.0.1.0.0.0.0.0.0.0.1
```

Now we fully understand why IPv6 is always used and shown in hexadecimal; the addresses are long even in that compressed format!

When we set up IPv4 networks, subnetting is extremely important because it is what enables us to have more than one collection of IP addresses within the same network. In the most basic form of networking, where you set up some IP addresses and run a /24 subnet, you are limited to 254 unique IP addresses. Ouch! Some companies have thousands of servers, without accounting for all of their client computers and devices that also need to connect to the network. Thankfully, we can build out many different subnets within a single IPv4 network to increase our usable IP address scope, but this takes careful planning and calculation of those subnets and address spaces and is the reason that we rely on experienced network administrators to manage this part of the network for us. One invalid subnet configuration in a routing table can tank network traffic flow. The administration of subnets in a large IPv4 network is not for the faint of heart.

When we talk about IPv6 addressing, the sky almost seems to be the limit. If you were to calculate all the unique IPv6 addresses available in the preceding 128-bit space, you would find that there are more than 340 undecillion addresses available to be created—in other words, 340 trillion, trillion, trillion addresses. This is the number being touted out there about how many available addresses there are on the IPv6 internet, but what does that mean for our internal networks?

To discuss the number of addresses we could have inside a typical internal network that runs IPv6, let's first step back and look at the address itself. The address I showed earlier is just something I made up, but we will break down the parts of it here:

```
2001:AABB:CCDD:AB00:0123:4567:8901:ABCD
```

Compared to 192.168.1.5, this thing looks like a monstrosity. That is because we are generally not accustomed to dealing with the hexadecimal format; it is just a different way of looking at data. As mentioned, this is a 128-bit address. It is broken into 8 sections, each sized at 16 bits, and each section is separated by a colon. The first 64 bits (the first half) of the address are routing information, and the latter 64 bits are the unique device ID on the network. Within the first part, we have two different components. The first 48 bits (three groups of hex) are an organizational prefix that will be the same on all of the devices in the network. Then, the fourth set of information, the next 16 bits, can be our subnet ID. This gives us the flexibility of still having many different subnets if we so desire in the future by using multiple numbers here as the subnet ID. After learning about the first half of the address, we now have the latter half to work with, the last 64 bits. These we can leave for device IDs. This part of the address will be different for every device on the network and will define the individual static IPv6 addresses that will be used for communication. Let's break down our example address into the following parts:

- **Overall IP address:** `2001:AABB:CCDD:AB00:0123:4567:8901:ABCD`
- **Organizational prefix:** `2001:AABB:CCDD`
- **Subnet ID:** `AB00`
- **Device ID:** `0123:4567:8901:ABCD` (this is one unique device ID)

How many devices can we have in our network with an IP schema such as this? Well, even in our example, where we only allocated one 16-bit section for subnetting and 64 bits for actual IP addresses, that would provide us with the capability to have more than 65,000 subnets and quintillions of unique device IDs in our IP range. Impressive, isn't it?

If we stick with this and use only a single subnet to contain all of our machines, the first half of our addresses will always be the same, making these long addresses much easier to remember and deal with. It is surprising how quickly you will get used to seeing these large hex numbers in your environment, but even though you will start to recognize them, you still are probably not going to quickly jump into servers or computers in your network anymore by using the static IP addresses. I know a lot of us are still in the habit of saying: "I need to jump into my web server; I'll just RDP into `192.168.1.5`." Even if you can remember an IPv6 address, the time that it takes to type out these addresses isn't generally worth it. IPv6 will bring with it a larger reliance on DNS to make it usable.

Now that we understand what sections of the address are going to be used for what purposes, how do we go about assigning the individual device ID numbers for all of the computers, servers, and other devices on our network? You could start with number 1 and go up from there. Another idea is to calculate the old IPv4 addresses into hex and use this as the last 32 bits of the address—open up Windows Calculator on your computer, drop down the menu, and change it into Programmer mode. This is a quick and easy tool that you can use to convert decimal into hexadecimal, and vice versa. Let's take the example of my web server that is running on `192.168.1.5`. I want to implement IPv6 inside my network, and I want my server's IPv6 addresses to reflect the original IPv4 address in the device ID section of the new address. In the calculator, if I type in 192 and then click on **HEX**, it will show me the corresponding hexadecimal for the decimal of 192, as shown in *Figure 8.2*:

Figure 8.2: Using Windows Calculator to convert decimal into hexadecimal

If we do that with each of the octets in our IPv4 address, we will see the following:

- 192 = C0
- 168 = A8
- 1 = 01
- 5 = 05

So, my `192.168.1.5` factors out to `C0A8:0105`. I can now utilize that in combination with the organizational prefix and the subnet ID to create a static IPv6 address for my web server:

`2001:AABB:CCDD:0001:0000:0000:C0A8:0105`

You'll notice in the preceding IPv6 address that I input the hex for the device ID at the end, but I also made a couple of other changes. Since we are leaving the last 64 bits available for the device ID, but my old IPv4 address only consumes 32 bits, I am left with the 32 bits in the middle. It would be kind of weird to have data in there that didn't mean anything to us, so we will simply make it all zeros to simplify the addressing scheme. In addition to that change, I also adjusted my subnet ID to the number 1, since this is the first subnet in my network.

Our new addressing is starting to look a little cleaner and makes more sense. Now that we see this new address for our web server laid out, we can see that there are some additional clean-up tasks we can perform on the address in order to make it look even better. Right now, the address listed earlier is 100% accurate. I could plug this IP address into the NIC properties of my web server and it would work. However, there are a whole lot of zeros in my address, and I don't need to keep them all. Anytime you have unnecessary zeros within a 16-bit segment that are preceding the actual number, they can simply be removed. For example, our subnet ID and the first 32 bits of our device ID have a lot of unnecessary zeros, so I can consolidate the address down to the following:

`2001:AABB:CCDD:1:0:0:C0A8:0105`

Then, to take it a step further, any time you have full 16-bit sections that are composed entirely of zeros, they can be fully consolidated into a double colon. So, the first 32 bits of my device ID that are all zeros, I can replace with `::`. The following is the full address and the consolidated address. These numbers look quite different. My consolidated address is much easier on the eye, but from a technological perspective, they are exactly the same number:

`2001:AABB:CCDD:0001:0000:0000:C0A8:0105`

`2001:AABB:CCDD:1::C0A8:0105`

In fact, if you set up a lab or want to quickly test IPv6, you can use addresses as simple as the following example. The two addresses that I will show you here are precisely the same:

`2001:0000:0000:0000:0000:0000:0000:0001`

`2001::1`

It is important to note that you can only use a double colon *once* within an IP address. If you had two places where it was applicable within the same address, you could only implement it in one of those places, and you would have to spell out the zeros in the other place. For example, changing `2001:AABB:0000:0000:0001:0000:0000:0123` into `2001:AABB::1::123` would cause your computer grief, as it would not know what to do with that second double-colon.

With the information provided here, you should be able to put together your own semblance of IPv6 and start issuing some IPv6 addresses to computers or servers in your network. There is so much more to be learned about this subject that an entire book could be written, and indeed, there are numerous offerings to choose from. Recent Windows computers and servers are well equipped to start using IPv6 right now inside NIC properties, but keep in mind that other types of devices on your network, especially older ones, may not have any knowledge of IPv6, nor have a field to even input an IPv6 address. Legacy devices could be a major deciding factor, or roadblock, on your journey toward IPv6.

Your networking toolbox

Whether you are a server administrator, a network administrator, or a combination of the two, there are a number of tools that are useful for testing and monitoring network connections within the Windows Server world. Some of these tools are baked right into the operating system and can be used from Command Prompt, PowerShell, or Terminal, and others are more expansive graphical interfaces that require installation before running. The following are the built-in Windows network tools that we are going to look at:

- ping
- tracert
- pathping
- Test-Connection
- telnet
- Test-NetConnection
- netstat

All of these tools are free and included out of the box, so you have no excuse to delay getting acquainted with these helpful utilities. Let's explore these, as well as some more enhanced options provided by special teams at Microsoft, or even third parties.

ping

Even the newest IT pros are usually familiar with this one. ping is a command that you can utilize from Command Prompt or PowerShell, and it is simply used to query a DNS name and/or IP address to find out whether it responds. ping is, and has always been, our go-to tool for testing network connectivity between two devices on a network. From my Windows 10 client on the LAN, I can open a prompt and use ping <IP_ADDRESS>. Alternatively, because I am using DNS in my environment, which will resolve names to IP addresses, I can also use ping <SERVERNAME>, as shown in *Figure 8.3*. You can see that my server replies to my ping, letting me know that it is online and responding:

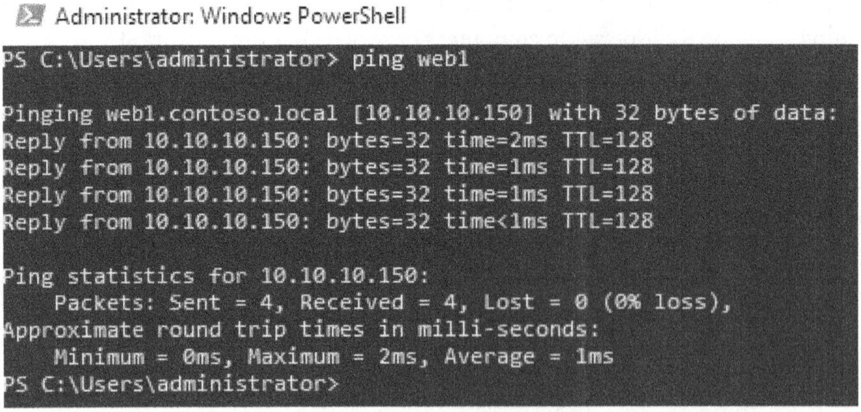

```
Administrator: Windows PowerShell

PS C:\Users\administrator> ping web1

Pinging web1.contoso.local [10.10.10.150] with 32 bytes of data:
Reply from 10.10.10.150: bytes=32 time=2ms TTL=128
Reply from 10.10.10.150: bytes=32 time=1ms TTL=128
Reply from 10.10.10.150: bytes=32 time=1ms TTL=128
Reply from 10.10.10.150: bytes=32 time<1ms TTL=128

Ping statistics for 10.10.10.150:
    Packets: Sent = 4, Received = 4, Lost = 0 (0% loss),
Approximate round trip times in milli-seconds:
    Minimum = 0ms, Maximum = 2ms, Average = 1ms
PS C:\Users\administrator>
```

Figure 8.3: Pinging a server

Ping traffic is technically called **ICMP traffic**. This is important because the ICMP protocol is blocked by default more and more often these days, with firewalls being turned on by default on so many of our systems and devices. Historically, `ping` was always a tool that we could count on to tell us with a fair degree of certainty whether connectivity was flowing between two devices, but that is no longer the case. If you build a brand-new Windows box and plug it into your network, that computer may communicate with the internet and all of the servers on your network just fine, but if you try to ping that new computer from another machine on your network, the ping will probably fail. Why would that happen? Because Windows has some security measures built into it by default, including blocking ICMP traffic in Windows Defender Firewall. In that case, you would need to either turn off the Windows firewall or provide it with an access rule that allows ICMP traffic. Once such a rule is enabled, pings will start replying from this new computer. Keep in mind, whenever building new systems or servers in your network, that `ping` is not always the most trustworthy tool to depend upon in today's security-focused world.

It's easy to allow ICMP responses by plugging a rule into Windows Defender Firewall with Advanced Security, though you still wouldn't want to have to remember to do this manually on every new system you introduce into a network. Thankfully, you already know how to utilize Group Policy to build a GPO and push it out to all machines on your network, and yes, you can absolutely place firewall rules inside that GPO. In fact, we will do exactly this in *Chapter 10, Hardening and Security*. This is a common way to allow or block ICMP throughout an entire organization, by issuing a firewall rule via Group Policy.

tracert

`tracert`, which is pronounced *trace route*, is a tool used to trace a network packet as it traverses your network. What it really does is report all of the places the packet bumps into before hitting its destination. These bumps in the road that a network packet encounters are called **hops**. `tracert` shows you all of the hops that your traffic takes as it moves toward the destination server or whatever it is trying to contact. My test lab network is very flat and boring, so using `tracert` wouldn't show me much of anything. However, if I open up a PowerShell prompt from an internet-connected machine and use `tracert` on a web service, such as Bing, we get some interesting results:

```
PS C:\WINDOWS\system32> tracert www.bing.com

Tracing route to any.edge.bing.com [204.79.197.200]
over a maximum of 30 hops:

  1     <1 ms     <1 ms     <1 ms   192.168.8.1
  2      1 ms     <1 ms     <1 ms   192.168.128.1
  3      8 ms      7 ms      5 ms   172.17.224.1
  4     11 ms      9 ms     15 ms   172.19.253.1
  5     10 ms      9 ms     11 ms   172.31.255.1
  6     20 ms      9 ms     13 ms   htl-max1-1.iserv.net [206.114.55.1]
  7     15 ms     12 ms      8 ms   69.87.144.9
  8     23 ms     18 ms     19 ms   888-2.iserv.net [206.114.40.2]
  9     23 ms     20 ms     15 ms   g5-0-0.core3.grr.iserv.net [206.114.51.20]
 10     19 ms     11 ms     19 ms   g5-0-0.core1.grr.iserv.net [206.114.51.2]
 11     21 ms     28 ms     19 ms   GigabitEthernet4-1.GW5.DET5.ALTER.NET [152.179.10.81]
 12     25 ms     28 ms     28 ms   0.ae1.XL3.CHI13.ALTER.NET [140.222.225.179]
 13     27 ms     37 ms     54 ms   TenGigE0-6-0-1.GW2.CHI13.ALTER.NET [152.63.65.133]
 14     36 ms     34 ms     34 ms   microsoft-gw.customer.alter.net [152.179.105.130]
 15     58 ms     50 ms     46 ms   104.44.81.58
 16     34 ms     33 ms     36 ms   10.201.194.219
 17     26 ms     29 ms     29 ms   a-0001.a-msedge.net [204.79.197.200]

Trace complete.
PS C:\WINDOWS\system32>
```

Figure 8.4: Using tracert

If you utilize tracert but are not interested in seeing all of the DNS information provided in the output, use tracert -d to focus only on the IP addresses.

This information can be extremely useful when trying to diagnose a connection that is not working. If your traffic is moving through multiple hops, such as routers and firewalls, before it gets to the destination, tracert can be essential in figuring out where in the connection stream things are going wrong. Given that the preceding screenshot shows a successful tracert to Bing, now let's see what it looks like when things are broken. I will unplug my internet modem and run the same tracert www.bing.com again, and now we can see that I am still able to communicate with my local router, but not beyond it:

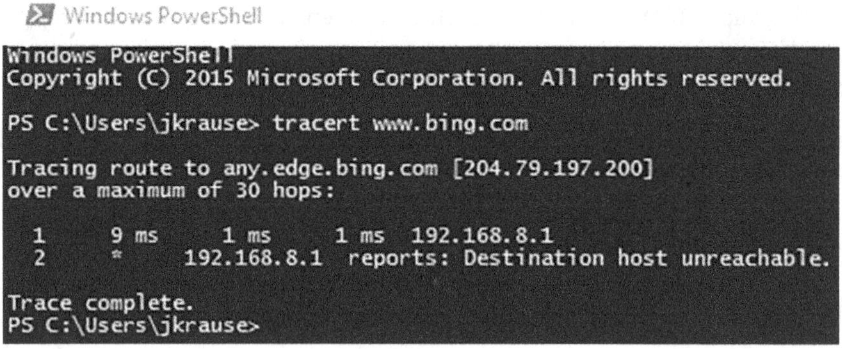

```
Windows PowerShell

Windows PowerShell
Copyright (C) 2015 Microsoft Corporation. All rights reserved.

PS C:\Users\jkrause> tracert www.bing.com

Tracing route to any.edge.bing.com [204.79.197.200]
over a maximum of 30 hops:

  1      9 ms     1 ms     1 ms  192.168.8.1
  2       *              192.168.8.1  reports: Destination host unreachable.

Trace complete.
PS C:\Users\jkrause>
```

Figure 8.5: Using tracert

It is important to note that tracert relies on ICMP to receive responses back from the network devices that it contacts. If those network devices don't permit an ICMP response, you won't receive information back from those hops.

pathping

tracert is useful and seems to be the *de facto* standard for tracing packets around your network, but this next command is even more powerful in my opinion. pathping essentially does the same thing as tracert, except that it provides one additional piece of crucial information. Most of the time, with either of these commands, you are only interested in figuring out where in the chain of hops something is broken. Often, though, when I'm setting up networking on new servers, I am working with servers and hardware that have many different network cards. When dealing with multiple NICs in a system, the local routing table is just as important as the external routers and switches, and I often want to check out the path of a network packet to see which local NIC it is flowing out of. This is where pathping becomes more powerful than tracert. The first piece of information that tracert shows you is the first hop away from the local server that you are traversing. However, pathping also shows you which local network interface your packets are flowing out of.

Let me give you an example: I often set up remote access servers with multiple NICs, and during this process, I create many routes on the local server so that it knows what traffic needs to be sent in which direction, such as what traffic needs to go out the internal NIC, and what traffic needs to go out the external NIC. After completing all of the routing statements for the internal NIC, I test them by pinging a server inside the network. Perhaps that ping fails, and I'm not sure why. I can try a tracert command, but it's not going to provide me with anything helpful because it simply cannot see the first hop; it just times out. However, if I use a pathping command instead, the first hop will still time out, but I can now see that the traffic is attempting to flow out of my *external NIC*. Whoops! I must have set something up incorrectly with the static route on this server. pathping can be the key to realizing that I need to delete that route and recreate it to make this traffic flow through the internal NIC instead.

The following is the same PowerShell prompt from the same computer that I used in my tracert screenshot. You can see that a pathping command shows me the local IP address on my laptop where the traffic is attempting to leave the system, whereas the tracert command did not show this information:

```
PS C:\Users\jkrause> pathping www.bing.com

Tracing route to any.edge.bing.com [204.79.197.200]
over a maximum of 30 hops:
  0  IVO-PC-328 [192.168.8.113]
  1  192.168.8.1
  2  192.168.128.1
  3    *        192.168.8.1  reports: Destination host unreachable.

Computing statistics for 75 seconds...
            Source to Here   This Node/Link
Hop  RTT    Lost/Sent = Pct  Lost/Sent = Pct  Address
  0                                            IVO-PC-328 [192.168.8.113]
                                0/ 100 =  0%   |
  1   1ms      0/ 100 =  0%    0/ 100 =  0%   192.168.8.1
                              100/ 100 =100%   |
  2   ---    100/ 100 =100%    0/ 100 =  0%   192.168.128.1
                                0/ 100 =  0%   |
  3   ---    100/ 100 =100%    0/ 100 =  0%   IVO-PC-328 [0.0.0.0]

Trace complete.
PS C:\Users\jkrause>
```

Figure 8.6: pathping shows the source NIC

Test-Connection

The commands we have discussed so far can be run from Command Prompt or PowerShell, but now it's time to dive into a newer one that can only be run from the PowerShell prompt (or Terminal, of course, which can run PowerShell all day): a cmdlet called Test-Connection; it is sort of like ping on steroids. If we open a PowerShell prompt in the lab and run Test-Connection WEB1, we see output that is very similar to what we'd get with a regular ping, but the information is laid out in a way that I think is a little easier on the eyes. There is also an unexpected column of data here called Source:

```
Administrator: Windows PowerShell
PS C:\Users\Administrator> Test-Connection WEB1

Source          Destination      IPV4Address        IPV6Address
------          -----------      -----------        -----------
DC1             WEB1             10.10.10.150
DC1             WEB1             10.10.10.150
DC1             WEB1             10.10.10.150
DC1             WEB1             10.10.10.150


PS C:\Users\Administrator>
```

Figure 8.7: Using Test-Connection

That is interesting. I was logged into my DC1 server when I ran this command, so the source computer for this command was DC1. But does this mean that I can manipulate the source computer for the Test-Connection cmdlet? Yes, this is exactly what it means.

As with everything in Windows Server 2025 management, the need to be logged in to a local server is decoupled. Specific to the Test-Connection cmdlet, this means you can open a PowerShell prompt anywhere on your network and test connections between two different endpoints, even if you are not logged in to either of them. Let's test that out.

I am still logged in to my DC1 server, but I am going to use a Test-Connection cmdlet to test connections between a number of my servers in the network. You see, not only can you specify a source computer other than the one you are currently logged in to, but you can also take it a step further and specify multiple sources and destinations with this powerful cmdlet. So, if I want to test connections from a couple of different source machines to a couple of different destinations, that is easily done with the following command:

```
Test-Connection -Source DC1, DC2 -ComputerName WEB1, FS01
```

You can see in *Figure 8.8* that I have ping statistics from both DC1 and DC2 to each of the WEB1 and BACK1 servers in my network. Test-Connection has the potential to be a very powerful monitoring tool:

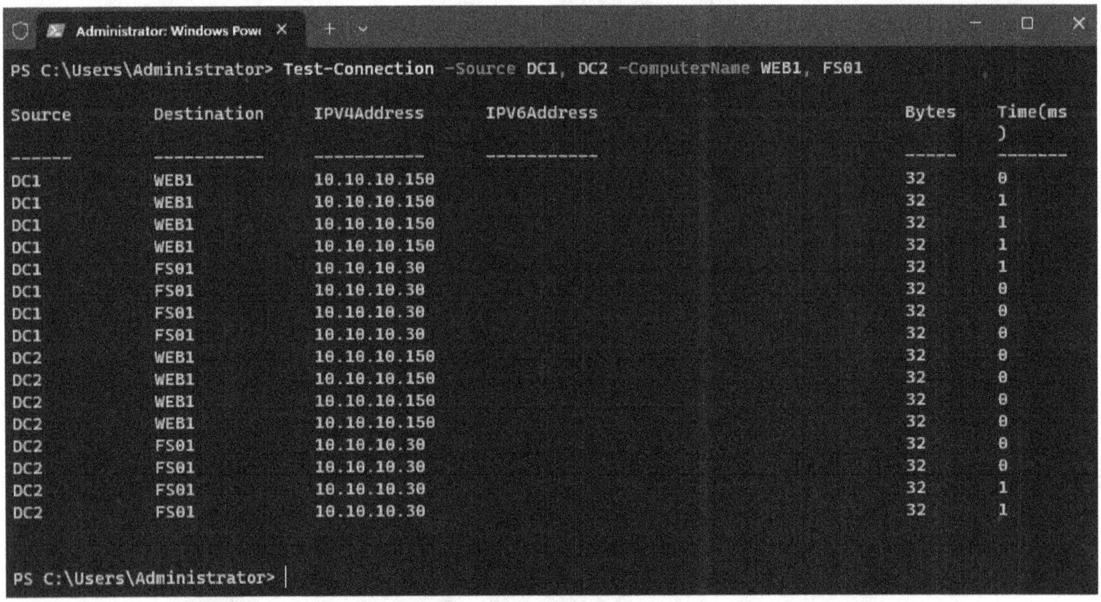

Figure 8.8: Multiple sources and destinations using Test-Connection

One more useful function to point out is that you can clean up the output of the command by using the -Quiet switch. By adding -Quiet to a Test-Connection command, it sanitizes the output and only shows you a simple True or False for whether the connection was successful, instead of showing you each individual ICMP packet that was sent. Unfortunately, you cannot combine both the -Source switch and the -Quiet switch, but if you use Test-Connection from the original source computer that you are logged in to, like most of us will be doing anyway, -Quiet works great. Most of the time, all we really care about is yes or no as to whether these connections are working, and don't necessarily want to see all four attempts. By using -Quiet, we get exactly that:

```
Test-Connection -Quiet -ComputerName WEB1, DC2, CA1, FS01
```

If I were to use Test-Connection in the standard way to try to contact all of the servers in my network, that would turn into a whole lot of output. But by using the -Quiet switch, I get back a simple True or False on whether each individual server could be contacted:

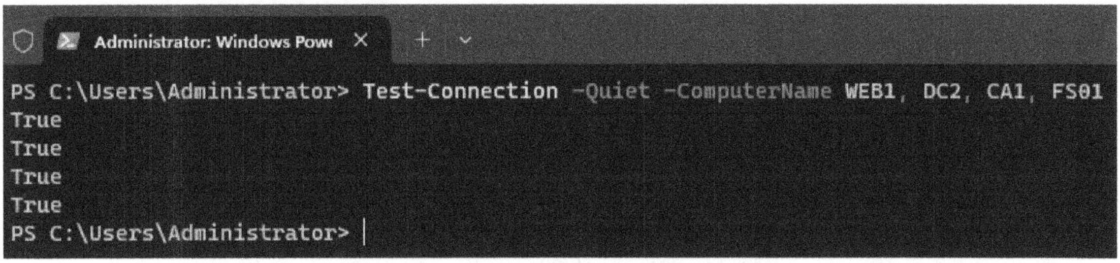

Figure 8.9: Using the -Quiet switch

telnet

telnet provides quite a bit of remote management capability; it essentially offers the ability to make a connection between two computers to manipulate the remote machine through a virtual terminal connection. What I find telnet most useful for is as a simple connection testing tool, usually to verify that a server is listening on a certain port and that my client can connect to that port.

When we discussed ping, we talked about the downside of ICMP: it is easily blocked, and it's more common in today's networks for pings not to be successful, even if the destination server is online. This is unfortunate since ping has always been the most common form of network connection testing, but the reality is that if ping makes our lives easier, it also makes the lives of hackers easier. If we cannot rely on ping to tell us with certainty whether we can contact a remote system, what do we use instead? Another case that I see often is where a server might be responding correctly, but a particular service running on that server has a problem and is not responding. A simple ping may show the server to be online, but it can't tell us anything about the service specifically. By using the **Telnet Client** commands, we can easily query a server remotely. Even more importantly, we can opt to query an individual service on that server to make sure it is listening as it is designed to do. Let me give you an example that I use all the time.

I often set up new internet-facing web servers. After installing a new web server, it makes sense that I would want to test access to it from the internet to make sure it's responding, right? But maybe the website itself isn't online and functional yet, so I can't browse it with Edge or any other browser. It is quite likely that I disabled pings on this server or at the firewall level because blocking ICMP over the internet is very common for lowering the security vulnerability footprint on the web. So, my new server is running, and I think I have the networking all squared away, but I cannot test pinging my new server because, by design, it fails to reply. What can I use to test this? telnet. By issuing a simple telnet command, I can tell my computer to query a specific port on my new web server and find out whether it connects to that port. Doing this establishes a TCP socket connection to the port on that server, which is much more akin to real user traffic than a ping would be.

If a `telnet` command connects successfully, you know your traffic is making its way to the server, and the server service running on the port you queried seems to be responding properly.

The ability to use `telnet` is not installed by default in Windows Server 2025 or any other Windows operating system, so we first need to head into **Server Manager** and then **Add Roles and Features** to install the feature called **Telnet Client**:

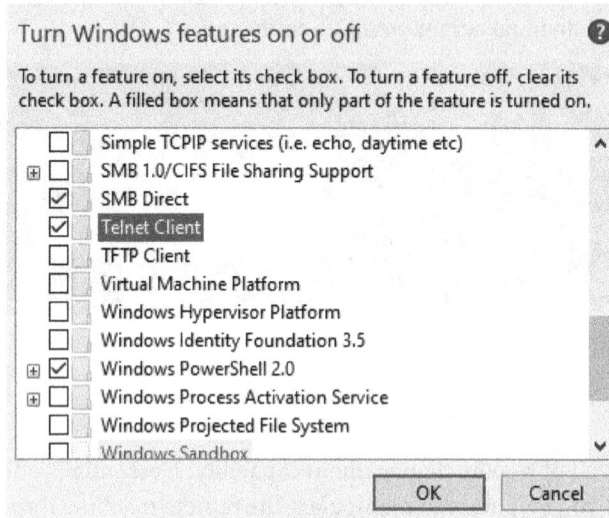

Figure 8.10: Installing Telnet Client

You only need to install **Telnet Client** on the machine from which you want to do command-line testing. You do not have to do anything on the remote server that you are connecting to. In the preceding screenshot, I am installing this feature onto a workstation in my test lab.

Now that the **Telnet Client** feature has been installed, we can utilize it from Command Prompt or PowerShell to do the work for us by attempting to make socket connections from our computer to the remote service. All we need to do is tell it what server and port to query. Then, `telnet` will simply connect or time out, and based on that result, we can see whether that particular service on the server is responding. Let me try it with my web server. For this example, I have turned off the website inside IIS, so I am now in the position where the server is online but the website is dead. If I ping `WEB1`, I can still see it happily responding. You can see where server-monitoring tools that rely on ICMP would show false positives, indicating that the server is online and running even though the website is in-accessible. Just below the successful ping in *Figure 8.11*, you can see that I also tried querying port 80 on the `WEB1` server. The command that I used for that was `telnet web1 80`. That timed out. This shows us that the website, which is running on port `80`, is not responding:

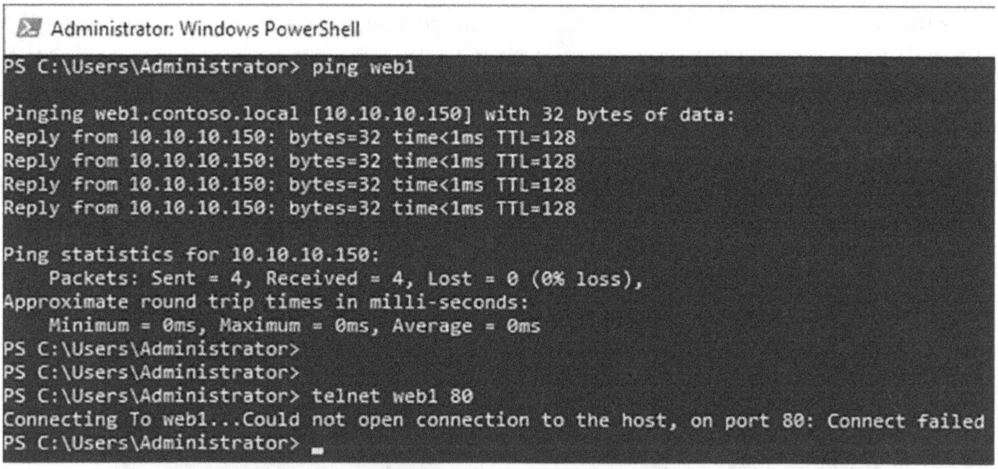

Figure 8.11: Failed connection on port 80

If I turn the website back on, I can try `telnet web1 80` again, and this time, I do not get a timeout message. This time, my PowerShell prompt wipes itself clean and sits waiting on a flashing cursor at the top. While it doesn't tell me, *"Yay, I'm connected!"* the flashing cursor indicates that a successful socket connection has been made to port 80 on my web server, indicating the website is online and responding:

Figure 8.12: A flashing cursor signals a successful connection

After creating a successful `telnet` socket connection, you may be wondering how to get back to the regular PowerShell interface. Press the *Ctrl +]* keys together (that second one is a closed bracket key, usually next to the backslash key on your keyboard), type the word `quit`, and then press *Enter*. This should return you to a regular prompt. Or simply close the PowerShell prompt and open a fresh one.

Test-NetConnection

If `ping` has an equivalent and improved PowerShell cmdlet called `Test-Connection`, does PowerShell also contain an improved tool that works similarly to `telnet` for testing socket connections to resources? It sure does. `Test-NetConnection` is another way to query particular ports or services on a remote system, and the displayed output is friendlier than that of `telnet`.

Let's walk through the same tests, once again querying port 80 on WEB1. You can see in the following screenshot that I have run the command twice. The first time, the website on WEB1 was disabled, and my connection to port 80 failed. The second time, I re-enabled the website, and I now see a successful connection:

```
Test-NetConnection WEB1 -Port 80
```

```
Administrator: Windows PowerShell

PS C:\Users\Administrator> Test-NetConnection WEB1 -Port 80
WARNING: TCP connect to (10.10.10.150 : 80) failed


ComputerName            : WEB1
RemoteAddress           : 10.10.10.150
RemotePort              : 80
InterfaceAlias          : Ethernet
SourceAddress           : 10.10.10.10
PingSucceeded           : True
PingReplyDetails (RTT)  : 1 ms
TcpTestSucceeded        : False


PS C:\Users\Administrator>
PS C:\Users\Administrator> Test-NetConnection WEB1 -Port 80


ComputerName      : WEB1
RemoteAddress     : 10.10.10.150
RemotePort        : 80
InterfaceAlias    : Ethernet
SourceAddress     : 10.10.10.10
TcpTestSucceeded  : True


PS C:\Users\Administrator>
```

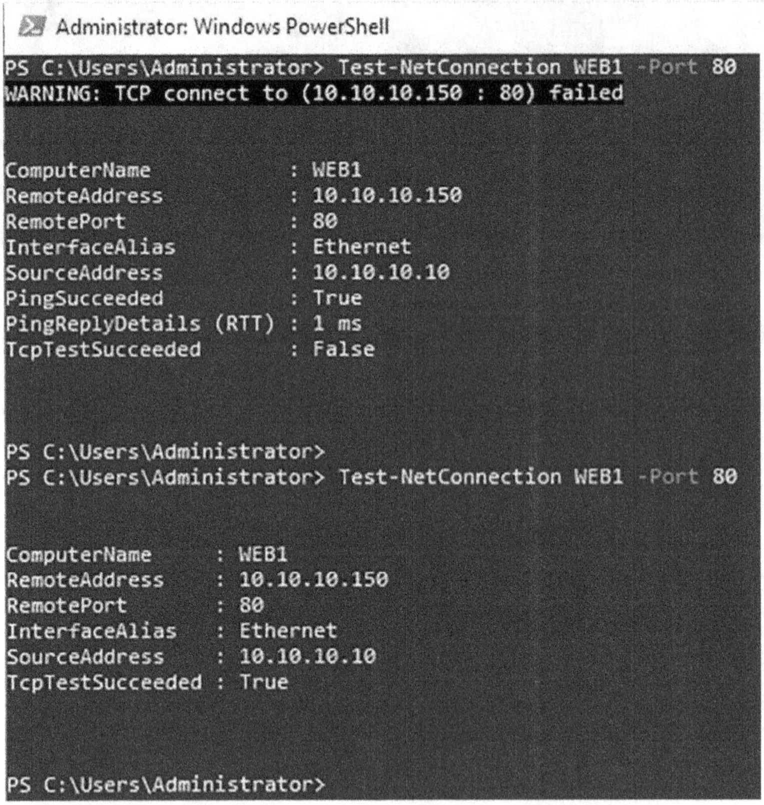

Figure 8.13: Using Test-NetConnection to test individual port connections

Packet tracing with Wireshark

Eventually, you might need to look a little deeper into your network packets. Now, we are entering territory where your network team may also be involved, but if you are familiar with these tools, you may be able to solve the problem before needing to call for assistance. Making use of command-line tools to check on the status of servers and services is very useful, but occasionally, it may not be enough. For example, you have a client application that is not connecting to the application server, but you don't know why. Utilities such as ping and even telnet might be able to connect successfully, indicating that network routing is set up properly, yet the application fails to connect when it opens. If the application's own event logs don't help you troubleshoot what is going on, you might want to take a deeper look inside the network packets that the application is trying to push toward the server.

This is where the **Wireshark** application comes in handy. Microsoft used to supply and support a couple of self-developed tools called NetMon and Message Analyzer that served similar functions, but both have now been officially retired. Probably because Wireshark is great, and it's free! This tool captures network traffic as it leaves from or arrives into a system, and captures the information *inside* the packets so that you can take a deeper look into what is going on. In our example of an application that cannot connect, we could run Wireshark on the client computer to watch outgoing traffic, and also on the application server to watch for incoming traffic from the client.

There is a whole lot of functionality inside Wireshark, and we don't have the space to cover all of it here, so I will leave you with a link from which to grab this tool so you can start testing it out for yourself: https://www.wireshark.org/download.html.

PsPing

In *Chapter 17*, we will discuss SysInternals tools, what they are, and the history behind their existence. One of these tools is called PsPing, and is useful for enhanced network pings and connectivity testing. Not only can it be used to ping resources for simple connectivity checks and to check latency between endpoints, but it can even be used to measure bandwidth between devices! PsPing is a standalone executable file that you must download and store on your Windows machine before you can make use of it via the command line. Go ahead and grab it from here, and then we will look at a few of the most common uses of PsPing: https://learn.microsoft.com/en-us/sysinternals/downloads/psping.

To simply check for the ICMP response between one device and another, throw something like this into the command line:

```
psping WEB1
```

You could tell PsPing to throw packets at a public DNS name, an internal DNS name, or an IP address, of course.

Now, let's get a little bit fancier and use PsPing to test TCP port connection, quite like we did with Test-NetConnection a few minutes ago:

```
Psping WEB1:80
```

This reaches out to the WEB1 server, querying whether it can make a successful connection to port 80. You can see the results of both commands in the following screenshot, where our first command was testing quick connectivity via ICMP, and the second command, which queried port 80, shows multiple connection attempts, all successful, using TCP connections to port 80 on WEB1.

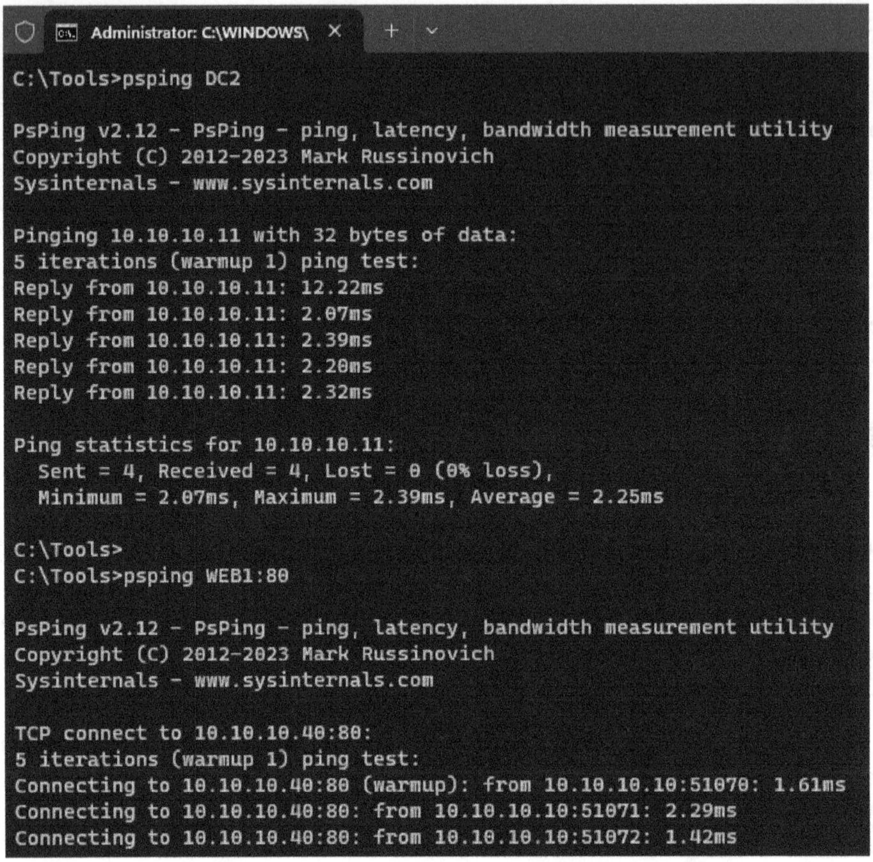

Figure 8.14: Using PsPing to test the connection between endpoints

TCPView

The tools that we have discussed so far are great and can be used daily for poking and prodding individual resources that you want to test, but sometimes there are situations where you need to step back and figure out what it is you are looking for in the first place. Maybe you are working with an application on a computer and are not sure what server it is talking to. Or perhaps you suspect a machine has a virus and is trying to "phone home" somewhere on the internet, and you would like to identify the location that it is trying to talk to or the process that is making the call. In these situations, it would be helpful if there were a tool that you could launch on the local computer that showed you all of the network traffic streams that were active on this computer or server clearly and concisely. That is exactly what **TCPView** does. TCPView is another tool created by SysInternals; you may have heard of some of their other tools, such as ProcMon and FileMon, and of course PsPing, which we mentioned only a moment ago. Running TCPView on a machine displays all of the active TCP and UDP connections happening on that computer in real time. Also important is the fact that you do not need to install anything to make TCPView work; it is a standalone executable, making it extremely easy to use and later clear off a machine when you are finished with it.

You can download TCPView from `https://learn.microsoft.com/en-us/sysinternals/downloads/tcpview`.

Simply copy the file onto the computer or server that you want to monitor and double-click on it. *Figure 8.15* shows the TCPView interface running on my local computer, displaying all of the connections that Windows and my applications are currently making. You can pause this output to take a closer look, and you can also set filters to pare down the data and find what you are really looking for. Filters get rid of the *noise*, so to speak, and enable you to look more closely at a particular destination or a specific **process ID (PID)**:

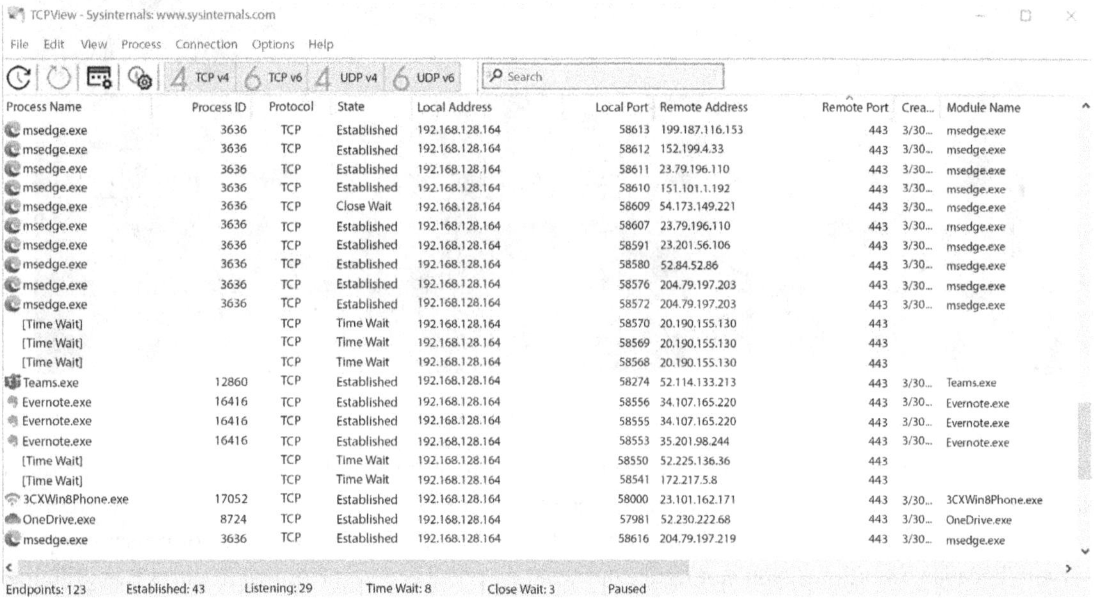
TCPView - Sysinternals: www.sysinternals.com
File Edit View Process Connection Options Help
4 TCP v4 6 TCP v6 4 UDP v4 6 UDP v6
Search
Process Name Process ID Protocol State Local Address Local Port Remote Address Remote Port Crea... Module Name
msedge.exe 3636 TCP Established 192.168.128.164 58613 199.187.116.153 443 3/30... msedge.exe
msedge.exe 3636 TCP Established 192.168.128.164 58612 152.199.4.33 443 3/30... msedge.exe
msedge.exe 3636 TCP Established 192.168.128.164 58611 23.79.196.110 443 3/30... msedge.exe
msedge.exe 3636 TCP Established 192.168.128.164 58610 151.101.1.192 443 3/30... msedge.exe
msedge.exe 3636 TCP Close Wait 192.168.128.164 58609 54.173.149.221 443 3/30... msedge.exe
msedge.exe 3636 TCP Established 192.168.128.164 58607 23.79.196.110 443 3/30... msedge.exe
msedge.exe 3636 TCP Established 192.168.128.164 58591 23.201.56.106 443 3/30... msedge.exe
msedge.exe 3636 TCP Established 192.168.128.164 58580 52.84.52.86 443 3/30... msedge.exe
msedge.exe 3636 TCP Established 192.168.128.164 58576 204.79.197.203 443 3/30... msedge.exe
msedge.exe 3636 TCP Established 192.168.128.164 58572 204.79.197.203 443 3/30... msedge.exe
[Time Wait] TCP Time Wait 192.168.128.164 58570 20.190.155.130 443
[Time Wait] TCP Time Wait 192.168.128.164 58569 20.190.155.130 443
[Time Wait] TCP Time Wait 192.168.128.164 58568 20.190.155.130 443
Teams.exe 12860 TCP Established 192.168.128.164 58274 52.114.133.213 443 3/30... Teams.exe
Evernote.exe 16416 TCP Established 192.168.128.164 58556 34.107.165.220 443 3/30... Evernote.exe
Evernote.exe 16416 TCP Established 192.168.128.164 58555 34.107.165.220 443 3/30... Evernote.exe
Evernote.exe 16416 TCP Established 192.168.128.164 58553 35.201.98.244 443 3/30... Evernote.exe
[Time Wait] TCP Time Wait 192.168.128.164 58550 52.225.136.36 443
[Time Wait] TCP Time Wait 192.168.128.164 58541 172.217.5.8 443
3CXWin8Phone.exe 17052 TCP Established 192.168.128.164 58000 23.101.162.171 443 3/30... 3CXWin8Phone.exe
OneDrive.exe 8724 TCP Established 192.168.128.164 57981 52.230.222.68 443 3/30... OneDrive.exe
msedge.exe 3636 TCP Established 192.168.128.164 58616 204.79.197.219 443 3/30... msedge.exe
Endpoints: 123 Established: 43 Listening: 29 Time Wait: 8 Close Wait: 3 Paused

Figure 8.15: TCPView interface

netstat

For anyone who may not be a fan of downloading and running an executable, or just for anyone on the lookout for similar functionality via a built-in Microsoft command, `netstat` is a command-line tool that has been around for ages and displays similar (if not quite as useful) information to that of TCPView. `netstat` will also show you per-port and per-process connection information on what is happening on the machine where you run the command. There are various switches that can be used to manipulate or enhance the `netstat` command output; if you open Command Prompt and utilize `netstat /?`, you will be presented with a full list of optional switches and their descriptions.

My go-to method of utilizing `netstat` is by adding `-ano`. Open Command Prompt on any computer or server and run the command; take a look at the output of `netstat -ano`, as seen in the following screenshot.

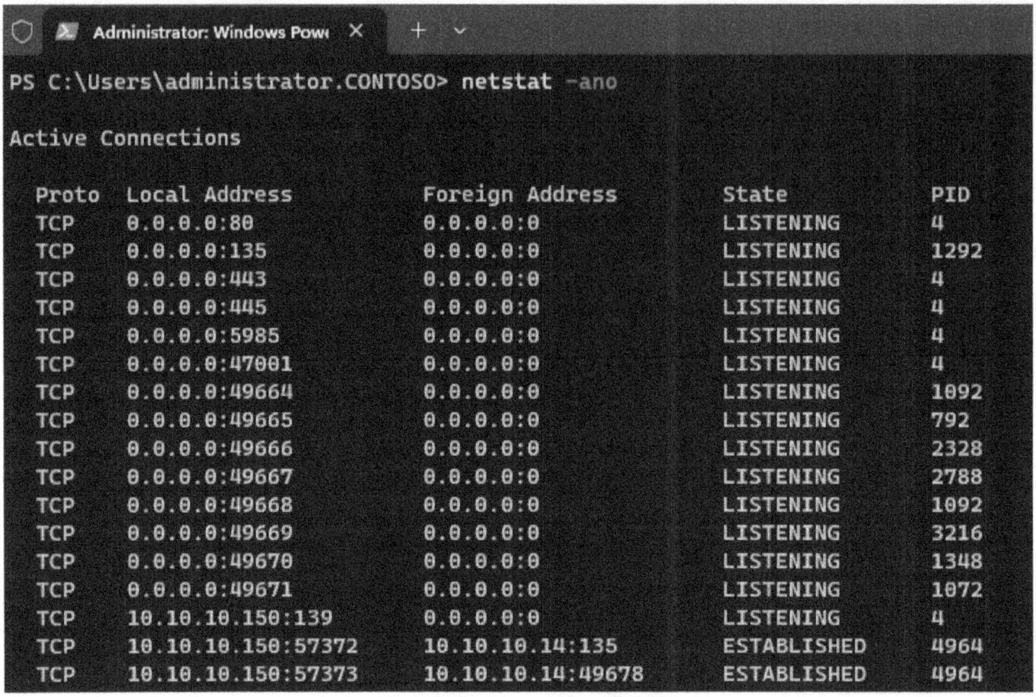

Figure 8.16: netstat displays open connections on my web server

After running your command, scroll back to the top of the output, and look at all those connections showing a Local Address value of 0.0.0.0. These are the different ports that your server is currently using to listen for incoming connections. I utilize this output all the time when decommissioning old servers because oftentimes, you can figure out what a server is doing from what ports it is utilizing. In the preceding screenshot, you can see at a glance that this server is listening on ports 80, 443, and 445, most likely indicating that it is being used as a web server running HTTP and HTTPS connections, and file services over SMB. Over to the right side of the output, visible here due to my use of the -o switch, you can also see which Windows PIDs own the ports being used.

netstat generates a ton of information, almost always multiple pages of IP address and port information. A lot of the time, when utilizing netstat, what you are really trying to do is narrow in on a specific port number or PID, to discover whether that port or process is correctly listening for connections, or perhaps already has established connections on this system. Thankfully, a little bit of extra syntax can be added to our netstat command to narrow in on any flavor of specific information:

```
Netstat -ano | Select-String "text"
```

Replace "text" with any information you are searching for. If you are trying to figure out what connections are occurring for a process running on PID 1128, try netstat -ano | Select-String "1128". Or another example, if you are trying to quickly figure out whether this system is listening for web connections on port 443, you can run the following: netstat -ano | Select-String "443".

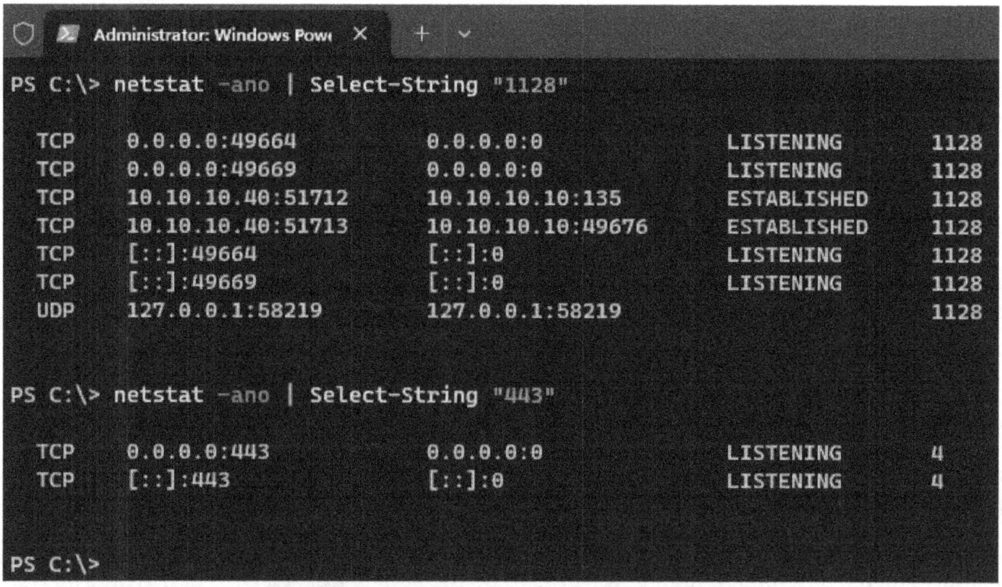

```
PS C:\> netstat -ano | Select-String "1128"

    TCP    0.0.0.0:49664           0.0.0.0:0              LISTENING       1128
    TCP    0.0.0.0:49669           0.0.0.0:0              LISTENING       1128
    TCP    10.10.10.40:51712       10.10.10.10:135        ESTABLISHED     1128
    TCP    10.10.10.40:51713       10.10.10.10:49676      ESTABLISHED     1128
    TCP    [::]:49664              [::]:0                 LISTENING       1128
    TCP    [::]:49669              [::]:0                 LISTENING       1128
    UDP    127.0.0.1:58219         127.0.0.1:58219                        1128


PS C:\> netstat -ano | Select-String "443"

    TCP    0.0.0.0:443             0.0.0.0:0              LISTENING       4
    TCP    [::]:443                [::]:0                 LISTENING       4


PS C:\>
```

Figure 8.17: Searching for unique information within netstat

Now that we have discovered and tested some tools that are useful for testing connections, let's move on to a new topic where we will begin to manipulate the flow of network traffic from our servers. Follow along as we learn about the Windows routing table.

The Windows routing table

When you hear the term **routing table**, it is easy to pass that off as something the network folks need to deal with, something that is configured within the network routers and firewalls. It doesn't apply to server admins, right? Networking servers together has been made easy for us by only requiring an IP address, subnet mask, and default gateway, and we can instantly communicate with everything inside the rest of our network.

While there is indeed a lot of networking magic going on under the hood that has been provided to us by networking equipment and network administrators, it is important to understand how routing inside Windows works because there will be some cases when we need to modify or build out a routing table directly on a Windows server.

Multi-homed servers

Running multi-homed servers is a case where you would certainly need to understand and work with a local Windows routing table, so let's start here. If you think this doesn't apply to you because you've never heard of "multi-homed" before, think again. Multi-homed is just a funny-looking word meaning your server has more than one NIC. This could certainly be the case for you, even if you are a small shop that doesn't have a lot of servers. Often, small businesses or essential servers have multiple network interfaces, separating internal LAN traffic from internet traffic. Another instance of a multi-homed server would be a remote access server that provides DirectAccess, VPN, or proxy capabilities at the edge of your network. Yet another reason to be interested in and understand multi-homing is Hyper-V servers. It is very common for Hyper-V servers to make use of multiple NICs because the VMs that run on that server might need to tap into different physical networks within your organization.

Now that we have established what a multi-homed server is, you might still be wondering why we are discussing this. If we have more than one NIC, don't we simply configure each NIC individually inside Windows, giving each one an IP address, just like we would for any NIC on any server? Yes and no. Yes, we configure a distinct IP address on each NIC, because it needs that for the identification and transport of packets on the network. No, we do not set up all of the NICs on your server in the same way. There is one critical item that we need to keep in mind and adhere to in order to make traffic flow properly on our multi-homed server.

Only one default gateway

This is the golden ticket. When you multi-home a server by having multiple NICs, you can only have one default gateway: one for your entire server. This means you will have one NIC with a default gateway, and one or many NICs that do *not* have a default gateway inside their TCP/IP settings. This is extremely important. The purpose of a default gateway is to be the *path of last resort*. When Windows wants to send a packet to a destination, it browses over the local routing table—yes, there is a routing table even if you haven't configured it or ever looked at it—and checks to see whether a specific, static route exists for the destination subnet where this packet needs to go. If a route exists, it shoots the packet out of that route and network interface to the destination. If no static route exists in the routing table, it falls back to using the default gateway and sends the traffic to that default gateway address. On all single NIC servers, the default gateway is a router that is designated with all the routing information for your network, so the server simply hands it to the router, and the router does the rest of the work.

When we have multiple NICs on a Windows server, we cannot give each one a default gateway because it will confuse the traffic flow from your server. Which default gateway is the right default gateway? This becomes a crapshoot for every network transmission. I have helped many people troubleshoot servers in the field with exactly this problem.

Usually, this situation appears when an admin needs to use their server as a bridge between two networks, or has the server plugged into multiple different networks for whatever reason, and is struggling because sometimes the traffic seems to work and sometimes it doesn't. We start looking through the NIC properties only to discover that every NIC has its own default gateway address in the TCP/IP properties. Bingo, that's our problem. The system is completely confused when it tries to send out traffic because it doesn't know which gateway it needs to use when.

If you have ever tried adding default gateways to more than one NIC on the same server, you are probably familiar with the warning prompt that is displayed when you do this. Let's give it a try. I have added another NIC to one of my servers and have IP settings configured on just one of the NICs. Now, I will add a new IP address, subnet mask, and default gateway onto my second NIC. When I click on the **OK** button to save those changes, I am presented with the following popup:

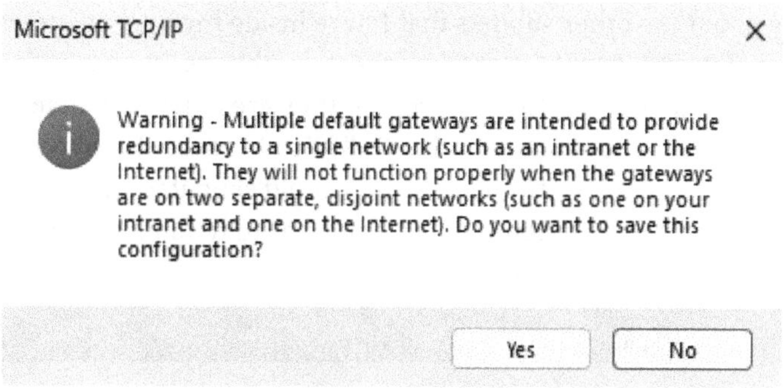

Figure 8.18: Warning message when configuring multiple default gateways

This is one of those warnings that is easy to misread because of its slightly cryptic nature, but you get the essence of it: proceed at your own risk! And then what do most admins do at this point? Simply click through it and save the changes anyway. Then, the routing problems begin. Maybe not today, maybe not tomorrow, but perhaps the next time you reboot that server, or maybe three weeks down the road, but at some point, your server will start to send packets to the wrong destinations and cause you trouble.

Building a route

So, what is our answer to all of this? Building a static routing table. When you have multiple NICs on a server, thereby making it multi-homed, you must tell Windows which NIC to use for what traffic inside the routing table. This way, when network traffic needs to leave the server for a particular destination, the routing table is aware of the different directions and paths that the traffic will need to take in order to get there and will send it out accordingly. You will still rely on routers to take the traffic the rest of the way, but getting the packets to the correct router by sending them out via the proper physical NIC is key to making sure that traffic flows quickly and appropriately from your multi-homed server.

Now that we understand why the routing table is important and conceptually how we need to use it, let's dig in and add a couple of routes to my dual-NIC server. We will add a route using Command Prompt, and we will also add one using PowerShell, since this task can be accomplished from either platform, but the syntax used is different depending on which you prefer.

Adding a route with Command Prompt

Before we can plan our new route, we need to get the lay of the land for the current networking configuration on this server. It has two NICs: one is plugged into my internal network and one is plugged into my **demilitarized zone (DMZ)** that faces the internet. Since I can only have one default gateway address, it goes onto the DMZ NIC because there is no way that I could add routes for every subnet that might need to be contacted over the internet. By putting the default gateway on my DMZ NIC, the internal NIC does not have a default gateway and is very limited in what it can contact at the moment. The internal subnet that I am physically plugged into is 10.10.10.0/24, so I can currently contact anything in this small network from 10.10.10.1 through 10.10.10.254. This is known as an **on-link** route; since I am plugged directly into this subnet, my server automatically knows how to route traffic inside this subnet. However, I cannot contact anything else through my internal NIC because the routing table knows nothing about the other subnets that I have inside my internal network. For example, I have an additional subnet, 192.168.16.0/24, and there are some servers running within this subnet that I need to be able to contact from this new server. If I were to try to contact one of those servers right now, the packets would shoot out from my DMZ NIC because the routing table on my server has no idea how to deal with 192.168 traffic, and so it would send it toward the default gateway. The following is the general syntax of the route statement we need to follow in order to make this traffic flow from our server into the new subnet:

```
Route add -p <SUBNET_ID> mask <SUBNET_MASK> <GATEWAY> IF <INTERFACE_ID>
```

Before we can type out our unique route statement for adding the 192.168 network, we need to do a little detective work and figure out what we are going to use in these fields. The following is a breakdown of the parts and pieces that are required to build a route statement:

- -p: This makes the command persistent. If you forget to put -p in the route add statement, this new route will disappear the next time you reboot the server. Not good.
- SUBNET_ID: This is the subnet we are adding; in our case, it is 192.168.16.0.
- SUBNET_MASK: This is the subnet mask number for the new route, 255.255.255.0.
- GATEWAY: This one is a little confusing. It is very common to think it means you need to enter the gateway address for the new subnet, but that would be incorrect. What you are actually defining here is the first hop that the server needs to hit in order to send out this traffic. Or, in other words, if you *had* configured a default gateway address on your internal NIC, what would that address have been? For our network, it is 10.10.10.1. This effectively instructs the server, "for any traffic destined for this route (192.168.16.0/24), shoot those packets at 10.10.10.1 (whom you already know how to contact) and that guy will figure out what to do."
- INTERFACE_ID: Specifying an interface ID number is not entirely necessary to create a route, but if you do not specify it, there is a chance that your route will bind itself to the wrong NIC and send traffic out the wrong direction. I have seen it happen before, so I always specify a NIC interface ID number. This is typically a one- or two-digit number that is the Windows identifier for the internal NIC itself. We can figure out what the interface ID number is by looking at the route print command:

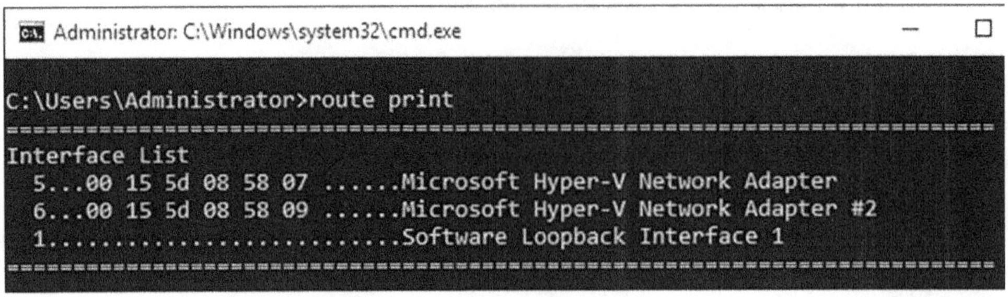

Figure 8.19: Acquiring the interface ID number

At the top of `route print`, you see all of the server's NICs. In our case, the internal NIC is the top one on the list. I identified it by running an `ipconfig /all` command and then comparing my internal NIC's MAC address against the MAC addresses listed here. As you can see, my internal NIC's interface ID number is 5. So, in my `route add` statement, I am going to use `IF 5` at the end of my statement to make sure my new route binds itself to that internal physical NIC.

The following is our completed `route add` statement:

```
route add -p 192.168.16.0 mask 255.255.255.0 10.10.10.1 if 5
```

```
Administrator: C:\Windows\system32\cmd.exe

C:\>route add -p 192.168.16.0 mask 255.255.255.0 10.10.10.1 if 5
OK!

C:\>
```

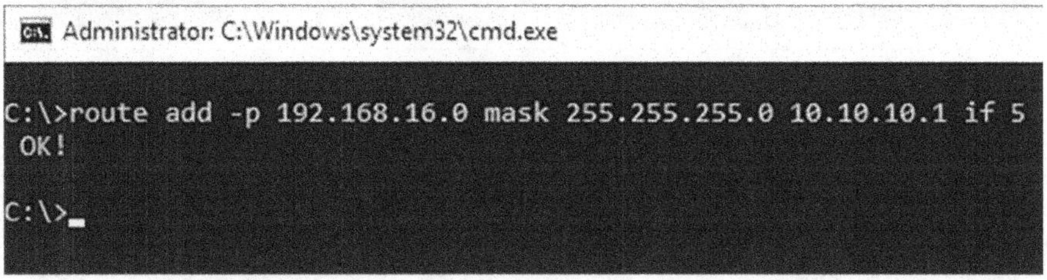

Figure 8.20: Running the complete route add statement

If you now run a `route print` command, you can see our new `192.168.16.0` route listed in the `Persistent Routes` section of the routing table, and we can now send packets into that subnet from this new server. Whenever our server has traffic that needs to go into the `192.168.16.x` subnet, it will send that traffic out via the *internal* NIC, toward the router running on `10.10.10.1`. The router then picks up the traffic from there and brings it into the `192.168.16.0` subnet:

```
===============================================================
Persistent Routes:
  Network Address          Netmask  Gateway Address  Metric
          0.0.0.0          0.0.0.0      10.10.10.1  Default
     192.168.16.0    255.255.255.0      10.10.10.1        1
===============================================================
```

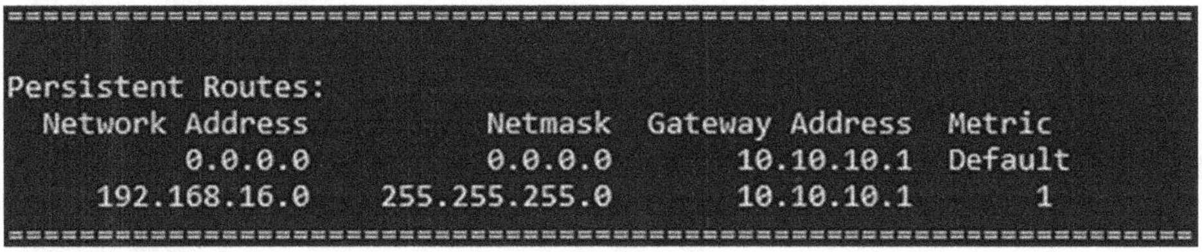

Figure 8.21: Sending traffic to the 192.168.16.0 subnet

Deleting a route

Occasionally, you may key in a route statement incorrectly. The best way to handle this is to simply delete the bad route and then rerun your `route add` statement with the correct syntax. There are possibly other reasons why you might need to delete routes every now and then, so you'll want to be familiar with this command. Deleting routes is much simpler than adding new ones. All you need to know is the subnet ID for the route that you want to remove and then simply use `route delete <SUBNET_ID>`. For example, to get rid of the `192.168.16.0` route that we created while we were working inside Command Prompt, I would simply issue this command:

```
route delete 192.168.16.0
```

Adding a route with PowerShell

Since PowerShell is king when it comes to most command-line-oriented tasks inside Windows Server, we should accomplish the same mission from this interface as well. You can utilize the same route add command from inside the PowerShell prompt and that will work just fine, but there is also a specialized cmdlet that you can use. Let's utilize New-NetRoute to add yet another subnet to our routing table. This time, we are going to add 192.168.17.0. The following is a command we can utilize:

```
New-NetRoute -DestinationPrefix "192.168.17.0/24" -InterfaceIndex 5 -NextHop
10.10.10.1
```

```
PS C:\> New-NetRoute -DestinationPrefix "192.168.17.0/24" -InterfaceIndex 5 -NextHop 10.10.10.1

ifIndex DestinationPrefix                          NextHop                        RouteMet
                                                                                       ric
------- -----------------                          -------                        --------
5       192.168.17.0/24                            10.10.10.1                          256
5       192.168.17.0/24                            10.10.10.1                          256

PS C:\>
```

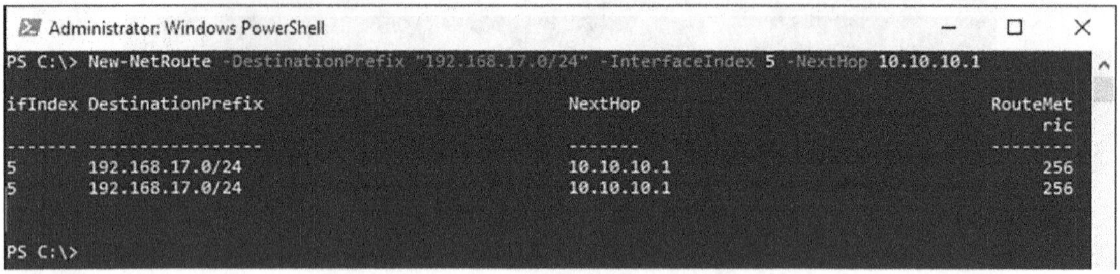

Figure 8.22: Adding another subnet to our routing table

I already knew that my interface number was 5 for this NIC because of my route print output earlier. If you do not know that information and want to stick with PowerShell cmdlets to find it, a quick Get-NetAdapter will tell you everything you need to know.

You can see that the structure is similar, but a little bit friendlier. Instead of having to type the word mask and specify the whole subnet mask number, you can use the *slash* method (CIDR) to identify the subnet and mask within the same identifier. Also, where before we were specifying the *gateway*, which is always a little confusing, with the New-NetRoute cmdlet, we instead specify what is called NextHop. This makes a little bit more sense to me.

Where we previously utilized route print to see our full routing table, the PowerShell cmdlet to display that table for us is simply Get-NetRoute:

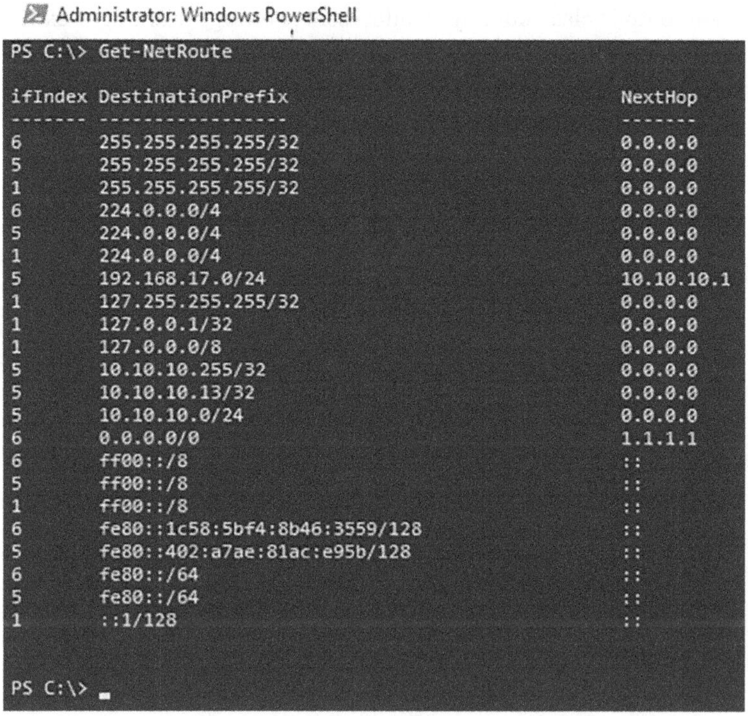

Figure 8.23: Displaying our full routing table

Building routing tables is essential knowledge for any server admin who encounters a server with multiple network interfaces that are connected to different networks. Now, let's discuss another use case where you may find multiple network cards on the same server, but this time, connected to the same network.

NIC teaming

Moving on to another network topic that is becoming more and more popular on server hardware, let's walk through the steps to create NIC teaming. The ability to team NICs essentially consists of binding two or more physical network interfaces together so that they behave as if they were a single network interface within Windows. This allows you to plug two physical cables into two different switch ports, all using the same settings. That way, if one NIC port, switch port, or patch cable goes bad, the server continues working and communicating without hesitation, because teaming allows the NIC that is still working to handle the network traffic.

NIC teaming itself is nothing new. It has been around for more than 10 years inside the Windows Server operating system. However, early versions were problematic, and in the field, I find that Server 2019 is the earliest server operating system most IT personnel consider to be stable enough to use NIC teaming in production.

To begin teaming together your NICs, you need to make sure that you have multiple network cards on your server. I currently have four NIC ports on this machine. I have plans to create two teams: my first and second NICs will be bound together to become an **internal network team**, and my third and fourth NICs will become a **DMZ network team**. This way, I have network card redundancy on both sides of my network flow on this server.

The first thing I want to do is clear out any IP addressing settings that might exist on my NICs. You see, once you tie together multiple NICs into a team, you will configure IP addressing settings for the team—you will no longer dive into individual NIC properties to assign IP addresses. So, open up the properties of each NIC and make sure they are clear of static IP information, like so:

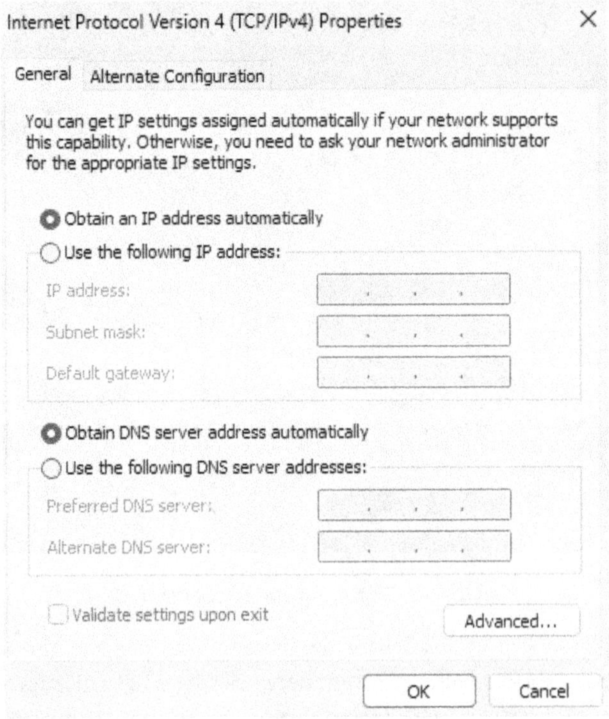

Figure 8.24: Clearing the static IP addresses of each NIC

Now, open **Server Manager** and click on **Local Server.** Looking inside the properties information for your server, you will see listings for each of your NICs, as well as an option called **NIC Teaming**, which is currently set to **Disabled:**

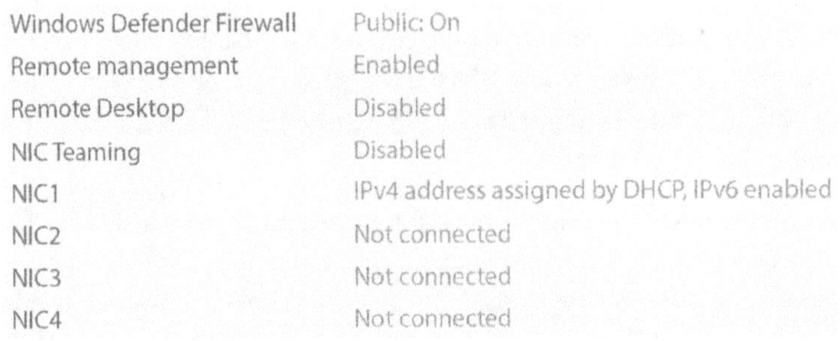

Windows Defender Firewall	Public: On
Remote management	Enabled
Remote Desktop	Disabled
NIC Teaming	Disabled
NIC1	IPv4 address assigned by DHCP, IPv6 enabled
NIC2	Not connected
NIC3	Not connected
NIC4	Not connected

Figure 8.25: NIC Teaming is initially disabled

Go ahead and click on the word **Disabled**, and now look for a section entitled **Teams**. Click on the **Tasks** button and choose to create a new team.

Give your new team an appropriate name and select the NICs that you want to be part of this team. Once finished, you can walk through the same steps as many times as you need to create additional teams with your remaining NICs:

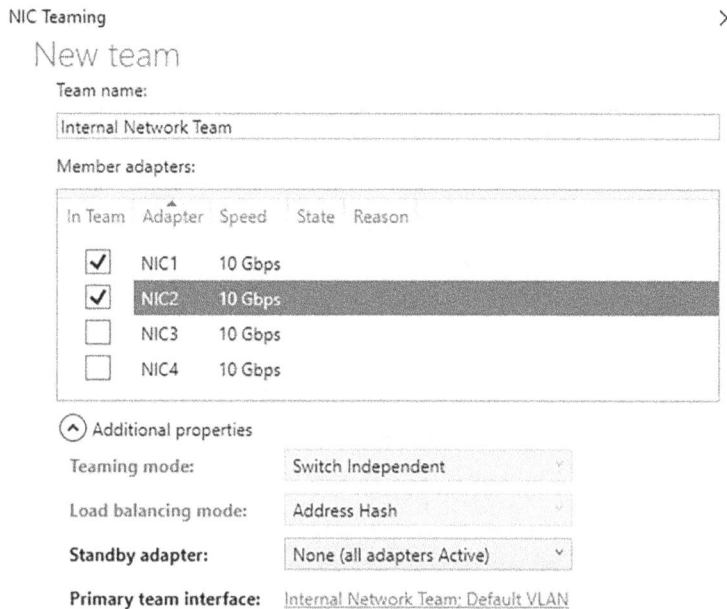

Figure 8.26: Creating a new NIC team

Dropping down the **Additional properties** arrow, you will notice some optional settings that require a little bit of explanation. Depending on what type of system you are running (virtual or physical servers), you may not be able to see or use all of these options:

- **Teaming mode: Switch Independent** is the default, and usually the route you want to travel. This selection means your NICs that are about to be teamed together can be plugged into different switches. Alternatively, **Switch Dependent** mode does require all NICs to be connected to the same switch and comes with some additional options that need to pair up with your switch configuration.
- **Load balancing mode:** There are three options to choose from here. **Address Hash** is the default and indicates that packets will be assigned a hash value that is used to direct them toward particular adapters. **Hyper-V Port**, on the other hand, uses VM MAC addresses to distribute traffic. The third option, **Dynamic**, sort of meshes the other two options, with outbound traffic using the address hash and incoming traffic being distributed based on the MAC address.
- **Standby adapter:** Your NIC team will be created so that both NICs are handling traffic unless you visit this option and choose differently. Here, you could specify for one of your NICs in a team to run in standby mode, meaning that it will not process network traffic unless one of the other NICs fails.

Once finished, you will see your teams listed inside **Server Manager**. After opening the **Network Connections** screen inside Windows, you can see in *Figure 8.27* that, in addition to the four physical NICs, I now have two new entries listed here, which are the configuration locations for our new teams. From here, I can right-click on each of my network teams and configure IP addressing information just like I would have done for a single NIC. IP information input into the team properties will be in effect on all NICs that are part of the team:

Figure 8.27: NIC teams are listed as additional adapters inside Network Connections

The items we have discussed so far in this chapter are useful for any environment utilizing Windows Server 2025 and can also be applied to many previous versions of the Windows Server operating system. Next, we will move on to a topic that some of you may already be living with, but many others may have never even heard of—**software-defined networking**, or **SDN**.

Software-defined networking

The flexibility and elasticity of cloud computing cannot be denied, and most technology executives are currently exploring their options for utilizing cloud technologies. One of the big stumbling blocks with adoption is trust. Cloud services provide enormous computing power, immediately accessible at the press of a button. For companies to store their data on these systems, the level of trust that your organization has in that cloud provider must be very high. After all, you don't own any of the hardware or networking infrastructure that your data is sitting on when it's in the cloud, and so your control of those resources is limited at best. Seeing this hurdle, Microsoft has made many efforts in recent updates to bring cloud-like technology to the local datacenter. Introducing server elasticity into our datacenters means virtualization. We have virtualized servers for many years now, although the capabilities there are continually being improved. Now that we have the ability to spin up new servers so easily through virtualization technologies, it makes sense that the next hurdle will be our ability to easily move these virtual servers around whenever and wherever we need to.

Do you have a server that you want to move into a datacenter across the country? Are you thinking of migrating an entire datacenter into a new co-location across town? Maybe you have recently acquired a new company and need to bring its infrastructure into your network but have an overlapping network configuration. Have you bought into some space at a cloud service provider and are now trying to wade through the mess of planning the migration of all your servers to the cloud and onto the cloud provider's infrastructure? These are all questions that require an answer, and that answer is SDN.

SDN is a broad, general term that encompasses many technologies working together to make this idea possible. Boiled down to one line, SDN takes the layers at play in any network interaction and manages them using software. For example, inside a switch, you have the infrastructure layer, where the work of moving packets around is happening. You also have the control layer, where the switch remembers all of the information that it needs to correctly tell the infrastructure layer what to do, and then you have the application layer, where you, as an administrator, manage the switch configuration. SDN takes these layers and breaks each one out in a way that is defined and managed by software. This software is centrally administered by a network controller of some sort. SDN enables you to extend your network boundaries whenever and wherever you need. Let's take a look at some of the parts and pieces available in Windows Server 2025 that work in tandem to create a virtual networking environment, the first step in adopting our SDN ideology.

Hyper-V Network Virtualization

Hyper-V contains integral components for SDN, allowing you to pick up your networks and servers and slide them around on a layer of virtualization. This makes sense because this is the same platform that we utilize to virtualize servers. With Hyper-V Network Virtualization, we create a separation between virtual networks and physical networks. You no longer need to accommodate IP scheme limitations on the physical network when you set up new virtual networks because the latter can ride on top of the physical network, even if the configurations of two or more networks would normally be incompatible.

This concept is slightly difficult to wrap your head around if this is the first time you are hearing about it, so let's discuss some real-world situations that would benefit from this kind of separation.

Private clouds

Private clouds are steamrolling through datacenters around the world because they make a tremendous amount of sense. Anyone interested in bringing the big benefits of the cloud into their environments, while at the same time staying away from cloud negatives, can benefit from this.

Building a private cloud gives you the ability to have dynamically expanding and shrinking compute resources and the ability to host multiple tenants or divisions within the same compute infrastructure. It provides management interfaces directly to those divisions so that the nitty-gritty setup and configuration work can be done by the tenant and you don't have to expend time and resources on the infrastructure-provider level, making small, detailed configurations.

Private clouds enable all of these capabilities while staying away from the big scare of your data being hosted in a cloud service provider's datacenter, which you have no real control over, and all of the privacy concerns surrounding that.

To provide a private cloud inside your infrastructure, particularly one where you want to provide access to multiple tenants, the benefits of network virtualization become apparent, and even a requirement. Let's say you provide computing resources to two divisions of a company, and they each have their own needs for hosting some web servers. No big deal, but these two divisions both have administrative teams who want to use IP schemes that are within 10.0.0.0. They both need to be able to use the same IP addressing subnets on the same physical core network that you are providing, yet you need to keep all their traffic completely segregated and separated. These requirements would have been impossible on a traditional physical network without creating physical separation between those divisions, but by employing the power of network virtualization, you can easily grant IP subnets and address schemes of whatever caliber each division chooses. They can run servers on whatever subnets and IP addresses they like, and all of the traffic is encapsulated uniquely so that it remains separated, completely unaware of the other traffic running around on the same physical core network that runs beneath the virtualization layer. This scenario also plays out well for corporate acquisitions. Two companies that are joining forces at the IT level often have conflicts with domains and network subnetting. With network virtualization, you can allow the existing infrastructure and servers to continue running with their current network config, but bring them within the same physical network by employing Hyper-V Network Virtualization.

Another example is one where you simply want to move a server within a corporate network. Maybe you have a legacy **line-of-business (LOB)** server that many employees still need access to, and their daily workload includes the requirement for that LOB application to be working at all times. The problem with moving the server is that the LOB application on the client computers has a static IPv4 address configured, through which it communicates with the server. When the user opens their app, it does something such as *talk to the server at* 10.10.10.10. Traditionally, that could turn into a deal-breaker for moving the server because moving that server from its current datacenter into a new location would mean changing the IP address of the server, and that would break everyone's ability to connect to it. With virtual networks, this is not an issue. With the ability to ride network traffic and IP subnets on the virtualization layer, that server can move from New York to San Diego and retain all of its IP address settings because the physical network running underneath doesn't matter at all. All of the traffic is encapsulated before it is sent over the physical network, so the IP address of the legacy server can remain at 10.10.10.10, and it can be picked up and moved anywhere in your environment without interruption.

Hybrid clouds

While adding flexibility to your corporate networks is already a huge benefit, the capabilities provided by virtualizing your networks expand exponentially when you do finally decide to start delving into real cloud resources. If and when you make the decision to move some resources to be hosted by a public cloud service provider, you will likely run a hybrid cloud environment. This means that you will build some services in the cloud, but you will also retain some servers and services on-site. In fact, some companies may remain in a hybrid cloud scenario for the rest of eternity, as a 100% movement to the cloud is simply not possible given the ways that many companies do business. So, now that we want to set up a hybrid cloud, we are again looking at all kinds of headaches associated with the movement of resources between our physical and cloud networks. When we want to move a server from on-site into the cloud, we need to adjust everything so that the networking configuration is compatible with the cloud infrastructure, right? Won't we have to reconfigure the NIC on our server to match the subnet that is running in our cloud network? Nope, not if we have our network virtualization infrastructure up and running. Once again, SDN saves the day, giving us the ability to retain the existing IP address information on our servers that are being moved and simply run them with those IP addresses in the cloud. Again, since all of the traffic is encapsulated before being transported, the physical network that is being provided by the cloud does not have to be compatible with, or distinct from, our virtual network, and this gives us the ability to seamlessly shuttle servers back and forth from on-premises to the cloud without having to make special accommodations for networking.

How does it work?

So far, it all sounds like a little bit of magic; how does this actually work and what pieces need to fit together in order to make network virtualization a reality in our organization? Something this comprehensive surely has many moving parts and cannot be turned on by simply flipping a switch. In any network where virtualization is functioning, there have been various components configured to make that successful. Let's do a little explaining here so that you have a better understanding of the technologies and terminology that you will be dealing with once you start your work with SDN.

System Center Virtual Machine Manager

Microsoft System Center is a key piece of the puzzle for creating your SDN model, particularly the **Virtual Machine Manager** (VMM) component of System Center. The ability to pick up IP addresses and move them to other locations around the world requires some coordination of your networking devices, and VMM is here to help. This is the component that you interface with as your central management point to define and configure your virtual networks. System Center is an enormous topic with many options and data points that certainly won't fit in this book, so I will leave you with a link as a starting point on VMM learning: `https://learn.microsoft.com/en-us/system-center/vmm/?view=sc-vmm-2025`.

Network Controller

Microsoft's Network Controller is a role that was initially introduced in Windows Server 2016, and as the name implies, it is used for control over network resources inside your organization. In most cases, it will be working side by side with VMM to make network configurations as centralized and seamless as possible. Network Controller is a standalone role and can be installed onto Server 2016, 2019, 2022, or 2025, and then accessed directly, without VMM, but I don't foresee many deployments leaving it at that. Interfacing with Network Controller directly is possible by tapping into its APIs with PowerShell, but is made even better by adding on a graphical interface from which you configure new networks, monitor existing networks and devices, or troubleshoot problems within the virtual networking model. The graphical interface that can be used is System Center VMM.

Network Controller can be used to configure many different aspects of your virtual and physical networks. You can configure IP subnets and addresses, configurations, and VLANs on Hyper-V switches, and you can even use it to configure NICs on your VMs. Network Controller also allows you to create and manage **access control list** (ACL)-type rules within the Hyper-V switch so that you can build your own firewalling solution at this level without needing to configure local firewalls on the VMs themselves or have dedicated firewall hardware. Network Controller can even be used to configure load balancing and provide VPN access through **Routing and Remote Access Service** (RRAS) servers.

Prior to Windows Server 2025, it was Microsoft's recommendation to never install Network Controller onto physical servers, and to keep this function on dedicated Hyper-V VMs. However, Server 2025's release moves the Network Controller function into failover cluster services, which you can utilize across physical server instances to provide the Network Controller functions.

Network Security Groups

If you have done any networking inside Azure, you are probably familiar with **network security groups** (**NSGs**). NSGs are sort of like virtual firewalls, keeping network traffic protected behind security rules that define what the NICs (which are part of the NSG) are and are not allowed to communicate with.

NSGs can also be used inside a virtualized network infrastructure, even on-premises. In fact, once you have SDN established and are virtualizing your networks, NSGs can be created and modified directly from Windows Admin Center, which is pretty slick.

Something new in Windows Server 2025 is that administrators can now utilize tags to associate NSGs and VMs, to control access. Security policies can then be applied to the tags, so that you no longer need to remember IP address ranges when creating your rules. This can be especially helpful when modifying rules that might apply to multiple IP addresses, as you can now modify one tag instead of visiting numerous rules to update IP ranges.

Generic Routing Encapsulation

Generic routing encapsulation (**GRE**) is just a tunneling protocol, but it's imperative in terms of making network virtualization happen successfully. Earlier, when I talked about moving IP subnets around and about how you can sit virtual networks on top of physical networks without regard for making sure that their IP configurations are compatible, I should add that all of that functionality is provided at the core by GRE. When your physical network is running 192.168.0.x but you want to host some VMs on a subnet in that datacenter, you can create a virtual network of 10.10.10.x without a problem, but that traffic needs to be able to traverse the physical 192.168 network for anything to work. This is where routing encapsulation comes into play. All of the packets from the 10.10.10.x network are encapsulated before being transported across the physical 192.168.0.x network. The 192.168.0.x network sees these packets as 192.168.0.x packets, but they are actually carrying payloads for the 10.10.10.x network.

There are two specific routing encapsulation protocols that are supported in our Microsoft Hyper-V Network Virtualization environment. Initially, Microsoft only configured Hyper-V to work with **Network Virtualization Generic Routing Encapsulation** (**NVGRE**) when setting up Network Virtualization. Another protocol, called **Virtual Extensible Local Area Network** (**VXLAN**), is a little bit newer to the Windows Server world, but has existed for quite some time in other technologies. Many network switches—particularly Cisco—that you have in your environment are more likely to support VXLAN than they are NVGRE. Now that VXLAN is a supported encapsulation protocol for Hyper-V Network Virtualization, it is more likely that you would select this option over NVGRE.

You don't necessarily have to understand how these GRE protocols work in order to make them work for you, since they will be configured for you by the management tools that exist in this Hyper-V Network Virtualization stack. But it is important to understand, in the overall concept of this virtual networking environment, that GRE exists, and that it is the secret to making all of this work.

Microsoft Azure Virtual Network

Once you have Hyper-V Network Virtualization running inside your corporate network and get comfortable with the mentality of separating the physical and virtual networks, you will more than likely want to explore the possibilities around interacting with cloud service provider networks. When you utilize Microsoft Azure as your cloud service provider, you tap into the ability to build a hybrid cloud environment that bridges your on-premises physical networks with remote virtual networks hosted in Azure. Azure's virtual network is the component within Azure that allows you to bring your own IP addresses and subnets into the cloud. You can get more info (and even sign up for a free trial for Azure Virtual Network) here: https://azure.microsoft.com/en-us/products/virtual-network/.

RAS gateways/SDN gateways

When you are working with physical networks, virtual networks, and virtual networks that are stored in cloud environments, you need a component to bridge those gaps, enabling the networks to interact and communicate with each other. This is where a RAS gateway (also called an **SDN gateway**) comes into play. This role has enjoyed a few different names over the years; you may also see these servers referred to as a Windows Server gateway or even the Hyper-V Network Virtualization gateway in some documentation. A RAS gateway's purpose is simple: to be the connection between a virtual network and some other network, most often, a gateway between a virtual network and a physical network. These virtual networks can be hosted in your local environment or in the cloud. In either case, when you want to connect networks, you will need to employ a gateway. When you are creating a bridge between on-premises and the cloud, your cloud service provider will utilize a gateway on their side, which you will tap into from the physical network via a VPN tunnel.

A RAS gateway can be a VM, or an entire pool of VMs, and is integrated with Hyper-V Network Virtualization. A single gateway or pool of gateways can be used to route traffic for many different customers, tenants, or divisions. Even though these different customers have separated networks that need to retain separation from the traffic of the other customers, cloud providers—public or private—can still utilize a RAS gateway to manage this traffic because the gateways retain complete isolation between those traffic streams. You can even run entire pools of gateways on a single public IP address, enabling multiple tenants to connect to the same IP, while still maintaining separation between all of those tenants' traffic streams.

The Windows Server gateway functionality existed back in Server 2016, but once it was put into practice, some performance limitations that restricted network traffic throughput were discovered. Those overheads have been increased dramatically in subsequent versions of Windows Server, meaning that you can flow more traffic and additional tenants through a single gateway than was previously possible.

Virtual network encryption

Security teams are continually concerned with the encryption of data. Whether that data is stored (at rest) or on the move, making sure that it is properly secured and safe from tampering is essential. Prior to Server 2019, getting inner-network traffic encrypted while it was moving was generally the responsibility of the software application, not the network's job. If your software can encrypt traffic while it is flowing between the client and server, or between the application server and the database server, great! If your application does not have native encryption capabilities, it is likely that the communications from that application are flowing in cleartext between the client and server. Even for applications that do encrypt, encryption ciphers and algorithms are often being cracked and compromised. Your application vendors may or may not be on top of the security game as new vulnerabilities are discovered, and even if your applications are protected today, it's possible they will not be tomorrow.

Fortunately, Windows Server 2025 brings us some comfort on this topic, provided within the boundaries of SDN. This capability is called **virtual network encryption**, and it does just what the name implies. In an SDN environment, when traffic moves between VMs and between Hyper-V servers (within the same network), entire subnets can be flagged for encryption, which means that all traffic flowing around those subnets is automatically encrypted at the virtual networking level. The VM servers and the applications that are running on those servers don't have to be configured or changed in any way to take advantage of this encryption, as it happens within the network itself, automatically encrypting all traffic that flows on that network.

With Server 2025 as the core of your SDN capabilities, any subnet in a virtual network can be flagged for encryption by specifying a certificate to use for that encryption. If the future happens to bring the scenario where current encryption standards are out of date or insecure, the SDN fabric can be updated to new encryption standards, and those subnets will continue to be encrypted using the newer methods, once again without having to make changes to your VMs or applications. If you are using SDN and virtual networks in your environment, enabling encryption on those subnets is a no-brainer!

Bridging the gap to Azure

Most companies that host servers in Microsoft Azure still have physical, on-premises networks, and one of the big questions that always needs to be answered is, *how are we going to connect our physical datacenter to our Azure datacenter?* Most businesses with comprehensive enough networking to be utilizing SDN will establish one of two different methods to make this happen.

A VPN gateway

Microsoft's VPN gateway is an SKU that you spin up in Azure, a virtual firewall of sorts that is capable of creating a connection between Azure and your on-premises firewalls or gateway servers using an IPsec site-to-site VPN tunnel. This establishes a continuous tunnel between the two networks, which is managed by you on your own servers or appliances. One benefit to this simple site-to-site VPN tunnel is that it is quick to set up as long as your on-prem equipment is stable and compatible. If your local ISP goes down, then, of course, your connection to Azure will go down with it. Most admins pursue building a VPN gateway for the purpose of connecting the entirety of on-premises infrastructure to Azure, but one other neat feature of the VPN gateway is that it also provides point-to-site VPN connection capability. When configured, client computers can connect directly to this Azure-located VPN gateway using SSTP, OpenVPN, or IPsec client VPN connectivity.

Azure ExpressRoute

VPN gateways are great, but they completely rely on traditional internet connections. Outages or latency can create significant issues with your connectivity to Azure. If you require higher bandwidth between a local datacenter and Azure, or a higher guaranteed percentage of uptime, Microsoft provides a service called **Azure ExpressRoute** that can be used for these more intense networking requirements. ExpressRoute is a dedicated connection between your building and Azure; the edge environments on both your side and the Azure side, as well as the connection itself, are dedicated and provided by a third party. ExpressRoute comes with a 99.99% availability **service-level agreement** (**SLA**) across the entire connection, which is pretty impressive. ExpressRoute is, of course, more expensive than setting up your own VPN, and you need to work with a third-party provider to build and maintain your ExpressRoute connection.

Third-party options

Microsoft partners with various vendors and third parties to provide additional connectivity options between your on-premises datacenter and Azure networks. As an example, the company that I work for deploys and maintains a lot of Cisco Meraki gear. Meraki firewalls have a unique SD-WAN capability that very easily ties all your sites together with constant site-to-site VPN tunnels. This can extend into the Azure environment as well if you place a Meraki firewall into your Azure network. How in the world would you do that? By deploying a Meraki vMX (virtual firewall) appliance into Azure. Once deployed, the vMX simply shows up as one more firewall to be managed and maintained inside your Meraki portal, and it taps into the rest of your Meraki infrastructure seamlessly.

There are other network vendors that provide similar services, but I have not personally tried them. I can tell you that the Meraki setup works well, and is often our preferred connectivity method to the cloud for small-to-medium businesses.

Azure Network Adapter

If you have an on-premises server that you need to quickly connect to your Azure environment, and you don't already have a permanent connection established between your physical and Azure sites, there is a hybrid cloud capability called **Azure Network Adapter** that can be attached to Windows Server. To use one of these network adapters, you must utilize Windows Admin Center to manage your servers.

Using Windows Admin Center, you can quickly add Azure Network Adapter to an on-premises server, which connects it straight to your Azure network using a point-to-site VPN connection. Cool! This capability is helpful for small businesses that have cloud resources and want to connect just a single on-premises server to Azure, or even within a branch office scenario at a larger company. Rather than creating site-to-site connections between your primary datacenter and every branch office, if your primary datacenter were already permanently connected to Azure, you could then connect branch office servers directly to Azure using Azure Network Adapter.

What Azure Network Adapter really does is configure a **point-to-site** (**P2S**) VPN for you on that server, connecting the server to Azure via a VPN tunnel. As you know, a VPN tunnel requires both client configuration and a VPN concentrator or gateway on the receiving side, which is exactly what Azure Network Adapter does. It configures the P2S client VPN on the server and spins up a virtual network gateway inside Azure to receive that connection.

Even better, this capability has been back-ported so that you can add one of these adapters not only to Server 2025 machines but also to Server 2022, Server 2019, Server 2016, and Server 2012 R2 machines as well.

To make this happen, there are a few requirements that need to be in place. You must have an active Azure subscription, and you need to have at least one Azure virtual network configured.

Next, you need to register your **Windows Admin Center (WAC)** with Azure. This is accomplished by opening **Windows Admin Center** and visiting **Settings**. Once inside, navigate to **Gateway | Register** and walk through the registration process:

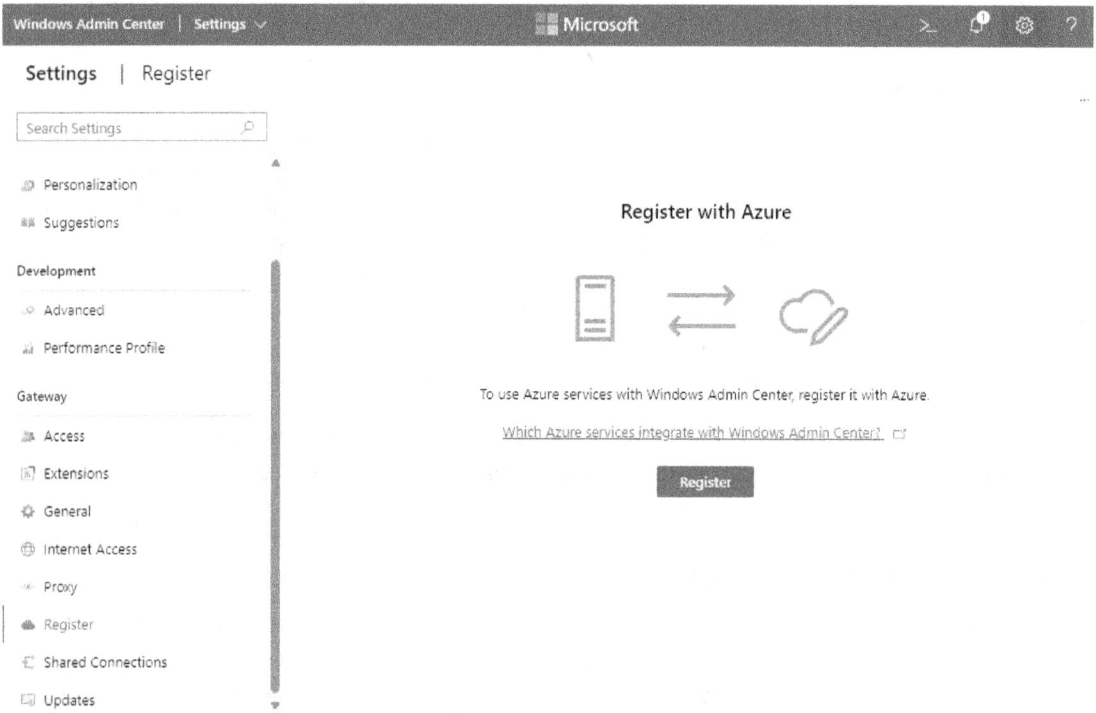

Figure 8.28: Registering Windows Admin Center with Azure

Now that WAC is registered with Azure, open the server that you are managing from inside WAC and head over to the **Networks** section. You will see any NICs that are present on your server listed here, and near the top of the window is an **+ Add Azure Network Adapter (Preview)** button:

You'll notice in this text and screenshots that the word "Preview" still exists in the title of this feature, but this capability has existed and continues to be titled "Preview" ever since it was released a few years ago. Microsoft documentation no longer declares this to be a preview feature; I believe they have simply forgotten to remove the word "Preview" from the text inside WAC.

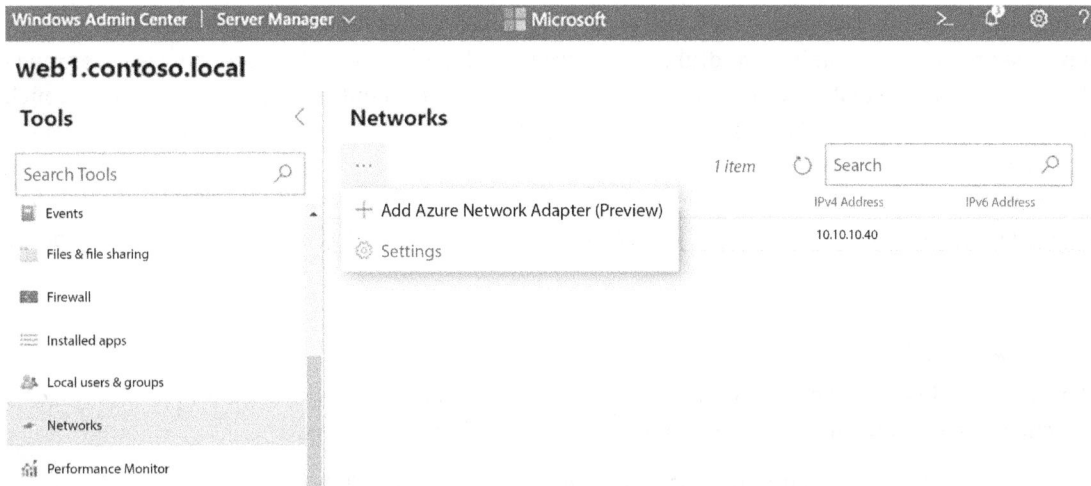

Figure 8.29: Adding Azure Network Adapter

You will find that all of the values Azure needs to make this connection are auto-populated for you, based on your Azure network and subscription. If you don't already have an Azure virtual network, this wizard can even create one for you. You also get the opportunity to specify your own certificate for authenticating this connection, and doing so would be a good practice if you planned for this to be a long-term connection to Azure; otherwise, you can proceed without any input by allowing WAC/Azure to generate a self-signed certificate and simply clicking on the **Create** button. Windows Admin Center will go ahead and create a connection between your on-premises server and the Azure virtual network. That was only a couple of mouse clicks! This is an ingenious way of creating ad hoc connections between your servers and Azure very quickly and without complications.

If you later need to disconnect this server from the Azure network, you can open **Network Connections** on that on-premises server, just like you would when modifying any NIC properties on your server, and you will find that what WAC has done under the hood is configure a point-to-site VPN connection, which is listed inside **Network Connections**. You can simply right-click on that Azure VPN connection and disconnect it.

Summary

Server administration and network administration have historically been different camps, but over time, those lines have blurred. There are numerous networking configurations and tasks that now need to be accomplished by Windows Server administrators without needing to involve a networking team, so it is important that you maintain a good understanding of how your infrastructure is connected. Familiarity with the tools laid out in this chapter will provide you with the ability to configure, monitor, and troubleshoot most Microsoft-centric networks.

Our introduction to SDN may have been partially confusing if you had never encountered this idea before, but hopefully, it has prompted you to dig a little deeper and prepare yourself for dealing with this in the future. Ready or not, the cloud is here to stay. Microsoft on-premises networks now have numerous ways to interact with Microsoft Azure, and it will soon be imperative that IT staff are familiar with these concepts. The idea of SDN will grow in popularity over the coming years. At the moment, it may seem daunting, but in a handful of years, we may all look back and wonder how we ever made things work with virtual networks, the same way we feel today about virtual servers. There is much more information both on Microsoft Learn and in published books about Hyper-V virtual networking and System Center VMM if you are interested in setting this up for yourself. For now, continue on to the next chapter, where we will discuss the componentry in Windows Server 2025 that is going to enable our employees to work remotely, which is particularly interesting in this new work-from-home world we are living in.

Questions

Put your knowledge to the test with the following questions. If you need a hand (or just want to double-check), you'll find all the answers in the *Appendix* section of the book.

1. What is the CIDR that represents a subnet mask of `255.255.255.0`?
2. Why could a corporate subnet of `192.168.1.0/24` cause problems for remote employees?
3. How many bits in length is an IPv6 address?
4. Rewrite the following IPv6 address in condensed form: `2001:ABCD:0001:0002:0000:0000:0000:0001`.
5. What is the name of the command that is similar to `tracert` but displays the local NIC that traffic is flowing out of?
6. True or False? On a server with multiple NICs, you should input a default gateway address onto each of those NICs.
7. What is the PowerShell cmdlet that can be used to create new routes on Windows Server?
8. Which Windows Server operating systems can be used with Azure Network Adapter in order to connect them directly to Azure virtual networks?
9. Which connectivity method between a local datacenter and Azure provides the fastest, most robust, and most reliable connection?

Join us on Discord

For discussions around the book and to connect with your peers, join us on Discord at `https://packt.link/discordcloud` or scan the QR code below:

9
Remote Access

Providing employees with the ability to remotely access corporate resources used to be a big benefit to most companies, but not necessarily a requirement. That little C-word, which shall not be named, changed everything, and quite suddenly, many companies in much of the world suddenly faced a need to grant access to employees who had to work from home. Indeed, as time progressed and some of the turbulence died down, companies realized that they could save quite a few expenses by offering continued work-from-home jobs, and since the year 2020, the working landscape has completely shifted. In fact, many remote workers took this idea and ran even further with it, where "work-from-home" is now "work-from-anywhere," and I have spoken with multiple remote workers who live and work from a travel trailer. They work by day, travel by night. Or sometimes the reverse. Interestingly, as I type these words, there are headlines in the news almost every day about another company that has issued a **return to office** (**RTO**) order. So far, this seems to be impacting large organizations and governmental entities, but it will certainly be interesting to watch as this progresses. Regardless of this recent backpedaling, most companies and employees now expect the option to tap into resources from wherever they happen to be. The technology most universally employed to grant remote workers the ability to do their jobs from home, coffee shops, hotels, or even campers is a **virtual private network** (**VPN**) connection.

Most VPNs in today's businesses are provided by products from companies other than Microsoft. I want you to know that the *Remote Access* role in Windows Server 2025 provides multiple ways to provide that access, without the need to involve a third party. With many improvements having been made to the VPN components right in Windows Server, it is now a feasible and secure platform for providing access to corporate resources from remote computers. In addition to VPN connectivity, we have a couple of more unique technologies baked into Windows Server 2025 that are also designed to provide remote access to corporate resources in a different way than traditional VPN. The topics that we will cover in this chapter are the following:

- Regular ol' VPN
- Always On VPN
- DirectAccess
- Remote Access Management Console

- DA, VPN, or AOVPN? Which is best?
- Web Application Proxy

Regular ol' VPN

A traditional VPN involves users clicking on a VPN connection that is configured on their local device, and that device then creates a secure virtual private networking connection to another device sitting in your datacenter, most often a firewall.

However, if your firewall doesn't provide VPN endpoint capabilities, or if you simply want to protect your VPN traffic in a different way, you can utilize a Windows Server to be the VPN termination device.

We already mentioned the *Remote Access* role, and indeed, this is a Windows Server role that is ready to be selected and installed on a fresh Windows Server instance. However, before making that leap, you want to formulate a plan for networking with this server. A VPN server can utilize a single NIC that is inside your corporate network, and in this case, you would need to configure your firewall to **network address translation** (NAT) traffic from a public IP address into that internal NIC's private IP address. This is necessary because your VPN clients are going to be creating connections from the internet to this VPN server. For that traffic stream to be successful, the client's traffic must land on the server.

Another option is to provide dual NICs on this server. One can be your internal NIC, connected to the internal network. The second NIC can be your external or DMZ NIC, and connected accordingly. This NIC could have its own public IP address and hang right on the internet, or it could be connected inside a DMZ with some protections around it, and traffic passed through to it there. The reasons you might go dual-NIC are security-related, so that this Windows Server and its traffic sit behind some layers of firewall protection. If you choose to employ dual NICs, you may want to reference back to our conversation about proper Windows routing table configuration, as you will be in a position to define a default gateway on your external NIC but not the internal, and will then be required to define static routes to navigate VPN traffic around your internal network.

Routing and Remote Access Service (RRAS)

Once networking has been established on your VPN server, it is time to install the *Remote Access* role. All the different connectivity components that we will discuss in this chapter are contained within this same role, so you will find that, upon installing the role, you will be asked for some further specifics about what role components you are trying to enable. For the purposes of VPN connectivity, as well as **DirectAccess**, which we will discuss shortly, simply check the top box and proceed.

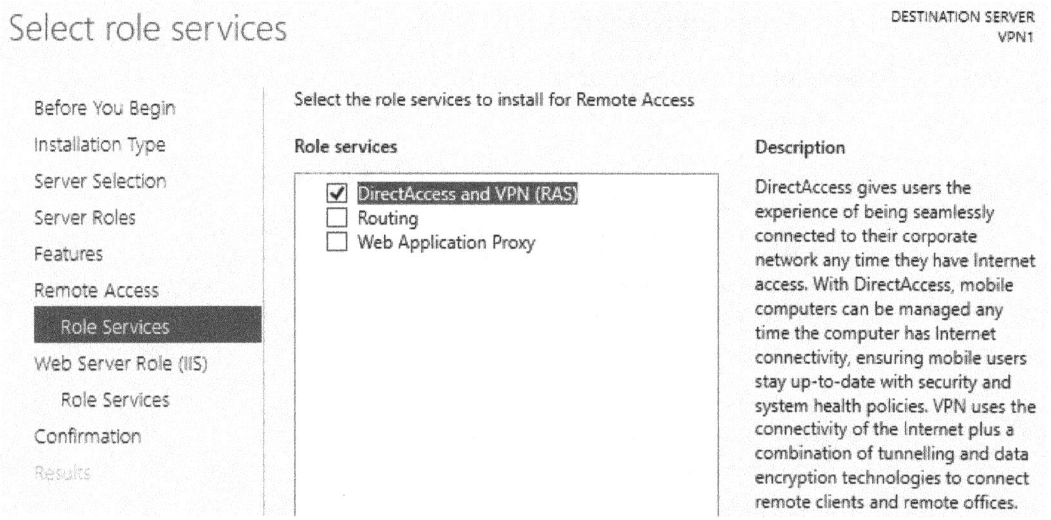

Select role services

Before You Begin

Installation Type

Server Selection

Server Roles

Features

Remote Access

   Role Services

Web Server Role (IIS)

   Role Services

Confirmation

Results

Select the role services to install for Remote Access

Role services

- [x] DirectAccess and VPN (RAS)
- [ ] Routing
- [ ] Web Application Proxy

Description

DirectAccess gives users the experience of being seamlessly connected to their corporate network any time they have Internet access. With DirectAccess, mobile computers can be managed any time the computer has Internet connectivity, ensuring mobile users stay up-to-date with security and system health policies. VPN uses the connectivity of the Internet plus a combination of tunnelling and data encryption technologies to connect remote clients and remote offices.

Figure 9.1: Installing the Remote Access role for VPN

After role installation is complete, you will find a couple of new tools available inside Server Manager. We will talk more about the **Remote Access Management Console** near the end of this chapter, as that toolset interacts with both VPN and DirectAccess, but when working on traditional VPN connectivity, we want to utilize the console called **Routing and Remote Access**.

Configuring VPN inside RRAS

Nothing is really happening inside RRAS by default; you can see the name of your server listed with a red arrow next to it, indicating that it is not active. To initiate a configuration wizard that will take us through VPN configuration, simply right-click on the name of your server and select **Configure and Enable Routing and Remote Access**. The first option we encounter is important. There are a few different uses for RRAS, including the routing of both incoming traffic (VPN) and outgoing traffic (proxy/ NAT). RRAS can also be used as a site-to-site connectivity platform! For our purposes today, the top option will suffice. We are going to configure **Remote access (dial-up or VPN)**.

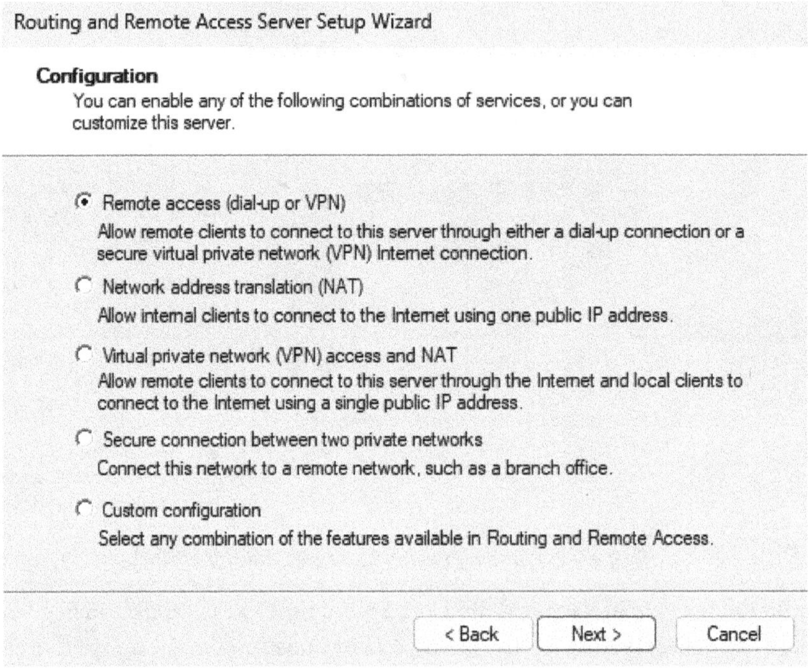

Routing and Remote Access Server Setup Wizard

Configuration
You can enable any of the following combinations of services, or you can
customize this server.

○ Remote access (dial-up or VPN)
  Allow remote clients to connect to this server through either a dial-up connection or a
  secure virtual private network (VPN) Internet connection.

○ Network address translation (NAT)
  Allow internal clients to connect to the Internet using one public IP address.

○ Virtual private network (VPN) access and NAT
  Allow remote clients to connect to this server through the Internet and local clients to
  connect to the Internet using a single public IP address.

○ Secure connection between two private networks
  Connect this network to a remote network, such as a branch office.

○ Custom configuration
  Select any combination of the features available in Routing and Remote Access.

< Back   Next >   Cancel

Figure 9.2: RRAS usage options

The screen is self-explanatory and kind of funny. Are we setting up a VPN or a dial-up connection? I haven't encountered anybody using dial-up internet in many, many years. This indicates just how long it has been since Microsoft put any work into updating the RRAS interface and wizards.

I suppose "if it ain't broke, don't fix it" applies here, because even though this interface looks like it came straight out of Server 2003, an RRAS VPN is still a stable and secure connection method, if configured properly.

At this point, you will realize that if you only have one NIC installed in your VPN server, you receive a message about RRAS expecting there to be two. It is possible to configure VPN or DirectAccess with a single NIC, but it is not Microsoft's default or recommended method. A proper Microsoft Remote Access server has dual NICs, separating the traffic coming in from the internet and the traffic that moves onward toward your internal network. That is, after all, the purpose of this role: *Routing* and Remote Access. Assuming you have two NICs on this server, one connected internally and one externally, the next screen will ask you to select the NIC that is facing toward the internet.

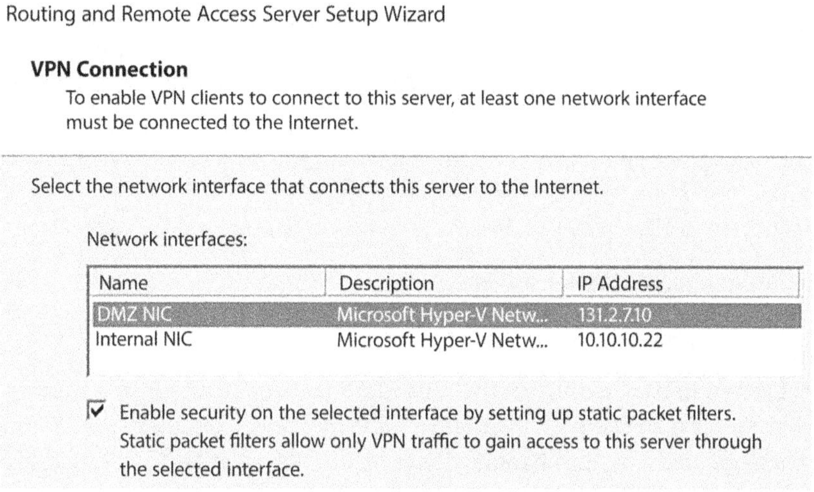

Routing and Remote Access Server Setup Wizard

VPN Connection
> To enable VPN clients to connect to this server, at least one network interface must be connected to the Internet.

Select the network interface that connects this server to the Internet.

Network interfaces:

Name	Description	IP Address
DMZ NIC	Microsoft Hyper-V Netw...	131.2.7.10
Internal NIC	Microsoft Hyper-V Netw...	10.10.10.22

☑ Enable security on the selected interface by setting up static packet filters. Static packet filters allow only VPN traffic to gain access to this server through the selected interface.

Figure 9.3: Defining internal and external NICs

The assignment of IP addresses to remote VPN client computers is our next configuration step, and the default option is to utilize DHCP for this purpose. You almost never want to use your normal DHCP server to provide IP addresses to VPN clients, because your network is then going to think that those remote computers are within your internal network, and routing packets back to those clients becomes problematic. Instead, it is recommended to choose the option to define your own range of IP addresses to assign to VPN client computers, and that this range of IP addresses be from a new subnet that you do not have in use at all inside your network currently. In my case, my internal network is 10.10.10.0/24, and I am going to define 172.16.1.0/24 as my VPN IP addressing subnet.

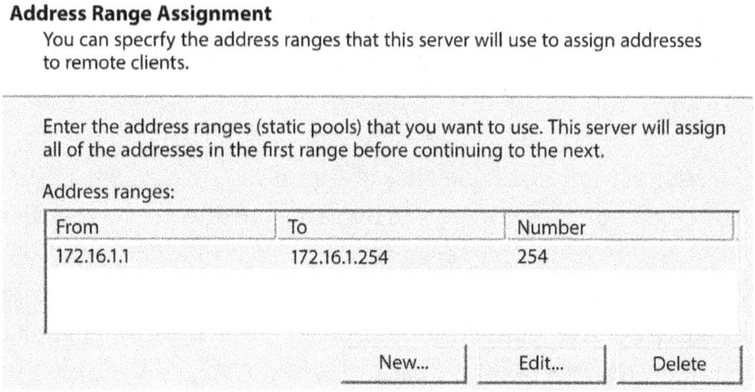

Address Range Assignment
> You can specrfy the address ranges that this server will use to assign addresses to remote clients.

Enter the address ranges (static pools) that you want to use. This server will assign all of the addresses in the first range before continuing to the next.

Address ranges:

From	To	Number
172.16.1.1	172.16.1.254	254

New... | Edit... | Delete

Figure 9.4: Best practice is to define a new subnet for VPN client IP addresses

Now, we define authentication for VPN connections. If you employ another Windows Server running the **Network Policy Server (NPS)** role, you can point RRAS at NPS to get very nitty-gritty with the authentication of remote computers. This is definitely a good thing, and it will enable you to allow only users who are part of a certain group to be able to connect to a VPN, or only during certain times. You can even use NPS to further enhance VPN connections by requiring MFA when NPS is tied in with an MFA provider. But in our test lab today, I do not have an NPS (RADIUS) server, and so I will proceed with the default option to allow RRAS to directly manage authentication for VPN connection requests.

RRAS VPN is now configured on your server!

Securing your VPN

Wait a minute. Let's wrap back to the fact that this RRAS management console appears to be lacking any updates over the past 20 years. While that is not technically true, there are many items in here that have not been updated with the changing times. Primarily, what I'm referring to are the different protocols that RRAS is listening on, which could be used to establish a VPN connection between the client and server. It is important to understand what these protocols are so that you can decide which connectivity options you intend to offer to client computers as they make connections. Prior to Windows Server 2025, all four of these protocols were enabled by default, but they are not all good ideas. I'll list them here in order of "strongest and more secure" all the way down to "don't touch this one!"

IKEv2

The newest, strongest, and all-in-all best way to connect your client computers via VPN or AOVPN, IKEv2 is the only way to connect the **Always On VPN (AOVPN)** device tunnel, which we will hear about in the next section of this chapter. IKEv2 requires machine certificates to be issued to your client computers in order to authenticate. This generally means that if you want clients to connect via IKEv2, those clients will be domain-joined. It is very important to note that IKEv2 uses UDP ports 500 and 4500 to make its connection, which is sometimes a hindrance and is blocked by firewalls.

SSTP

SSTP VPN uses an SSL stream to connect. Because of this, it requires an SSL certificate to be installed on the Remote Access server, but does not require machine certificates on the client computers. SSTP uses TCP port 443, so it is able to connect even from inside very restrictive networks where IKEv2 may fail (because of IKEv2's reliance on UDP). I have to say that SSTP is my favorite flavor of Windows RRAS-based VPN connectivity protocol, but it only works from Windows clients. If you have the requirement to connect other devices such as Macs, iPhones, Android devices, and so on, you'll want to jump to the *L2TP* subsection.

To enable SSTP VPN to be successful on your RRAS server, simply decide on a DNS name to point at your RRAS public IP address, and then acquire a standard SSL certificate for that name. For example, I might choose vpn.contoso.com and get an SSL certificate for the same name. Install that SSL certificate onto your VPN server, and then inside the RRAS console, follow these steps:

1. Right-click on the name of your server, and head into **Properties**.
2. Visit the **Security** tab.

3. Down near the bottom is a section called **SSL Certificate Binding**. Once your SSL certificate is installed on the server, simply use the drop-down menu here to select your certificate. This enables an SSTP VPN to work properly when clients connect and request SSTP.

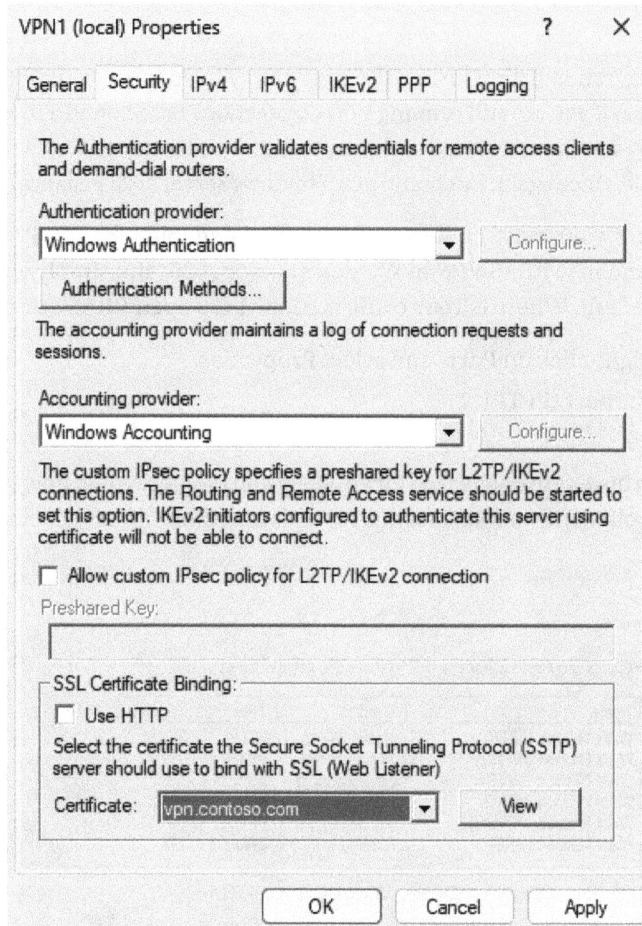

Figure 9.5: Selecting an SSL certificate to be used by SSTP VPN

L2TP

We have already discussed the two best VPN connectivity options—best from a security perspective, anyway. Now, we turn to the other two, which are no longer enabled by default in Windows Server 2025, but this one at least still serves a valid purpose.

Layer 2 Tunneling Protocol (L2TP) is able to establish VPN connections by using certificates or a **pre-shared key (PSK)**. If you are only connecting Windows clients to your VPN, stay away from this one and focus on SSTP. If you have a requirement to connect non-Windows devices to your VPN, utilizing L2TP to establish VPN connections through the use of a PSK is generally the approach that is taken. In my experience, it is quite rare to find a Windows Server hosting L2TP VPN, but it may be a common thing for you to interact with L2TP on client computers when connecting to other flavors of VPN. For example, if your firewall provides VPN connectivity for workstations, it is fairly common for those firewalls to utilize L2TP to build the initial tunnel. In these scenarios, L2TP itself does not encrypt data, but rather it will be combined with another tunnel (such as IPsec) to secure your traffic.

PPTP

While still a valid configuration option inside RRAS, stay away from this one! PPTP is no longer a secure method of tunneling, and if you are still running VPN connections based on PPTP, you need to treat those traffic streams as if they were unencrypted and clear-text over the internet. Replace this with something better as soon as possible. Once again, in a brand new Windows Server 2025 instance, PPTP will be disabled.

How can you find out if your existing RRAS VPN server is enabled for PPTP? Or perhaps you just finished creating a brand new RRAS VPN in Windows Server 2025, and simply want to verify that this really is disabled by default. Where is your confirmation? Let's open RRAS and take a peek...

1. Inside RRAS, right-click on **Ports** and select **Properties**.
2. Select **WAN Miniport (PPTP)**.
3. Click **Configure...**.
4. Verify that both boxes are unchecked (or go ahead and uncheck them now). The absence of these checkboxes is your confirmation that this server is not listening for VPN connections using PPTP.

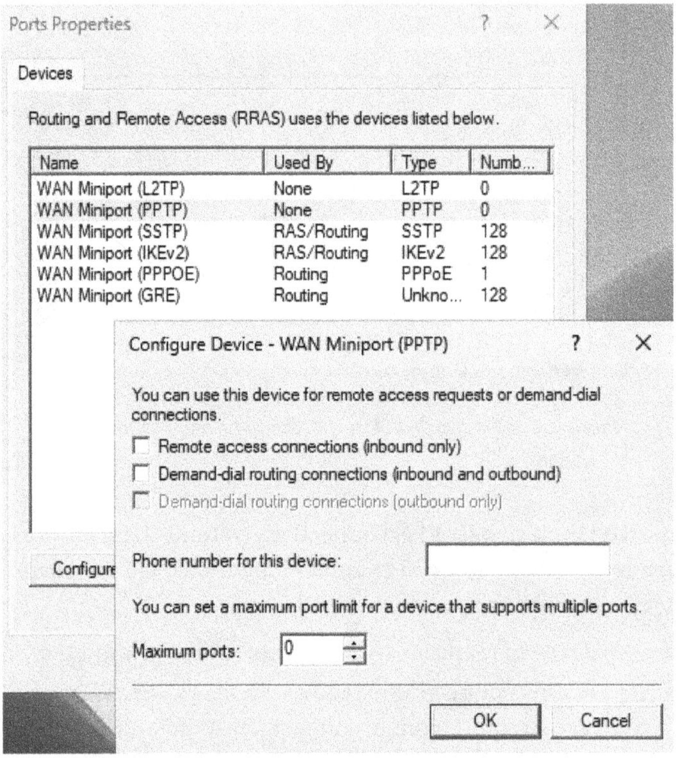

Figure 9.6: PPTP is disabled

Throughout these descriptions, I kept specifically mentioning whether these protocols were enabled by default or not. I did this because our behavior has changed as of the Windows Server 2025 release. Prior to our latest operating system, configuring RRAS-based VPN on any Windows Server would net you a VPN server listening for all four, even though they are not all secure. Installing a brand-new Server 2025 RRAS instance will now only provide you with IKEv2 and SSTP out of the box, but the others can be re-enabled if needed. Since a lot of us are currently in the middle of projects to in-place upgrade older versions of Windows Server to the 2025 flavor, it is also important to understand that an RRAS VPN server configured to allow L2TP or PPTP prior to the upgrade will still be offering those connectivity protocols following the upgrade. The server upgrade process will specifically retain those configurations so as not to break existing VPN client connections, and you need to decide whether they are really still in your best interests.

Configuring VPN on the client

Once the server side of VPN connectivity is established, how do computers create connections to this VPN? It is quite simple to configure a Windows client for VPN connectivity; you generally only need to know the name or IP address where your VPN server is running. Let's walk through the VPN configuration process on a Windows 11 computer to see the experience.

Click on your **Start** button, and type VPN. The top option is probably **VPN settings**, which is exactly where we want to go. Once inside, click the **Add VPN** button, and you're already half finished. Name this connection whatever you like, and input the public DNS name that is steering toward your VPN server. Remember earlier when I gave the example of vpn.contoso.com? Something like that. If you have not established a DNS name to resolve these connections, you can alternatively input the public IP address that lands on your VPN server, but doing so would imply that you cannot use SSTP VPN. The most advanced thing you will have to decide on this screen is what type of VPN connection you are creating, and by default, your Windows client computer will select **Automatic** here. If you know that your VPN server is only listening on SSTP (as an example), your VPN will connect slightly faster if you specify SSTP in this drop-down list. If you are unsure of the protocols that are available on your VPN server, or if you intentionally have multiple enabled, then leave it set to **Automatic**, and the client computer will cycle through the options in order of best to worst, to figure out what works.

The only alteration to this screen comes if you select **L2TP/IPsec with pre-shared key**. As with any technology that utilizes PSKs, obviously, you need to type in the PSK here, which must match the PSK established on your VPN server, and so a new field is displayed for you to enter that information. Otherwise, there isn't much to configure here on the screen to add a new VPN connection; however, both IKEv2 and L2TP/certificate require a special certificate to be installed on every computer before the VPN connection will work. While this VPN screen will certainly allow you to establish a VPN connection profile that includes these protocols, pursuing a successfully connected VPN using either IKEv2 or L2TP/certificate means you would need to do a little additional reading on requirements surrounding those specific protocols. Here is our completed **Add VPN** screen:

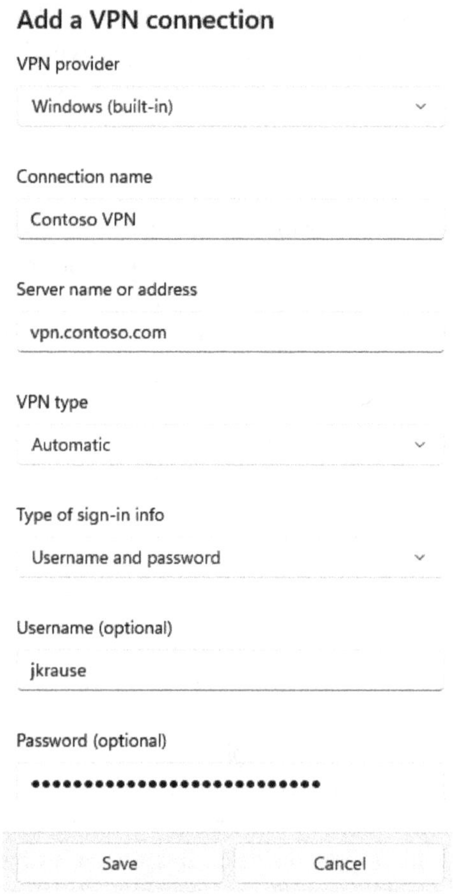

Add a VPN connection

VPN provider

Windows (built-in)   ⌄

Connection name

Contoso VPN

Server name or address

vpn.contoso.com

VPN type

Automatic   ⌄

Type of sign-in info

Username and password   ⌄

Username (optional)

jkrause

Password (optional)

•••••••••••••••••••••••••••••

Save   Cancel

Figure 9.7: Configuring VPN on a client computer

After completing the setup of a VPN connection, engaging this connection is as simple as clicking on it from inside VPN settings, or from the wireless connectivity option in the system tray. Rather than manually create VPN connections across hundreds or thousands of computers, you could certainly employ Group Policy or InTune to automatically create these connections for you!

Always On VPN

Providing users with access to VPN connectivity traditionally means providing them with a special network connection link (such as the one we just created) that they can launch and enter credentials to pass authentication to connect to their work environment's network and then communicate with company resources. After launching a VPN, users can open their email, find documents, launch their line-of-business applications, or otherwise work in the same ways that they can when physically sitting in their office. Also, when connected via a VPN, management of their laptop is possible, enabling a successful communication flow for systems such as Group Policy and Microsoft Configuration Manager (previously SCCM). VPN connections offer great connectivity back to your network, but (remember, we are talking about traditional, regular VPN connections here), they only work when the user manually launches them and tells them to work. Anytime a user has not connected to their VPN, they are navigating the internet with no connectivity back to the company datacenter. This also means that a traditional VPN connection has no form of connectivity on the Windows login screen because, until they get logged in to the computer and find their way to the Windows desktop, users have no way of launching that VPN tunnel. This means that anything that might attempt to happen on the login screen, such as live authentication lookups, or during the login process, such as Group Policy processing or logon scripts, will not function via a traditional, manual VPN.

AOVPN, as you have probably guessed based on the name, is simply the idea of making a VPN connection continuous and automatically connected. In other words, any time the user has their laptop outside the office walls and is connected to the internet, a VPN tunnel back to the corporate network is automatically established, ideally with zero user input to the process. This enables users to forget about the VPN altogether, as it is simply always connected and ready for them to use. They can log in to their machines, launch their applications, and start working. It also means that IT management functions such as security policies, updates, and installer packages can push out to client machines a greater percentage of the time, since we no longer wait for the user to decide when they want to connect back to work; it happens automatically and pretty much all the time.

There are three different ways in which AOVPN can be triggered on the client machine, and none of them involve the user having to launch a VPN connection:

- AOVPN can be configured to truly be always-on, meaning that as soon as internet access is available, it will always attempt to connect.
- Another option is **application triggering**, which means that you can configure AOVPN to launch itself only when specific applications are opened on the workstation.
- The third option is DNS name-based triggering. This calls the VPN connection into action when particular DNS names are called for, which generally happens when users launch specific applications or URLs.

Since you don't need AOVPN to be connected and working when your laptop is sitting *inside* the corporate network, we should also discuss the fact that AOVPN is smart enough to turn itself off when the user walks through those glass doors. AOVPN-enabled computers will automatically decide when they are inside the network, therefore disabling VPN components, and when they are outside the network and need to launch the VPN tunnel connection.

This detection process is known as **trusted network detection**. When configured properly, AOVPN components know what your company's internal DNS suffix is, and they monitor your NIC and firewall profile settings to establish whether that same suffix has been assigned to those components. When it sees a match, it knows you are inside the network and then disables AOVPN.

Types of AOVPN tunnels

Before we get started on the particulars of client and server components required to make AOVPN happen, there is an important core topic that needs to be understood to make appropriate decisions about how you want to utilize AOVPN in your company. There are two very different kinds of VPN tunnels that can be used with AOVPN: a **user tunnel** and a **device tunnel**. As you will learn later in this chapter, the ability to have two different kinds of tunnels is something included with AOVPN to bring it closer to feature parity with DirectAccess, which also has this dual-tunnel mentality. Let's take a minute and explore the purposes behind the two tunnels.

User tunnels

The most common way of using AOVPN in the wild involves a user tunnel being authenticated at the user level. User certificates are issued from an internal PKI to your computers, and these certificates are then used as part of the authentication process during connection. User tunnels carry all of the machine and user traffic, but it is very important to note that user tunnels cannot be established while the computer is sitting on the login screen because user authentication has not happened at that point. So, a user tunnel will only launch itself once a user has successfully logged in to the computer. With only a user tunnel at play, the computer will not have connectivity back to the corporate network for management functions until someone has logged in to the computer, and this also means that you will rely on cached credentials in order to pass through the login prompt.

Device tunnels

A device tunnel is intended to fill the gaps left by only running a user tunnel. A device tunnel is authenticated via a machine certificate, also issued from your internal PKI. This means that the device tunnel can establish itself even prior to user authentication. In other words, it works even while sitting on the Windows login screen. This enables management tools such as Group Policy and Microsoft Configuration Manager to work regardless of user input, and it also enables real-time authentication against domain controllers, enabling users to log in to a workstation they have never logged in to before, even when that computer is outside the office. This also enables real-time password expiry resets from any location.

Device tunnel requirements

A user tunnel can work with pretty much any Windows 10/11 machine, but there are some firm requirements to be able to make use of a device tunnel. To roll out a device tunnel, you need to meet the following criteria:

- The client must be domain-joined.
- The client must be issued a machine certificate.
- The client must be running Windows 10 1709 or newer.
- The client must be running Windows 10/11 Enterprise or Education SKUs. (Note that Pro is not included in this list.)
- A device tunnel can only be IKEv2. This is important to understand because, as you already know, IKEv2 utilizes UDP to make its connection. This means that computers that are sitting behind port-restricting firewalls may be unable to establish that device tunnel connection.

AOVPN client requirements

It is important to understand that the *Always On* part of Always On VPN is client-side functionality. You can utilize AOVPN on a client computer to connect to many kinds of VPN infrastructure on the backend. We will talk about that shortly, in the *AOVPN server components* section.

While creating regular, manual VPN connections has been possible on Windows client operating systems for 20+ years, AOVPN is a bit younger. Your workforce will need to be running Windows 10 or 11 to make this happen. Specifically, they will need to be running, at a minimum, Windows 10 version 1607.

The following are the supported SKUs:

*   Windows 10 1607+
*   Windows 10 1709+
*   Windows 10 1803+
*   Windows 11

Wait a minute—that doesn't make any sense. Why list those three Windows 10 versions separately if they are inclusive of one another? While AOVPN was technically introduced in Windows 10 1607, it has had some improvements along the way. Let's list those again, with a brief summary of what has changed over the years:

*   **Windows 10 1607**: The original capability to auto-launch a VPN connection, thus enabling AOVPN.
*   **Windows 10 1709**: Updates and changes included the addition of device tunnels. If you intend to run a device tunnel for computer management purposes (and most enterprises will), then consider 1709 to be your minimum OS requirement.
*   **Windows 10 1803**: Includes some major fixes that were discovered in 1709. In reality, what this means is that I never see anyone implementing AOVPN unless they are running 1803. Thankfully, the Windows 10 update platform is much improved, meaning that many more companies are rolling out newer versions of Windows 10 on an ongoing basis, and 1803 is now mostly in the dust, having long ago been replaced by even newer versions.

Whether you are running 1607, 1709, 1803, 1809, or whatever the latest and greatest version is, the particular SKU within those platforms does not matter. Well, it hardly matters. AOVPN works with Windows 10/11 Home, Pro, Enterprise, and all of the other flavors. That is, the *user tunnel* works with all of those.

It is important enough to point out once again: if you want to utilize a *device tunnel* with AOVPN, using domain-joined Windows 10/11 Enterprise or Education SKUs is a firm requirement.

Domain-joined

As we have already established, when you're interested in using the AOVPN device tunnel, your client computers must be domain-joined. However, if you are okay with only running the user tunnel for AOVPN access, then there are no domain membership requirements. Clients still need to be running Windows 10 1607 or newer, but they could be any SKU and could even be home computers that are joined to simple workgroups; no domain is required.

This is emphasized specifically in Microsoft documentation in many places because it enables AOVPN to be utilized (somewhat) by the **bring your own device (BYOD)** crowd. While this is interesting, I don't foresee it being at all common that companies would allow employees' personal computers to be connected to their VPN. Most organizations are trying to cater in a small way to the BYOD market by providing access to some resources via the cloud, such as Office 365 for email and documents. But connecting those personal computers and devices back to your network with a full-scale layer 3 VPN tunnel? I don't think so. That is security administrator nightmare fuel.

Rolling out the settings

Let's say you have all of the server-side parts and pieces ready to roll for VPN connectivity, and indeed, you have successfully established the fact that you can create ad hoc traditional VPN connections to your infrastructure with no problems. Great! Looks like you are ready from the infrastructural side. Now, what is necessary to get clients to start doing Always On connections?

Configuration of AOVPN policy settings isn't terribly difficult, but they need to be converted into a configuration file or script to run against other computers. A generalized method is that you can build a manual-launch VPN connection, tweak it with some specific security and authentication settings, and then run a utility that exports that configuration out to some configuration files. These VPN profile settings come in XML and PS1 (PowerShell script) flavors, and you may need one or both files in order to roll the settings around to your workforce. The following document from Microsoft outlines this in greater detail, with specific steps to follow: `https://learn.microsoft.com/en-us/windows-server/ remote/remote-access/tutorial-aovpn-deploy-configure-client`.

Once you have created your configuration files, you then face the task of pushing that configuration out to the clients. You ideally need to have a **mobile device management (MDM)** solution of some kind to roll the settings out to your workforce. While many technologies in the wild could be considered MDMs, the two that Microsoft is focused on are Microsoft Configuration Manager and Microsoft Intune.

If you have MCM on-premises, great! You can easily configure and roll out PowerShell-based configuration settings to your client computers and enable them for AOVPN.

Perhaps you don't have MCM, but you are cloud-focused, and you have all your computers tapped into Intune. Wonderful! You could alternatively use Intune to roll out those AOVPN settings via XML configuration. One of the benefits of taking the Intune route is that Intune can manage non-domain-joined computers, so you could theoretically include users' home and personal computers in your Intune-managed infrastructure and set them up to connect.

Microsoft Configuration Manager and Intune are great, but not everybody is running them. There is a third option for rolling out AOVPN settings via PowerShell scripting. While this is *plan B* from Microsoft (they would really prefer you to roll out AOVPN via an MDM solution), I'm afraid that PowerShell will be the reality for many SMB customers who want to utilize AOVPN. The biggest downside to using PowerShell to put AOVPN settings in place is that PowerShell needs to be run in elevated mode, meaning that it's difficult to automate because the logged-on user (for whom you need to establish the VPN connection) needs to be a local administrator for the script to run properly.

I am hopefully and anxiously waiting for the day that they announce a traditional Group Policy template for rolling out AOVPN settings, but so far, there is no word on whether or not that will ever be an option. Everyone has Group Policy; not everyone has MDM. You will read in a few moments that the rollout of Microsoft DirectAccess connectivity settings (an alternative to AOVPN) is done via Group Policy, which is incredibly easy to understand and manage. As far as I'm concerned, at the time of writing, DirectAccess holds a major advantage over AOVPN in the way that it handles the client-side rollout of settings. But, make sure you check out the Microsoft docs online to find the latest information on this topic, as AOVPN is being continuously improved, and there will likely be some changes coming to this area of the technology.

AOVPN server components

Now that we understand what is needed on the client side to make AOVPN work, what parts and pieces are necessary on the server/infrastructure side in order to allow these connections to happen? Interestingly, the *Always On* component of AOVPN has nothing to do with server infrastructure; the Always On part is handled completely on the client side. Therefore, all we need to do on the server side is make sure that we can receive incoming VPN connections. If you currently have a workforce that is making successful VPN connections, then there is a good chance that you already have the server infrastructure necessary for bringing AOVPN into your environment.

Remote Access server

Obviously, you need a VPN server to host VPN connections, right? Well, not so obviously. As we have already discussed, the Windows Server role that hosts VPN, AOVPN, and DirectAccess connections is called the **Remote Access** role, but you can actually get AOVPN working without Windows Server as your Remote Access server. Since the *Always On* part is client-side functionality, this enables VPN server-side infrastructures to be hosted by third-party vendors and firewalls. Even though that is technically accurate, it's not really what Microsoft expects, nor is it what I find in the field. In reality, those interested in using Microsoft AOVPN often use Microsoft Windows Server to host the Remote Access role, which will be the inbound system that our remote clients connect to.

A lot of people automatically assume that AOVPN is married to Windows Server 2022 or 2025 because it is a fairly new technology, but that is actually not the case at all. You can host your VPN infrastructure (the Remote Access role) on Server 2025, Server 2022, Server 2019, Server 2016, or even Server 2012 R2. It works the same on the backend, giving clients a place to tap into with their VPN connections.

The setup of your Remote Access server to handle AOVPN connections is really the same process that we already took in the last section of this chapter, configuring RRAS VPN for manual client VPN connections. These same VPN protocols are the ones that your AOVPN clients will be tapping into. The two VPN protocols most utilized by AOVPN are going to be IKEv2 and SSTP. IKEv2 is required for a successful device tunnel, but if you don't need device tunnels and are focused on more flexible user tunnels for AOVPN, then you can get away with running SSTP as a fallback tunneling method, which connects successfully from almost any internet connection.

Certification authority (CA)

Machine certificates, user certificates, SSL certificates... Oh, my! Clearly, you need to be familiar with working with and deploying certificates to make use of AOVPN. This is becoming more and more common with newer, well-secured technologies of any flavor. The major requirement here is that you will need to have PKI inside your environment and at least one Windows CA server to issue the necessary certificates. The following is a list of the places in which certificates could be used by an AOVPN infrastructure:

- **User certificates:** These are the certificates issued to your VPN users from an internal CA, used for authentication of the user tunnel.
- **Machine certificates:** These are certificates issued to your workstations (mostly laptops) from an internal CA, used for authentication of the device tunnel.
- **SSL certificates:** These are installed on your Remote Access server to validate the incoming traffic for SSTP VPN connections.
- **VPN and NPS machine certificates:** Your Remote Access server, as well as your NPS servers, which we will talk about in just a minute, require machine certificates issued by your internal CA.

Network Policy Server (NPS)

NPS is basically the authentication decision maker for VPN connections. When a VPN connection request comes in, the Remote Access server hands that authentication request over to an NPS server to validate who that user is, and also to verify that the user has permissions to log in via the VPN.

Most commonly, when working with Microsoft VPN connections, we configure NPS so that it allows only users who are part of a certain Active Directory security group. For example, if you create a group called VPN Users and then point NPS to that group, it will only allow users who you have placed inside that group to make successful VPN connections.

NPS is another Windows Server role that can be hosted on its own system or spread across multiple servers for redundancy. As with the Remote Access role, there is no Server 2025 requirement for NPS. You could easily deploy it on previous versions of Windows Server just as well.

Keep in mind that you should *not* install NPS onto the same server where you are running Remote Access. You need to spin up a second server for the purposes of NPS.

DirectAccess

Throughout our discussion about AOVPN, I mentioned Microsoft **DirectAccess (DA)** a couple of times. DA is another form of automatic VPN-like connectivity, but it takes a different approach compared to AOVPN. Where AOVPN simply uses expected, well-known VPN protocols and does some crafty magic to automatically launch those otherwise traditional VPN tunnels, DA tunnels are quite proprietary. Tunnels are protected by IPsec and are essentially impenetrable and unable to be impersonated. I find that security teams love the protection and complexity surrounding DA tunnels because they are a connection platform that attackers have no idea how to tamper with or how to replicate.

My personal experience in the Microsoft Remote Access space is that the number of DA customers outweighs the number of AOVPN customers as of right now. Indeed, I would say that DA is the most common reason that administrators deploy the Remote Access role on a Windows Server instance. As stated, the easiest way to think about DA is to think of it as an automatic VPN. Similar to a VPN, its purpose is to connect users' computers to a corporate network when they are outside the office. Different from a VPN, however, is the method that employees use to make this connection possible. DA is not a piece of software; it is a series of components that are already baked into the Windows operating system, working in tandem to provide completely seamless access to the user. What do I mean by **seamless**? In the same way that AOVPN connects without user interaction, there is nothing the user needs to do to make DA connect. It does that all by itself. As soon as a mobile computer receives an internet connection, whether that connection is home Wi-Fi, public internet at a coffee shop, or a cell phone hotspot connection, DA tunnels automatically build themselves using whatever internet connection is available, without any user input.

There is a bit of "fortunately/unfortunately" mixed in with recent news on DA. Fortunately, DA is alive and well in Windows Server 2025. Unfortunately, in June 2024, Microsoft added DA to the official list of deprecated Windows Server features. Deprecated does not equal dead, but it does mean that Microsoft has no plans to improve it in the future or add new features to it. It is possible that when Windows Server 2028 (?) is released, DA could be missing. Or...maybe not. Time will tell. As of this writing, DA continues to be a valid connectivity technology, and an impressive one at that. Given this truth, we are certainly going to discuss the ins and outs of DA so that you have a well-rounded understanding of what Microsoft offers in the remote access space.

Whether using AOVPN or DA, when your computer connects automatically, it saves you time and money. Time is saved because the user no longer has to launch a VPN connection. Money is saved because time equals money, but also because having an *always-on* connection means that patching, security policies, and the management of those remote computers always happen, even when the user is working remotely. You no longer have to wait for users to get back into the office or for them to choose to launch their manual VPN connection in order to push new settings and policies down to their computers; it all happens wherever they are, as long as they have internet access. Clearly, with the advent of two different remote access technologies that are both focused on automatic connectivity for remote users, Microsoft is clearing the way for a more productive workforce. The terms *user-friendly* and *VPN* have never gone hand-in-hand before, but in the latest versions of the Windows operating systems, that is exactly the goal.

DA has actually been around since the release of Windows Server 2008 R2, and yet I regularly bump into IT people who have never heard of it. In the early days, it was quite difficult to deploy and came with a lot of awkward requirements, but much has changed since inception, and DA is now easier than ever to deploy and more beneficial than ever to have running in your environment.

The truth about DA and IPv6

One of the awkward requirements I mentioned *used* to be the need for IPv6 inside your network. With the first version of DA, this was an unfortunate requirement. I say unfortunate because, even today, almost nobody runs IPv6 inside their corporate networks, let alone years ago when this technology was released—a lot of admins didn't even understand what IPv6 was. Fortunately, the requirement for IPv6 inside your networks is no more. I repeat, just in case anybody wasn't paying attention or is reading old, outdated TechNet documents—*you do not need IPv6 to use DA!* I have seen too many cases where DA was considered by a company, but the project was tossed aside because reading something on TechNet made them believe that IPv6 was a requirement, and they discarded DA as something that wouldn't work. You absolutely do not have to be running IPv6 in your network to make DA function, but it is important to understand how DA uses IPv6 because you will start to encounter traces of it once your deployment gets underway.

When I am sitting at home, working on my company laptop, DA connects me to the corporate network. My internal network at work has absolutely no IPv6 running inside of it; we are a completely IPv4 network. This is true for most companies today. However, when I open Command Prompt and ping one of my servers from my DA laptop, this is what I see—apologies for the sanitized output of the screenshot:

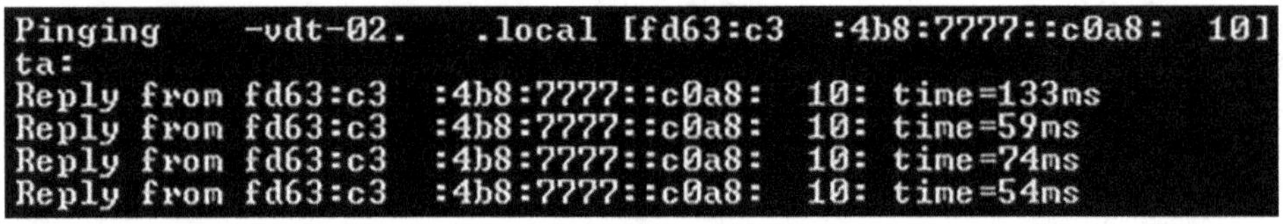

```
Pinging      -vdt-02.    .local [fd63:c3   :4b8:7777::c0a8:   10]
ta:
Reply from fd63:c3   :4b8:7777::c0a8:   10: time=133ms
Reply from fd63:c3   :4b8:7777::c0a8:   10: time=59ms
Reply from fd63:c3   :4b8:7777::c0a8:   10: time=74ms
Reply from fd63:c3   :4b8:7777::c0a8:   10: time=54ms
```

Figure 9.8: Pinging an internal server from a DA laptop

What in the world is that? Looks like IPv6 to me. This is where IPv6 comes into play with DA. All of the traffic that moves over the internet part of the connection, between my laptop and the DA server that is sitting in my datacenter, is IPv6 traffic. My internal network is IPv4, and my DA server only has IPv4 addresses on it, yet my DA tunnel is carrying my traffic using IPv6. This is the core of how DA works and cannot be changed. Your DA laptop sends IPsec-encrypted IPv6 packets over the internet to the DA server, and when the DA server receives those packets, it has the capability to spin them down into IPv4 in order to send them to the destination server inside the corporate network. For example, when I open Outlook and it tries to connect to my Exchange server, my Outlook packets flow over the DA tunnel as IPv6. Once these packets hit my DA server, that DA server reaches out to internal DNS to figure out whether my Exchange server is IPv4 or IPv6.

If you are actually running IPv6 inside the network and the Exchange server is available via IPv6, the DA server will simply send the IPv6 packets along to the Exchange server. Connection complete! If, on the other hand, you are running IPv4 inside your network, the DA server will only see a single A host record in DNS, meaning that the Exchange server is IPv4-only. The DA server will then manipulate the IPv6 packet, converting it into IPv4, and then send it on its way to the Exchange server. The two technologies that handle this manipulation of packets are DNS64 and NAT64, which you have probably seen in some of the documentation if you have read anything about DA online.

The purposes of these technologies are to change the incoming IPv6 packet stream into IPv4 for networks where it is required, which is pretty much every network at the moment, and spin the return traffic from IPv4 back up into IPv6 so that it can make its way back to the DA client computer over the IPv6-based IPsec tunnel that is connecting the DA client to the DA server over the internet.

It is important to understand that DA uses IPv6 in this capacity because any security policies that you might have in place that squash IPv6 on the client computers by default will stop DA from working properly in your environment. You will have to reverse these policies to allow the clients to push out IPv6 packets and get their traffic across the internet. However, it is also very important to understand that you do *not* need any semblance of IPv6 running *inside* the corporate network to make this work, as the DA server can spin all of the traffic down into IPv4 before it hits that internal network, and most DA implementations that are active today run in exactly this fashion.

Prerequisites for DA

DA has a lot of moving parts, and there are many different ways in which you can set it up. However, not all of these ways are good ideas. So, in this section, we are going to discuss some of the big decisions that you will have to make when designing your own DA environment.

Domain-joined

The first big requirement is that the systems involved with DA need to be domain-joined. Your DA server, or servers, all need to be joined to your domain, and all of the client computers that you want to be DA-connected need to be joined to a domain as well. Domain membership is required for authentication purposes, and also because the DA client settings that need to be applied to mobile computers come down to these computers via Group Policy. You can see here one reason why Microsoft is setting future sights more so on AOVPN than DA: flexibility in client computers. AOVPN can work on non-domain-joined computers, yet if you want to utilize AOVPN device tunnels (and you would want to), then the domain-join requirement remains.

I always like to point out this requirement early in the planning process, because it means that users who purchase their own laptops at a retail location are typically not going to be able to utilize DA—unless you are somehow okay with adding home computers to your domain—and so DA is really a technology that is designed for managing and connecting corporate assets that you can join to the domain. It is also important to understand this requirement from a security perspective since your DA server or servers will typically be facing the edge of your network. It is common for the external NIC on a DA server to sit inside a DMZ, but they also have to be domain-joined, which may not be something you are used to doing with systems in a perimeter network.

Supported client operating systems

Not all Windows client operating systems contain the components that are necessary to make a DA connection work. Enterprise does, which covers the majority of larger businesses that own Microsoft operating systems, but that certainly does not include everyone. I still see many small businesses using professional or even home SKUs on their client machines, and these versions do not include DA components. The following is a list of the operating systems that do support DA. During your planning, you will need to make sure that your mobile computers are running one of these:

- Windows 11 Enterprise
- Windows 10 Enterprise
- Windows 10 Education

- Windows 8.0 or 8.1 Enterprise
- Windows 7 Enterprise
- Windows 7 Ultimate

(I left these old operating systems listed for accuracy, but *please* don't allow your business to run computers this old!)

DirectAccess servers: one or two NICs?

One big question that needs to be answered even prior to installing the Remote Access role on your new server is, how many NICs are needed on this server? There are two supported methods for implementing DA.

Single NIC mode

Your DA server can be installed with only a single NIC. In this case, you would typically plug that network connection directly into your internal network so that it has access to all of the internal resources that the client computers are going to need to contact during the user's DA sessions. In order to get traffic from the internet to your DA server, you would need to establish a NAT from a public IP address to whatever internal IP address you have assigned to the DA server.

Many network security administrators do not like this method because it means creating a NAT that brings traffic straight into the corporate network without flowing through any kind of DMZ.

Dual NICs

Here, we have two network cards in the DA server. The internal NIC typically gets plugged right into the corporate network, and the external NIC's physical placement can vary depending on the organization. We will discuss the pros and cons of where to place the external NIC immediately after this section of the chapter. Edge mode with two NICs is the way that DA works best. As you may recall from earlier in the book, implementing a Windows Server instance with multiple NICs means that you will be multihoming this server, and you will need to set up network settings accordingly. With a Remote Access server, your external NIC is always the one that receives the default gateway settings, so you need to make sure you follow this rule and *do not configure a default gateway on the internal NIC*. On the other hand, you do want to configure DNS server addresses into the internal NIC properties, but you do *not* want to configure DNS servers for the external NIC. Since this server is multihomed, you will likely need to create some route statements to add your corporate subnets into the Windows routing table of this server before it can successfully send and receive traffic.

The only networks that would not need to accommodate adding static routes would be small networks, where all of your internal devices are on a single subnet. If this is the case, then you do not need to input static routes. But most corporate networks span multiple subnets, and in this case, you should refer back to *Chapter 8, Networking with Windows Server 2025*, where we discussed multihoming and how to build out those route statements.

More than two NICs

Nope, don't go there. If you are familiar with configuring routers or firewalls, you know that you have the potential to install many different NICs on a server and plug them all into different subnets. While there are many reasons why splitting up network access like this on a Remote Access server might be beneficial, it won't work how you want it to. The DA configuration itself is only capable of managing two different network interfaces.

As you can see in *Figure 9.9*, in the course of the setup wizards, you will have to define one NIC as external and the other as internal. Any more NICs that exist in that server will not be used by DA, unfortunately.

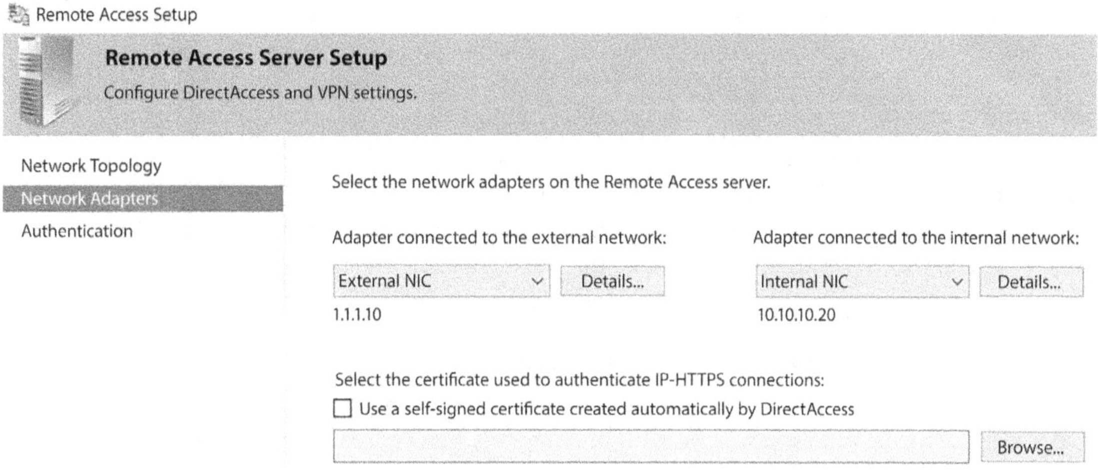

Figure 9.9: Defining NICs during DA configuration

To NAT or not to NAT?

Now that you have decided to roll with two NICs in your DA server, where do we plug in the external NIC? There are two common places that this external network interface can be connected to, but depending on which you choose, the outcome of your DA environment can be vastly different. Before we talk about the actual placement of the NIC, I would like to define a couple of protocols that are important to understand, because they pertain very much to answering this question about NIC placement. When your DA laptop makes a connection to the DA server, it will do so using one of the three IPv6 transition tunneling protocols. These protocols are **6to4**, **Teredo**, and **IP-HTTPS**. When the DA client connects its DA tunnels, it will automatically choose which of these protocols is best to use, depending on the user's current internet connection.

All three protocols perform the same function for a DA connection: their job is to take the IPv6 packet stream coming out of the laptop and encapsulate it inside IPv4 so that the traffic can make its way successfully across the IPv4 internet. When the packets get to the DA server, they are decapped so that the DA server can process these IPv6 packets.

6to4

DA clients will only attempt to connect using 6to4 when a remote laptop has a truly public internet IP address. This hardly ever happens these days, with the shortage of available internet IPv4 addresses, and so 6to4 is typically not used by any DA client computers. In fact, it can present its own set of challenges when users are connecting with cell phone cards in their laptops, and so it is common practice to disable the 6to4 adapter on client computers as a DA best-practice setting.

Teredo

When DA clients are connected to the internet using a private IP address, such as behind a home router or a public Wi-Fi router, they will attempt to connect using the Teredo protocol. Teredo uses a UDP stream to encapsulate DA packets, and so, as long as the user's internet connection allows outbound UDP 3544, Teredo will generally connect and is the transition protocol of choice for that DA connection.

IP-HTTPS

If Teredo fails to connect, such as in the case where a user is sitting in a network that blocks outbound UDP, then the DA connection will fall back to using IP-HTTPS, pronounced *IP over HTTPS*. This protocol encapsulates the IPv6 packets inside IPv4 headers, but then wraps them up inside an HTTP header and encrypts them with TLS/SSL, before sending the packet out over the internet. This effectively makes the DA connection an SSL stream, just like when you browse an HTTPS website.

Installing on the true edge — on the internet

When you plug your DA server's external NIC directly into the internet, you grant yourself the ability to put truly public IP addresses on that NIC. In doing this, you enable all three of the preceding transition tunneling protocols, so that DA client computers can choose between them for the best form of connectivity. When installing via the true edge method, you would put not only one but two public IP addresses on that external NIC. Make sure that the public IP addresses are consecutive, as this is a requirement for Teredo. When your DA server has two consecutive public IP addresses assigned to the external NIC, it will enable the Teredo protocol to be available for connections.

This NIC does not necessarily have to be plugged directly into the internet for this to work. Depending on your firewall capabilities, you might have the option to establish a *bridged DMZ* where no NAT is taking place. You need to check with your firewall vendor to find out whether or not that is an option for your organization. In this scenario, you are still able to configure truly public IP addresses on the external NIC of the server, but the traffic flows through a firewall first, to better protect and manage that traffic.

Installing behind a NAT

It is much more common for the networking team to want to place the external NIC of your DA server behind a firewall, inside a DMZ. This typically means creating a NAT to bring this traffic into the server. While this is entirely possible and better protects the DA server itself from the internet, it does come with a big downside. When you install a DA server behind a NAT, Teredo no longer works. In fact, the DA configuration wizards will recognize when you have a private IP address listed on the external NIC and will not even enable Teredo.

When Teredo is not available, all your DirectAccess clients will connect using IP-HTTPS. So why does it even matter if Teredo is unavailable? Because it is a more efficient protocol than IP-HTTPS. When Teredo tunnels packets, it simply encapsulates IPv6 inside IPv4. The DA traffic stream is already and always IPsec-encrypted, so there is no need for the Teredo tunnel to do any additional encryption. On the other hand, when IP-HTTPS tunnels packets, it takes the already-encrypted IPsec traffic stream and encrypts it a second time using TLS. This means all of the packets that come and go are subject to double encryption, which increases processing and CPU cycles and makes for a slower connection. It also creates additional hardware load on the DirectAccess server, because it is handling twice the amount of encryption processing.

This is a particularly apparent problem when you are running Windows 7 on client computers, as double encryption processing will cause a noticeably slower connection for users. DA still works fine, but if you sit a Teredo-connected laptop next to an IP-HTTPS-connected laptop, you will notice the speed difference between the two.

Thankfully, in Windows 8 and higher, there have been some countermeasures added to help with this speed discrepancy. These newer client operating systems are now smart enough that they can negotiate the SSL part of the IP-HTTPS tunnel by using the NULL encryption algorithm, meaning that IP-HTTPS doesn't do a second encryption, and IP-HTTPS performance is now essentially on par with Teredo.

However, this only works for the newer client operating systems (Windows 7 will always double-encrypt with IP-HTTPS), and it still doesn't work in some cases. For example, when you enable your DA server to also provide VPN connectivity, or if you choose to employ a **one-time password** (OTP) system alongside DA, then the NULL algorithm will be disabled because it is a security risk in these situations, and so even your Windows 8, 10, and 11 computers will perform double encryption when they connect via IP-HTTPS. You can see where it would be beneficial to have Teredo enabled and available so that any computers that can connect via Teredo will do so.

To summarize, you can certainly install your DA server's external NIC behind a NAT, but be aware that all DA client computers will connect using the IP-HTTPS protocol, and it is important to understand the potential side effects of implementing it in this way.

Network location server

This major component in a DA infrastructure is something that does not even exist on the DA server itself, or at least it shouldn't if you are setting things up properly. The **network location server** (NLS) is simply a website that runs inside the corporate network. This website does not need to be available for access over the internet; in fact, it should not be.

The NLS is used as part of the inside/outside detection mechanism on DA client computers, similar to the way that trusted network detection works for AOVPN. Every time a DA client gets a network connection, it starts looking for the NLS website. If it can see the site, then it knows that you are inside the corporate network, and DA is not required, so it turns itself off. However, if your NLS website cannot be contacted, it means you are outside the corporate network, and DA components will start turning themselves on.

This prerequisite is easily met; all you need to do is spin up a VM and install IIS on it to host this new website, or you can even add a new website to an existing web server in your network. There are only two things to watch out for when setting up your NLS website. The first is that it must be an HTTPS site, and so it requires an SSL certificate. We will discuss the certificates used in DA, including this one, in the next section of this chapter. In addition to making sure that this website is accessible via HTTPS, you must also make sure that the DNS name you are using to contact this website is unique. You want to do this because, whatever name you choose for the NLS website, that name will not be resolvable when client computers are outside the corporate network. This is by design because you obviously don't want your DA clients to be able to successfully contact the NLS website when they are working remotely, as that would then disable their DA connection.

The reason I bring up the unique DNS name is that I often see new DA admins utilizing an existing internal website as their NLS website. For example, if you have `https://intranet` running as a Share-Point site, you could simply use this in the DA config as the NLS server definition. However, once you set it up this way, you will quickly realize that nobody who is working remotely can access the `https://intranet` website. This is by design because the DA environment now considers your intranet website to be the NLS server, and you cannot resolve it while you are mobile. The solution to this problem? Make sure that you choose a new DNS name to use for this NLS website. Something like `https://nls.contoso.local` is appropriate.

The most important part about the NLS that I want to stress is that you should absolutely implement this website on a server in your network that is *not* the DA server itself. When you are running through the DA configuration wizards, you will see on the screen where we define NLS that it is recommended to deploy it on a remote web server, but it also gives you the option to self-host the NLS website right on the DA server itself. Don't do it! There are many things that can go wrong when you co-host NLS on the DA server. Running the NLS on your DA server also limits your DA potential in the future, because some of the advanced DA configurations require you to remove the NLS from the DA server anyway, so you might as well do it correctly the first time you set it up. Changing your NLS website after you are running DA in production can be very tricky, and often goes sideways. I have helped numerous companies move their NLS website after realizing that they cannot co-host NLS on the DA server if and when they want to add a second DA server for growth or redundancy. The following is a screenshot of the section in the DA configuration wizard where you choose the location of NLS. Make sure you stick with the top box!

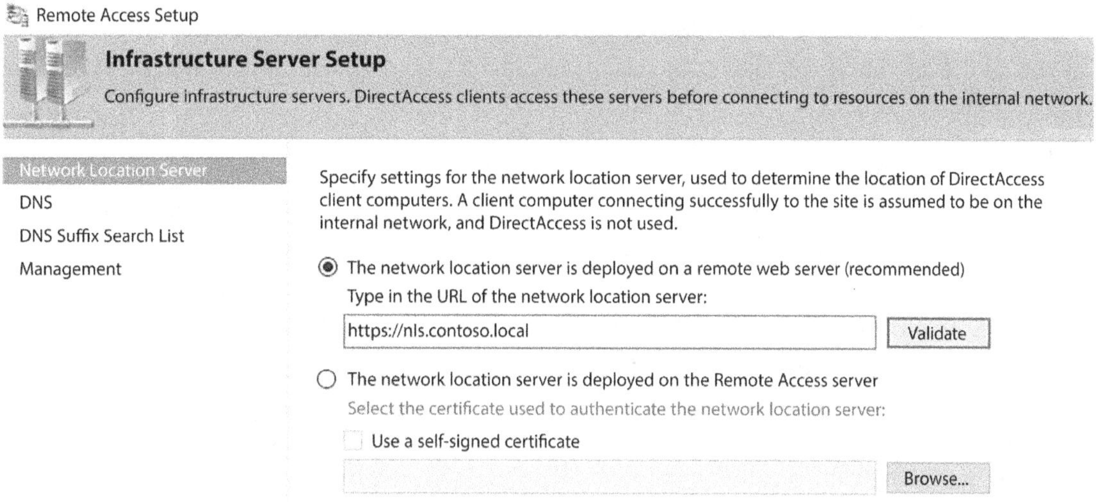

Remote Access Setup

Infrastructure Server Setup

Configure infrastructure servers. DirectAccess clients access these servers before connecting to resources on the internal network.

Network Location Server

DNS

DNS Suffix Search List

Management

Specify settings for the network location server, used to determine the location of DirectAccess client computers. A client computer connecting successfully to the site is assumed to be on the internal network, and DirectAccess is not used.

◉ The network location server is deployed on a remote web server (recommended)
Type in the URL of the network location server:

| https://nls.contoso.local | Validate |

○ The network location server is deployed on the Remote Access server
Select the certificate used to authenticate the network location server:

☐ Use a self-signed certificate

| | Browse... |

Figure 9.10: Defining the NLS

Certificates used with DirectAccess

Aside from reading and misunderstanding how DA uses IPv6, here is the next biggest "turn-off" for administrators who are interested in giving DA a try. Once you start to read about how DA works, you will quickly come to realize that certificates are required in a few different places. While VPNs generally also require the use of certificates, it is admittedly difficult to distinguish which certificates need to go where when you are wading through Microsoft DirectAccess documentation, so this section clears up any confusion that exists about DA certificates. It really is not very complicated, once you know what does and does not need to be done.

The core prerequisite is that you have a Windows CA server somewhere in your network. The stature of your PKI implementation is not that important to DA. We simply need the ability to issue certificates to our DA server and clients. There are only three places where certificates are used in DA, and two of them are SSL certificates.

SSL certificate on the NLS web server

As mentioned previously, your NLS website needs to be running HTTPS. This means that you will require an SSL certificate to be installed on the server that is hosting your NLS website. Assuming that you have an internal CA server, this certificate can be easily acquired from that internal CA, so there are no costs associated with this certificate. You do not need to purchase one from a public CA, because this certificate is only going to be accessed and verified from your domain-joined machines, the DA clients. Since domain-joined computers automatically trust the CA servers in your network, this certificate can simply be issued from your internal CA, and it will do exactly what we need it to do for the purposes of DA.

SSL certificate on the DirectAccess server

An SSL certificate is also required to be installed on the DA server itself, but this one *should* be purchased from your public CA. This certificate will be used to validate IP-HTTPS traffic streams coming in from the client computers because that is SSL traffic, and so we need an SSL certificate to validate it. Since the IP-HTTPS listener is facing the public internet, it is definitely recommended that you use a certificate from a public CA, rather than trying to use a certificate from your internal PKI.

If your company already has a wildcard SSL certificate, use it here to save costs!

Machine certificates on the DA server and all DA clients

The last and most complicated part of the DA certificate puzzle is machine certificates. Once you know what is required, though, it's really not hard at all. We simply require that a computer or machine certificate be installed on the DA server, as well as each of the DA client machines. This machine certificate is used as part of the authentication process for IPsec tunnels. It is a big part of the way in which DA verifies that you really are who you say you are when your computer makes that DA connection happen.

The best way to go about issuing these machine certificates is to log in to your CA server and create a new certificate template that is duplicated from the built-in **Computer** template. When setting up your new certificate template, just make sure that it meets the following criteria:

- The **common name** (subject) of the certificate should match the FQDN of the computer.
- The **subject alternative name** (**SAN**) of the certificate should equal the DNS name of the computer.
- The certificate should serve the intended purposes (enhanced key usage) of both client authentication and server authentication.

I should note here, though I don't really want to, that issuing these certificates is not absolutely necessary to make DA work. If you are running Windows 8 or higher on the client side, then it is possible to get DA working without machine certificates. It is possible for client computers running without machine certificates to instead utilize something called **Kerberos Proxy** for their computer authentication when the IPsec tunnels are being built, but I highly recommend sticking with certificates. Using certificates as part of the authentication process makes the connection more stable and more secure. Additionally, as with the placement of NLS, if you want to perform any advanced functions with DA, such as load balancing or multisite, or even if you simply want to make some Windows 7 computers connect through DA, then you will be required to issue certificates anyway. So, stick with best practices and issue these certificates before you even get started with testing DA.

Do not use the Getting Started Wizard (GSW)!

After making the necessary design decisions and implementing the prerequisites we have talked about so far, it is finally time to install the Remote Access role on your new DA server! After you have finished installing the role, similar to many roles in Windows Server 2025, you will be shown a message informing you that additional configuration is required to use this role. If you follow the yellow exclamation mark inside Server Manager, the only option that you are presented with is **Open the Getting Started Wizard**. Ugh! This is *not* what you want to click on:

⚠ Post-deployment Configuration

Configuration required for DirectAccess and VPN
(RAS) at RA1
Open the Getting Started Wizard

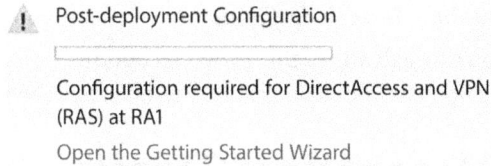

Figure 9.11: Do not click on this!

Don't do it!

Your home for DA configurations is the **Remote Access Management Console**, which is available from inside the **Tools** menu of Server Manager now that our Remote Access role has been installed. Go ahead and launch that, and now we are presented with a choice:

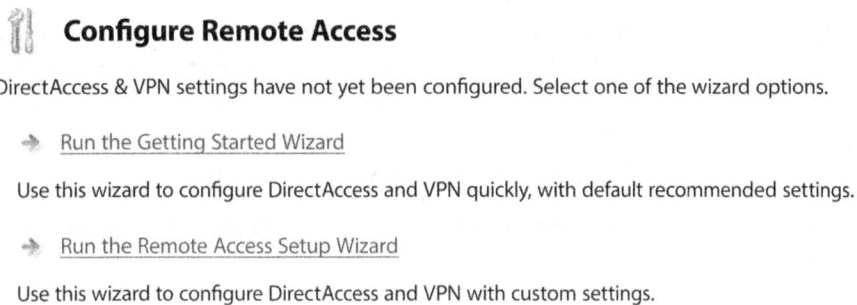

🔧 Configure Remote Access

DirectAccess & VPN settings have not yet been configured. Select one of the wizard options.

➡ Run the Getting Started Wizard

Use this wizard to configure DirectAccess and VPN quickly, with default recommended settings.

➡ Run the Remote Access Setup Wizard

Use this wizard to configure DirectAccess and VPN with custom settings.

Figure 9.12: Configuring Remote Access

Do *not* click on **Run the Getting Started Wizard**! The GSW is a shortcut method for implementing DA, designed only for getting DA up and running as quickly as possible, perhaps for a quick proof of concept. Under no circumstances should you trust the GSW for your production DA environment, because in an effort to make configuration quick and easy, many configuration decisions are made for you that are not best practices.

You want to make sure you click on **Run the Remote Access Setup Wizard** when you are first prompted in the console; this will invoke the full set of DA configuration screens. The DA setup consists of a series of four steps, each containing a handful of screens that you will navigate through to choose your appropriate configuration options. There is a good amount of detail on these screens as to what each one of them means and what your options are, so don't be afraid to dive in and set this up in the proper way. If you have already configured DA and used the **Getting Started Wizard**, DA may be working for you, but it will not be running as efficiently or securely as it could be. The following is a quick list of the reasons why the GSW is not in your best interests. These are the things that it does that go directly against a best-practice DA installation, with accompanying *peanut gallery* commentary from yours truly:

- GSW co-hosts the NLS website on the DA server—*bad*
- GSW applies the DA client GPO settings to all domain computers—*this is a terrible idea*
- GSW utilizes self-signed certificates—*a Security 101 level no-no*

- GSW automatically disables Teredo—*inefficient*
- GSW does not walk you through any of the advanced options for DA, probably because the way that it sets everything up invalidates your ability to even use the advanced functions—*lame*

Remote Access Management Console

You are well on your way to giving users remote access capabilities on this new server. As with many networking devices, once you have established all of your configurations on a Remote Access server, it is pretty common for admins to walk away and let it run. There is no need for a lot of ongoing maintenance or changes to that configuration once you have it running well. However, the **Remote Access Management Console (RAMC)** in Windows Server 2025 is useful not only for the configuration of remote access parts and pieces but for monitoring and reporting as well.

When working with DA, this is your home for pretty much everything: configuration, management, monitoring, and troubleshooting. On the VPN/AOVPN side of the Remote Access toolset, you will be making many of the VPN configuration decisions inside RRAS, but the RAMC is the place to go when checking over server-side monitoring, client-connection monitoring, and reporting statistics. Whether you use DA, VPN, or a combination of the two, the RAMC is a tool you need to be comfortable with.

Let's take a look inside this console so that you are familiar with the different screens you will be interacting with:

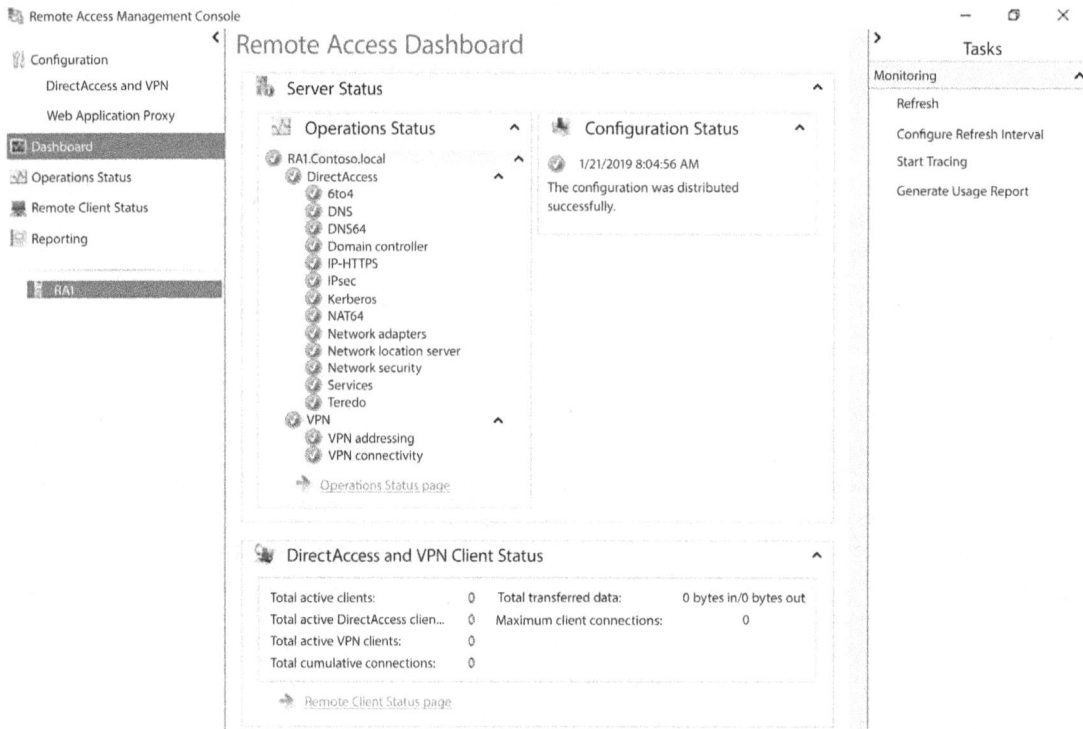

Figure 9.13: Remote Access Dashboard

Configuration

The **Configuration** screen is pretty self-explanatory; this is where you create your initial remote access configuration and where you update any settings in the future. As you can see in *Figure 9.13*, you can configure **DirectAccess and VPN**, and even **Web Application Proxy (WAP)**, right from **Remote Access Management Console**.

Do not follow my lead with this screenshot. I have installed the DA/VPN portion of the Remote Access role alongside the WAP portion of the same role, but it is not recommended to run both DA/VPN and WAP together on the same server. I did it simply for the purpose of creating screenshots in my test lab.

There is not a lot to configure as far as the VPN goes; you really only have one screen of options where you define what kinds of IP addresses are handed down to the VPN clients connecting in, and how to handle VPN authentication. It is not immediately obvious where this screen is, so I wanted to point it out. Inside the **DirectAccess and VPN** configuration section, if you click on **Edit...** under **Step 2**, this will launch the **Step 2** mini-wizard. The last screen in this mini-wizard is called **VPN Configuration**. This is the screen where you configure these IP addresses and authentication settings for your VPN connections. The remainder of your VPN configuration duties will fall within the traditional VPN configuration console, called RRAS. However, everything about DA connections is configured right from inside **Remote Access Management Console** and those four mini-wizards:

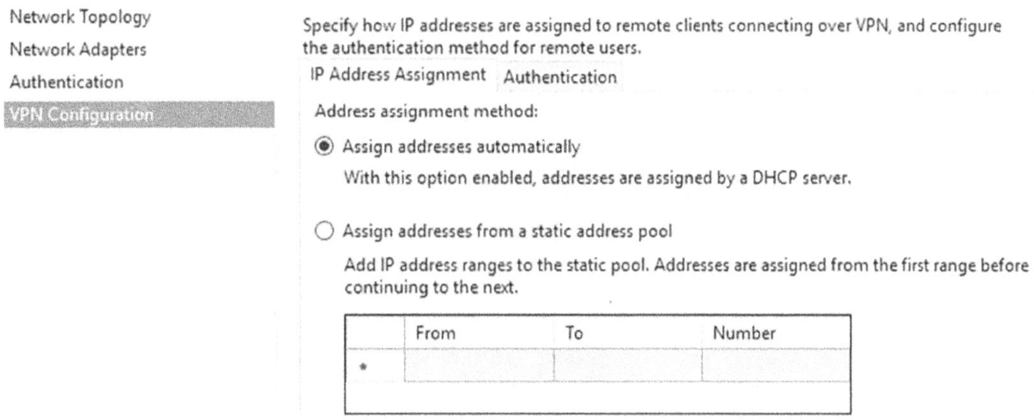

Network Topology

Network Adapters

Authentication

VPN Configuration

Specify how IP addresses are assigned to remote clients connecting over VPN, and configure the authentication method for remote users.

IP Address Assignment   Authentication

Address assignment method:

◉ Assign addresses automatically

With this option enabled, addresses are assigned by a DHCP server.

○ Assign addresses from a static address pool

Add IP address ranges to the static pool. Addresses are assigned from the first range before continuing to the next.

	From	To	Number
*			

Figure 9.14: VPN configuration settings inside RAMC

Dashboard

Remote Access Dashboard gives you a 30,000-foot view of the Remote Access server status. You can view a quick status of the components running on the server, whether or not the latest configuration changes have been rolled out, and some summary numbers near the bottom about how many DA and VPN connections are ongoing:

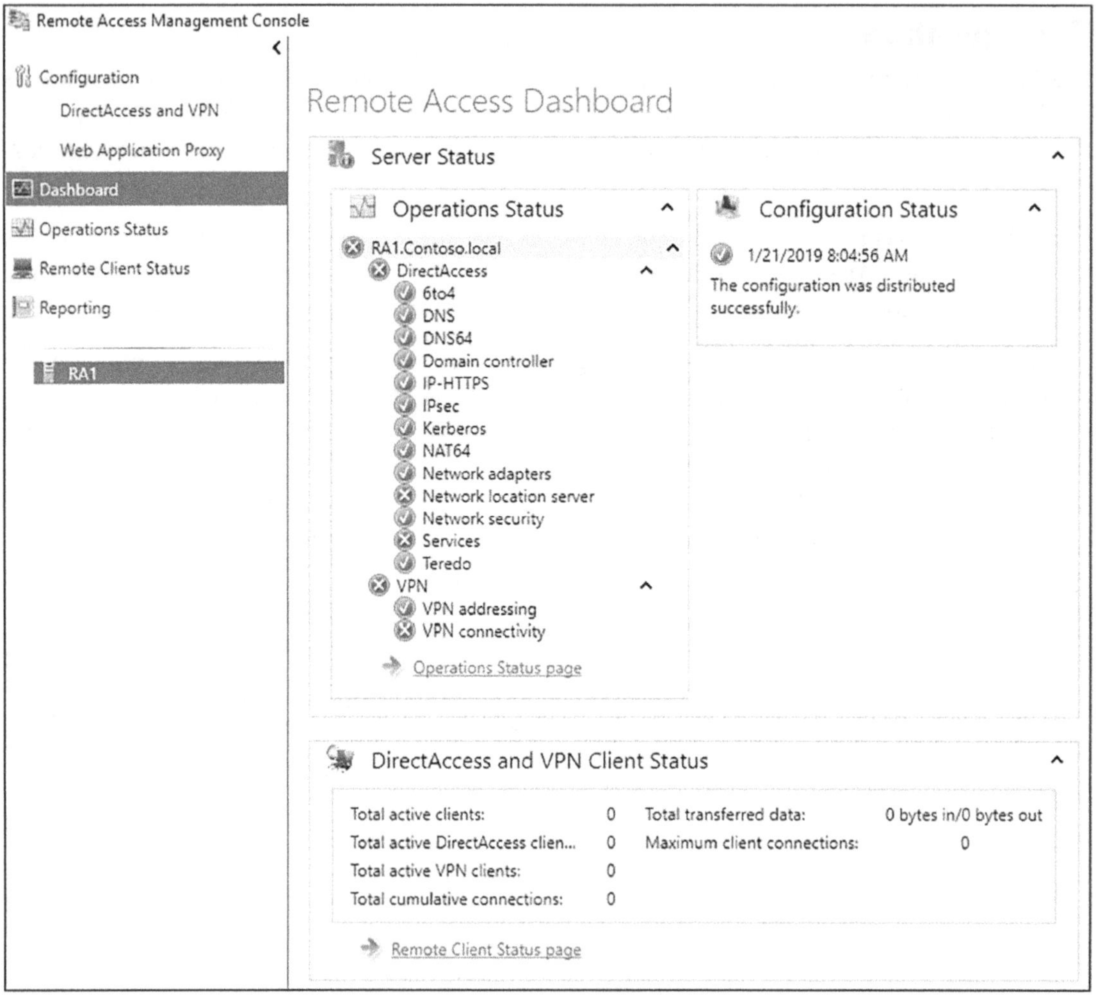

Figure 9.15: Summary stats on Remote Access Dashboard

Operations Status

If you want to drill down further into what is happening on the server side of the connections, that is what the **Operations Status** page is all about. Here, you can see more details on each of the components that are running under the hood to make your DA and VPN connections happen. If any of them have an issue, you can click on the specific component to get a little more information. For example, as a test, I have turned off the NLS web server in my lab network, and I can see on the **Operations Status** page that the NLS is flagged with an error. Clicking on that component gives me additional information about what is happening so that I can resolve it:

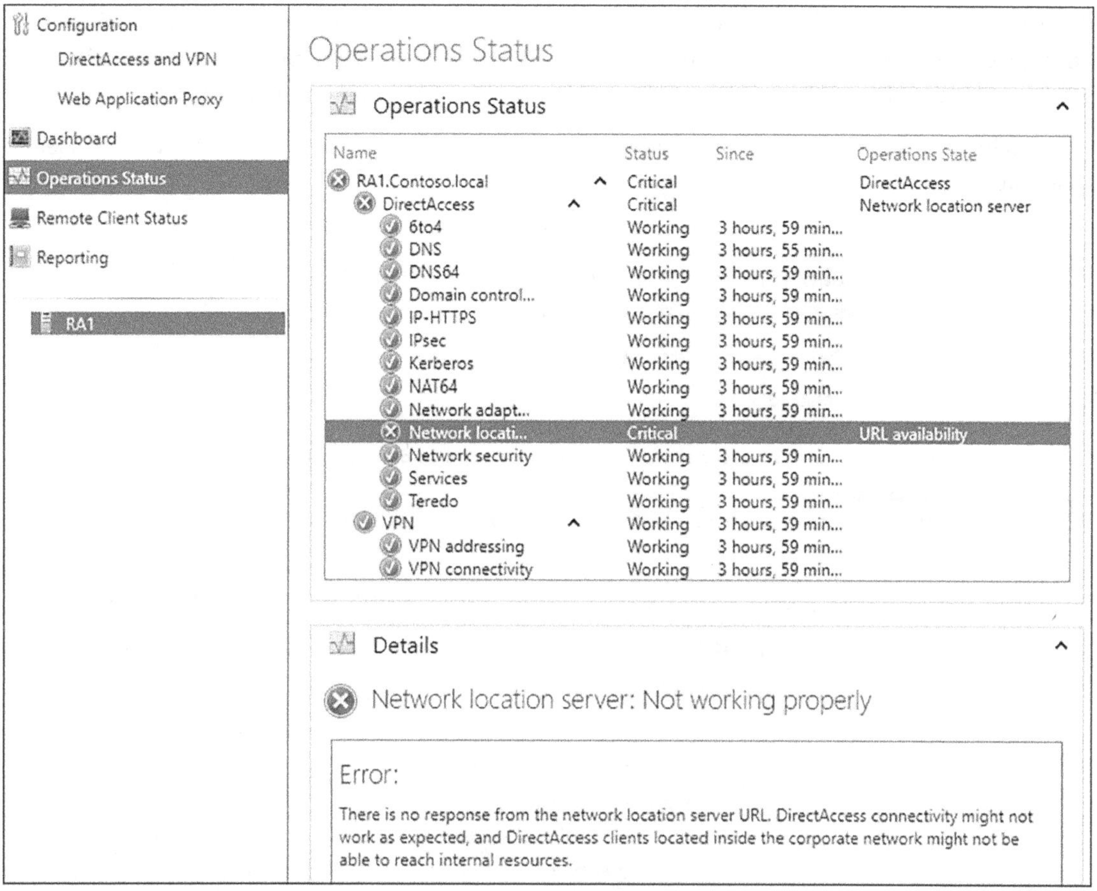

Figure 9.16: The Operations Status page displays information about server components

Remote Client Status

Next up is the **Remote Client Status** screen. As indicated, this is the screen where we monitor client computers that are connected. It will show us both DA and VPN connections here. We can see computer names, usernames, and even the resources they are utilizing during their connections. Information on this screen can be filtered by simply putting any criteria into the **Search** bar at the top of the window.

It is important to note that the **Remote Client Status** screen only shows live, active connections. There is no historical information stored here.

Reporting

You guessed it: this is the window to visit if you want to see historical remote access information. This screen is almost exactly the same as the **Remote Client Status** screen, except that you have the ability to generate reports for historical data pulled from date ranges of your choosing. Once the data is displayed, you have the same search and filtering capabilities that you had on the **Remote Client Status** screen.

Reporting is disabled by default, but you simply need to navigate to the **Reporting** page and click on **Configure Accounting**. Once that is enabled, you will be presented with options for storing historical information. You can choose to store the data in the local WID or on a remote RADIUS server.

You also have options here for how long to store logging data and a mechanism that can be used to clear out old data:

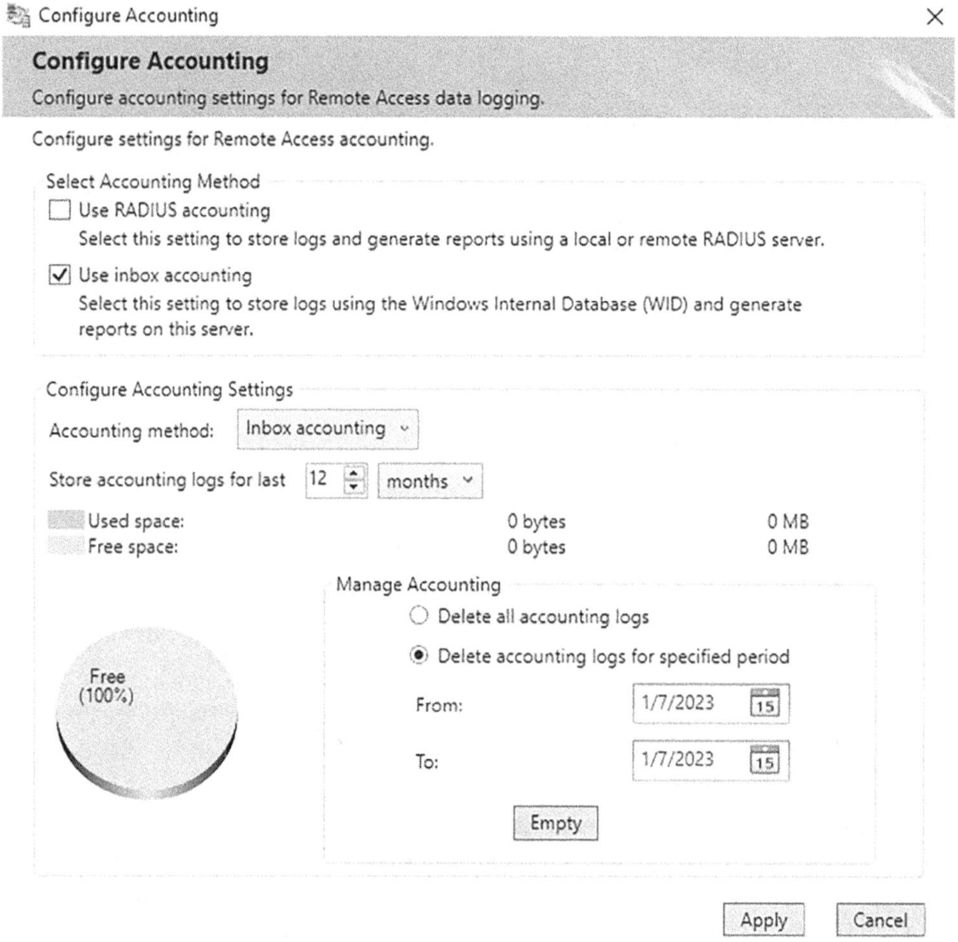

Figure 9.17: Configure Accounting (reporting) settings

Tasks

The last window pane in **Remote Access Management Console** that I want to point out is the **Tasks** bar on the right-hand side of your screen. The actions and options that are displayed in this taskbar change depending on what part of the console you are navigating through. Make sure you keep an eye on this side of your screen to set up some more advanced functions. Some examples of available tasks are creating usage reports, refreshing the screen, enabling or disabling VPNs, and configuring network load balancing or multisite configurations if you are running multiple Remote Access servers.

DA, VPN, or AOVPN? Which is best?

VPNs have been around for a very long time, making them familiar territory to anyone working in IT. AOVPN certainly brings its share of new capabilities, but under the hood, what AOVPN is doing is launching a traditionally configured VPN connection, so the connection flow is similar to what we have always known. In this chapter, we have also discussed quite a bit about DA in order to bring you up to speed on this alternative method of automatically connecting your remote clients back to the datacenter. Now that you know there are two great connectivity platforms built into Windows Server 2025 for enabling your mobile workforce, which one is better?

You don't have to choose! You can run both of these technologies side by side, even on the same Remote Access server. Each technology has its pros and cons, and the ways that you use each, or both, will depend upon many variables. Your users, your client computers, and your organization's individual needs must be factored into your decision-making process. Let's discuss some of the differences between DA and VPN so that you can make intelligent decisions on which connectivity platforms fit into your organization.

Domain-joined or not?

One of the biggest requirements for a DA client computer is that it must be domain-joined. While this requirement in and of itself doesn't seem so major, it carries implications. Trusting a computer enough to join it to your domain more than likely means that the laptop is owned by the company. It also probably means that this laptop was initially built and prepped by the IT team. Companies that are in the habit of allowing employees to purchase their own computers to be used for work purposes may not find that DA fits well with that model. DA is also not ideal for situations where employees use their existing home computers to connect to work remotely.

In these kinds of situations, such as home and personally owned computers, a VPN may be better suited to the task. Don't get me wrong, allowing employees to connect a personally owned computer to your corporate network via VPN is a terrible idea from a security perspective. But technically, you *can* connect to a VPN (including AOVPN) from a non-domain-joined Windows machine, and you can even establish VPN connections (manual connections) from many non-Microsoft devices. iOS, Android, and macOS—all these platforms have a VPN client built into them, which can be used to tap into a VPN listener on a Windows Server 2025 Remote Access server. If your only remote access solution were DA, you would not be able to provide non-domain-joined devices with a connectivity platform.

Keep in mind that, while the AOVPN user tunnel is more flexible than DA in this regard, if you intend to use the AOVPN *device tunnel*, then your machines will still need to be domain-joined.

Auto or manual launch

There are multiple ways to look at this one. When discussing whether DA or a traditional VPN is better, DA is the clear winner. Nobody wants to make their users open a connection and manually launch it to establish VPN connectivity when an automated platform is available to use.

AOVPN, however, brings automated and seamless connectivity to the VPN world. AOVPN is almost as seamless as DA in this regard. I say *almost* because it is not the easiest thing in the world to make a device tunnel work well. This means that most companies rolling out AOVPN only use the user tunnel. In the user tunnel scenario, the VPN does launch automatically, but not until the user has already passed the login screen. That means in these situations, DA still holds an advantage over AOVPN because DA connects seamlessly *at* the login screen. This enables password resets and new domain users to log in to DA-connected machines. I hope that future improvements will enable AOVPN devices and user tunnels to co-exist in a stable way, which will give true, always-on connectivity to AOVPN clients.

Software versus built-in

I'm a fan of Ikea. They do a great job of supplying quality products at a low cost, and somehow package up these products inside incredibly small boxes. After you pay for the product, unbox it, put it together, and then test it to make sure it works—it's great. If you can't see where this is going, I'll give you a hint: it's an analogy for traditional, third-party VPNs. In other words, you typically pay a vendor for their VPN product, unbox it, implement it at more expense, and then test the product. That VPN software has the potential to break and need reinstallation or reconfiguration, and will certainly come with software updates that need to be accomplished down the road. Maintenance, maintenance, maintenance.

Maybe I have watched too many home improvement shows lately, but I am a fan of houses with built-ins. Built-ins are essentially furniture that is permanent to the house, built right into the walls, corners, or wherever it happens to be. It adds value, and it integrates into the overall house much better than furniture that was pieced together separately and then stuck against the wall in the corner.

DA and AOVPN are built-ins. They live inside the operating system. There is no software to install, no software to update, and no software to reinstall when it breaks. Everything that DA and AOVPN need is already in Windows today; you just aren't using it. Oh, and it's free! Well, built into the cost of your Windows license anyway. There are no user CALs, and no ongoing licensing costs related to implementing one of Microsoft's Remote Access solutions.

While third-party enterprise-grade VPN solutions can offer different levels of flexibility and more options for high availability, if your workforce consists of Windows 10 and 11 machines, there are some major factors that show Microsoft DA and Microsoft AOVPN should be near the top of your considerations list when designing a remote access solution.

Password and login issues with traditional VPNs

If you have ever worked on the help desk for a company that uses a VPN, you know what I'm talking about. There are a series of common troubleshooting calls that happen in the VPN world related to passwords. Sometimes, the user forgets their password. Perhaps their password has expired and needs to be changed—ugh! A VPN doesn't handle this scenario very well either. Or perhaps the employee changed their expired password on their desktop before they left work for the day, but are now trying to log in remotely from their laptop, and it isn't working.

What is the solution to password problems with a VPN? Reset the user's password in Active Directory, and then ask the user to come into the office for the laptop to re-sync with the domain and recognize the new password. Yup, this kind of phone call still happens every day. This is unfortunate, but a real potential problem with old-school VPNs.

What's the good news? New Microsoft Remote Access solutions don't have these kinds of problems! Since DA and AOVPN are part of the operating system, they have the capability to be connected anytime that Windows is online. This includes the login screen! Even if I am sitting on the login or lock screen, and the system is waiting for me to input my username and password, as long as I have internet access, I also have a DA tunnel or an AOVPN device tunnel. This means that I can actively do password management tasks. If my password expires and I need to update it, no problem. If I forgot my password and I can't get into my laptop, I can call the help desk and simply ask them to reset my password. I can then immediately log in to my DA or AOVPN laptop with the new password, right from my house.

Another cool function that this seamlessness enables is the ability to log in with new user accounts. Have you ever logged in to your laptop as a different user account to test something? Yup, that works over DA and AOVPN as well. For example, I am sitting at home, and I need to help one of the salespeople troubleshoot some sort of file permission problem. I suspect it's got something to do with their user account, so I want to log in to my laptop as them in order to test it. The problem is that their user account has never logged in to my laptop before. With a classic VPN, not a chance; this would never work. With DA, piece of cake! I simply log off, type in their username and password, and bingo. I'm logged in while still sitting at home in my pajamas.

It is important to note that you can run both DA and VPN connections on the same Windows Server 2025 Remote Access server. This enables you to host clients who are connected via DA, via AOVPN, and also via traditional VPN connections if you have non-Windows machines that need to connect. If any of these connectivity technologies have capabilities that you could benefit from, use them all!

Port-restricted firewalls

One of the other common VPN-related helpdesk calls has always been *My VPN won't connect from this hotel*. Unfortunately, most protocols that VPNs use to connect are not firewall-friendly. Chances are that your router at home allows all outbound traffic, and so, from your home internet connection, everything is fine and dandy when connecting with a VPN. But take that same laptop and connection over to a public coffee shop, a hotel, or an airport, and suddenly the VPN fails to connect, with a strange error. This is usually caused by the public internet connection flowing its traffic through a port-restricting firewall. These firewalls restrict outbound access, oftentimes blocking things such as ICMP and UDP, which can interfere with VPN connections. In the most severe cases, these firewalls may only allow two outbound ports: TCP 80 for HTTP and TCP 443 for HTTPS website traffic. Then, they block everything else.

In the event that you are sitting behind a port-restricted firewall, how do these newer remote access technologies handle connectivity?

DA is built to handle this scenario out of the box. Remember those three different protocols that DA can use to connect? The *fallback* option is called IP-HTTPS, and it flows its traffic inside TCP 443. So, even while sitting behind the most severe firewalls, DA will generally connect automatically and without hesitation.

AOVPN is generally deployed (as it should be) with best practices in mind, which includes prioritizing IKEv2 as the VPN connectivity protocol. In fact, some companies deploy AOVPN with only IKEv2. For these folks, a port-restricting firewall would be detrimental to that user's VPN connection, as IKEv2 uses UDP ports to connect. It wouldn't work. So, hopefully, the main point you take from this is that when setting up AOVPN, make sure that you take the necessary steps to also enable SSTP VPN connectivity as a fallback method. SSTP flows traffic inside TCP 443, which can connect even through hardcore firewalls.

> **Super important note:**
>
> The AOVPN device tunnel can only use IKEv2. If you are behind a port-restricting firewall and are relying on a device tunnel for connectivity, it's not going to work. The AOVPN user tunnel is the only one capable of doing SSTP fallback.

In fact, I have worked through the decision process for using DA or AOVPN with customers many times. To pull out one example from the memory banks, I was talking with a company that manages computers for numerous hospitals and doctors' offices, and they did not have WAN links to those offices. The offices did have internet access, though, and needed the ability to keep those computers automatically connected back to the main datacenter at all times. So far in the scenario, either DA or AOVPN would fit the bill. Then, during testing, we discovered that many hospital networks restrict outbound internet access. The only way that DA would connect was via IP-HTTPS, and the only way that AOVPN would connect was via SSTP. Not a problem, right? Except that it was. You see, these remote workstations are often treated as kiosks, walk-up machines, where dozens of different employees could walk up at any moment and log in to them. Oftentimes, this means that users who have never logged in to these machines before are now logging in to them, so they don't have cached credentials on those computers.

If you haven't figured it out already, we had no choice but to go with DA in this scenario. DA is always connected at the login screen, even when using its *fallback* IP-HTTPS method. AOVPN, however, can only do IKEv2 at the login screen, because the device tunnel requires IKEv2. This uses UDP and was blocked by the firewall, so the only way that AOVPN would connect was by using SSTP, but that wasn't available until the user tunnel could launch, which was only after the user had logged in to the machine. It was an extremely interesting real-world use case that helped shed some light on the decision-making process you may need to take for your own environment.

Manual disconnect

If you aren't already convinced that old-school, traditional VPNs are yesterday's news, let's throw another point at you. When you use VPNs that require the user to manually launch the connection, you are relying on the user themself to keep that machine managed, patched, and up to date. Sure, you may have automated systems that do these things for you, such as WSUS, SCCM, and Group Policy. But when the laptop is out and about, roaming around away from the LAN, those management systems can only do their jobs when the user decides to establish a VPN connection. It's very possible that a laptop could spend weeks completely outside the corporate network, connecting to dozens of insecure hotspots while that employee works their way around the Caribbean on a cruise ship.

After weeks of partying and Netflix, they connect back into the LAN or via VPN to do some work, and wouldn't you know it, that machine has been offline for so long that it's picked up all kinds of fun and creative new software that you now have to deal with.

Not so with the Microsoft Remote Access tools! Providing automatic connectivity via AOVPN or DA means that the laptop would have been connected and receiving all of its security policies and patches during that entire vacation.

In fact, to take it one step further, on a DA-connected machine, the user cannot disable their DA tunnels even if they want to. You do have the ability to provide them with a **Disconnect** button, but that basically just fakes out the connection from the user's perspective to make it feel to them like DA is offline. In reality, the IPsec tunnels are still flowing in the background, always allowing management-style tasks to happen.

Native load-balancing capabilities

Long story short, DA is the winner here. The Remote Access Management Console has built-in capabilities for configuring and managing arrays of DA servers. You can stack multiple DA servers on top of each other, tie them together in load-balanced arrays, and provide redundancy and resiliency right from inside the console, without any extra hardware or traditional load-balancer consideration. You can even configure something called **DirectAccess Multisite**, where you tie DA servers that reside in different geographical locations together in arrays, giving cross-site resiliency. Almost every company that runs DA configures a redundant environment, providing either inner-site load balancing or multisite, or sometimes both, because these capabilities are built in and easy to configure.

Unfortunately, these capabilities are not (not yet, anyway) ported over into the Microsoft VPN world. Whether you are connecting Windows 7 clients via traditional VPN connectivity or getting Windows 10 clients to connect using AOVPN, the backend infrastructure of an RRAS VPN is the same and has no built-in accommodation for multiple servers or sites. It is certainly possible to do so, making that VPN system redundant, but that would require you to set it up on your own by using external load balancers and, oftentimes, would require the use of global site/server load balancers to make that traffic flow properly.

Anyone who has set up load-balanced VPNs of any flavor in the past may be well aware of this process and be able to configure that easily, and that is great. But this is a limiting factor for small business customers who have a limited number of servers, network equipment, and IT experience. All in all, the extra capabilities built into the console related to DA put it a step ahead of any VPN solution in terms of building up your remote access infrastructure to be resilient to failure.

Distribution of client configurations

The last primary consideration that you need to consider when deciding which direction you want to go for remote access is the method by which client-side settings get pushed down to their respective computers:

- **Third-party VPN:** We have already discussed the downsides of dealing with software applications for third-party VPN vendors. If you can use something baked into the Windows operating system instead, that seems like a no-brainer.

- **Always On VPN**: The recommended way to roll out AOVPN settings to client computers is through the use of an MDM solution, namely either MCM/SCCM or Intune. If you have one of these systems and your client computers are joined to it, rolling out AOVPN settings to your workforce is a breeze. If you do not have one of those systems, it is still possible, but not a straightforward process.
- **DirectAccess**: When working in a traditional infrastructure, Active Directory and on-prem servers, DA's approach to client settings distribution is the easiest to work with. You have to keep in mind that DA is only for your domain-joined systems. Given that you can expect all clients to be domain-joined, you have access to rolling out DA connectivity settings via Group Policy, which exists inside any Microsoft-driven infrastructure.

I genuinely hope that we will see a Group Policy distribution option added in the future for AOVPN configuration rollouts. There is at least one third-party company that has created an add-on module to do such a thing, but my opinion is that if Microsoft were to release native ADMX for AOVPN profile creation, many people would flock to it.

To summarize this whole topic, when comparing DA against traditional, manual-launch VPNs, DA cleanly takes first prize. There really is no comparison. Now that we have AOVPN at our disposal, the benefits of one over the other (DA or AOVPN) are quite fuzzy. They both accomplish a lot of the same things, but in different ways. My personal experience in working with these technologies for many years is that the primary deciding factors for most customers have always been client-side rollout capabilities, whether or not they have access to an MDM solution, and how important device tunnel connectivity is to them. Microsoft's goal is for AOVPN to have feature parity with DA, and it's close. AOVPN also has some advanced authentication features that DA does not have, such as integration with Windows Hello for Business or Azure MFA. Ultimately, Microsoft's DirectAccess deprecation announcement seems to have set a firm path forward. Many will still deploy and make use of DA in the future, as Windows Server 2025 is just beginning life and will have some form of support for approximately 10 years, but Microsoft is going to encourage people to lean toward AOVPN. I will happily agree with that blanket recommendation, as soon as they enhance AOVPN to have actual feature parity with DA. Until then, each continues to have advantages and disadvantages.

Web Application Proxy

DA and VPN are both great remote access technologies, and combining the two of them can provide a complete remote access solution for your organization, without having to pay for or work with a third-party solution. Better still, in Windows Server 2025, there is yet another component of the Remote Access role available to use. This third piece of the remote access story is **Web Application Proxy** (**WAP**). This is essentially a reverse-proxy mechanism, giving you the ability to take some HTTP and HTTPS applications that are hosted inside your corporate network and publish them securely to the internet. Any of you who have worked with Microsoft technologies in the perimeter networking space over the last decade will probably recognize a product called Forefront **Unified Access Gateway** (**UAG**), which accomplished similar functionality. UAG was a comprehensive SSL VPN solution, also designed for publishing internal applications to the internet via SSL. It was considerably more powerful than a simple reverse proxy, including components such as pre-authentication, SSTP VPN, and RDS gateway; DA itself could even be run through UAG.

If all of your mobile workers have access to use either DA or VPN, then you probably don't have any use for WAP. However, with the growing cloud mentality, it is quite common for users to expect that they can open a web browser from any computer, anywhere, and gain access to some of their applications.

Document access is now often provided by web services such as SharePoint. Email access is available remotely, from any computer, by tapping into Outlook Web Access. Universal access to SharePoint and Exchange Online is extremely easy to accomplish when using cloud services such as Azure and Microsoft 365, but many don't realize that this can also be true of on-premises Exchange and SharePoint services.

So many applications and so much data can be accessed through only a web browser, and this enables employees to access this data without needing to establish a full-blown corporate tunnel such as a VPN. So, what is the real-world use case for WAP? Home computers that you do not want to be VPN-connected. This way, you don't have to worry as much about the health and status of the home or user-owned computers, since the only interaction they have with your company is through a web browser. This limits the potential for sinister activity to flow into your network from these computers. As you can see, technology such as WAP certainly has its place in the remote access market.

I have hopes that, over time, WAP will continue to be improved and evolve into a true replacement for UAG. UAG ran on Windows Server 2008 R2 and has long been discontinued as a Microsoft product. The closest solution Microsoft has to UAG now is the WAP role. It is not yet nearly as comprehensive, but they are working on improving it. Currently, WAP is useful for publishing access to simple web applications. You can also publish access to rich clients that use basic HTTP authentication, such as Exchange ActiveSync, although, more recently, basic authentication has been put on the naughty list by security teams, and so I don't see this one being utilized very often. Also included is the ability to publish data to clients that use MSOFBA, such as when users try to pull down corporate data from their Word or Excel applications running on the local computer.

WAP can be used to reverse-proxy (publish) remote access to things such as Exchange and SharePoint environments. This is no small thing, as these are technologies that almost everyone uses, so it can certainly be beneficial to your company to implement WAP for publishing secure access to these resources; it's certainly better than implementing NAT directly to your Exchange server.

WAP as AD FS Proxy

Another useful way in which you can utilize a WAP server is when setting up **Active Directory Federation Services (AD FS)** in your network (this is perhaps the most common use for WAP right now). AD FS is a technology designed to enable **single sign-on (SSO)** for users and federation with other companies, and so it involves taking traffic coming in from the internet and passing it into your internal network. In the past, there was a Windows Server role component that accompanied AD FS, called the AD FS Proxy. In the latest versions of AD FS, this separate role no longer exists and has been replaced by the WAP component of the Remote Access role. This better unifies the remote access solution, bringing your inbound AD FS traffic through the official Remote Access server, rather than needing a separate AD FS Proxy server. Anyone implementing outward-facing AD FS in their environments will likely find themselves required to deploy WAP at some point.

Requirements for WAP

Unfortunately, the ability to make use of WAP comes with an awkward requirement: you must have AD FS installed in your environment to be able to use it, even to test it, because the WAP configuration is stored inside AD FS.

None of the WAP configuration information is stored on the Remote Access server itself, which makes for a lightweight server that can be easily moved, changed, or added to. The downside to this is that you must have AD FS running in your environment so that WAP can have a place to store that configuration information.

While a tight integration with AD FS does mean that we have better authentication options, and users can take advantage of AD FS SSO to their applications that are published through WAP, so far, this has proven to be a roadblock to implementation for smaller businesses. Many folks are not yet running AD FS, and if the only reason they are looking into implementing AD FS is so that they can use WAP to publish a few web applications to the internet, they may not choose to invest the time and effort just to make that happen.

One thing to keep in mind if you are interested in using WAP and are, therefore, looking at the requirement for AD FS is that AD FS can certainly be used for other functions. In fact, one of its most common uses at present is integration with Office 365. If you are thinking of incorporating Office 365 into your environment, AD FS is a great tool that can enhance the authentication capabilities for that traffic.

Latest improvements to WAP

WAP was introduced in Server 2012 R2 and had many improvements when Windows Server 2016 was released. There have been a few major modifications since that time, but it is still important to point out the latest benefits that have been rolled into this feature to show that it is still learning to do new things. Let's discuss some of the more recent improvements to WAP.

Pre-authentication for HTTP Basic

There are two ways that users can authenticate to applications that are being published by WAP: pre-authentication or pass-through authentication. When publishing an application with pre-authentication, this means that users will have to stop by the AD FS interface to authenticate themselves before they are allowed through to the web application itself.

In my eyes, pre-authentication is a critical component of any reverse proxy, and I would have to be stuck between a rock and a hard place to externally publish an application that did not require pre-authentication. However, the second option is to do pass-through authentication, and it does exactly that. When you publish access to an application and choose pass-through authentication, all WAP is doing is shuttling the packets from the internet to the application server, in true reverse proxy form. Users can get to the web application without authentication, so in theory, anyone on the internet can hit the web frontend of your application. From there, the application will likely require the user to authenticate, but there is no man-in-the-middle protection happening; that web application is available for the public to view. As you can tell, I do not recommend taking this route.

We already know that WAP can pre-authenticate web applications, but the original version could not do any form of pre-authentication on HTTP Basic applications, such as when a company wanted to publish access to Exchange ActiveSync.

This inability leaves ActiveSync a little bit too exposed to the outside world and is a security risk. Thankfully, this changed in Windows Server 2016 and continues to be a benefit today—you can now pre-authenticate traffic streams that use HTTP Basic.

HTTP to HTTPS redirection

Users don't like going out of their way or wasting time by having to remember that they need to enter `https://` in front of the URL when they access applications. They would rather just remember `email.contoso.com`. The inability of WAP to do HTTP to HTTPS redirection was an annoyance and a hindrance to adoption, but that has since changed. WAP now includes the capability for WAP itself to handle HTTP to HTTPS redirection, meaning that users do not need to type `https` into their browser address bar any longer; they can simply type in the DNS name of the site and let WAP handle the translations.

Wildcard domain publishing

Early versions of WAP didn't play nicely with some SharePoint environments because of limitations in the way that WAP handled domain names. The external URL utilized for publishing an application through WAP can now include a wildcard identifier, which enables the newer versions of on-premises SharePoint to be successfully published to the internet via WAP. This will simplify SharePoint publishing over WAP, making it successful in more cases.

Client IP addresses forwarded to applications

In the reverse proxy and SSL VPN world, we occasionally run across applications that require knowing the client's local IP address. While this requirement doesn't happen very often and is typically segregated to what we would call legacy applications, it does still happen. When the backend application needs to know what the client's IP address is, this presents a big challenge with reverse-proxy solutions. When the user's traffic flows through WAP or any other reverse proxy, it is similar to a NAT, where the source IP address information in these packets changes. The backend application server is unable to determine the client's own IP address, and trouble ensues. WAP now has the ability to propagate the client-side IP address through to the backend application server, alleviating this problem.

Publishing Remote Desktop Gateway apps

One of the items that UAG was commonly used for was publishing access to Remote Desktop Services. UAG was essentially its own Remote Desktop Gateway, which gave you the ability to publish access to RDSH servers, individual RDP connections to desktop computers, such as in a VDI implementation, and even access to RemoteApp applications. Unfortunately, WAP cannot do any of this, even in the new version, but the fact that Microsoft added a little bit of functionality here means movement in the right direction is happening.

What has been improved regarding WAP and Remote Desktop is that you can now use WAP to publish access to a Remote Desktop Gateway server. Traditionally, a Remote Desktop Gateway sits on the edge of the network and connects external users to internal Remote Desktop servers or RemoteApps. Remote Desktop Gateway servers are a common attack vector, and placing WAP in front of the Remote Desktop Gateway allows stronger pre-authentication for Remote Desktop Services and creates a bigger separation between the internal and external networks.

All of my fingers are crossed that we will continue to see improvements in this area and that WAP can be expanded to handle traffic such as Remote Desktop natively, without even needing a Remote Desktop Gateway in the mix.

Improved administrative console

The original version of WAP inside Windows Server 2012 R2 was best served using PowerShell to implement it. You can certainly still use PowerShell to create your publishing rules if you choose, but the Remote Access Management Console has now been improved in terms of how it relates to WAP. Before you can find WAP in the Remote Access Management Console, you need to make sure that the appropriate box was checked during the Remote Access role installation. If you did not select **Web Application Proxy** when you first installed that role, revisit the add/remove roles function inside Server Manager to add WAP to this server:

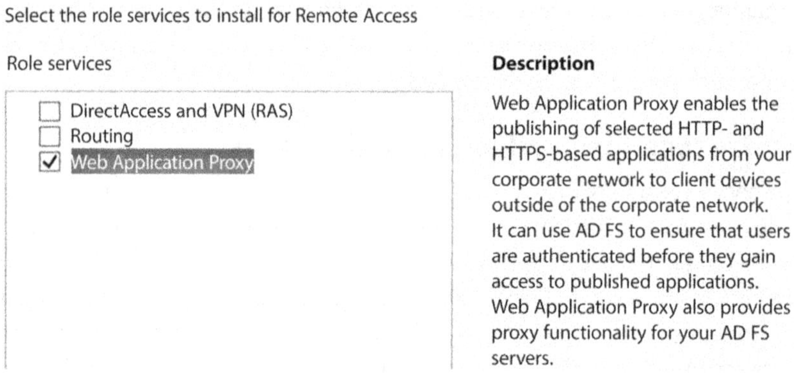

Select the role services to install for Remote Access

Role services

- [ ] DirectAccess and VPN (RAS)
- [ ] Routing
- [x] Web Application Proxy

Description

Web Application Proxy enables the publishing of selected HTTP- and HTTPS-based applications from your corporate network to client devices outside of the corporate network. It can use AD FS to ensure that users are authenticated before they gain access to published applications. Web Application Proxy also provides proxy functionality for your AD FS servers.

Figure 9.18: Adding WAP to a server

Note that, while WAP is a component of the same Remote Access role that houses DA and VPN, it is not recommended to run WAP alongside DA and VPN on the same server. As you already know, you can co-host DA and VPN connections together, simultaneously, on a single Remote Access server. But once you make the foray into WAP, this should be a standalone component. Do not run WAP on a DA/VPN server, and do not run DA/VPN on a WAP server.

Now that we have added **Web Application Proxy** to our server, you can open the RAMC and see it listed inside the **Configuration** section. From here, you launch the **Web Application Proxy** Configuration Wizard and start walking through the steps to define your AD FS server, the certificates you are planning to use, and other criteria needed for the role:

Remote Access Management Console

<

Configuration

Web Application Proxy

WAP1

Configure Web Application Proxy

To set up Web Application Proxy, you must run the Web Application Proxy Configuration Wizard.

↪ Run the Web Application Proxy Configuration Wizard

After you run the Web Application Proxy Configuration Wizard, it will no longer be available through the Remote Access Management console. After you complete this wizard, to edit Web Application Proxy settings, in the navigation pane, select Web Application Proxy.

Figure 9.19: Configuring WAP from the RAMC

Summary

The nature of the world today demands that most companies enable their employees to work from wherever they are. Working from home has become normal over the past few years; with a worldwide pandemic, we have seen staggering increases in the percentage of employees who work outside of an office building. Companies need a secure, stable, and efficient way to provide access to corporate data and applications for these mobile workers. The Remote Access role in Windows Server 2025 is designed to do exactly that. With three different ways of providing remote access to corporate resources, IT departments have never had so much remote access technology available at their fingertips, built right into the Windows operating system that they already own. If you are still supporting a third-party or legacy VPN system, you should at least explore the capabilities provided here.

DirectAccess and Always On VPN are particularly impressive and compelling connectivity options—a fresh way of looking at remote access. Automatic connectivity means your machines are constantly patched and updated because they are always connected to your management servers. You can improve user productivity and network security at the same time. These two things are usually oxymorons in the IT world, but with the Microsoft Remote Access stack, they hold hands and sing songs together.

In the next chapter, we are going to look at some of the security functions built into your Windows Server 2025 operating system, and at some of the ways that your servers can be hardened to provide even better security than what comes out of the box.

Questions

Put your knowledge to the test with the following questions. If you need a hand (or just want to double-check), you'll find all the answers in the *Appendix* section of the book.

1. What two VPN protocols are no longer enabled by default in Windows Server 2025?
2. What does AOVPN stand for?
3. What are the two primary protocols used for connecting AOVPN clients?

4. In which version of Windows 10 was AOVPN released?

5. In what special instance would an AOVPN client be required to be joined to your domain?

6. Does DirectAccess require your corporate internal network to be running IPv6?

7. What is the name of the internal website that DirectAccess clients check in with to determine when they are inside the corporate network?

8. What ports are used by Teredo and IP-HTTPS?

9. How do you provision DirectAccess configuration settings to the client machines?

10. What role does a Web Application Proxy server hold in a federation environment?

Unlock this book's exclusive benefits now   **UNLOCK NOW**

Scan this QR code or go to `https://packtpub.com/unlock`,
then search for this book by name.

Note: Keep your purchase invoice ready before you start.

10
Hardening and Security

10.93 million dollars. Apparently, inflation has even hit Austin Powers' world, and for anyone who read that in the voice of Dr. Evil, you're my kind of people. Joking aside, that number is very real and very serious to IT security. Why? Because $10.93 million is the average cost of a data breach for a US-based organization, according to IBM's *Cost of a Data Breach Report 2024*. This number has grown significantly since the first time I heard it, sitting at a Microsoft conference in Redmond. Here's another statistic that could help you secure a bump in your security budget: *204 days*. That is the **average dwell time** that an attacker sits inside your network, hanging around among your files and infrastructure before they act. More than six months of poking, prodding, and exfiltrating your sensitive data.

Another important number is 79%—as in, the percentage of network intrusions that happen as a result of **compromised user credentials**. Almost four out of five breaches begin with somebody clicking on a bad link, reusing a password, or getting socially engineered. Furthermore, it is becoming more and more difficult to identify these attacks early because attackers use legitimate IT tools to grab what they want. For instance, an attacker could socially engineer their way into the trust of a single employee and leverage that trust to get a remote access connectivity tool installed on the user's work computer. Why use malware when you can install a valid remote connection tool that is going to fly under the radar of intrusion detection systems? Makes sense to me.

Modern attacks don't need to break down the door. They just need someone to open it. Data security, network security, credential and identity security—these things are all becoming harder to accomplish, but there are always new tools and technologies coming out that can help you fight off the bad guys. Windows Server 2025 is the most secure server OS that Microsoft has produced; in this chapter, we'll discuss some of the functionality included that makes that statement true:

- Microsoft Defender Antivirus
- Windows Defender Firewall: no laughing matter
- Encryption technologies
- Microsoft Entra Password Protection
- Fine-grained password policy
- Windows LAPS

- Advanced Threat Analytics: end of support
- General security best practices

Microsoft Defender Antivirus

The name *Windows Defender* has been around for many years, but its terminology and capabilities have evolved numerous times during OS releases. We originally discovered Defender around 2005, as a very basic anti-spyware tool. The Windows 8 era introduced a staggering change for Windows users, including Windows Defender in the OS, free and out of the box. Although this sounds great on paper, Defender's capabilities were not taken too seriously by the IT population, and everyone ignored Defender in lieu of a commercial antivirus product. Fast forward to today, however, and what is now known as **Microsoft Defender Antivirus** is a much-improved antimalware/antivirus that is running on millions of Windows 10 and 11 client computers as well as, you guessed it, current versions of Windows Server. Defender Antivirus exists in the OS and is enabled by default, and as a result, has a level of integration and responsiveness that is hard for third-party vendors to match. I can't tell you how many times I have tracked memory leaks and random server reboots back to poorly functioning third-party antivirus software, which is unacceptable in today's server world. Some still consider the antivirus capabilities provided by Defender to be lackluster, perhaps only because it is free, but it certainly carries some advantages over third-party antivirus solutions. I have yet to see a Windows Defender product tank a workstation or server.

You may also be familiar with Windows Defender **Advanced Threat Protection** (**ATP**), which has since been rebranded as **Microsoft Defender for Endpoint**. This product is part of the broader Microsoft Defender family, protecting against threats, investigating rogue behavior, and responding to attacks.

The first server OS that we found with built-in Defender for Antivirus was Server 2016. Many servers running in production for companies around the world are still Server 2012 R2 at this point (I know because I work on them every day), and so the improved existence of the Defender toolset in Server 2025 is yet another reason to start planning your migration today.

We simply do not have enough page space to dive into every aspect of Windows Defender, and it is being continually improved upon. One of the latest advancements of the Microsoft Defender family comes in the form of **Microsoft Defender for Cloud**, working to protect your cloud-based applications, and an interesting topic for the DevSecOps community. What we will do in this chapter is explore some of the interfaces, make sure you know how to use the most common components that don't require policy-level manipulation or centralized administration, and expand your knowledge of some of the more advanced features that are available for further learning and digging.

Installing Microsoft Defender Antivirus

You're done! Microsoft Defender Antivirus is installed by default in Windows Server 2025. In fact, unless you have somehow changed it, not only is it installed, but it also automatically protects your system as soon as the OS is installed. But don't take my word for it: if you open **Server Manager**, choose **Add roles and features**, and click ahead to the **Select features** page, you should find a checkbox already selected next to **Microsoft Defender Antivirus**:

Select features

Before You Begin

Installation Type

Server Selection

Server Roles

Features

Confirmation

Results

Select one or more features to install on the selected server.

Features

- [ ] Media Foundation
  - ▷ [ ] Message Queuing
  - [✓] Microsoft Defender Antivirus (Installed)
  - [ ] Multipath I/O
  - ▷ [ ] MultiPoint Connector
  - [ ] Network ATC
  - [ ] Network Load Balancing
  - [ ] Network Virtualization

Description

Microsoft Defender Antivirus helps protect your machine from malware.

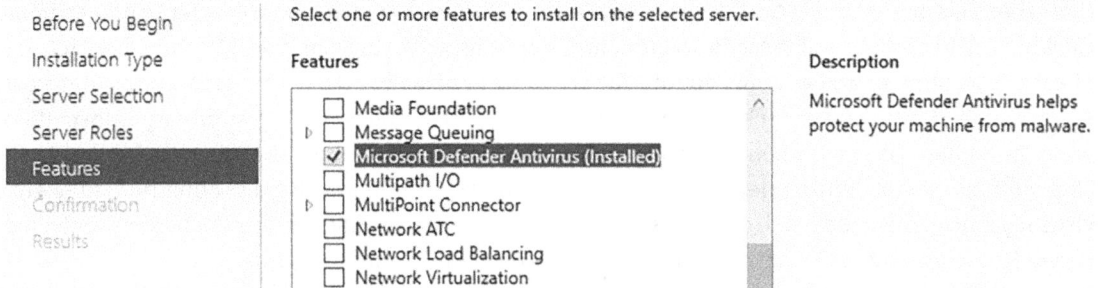

Figure 10.1: Microsoft Defender Antivirus is preinstalled

If it's not already checked for some reason, then this is exactly the place to visit to get it installed and working.

Exploring the user interface

The interface for the Microsoft Defender toolset is the same as within the latest versions of Windows 11, but if you haven't explored that yet, we will take a quick look at it here. Go ahead and launch **Settings** from inside the **Start** menu, then click on **Privacy & security**.

Once inside that section, you will see **Windows Security** listed on the right. Here, you get an overhead view of the different Defender components that are working together to protect your system.

Remember, you have done nothing to enable any of this functionality; these are all out-of-the-box capabilities:

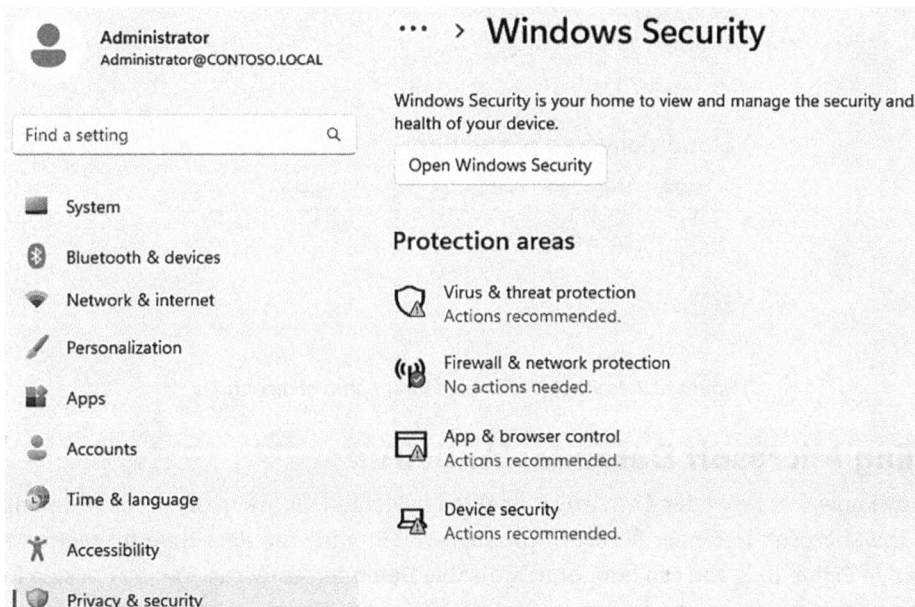

Administrator
Administrator@CONTOSO.LOCAL

Find a setting

··· > **Windows Security**

Windows Security is your home to view and manage the security and health of your device.

Open Windows Security

- System
- Bluetooth & devices
- Network & internet
- Personalization
- Apps
- Accounts
- Time & language
- Accessibility
- Privacy & security

Protection areas

Virus & threat protection
Actions recommended.

Firewall & network protection
No actions needed.

App & browser control
Actions recommended.

Device security
Actions recommended.

Figure 10.2: Microsoft Defender capabilities

You'll notice in *Figure 10.2* that some of my security components are unhappy, displaying small warning symbols. This is largely due to the fact that my test lab does not have internet connectivity, and so this server has not been able to check in with Microsoft for definition updates or other configurations. Clicking further into any of these **Protection areas** options will bring you more detailed descriptions of each capability, as well as many options for enabling or disabling particular protections that exist. For example, if you were to click on **Virus & threat protection**, you would see summary information about Defender Antivirus, when its definition files were updated, what it's scanning, and so on. Then, clicking further into a link called **Manage settings** will give you options for disabling Defender Antivirus if you ever have the need, as well as numerous other options that can be selected or deselected. *Figure 10.3* shows you a few of the settings available inside Defender Antivirus:

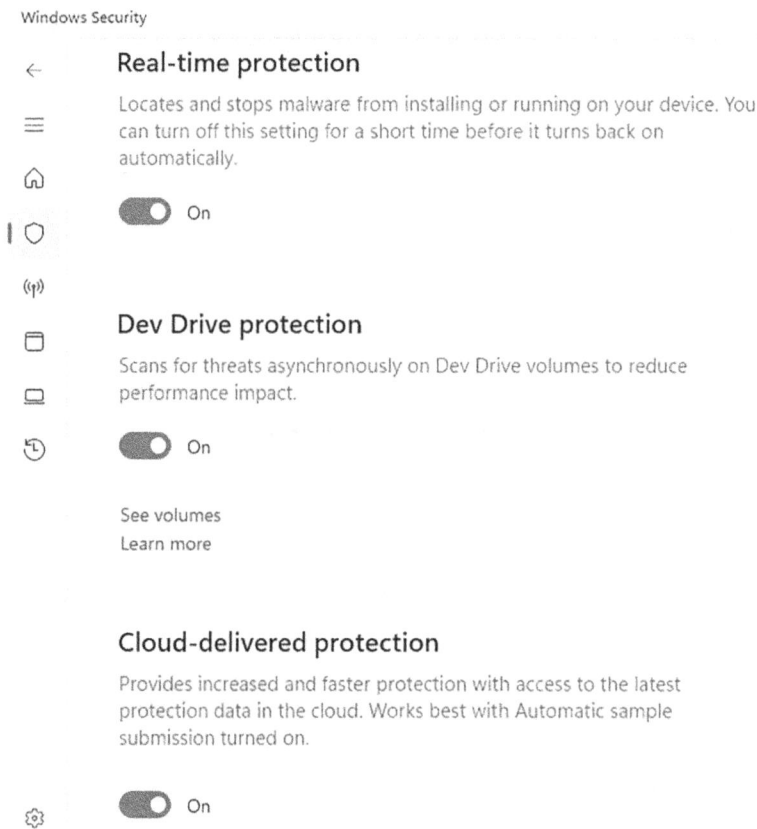

Windows Security

Real-time protection

Locates and stops malware from installing or running on your device. You can turn off this setting for a short time before it turns back on automatically.

On

Dev Drive protection

Scans for threats asynchronously on Dev Drive volumes to reduce performance impact.

On

See volumes
Learn more

Cloud-delivered protection

Provides increased and faster protection with access to the latest protection data in the cloud. Works best with Automatic sample submission turned on.

On

Figure 10.3: Managing virus and threat protection options

Disabling Microsoft Defender Antivirus

You already know that Defender Antivirus is enabled by default, as are many other components that make up the Microsoft Defender family of products. By flipping the **Real-time protection** radio option shown in *Figure 10.3*, you can temporarily disable Defender Antivirus. Taking it a step further, if you are absolutely sure that you do not want to use Defender Antivirus because you have your own antivirus software that you have already paid for, you have two different avenues that could be taken.

First, Defender Antivirus is designed to automatically step down when another antivirus is installed. More than likely, all you need to do is install your other third-party antivirus tool, and after the server finishes restarting, Defender Antivirus will stand down and allow the third-party product to run, so that they don't conflict with each other. This is important because a fact that even many computer technicians don't realize is that running multiple antivirus programs on a single system is generally a terrible idea. They often cause conflicts with each other, have memory allocation errors, and cause otherwise slow and strange behavior on the system.

By default, Microsoft Defender runs in what is known as **Active mode**, which makes a lot of sense. If you employ an additional capability in the Defender family called **Microsoft Defender for Endpoint**, when a third-party antivirus product is installed, Defender changes gears and enters **Passive mode**. In this instance, Defender Antivirus is not the primary antivirus. It may still scan some files and detect threats if it sees them, but Defender now takes no action to remediate these potential threats.

If you are planning to utilize your own antivirus and want to make sure Defender is *completely* removed, it is possible to uninstall the Defender feature from your server. This is most easily done via PowerShell, with the following command:

```
Uninstall-WindowsFeature -Name Windows-Defender
```

```
Administrator: Windows PowerShell                                    —   □   ×
Windows PowerShell
Copyright (C) Microsoft Corporation. All rights reserved.

 Install the latest PowerShell for new features and improvements! https://aka.ms/PSWindows

       PS C:\Users\Administrator.CONTOSO> Uninstall-WindowsFeature -Name Windows-Defender
Success Restart Needed Exit Code      Feature Result
------- -------------- ---------      --------------
True    Yes            SuccessRest... {Microsoft Defender Antivirus}
WARNING: You must restart this server to finish the removal process.

PS C:\Users\Administrator.CONTOSO>
```

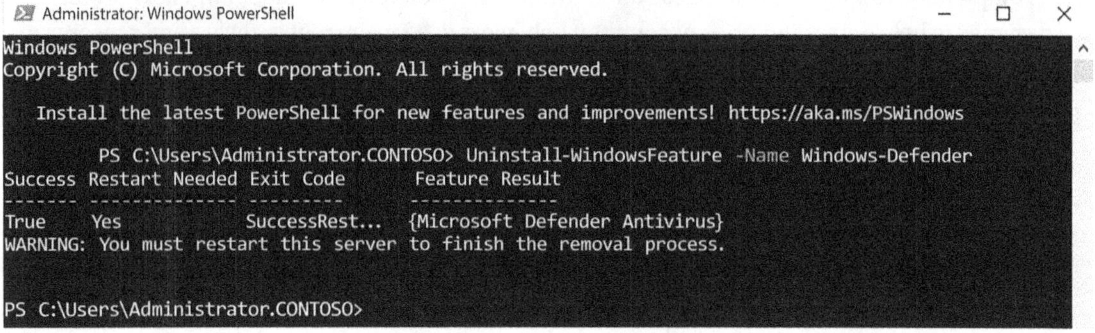

Figure 10.4: Uninstalling Defender

Microsoft Defender for Endpoint

Microsoft Defender for Endpoint is the new name for Microsoft Defender ATP. Whether you engage Microsoft Defender for antivirus capabilities or you are running a third-party antivirus, it can still be beneficial to your overall security footprint to leave the Defender components installed on your computers and servers, and make use of this paid service.

Defender for Endpoint is a cloud-managed endpoint security platform that serves the purpose of an **endpoint detection and response (EDR)** system. Defender for Endpoint is licensed for use via Microsoft 365 licensing, and when engaged, makes use of the Defender components baked into Windows to detect threats, learn from those threats, and take remedial action against threats across your entire workforce. By leveraging Defender components across your endpoints, you are effectively crowd-sourcing information about new threats and allowing Microsoft to further protect your systems based on behavioral patterns seen elsewhere.

Defender for Endpoint can integrate with third-party EDR/MDR solutions as well, giving even larger and more granular capabilities for administration. Whatever the flavor of management platform being used, Defender itself is at the center of the action, doing the work to protect your systems against malware, exploits, and ransomware.

Office 365 does this kind of data handling as well, to identify and block exploits. For example, if an email address within a company is suddenly sending emails to a large group of people, and that email contains a macro-enabled Word document, which is something that a user does not typically do, Office 365 can very quickly take that document offline into a secure zone, open it (or launch it if the attachment happened to be an executable), and discover whether or not this file is malware of some kind. If it is, Office 365 will immediately start blocking that file, thereby stopping the spread of this potentially disastrous behavior. All of this happens without input from the user or the company's IT staff. This is not even inner-company-specific. If one of my users' emails is the first to receive a new virus and it is identified by Microsoft, that discovery will help to block the new virus for other customers who also host their email in Microsoft's cloud. This is pretty incredible stuff!

Windows Defender Exploit Guard

The name *Exploit Guard* sounds singular and specific, but **Exploit Guard** is not a single feature; rather, it is a comprehensive suite of capabilities built into Microsoft Defender for Endpoint. These protections are designed to help detect and prevent common behaviors used in current malware and ransomware attacks.

Here are the four primary components of Defender Exploit Guard:

- **Attack surface reduction (ASR)**: ASR is a series of rules and controls that block certain types of files from running. This can help mitigate malware being installed by users clicking on email attachments or prevent the opening of certain kinds of Office files. We are quickly learning as a computer society that we should never click on files in an email that appear to be executables, but often, a standard computer user won't know the difference between an executable and any other kind of file. Just last week, I received a forwarded email from somebody that contained some incredibly sketchy-looking attachments. Rather than question the email, this person had forwarded the request, simply asking, "My computer won't let me open these files; can you open them and send me back the contents?" ASR can help to block the running of any executable or scripting file from inside an email.

- **Network protection:** This enables **Windows Defender SmartScreen**, which can block potential malware from phoning home, communicating back to the attacker's servers to siphon or transfer company data outside of your company. Websites on the internet have reputation ratings, deeming sites or IP addresses to be trusted or not trusted, depending on the types of traffic that have headed to that IP address in the past. SmartScreen taps into those reputation databases to block outbound traffic from reaching bad destinations.

- **Controlled folder access:** Ransomware protection! This one is intriguing because ransomware is a top concern for any IT security professional. If you're not familiar with the concept, ransomware is a type of malware that installs an application onto your computer that then encrypts files on your computer. Once encrypted, you can't open or repair those files without the encryption key, which the attackers will (most of the time) happily hand over to you for lots of money. Every year, many companies end up paying that ransom (and therefore engaging in passive criminal behavior themselves) because they do not have good protections or good backups from which to restore their information. Controlled folder access helps to protect against ransomware by blocking untrusted processes from gaining access to areas of your hard drive that have been deemed protected.

- **Exploit protection:** Generalized protection against many kinds of exploits that might take place on a computer. Originally a component of the **Enhanced Mitigation Experience Toolkit (EMET)**, which no longer formally exists, exploit protection mitigates against rogue system processes as well as application executables.

These controls, particularly exploit protection controls, can be managed in many ways. They can be rolled out in a centralized fashion via Intune, Group Policy, or Microsoft Endpoint Configuration Manager. Additionally, they can be configured on a per-machine basis by using PowerShell or the Windows Security app, which is built into every current Windows version.

Let's take a peek at the settings on an individual instance of Windows Server 2025. Open **Windows Settings | Privacy & security | Windows Security**. Inside, click **App & browser control**. On this screen, you have options for configuring **Reputation-based protection**, which is the section where the configuration of SmartScreen URL-based protection is accomplished, and a section for **Exploit protection**. Clicking on **Exploit protection settings**, we now get into the nitty gritty of these protection mechanisms, as you can see in *Figure 10.5*.

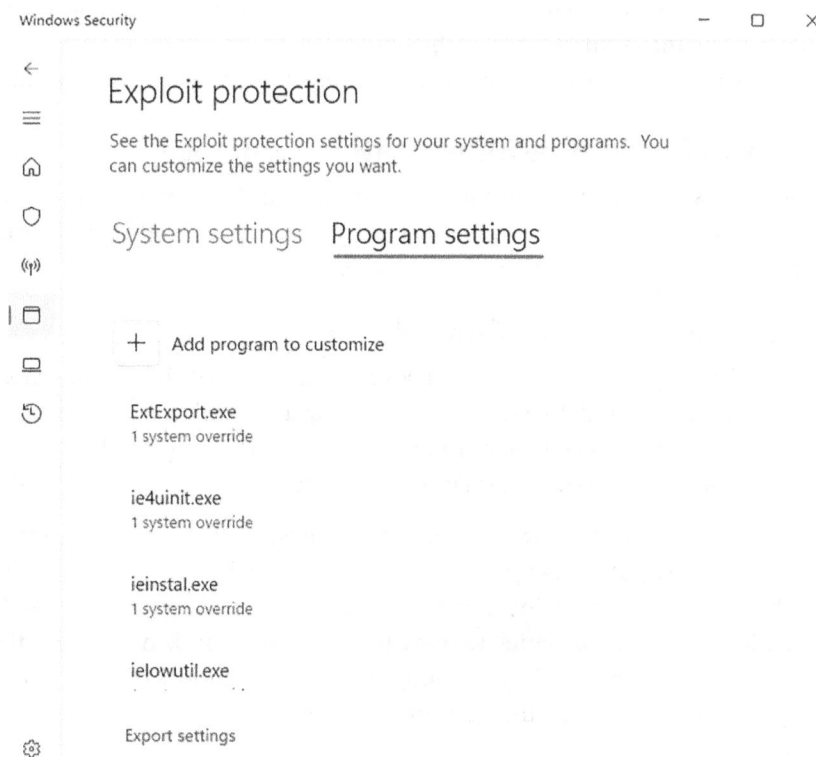

Figure 10.5: Exploit protection settings

Many different pieces of exploit protection can be globally enabled or disabled (many are enabled by default), and clicking on **Program settings** allows you to get granular, defining to what extent exploit protection handles individual programs.

Windows Defender Firewall: no laughing matter

Let's play a word association game. I will say something, and you say the first word that comes to mind.

Network security.

Did you say *firewall*? I would have. When we think of securing our devices at the network level, we think of perimeters. Those perimeters are defined and protected by firewalls, mostly at the hardware level, with specialized networking devices made to handle that particular task in our networks. Today, we are here to talk about another layer of firewalling that you can and should be utilizing in your environments. Yes, we are talking about Windows Firewall. Stop laughing, it's rude!

It is easy to poke fun at Windows Firewall based on its history. In the days of Windows XP and Server 2003, it was almost useless and caused way more headaches than it solved. These feelings were so common that I still today find many companies that completely disable Windows Firewall on all their domain-joined systems as a matter of default policy. If you ask them, there is usually no specific reason they are doing this—"*It's always been this way*," or "*It's in our written security policy*" are standard replies. This is a problem because the **Windows Defender Firewall with Advanced Security** (**WFAS**) that exists in the Windows OSs of today is much more robust and advanced than ever before, and can absolutely be used to enhance your security architecture. I would go as far as to say that it is entirely silly to disable WFAS on a current OS, unless you have a very good, very specific reason to do so.

Three Windows Firewall administrative consoles

It is important to understand that there are three different consoles from which you can configure Windows Firewall settings. Two of these consoles are redundant with each other, and the third is much more capable than the others. Let's take a quick look at each one.

Windows Defender Firewall (Control Panel)

When trying to launch any application or setting in Windows Server 2025, it is usually most efficient to simply click on the **Start** button and then type a word relating to the task you are trying to accomplish. In my case, I clicked on **Start** and typed the word `firewall`. One of the top matches that was provided in my search results was **Windows Defender Firewall**, so I went ahead and clicked on that.

Interestingly, this link opens the Windows Defender Firewall configuration console from inside **Control Panel**, the old-school way of doing system settings. This console is still online and fully capable of manipulating basic firewalling functions, such as enabling or disabling the Windows Firewall, but since this tool resides inside **Control Panel**, we have to assume that this is not the tool that Microsoft intends for us to utilize. Remember, all new configuration capabilities have been migrated to the **Windows Settings** screens, rather than the old **Control Panel**:

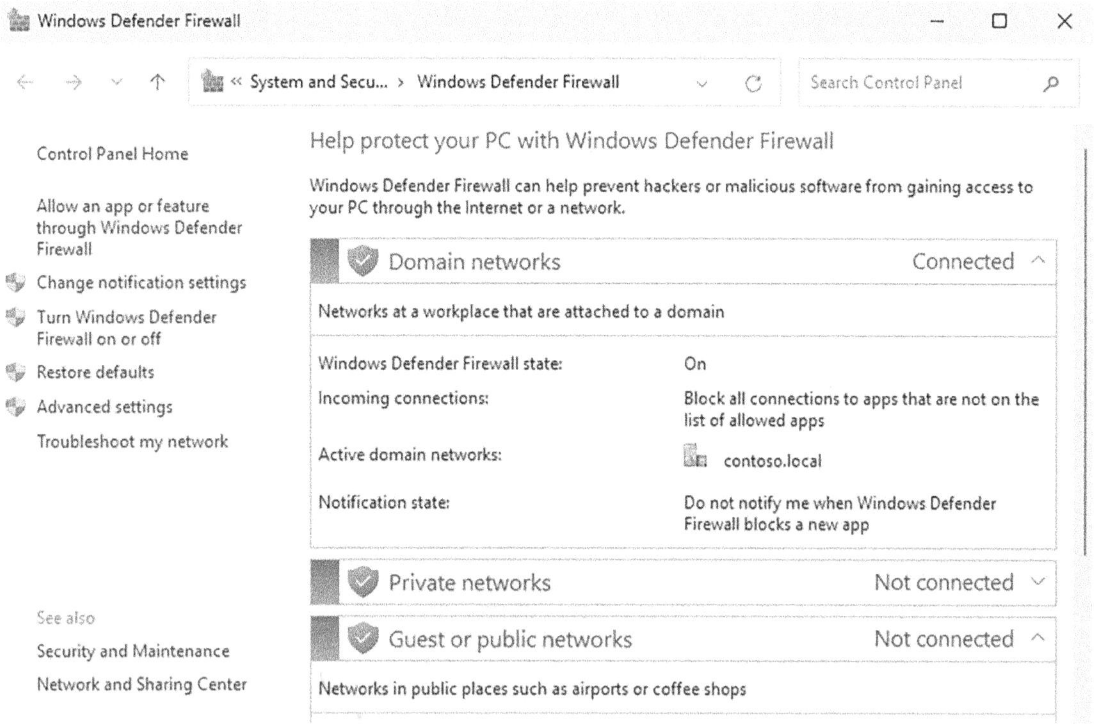

Figure 10.6: Firewall settings inside Control Panel

Firewall & network protection (Windows Security Settings)

While the **Control Panel**-based tools were always the proper place to make these changes in past versions of the OS, we already know that there are many Windows Defender options stored inside **Windows Settings.** Could it be the case that there are also Windows Defender Firewall configuration settings stored inside the **Windows Security** section of **Settings**?

Yes, there definitely are. Open **Windows Settings** and click on **Privacy & Security**, then on **Windows Security.** You've been here before—this is the screen that gives a quick summary of the Windows Defender components. Sure enough, there is one here called **Firewall & network protection.**

Click on that button, and you will be taken to a newer configuration platform for the Windows Firewall functions that was new starting with Windows Server 2022:

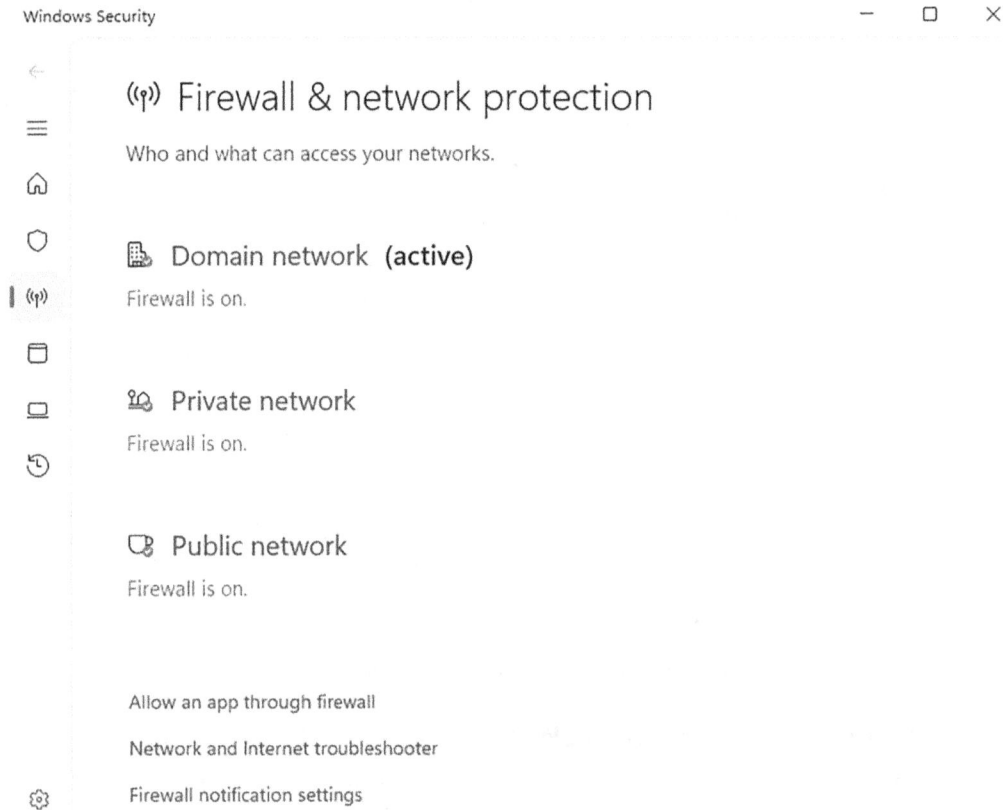

Figure 10.7: Firewall settings inside Windows Settings

Clicking any of the links provided here will open additional configuration options. For example, if you wanted to quickly enable or disable particular firewall profiles (we will learn about those shortly), you could click on the profile you wanted to configure, such as the **Domain network** profile, and from there, easily turn off the firewall for this networking profile. Many companies disable the domain network profile on their machines so that the firewall is not protecting traffic that happens inside a corporate LAN network.

While disabling the firewall is generally a bad idea, sometimes it is required to fit your business model. For example, if all of your computers sit behind an enterprise-class corporate firewall, you may deem it unimportant and redundant to also have the Windows Firewall engaged on workstations:

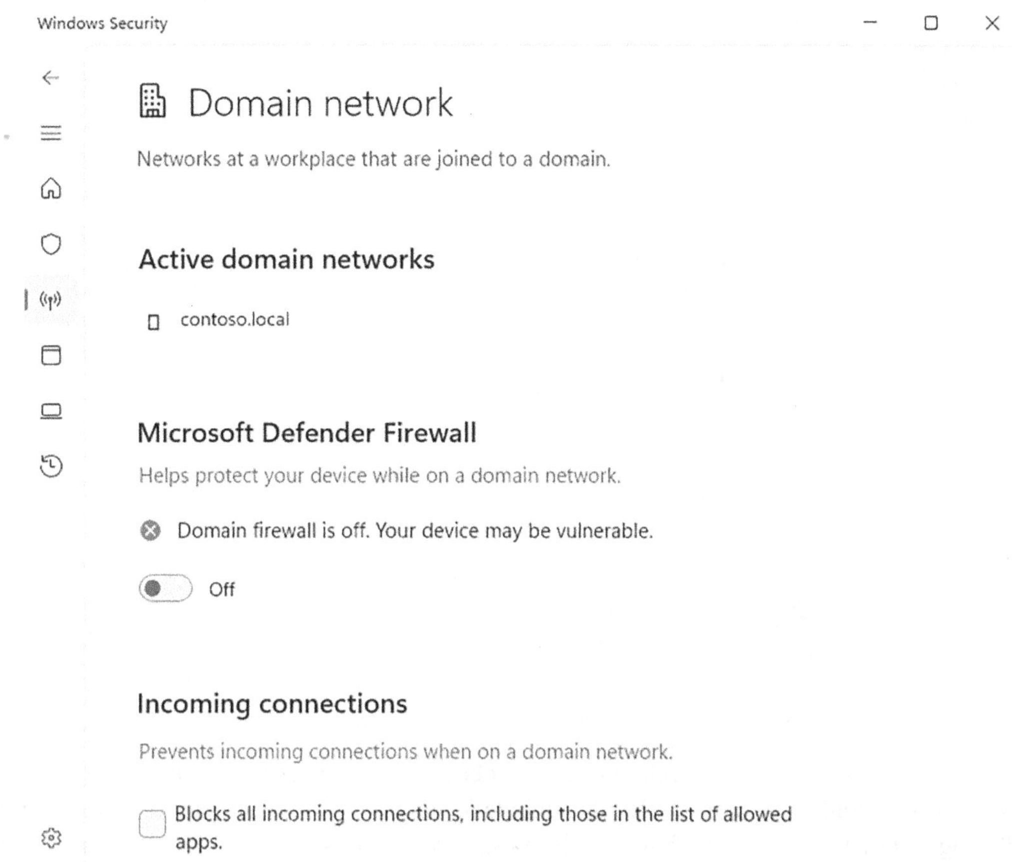

Figure 10.8: Disabling the Windows Firewall while on Domain network

The firewall configuration screen available inside **Windows Settings** is a good place to make simple, overhead decisions about Windows Defender Firewall, but this interface is limited in capabilities. For any deep utilization of firewall functionality or configuration...

Windows Defender Firewall with Advanced Security (WFAS)

If you are anything like me, you won't be satisfied with the firewall information provided inside **Windows Settings**, and you will want to see what is going on under the hood, so you will want a little more information than the basic Windows Firewall tools alone can give you. You can either click on one of the **Advanced settings** links shown in previous screenshots or simply open Command Prompt or a **Start | Run** prompt and type wf.msc. Either of these functions will launch the full WFAS administration console:

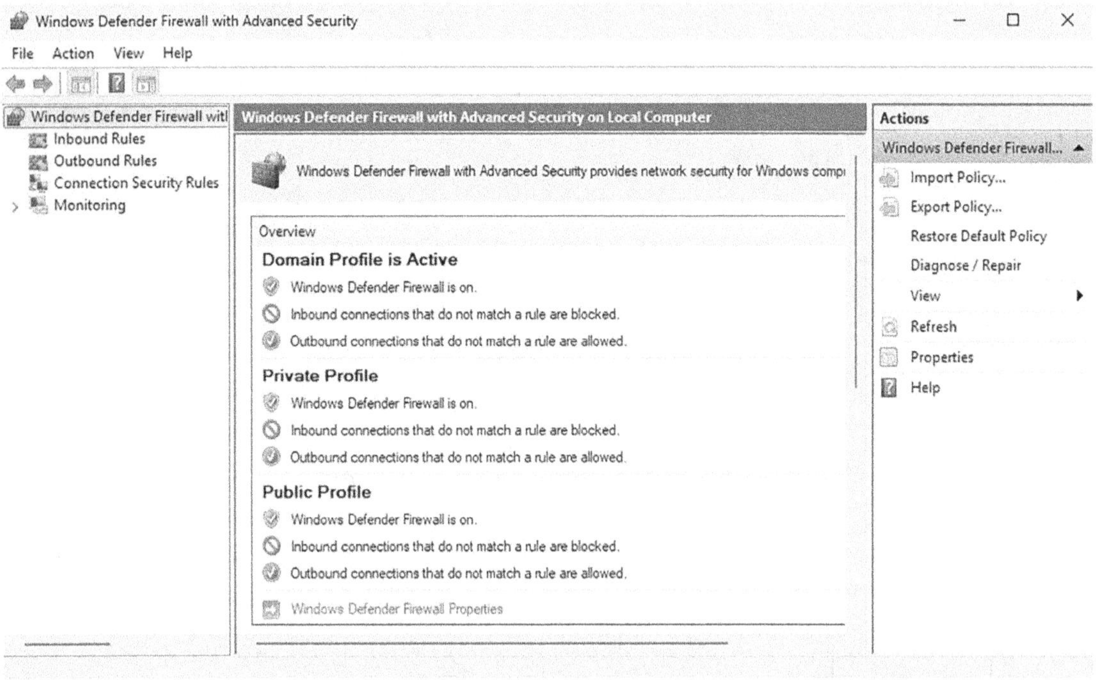

Figure 10.9: Windows Defender Firewall with Advanced Security

Here, you can see much more in-depth information about the activity and rules that are at play with Windows Firewall and make more acute adjustments in your allowances and blocks. There is also a **Monitoring** section where you can view actively engaged rules, including **Connection Security Rules**. This is an important section because it highlights the fact that WFAS does much more than block network traffic. It is not only a firewall; it is also a connectivity platform. If you plan to utilize IPsec for the encryption of network traffic, whether it be native IPsec inside your network or through the remote access technology DirectAccess, you will see rules populated in this section that are the definitions of those IPsec tunnels.

Believe it or not, Windows Firewall is responsible for making those encrypted connections and tunnels happen. This is way more advanced than the Windows Firewall of yesteryear.

Three firewall profiles

When any NIC on a computer or server is connected to a network, Windows Firewall will assign that connection to one of the three possible firewall profiles. You have probably interfaced with this decision-making process before without even realizing it. When you connect your laptop to the Wi-Fi at your local coffee shop, did Windows ask you whether you were connecting to a home, work, or public network? Or in more recent versions of Windows, it asks you a question more along the lines of, "Would you like to allow your computer to be discoverable on this network—yes or no?" This is your Windows Firewall asking you which profile you would like to assign to the new network connection.

The reason that you can assign NICs and network connections to different firewall profiles is that you can assign different access rules and criteria for what is or is not allowed over those different profiles. Effectively, it is asking you, *How much do you trust this network?* For example, when your laptop is connected to the corporate network, you can relax your rules compared to the times when that same laptop is connected at a hotel across the country. By assigning more intense firewall rules to the profile that is active when you are in the hotel, you build bigger walls for attackers to face when you are out working on that public internet. Let's look at the three different types of profiles that are available, with a quick description of each:

- **Domain profile:** This is the only one that you cannot choose to manually assign. The domain profile is only active when you are on a domain-joined computer that is currently connected to a network where a domain controller for your domain is accessible. So, for any corporate machine inside the corporate network, you can expect that the domain profile will be active. The detection of this domain connectivity happens automatically, via a Windows service called **Network Location Awareness (NLA)**.

- **Private profile:** When connecting to a new network and you are prompted to choose where you are connected, if you choose either **Home** or **Work**, that connection will be assigned the private profile.

- **Public profile:** When prompted, if you choose **Public**, then, of course, you are assigned the public firewall profile. Also, if you are not prompted for some reason, or if you do not choose an option at all and simply close the window that is asking you what to assign to your new connection, this public profile will be the default profile that is given to any connections that do not have a different profile already assigned.

> In the more recent versions of Windows (particularly in Win10/11), you don't usually get the prompt asking what kind of network it is; instead, you get that prompt asking whether or not you want to allow your computer to communicate with other devices on the new network. Effectively, this is the same prompt, and the decision you make at that prompt will assign your connection to either the public or private firewall profile.

Each network connection gets assigned its own profile definition. You could certainly have more than one firewall profile active at the same time on the same system. For example, my RA1 server that we used in the last chapter is connected to both the corporate network as well as the public internet. Inside WFAS, you can see that both the domain profile and public profile are active:

Windows Defender Firewall with advanced Security provides network security

Overview

Domain Profile is Active

Windows Defender Firewall is on.

Inbound connections that do not match a rule are blocked.

Outbound connections that do not match a rule are allowed.

Private Profile

Windows Defender Firewall is on.

Inbound connections that do not match a rule are blocked.

Outbound connections that do not match a rule are allowed.

Public Profile is Active

Windows Defender Firewall is on.

Inbound connections that do not match a rule are blocked.

Outbound connections that do not match a rule are allowed.

Figure 10.10: Multiple NICs can mean multiple active firewall profiles

Alternatively, if you open **Network and Sharing Center** on this server, you can also see the profiles listed here, and you can easily tell which NIC is using which profile:

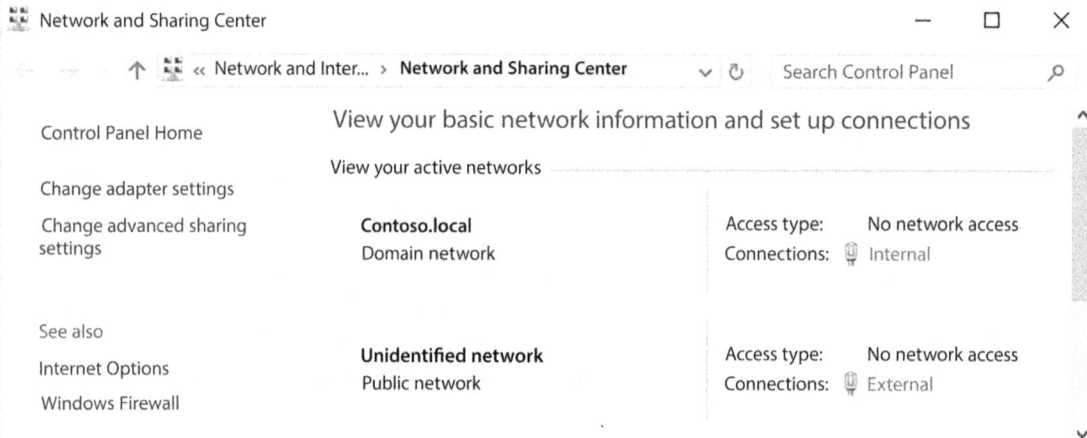

Network and Sharing Center   —   □   ✕

↑ « Network and Inter... > **Network and Sharing Center**   ∨ ↻   Search Control Panel   ⌕

Control Panel Home   View your basic network information and set up connections

                            View your active networks
Change adapter settings

Change advanced sharing   **Contoso.local**   Access type: No network access
settings   Domain network   Connections: 🖵 Internal

See also
                            Unidentified network   Access type: No network access
Internet Options   Public network   Connections: 🖵 External
Windows Firewall

Figure 10.11: Firewall profiles assigned to each NIC

Building a new inbound firewall rule

Now, knowing that the real meat and potatoes of Windows Firewall is inside the WFAS console, let's use WFAS to build ourselves a new rule. On this RA1 server, I have enabled RDP access so that I can more easily manage this server from my desk. However, by turning on RDP, I have now allowed RDP access from all the networks connected to this server. That means I can RDP into RA1 from inside the network, but I can also RDP into RA1 from the internet, since this is a remote access server and happens to be connected directly to the internet. This is a big problem because, now, any yahoo on the internet could potentially find my server, find the RDP login prompt, and try to brute-force their way into RA1. I am almost begging to be ransomwared in this scenario.

To alleviate this problem, I want to squash RDP only on my external NIC. I want it to remain active on the inside so that I can continue to access the server from my desk, but is there an easy way inside WFAS to create a firewall rule that blocks RDP access only from the outside? Yes, there certainly is.

Open wf.msc to launch WFAS, navigate to the **Inbound Rules** section, and you will see all of the existing inbound firewall rules that exist on this server (there are many rules listed here even if you have never visited this console before; these rules are installed with the OS). Right-click on **Inbound Rules** and choose **New Rule....** This launches a wizard from which we will create our new firewall rule. The first screen is where we identify what kind of rule we want to create. You can create a rule that modifies traffic for a particular program or port number, or you can look through a list of predefined protocols.

I like knowing exactly what my rule is doing because of the way that *I* defined it, not because of a pre-existing protocol definition, and I know that RDP runs over TCP port 3389. So, I am going to choose **port** on this screen, and after I click on **Next**, I will define 3389 as the specific port that I want to modify:

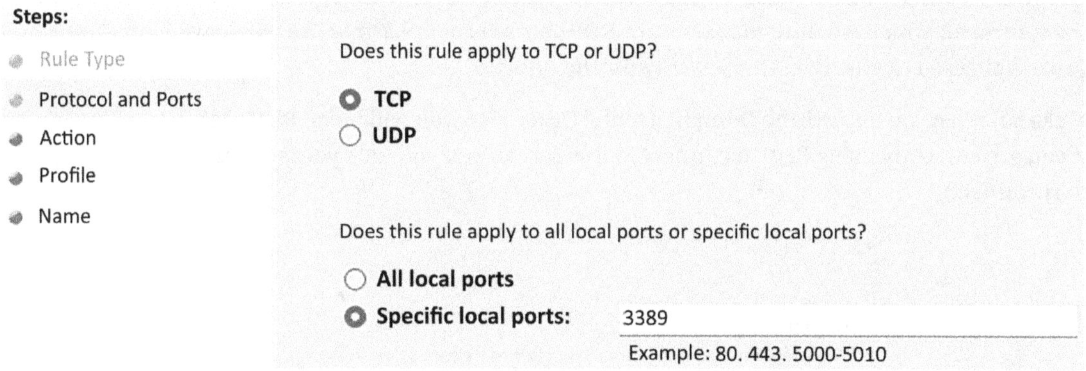

Steps:

Rule Type	Does this rule apply to TCP or UDP?
Protocol and Ports	◉ **TCP**
Action	○ **UDP**
Profile	
Name	

Does this rule apply to all local ports or specific local ports?

○ **All local ports**

◉ **Specific local ports:**   3389

Example: 80. 443. 5000-5010

Figure 10.12: This firewall rule is going to manipulate port 3389 (RDP) traffic

The third step is to decide whether we want to allow or block this port. There is a third option listed about only allowing the connection if it is authenticated by IPsec, which is a powerful option, but necessitates having IPsec established in our network already. Because of that requirement, this option doesn't apply to most people.

For our example, we already have RDP working, but we want to block it on one of the NICs, so I am going to choose **Block the connection**:

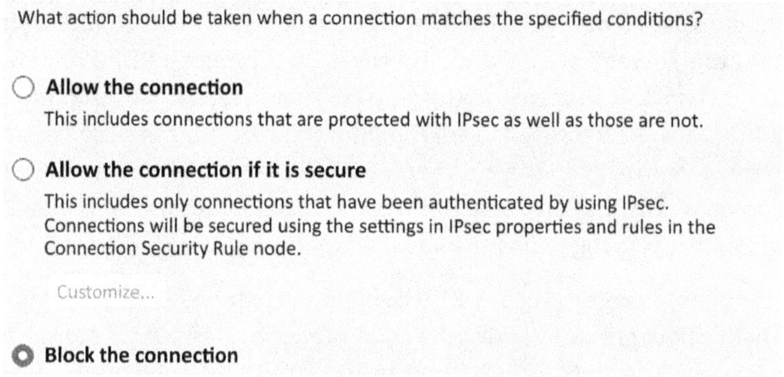

What action should be taken when a connection matches the specified conditions?

○ **Allow the connection**
This includes connections that are protected with IPsec as well as those are not.

○ **Allow the connection if it is secure**
This includes only connections that have been authenticated by using IPsec. Connections will be secured using the settings in IPsec properties and rules in the Connection Security Rule node.

    Customize...

◉ **Block the connection**

Figure 10.13: Blocking port 3389

We don't want to block RDP for *all* of the NICs, though, so this next screen is very important. Here, we need to reference back to our knowledge about those firewall profiles we talked about. Remember that internal NICs connected to our domain network will have the domain profile assigned to them. But any NICs that are not connected to an internal network where a domain controller resides will have either public or private profiles active. That is the knowledge we need to employ on this screen. If we want to disable RDP only on the external NIC, we need this rule to be active for only the private profile and public profile. In fact, in looking back through previous screenshots, we can see that the external NIC is assigned to the public profile specifically, and so we could check only the **Public** checkbox here, and RDP would then be blocked on the external NIC. But in case we add more NICs to this server in the future, for which we want to make sure RDP access is not possible, we will leave both **Public** and **Private** checked to ensure better security for the future.

Make sure that you *uncheck* the **Domain** profile! Otherwise, you will block RDP access completely, and if you are currently using RDP to connect to this server, you will kick yourself out of it and be unable to reconnect:

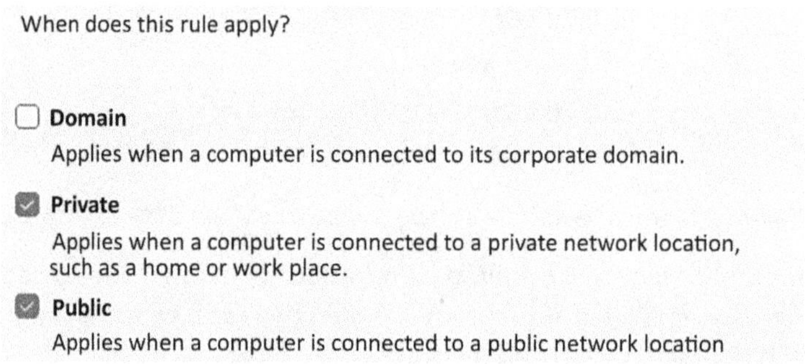

When does this rule apply?

☐ **Domain**
Applies when a computer is connected to its corporate domain.

☑ **Private**
Applies when a computer is connected to a private network location, such as a home or work place.

☑ **Public**
Applies when a computer is connected to a public network location

Figure 10.14: Blocking RDP only on our external NIC

And now, we simply create a name for our new rule, and we are done! Our ability to RDP into this server from the internet has immediately been disabled, and we can rest much easier tonight.

Creating a rule to allow pings (ICMP)

Very often, I find myself needing to create either an allow or a block rule for ICMP. In other words, I often find myself needing to adjust the firewall on servers in order to enable or disable their ability to reply to ping requests. You've probably noticed with newer server OSs that it is normal for the firewall to automatically block pings (ICMP) out of the box.

This is a problem for environments where pinging is the standard method for testing whether an IP address is consumed or available. You may be laughing, but trust me, there are still plenty of IT administrators out there who don't keep track of which IP addresses they have used inside their networks, and when faced with the need to set up a new server and decide what IP address to give it, they simply start pinging IP addresses in their network until they find one that times out! I have seen this so many times. While this is obviously not a good way to manage IP addresses, it happens. Unfortunately, this method encounters big problems because most new Windows installations are designed to block ICMP responses out of the box, which means that you may ping an IP address and receive a timeout, but there could still be another server or PC running on that IP address.

So, back to the point. You may have a need to enable ICMP on your new server, so that it responds when someone tries to ping it. When we need to create a new rule that allows pings to happen, we set up a rule just like we did for RDP, but there is one big catch. On that very first **Rule Type** screen when creating the new rule, where you identify what kind of rule you are creating, there are no options or predefinitions for ICMP. I find this strange because this is a very common type of rule to put into place, but alas, choosing **ICMP** from the drop-down list would just be too easy. Instead, what you need to do is create a new inbound rule like we did for RDP, but at the very first screen for **Rule Type**, make sure you select the option that says **Custom**.

Next, leave the option selected to define this rule for **All programs**. Click **Next** again, and now you have a drop-down box called **Protocol type**. This is the menu where you configure your new rule to manipulate ICMP traffic. As you can see in *Figure 10.15*, you can choose **ICMPv4** or **ICMPv6**, depending on what your network traffic looks like. My test lab is IPv4-only, so I am going to choose **ICMPv4**:

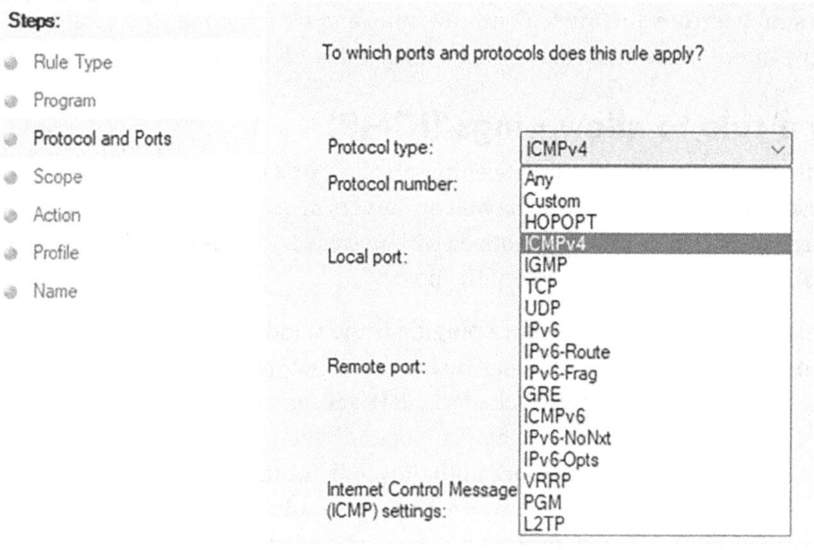

Steps:

- Rule Type
- Program
- Protocol and Ports
- Scope
- Action
- Profile
- Name

To which ports and protocols does this rule apply?

Protocol type: ICMPv4

Protocol number:

Local port:

Remote port:

Internet Control Message (ICMP) settings:

Any
Custom
HOPOPT
ICMPv4
IGMP
TCP
UDP
IPv6
IPv6-Route
IPv6-Frag
GRE
ICMPv6
IPv6-NoNxt
IPv6-Opts
VRRP
PGM
L2TP

Figure 10.15: Applying firewall rules to specific protocols

For the rest of the ICMP rule creation, follow the same procedures outlined when we created the RDP rule, choosing to either allow or block this traffic, and for which firewall profiles. Once finished, your new ICMPv4 rule is immediately enacted, and if you have configured an **Allow** rule, your new server will now successfully respond to ping requests:

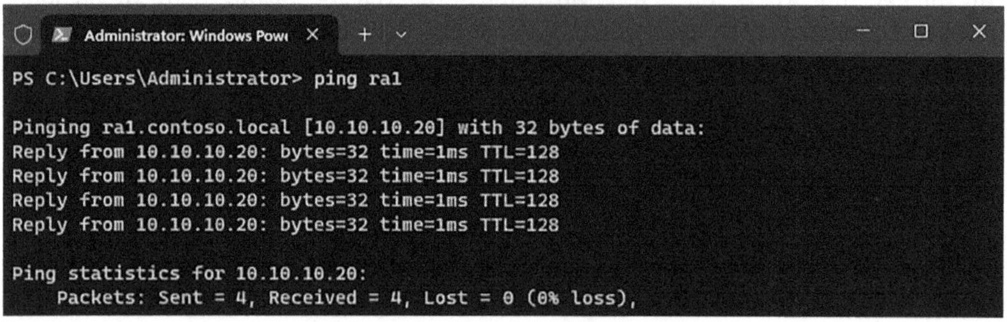

```
Administrator: Windows Powe  X   +  v                                    —    □    ×

PS C:\Users\Administrator> ping ra1

Pinging ra1.contoso.local [10.10.10.20] with 32 bytes of data:
Reply from 10.10.10.20: bytes=32 time=1ms TTL=128
Reply from 10.10.10.20: bytes=32 time=1ms TTL=128
Reply from 10.10.10.20: bytes=32 time=1ms TTL=128
Reply from 10.10.10.20: bytes=32 time=1ms TTL=128

Ping statistics for 10.10.10.20:
    Packets: Sent = 4, Received = 4, Lost = 0 (0% loss),
```

Figure 10.16: Pinging your server and now receiving an ICMP response

If ever you need to modify a rule or dig into more advanced properties of a firewall rule, back on the **Inbound Rules** screen, you can right-click on any individual firewall rule and head into **Properties**. Inside these tabs exists the opportunity to modify any criteria about the rule. For example, you could accommodate additional ports, you could modify which firewall profiles it applies to, or you could even restrict which specific source or destination IP addresses this rule applies to through the use of the **Scope** tab.

This enables you to apply your firewall rule only to traffic coming or going from a specific portion of your network, or a certain subset of machines. For example, here I have modified my **Scope** tab to reflect that I only want this firewall rule to apply to traffic that is coming in from the 192.168.0.0/16 subnet:

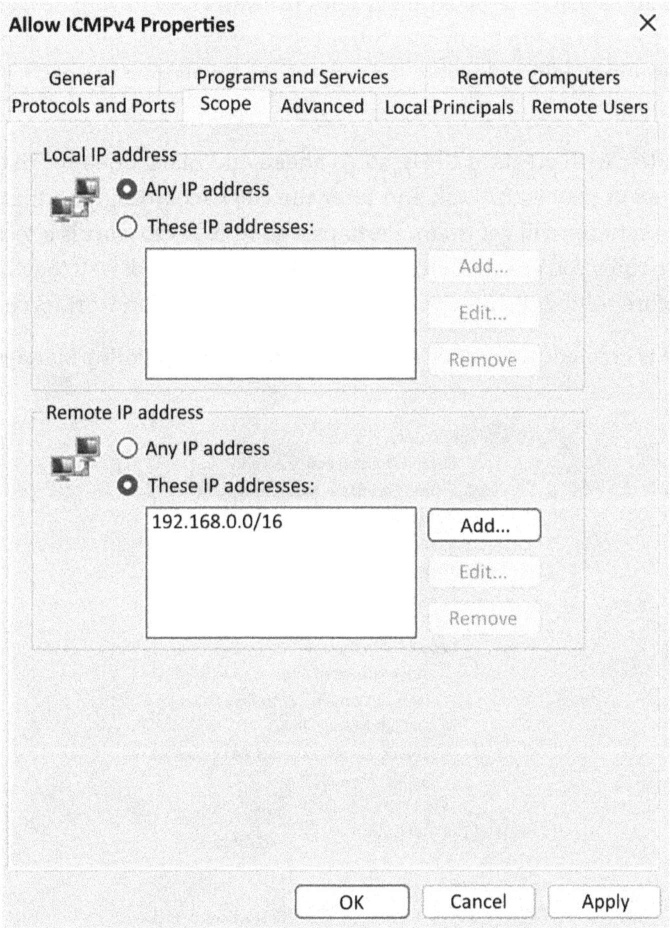

Figure 10.17: Scoping a firewall rule to specific IP addresses or subnets

Managing WFAS with Group Policy

Managing firewall rules on your servers and clients can be a huge step toward a more secure environment for your company. The best part? This technology is enterprise-class and free to use since it's already built into the OSs that you use. The only cost you have associated with firewalling at this level is the time it takes to put all these rules in place, which would be an administrative nightmare if you had to implement your entire list of allows and blocks on every machine individually.

Thank goodness for **Group Policy**. As with most settings and functions inside the Microsoft Windows platform, setting up a firewall policy that applies to everyone is a breeze for your domain-joined machines. You can even break it up into multiple sets of policies, creating one GPO that applies firewall rules to your clients and a separate GPO that applies firewall rules to your servers, however you see fit. The point is that you can group many machines together into categories, create a GPO ruleset for each category, and automatically apply it to every machine by making use of Group Policy's powerful distribution capabilities.

You are already familiar with creating GPOs, so go ahead and make one now that will contain some firewall settings for us to play with. Link and filter the GPO accordingly so that only the machines you want to have the settings will get them. Perhaps a good place to start is a testing OU, so that you can make sure all the rules you are about to place inside the GPO work well together and with all your existing policies, before rolling the new policy out to your production workforce.

Once your new GPO is created, right-click on it from inside **Group Policy Management Console** and click on **Edit...**:

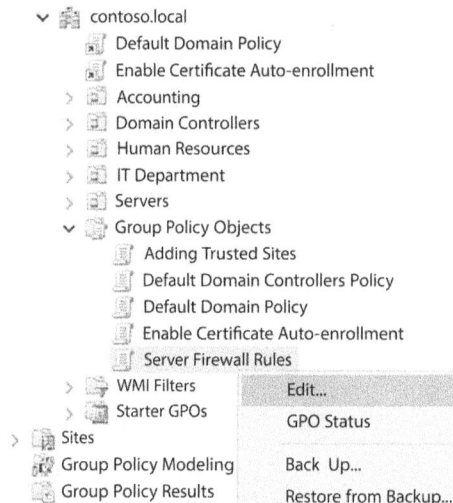

Figure 10.18: Using Group Policy to centrally manage Windows Firewall rules

Now that we are looking at the insides of this new GPO, we just need to figure out where the correct location is for us to create some new firewall rules. When you are looking inside the rules on the local machine itself, everything is listed under a **Windows Defender Firewall with Advanced Security** heading, and that is located at **Computer Configuration | Policies | Windows Settings | Security Settings | Windows Defender Firewall with Advanced Security | Windows Defender Firewall with Advanced Security**:

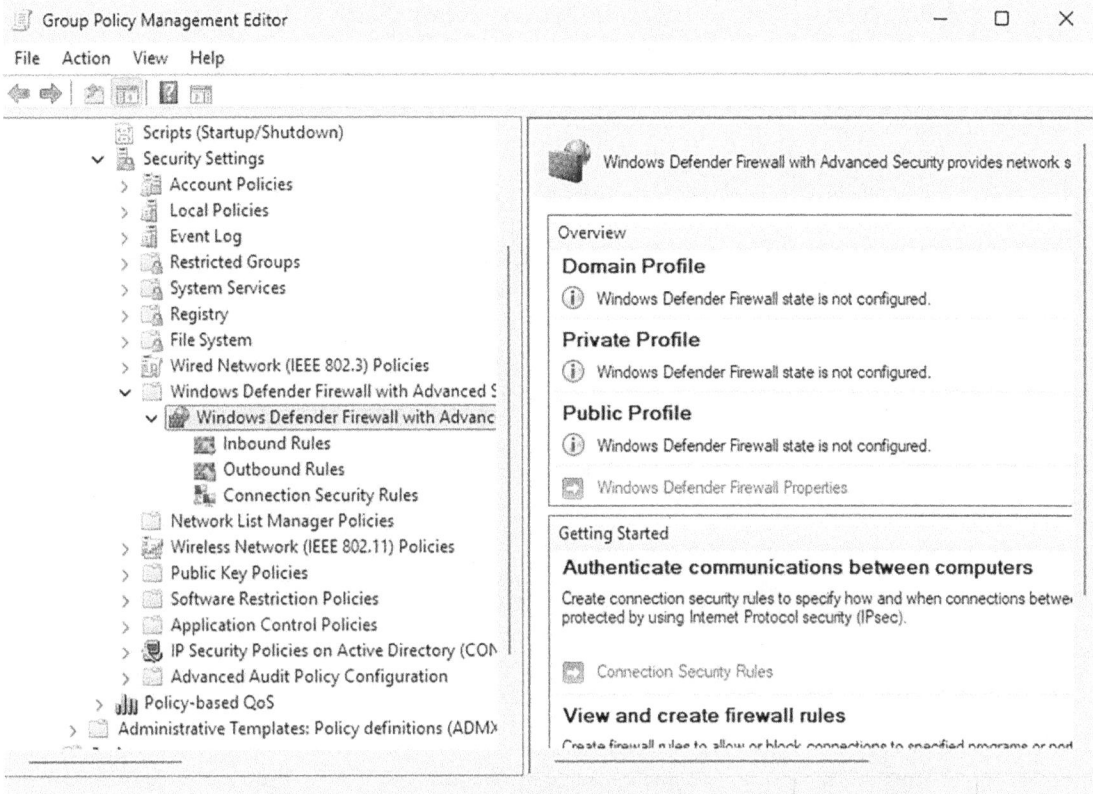

Figure 10.19: Location of firewall rule settings inside a GPO

As you can see, this is also the place to go when you want to make sure that particular firewall profiles, or Windows Firewall as a whole, are specifically turned on or off. So, this is the same place that you would go to if you wanted to disable Windows Firewall for everyone.

By clicking on the **Windows Defender Firewall Properties** link shown in *Figure 10.19*, you can determine the status of each firewall profile individually:

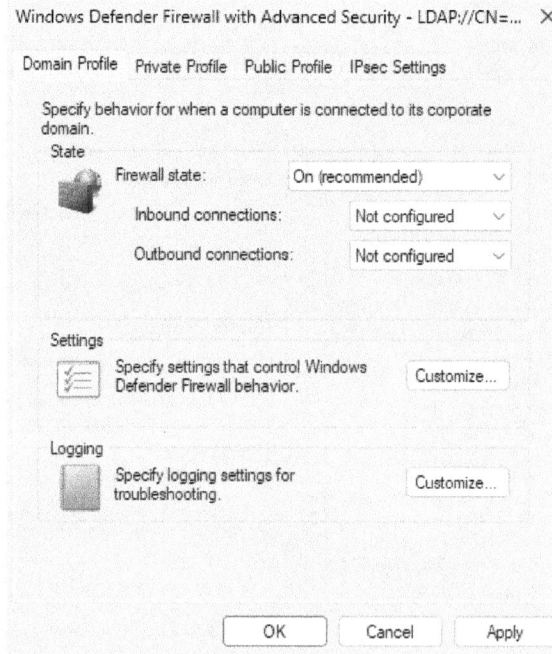

Figure 10.20: Separate tabs to modify each firewall profile's behavior

Once you are finished setting your profiles according to your needs, click on **OK,** and you will find yourself back at the WFAS part of the GPO. Just like inside the local WFAS console, you have categories for **Inbound Rules** and **Outbound Rules.** Simply right-click on **Inbound Rules** and click on **New Rule...** to get started with building a rule right into this GPO. Walk through the same wizard that you are already familiar with from creating a rule in the local WFAS console, and when you are finished, your new inbound firewall rule is shown inside the GPO:

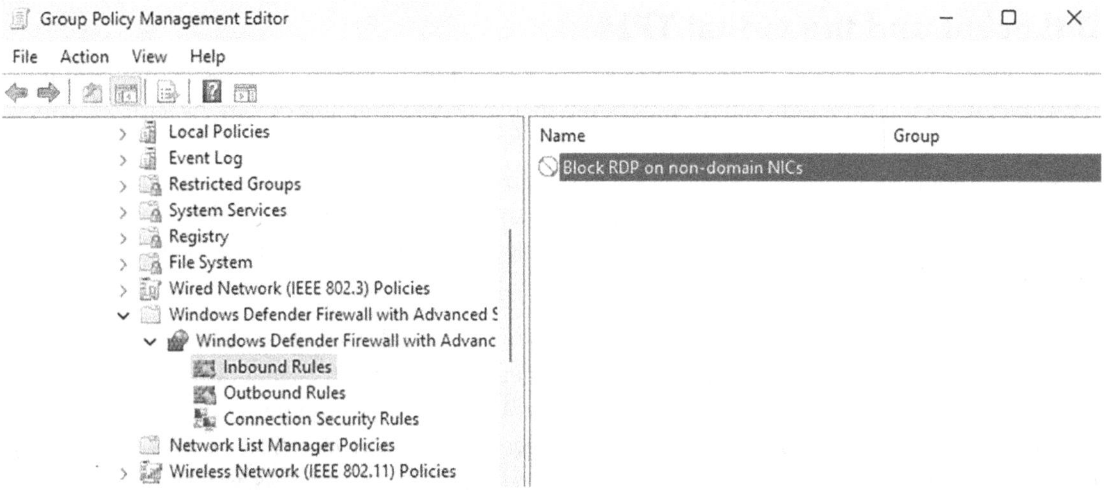

Figure 10.21: A successfully implemented firewall rule, inside the GPO

Faster than you can say Jack Robinson, this new firewall rule is already making its way around Active Directory and installing itself onto those computers and servers that you defined in the policy's links and filtering criteria.

Encryption technologies

Not too many years ago, the idea of encrypting data was something best left to action movies. Tom Cruise might have been able to do it, but many of us sat back and left this to the experts. Times have certainly changed, and data being encrypted both on the move and at rest is commonplace. Most of us have been encrypting our website traffic for many years by using HTTPS websites, but even in that realm, there are surprising exceptions, with a lot of the cheap web-hosting companies still providing login pages that transmit traffic in clear text. This is terrible, because for anything that you submit over the internet now using regular HTTP or an unencrypted email, you *have to assume* that it is being read by someone else. Chances are you are being paranoid and nobody is actually intercepting and reading your traffic, but you need to know that if you are accessing a website that says HTTP in the address bar, or if you are sending an email from any of the free email services, any data that is being entered on that web page or in that email can easily be stolen by someone halfway around the world. Data encryption is an absolute requirement for corporate information that needs to traverse the internet.

While we are getting better and better at protecting internet browser and web traffic, we traditionally are still not paying a lot of attention to data that is "safe" within the walls of our organization. The bad guys aren't dumb, and they have a very large toolbox of tricks to socially engineer their way into our networks. Once inside, what do they find? In most cases, it's a big free-for-all. Get hold of one user account or one computer, and you've got keys to a large part of the kingdom. Fortunately, there are several technologies built into Windows Server 2025 that are designed to combat these intrusions and protect your data even while it sits within the four walls of your datacenter. Let's look at some information on them so that you can explore the possibility of using these encryption technologies to further protect your data.

BitLocker and the virtual TPM

BitLocker is a technology that has become familiar to see on our client systems within corporate networks. It is a full-drive encryption technology, giving us the advantage of making sure our data is fully protected on laptops or computers that might be stolen. If a thief gets their hands on a company laptop, claws out the hard drive, and plugs it into their computer... sorry, Charlie, no access. The entire volume is encrypted. This makes all kinds of sense for mobile hardware that could be easily lost or stolen. But in the beginning stages of this technology, there was never real consideration of using BitLocker to protect our servers.

With the escalated adoption of cloud computing resources, it suddenly makes much more sense to want BitLocker on our servers. More particularly, when talking about the cloud, what we really want is BitLocker on our **virtual machines** (**VMs**), whether they be client or server OSs. Whether you are storing your VMs in a true cloud environment provided by a public cloud service provider or hosting your own private cloud where tenants log in to create and manage their own VMs, without the possibility of encrypting those virtual hard drives—the VHD and VHDX files—your data is absolutely **not** secure.

Why not? Because anyone with administrative rights to the virtualization host platform can easily gain access to any data sitting on your server's hard drives, even without any kind of access to your network or user account on your domain. All they have to do is take a copy of your VHDX file (the entire hard drive contents of your server), copy it to a USB stick, bring it home, mount this virtual hard disk on their own system, and bingo—they have access to your server hard drive and your data. This is a big problem for data security compliance.

Why has it historically not been feasible to encrypt VMs? Because BitLocker comes with an interesting requirement. The hard drive is encrypted, which means that it can't boot without the encryption being unlocked. How do we unlock the hard drive so that our machine can boot? One of two ways.

The best method is to store the **unlock keys** inside a **Trusted Platform Module** (**TPM**). This is a physical microchip that is built right into most computers that you purchase today. Storing the BitLocker unlock key on this chip means that you do not have to connect anything physically to your computer to make it boot; you simply enter a PIN to gain access to the TPM, and then the TPM unlocks BitLocker. On the other hand, if you choose to deploy BitLocker without the presence of a TPM, to unlock a BitLocker volume and make it bootable, you need to plug in a physical USB stick that contains the BitLocker unlock keys. Do you see the problem with either of these installation paths in a VM scenario? VMs cannot have a physical TPM chip, and you also have no easy way of plugging in a USB stick! So, how do we encrypt those VMs so that prying eyes at the cloud hosting company can't see all our stuff?

Enter the **virtual TPM**. This capability came to us brand new in Windows Server 2016; we now have the ability to give our virtual servers a virtual TPM that can be used for storing these keys! This is incredible news and means that we can finally encrypt our servers, whether they are hosted on physical Hyper-V servers in our datacenter or sitting in the Azure cloud.

Shielded VMs

Using BitLocker and virtual TPMs to encrypt and protect virtual hard drive files produces something called **shielded VMs**. Shielded VMs are a capability first introduced in Windows Server 2016 and were improved quite a bit in Server 2019. With Microsoft's redirected focus on cloud hosting and Azure-supported servers, it is likely that Microsoft won't be adding additional development or capabilities to on-prem shielded VMs in the future, but they still exist in Server 2025 and are still fully supported.

We will cover more details of shielded VMs in *Chapter 15, Hyper-V*.

Encrypted virtual networks

Wouldn't it be great if we could configure, control, and govern our networks from a graphical administrative interface, rather than looking at router CLIs all day? Would we not benefit from the networking flexibility to move servers and workloads from one subnet to another, without having to change IP addressing or routing on those servers? Couldn't we find some way to automatically encrypt all of the traffic that is flowing between our servers, without having to configure that encryption on the servers themselves?

Yes, yes, and yes! Through the use of **software-defined networking** (SDN) and a capability called **encrypted virtual networks**, we can accomplish all of these things. This section of text is really just a reference point, a place to steer you back toward *Chapter 8, Networking with Windows Server 2025*, if you skipped over it and landed here instead. We have already discussed SDN and its capability to create and automatically encrypt virtual networks that flow between Hyper-V VMs and Hyper-V host servers, so if this idea intrigues you, make sure to head back and revisit that chapter.

Encrypted File System

Encrypted File System (EFS) is a component of Microsoft Windows that has existed on both client and server OSs for many years. Whereas BitLocker is responsible for securing an entire volume or disk, EFS is a little more particular. When you want to encrypt only certain documents or folders, this is the place you turn to. When you choose to encrypt files using EFS, it is important to understand that Windows needs to utilize a user certificate as part of the encryption/decryption process, and so the availability of an internal PKI is key to a successful deployment. Also important to note is that authentication keys are tied to the user's password, so a fully compromised user account could negate the benefits provided by EFS.

I think that many companies don't employ EFS because you leave the decision on what documents to encrypt up to the user. This also means that you depend on them to remember to do the encryption in the first place, which means they will have to understand the importance of it to make it worthy of their time. I wanted to mention EFS because it is still alive and is still a valid platform for which you can encrypt data, but most administrators land on BitLocker as a better solution.

The lack of responsibility on the user's part and a good centralized management platform put BitLocker a solid step ahead of EFS. The technologies could certainly co-exist, though, keeping data safe at two different tiers instead of relying on only one of the data encryption technologies available to you.

IPsec

A lot of the encryption technology built into OSs revolves around data at rest. But what about our data on the move? We talked about using SSL on HTTPS websites as a way of encrypting web browser data that is on the move across the internet, but what about data that is not flowing through a web browser?

And what if I'm not even concerned about the internet? What if I am interested in protecting traffic that could even be flowing from point to point *inside* my corporate network? Is there anything that can help with these kinds of requirements? Certainly.

IPsec is a protocol suite that can be used for authenticating and encrypting the packets that happen during network communication. IPsec is not a technology that is particular to the Microsoft world, but there are various ways in Windows Server 2025 that IPsec can be utilized in order to secure data that you are shuttling back and forth between machines.

The most common place where IPsec interaction shows up on Windows Server is when using the **Remote Access (RA)** role. When configuring VPN on your RA server, you will find several different connection protocols that VPN clients can use to connect to the VPN server. Included in this list of possible connection platforms are IPsec (IKEv2) tunnels. The second remote access technology that uses IPsec is DirectAccess.

When you establish DirectAccess in your network, every time a client computer creates a DirectAccess tunnel over the internet to the DirectAccess server, that tunnel is protected by IPsec. Thankfully, the Remote Access Management console that you use to deploy both VPN and DirectAccess is smart enough to know everything that is needed to make IPsec authentication and encryption work, and you don't need to know a single thing about IPsec to make these remote access technologies work for you!

The big missing factor with IPsec provided by the Remote Access role is traffic *inside* your network. When you are talking about VPN or DirectAccess, you are talking about traffic that moves over the internet. But what if you simply want to encrypt traffic that moves between two different servers inside the same network? Or the traffic that is flowing from your client computers inside the office to their local servers, also located in the office? This is where some knowledge of the IPsec policy settings comes in handy because we can specify that we want traffic moving around inside our corporate networks to be encrypted using IPsec. Making that happen is simply a matter of putting the right policies in place.

Configuring IPsec

There are two different places where IPsec settings can be configured in a Microsoft Windows environment. Both current and very old systems can be supplied with IPsec configurations through the traditional **IPsec Security Policy snap-in**. If you are running all systems that are Windows 7 and Server 2008 or newer (and hopefully you are!), then you can alternatively employ WFAS for setting up your IPsec policies. WFAS is the most flexible solution, but it isn't always an option depending on the status of legacy systems in your environment.

First, let's take a glance at the older IPsec policy console. We will start here because the different options available will help to build a baseline for us to start wrapping our minds around the way that IPsec interaction works between two endpoints. There are three different classifications of IPsec policy that can be assigned to your machines that we will encounter in this console. Let's take a minute to explain each one, because the policy names can be a little bit misleading. Understanding these options will put you a step ahead in understanding how the settings inside WFAS work as well.

Server policy

Server policy should probably be renamed *Requestor* policy because that is really what this one does. When a computer or server makes a network request outbound to another computer or server, it is requesting to establish a network connection. On these requesting computers—the ones initiating the traffic—this is where we tell the IPsec Server policy to apply. Once applied, the Server policy tells that computer or server to request IPsec encryption for the communication session between the initiating machine and the remote computer. If the remote system supports IPsec, then the IPsec tunnel is created to protect traffic flowing between the two machines. The Server policy is pretty lenient, though, and if the remote computer does not support IPsec, then the network connection is still successful but remains unencrypted.

Secure Server policy

Creating and assigning a Secure Server policy is very similar to a normal Server policy, except that the Secure Server policy *requires* IPsec encryption before allowing network communication to happen. The regular Server policy that we talked about earlier will encrypt with IPsec when possible, but if not possible, it will continue to flow the traffic unencrypted. The Secure Server policy, on the other hand, will fail to establish the connection at all if IPsec cannot be negotiated between the two machines.

Client policy

Our third flavor of IPsec policy that can be created and assigned, the Client policy, really should be renamed the *Response* policy, because this one is on the other end of the connection. The Client policy does not care about *requesting* an IPsec session; it only cares about *receiving* one. When a computer makes a network request to a server, having a Server policy assigned to that computer will force it to request an IPsec-encrypted connection. That computer might be reaching out to a server for information, and if the server has a Client policy assigned to it, that computer and server will be able to establish an encrypted tunnel between themselves.

The reality is that you will generally have both requesting and receiving types of policies assigned to both the workstation and server involved with your network communication. That way, if a client reaches out to a server, it can build an IPsec tunnel. Alternatively, if the server needs to reach out to the client workstation, that direction of tunneling works as well.

IPsec Security policy snap-in

The original console for manipulating IPsec settings is accessed via MMC. Open that, and add the **IP Security Policy Management** snap-in. Interestingly, when adding this snap-in, you will notice that you can view either the local IPsec policy of the machine that you are currently logged in to, or you can open the IPsec policy for the domain.

If you are interested in configuring a domain-wide IPsec implementation, this would be your landing zone for working on those settings. But for the purpose of just sticking our head in here to poke around a little, you can choose **Local computer** to take a look at the console:

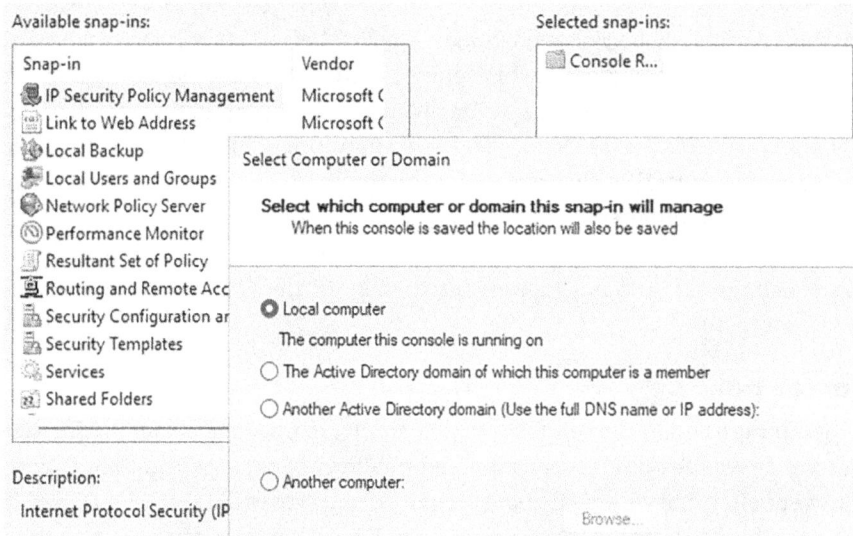

Figure 10.22: Exploring IPsec configuration for our local server

Once inside, you can see any existing IPsec policies that might be in place, or you can start creating your own by using the **Create IP Security Policy...** action available when right-clicking on **IP Security Policies**. Doing this will invoke a wizard that will walk you through the configuration of your own IPsec policy:

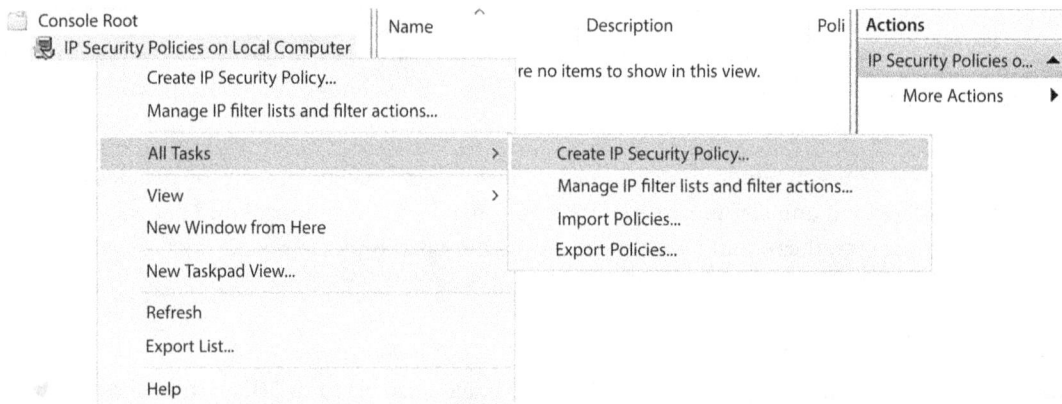

Figure 10.23: Creating an IP security policy

Using WFAS instead

The newer platform used for establishing IPsec connection rules is WFAS. Go ahead and open that up, as you are already familiar with doing. Once inside, navigate to the **Connection Security Rules** section, which is listed immediately below **Inbound Rules** and **Outbound Rules. Connection Security Rules** is where you define IPsec connection rules. If you right-click on **Connection Security Rules** and choose **New Rule...,** you will then walk through a wizard similar to the one for creating a firewall rule:

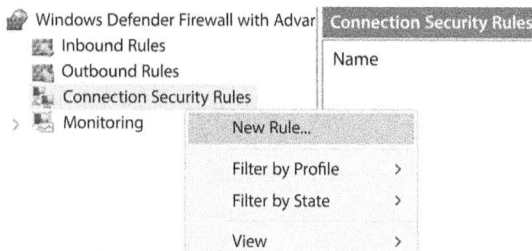

Figure 10.24: WFAS can also be used to create IPsec policy rules

Once inside the wizard to create your new rule, you start to see that the options available to you are quite different from the ones shown when creating a new firewall rule. This is the platform from which you will establish IPsec connection security rules, which define what the IPsec tunnels look like and on which machines or IP addresses they need to be active:

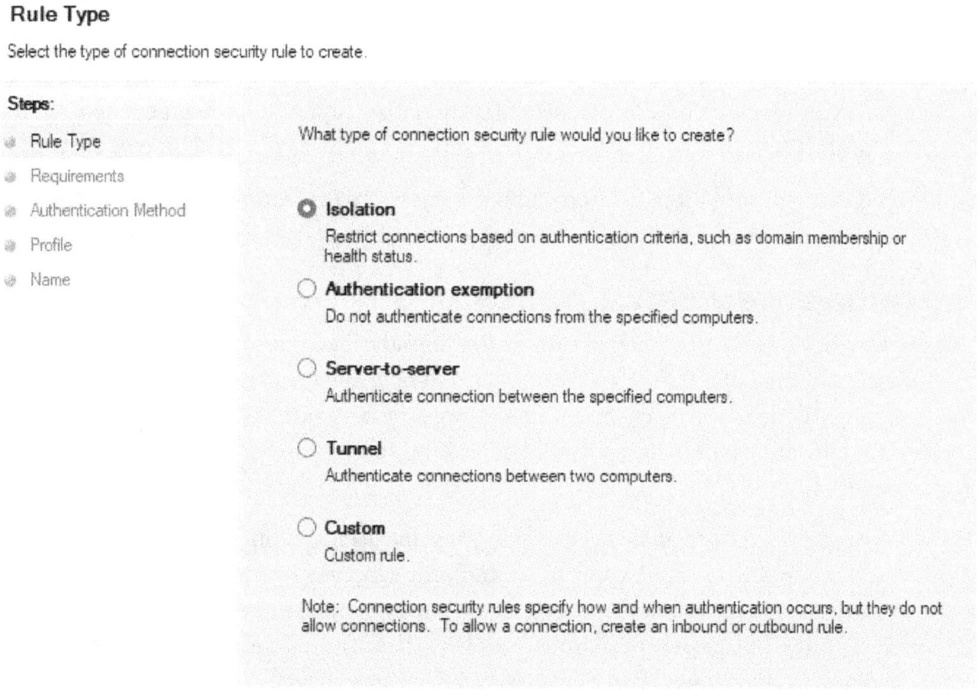

Figure 10.25: Types of connection security rules

We do not have space here to cover all available options in this wizard, but I recommend picking up from here and taking it a step further with the following Microsoft Learn article. While I find that few companies make use of inner-network encryption, there are some real security benefits to doing so, and even though this method for utilizing IPsec has been around for more than 10 years, it still serves valid use cases: https://learn.microsoft.com/en-us/previous-versions/windows/it-pro/windows-server-2012-r2-and-2012/hh831807(v=ws.11).

Microsoft Entra Password Protection

If you are a Microsoft Entra customer, you already have access to this new function called **Microsoft Entra Password Protection** (formerly called **Azure Active Directory Password Protection**), still formerly known as **banned passwords**. The idea is this: Microsoft maintains a global, ongoing list of commonly bad passwords (such as the word password) and automatically blocks all variants of that password, such as P@ssword, Password123, and so on. Any of these potential passwords would be blocked altogether if a user ever tried to create one as their own password. You also have the ability to add your own custom banned passwords inside the Entra interface. Once you have banned passwords up and running in Azure, this capability can then be ported to your on-premises Active Directory environment as well, by implementing the Microsoft Entra Password Protection proxy service (whew, that's a mouthful).

This proxy is an agent that gets installed onto your local domain controller servers and pulls down password policies from Entra (formerly Azure Active Directory), ensuring all passwords that users attempt to put into place on your local domain controllers fit within the rules defined by Azure's banned password algorithms.

To use this technology, you must, of course, be utilizing Entra, so this isn't for everyone. However, if you do have and sync accounts into Microsoft Entra, then this capability is even backported to older versions of on-premises domain controllers. These servers can be as old as Windows Server 2012.

Here is a link to further information on Microsoft Entra Password Protection for AD DS: https://learn.microsoft.com/en-us/entra/identity/authentication/concept-password-ban-bad-on-premises.

Fine-grained password policy

As promised way back during our discussion of the domain-level password policy, we are here to walk through the building of a fine-grained password policy. Most organizations do require specific password complexity for their users, but almost always by way of the default domain policy GPO, which means that the password complexity and expiration settings are exactly the same for everyone within the domain.

What if you have requirements to enable complexity on some user accounts but not on others? Perhaps you have sales personnel who travel constantly, and requiring very strong and complex passwords makes a lot of sense for them. But let's say you also have a machine shop where users have to log in to computers every day, but those computers never leave the office, and the users never type in their credentials into any systems other than those physically secure devices.

Is it really necessary for those machine shop users to have the same level of password complexity as the traveling sales personnel? Should they also be required to update their password every 30 days simply because you also ask it of your sales folks?

Starting with Windows Server 2012, log in to any domain controller server and launch Server Manager, and at the very top of your **Tools** list, you will see something called **Active Directory Administrative Center (ADAC)**. This ADAC tool can be used to manipulate many things within Active Directory, but most importantly for our purposes today, this new tool is the mechanism that enables you to create a **fine-grained password policy (FGPP)**. An FGPP enables the scenario we alluded to a paragraph ago: the ability to create multiple password policies and assign those policies to different classes of users and user accounts.

Log in to a domain controller as a domain admin and open ADAC. In the left navigation pane, expand the name of your internal domain, then go to **System | Password Settings Container**. In my lab environment, I am clicking on **contoso (local) | System | Password Settings Container**. Currently, **Password Settings Container** is empty, but using the **New | Password Settings** task will get things rolling:

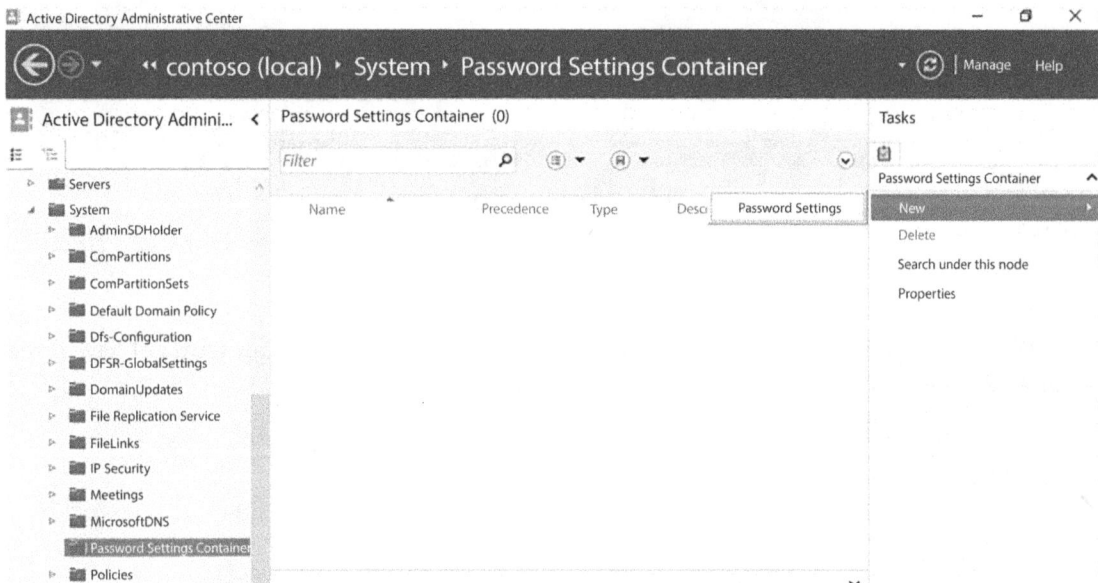

Figure 10.26: Fine-grained password policies are configured inside ADAC

The **Password Settings** screen is fairly self-explanatory. Here, you define the same types of password complexity, length, and expiration criteria that you would normally configure inside the default domain policy GPO. You can see in *Figure 10.27* that I have created a **Password Settings** policy called `Sales Users`, with a number of specific criteria.

I was able to configure password settings as well as account lockout settings (another security setting commonly done globally via a GPO), and filtered this password policy so that it only applies to users that are inside my AD group called **Sales Users**:

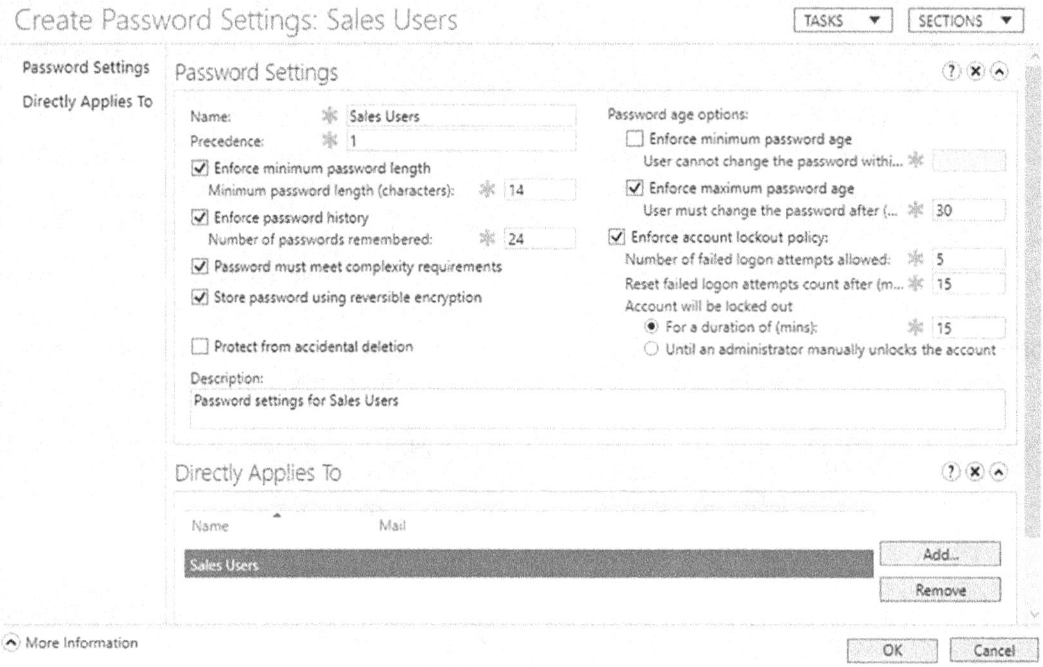

Figure 10.27: Creating new Password Settings policies

Now, I'm going to repeat the process a couple more times, after which you can see that I have three separate **Password Settings** policies inside my ADAC container:

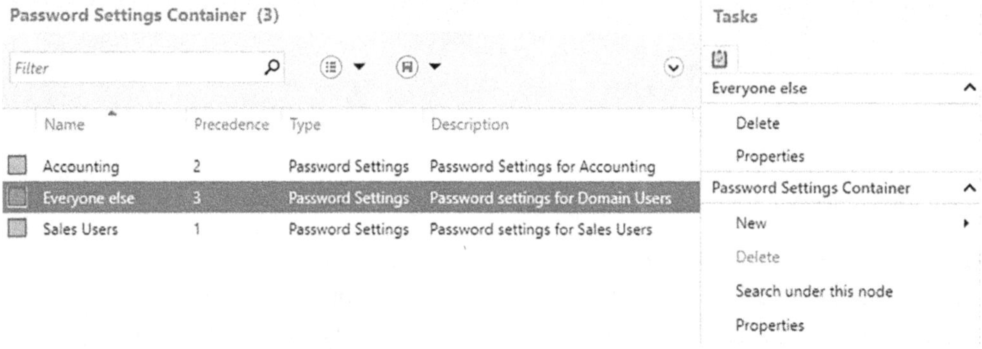

Figure 10.28: Creating more than one Password Settings policy

Something important to note here is that each Password Settings policy has a **Precedence** declaration. Since we apply these password settings to groups, it is certainly possible that a particular user could be part of multiple groups, which would give them multiple password policies. The **Precedence** number helps FGPPs to distinguish which settings should apply.

That's it! As soon as you have defined a fine-grained password policy inside ADAC, these new password settings will now take priority over settings inside the default domain policy GPO. Rather than pushing password settings via Group Policy, using a fine-grained password policy utilizes its own objects inside Active Directory to do its work. These objects are called **Password Settings objects (PSOs)**. If you want to see a little bit further under the hood of a PSO, now that you have created an FGPP inside ADAC, head over to **Active Directory Users and Computers** and enable **Advanced Features** under the **View** menu. Once **Advanced Features** is enabled, you can navigate to **Domain | System | Password Settings Container** and see the new PSOs that you created a minute ago.

Double-clicking on any of these objects and then visiting the **Attribute Editor** tab will display details on the password criteria for that object:

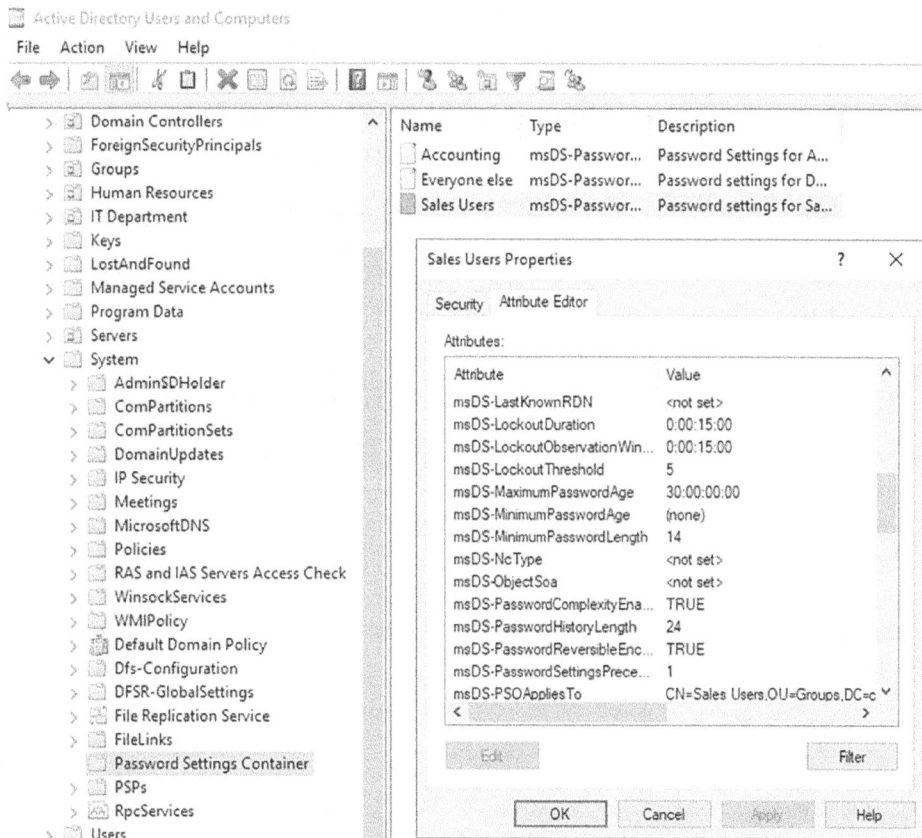

Figure 10.29: Viewing password criteria outside of ADAC

There is no *need* to visit these objects from inside ADUC, as you can always make tweaks and changes to your FGPP from inside the ADAC console, but seeing these PSOs helps us to understand how Active Directory is storing and processing these policies.

Windows LAPS

Current admins may recognize the term *LAPS,* but you are probably thinking about Microsoft LAPS, the original iteration of this technology. That original Microsoft LAPS came to us in the year 2016, but was deprecated in 2023.

Replacing one keyword in its name, **Windows Local Administrator Password Solution (Windows LAPS)** is the improved replacement. The old Microsoft LAPS required software to be installed, and only worked on domain-joined workstations. The newer Windows LAPS is built into the Windows operating system, no more software to install or maintain, and can benefit domain-joined, Entra-joined, or hybrid-joined computers.

The whole idea of Windows LAPS is this: a system that automatically rotates local administrator passwords on your workstations and stores those passwords securely inside either AD or Entra. By making use of LAPS, you will no longer have a single local administrator password that can be used on every computer, because each one will maintain a unique password for that account, which updates itself on whatever cadence you desire. This greatly helps to protect against pass-the-hash or other lateral attacks.

When Windows LAPS is implemented, domain-joined computers can store these passwords in Active Directory, Entra-joined computers store in Entra, and hybrid-joined computers (joined to both AD and Entra) can store their local administrator passwords in either AD or Entra—but not both. You can only store LAPS passwords in one place or the other.

Windows LAPS works with Windows 10 or Windows 11, as long as they are running at least the April 11, 2023, update. It also works with Windows Server 2019 or newer operating systems.

LAPS can also be used to securely store Active Directory DSRM account passwords. When initially implementing AD, you may remember that we had to specify a disaster recovery (DSRM) account that would be necessary in the event that we ever need to recover AD. Once an AD domain is established, it very well may run for 10 years before you ever need to think about the DSRM passwords again, but when you need them, suddenly you need them really badly. Rather than keep a sticky note locked in a safe for years, Windows LAPS can store the DSRM account passwords as well, giving you a central place to find them later, if ever needed.

Implementing LAPS

Windows LAPS can be implemented via Group Policy or Intune. Since the focus of this book is primarily localized Windows Server tasks, we will take the Group Policy approach. If you are running a current AD schema, you should already have LAPS configuration settings waiting for you inside Group Policy; you simply need to know where to find them. If you are running older infrastructure, you may need to download the LAPS.admx template and inject it into Group Policy. The setup for LAPS is fairly quick and painless, but in addition to rolling out client settings via GPO, you must begin this journey with a couple of PowerShell commands to prep your domain environment to accept Windows LAPS.

Prepping the environment

An important note before I forget: it is in your best interests when using LAPS for your AD functional levels to be at least Server 2016. Anything earlier than that, and you won't be able to configure the option for AD to encrypt these administrator passwords.

First, we need to ensure that the AD schema is expanded to include the LAPS attributes. This is easily accomplished via a single PowerShell command:

```
Update-LapsADSchema
```

Once finished, you should be able to open any computer object inside Active Directory Users and Computers, and find a new tab called **Local Administrator Password Solution**.

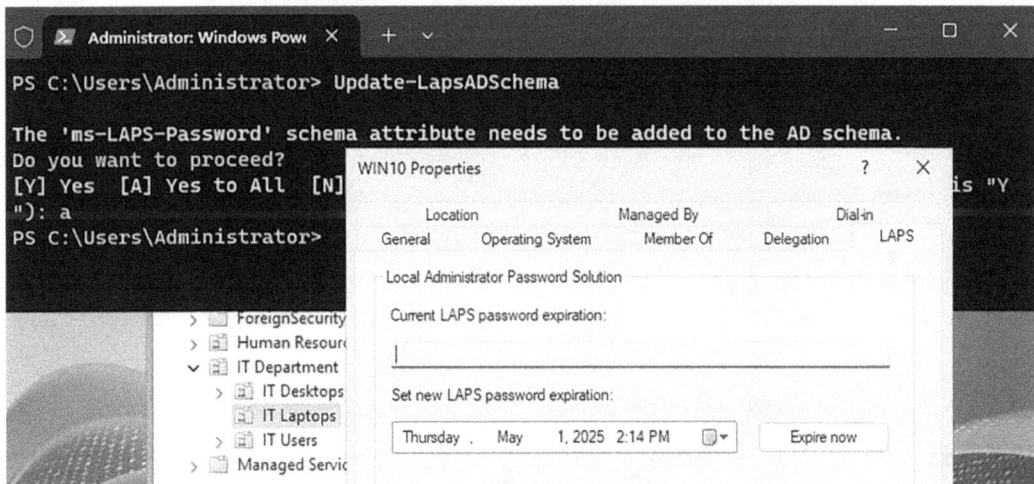

Figure 10.30: Preparing the AD schema for LAPS

Next, we must tweak permissions for the OU(s) where our computer accounts live. For any OUs where workstations reside, workstations that you want to take advantage of LAPS, a PowerShell command needs to be run to set permissions accordingly, granting computers the ability to self-update local administrator passwords inside AD. This command does apply to nested OUs, so if all of your computers are under a single high-level OU, you can get away with a single command here:

```
Set-LapsADComputerSelfPermission -Identity "ou=IT Laptops,
ou=IT Department,dc=contoso,dc=local"
```

(You will want to replace my OU identity name with your own, of course.)

After running this command against any relevant OUs, we are now ready to configure and push settings to our client computers via Group Policy.

Configuring the clients

Create yourself a new GPO, and navigate to the following location:

Computer Configuration | Policies | Administrative Templates | System | LAPS

Here you will find configurable options related to LAPS.

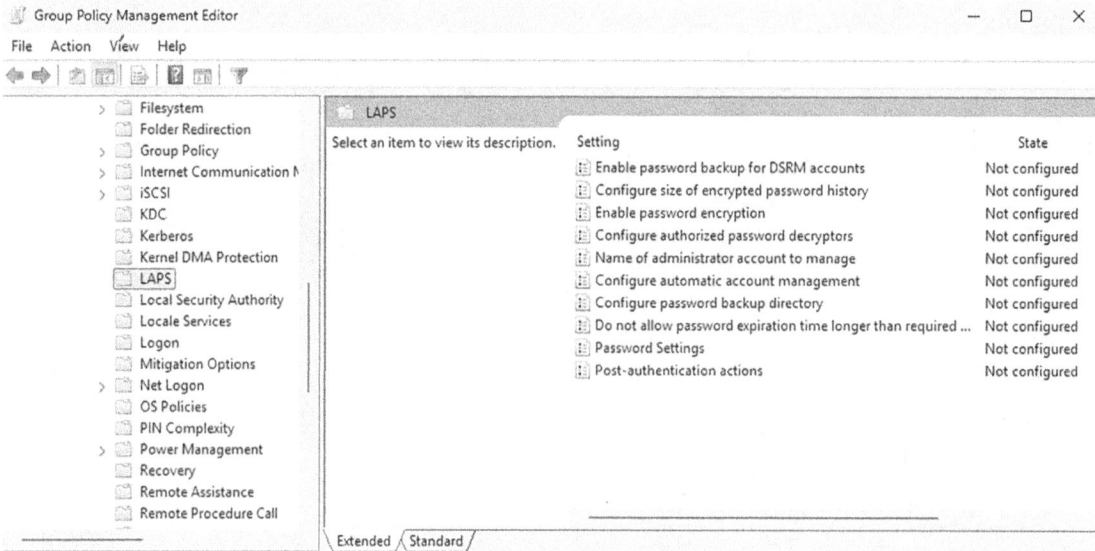

Figure 10.31: Configuring Windows LAPS via Group Policy

Let's discuss some of the most common settings to configure, to fill out extra details about LAPS capabilities:

- **Name of administrator account to manage:** If you are using a custom local administrator account on all computers, you can tell LAPS to focus on that account. Remember that it is your responsibility to ensure this account actually exists on all computers. However, most people are using the built-in administrator local account, and if that is true for you, there is no need to configure this setting. LAPS will focus on *administrator* by default.

- **Password Settings:** This is a key component to crafting your LAPS policy, configuration of the password options you would expect, such as complexity, length, and age.

- **Configure password backup directory:** Use this to tell LAPS whether passwords need to be stored inside AD or Entra. This is a key trigger to making LAPS work. Without configuring this setting, LAPS will not manage your local administrator passwords at all.

- **Configure size of encrypted password history:** Tell LAPS how many previous versions of the administrator password to retain. This can be really useful if you ever restore computers back to previous states or backups, thus invalidating their newest instance of local administrator password.

- **Enable password encryption:** This is the option to tell LAPS to encrypt these administrator passwords. Remember that in order to do this, you must be running a domain functional level of at least Server 2016.

There are clearly more settings available here, and each has a good description right inside the policy about what they are for. I am going to test LAPS in my lab environment, and I have taken a simple approach by configuring only these two options:

- **Configure password backup directory:** 2 (AD)
- **Password Settings:** Level 4 complexity (default), password length of 14, password age of 30 days, and passphrase length of 6 words. These are all the default/recommended options in this setting; I simply had to flip it to **Enabled.**

After configuring this GPO with my two specific LAPS requirements, I created a link to the OU where my WIN10 workstation is sitting; for now, I am only going to test LAPS on this machine. You can link and filter your own GPO appropriately, so that it applies to whichever workstations or servers you need it to touch. Our new LAPS GPO is now successfully applying settings to my WIN10 computer.

Finding a password

If the local administrator password is going to be different per workstation, and indeed if they update themselves on a regular basis, doesn't that mean it is now much more difficult to log in to computers as that local admin account? Yes—yes it is. That is the whole point! Using Windows LAPS does mean that legitimate sysadmins who are trying to log in to a computer with the local administrator account will have some extra hoops to jump through, but it also means that attackers will have a far more difficult time making use of these accounts, and they don't have your tools at their disposal.

To find an administrator password for a Windows system protected by LAPS, simply utilize the following PowerShell command:

```
Get-LapsADPassword -Identity WIN10 -AsPlainText
```

Or, perhaps even easier, head into **AD Users and Computers**, find the object of the computer to which you need to log in, and visit that new **LAPS** tab. Now that my GPO has baked for a while and WIN10 should have adjusted its own administrator password and recorded it inside AD, I log in to my DC1 server and check both PowerShell and GUI avenues to find that, yes indeed, my unique and complex password for the local administrator account is sitting right here, waiting for me to copy and use it.

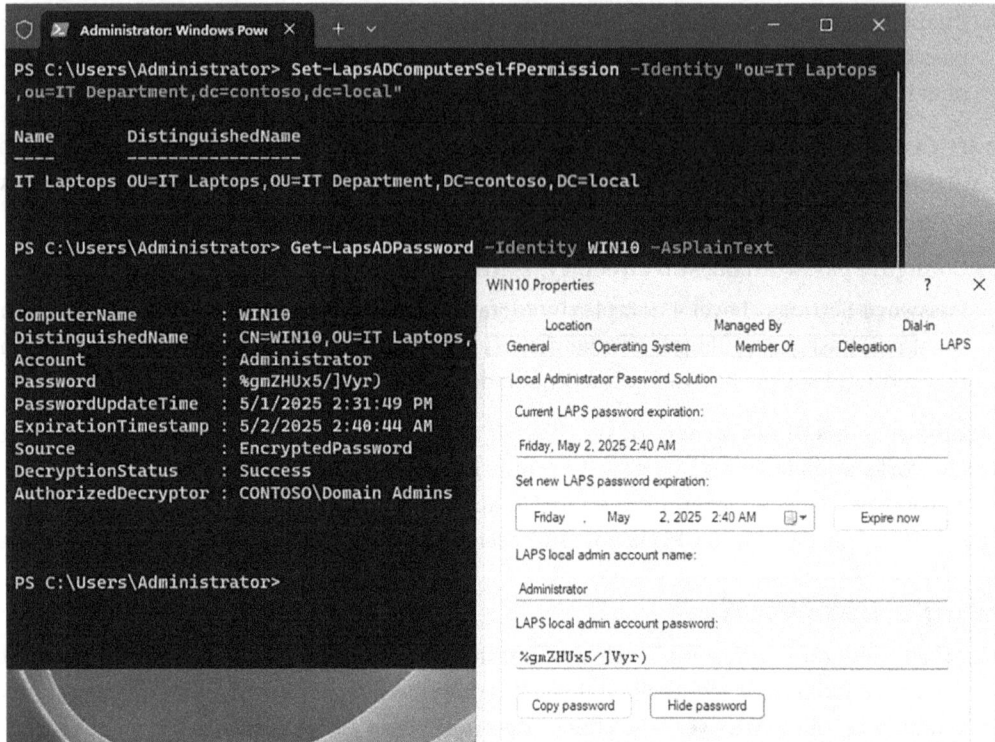

Figure 10.32: Grabbing the local administrator password via PowerShell or ADUC

Finding a password in Entra

My test lab is primarily focused on local AD, but we discussed how LAPS can alternatively store passwords inside Entra, for Entra-joined or hybrid-joined environments. If you are working within such an environment and configure LAPS to store administrator passwords inside Entra instead of AD, there is a fast and simple way to find those LAPS passwords whenever you need them:

M365 Admin Center | Identity (entra.microsoft.com) | Devices

Find the workstation for which you need to know the local administrator password, and click on that computer name. Once inside the **Properties** section of that computer, there is an option on the left called **Local administrator password recovery**. Simply click here, and then on the link that says **Show local administrator password**.

Rotating a password

You can see in our last screenshot that a LAPS password expiration timestamp is specified. Computers configured to store their local administrator password inside AD are triggered once every hour to check in with AD and find out whether it is time for them to rotate this password. As soon as the new password is implemented, it is, of course, updated inside AD and visible from there.

Occasionally, you may need to jumpstart this process and cause LAPS to create and record a new password sooner than the planned expiration date. Most commonly, you would need to do this in the event of a compromised computer or as part of troubleshooting. Thankfully, it is very easy to tell a computer to generate a new LAPS password, using either that **Expire now** button shown in *Figure 10.32*, or by using the following PowerShell command on your domain controller:

```
Set-LapsADPasswordExpirationTime -Identity WIN10
```

This command sets WIN10's LAPS password expiration time to the current time, causing the computer to recognize that it has hit the expiration period, it will generate a new password and store it inside AD.

Advanced Threat Analytics: end of support

In my opinion, one of the coolest security features to have ever existed at Microsoft is **Advanced Threat Analytics (ATA)**, and yet I have hardly heard anyone talk about it. Perhaps because they never went so far as to add it as a native feature built into the Windows Server OS. ATA is an on-premises software that rides on top of Windows to produce some amazing functionality. Essentially, what ATA does is monitor all of your AD traffic and warn you of dangerous or unusual behavior in real time, immediately as it is happening.

Unfortunately, ATA reached the end of mainstream support in January 2021. Extended support will continue until 2026, however, and so I am choosing to retain information in this latest book edition. There is additional information at the end of this section regarding the ATA roadmap.

What is (was) ATA?

The idea of ATA is simple to understand and makes so much sense that we are all going to wonder why it took so many years for someone to come up with this idea. AD has been around for a very long time, and attacks against your environment utilizing user accounts for just as long. Discovering and troubleshooting attacks within the directory is complicated and messy; there is so much information being logged all the time inside AD that it is almost impossible to catch or track bad guys as they do their worst. Following some form of attack, you can certainly pore over log data from multiple domain controllers and piece together some semblance of what happened, but being able to identify an attack *as it is happening* is just a pipe dream. Or is it...?

ATA is an advanced form of AD monitoring that uses machine learning. This is the coolest part of ATA. You configure your network so that all traffic flowing in or out of your domain controllers also lands in the ATA system. The most secure way to accomplish this is at the networking level, establishing port mirroring so that all of the domain controller packets also make their way to ATA, but at a level that an attacker would not be able to see.

This way, even if someone nefarious is inside your network and is on the lookout for some kind of protection working against them, ATA remains invisible to their prying eyes. However, port-mirroring that traffic is something that smaller companies may not be able to do or may be too complex for an initial setup, and so a second option exists to install an ATA lightweight agent right onto the domain controllers themselves. This agent then sends the necessary information over to the ATA processing servers.

In either case, those ATA processing servers receive all this data and start finding patterns. If Betty uses a desktop computer called **BETTY-PC** and a tablet called **BETTY-TABLET**, ATA will recognize that pattern and associate her user account with those devices. It also watches for her normal traffic patterns. Betty usually logs in at around 8 a.m., and her traffic usually stops somewhere around 5 p.m. She typically accesses a few file servers and a SharePoint server. After a week or so of collecting and monitoring data, ATA has a pretty good idea of Betty's standard MO.

Now, one night, something happens. ATA sees a bunch of password failures against Betty's account. That in itself might not be something to get too excited about, but then all of a sudden, Betty logs in to a terminal server that she doesn't typically access. From there, her credentials are used to access a domain controller. Uh oh, this clearly sounds like an attack to me. With the tools built into AD that we currently have at our disposal, what do we know? Nothing, really. We might see the password failures if we dig into the event logs, and based on that, we could try poking around other servers' event logs in order to find out what that account was accessing, but we really wouldn't have any reason to suspect anything, nor any prompts or warnings that anything was happening whatsoever. This could be the beginning of a very large breach, and we would never see it. Thankfully, ATA knows better.

The management interface for ATA is like a social media feed, updated almost in real time. During the events I have just laid out, if we had been looking at the ATA media feed, we would have seen these items happen, as they happened, and it would be immediately obvious that someone compromised Betty's account and used it to gain access to a domain controller. When ATA was released, there had never been a technology that watched AD traffic so intensely, and there had certainly never been anything that learned patterns and behavioral diversions like this. It is truly an amazing technology, and I don't say that only because I happen to know the guys who built it. But since I do, I can tell you that they are brilliant, which is already obvious since Microsoft scooped them up.

Even though this technology is now being morphed into something at the cloud level, let's take a few minutes and review a couple of screenshots from the ATA interface so you have an idea of what this social media-style feed looks like. This screenshot was taken from a Microsoft demo where they purposefully stole the Kerberos ticket from a user and then utilized it on another computer to access some confidential files that only Demi Albuz should have been able to access. While ATA did not stop this activity, it immediately—and I mean within seconds—alerted inside this feed to show the **pass-the-ticket attack:**

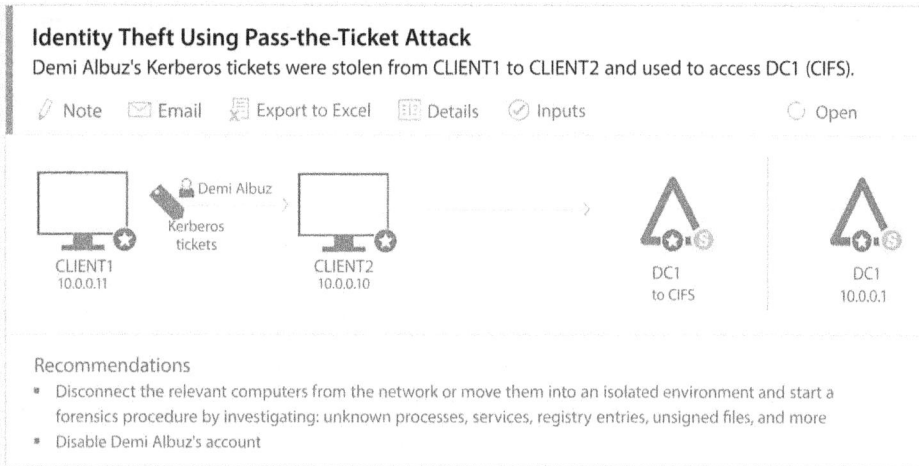

Identity Theft Using Pass-the-Ticket Attack
Demi Albuz's Kerberos tickets were stolen from CLIENT1 to CLIENT2 and used to access DC1 (CIFS).

Note   Email   Export to Excel   Details   Inputs   Open

CLIENT1   Demi Albuz   CLIENT2   DC1   DC1
10.0.0.11   Kerberos   10.0.0.10   to CIFS   10.0.0.1
               tickets

Recommendations
* Disconnect the relevant computers from the network or move them into an isolated environment and start a
  forensics procedure by investigating: unknown processes, services, registry entries, unsigned files, and more
* Disable Demi Albuz's account

Figure 10.33: ATA identifying a pass-the-ticket attack

Here's another example where a user named Almeta Whitfield suddenly accessed 16 computers that she does not usually access, another big red flag that something is going on with her user account:

Suspicion of identity theft based on abnormal behavior   OPEN ⋮

Almeta Whitfield exhibited abnormal behavior when performing activities that were not seen over the last month and are also not in accordance with the activities of other accounts in the organization. The abnormal behavior is based on the following activities:

○ Performed interactive login from 16 abnormal workstations.
○ Requested access to 5 abnormal resources.

Almeta Whitfield   On   9 normal   16 abnormal   Accessed   13 normal   5 abnormal
Software Engineer   computers   computers   resources   resources

Figure 10.34: ATA alerts on abnormal behavior

Microsoft Defender for Identity

While ATA is an on-premises solution, its replacement lives in the cloud. **Microsoft Defender for Identity** is our new home for this type of technology, hosted, of course, within Microsoft Azure and M365 environments. Defender for Identity was not always named as such, and you will still find some documentation about this technology labeled as **Azure Advanced Threat Protection**, the name for what was to have been the direct ATA replacement, before Microsoft slid the capabilities under the Defender umbrella. Defender for Identity still works to protect your local on-premises AD environment by utilizing "sensors" installed on your domain controllers to shuttle this information into Defender, and from that cloud interface, take advantage of capabilities originally introduced via ATA.

Documentation is still online for ATA, and further learning materials can be found here: `https://learn.microsoft.com/en-us/advanced-threat-analytics/what-is-ata`.

For more information on the new Microsoft Defender for Identity, the following link is a good starting point: `https://learn.microsoft.com/en-us/defender-for-identity/`.

General security best practices

Sometimes we need only to rely on ourselves, and not necessarily on functionality provided by the OS, to secure our systems. There are many common-sense approaches to administratorship (part of the fun sitting behind this keyboard: I get to make up new words all day long) that are easy to accomplish but are rarely used in the field.

The following are a few tips and tricks that I have learned over the years and have helped companies implement. Hopefully, you have even more to add to this list as to what works well for you, but if nothing else, this section is intended to jog your thinking into finding creative ways with which you can limit administrative capability and vulnerability within your network.

Getting rid of perpetual administrators

Do all of your IT staff have domain admin rights on the day they are hired? Do any of your IT staff have access to the built-in domain administrator account password? Do you have regular users whose logins have administrative privileges on their own computers? You know where I'm going with this—these are all terrible ideas!

Unfortunately, that was the status quo for many years in almost every network, and the trend continues today. I still regularly watch engineers use the *administrator* domain account for many tasks when setting up new servers. This means they not only have access to potentially the most important account in your network and use it for daily tasks, but it also means that anything that is set up with this user account is not accountable. What do I mean by that? When I set up a new server or make changes to an existing server using the general administrator account, and I end up causing some kind of big problem, nobody can prove that I did it. Using generalized user accounts is a sure way to thwart responsibility in the event that something goes wrong. I'm not trying to imply that you are always on the lookout for "who dunnit," but if I mess something up on an application server that I don't normally administer, it would be nice if the people trying to fix it could easily figure out that it was me and come ask me what I did so that they can reverse it. There are many reasons that using the built-in administrator account should be off-limits for all of us.

To address the client side, do your users really need administrative rights on their computers? *Really?* I think you could probably find ways around it. Bringing regular users down to user or even power user rights on their systems can have a huge impact on the security of those computers. It gives viruses a much harder time installing themselves if the user needs to walk through a prompt asking for admin privileges before they can proceed with the installation. It also keeps all your machines in a much more consistent behavioral pattern, without new and unknown applications and settings being introduced by the user. Even if you find some applications that truly require administrative permissions to run successfully, there are now third-party tools that allow you to automatically elevate specific executable files to always run as admin, even when the user is not an admin.

Using distinct accounts for administrative access

This idea piggybacks off the last one and is something that I have started employing even on all of the home computers that I install for friends and family members. It really boils down to this: utilize two different user accounts, one with administrative access and one without. When you are logged in for daily tasks and chores, make sure that you are logged in with your regular user account that does not have administrative privileges, either on the local computer or on the domain. That way, if you attempt to install anything, or if something attempts to install itself, you will be prompted by the **User Account Control (UAC)** box asking you to enter an administrative username and password before the installer is allowed to do anything. I can tell you that this works, as I have stopped a number of viruses and/or bloatware software on my own computer from installing themselves as I browsed around the internet, trying to do research for one project or another. If I get a UAC prompt asking me for an admin password and I haven't intentionally clicked on an installer file, I know it's something I don't want. All I have to do is click on **No**, and that installer will be stopped before it gets hold of my computer. On the other hand, if it is something that I am intending to install, then it is a minor inconvenience to simply enter the password of my administrative account and allow the installer to continue.

Maintaining two separate accounts allows you to work your way through most daily tasks while putting your mind at ease that you do not have the right to inadvertently do something bad to your system. This mindset also naturally limits the amount of activity or changes performed on any given computer by an administrative account, meaning that the logging and tracking of changes by those accounts becomes easier. This results in greater accountability and better change management processes.

Using a different computer to accomplish administrative tasks

If you want to progress further still with the idea of separate user accounts, you could make your computing experience even more secure by utilizing a separate computer altogether when accomplishing administrative-level tasks: one computer for regular knowledge worker tasks and another computer for administration. This would certainly help to keep your administrative system secure, as well as the remote systems that it has access to. And while it does seem cumbersome to have two physical computers at your desk, remember that with many SKUs in Windows 10/11, we can run Hyper-V right on our desktop computers.

I do exactly this with my own computer. I have a computer that is running Windows 11, and inside that computer, I am running a VM via Hyper-V from which I do all administrative tasks on the sensitive servers. This way, a compromise of my day-to-day OS doesn't mean a compromise of the entire environment.

You could also employ this idea in reverse. When needing to test some new software, functionality, or link, you could spin up a VM in Hyper-V on your workstation, keep it fully disconnected from any networks so that it is sandboxed away, and test out whatever new or sketchy thing it is that you need to test. If it bombs your VM, no big deal. Just delete it and create a new one.

Whether you choose to split up administrative access at the user account level or the computer level, remember this simple rule: *never administer Active Directory from the same place that you browse Facebook*. I think that pretty well sums this one up.

Never browse the internet from servers

Seems like a no-brainer, but everyone does it. We spend all day working on servers and very often have to reach out and check something from a web browser. Since Edge and Internet Explorer exist on Windows servers, sometimes it is quicker and easier to check whatever it is that we need to check from the server console where we are working, rather than walk back over to our desks or minimize the RDP window. Sometimes (perhaps oftentimes) we even take the extra step, consciously installing a different, better browser onto servers just so it's there if ever we need it. Resist the temptation! It is so easy to pick up bad things from the internet, especially on servers, because if any machines in our network are running without antivirus protection, it is probably on the server side. The same is true for internet filters. We always make sure that client traffic is flowing through our corporate proxy (if we have one) or other protection mechanisms, but we don't always care whether server traffic is moving outward the same way.

Don't even do it for websites that you trust. A man-in-the-middle attack or a compromise of the website itself can easily corrupt your server, or worse, give someone access to it and therefore the rest of your network. It's much easier to rebuild a client computer than it is a server.

Role-Based Access Control

The phrase **Role-Based Access Control** (RBAC) is not one that is limited to Microsoft environments. It is also not a particular technology that can be utilized inside Windows Server 2025, but rather it is an ideology about separating job roles and duties.

When we think about separating our employees' job roles from an IT perspective, we traditionally think in terms of AD groups. While adding user accounts to groups does solve many problems about splitting up levels of permissions and access, it can be complicated to grow in this mentality, and ultimately, AD groups still empower administrators with full access to the groups themselves. RBAC technologies divide up roles at a different level, caring about more than permissions. RBAC focuses more on employee job descriptions than access restrictions. There are a number of different technologies that take advantage of RBAC tools integrated into them, and there are even third-party RBAC solutions that ride on top of all your existing infrastructure, making it widely accessible across your entire organization and not restricted to working in the confines of a single domain or forest.

Just Enough Administration

A great example of an RBAC technology that is included in Windows Server 2025 is **Just Enough Administration** (JEA), which is part of PowerShell. JEA provides you with a way to grant special privileged access for people, without needing to give them administrative rights, which would have been required to accomplish the same duties in the past. The necessity to add someone to the administrators group on a server so that they can do their job is quite common, but JEA is a first step away from that necessity.

In our old way of thinking, it might be easy to think of JEA as doing something like allowing users to have administrative access within PowerShell even when they don't have administrative access to the OS itself, but it's even more powerful than that. The design of JEA is such that you can permit users to have access only to run particular PowerShell commands and cmdlets at an administrative level, leaving in the dark other commands that they do not need to access.

In fact, if a user is working within a JEA context of PowerShell and they try to invoke a cmdlet that is not part of their **allowed** cmdlets, PowerShell pretends as though it doesn't even recognize that cmdlet. It doesn't say, *Sorry, you can't do this*—it just ignores the command! This helps to keep prying fingers out of the cookie jar, unless you want to let them in.

Here's an example scenario that helps portray the JEA capability. Maybe you are a DNS administrator, and you might occasionally need to restart DNS services. Since we are adopting the JEA/RBAC mentality, you are not going to have administrative rights on the OS of that DNS server, but you will have JEA-based rights within PowerShell so that you can run the tools that you need in order to do your work.

Restarting the DNS service requires access to use the `Restart-Service` cmdlet, right? But doesn't that mean I would be able to restart any service on that server and could potentially do all sorts of things that I don't need to do? JEA is even powerful enough to deal with this scenario. When setting up the level of access that a user needs, you can dive into particular cmdlets and divide up permissions. In our example, you could provide your DNS administrator with access to use the `Restart-Service` cmdlet, but only give permissions to restart particular services, such as those pertaining to DNS. If your admin tried `Restart-Service` on WinRM, they would be denied.

Adjusting RDP away from 3389

Any IT engineer is familiar with RDPing into Windows Servers, and very likely, this is the approach that *you* most often take when remotely controlling servers in your environment. Any hacker worthy of the title is also familiar with this and would know that every single Windows machine, be it a client workstation or a server, listens by default on TCP port 3389 for those RDP connections to flow in. What is the point of this statement? If an attacker has gained access to a computer on your network, they have very quick and easy tools to discover the names of servers in your network. They can immediately attempt to start connecting to your servers via RDP by simply typing the server name and using the default port 3389. If they have already gained credentials in your network, they could potentially access all of your critical servers within seconds of entering the environment.

One barrier you can put in the bad guys' way is the use of ambiguous port numbers for RDP connectivity. There are still plenty of bad things they can do without RDPing into servers, and ultimately, they will still eventually seek out these randomized RDP ports if they really want to, but you certainly will have slowed the process way down if each of your servers listens for RDP connections on a different port number.

Won't it become an annoyance and a burden on our IT administration team if they now have to document or remember all of these differing port numbers? You bet it will. But it will also annoy and burden your enemies, which is the point.

Many of you reading this may have had no idea this was even possible, and how would you unless you had done it before? There is no graphical-based setting for changing RDP port numbers, but this capability has existed for many generations of the Windows operating system.

Let's demonstrate. RDP is enabled on my WEB1 server. Currently, I can connect to it easily by opening MSTSC.EXE, typing WEB1, and clicking **Connect**. After entering credentials, I am immediately connected to WEB1 and driving its interface. The **Remote Desktop Connection** tool (MSTSC) is smart enough to know that if I don't specify a port number along with my server name, I intend to use the default port 3389 for connectivity. To change the port number that WEB1 uses to listen for RDP connections, I need to edit the registry and visit the following key:

```
HKEY_LOCAL_MACHINE\SYSTEM\CurrentControlSet\Control\
Terminal Server\WinStations\RDP-Tcp
```

Inside that key, the registry value we want to change is called PortNumber. If you have never modified this before, you will find 3389 specified in decimal form.

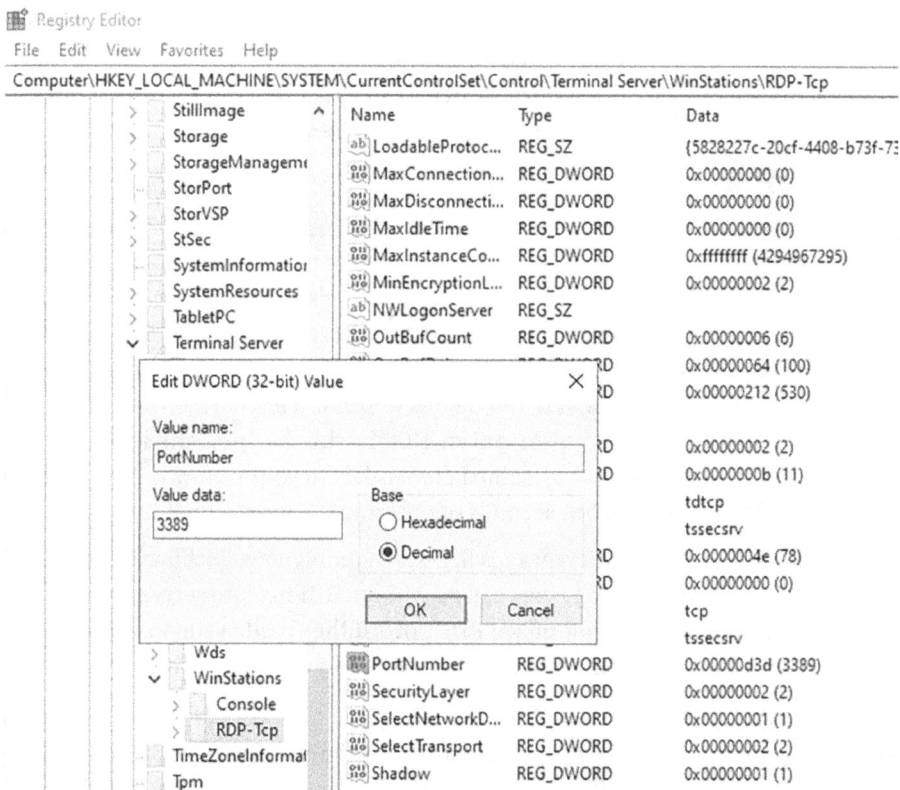

Figure 10.35: Updating the RDP port number inside the registry

All you need to do is enter a new port number (make sure it isn't one that your server is already using by reviewing a netstat command output), and then reboot the server. Now that my WEB1 server is back up and running, you can see in the following screenshot that I can no longer create an RDP connection to WEB1 by simply using the server name; I now have to manually specify the new port number that I used (4095) to create that connection.

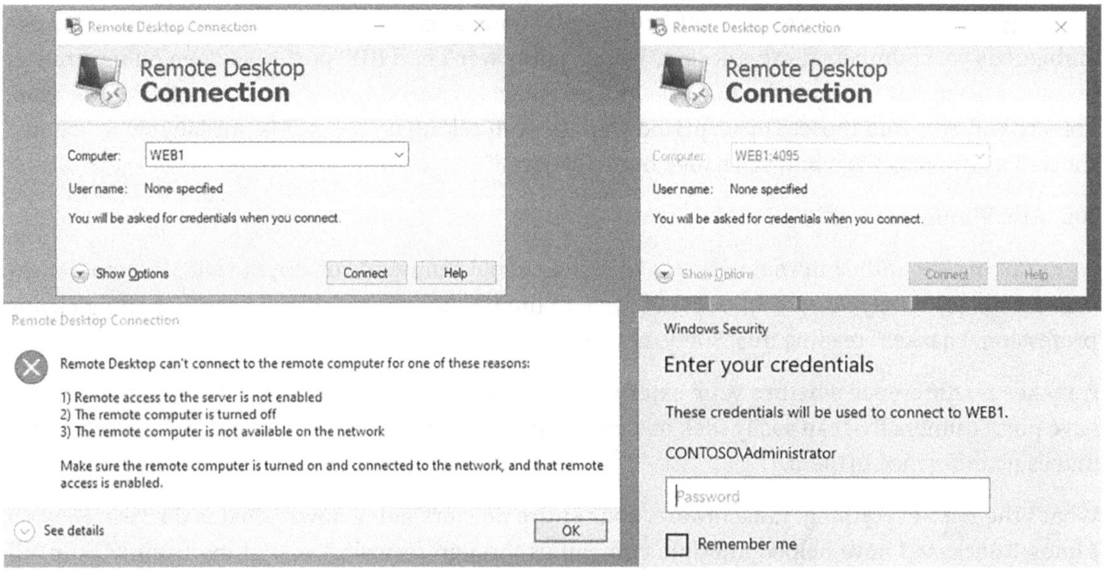

Figure 10.36: WEB1 is now listening on port 4095

Disable external RDP… NOW

We all know how to RDP into servers, and indeed, I bet 99% of everyone reading this RDPs into servers most days of the week. Doing so from inside the corporate network is a fast and easy way to interact with servers, and it makes a lot of sense that we employ this technology. Have you ever thought about the possibility of allowing RDP access over the internet? Wouldn't it be nice if you could simply open up MSTSC on your home computer and hop right into your servers without having to first establish a cumbersome VPN? Have you done it? Do you have servers that right now have NAT rules configured in your firewall so that you can hit a certain port using RDP from anywhere in the world and RDP directly into your server?

Stop it right now!

Shut down the port, delete the NAT rule, do not pass Go, do not collect $200.

This is the absolute worst idea, and yet I discover NAT rules just like this on a very regular basis. When engaging with a company I have never worked with before, preparing to support various parts of their infrastructure and running through a discovery process of these client networks, we always check over the firewall rules. It is truly amazing how many places in the world have RDP access to servers open to the entire internet.

Now, perhaps you're saying to yourself, "Of course I don't do that! Well, I do, but I am tricky and use ambiguous port numbers for this access. You certainly won't find RDP port 3389 open on my firewall because I set up my NAT rules so that you must connect to crazy things such as port 33343 and 5896; nobody will ever find those. I'm surprised you are even asking us about this, Jordan, since you just showed us two pages ago how to change our RDP ports!"

You. Are. Wrong.

We're talking about the internet here. We're talking about thousands of 12-year-old Minecraft aficionados with absolutely infinite amounts of time on their hands. Oh no, I may have just offended any "professional hacker" reading this. Sorry, not sorry.

It makes no difference whether your external ports are 3389 or 12345, or anything else. Attackers have port scanners that can easily seek out any open RDP channels; the port those RDP channels use makes no difference to them.

What's the risk? Everything: ransomware, your entire network going down—that is the risk. How do I know? Because I have helped multiple companies through restoring everything from backup, all of their servers, because of one little NAT rule that allowed RDP access into a single server from the internet. Just one little rule to one little server, and the entire infrastructure was locked down by ransomware overnight.

If you allow RDP connections to flow into your network from a NAT rule that allows communication from the internet, it is only a matter of time before someone bad is inside your network. It will happen. The fact that it has not happened yet is simply luck.

Delete the firewall rules and lock it down immediately, and then look into a better way of providing RDP access remotely. This could mean launching a VPN from your client, or it could mean setting up an RD Gateway server in your environment. RD Gateways are far more secure than open NATs, but even RD Gateways are finding themselves under regular attacks these days.

Disable insecure encryption protocols

Those of you who have managed web servers in recent years are likely familiar with disabling certain protocols, ciphers, and encryption algorithms that are old, out of date, and no longer secure by today's security standards. Anyone new to IT or server administration may have never even heard of these things, so let's talk about them now. When information crosses the internet between your users' computers and your servers, *hopefully*, there is encryption happening on that traffic. If there is not, then you have bigger worries than what we are talking about right now.

Assuming there is encryption happening, it is quite likely that your traffic is using some flavor of encryption technology that has both old versions and new versions. The kinds of things I am talking about are SSL, TLS, AES, DES, Triple DES, SHA, Diffie-Hellman... the list goes on and on. These funny acronyms are the inner workings of how your traffic transports itself securely between the client and the server. Sometimes, these things fall out of date and out of support. As a couple of good real-world examples, SSL 3.0 and TLS 1.0 are still valid protocols, but they have become bad news over the past few years.

These protocols have been replaced with newer versions, and the old ones are no longer being supported or patched in any way. If you have websites or applications making use of these old protocols, all of that traffic is in real danger of compromise.

It is a fairly common service desk ticket to receive communication from a software vendor, or from your PCI compliance vendor, asking you to review your such-and-such system and make sure that some of these protocols or ciphers are disabled. If they are disabled on your servers, no clients (good or bad) will be able to tap into them. When you receive such a request and need to make sure that the old, bad protocols are disabled, where do we even start with making a change like this?

Windows registry

On Windows Server, you can enable or disable these protocols and ciphers by modifying the registry. This is fairly straightforward once you have the locations saved and have been through the process a few times, but no matter how many times I do it this way, I am never left feeling 100% confident that I accomplished the change properly. In any case, to round out knowledge on this baseline way to adjust protocols in Windows Server, here is the primary registry location from which you can add or remove registry values to enable or disable specific protocols and cipher suites:

```
HKEY_LOCAL_MACHINE\SYSTEM\CurrentControlSet\Control\SecurityProviders\
SCHANNEL\Protocols
```

It would take many pages to type up all of the different exact registry values that pertain to different protocols and suites, so I am not going to do that. Instead, here is a link to a Microsoft article that outlines many of the possible settings for an AD FS server:

https://learn.microsoft.com/en-us/windows-server/identity/ad-fs/operations/manage-ssl-protocols-in-ad-fs.

Take a look over all the possible registry changes here, and I think you'll agree with me that it quickly becomes a muddy mess of confusion. So, while it is absolutely possible to disable old and insecure ciphers using the registry method, I strongly recommend...

IIS Crypto

This free tool, created by Nartac Software, makes protocol, cipher, hash, and key exchange adjustments *so much easier* than editing the registry. All you need to do is search the web for a quick download and run this program on the server for which you want to make changes. It is a standalone executable; no need to install software to make this happen. As soon as IIS Crypto opens, it will show you all of the different protocols and ciphers that could be used on this server, with checkboxes next to each one.

To enable or disable each protocol, simply check or uncheck the box next to its name. It's that easy! What this tool is really doing is making the registry changes for you, so that you don't have to worry about finding them and inputting the correct syntax. When you check a box, it creates the corresponding registry value and sets it to enabled. When you uncheck a box, it changes the registry key to disabled. You'll notice a lot of gray checks when you first launch IIS Crypto; those indicate that there is currently no registry value whatsoever for that particular protocol, which is the default state on any server. When you check or uncheck a box and click the **Apply** button, it then creates the registry key and sets its value accordingly.

You can see in the following screenshot that I have some protocols disabled on this server, including SSL 3.0 and TLS 1.0:

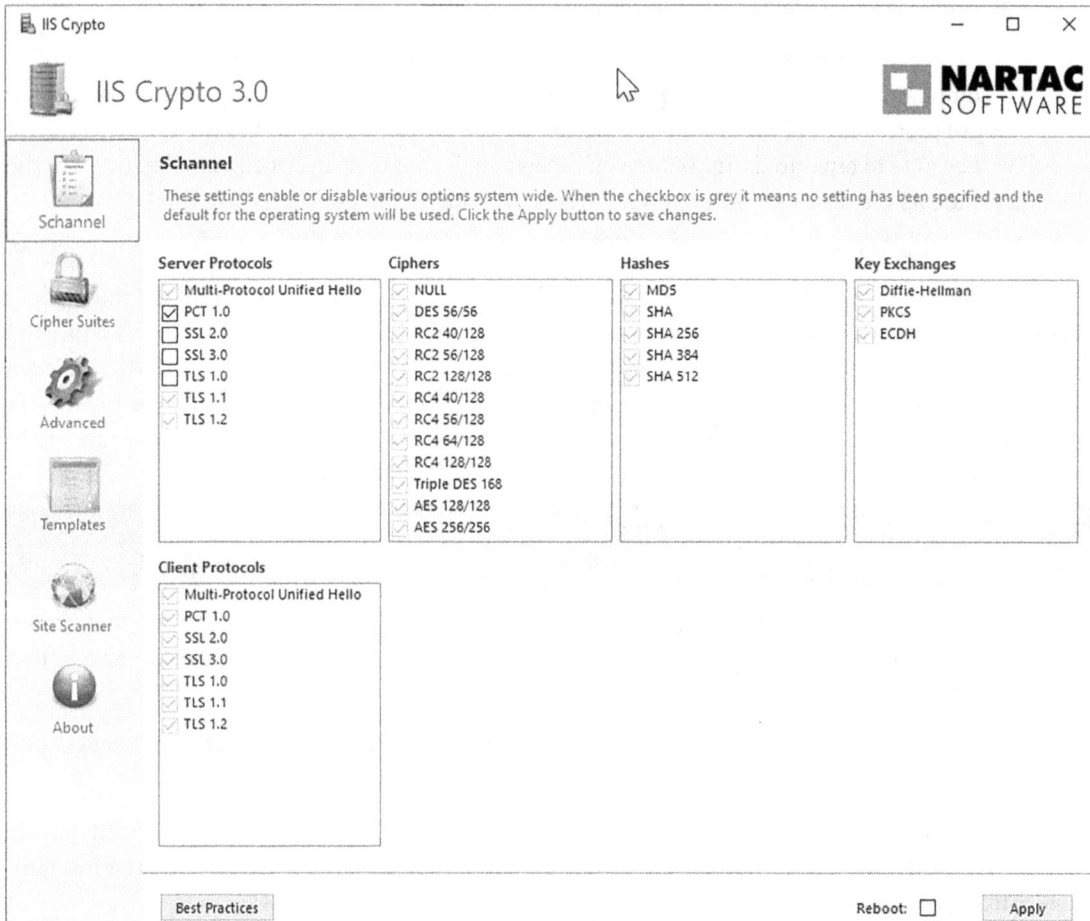

Figure 10.37: IIS Crypto is an easy way to implement protocol security

Any changes that you make, whether they be via IIS Crypto or taking the hard road and modifying the registry yourself, will be active the next time you restart your server. Remember, a restart is necessary before you can consider your security changes to be working!

Summary

The number one agenda item for many CIOs is security. Security for your client machines, security for your networks, security for your cloud resources, and most importantly, security for your data. There is no single solution for securing your infrastructure; it requires many moving parts and many different technologies all working together to provide safety for your resources. The purpose of this chapter was to provide examples of security measures and technologies that can be utilized in anyone's environment, as well as to reprioritize the importance that security has in today's IT world. Concerns about privacy and security need to be discussed for any and every technological solution that we put into place.

Too many times, I find new applications being implemented inside organizations without any regard for how secure that application platform is. Applications that transmit or store data unencrypted need to be modified or dumped. Protection of information is essential to the longevity of our businesses.

We cannot complete a discussion about security in Windows Server 2025 without discussing the other OS installation option that we have thus far ignored throughout this book. In the next chapter, we'll dive into Server Core, the headless and less vulnerable version of Windows Server.

Questions

Put your knowledge to the test with the following questions. If you need a hand (or just want to double-check), you'll find all the answers in the *Appendix* section of the book.

1. What is the name of the antimalware product built into Windows Server 2025?
2. When a domain-joined computer is sitting inside the corporate LAN, which Windows Defender Firewall profile should be active?
3. Other than the domain profile, what are the other two possible firewall profiles inside Windows Defender Firewall?
4. When creating a firewall rule to allow IPv4 ping replies, what protocol type must you specify inside your inbound rule?
5. What is the easiest way to push standardized Windows Defender Firewall rules to your entire workforce?
6. A virtual machine whose virtual hard disk file is encrypted is called a...?
7. True or False? LAPS passwords can be stored only in Active Directory.
8. What is the name of the (deprecated) Microsoft technology that parses domain controller information in order to identify pass-the-hash and pass-the-ticket attacks?
9. Which inbound RDP port number is considered safe to open on your external firewall?
10. What third-party tool can you use to disable TLS 1.0 on Windows Server?

Join us on Discord

For discussions around the book and to connect with your peers, join us on Discord at `https://packt.link/discordcloud` or scan the QR code below:

11

Server Core

Honey, I shrunk the server! Another chapter, another outdated movie reference. Over the past 25 years or so, we have seen nothing but growth from Microsoft operating systems. Growth can be good; new features and enhancements make our lives easier. But growth can also be bad, such as bloated file structures and memory-hogging graphical interfaces. If you were to chronologically graph Windows and Windows Server operating system footprints through the years, based on factors such as disk space consumption and memory requirements, it would show a steady upward slope. Every new release seems to require just a little more processing power and just a little more hard drive space than the previous version. I always find it intriguing how many critical pieces of the operating system are still hanging around in locations and folders left over from Server 2003 or even earlier. Even on a brand-new Windows Server 2025 instance, you will find all kinds of important things inside `C:\Windows\System32`. System32, but Server 2025 is only available in a 64-bit flavor. We're not even going to talk about what's in the registry. I suppose that moving, renaming, or changing these core components could prove to be detrimental to many aspects of Windows, and so they may remain the same forevermore. This limits the amount of cleanup and downsizing that could ever happen, unless a fairly drastic approach were to be taken by approaching Windows Server as a completely different type of operating system platform.

Here, we are going to talk about an alternative way to use Windows Server 2025 on a much, much smaller scale. Server Core has been around for quite some time now, but I'm hard-pressed to find people who actually use it. This miniaturized version of Windows Server has been built to provide you with a smaller, more efficient, and more secure server platform.

We will cover the following topics in this chapter:

- Why use Server Core?
- Interfacing with Server Core
- Using Windows Admin Center to manage Server Core
- The `Sconfig` utility
- Roles available in Server Core
- Building a Server Core domain controller

- What happened to Nano Server?
- Can we run Server Core in Azure?

Why use Server Core?

Why am I even talking about Server Core? Hasn't it been around since 2008? Yes, and it is also true that nothing has really changed with regard to Server Core in this latest version of Windows. Server Core instances in Server 2022 and Server 2025 are effectively the same, although the newest improvements in Active Directory and Azure Arc management can benefit these latest instances. The fact that Server Core has been around since 2008, yet many of you reading these words have never touched it, is exactly why I *am* talking about it. The Server Core variant of the Windows Server operating system has been around for quite some time, but it seems like many admins are afraid to use it. I work with many different companies from many different industries. Most of them have one big thing in common: they use a lot of Windows Servers, and all of those Windows Servers run the full GUI (Desktop Experience). Have they heard of Server Core? Sure. Have they tested it out in a lab? Sometimes. Everyone seems to have a slightly different experience level with Core, but it's quite rare to find one in production. Maybe I'm just talking to the wrong people, but I have to assume that there are many of us out there, myself included, who need to start using Server Core on a more regular basis.

Why do we need to start using Server Core? Because GUI-less servers are the future, says Microsoft. Would you believe that in the pre-release copies of Windows Server 2016, the Desktop Experience option didn't even exist? You couldn't run a full GUI desktop shell on Server 2016 even if you wanted to (which everyone did), other than a mini shell that could be plopped on top of Server Core. Microsoft received so much flak about this that the full Desktop Experience was added back during one of the technical preview rollouts. Even so, since that time, you have probably noticed that Server Core is the default option when installing any Windows Server operating system. Remember the beginning of our book, where we first installed Windows Server 2025 together? The default option for installation is not Desktop Experience; rather, the top option in *Figure 11.1* is the one to install command-line-driven Server Core. It is clearly stated on this page that Server Core is Microsoft's recommended installation option:

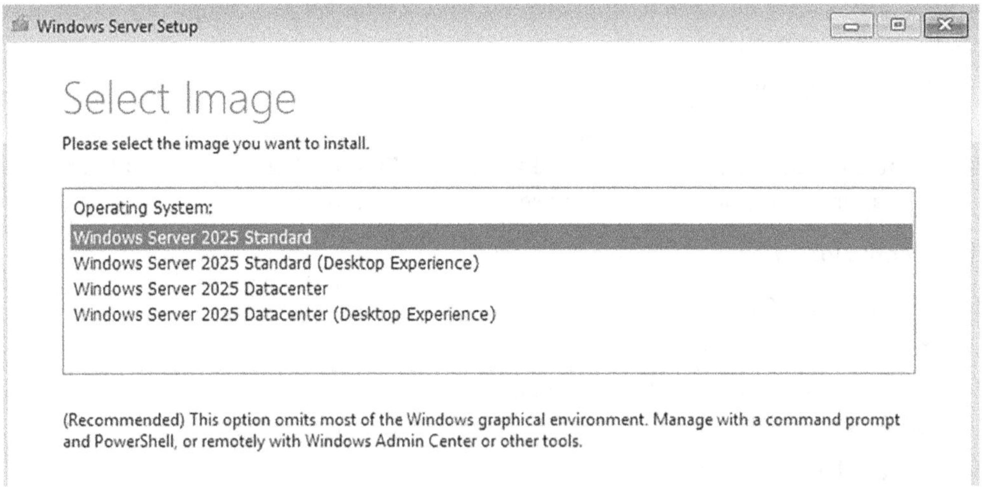

Figure 11.1: The default installation option is Server Core

One of the reasons for moving away from the graphical interface is increased capabilities for automation and scalability. When all our servers are built similarly, it means that we can use more cloud-like functions with them. Automatic spinning up and down of resources as they are needed, rolling out dozens of servers at the flip of a switch—this kind of automation and sizing is possible in the cloud, but it is only possible because the infrastructure is set up in a way that it is so standardized and repeatable. Cloud hardware resources need to be so streamlined that operations and automation tools can make them do what is needed, without worrying about all of the variables that would be present in a user-tweaked graphical interface.

There are other obvious advantages to running all of your servers on this limited, restricted version. Server Core boasts reduced hard drive space, reduced memory consumption, and a reduced attack surface when compared to a traditional, full-blown server experience. Now you can see why I made the hefty statements a minute ago about how we all need to start becoming more comfortable with Server Core! In fact, let's take a look at that reduced footprint. Base Server 2025 Standard running Desktop Experience consumes almost 15 GB of hard drive space; I just verified this by looking at the properties of my virtual hard disk file being used by my RDSH1 server, where I have installed the operating system, but have done nothing else yet with this server. RDSH1 is standard Windows Server 2025 running the full Desktop Experience. Now, I have just finished running through the installation for my first Server Core 2025 operating system, and we can see in *Figure 11.2* that the VHDX file being used by this new VM is only 4.78 GB, a huge reduction in space:

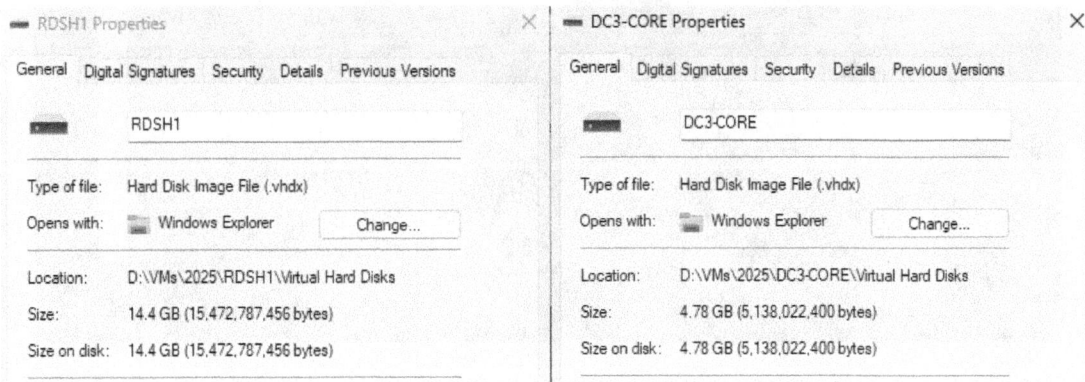

Figure 11.2: Server Core has a much smaller footprint than Desktop Experience

Fun fact: Microsoft says that, on average, a Server Core instance will consume roughly 4 GB less space than a similar Desktop Experience build, when comparing servers that are hosting the same roles and features.

No more switching back and forth

There is a very important note that I wanted to make here: those of you who worked with Server Core in Windows Server 2012 R2 know that we had the option of changing a server *on the fly*. What I mean is that if you created a new server as the full Desktop Experience, you could later change it to Server Core. The opposite approach was equally possible; you could take Server Core and flip it over to the full Desktop Experience. While this capability existed, it naturally enabled more people to use Server

Core because it meant that even if you knew nothing about interfacing with Server Core, you could build a new server in a graphical way as you would with any other server, install roles and get them configured, and when you were finished, switch it to Server Core, effectively disabling the graphical interface.

Not anymore! This capability to move servers back and forth between platforms has been removed. I repeat, *this is no longer possible*. So, plan carefully from here on out when installing these operating systems. If you implement a server as Server Core, that guy is going to remain a Server Core for its lifetime.

Interfacing with Server Core

After running through your first installation of Server Core, your server console window will be a simple black screen, presenting the following prompt (accessing this screen always makes me feel like I'm Harold in the show *Person of Interest*):

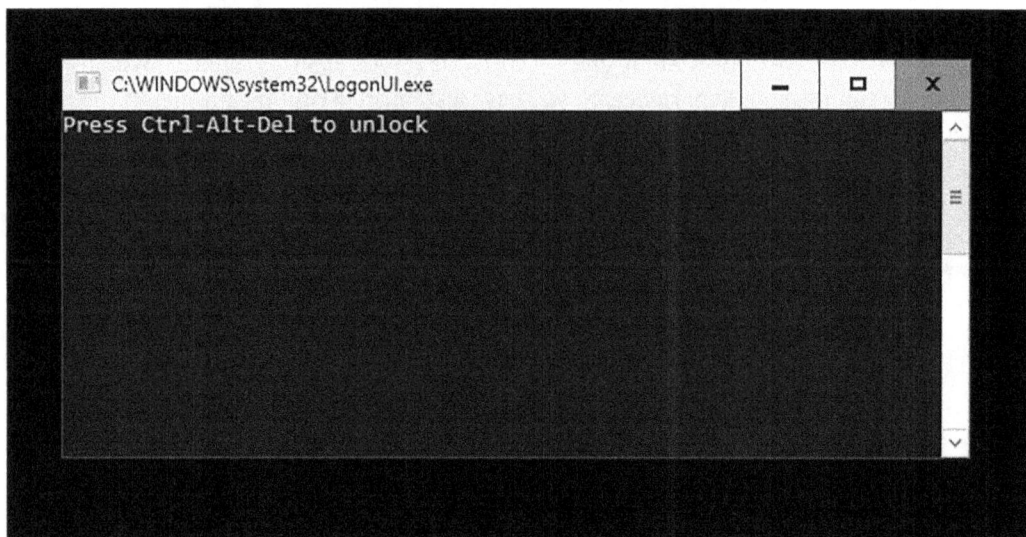

Figure 11.3: Server Core lock screen

Is that really a Command Prompt window that says **Press Ctrl-Alt-Del to unlock**? Yes, yes, it is. This usually gets a few chuckles when an admin sees it for the first time. I know it did for me, anyway. It reminds me a little of when we used to code if/then games on our TI-83 calculators during high school math class. Press *Ctrl + Alt + Del*, and you will be prompted to change your administrator password for the first time, which is the same task that must always be performed first inside GUI versions of Windows Server. Except, of course, that you do it all from within the Command Prompt window using only your keyboard. After configuring your administrator account password, the login process continues, and you'll even notice some familiar things fly past on this Command Prompt window, such as **Preparing Windows** and **Applying settings**.

If you are installing Server Core in earlier versions of Windows Server, such as 2019 or 2016, then you will find yourself now looking at a standard blinking Command Prompt cursor, awaiting your input. The operating system is loaded in the background, and it presents you with this simple interface from which you can run any standard commands as you wish.

One of the common things for administrators to run from this Command Prompt window is a configuration utility called Sconfig. We will talk more about what exactly Sconfig is and can do for you later in this chapter, but the primary point to mention here is that, starting with Windows Server 2022, Server Core now launches Sconfig automatically upon login, as you can see in *Figure 11.4*.

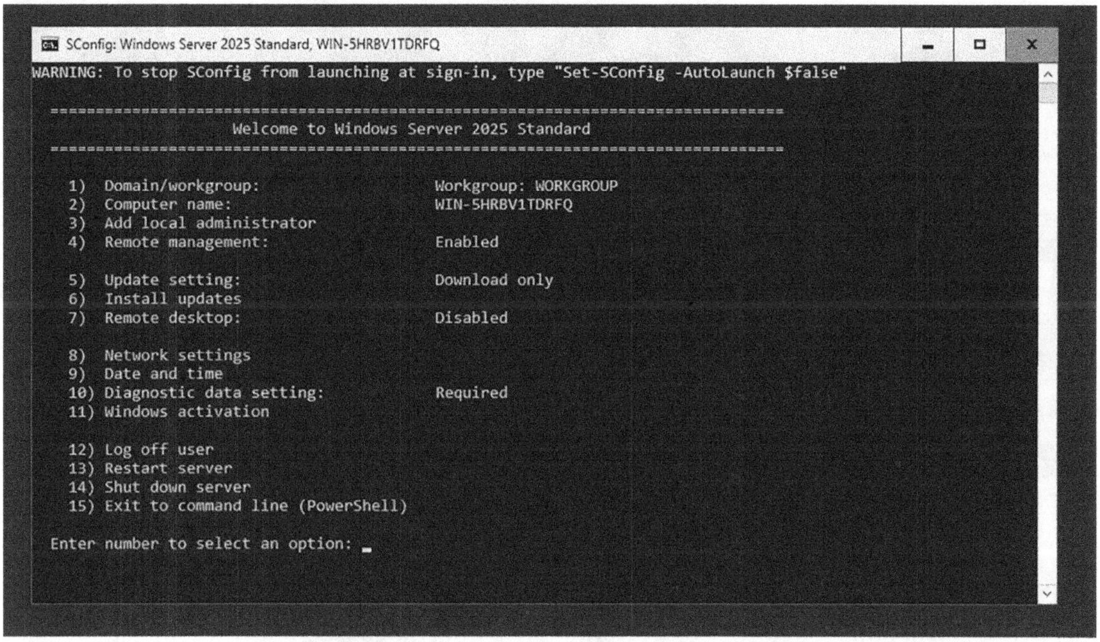

```
SConfig: Windows Server 2025 Standard, WIN-5HRBV1TDRFQ                          _  □  x
WARNING: To stop SConfig from launching at sign-in, type "Set-SConfig -AutoLaunch $false"

=========================================================================================
                         Welcome to Windows Server 2025 Standard
=========================================================================================

     1)  Domain/workgroup:              Workgroup: WORKGROUP
     2)  Computer name:                 WIN-5HRBV1TDRFQ
     3)  Add local administrator
     4)  Remote management:             Enabled

     5)  Update setting:                Download only
     6)  Install updates
     7)  Remote desktop:                Disabled

     8)  Network settings
     9)  Date and time
    10)  Diagnostic data setting:       Required
    11)  Windows activation

    12)  Log off user
    13)  Restart server
    14)  Shut down server
    15)  Exit to command line (PowerShell)

Enter number to select an option: _
```

Figure 11.4: Server Core now auto-launches Sconfig

Interestingly, this Command Prompt window doesn't consume our entire screen real estate; it is clear that there is a black background and cmd.exe is riding on top of it. I find this interesting because you can tell that the Core operating system itself is something other than Command Prompt, and that cmd.exe is just an application that auto-launches upon login. You can even utilize the mouse here and resize or move that Command Prompt window around.

Even more interesting and good to know is that you can launch some GUI-like applications from this prompt. The easiest way to do this is to exit the Sconfig utility by typing option 15 and pressing *Enter*. This will eject your Sconfig session and bring you back to a standard Command Prompt.

From here, you can do something such as opening **Notepad** and utilize it with both a keyboard and mouse, just like you would from any version of Windows. If you have Notepad open, create a note and then save it; you can see that there is a real file structure and a set of relatively normal-looking system folders.

So, rather than some form of black magic, Server Core is actually the real Windows Server operating system, wrapped up in a smaller and more secure package:

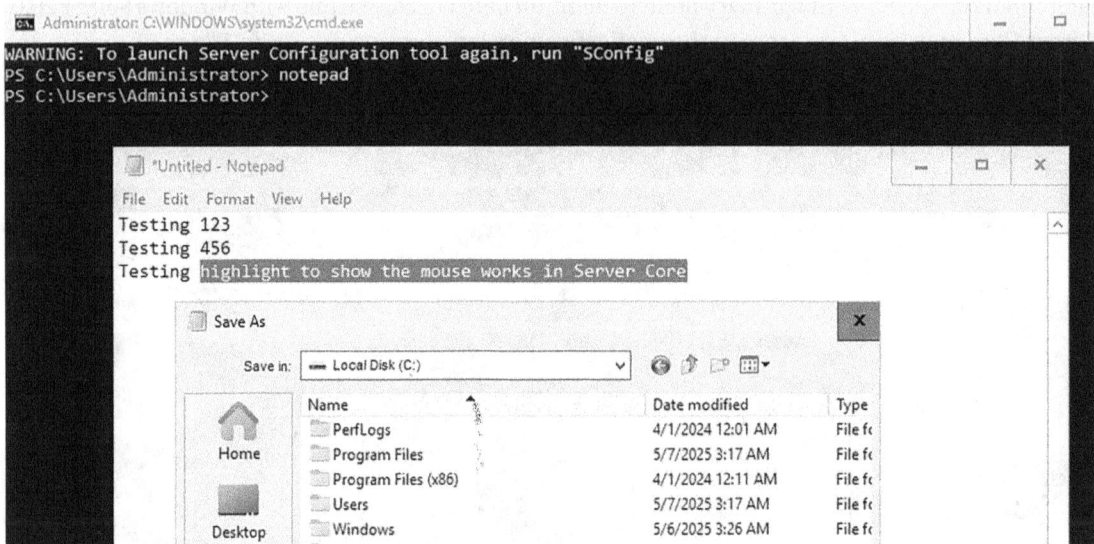

Figure 11.5: Opening Notepad on Server Core

PowerShell

To manage Server Core, you can obviously work straight from the console and use Command Prompt to accomplish many things on this server. In reality, the commands and functions available from inside Command Prompt will be limited. If you are working from the console of a Windows Server Core box, it makes much more sense to use Command Prompt for just one purpose—to invoke PowerShell and then use PowerShell to accomplish whatever tasks you need to do on that server. The quickest way I know to move into PowerShell from the basic Command Prompt is to simply type the word powershell and press *Enter*. This will bring PowerShell capabilities right into your existing Command Prompt window so that you can start interfacing with the PowerShell commands and cmdlets that you need, in order to really manipulate this server:

```
 Administrator: C:\WINDOWS\system32\cmd.exe                                    —  □  X

WARNING: To launch Server Configuration tool again, run "SConfig"
PS C:\Users\Administrator> notepad
PS C:\Users\Administrator> powershell
Windows PowerShell
Copyright (C) Microsoft Corporation. All rights reserved.

Install the latest PowerShell for new features and improvements! https://aka.ms/PSWindows

PS C:\Users\Administrator> Get-Command

CommandType     Name                                         Version     Source
-----------     ----                                         -------     ------
Alias           Add-AppPackage                               2.0.1.0     Appx
Alias           Add-AppPackageVolume                         2.0.1.0     Appx
Alias           Add-AppProvisionedPackage                    3.0         Dism
Alias           Add-MsixPackage                              2.0.1.0     Appx
Alias           Add-MsixPackageVolume                        2.0.1.0     Appx
Alias           Add-MsixVolume                               2.0.1.0     Appx
Alias           Add-ProvisionedAppPackage                    3.0         Dism
Alias           Add-ProvisionedAppSharedPackageContainer     3.0         Dism
Alias           Add-ProvisionedAppxPackage                   3.0         Dism
Alias           Add-WindowsFeature                           2.0.0.0     ServerManager
Alias           Apply-WindowsUnattend                        3.0         Dism
Alias           Disable-PhysicalDiskIndication               2.0.0.0     Storage
Alias           Disable-PhysicalDiskIndication               1.0.0.0     VMDirectStorage
```

Figure 11.6: Loading PowerShell inside Server Core

What is the first thing we typically do on new servers? Give them IP addresses, of course. Without network connectivity, there isn't much that we can do on this server. You can assign IP address information to NICs using PowerShell on any newer Windows Server instance, but most of us are not in the habit of doing so. Since we can't just open up **Control Panel** and get into the Network and Sharing Center like we can from inside the Desktop Experience GUI of Windows Server, where do we begin to get network connectivity on this new Server Core?

Using cmdlets to manage IP addresses

There are cmdlets that you can use to view and manipulate IP address settings from within PowerShell. Again, these same cmdlets can be used in the full GUI version of Windows Server or from within Server Core.

As we are currently working from Server Core, where we only have command-line interfacing available to us, these cmdlets are essential to get network connectivity flowing on our new server:

- Get-NetIPConfiguration: This displays the current networking configuration.
- Get-NetIPAddress: This displays the current IP addresses.
- Get-NetIPInterface: This shows a list of NICs and their interface ID numbers. This number is going to be important when setting an IP address because we want to make sure we tell PowerShell to configure the right IP on the right NIC.
- New-NetIPAddress: This is used to configure a new IP address.
- Set-DNSClientServerAddress: This is used to configure DNS server settings in the NIC properties.

Let's quickly walk through the setup of a static IP address on a new Server Core instance to make sure this all makes sense. I want to assign the 10.10.10.12 IP address to this new server, but first, we need to find out which NIC interface ID number it needs to be assigned to. The output of Get-NetIPInterface tells us that ifIndex for my Ethernet NIC is 6:

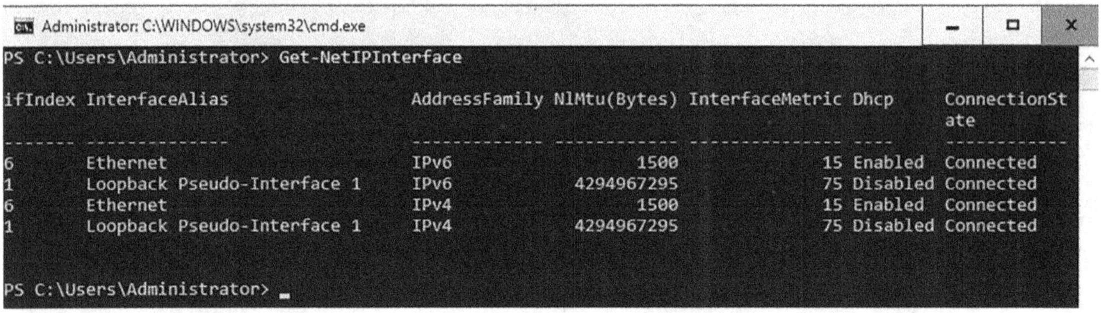

```
Administrator: C:\WINDOWS\system32\cmd.exe                                         _   □   X

PS C:\Users\Administrator> Get-NetIPInterface

ifIndex InterfaceAlias                  AddressFamily NlMtu(Bytes) InterfaceMetric Dhcp      ConnectionSt
                                                                                            ate
------- --------------                  ------------- ------------ --------------- ----      ------------
6       Ethernet                        IPv6                  1500              15 Enabled   Connected
1       Loopback Pseudo-Interface 1     IPv6            4294967295              75 Disabled  Connected
6       Ethernet                        IPv4                  1500              15 Enabled   Connected
1       Loopback Pseudo-Interface 1     IPv4            4294967295              75 Disabled  Connected


PS C:\Users\Administrator> _
```

Figure 11.7: Finding the interface ID number for your NIC

Alternatively, or as a double-check, you could also run route print and verify your interface ID number near the top of that output. You can see in *Figure 11.8* that my Hyper-V NIC on this Server Core VM is interface 6 (shown at the left of the output):

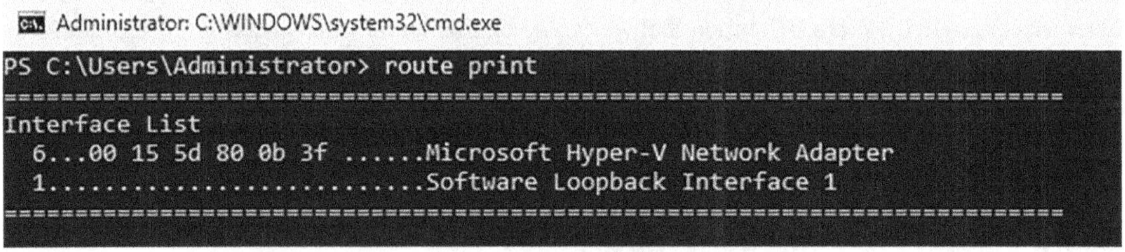

```
Administrator: C:\WINDOWS\system32\cmd.exe

PS C:\Users\Administrator> route print
===========================================================================
Interface List
  6...00 15 5d 80 0b 3f ......Microsoft Hyper-V Network Adapter
  1...........................Software Loopback Interface 1
===========================================================================
```

Figure 11.8: Confirming the interface ID via route print

Now, knowing the interface number, let's build the commands that are going to assign my new IP address settings to the NIC. I am going to use one command to assign the IP address, subnet mask prefix, and default gateway. I will use a second command to assign DNS server addresses:

```
New-NetIPAddress -InterfaceIndex 6 -IPAddress 10.10.10.12 -PrefixLength 24
-DefaultGateway 10.10.10.1
Set-DNSClientServerAddress -InterfaceIndex 6 -ServerAddresses
10.10.10.10,10.10.10.11
```

Figure 11.9 shows us the resulting output:

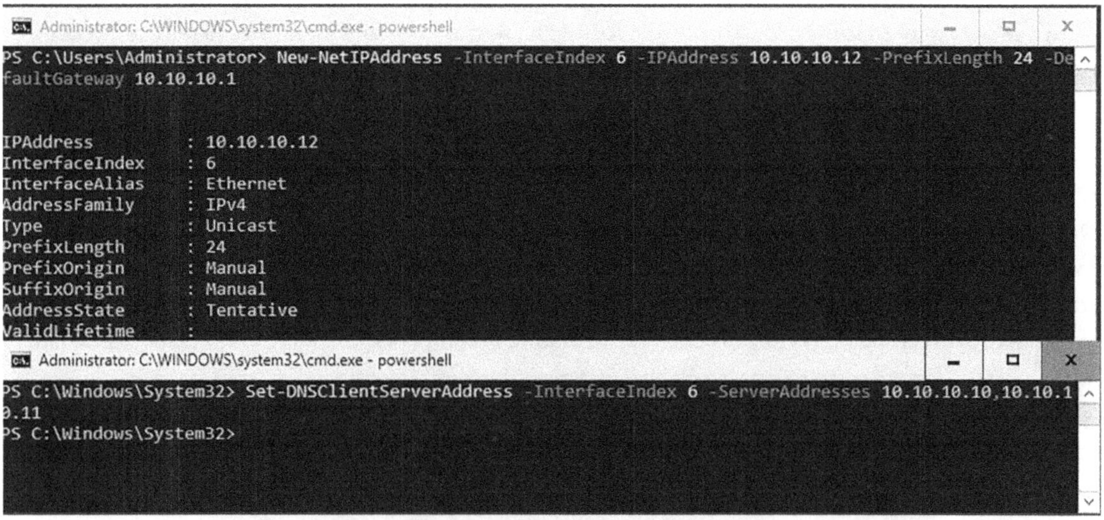

```
Administrator: C:\WINDOWS\system32\cmd.exe - powershell                          _   □   X
PS C:\Users\Administrator> New-NetIPAddress -InterfaceIndex 6 -IPAddress 10.10.10.12 -PrefixLength 24 -De
faultGateway 10.10.10.1


IPAddress          : 10.10.10.12
InterfaceIndex     : 6
InterfaceAlias     : Ethernet
AddressFamily      : IPv4
Type               : Unicast
PrefixLength       : 24
PrefixOrigin       : Manual
SuffixOrigin       : Manual
AddressState       : Tentative
ValidLifetime      :
```
```
Administrator: C:\WINDOWS\system32\cmd.exe - powershell                          _   □   X
PS C:\Windows\System32> Set-DNSClientServerAddress -InterfaceIndex 6 -ServerAddresses 10.10.10.10,10.10.1
0.11
PS C:\Windows\System32>
```

Figure 11.9: Assigning IP and DNS server addresses

Hold the phone! How did I get two PowerShell prompts open at the same time within the Server Core interface? Make sure to read the *Accidentally closing Command Prompt* section later in this chapter to discover how you can launch multiple windows and tools inside the Server Core console.

Now, all of these IP settings should be in place on the NIC. Let's double-check that with the Get-NetIPConfiguration command, seen in *Figure 11.10*. As you can see in the screenshot, here is yet another command you could utilize to discover that InterfaceIndex NIC identification number. Alternatively, you could use good old ipconfig to check these settings, but where's the fun in that?

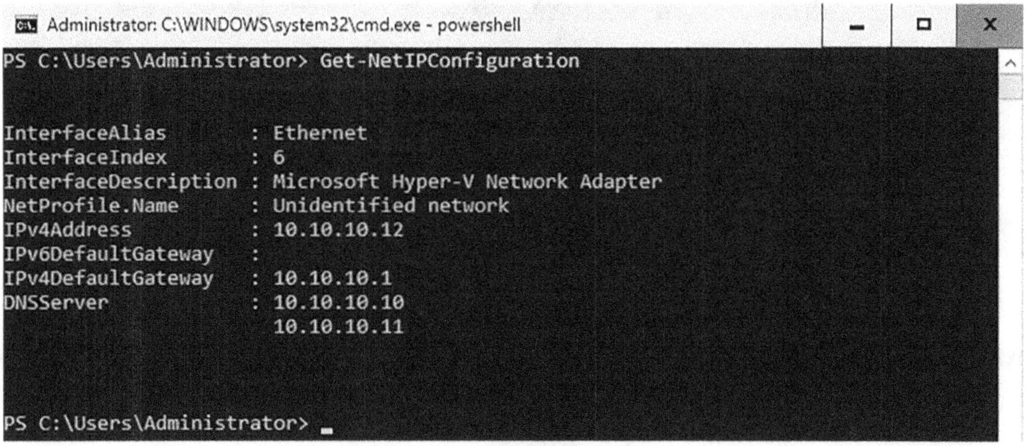

```
Administrator: C:\WINDOWS\system32\cmd.exe - powershell                          _   □   X
PS C:\Users\Administrator> Get-NetIPConfiguration


InterfaceAlias       : Ethernet
InterfaceIndex       : 6
InterfaceDescription : Microsoft Hyper-V Network Adapter
NetProfile.Name      : Unidentified network
IPv4Address          : 10.10.10.12
IPv6DefaultGateway   :
IPv4DefaultGateway   : 10.10.10.1
DNSServer            : 10.10.10.10
                       10.10.10.11


PS C:\Users\Administrator>
```

Figure 11.10: Checking IP configuration

Remember, you can always utilize DHCP reservations to make this a little bit easier. If you were to simply run `ipconfig /all` from Server Core and jot down the MAC address of your NIC, you could use this address to create a reservation in DHCP and assign a specific IP address to the new server that way.

Setting the server hostname

Now that we have network connectivity, a good next step is setting the hostname of our server and joining it to the domain. First things first, let's see what the current name of the server is, and change it to something that fits our standards. When you freshly install Windows, it self-assigns a random hostname to the server. You can view the current hostname by simply typing `hostname` and pressing *Enter*:

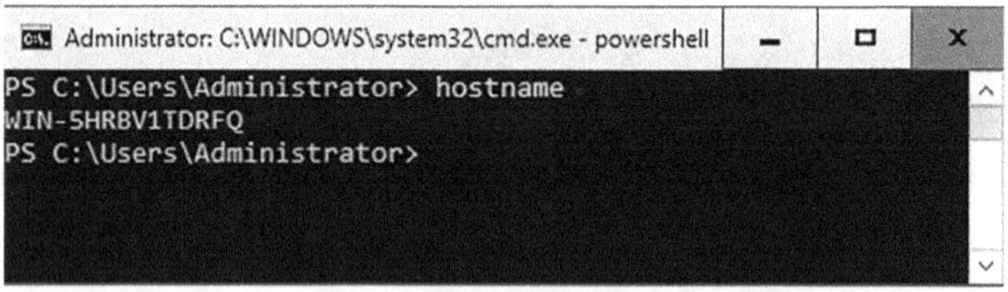

```
Administrator: C:\WINDOWS\system32\cmd.exe - powershell        —    □    X
PS C:\Users\Administrator> hostname
WIN-5HRBV1TDRFQ
PS C:\Users\Administrator>
```

Figure 11.11: Checking the current server hostname

To change the hostname of your server, we need to use PowerShell. Bring yourself into a PowerShell prompt if not already there, and all we need to do is use the `Rename-Computer` cmdlet to set our new hostname. I have decided to name this new server WEB4 because, later, we will install the Web Services role on it and host a website. Remember, after renaming your computer, just like in the GUI version of Windows Server, a system restart is necessary to put that change into action. So, following the `Rename-Computer` command, you can issue a `Restart-Computer` command to reboot the VM:

```
Rename-Computer WEB4
Restart-Computer
```

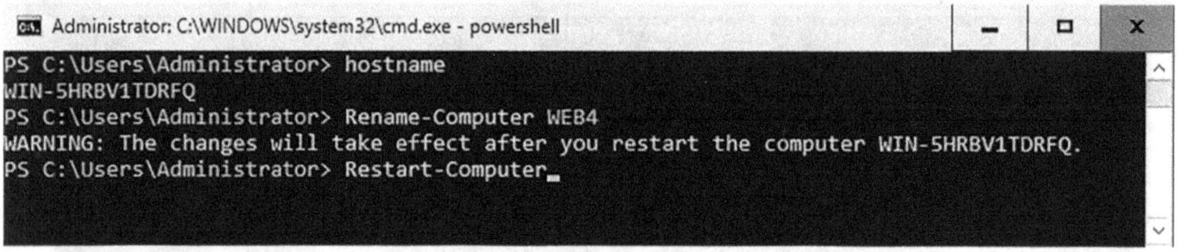

```
Administrator: C:\WINDOWS\system32\cmd.exe - powershell        —    □    X
PS C:\Users\Administrator> hostname
WIN-5HRBV1TDRFQ
PS C:\Users\Administrator> Rename-Computer WEB4
WARNING: The changes will take effect after you restart the computer WIN-5HRBV1TDRFQ.
PS C:\Users\Administrator> Restart-Computer
```

Figure 11.12: Changing the hostname and restarting your system

Joining your domain

The next logical step is, of course, joining this new server to your domain. These are the standard functions that we would perform on any new server in our environment, but done in a way that you may have never encountered before, since we are doing all of this strictly from the Command Prompt and PowerShell interfaces.

To join Server Core to your domain, head into PowerShell and then use the Add-Computer cmdlet. You will be asked to specify both the domain name and your credentials for joining the domain—the same information you would have to specify if you were joining Windows Server 2025 in Desktop Experience mode to a domain.

First, you must specify the credentials that will be used to accomplish this domain join:

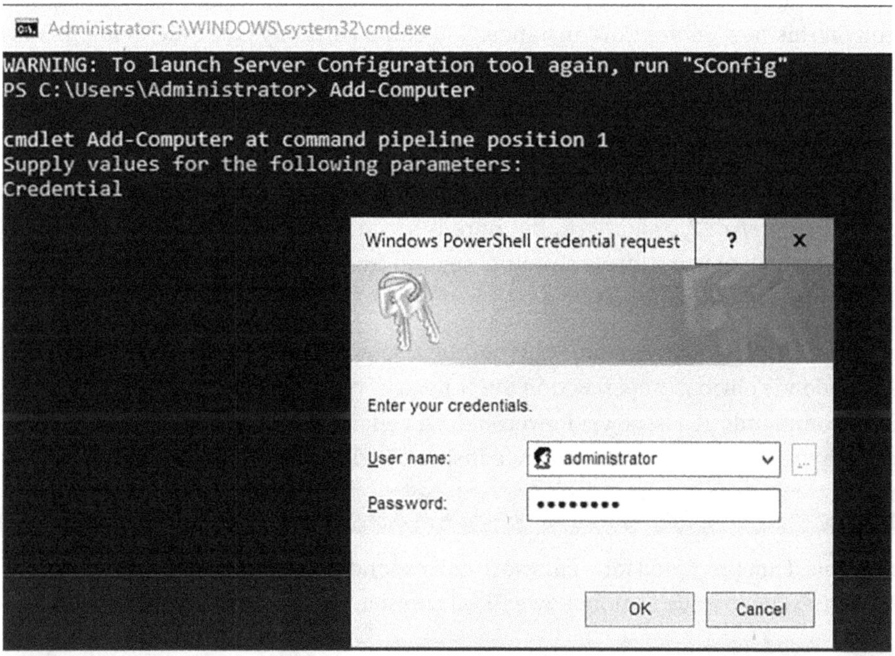

Figure 11.13: Entering credentials authorized to join this system to your domain

Then you tell it what domain you would like to join:

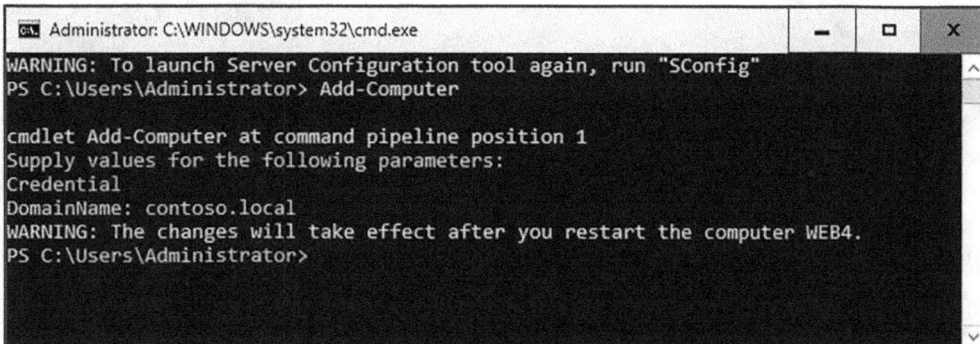

Figure 11.14: Specifying the domain to join

Alternatively, you could utilize the `-DomainName` parameter in combination with the original `Add-Computer` cmdlet to specify the name of the domain as part of the original command. And of course, after joining the domain, you need to utilize `Restart-Computer` once again to finalize this change.

Remote PowerShell

Once the new server is IP-addressed, named, and domain-joined, we can start doing some real administration on this new Server Core instance. You could certainly continue to log in and interface directly with the console, but as with managing any other server in your environment, there must be ways to handle this remotely, right? One of the ways that you can manipulate Server Core without having to sit in front of it is by using a remote PowerShell connection.

We will cover the process to use remote PowerShell to manipulate servers (both GUI and headless) in more detail in *Chapter 12, PowerShell*, but here is a glimpse of the commands necessary and the capabilities present when you achieve a remote session from a PowerShell prompt, on a workstation inside a domain-joined environment.

Open PowerShell from another system—this can be a server or even a client operating system. This PowerShell window is obviously open within the context of whatever machine you are currently logged in to, and any commands you issue via PowerShell will elicit a response from the local system. To tap PowerShell into the WEB4 Server Core instance instead, I will issue the following command:

```
Enter-PSSession -ComputerName WEB4 -Credential administrator
```

After running this, I am prompted for a password corresponding to the administrator account on WEB4, and I will then be able to issue remote PowerShell commands against Server Core:

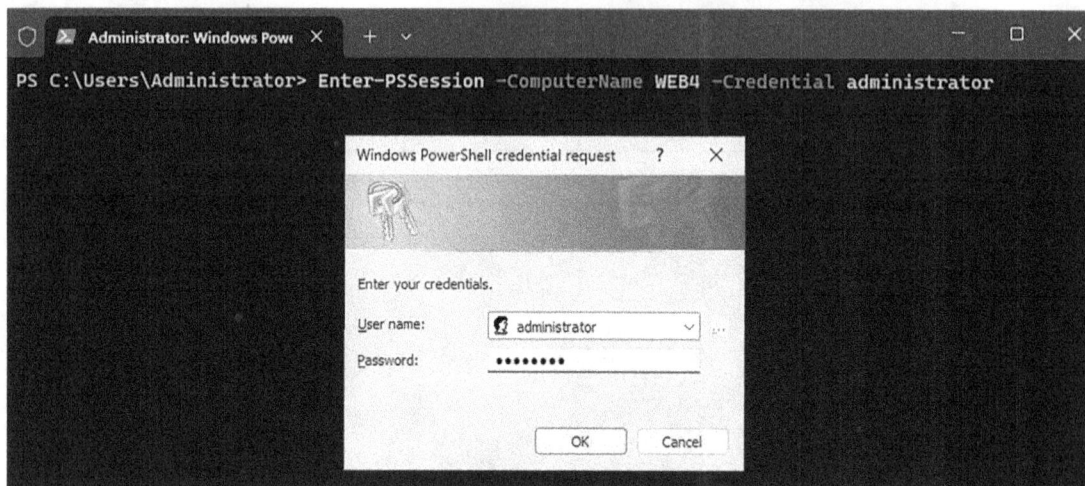

Figure 11.15: Using Enter-PSSession to remotely connect to WEB4

Now we are sitting at a PowerShell prompt, remotely connected to the WEB4 Server Core box. You can see this by [WEB4] being listed to the left of our prompt. Perhaps you don't trust that little identifier, and you want to make sure that this PowerShell window now accesses and manipulates the remote WEB4 server?

Let's issue a couple of quick commands, such as `hostname` and `ipconfig`, to prove that the information being given to us in this PowerShell session really comes from the new WEB4 server, even though I am running this PowerShell session from my DC1 server:

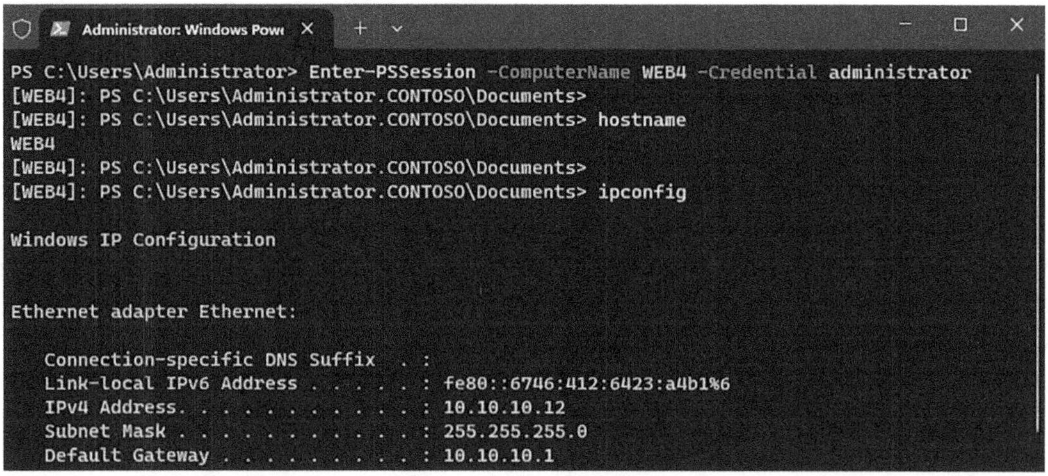

Figure 11.16: PowerShell now responds as if I were logged in to WEB4

Now that we have a remote PowerShell connection to this new Server Core, we can do pretty much whatever we want to that server, right from this console. Commands and cmdlets issued inside this remote PowerShell session will manipulate WEB4, rather than our local workstation.

Server Manager

While the initial configuration of your server will be handled to a degree from the command-line interfaces available at the console, once your server has been established on the network, it will likely be more advantageous for you to expand your horizons a little. You could probably find PowerShell cmdlets that allow you to manage and manipulate anything in your new server, but we are generally more accustomed to using graphical tools such as Server Manager. You already know that Server Manager can be used to manage multiple servers, local and remote, and is a piece of the Microsoft *centralized management* puzzle. This remote management capability in Server Manager, which we explored earlier in the book, allows you to tap into not only GUI-based Windows Server but also Server Core instances.

I want to install a role on my new WEB4 server. I could do that with PowerShell right on the server console, but instead, let's try adding WEB4 into Server Manager, which runs on another one of my servers. I am going to log in to WEB3 and use Server Manager from there. As we have already experienced, I can add a new server to Server Manager by using the **Manage** menu and choosing **Add Servers**:

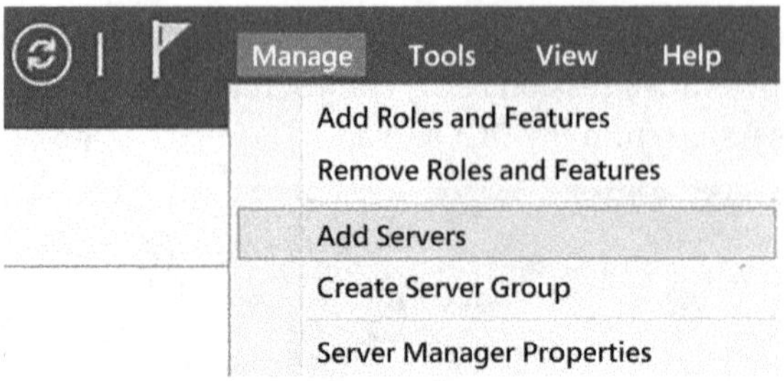

Figure 11.17: Adding new servers to be managed inside Server Manager

Let's add the new WEB4 server to our list of managed machines, and it is now manageable from inside this instance of Server Manager. Getting back to what my original intentions were, I want to install the Web Server (IIS) role on WEB4. If I use the **Add roles and features** function inside Server Manager, I can now choose to manipulate the WEB4 server:

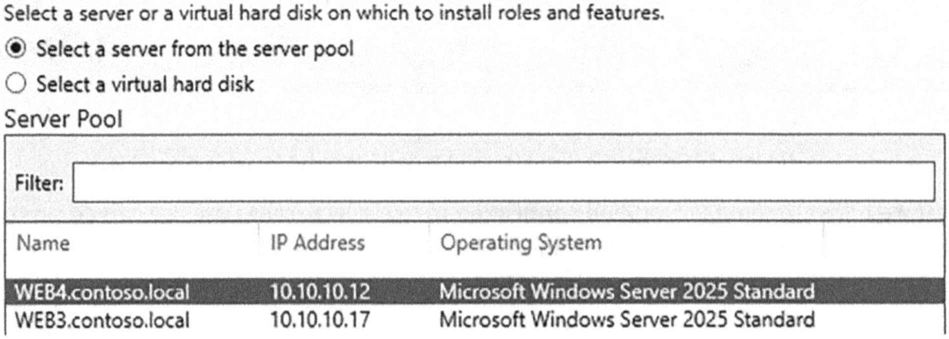

Figure 11.18: Modifying WEB4 from WEB3's Server Manager

As with any server running the full Desktop Experience version of Windows Server, we can now finish walking through the role installation wizard, and the Web Server role will be installed on WEB4.

Remote Server Administration Tools

Also true is the fact that you can manage Server Core instances with the **Remote Server Administration Tools (RSAT)** in Windows 10/11. RSAT is essentially just a copy of Server Manager and accompanying administrative tools that are designed to run on the client operating system. In our case, I already have a Windows workstation on which I installed RSAT earlier in the book, so I will test this by logging in to that guy and adding WEB4 to the interface. I just finished installing the IIS role on WEB4 in our previous task, so I should be able to see that listed inside RSAT when I connect it to WEB4.

f you haven't used RSAT before and haven't read over that section of text, it is important to know that there is no application called **Remote Server Administration Tools**. Instead, after the RSAT installation has been completed, take a look inside your **Start** menu for the application called **Server Manager**. This is how you utilize a Windows 10/11 client to remotely manage Windows Server 2025 (or other version) instances:

Figure 11.19: Server Manager on a Windows client, courtesy of RSAT

Precisely as you would do from a Server Manager interface of Windows Server 2025, go ahead and walk through the wizard to add other servers to manage. Once I have added WEB4 as a managed server in my Windows 11 Server Manager, I can see IIS listed inside my **Dashboard**. This indicates that the IIS service running on WEB4 is visible, accessible, and configurable right from my Windows 11 desktop computer. For most of the tasks that I need to accomplish on WEB4, I will never have to worry about logging in to the console of that server.

If I right-click on the WEB4 server name from within this RSAT console, you can see that I have many features available to me that I can use to manage this remote Server Core instance:

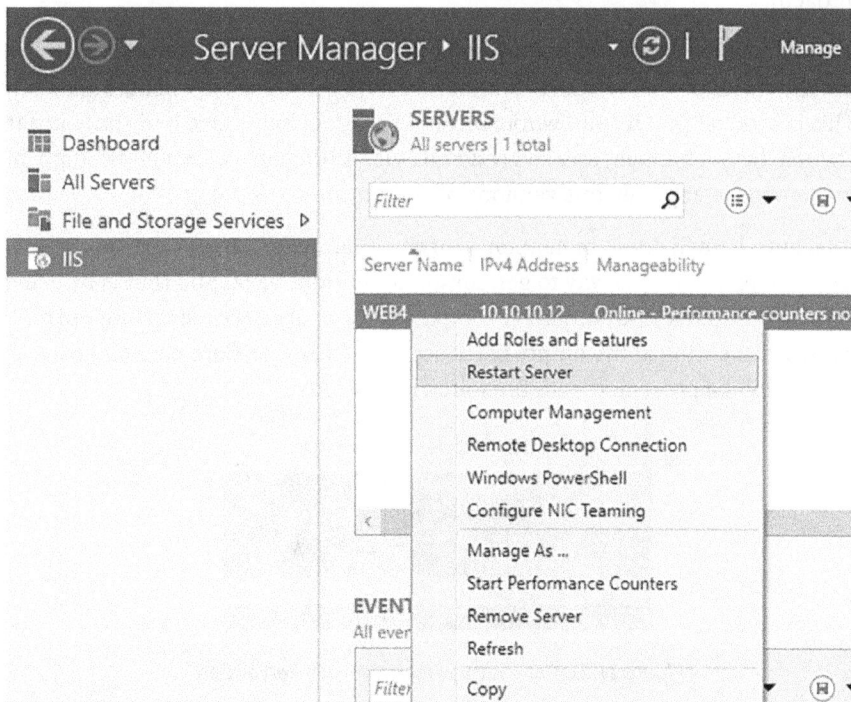

Figure 11.20: Interacting with remote servers via Server Manager

Clearly, there are ways to use the GUI tools to manage our GUI-less instances of Windows Server. Doing so is a matter of putting your mind in a place where you think of servers as headless, and that tools such as PowerShell or Server Manager really don't care at all whether the server they are changing is local or remote. The processes and tools are the same either way. You can see in the previous screenshot that I could even click from here to launch a remote PowerShell connection to WEB4. Clicking on this button immediately launches a PowerShell prompt that is remotely tied to the WEB4 server, even though I am currently only logged in to my Windows 11 workstation. This is even easier than issuing the Enter-PSSession cmdlet from inside PowerShell.

Accidentally closing Command Prompt

Let's turn back to my console session of Server Core and explore one more common obstacle that many admins find themselves in the middle of. We tend to close windows and applications that are no longer being used, so you might unconsciously close the Command Prompt window that serves your entire administrative existence within a Server Core console session. In early editions of Server Core, accidentally closing the one-and-only Command Prompt interface would leave you staring at a large blank screen, with seemingly no interface and nowhere to go from here.

How do you get back to work on this server? Do we have to turn the server off and back on to reset it? That would interrupt any roles or traffic that this server might serve up to users, so obviously it isn't the ideal approach.

New as of Windows Server 2022 (and continuing into Server 2025) is a feature where, if an administrator accidentally closes the Server Core Command Prompt instance, it will automatically re-launch a new one. This is so nice! And it even works most of the time, but I have had some instances where the auto-re-launch did not happen, and so I was still stuck sitting on a completely empty black screen, just like what happens in any previous versions of Server Core.

In the event that auto-launch does not happen, or if you administer Server Core on an older version of Windows Server, there is a simple way to get Command Prompt back, and that is by using **Task Manager** to launch a new instance of Command Prompt. After mistakenly closing your current Command Prompt window, when sitting at the empty black screen of a Server Core console, you can press *Ctrl + Alt + Del* and you will be presented with the following options:

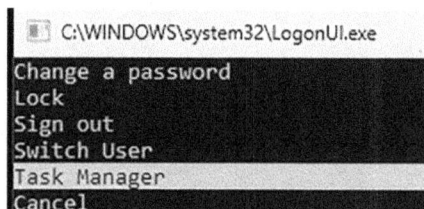

Figure 11.21: Ctrl + Alt + Del works inside Server Core

There are a few different functions you can perform here, which is pretty neat. But to get our Command Prompt window back, arrow down to **Task Manager** and press *Enter*. This will launch the **Task Manager** application that we are all familiar with. Drop down the **File** menu, and then click on **Run new task**:

Figure 11.22: Running a new task via Task Manager

In the **Create new task** box, type cmd and then click **OK**:

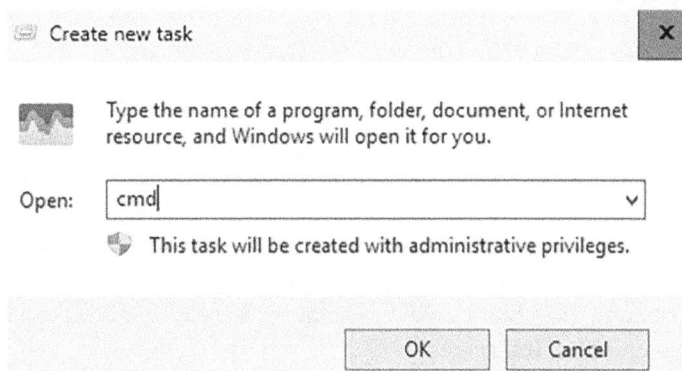

Figure 11.23: Launching a new instance of Command Prompt

Alternatively, you could specify to launch any application directly from this **Create new task** prompt. If you were interested in moving straight into PowerShell, instead of typing cmd, you could instead simply type powershell into that prompt, and it would open directly:

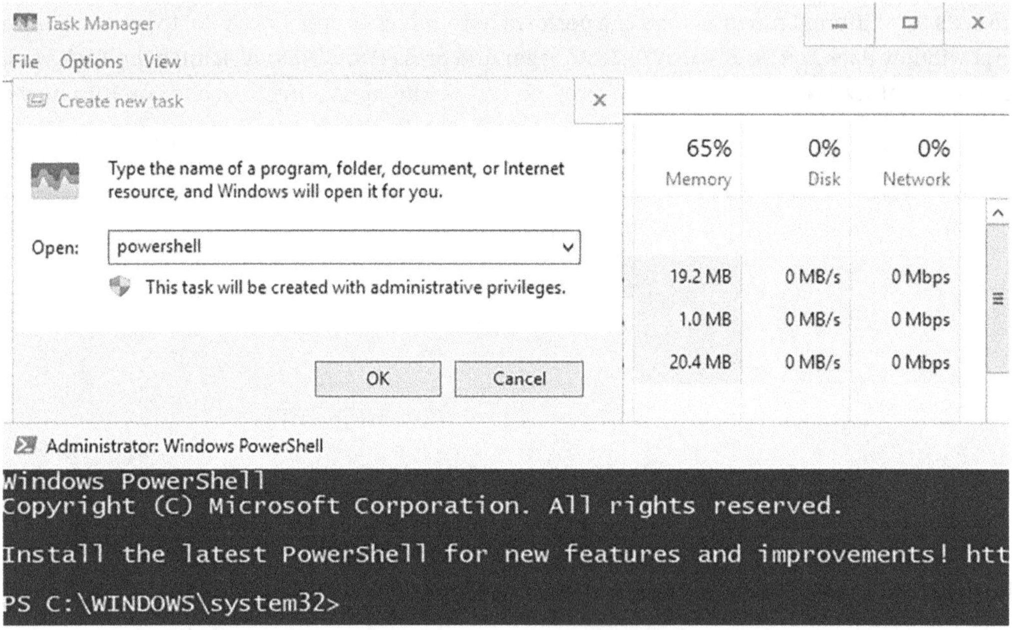

Figure 11.24: Opening PowerShell in Server Core

Using Windows Admin Center to manage Server Core

While Command Prompt from the console, remote PowerShell connections, remote Server Manager administration, and even the RSAT tools running on a Windows 10/11 workstation are all valid and powerful tools to administer our Server Core instances, they have all now been upstaged by the release of **Windows Admin Center (WAC)**. You already learned what WAC can do to centrally manage your entire server infrastructure, but what we need to point out here is that WAC can be used for servers both with and without graphical interfaces.

I have spoken with many Windows Server administrators about the topic of Server Core, and one of the biggest blocks to implementing these more efficient and secure server platforms is an apprehension that, once configured, ongoing administration and maintenance of these servers will be more difficult to handle. Admins who are familiar and comfortable working with the Windows Server Desktop Experience know exactly what needs to be done to accomplish their daily tasks, but remove that point-and-click interface, and suddenly the workday gets a lot more complicated.

Thankfully, you don't have to memorize the PowerShell handbook to use Server Core! WAC treats Server Core instances in the same way that it does a server running Desktop Experience. It just works!

We already have WAC installed on a server in our test lab, so let's open it up, add the new WEB4 server to be administered, and take a look at what options are available for the ongoing maintenance of this server.

When we first connect to WEB4 via the WAC console, there is nothing in here that even indicates this is a Server Core instance. We have all of the WAC tools and utilities available to click on:

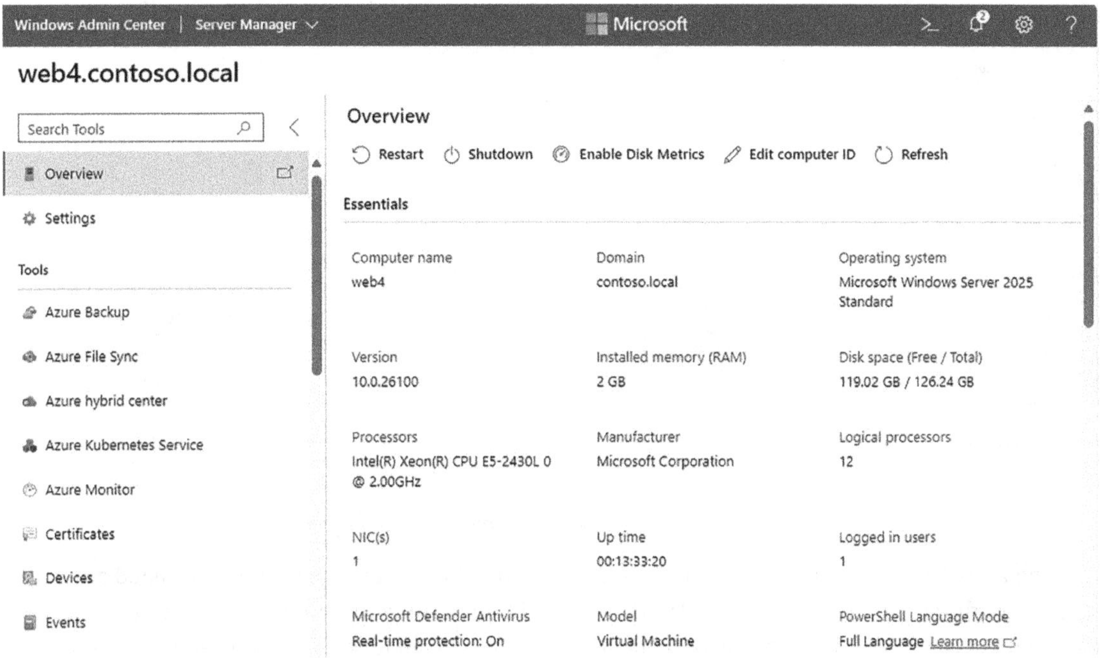

Figure 11.25: WAC overview of WEB4

Let's try a couple of things from WAC. You have power controls right near the top of the screen from which you can easily shut down or restart the server. That is much easier and faster than having to establish a remote PowerShell connection from which you can issue commands to accomplish the same actions. There are also performance metrics on the home screen (if you scroll down), showing your consumed **CPU**, **Memory**, and **Networking** resources. Without WAC, you would need to log in to WEB4 and launch **Task Manager** to see these statistics:

web4.contoso.local

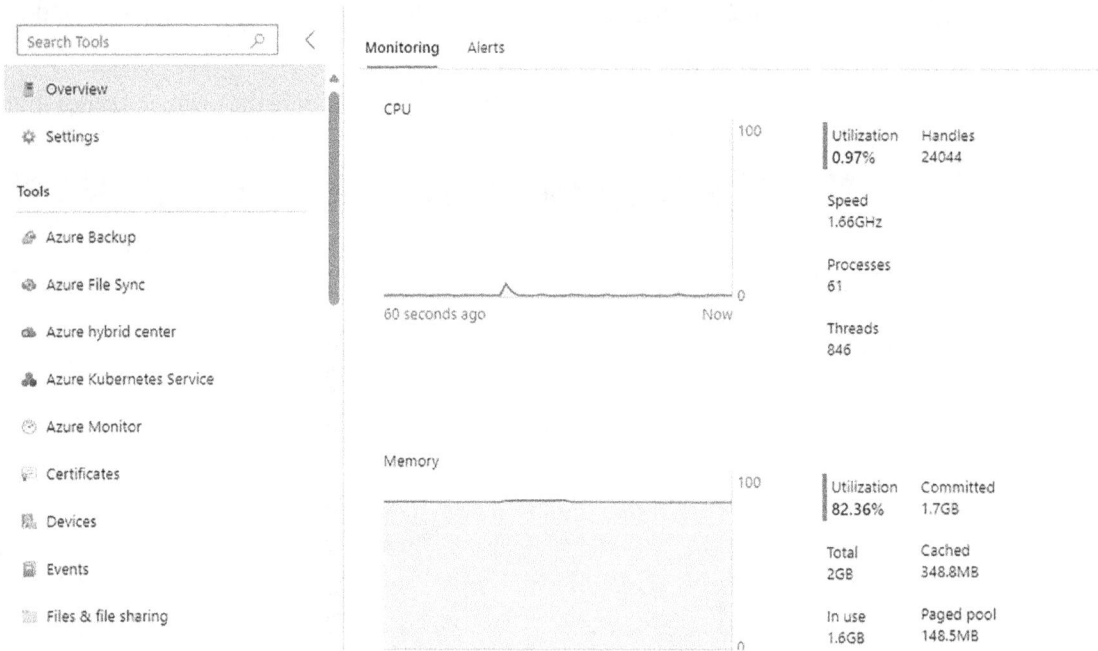

Figure 11.26: Server performance metrics at your fingertips

Moving away from the home screen, as useful as it is, try clicking on one of the tools listed along the left side of the screen, such as **Events**. Without WAC, if you wanted to troubleshoot an issue on Server Core, you may struggle figuring out a way to view Windows event logs on that server. How can you do that via the command line? I suppose you could have logged on to the Server Core console and used **Task Manager** to launch EventVwr, but opening WAC and simply clicking on **Events** is much easier:

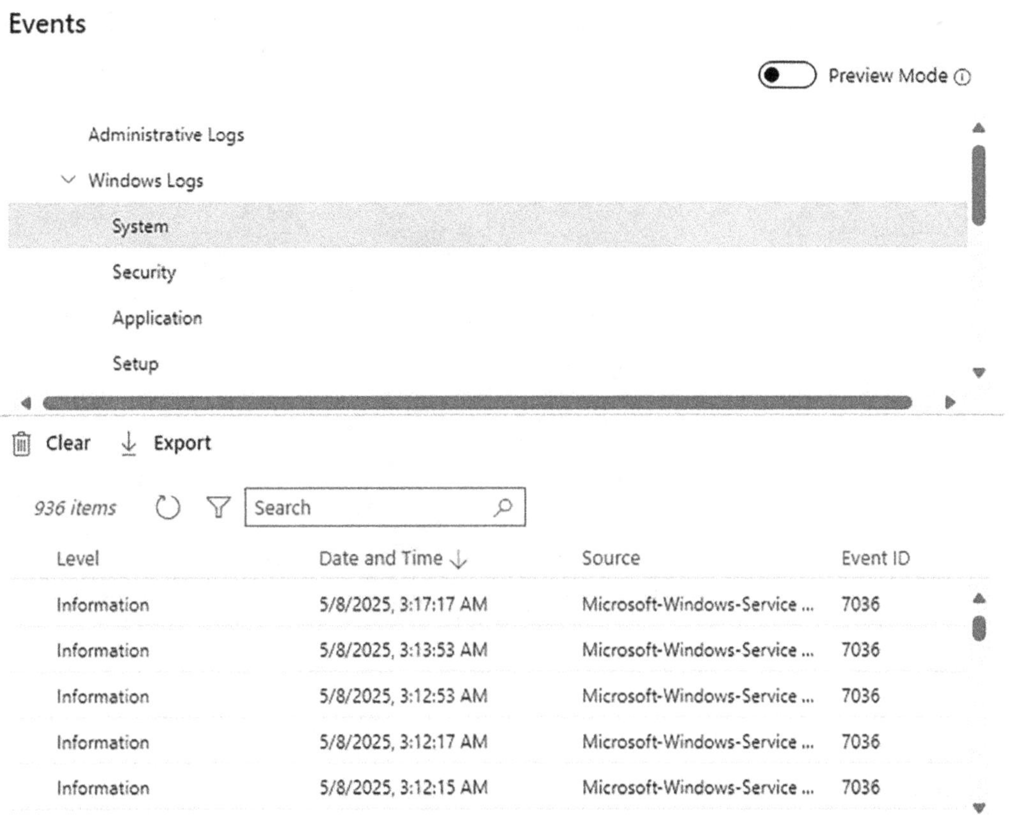

Events

Preview Mode ⓘ

Administrative Logs

∨ Windows Logs

    System

    Security

    Application

    Setup

🗑 Clear   ↓ Export

936 items ○ ▽ Search

Level	Date and Time ↓	Source	Event ID
Information	5/8/2025, 3:17:17 AM	Microsoft-Windows-Service ...	7036
Information	5/8/2025, 3:13:53 AM	Microsoft-Windows-Service ...	7036
Information	5/8/2025, 3:12:53 AM	Microsoft-Windows-Service ...	7036
Information	5/8/2025, 3:12:17 AM	Microsoft-Windows-Service ...	7036
Information	5/8/2025, 3:12:15 AM	Microsoft-Windows-Service ...	7036

Figure 11.27: System event logs

Other examples of useful functions inside WAC, particularly when working with a Server Core instance, are using **Files & file sharing** to navigate the file and folder structure of the hard drive of WEB4 or using the **Firewall** function here to create or remove Windows firewall rules on WEB4. There is also a **Networks** tool, from which you can manipulate IP addressing configurations.

While many more tools exist inside WAC, the last thing I want to point out is that, once again, we have a **PowerShell** option (similar to what we can launch from inside Server Manager). This **PowerShell** button will invoke and display a remote PowerShell connection to the WEB4 Server Core instance, for if ever we can't find a function that is needed inside WAC and need to dive a little further under the hood to accomplish something from a command-line interface. And the best part is that you never actually have to launch PowerShell! This all happens from within your internet browser window:

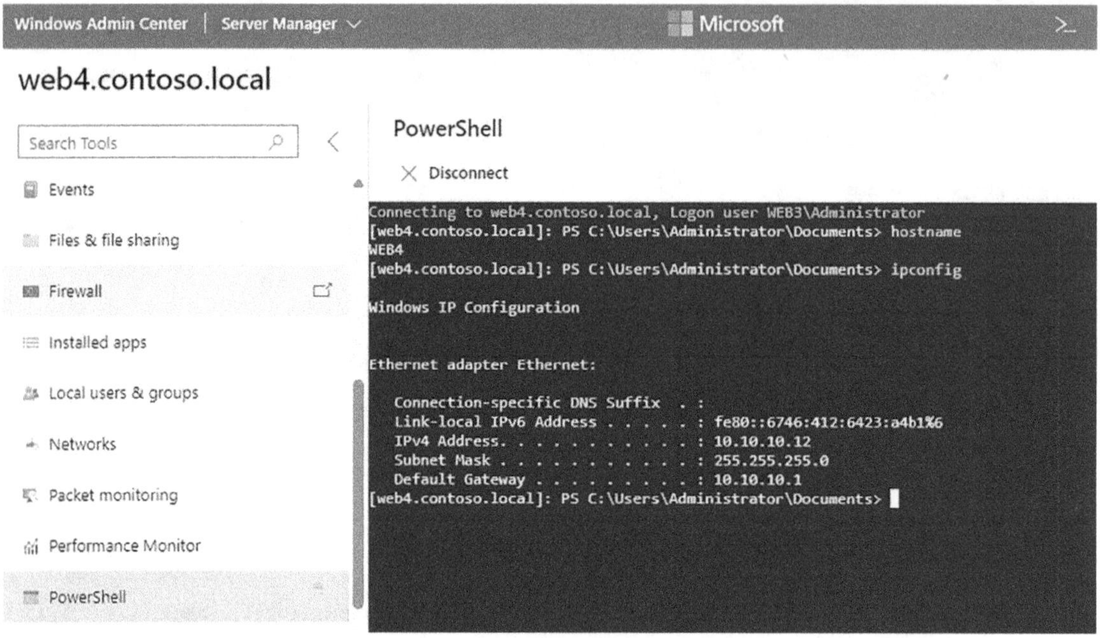

Windows Admin Center | Server Manager ∨   ▦ Microsoft   >_

web4.contoso.local

Search Tools	🔍	<

📋 Events

🗄 Files & file sharing

▦ Firewall   ⌷

☰ Installed apps

👥 Local users & groups

✦ Networks

🖫 Packet monitoring

᰼ Performance Monitor

▦ PowerShell

PowerShell

✕ Disconnect

```
Connecting to web4.contoso.local, Logon user WEB3\Administrator
[web4.contoso.local]: PS C:\Users\Administrator\Documents> hostname
WEB4
[web4.contoso.local]: PS C:\Users\Administrator\Documents> ipconfig

Windows IP Configuration

Ethernet adapter Ethernet:

   Connection-specific DNS Suffix  . :
   Link-local IPv6 Address . . . . . : fe80::6746:412:6423:a4b1%6
   IPv4 Address. . . . . . . . . . . : 10.10.10.12
   Subnet Mask . . . . . . . . . . . : 255.255.255.0
   Default Gateway . . . . . . . . . : 10.10.10.1
[web4.contoso.local]: PS C:\Users\Administrator\Documents> █
```

Figure 11.28: Using PowerShell inside WAC

There is so much more that can be accomplished from inside WAC—editing **Registry**, adding to **Roles & Features**, checking the status of **Services**, and even interfacing with Windows Update. If you aren't already using WAC, you're missing the boat!

The SConfig utility

Now we will take a step back from the idea of centralized administration, and check out a tool that is available inside Server Core, but one that is generally only useful when working on the console of your server. We mentioned SConfig earlier in the chapter, but breezed right past it at the time, so that you could focus on getting to know Server Core a little bit more intimately from Command Prompt and PowerShell. While you can certainly ignore SConfig completely and make all configurations and adjustments to Server Core from the traditional command-line interfaces and centralized administration tools, SConfig is a very nice utility to make initial networking, hostname, and domain membership changes to your new server.

SConfig has existed for most versions of Server Core, but in early versions, you always had to intentionally launch it to make use of the capabilities within. Windows Server 2022 was the first time we saw SConfig auto-launch when your server boots, and that idea continues into Server 2025. If you built your own Server Core version of Server 2025 while reading through this chapter, you certainly have already seen the SConfig interface, as it launches immediately after logging into Server Core.

We will soon be configuring a new Server Core Domain Controller, so I have spun up a brand-new instance of Server Core, which currently has no name, domain membership, or IP settings.

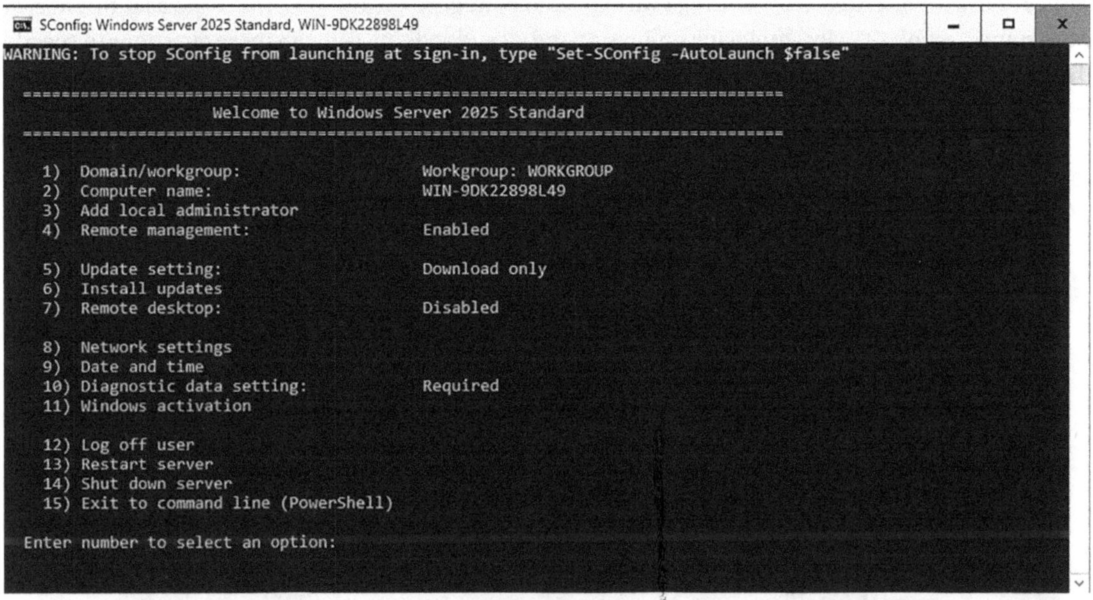

Figure 11.29: Sconfig auto-launches upon server login

The options available inside SConfig are fairly self-explanatory, but we'll cover those few tasks that are common to building any new server. Again, these are all things that you could instead accomplish via PowerShell cmdlets, but I find it easier to take the SConfig approach. The most common uses of this interface are to configure initial networking settings by pressing *8,* and to configure the server hostname and domain membership by using options *2* and *1.*

Beginning with network configuration, press *8* and *Enter*, and you'll find yourself on the **Network settings** screen displaying this server's current IP address, which was assigned via DHCP. Not only can we see the current IP address here, but also the interface index # for my network card, which you remember is important information to know whenever using command-line interfaces to update network card settings. On this new server, my current IP is 10.10.10.112 and my index # is 6.

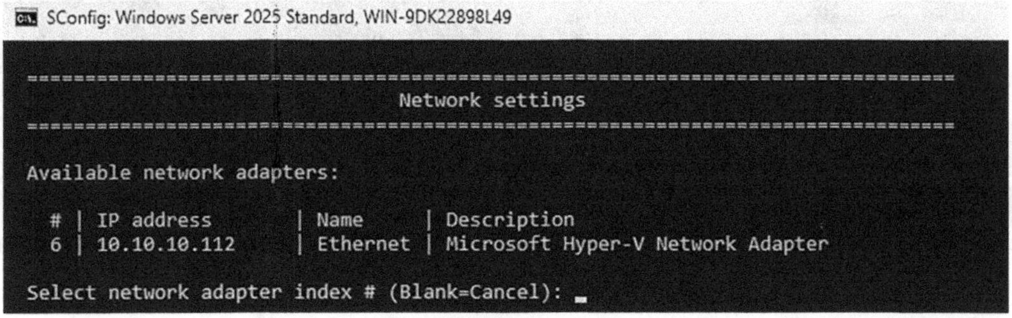

Figure 11.30: This NIC is index #6

To manipulate #6, simply type 6 and press *Enter*. You will, of course, need to select the correct index for your own server. Next, we find additional options for configuring network adapter addressing and DNS server addressing. These are the things we expect to configure on any NIC, the same as if this server were running a full GUI. By employing options #1 and #2 and walking through these questions to specify that I want a static IP address, what that IP should be, as well as defining a subnet mask and default gateway, you can see in *Figure 11.31* that this server is now properly IP-addressed as I want it to be.

```
SConfig: Windows Server 2025 Standard, DC3

==================================================================================
                          Network adapter settings
==================================================================================

NIC index:     6
Name:          Ethernet
Description:   Microsoft Hyper-V Network Adapter
IP address:    169.254.106.153,
               10.10.10.12,
               fe80::46e6:11c2:8dc4:a315
Subnet mask:   255.255.0.0
DHCP enabled: False

Default gateway: 10.10.10.1
1st DNS server:  10.10.10.10
2nd DNS server:  10.10.10.11
3rd DNS server:

  1) Set network adapter address
  2) Set DNS servers
  3) Clear DNS server settings
  4) Rename network adapter

Enter selection (Blank=Cancel): 1
Select (D)HCP or (S)tatic IP address (Blank=Cancel): S
Enter static IP address (Blank=Cancel): 10.10.10.23
Enter subnet mask (Blank=255.255.255.0): 255.255.255.0
Enter default gateway (Blank=Cancel): 10.10.10.1
Setting NIC to static IP...
Successfully enabled static addressing. DHCP for this network adapter is disabled.
Successfully set gateway.
Successfully set network adapter address.
(Press ENTER to continue): _

  1) Set network adapter address
  2) Set DNS servers
  3) Clear DNS server settings
  4) Rename network adapter

Enter selection (Blank=Cancel): 2
Enter 1st DNS server (Blank=Cancel): 10.10.10.10
Enter 2nd DNS server (Blank=None): 10.10.10.11
Enter 3rd DNS server (Blank=None):
Successfully assigned DNS server(s).
(Press ENTER to continue):
```

Figure 11.31: Using SConfig to set IP addressing information

NIC now configured, pressing *Enter* a couple of times will bring you back to the main SConfig menu. From here, we can use option #2 to rename this computer to DC3, reboot, and then use option #1 to join this server to our contoso.local domain. These actions are shown in *Figure 11.32*:

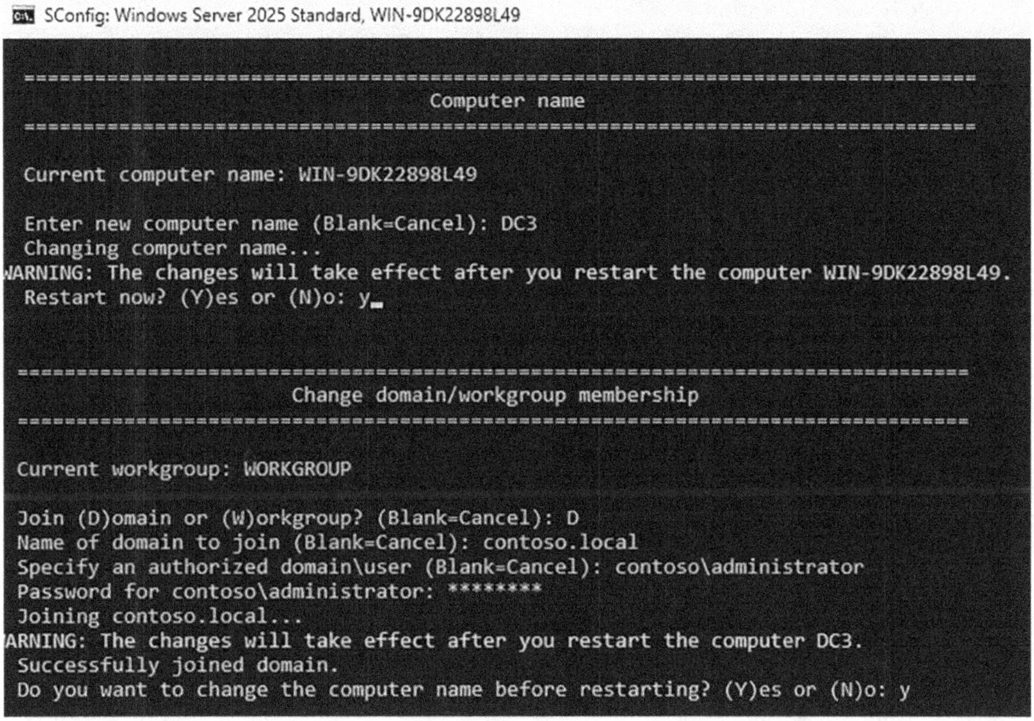

```
SConfig: Windows Server 2025 Standard, WIN-9DK22898L49

==============================================================================
                                 Computer name
==============================================================================

Current computer name: WIN-9DK22898L49

Enter new computer name (Blank=Cancel): DC3
Changing computer name...
WARNING: The changes will take effect after you restart the computer WIN-9DK22898L49.
Restart now? (Y)es or (N)o: y_



==============================================================================
                      Change domain/workgroup membership
==============================================================================

Current workgroup: WORKGROUP

Join (D)omain or (W)orkgroup? (Blank=Cancel): D
Name of domain to join (Blank=Cancel): contoso.local
Specify an authorized domain\user (Blank=Cancel): contoso\administrator
Password for contoso\administrator: ********
Joining contoso.local...
WARNING: The changes will take effect after you restart the computer DC3.
Successfully joined domain.
Do you want to change the computer name before restarting? (Y)es or (N)o: y
```

Figure 11.32: Naming and domain-joining this new Server Core

Common tasks for any fresh server are to configure a static IP address, set a hostname, and then join the server to your domain. For anyone who has never used Server Core before, these simple tasks can feel intimidating, but I hope that this walk-through has given you the courage to set one up for yourself! After finishing these quick configurations, we will now be able to manipulate DC3 using remote administration tools such as WAC, Server Manager, or a remote PowerShell session, as we have already discussed.

Roles available in Server Core

Server Core is obviously a restricted form of the operating system, and some of the roles inside Windows Server are just not designed to work properly within that limited context. Fortunately for us, most of them are, which enables Server 2025 administrators to deploy most of their critical infrastructure via the more secure Server Core platform. Here is a list of the roles that are currently supported to run on a Windows Server 2025 Server Core instance, and I have marked the ones in bold that I see most often used within the businesses I work with:

- Active Directory Certificate Services
- **Active Directory Domain Services**

- Active Directory Federation Services
- Active Directory Lightweight Directory Services
- Active Directory Rights Management Services
- Device Health Attestation
- **DHCP Server**
- **DNS Server**
- **File and Storage Services**
- Host Guardian Service
- **Hyper-V**
- Print and Document Services
- Remote Access
- Remote Desktop Services*
- Volume Activation Services
- **Web Server (IIS)**
- **Windows Server Essentials Experience**
- Windows Server Update Services

You'll notice that I placed a * next to Remote Desktop Services in the preceding list. While you can install the RDS role on Server Core, you cannot perform *all* the functions of Remote Desktop with a Server Core instance. You can use Server Core to be your RDS Connection Broker or RDS Licensing server, but you cannot use Server Core as a Remote Desktop Session Host. Similar limitations exist for other roles as well.

For an always-updated, comprehensive list of which parts and pieces of which roles and features are supported on Server Core, check out the following Microsoft document: `https://learn.microsoft.com/en-us/windows-server/administration/server-core/server-core-roles-and-services?tabs=roles`

Building a Server Core domain controller

You are now equipped to spin up Server Core instances, configure them with hostnames, IP addresses, and domain memberships, and administer these new servers using various administrative toolsets. One of the most frequent uses of Server Core that I have seen in production environments is as a secondary or tertiary domain controller. Let's walk through the process of setting one up so that you have the exact steps if ever this situation applies to you.

Begin by prepping the new server. You already know all of this, but here is the basic outline of steps that you want to accomplish before thinking about turning this server into a domain controller:

1. Spin up the new server and install Server Core.
2. Use SConfig or PowerShell from the console to configure a static IP address and a permanent hostname. Remember, once you turn this server into a domain controller, it no longer supports name changes, and it is not so easy to change the IP – so choose wisely. I have named mine DC3 since I already have DC1 and DC2 in my lab.

3. Make sure to specify an existing domain controller as the NIC's DNS server address.

4. Use SConfig or PowerShell to join this new server to your existing domain.

5. At this point, your server is online and communicable on the network but has no roles installed. You could proceed from here with the installation of any role to serve any purpose.

Installing the AD DS role

There are numerous ways in which this step could be accomplished. Using WAC or remotely manipulating the new server via Server Manager on another machine would be valid ways of installing the new role. You should already be familiar with those processes based on what we have covered in this chapter so far.

Instead, let's stick to pure PowerShell to convert this new Server Core into a headless domain controller. From the console of DC3, make sure that you are logged in to a Domain Admin account. Then, use the powershell command to change Command Prompt into a PowerShell prompt. Finally, run the following command to install the AD DS role on the new server:

```
Install-WindowsFeature -Name AD-Domain-Services -IncludeManagementTools
```

If you want this server to respond to DNS lookups (as most domain controllers do), also install the DNS role with the following command:

```
Install-WindowsFeature DNS
```

```
Administrator: C:\WINDOWS\system32\cmd.exe                                        _  □  x
WARNING: To launch Server Configuration tool again, run "SConfig"
PS C:\Users\administrator.CONTOSO> powershell
Windows PowerShell
Copyright (C) Microsoft Corporation. All rights reserved.

Install the latest PowerShell for new features and improvements! https://aka.ms/PSWindows

PS C:\Users\administrator.CONTOSO> Install-WindowsFeature -Name AD-Domain-Services -IncludeManagementTools

Success Restart Needed Exit Code    Feature Result
------- -------------- ---------    --------------
True    No             Success      {Active Directory Domain Services, Group P...

PS C:\Users\administrator.CONTOSO> Install-WindowsFeature DNS

Success Restart Needed Exit Code    Feature Result
------- -------------- ---------    --------------
True    No             Success      {DNS Server}

PS C:\Users\administrator.CONTOSO> _
```

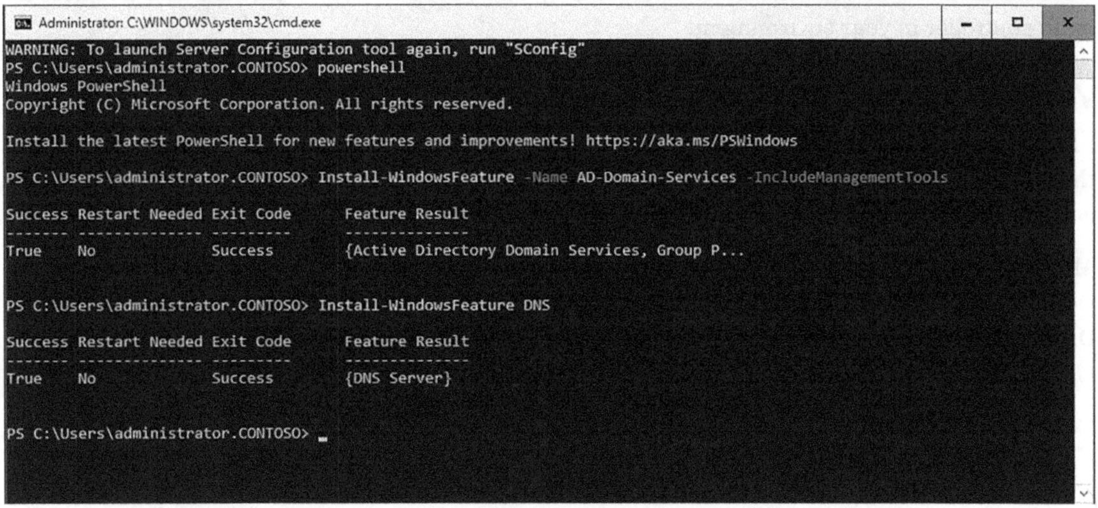

Figure 11.33: Installing AD DS and DNS roles on Server Core

Promoting this server to a domain controller

With roles installed, we are now ready to promote this server to a domain controller. The old dcpromo command still exists and could be used to perform this function, or we could, of course, utilize one of the graphical administrative tools to handle this remotely as well. Since we started with PowerShell, though, we'll finish the process using it:

```
Install-ADDSDomainController -InstallDns -DomainName "contoso.local"
```

(Replace contoso.local with your own domain name, of course.)

As this command runs, you will be asked to input required information, such as the AD SafeMode password, and administrative credentials with permission to create a new domain controller:

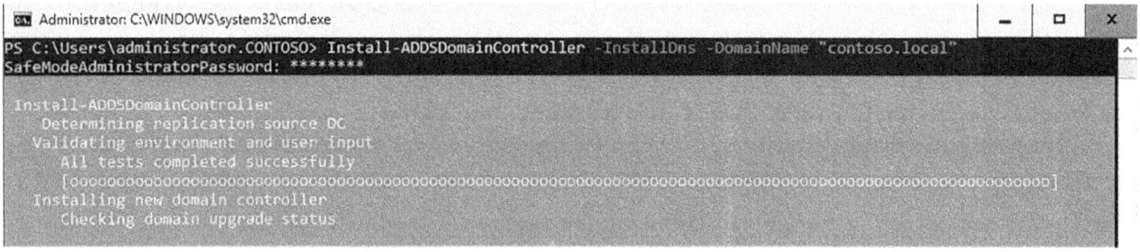

```
Administrator: C:\WINDOWS\system32\cmd.exe
PS C:\Users\administrator.CONTOSO> Install-ADDSDomainController -InstallDns -DomainName "contoso.local"
SafeModeAdministratorPassword: ********

Install-ADDSDomainController
    Determining replication source DC
    Validating environment and user input
        All tests completed successfully
        [oooooooooooooooooooooooooooooooooooooooooooooooooooooooooooooooooooooooooooooooooooooooooooooooooooooo]
    Installing new domain controller
        Checking domain upgrade status
```

Figure 11.34: Creating your first Server Core DC

Once finished, the server will restart automatically, and your new Server Core is now a headless domain controller in your environment!

Verifying that it worked

I know you trust me implicitly, but just for the sake of argument, what if we wanted to verify that those simple PowerShell commands really did what they said they did? Let's verify that DC3 really is a domain controller now servicing our infrastructure.

All domain controllers in an environment automatically get their computer object moved into the **Domain Controllers** OU inside Active Directory. Logging in to any DC in your network, open **Active Directory Users and Computers**, and navigate to the **Domain Controllers** OU. You can see in *Figure 11.35* that DC3 is now inside this container, indicating that it is a DC for my domain:

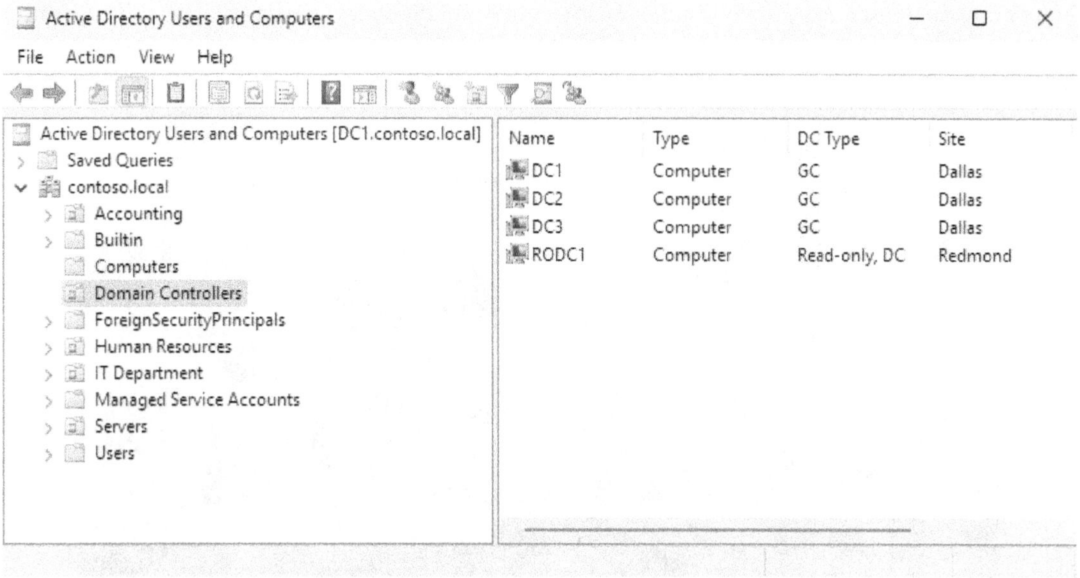

Figure 11.35: Verification that DC3 is a domain controller

To verify the DNS side of things, you can now open the **DNS Management** console from inside your network and go into **Properties** of your primary internal DNS zone. In my case, that is contoso.local. Opening those properties, I can see that my **Name Servers** tab now displays DC3-CORE as a name server for this zone:

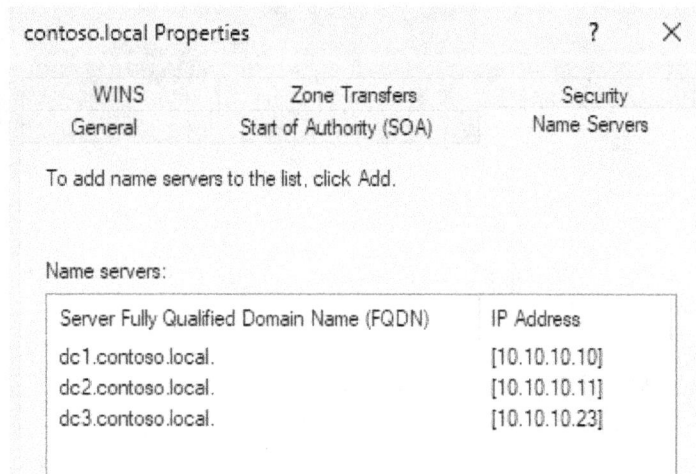

Figure 11.36: DC3 is a confirmed DNS server

There's one final test and verification. Let's use a command that queries and displays the replication status between domain controller servers in our environment. Open Command Prompt or PowerShell on any DC and run the following command:

```
Repadmin /showrepl
```

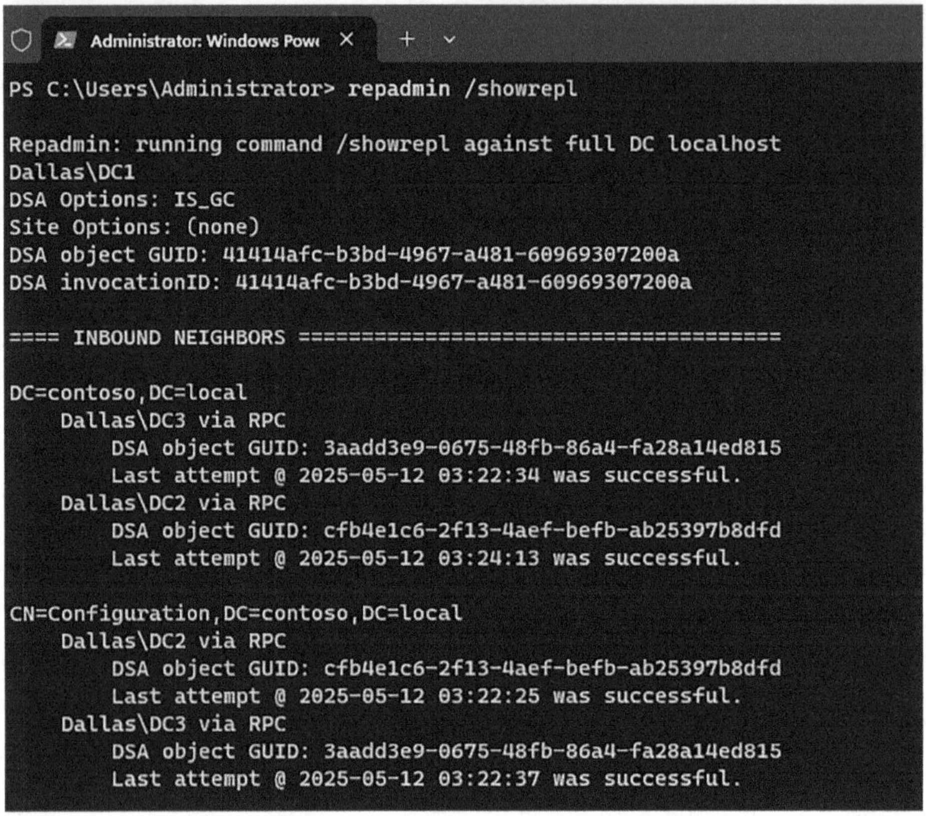

```
PS C:\Users\Administrator> repadmin /showrepl

Repadmin: running command /showrepl against full DC localhost
Dallas\DC1
DSA Options: IS_GC
Site Options: (none)
DSA object GUID: 41414afc-b3bd-4967-a481-60969307200a
DSA invocationID: 41414afc-b3bd-4967-a481-60969307200a

==== INBOUND NEIGHBORS ======================================

DC=contoso,DC=local
    Dallas\DC3 via RPC
        DSA object GUID: 3aadd3e9-0675-48fb-86a4-fa28a14ed815
        Last attempt @ 2025-05-12 03:22:34 was successful.
    Dallas\DC2 via RPC
        DSA object GUID: cfb4e1c6-2f13-4aef-befb-ab25397b8dfd
        Last attempt @ 2025-05-12 03:24:13 was successful.

CN=Configuration,DC=contoso,DC=local
    Dallas\DC2 via RPC
        DSA object GUID: cfb4e1c6-2f13-4aef-befb-ab25397b8dfd
        Last attempt @ 2025-05-12 03:22:25 was successful.
    Dallas\DC3 via RPC
        DSA object GUID: 3aadd3e9-0675-48fb-86a4-fa28a14ed815
        Last attempt @ 2025-05-12 03:22:37 was successful.
```

Figure 11.37: DC3 is part of domain controller replication

There you go! Proof in three different flavors that our DC3 Server Core instance really is a domain controller and DNS server in our domain. How cool is that?!

What happened to Nano Server?

This story about small-footprint Windows Server platforms hasn't always ended with Server Core. Anyone who kept tabs on the new features coming out with Server 2016 is aware that there was another installation option for the Server 2016 operating system, called Nano Server. The premise of Nano Server was an even smaller, more secure, more efficient, and super-tiny operating system that could run a very limited set of roles. Though limited, it could still be installed on a physical or virtual server platform, run as a true server operating system, and still host traditional workloads on it.

Unfortunately for Nano Server enthusiasts, and especially for anyone who already did the work of installing and using it, the story behind Nano Server has flipped around completely over the last few years. To cut a long story short, you can no longer use Nano Server for anything that a traditional server can do. You cannot install it on physical hardware; you cannot even install Nano on a VM. Additionally, management functionalities, such as PowerShell and WinRM, have been removed from Nano Server, and you cannot install any of the Microsoft infrastructural roles on it.

With all of this functionality ripped out of Nano Server's scope, what is left? Is it dead? Can Nano Server do *ANYTHING*?

The answer is **containers**. If you are interested in utilizing containers to build and host cloud-ready and scalable applications, this is where Nano is now focused. We will cover more information about containers and the fact that Nano Server is completely married to them in *Chapter 14, Containers*, but suffice it to say that downloading container images from Microsoft will now be the *only* place where you will find Nano Server.

Can we run Server Core in Azure?

Yes! When working through the Azure steps to build a new server, one of those steps is the selection of a marketplace image from which to build your new server. Microsoft and others have provided images in that marketplace for Server Core instances, ranging all the way from Server 2016 to Server 2025.

The same management methods and limitations are true of Server Core inside Azure as if it were on-premises. Your Azure-based Server Core instances will have no GUI, and you will have to use remote toolsets to manage those servers, just as we have shown throughout this chapter when working with on-prem Server Core instances.

Summary

I said it in previous versions of this book, and I'll say it again now—writing this chapter has been the (re-)kick in the pants that I needed to start thinking about shrinking my own servers. I am in the same boat as many of you—I know what Server Core is and have played around with it, have worked through the exercises in this book numerous times, and have even supported a handful of them in customer environments, to a limited extent. But I have never attempted to change my default mindset when spinning up new servers within production environments that I support. Now that tools such as SConfig and the new WAC are available to us, we have officially run out of excuses as to why we shouldn't at least consider using Server Core for new instances of Windows Server in our environments.

In fact, as I was building out the new DC3 server, I realized just how much faster it is to get a Server Core instance off the ground compared to the full graphical interface. Reboots are faster, and using SConfig to set the IP address, hostname, and domain membership all took me about 2 minutes in total. I was also re-impressed with how quickly you can copy/paste PowerShell commands to cause this DC3 to become a domain controller, all in a matter of seconds.

While it never hurts to learn something new, using Server Core no longer comes with the requirement that you must be fluent in PowerShell. The early days of Server Core came with a requirement to be really good with PowerShell, as this was the only reliable way to configure and interface with your tiny servers, but the tools we have learned about in this chapter allow us to utilize a smaller platform and administer it without memorizing a bunch of new cmdlets.

Security is the primary reason that we should all consider Server Core as our new standard. The Windows graphical interface adds a lot of code and grants a lot of ability to those logged in to the servers, such as the ability to browse the internet. This opens all kinds of doors to vulnerabilities that simply don't exist in Server Core.

Questions

Put your knowledge to the test with the following questions. If you need a hand (or just want to double-check), you'll find all the answers in the *Appendix* section of the book.

1. True or False? Server Core is the default installation option for Windows Server 2025.

2. True or False? You can utilize PowerShell to change Server 2025 from *Server Core* mode to *Desktop Experience* mode.

3. True or False? You can utilize PowerShell to change Server 2019 from *Server Core* mode to *Desktop Experience* mode.

4. Bonus points: What is the last version of Windows Server that allowed for on-the-fly changing of a server back and forth between Server Core and Desktop Experience?

5. When sitting in front of the console of a freshly booted Windows Server 2025 Server Core instance, what application do you see on the screen?

6. When sitting in front of the console of a freshly booted Windows Server 2019 Server Core instance, what application do you see on the screen?

7. What cmdlet can be used to view the current networking configuration on Server Core?

8. Which PowerShell cmdlet can be used to configure the hostname of a Server Core?

9. Name some of the management tools that can be used to remotely interface with Server Core.

10. What is the name of the utility built into Server Core that can be launched from a console to provide quick task links to configure IP addresses, hostnames, and domain membership?

11. What movie reference did I make at the beginning of this chapter?

12

PowerShell

If you've had some drive time with Windows 11, you may be wondering, "Why are we reading about PowerShell when it has been replaced by Windows Terminal?" The "replacement" of PowerShell with Windows Terminal inside Windows 11 has generated a little bit of confusion among the user population, but they are not at all the same thing, nor is Terminal an actual replacement for PowerShell. PowerShell is much more than a console screen from which you run commands. It is integrated into all facets of Windows itself. We will discuss Windows Terminal a little bit more near the end of this chapter, but for the purposes of PowerShell learning, we can safely leave Terminal out of scope.

So far, we've been talking about PowerShell and Terminal, but let's be honest, many of us are still using Command Prompt on a daily basis. If you have moved over and are using the PowerShell prompt as a total replacement for Command Prompt, I applaud you! I, however, still use a pretty good mix of both and tend to open cmd.exe as a matter of lazy habit. Adjusting this behavior within myself is in part what I hope to accomplish with this chapter, and we are going to explore some of the reasons why you should do so, too. PowerShell is more useful and powerful than Command Prompt could ever dream of being.

In this chapter, we will cover the following topics:

- Why move to PowerShell?
- Working within PowerShell
- Importing a module
- Using a pipeline
- PowerShell Integrated Scripting Environment
- Remotely managing a server
- Desired State Configuration
- WinGet application management
- PowerShell for M365
- Windows Terminal in Server 2022

Why move to PowerShell?

I don't think there is any question in people's minds that PowerShell is indeed the evolution of Command Prompt, but the reason that many of us still default to the old interface is that it still contains all of the functionality required to accomplish what we historically have needed to do on our servers. What Command Prompt really contains is the ability to do the same things, in the same ways, that we have always done from Command Prompt, and nothing else. Without realizing it, there are a lot of functions that you use the GUI to accomplish that cannot be done well from within a Command Prompt window.

The limitations within Command Prompt that force you into using your mouse to interface with the GUI do not exist with PowerShell. It is fully comprehensive and capable of modifying almost any aspect of the Windows operating system. How did PowerShell become so much more powerful than Command Prompt? It differs from any classic I/O shell in that it is built on top of .NET and runs much more like a programming language than simple input and output commands.

PowerShell is also built with centralized computing in mind. Running ad hoc commands is great if you are logged directly into one server and only need to make changes on that one server. Most server administrators are responsible for maintaining dozens or even hundreds of servers, and PowerShell scripting can be formulated to centrally monitor or manipulate all of them from the same console interface, and all at the same time. This can be an incredible timesaver and tool of efficiency in day-to-day chores.

Cmdlets

Most of the functionality that a traditional server admin will use within PowerShell comes in the form of **cmdlets** (pronounced *command-lets*). These are commands that you run from within the PowerShell prompt, but you can think of them as tools rather than simple commands. Cmdlets can be used to both get information from a server and set information and parameters on a server. Many cmdlets have intuitive names that begin with Get or Set, and similar to the way that most **command-line interfaces** (CLIs) work, each cmdlet has various switches or variables that can be configured and flagged at the end of the cmdlet to make it do special things. It is helpful to understand that cmdlets are always built using a verb-noun syntax. You specify the action you want to accomplish, such as Get or Set, and then your noun is the piece inside Windows that you are trying to manipulate. Here are a few simple examples of cmdlets in PowerShell to give you an idea of what they look like and how they are named in a fairly simple way:

- `Get-NetIPAddress`: With this cmdlet, we can see the IP addresses on our system
- `Set-NetIPAddress`: We can use this one to modify an existing IP address
- `New-NetIPAddress`: This cmdlet allows us to create a new IP address on the computer
- `Rename-Computer`: As we saw earlier in the book, this is a quick and easy way to set the computer hostname of a system
- `Add-Computer`: This is used to add local or remote computers to a domain or workgroup

If you're ever struggling to come up with the name or syntax of a particular command, the online Microsoft Learn platform (formerly and sometimes still called either Microsoft Docs or Microsoft TechNet) has a full page of information dedicated to each cmdlet inside PowerShell. That can be incredibly useful, but sometimes you don't want to take the time to pop onto the internet just to find the name of a command that you are simply failing to remember while you sit in front of a server console.

One of the most useful cmdlets in PowerShell shows you a list of all available cmdlets. Memorizing the names of cmdlets isn't critically important, as long as you commit this one, Get-Command, to permanent memory:

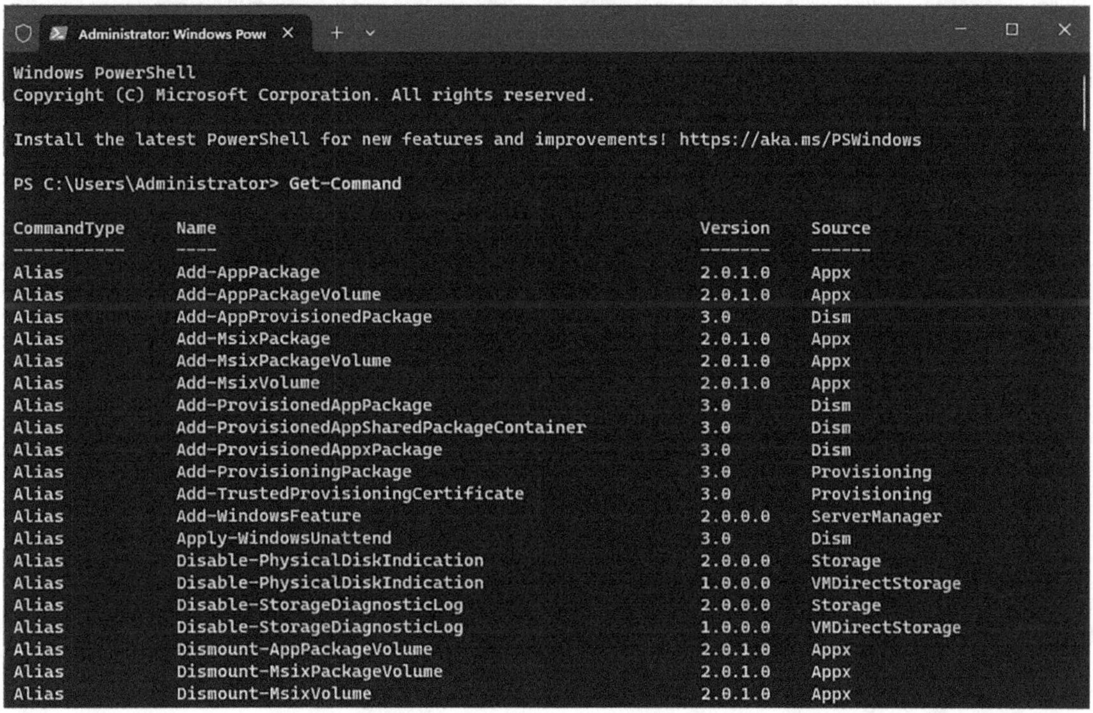

Figure 12.1: Results of Get-Command

Whoa, there are pages and pages and pages of cmdlets! Rather than scrolling through the entire list to find the one you are looking for, it is easy to filter this list based on any criteria that you would like. If we were interested in seeing only the commands that deal with IP addressing, we could give this a try:

```
Get-Command -Name *IPAddress
```

The Get-Command cmdlet, combined with the -Name parameter, allows you to selectively search for useful items in PowerShell that relate to any name or portion of a name:

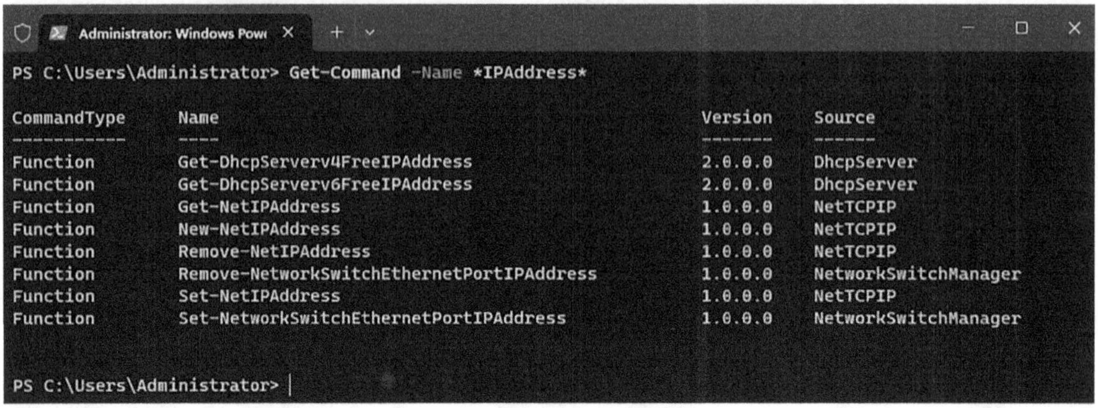

```
PS C:\Users\Administrator> Get-Command -Name *IPAddress*

CommandType     Name                                      Version     Source
-----------     ----                                      -------     ------
Function        Get-DhcpServerv4FreeIPAddress             2.0.0.0     DhcpServer
Function        Get-DhcpServerv6FreeIPAddress             2.0.0.0     DhcpServer
Function        Get-NetIPAddress                          1.0.0.0     NetTCPIP
Function        New-NetIPAddress                          1.0.0.0     NetTCPIP
Function        Remove-NetIPAddress                       1.0.0.0     NetTCPIP
Function        Remove-NetworkSwitchEthernetPortIPAddress 1.0.0.0     NetworkSwitchManager
Function        Set-NetIPAddress                          1.0.0.0     NetTCPIP
Function        Set-NetworkSwitchEthernetPortIPAddress    1.0.0.0     NetworkSwitchManager


PS C:\Users\Administrator>
```

Figure 12.2: Searching with Get-Command

As with many toolsets, PowerShell utilizes * as a wildcard indicator. In the search we just accomplished, and in truth, for almost any cmdlet search that I ever run, using the * wildcard on both ends of the term I am searching for helps to display any results that contain that term.

PowerShell is the backbone

As you will discover in this chapter, interfacing with PowerShell puts all kinds of power at your fingertips. What we sometimes find, though, is that admins don't fully trust PowerShell because they are used to taking these actions and making these changes from a graphical interface. After running a single PowerShell cmdlet to set a configuration that would have taken you a dozen mouse clicks to accomplish the same thing, it is easy to think that it must not have actually done anything. That was too easy, and it processed my command way too quickly, right? I'd better go into that graphical interface anyway, just to double-check that PowerShell actually did the job.

When I started using PowerShell, I was tempted to do exactly that all the time. But the more I used it, and the more I started digging into those graphical interfaces themselves, the more I realized that I'm not the only one using PowerShell. A lot of the administrative tool GUIs use PowerShell too! Without even realizing it, you use PowerShell for quite a few graphically driven tasks inside the Windows Server operating system. When you open that management console for whatever you happen to be changing on the server, make your configurations, and then click on the **Go**, **Finish**, or **Apply** button, how does that graphical console put your configuration into place? With PowerShell. Under the hood, in the background, the console is taking the information that you input, plugging that information into PowerShell cmdlets, and running them to do the actual configuration work.

Many of the administrative tools that we run from inside Server Manager take this approach, accepting changes and configurations from you and then formulating those settings into PowerShell commands that run in the background to push the changes into action.

So, if you're hesitant to start using PowerShell because it just feels different, or you don't trust the process to be uniform with the way that it would have worked in the GUI, forget all of that. Because often, when you are using mouse clicks to change settings on your server, you are invoking PowerShell cmdlets to do the work.

Scripting

The more you use PowerShell, the more powerful it becomes. In addition to running ad hoc single commands and cmdlets, you can build extensive scripts that can accomplish all sorts of different things. I mentioned that PowerShell has similarities to a regular programming language, and scripting is where we start to navigate into that territory. PowerShell provides the ability to create script files, which we will do for ourselves shortly, saving scripts for easy running time after time. You can also use variables, as in other forms of coding, so that you can provide variable input and objects that scripts can use to make them more flexible and squeeze even more functionality out of them.

Server Core

If there is any one area where I think we, as server admins, could do a better job of using the technology at our disposal, it is using PowerShell to fulfill the Microsoft model of centralized management. When we have a task that needs to be accomplished on a server, it is our default tendency to log in to that server (usually via RDP), then use our mouse to start clicking around and doing the work. Logging in to the server is becoming more and more unnecessary, and we could save a lot of time by using the central management tools that are available to us. PowerShell is one of these tools. Rather than RDPing into that server, simply use the PowerShell prompt on your local machine to reach out and change that setting on the remote server.

This kind of remote management becomes not only efficient but also necessary as we start dealing more with headless servers. I hope to see increased utilization of Server Core in our organizations in the coming years, and interacting with these servers is going to require a shift in your administrative mindset. By becoming familiar with accomplishing daily tasks from inside PowerShell now, you will better equip yourself for the future administration of these headless machines, which will require you to interface with them differently from how you are comfortable doing today. If you have skipped ahead to this chapter and missed out on our discussion of Server Core, make sure to circle back to *Chapter 11*, where we worked together to remotely connect to and administer a Server Core instance, using PowerShell.

Working within PowerShell

The first step to doing real work with PowerShell is getting comfortable interfacing with the platform and becoming familiar with the daily routines of working from this CLI, rather than relying on your mouse pointer. Here, we will explore some of the most common ways that I have seen server administrators make use of PowerShell to enhance their daily workflow.

We will be working, throughout this chapter, inside the version of PowerShell that comes out of the box with Windows Server 2025, PowerShell 5.1. This version number may come as a surprise, because PowerShell 7 has been available for multiple years at this point.

If you are familiar with this and already utilizing it, everything that we discuss will work perfectly well on that updated platform. To administer a Windows Server instance, the differences between versions won't have much of a bearing. Installing PowerShell 7 will not update PowerShell 5.1, but rather, they will run side by side. This is in part because PowerShell 5.1 is built upon the .NET Framework, while PowerShell 7.x runs on .NET Core. Having foundations in the open source .NET Core means that PowerShell 7 comes with the ability to work cross-platform, with Windows, Linux, and even macOS (gasp!). It also includes some additional support for working with Docker containers. I imagine that Microsoft has had many internal discussions about moving all PowerShell into the 7.x territory, but until all components of Windows are no longer based on .NET and able to be manipulated by .NET Core, we continue to use traditional PowerShell 5.1 for normal interfacing with the Windows operating system. If you would like to seek out and install PowerShell 7, there are a variety of different ways you could do so. The following Microsoft article outlines them all: `https://learn.microsoft.com/en-us/powershell/scripting/whats-new/migrating-from-windows-powershell-51-to-powershell-7?view=powershell-7.5`.

For those of you following the path toward PowerShell 7 installation, keep in mind that this shell is entirely separate from our "normal" PowerShell and is launched by a different executable. This may be a helpful quick reference to ensure you are launching the shell that you intend:

- PowerShell 5.1: `powershell.exe`
- PowerShell 7.x: `pwsh.exe`

Launching PowerShell...err...Windows Terminal?

The first thing we need to do is get PowerShell open to start using it. The PowerShell console is installed by default in all recent versions of Windows, so you can run it from the **Start** menu, pin it to the Desktop, or access it in any way that you normally open any application.

Since I tend to prefer using my keyboard for everything, the way that I normally open PowerShell is to hold down the *Windows* key and press *R* to open a **Run** prompt, type the word `powershell`, and press *Enter*:

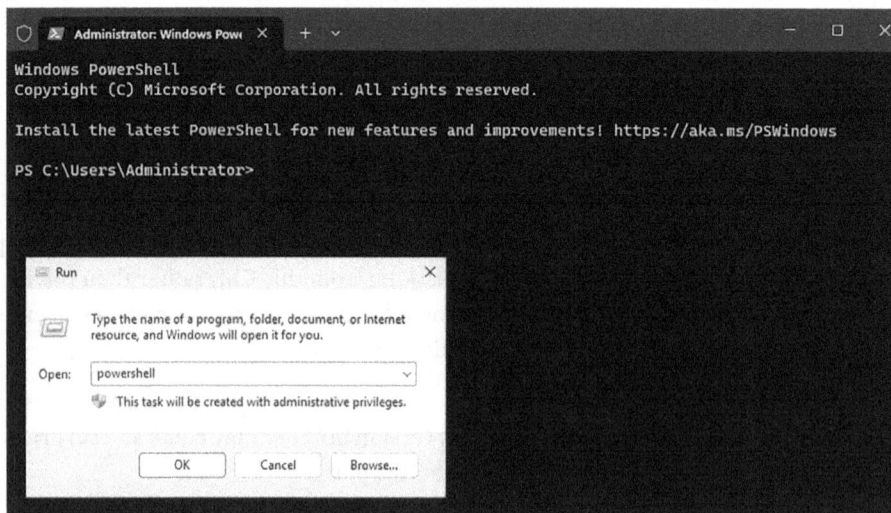

Figure 12.3: Launching PowerShell via the keyboard

What is that?? If you don't have a lot of experience working with past versions of Windows Server, you have no idea why I am so excited. A Windows 11 admin sees the Windows Terminal prompt and thinks nothing of it, because they are used to the fact that Windows Terminal has now replaced the older PowerShell and Command Prompt interfaces by default. But this behavior is brand-new for the Windows Server world! Windows Server 2025 is the first server operating system to include the updated Win11-ish graphical interface, updated Taskbar with icons in the middle, and also, yes, the first Server OS to include Windows Terminal out of the box.

For anyone who hasn't had the pleasure of working within Windows Terminal before, it brings two huge benefits over the older Command Prompt and PowerShell prompts. First, it is "one command-line interface to rule them all." Microsoft has tried very hard to make sure that Terminal can be your one-stop shop for any kind of commands you are throwing around inside a Windows system. Second, as evidenced in screenshots throughout this chapter, Terminal includes the ability to maintain many different tabs within one Terminal instance. Similar to running multiple tabs inside a web browser, which all of us rely upon every single day, taking the idea of tabs into the command-line world is a game-changer for anybody who regularly works from a CLI.

> Sidenote: Windows Server 2022 is still a new idea to many businesses, let alone 2025, and it may be helpful to have Windows Terminal on your Server 2022 instances as well (it's not there by default). Navigate your way to the end of this chapter for further information about how to get Windows Terminal working on your Windows Server 2022 instances.

Getting over the excitement of seeing Windows Terminal here, look back at *Figure 12.3*. As you can see, since I am logged in to an administrative account on my server, my Terminal/PowerShell prompt has been opened with elevated permissions. The word `Administrator` is listed in the top toolbar of the PowerShell window. It is important to note that, just like Command Prompt, you can open a PowerShell prompt with either regular user permissions or elevated administrator privileges. It is generally safer to work from within a regular PowerShell session that does not have elevated rights unless the task that you are trying to accomplish requires those extra permissions.

Another quick and easy way to open Terminal/PowerShell on any newer Windows platform is by right-clicking on the **Start** button and selecting it directly from the quick tasks list that is presented. As you can see in *Figure 12.4*, I have right-clicked on the **Start** button of one of my new Server 2025 machines and can choose from here to open Terminal or even an elevated (administrative) Terminal prompt:

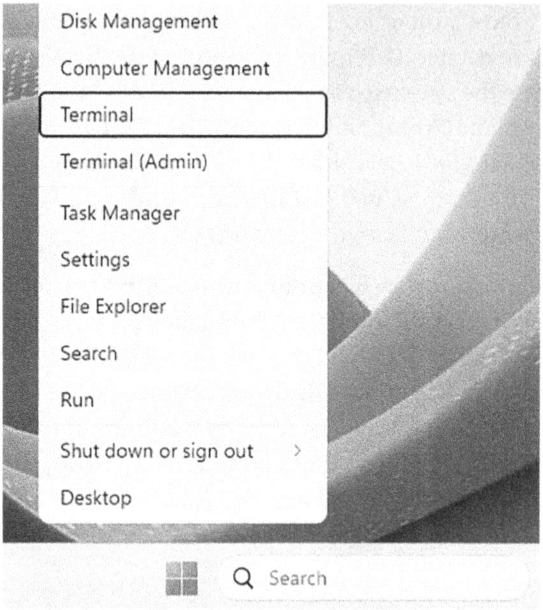

Figure 12.4: Launching Terminal/PowerShell from the quick admin tasks menu

You also have the option of entering into a PowerShell prompt from inside an existing Command Prompt window. With Windows Terminal at our fingertips, you may be wondering why in the world we would ever use the classic Command Prompt window, but we are creatures of habit. When I am logged in to a server and need to perform a quick task from a command line, my instinct is not to right-click the **Start** button and launch Windows Terminal. Instead, I press *WinKey + R* and type cmd to open the old Command Prompt window. It's a decades-old habit at this point. In this circumstance, staring at a classic Command Prompt window, I cannot make any use of PowerShell cmdlets, and need to take an extra action to invoke PowerShell. Let's go ahead and give this a shot. Open an administrative Command Prompt window and try to type in the name of one of the cmdlets we mentioned earlier. Perhaps type Get-NetIPAddress to show us what IP addresses reside on this system. Even though launching cmd. exe in Windows Server 2025 looks and feels like Windows Terminal, it is Windows Terminal *without* PowerShell modules loaded. Thus, our command fails because Command Prompt doesn't recognize the Get-NetIPAddress cmdlet.

Now type the word powershell and press *Enter*. Instead of opening a separate PowerShell window, your prompt changes, but the application window itself remains the same. You have now entered the PowerShell shell from inside the traditional Command Prompt window, and you can start utilizing cmdlets as you wish. Running Get-NetIPAddress again now produces some information:

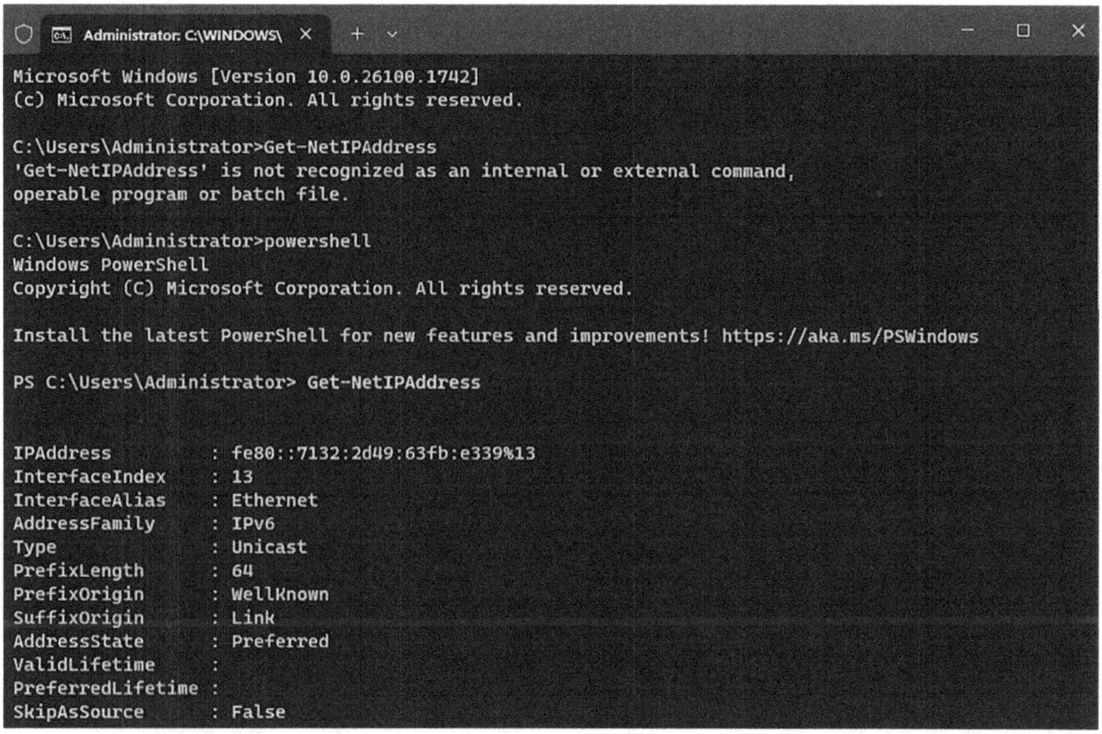
Administrator: C:\WINDOWS\
Microsoft Windows [Version 10.0.26100.1742]
(c) Microsoft Corporation. All rights reserved.
C:\Users\Administrator>Get-NetIPAddress
'Get-NetIPAddress' is not recognized as an internal or external command,
operable program or batch file.
C:\Users\Administrator>powershell
Windows PowerShell
Copyright (C) Microsoft Corporation. All rights reserved.
Install the latest PowerShell for new features and improvements! https://aka.ms/PSWindows
PS C:\Users\Administrator> Get-NetIPAddress
IPAddress : fe80::7132:2d49:63fb:e339%13
InterfaceIndex : 13
InterfaceAlias : Ethernet
AddressFamily : IPv6
Type : Unicast
PrefixLength : 64
PrefixOrigin : WellKnown
SuffixOrigin : Link
AddressState : Preferred
ValidLifetime :
PreferredLifetime :
SkipAsSource : False

Figure 12.5: Invoking PowerShell from within Command Prompt

You can move from PowerShell mode back to regular Command Prompt mode by typing `exit`.

Default execution policy

When you are working with the PowerShell CLI directly, you can simply open up PowerShell, start typing cmdlets, and get work done. However, one of the big advantages of using PowerShell comes when you start playing around with creating, saving, and running scripts. When first creating and running a PowerShell script, you may find that it fails with a big, messy error message, such as this one:

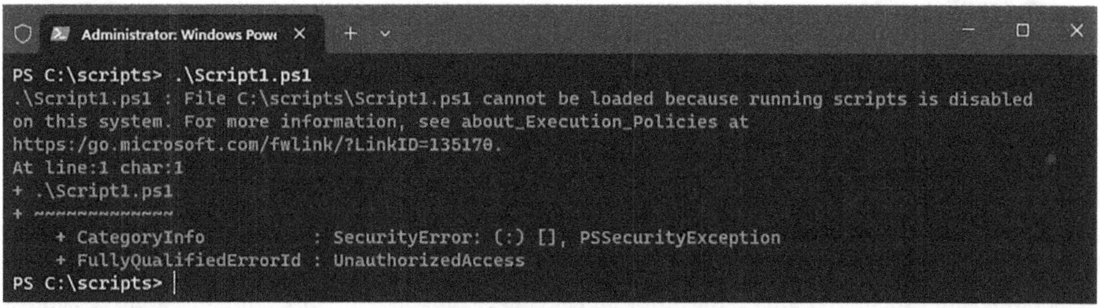
Administrator: Windows Pow
PS C:\scripts> .\Script1.ps1
.\Script1.ps1 : File C:\scripts\Script1.ps1 cannot be loaded because running scripts is disabled
on this system. For more information, see about_Execution_Policies at
https:/go.microsoft.com/fwlink/?LinkID=135170.
At line:1 char:1
+ .\Script1.ps1
+ ~~~~~~~~~~~~~
+ CategoryInfo : SecurityError: (:) [], PSSecurityException
+ FullyQualifiedErrorId : UnauthorizedAccess
PS C:\scripts>

Figure 12.6: A common PowerShell script execution error

This shouldn't happen on a fresh instance of Windows Server 2025, but could if you have any GPOs being applied to your new server or if you are using a different operating system and are trying to run some PowerShell scripts; you might find yourself stuck at one of these error messages right out of the gate. While the nature of some versions of Windows to block the running of scripts by default is a security enhancement, it can be a nuisance to work around when you are trying to get something done. Thankfully, if you do encounter this problem, the resolution is easy: you simply need to adjust the **default execution policy (DEP)** inside PowerShell so that it allows the execution of scripts to happen properly.

This is not a simple on/off switch. There are five different levels within the DEP, and it is important to understand each one so that you can set your DEP accordingly, based on the security that you want in place on your servers and even workstations. Here are descriptions of each level, in order of most to least secure.

Restricted

The Restricted policy allows individual commands and cmdlets to be run, but stops the running of scripts altogether.

AllSigned

This requires that any script being run is signed by a trusted publisher. When set to AllSigned, even scripts that you write yourself will have to be put through a validation process and signed before they will be allowed to run.

RemoteSigned

RemoteSigned is the default policy in Windows Server 2025. For scripts that have been downloaded from the internet, this policy requires that these scripts be signed with a digital signature from a publisher that you trust. However, if you choose to create your own scripts, it will allow these local scripts to run without requiring that digital signature.

Unrestricted

Scripts are allowed to run, signed or unsigned. You do still receive a warning prompt when running scripts that have been downloaded from the internet.

Bypass mode

In Bypass mode, nothing is blocked, and no warnings are given when you run scripts. In other words, you're on your own.

Sometimes a single execution policy doesn't meet all of your needs, depending on how you utilize PowerShell scripts. DEPs can be further enhanced by setting an execution policy scope that allows you to set different execution policies for different aspects of the system. For example, the three scopes that you can manipulate are Process, CurrentUser, and LocalMachine. By default, the DEP affects LocalMachine so that any scripts running adhere to the DEP. But if you need to modify this behavior so that different DEPs are set for CurrentUser or even an individual process, you have the ability to do that.

If you are unsure about the current status of your DEP or suspect that someone may have changed it, you can easily view the currently assigned execution policy with a simple cmdlet called Get-ExecutionPolicy. As you can see in *Figure 12.7*, mine is set to Restricted, which explains my earlier error message when I tried running a script:

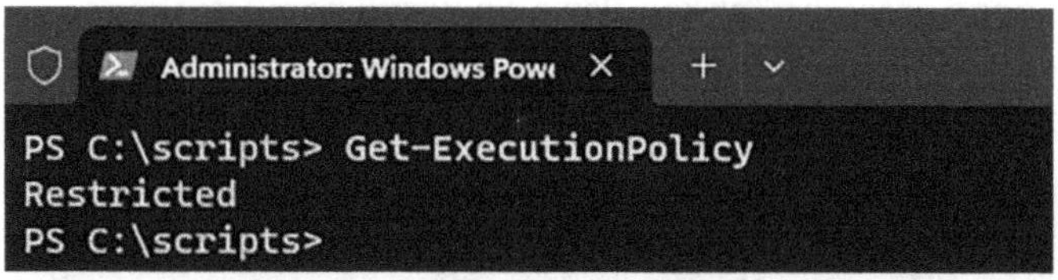

Figure 12.7: ExecutionPolicy is currently set to Restricted

Once you have decided on the level of DEP that you want on your server or workstation, you can set it accordingly with a quick cmdlet. For this particular server, I want it configured back to the default setting of RemoteSigned. Here is my command for doing just that:

```
Set-ExecutionPolicy RemoteSigned
```

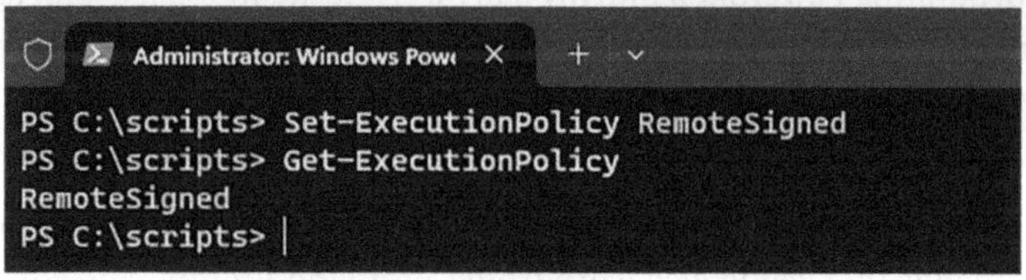

Figure 12.8: Setting ExecutionPolicy to RemoteSigned

Remember, right now, we are running PowerShell on this local system (I happen to be logged in to my WEB3 server), so the only execution policy I am setting is the local one for my WEB3 system. If I wanted to change this setting globally or for a group of machines at the same time, I could utilize Group Policy for that change. The location inside Group Policy for configuring the PowerShell script execution policy is **Computer Configuration | Policies | Administrative Templates | Windows Components | Windows PowerShell | Turn on script execution**.

Using the Tab key

Before we get started navigating inside PowerShell, there is one important thing I want to point out: get used to pressing the *Tab* key when you are inside the PowerShell prompt! If you type the first few letters of any command or cmdlet or even an added variable to a cmdlet and then press *Tab*, the remainder of the cmdlet name or option will be automatically populated on the screen.

If we type get-co and then press *Tab*, the prompt automatically populates the full Get-Command cmdlet. Since there are multiple cmdlets that start with get-co, if you press *Tab* numerous times, you can see that it cycles through all of the available cmdlets that start with those letters.

Tab also works with file and folder names. For example, say I download a hotfix that needs to be installed on a server. I want to launch this hotfix using the PowerShell prompt that I already have open, but I don't want to spend an entire minute or more trying to type out the huge filename of this hotfix. I have already navigated to the folder where my hotfix resides, and now if I simply type the first few letters of the filename and press the *Tab* key, PowerShell will populate the remainder of the filename. From there, all I need to do is press *Enter* to launch that installer. In the following screenshot, I navigated to the Hotfixes folder and then typed the letter a and pressed *Tab* to generate the following:

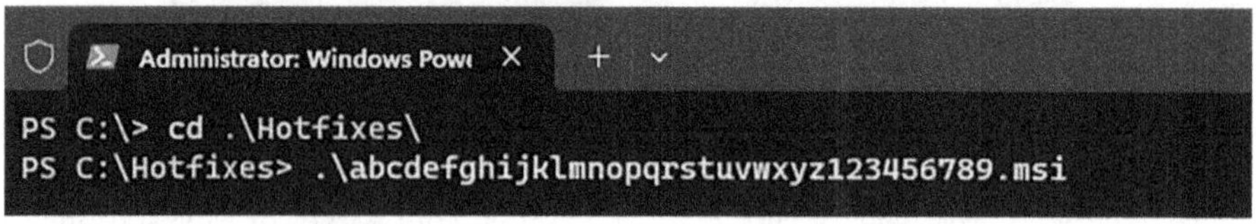

Figure 12.9: The Tab key auto-fills file or command names, so you don't have to

Useful cmdlets for daily tasks

When I started incorporating PowerShell into my daily workflow, I found it useful to keep a list of commonly used commands and cmdlets handy. Until you get to the point where they become memorized and second nature, if you don't have a quick and easy way to recall those commands, chances are you aren't going to use them and will revert to the old method of configuring your servers.

Here is a list of some of the items I use regularly when I'm building or troubleshooting servers. Some are traditional commands that would also work from Command Prompt, and some are cmdlets, but they are all useful when working inside a PowerShell window:

- Get-Command: This is useful for finding additional commands or cmdlets that you may want to run or research.

- Get-Command -Name *example*: This enhances the usefulness of Get-Command by adding the -Name switch to the end of it, so that you can filter results to whatever types of cmdlets you are searching for.

- GCM: This is simply a short alias for Get-Command. I only wanted to point this one out because many of the PowerShell cmdlets have aliases, such as gcm, that allow you to launch these commonly used cmdlets with fewer keystrokes.

- Get-Alias: Since we just mentioned the gcm alias for Get-Command, you may be wondering what other aliases are available inside PowerShell. To see a complete list, simply plug in the Get-Alias cmdlet. Using aliases rather than full cmdlet names can greatly reduce the number of characters you type inside PowerShell.

- Rename-Computer: This allows you to set a new hostname for the server.

- Add-Computer: Use the Add-Computer cmdlet to join servers or computers to a domain.

- hostname: This displays the name of the system you are currently working on. I use hostname all the time to make sure that I really am working on the server that I think I am. Have you ever rebooted the wrong server? I have. By running a quick hostname command prior to issuing your restart command, you can get peace of mind that the function you are about to perform is really happening on the correct system.

- $env:computername: This also presents you with the hostname of the system you are working on, but I'm calling it out to show that PowerShell can easily tap into your environment variables in order to pull out information. The simpler hostname command is useful when you are logged in to a local system and are simply trying to verify its name, but the ability to pull information from a variable, such as $env:computername, will be much more useful when creating scripts or trying to perform a function against a remote system.

- Get-ComputerInfo -Property csname: The Get-ComputerInfo cmdlet outputs tons of information about your system, and buried in the middle of that output is the name of your computer or server. If you wanted to use a true cmdlet for finding the name of your server rather than a traditional command or environment variable, here's your answer. I included -Property csname in this cmdlet because adding that specification will output only the computer name. Another interesting property to query is -Property WindowsInstallDateFromRegistry, showing you the date Windows was installed on this system. I often look for this information during server troubleshooting.

- Logoff: The name is self-explanatory; Logoff just logs you out of the system. Rather than trying to find the **Sign out** function by clicking around inside your server's **Start** menu (which carries with it the very real possibility of accidentally clicking **Restart**), you can throw a quick Logoff command into either a Command Prompt or PowerShell window, and you will be immediately logged out of that server. I use this one all the time when closing out RDP connections.

- Install-WindowsFeature: Use PowerShell to simplify the addition of new roles or features on your servers.

- Test-NetConnection: As mentioned in a previous chapter, this cmdlet is extremely useful for testing TCP connectivity between two systems.

- Get-Service: This one displays all Windows services, along with their current running status. You can also use Set-Service to manipulate those services.

Both shutdown and Restart-Computer are useful for shutting down or restarting a server. In my own workflows, these commands are most commonly preceded by the hostname command. When rebooting a server, you want to take special care that you restart the correct machine, so I find it best to open a PowerShell prompt, do a quick hostname check, and then run a Restart-Computer command from that same prompt. This ensures that I am restarting the server that was returned in the hostname output:

```
shutdown /r /t 0
```

If, for some reason, you are opposed to running Restart-Computer, or if you are in a simpler Command Prompt window and unable to launch cmdlets, you can utilize shutdown /r /t 0 to immediately restart any computer or server.

In the preceding command, I have told the `shutdown` command that I want to restart instead of shutting down; that is what /r does. I have also told it to wait zero seconds before performing this restart. This way, it happens immediately. If you wanted to delay the restart for some reason, replace the zero with a desired number of seconds. The server will count down before restarting.

> Pro tip: Try playing around with `shutdown /i`. The special /i switch prompts a graphical interface from which you can select various options and impress your IT friends!

Query user or quser

Most useful in RDS environments, the `quser` command will display all of the users that are currently logged in to a server, including statistics about whether they are logged in locally or remotely, and how long their session has been active. I commonly use `quser` to discover RDS sessions that have been sitting around idle for a long time, so that I can end those sessions and free up resources on the server:

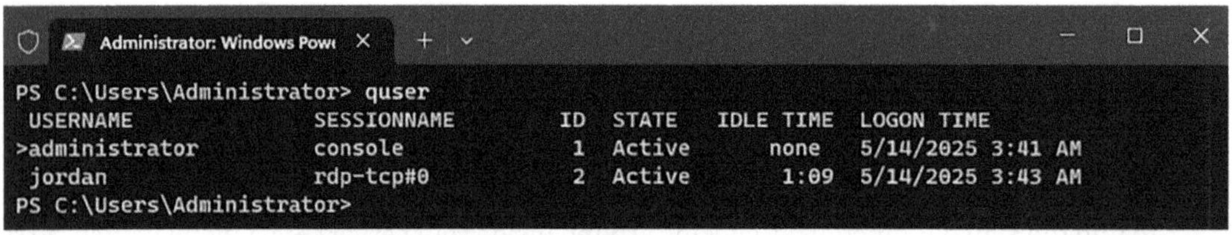

```
PS C:\Users\Administrator> quser
 USERNAME              SESSIONNAME       ID  STATE   IDLE TIME  LOGON TIME
>administrator         console            1  Active      none  5/14/2025 3:41 AM
 jordan                rdp-tcp#0          2  Active      1:09  5/14/2025 3:43 AM
PS C:\Users\Administrator>
```

Figure 12.10: The quser command displays logged-in sessions

```
quser /server:WEB1
```

Using `quser` in combination with the /server switch allows you to see the currently logged-in users on a remote system. This way, you can remain logged in to a single server in your RDS farm but can check on the user sessions for all of your systems without having to log in to them. You could even write a script that runs this command against each of your session host servers and outputs the data to a file. This output could then be run on a schedule and used as a reporting mechanism for keeping track of which users were logged in to which RDS session host servers at any given time, which is a level of reporting that Microsoft doesn't offer out of the box for RDS servers.

IP addressing cmdlets

When we built a Server Core instance together earlier in this book, we utilized the SConfig tool to define IP addressing for that server. While that was a quick and easy way to accomplish such a task, let's define the PowerShell cmdlets that are used for the configuration of IP addressing information on a server NIC:

```
New-NetIPAddress -InterfaceIndex 12 -IPAddress 10.10.10.40 -PrefixLength 24
 -DefaultGateway 10.10.10.1
```

This is just an example command with some sample numbers; the point here is that we can use New-NetIPAddress to assign IP addresses to NICs on our servers, and the preceding syntax is the correct way to go about doing it.

Often used in combination with New-NetIPAddress, use the following command to set the DNS server addresses in your NIC properties:

```
Set-DnsClientServerAddress -InterfaceIndex 12 -ServerAddresses
10.10.10.10,10.10.10.11
```

Using Get-Help

How many hundreds of times have you used the /? switch in Command Prompt to pull some extra information about a command that you want to run? The extra information provided by this help function can sometimes be the difference between a command saving the day or being completely useless. PowerShell cmdlets have a similar function, but you cannot simply add /? at the end of a PowerShell cmdlet because a space following a cmdlet in PowerShell indicates that you are about to specify a parameter to be used with that cmdlet. For example, if we try to use /? with the Restart-Computer cmdlet to find more information about how to use Restart-Computer, it will fail to recognize the question mark as a valid parameter, and our output will be as follows:

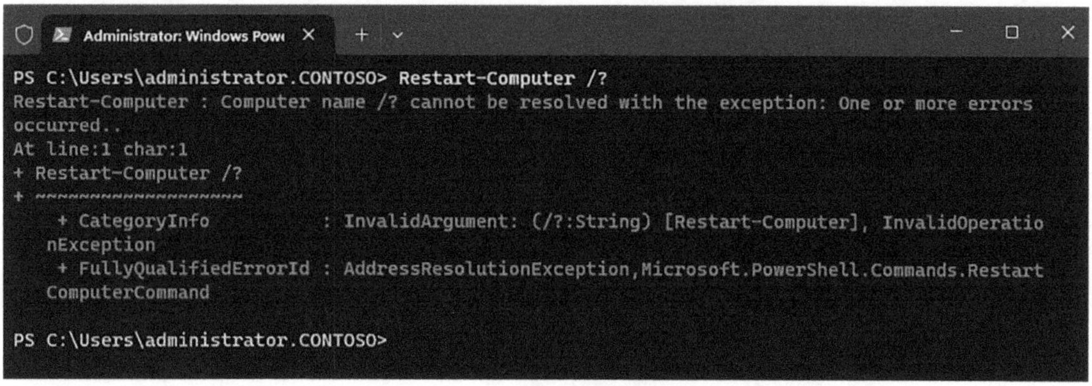

```
PS C:\Users\administrator.CONTOSO> Restart-Computer /?
Restart-Computer : Computer name /? cannot be resolved with the exception: One or more errors
occurred..
At line:1 char:1
+ Restart-Computer /?
+ ~~~~~~~~~~~~~~~~~~~~
    + CategoryInfo          : InvalidArgument: (/?:String) [Restart-Computer], InvalidOperatio
  nException
    + FullyQualifiedErrorId : AddressResolutionException,Microsoft.PowerShell.Commands.Restart
  ComputerCommand

PS C:\Users\administrator.CONTOSO>
```

Figure 12.11: PowerShell cmdlets do not work with /?

Instead, there is an even more powerful help function inside PowerShell. Get-Help is a cmdlet itself, and like any cmdlet, we need to use parameters following the cmdlet to specify and pull the information that we are looking for. So, instead of using Get-Help at the end of a command, like we used to do with the question mark, we use it as its own entity.

Running Get-Help by itself only gives us more information about the Get-Help command, which may be useful to look over, but right now, we are more interested in finding out how we can use Get-Help to give us additional information for a cmdlet we want to run, such as the Restart-Computer function. What we need to do is use Get-Help as a cmdlet, and then specify the other cmdlet as a parameter to pass to Get-Help by placing a space between them:

```
Get-Help Restart-Computer
```

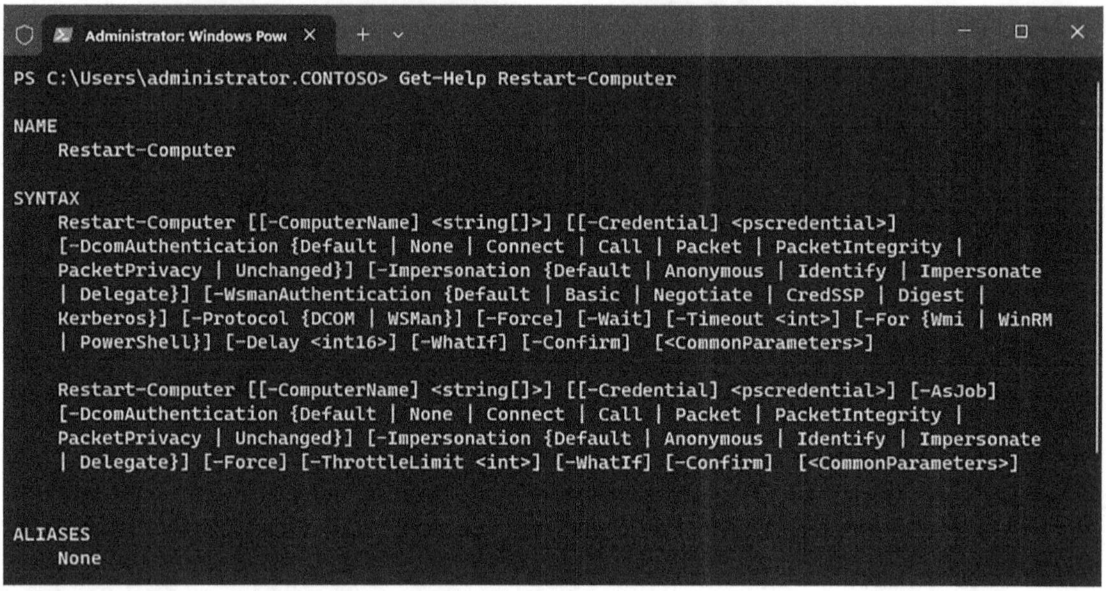

```
⬡  ⬛ Administrator: Windows Pow  ✕   +  ⌄                                                        ─    ☐    ✕
PS C:\Users\administrator.CONTOSO> Get-Help Restart-Computer

NAME
    Restart-Computer

SYNTAX
    Restart-Computer [[-ComputerName] <string[]>] [[-Credential] <pscredential>]
    [-DcomAuthentication {Default | None | Connect | Call | Packet | PacketIntegrity |
    PacketPrivacy | Unchanged}] [-Impersonation {Default | Anonymous | Identify | Impersonate
    | Delegate}] [-WsmanAuthentication {Default | Basic | Negotiate | CredSSP | Digest |
    Kerberos}] [-Protocol {DCOM | WSMan}] [-Force] [-Wait] [-Timeout <int>] [-For {Wmi | WinRM
    | PowerShell}] [-Delay <int16>] [-WhatIf] [-Confirm]  [<CommonParameters>]

    Restart-Computer [[-ComputerName] <string[]>] [[-Credential] <pscredential>] [-AsJob]
    [-DcomAuthentication {Default | None | Connect | Call | Packet | PacketIntegrity |
    PacketPrivacy | Unchanged}] [-Impersonation {Default | Anonymous | Identify | Impersonate
    | Delegate}] [-Force] [-ThrottleLimit <int>] [-WhatIf] [-Confirm]  [<CommonParameters>]


ALIASES
    None
```

Figure 12.12: Displaying help information for any cmdlet

The information provided by Get-Help is very comprehensive; in some cases, it contains all of the same information that you can find on Microsoft Learn. Using Get-Help is a quick way of finding example syntax for commands and cmdlets that you may be unfamiliar with, and negates the need for you to launch a web browser to find that information. Make sure to start utilizing Get-Help to further your knowledge of any cmdlet in PowerShell!

> 💡 When using PowerShell on a fresh system, or one that you haven't worked on in a while, take a minute to run a command called Update-Help. This will cause PowerShell to reach out to Microsoft and download the latest versions of help files, so that you know you are viewing the most up-to-date information when using Get-Help.

Formatting the output

When searching for information in PowerShell, I often encounter cases where so much information is provided to me that it's difficult to sort through. Are you trying to find useful cmdlets from Get-Command, or maybe track down a particular alias with Get-Alias? The output from these cmdlets can be staggeringly long. While we have discussed some parameters you can use to whittle down this output, such as specifying particular -Name parameters, there are a couple of formatting parameters that can also be appended to cmdlets, to modify the data output.

Format-Table

The purpose of Format-Table is simple: it takes the data output from a command and puts it into a table format. This generally makes the information much easier to read and work with. Let's look at an example. We have used Get-NetIPAddress a couple of times, but let's be honest, its output is a little messy. Running the cmdlet by itself on my virtual server, which only has a single NIC assigned to it, results in four pages of data inside my PowerShell window, with all kinds of informational fields that are either empty or not important for finding the IP addresses assigned to my server:

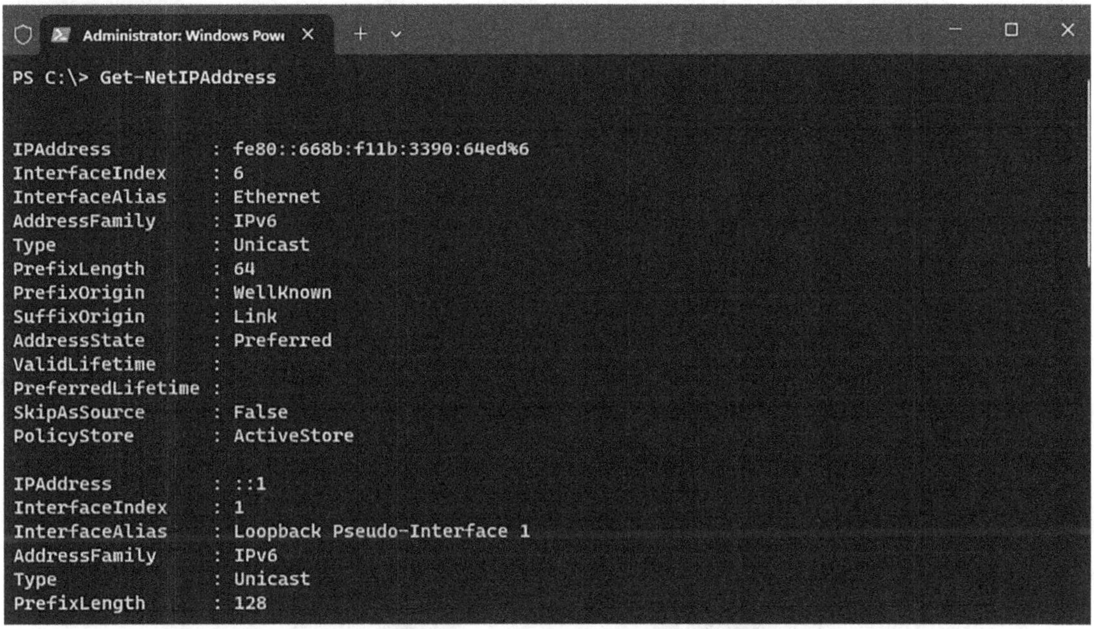

```
○  ▨ Administrator: Windows Powe  ×   + ∨                                          —    □    ×

PS C:\> Get-NetIPAddress


IPAddress            : fe80::668b:f11b:3390:64ed%6
InterfaceIndex       : 6
InterfaceAlias       : Ethernet
AddressFamily        : IPv6
Type                 : Unicast
PrefixLength         : 64
PrefixOrigin         : WellKnown
SuffixOrigin         : Link
AddressState         : Preferred
ValidLifetime        :
PreferredLifetime    :
SkipAsSource         : False
PolicyStore          : ActiveStore

IPAddress            : ::1
InterfaceIndex       : 1
InterfaceAlias       : Loopback Pseudo-Interface 1
AddressFamily        : IPv6
Type                 : Unicast
PrefixLength         : 128
```

Figure 12.13: Default output from Get-NetIPAddress

If I simply add `Format-Table` to the end of my `Get-NetIPAddress` cmdlet, the generated data is much easier on the eyes, while still giving me the important information that I am really looking for, that is, the IP addresses being used on the system:

```
Get-NetIPAddress | Format-Table
```

```
○  ▨ Administrator: Windows Powe  ×   + ∨                                          —    □    ×

PS C:\> Get-NetIPAddress | Format-Table

ifIndex IPAddress                             PrefixLength PrefixOrigin SuffixOrigin
------- ---------                             ------------ ------------ ------------
6       fe80::668b:f11b:3390:64ed%6                     64 WellKnown    Link
1       ::1                                            128 WellKnown    WellKnown
6       10.10.10.17                                     24 Manual       Manual
1       127.0.0.1                                        8 WellKnown    WellKnown


PS C:\>
```

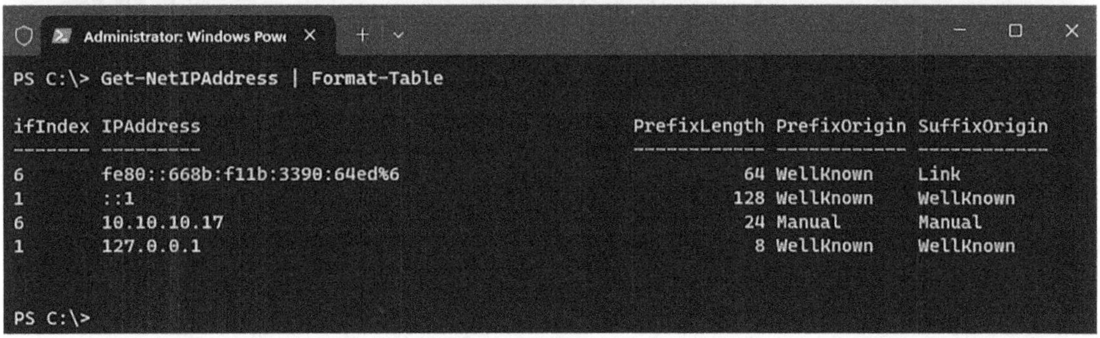

Figure 12.14: Formatted output of Get-NetIPAddress

And since nobody wants to type more characters than is necessary, `Format-Table` can be further shortened to simply `FT`. The following command would accomplish exactly the same output:

```
Get-NetIPAddress | FT
```

Some of you may be familiar with a cmdlet called `Select-Object`, which can perform the same functions as `Format-Table`. While `Select-Object` seems to be the more widely known cmdlet, in my experience, it is less powerful than `Format-Table`, so I suggest you spend some time playing around with the one we have discussed here.

Format-List

Similar to the way that `Format-Table` works, you can utilize `Format-List` to display command output as a list of properties. Let's give it a quick try. We already know that `Get-Command` gives us the available cmdlets within PowerShell, and by default, it gives them to us in a table format.

If we wanted to view that output in a list instead, with more information being provided about each cmdlet, we could tell `Get-Command` to output its data in list format, with the following command:

```
Get-Command | Format-List
```

```
PS C:\> Get-Command | Format-List


DisplayName        : Add-AppPackage
CommandType        : Alias
Definition         :
ReferencedCommand  :
ResolvedCommand    :

DisplayName        : Add-AppPackageVolume
CommandType        : Alias
Definition         :
ReferencedCommand  :
ResolvedCommand    :

DisplayName        : Add-AppProvisionedPackage
CommandType        : Alias
Definition         :
ReferencedCommand  :
ResolvedCommand    :

DisplayName        : Add-MsixPackage
CommandType        : Alias
```

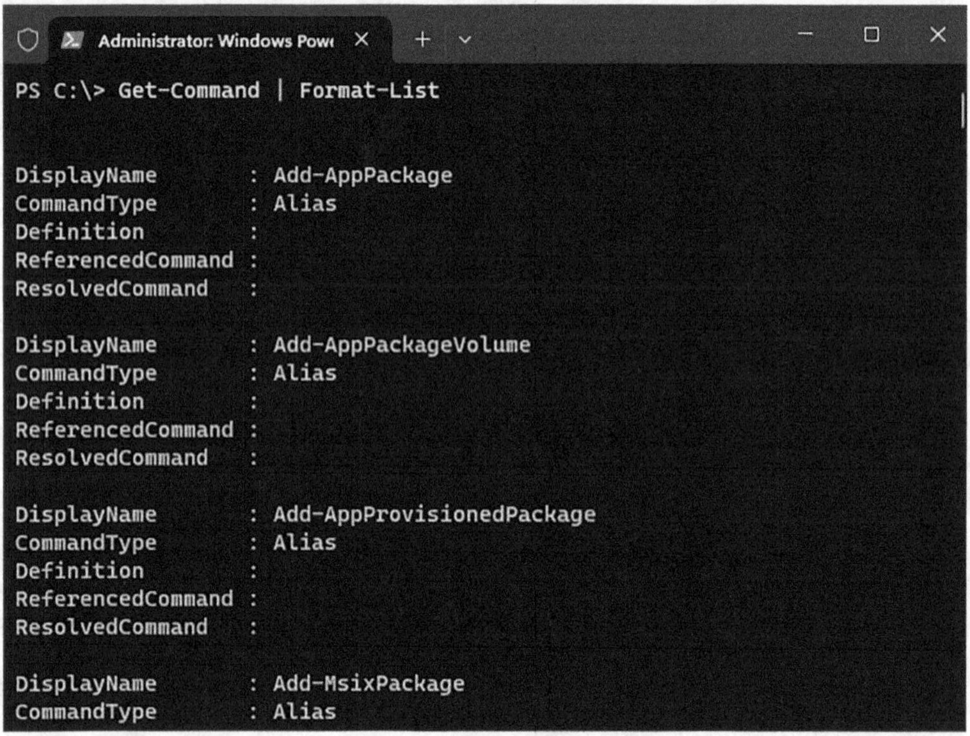

Figure 12.15: Using Format-List to modify cmdlet output

In a similar fashion to `Format-Table` being shortened to `FT`, rather than spell out `Format-List`, you could instead shorten that to `FL`, as you can see in *Figure 12.16*. Using `Format-List` in this instance results in a tremendously long output of information, so long in fact that my PowerShell window had a problem displaying it all. Maybe we need to whittle that info down a little bit by narrowing our focus. Let's search for all of the cmdlets that include the word `Restart` while displaying them in list format, and additionally, I will add another designation following `FL`, so that the outputted information only displays the Name field for each cmdlet:

```
Get-Command -Name *Restart* | FL Name
```

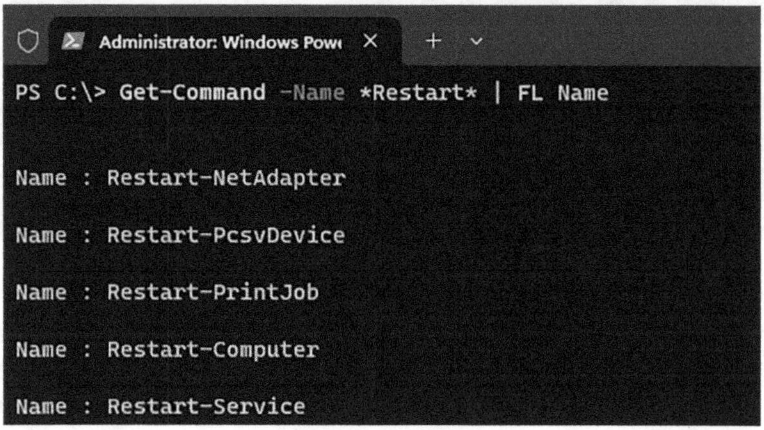

Figure 12.16: List format information about Restart-related cmdlets

Visual customizations

PowerShell has been around for a long time, and exists in all current versions of Windows, both client and server. If you are viewing this chapter in color, you probably noticed that all screenshots are a black backgrounded Terminal window, because that is the default way to utilize PowerShell in Windows Server 2025. However, working with PowerShell in many other versions of Windows lands you on the classic PowerShell blue colored background, and ultimately, what I'm trying to say here is that color doesn't matter, and is customizable. Indeed, many visual aspects of the PowerShell and Terminal windows are customizable. Let's toy around with some color settings inside Terminal.

You already know that you can run many tabs within Terminal at the same time, each tab serving a different purpose, or maybe you even run Terminal with multiple tabs so that each tab can be remotely interacting with a different server. In this case, it could be helpful to quickly distinguish between the tabs by giving each one a different color. This is easily accomplished by right-clicking on the tab and clicking on **Color...** to select a new one. In *Figure 12.17*, you can see that I have gone a little color-crazy with my tabs to showcase this ability:

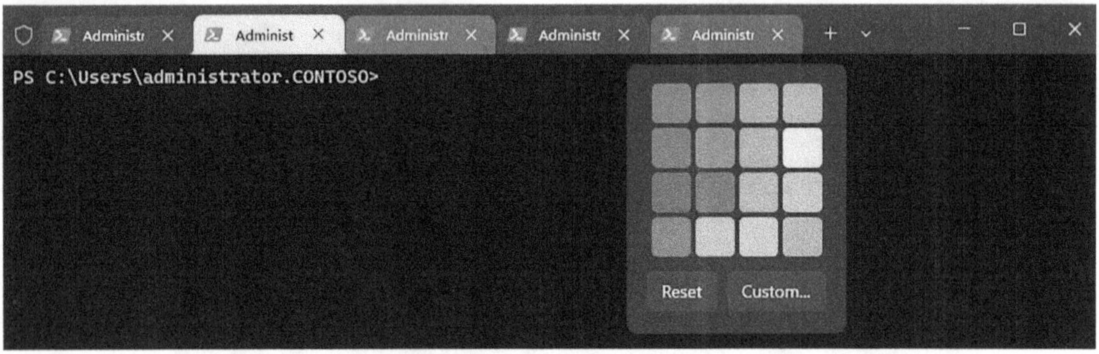

Figure 12.17: The tab rainbow

Furthermore, the interior background color and text color of your tabs can be customized by right-click-ing in the main space of the Terminal header and visiting **Settings**. Once inside **Settings** (which opens inside its own tab), find the **Color schemes** settings, and here you can select from predefined color schemes or create your own.

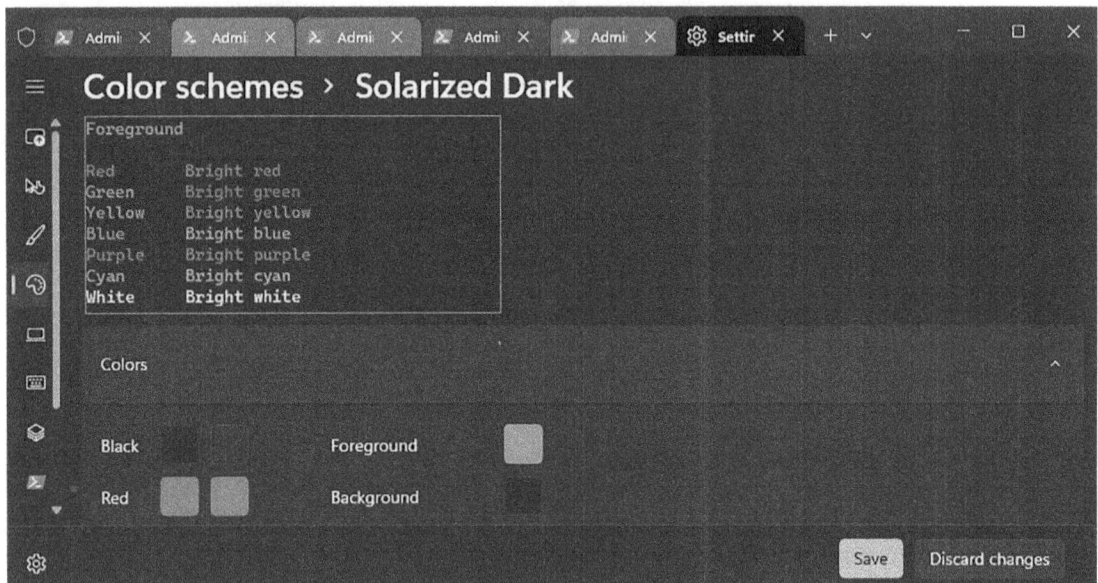

Figure 12.18: Configuring Terminal color schemes

Importing a module

A PowerShell module is a grouping of items and cmdlets that are generally all related to a particular technology, and add a set of new functionality to your PowerShell session. You see, PowerShell can't have everything in the world installed into it by default, or it would be enormous! So, it operates with a standard set of items, and when you need to work with specific pieces of technology, such as Active Directory, remote access, or Office 365, there are modules offered by Microsoft that bring those func-tions into PowerShell. Importing a module most often gives you access to additional cmdlets, but it could also include aliases, variables, assemblies, or workflows.

Active Directory (AD) is super common, so let's look at some AD-related cmdlets and prove that PowerShell doesn't know what to do with them by default. Once we import a module into our PowerShell session, however, we will find more functionality than before. Here are some AD-related cmdlets that are useful for the administration of AD. There are many, many more available:

- `Get-ADDomain`: Queries information about the current AD domain.
- `Get-ADForest`: Queries information about the current AD forest.
- `Get-ADUser`: Queries and displays information about AD users as specified by parameters, such as `Get-ADUser -Filter 'Name -like "*admin*"'`.
- `Get-ADComputer`: Queries information about AD computers as specified. For example, to see all computers joined to the domain, use `Get-ADComputer -Filter *`.
- `Get-ADDefaultDomainPasswordPolicy`: Outputs the currently configured password policy settings from the domain.

If you log in to a domain controller, launch Terminal, and then run these commands, it may seem like I am lying to you because they will work, without importing a module! In this scenario, you are unintentionally cheating because the AD PowerShell module gets installed when you install the AD DS role onto that server, so the commands already exist.

Logging in to any other server that is not a domain controller, however, and running any of these commands will present you with a whole lot of nothing, except error messages.

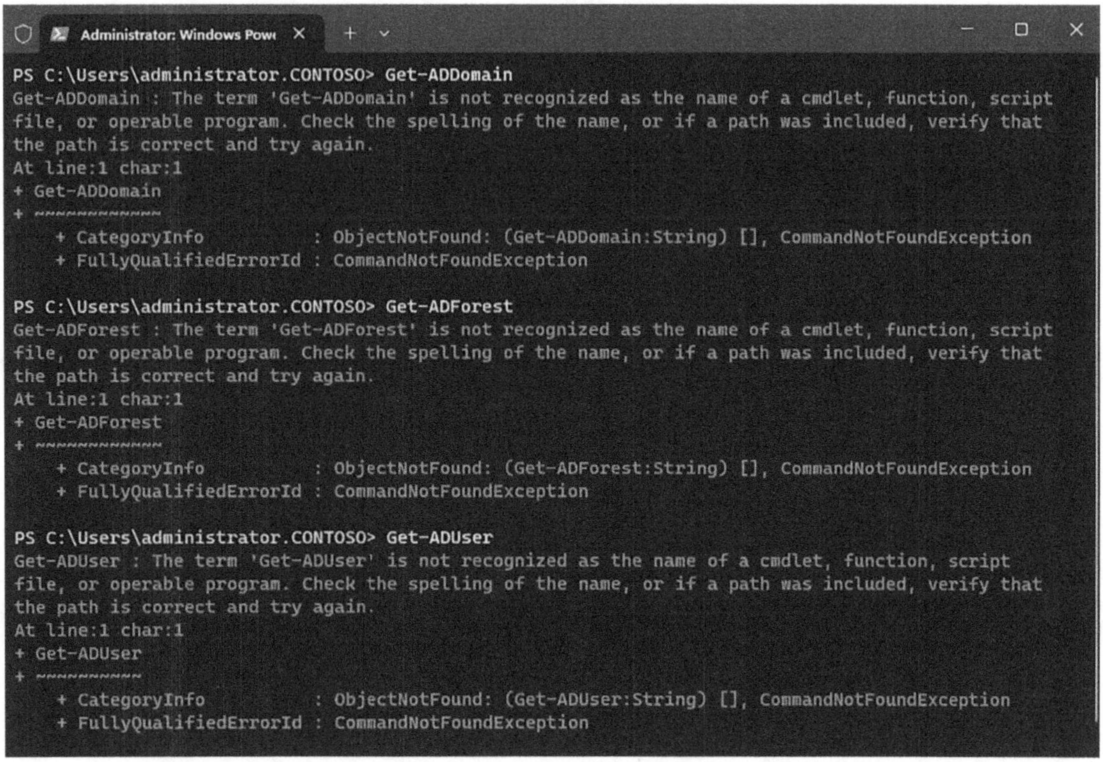

Figure 12.19: Prior to the AD module being installed

Let's change that. The process to implement PowerShell modules for Windows Server roles is pretty simple, and exists in the same place where you would go to install a role or feature into the operating system. Open Server Manager, and use the **Add Roles and Features** option. Navigate all the way to the **Features** screen, and here you will find a Windows feature called **Remote Server Administration Tools**. Drop down the menu on that, and then expand **Role Administration Tools**. At the top of this list is **AD DS and AD LDS Tools,** and finally, listed under that category is **Active Directory module for Windows PowerShell.**

Select features

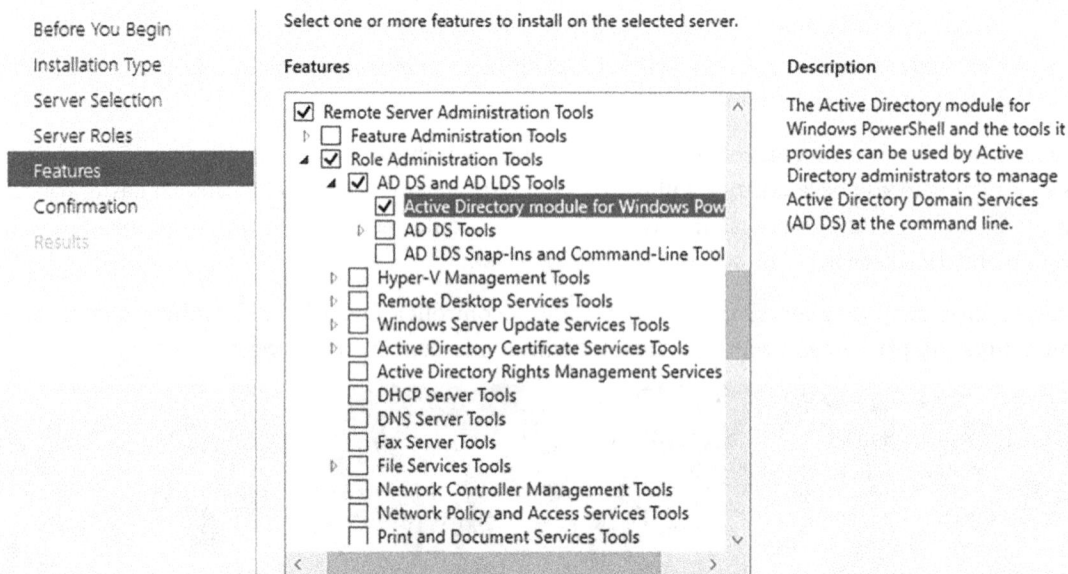

Before You Begin

Installation Type

Server Selection

Server Roles

Features

Confirmation

Results

Select one or more features to install on the selected server.

Features

- ☑ Remote Server Administration Tools
  - ▷ ☐ Feature Administration Tools
  - ▲ ☑ Role Administration Tools
    - ▲ ☑ AD DS and AD LDS Tools
      - ☑ Active Directory module for Windows Pow
      - ▷ ☐ AD DS Tools
      - ☐ AD LDS Snap-Ins and Command-Line Tool
  - ▷ ☐ Hyper-V Management Tools
  - ▷ ☐ Remote Desktop Services Tools
  - ▷ ☐ Windows Server Update Services Tools
  - ▷ ☐ Active Directory Certificate Services Tools
  - ☐ Active Directory Rights Management Services
  - ☐ DHCP Server Tools
  - ☐ DNS Server Tools
  - ☐ Fax Server Tools
  - ▷ ☐ File Services Tools
  - ☐ Network Controller Management Tools
  - ☐ Network Policy and Access Services Tools
  - ☐ Print and Document Services Tools

Description

The Active Directory module for Windows PowerShell and the tools it provides can be used by Active Directory administrators to manage Active Directory Domain Services (AD DS) at the command line.

Figure 12.20: Installing the AD PowerShell module via RSAT

Once this feature has finished installing, you will find that all of your AD-related PowerShell cmdlets now come to life on this non-domain controller server!

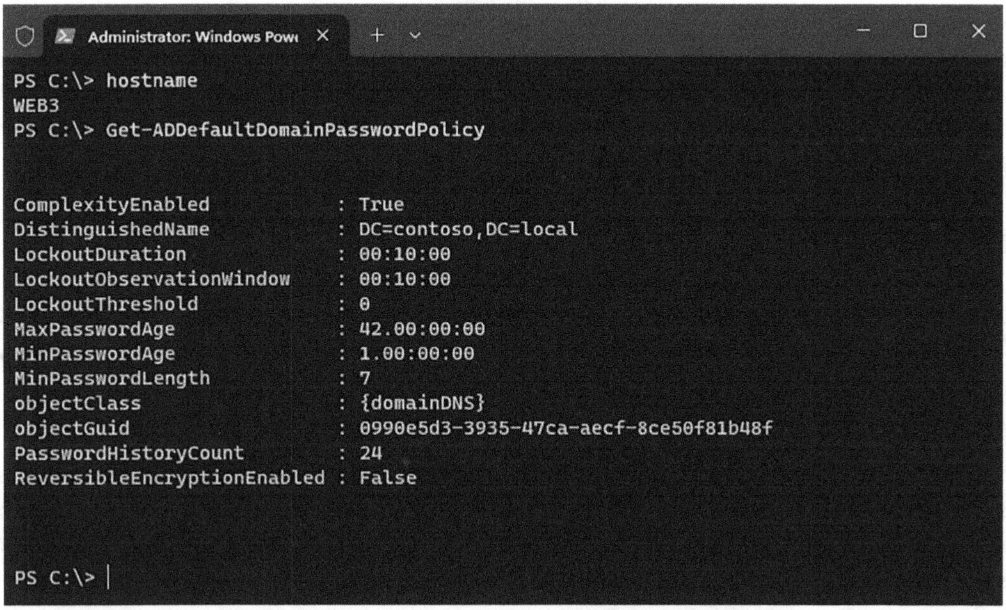

```
○  ⯈ Administrator: Windows Powe  ╳    +  ⌄                                    ─   □   ╳

PS C:\> hostname
WEB3
PS C:\> Get-ADDefaultDomainPasswordPolicy


ComplexityEnabled            : True
DistinguishedName            : DC=contoso,DC=local
LockoutDuration              : 00:10:00
LockoutObservationWindow     : 00:10:00
LockoutThreshold             : 0
MaxPasswordAge               : 42.00:00:00
MinPasswordAge               : 1.00:00:00
MinPasswordLength            : 7
objectClass                  : {domainDNS}
objectGuid                   : 0990e5d3-3935-47ca-aecf-8ce50f81b48f
PasswordHistoryCount         : 24
ReversibleEncryptionEnabled  : False



PS C:\> |
```

Figure 12.21: The AD module is now installed on WEB3

Even easier than plugging your way all through that installation wizard, you can accomplish the same thing with the following simple PowerShell command:

```
Install-WindowsFeature -Name "RSAT-AD-PowerShell"
 -IncludeAllSubFeature
```

Using a pipeline

Following the last couple of example cmdlets that we ran, you may be thinking to yourself, "I see that he is using that vertical line on the key above *Enter* on my keyboard, but why?"

Great question. In Command Prompt, we generally issue one command at a time. The same is often true for PowerShell when we are manually interacting with it, but in PowerShell, we have the potential for so much more power. One of those items of power is the ability to create a pipeline of commands. In other words, you can connect, or chain, commands together. This is commonly referred to as *piping* information from one cmdlet to another cmdlet and is done by using that little |.

Cmdlets often output data. If you then want to utilize that set of data against another cmdlet, this is where the pipe comes in handy. In our last example command, we told PowerShell to gather all of the commands that included the word Restart by performing Get-Command -Name *Restart*.

Then we **piped** that output to `Format-List`. PowerShell took the outputted dataset and threw it at `Format-List` to display a different set of output. The pipe is used very often in PowerShell commands. Keep in mind, when using a pipe, that the parameter defined needs to be something that knows how to accept the data you are piping toward it. If ever you try piping and it doesn't work, you may be attempting syntax that is unacceptable.

Exporting to CSV

One common way to use a pipe is when grabbing information via PowerShell that you want to retain, document, or send to somebody else. A common method for storing output data is within CSV files, a popular enough request that Microsoft has baked a cmdlet in for just that purpose. Let's work with another cmdlet that is very useful, `Get-EventLog`, and combine it with `Export-CSV` to show off this capability.

Event logs are essential information in a Windows Server environment. Troubleshooting issues on a server almost always involves a step of reviewing the Windows event logs. There is, of course, a graphical interface from which to accomplish this, but filtering and searching within that GUI is not as useful as it should be. Instead, we can turn to PowerShell to output event log information, such as the following:

```
Get-EventLog System
```

```
PS C:\> Get-EventLog System

Index Time              EntryType    Source            InstanceID Message
----- ----              ---------    ------            ---------- -------
41770 May 14 06:56      Information  Service Control M...  1073748860 The Network Setup Servic...
41769 May 14 06:54      Information  Service Control M...  1073748860 The Network Setup Servic...
41768 May 14 06:53      Information  Service Control M...  1073748860 The Windows Camera Frame...
41767 May 14 06:53      Information  Service Control M...  1073748860 The Windows Camera Frame...
41766 May 14 06:53      Information  Service Control M...  1073748860 The Windows Camera Frame...
41765 May 14 06:53      Information  Service Control M...  1073748860 The Windows Camera Frame...
41764 May 14 06:53      Information  Microsoft-Windows...         566 The description for Even...
41763 May 14 06:36      Information  Service Control M...  1073748860 The AppX Deployment Serv...
41762 May 14 06:34      Information  Service Control M...  1073748860 The Network Setup Servic...
41761 May 14 06:31      Information  Service Control M...  1073748860 The Network Setup Servic...
41760 May 14 06:31      Information  Service Control M...  1073748860 The AppX Deployment Serv...
41759 May 14 06:26      Information  Service Control M...  1073748860 The Windows Camera Frame...
41758 May 14 06:26      Information  Service Control M...  1073748860 The Network Setup Servic...
41757 May 14 06:25      Information  Service Control M...  1073748860 The Windows Camera Frame...
41756 May 14 06:25      Information  Microsoft-Windows...         566 The description for Even...
41755 May 14 06:24      Information  Service Control M...  1073748860 The Network Setup Servic...
41754 May 14 06:20      Information  Service Control M...  1073748860 The Network Setup Servic...
41753 May 14 06:18      Information  Service Control M...  1073748860 The Network Setup Servic...
41752 May 14 06:18      Information  Service Control M...  1073748860 The Windows Modules Inst...
```

Figure 12.22: Viewing the system event logs in PowerShell is messy

As you can see, the system event logs on this server contain a lot of information, and reading through it all within the PowerShell window could take the next three years. Filtering and searching are key to making this data useful, so let's see what this does instead:

```
Get-EventLog System | Export-CSV C:\Logs\SysLog.csv
```

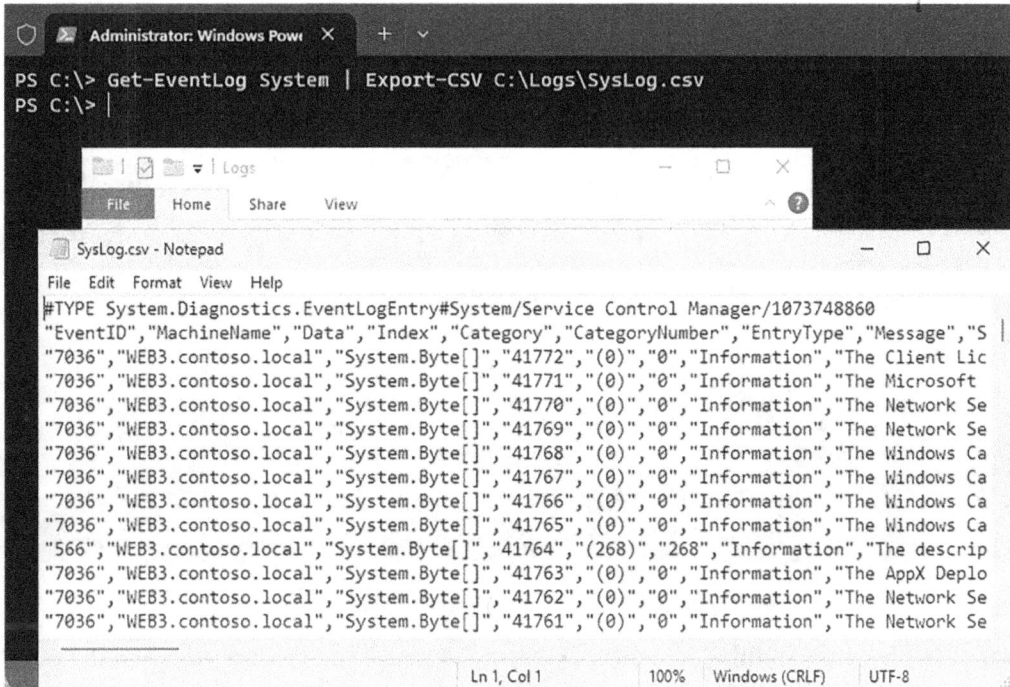

Figure 12.23: Piping output to a CSV file

PowerShell grabbed all of the information from the system event logs and spat that info into a CSV file for us. We can now take that CSV file, open it inside a program such as Microsoft Excel, and easily sort, filter, or search on these events in a much easier way than we could do from within the default Windows Event Viewer.

You can also export to XML or HTML, or even pipe output directly to a printer!

Pipes can invoke action

So far, we have only seen pipes modify outputted data. This is very useful, but I don't want you to walk away from this thinking that pipes are only useful for generating information. They can also take the output from one command and throw it at another command, but perhaps a command that actually causes a change or action to be performed. A good example is stopping a process or service. Let's pretend that, for some reason, you want to have a way to immediately stop all of the Hyper-V services on a server. Those services all have a DisplayName value that begins with the word Hyper-V. We can verify that by using the following command to view all of those services:

```
Get-Service -DisplayName hyper*
```

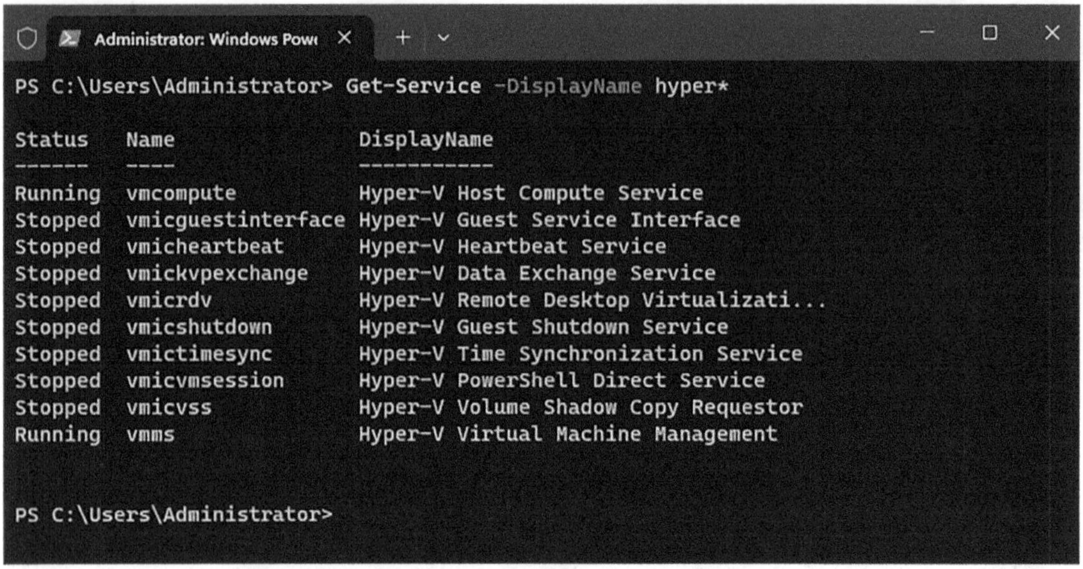

```
Administrator: Windows Powe    X    +    ∨

PS C:\Users\Administrator> Get-Service -DisplayName hyper*

Status    Name                DisplayName
------    ----                -----------
Running   vmcompute           Hyper-V Host Compute Service
Stopped   vmicguestinterface  Hyper-V Guest Service Interface
Stopped   vmicheartbeat       Hyper-V Heartbeat Service
Stopped   vmickvpexchange     Hyper-V Data Exchange Service
Stopped   vmicrdv             Hyper-V Remote Desktop Virtualizati...
Stopped   vmicshutdown        Hyper-V Guest Shutdown Service
Stopped   vmictimesync        Hyper-V Time Synchronization Service
Stopped   vmicvmsession       Hyper-V PowerShell Direct Service
Stopped   vmicvss             Hyper-V Volume Shadow Copy Requestor
Running   vmms                Hyper-V Virtual Machine Management


PS C:\Users\Administrator>
```

Figure 12.24: Viewing services related to Hyper-V

We can take the output of this Get-Service cmdlet and pipe it to Stop-Service, and the resulting command will immediately stop all services that begin with the word Hyper:

```
Get-Service -DisplayName hyper* | Stop-Service
```

> Obviously, you'll want to be careful with this particular cmdlet piping! It would be easy to bomb an entire server by stopping all of its services with one little command.

PowerShell Integrated Scripting Environment

Most server administrators are familiar with the concept of creating batch files for use in the Command Prompt world. Have a series of commands that you want to run in sequence? Need to run this sequence of commands multiple times across different servers or repeatedly in the future? Throwing multiple commands inside a text document and then saving it with the .BAT file extension will result in a batch file that can be run on any Windows computer, issuing those commands in sequence, which saves you the time and effort of having to plunk out these commands over and over inside the CLI.

Scripting in PowerShell is the same idea, but is much more powerful. Commands in Command Prompt are useful but limited, while PowerShell cmdlets can manipulate anything within the operating system. With PowerShell, we can reference items from inside environment variables or the registry, we can easily issue commands to remote systems, and we can even utilize variables inside a PowerShell script, just like you would do with any full programming language.

Let's explore a couple of different ways that can be used to start creating your first PowerShell scripts.

PS1 files

Creating a simple .PS1 file (a PowerShell script file) is almost the same as creating a .BAT file. Simply open a text document using your favorite editor, throw in a series of commands or cmdlets, and then save the file as FILENAME.PS1. As long as your PowerShell environment allows the running of scripts (see earlier in the chapter about the DEP), you now have the ability to double-click on that .PS1 file, or launch it from any PowerShell prompt, to run the series of cmdlets inside that script. Let's give it a try and prove that we can get a simple script up and operational.

Since you are only going to create scripts that serve a purpose, let's think of a real-world example. I work with terminal servers quite a bit—pardon me, RDS servers—and a common request from customers is a log of which users logged in to which servers.

A simple way to gather this information is to create a logon script that records information about the user session to a file as they log in. To do this, I need to create a script that I can configure to run during the logon process. To make the script a little bit more interesting and flexible down the road, I am going to utilize some variables for my username and the current date and time, and record the name of the RDS server being logged into. That way, I can look at the collective set of logs down the road and easily determine which users were on which servers. I am going to use Notepad to create this script. I have opened a new instance of Notepad and entered the following commands, and am now saving this as C:\Scripts\UserReporting.ps1:

```
$User = $env:username
$RDSH = $env:computername
$Date = Get-Date
```

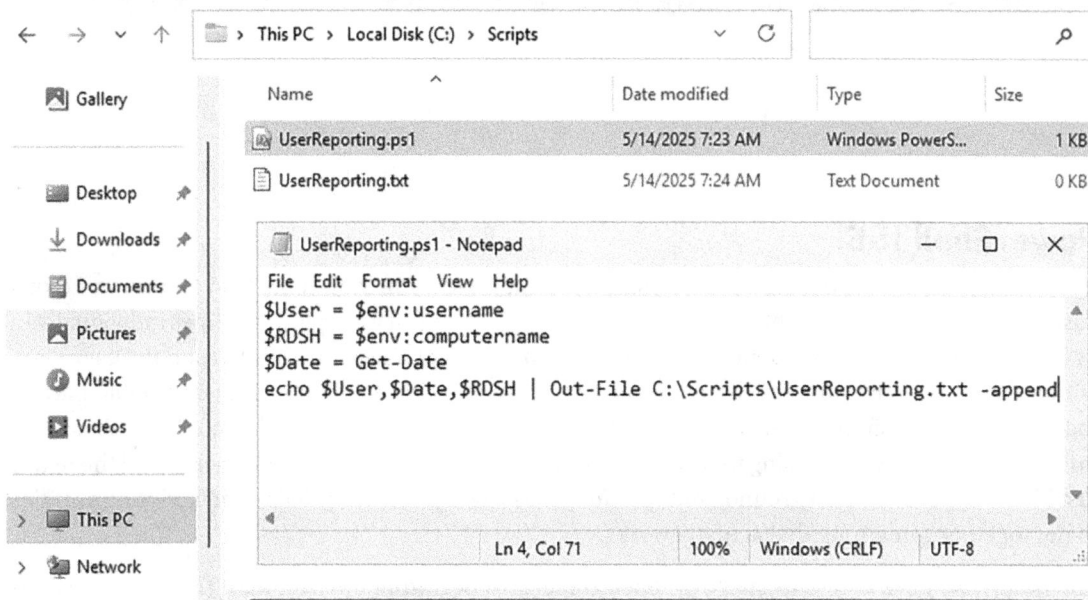

Figure 12.25: Creating a simple PS1 script

You can probably already tell what this script is doing, but let's walk through it anyway. First, we are defining three variables. I am telling the script that $User needs to equal the environment variable username. This will give me the username of the person who is signing in. $RDSH is going to be the name of the server where the user is logging in, also pulled by accessing the server's environment variables. The third variable defined is $Date, which simply pulls the current system date by calling a PowerShell cmdlet named Get-Date.

After pulling all of the information into the PowerShell variables, I am then outputting these three items into a text file that is sitting on my server's hard drive.

If I run this script a few times, I can open my UserReporting.txt file and see that every time the script is run, it successfully logs my specified variables into this report file:

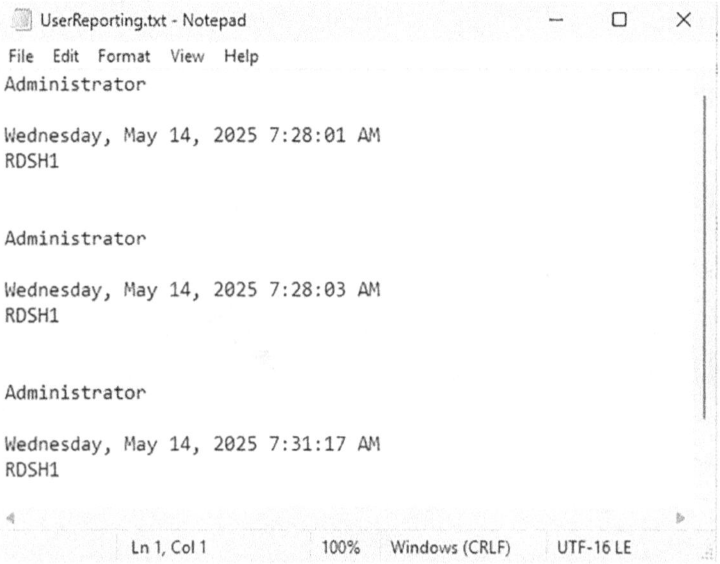

Figure 12.26: Results of our PowerShell script

PowerShell ISE

If I'm being honest, putting together that simple script we just ran took some trial and error. I didn't have a copy of it readily available to work from, and I needed to test a couple of the lines individually in PowerShell before I was confident they would work in my script. I also first tried to pull the username without using the environment variable, and it didn't work. Why did I have so much trouble putting together just a few simple lines of code? Because as I typed those lines in Notepad, I had absolutely no idea whether they were going to work when I saved and attempted to run that script. All the text is just black with a white background, and I am fully trusting my own knowledge and scripting abilities to put together something that actually works.

Thankfully, we have access to the PowerShell **Integrated Scripting Environment** (ISE). This is a program that is installed by default in Windows Server 2025; it is a scripting shell that allows you to write PowerShell scripts and provides help along the way. Let's go ahead and open it up. If you have any PS1

PowerShell script files, you can simply right-click on one of them and choose **Edit**. Otherwise, hit up the **Start** menu and search for ISE to find and launch this application.

Now, inside ISE and working within the **Scripting** section, if we start typing in the same script information that I used in Notepad a few minutes ago, you can see that even as we type, we get popups and prompts that help us decide which cmdlets or variables we want to utilize. Similar to the way that auto-complete keyboards on our smartphones work, ISE will give suggestions about what you are starting to type, so that you don't necessarily have to remember what the cmdlets or parameters are called; you can take an educated guess on what letter it starts with and then choose one from the list that is presented. There is also a list off to the right of all the commands available, and it is searchable! That is a great feature that really helps to get these scripts rolling:

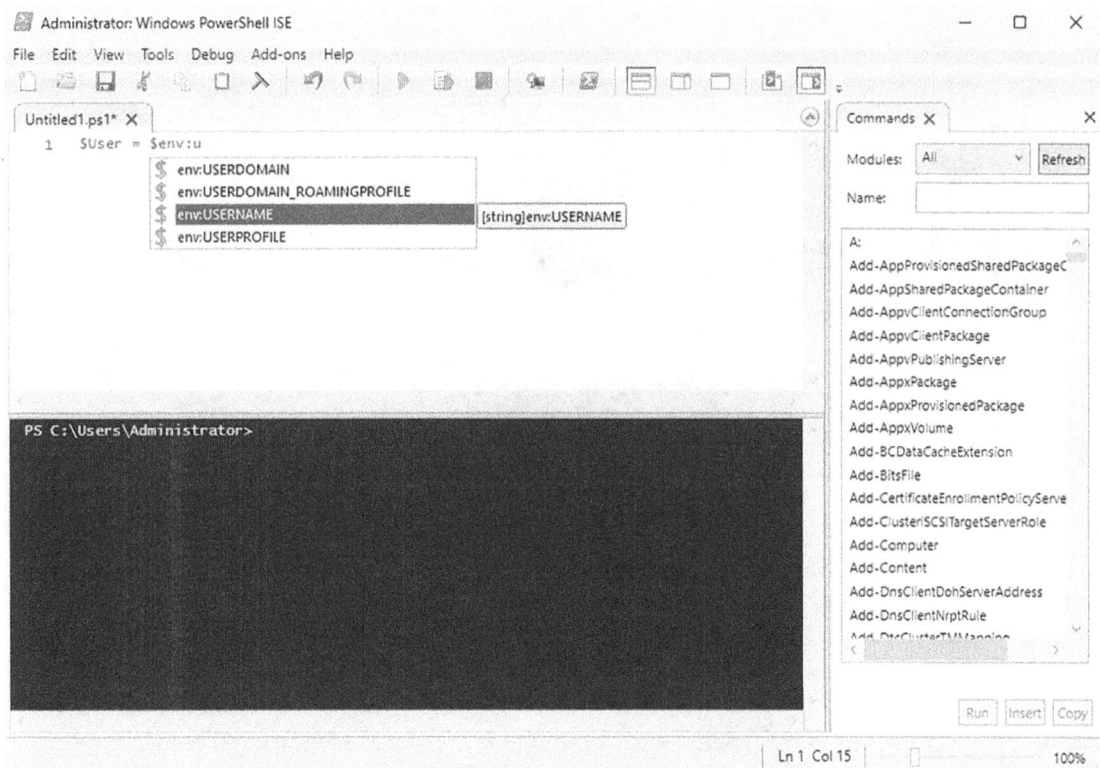

Figure 12.27: ISE provides suggestions for cmdlets and variables as you type them

Also useful is the blue PowerShell mini screen that consumes the bottom half of the development window inside ISE. Basically, when you type in some commands, ISE helps to make sure they are all going to work by color-coding the cmdlets and parameters for easy identification, and then you can click on the green arrow button in the taskbar that is labeled **Run Script (F5)**. Even if you haven't saved your script anywhere yet, ISE launches through your commands and presents the output in the following PowerShell prompt window. This allows you to test your script, or test changes that you are making to an existing script, without having to save the file and then launch it separately from a traditional PowerShell window:

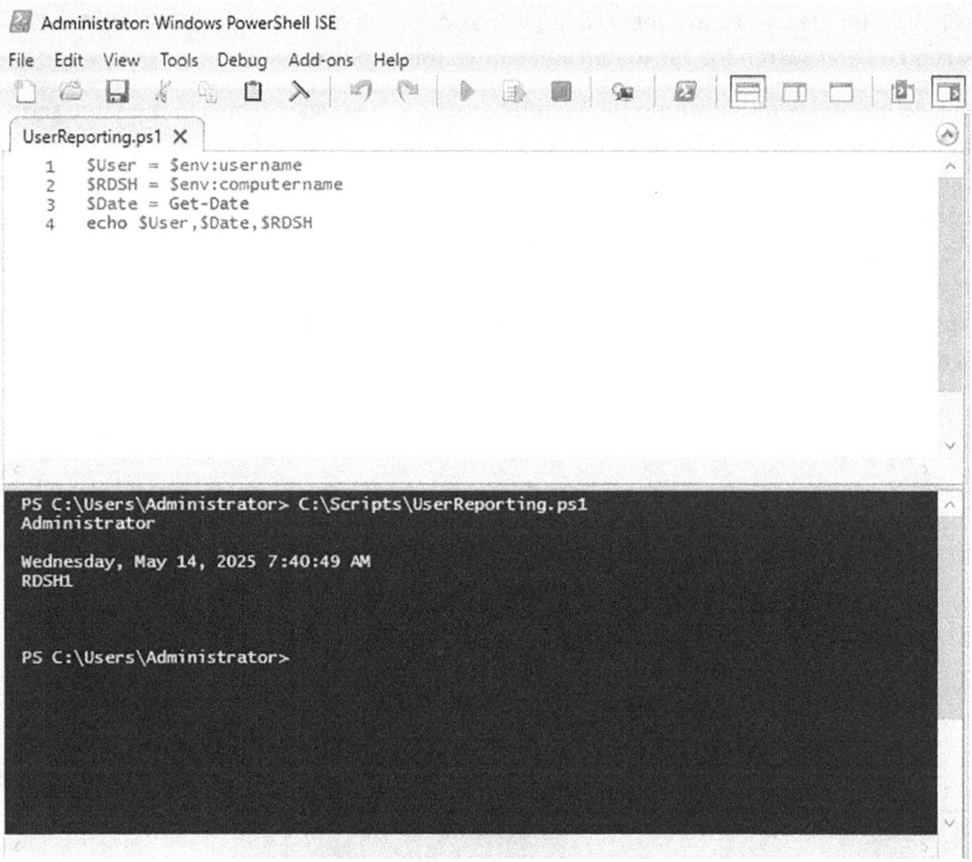

Figure 12.28: Testing the script inside ISE

What's even better is that you can highlight sections of your script and choose to run only isolated pieces of the code. This allows you to test certain sections of a script, or do something creative, such as keep one big PS1 script file that is full of common PowerShell commands that you might use on a daily basis. When you need to run just one of them, you can simply highlight the text that you want to run and click on the **Run Selection (F8)** button. By highlighting text before running the script from within ISE, only the selected cmdlet(s) will be put into action. In the following screenshot, you can see that I have numerous cmdlets listed inside my script file, but only the one that is highlighted ran when I pressed *F8*:

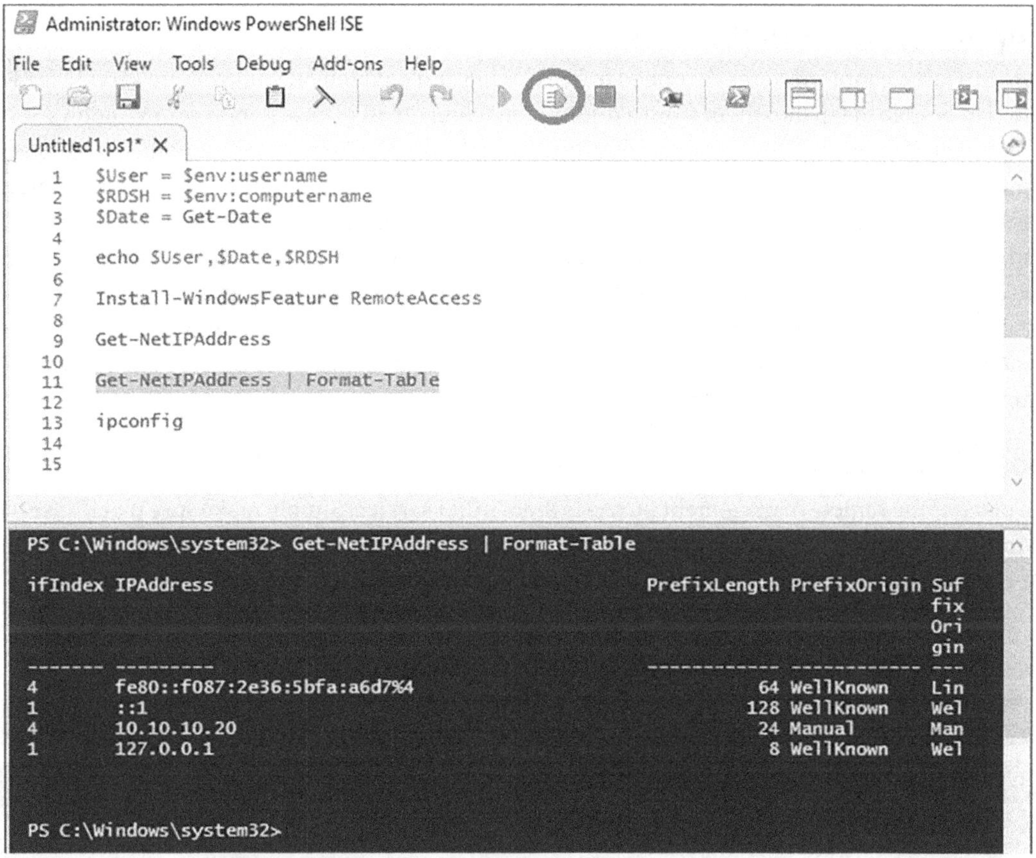

Figure 12.29: Running only highlighted commands in ISE

Remotely managing a server

Now that we have worked a little bit in the local instance of PowerShell and have explored a couple of methods that can be used to start creating scripts, it is time to take a closer look at how PowerShell fits into your centralized administration needs. If you start using PowerShell for server administration but are still RDPing into the servers and then opening PowerShell from there, you're doing it wrong. We already know that you can tap remote servers into Server Manager so that they can be managed centrally.

We also know that the tools inside Server Manager are, for the most part, just issuing a series of PowerShell cmdlets when you click on the buttons. Combine those two pieces of information, and you can surmise that PowerShell commands and cmdlets can be easily run against remote systems, including ones that you are not currently logged into.

Taking this idea and running with it, we are going to look over the criteria necessary to make this happen in our own environment. We are going to make sure that one of our servers is ready to accept remote PowerShell connections, and then use a PowerShell prompt on a different machine to pull information from and make changes to that remote server.

Preparing the remote server

There are just a couple of items that need to be running and enabled on your remote servers for PowerShell to be able to tap into them from a different machine. If all of your servers are Windows Server 2025 (in fact, if they are all Windows Server 2012 or higher), then PowerShell remoting is enabled by default, and you may be able to skip the next couple of sections. However, if you try to use PowerShell remoting and it's not working for you, it is important that you understand how it works under the hood. This way, you can troubleshoot it and manually establish remote capabilities if you run into problems or are running some older operating systems where these steps may be necessary. It is also possible that you have pre-existing security policies that are disabling components used by the remote connection capabilities of PowerShell, so if you find your remote access to be blocked, these are the items to investigate on those systems.

The WinRM service

One piece of the remote management puzzle is the WinRM service. Simply make sure that this service is running. If you have stopped it as some sort of hardening or security benefit, you will need to reverse that change and get the service back up and running to use PowerShell remoting.

You can check the status of the WinRM service from `services.msc`, of course, or since we are using PowerShell in this chapter, you could check it with the following command:

```
Get-Service WinRM
```

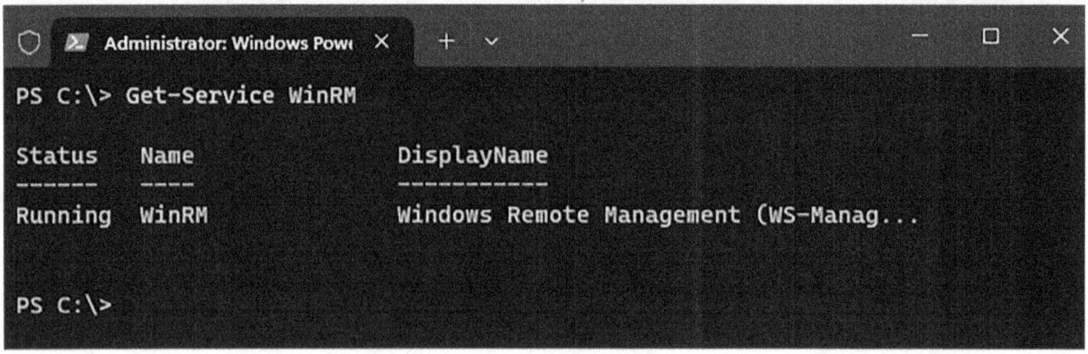

```
Administrator: Windows Powe  ×    +   ∨                                    —      □      ×

PS C:\> Get-Service WinRM

Status    Name                DisplayName
------    ----                -----------
Running   WinRM               Windows Remote Management (WS-Manag...


PS C:\>
```

Figure 12.30: Ensuring that the WinRM service is running

Enable-PSRemoting

Typically, the only other thing that needs to be accomplished on your remote server is to run a single, simple cmdlet. Well, the server needs to have network access, of course, or you won't be able to see it on the network at all. But other than making sure network connectivity and flow are working directly from the console of your new server, you are then ready to issue the PowerShell command that enables this server to be able to accept incoming, remote PowerShell connections. Once again, you only need to take these actions if you discover that remote PowerShelling is not already working for you:

```
Enable-PSRemoting -Force
```

Using `-Force` at the end of the `Enable-PSRemoting` command causes the command to roll without asking you for confirmation. There are a few different things that `Enable-PSRemoting` is doing in the background here. First, it is attempting to start the WinRM service. Why did I already specify that you should check it manually? Because if you have it disabled as part of a lockdown strategy, you will interfere with this process. Checking WinRM before using `Enable-PSRemoting` increases your chances of success when running the `Enable-PSRemoting` cmdlet. There are two other things that this command is doing: starting the listener for remote connections and creating a firewall rule on the system to allow this traffic to pass successfully.

If you intend to use PowerShell remoting on a large scale, it is daunting to think about logging in to every single server and running this command. Thankfully, you don't have to! As with most functions in the Windows world, we can use Group Policy to make this change for us automatically. Create a new GPO, link and filter it appropriately so that it only applies to those servers that you want to be centrally managed, and then configure this setting: **Computer Configuration | Policies | Administrative Templates | Windows Components | Windows Remote Management (WinRM) | WinRM Service**.

Set **Allow remote server management through WinRM** to **Enabled**, as follows:

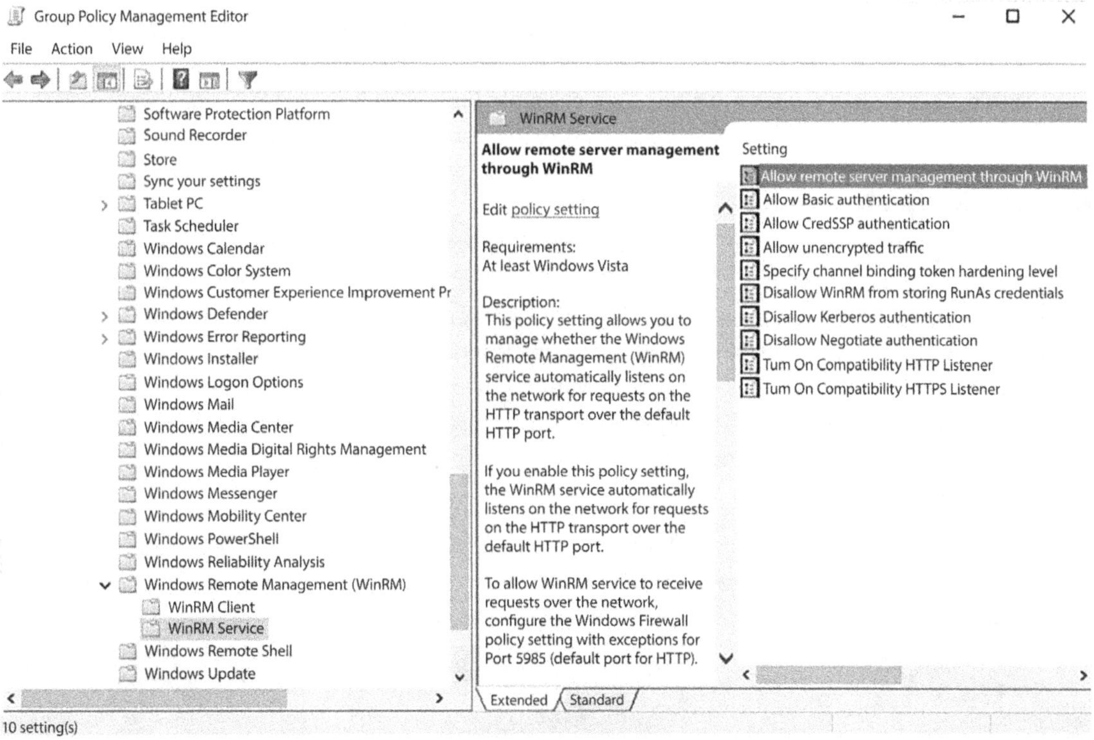

Figure 12.31: Enabling remote management via GPO

Allowing machines from other domains or workgroups

If you are working with servers that are all part of the same corporate domain, which will most often be the case, then authentication between machines is easy to accomplish. They automatically trust each other at this level. However, on the server you are prepping to accept remote connections, if you expect those remote computers will be members of a different domain that is not trusted, or even members of a workgroup, then you will have to issue another command to manually trust the individual computers that are going to be connecting. For example, if I were planning to manage all of my servers from a client computer called `Win10Client` that is not trusted by the servers, I would need to run the following command on these servers:

```
Set-Item wsman:\localhost\client\trustedhosts Win10Client
```

If you wanted to allow *any* machine to connect remotely, you could replace the individual computer name with a * character, but in general, this wouldn't be a good practice, as you may be inviting trouble by allowing *any* machine to connect to your server in this way.

Connecting to the remote server

I typically see administrators utilize remote PowerShell in two different ways. You can perform some commands against remote systems on an ad hoc basis while your PowerShell prompt is still running in a local context, or you can launch a full-blown remote PowerShell session to make your PowerShell prompt behave as if it is running directly on that remote system. Let's take a look at both options.

Using -ComputerName

Many of the cmdlets available in PowerShell, particularly ones that begin with `Get-`, can be used with the `-ComputerName` parameter. This specifies that the command you are about to run needs to execute against the remote system that you specify in the `-ComputerName` section. For our remote PowerShell examples, I will be using a PowerShell prompt on my Windows 10 client computer to access information on some of my servers in the network. I want to query the WinRM service to make sure that it is up and running. For the sake of proving to you that I am remotely communicating with `WEB3`, you will see in the output that I have first queried my local WinRM service, which I happened to disable on my Windows 10 workstation.

You see in *Figure 12.32* that my local WinRM service shows as `Stopped`, but when I issue the same command specifying to query `-ComputerName` of `WEB3`, it reaches out and reports back to me that the WinRM service is indeed running successfully on the `WEB3` server:

```
Hostname
Get-Service WinRM
Get-Service WinRM -ComputerName WEB3
```

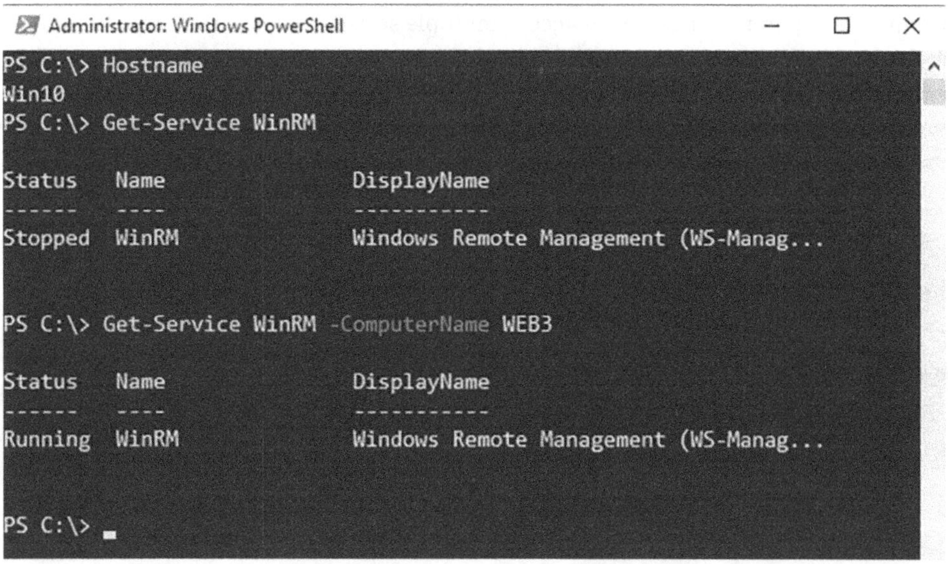

Figure 12.32: Using -ComputerName to query a remote system

Alternatively, perhaps I want to query the new Server Core instance we set up a little while ago and check which roles are currently installed on WEB4:

```
Get-WindowsFeature -ComputerName WEB4 | Where Installed
```

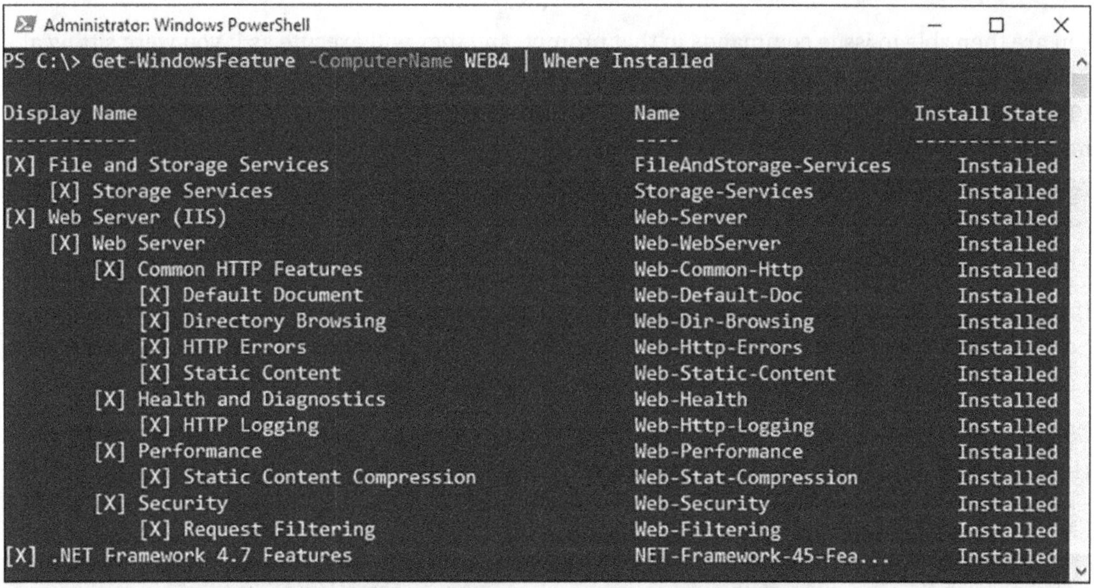

Figure 12.33: Roles and features installed on WEB4

The -ComputerName parameter can even accept multiple server names at the same time. If I wanted to check the status of the WinRM service on a few of my servers, by using a single command, I could do something such as this:

```
Get-Service WinRM -ComputerName WEB1,WEB2,DC1
```

```
Administrator: Windows PowerShell                                    —    □    ×
PS C:\> Get-Service WinRM -ComputerName WEB1,WEB2,DC1

Status     Name                DisplayName
------     ----                -----------
Running    WinRM               Windows Remote Management (WS-Manag...
Running    WinRM               Windows Remote Management (WS-Manag...
Running    WinRM               Windows Remote Management (WS-Manag...


PS C:\>
```

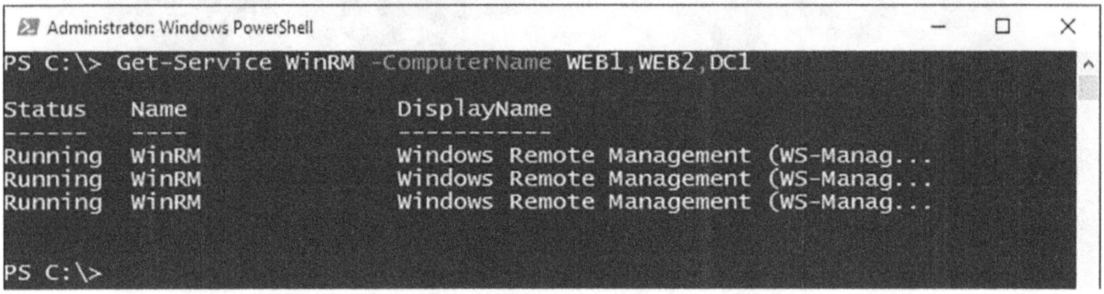

Figure 12.34: Remote PowerShell running against multiple machines

Using Enter-PSSession

On the other hand, sometimes you have many different cmdlets that you want to run against a particular server. In this case, and also because doing it this way just makes more sense to my brain, we can invoke a fully capable, fully remote PowerShell instance on that remote server. If you open PowerShell on your local system and utilize the Enter-PSSession cmdlet, your PowerShell prompt will be a full remote representation of PowerShell on that remote server.

You are then able to issue commands in that prompt, and they will execute as if you were sitting at a PowerShell prompt from the console of the remote server. Once again, I am logged in to my Windows 10 client computer and have opened PowerShell. I then use the following command to remotely connect to my WEB4 server:

```
Enter-PSSession -ComputerName WEB4
```

The prompt will change, indicating that I am now working in the context of the WEB4 server.

If your user account does not have access to the server, you can specify alternative credentials to be used when creating this remote connection. Simply append your Enter-PSSession cmdlet with -Credential USERNAME to specify a different user account.

Commands that I issue from this point forward will be executed against WEB4. Let's verify this. If I check a simple $env:computername, you can see that it presents me with the WEB4 hostname:

```
Administrator: Windows PowerShell                                    —    □    ×
PS C:\> Enter-PSSession -ComputerName WEB4
[WEB4]: PS C:\Users\Administrator.CONTOSO\Documents> $env:computername
WEB4
[WEB4]: PS C:\Users\Administrator.CONTOSO\Documents>
```

Figure 12.35: PowerShell is remotely connected to WEB4

And to further verify this, if I check the installed Windows roles and features, you can see that I have the Web Server role installed, as we accomplished when we initially configured this Server Core to be a web server. Clearly, I do not have the Web Server role installed on my Windows 10 workstation; PowerShell is pulling this data from the WEB4 server:

```
Get-WindowsFeature | Where Installed
```

```
Administrator: Windows PowerShell                                                      —    □    ×
[WEB4]: PS C:\Users\Administrator.CONTOSO\Documents> Get-WindowsFeature | Where Installed

Display Name                                      Name                          Install State
------------                                      ----                          -------------
[X] File and Storage Services                     FileAndStorage-Services           Installed
    [X] Storage Services                          Storage-Services                  Installed
[X] Web Server (IIS)                              Web-Server                        Installed
    [X] Web Server                                Web-WebServer                     Installed
        [X] Common HTTP Features                  Web-Common-Http                   Installed
            [X] Default Document                  Web-Default-Doc                   Installed
            [X] Directory Browsing                Web-Dir-Browsing                  Installed
            [X] HTTP Errors                       Web-Http-Errors                   Installed
            [X] Static Content                    Web-Static-Content                Installed
        [X] Health and Diagnostics                Web-Health                        Installed
            [X] HTTP Logging                      Web-Http-Logging                  Installed
        [X] Performance                           Web-Performance                   Installed
            [X] Static Content Compression        Web-Stat-Compression              Installed
        [X] Security                              Web-Security                      Installed
```

Figure 12.36: Roles and features installed on WEB4

This is pretty powerful stuff. We are sitting at our local desktop computer, have a remote PowerShell session running to the WEB4 server, and are now able to pull all kinds of information from WEB4 because it is as if we are working from PowerShell right on that server. Let's take it one step further and try to make a configuration change on WEB4, just to verify that we can. Maybe we can install a new feature on this server. I use Telnet Client quite a bit for network connectivity testing, but can see that it is currently not installed on WEB4:

```
Get-WindowsFeature -Name *telnet*
```

```
Administrator: Windows PowerShell                                                      —    □    ×
[WEB4]: PS C:\> Get-WindowsFeature -Name *telnet*

Display Name                                      Name                          Install State
------------                                      ----                          -------------
[ ] Telnet Client                                 Telnet-Client                     Available


[WEB4]: PS C:\> _
```

Figure 12.37: Telnet Client is currently not installed on WEB4

By using the Add-WindowsFeature cmdlet, I should be able to make quick work of installing that feature:

```
Add-WindowsFeature Telnet-Client
```

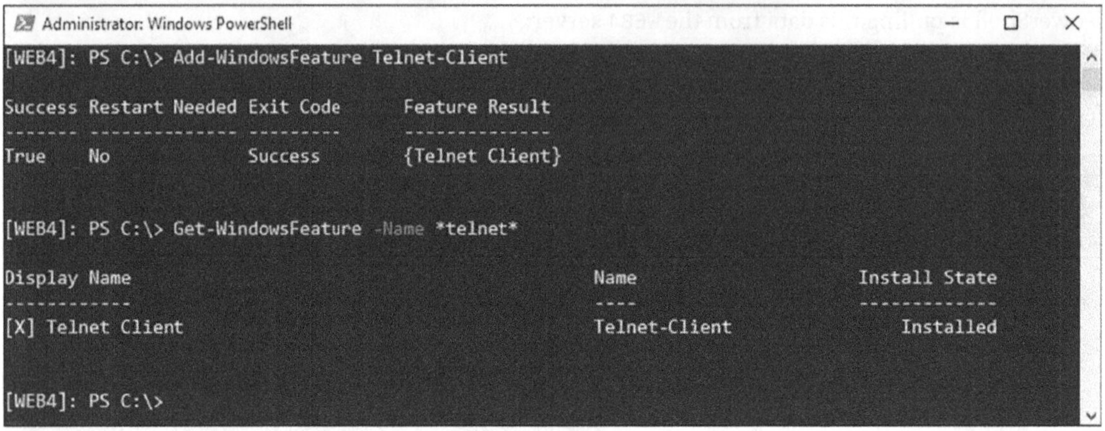

Figure 12.38: Installing Telnet Client on WEB4 via remote PowerShell

There is a ton of potential in utilizing remote PowerShell daily, not only for your servers running the full-blown Desktop Experience graphical interface but also for interacting with your security-focused Server Core deployments. Becoming familiar with working in remote PowerShell sessions will be essential to a successful deployment of Server Core in your infrastructure.

Desired State Configuration

There is some powerful functionality in the more recent versions of PowerShell, provided by something called **Desired State Configuration** (DSC). DSC is a management platform plugged into PowerShell, which provides new functions and cmdlets that you can take advantage of in your scripts to enable some really cool features. As the name implies, it allows you to build configurations inside PowerShell that will provide a *desired state*. What do I mean by that? Well, in a basic sense, DSC makes sure that the PowerShell scripts you build will always work the same way across all of the servers where you apply them by making sure the servers themselves are configured in the same way. It is quite easy to build a script that works correctly on the server you are logged into. But, if you try to roll that same script out to a different server that might reside in a different **organizational unit** (OU), or have different items installed on it to begin with, then the script could produce different results from what it was originally intended to do. DSC was built to counteract these differences.

In building your DSC configuration, you identify particular roles, settings, functions, accounts, variables, and so on that you want to retain in your specific desired state. Once you identify and configure these variables, DSC will work to ensure they stay where you have them set and that they remain uniform according to your DSC configuration policy, which means they are uniform across the other servers where you have run this script.

DSC also helps to prevent unwanted changes on servers. If your DSC-enabled script has identified that a particular service should be running all the time on your servers, and that service stops for some reason, DSC can be there to help spin it back up so that you don't experience an outage. Alternatively, perhaps you have a script that configures a server to a particular set of standards, and another person in IT comes along and adjusts a configuration on the server—perhaps they log in and stop a service purposefully for some reason. Normally, this could result in an outage for that server, but DSC will get that service running again to maintain your originally configured *desired state* for this server. DSC is your *scripting nanny*, so to speak. It helps to build configurations that will remain uniform across multiple platforms and will then work to ensure these configurations are always true. You can then be confident that your servers are always running within the context of your specified desired state.

After building a configuration that identifies the items you want to be installed or monitored, an engine called the **Local Configuration Manager (LCM)** works to ensure the resources remain within the configuration specifications. LCM polls the system regularly, watching for irregularities and changes, and takes action when needed to bring your servers back into DSC.

The ultimate goal of DSC is to keep everything constant and consistent across your servers and services. DSC's capabilities and access to reach more and more places in the operating system grow constantly, as roles are rewritten to accept DSC parameters and monitoring. This technology helps to ensure that servers are always working with your defined standards, helping to maintain your 99.999% uptime status.

There is a lot to learn about DSC, and I encourage you to explore this topic more once you are familiar with creating and using PowerShell scripts. Here are some great starting points for learning more about DSC:

- https://learn.microsoft.com/en-us/powershell/scripting/dsc/overview?view=powershell-7.5
- https://learn.microsoft.com/en-us/powershell/dsc/getting-started/wingettingstarted?view=dsc-1.1
- https://learn.microsoft.com/en-us/shows/getting-started-with-powershell-dsc/?l=zwhuclg1_2504984382

WinGet application management

This is technically a diversion from the topic of PowerShell, but I'm really excited about WinGet, and I couldn't think of a better place to discuss it in this book other than the chapter where we are already living inside a CLI.

WinGet is a command-line-only tool that enables administrators to seek out, install, remove, and even upgrade applications inside Windows 10, Windows 11, and Windows Server 2025. Can you imagine leaving the idea of application installer packages in the dust, and running single commands to install or upgrade software? That is exactly what WinGet is all about! WinGet is an application package manager, and your entire interaction with installing applications via WinGet happens from inside a simple CLI, usually Windows Terminal.

WinGet is installed by default when you first log in to a new Windows 10 (at least 1709), Windows 11, or Windows Server 2025; to test it, all you need is access to Windows Terminal or PowerShell and an internet connection.

Let's see what kind of applications are available via WinGet, and install one together. After launching an administrative copy of either Terminal or PowerShell, you can immediately begin searching for applications to install by using the following command:

```
Winget search <appname>
```

Once you have found an application you want to install, simply...

```
Winget install <appname>
```

For example, I just finished reinstalling Windows 11 on a laptop for my neighbor (are you all the "friends and family" IT person, too?), and I have not yet installed any applications on here, but I know that she prefers Google Chrome for a web browser. Historically, I would visit google.com, ask for a Chrome downloader, click on the downloader, wait for it to download, run the installer, click **Next**, **Next**, **Next**... you get the picture. While this process doesn't take an extravagant amount of time, it does require multiple actions and minutes of time. What if I could install Google Chrome with one single, simple command?

```
Winget search chrome
```

This command seeks out any application installer packages available to WinGet that include the word Chrome. There are a lot of them.

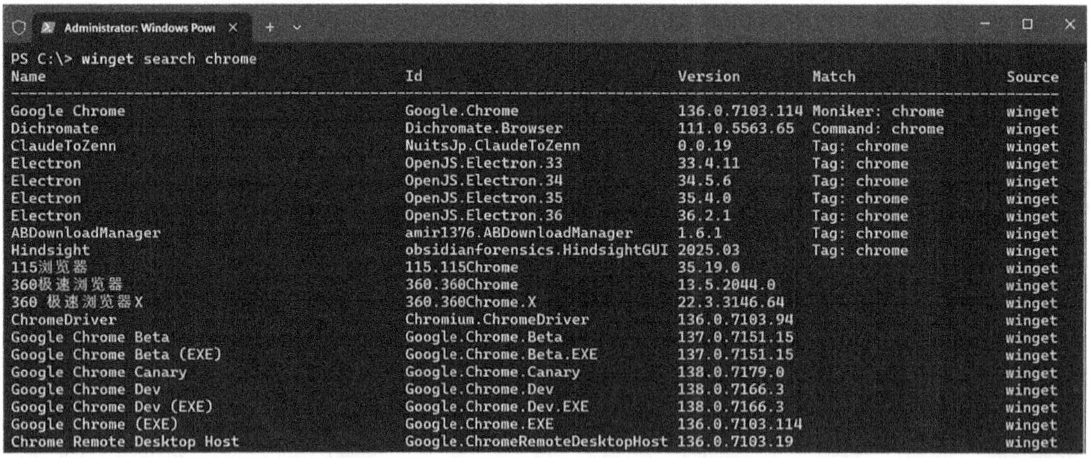

Figure 12.39: Searching for applications via WinGet

Up at the very top of this list, the one simply titled `Google Chrome` seems like the one we are looking for. Let's install it:

```
Winget install Google.Chrome
```

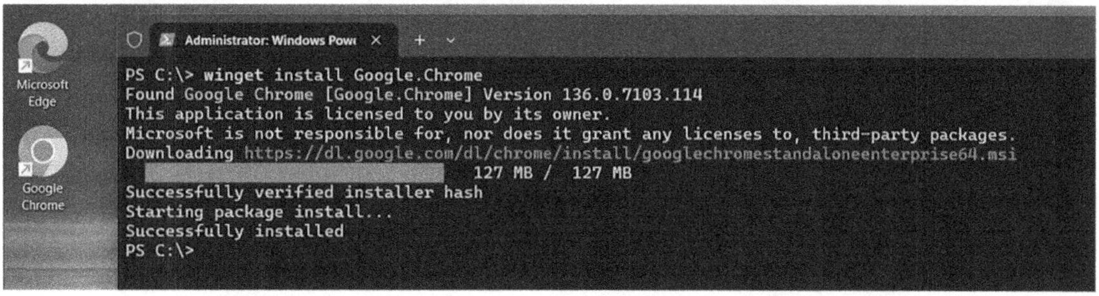

Figure 12.40: WinGet has installed Google Chrome!

That's it! Google Chrome is downloaded and installed with this one WinGet command. Removal of applications is just as easy, and WinGet can be used to upgrade applications as well. You can throw individual commands around to update applications one at a time, such as `Winget upgrade Google.Chrome`, or you can toss out one powerful command that seeks out any application on your system that is upgradable by WinGet, and updates them all at once:

```
Winget upgrade --all
```

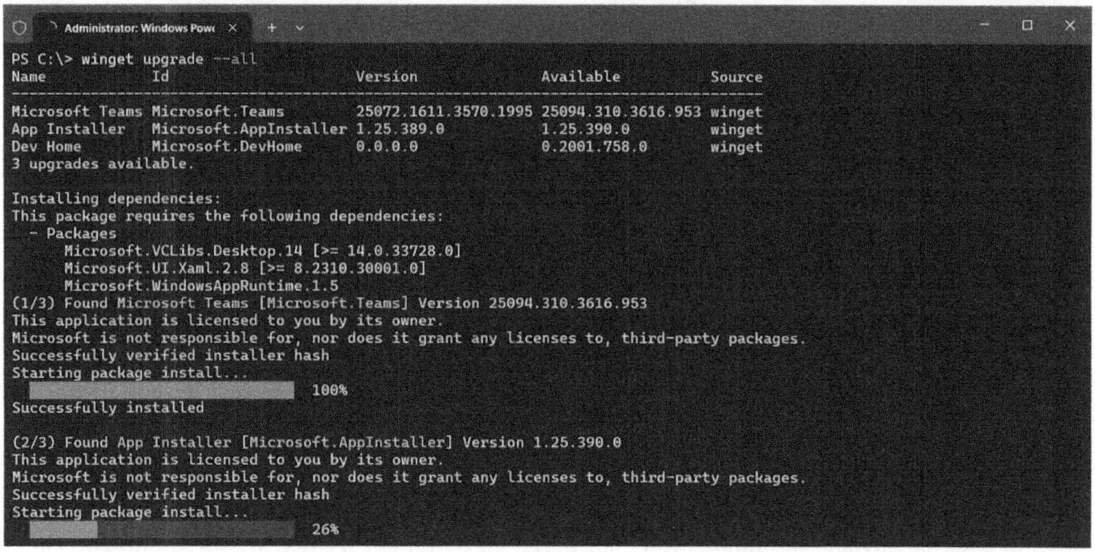

Figure 12.41: Upgrading all WinGet applications with one command

PowerShell for M365

Increasingly common is the need to utilize PowerShell to monitor and adjust configurations inside the Microsoft 365 world. Most businesses utilize M365 for email, and it is likely that anyone reading this book has at least some level of experience in the M365 admin consoles via a web browser. You may have found that there are certain functions that simply do not exist inside those admin portals, and when researching, have discovered that creating a PowerShell connection into that M365 environment is the secret sauce necessary to find and perform the function that you are trying to accomplish.

One regular support item that lands us inside M365 PowerShell is the requirement to adjust calendar permissions. For example, granting a user the ability to edit another user's calendar, such as is a common scenario for an executive assistant type of position. For a reason I do not understand, this very common task is not able to be executed from inside the M365 admin portals; you must turn to PowerShell to accomplish it from the backend.

While the PowerShell command to grant calendar access is a one-liner, the longer and trickier part of accomplishing this task is connecting your PowerShell window to the M365 environment in the first place. The process involved with launching a PowerShell window and tapping into M365 has changed numerous times over the years. Early on, you even had to do squirrely things such as log in to the M365 admin portal and visit a special section in order to launch this PowerShell connection. Thankfully, today, the process is much simpler. Let's walk through this together, connecting PowerShell to M365 and adjusting a calendar permission setting.

Installing and importing the module for the first time

Step one: open PowerShell. This can be a standard blue PowerShell window, or it can be the newer and sleeker Windows Terminal that is PowerShell-enabled by default. Either is fine.

If you have never used PowerShell on this computer to interact with M365 before, as with many functions in PowerShell, we must load the Exchange Online module so that our toolset is populated with cmdlets pertaining to Exchange Online (365) administration. This is accomplished by running the following two commands:

```
Install-Module -Name ExchangeOnlineManagement
Import-Module ExchangeOnlineManagement
```

Connecting to M365

Now, having imported our cmdlets and tools, we are ready to issue a command that causes PowerShell to reach out to M365 (Exchange Online) and create a connection. You would never expect M365 to allow any user anywhere to have the ability to connect to your M365 tenant, and so, of course, authentication is part of this process. There are various ways to streamline this PowerShell cmdlet with variables to bake authentication into the command, but I find it easiest for my brain to remember the simple `Connect-ExchangeOnline` command:

```
Connect-ExchangeOnline
```

By running this command without any parameters defined, you will be presented with a pop-up authentication window, asking for your username, password, and MFA to connect to your M365 tenant:

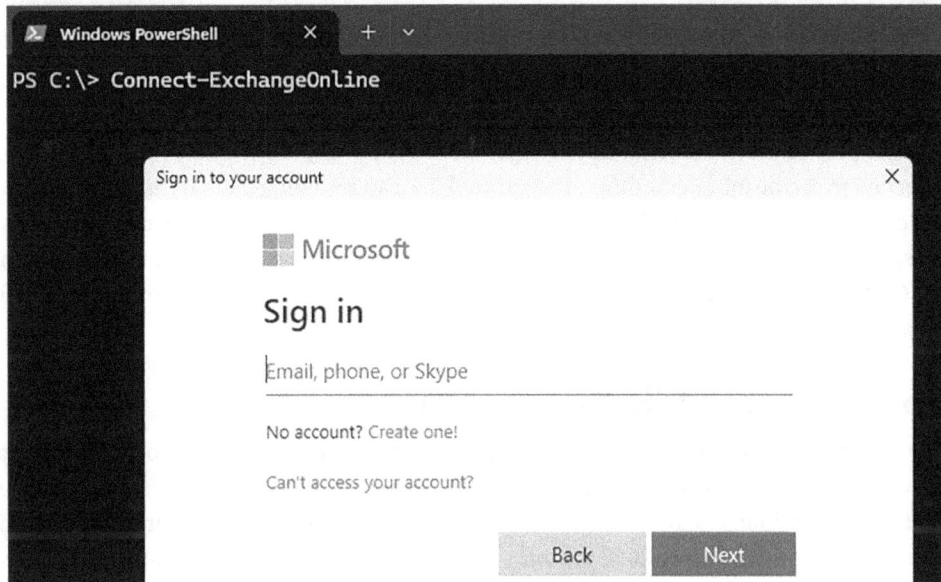

Figure 12.42: Connecting PowerShell to Exchange Online (M365)

Issuing commands

Assuming you used an administrative credential to connect, you now have access to seek or change any configurations inside your M365 tenant! The sky is the limit with this; you have only to figure out what information you are looking for and then research the appropriate PowerShell commands to get the job done. As with everything in PowerShell, your commands to seek out information are generally going to begin with `Get-`, and those commands used to make changes will be `Set-` or `Add-`.

Remember that you are now connected to your M365 tenant with full global administrator access (if these are the permissions your admin account has), which means that a misstep with a command could indeed delete information or break things. Take care when crafting those cmdlets! Thankfully, Microsoft has great documentation about each of the available PowerShell cmdlets used by M365 on the Microsoft Learn sites, and any task you want to accomplish via PowerShell is simply a web search away.

As an example, let's round out the scenario we discussed earlier and give Lorien access to Jackson's calendar. To do this, we need to make a permission adjustment on Jackson's calendar, granting Lorien's account access to edit that calendar. In the M365 world, calendar permissions have predefined roles, and so what we specifically are trying to do here is adjust Jackson's calendar so that Lorien has `Editor` permissions to it:

```
Set-MailboxFolderPermission -Identity Jackson@contoso.com:\Calendar -user
Lorien@contoso.com -Accessrights Editor
```

If you later wanted to check your work, or for any reason wanted to view the currently configured permissions on Jackson's calendar, that is easily accomplished with the following command:

```
Get-MailboxFolderPermission -Identity Jackson@contoso.com:\Calendar
```

This calendar permission adjustment is one simple example of a common task that cannot be accomplished through the M365 web portal, but easily finished if you are familiar with tapping PowerShell into M365. It is possible to administer anything in M365 via PowerShell; you have only to seek out the cmdlets needed to do the job. Remember, PowerShell ISE can be a huge help here! As you continue to build your comfort level driving in PowerShell, you will find yourself saving large quantities of sample commands, because copy/paste is far easier than re-researching commands every time you need to run them. Create a dummy script file in ISE, storing all your commonly used commands, so that you can very easily find and execute them again and again.

Windows Terminal in Server 2022

We already covered Windows Terminal, but earlier I referenced this section as a sort of mini-appendix, and we have finally made our way to the end of this chapter. Using Windows Terminal on Windows Server 2025 is a no-brainer, because it comes installed out of the box! However, many companies are still working through their Server 2022 rollouts, and won't even be thinking about Server 2025 for a few more years. Is there a way to make use of Windows Terminal on Server 2022?

Yes indeed! It just takes a little bit of manual work. With a couple of quick download and package installation commands, we are going to add Windows Terminal to a brand-new Windows Server 2022 right now.

First, we need to know exactly what we are downloading. Microsoft releases new versions of Windows Terminal occasionally, and we want to make sure we grab the latest. This URL will bring you to the GitHub site to identify the latest version hash number: `https://github.com/microsoft/terminal/releases`.

I am going to download the latest release, currently v1.22.11141.0. Don't download it just yet; you'll see in a minute that we can handle the download process via PowerShell. Windows Terminal also relies on the XAML framework, so I actually need to download and install two packages onto my Server 2022: first XAML, then the Windows Terminal application. Use the GitHub page to find the installation package you want to download, right-click on it to copy the URL, and then utilize the URL in the following PowerShell commands that you are going to run from your Server 2022:

1. Download XAML:

```
Invoke-WebRequest -Uri https://github.com/microsoft/microsoft-ui-xaml/
releases/download/v2.8.5/Microsoft.UI.Xaml.2.8.x64.appx
-outfile Microsoft.UI.Xaml.2.8.x64.appx
```

2. Download Windows Terminal:

```
Invoke-WebRequest -Uri https://github.com/microsoft/
terminal/releases/download/v1.22.11141.0/Microsoft.
WindowsTerminal_1.22.11141.0_8wekyb3d8bbwe.msixbundle
-outfile Microsoft.WindowsTerminal_1.22.11141.0_8wekyb3d8bbwe.msixbundle
```

3. Install XAML:

```
Add-AppxPackage Microsoft.UI.Xaml.2.8.x64.appx
```

4. Install Windows Terminal:

```
Add-AppxPackage Microsoft.WindowsTerminal_1.22.11141.0_8wekyb3d8bbwe.
msixbundle
```

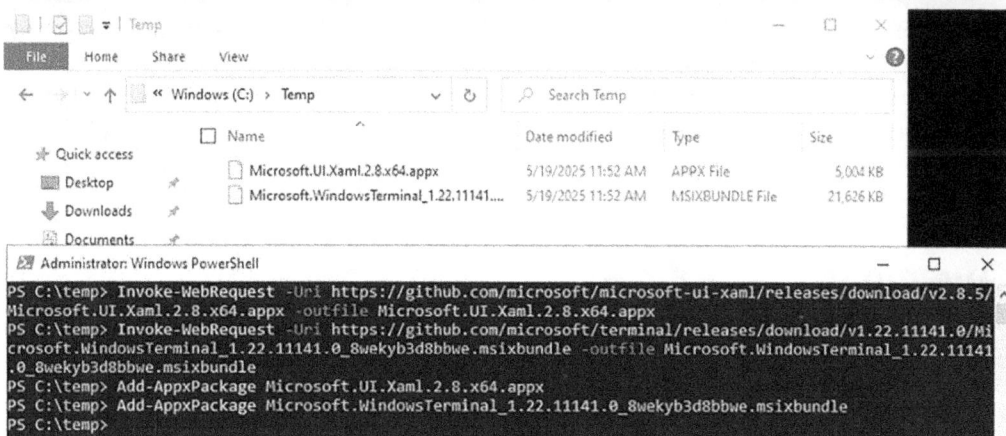

Figure 12.43: Downloading and installing application packages

And just like that, Windows Terminal is installed on this server. Click on the **Start** button and check near the top, and you should see **Terminal** listed as a recently added application!

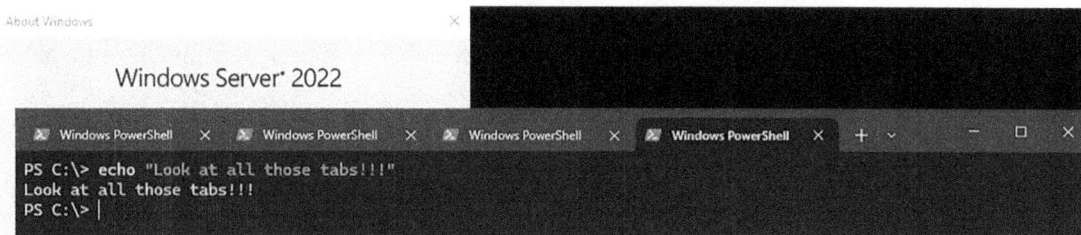

Figure 12.44: Windows Terminal running on Windows Server 2022

Summary

In this chapter, we found that Windows Server 2025 can be completely administered with PowerShell. In fact, whether utilizing the newer Windows Terminal or "old blue" (the original PowerShell prompt), you can completely manage many versions of Windows Server via the CLI. Since management GUIs are now just shells running PowerShell scripts and the default installation option for Windows Server is Server Core, we can assume that headless, command-line-oriented servers are expected to be our servers of the future. Even though PowerShell has been at the core of our operating system functionality since Windows Server 2012, I believe that, so far, PowerShell is still viewed by many admins as simply an alternative way of managing servers. "Yeah, I know it exists and that I should start using it, and the scripting looks pretty cool, but I can still do anything I want to with the old Command Prompt or my mouse button." That old mentality should be quickly changing; the only thing that is stopping you from using it is you!

Now that we are experiencing an onset of new technologies, such as DSC and open source PowerShell 7.x, we can see that PowerShell is starting to develop functionality that simply does not exist anywhere else in the operating system. This, combined with the remote management accessibility provided by the standardized PowerShell platform that can be used across all of your current Windows devices (even against servers sitting inside Azure!), means that we will definitely be seeing more and more PowerShell in subsequent Microsoft operating systems and services.

Questions

Put your knowledge to the test with the following questions. If you need a hand (or just want to double-check), you'll find all the answers in the *Appendix* section of the book.

1. What is the fastest way to get from Command Prompt to PowerShell?
2. What is the cmdlet that will display all available PowerShell cmdlets?
3. What PowerShell cmdlet can be used to connect your PowerShell prompt to a remote computer?
4. What file extension does a PowerShell scripting file have?
5. To which setting is the Default Execution Policy configured on a fresh Windows Server 2025 instance?
6. What key on your keyboard can be used to auto-populate the remainder of a cmdlet or filename when working in a PowerShell prompt?
7. Which service must be running on a system before it can be connected to by a remote PowerShell connection?
8. Why do you think Windows Terminal is not installed in Windows Server 2022 by default?
9. What command triggers an update for all applications that WinGet is capable of managing?
10. With modules installed, what cmdlet is used to tap PowerShell into Microsoft 365?

13

Redundancy in Windows Server 2025

Multiply that by two. What does redundancy look like? How many can run side-by-side? Let's make sure this never goes offline… These are phrases and questions I hear all the time when planning server deployments. I'm sure you have as well. Any time you are rolling out new technology, you want to plan that rollout very carefully. Figure out what servers you need, where they need to be placed, and how the networking needs to be configured. Once the planning is done, order two of everything, in case one breaks. We live in a world of always-on technology. Services going down is unacceptable, particularly if we are hosting cloud or private cloud services. Any application or service that our users depend on to get their work done is mission-critical and needs 100% uptime, or darn close to it. The problem with redundancy is that it's much easier to talk the talk than to walk the walk. Maybe one day we will be blessed with a magic **Press here to make this server redundant** button—some DevOps and container functions are getting close—but today is not that day for us infrastructure nerds. We need to understand the technologies that are available to us that enable us to provide redundancy in our systems. This chapter will introduce us to some of those technologies. This book is focused on Server 2025 used on-premises, so the technologies we cover are ones that you can utilize in your local datacenters on real (physical or virtual) servers that you are responsible for building, configuring, and maintaining. Yes, the cloud can provide us with some magical scalability and redundancy options, but those are easy, and often, we don't even need to understand how they work. When we use our servers within our own walls, how can we add some increased reliability to our systems?

We will cover the following topics in this chapter:

- Network Load Balancing
- Configuring a load-balanced website
- Failover clustering
- Clustering tiers
- Setting up a failover cluster
- Clustering improvements in Windows Server

- Storage Replica
- Storage Spaces Direct

Network Load Balancing

Often, when I hear people discussing redundancy on their servers, the conversation includes many instances of the word *cluster*, such as, *"If we set up a cluster to provide redundancy for those servers..."* or *"Our main website is running on a cluster..."* or *"This situation is a real cluster..."* (oh wait, that is something else entirely). While it is great that there is some form of resiliency being used on the systems to which these conversations pertain, it is often the case that *clustering* is not actually involved anywhere. When we boil down the particulars of how their systems are configured, we discover that it is some form of **network load balancing (NLB)** doing this work for them. We will discuss real clustering further along in this chapter, but first, I wanted to start with the more common approach to making many services redundant. NLB distributes traffic at the TCP/IP level, meaning that the server operating systems themselves are not completely aware of or rely on each other, with redundancy instead being provided at the network layer. This can be particularly confusing—NLB versus clustering—because sometimes Microsoft refers to something as a cluster when, in fact, it is using NLB to make those connections happen. Prime examples are the Microsoft remote access technologies. When you have two or more remote access servers together in an array, there are Microsoft documents and even places inside the console where it is referred to as a cluster. But there is no failover clustering going on here; the technology under the hood that is making connections flow to both nodes is actually Windows NLB.

You've probably heard some of the names in the hardware load balancer market—F5, Cisco, Kemp, Barracuda, and many more. These companies provide dedicated hardware or virtual appliances that can take traffic headed toward a particular name or destination and split that traffic between two or more application servers. While this is generally the most robust way that you can establish NLB, it is also the most expensive and makes the overall environment more complex. One feature these guys offer that the built-in Windows NLB cannot provide is SSL termination, or SSL offloading, as we often call it.

These specialized appliances are capable of receiving SSL website traffic from user computers and decrypting the packets before sending them on their way to the appropriate web server. This way, the web server itself is doing less work, since it doesn't have to spend CPU cycles encrypting and decrypting packets. It's important for you to know that hardware load balancer solutions exist, but today, we are not going to talk about hardware load balancers at all, but rather the NLB capabilities that are provided right inside Windows Server 2025.

Now that we just teed up a relevant summary of what NLB is and does, I'm afraid I have to tell you another Microsoft-induced disclaimer at this point. Windows NLB is officially stamped as "deprecated" with the release of Windows Server 2025. Please don't misunderstand; NLB is alive and well inside Server 2025, and as such, we are still going to discuss it here. But as we already discussed, a technology being deprecated means that Microsoft doesn't have plans to make it better (to be honest, it hasn't changed in the last 10 years anyway), and at some point in a future release, it might disappear from the Windows Server operating system. *Might* is the keyword here; we don't know if or when that will happen, and until that day, NLB continues to be a valid network traffic distribution tool.

If NLB eventually disappears, what is Microsoft's answer to load balancing? We will discuss failover clustering shortly, which is one answer to the question that fits some scenarios. Alternatively, Microsoft expects there to be more emphasis on **Software Load Balancing (SLB)** for **software-defined networking (SDN)** in the future. What is quite interesting is that SLB for SDN utilizes very similar structure and traffic paths that NLB has always used. SLB continues to make use of **Virtual IP Addresses (VIPs)** and **Dedicated IP Addresses (DIPs)**, which we will talk about in just a few pages. By deploying SDN inside your environment and using it to configure SLB, you will find yourself with the ability to distribute traffic among virtual network resources in your environment. Multiple servers can host the same workloads (websites, etc.), and SLB will handle the distribution of traffic between them. This, in a nutshell, is exactly what NLB does today. A core difference is that SLB involves many SDN components, such as a dedicated network controller. NLB, on the other hand, is configured completely from the servers hosting those workloads, more like the ideology of failover DHCP servers.

Let's continue forward with our discussion on NLB, as it is still a relevant technology that you can make use of immediately in your own environments.

Not the same as round-robin DNS

I have discovered over the years that some people's idea of NLB is really round-robin DNS. Let me give an example of that: say you have an intranet website that all your users access daily. It makes sense that you would want to provide some redundancy to this system, and so you set up two web servers in case one goes down. However, in the case that one does go down, you don't want to require manual cutover steps to fail over to the extra server; you want it to happen automatically. In DNS, it is possible to create two host A records that have the same name but point to different IP addresses. If Server01 is running on 10.10.10.5 and Server02 is running on 10.10.10.6, you could create two DNS records, both called INTRANET, pointing one host record at 10.10.10.5 and the other host record at 10.10.10.6. This would provide round-robin DNS, but not any real load balancing. Essentially, what happens here is that when the client computers reach out to INTRANET, DNS will hand them one or the other IP address to connect.

The problem with this scenario is that DNS doesn't care whether the website is actually running; it simply responds with an IP address. So even though you might set this up and it appears to be working flawlessly because you can see that clients are connecting to both Server01 and Server02, be fore-warned. In the event of a server failure, you will have many clients who still work, and many clients who are suddenly getting **Page cannot be displayed** when DNS decides to send them to the IP address of the server that is now offline.

NLB is much more intelligent than this. When a node in an NLB array goes down, traffic moving to the shared IP address will only be directed to the node that is still online. We'll get to see this for ourselves shortly when we set up NLB on an intranet website of our own.

What roles can use NLB?

NLB is primarily designed for *stateless* applications, in other words, applications that do not require a long-term memory state or connection status. In a stateless application, each request made from the application could be picked up by Server01 for a while, then swing over to Server02 without inter-rupting the application. Some applications handle this very well (such as websites), and some do not.

Web services (IIS) benefit the most from the redundancy provided by NLB. NLB is easy to configure and provides full redundancy for websites that you have running on your Windows Servers, without incurring any additional cost. NLB can additionally be used to enhance FTP, firewall, and proxy servers.

Another role that commonly interacts with NLB is the remote access role. Specifically, DirectAccess can use the built-in Windows NLB to provide your remote access environment with redundant entry-point servers. When setting up DirectAccess to make use of load balancing, it is not immediately obvious that you are using the NLB feature built into the operating system because you configure the load-balancing settings from inside the **Remote Access Management** console, rather than the NLB console. When you walk through the **Remote Access Management** wizards to establish load balancing, that remote access console is reaching into the NLB mechanism within the operating system and configuring it, so that its algorithms and transport mechanisms are the pieces being used by DirectAccess in order to split traffic between multiple servers.

One of the best parts about using NLB is that you can make changes to the environment without affecting the existing nodes. *Want to add a new server to an existing NLB array?* No problem. Slide it in without any downtime. *Need to remove a server for maintenance?* No issues here either. NLB can be stopped on a particular node, allowing another node in the array to pick up the slack. In fact, NLB is NIC-particular, so you can run different NLB modes on different NICs within the same server. You can tell NLB to stop on a particular NIC, removing that server from the array for the time being. Even better, if you have a little bit of time before you need to take the server offline, you can issue a `drainstop` command instead of an immediate stop. This allows the existing network sessions that are currently live on that server to finish cleanly. No new sessions will flow to the NIC that you have drain-stopped, and old sessions will evaporate naturally over time. Once all sessions have been dropped from that server, you can then yank it and bring it down for maintenance with zero user interruption.

Virtual and dedicated IP addresses

It is important to understand how NLB utilizes IP addresses on your servers. First of all, any NIC on a server that is going to be part of a load-balanced array must have a static IP address assigned to it. NLB does not work with DHCP addressing. In the NLB world, a static IP address on a NIC is referred to as a **Dedicated IP Address (DIP)**. These DIPs are unique per NIC, obviously meaning that each server has its own DIP. For example, in my environment, WEB1 is running a DIP address of 10.10.10.40, and my WEB2 server is running a DIP of 10.10.10.41.

Each server hosts the same website on its own respective DIP addresses. It's important to understand that when establishing NLB between these two servers, I need to retain the individual DIPs on the boxes, but I will also be creating a new IP address that will be shared between the two servers. This shared IP is called the **Virtual IP Address (VIP)**. When we walk through the NLB setup shortly, I will be using the IP address 10.10.10.42 as my VIP, which is so far unused in my network. Here is a quick layout of the IP addresses that are going to be used when setting up my network load-balanced website:

```
WEB1 DIP = 10.10.10.40
WEB2 DIP = 10.10.10.41
Shared VIP = 10.10.10.42
```

When establishing my DNS record for `intranet.contoso.local`, which is the name of my website, I will be creating a single host A record, and it will point to my `10.10.10.42` VIP.

NLB modes

Shortly, we will find ourselves in the actual configuration of our load balancing and will have a few decisions to make within that interface. One of the big decisions is what NLB mode we want to use. Unicast is chosen by default and is the way that I see most companies set up their NLB, perhaps because it is the default option and they've never thought about changing it. Let's take a minute to discuss each of the available options, to make sure you can choose the one that is most appropriate for your networking needs.

Unicast

Here, we start to get into the heart of how NLB distributes packets among the different hosts. Since we don't have a physical load balancer that is receiving the traffic first and then deciding where to send it, how do the load-balanced servers decide who gets to take which packet streams?

To answer that question, we need to back up a little bit and discuss how traffic flows inside your network. When you open a web browser on your computer and visit `HTTP://WEB1`, DNS resolves that name to an IP address, such as `10.10.10.40`. When the traffic hits your switches and needs to be directed somewhere, the switches need to decide where `10.10.10.40` traffic needs to go. Remembering back to our chapter on networking, we then dive into the MAC address layer.

Each NIC has a MAC address, and when you assign an IP address to a NIC, it registers its own MAC address and IP with the networking equipment. These MAC addresses are stored inside an ARP table, which is a table that resides inside most switches, routers, and firewalls.

When my `WEB1` server was assigned the `10.10.10.40` IP address, it registered its MAC address corresponding to `10.10.10.40`. When traffic needs to flow to `WEB1`, the switches realize that traffic destined for `10.10.10.40` needs to go to that specific NIC's MAC address and shoot it off accordingly.

In the NLB world, when you are sending traffic to a single IP address that is split between multiple NICs, how does that get processed at the MAC level? The answer with unicast NLB is that the physical NIC's MAC address gets replaced with a virtual MAC address, and this MAC is assigned to all of the NICs within the NLB array. This causes packets flowing to that MAC address to be delivered to all of the NICs, and therefore all of the servers, in that array. If you think that sounds like a lot of unnecessary network traffic is moving around the switches, you would be correct. Unicast NLB means that when packets are destined for the virtual MAC address of an array, that traffic is basically bounced through all ports on the switch (or at least on the VLAN) before finding and landing on their destinations.

The best part about unicast is that it works without having to make any special configurations on the switches or networking equipment in most cases. You set up the NLB configuration from inside the Windows Server tools, and it handles the rest. A downside to unicast is that, because the same MAC address exists on all NLB server nodes, it causes some intra-node communication problems. In other words, the servers that are enabled for NLB will have trouble communicating with each other's IP addresses. Often, this doesn't really matter because `WEB1` would rarely have reason to communicate directly with WEB2. But if you really need those web servers to be able to talk with each other consistently and reliably, the easiest solution is to install a separate NIC on each of those servers and use that NIC for those intra-array communications, while leaving the primary NICs configured for NLB traffic.

The other downside to unicast is that it can create some switch flooding. The switches are unable to learn a permanent route for the virtual MAC address because we need it to be delivered to all of the nodes in our array. Since every packet moving to the virtual MAC is being sent down all avenues of a switch so that it can hit all of the NICs where it needs to be delivered, it has the potential to overwhelm the switches with this flood of network packets. If you are concerned about that or are getting complaints from your networking people about switch flooding, you might want to check out one of the multicast modes for your NLB cluster.

An alternative method for controlling unicast switch flooding is to get creative with VLANs on your switches. If you plan an NLB server array and want to ensure that the switch traffic being generated by this array will not affect other systems in your network, you could certainly create a small VLAN on your switches and plug only your NLB-enabled NICs into that VLAN. This way, when the planned flood happens, it only hits that small number of ports inside your VLAN, rather than segmenting its way across the entire switch.

Multicast

Choosing multicast as your NLB mode comes with some upsides and some headaches. The positive is that it adds an extra MAC address to each NIC. Every NLB member then has two MAC addresses: the original and the one created by the NLB mechanism. This gives the switches and networking equipment an easier job of learning the routes and sending traffic to its correct destinations, without an overwhelming packet flood. To do this, you need to tell the switches which MAC addresses need to receive this NLB traffic; otherwise, you will cause switch flooding, just like with unicast.

Telling the switches which MACs need to be contacted is done by logging in to your switches and creating some static ARP entries to accommodate this. For any company with a dedicated networking professional, usually proficient in Cisco equipment, this will be no sweat. If you are not familiar with modifying ARP tables and adding static routes, it can be a bit of a nuisance to get it right. In the end, multicast is generally better than unicast, but it can be more of an administrative headache. My personal preference still tends to be unicast, especially in smaller businesses. I have seen it used in many different networks without any issues, and going with unicast means we can leave the switch programming alone.

Multicast IGMP

Better yet, but not always an option, is multicast with **Internet Group Management Protocol (IGMP)**. Multicast IGMP really helps to mitigate switch flooding, but it only works if your switches support IGMP snooping. This means that the switch has the capability to look inside multicast packets to determine where exactly they should go. So, where unicast creates some amount of switch flooding by design, multicast can help to lower that amount, and IGMP can get rid of it completely.

The NLB mode that you choose will depend quite a bit on the capabilities of your networking equipment. If your servers have only a single NIC, try to use multicast, or you will have intra-array problems. On the other hand, if your switches and routers don't support multicast, you don't have a choice—unicast will be your only option for configuring Windows NLB.

Configuring a load-balanced website

Enough talk; it's time to set this up for ourselves and give it a try. I have two web servers running on my lab network, WEB1 and WEB2. They both use IIS to host an intranet website. My goal is to provide my users with a single DNS record for them to access, but have all of that traffic split between the two servers with some real load balancing. Follow along as we set up this scenario.

Enabling NLB

First things first, we need to make sure that WEB1 and WEB2 are prepared to do NLB because it is not installed by default. NLB is a feature available in Windows Server 2025, and you add it just like any other role or feature, by running through the **Add Roles and Features** wizard. Add this feature to all the servers that you want to be part of the NLB array:

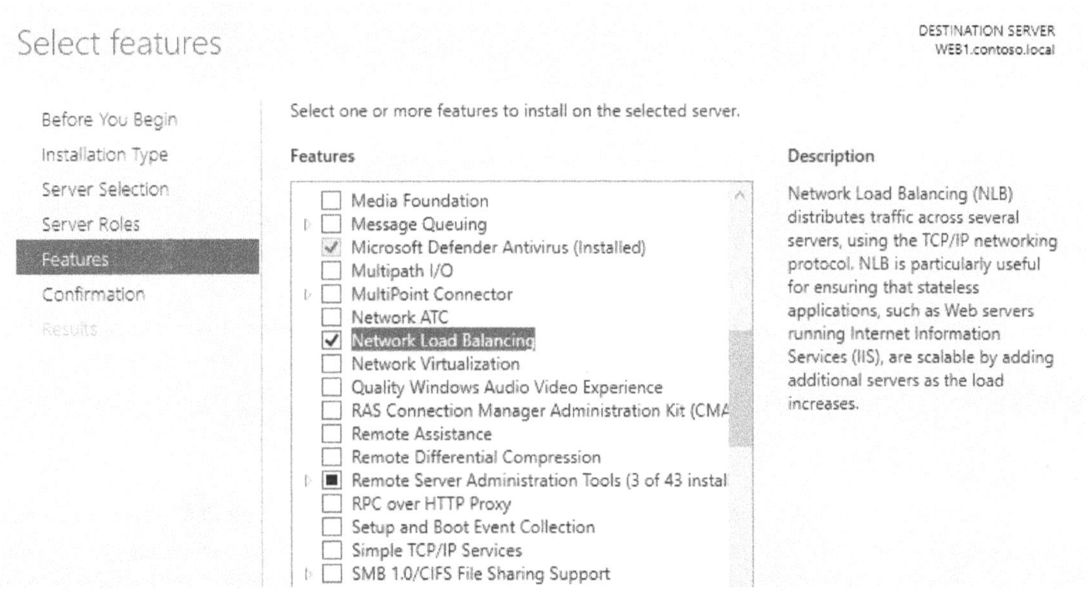

Figure 13.1: Adding NLB to your servers

Enabling MAC address spoofing on VMs

Remember when we talked about unicast NLB and how the physical MAC address of the NIC gets replaced with a virtual MAC address that is used for NLB array communications? Yeah, VMs don't like that. If you are load balancing physical servers with physical NICs, you can skip this section. But many of you will be running web servers that are VMs. Whether they are hosted with Hyper-V, VMware, or some other virtualization technology, there is an extra option in the configuration of the VM that you will have to choose so that your VM will happily comply with this MAC addressing change.

The name of this setting will be something along the lines of **Enable MAC address spoofing**, though the specific name of the function could be different depending on what virtualization technology you use. The setting should be a simple checkbox that you have to enable in order to make MAC spoofing work properly. Make sure to do this for *all* of your virtual NICs upon which you plan to utilize NLB. Keep in mind, this is a per-NIC setting, not a per-VM setting. If you have multiple NICs on a VM, you may have to check the box for each NIC if you plan to use them all with load balancing.

Depending on how old your hypervisor is, the VM may need to be shut down to make this change. Other than that potential gotcha, all we need to do is find the checkbox and enable it. Since everything that I use is based on Microsoft technology, I am, of course, using Hyper-V as the platform for my VMs here in the lab. Within Hyper-V, if I right-click on my WEB1 server and head into the VM's settings, I can then click on my network adapter to see the various pieces that are changeable on WEB1's virtual NIC. In the latest versions of Hyper-V, this setting is listed underneath the NIC properties, inside the section titled **Advanced Features**. And there it is, my **Enable MAC address spoofing** checkbox. Simply click on that to enable it, and you're all set:

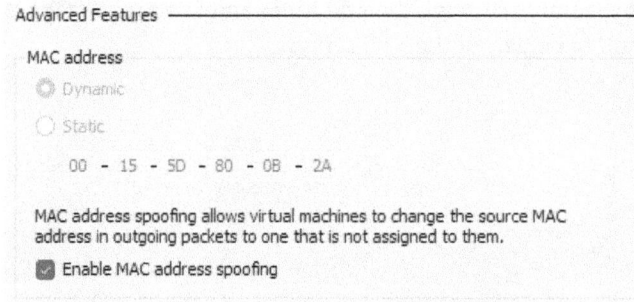

Figure 13.2: Enabling MAC address spoofing

If **Enable MAC address spoofing** is grayed out, remember that the VM may need to be completely shut down before the option appears. Shut it down, then open **Settings** and take another look. The option should now be available to select.

Configuring NLB

Let's summarize where we are at this point. I have two web servers, WEB1 and WEB2, and they each currently have a single IP address. Each server has IIS installed, which is hosting a single website. I have enabled MAC address spoofing on each (because these servers are VMs), and I just finished installing the NLB feature on each web server. We now have all of the parts and pieces in place to be able to configure NLB and get that web traffic split between both servers.

I will be working from WEB1 for the initial configuration of NLB. Log in to this, and you will see that we have a new tool in the list of tools that are available inside **Server Manager**, called **Network Load Balancing Manager**. Go ahead and open that console. Once you have NLB Manager open, right-click on **Network Load Balancing Clusters** and choose **New Cluster**, as shown in *Figure 13.3*:

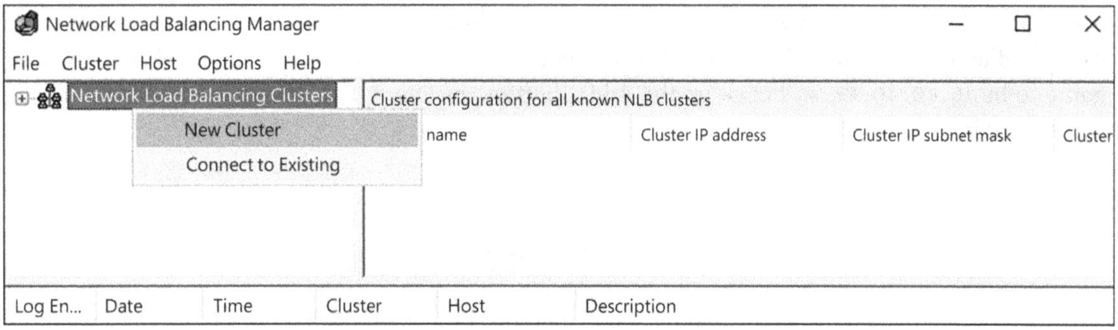

Figure 13.3: Creating a new NLB cluster

When you create a new cluster, it is important to note that, currently, there are zero machines in this cluster. Even the server where we are running this console is not automatically added to the cluster, and we must remember to manually place it into this screen. First, I am going to type in the name of my WEB1 server and click on **Connect**. After doing that, the NLB Manager will query WEB1 for NICs and will give me a list of available NICs upon which I could potentially set up NLB:

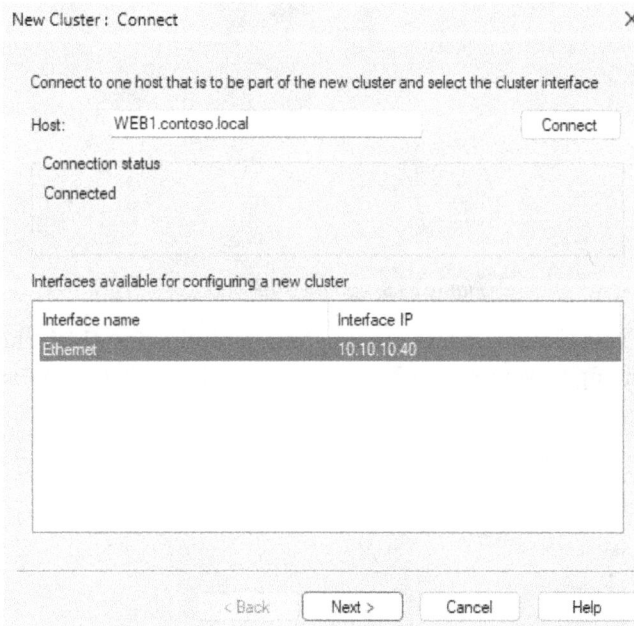

Figure 13.4: Choosing a NIC to establish NLB

Since I only have one NIC on this server, I simply leave it selected and click **Next**. The following screenshot gives you the opportunity to input additional IP addresses on WEB1, but since we are only running one IP address, I will leave this screen as-is and click **Next** again.

Now, we have moved on to a window asking us to input cluster IP addresses. These are the VIPs that we intend to use to communicate with this NLB cluster. As stated earlier, my VIP for this website is going to be `10.10.10.42`, so I click on the **Add...** button and input that IPv4 address along with its corresponding subnet mask:

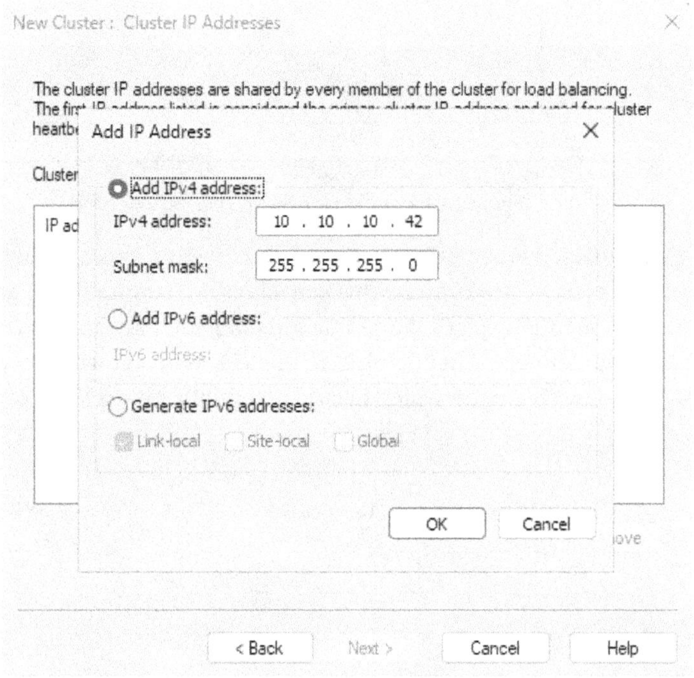

Figure 13.5: Adding a VIP address

One more click of the **Next** button, and we can now see our option for which cluster operation mode we want to run. Depending on your network configuration, choose between **Unicast**, **Multicast**, and **IGMP multicast**:

Figure 13.6: Choosing a cluster operation mode

The following screenshot of our NLB wizard allows you to configure port rules. By default, there is a single rule that tells NLB to load balance any traffic coming in on any port, but you can change this if you want. I don't see a lot of people in the field specifying rules here to distribute specific ports to specific destinations, but one neat feature in this screenshot is the ability to disable certain ranges of ports.

That function could be very useful if you want to block unnecessary traffic at the NLB layer. For example, *Figure 13.7* shows a configuration that would block ports 81 and higher from being passed through the NLB mechanism:

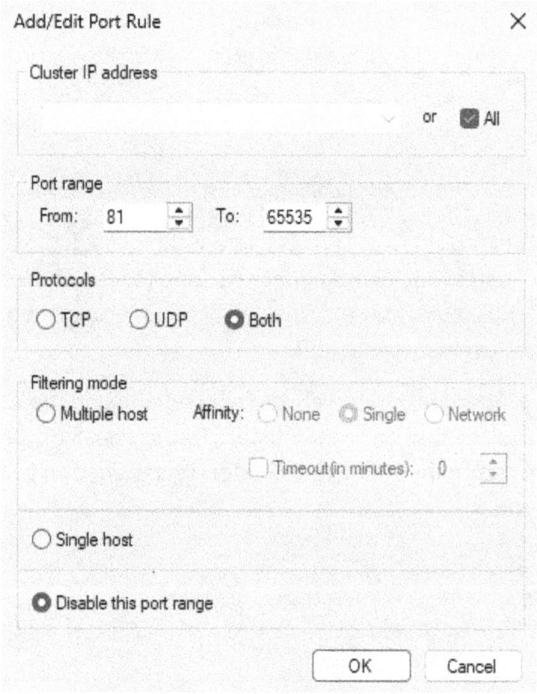

Figure 13.7: Blocking specific traffic

Finish that wizard, and you have now created an NLB cluster! However, at this point, we have only specified information about the VIP and about the WEB1 server. We have not established anything about WEB2. We are running an NLB array, but currently, that array has just a single node inside of it, so traffic to the array is all landing on WEB1. Right-click on the new cluster and select **Add Host To Cluster:**

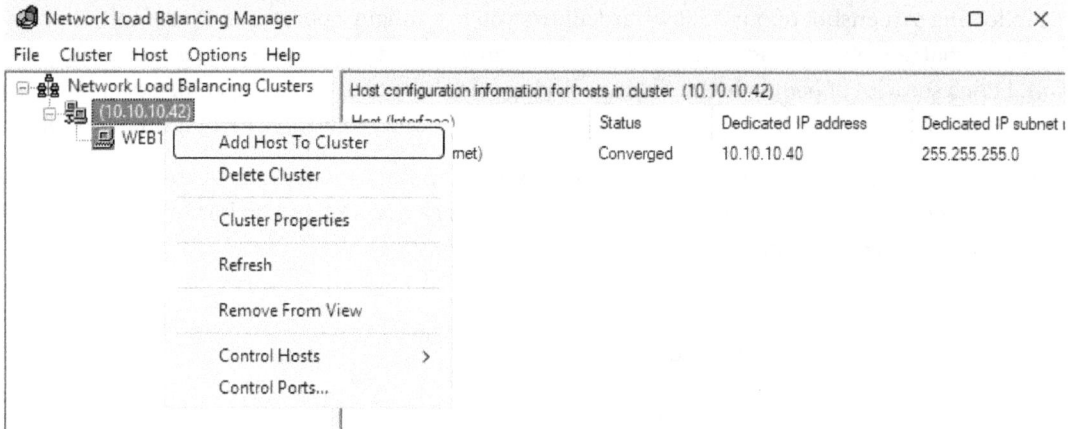

Figure 13.8: Adding another host to the new cluster

Input the name of our WEB2 server, click on **Connect,** and walk through the wizard to add the secondary NLB node of WEB2 into the cluster. Once both nodes are added to the cluster, our NLB array, or cluster, is online and ready to use. (See, I told you that the word *cluster* is used in a lot of places, even though this is not talking about a failover cluster at all!)

If you look inside the NIC properties of our web servers and click on the **Advanced** button inside the TCP/IPv4 properties, you can see that our new cluster IP address of 10.10.10.42 has been added to the NICs. Each NIC will now contain both the DIP address assigned to it, as well as the VIP address shared in the array:

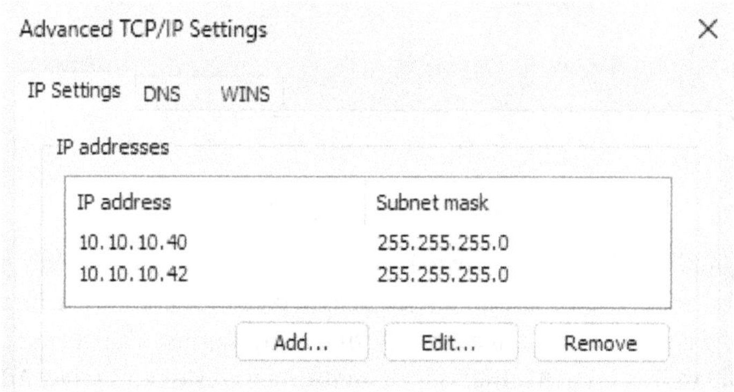

Figure 13.9: NLB has updated IP addresses on the NIC

The traffic that is destined for the 10.10.10.42 IP address is now starting to be split between the two nodes, but right now, the websites that are running on the WEB1 and WEB2 servers are configured to only be running on the dedicated 10.10.10.40 and 10.10.10.41 IP addresses, so we need to make sure to adjust that next.

Configuring IIS and DNS

Just a quick step within IIS on each of our web servers should get the website responding on the appropriate VIP address. Now that the NLB configuration has been established and we have confirmed that the new 10.10.10.42 VIP address has been added to our NICs, we can use that IP address as a website binding. Open the IIS management console and expand the **Sites** folder so that you can see the properties of your website. Right-click on the site name, and choose **Edit Bindings...**:

Figure 13.10: Editing website bindings

Once inside **Site Bindings**, choose the binding that you want to manipulate, and click on the **Edit...** button. This intranet website is just a simple HTTP site, so I am going to choose my HTTP binding for this change. The binding is currently set to 10.10.10.40 on WEB1, and 10.10.10.41 on WEB2. This means that the website is only responding to traffic that comes in on these IP addresses. All I have to do is change that **IP address** drop-down menu to the new VIP, which is 10.10.10.42. After making this change (on both servers) and clicking **OK**, the website immediately begins responding to traffic coming in through the 10.10.10.42 IP address:

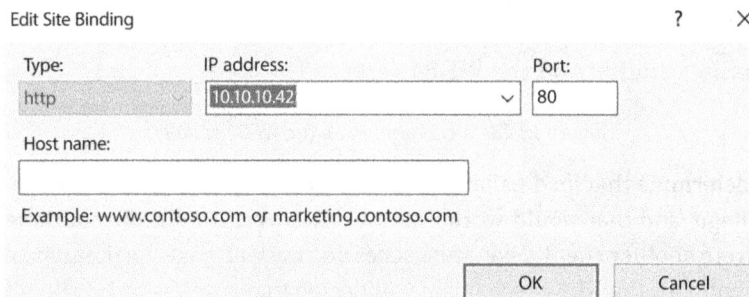

Figure 13.11: Updating your website binding to run on your new VIP

Now, we come to the last piece of the puzzle: DNS. Remember, we want users to have the ability to simply enter `http://intranet` into their web browsers to browse this new NLB website, so we need to configure a DNS host A record accordingly. That process is exactly the same as any other DNS host record; simply create one and point `intranet.contoso.local` to `10.10.10.42`:

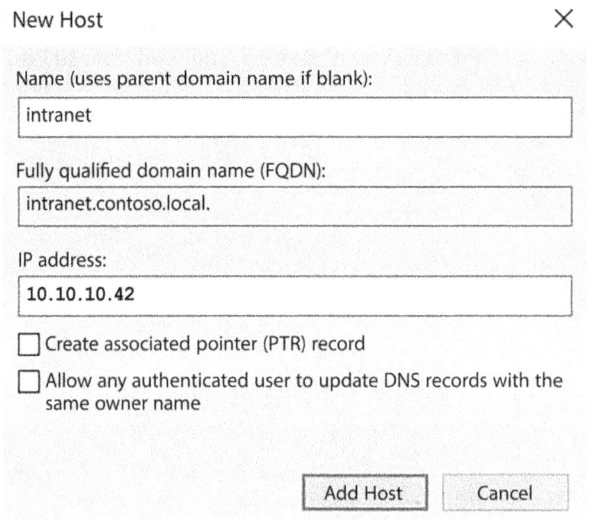

New Host   ✕

Name (uses parent domain name if blank):

intranet

Fully qualified domain name (FQDN):

intranet.contoso.local.

IP address:

10.10.10.42

☐ Create associated pointer (PTR) record

☐ Allow any authenticated user to update DNS records with the
   same owner name

Add Host   Cancel

Figure 13.12: Configuring the DNS record

Testing it out

NLB configured? Check.

IIS bindings updated? Check.

DNS record created? Check.

We are ready to test this thing out. If I open an internet browser on a client computer and browse to `http://intranet`, I can see the website:

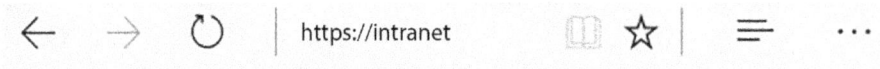

←   →   ↻ | https://intranet   ▢ ☆ | ≡   ...

This is Site1 running on the WEB1 server.

Figure 13.13: Site 1 running on the WEB1 server

But how can we determine that load balancing is really working? I could shut down the WEB1 server, simulating an outage, and that would work fine. Alternatively, if I simply continue refreshing the page, or browse from another client, I continue accessing my web page via the same name of `http://intranet`, and eventually, the NLB mechanism will decide that a new request should be sent over to WEB2, instead of WEB1. When this happens, I am presented with this page instead:

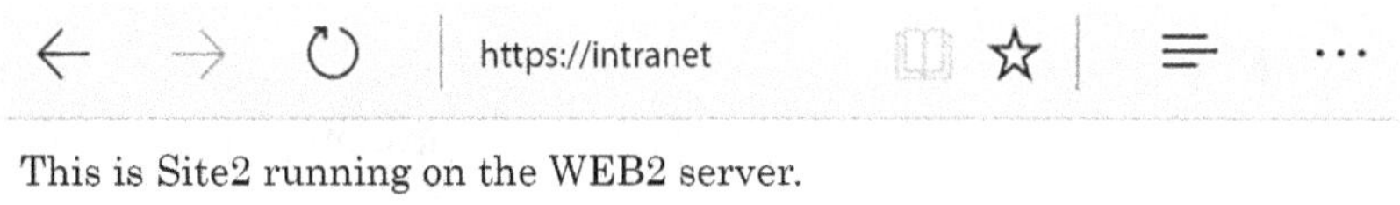

This is Site2 running on the WEB2 server.

Figure 13.14: Site 2 running on the WEB2 server

As you can see, I modified the content between WEB1 and WEB2 so that I could distinguish between the different nodes, just for the purposes of this test. If this were a real production intranet website, I would want to make sure that the content of both sites was exactly the same, so that users were completely unaware of the NLB happening. All they need to know is that the website is going to be available and working all the time.

Flushing the ARP cache

Earlier, we had a little discussion about how switches keep a cache of ARP information, which lessens the time those switches take when deciding where packets should flow. When you assign an IP address to a NIC, the MAC address of that NIC gets associated with the IP address inside the ARP table of certain pieces of networking equipment.

Switches, routers, and firewalls—these tools commonly have what we refer to as an ARP table, and they have a set of data in that table that is known as the ARP cache.

When configuring NLB, particularly unicast, the NIC's physical MAC address gets replaced with a new, virtual MAC address. Sometimes, the switches and networking equipment are very quick to catch on to this change, and they associate the new MAC address with the new IP address, and everything works just fine. However, I find that when configuring NLB, the following is generally true: *The smarter and more expensive your networking equipment is, the dumber it gets when configuring NLB*. What I mean is that your networking equipment might continue to hold onto the old MAC address information that is stored in its ARP table, and doesn't get updated to reflect the new virtual MAC addressing.

What does this look like in real life? Network traffic will stop flowing to or from those NICs. Sometimes, when you establish NLB and it turns itself on, all network traffic will suddenly stop cold to or from those network interfaces. *What do you need to do to fix this situation?* Sometimes you can wait it out, and within a few minutes, hours, or even a few days, the switches will drop the old ARP info and allow the new virtual MACs to register themselves in that table. *What can you do to speed up this process?* Flush the ARP cache.

The procedure for doing this will be different depending on what kind of networking equipment you are working on—whether it is a switch or router, what brand it is, what model it is, and so on. But each of these should have this capability, and it should be named something along the lines of *flushing the ARP cache*. When you run this function on your equipment, it cleans out that ARP table, getting rid of the old information that is causing you problems and allowing the new MAC addresses to register themselves appropriately in the fresh table.

I only wanted to point this out in the event that you configure NLB, only to see traffic flow cease on your server. More than likely, you are dealing with the ARP cache being stuck on one or more pieces of network equipment that are trying to shuttle traffic to and from your server.

Failover clustering

We have established that NLB is a great solution for stateless applications, with a prime example being websites that you want to make highly available. What about other server roles or functions that you want to make redundant? Well, the opposite of *stateless* is *stateful*, so how about giving high availability to stateful pieces of technology?

Failover clustering provides this level of capability and can be used in cases where the nodes within the cluster are accessing shared data. This is a key factor in the way failover clustering is designed. The storage used by the cluster nodes must be shared and accessible by each node that needs it. There are many different roles and services that can take advantage of failover clustering, but there are four specific technologies that seem to make up the majority of clusters running in datacenters today: Hyper-V, file services, Exchange, and SQL. If you are working with any of these technologies – and chances are that you work with all of them – you need to investigate the high-availability capabilities that can be provided for your infrastructure by the use of failover clustering.

While failover clustering provided by Windows Server is Microsoft-built and has the capacity to work very well out of the box with many Microsoft roles and services, it is important to note that you can establish failover clustering for non-Microsoft applications as well.

Third-party applications that run on Windows Server in your environment, or even homegrown applications that have been built in-house, can also take advantage of failover clustering. As long as that application uses shared storage and you can specify the tasks that it needs to be able to perform against those applications for the clustering administration tools – how to start the service, how to stop the service, how to monitor the service health, and so on – you can interface these custom services and applications with failover clustering and provide some major redundancy for just about any type of application.

Clustering Hyper-V hosts

One of the most powerful examples of failover clustering is displayed when combining clustering with Hyper-V. It is possible to build out two or more Hyper-V servers, cluster them together, and give each of them the capability to host all VMs that are stored in that virtual environment. By giving all the Hyper-V host servers access to the same shared storage where the virtual hard disks are stored and configuring failover clustering between the nodes, you can create an incredibly powerful and redundant virtualization solution for your company. When a Hyper-V server goes down, the VMs that were running on that Hyper-V host will fail over to another Hyper-V host server and spin themselves up there instead.

After minimal service interruption while the VMs spin up, everything is back online automatically, without any administrative input. Even better, *how about when you need to patch or otherwise take a Hyper-V host server offline for maintenance?* You can easily force the VMs to run on a different member server in the cluster; they are live-migrated over to that server, so there is zero downtime, and then you are free to remove the node for maintenance and finish working on it before reintroducing it to the cluster. We use VMs and servers for all kinds of workloads, so *wouldn't it be great if you could get rid of any single point of failure within that virtualization environment?* That is exactly what failover clustering can provide.

VM load balancing

In fact, not only is a Hyper-V cluster able to quickly self-recover in the event of a Hyper-V server node going offline, but we now have some smart load-balancing logic working along with these clustered services. If your Hyper-V cluster is becoming overloaded with VMs, it makes sense that you would add another node to that cluster, giving the cluster more capability and computing power. But once the node is added, *how much work is involved in sliding some of the VMs over to this new cluster node?*

None! As long as you have VM load-balancing enabled, the cluster's weights will be evaluated automatically, and VM workloads will be live-migrated, without downtime, on the fly, in order to better distribute the work among all cluster nodes, including the new host server. VM load-balancing can be run and evaluated on demand, whenever you deem fit, or can be configured to run automatically, where clustering services review the environment every 30 minutes, automatically deciding whether any workloads should be moved around.

Clustering for file servers

Clustering for file servers has been available for quite a while; this was one of the original intentions behind the release of failover clustering. Originally, file server clustering was only useful for document and traditional file utilization—in other words, when knowledge worker types of users need to access files and folders daily, and you want those files to be highly available. To this day, this general-purpose file server clustering works in an active-passive scenario. When multiple file servers are clustered together for general-purpose file access, only one of those file server nodes is active and presented to the users at a time. Only in the event of downtime on that node does the role get flipped over to one of the other cluster members.

Scale-Out File Server

While general file server clustering is great for ad hoc access of files and folders, and fits the bill perfectly for most user-initiated file access, it isn't comprehensive enough to handle files that are continuously open or being changed. A prime example of these files is virtual hard disk files used by Hyper-V VMs.

There is a need for virtual hard disk files to be redundant; losing these files would be detrimental to our businesses. Thankfully, hosting application data workloads such as this is exactly what **Scale-Out File Server (SOFS)** does. If you plan to host VMs using Hyper-V, you will want to check out the failover clustering capabilities that are available to use with Hyper-V services. Furthermore, if you intend to use clustered Hyper-V hosts, you should check out SOFS as an infrastructure technology to support that highly available Hyper-V environment.

SOFS helps support failover clustering by providing file servers with the capability to have multiple nodes online (active-active) that remain persistent between each other constantly. This way, if one storage server goes down, the others are immediately available to pick up the slack without a cutover process that involves downtime. This is important when looking at the difference between storing static data, such as documents, and storing virtual hard disk files accessed by VMs. The VMs can stay online during a file server outage with SOFS, which is pretty incredible!

Clustering tiers

An overhead concept to failover clustering that is important to understand is the different tiers at which clustering can benefit you. There are two levels upon which you can use clustering: you can take an either/or approach and use just one of these levels of failover clustering, or you can combine both to really impress your high-availability friends.

Application layer clustering

Clustering at the application level typically involves installing failover clustering onto VMs. Using VMs is not a firm requirement, but it is the most common installation path. You can mix and match VMs with physical servers in a clustering environment, as long as each server meets the installation criteria. This application mode of clustering is useful when you have a particular service or role running within the operating system that you want to make redundant. Think of this as more of a microclustering capability, where you are really digging in and making one specific component of the operating system redundant with another server node that is capable of picking up the slack in the event that your primary server goes down.

Host layer clustering

If application clustering is *micro*, clustering at the host layer is more *macro*. The best example I can give of this is the one that gets most admins started with failover clustering in the first place: Hyper-V. Let's say you have two physical servers, both hosting VMs in your environment. You want to cluster these servers together so that all of the VMs being hosted on these Hyper-V servers can be redundant between the two physical servers. If a whole Hyper-V server goes down, the second one can spin up the VMs that had been running on the primary node. And after a minimal interruption of service, your VMs that are hosting the actual workloads in your environment will be back up and running, available for users and their applications to tap into.

A combination of both

These two modes of using failover clustering mentioned earlier can certainly be combined for an even better and more comprehensive high-availability story. Let's let this example speak for itself: you have two Hyper-V servers, each one prepared to run a series of VMs. You are using host clustering between these servers, so if one physical box goes down, the other picks up the slack. That in itself is great, but you use SQL a lot, and you want to make sure that SQL is also highly available. You can run two VMs, each one a SQL server, and configure application-layer failover clustering between those two VMs for the SQL services specifically. This way, if something happens to a single VM, you don't have to fail over to the backup Hyper-V server; rather, your issue can be resolved by the second SQL node taking over. There is no need for a full-scale Hyper-V takeover by the second physical server, yet you utilize failover clustering to ensure that SQL is always online. This is a prime example of clustering on top of clustering, and by thinking along those lines, you can start to get pretty creative with all of the different ways that you can make use of clustering in your network.

How does failover work?

Once you have configured failover clustering, the multiple nodes remain in constant communication with each other. This way, when one goes down, they are immediately aware and can flip services over to another node to bring them back online. Failover clustering uses the registry to keep track of many per-node settings. These identifiers are kept synced across the nodes, and when one goes down, those necessary settings are blasted around to the other servers, and the next node in the cluster is told to spin up whatever applications, VMs, or workloads were being hosted on the primary box that went offline. There can be a slight delay in services as the components spin up on the new node, but this process is all automated and hands-off, keeping downtime to an absolute minimum.

When you need to cut services from one node to another as a planned event, such as for patching or maintenance, there is an even better story here. Through a process known as **live migration**, you can flip responsibilities over to a secondary node with zero downtime. This way, you can take nodes out of the cluster for maintenance or security patching, or whatever reason, without affecting the users or system uptime in any way. Live migration is particularly useful for Hyper-V clusters, where you will often have the need to manually decide which node your VMs are being hosted on so that you can accomplish work on the other node or nodes.

In many clusters, there is the idea of a **quorum**. This means that if a cluster is split, for example, if a node goes offline or if there are multiple nodes that are suddenly unavailable through a network disconnect of some kind, then quorum logic takes over to determine which segment of the cluster is the one that is still online. If you have a large cluster that spans multiple subnets inside a network, and something happens at the network layer that breaks cluster nodes away from each other, all the two sides of the cluster know is that they can no longer communicate with the other cluster members, and so both sides of the cluster would automatically assume that they should now take responsibility for the cluster workloads.

Quorum settings tell the cluster how many node failures can happen before action is necessary. By the entire cluster knowing the quorum configuration, it can help provide answers to those questions about which section of the cluster is to be primary when the cluster is split. In many cases, clusters provide quorum by relying on a third party, known as a **witness**. As the name implies, this witness watches the status of the cluster and helps to make decisions about when and where failover becomes necessary.

There is a lot more information to be gained and understood if you intend to create clusters large enough for quorum and witness settings. If you're interested in learning more, check out the following link: `https://learn.microsoft.com/en-us/windows-server/storage/storage-spaces/quorum`.

Setting up a failover cluster

We are going to take a few minutes to set up a small cluster of servers so that you can experience the management tools and the places that have to be visited to accomplish this. I already have multiple file servers in this test lab, but they are on deck to be used for Storage Replica configuration later in this chapter. Leaving those alone, I just finished building a couple of new servers, **FS03** and **FS04**. Let's create our first failover cluster and add both servers to that cluster.

Building the servers

We have two servers already running with Windows Server 2025 installed. Nothing special has been configured on these servers, but they do have static IP addresses and are joined to my domain. I have added the **File Server** role to both of them because, eventually, I will utilize these as a cluster of file servers. The key point here is that you should have the servers as identical as possible, with the roles already installed that you intend to make use of within the cluster.

One other note during the building phase: if possible, it is a best practice with clustering that member servers belonging to the same cluster reside within the same **organizational unit** (**OU**) in **Active Directory** (**AD**). The reason for this is twofold: first, it ensures that the same GPOs are being applied to the set of servers, in an effort to make their configurations as identical as possible. Second, during cluster creation, some new objects will be auto-generated and created in AD, and when the member servers reside in the same OU, these new objects will be created in that OU as well. It is very common with a running cluster to see all of the relevant objects in AD be part of the same OU, and for that OU to be dedicated to this cluster:

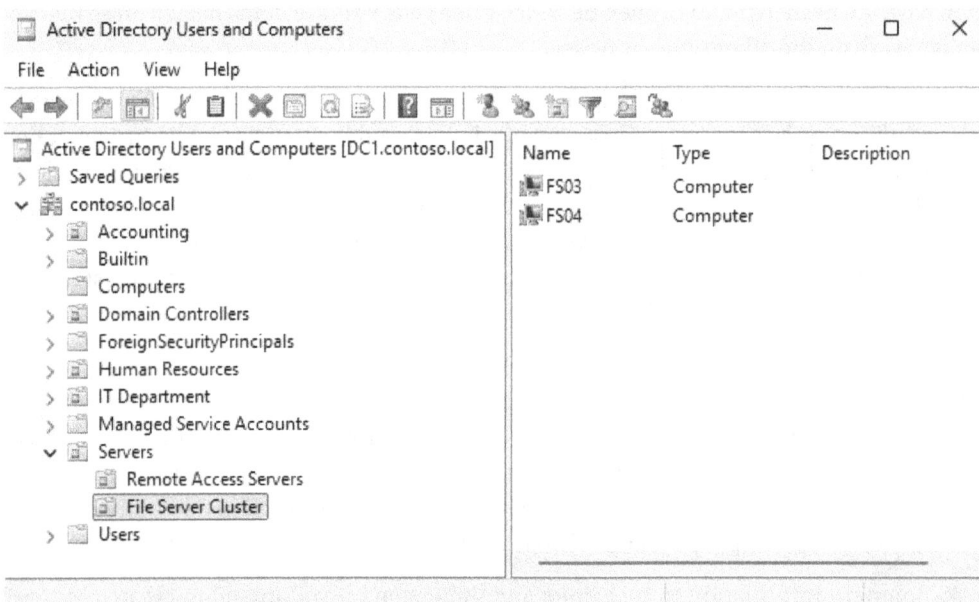

Figure 13.15: Cluster servers should be stored in the same OU

Installing the feature

Now that our servers are online and running, we want to install the clustering capabilities on each of them. **Failover Clustering** is a *feature* inside Windows Server, so open the **Add roles and features** wizard and add it to all of your cluster nodes:

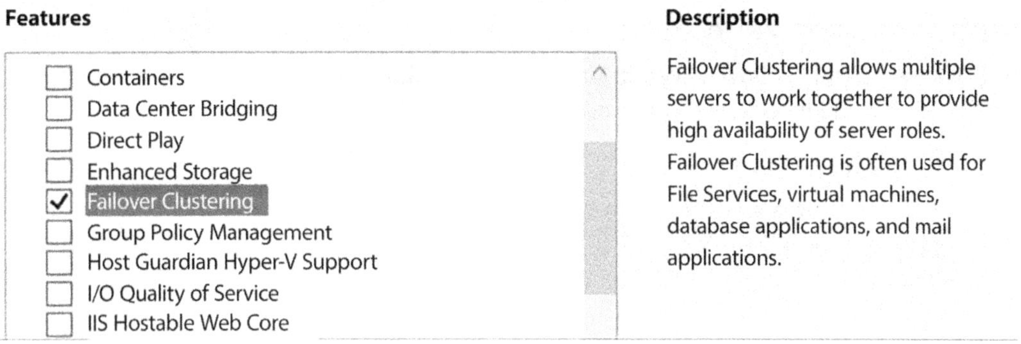

Features	Description
Containers Data Center Bridging Direct Play Enhanced Storage ☑ Failover Clustering Group Policy Management Host Guardian Hyper-V Support I/O Quality of Service IIS Hostable Web Core	Failover Clustering allows multiple servers to work together to provide high availability of server roles. Failover Clustering is often used for File Services, virtual machines, database applications, and mail applications.

Figure 13.16: Adding Failover Clustering to your cluster nodes

Running Failover Cluster Manager

As is the case with most roles or features that can be installed on Windows Server 2025, once implemented, you will find a management console for it inside the **Tools** menu of Server Manager. If I look inside there on FS03 now, I can see that a new listing for **Failover Cluster Manager** is available for me to click on. I am going to open that tool and start working on the configuration of my first cluster from this management interface:

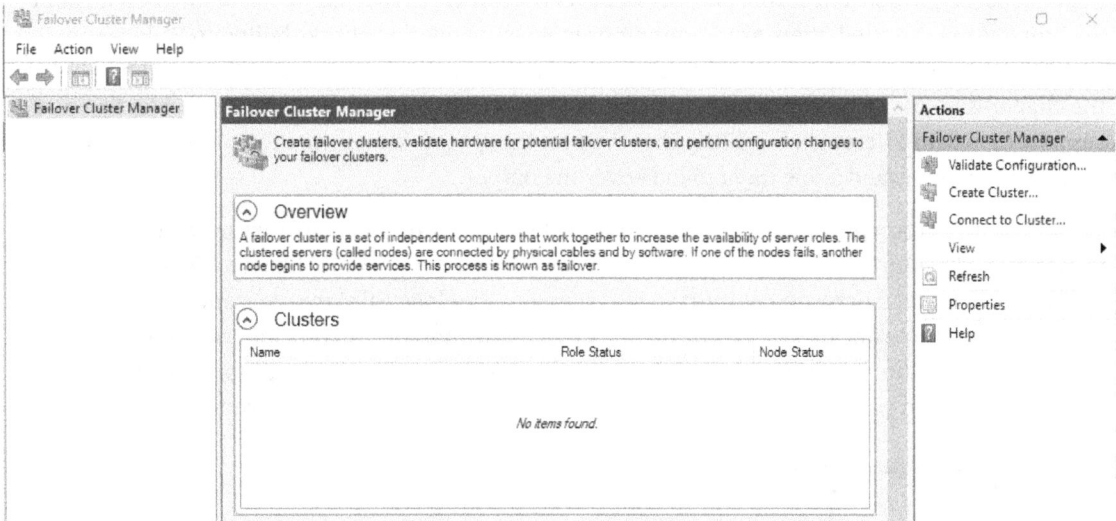

Figure 13.17: Failover Cluster Manager

Running cluster validation

Now that we are inside **Failover Cluster Manager,** you will notice a list of tasks available to launch under the **Management** section of the console, near the middle of your screen:

> (∧) Management
>
> To begin to use failover clustering, first validate your hardware configuration, and then create a cluster. After these steps are complete, you can manage the cluster. Managing a cluster can include copying roles to it from a cluster running Windows Server 2025 or supported previous versions of Windows Server.
>
> Validate Configuration...
>
> Create Cluster...
>
> Connect to Cluster...

Figure 13.18: Cluster configuration tasks

Before we can configure the cluster or add any server nodes to it, we must first validate our hardware configuration. Failover clustering is a complex set of technologies, and there are many places where misconfigurations or inconsistencies could set the whole cluster askew. Your intentions behind setting up a cluster are obviously for reliable redundancy, but even a simple mistake in the configuration of your member servers could cause problems large enough that a node failure would not result in automated recovery, which defeats the purpose of the cluster in the first place. To make sure that all our *t's* are crossed and *i's* dotted, there are some comprehensive validation checks built into Failover Cluster Manager, sort of like a built-in best practices analyzer. These checks can be run at any time—before the cluster is built or after it has been running in production for years. In fact, if you ever do open a support case with Microsoft, it is likely that the first thing they will ask you to do is run the **Validate Configuration** tools and allow them to look over the output.

To start the validation process, click on the **Validate Configuration...** link. We are now launched into a wizard that allows us to select which pieces of cluster technology we would like to validate. Once again, we must put on our Microsoft centralized management theology thinking caps and realize that this wizard doesn't know or care that it is running on one of the member servers that we intend to be part of the cluster. We must identify each of the server nodes that we want to scan for validation checks, so in my case, I am going to tell it that I want to validate the FS03 and FS04 servers:

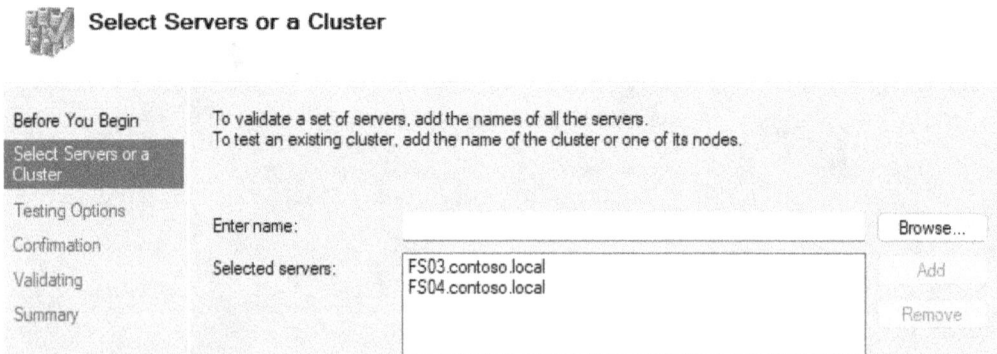

Figure 13.19: Selecting server nodes for cluster validation checks

The **Testing Options** screen allows you to choose the **Run only tests I select** radio button, and you will then be able to run only particular validation tests. Generally, when setting up a new cluster, you want to run *all* of the tests so that you can ensure everything measures up correctly. On a production system, however, you may choose to limit the number of tests that run. This is particularly true with respect to tests against **Storage**, as those can take the cluster offline temporarily while the tests are being run, and you wouldn't want to interfere with your online production services if you are not working within a planned maintenance window:

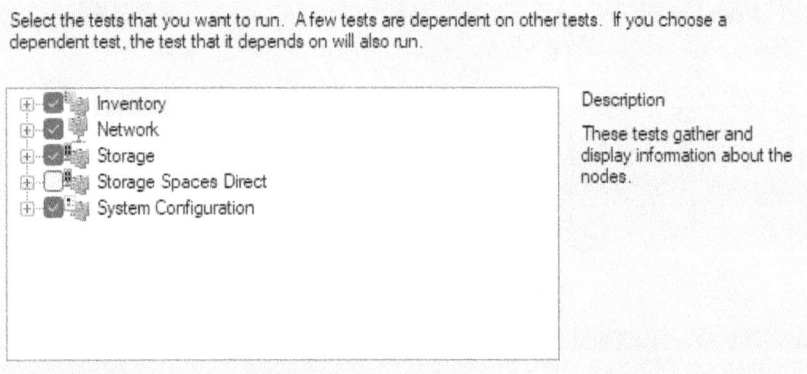

Select the tests that you want to run. A few tests are dependent on other tests. If you choose a dependent test, the test that it depends on will also run.

Inventory	Description
Network	These tests gather and
Storage	display information about the
Storage Spaces Direct	nodes.
System Configuration	

Figure 13.20: You have the option of selecting individual validations

Since I am setting up a new cluster, I am going to let all of the tests run. So, I will leave the recommended option selected, **Run all tests (recommended)**, and continue:

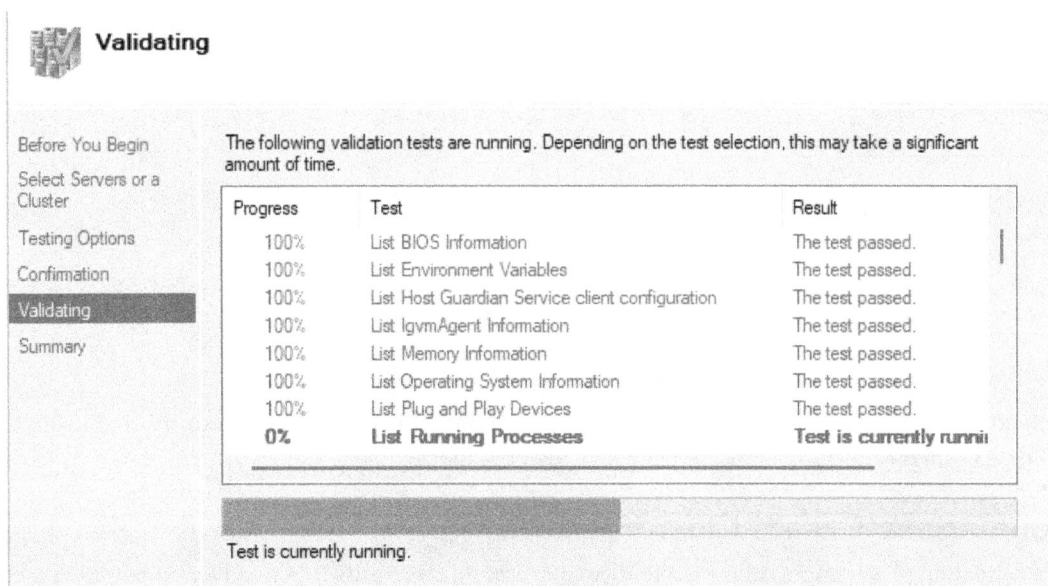

Validating

Before You Begin

Select Servers or a Cluster

Testing Options

Confirmation

Validating

Summary

The following validation tests are running. Depending on the test selection, this may take a significant amount of time.

Progress	Test	Result
100%	List BIOS Information	The test passed.
100%	List Environment Variables	The test passed.
100%	List Host Guardian Service client configuration	The test passed.
100%	List IgvmAgent Information	The test passed.
100%	List Memory Information	The test passed.
100%	List Operating System Information	The test passed.
100%	List Plug and Play Devices	The test passed.
0%	**List Running Processes**	**Test is currently runni**

Test is currently running.

Figure 13.21: Running all tests

Once the tests have completed, you will see a summary output of their results. You can click on the **View Report...** button to see a lot of detail on everything that was run. Keep in mind that there are three tiers of pass/fail. Green is *good* and red is *bad*, but yellow is more like *it'll work, but you're not running best practices*. For example, I only have one NIC in each of my servers; the wizard recognizes that, and for my setup to be truly redundant in all aspects, I should have at least two. It'll let this slide and continue to work, but it is warning me that I could make this cluster even better by adding a second NIC to each of my nodes.

If you ever need to reopen this report or grab a copy of it off the server for safekeeping, it is located on the server where you ran the tests, inside `C:\Windows\Cluster\Reports`:

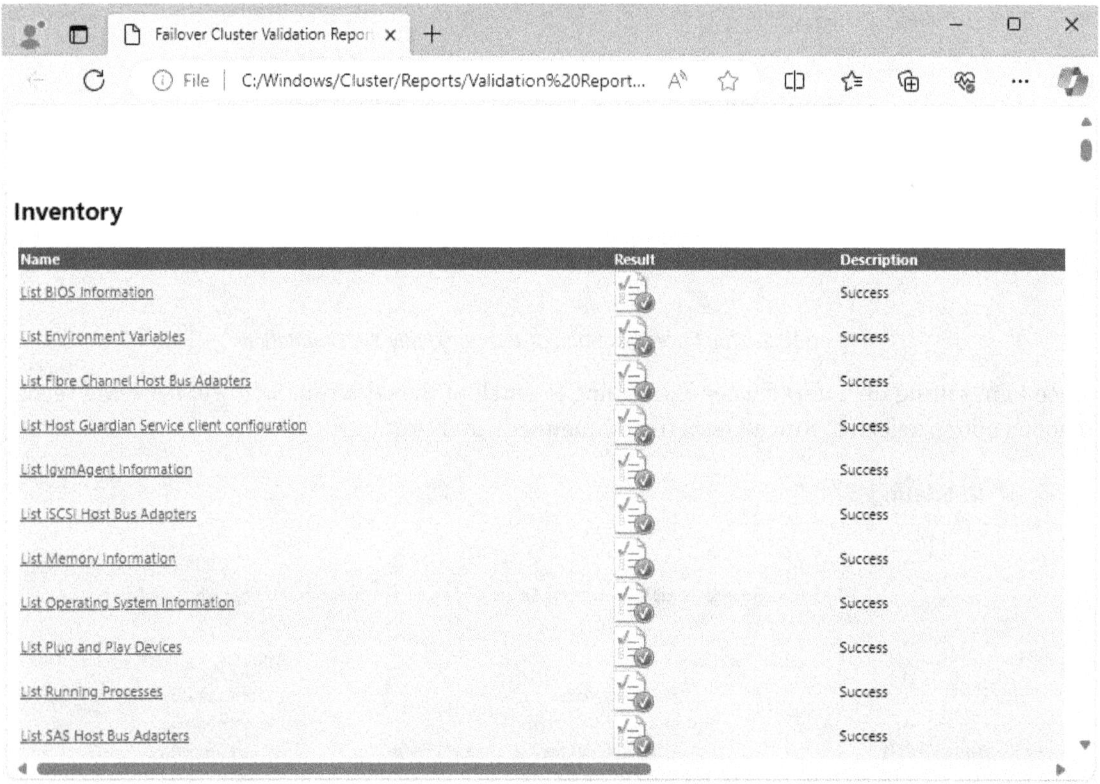

Figure 13.22: Cluster validation report

Remember, you can rerun the validation processes at any time to test your configuration using the **Validate Configuration...** task inside Failover Cluster Manager.

Running the Create Cluster wizard

The validation phase might take a while if you have multiple results that need fixing before you can proceed, but once your validation check comes back clean, you are ready to build out the cluster. For this, click on the next action that we have available in our **Failover Cluster Manager** console: **Create Cluster...**.

Once again, we must first specify which servers we want to be part of this new cluster, so I am going to input my FS03 and FS04 servers. After this, we don't have a whole lot of information to input about setting up the cluster, but one very key piece of information is on the **Access Point for Administering the Cluster** screen. This is where you identify the unique name that will be used by the cluster and shared among the member servers. This is known as a **Cluster Name Object (CNO)**, and after completing your cluster configuration, you will see this name show up as an object inside AD. Also required on this screen is the specification of an IP address in your network that will be used for cluster communications. Similar to the way that I structured DIPs and VIPs in the NLB world, each of my cluster nodes has a static IP address, and here I am specifying a separate, currently unused IP address that this cluster can make use of:

Access Point for Administering the Cluster

Before You Begin	Type the name you want to use when administering the cluster.
Select Servers	
Access Point for Administering the Cluster	Cluster Name: FileCluster
Confirmation	The NetBIOS name is limited to 15 characters. One or more IPv4 addresses could not be configured automatically. For each network to be used, make sure the network is selected, and then type an address.
Creating New Cluster	
Summary	

	Networks	Address
☑	10.10.10.0/24	10.10.10.34

Figure 13.23: Setting a cluster name and IP address

After finishing the wizard, you can see the new cluster inside the **Failover Cluster Manager** interface and can drill down into more particular functions within that cluster. There are additional actions for things such as **Configure Role...**, which will be important for setting up the actual function that this cluster is going to perform, and **Add Node...**, which is your spot to include even more member servers in this cluster down the road:

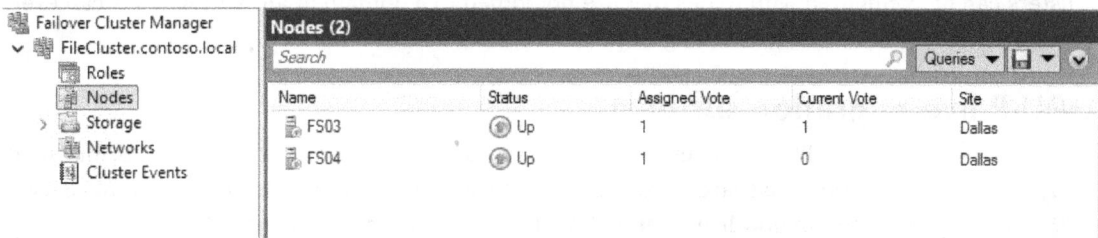

Failover Cluster Manager	**Nodes (2)**				
∨ FileCluster.contoso.local	*Search*				Queries ▼
Roles					
Nodes	Name	Status	Assigned Vote	Current Vote	Site
> Storage	FS03	Up	1	1	Dallas
Networks	FS04	Up	1	0	Dallas
Cluster Events					

Figure 13.24: Viewing nodes in our first cluster

As you have seen, creating a cluster isn't terribly complicated, but it is somewhat of a lengthy process. Every technology that you may want to cluster will come with some flavor of unique requirements as to how exactly the cluster is configured, so make sure to dig into advanced reading within Microsoft's Learn documentation to find the particulars for the role you are working with.

Clustering improvements in Windows Server

The clustering feature has been around for a while, and every new release of Windows Server comes with some improvements and new features, but they often fly under the radar. There were some good changes in 2019, and more followed in 2022. Some of these improvements were wrapped into Server 2022 directly from Azure Stack HCI (now Azure Local), bringing cloud capability into our datacenters. Let's review some of the recent enhancements within Failover Clustering, so you can see the ways that Microsoft continues to be committed to improving our datacenter resiliency.

Cluster rolling OS upgrades

The idea of rolling OS upgrades is not new; in fact, it dates back more than 10 years. However, every new version of the Windows Server operating system makes this process a little bit easier, a little bit more automated. Windows Server 2025 is no exception, making cluster upgrades easier than ever before. The "rolling" part of these upgrades is the secret sauce here. When tasked with upgrading the operating systems of a failover cluster, rolling upgrades is a process that upgrades cluster nodes, for example, from Server 2022 to Server 2025, in sequence. The process will drop one node at a time out of the cluster group, upgrade the operating system on that node, and then reintroduce the node into the cluster. This ultimately enables live upgrades of your failover cluster workloads, moving to a completely new operating system on all cluster nodes, with zero minutes of downtime! In a few pages, you will find some more historical information about rolling cluster OS upgrades, if the backstory on this is interesting to you.

Workgroup cluster live migration

Failover Clustering is a Windows Server technology, and most things in the Windows Server world simply work best, better, or sometimes only work at all if the servers involved are joined to a classic Active Directory domain. While this was originally true of failover clustering, times are changing! Clusters can be configured with nodes that are not joined to a domain at all, and now we can even configure live migration between workgroup-based cluster nodes.

GPU-P live migration support

GPU Paravirtualization (GPU-P) is a new Hyper-V technology, enabling powerful GPUs to be installed in Hyper-V host servers and that card's resources shared among multiple VMs. With Windows Server 2025, failover clustering can now live-migrate VMs that are taking advantage of GPU-P.

AutoSites

Many administrators don't even pay attention to Active Directory Sites and Services because many only have one site to deal with, but even if you have multiple physical sites that include servers, it is often true that most Windows Server technology will work just fine if you leave all of your servers plugged into the default AD site. Failover clustering is one of the roles that can now take advantage of properly configured AD sites. If you configure your physical sites and ensure that your failover cluster nodes are assigned to the proper sites in AD, failover clustering will automatically create site fault domains according to the names of your sites and place failover nodes into the appropriate locations.

Clustering Affinity

Prior to Windows Server 2022, failover clustering had the capability of AntiAffinity rules. AntiAffinity is a way to specify roles (like VMs) within a failover cluster and create rules for these roles to keep them away from each other—for example, if you wanted to ensure that two servers that were part of the same failover cluster remained separated and running on different Hyper-V host servers.

What is new in 2022 is that we can now configure Affinity rules in addition to AntiAffinity rules. Affinity rules work the same way but in reverse. It is a more common-sense approach to grouping roles or nodes together, by specifying that you want certain ones to remain within the same host or site, rather than needing to think backward and decide which ones to keep apart from each other.

Improvements to BitLocker protected cluster storage

You know that failover cluster servers must share the same storage for the cluster to be successful, and you are likely aware that BitLocker is a very common way to encrypt and protect any Windows-based data volume. In prior versions of Windows Server, BitLocker-encrypting a shared cluster storage volume would be risky, as the BitLocker key always needed to be pulled live from Active Directory to allow access to that storage and successfully mount the drive. If a domain controller was not available, it could result in your cluster resource failing to start. As of Server 2022, there is now an additional key protector specific to the cluster itself. During the boot or unlocking of that volume, it will always reach out and *try* to contact Active Directory for the real unlock information. If AD happens to be unavailable, the cluster can still be successfully launched by utilizing a locally stored unlock key to mount the drive.

Slightly older improvements (but still cool)

It's always difficult to decide whether "new releases" that came with a previous version of Windows Server should remain in an updated book, but I believe that understanding anything requires knowing where it came from. Here are some new-ish components of clustering that came to us by way of Windows Server 2019 or earlier, and remain as helpful technology to this day.

Cluster administration via Windows Admin Center

Now that **Windows Admin Center (WAC)** exists, one way to pull good value out of this tool is the configuration of your clusters. As you witnessed in this chapter, the local Failover Cluster Manager is looking a little long in the tooth. You can certainly configure clustering via PowerShell, but for those less in-tune with their CLI side, WAC can be instrumental to getting cluster services established. What's more, you can even configure workgroup-based clustering from inside WAC!

True two-node clusters with USB witnesses

When configuring quorum for a failover cluster, prior to Server 2019, a two-node cluster required three servers, because the witness for quorum needed to reside on a witness share of some kind, usually a separate file server.

Starting in 2019, that witness can now be a simple USB drive, and it doesn't even have to be plugged into a Windows Server! There are many pieces of networking equipment (switches, routers, and so on) that can accept USB-based file storage media, and a USB stick plugged into such a networking device is now sufficient to meet the requirements for a cluster witness. This is a win for enhanced clustering in small environments.

Higher security for clusters

Several security improvements were made to failover clustering in Windows Server 2019. Previous versions relied on **New Technology LAN Manager (NTLM)** for authentication of intra-cluster traffic, but many companies are taking proactive steps to disable the use of NTLM (at least the early versions) within their networks. Failover clustering can now do intra-cluster communication using Kerberos and certificates for validation of that networking traffic, removing the requirement for NTLM.

Another security/stability check that has been implemented when establishing a failover cluster file share witness is the blocking of witnesses stored inside DFS. Creating a witness inside a DFS share has never been supported, but the console previously allowed you to do so, which meant that some companies did exactly this and paid the price for it, as this can cause cluster stability issues. The cluster management tools have been updated to check for the existence of a DFS namespace when creating a witness and will no longer allow it to happen.

Multi-site clustering

Can I configure failover clustering across subnets? In other words, if I have a primary datacenter and I also rent space from a CoLo down the road, or I have another datacenter across the country, are there options for me to set up clustering between nodes that are physically separate? There's a quick, easy answer here: yes, failover clustering doesn't care! Just as easily as if those server nodes were sitting right next to each other, clustering can take advantage of multiple sites that each host their own clustered nodes and move services back and forth across these sites.

Cross-domain or workgroup clustering

Historically, we were only able to establish failover clustering between nodes that were joined to the same domain. Windows Server 2016 brought the ability to move outside of this limitation, and we can even build a cluster without Active Directory being in the mix at all. In Server 2016 and 2019, you can, of course, still create clusters where all nodes are joined to the same domain, and I expect this will be the majority of installations out there. However, if you have servers that are joined to different domains, you can now establish clustering between those nodes. Furthermore, member servers in a cluster can now be members of a workgroup and don't need to be joined to a domain at all.

Migrating cross-domain clusters

Although establishing clusters across multiple domains has been possible for a few years, migrating clusters from one AD domain to another was not an option. Starting with Server 2019, this changed. We have more flexibility in multi-domain clustering, including the ability to migrate clusters between those domains. This capability will help administrators navigate company acquisitions and domain consolidation projects.

Cluster operating system rolling upgrades (a history lesson)

This capability, given to us originally with Windows Server 2016, has a strange name but is a really cool feature. It's something designed to help those who have been using failover clustering for a while be able to improve their environment. If you are running a cluster currently, and that cluster is Windows Server 2012 R2, this is definitely something to look into. Cluster operating system rolling upgrade enables you to upgrade the operating systems of your cluster nodes from Server 2012 R2 to Server 2016, then to Server 2019, and again to Server 2022, and now of course to Server 2025, *all without downtime*. There's no need to stop any of the services on your Hyper-V or SOFS workloads that are using clustering; you simply utilize this rolling upgrade process, and all your cluster nodes will soon be running the newer version of Windows Server. The cluster is still online and active, and nobody knows that it even happened. Except you, of course.

This is vastly different from the previous upgrade process, where, in order to bring your cluster up to Server 2012 R2, you needed to take the cluster offline, introduce new server nodes running 2012 R2, and then re-establish the cluster. There was plenty of downtime and plenty of headaches associated with these upgrades.

The trick that made this seamless upgrade possible is that the cluster itself remains running at the 2012 R2 functional level until you issue a command to flip it over to the Server 2016 functional level. Until you issue that command, clustering runs on the older functional level, even on the new nodes that you introduce, which are running the Server 2016 operating system. As you upgrade your nodes one at a time, the other nodes that are still active in the cluster remain online and continue servicing the users and applications, so all systems are running as normal from a workload perspective. As you introduce new Server 2016 boxes into the cluster, they start servicing workloads like the 2012 R2 servers, doing so at a 2012 R2 functional level. This is referred to as **mixed mode**. This enables you to take down even that very last 2012 R2 box, change it over to 2016, and reintroduce it, all without anybody knowing. Then, once all of the OS upgrades are complete, issue the `Update-ClusterFunctionalLevel` PowerShell command to flip over the functional level, and you have a Windows Server 2016 (or 2019, or whatever) cluster that has been seamlessly upgraded with zero downtime.

Storage Replica

Storage Replica (SR) is a modern way to synchronize data between servers. It is a data-replication technology that provides the ability for block-level data replication between servers, even across different physical sites. SR is a type of redundancy that we had never seen in a Microsoft platform prior to Windows Server 2016; in the past, we had to rely on third-party tools for this kind of capability. SR is also important to discuss on the heels of failover clustering because SR is the secret sauce that enables multi-site failover clustering to happen.

When you want to host cluster nodes in multiple physical locations, you need a way to make sure that the data used by those cluster nodes is synced continuously, so that failover can really be successful. This data flow is provided by SR.

One of the neat data points about SR is that it finally allows a single-vendor solution (that vendor being Microsoft, of course) to provide the end-to-end technology and software for storage and clustering. It is also hardware-agnostic, giving you the ability to utilize your own preference for storage media.

SR is meant to be tightly integrated and one of the supporting technologies of a solid failover clustering environment. In fact, the graphical management interface for SR is located inside the Failover Cluster Manager software—but is, of course, also configurable through PowerShell—so make sure that you look into failover clustering and SR as a *better together* story for your environment.

Originally, SR required the Datacenter edition of Windows Server, which was prohibitive to some implementations. Starting with Server 2019 and continuing to 2022 and 2025, SR is now available inside the Standard edition. Administration of SR is also now available inside the new WAC. Let's put together an SR environment, so you can see how quick and easy it is to create storage redundancy.

Configuring Storage Replica

I already have multiple file servers in my lab, but for SR configuration, I will utilize FS01 and FS02. These servers are joined to my domain, and there are a few important things I have done with them:

1. Attached a new disk to each VM, to be used for data storage. Windows is running on a normal virtual disk on my server, but I added a second one that will be dedicated to storage. The important part here is that the data disk must be initialized with GPT.

2. Created a volume to contain data. This volume in Windows is labeled as the S: drive (I chose a drive letter at random) and, once again, I am making sure that this data volume resides on a GPT-initialized disk.

3. Created a separate volume to contain SR logging data. When creating the SR replication set shortly, we will need to define a location for keeping SR logs, and it is easiest to do so on its own drive letter. I have called mine the L: drive. It also resides on my GPT-initialized data disk. The volume used for logs must be a minimum of 9 GB.

4. Installed the SR feature inside Windows, on both servers.

Initializing disks as GPT

If you're not familiar with the process stated above to initialize your new data disk as GPT, let's cover that for a minute. After attaching a new disk to your server, right-click on the **Start** button and head into **Disk Management**. This tool should automatically recognize the new disk and ask whether you want to initialize it using MBR or GPT. Make sure to select **GPT** here:

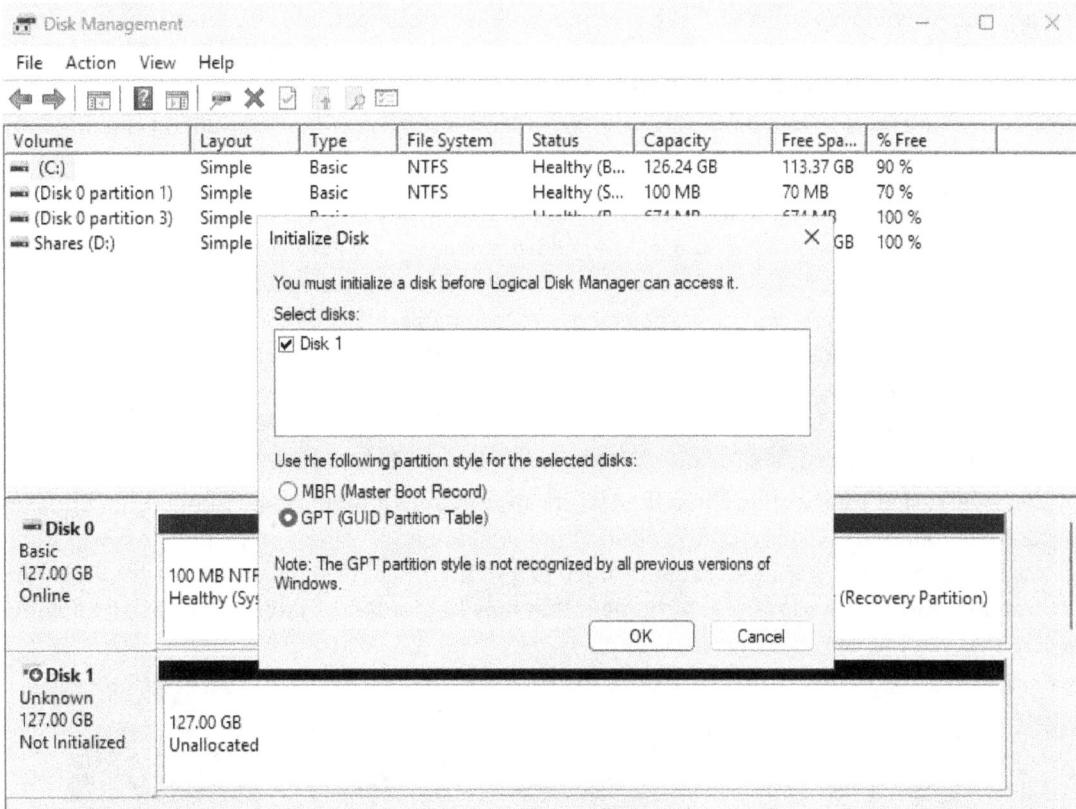

Figure 13.25: Initializing a new disk as GPT

Testing preparedness for Storage Replica

We now have two file servers, each with a new GPT data disk that contains two new volumes. One will be used for SR data storage, and the other for SR logs. Here's a quick look at the volumes I have. They are set up exactly the same on both servers:

Figure 13.26: Volumes created on the servers

At this point, we could plow forward with creating the SR environment, and since these are brand-new servers with identical configurations, it would most likely work. However, you will often be configuring SR on servers that have already been running in production for a while, or at least the primary file server where your source data is going to be located. Knowing whether or not SR is going to be successful would be comforting knowledge.

Thankfully, there is a testing process that SR can run before putting your configurations into place. Using PowerShell, let's issue a big, long command from our primary FS01 server. The following is the command I am running. You will, of course, have to adjust it to accommodate your own server names and volume letters. As you can see at the end of the command, I specify for the output to be placed inside the C:\SR_TEST folder, so make sure that folder exists on your server:

```
Test-SRTopology -SourceComputerName FS01 -SourceVolumeName S:
 -SourceLogVolumeName L: -DestinationComputerName FS02 -DestinationVolumeName S:
```

This test will gather information about the servers and volumes and run some sample data transfers in the background for 10 minutes (as specified in the command). After completion, you will find a results file inside C:\SR_TEST that should launch in a web browser to show you all kinds of resulting information. Any issues with the environment that may hinder SR's ability to work will be detailed here so that you can go resolve those issues:

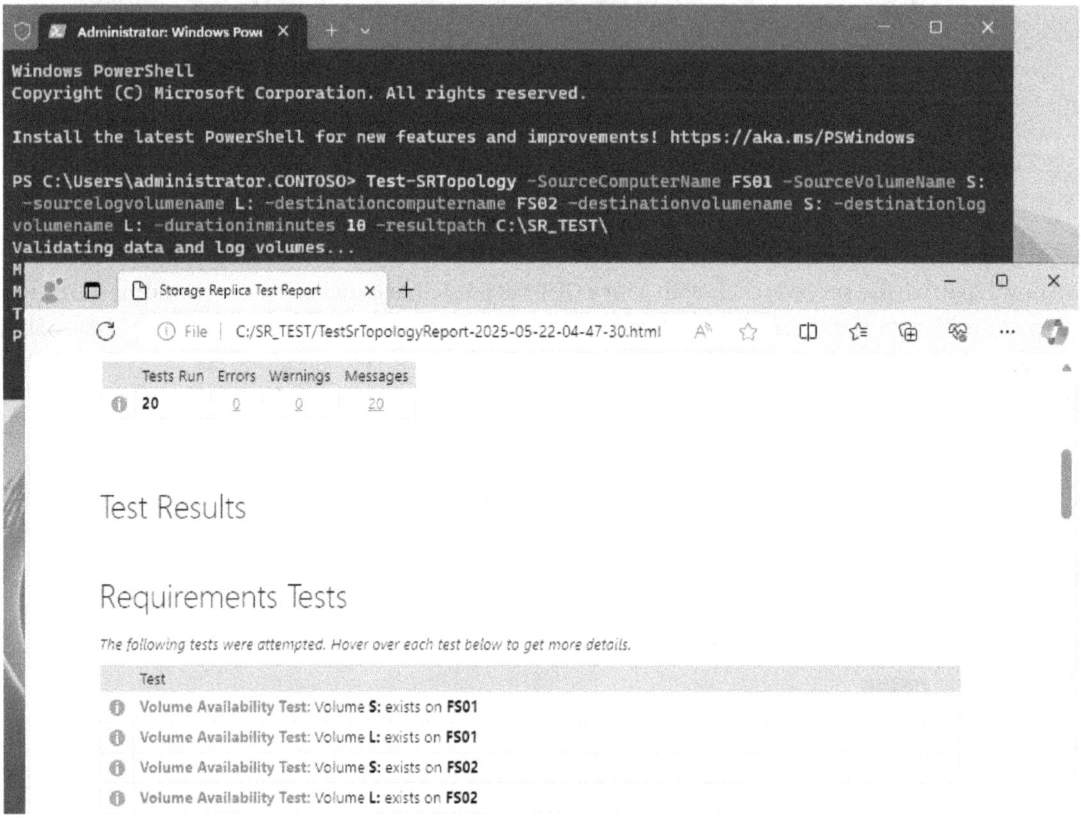

Figure 13.27: Storage Replica Test Report

Having validated that FS01 and FS02 are configured properly for SR to function, let's move on to the fun part!

Configuring Storage Replica

Now that our servers are prepped and tested, it's time to build the real deal! Since we have met all pre-requisites and built out our servers with SR in mind, all it takes is one PowerShell command to get this SR partnership started. I will list the following command, which is pretty self-explanatory. The only pieces that may be slightly unfamiliar are SourceRGName and DestinationRGName. The **RG** stands for **replication group**, which is simply a name you must define for the replication group on each server:

```
New-SRPartnership -SourceComputerName FS01 -SourceRGName RepGroup1
 -SourceVolumeName S: -SourceLogVolumeName L: -DestinationComputerName FS02
 -DestinationRGName RepGroup2 -DestinationVolumeName S:
```

Boom! Just like that, SR is configured with FS01's S: drive being the primary storage, automatically and synchronously replicated to FS02's S: drive. Depending on performance and networking specs, the initial sync between volumes can take a bit of time, during which you will see ReplicationState: InitialBlockCopy in the results of the Get-SRGroup command. Once the initial sync has completed, that field will instead show ReplicationState: ContinuouslyReplicating, as you can see in *Figure 13.28*. Any data that is stored on FS01's S: drive is automatically replicated over to FS02:

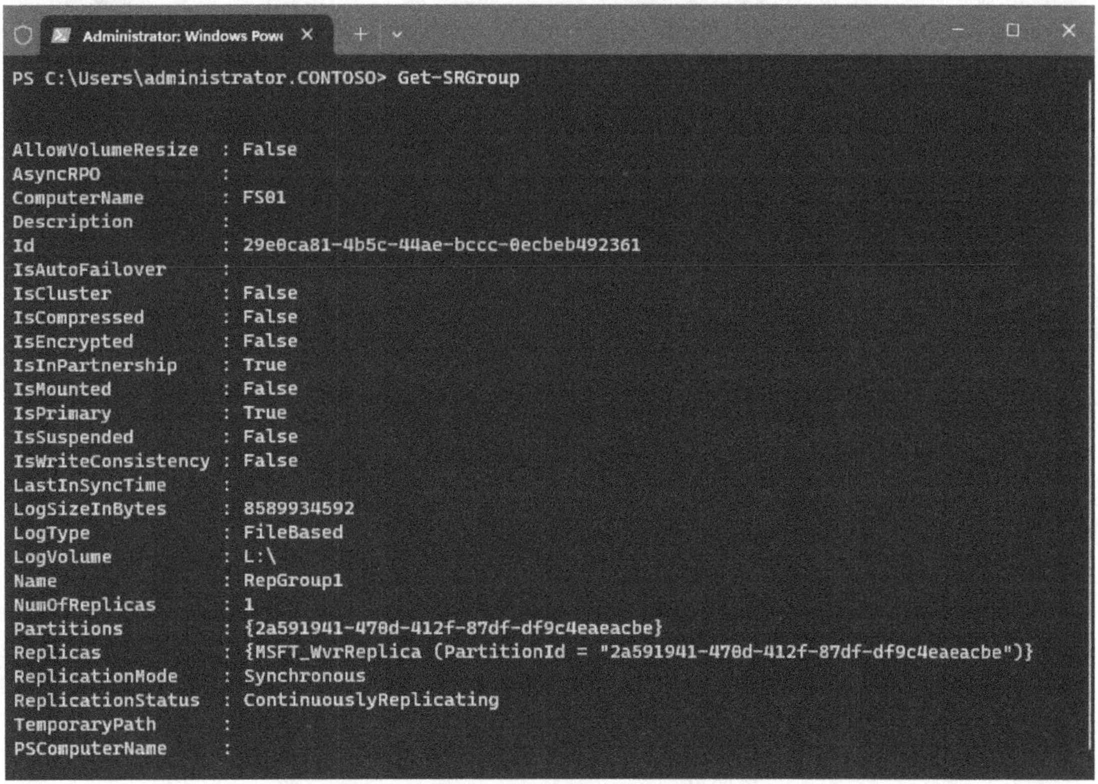

```
PS C:\Users\administrator.CONTOSO> Get-SRGroup


AllowVolumeResize  : False
AsyncRPO           :
ComputerName       : FS01
Description        :
Id                 : 29e0ca81-4b5c-44ae-bccc-0ecbeb492361
IsAutoFailover     :
IsCluster          : False
IsCompressed       : False
IsEncrypted        : False
IsInPartnership    : True
IsMounted          : False
IsPrimary          : True
IsSuspended        : False
IsWriteConsistency : False
LastInSyncTime     :
LogSizeInBytes     : 8589934592
LogType            : FileBased
LogVolume          : L:\
Name               : RepGroup1
NumOfReplicas      : 1
Partitions         : {2a591941-470d-412f-87df-df9c4eaeacbe}
Replicas           : {MSFT_WvrReplica (PartitionId = "2a591941-470d-412f-87df-df9c4eaeacbe")}
ReplicationMode    : Synchronous
ReplicationStatus  : ContinuouslyReplicating
TemporaryPath      :
PSComputerName     :
```

Figure 13.28: Details of our SR group

Shifting the primary server to FS02

After poking around on the file servers, you'll notice that you can see data on FS01's S: drive, but if you try to browse FS02's S: drive, you are met with an error message – "S:\ is not accessible. The device is not ready." This is by design. You are unable to browse and see data on the destination SR server until you run another command to make it primary, such as in the event of a disaster recovery scenario. To prove that SR is really working, let's follow that step to make sure data is automatically replicating from FS01 to FS02.

I have created some sample text files on FS01's S: drive, but I am unable to verify that they exist on FS02. Let's pretend that FS01 has gone offline or is having some other kind of issue, and I need to make FS02 my new primary file server. All I need to do is run the following PowerShell command on FS02 to flip roles, turning FS02 into the new primary SR partner:

Immediately after running this command, I can now see and browse through the data on FS02's S: drive, which means that it is now the primary SR member, and also proves to me that SR was working in the first place:

```
Set-SRPartnership -NewSourceComputerName FS02 -SourceRGName RepGroup2
 -DestinationComputerName FS01 -DestinationRGName RepGroup1
```

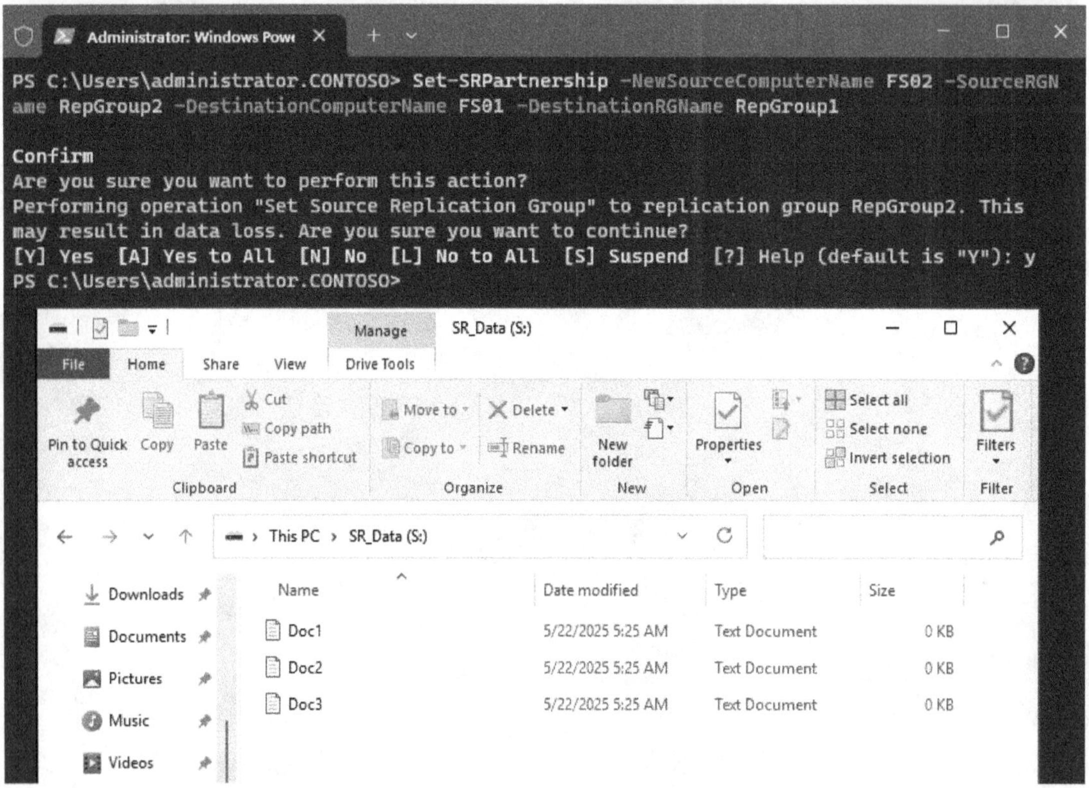

Figure 13.29: We have shifted primary drive access to FS02

And as expected, if I attempt to open and browse the S: drive on FS01, I now receive the error message on that node instead.

Storage Spaces Direct

Storage Spaces Direct (S2D) is a clustering technology, but I list it here separately from general failover clustering because S2D is a core component of the **software-defined data center** (SDDC) and has had so much focus on improvements over the past few years that it really is in a category of its own. As a forewarning, I am in no way going to be able to cover the entirety of S2D in this chapter; it really deserves its own book. There are links at the end of this section that will bring you into the swaths of documentation that accompany S2D.

In a nutshell, S2D is a way to build an extremely efficient, redundant, scalable, centralized, network-based storage platform entirely from Windows Servers containing normal hard drives. While serving the same general purpose (file storage) as a traditional NAS or SAN device, S2D takes an entirely different approach in that it does not require specialized hardware, nor special cables or connectivity between nodes of the S2D cluster.

To build S2D, all you need are Windows servers (the faster, the better), but they could be normal, every-day servers. They do need to be Windows Server Datacenter Edition, but you could run S2D on either Desktop Experience or Server Core nodes. These servers must be connected through networking, and that networking needs to be pretty serious for S2D to work properly. You will need high bandwidth and low latency between servers to make this successful—a minimum of 10 GB is what we're talking about here. Once you have these servers running and connected, you can utilize clustering technologies or WAC to bind these servers together into S2D arrays.

S2D is part of the overall **Hyper-Converged Infrastructure** (HCI) story and is a wonderful way to provide extremely fast and protected storage for anything, especially for workloads such as clusters of Hyper-V servers. As you already know, when building a Hyper-V Server cluster, the nodes of that cluster must have access to shared storage upon which the VM hard disk files will reside. S2D is the best way to provide that centralized storage.

S2D will take the hard drives inside your S2D cluster node servers and combine all of their space together into software-defined pools of storage. These storage pools are configured with caching capabilities and even built-in fault tolerance. You obviously wouldn't want a single S2D node, or even a single hard drive, going offline to cause a hiccup in your S2D solution, and of course, Microsoft doesn't want that to happen either. So, when you group servers and all their hard drives together into these large pools of S2D storage, they are automatically configured with parity among those drives so that particular components going offline do not result in lost data or even a slowdown of the system.

S2D is the best storage platform for both SOFS and Hyper-V clusters.

While early versions of S2D were configured mostly through PowerShell (which unfortunately means that a lot of administrators haven't tried it yet), our current version of WAC includes built-in options for configuring an S2D environment:

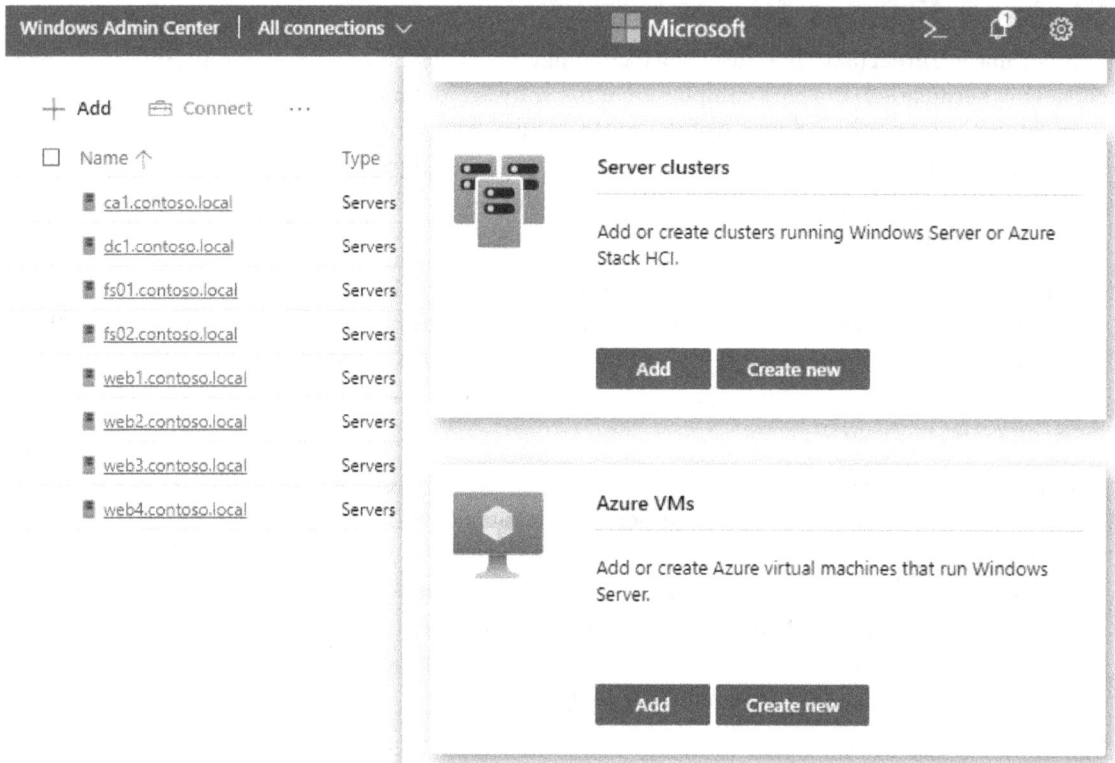

Figure 13.30: Using WAC to add new server clusters

As mentioned, S2D is one of those technologies that warrants its own book, but anyone looking to try out or get started with this amazing storage technology should start at

`https://learn.microsoft.com/en-us/windows-server/storage/storage-spaces/storage-spaces-direct-overview.`

Recent enhancements in S2D

Many great changes have come to S2D over the past few years, through the releases of Windows Server 2019, 2022, and now 2025. Moving forward, Microsoft is focusing primarily on S2D changes to hit Azure Local (Azure Stack HCI), as they really expect most companies to utilize that technology stack to support S2D. As new features are introduced to Azure Local, some or all of those then get ported down to the latest version of Windows Server as well.

Most of the enhancements in S2D that are new for Windows Server 2025 relate to S2D's interoperability with newer and faster hard disks and filesystems. Hardware continues to evolve; S2D's capabilities must evolve with it:

- **NVMe performance:** The numbers surrounding S2D and server disk speed in general astound me. Depending on what source you use, I found stats that the speed of disk access (usually measured in IOPS) has grown anywhere from 60% to 90% with the release of Windows Server 2025! This will be useful, of course, for virtualization workloads as well as the continually growing AI application space.

- **S2D thin-provisioned volumes:** Those familiar with building VMs already know about thin-provisioned disks, starting small and growing as needed. Server 2025 brings us thin provisioning for S2D-based volumes.

- **NVMe over Fabrics (NVMe-oF):** Windows Server 2025 now supports NVMe-oF, all in an effort to continually improve speed and efficiency, with the ability for it to make network connections to NVMe SANs.

- **ReFS deduplication and compression:** Deduplication and compression save space, especially on storage systems that house many instances of redundant data, such as numerous Windows operating systems sitting in virtual disks that are used by virtual machines. Deduplication and compression are now natively supported for the **Resilient File System (ReFS)**.

Prior to Windows Server 2025, there were enhancements made for S2D that are still relevant today:

- **Adjustable storage repair speed:** S2D's capability to self-repair data copies between servers is not a new thing, but starting with Windows Server 2022, you now have options for controlling how many workload resources are dedicated to this task.

- **Storage Spaces tiering:** You already know that S2D is all about taking storage from multiple servers and combining them together. Stepping back a bit from that idea, you have probably heard of **Storage Spaces**, which is a similar but different technology that is used on a per-server basis. Storage Spaces uses software to combine multiple drives in a single server to create a larger usable storage space, and this new feature is specifically for Storage Spaces. We now have the option of tiering storage, giving us access to utilize SSD drives for caching.

- **WAC:** WAC now includes tools and functionality for defining and managing S2D clusters. This will make adoption much easier for folks who are not overly familiar with PowerShell.

Summary

Redundancy is a critical component in the way that we plan infrastructure and build servers in today's world. Windows Server 2025 has powerful capabilities built right into it that you can utilize in your own environments, starting today! I hope that by gleaning a little information about both NLB and failover clustering, you will be able to expand the capabilities of your organization by employing these techniques and stretching the limits of your service uptime. Failover Clustering, in particular, seems to be a scary place for many server administrators, and familiarity with the capabilities provided by clustering will not only enhance your current workplace but also open doors for enhanced employment in the future.

Even for a small to medium-sized business, there are some great replication options in Windows Server, made possible with a limited set of servers. You could use SR to replace many other third-party options that currently exist in these environments, giving you redundant file servers in a quick and easy fashion, without extra cost. For any enterprise-class organization that hasn't tested the waters with S2D yet, what's stopping you? Let's get serious about resiliency for your Hyper-V infrastructure. HCI will change the way you work and give you peace of mind that you didn't think was possible in a world aiming for 99.999% uptime.

Questions

Put your knowledge to the test with the following questions. If you need a hand (or just want to double-check), you'll find all the answers in the *Appendix* section of the book.

1. Which technology is more appropriate for making web server traffic redundant: Network Load Balancing or failover clustering?
2. Is website traffic generally stateful or stateless?
3. In Network Load Balancing, what do the acronyms DIP and VIP stand for?
4. What are the three NLB modes?
5. In Windows Server 2025, is Network Load Balancing a role or a feature?
6. What roles are most often used with failover clustering?
7. What are cluster rolling OS upgrades?
8. True or False? Storage Spaces Direct requires the use of SSD hard drives.
9. What is the difference between Storage Spaces and Storage Spaces Direct?

14

Containers

Many technologies included in Windows Server 2025 are designed to reflect capabilities provided by cloud computing, bringing your private and hybrid clouds to life and granting you the ability to produce the same solutions given to you by public cloud providers within your physical infrastructure. The last few iterations of the Windows Server operating system have also revolved around virtualization, and the idea of application containers is something that taps into both of these mindsets. Application containers will make the deployment of applications more streamlined, more secure, and more efficient. Containers have been around longer than Microsoft has been working with them, and outside of conversations about DevOps, I haven't heard many IT admins talking about them. Containers and container orchestration have been enhancing Linux computing for a while now, and our recent Windows Server operating systems bring these technologies a little bit closer to home for us Microsoft-centric shops.

Application developers will be very interested in application containers provided by Windows Server 2025, and in truth, they probably understand the concepts behind containers much better than a traditional server administrator. While the premise of this book is not focused on development opportunities and is clearly not focused on Linux, we will discuss containers because the benefits provided are not only for developers. We, being responsible for system operations, will also benefit from using containers, and if nothing else, it is going to be important for us to know and understand how to conceptualize and spin up containers, so that we can provide the infrastructure that our developers are going to require as they begin to build modern, scalable applications.

In this chapter, we will cover the following topics dealing with application containers; hopefully, this will help prepare your administrators to support this technology in your datacenters:

- Understanding application containers
- Container base images
- Windows Server containers versus Hyper-V containers
- Docker and Kubernetes
- Working with containers
- Where is Azure in all this?

Understanding application containers

What does it mean to *contain* an application? We have a pretty good concept these days of containing servers through virtualization. Taking physical hardware, turning it into a Hyper-V virtualization host, and then running many **virtual machines (VMs)** on top of it is a form of containment for those VMs. We are essentially tricking them into believing that they are their own entity, completely unaware that they are sharing resources and hardware with other VMs running on that host. Although we share hardware resources, we can provide strong layers of isolation between VMs because we need to make sure that access and permissions cannot bleed across VMs, particularly in a cloud provider scenario, as that would spell disaster.

Application containers are the same idea, at a different level. While VMs are all about virtualizing hardware, containers are more like virtualizing an operating system. Rather than creating VMs to host our applications, we can create containers, which are much smaller. We then run applications inside those containers, and the applications are tricked into thinking that they are running on top of a dedicated instance of the operating system.

A huge advantage of using containers is the unity that they bring to the development and operations teams. We hear the term *DevOps* all the time, which is a combination of *development* and *operations* processes working together to make the entire application rollout process more efficient. The utilization of containers is core to creating a successful DevOps mentality since developers can now do their job (developing applications) without needing to accommodate the operations and infrastructure side of things. Developers create applications inside containers, knowing that their application will run anywhere that the container can run. Once the application is built, operations can take the container within which the application resides and simply spin it up inside their container infrastructure, without any worries that the application is going to break servers or experience compatibility problems.

The potential is real for containers to take the place of many VMs, but this will only happen if admins jump in and try it out for themselves. Let's discuss a few benefits that containers bring to the table.

Sharing resources

Similar to the ideology of splitting hardware among VMs, application containers mean that we take physical chunks of hardware and divide them up among containers. This allows us to run many containers from the same server, be it a physical or virtual server.

However, in that alone, there is no benefit over VMs, because they simply share hardware as well. Where we really start to see the benefits of using containers rather than separate VMs for each of our applications is that all of our containers can share the same base operating system. Not only are they spun up from the same base image, which makes it extremely fast to bring new containers online, but they also share the same kernel resources. Every instance of an operating system has its own set of user processes. Often, it is tricky business to run multiple applications together on servers because those applications traditionally have access to the same set of processes and have the potential to be negatively affected by those processes. In other words, it's the reason that we tend to spin up so many servers, keeping each application on its own server so that they cannot negatively impact each other. Sometimes apps simply do not like to mix. The kernel in Windows Server 2025 has been enhanced so that it can handle multiple copies of the user-mode processes.

This means you not only have the ability to run instances of the same application over many different servers but can also run many different applications, even if they don't typically like to coexist, on the same server.

Isolation

One of the huge benefits of application containers is that developers can build their applications within a container running on their own workstation! A machine that hosts containers can be a Windows Server instance, or it can be a Windows 10 or 11 workstation. When coding within this container sandbox, developers will know that their application contains all the parts, pieces, and dependencies that it needs to run properly, and that it runs in a way that doesn't require extra components from the underlying operating system. This means the developer can build the application, make sure it works in their local environment, and then easily slide that application container over to the hosting servers, where it will be spun up and ready for production use. That production server might be an on-premises container server that an IT admin has built, or it could even be a cloud-provided resource—the application doesn't care. The isolation of the container from the operating system helps to keep the application standardized in a way that is easily mobile and movable, saving the developer time and headaches, since they don't have to accommodate differences in underlying operating systems during the development process.

The other benefit of isolation is increased security. This is the same story as multiple VMs running on the same host, particularly in a cloud environment. You want security boundaries to exist between those machines; in fact, most of the time, you do not want them to be aware of each other in any way. You even want isolation and separation between the VMs and the host operating system because you sure don't want your public cloud service provider snooping around inside your VMs. The same idea applies to application containers.

The processes running inside a container are not visible to the hosting operating system, even though you are consuming resources from that operating system. Containers maintain two different forms of isolation:

- There is namespace isolation, which means the containers are confined to their own filesystem and registry.
- Then, there is also resource isolation, meaning that we can define what specific hardware resources are available to the different containers, and they are not able to steal from each other.

Shortly, we will discuss two different categories of containers: Windows Server containers and Hyper-V containers. These two types of containers handle isolation in different ways, so stay tuned for more info on that topic.

We know that containers share resources and are spun up from the same base image, while still keeping their processes separated so that the underlying operating system can't negatively affect the application, and also so that the application can't tank the host operating system. But how is that isolation handled from a networking aspect? Well, in the Windows Server world, application containers utilize technology from the Hyper-V virtual switch to keep everything straight on the networking side. In fact, as you start to use containers, you will quickly see that each container has a unique IP address assigned to it, helping to maintain network isolation.

Scalability

The combination of spinning up from the same base image and the isolation of the container makes a very compelling scalability and growth story. Think about a web application you host whose use might fluctuate greatly from day to day. Providing enough resources to sustain this application during busy times has traditionally meant overpaying for compute resources when that application is not being heavily used. Cloud technologies provide dynamic scaling for these modern kinds of applications, but they often do so by spinning up or down entire VMs. There are three common struggles with dynamically scaling applications like this:

- First is the time that it takes to produce additional VMs; even if that process is automated, your application may be overwhelmed for a period of time while additional resources are brought online.

- The second challenge is the struggle that the developer needs to go through to make that application so agnostic that it doesn't care whether there are inconsistencies between the different machines upon which their application might be running. Creating non-dependent applications should be a requirement for any modern developer, yet in some industries, I still regularly find new software releases that are coded in poor ways from many years ago, requiring us, as administrators, to take great care in making sure the environment matches up with what the application needs.

- The third challenge with scaling applications is cost—not only a hardware resource cost, as new VMs coming online will each consume an entire set of kernel resources, but monetary costs as well. Spinning VMs up and down in your cloud environment can quickly get expensive.

These are all hurdles that do not exist when you utilize containers as your method to deploy applications.

Since application containers use the same underlying kernel and the same base image, their time to live is extremely fast. New containers can be spun up or down very quickly and in batches, without having to wait for the boot and kernel mode processes to start. Also, since we have provided the developer with this isolated container structure within which to build the application, we know that our application is going to be able to run successfully anywhere that we spin up one of these containers. No more worries about whether the new VM that is coming online will be standardized correctly, because containers for a particular application are always the same and contain all of the important dependencies that the application needs, right inside that container.

Latest enhancements for containers

Containers have been included in Windows Server for a few versions, but every release includes some additional or changed features. Here are highlights of the latest enhancements related to containers in the Windows Server world.

32-bit applications in Nano Server

We will be talking about Nano Server shortly, but as the name implies, Nano is a super tiny instance of a Windows Server. Microsoft worked on making Nano Server so small that they ended up removing components necessary for 32-bit applications to run at all, and so up until this point, Nano Server containers have only been able to run 64-bit applications. With the release of Windows Server 2025, Nano Server can now be enhanced (even if it means a larger footprint) to also run 32-bit applications.

Nano Server Features on Demand (FoD)

Nano Server is still very small by default, but the addition of FoD means that you can optionally add more components onto Nano Server, increasing its size but also increasing its potential. FoD is the mechanism through which you can enable Nano Server to run 32-bit applications, among other things.

Smaller image size for Server Core

When starting a container instance, the container image base layers need to be downloaded and extracted on the host. Many of the containers in use today are based on a Server Core image, and Microsoft has worked hard to reduce the RTM portion of this image by approximately 33% when compared to the Server Core container base image from Windows Server 2019.

Virtualized time zones

New as of Windows Server 2022 is the ability for each Windows container instance to maintain its own virtualized time zone, separated from the container host server upon which it is running.

Initial IPv6 support

While there is still development being made for full IPv6 support in Windows container land, improvements in Kubernetes now give us the ability to start making use of this newer networking stack.

HostProcess containers

There are two primary types of containers in the world of Windows Server container hosts, which we will discuss later in this chapter. New in Server 2022, and still being enhanced with the 2025 release, is a third container type that is not exactly brand-new but rather an extension of Windows Server containers. **HostProcess containers** enable enhanced cluster management scenarios through Kubernetes. When orchestrating many nodes and groupings of containers, administrative tasks within those containers can be made more efficient using HostProcess containers. These special containers don't maintain their own filesystem or processes, but share the host's resources directly.

Enhanced management through Windows Admin Center (WAC)

Limited container management was already available via WAC, primarily helpful to containerize web applications. The latest version of WAC now includes integration with Azure Container Registry to upload container images to that registry, as well as the ability to start and stop container instances.

A new base image option

In the very next section of this chapter, we will talk more in depth about container base images and why they matter. Historically, with LTSC versions of Windows Server (2016 and 2019), there were only two base images from which containers could be built. New in Windows Server 2022 and continuing into Server 2025 is a third option, somewhat confusingly called... "Windows Server." We'll discuss this further in a moment.

Container base images

This topic brings us full circle to our discussion about Server Core and Nano Server. If you have worked with Windows Server for many years, you have probably wondered why Microsoft introduced a new installation option called Nano Server, only to remove it during the next LTSC release. This change happened right around the same time that Microsoft started diving into using Windows Servers as container host servers, and this information directly relates to the question, "What happened to Nano Server?".

Nano Server is now only useful for containers. In fact, you cannot install a Nano Server instance outside of a container. This is its purpose. You do not *have* to use Nano inside your containers, but it's one of the options.

Containers are sort of like VMs, but at a different level. With VMs, you share hardware among multiple full instances of the Windows operating system. Each VM maintains a completely separated kernel from the others, creating strong isolation between VMs and between the VMs and the host server. Microsoft has some great diagrams to describe these differences, which I am going to use here and show you.

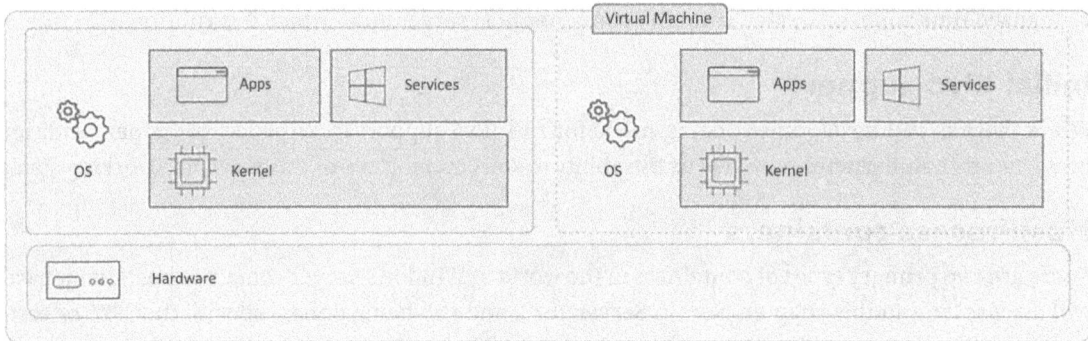

Figure 14.1: Layers of a Windows virtual machine

Windows Server containers, on the other hand, are like multiple individual instances of the Windows operating system running on a host server, except they share not only hardware resources but also the Windows kernel itself. Thanks again to *Microsoft Learn* documentation, here is a screenshot displaying the makeup of a Windows Server container; you can see here how it differs from a true virtual machine:

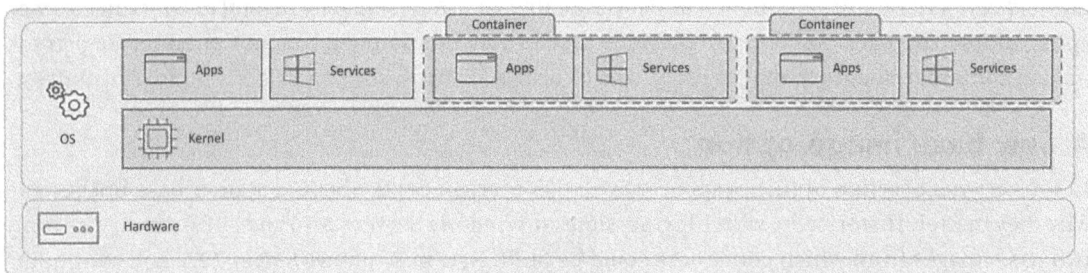

Figure 14.2: Layers of a Windows container environment

Each container is comprised of multiple layers that lie on top of each other to make up a fully functioning container. This container will have an operating system, roles and services, and the application for which the container is purposed. When deploying a container, the core layer of that container is the base operating system that will run within the container, and that is always provided by a container base image.

In Windows Server 2016 and 2019, there were only two base images available to use for containers: **Server Core** and **Nano Server**. If you're familiar with **semi-annual channel** (**SAC**) versions of Windows Server (also only used for container purposes), you may know that there was a third flavor of container image specific to these versions of the operating system, called **Windows**. We are not going to focus any attention on this one, because SAC versions of Windows Server are a moot point for the future as Microsoft moves away from using them. However, as described when we talked about container improvements in Windows Server 2025, we do now have a third option for container base images, somewhat confusingly called **Windows Server**. Let's spend some time discussing these three types of base container images.

Nano Server

While Server Core is a great operating system to build small and efficient servers, it is still a heavy-weight compared to Nano Server.

Nano is so incredibly different, and so incredibly tiny, that it really isn't a comparison. You may remember earlier when we installed Server Core and came out with a hard drive size of around 6 GB. While that is much smaller than a Desktop Experience version of Windows Server, think about this—a Nano Server base image can be less than 500 MB!

That is amazingly small. Additionally, updates to Nano Server are expected to be few and far between. This means you won't have to deal with monthly patching and updates on your application containers. In fact, there is technically no patching component inside containers. Since containers include all that they need to run the applications hosted on them, it is generally expected that when you need to update something about a container or the software contained within, you'll just go ahead and build out a new container image that includes your patches or changes, rather than update existing ones. If Nano Server receives an update, just build out a new container, install and test the application on it, and roll out container instances based on the new image. Need to make some changes to the application itself? Rather than figuring out how to update the existing container image, it's quick and easy to build a new one, test it outside of your production environment, and once it is ready, simply start deploying and spinning up the new container image into production, letting the old version fall away.

Nano Server is now only used as a base operating system for containers. This is a major change since the release of Server 2016, when the scope that Nano was expected to provide was much larger. If you are somehow utilizing Nano Server for workloads outside of container images, you need to start working on moving those workloads into more traditional servers, such as Server Core.

Server Core

You may be wondering, "Why would anybody use Server Core as the base for a container image if Nano Server is available?". The easiest answer to that question is application compatibility. Nano Server is incredibly small, and as such, it is obviously lacking much of the code that exists inside Server Core. When you start looking into utilizing containers to host your applications, it's a great idea to utilize the smaller Nano Server as a base *if possible*, but often, your applications simply won't be able to run on that platform, and in these cases, you may need to call on Server Core as the base operating system.

.NET applications can help to portray scenarios when one type of container must be used over another. If the app you are building is based on .NET Core, a Nano Server container image likely includes all of the needed dependencies to run that application. This will provide you with the smallest possible footprint for your container and will run most efficiently. However, if you find yourself building an app that requires the full .NET framework, Nano Server won't cut it. You will have to change gears and utilize a Server Core container to bring your application to life.

What may be a decent general rule of thumb is that if anybody builds out a new modern cloud application that you want to be as scalable and efficient as possible, focus that development around containers based on Nano Server. This way, you can code around those restrictions in Nano and end up with an app that can work on these incredibly small and lightweight containers.

If, instead, you find yourself faced with the task of taking existing application code and moving it into containers, it is pretty likely that you will have to shift over to Server Core-based containers to give yourself the extra flexibility to get those applications to work.

Windows Server

There are some tasks that DevOps engineers call on containers to perform that even Server Core cannot handle. Or, in some cases, there are limitations and restrictions even in Server Core that an application may need to overcome in order to work successfully. Up until Server 2022, the answer to this was a third container image type called Windows, which used a more significant code base of the Windows operating system. This was, of course, a heavier footprint than Nano Server or Server Core, but it enabled more things to be possible. The Windows container image type was exclusive to SAC versions of Windows Server, those special versions of Windows Server that were released twice per year, but which you already know are being deprecated. So, what is there to fill in that gap? Windows Server 2022 and 2025 come with a new container base image type called **Windows Server**. This container image is essentially based on a full Windows Server edition; in fact, the code is based on Windows Server 2025 Desktop Experience. Now, don't take that the wrong way; no container includes a GUI. This is core to what containers are. But with the code coming from the Desktop Experience version, doors are open in this container type that would normally be closed in a Nano or Server Core container.

Windows Server container base images have fewer restrictions inside IIS than Server Core instances, and they have a broader API support scope. Since they are based on LTSC code, containers based on the Windows Server container image are supported as standard for five years, which is considerably different and longer than SAC versions ever were.

Windows Server containers versus Hyper-V containers

When spinning up your containers, it is important to know that there are two categories of containers that you can run in Windows Server 2025. I know this is all a bit confusing, since we just talked about how there are three (or four, depending on how you view SAC) different container base image types. Those are all about what OS runs *within* the container. Here, we are talking about what different *types* of containers there are, which is more so from the perspective of the container *host* operating system, and what functionality your containers as a whole will have. All aspects of application containers that we have been talking about so far apply to either Windows Server containers or Hyper-V containers. Hyper-V containers can run the same code or images as Windows Server containers, while keeping stronger isolation guarantees to make sure the important stuff stays separated. The decision on whether to use Windows Server containers or Hyper-V containers will likely boil down to what level of security you need your containers to maintain. Let's discuss the differences between the two so that you can better understand the choice you are facing.

Windows Server containers

Like Linux containers, Windows Server containers share their host operating system kernel files in order to make the containers efficient. What this means, however, is that while namespace, filesystem, and network isolation are in place to keep the containers separated from each other, there is some potential for vulnerability between the different Windows Server containers running on a host server. For example, if you were to log in to the host operating system on your container server, you would be able to see and manipulate the running processes of each container.

The container cannot see the host or other containers and is still isolated from the host in various ways, but knowing that the host can view the processes within the container shows us that some interaction does exist with this level of sharing. Windows Server containers will be most useful in circumstances where your container host server and the containers themselves are within the same *trust boundary*. In most cases, this means that Windows Server containers are going to be most useful for company-owned servers that only run containers owned and trusted by the company. If you trust both your host server and your containers, and are okay with those entities trusting each other, deploying regular Windows Server containers is the most efficient use of your hardware resources.

HostProcess containers

As previously mentioned, a new container type is coming to town, called HostProcess containers. I'm including this as a subheading under *Windows Server containers* because HostProcess containers are essentially Windows Server containers that can be centrally managed and orchestrated in better ways. As more and more companies get more involved in working with containers, Microsoft has expectations that containers being used to run modern applications will likely be hosted in Azure or Azure Local, and that they will be orchestrated by something like Kubernetes. HostProcess containers come with advantages over classic Windows Server containers when used in this way.

In contrast to Windows Server containers, which do isolate themselves in the ways we have already discussed, HostProcess containers run directly on the container host as processes. They do not have isolation of filesystem, networking, or processing, which makes them more flexible but means that you would only ever run these types of containers on systems residing well within that trust boundary we mentioned.

Hyper-V containers

If you're looking for an increased amount of isolation and stronger boundaries, it's worth foraying into Hyper-V containers. Hyper-V containers are more like a super-optimized version of a VM. While kernel resources are still shared by Hyper-V containers, making them much more performant than full VMs, each Hyper-V container gets its own dedicated Windows shell within which a single container can run. This means you have isolation between Hyper-V containers that is more on par with isolation between VMs, and yet you are still able to spin up new containers at will and very quickly because the container infrastructure is still in place underneath. Hyper-V containers are more useful in multitenant infrastructures, where you want to make sure no code or activity can be leaked between the container and host, or between two different containers that might be owned by different entities. Earlier, we discussed how a host operating system can see the processes running within a Windows Server container, but this is not the case with Hyper-V containers. The host operating system is completely unaware of and unable to tap into the services running within the Hyper-V containers. These processes are now invisible to prying eyes.

The availability of Hyper-V containers means that even if you have an application that must be strongly isolated, you no longer need to dedicate a full Hyper-V VM to this application. You can now spin up a Hyper-V container, run the application in that container, and maintain full isolation for the application, while continuing to share resources and provide a better, more scalable experience for that application.

A special note on the topic of Hyper-V containers – since a Hyper-V container is essentially a full VM running on your host server, each one counts as a VM from a licensing perspective. If your container host server is Windows Server 2025 Standard, you are restricted to running two Hyper-V containers, which is probably not going to be very helpful. Windows Server 2025 Datacenter edition allows an unlimited number of VMs to run, including Hyper-V container VMs.

Docker and Kubernetes

Docker started as an open source project—a toolset, really—that was originally designed to assist with the running of containers on Linux operating systems. Wait a minute, what? The words **Linux** and **open source** have been written once again inside a Microsoft book! What is this world coming to? You see, containers are quickly becoming a big deal, and rightfully so. In Server 2016, Microsoft took some steps to start reinventing the container wheel, with the inclusion of PowerShell cmdlets that could be used to spin up and control containers running on your Windows Server, but the Docker platform has grown at such a fast rate that Microsoft now expects that anyone who wants to run containers on their Windows machines is probably going to do so via the Docker toolset. If you want to utilize or even test containers in your environment, you'll need to get **Docker for Windows** to get started.

Docker is a container *platform*. This means that it provides the commands and tools needed to download, create, package, distribute, and run containers. Docker for Windows is fully supported to run on both Windows 11 and Windows Server 2025. By installing Docker for Windows, you acquire all the tools needed to begin using containers to enhance your application's isolation and scalability.

Developers can use Docker to create an environment on their local workstation that mirrors a live server environment, so that they can develop applications within containers and rest assured that those applications will function when those containers are moved to their final destination server. Docker is the platform that provides pack, ship, and run capabilities for your developers. Once finished with development, the container package can be handed over to the system administrator, who spins up the container(s) that run the application and deploys it accordingly. The developer doesn't know or care about the container host infrastructure, and the admin doesn't know or care about the development process or compatibility with their servers, because the application's dependencies live within the container.

Linux containers

When running containers on a Windows Server, it makes common sense that your containers would need to be running an instance of the Windows operating system as well, since containers share kernel resources from the host. However, containers in general have been used in the Linux world for much longer than in the Microsoft world, and a lot of today's containerized infrastructure is based on Linux operating systems. There are various ways that Microsoft and third parties craft ways to run Linux containers on top of a Windows Server container host. This functionality, of course, includes the isolation of those kernel resources. For example, if your Windows container host server natively runs some Windows Server containers, and then also runs a VM that is then used to host Linux-based containers, this could be one scenario where you run Windows and Linux containers on the same host, even though those systems could never share source code or a kernel.

This topic is ever-evolving, and some of the capabilities are still considered "experimental." If this is a topic that interests you, a good term to start searching for and reading about is **Linux Containers on Windows (LCOW)**. The following link is a good starting point to begin your investigation of this space: `https://learn.microsoft.com/en-us/virtualization/windowscontainers/deploy-containers/set-up-linux-containers`.

Docker Hub

When you work with containers, you build container images that are usable on any server instance running the same host operating system—that is the essence of what containers enable you to do. When you spin up new instances of containers, you just pull new copies of that exact image, which is all-inclusive. This kind of standardized imaging mentality lends well to a shared community of images—a repository, so to speak, of images that people have built that might benefit others. Docker's history is open source, after all. Does such a sharing resource exist, one that you can visit to grab container image files for testing, or even to upload images that you have created and share them with the world? Absolutely! It is called **Docker Hub** and is available at `https://hub.docker.com`.

Visit this site and create a login, and you will immediately have access to thousands of container base images that the community has created and uploaded. This can be a quick way to get a lab up and running with containers, and many of these container images could even be used for production systems, running the applications that the folks here have pre-installed for you inside these container images. Alternatively, you can use Docker Hub to upload and store your own container images:

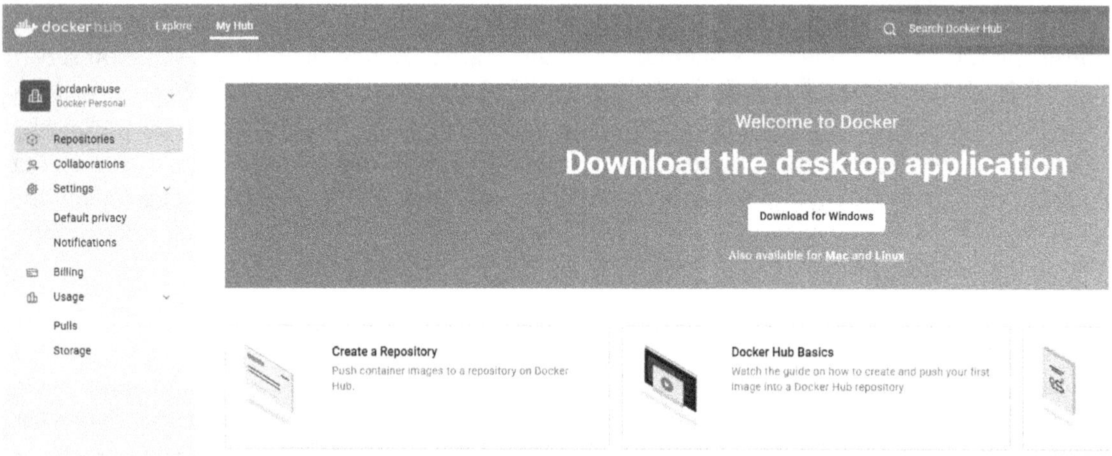

Figure 14.3: Docker Hub

Public and private repositories

The first reason you will likely visit Docker Hub is to find a container image that somebody else created, download it, and test things out for yourself. We also mentioned that you can upload your own container images to Docker Hub. Both options sound awfully "public," and they are. Uploading your container images to Docker Hub in a public repository means that other Docker Hub users can find and utilize them.

If you're anything like me, putting my information in a public repository sounds scary and insecure, and most businesses would agree. Thus, Docker Hub private repositories now exist for the safekeeping of your own container images, in a way and place that other users are not able to access your images.

You really should go ahead and create an account for Docker Hub now because if you want to follow along later in the chapter and try out implementing a container with Docker, you'll need a login to do it.

Docker Trusted Registry (where'd it go?)

Docker Hub originally lacked a way to privately store container images, only offering options for sharing container images with your friends (and enemies) all around the world. In those days, the **Docker Trusted Registry** (**DTR**) was one of the few ways to securely store Docker images. One key feature of DTR was that you could build a repository within your own data center, behind your firewalls and security systems. DTR is now end of life, no longer being sold or supported by Docker. There has been so much advancement in internet connections and internet security over the past few years that they really expect everyone to store these images in a cloud-based repository such as Docker Hub or Azure Container Registry (more on that in a few minutes).

Kubernetes

While Docker is our primary interface to build and host containers, allowing us to create platforms within which we can host applications in this new and exciting way, the real magic comes after we are finished with the container's setup. Let's peek into the future a little and assume that you have an application now successfully hosted inside a container. This container can be spun up on a container host server in your environment or even slid over to an Azure container host very easily. This provides easy interaction with the infrastructure needed to seamlessly scale this application up or down, but there is a missing piece to this scalability: **orchestration**.

Kubernetes, often referred to as **K8s**, is a container orchestration solution. This means that Kubernetes orchestrates, or facilitates, how the containers run. It is the tool that enables many containers to run together, in harmony, as if they were one big application. If you intend to use containers to create scaling applications that can spin up new containers whenever additional resources are needed, you will absolutely need to have a container orchestrator, and Kubernetes is one of the most popular.

Microsoft recognized this popularity and has taken steps to ensure that Kubernetes is fully supported on Windows Server 2025. In fact, as you know, our latest version of Windows Server includes a new class of Windows containers called HostProcess containers, which are specifically designed to allow Kubernetes to have better control over these containers. Previously, administering Windows containers involved a lot of logging in to the containers directly to manage parts and pieces, but HostProcess containers enable direct management from the Kubernetes administration platform.

The combination of these latest Windows containers and Kubernetes means that you can run hundreds of container nodes on a single server.

As with any software, Kubernetes is not the only name in the game. Docker has its own orchestration platform, called **Docker Swarm**. While it might make sense that Docker and Docker Swarm would work together better than Docker and any other orchestrator, they serve slightly different audiences. Docker Swarm works great for smaller environments and is built right into Docker. However, most organizations making solid use of containers are larger and have a significant purpose behind their orchestration needs, and Kubernetes is better at dealing with large and more comprehensive container environments. Kubernetes even has a specific integration with Azure, which we will outline near the end of this chapter.

As I mentioned earlier, tools such as containers, Docker, and Kubernetes are part of a cloud-first vision for your applications. While the use of containers for most companies will start on-site, using their own servers and infrastructure to host containers, this is a technology that is already capable of extending to the cloud. Because the containers themselves are so standardized and fluid—making them easy to expand and move around—sliding them into a cloud environment is easily done.

Working with containers

There are a lot of moving pieces that work together to make containers a reality in your environment, but it's not too difficult to get started. Let's walk through the initial setup of turning Windows Server 2025 into a container-running mega-machine.

Installing the role and feature

The amount of work that you need to accomplish here depends on whether you want to run Windows Server containers, Hyper-V containers, or both. The primary feature that you need to make sure that you install is **Containers**, which can be installed by using either the **Add roles and features** link from inside Server Manager, or by issuing the following PowerShell command:

```
Add-WindowsFeature Containers
```

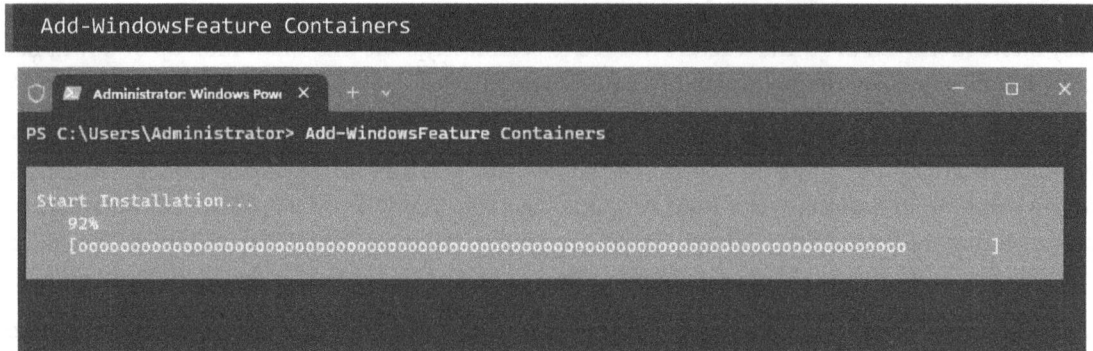

Figure 14.4: Installing the Containers feature

Additionally, if you intend to run Hyper-V containers, you need to ensure that the underlying Hyper-V components are also installed on your container host server. To do that, install the **Hyper-V role** and accompanying management tools onto this same server.

As indicated, following the role and feature installation, make sure to restart your server after these changes.

At this point, you may be wondering, "If my container host server needs to have the Hyper-V role installed, doesn't that mean it must be a physical server? You can't install the Hyper-V role on a virtual machine, right?". *Wrong*. Windows Server 2025 supports something called **nested virtualization**, which was added primarily for containers. You see, requiring physical hardware is becoming a limiting factor for IT departments these days, as almost everything is done from VMs. It makes sense that companies would want to deploy containers, but they may also want their container host servers to be VMs, with multiple containers being run within that VM. Therefore, nested virtualization was required to make this possible. If you run a Windows Server 2022 or 2025 physical hypervisor server and a Windows Server 2022 or 2025 VM inside that server, you will now find that you can successfully install the Hyper-V role directly onto that VM. I told you VMs were popular, so much so that they are now being used to run other VMs!

Remember that we can also host and run containers on our Windows 10 and 11 machines! To prep a Windows client for this purpose, simply add the Windows feature called Containers, just like on the server operating system. Keep in mind that the Containers feature is only available in the more business-class SKUs of Windows. If you run Windows Pro, Enterprise, or Education, you will be able to make use of this feature.

Installing Docker for Windows 10/11

Now that our container host server is prepped with the necessary Windows components, we need to grab Docker for Windows from the internet. The Docker interface will provide us with all the commands that are needed to start building and interacting with our containers.

This is the point where the Docker Hub login becomes important. If you are following along with this chapter to test containers on your own workstation and need to install Docker Desktop for Windows on your Windows 10 or 11 *client*, the easiest way is to visit Docker Hub, log in, and search for the Docker Desktop client software. Here is a general link to that software (again, this is the tool you need to use if you install it on Windows 10 or 11, for container development purposes): https://www.docker.com/products/docker-desktop/.

Alternatively, here is another page of Docker Desktop downloads that includes more information about installing from a command line: https://docs.docker.com/desktop/setup/install/windows-install/.

Installing Docker for Windows Server 2025

If you tested containers running on a Windows Server at some point in the last few years, it is likely that the process you took is no longer applicable. Running containers on a Windows Server requires Docker toolsets, as well as a runtime environment for containers. Microsoft used to maintain its own runtime called **Docker Enterprise Edition (Docker EE)**, and licensing for it was included with Windows Server licensing, but Microsoft has since decided to pull its resources from the container runtime game and ask you to utilize a third party for these functions. The most direct replacement for Docker EE is Mirantis Container Runtime, which provides a lot of capabilities but comes at a cost. For any enterprise customer who is going to make use of containers in production, you will almost certainly utilize Azure management tools or Azure Local to deploy containers and tap into Mirantis for runtime capabilities, but for my offline test lab where I simply want to prove the use of containers, I am going to employ **Docker Community Edition (Docker CE)**, which is part of an open source project called **Moby**.

Docker CE/Moby runtime installation

Thankfully, the power of PowerShell makes this installation quick and easy! I have already installed the Containers feature on my new server called CTNR1, and will now run these two simple commands to pull down an installer script and then run that script, as shown in the figure that follows:

```
Invoke-WebRequest -UseBasicParsing "https://raw.githubusercontent.com/
microsoft/Windows-Containers/Main/helpful_tools/Install-DockerCE/install-
docker-ce.ps1" -o install-docker-ce.ps1
.\install-docker-ce.ps1
```

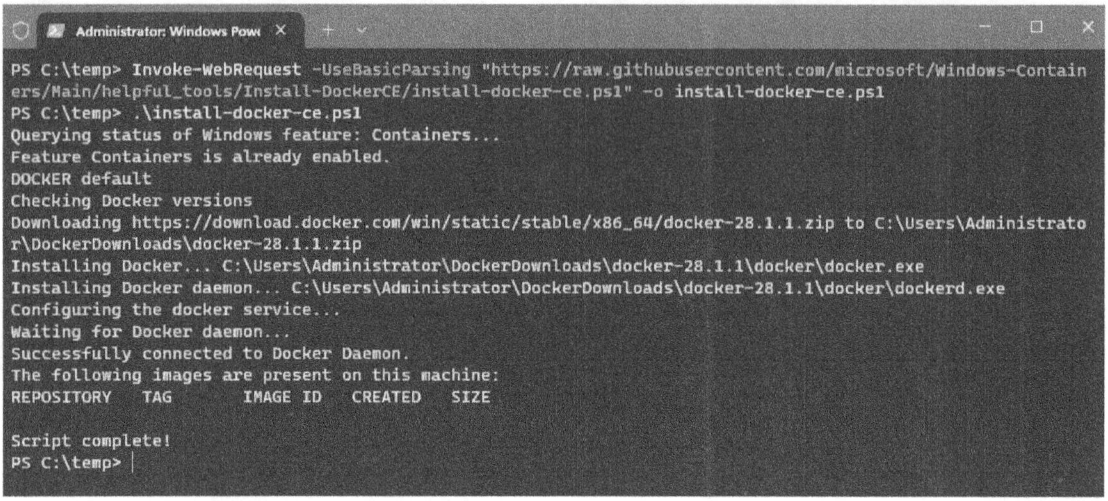

```
Administrator: Windows Pow     X     +   v                                  —   □   ×
PS C:\temp> Invoke-WebRequest -UseBasicParsing "https://raw.githubusercontent.com/microsoft/Windows-Contain
ers/Main/helpful_tools/Install-DockerCE/install-docker-ce.ps1" -o install-docker-ce.ps1
PS C:\temp> .\install-docker-ce.ps1
Querying status of Windows feature: Containers...
Feature Containers is already enabled.
DOCKER default
Checking Docker versions
Downloading https://download.docker.com/win/static/stable/x86_64/docker-28.1.1.zip to C:\Users\Administrato
r\DockerDownloads\docker-28.1.1.zip
Installing Docker... C:\Users\Administrator\DockerDownloads\docker-28.1.1\docker\docker.exe
Installing Docker daemon... C:\Users\Administrator\DockerDownloads\docker-28.1.1\docker\dockerd.exe
Configuring the docker service...
Waiting for Docker daemon...
Successfully connected to Docker Daemon.
The following images are present on this machine:
REPOSITORY     TAG        IMAGE ID    CREATED     SIZE

Script complete!
PS C:\temp> |
```

Figure 14.5: Docker CE runtime is installed with two simple commands

Just like that, this server is prepared to run containers and has the Docker toolsets installed. Now... how do we interact with Docker?

Docker commands

Once Docker is installed on your system, whether you are working with a Windows Server 2025 or Windows 10/11 machine, you now have Docker Engine running on your machine, and it is ready to accept some commands to begin working with containers. If there is a single word to remember when it comes to working with containers, it is **Docker**. That is because every command that you issue to interact with containers will begin with the word docker. Let's look at some of the common commands that you will be working with.

docker version

Certain container images that you want to run may require particular versions of Docker Engine to be successful. When in doubt about what your current Docker environment is running, you can easily check version numbers anytime by running docker version.

docker info

While docker version displays version numbers of Docker Engine, docker info steps back and gives some general info and statistics about your Docker container host server. Here you can see a Docker versioning number as well as the current Windows operating system version numbers, along with stats about the server itself, such as allocated memory. Probably the most interesting numbers shown in the docker info output are counters for how many containers are on this server, with breakdowns on how many of those containers are running, paused, or stopped.

docker –help

This is sort of like issuing docker /?, if that were a real command. The help function of Docker generates a list of the possible Docker commands that are available to run. This is a good reference point as you get started.

docker images

After downloading some container images from a repository (we will do this for ourselves in the next section of this chapter), you can use the docker images command to view all of the images that are available on your local system.

docker search

Utilizing the search function allows you to search through container repositories (such as Docker Hub) for base container images that you might want to utilize in your environment. For example, to search and find images related to "Windows" inside the Docker Hub repository, you would run the following command, which would produce the output shown in the figure that follows:

```
docker search Windows
```

```
PS C:\> docker search windows
NAME                            DESCRIPTION                                      STARS     OFFICIAL
dockurr/windows                 Windows inside a Docker container.               426
actiontestscript/windows        ATS Docker Windows image ready to launch ATS…    0
calico/windows                                                                   3
mgba/windows                    Windows autobuilds                               2
toxchat/windows                                                                  0
toktoknet/windows               Windows cross compilers: i686 and x86_64.        0
spellegrino021/windows                                                           2
zixia/windows                   Run Windows Application in a Linux Docker Co…    3
dcoswindowsci/windows           CI Nano Server Image                             0
hchandawad1/windows                                                              0
oufqatu/windows                 This is just a testing windows image             0
ironsoftwareofficial/windows    Pre-configured Windows containers for runnin…    0
cdaf/windows                    Base on Windows Server 2022                      0
njawalequalys/windows                                                            1
jklaassen/windows                                                                0
metthal/windows                 Unofficial Windows images with MSVC, CMake a…    0
h3llix/windows                                                                   0
jerbi/windows                                                                    0
kpack/windows                                                                    0
kwaziio/windows                 STIG-Hardened Windows Docker Images Based on…    0
newbe36524/windows                                                               0
seokjunyoon/windows             Windows Containers                               0
cloudhack01/windows             windows                                          0
microsoft/windows               The official Windows base image for containe…    39
atxwebdesigner/windows                                                           0
PS C:\>
```

Figure 14.6: Searching the container repository

You'll notice in *Figure 14.6* that there are numerous container images stored in Docker Hub that contain the word Windows, and most of them are published by entities that have nothing to do with Microsoft, the company. Searching for container images via the command line using docker search can be confusing and frustrating to figure out whether container images are from proper sources. Rather than make sense of these from inside PowerShell, I prefer using Docker Hub in a web browser to seek out the image I want. Docker Hub is easily searchable, and you can visit one URL to begin your search through the Microsoft-official container images: `https://hub.docker.com/u/microsoft`.

In fact, here is a screenshot of a specific container image that I want to download. I found this by visiting Microsoft's Docker Hub repository, and from there, searching for `servercore`.

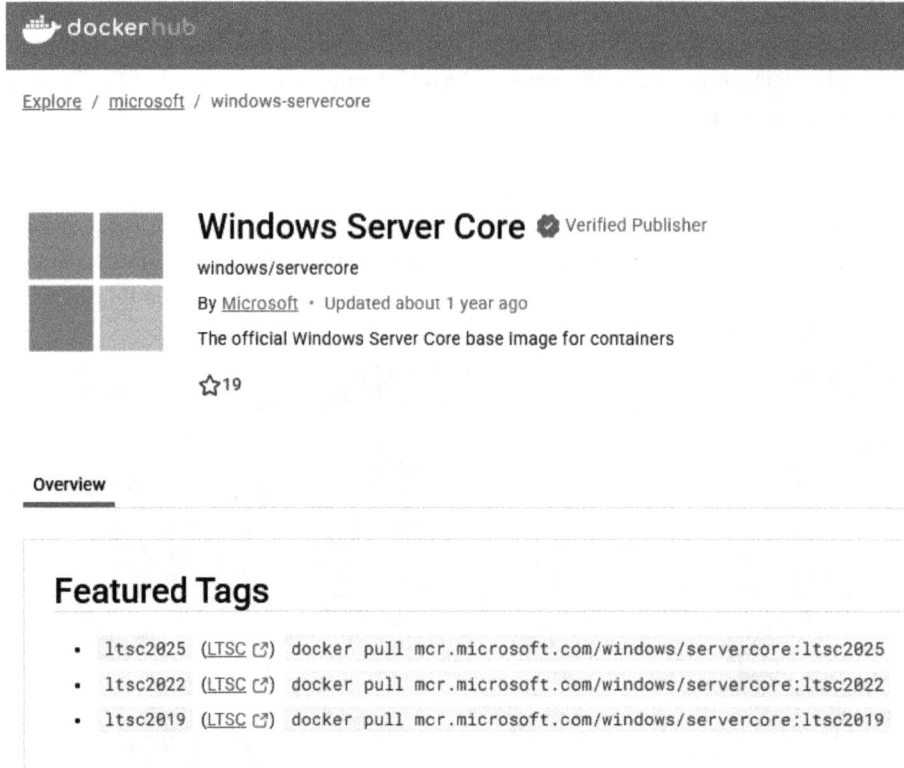

Figure 14.7: Discovering container images inside Docker Hub

Now that we have found a container image that sounds interesting, what do we do with this information? You'll notice near the bottom of *Figure 14.7* some docker pull commands, let's explore those…

docker pull

We use docker pull to pull down container images from online repositories. There are multiple repositories from which you can get container images. Most often, when seeking out container images that were created by Microsoft directly, you will work with images from Docker Hub or Microsoft's own **Microsoft Container Registry (MCR)**. docker pull commands run directly on your container server and immediately begin downloading the specified container image and storing it on your server, prepared to be used for running a container based on that image. The docker pull commands shown in *Figure 14.7* are clearly pulling from MCR, and there are three Server Core container options to choose from: Server Core based on Windows Server 2019, 2022, or 2025.

Here are some sample `docker pull` commands that show you how to pull container images from Docker Hub, as well as MCR:

```
docker pull Microsoft/nanoserver
docker pull Microsoft/windowsservercore
docker pull mcr.microsoft.com/windows/servercore:ltsc2025
```

docker run

This is the command to start a new container from a base image. You will find that you can retain multiple container images in your local repository that are all based on the same original container image. For example, as you add new things to your containers or update the application inside your containers, you may be building new container images that are now a subset of an existing container image. You may have numerous container images that are all named windowsservercore, for example. In this case, container tags become very important, as they help you to distinguish between different versions of those container images. As an example, here is a command that would start a container based on a windowsservercore image, with which I associated the ltsc2019 tag:

```
docker run -it --rm Microsoft/windowsservercore:ltsc2019
```

In the preceding command, the `-it` switch creates a shell from which we can interact with a container, which is useful to build and test containers, but you generally wouldn't need that switch to launch production containers that were 100% ready to serve up applications. `--rm` is a cleanup switch, meaning that once this particular container exits, the container and its filesystem will be automatically deleted.

docker ps -a

You utilize `docker ps -a` when you want to view the containers currently running on your system.

Downloading a container image

The first command we will run on our newly created container host is `docker images`, which shows us all of the container images that currently reside on our system. I will also throw in `docker ps -a` to view any currently running containers. For our brand-new container server, there are exactly zero of these items:

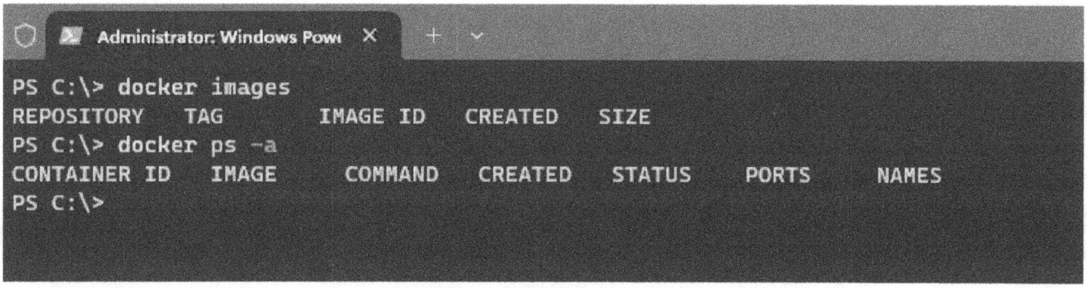

Figure 14.8: Zero container images on our system

Of course, there are no container images yet as we haven't downloaded any. Let's grab a couple so that we can test this out. In addition to base container images that only contain the operating system, Microsoft also provides sample container image files that showcase running .NET applications inside a Nano Server container—that sounds like a fun way to get started with verifying that we can successfully run containers on this new host server.

Once we know the image that we want to download, we can use docker pull to download it onto our server. You can see in the following commands and screenshot that I have downloaded the 2022 version image of Nano Server and the Server Core 2025 image as well. After "pulling" these down to my system, I verified they are visible on my server by using docker images. As you can imagine, the Nano Server base container image downloaded in a matter of seconds, while the Server Core instance took probably 20 times longer to download and extract. Once again, what an amazing thing Nano Server is!

```
docker pull mcr.microsoft.com/windows/nanoserver:ltsc2022
docker pull mcr.microsoft.com/windows/servercore:ltsc2025
docker images
```

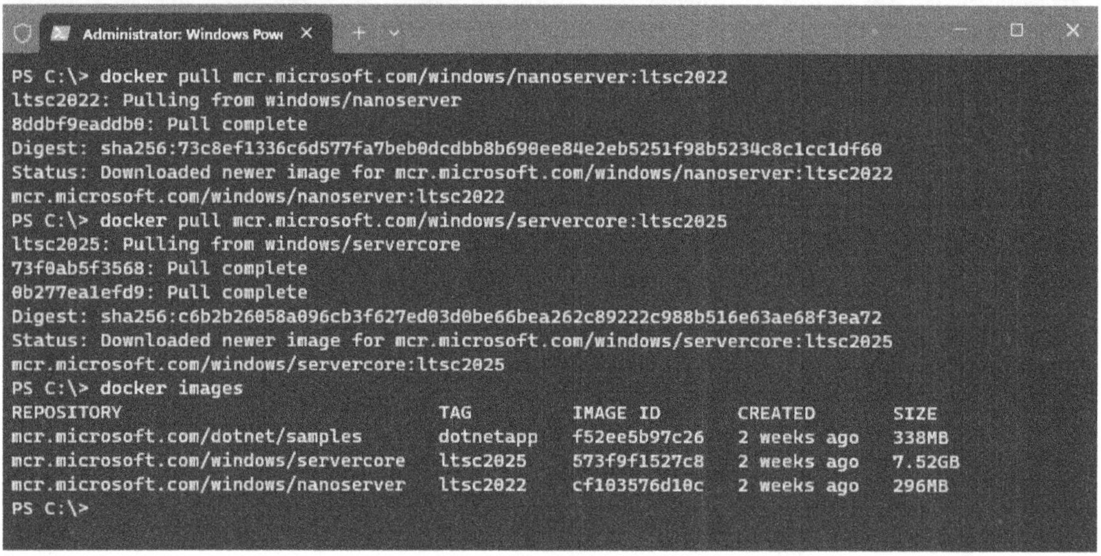

```
PS C:\> docker pull mcr.microsoft.com/windows/nanoserver:ltsc2022
ltsc2022: Pulling from windows/nanoserver
8ddbf9eaddb0: Pull complete
Digest: sha256:73c8ef1336c6d577fa7beb0dcdbb8b690ee84e2eb5251f98b5234c8c1cc1df60
Status: Downloaded newer image for mcr.microsoft.com/windows/nanoserver:ltsc2022
mcr.microsoft.com/windows/nanoserver:ltsc2022
PS C:\> docker pull mcr.microsoft.com/windows/servercore:ltsc2025
ltsc2025: Pulling from windows/servercore
73f0ab5f3568: Pull complete
0b277ea1efd9: Pull complete
Digest: sha256:c6b2b26058a096cb3f627ed03d0be66bea262c89222c988b516e63ae68f3ea72
Status: Downloaded newer image for mcr.microsoft.com/windows/servercore:ltsc2025
mcr.microsoft.com/windows/servercore:ltsc2025
PS C:\> docker images
REPOSITORY                              TAG          IMAGE ID       CREATED        SIZE
mcr.microsoft.com/dotnet/samples        dotnetapp    f52ee5b97c26   2 weeks ago    338MB
mcr.microsoft.com/windows/servercore    ltsc2025     573f9f1527c8   2 weeks ago    7.52GB
mcr.microsoft.com/windows/nanoserver    ltsc2022     cf103576d10c   2 weeks ago    296MB
PS C:\>
```

Figure 14.9: Using docker pull to grab container images from MCR

The preceding commands downloaded a copy of base images, and we could spin up containers based on these images all day long. But earlier, I mentioned that Microsoft has put some sample container images out there, which are prebuilt to do some fun things. Here is a command to download a sample .NET application container image from Microsoft's container repository:

```
docker pull mcr.microsoft.com/dotnet/samples:dotnetapp
```

Figure 14.10: Downloading a .NET sample container image

After the downloads are finished, running docker images once again shows us the container base images that were downloaded, alongside the sample .NET image:

Figure 14.11: Local container image repository

From these base images, we are now able to launch and run a real container.

Running a container

We are so close to having a container running on our host! Now that we have installed the service, implemented Docker, and downloaded a base container image, we can finally issue a command to launch a container from that image. Let's run the .NET container that we downloaded before, with the following command:

```
docker run --rm mcr.microsoft.com/dotnet/samples:dotnetapp
```

The container starts and runs through its included code, and we see some fun output:

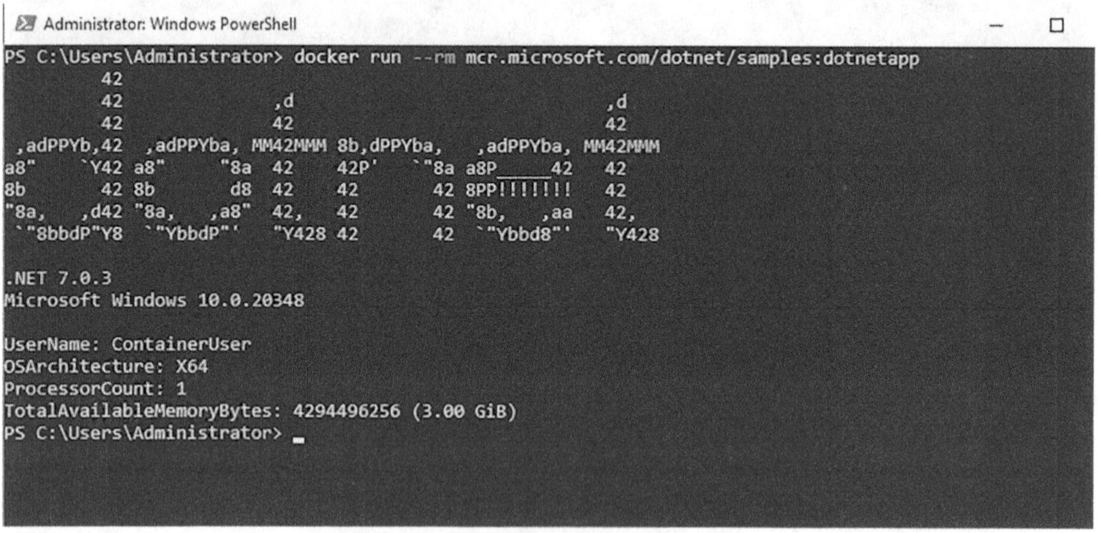

```
Administrator: Windows PowerShell                                    —    □
PS C:\Users\Administrator> docker run --rm mcr.microsoft.com/dotnet/samples:dotnetapp
          42
          42                       ,d                        ,d
          42                       42                        42
  ,adPPYb,42  ,adPPYba, MM42MMM 8b,dPPYba,    ,adPPYba, MM42MMM
a8"     `Y42 a8"     "8a 42    42P'   `"8a a8P_____42    42
8b       42 8b      d8 42    42       42 8PP!!!!!!!   42
"8a,   ,d42 "8a,   ,a8" 42,   42       42 "8b,   ,aa   42,
 `"8bbdP"Y8 `"YbbdP"'  "Y428 42       42 `"Ybbd8"'   "Y428

.NET 7.0.3
Microsoft Windows 10.0.20348

UserName: ContainerUser
OSArchitecture: X64
ProcessorCount: 1
TotalAvailableMemoryBytes: 4294496256 (3.00 GiB)
PS C:\Users\Administrator>
```

Figure 14.12: Our first container is up and running!

This container showcases that *all* components necessary for this .NET application to run are included *inside* the container. This container is based on Nano Server, which means it has an incredibly small footprint. In fact, looking back a few pages at the last docker images command that we ran, I can see that this container image is only 338 MB! What a resource saver this is, compared with running this application on a traditional IIS web server.

The main resource for Microsoft documentation on containers is https://aka.ms/windowscontainers. The tools used to interact with containers constantly change, including changes to Docker and Kubernetes. Make sure to check over the Microsoft Learn site to find the latest best practices and approved installation path to prepare your container host servers.

Where is Azure in all this?

This book is focused primarily on functionality provided natively inside the Windows Server operating system, most often utilized on-premises. Our chapter on containers has obviously followed suit. Containers are part of a cloud-first mentality, and there is certainly much to learn on the topic of utilizing Windows containers inside Azure, rather than on classic servers. While this is not our core focus, here is some information regarding ways that containers intersect with Azure.

Azure Container Registry

Earlier in this chapter, we looked into Docker Hub and pulled some container images from MCR. Both of these systems are live and ready to use, but they may be too public-facing for your enterprise's taste. A third option that may be more appropriate when working with containers hosted in Azure is another container registry, useful for the *private* storage of container images, **Azure Container Registry**.

Azure Kubernetes Service (AKS)

I told you that Kubernetes was becoming well adopted by Microsoft, so much so that there is a dedicated Azure service that is completely interwoven with K8s. If your intentions are to move cloud-ward with your containers, and you're thinking about running those containers inside Azure, AKS can provide the toolset to manage and scale those containers through its powerful orchestration capabilities. Think about the possibilities here. Store your container images in Azure Container Registry, and then engage AKS to spin up hundreds or even thousands of container instances on Azure VMs at will.

AKS on Azure Local

Azure Local (formerly Azure Stack HCI) is all about taking Azure infrastructure and scaling capabilities and bringing them locally into your data center, so that you retain more direct control over those resources. For companies implementing Azure Local, it is important to know that you can also run AKS within this environment, providing on-premises container solutions that mirror the capabilities of pure Azure. AKS on Azure Local utilizes Azure Arc, allowing you to use the Azure portal to create and manage containers that are running inside your on-premises environment.

Summary

Containers are revolutionizing the way that we build and host modern applications. By containerizing apps, we can run many more applications on each physical server, because they are capable of being fully isolated from each other. Additionally, the container mentality allows the development of applications to happen in a much more fluid fashion. App developers can build their applications inside containers running on their own laptops and, once finished, simply hand them over to the infrastructure team to slide that container image onto a production container host server. That host server could be on-premises or cloud-based. Orchestration tools such as Kubernetes can then be leveraged to scale that application, increasing or decreasing resource capacity and the number of running containers, based on load or other factors. The usability of containers in the real world has been expanded greatly by the Docker project. The folks at Docker are clearly the frontrunners in this space, enough that Microsoft has decided to incorporate the use of Docker, an open source project developed for Linux, straight into Windows Server 2025. We can now utilize both Docker Engine to run containers on our Windows servers, and the Docker client toolset to manage and manipulate containers inside Windows in the same way we work with containers in the Linux world.

Linux containers and Windows Server containers have a lot in common and function in essentially the same way. Microsoft's ingenious idea to create an additional container scope, the Hyper-V container, brings a solid answer to a lot of common security questions that present themselves when approaching the idea of containers in general. Everyone uses VMs heavily these days; I don't think anybody can disagree with that. Assuming the use of containers evolves into something easy to implement and administer, Hyper-V containers could replace many of our existing Hyper-V VMs in the coming years. This will save time, money, and server space.

Speaking of Hyper-V, it has become an integral part of so many of our corporate networks today. In the next chapter, we will learn more about this amazing virtualization technology.

Questions

Put your knowledge to the test with the following questions. If you need a hand (or just want to double-check), you'll find all the answers in the *Appendix* section of the book.

1. There are three base operating systems that can be used for a Windows Server 2025 container. What are they?

2. Compared to a Windows Server container, what type of container provides even greater levels of isolation?

3. True or False? In Windows Server 2016, you can run both Windows and Linux containers on the same Windows Server host platform.

4. What is the Docker command to see a list of container images on your local system?

5. What is currently the most popular container orchestration software that integrates with Windows Server 2025?

6. True or False? Developers can install Docker onto their Windows 10 workstations to start building applications inside containers.

7. What is a common reason that a developer may need to utilize Server Core containers, rather than Nano Server?

8. What service allows you to manage on-premises containers from inside the Azure portal?

Join us on Discord

For discussions around the book and to connect with your peers, join us on Discord at `https://packt.link/discordcloud` or scan the QR code below:

15

Hyper-V

I've always been a country boy. Driving along dirt roads, working on cars, and hunting are all ways that I prefer to fill my free time. Traveling to cities always hits me with a bit of culture shock. All those skyscrapers and tall apartment buildings serve an important purpose, though, and serve to fulfill my metaphor: if there isn't enough land to grow outward, you have to build up. The vertical ascension of large cities portrays what we have seen happening in our datacenters over the past decade. Cities need more and more space for people and businesses, just like we need to house more and more servers every year. Rather than horizontal expansion, with enormous server rooms filled with racks and racks of hardware, we are embracing the skyscraper mentality and virtualizing everything. We build considerably fewer servers but make them incredibly powerful. Then, on top of these super-computers, we can run dozens, if not hundreds, of virtual servers. The technology that provides this hypervisor layer, the ability to run **virtual machines** (**VMs**) in Microsoft-centric shops, is the **Hyper-V** role in Windows Server. This is one of the most critical roles to understand as a server administrator because if your organization is not yet making use of server virtualization, you've been left behind. Virtualization is no longer the way of the future; it is the implied expectation of every datacenter in the world. The following are some topics we are going to explore so that you can become familiar with the virtualization capabilities provided by Microsoft in Windows Server 2025:

- Designing and implementing Hyper-V server
- What's new in 2025?
- Virtual switches
- Implementing a virtual server
- Managing a virtual server
- Shielded VMs
- Integrating Hyper-V with Linux
- Resilient Filesystem (ReFS) deduplication
- Hyper-V server...2019?

Designing and implementing Hyper-V server

Creating your own Hyper-V server is usually simple: build a server, install an operating system, install the Hyper-V role, and you're ready to get started. In fact, you can even install the Hyper-V role on a Windows 10 or 11 Pro or Enterprise computer if you need to run some VMs from your own desktop. While most hardware that is created these days fully supports the idea of being a hypervisor provider, some of you may try installing the Hyper-V role only to end up with the following error message:

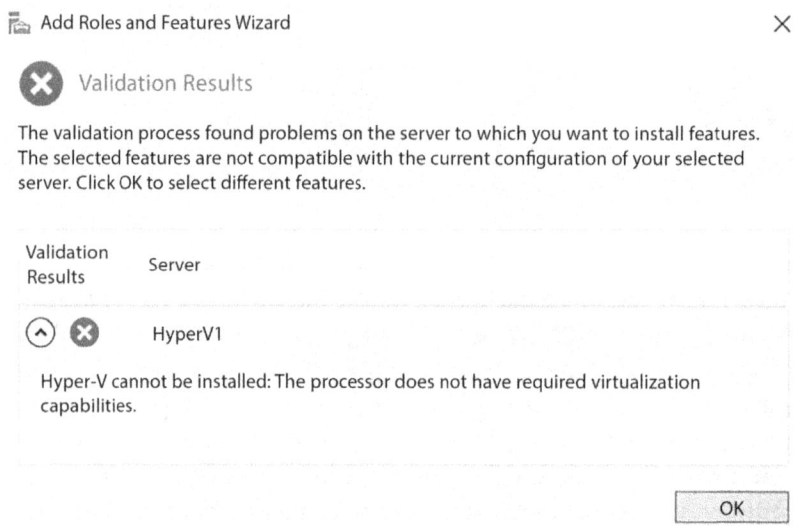

Figure 15.1: Hyper-V compatibility error

Uh oh, that's not good. This means one of two things: either my CPU really doesn't support virtualization, or I simply have some settings turned off inside the BIOS on my server that prevent this from working. There are three considerations you should check on your server to make sure it is ready to run Hyper-V:

- First, you need to be running an x64-based processor. This is kind of a given since Windows Server 2025 only comes in 64-bit anyway. If you don't have an x64 processor, you're not going to be able to install the operating system in the first place.

- Second, your CPUs need to be capable of hardware-assisted virtualization. This is typically called either **Intel Virtualization Technology (Intel VT)** or **AMD Virtualization (AMD-V)**.

- Finally, you must have **Data Execution Prevention (DEP)** available and enabled on your system. If you have investigated the hardware itself and it seems to be virtualization-capable, but it's still not working, it is likely that you have DEP currently disabled inside the BIOS of that system. Boot into the BIOS settings and enable DEP, along with any other more user-friendly-named settings that might indicate they are currently blocking your ability to run VMs.

As long as your processors are happy to run VMs, you can turn just about any size of hardware into a hypervisor by installing the Hyper-V role. It is not important to think about *minimum* system requirements because you want your system hardware to be as large as possible in a Hyper-V Server.

The more CPU cores, RAM, and hard drive space you can provide, the more VMs you will be able to run. Even the smallest Hyper-V servers I have seen in production environments are running hardware such as dual Xeon processors, 96 GB of RAM, and many terabytes of storage space. While 96 GB of RAM may seem like a lot for a single system, if your standard workload server build includes 8 GB of RAM, which is a pretty low number, and you want to run 12 servers on your Hyper-V server, you are already beyond the capabilities of a Hyper-V server with only 96 GB of RAM, as 8 x 12 is 96, and you haven't left any memory for the host operating system to use! The moral of the story? Go big or go home!

Installing the Hyper-V role

Hyper-V is just another role in Windows Server 2025, but during the installation of that role, you will be asked a few questions, and it is important to understand what they are asking so that you can be sure your new Hyper-V server is built to last and to work in an efficient manner. First, you will need to have Windows Server 2025 already installed, and use the **Add Roles and Features** function in order to install the role called **Hyper-V**:

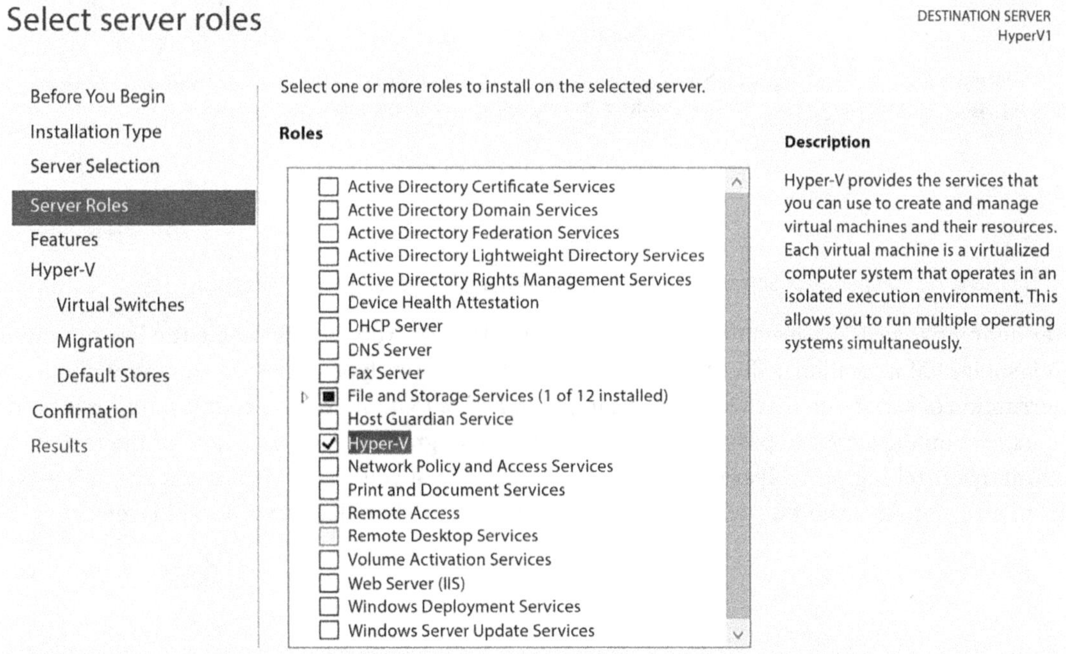

Select server roles

DESTINATION SERVER
HyperV1

Before You Begin

Installation Type

Server Selection

Server Roles

Features

Hyper-V

   Virtual Switches

   Migration

   Default Stores

Confirmation

Results

Select one or more roles to install on the selected server.

Roles

- [ ] Active Directory Certificate Services
- [ ] Active Directory Domain Services
- [ ] Active Directory Federation Services
- [ ] Active Directory Lightweight Directory Services
- [ ] Active Directory Rights Management Services
- [ ] Device Health Attestation
- [ ] DHCP Server
- [ ] DNS Server
- [ ] Fax Server
- [■] File and Storage Services (1 of 12 installed)
- [ ] Host Guardian Service
- [x] Hyper-V
- [ ] Network Policy and Access Services
- [ ] Print and Document Services
- [ ] Remote Access
- [ ] Remote Desktop Services
- [ ] Volume Activation Services
- [ ] Web Server (IIS)
- [ ] Windows Deployment Services
- [ ] Windows Server Update Services

Description

Hyper-V provides the services that you can use to create and manage virtual machines and their resources. Each virtual machine is a virtualized computer system that operates in an isolated execution environment. This allows you to run multiple operating systems simultaneously.

Figure 15.2: Installing the Hyper-V role is quite simple, as long as you meet the prerequisites

As you continue working through the wizard to install the role, you'll come across a screen labeled **Create Virtual Switches**. We will discuss networking in Hyper-V a little bit more in the next section, but what is important here is that you get to define which of your server's physical NICs will be tied into Hyper-V and available for your VMs to use. It is a good idea for each Hyper-V server to have multiple NICs. You want one NIC dedicated to the host itself, which you would not select on this screen. Leave that one alone for the hypervisor's own communications. In addition to that NIC, you will want at least one network card that can bridge the VMs into the corporate network.

You would select at least this one, as you can see in *Figure 15.3*. If you will be hosting many different VMs on this server, and they need to be connected to different physical networks, you might have to install many different NICs on your Hyper-V server:

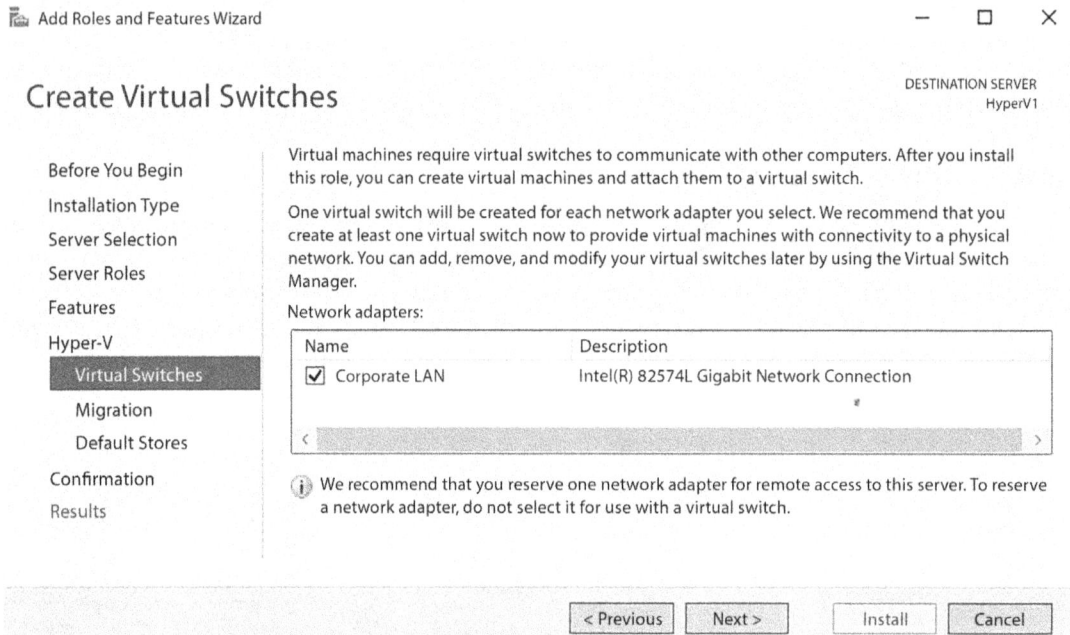

Add Roles and Features Wizard — □ ✕

Create Virtual Switches

DESTINATION SERVER
HyperV1

Before You Begin
Installation Type
Server Selection
Server Roles
Features
Hyper-V
   Virtual Switches
   Migration
   Default Stores
Confirmation
Results

Virtual machines require virtual switches to communicate with other computers. After you install this role, you can create virtual machines and attach them to a virtual switch.

One virtual switch will be created for each network adapter you select. We recommend that you create at least one virtual switch now to provide virtual machines with connectivity to a physical network. You can add, remove, and modify your virtual switches later by using the Virtual Switch Manager.

Network adapters:

Name	Description
☑ Corporate LAN	Intel(R) 82574L Gigabit Network Connection

ⓘ We recommend that you reserve one network adapter for remote access to this server. To reserve a network adapter, do not select it for use with a virtual switch.

< Previous   Next >   Install   Cancel

Figure 15.3: Selecting the physical NICs that will be available for VMs to use

After defining the NICs, we get to decide whether this Hyper-V server will handle the live migration of VMs. Live VM migration is the ability to move a VM from one Hyper-V host to another without any interruption of service on that VM. As you can see in *Figure 15.4*, there are a couple of different ways you can set up the server to prepare it for handling live migrations, and take note of the text at the bottom that is telling you to leave this option alone for now if you plan to make this Hyper-V server part of a cluster. In clustered environments, these settings are handled at a different layer:

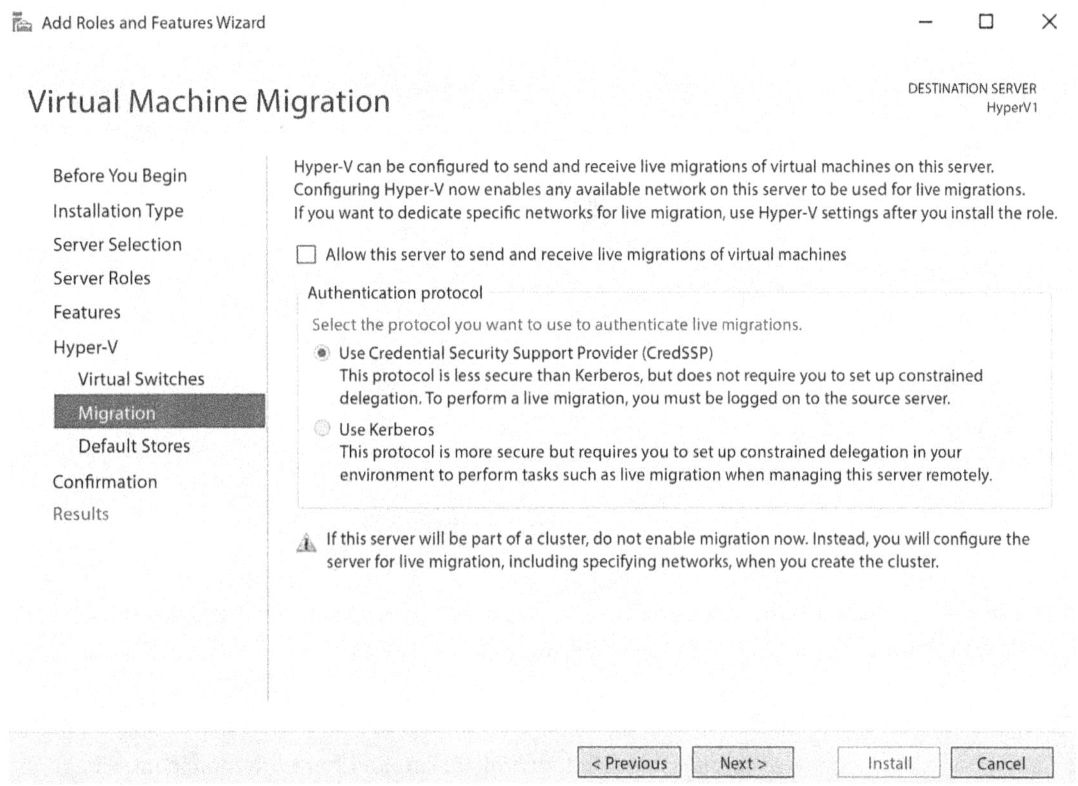

Figure 15.4: Deciding whether you need live migration capabilities

The last screen that I want to point out is the definition of storage locations for your VM data. After creating VMs and digging into what they look like at the hard-disk level (looking at the actual files that are created per VM), you will find that there are two key aspects to a VM: the **virtual hard-disk** (**VHD** or **VHDX**) file and a folder that contains the configuration files for that VM.

As you can see in *Figure 15.5*, the default locations for storing these items seem to be more in line with a piece of software you were installing on a laptop. It always surprises me that these are the default locations specified by Microsoft, as I would assume something as heavy as Hyper-V should have some best practices surrounding storage locations for your VM files and disks, not a shared-user Documents folder. I suppose since Microsoft doesn't know the configuration of your server, it can't make any real guesses as to where you want to store that data, and so it sets the default to be something that would work technically but should probably be changed as a matter of best practice. Many Hyper-V servers will have dedicated storage, even if only a separate hard disk, on which these files are planned to be stored. Make sure you take a minute on this screen and change the default storage locations of your VM files:

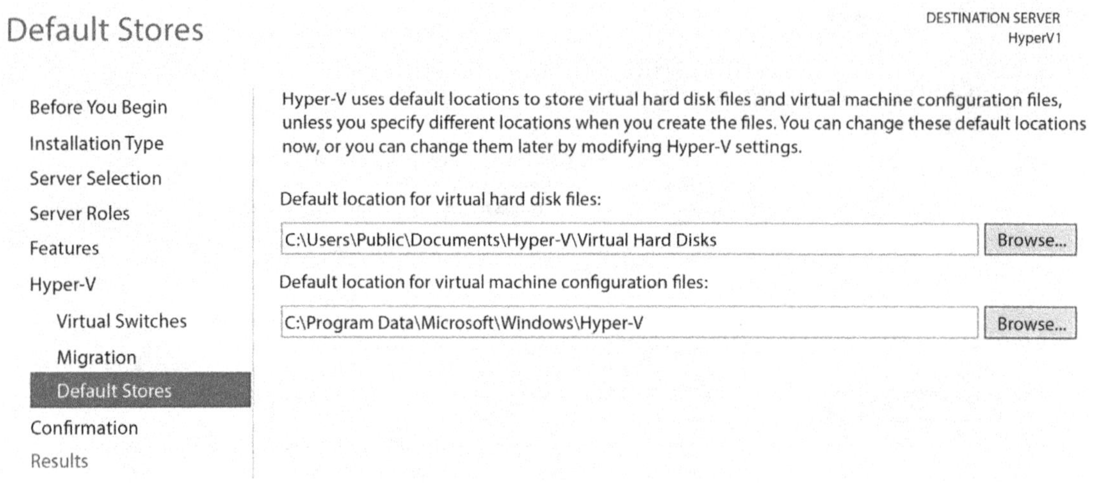

Default Stores

Before You Begin

Installation Type

Server Selection

Server Roles

Features

Hyper-V

   Virtual Switches

   Migration

   Default Stores

Confirmation

Results

Hyper-V uses default locations to store virtual hard disk files and virtual machine configuration files, unless you specify different locations when you create the files. You can change these default locations now, or you can change them later by modifying Hyper-V settings.

Default location for virtual hard disk files:

C:\Users\Public\Documents\Hyper-V\Virtual Hard Disks   [Browse...]

Default location for virtual machine configuration files:

C:\Program Data\Microsoft\Windows\Hyper-V   [Browse...]

Figure 15.5: Defining default storage locations for VM files

Remember that the version of Windows Server 2025 you are running determines how many VMs you will be able to run on top of this host. Server 2025 Standard limits you to running two VMs, while the Datacenter edition gives you access to launch as many as you can fit on the hardware.

Nested virtualization

In *Chapter 14, Containers*, we mentioned **nested virtualization**, and here the topic comes back into play. Usually, when talking about installing the Hyper-V role on a server, we are talking about installing it onto physical hardware. This hardware becomes your Hyper-V host server, and virtualization prerequisites such as DEP are all related to the hardware itself. There are some circumstances, both related to containers and separately, where you may find yourself wondering, *Do you suppose I could install the Hyper-V role onto...a VM?* The answer is yes! And indeed, this is the very definition of nested virtualization.

In fact, if you remember back to the first screenshot in this chapter, where I portrayed an error message encountered when attempting to install the Hyper-V role, that error was because I was attempting to install Hyper-V on a VM. I had simply created a new VM on my physical host, spun up Windows Server 2025 on it, and then tried clicking the box to install Hyper-V on it. But it failed. Why?

New VMs are not prepared by default to host other VMs. If you've worked within Hyper-V at all before, you probably remember that there are some BIOS-level settings available for each VM, and you may be thinking that is where you would visit to enable a VM to be able to do nested virtualization, but the option is not available from inside the Hyper-V management GUI whatsoever. Instead, we must turn to PowerShell on the physical host server to enable nested virtualization on our VM.

Launching PowerShell on my Hyper-V physical host, I simply execute the following command to enable my new HyperV1 VM to be able to do nested virtualization and host additional VMs:

```
Set-VMProcessor -VMName HyperV1 -ExposeVirtualizationExtensions $true
```

Your VM must be powered off for this command to be successful, but following this simple adjustment, your VM will now be prepared to install the Hyper-V role and serve the purposes of nested virtualization in your environment.

AMD processors are now supported

When running nested virtualization by installing the Hyper-V role on a VM, prior to Windows Server 2022, you were limited on the type of physical processor that could support this scenario. We can now successfully run nested virtualization on top of AMD processors as well as Intel.

What's new in 2025?

Microsoft introduces new improvements and tidbits for Hyper-V in almost every release of Windows Server, but they often go unnoticed, working silently in the background to make your life easier. Let's take a minute to look over what Windows Server 2025 brings to the table.

Generation 2 by default

As you will see for yourself in just a few pages, every Hyper-V VM can be configured as a **Generation 1 (Gen1)** or **Generation 2 (GEN2)** VM. The details behind these differing version numbers will be visible shortly, when we implement our first VM together, but suffice it to say that Gen2 is better in almost every way. Gen2 VMs have been around for multiple versions of Windows Server, but surprisingly, Microsoft's default for new VMs has always been Gen1, until now. This is not a shock-and-awe improvement in Hyper-V-land, but the console now defaults to creating new VMs as Gen2, as they should be.

GPU-P

GPU partitioning (GPU-P) is a new feature for the Hyper-V role in Windows Server 2025, which allows you to share a physical GPU across multiple VMs. When utilizing GPU-P, your VMs can each receive a dedicated fraction of the GPU, not a simple pass-through of hardware to the VM. This may sound similar to functionality that already existed, previously provided by **Discrete Device Assignment (DDA)**, but there are some key differences. The older DDA can intentionally allocate dedicated GPU resources to VMs, but on a 1:1 ratio. DDA can assign an entire GPU to a VM. GPU-P, on the other hand, allows you to chop up those massive GPU cards and assign segments (fractions) of them to VMs, allowing you to utilize large GPUs and spread that processing load across many servers.

GPU-P is going to be useful for VDI-type environments, especially where you need high rendering capacity. DDA is cool, but it requires many physical GPUs if you need multiple high-powered VMs. GPU-P widens this bottleneck, allowing you to do more with less physical hardware. Keep in mind that you cannot share GPUs via both DDA and GPU-P at the same time!

Live migration for Workgroup clusters

I imagine most Hyper-V clusters around the world to be handling domain-joined systems, but some organizations will certainly want to make use of Hyper-V servers that are not joined to a domain. The idea of Workgroup clusters is not new; Windows Server 2016 already included functionality to build failover clusters without a requirement for Active Directory. However, Hyper-V has never been able to take advantage of live migration in a Workgroup scenario... until now. Windows Server 2025 allows for certificate-based live migration of VMs among multiple Hyper-V hosts in a cluster, even when those hosts are only Workgroup-joined.

Hyper-V performance

As you would expect, a Hyper-V server should be capable of managing many virtual CPUs and very large quantities of RAM. Most often, what I see in the wild are high-powered Hyper-V host servers, servicing fairly normal-looking VMs. What I mean by that is a Hyper-V server with lots of resources might be serving up many dozens of different servers, but each of those servers is pretty standard with 2–4 vCPUs and 8–16 GB of RAM. Sometimes, however, you find a need to build a VM to be much, much larger. Is this possible in Hyper-V? Yes, of course, but there are limits on the quantity of CPU and RAM resources that you can allocate to a single VM. The ceiling on these limits has been raised with Windows Server 2025 running Hyper-V, as Microsoft has taken some of Azure's capabilities and algorithms into your on-premises Hyper-V servers. I love looking at these numbers because it always amazes me how much growth we can find from one version of the operating system to the next!

In Windows Server 2025, here are your *per-VM* maximums, and how they compare to Server 2022:

- **Virtual CPUs per VM**: 2,048 (this is more than 8x Server 2022's capabilities)
- **Memory per VM**: 240 terabytes (this is 10x Server 2022's capacity)

Virtual switches

Upon completion of the Hyper-V role installation, your first inclination may be to jump right in and start creating VMs, but you should take a minute to make sure that the networking capabilities of your Hyper-V server are adequate to meet your needs. During the role installation process, we selected the physical NICs that are to be passed through into Hyper-V, and that screen told us it was going to establish a virtual switch for each of these NICs. But what does that look like inside the console? And what options do we have for establishing networking between our VMs?

To answer these questions, we need to open the management interface for Hyper-V. As with any administrative tool of a Windows role, check inside the **Tools** menu of Server Manager, and now that the role has been installed, you will see a new listing for **Hyper-V Manager**. Launch that, and you are now looking at the primary platform from which you will be managing and manipulating every aspect of your Hyper-V environment:

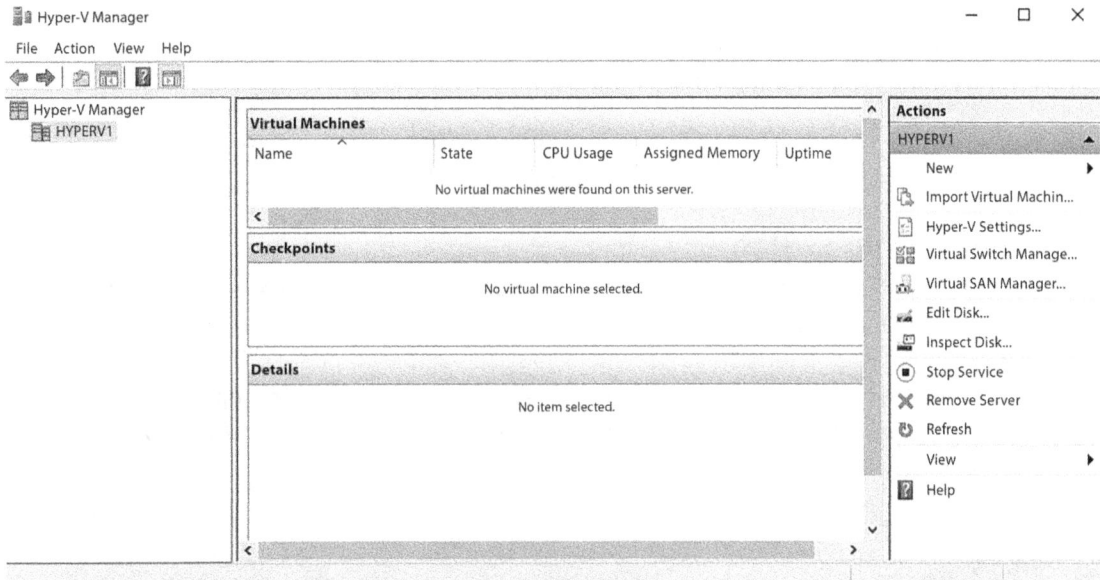

Figure 15.6: First look at Hyper-V Manager

We currently have a lot of blank space in this console because we don't have any VMs running yet. Over on the right side of **Hyper-V Manager**, you can see a link that says **Virtual Switch Manager....** Go ahead and click on that link to be taken to the settings for our virtual switches and networking:

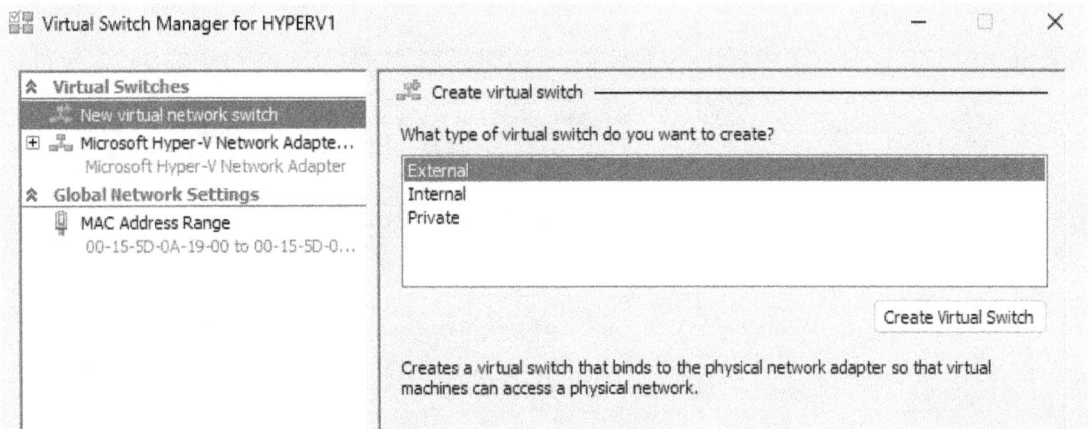

Figure 15.7: Managing virtual switches inside Hyper-V

Toward the left, you see a list of current virtual switches. On my server, there is only one switch listed there at the moment, which is named after the physical NIC to which it is connected. This is the virtual switch that the role installation process created for us when we selected the NIC to be included with Hyper-V. If you selected multiple NICs during the role installation, you will have multiple virtual switches available here, each corresponding to a single physical NIC. Every VM you create will have one or more virtual NICs, and you will see shortly that you can choose where each of those virtual NICs gets connected. If there are five different physical networks that your VMs might need to contact, you can use five physical NICs in the Hyper-V server, plug each one into a different network, and then have five virtual switches here in the console that your VM NICs can be *plugged* into.

As you can see in *Figure 15.7*, we have a button named **Create Virtual Switch**, which is self-explanatory. This is where we go to create new switches, but there are three different types of switches that you can create. Let's take just a minute to discuss the differences between them.

External virtual switch

The external virtual switch is the most common type to use for any VMs that need to contact a production network. Each external virtual switch binds to a physical NIC that is installed on the Hyper-V Server. If you click on an external virtual switch, you can see that you have some options for configuring this switch and that you can even change the switch type. In the following screenshot, I have renamed my external virtual switch so that it is easier to identify when I decide to add additional NICs to this server in the future:

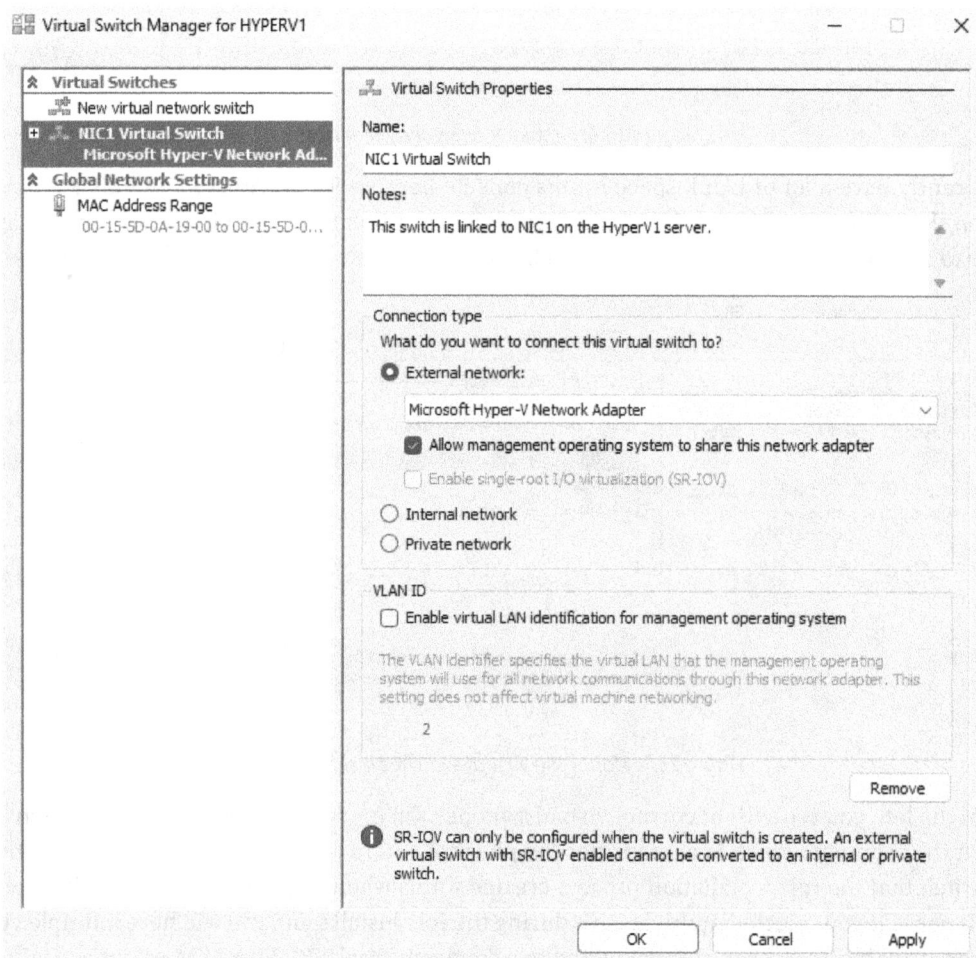

Figure 15.8: Renaming an external virtual switch for easy identification

Internal virtual switch

Internal virtual switches are not bound to a physical NIC, so if you create an internal virtual switch and connect a VM to it, that VM will not be able to contact a physical network outside the Hyper-V host server. It's sort of a middleman between the other two types of switches; using an internal virtual switch is useful when you want the VM traffic to remain within the Hyper-V environment but still provide network connectivity between the VMs and the Hyper-V host itself. In other words, VMs connected to an internal virtual switch can talk to each other and talk to the Hyper-V server, but not beyond.

Private virtual switch

The private virtual switch is just what the name implies: private. VMs plugged into the same private virtual switch can communicate with each other, but not beyond. Even the Hyper-V host server does not have network connectivity to a private virtual switch. Test labs are a great example of a use case for private virtual switches, which we will discuss immediately following this section when we create a new virtual switch of our own.

Creating a new virtual switch

The following is an example I use often. I am running a new Hyper-V server, which is connected physically to my corporate network, so I can spin up new VMs, connect them to my external virtual switch, and have them communicate directly with the corporate network. This allows me to domain-join them and interact with them like I would any server on my network. Maybe I need to create some VMs that I want to talk with each other, but I do *not* want them to communicate with my production network. A good example of this scenario in the real world is when building a test lab or sandbox environment. In fact, I am taking this exact approach for all of the servers that we have used throughout this book. My physical Hyper-V server is on my production network, yet my entire Contoso.local network, and all of the VMs running within it, are on their own separate network, which is completely segregated from my real network. I did this by creating a new private virtual switch. Remember from the description that when you plug VMs into this kind of switch, they can communicate with other VMs that are plugged into that same virtual switch, but they cannot communicate beyond that switch.

Inside **Virtual Switch Manager**, all I must do is choose the kind of virtual switch that I want to create (**Private network**, in this case) and click on the **Create Virtual Switch** button. I can then provide a name for my new switch, and I am immediately able to connect VMs to this switch. You can see in *Figure 15.9* that I have created two new private virtual switches: one to plug my test lab VM's internal NICs into, and another switch that will act as my test lab's DMZ network:

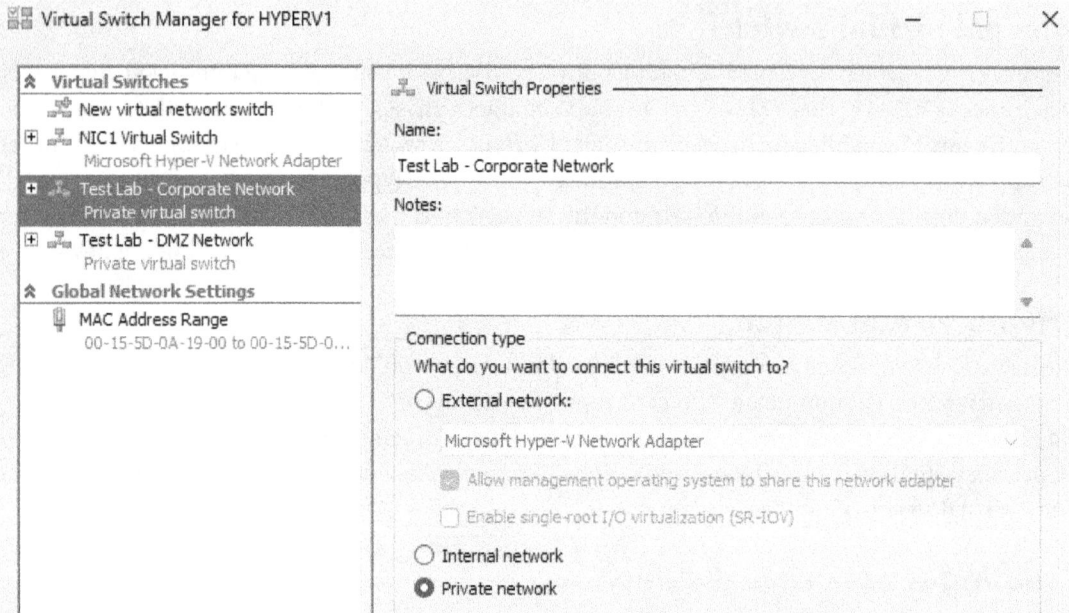

Figure 15.9: Creating new private virtual switches

Implementing a virtual server

Now, we are ready to spin up our first virtual server! Similar to creating new virtual switches, the process for creating a new VM is straightforward, but there are some steps along the way that might need explanation if you haven't been through this process before. We start with the same management interface from which we do everything in the Hyper-V world. Open **Hyper-V Manager** and right-click on the name of your Hyper-V server. Navigate to **New** | **Virtual Machine...** to launch the wizard:

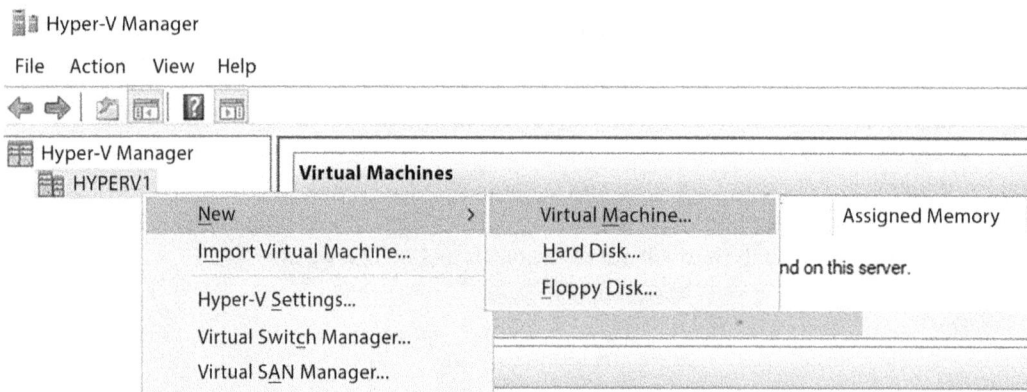

Figure 15.10: Creating a new VM

The first screen where we need to make some decisions is **Specify Name and Location**. Create a name for your new VM, which is easy enough. Then, you also have the chance to store your VM in a new location. If you set a good default location for your VMs during Hyper-V role installation, chances are that you won't have to modify this field. But in my case, I chose the default options when I installed the role, and so this wizard was going to place my VM somewhere inside C:\ProgramData, and I didn't like the look of that. So, I selected the checkbox and chose a location that I like for my VM. You can see that I am using a dedicated disk to store my VMs, which is generally a good practice. An even better practice in a larger network would be to utilize resilient disk space that was accessed through the network, such as a Storage Spaces Direct infrastructure or some kind of SAN:

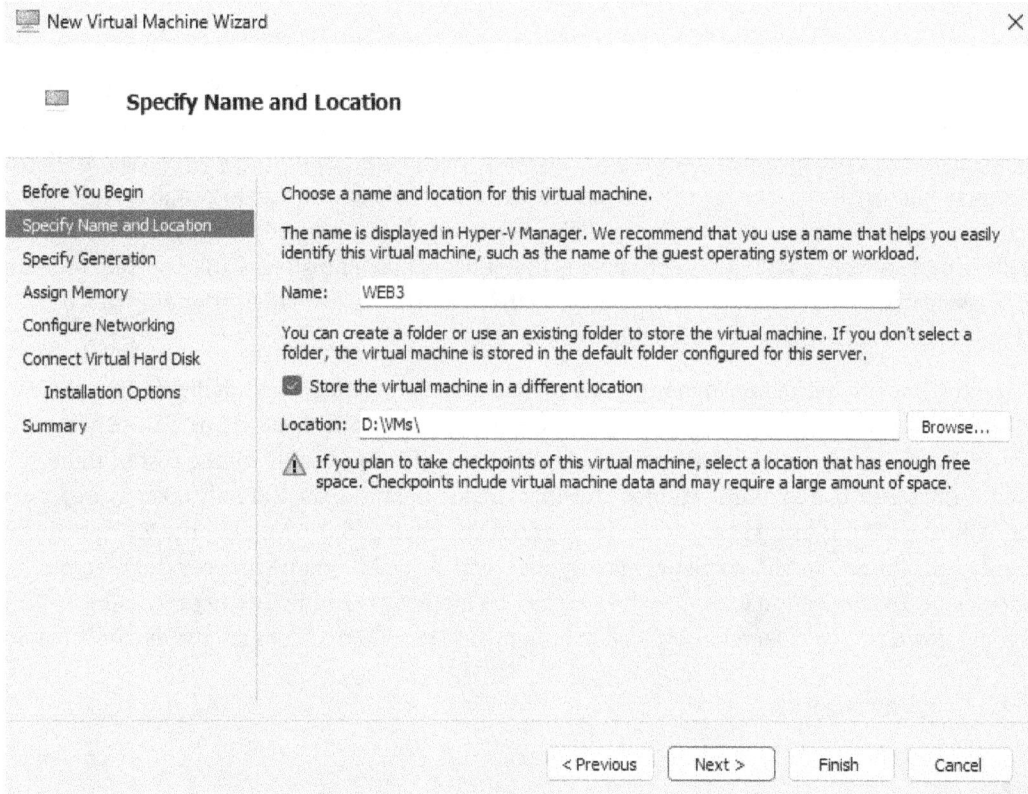

Figure 15.11: Specifying a storage location for a new VM

Next, you have to decide whether you are creating a **Generation 1** or **Generation 2** VM. You already know that one of Windows Server 2025's Hyper-V enhancements is to now default new VMs to Gen2, which are more comprehensive and more powerful than Gen1 VMs. However, Gen1 still has its place, especially for legacy systems or operating systems. *Figure 15.12* portrays good detail about the differences between these two types of VMs. If your VM is going to be running an older operating system, you should likely go with **Generation 1** to ensure compatibility. Alternatively, if you are planning for a recent operating system to be installed on this new VM, selecting **Generation 2** is in your best interests from a new features and security perspective:

Choose the generation of this virtual machine.

○ Generation 1

This virtual machine generation supports 32-bit and 64-bit guest operating systems and provides virtual hardware which has been available in all previous versions of Hyper-V.

◉ Generation 2

This virtual machine generation provides support for newer virtualization features, has UEFI-based firmware, and requires a supported 64-bit guest operating system.

⚠ Once a virtual machine has been created, you cannot change its generation.

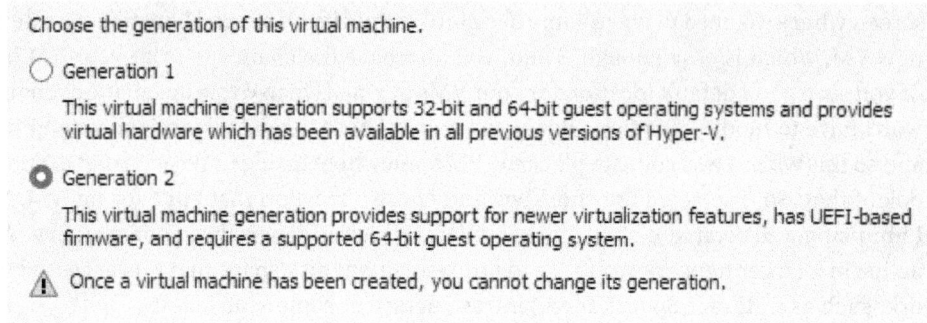

Figure 15.12: Each VM can be either Generation 1 or Generation 2

Now, define how much memory you want to assign to this particular VM. Keep in mind that this setting is adjustable in the future, so you don't have to plan too hard for this. The amount of RAM you dedicate to this VM will depend on how much RAM you have available in the Hyper-V host system and how much memory is required to run whatever roles and services you plan to install on this VM. You can specify any amount of memory in this field. For example, if I wanted roughly 4 GB, I could type in 4000 MB. However, what I find in the field is that most people still stick with the actual amount of MB, because that is what we have always done with hardware. So instead of rounding to 4,000, I am going to set my 4 GB VM to an *actual 4* GB, or 4096 MB.

Leaving the box unchecked for dynamic memory means that Hyper-V will dedicate 4,096 MB of its physically available RAM to this specific VM. Whether the VM is using 4,096 MB or 256 MB at any given time, the full 4,096 MB will be dedicated to the VM and will be unusable by the rest of the Hyper-V server. If you select **Use Dynamic Memory for this virtual machine**, the VM only takes away from the Hyper-V host what it is using at any given moment. If you set it to 4,096 MB, but the VM is sitting idle and only consuming 256 MB, it will only tax Hyper-V with a 256 MB load. This sounds great, but there is a downside. Dynamically expanding and contracting memory consumes extra processing resources and could slow down your server's performance, compared to a VM that does not use dynamic memory:

Assign Memory

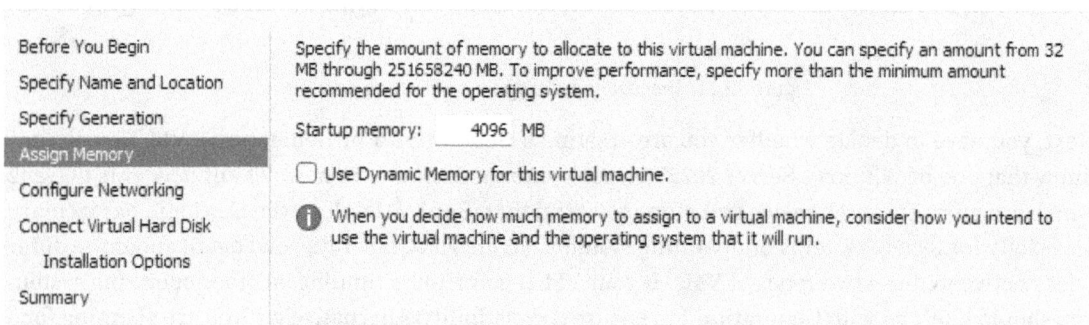

Before You Begin
Specify Name and Location
Specify Generation
Assign Memory
Configure Networking
Connect Virtual Hard Disk
Installation Options
Summary

Specify the amount of memory to allocate to this virtual machine. You can specify an amount from 32 MB through 251658240 MB. To improve performance, specify more than the minimum amount recommended for the operating system.

Startup memory: 4096 MB

☐ Use Dynamic Memory for this virtual machine.

ⓘ When you decide how much memory to assign to a virtual machine, consider how you intend to use the virtual machine and the operating system that it will run.

Figure 15.13: Defining memory allocation for the new VM

Configure Networking is the next screen we are presented with, and here we simply choose which virtual switch our VM's NIC gets plugged into. We do have the ability to add additional NICs to this VM later, but for now, we get a standard single NIC during the creation of our new VM, and we simply need to choose where it needs to be connected. For the time being, this new web server I am building will be connected to my Test Lab internal corporate network, so that I can build my web app and test it out before introducing it into a real production network. If I drop down a list of available connections here, you will see that my original external virtual switch, as well as the two new private virtual switches that I created, are available to choose from:

Each new virtual machine includes a network adapter. You can configure the network adapter to use a virtual switch, or it can remain disconnected.

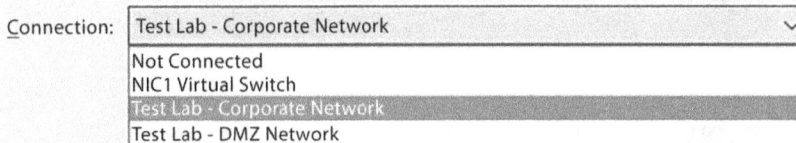

Connection: Test Lab - Corporate Network   ∨

Not Connected
NIC1 Virtual Switch
Test Lab - Corporate Network
Test Lab - DMZ Network

Figure 15.14: Plugging the new VM into a virtual switch

A few details are also needed so that this new VM can have a hard drive. Most commonly, you will utilize the top option here so that the new VM gets a brand-new hard drive. There are also options for using an existing virtual hard disk if you are booting from an existing file, or attaching a disk later if you aren't yet prepared to make this decision. We are going to allow the wizard to generate a new virtual hard disk, and the default size is 127 GB. I can set this to whatever I want, but it is important to know that it does not consume the full 127 GB of space. VHDX files are dynamically expanding; thus, the actual disk size will only be as large as what is being used on the disk. When this server is first running, only a fraction of that 127 GB will be used. I mention this to point out that the number you specify here is more of a *maximum* size, so make sure to plan your disks appropriately, specifying enough size so that you and your applications have the necessary room to grow:

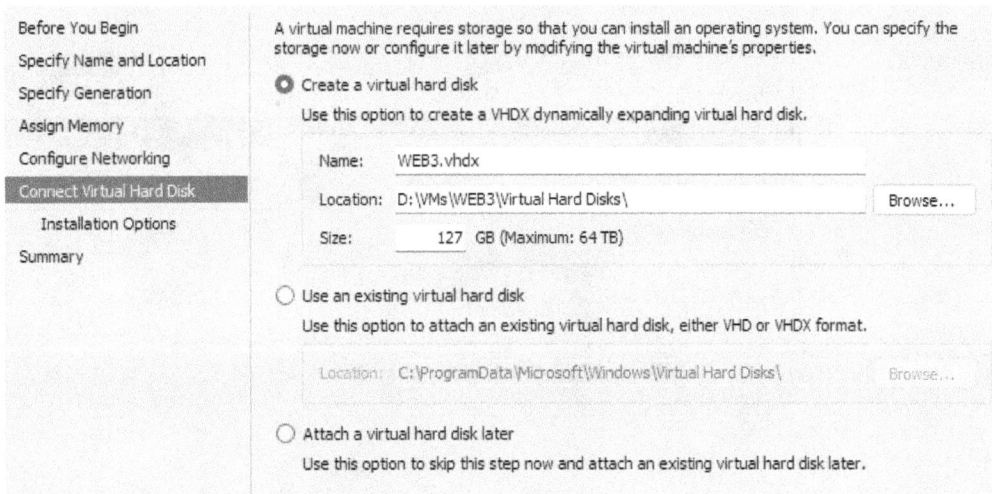

Before You Begin	A virtual machine requires storage so that you can install an operating system. You can specify the storage now or configure it later by modifying the virtual machine's properties.
Specify Name and Location	
Specify Generation	● Create a virtual hard disk
Assign Memory	Use this option to create a VHDX dynamically expanding virtual hard disk.
Configure Networking	Name: WEB3.vhdx
Connect Virtual Hard Disk	Location: D:\VMs\WEB3\Virtual Hard Disks\ Browse...
Installation Options	Size: 127 GB (Maximum: 64 TB)
Summary	
	○ Use an existing virtual hard disk
	Use this option to attach an existing virtual hard disk, either VHD or VHDX format.
	Location: C:\ProgramData\Microsoft\Windows\Virtual Hard Disks\ Browse...
	○ Attach a virtual hard disk later
	Use this option to skip this step now and attach an existing virtual hard disk later.

Figure 15.15: Allowing the wizard to create a new virtual hard disk

The last screen of options in the wizard allows us to define the specifics of the operating system our new VM is going to run on, or rather, where that operating system will be installed from. We are going to purposefully leave this set to **Install an operating system later** because that is the default option, and it will give us the chance to see what happens when you do not specify any settings on this screen:

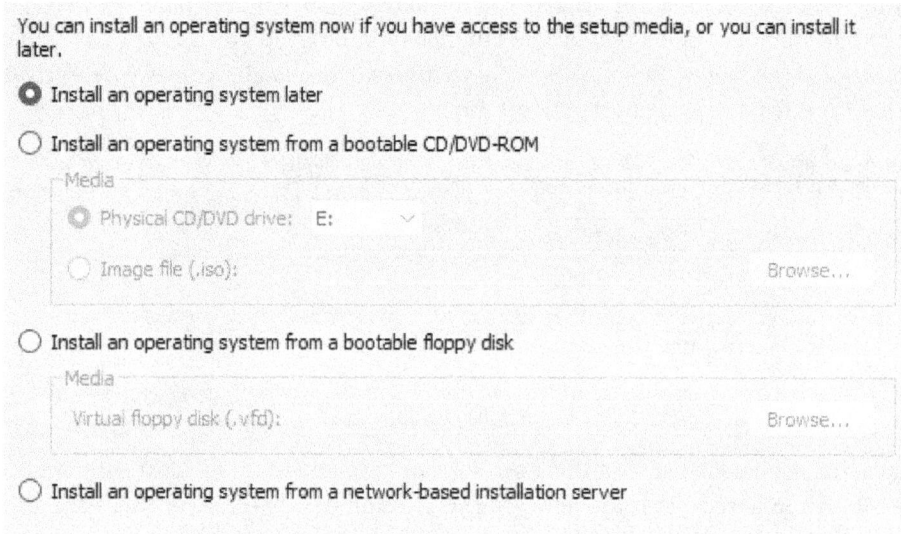

Figure 15.16: Decisions to be made regarding operating system installation

Starting and connecting to the VM

We have now created a VM, which you can see inside the **Hyper-V Manager** console. Starting the VM is as simple as right-clicking on it and then selecting **Start**. After selecting the option to start the VM, right-click on it again and click on **Connect**. This will open a console window from which you can watch the boot process of your new server:

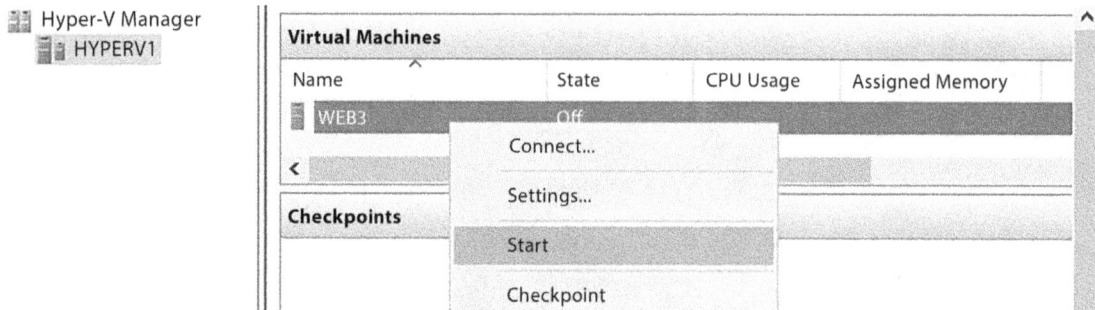

Figure 15.17: Starting our new VM

Now that our new VM has been started, what can we expect to see inside the console window? A boot failure error, of course:

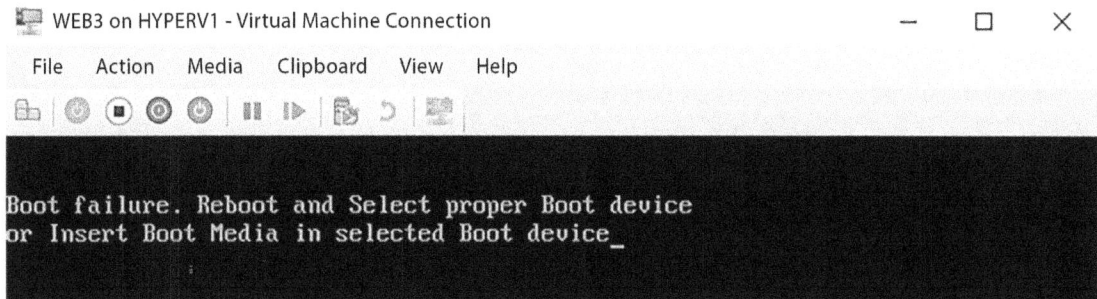

Figure 15.18: The initial start of this VM was not so successful

Installing the operating system

We received a boot failure message because we didn't specify any operating system media during our wizard, and so Hyper-V has created our VM and our new hard disk, but just like when you build a new server out of fresh hardware, you need software to be installed on that hard disk in order for it to do something. Luckily, installing an operating system on a VM is even easier than installing it on a physical server. Heading back into the **Hyper-V Manager** console, right-click on the name of your new VM and go to **Settings...**.

Inside **Settings**, you will see that this VM has a DVD drive automatically listed in **IDE Controller 1**. If you click on **DVD Drive**, you can easily tell it to mount any ISO to that drive. Copy the ISO file of the operating system installer you wish to run to the hard drive of your Hyper-V server.

I typically place all my ISOs inside a dedicated folder called ISOs, right alongside my VMs folder, and then browse to it from this screen using the **Browse...** button. Connecting an ISO to your VM is the same as if you were plugging a physical installation DVD into a physical server:

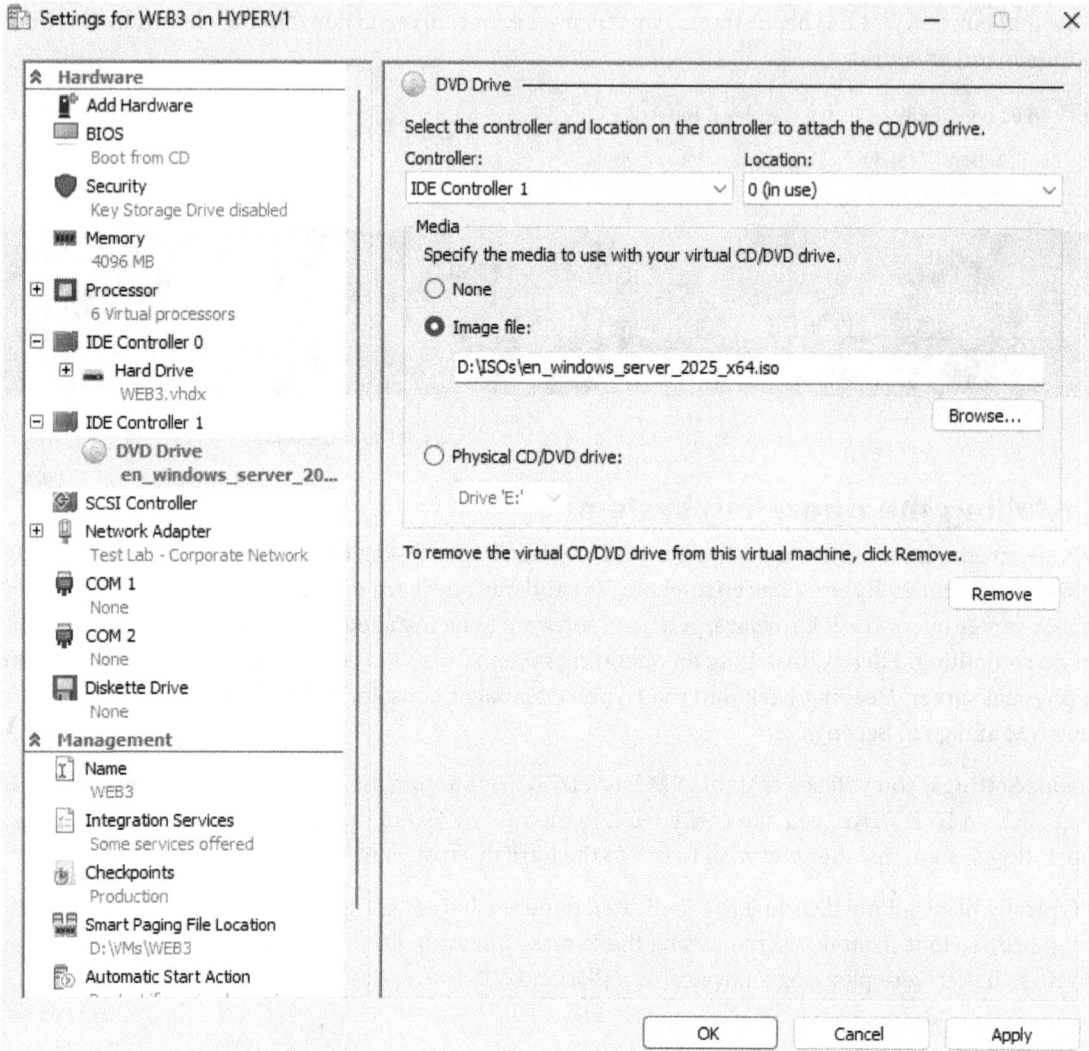

Figure 15.19: Providing operating system installation media to our new VM

After mounting the media, restart your VM, and you will see that our operating system installer kicks off automatically:

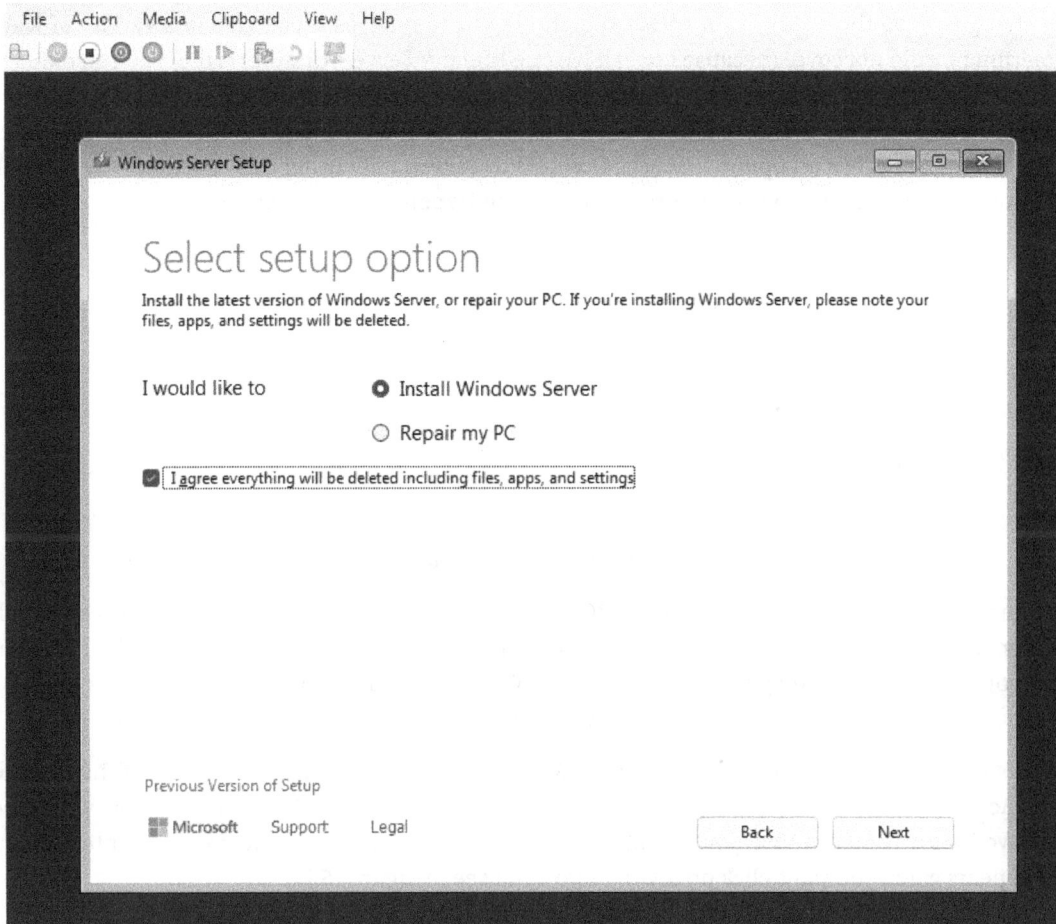

Figure 15.20: The VM is now booting to the installation ISO

Managing a virtual server

We have made use of Hyper-V Manager to manage our virtual switches and to create a VM. This tool is all-powerful when it comes to manipulating your VMs, and I find myself accessing it frequently in my daily job. Let's take a look at a few of the other things you can do from inside Hyper-V Manager, as well as discuss other methods that can be used to work with the new VMs that are being created on your Hyper-V server.

Hyper-V Manager

As you know, Hyper-V Manager is the primary tool for managing a Hyper-V server. It is a nice console that gives you the status of your VMs and allows you to manage those VMs in a variety of ways. Something we did not cover (because I only have one Hyper-V Server running) is that you can manage multiple Hyper-V servers from a single **Hyper-V Manager** console. Just like any MMC-style console in the Microsoft world, you can right-click on the words **Hyper-V Manager** near the top-left corner of the screen and select an option that says **Connect to Server...** By using this function, you can pull information from other Hyper-V servers into this same **Hyper-V Manager** console:

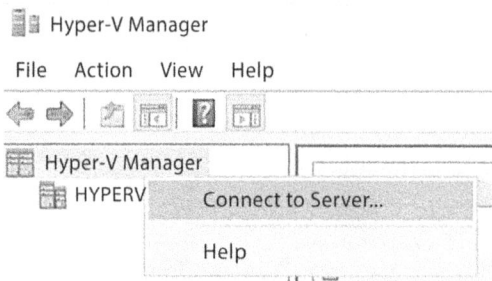

Figure 15.21: Connecting Hyper-V Manager to remote Hyper-V hosts

Furthermore, this enables you to run **Hyper-V Manager** software on a client computer. You can install the Hyper-V role on a Windows 10/11 machine, which will also install this console, and then use that local copy of **Hyper-V Manager** running on your Windows 10/11 desktop to manage your Hyper-V servers, without needing to log in to those servers directly.

Some of the most useful actions inside **Hyper-V Manager** are listed along the right side of the console in the **Actions** pane—features such as **Virtual Switch Manager** and the ability to create a new VM. Once you have VMs up and running, you will find a lot of useful functions listed inside the context menu that appears when you right-click on a VM, as you can see in *Figure 15.22*:

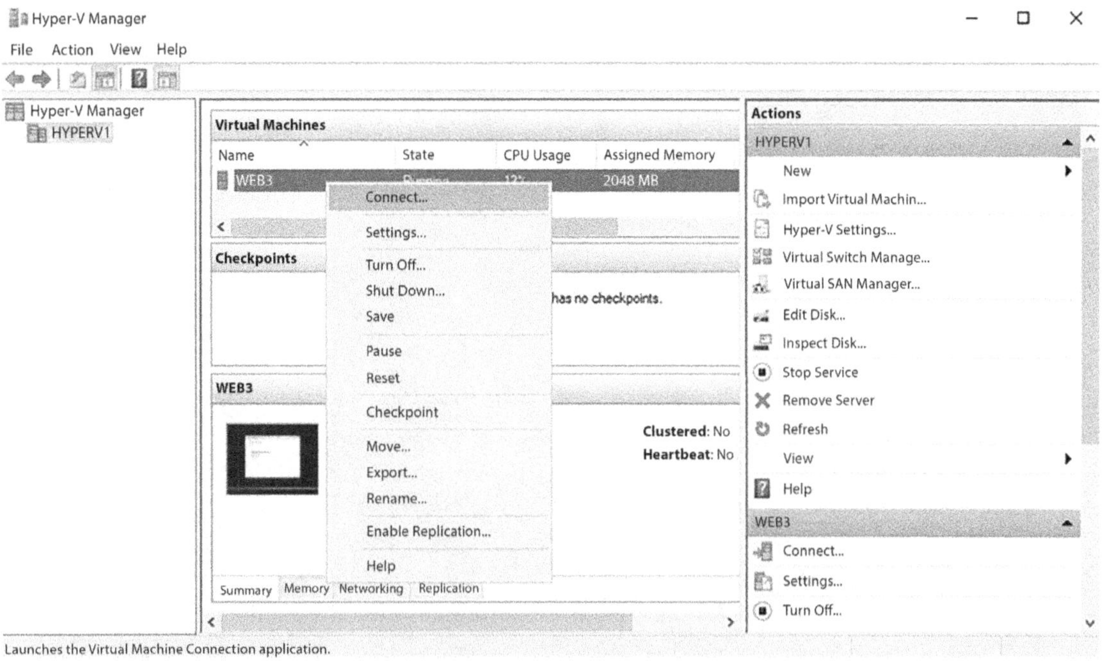

Figure 15.22: Hyper-V management tasks via the Actions pane

Some of these are self-explanatory, and some are worth playing around with. We have already used **Connect…** to connect to our VM's console. **Settings…** opens up a ton of possibilities, and we will take a look further inside the **Settings** menu immediately following this section. One of the most common reasons I open this right-click menu is for power functions on my VMs. Here, you find the ability to turn off or shut down your VM. Turning it off is like yanking the power cord on a server: it cuts off the power immediately to that server and will cause Windows some grief when doing so. The shutdown function, on the other hand, initiates a clean shutdown, at least when you are using Microsoft operating systems on the VMs. Shutting down a server is no big deal, but the real power here comes from the fact that you can shut down multiple VMs at the same time. For example, if I were running a dozen different VMs for all of my test labs, and I decided that my lab was taking up too many resources and causing problems on my Hyper-V server, I could select all of my VMs at the same time, right-click on them, then click on **Shut Down…** just once, and it would immediately kick off the shutdown process on all of the VMs that I had selected. Once a VM is shut down or turned off, right-clicking on that VM will give you a **Start** function; you can also select many servers and start them all at once by using this right-click menu.

The Settings menu

Making in-depth modifications to any of your VMs typically means right-clicking on that VM and then navigating to **Settings…** for that particular VM. Inside **Settings**, you can adjust any aspect of your VM's hardware, which is the most common reason to visit this screen. Immediately upon opening **Settings**, you have the option to add hardware to your VM. This is the place you would visit to add more hard drive controllers or NICs to your virtual server:

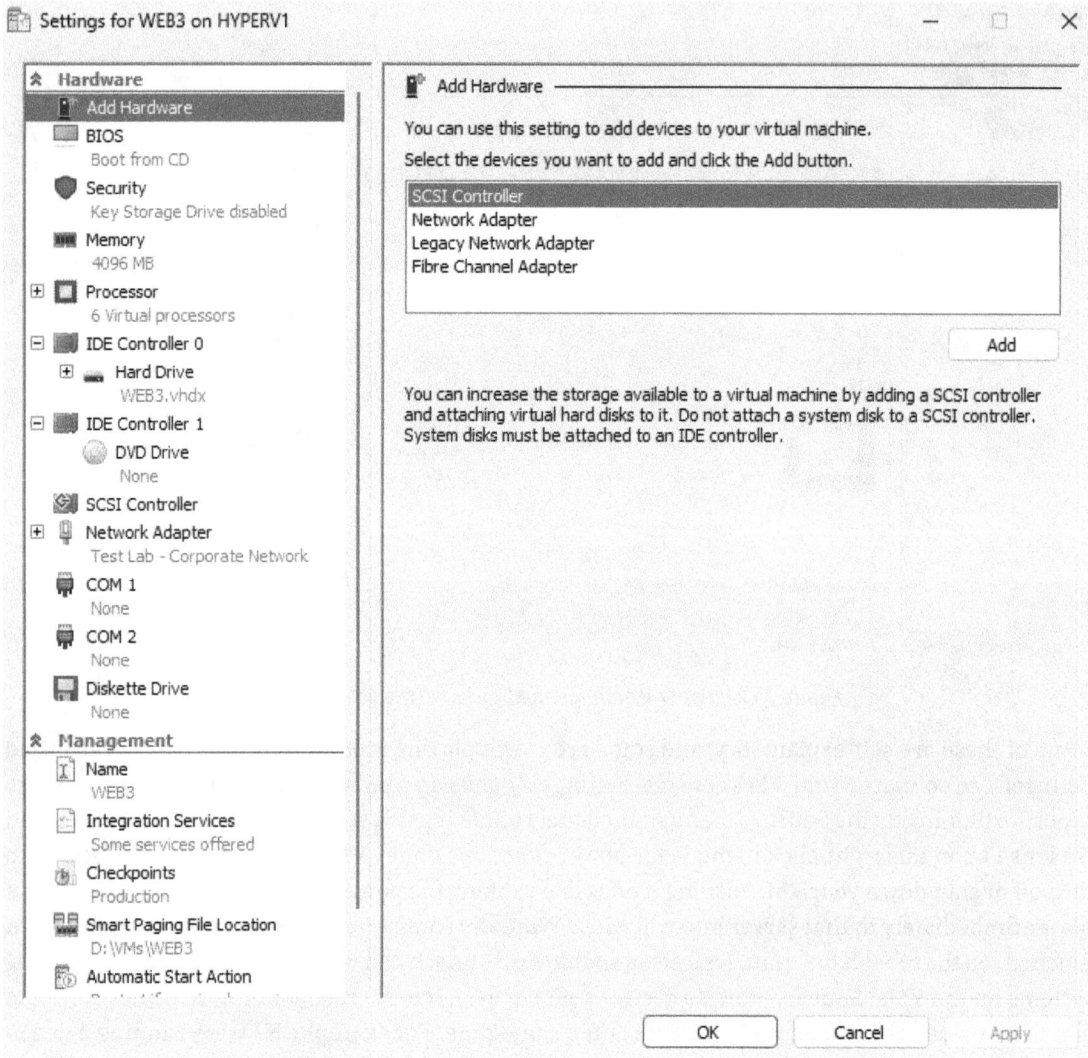

Figure 15.23: Adding new hardware to an existing VM

I don't know whether you can tell from the preceding screenshot, but the **Add** button is currently grayed out. This is important. Many functions inside **Settings** can be manipulated on the fly, while the VM is running. Some functions cannot be accomplished unless the VM is turned off. Adding hardware is one of those functions. If you want to add a new hard drive or NIC to your VM, you will need to shut down that VM before you can do it.

Next, we should talk about the **Memory** screen. This one is fairly painless, right? Simply input the amount of RAM that you want assigned to this VM. The reason that I want to point it out is that a major improvement has been made in this functionality since the early days of Hyper-V. Starting with Windows Server 2016 Hyper-V, you can now adjust the amount of RAM that a VM has allocated *while it is running*! In previous versions of Hyper-V, you were required to shut down the VMs to change their memory allocation, but even though my WEB3 server is currently running and servicing users, I can pop in here and increase RAM at will.

Let's say my 4 GB isn't keeping up with the task load, and I want to increase it to 8 GB. I leave the server running, open the **Hyper-V Manager** settings for the VM, and adjust the relevant setting to 8192 MB:

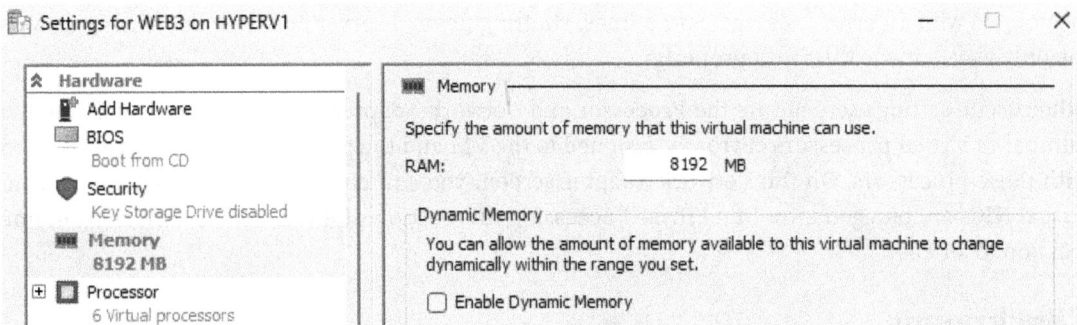

Figure 15.24: Increasing memory while the VM is running

The amount of memory immediately adjusts, and if I open system properties inside the WEB3 server, I can see that the operating system has updated to reflect the 8 GB of RAM now installed:

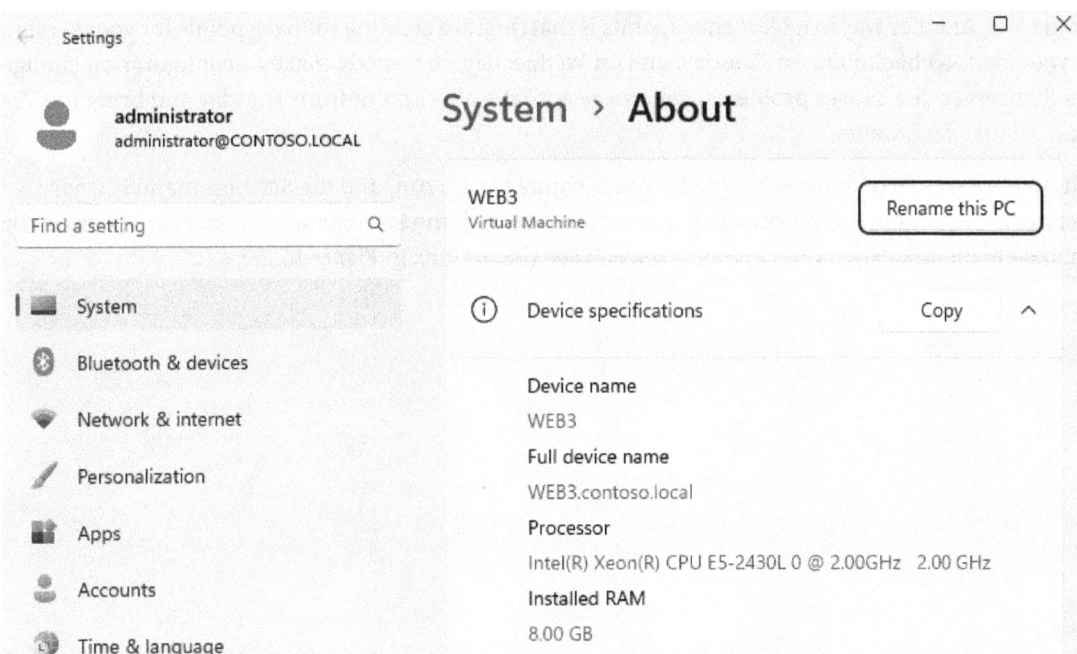

Figure 15.25: WEB3 is immediately increased to 8 GB of memory

RAM assigned to a VM can also be decreased on the fly, while the server is running. This can be helpful if you are running out of resources on your host and need to make some adjustments to already-running VMs, stealing from them to be able to spin up a new server. However, decreasing RAM on VMs is not always something that Hyper-V can engage in. If the VM is using less memory than it is allocated, you will be allowed to decrease. If the VM is utilizing memory that you try to remove, however, you'll be stopped with an error message. Sometimes, shutting down a server and then decreasing RAM is the only way to make this work properly.

Other useful settings screens are the **Processor** and **Network Adapter** sections. Here, you define the number of virtual processors currently assigned to the VM and the performance weights associated with these processors. On the **Network Adapter** screen, you can change which virtual switch your virtual NICs are plugged into. I find myself accessing this section often as I move servers from one location to another.

Checkpoints

Another important function inside the **Settings** menu is called **checkpoints**. These were formerly called **snapshots**, which is also the name used by VMware for this capability, but the word "checkpoint" is a little bit more accurate to what these actually are. Checkpoints are a function that you can invoke from Hyper-V Manager by right-clicking on one or more VMs. It essentially creates a *snapshot in time* of the VM. Another way to look at checkpoints is that they are creating rollback points for your servers. If you create a checkpoint on Tuesday, and on Wednesday, somebody makes a configuration change on that server that causes problems, you can restore the checkpoint from Tuesday and bring the VM back to that day's status.

There are a couple of different ways that checkpoints can be run, and the **Settings** menu is where we define those particulars. Simply right-click on any VM, visit the **Settings** screen, and then click on the management task called **Checkpoints**. You can see the options in *Figure 15.26*:

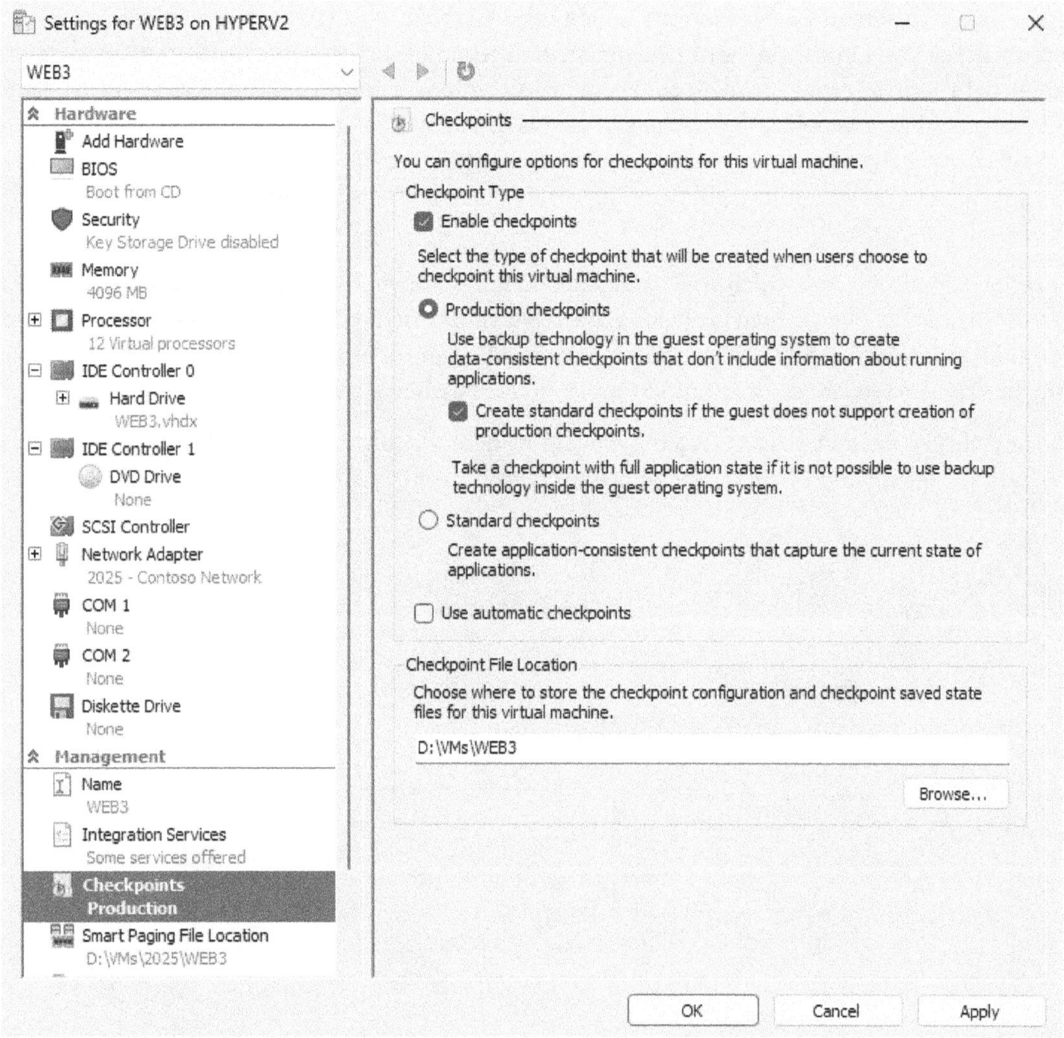

Figure 15.26: Options for configuring checkpoints

These settings are individual for each VM you are running; you could treat checkpoints for WEB1 differently from WEB2, for example. The default way to handle these snapshots in time is called **Production checkpoints**. This is generally the preferred method for creating these quick images of your servers, as it is the cleanest method. When choosing to generate a production checkpoint, Hyper-V invokes Windows backup functions inside the VM's operating system to create a backup of that server. This would be similar to you logging in to that VM and manually launching an operating system backup task. Keep in mind that, when you do this, and therefore when Hyper-V does this for you, it is not a block-by-block identical backup of the VM, but rather a backup file that can then be restored in the future to bring the operating system files back to this point in time. In other words, a production checkpoint brings Windows back to the previous state, but any applications and data that are constantly changing on the server are not captured in the checkpoint, nor restored when the checkpoint is rolled back into place.

Alternatively, the **Standard checkpoints** option does just that. This takes more of a quick-and-dirty capture of the VM, kind of like right-clicking on the VHDX file and choosing to copy and then paste it somewhere else. Restoring standard checkpoints can be a messier process. Suppose your checkpoint was created while an application on the server was in the middle of an important function, such as a database write. Restoring that checkpoint would bring the server right back to the moment in time that the application was in the middle of that database write. This has the potential to cause issues inside that database.

Once you have decided on which kind of checkpoint is best for your VM, invoking checkpoints is very simple. Back at the main screen in Hyper-V Manager, simply right-click on your VM and select **Checkpoint**. After performing this task, you will see the middle pane of Hyper-V Manager receive some new information in a section you may not have even noticed earlier: **Checkpoints**.

The new checkpoint that we just created is now sitting here, waiting to be restored if the need arises. In the future, right-clicking on this checkpoint and choosing **Apply...** will initiate the restoration process:

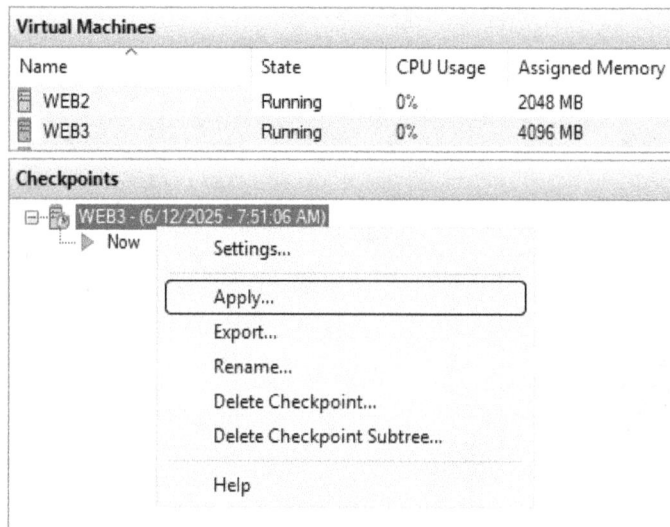

Figure 15.27: Viewing and recovering from a previous checkpoint

After reading this section, you may be tempted to think that Hyper-V checkpoints could be a replacement for normal server backups. Please don't let your mind wander down this path! Checkpoints are great for temporary use, but they should be cleaned up when finished. The more checkpoints you add for a server, the messier Hyper-V metadata gets when dealing with that VM. If you find yourself adding more and more checkpoints to VMs, and not deleting them when you are finished with them, you may find that the VM or your entire Hyper-V host begins to slow down with the extra baggage it now carries. Leave backups to real backup platforms. Checkpoints are very useful for taking a quick check-in of a server before making major changes to it, so you have a fast fallback path to revert those changes, but they should never be a replacement for real server backups.

Configuring auto stop and start

VMware is another very popular hypervisor host platform (competing with Hyper-V in the space), and while this chapter is not in any way a comparison of VMware and Hyper-V, I mention it here to point out a common issue that I encounter in the VMware world. What happens to your VMs when the physical host server is shut down, restarted, or even loses power temporarily?

While a sudden loss of power is going to be an interruption to both the physical host and VMs no matter what platform you are running, hopefully you have spent some money on a smart UPS system to keep your host server running during a power outage and it is perhaps even capable of cleanly shutting down that physical host if the power remains offline for an extended period of time.

Assuming a clean shutdown of the physical host occurs, what happens to your VMs? Do they all need to be individually shut down before shutting down the physical host? That may take a long time, yet I see many IT admins do exactly this because they think it is necessary and are worried about messing up the operating systems of their VMs by initiating a shutdown of the host server. Fortunately, you do not have to worry about shutting down VMs in this scenario, and there are options inside Hyper-V Manager to declare what happens with each VM when the host shuts down.

Inside **Settings** for any VM, scroll down to the bottom option called **Automatic Stop Action**. Here, you can see that there are three options available to declare what happens with a VM when the host shuts down. The VM can be cleanly shut down by Hyper-V, the VM can simply be turned off (which may negatively impact Windows on the VM), or Hyper-V can save the VM's state. You'll notice the save option is the default for every new VM and is likely the option you want to leave selected.

With this option in place, when your Hyper-V host server shuts down, the VMs are saved (another way to think about it is that they are being paused) so that when the host is powered back on, those VMs will resume from exactly where they were prior to the host shutdown:

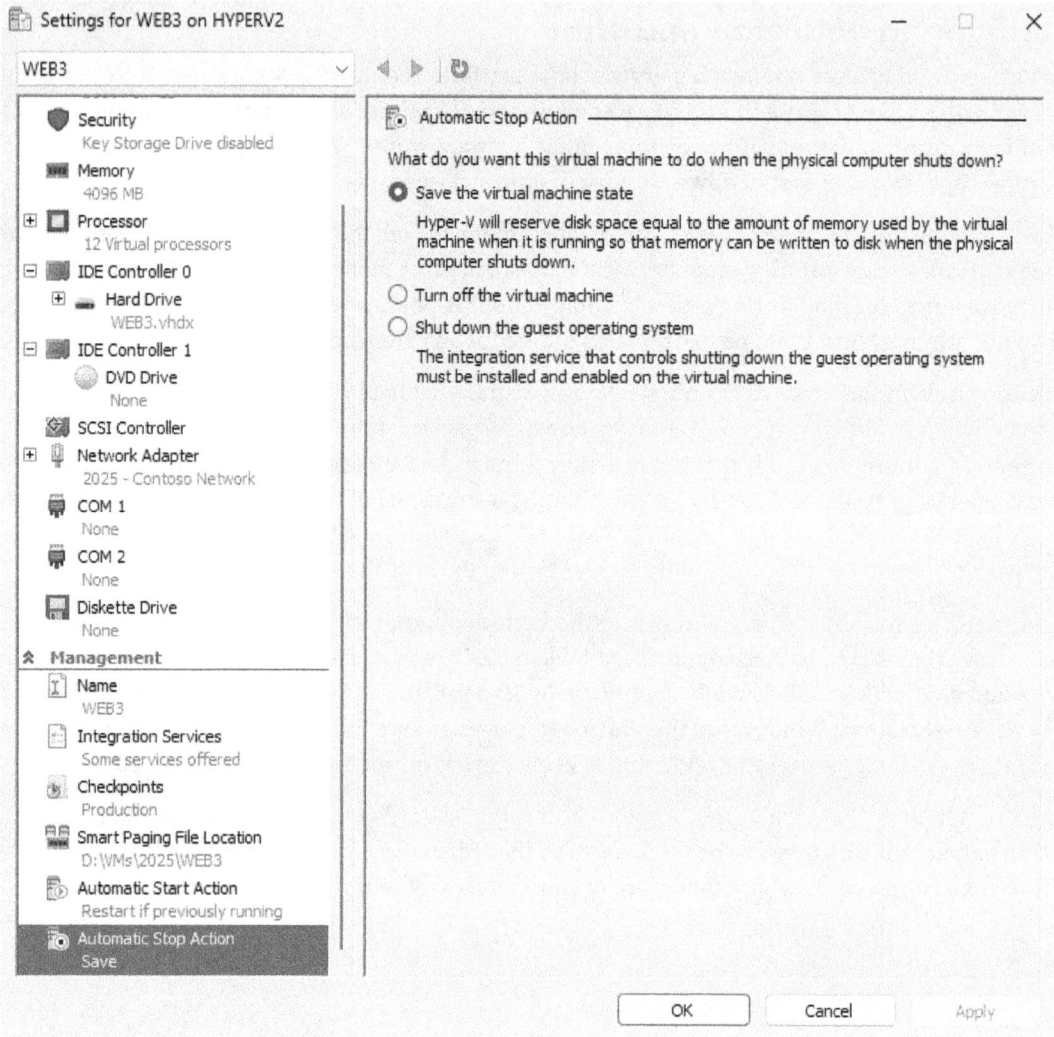

Figure 15.28: Automatic Stop Action settings

Clicking just one option higher on the **Settings** screen for any VM, you will also find **Automatic Start Action** options. As you have likely surmised, these are your options for handling each VM when a Hyper-V host server resumes power after having been powered off. Here, you can instruct Hyper-V to leave the VM powered off, to always start this VM when the host starts, or for Hyper-V to decide whether or not the VM was running prior to the host shutdown and to start up the VM only if it was previously running. This is the default option for each VM.

Also available on this screen is a **Startup delay** selection. This is useful when you need certain servers (VMs) to boot before others. For example, you want your domain controller to be online before any domain member servers attempt to boot. You could configure a startup delay of 30 or 60 seconds for any non-domain-controller servers, which would cause them to start after the domain controller starts:

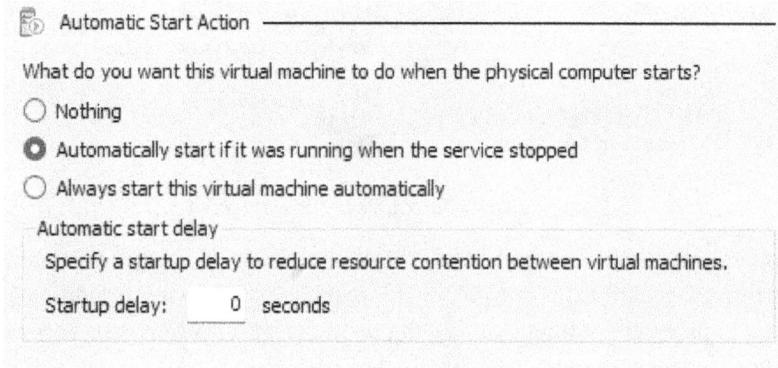

Figure 15.29: VM auto-start settings

Now you know where options live for configuring auto-stop and auto-start settings on each VM, and it would seem that retaining the default settings and never even visiting these options would produce VM shutdown and startup procedures that fit most environments. Wrapping this topic back to my opening statement about a common problem in VMware, what I find in the wild is that VMware host systems are rarely configured with correct auto-start settings. It is a rare occurrence that host servers go offline. I have seen hosts with uptimes longer than 1,000 days. Someday, however, you will encounter a situation where your host shuts down unexpectedly, and when that happens, do you know with certainty what your hypervisor is going to do with its VMs? Many of the VMware environments I encounter do not have auto-start settings configured for VMs, and so when the power goes off and comes back online, servers remain offline until you give them some manual attention.

No matter your hypervisor platform, spend a few minutes reviewing your VM auto-stop and auto-start procedures to ensure they fall in line with your expectations!

Check the host BIOS! It's easy enough to check over VM settings to make sure they auto-start following a power outage, but do you know whether or not the host server itself is going to auto-power on? This option is typically configured inside the BIOS on your physical server.

Expanding a virtual disk

Hardware changes to VMs are quick and easy, due to the nature of VMs and the use of all virtual resources that can be expanded or condensed with simple clicks of the mouse. Increasing or decreasing CPU cores and RAM resources is very self-explanatory and happens from inside the **VM Settings** menu. One other specific task that is a very normal procedure, but is not quite so straightforward, is the expansion of a virtual hard disk upon which a VM is running.

You can see in the following screenshot that my WEB3 server has a D: volume, but some yahoo (me) only allocated 5 GB initially, and it's almost full.

Figure 15.30: My data drive needs more room

On a physical server, this could be complicated, installing a newer and bigger drive and then needing to migrate everything to it. Since this is a VM, could we make things easier by adding a new disk that is larger and then copying everything over, saving us the step of dealing with hardware? Certainly. But there is a much simpler way, even than that, to deal with disks running out of space. Let's expand the existing data disk! The best part is that this only takes a few minutes.

Open **Hyper-V Manager**, and under **Actions** on the right side of the screen, select **Edit Disk….**

Run through the **Edit Disk** wizard, specifying the VHDX file that you want to manipulate, and on the third screen of the wizard, select the option to expand this disk. Following the **Expand** selection, you will be presented with the current size of the disk and a field where you can populate the new size. I'll go ahead and quadruple the size of this disk from 5 GB to 20 GB:

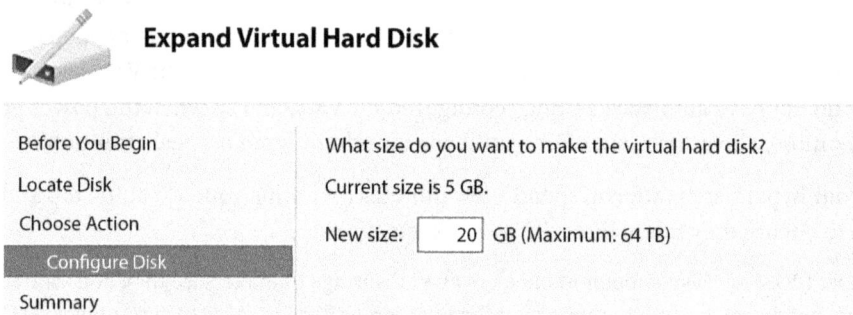

Figure 15.31: Expanding my data disk on the fly

After finishing that wizard, I revisit WEB3 and, lo and behold... my D: volume is still sitting at 5 GB. What gives? Even though we have now successfully expanded the virtual disk to 20 GB, the D: volume inside Windows has only ever been configured for 5 GB, and the Windows instance inside the VM has no idea what you want to accomplish with this extra free space. Perhaps we intend to expand the D: volume, or we could even use this new space to create a new E: volume, should we have the need.

Inside the VM, right-click on the **Start** menu and open **Disk Management**. Inside, you will see the status of disks plugged into the VM, where it is clear that the second disk has now been expanded to the larger size:

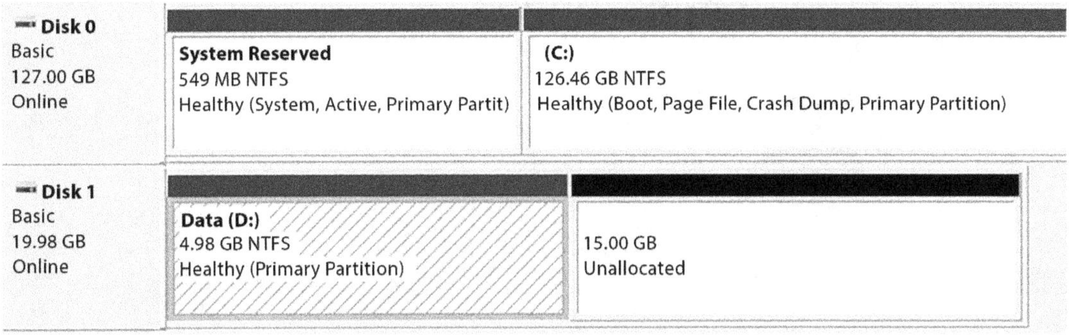

Figure 15.32: Disk 1 has now been expanded

Simply right-clicking on the D: volume and choosing **Extend Volume...** will walk through a very short wizard, after which the D: drive will have been extended to consume the entirety of our newly expanded disk:

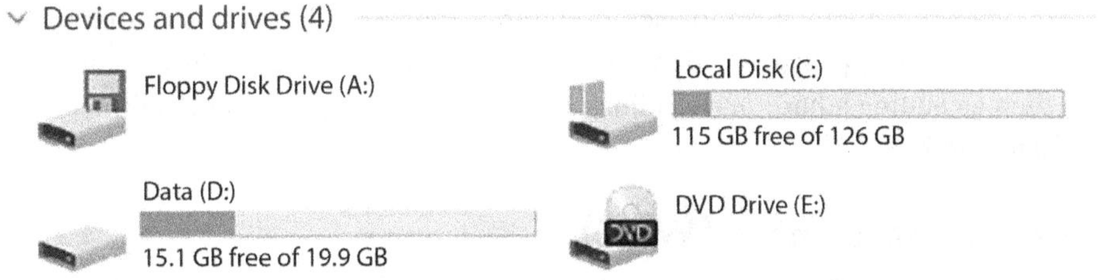

Figure 15.33: The data volume is now expanded

Hyper-V console, Remote Desktop Protocol (RDP), or PowerShell

While hardware adjustments to VMs need to be made through Hyper-V Manager, your daily interaction with these VMs running as servers in your environment does not necessarily mean you have to log in to your Hyper-V server. If you happen to be inside Hyper-V Manager anyway, you can quickly and easily use that **Connect** function to interact with the console of your servers through the use of the Hyper-V console tool. Accessing your servers this way is beneficial if you need to see something in the BIOS or otherwise outside of the Windows operating system that is running on that VM, but it's not often that you require this level of console access.

When you have Windows servers running as VMs, it is much more common to interact with these servers in the same way that you would interact with physical servers on your network. While I have been accessing my WEB3 server through the Hyper-V console in this chapter, now that I have Windows Server 2025 installed on WEB3 and I have enabled the RDP capabilities on it, there is no reason why I couldn't just pop open MSTSC and log in to WEB3 that way, directly from my workstation desktop:

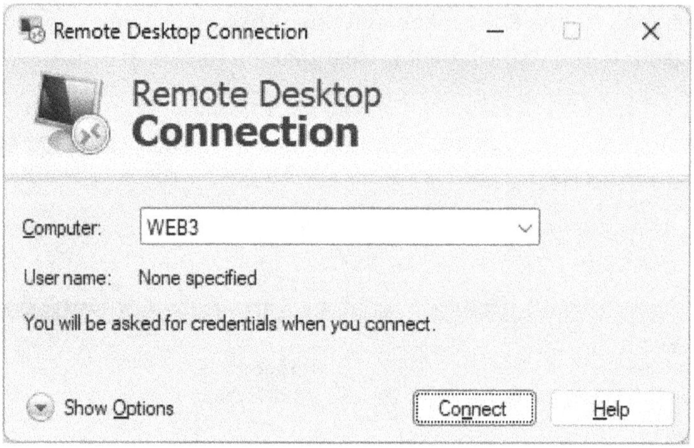

Figure 15.34: Using normal support tools to connect to VMs

The same is true for PowerShell or any other traditional way of remotely accessing services on any other server. Since this VM is fully online and has the server operating system installed, I can use PowerShell remoting to manipulate my WEB3 server as well, from another server or from my desktop computer. Once you are finished building out the hardware and installing the operating system on a VM, it's rare that you actually need to use the Hyper-V console to interact with that server. The primary reasons for opening up Hyper-V Manager to reach a VM are to make hardware-level changes on that server, such as adding a hard drive, adjusting RAM, or moving a network connection from one virtual switch to another.

Windows Admin Center (WAC)

We have seen WAC scattered throughout this book, and for good reason. WAC is the new super-tool that Microsoft wants server administrators to start using to interact with and manage almost every single one of their servers. VM servers hosted in Hyper-V are no exception; you can make use of the WAC toolset to administer servers running on your Hyper-V hosts and use WAC to manage the host servers themselves.

Copying files into VMs without network connectivity

Most often, your Hyper-V VMs will be running and connected to a Hyper-V *external* switch, which then gives them true network connectivity to your production network. If you find yourself needing to copy files to or from this VM, you can utilize any normal tool to perform that function. Maybe you RDP into the VM and copy/paste what you need. Otherwise, if the VM's firewall allows it, you could probably even grab what you need directly from File Explorer by visiting \\VMNAME\C$ and navigating to the files you are trying to access.

This all relies on that VM being connected to the network in a way that your workstation can route to it. How about VMs that are offline, disconnected from the network, maybe sitting in a test lab that is intentionally disconnected from your production network? Or perhaps you are working on a VM that is failing to boot into Windows, but this VM contains some really important files that your CEO needs *right now*. Let me show you a trick for very quickly connecting directly to this VM's hard disk files, so that you can browse through them. This can be useful for pulling information from those VDHX files or for pushing information into them.

Log in to your Hyper-V server, and shut down the VM that you need to access. You must shut this server down because the VHDX hard drive file would be in use when the server is running, and to gain access to that virtual disk, you must free it up.

Once the VM is shut down, use File Explorer on the Hyper-V host server and navigate to the location where that VHDX file sits. Simply right-click on the file and choose the **Mount** option. This will mount the VHDX as a new drive letter on the host operating system, where you can simply click into it and navigate through the entirety of that virtual hard drive. Copy or paste any files that you need this way. You can see in *Figure 15.35* that I have navigated to the VHDX file used by my WEB3 server, mounted it, and can now successfully browse through its information, even though WEB3 is not connected to my network whatsoever.

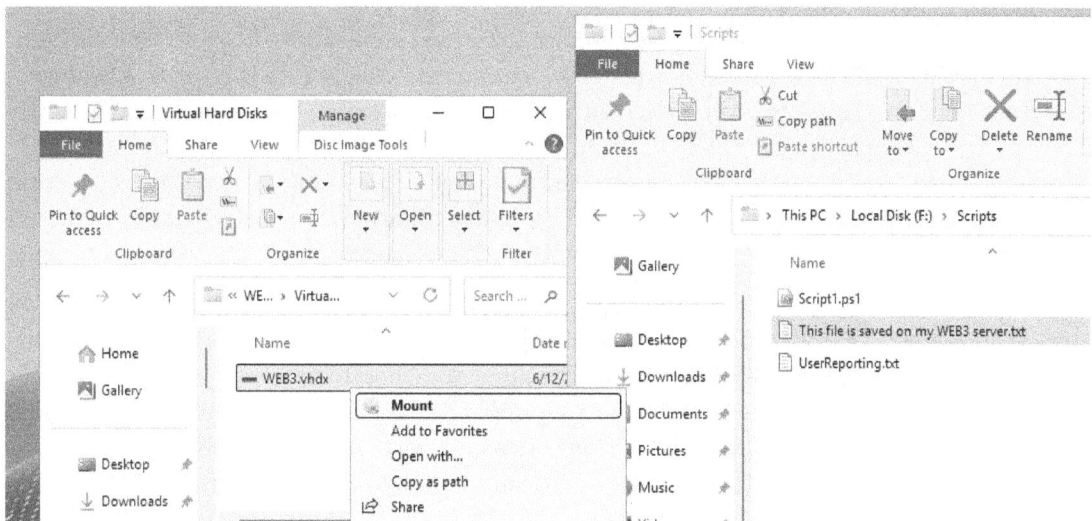

Figure 15.35: Mounting and browsing a VM's virtual disk from the Hyper-V server

Once you are finished shuffling data around, make sure to unmount that drive. Simply find the drive letter being used by the mount (F: in my case), right-click on it, and choose **Eject**. The VM can now be successfully restarted from the Hyper-V Manager console.

Shielded VMs

If your day job doesn't include work with Hyper-V, it's possible that you have never heard of shielded VMs. The name does a pretty good job of explaining this technology at a basic level. If a VM is a virtual machine, then a shielded VM must be a virtual machine that is *shielded* or protected in some way, *right?*

A shielded VM is essentially a VM that is encrypted. Rather, the hard drive file itself (the VHDX) is encrypted, using BitLocker. It sounds simple, but there are some decent requirements for making this happen. For the BitLocker encryption to work properly, the VM is injected with a virtual **Trusted Platform Module (TPM)** chip. TPMs are now commonplace at a hardware level, but actually using them is still a mysterious black box to many administrators. Shielded VMs can also be locked down so that they can only run on healthy and approved host servers, which is an amazing advantage to the security-conscious among us. This capability is provided by a couple of different attestation options, which we will discuss shortly.

To explain the benefits that shielded VMs bring to the table, we are going to look at an example of what happens when VMs are *not* shielded. Keep in mind that the idea of shielded VMs is quite a bit more important when you think in the context of servers being hosted in the cloud, where you don't have any access to the backend, or hosted by some other division inside your company, such as inside a private cloud. Unless you have already taken the time to roll out all shielded VMs in your environment, what I am about to show you is currently possible on *any* of your existing VMs. Indeed, we just finished talking about accessing your VHDX files from the Hyper-V host directly, by mounting them. We used this to our advantage a few minutes ago, for a specific purpose that contained no malice. Now, let's think along those same lines, but from an attacker's point of view.

You already know that I am running a Hyper-V host server, and on that host, I have a VM called WEB3. Now, let's pretend that I am a cloud-hosting provider and that WEB3 is a web server that belongs to one of my tenants. I have provided my tenant with a private virtual switch for networking so that they can manage the networking of that server, and I don't have access to that VM at the networking level. Also, it is a fact that this WEB3 server is joined to my tenant's domain and network, and I, as the cloud host, have absolutely no access to domain credentials or any other means that I can utilize to log in to that server.

Sounds pretty good so far, right? You, as a tenant, certainly wouldn't want your cloud provider to be able to snoop around inside your VMs that are being hosted on that cloud. You also wouldn't want any other tenants who might have VMs running on the same cloud host to be able to see your servers in any way. This same mentality holds true in private clouds as well. If you are hosting a private cloud and are allowing various companies or divisions of a company to have segregated VMs running in the same fabric, you will want to ensure those divisions have real security layers between the VMs and between the VMs and the host.

Now, let's have a little fun and turn villain. I am a rogue cloud-host employee, and I decide that I'm going to do some damage before I walk out the door. It would be easy for me to kill off that WEB3 server completely since I have access to the host administrative console. However, that would probably throw a flag somewhere, and the tenant would just spin up a new web server or restore it from a backup. So, even better than breaking the VM, I'm going to leave it running and then change the content of the website itself. Let's give this company's clients something to talk about!

To manipulate my tenant's website running on WEB3, I don't need any real access to the VM because I have direct access to the virtual hard drive file. All I need to do is tap into that virtual hard disk file, modify the website, and I can make the website display whatever information I want.

This is going to sound familiar. First, I log in to the Hyper-V server (remember, this is owned by me since I am the host), and browse to the location of the VHDX file that WEB3 is using. This is all on the backend, so I don't need any tenant credentials to get here. Furthermore, nothing is logged with these actions, and the tenant will have no way of knowing that I am doing this. I simply right-click on that VHDX and select **Mount**:

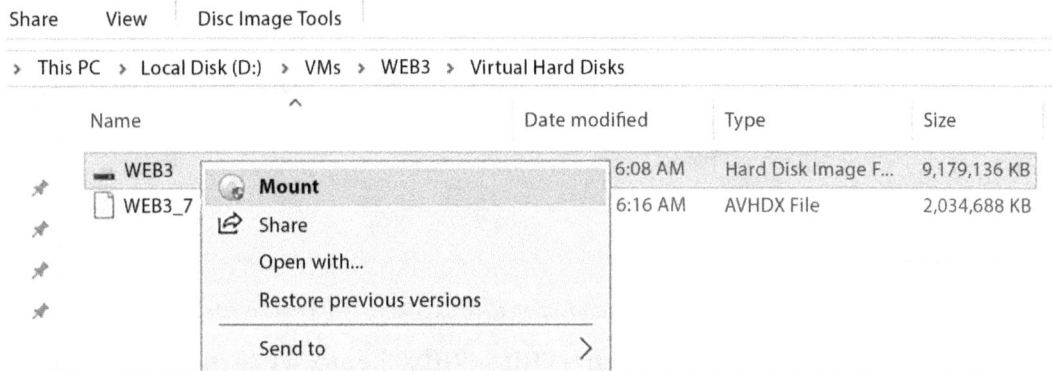

Figure 15.36: Silently mounting a connection to this virtual hard disk file

Now that the VHDX has been mounted to the host server's operating system directly, I can browse that VM's hard drive as if it were one of my own drives. Navigate to the wwwroot folder to find the website files, and change the default page to display whatever you want:

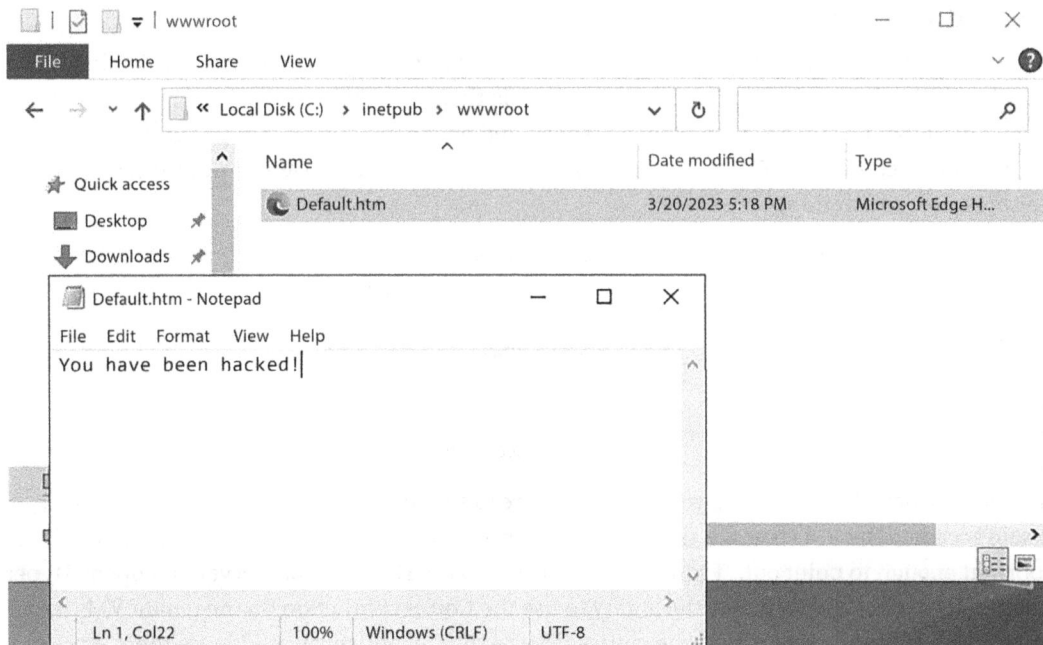

Figure 15.37: Editing content inside a customer VM

When I'm finished playing around with the website, I can open up **Disk Management**, right-click on that mounted disk, and select **Detach VHD** to cover my tracks:

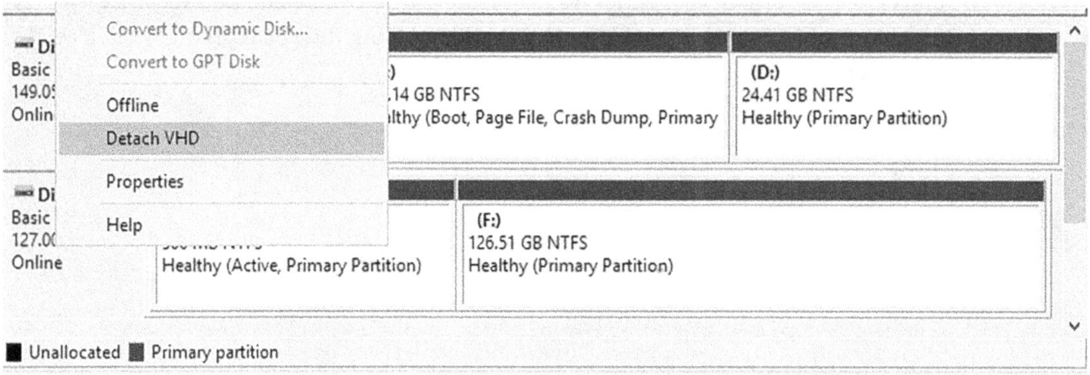

Figure 15.38: Removing the connection to this VHD, my work here is done

And then, just for the fun of it, I copy the entire VHD or VHDX file onto a USB stick so that I can take it with me and mess around with it more later.

This example cuts to the core of why so many companies are hesitant about server hosting platforms, and is precisely why Microsoft began crafting something known as **shielded VMs**. The ability to mount and interact with a virtual hard disk file can be used for good, and it can be used for evil...

Encrypting VHDs

The idea behind shielded VMs is quite simple. Microsoft already has a great drive-encryption technology, called BitLocker. Shielded VMs are Hyper-V VMs that have BitLocker drive encryption enabled. When your entire VHD file is protected and encrypted with BitLocker, nobody is going to be able to gain backdoor access to that drive. Attempting to mount the VHD as we just did would result in an error message, and nothing more:

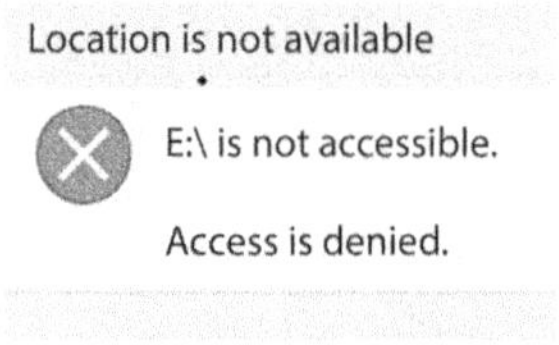

Figure 15.39: Access denied!

Even better is that when you set up your infrastructure to support shielded VMs, you also block Hyper-V console access to the VMs that are shielded. While this isn't as big a deal as drive encryption, it's still important enough to point out. If someone has access to the Hyper-V host server and opens **Hyper-V Manager**, they will generally have the ability to use the **Connect** function on the tenant VMs in order to view whatever was currently on the console. More than likely, this would leave them staring at a login screen that they, hopefully, would not be able to breach. But if that VM's console had somehow been left in a logged-in state, they would have immediate access to manipulating the VM, even if the drive was encrypted.

When you create a shielded VM, it not only encrypts the VHD using BitLocker technology but it also blocks all access to the VM's console from Hyper-V Manager.

Does this hardcore blocking have the potential to cause you problems when you are trying to legitimately troubleshoot a VM? What if you need to use the Hyper-V console to figure out why a VM won't boot or something like that? Yes, that is a valid point and one that you need to consider. Shielded VMs are much more secure. So much so that you could, in fact, lock yourself out from being able to troubleshoot issues on that server. As is often the case with everything in the IT world, we are trading usability for security.

Infrastructure requirements for shielded VMs

There are a couple of important pieces in this puzzle that you need to be aware of if you are interested in running shielded VMs.

Guarded hosts

You will need to run one or more guarded host servers to house your shielded VMs. Guarded hosts are essentially Hyper-V servers on steroids. They will host VMs like any other Hyper-V server, but they are specially crafted and configured to host these encrypted shielded VMs and to attest their own health as part of this overall security strategy.

Guarded hosts must be running Server 2016, 2019, 2022, or 2025 Datacenter, and generally, you want them to boot using UEFI and to contain a TPM 2.0 chip. While TPM 2.0 is not a firm requirement, it is certainly recommended.

These guarded host servers then take the place of your traditional Hyper-V servers. It is their job to host your shielded VMs.

Host Guardian Service (HGS)

HGS is a service that runs on a server, or more commonly, a cluster of three servers, and handles the attestation of guarded hosts. When a shielded VM attempts to start/boot on a guarded host server, that host must reach over to HGS and attest that it is safe and secure. Only once the host has passed the HGS attestation and health checks will the shielded VM be allowed to start.

HGS is *critical* to making a guarded fabric work. If HGS goes down, *none* of your shielded VMs will be able to start!

There are different requirements for HGS, depending on what attestation mode your guarded hosts are going to utilize. We will learn about those modes in the next section of this chapter. HGS will have to be running Server 2016 or newer, and most commonly, you want to use physical servers running in a three-node cluster for this service.

I also want to point out a more recent capability related to HGS that came via Windows Server 2019: **HGS cache**. A previous limitation of Server 2016 shielded VMs was that HGS needed to be contacted every time *any* guarded host wanted to spin up *any* shielded VM. This can become problematic if HGS is unavailable for some temporary reason. New in Server 2019 is the HGS cache for VM keys so that a guarded host is able to start up approved VMs based on keys in the cache, rather than always having to check in with a live HGS.

This can be helpful if HGS is offline (although HGS being completely offline probably means that you have big problems), but the HGS cache has a more valid use case in branch office scenarios where a guarded host might have a poor network connection to HGS.

Host attestations

Attestation of the guarded hosts is the secret to using shielded VMs. This is the basis of security in wanting to move forward with such a solution in your own environment. The ability of your hosts to attest their health and identity gives you peace of mind in knowing that those hosts are not being modified or manipulated without your knowledge, and it ensures that a malicious host employee cannot copy all of your VM hard drive files onto a USB, bring them home, and boot them up. Those shielded VMs are only ever going to start on the guarded hosts in your environment, nowhere else.

There are two different modes that guarded hosts can use to pass attestation with HGS. Well, actually, there are three, but one has already been deprecated. Let's take a minute to detail the different modes that can be used between your guarded hosts and your HGS.

TPM-trusted attestations

This is the best way! TPM chips are physical chips installed on your server's motherboard that contain unique information. Most importantly, this information cannot be modified or hacked from within the Windows operating system. When your guarded host servers are equipped with TPM 2.0 chips, this opens the door to doing some incredibly powerful host attestation. The host utilizes Secure Boot and some code integrity checks that are stored inside the TPM to verify that it is healthy and has not been modified. HGS then cross-checks the information being submitted from the TPM with the information that it knows about when the guarded host was initially configured, to ensure that the requesting host is really one of your approved guarded hosts and that it has not been tampered with. If you are configuring new Hyper-V servers, make sure they contain TPM 2.0 chips so that you can utilize these features.

Host key attestations

If TPMs aren't your thing or are beyond your hardware abilities, we can do a simpler host key attestation. The ability of your guarded hosts to generate a host key that can be known and verified by HGS is new as of Windows Server 2019. This uses asymmetric key-pair technology to validate the guarded hosts. Basically, you will either create a new host-key pair or use an existing certificate, and then send the public portion of that key or certificate over to HGS. When guarded hosts want to spin up a shielded VM, they reach out to attest with HGS, and that attestation is approved or denied based on this key pair.

This is certainly a faster and easier way to make shielded VMs a reality in your network, but it is not as secure as TPM-trusted attestation.

Admin-trusted attestation – deprecated in 2019

If your environment is recent and based on Server 2022 or 2025, don't pay any attention to this one. However, there are folks who are running shielded VMs within a Windows Server 2016 infrastructure, and in that case, there was an additional option for attestation.

Commonly known as admin-trusted attestation, this was a very simple (and not very secure) way for your hosts to attest to HGS that they were approved. Basically, you created an **Active Directory** (**AD**) security group, added your guarded hosts into that group, and then HGS considered any host that was part of that group to be guarded and approved to run shielded VMs.

Resilient Filesystem (ReFS) deduplication

While filesystems and deduplication features are technologies that you may not expect to be discussed when it comes to Hyper-V, the improvements in Server 2022 and 2025 related to ReFS and the deduplication of data carry some huge advantages for Hyper-V Servers. In case these are unfamiliar terms, let's take a minute and define ReFS and deduplication.

ReFS

Anyone who has worked on computers for a while will recognize FAT, FAT32, and NTFS. These are filesystems that can be used when formatting hard drives. These different versions of filesystems translate into different capabilities of how you can utilize that hard drive. For several years, NTFS has been the *de facto* standard for all hard disks connected to Windows machines.

That is…until Windows Server 2016 came along. We now have a new filesystem option called ReFS. Even if you work in an IT department every day, you may have never heard of ReFS because, so far, it isn't getting used all that much. It is primarily used in servers that are involved with **Storage Spaces Direct** (**S2D**). If it's the latest and greatest filesystem from Microsoft, *why isn't it being used as the default option on any new system?* Primarily because ReFS is not a bootable filesystem. That immediately cancels out the capability of systems with a single hard disk to run ReFS on the whole drive. What that implies is that ReFS is designed for secondary volumes on servers, perhaps volumes intended to hold large amounts of data.

In those instances where you format a second volume to be ReFS and store data on it, there are some great resiliency and performance advantages to using ReFS instead of NTFS. These advantages were designed to make S2D implementations more efficient.

Data deduplication

Data deduplication is simply the ability of a computing system to discover multiple bits of data on a drive that are identical and *clean them up*. If there were six copies of the exact same file on a system, deduplication could delete five of them, retaining one for the purposes of all six locations. This idea enables some major space-saving. Data deduplication itself is not new; we had some capabilities introduced way back in Server 2012 regarding this.

Windows Server 2019 was the first platform where it became possible to enable data deduplication on a volume that is formatted via ReFS, and the combination of these two technologies continues to improve efficiency and performance to this day.

Why is this important to Hyper-V?

Data deduplication can be incredibly advantageous to run on a volume that stores Hyper-V VM hard drive files because, as you can imagine, there will be a ton of information that is duplicated over and over and over again when you are running dozens of VMs. Think about all of those Windows operating system files that will be identical among all of your VMs running on the Hyper-V host. It's obvious why it would be beneficial to enable data deduplication on a volume that stores VHDX files.

ReFS has some big resiliency and performance advantages over NTFS, so it is also obvious that VHDX files would be best served by being stored on a ReFS volume.

Windows Server 2022 and 2025 are the first platforms where you can have your cake and eat it too. We now have the ability to create a ReFS volume for storing VM hard drives and enable data deduplication on that same volume.

The future of shielded VMs

HGS, attestation modes, and shielded VMs are pieces of technology that exist in Windows Server 2025, and Microsoft's documentation has been updated to reflect Server 2025 as included and supported for the use of shielded VMs. However...

Microsoft has also announced that Guarded Fabric and shielded VMs are officially on their list of "features we're no longer developing." This does not mean they are no longer viable, as they will continue to support the use of shielded VMs, including on Server 2025, but they are ceasing to pour development resources into this on-premises technology. This is largely due to Microsoft's continued improvements in the Azure space, specifically Azure confidential computing, and their assumption that hyper-secure workloads will more commonly be hosted in Azure or on-premises through Azure Local, rather than on traditional Hyper-V servers.

Integrating Hyper-V with Linux

Many companies utilize Linux in some capacity. The use of Linux may even be poised to make a grander entrance into the Windows Server world now that we have this higher level of integration possible inside Windows Server 2025. There are multiple ways in which your Server 2025 Hyper-V can now be used to interact with Linux VMs:

- **Running in Hyper-V:** VMs hosted on a Hyper-V server used to be limited to Windows-based operating systems. This is no longer the case. The scope of the Hyper-V virtualization host has now been expanded to accommodate running Linux-based VMs in Hyper-V Manager. There is even good integration with the keyboard and mouse!

- **Linux-shielded VMs:** You now know about running shielded VMs in Hyper-V, and you also know about running Linux-based VMs inside Hyper-V. *Does this mean we can combine those two ideas and run a Linux VM that is also shielded?* Why yes, we certainly can. This capability was introduced in SAC version Windows Server 1709 and also exists in the newest LTSC release of Windows Server 2025.

- **Running in containers:** While most server and Hyper-V administrators won't be chomping at the bit to install Linux on their systems because they simply have no reason to do so, there will definitely be a lot more Linux-y talk coming from anyone on the DevOps side of the IT house. When building scalable, modern applications that are destined for the cloud, we often talk about running these applications inside containers. In the past, hosting containers on a Windows server meant that the container itself had to be running Windows, but no more.

You can now host Linux-based containers on top of Windows Server 2025. This allows great flexibility in the application development process and will be an important consideration for the future of containers.

Hyper-V Server...2019?

It's very easy to get excited about virtualization. Build some hardware, install Windows Server 2025, implement the Hyper-V role, and bam! You're ready to start rolling out hundreds and hundreds of VMs in your environment... *right?*

Not necessarily. We haven't talked about licensing yet, and too often our technological prowess is limited by licensing requirements. The same is true with Hyper-V. Every VM that you spin up needs to have its own operating system license, of course. That requirement makes sense. What isn't as obvious, however, is the fact that you can only run a certain number of VMs on your Hyper-V server, depending on what SKU you use for the host operating system.

The biggest *gotcha* is that using Windows Server 2025 Standard edition as your Hyper-V server will result in the ability to run only two VMs. Two! That's it, no more. You will be able to launch a couple of VMs and will then be prevented from running any more. Clearly, the Standard edition SKU isn't designed to be used as a Hyper-V server.

That leaves you with Windows Server 2025 Datacenter edition. Fortunately, Datacenter allows you to run *unlimited* VMs! This is great news! Except for one thing: the Datacenter edition usually costs many thousands of dollars. This can be a limiting factor for deployments of Hyper-V servers in smaller businesses.

All of this talk about licensing and how messy or expensive it can be leads to one point: **Hyper-V Server**. Wait a minute, what are you talking about, Jordan? *Isn't that what this whole chapter has been about? Isn't that just a Windows Server 2022 or 2025 with the Hyper-V role installed?* No, not at all.

"Hyper-V Server" is its own animal. It has its own installer and a whole different user interface from a traditional server. Installing Hyper-V Server onto a piece of hardware will result in a server that can host an *unlimited* number of Hyper-V VMs, but can do nothing else. You cannot use this as a general-purpose server to host other roles or services. Hyper-V Server also **does not have a graphical user interface**.

Hyper-V Server 2019 has one *huge* benefit: it's free! You are still responsible for licenses on each of the VMs, of course, but to have a free host operating system that can run an unlimited number of VMs, now that is something my wallet can really get behind.

Back the train up. Did I forget to update "2019" in the previous paragraph to say "2025"? Nope. We are talking here about **Hyper-V Server 2019** because, sadly, this is going to be the last version released for this special flavor of Hyper-V Server. Microsoft had been releasing this little-known Hyper-V Server installer alongside Windows Server editions for many years, but starting with Windows Server 2022, they are no longer creating a Hyper-V Server offering. Once again, this has nothing at all to do with installing Windows Server 2025 and then installing the Hyper-V role on top of it, which, of course, is still fully relevant and what we have been talking about throughout this entire chapter.

This particular section of the chapter, however, is focused on the alternate installation method specifically for "Hyper-V Server 2019," as there is no "Hyper-V Server 2022" or "Hyper-V Server 2025." This is unfortunate, and Microsoft's recommendation to those seeking the special Hyper-V Server installer is to continue using Hyper-V Server 2019 or to trial run Azure Local, but that comes at a cost. So we're going to move forward with the former option, as Hyper-V Server 2019 will continue to be viable and supported until the year 2029, and make use of it here today.

If you're following along on these topics within your own lab or network, here is a landing page for downloading a Hyper-V Server 2019 installer: `https://www.microsoft.com/en-us/evalcenter/download-hyper-v-server-2019`.

I have burned the ISO installer for Hyper-V Server 2019 onto a DVD (thankfully, this one is small enough to actually fit!), and just finished installing it onto my hardware. The installation of the operating system itself was completely familiar: all of the installation screens and options were the same as if I were installing the full version of Windows Server 2019. However, now that the installer has finished and I have booted into the operating system of my Hyper-V Server 2019, everything looks completely different:

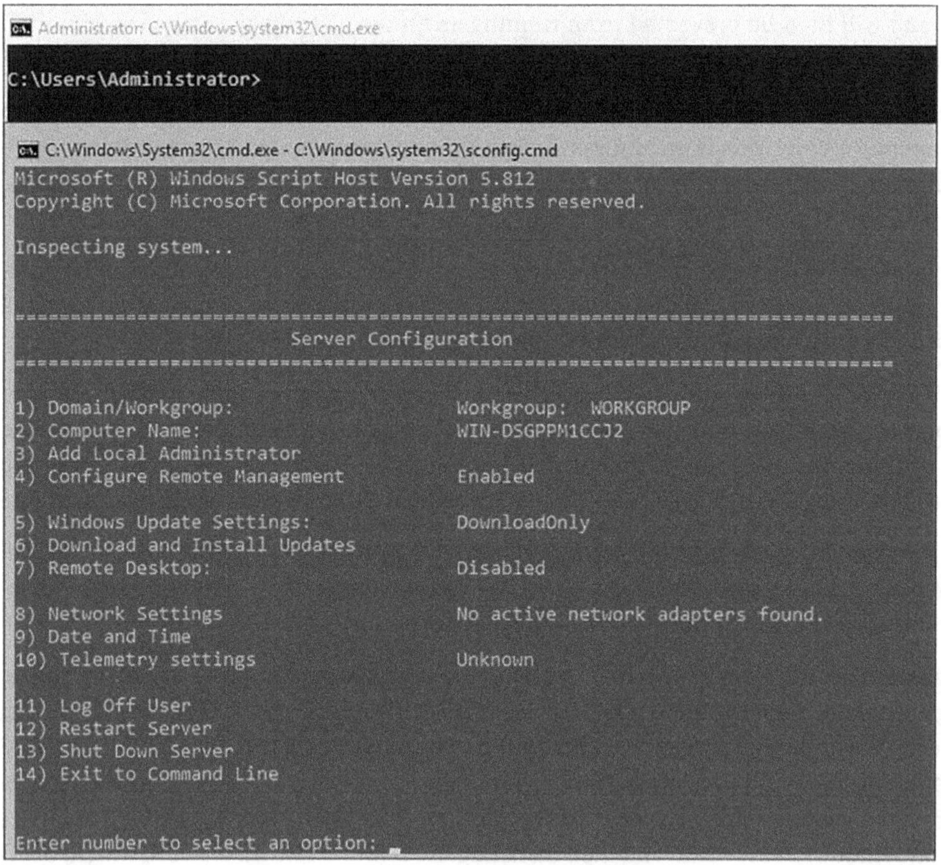

Figure 15.40: Interfacing with Hyper-V Server 2019

We are presented with only a Command Prompt, and inside that prompt, it has auto-launched a configuration utility called **SConfig**. If you read through our chapter on Server Core, you are already familiar with SConfig's capabilities. By using the keyboard here, I can do things such as set the hostname of this server, join it to a domain, and change networking settings. Once you have finished using this CLI to set the basic requirements on the server and get it communicating with the network, you really don't need to access the console of this Hyper-V server again, unless you need to backtrack and revisit this configuration screen to change something. Instead, after configuring Hyper-V Server, you simply utilize Hyper-V Manager or PowerShell on another server or desktop inside your network to tap remotely into the management of VMs that are running on this Hyper-V server.

In *Figure 15.41*, you can see that I have launched **Hyper-V Manager**. I am running this instance of Hyper-V Manager from my Windows 11 machine, where I have the Hyper-V role installed. From here, I right-click on **Hyper-V Manager** and choose **Connect to Server....** I then input the name of my new Hyper-V server, and the console creates a remote connection. From this remote connection, I can now utilize all functionality inside my Windows 11 Hyper-V Manager as if I were logged directly into the new Hyper-V server:

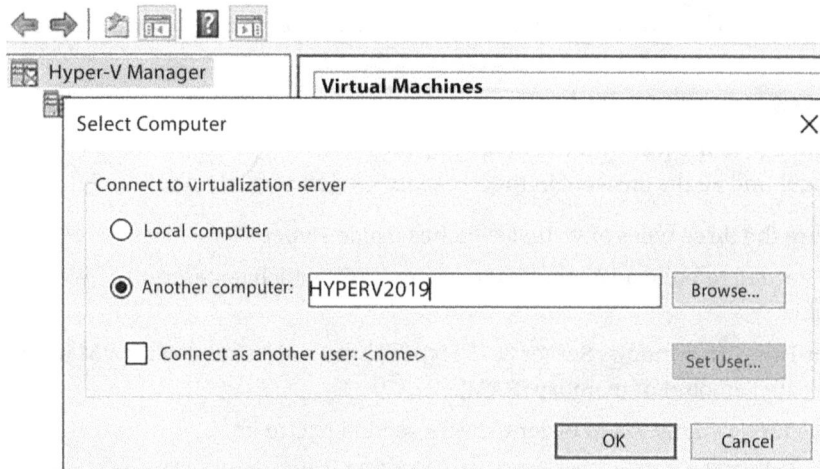

Figure 15.41: Remotely connecting to a Hyper-V server

Similar to the way that most tasks performed on Server Core are handled remotely (using remote consoles or PowerShell), we make all ongoing maintenance and administration of this Hyper-V server happen from a remote Hyper-V Manager console.

Hyper-V Server gives you the security benefits of a GUI-less interface, combined with the flexibility benefits of hosting an unlimited number of virtual machines, at a price point that nobody can argue with!

Summary

I don't have official numbers, but I will take a risk and say that today, there are already more virtual servers running than physical servers to keep our world online. While the battle continues to rage about which hypervisor platform is the best, typically the argument is split between Hyper-V and VMware, you cannot ignore the fact that virtualization is here to stay.

Microsoft puts great quantities of time and resources into making sure that Hyper-V always stays ahead of the competition and introduces more and more features with every release, so that you can keep your virtualized infrastructure up and running perfectly all the time. Is the capacity for cloud virtualization even more powerful than on-premises Hyper-V Server? I would say yes because the infrastructure that is in place at a cloud service provider is going to be the all-powerful Oz compared to what a single company can provide in its own datacenter. *Does this mean you can forget about Hyper-V altogether and just use cloud-provided servers?* Possibly, but there are a lot of factors that make the answer to that question unique for each company. The general concepts outlined in this chapter for working with VMs apply to Azure, Amazon, Google, and most of the other public cloud providers. Once you understand the ideas behind virtual servers, shared resources, and administration of those things, you can navigate your way through any type of server hosting scenario. Microsoft is also putting a lot of recent emphasis on Azure Local, which is essentially a miniaturized instance of Azure that runs within your datacenter. The need for on-premises servers and services is still immense, and some industries are simply never going to permit their data and applications to be hosted by a third party. In some cases, regulatory compliance reasons will make the decision for you. Understanding the capabilities of Hyper-V and being able to build this infrastructure from the ground up will give you a major advantage when looking for a technology job in a Microsoft-centric organization.

Questions

Put your knowledge to the test with the following questions. If you need a hand (or just want to double-check), you'll find all the answers in the *Appendix* section of the book.

1. What are the three types of virtual switches inside Hyper-V?
2. If you needed to build a VM that boots using UEFI, which generation of VM would you need to create?
3. True or False? In Windows Server 2025 Hyper-V, you must shut down a VM in order to change its allocated amount of memory (RAM).
4. Must I shut down my VM in order to add a second NIC to it?
5. True or False? The only way to interact with a VM is through the Hyper-V console.
6. What is the name of the technology inside Hyper-V that allows you to take snapshot images of VMs that can later be restored?
7. When running shielded VMs in your environment, what is the name of the role that handles the attestation of your Hyper-V host servers?
8. Which is the most comprehensive attestation method for shielded VMs: host key attestation, TPM trusted attestation, or admin trusted attestation?
9. How many VMs can run on top of a Windows Server 2025 Standard edition host?
10. What editions of Windows Server allow me to run an unlimited number of VMs?

16

Remote Desktop Services

The words *remote desktop* usually bring to mind the simple Remote Desktop Connection client that we have utilized for decades to remotely control servers and workstations. **Remote Desktop Services (RDS)** is much more powerful and has also been around for many years, but it was originally known as **Terminal Services**. By crafting an RDS environment, ideally comprising multiple Windows Server instances, you are taking your first steps into the world of virtualized desktops and centralized computing. An RDS **farm**, as it is often lovingly called, provides users with access both inside and outside of the office to a secure virtual session, within which they can run the applications they need and access the data they require in order to do their jobs. Implementing RDS can be a way to provide work-from-home capabilities, even from personal devices, and can allow companies to utilize cheaper, thin-client workstations instead of standard desktops and laptops if their workforce can truly function completely within the RDS environment. This chapter is all about the components that make up RDS and how you can immediately start using it in your own networks, covering the following topics:

- Wherefore art thou, role?
- Components of an RDS environment
- Publishing RDS sessions
- RDS licensing
- RDS user profiles
- RemoteApp
- RDS maintenance considerations
- Azure Virtual Desktop

Wherefore art thou, role?

What is the first thing you typically need to accomplish on a Windows Server instance to make it do any kind of real work? Oh yeah, install a role. The trouble with this is that our fingers get so used to muscle-memorying their way through the **Add Roles and Features Wizard** screens that you may already be three steps ahead of me, staring at the list of Windows Server roles and getting ready to click on the one called **Remote Desktop Services**. Stop!

Back up. If you slow down and pay attention when you launch the wizard to install your new role, you will notice that you normally blow right past a screen that asks whether you want to install an RDS component or any other Windows Server component. RDS has an entirely separate section in **Add Roles and Features Wizard**. The easiest way to deploy RDS is to make use of this second option and continue forward from here.

Select installation type

DESTINATION SERVER
No servers are selected.

Before You Begin

Installation Type

Deployment Type

Deployment Scenario

Role Services

RD Connection Broker

RD Web Access

RD Virtualization Host

Confirmation

Completion

Select the installation type. You can install roles and features on a running physical computer or virtual machine, or on an offline virtual hard disk (VHD).

○ **Role-based or feature-based installation**
Configure a single server by adding roles, role services, and features.

◉ **Remote Desktop Services installation**
Install required role services for Virtual Desktop Infrastructure (VDI) to create a virtual machine-based or session-based desktop deployment.

Figure 16.1: Initial configuration wizard for RDS

Now that you are navigating down the correct role installation road, we must choose which of the RDS components we would like to install on which server. While possible to place all RDS parts and pieces onto one server, creating a sort of "all-in-one RDS," it is not generally recommended to do so. The next section of this chapter covers descriptions and differences of the RDS components, but it's important to note that RDSH servers should only ever be RDSH servers, while all other RDS roles can exist together on a single RDS management or administration server. In our lab environment throughout this chapter, I will be utilizing four RDS-related servers. Three of them will simply be RDSH servers, and the fourth is an RDS-MGMT server that contains all other RDS-related pieces installed on it. Prior to running **Add Roles and Features Wizard** on my first RDS server, I want to make sure that I have all my RDS servers spun up, so that this wizard can tap into all four of them to configure the components that I specify.

If you are adding a node to an existing RDS infrastructure, then there is no need to run this special version of the role installation wizard. We will talk in more depth about this later in the chapter.

Components of an RDS environment

RDS contains many moving parts, and you may get your fingers stuck in them if you aren't clear on which component serves which purpose. Let's take a few pages to describe the different RDS server roles that we are going to be working with.

Remote Desktop Session Host

The most common type of RDS server is called a **Remote Desktop Session Host (RDSH)**. These are the most common because there are usually more RDSH servers than there are servers of any other RDS component type. All user sessions will land on an RDSH server. These are the servers doing the real grunt work: everybody logs in to RDS, and they land within virtual sessions that are running on top of RDSH servers. Very much like when you use a simple RDP connection to remotely connect to another desktop computer, RDSH servers offer up that same ability to many users all at the same time. Each person making a connection to an RDSH ends up looking at a Windows desktop instance, with all of the applications, drive mappings, printers, and so on that they need in order to do their work. This virtual instance of Windows is running on one of the RDSH servers in the farm that shares the user login load with the other. Since every user login consumes resources (CPU, RAM, etc.) and in almost all cases an RDSH server is intended to host multiple user sessions at once, RDSH servers are typically configured to have more resources than other RDS server types.

It is important to note that you usually want an RDSH server to be an RDSH server and nothing else. Do not install RDS *Connection Broker*, *License Manager*, *Gateway*, or any other roles on these servers.

Remote Desktop Connection Broker

A good way to think of Remote Desktop Connection Broker is as a built-in load balancer for RDS sessions. New user logins coming into an RDS farm will be distributed across multiple RDSH servers based on weights that are defined within the Remote Desktop Connection Broker properties, and Remote Desktop Connection Broker is also what enables users to disconnect their RDS sessions and be automatically reconnected to the same session when they reconnect later that day. Remote Desktop Connection Broker makes the decisions about who will land upon which RDSH server.

Remote Desktop License Manager

This one is pretty self-explanatory. Remote Desktop License Manager is the role and toolset that defines RDS licensing. What can get tricky about this topic is the different types of RDS licenses available, which we will discuss later in this chapter.

As you move forward into RDS administration, you are going to quickly realize that almost everything that needs to be configured in the RDS world happens inside Server Manager. This is only partially true of RDS licenses. It is true that you will be defining which server contains the RDS licensing components from within Server Manager, but there is a more specific management tool that is installed in the RDS license server that needs to be used to import RDS **client access licenses (CALs)**.

Remote Desktop Web Access

Remote Desktop Web Access is a web portal that users can log in to from a browser and gain access to their applications or virtual desktops published by RDS. The *Web Access* component is published by IIS, so you will find the Web Server role installed on any RDS server that hosts Remote Desktop Web Access. It is common to combine this with Remote Desktop Gateway, which we will discuss next. If you are going to be working with Remote Desktop environments regularly, you might as well memorize the term rdweb. This is the last portion of the URL that makes up access to the Web Access portal. For example, if the DNS name you are using for your RDS environment is gateway.contoso.com, then your Remote Desktop Web Access portal will be https://gateway.contoso.com/rdweb.

Remote Desktop Gateway

I almost never find an RDS environment that does not also include a **Remote Desktop Gateway** instance. Remote Desktop Gateway is the secret ingredient that ties together on-premises and remote employees. Building an RDS farm inside a network and licensing it and allowing the connection broker to take care of distributing user sessions across all of the farm servers is great, but if you are already providing users with a virtual desktop session to do their work, why wouldn't you give them access to also log in to that virtual desktop from outside the office, such as from their homes?

RD Gateway does exactly this. It is designed to listen for incoming connections from the internet on port 443 (although this can be adjusted), so that remote users can utilize a simple RDP icon file on their computers that is designed to flow traffic through the gateway and into the RDS farm that is sitting inside your datacenter.

Alternatively, you can even utilize Remote Desktop Gateway without an RDSH farm to connect users directly to workstations sitting inside the office! In some cases, I find that the only RDS server a company has is a single Remote Desktop Gateway server. The purpose of this server, in these cases, is to take incoming connections from remote workers and securely shuttle their RDP connections into their workstation computers within your company's walls. This enables users to have a work desktop computer that is always in the office, and when working remotely, they can launch a Remote Desktop Gateway connection that RDPs them securely into that work desktop, perhaps from a personal laptop (maybe even a Mac!).

RD Gateway is another one of the RDS components that has two different homes for configuration. The primary functionality is configured inside Server Manager, while a separate Remote Desktop Gateway Manager is also installed for deeper levels of configuration.

In a large and robust RDS environment, all of the roles we just discussed would be installed on different servers, with any of them having redundancy capabilities so that you could painlessly survive the failure of a single server. However, most businesses that use RDS do not go so extreme when creating resiliency on these servers, and we will follow the majority with the remaining pages of this chapter as we set up our own RDS environment in a test lab. The configuration steps I follow in these pages will closely reflect the production environments that I most often find in the SMB market.

Publishing RDS sessions

RDS is all about creating a centralized computing environment for users to take advantage of and leaving resource assignment and utilization to the servers, which greatly reduces the need to care about what kind of workstation or laptop somebody is using to connect. Two primary types of connections exist in an RDS environment: publishing full virtual desktops and publishing individual applications, which we will discuss near the end of this chapter.

We are going to build an RDS environment that contains all of the components we outlined earlier, and we are going to use this RDS farm to publish full virtual desktop sessions that users will be able to log in to and work from.

When building a fresh RDS environment, it is helpful to have all of the servers you intend to include already running and initially prepped. These servers should have a final hostname, have reserved or static IP addresses, and already be joined to your domain. For my lab today, I am going to be using the following servers:

- RDS-MGMT: This server will be my Swiss Army knife, doing everything other than hosting user sessions. Upon it, we will implement Remote Desktop Gateway, Remote Desktop Connection Broker, Remote Desktop Licensing, and Remote Desktop Web Access.

- RDSH1: This will be one of my initial session host servers, upon which we will install applications and host user virtual sessions.

- RDSH2: Another RDSH server, this one and RDSH1 will be the initial members of my RDS "farm." User sessions will be load-balanced (or brokered) between these two.

- RDSH3: Later, I will add this third node to my farm, so that we can take a real look at what it takes to expand an RDS environment that is already up and running.

Creating an RDS environment

My four servers are already up and running, but at this point, I have not installed any roles or RDS components onto them. Here, we are going to walk through the steps necessary to build this RDS farm, which can all happen from a single instance of Server Manager. It is important to make sure that all of the servers you intend to manipulate are already added to Server Manager before you start the wizard. You already know how to add multiple servers to the same instance of Server Manager, but if you need a refresher, simply click **Manage** > **Add Servers** and add all the related servers that you are going to modify. This will be important later in the wizard when you need to define these servers to own the different RDS components.

Logging in to RDS-MGMT, I will utilize the **Add Roles and Features** function and make sure to select that second installation type we looked at earlier, **Remote Desktop Services installation**. On the following screen, you will notice an option for **Quick Start**, which is interesting in that there is a shortcut method to create an all-in-one RDS environment on a single server, but this is rarely what a business would want to do in production, and so we will not perform that here either. Instead, continue forward with the option for **Standard deployment**.

Now, on the **Deployment Scenario** screen, we are presented with an interesting option. It is easy to intermingle the terms *virtual desktop*, *session*, and *virtual session*. Here, we face a fork in the road. The first option, **Virtual machine-based desktop deployment**, is not very common; this is a more classic VDI-type environment, where you may have entire **virtual machines** (**VMs**) dedicated to each user. Instead, when talking about RDS, we are almost always talking about publishing virtual desktop *sessions* to users, where multiple users are going to be logged in to the same RDSH server, sharing hardware resources. This is the direction we want to pursue today, and most likely what you will find in your corporate environments. Therefore, go ahead and select **Session-based desktop deployment**.

The wizard now summarizes for us that, based on our selections so far, it is going to install **Remote Desktop Connection Broker**, **Remote Desktop Web Access**, and **Remote Desktop Session Host**.

Figure 16.2: Building an RDS session host infrastructure

For each of those three components, the next screens in the wizard are pretty simple. Select the server that you want to host each RDS role, and slide it to the right side of the screen. For example, here I have specified that I would like **RD Connection Broker** to reside on **RDS-MGMT**.

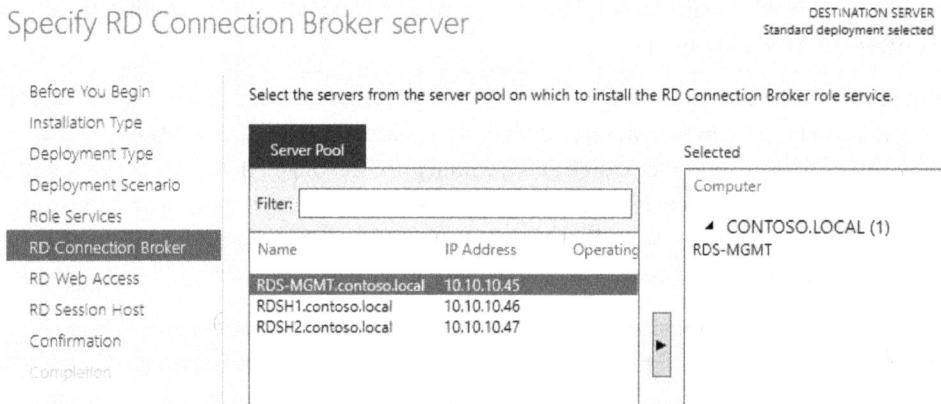

Figure 16.3: Specifying the RD Connection Broker

Follow suit for defining the home for RD Web Access, which I am also placing on top of RDS-MGMT, and now we visit the last screen asking us to make decisions on which servers are going to be our RD Session Host servers. I do not want RDS-MGMT to host user sessions, because it will be busy doing all other functions, so I am declaring that RDSH1 and RDSH2 are to be my RD Session Host servers. The configuration wizard here is going to reach out to those servers and configure them as needed to be RDSH servers.

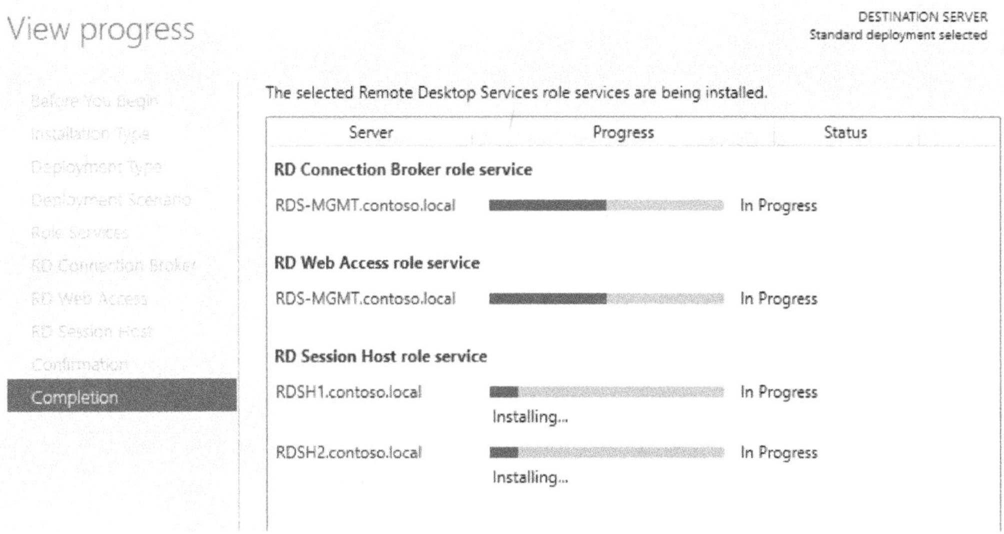

View progress

The selected Remote Desktop Services role services are being installed.

Server	Progress	Status
RD Connection Broker role service		
RDS-MGMT.contoso.local		In Progress
RD Web Access role service		
RDS-MGMT.contoso.local		In Progress
RD Session Host role service		
RDSH1.contoso.local		In Progress
	Installing...	
RDSH2.contoso.local		In Progress
	Installing...	

Before You Begin
Installation Type
Deployment Type
Deployment Scenario
Role Services
RD Connection Broker
RD Web Access
RD Session Host
Confirmation
Completion

Figure 16.4: Server Manager doing the work for you

Once this configuration wizard is finished installing roles and feature sets onto your RDS environment's servers, you will find that they are prepared to do exactly nothing for you. Our next critical step in the build of this RDS farm is to configure the farm itself, or more accurately, the **RDS collection**.

Your first RDS collection

Throughout this book, we have installed numerous roles in Windows Server, and you know firsthand that installing roles does not result in functionality until you invest a little more time and effort to configure those roles. RDS is no different. Now that you have rolled out the roles, go ahead and open Server Manager, and once again, make sure that all of your RDS servers are added into Server Manager, so that it can reach out to any of them to pull or push information as needed. I will be using Server Manager on RDS-MGMT, since I plan for this server to be my primary RDS administration center point.

An RDS collection is generally thought of as a group of RDSH servers that are part of a pool, or farm, as we keep mentioning. A collection actually consists of quite a bit more than the servers themselves; a collection also includes all configurations and settings that the servers involved are going to adhere to.

Whenever you have Server Manager tapped into servers with RDS components installed, you will find that your primary management functionality of RDS is found by clicking on the words **Remote Desktop Services** listed along the left side of Server Manager. This is your home for the configuration of RDS collections (yes, you can have multiple collections), adding or removing RDSH servers from those collections, and adjusting collection settings; it's also your home for tacking on the additional RDS components that we never got a chance to add during the initial role installation wizard. You'll notice green plus symbols next to **RD Gateway** and **RD Licensing**, which you will click to install these two components, since the initial wizard did not ask for information about these. In fact, let's do that now.

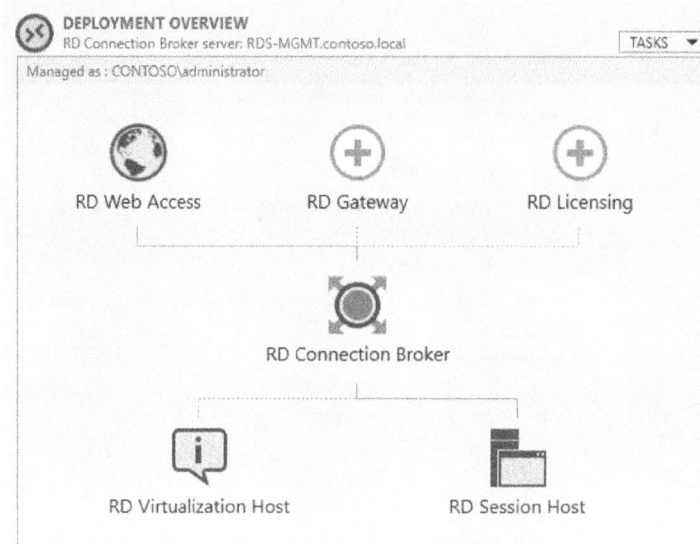

Figure 16.5: RD Gateway and RD Licensing are not yet installed

Adding RD Gateway and RD Licensing

Clicking on the plus symbols next to **RD Gateway** and **RD Licensing** will invoke mini-wizards very much like the ones we used a few minutes ago to specify the broker and RDSH servers. Simply select the server that you want to contain each of these roles; I am going to place them both on RDS-MGMT.

You'll have to make a few additional decisions about how the Gateway and Licensing components function. Utilizing Remote Desktop Gateway means that you will be accepting traffic that flows in from outside of the network, and those client computers will be reaching out to a DNS name such as gateway.contoso.com. To properly protect that traffic, you will, of course, want to decide on a name, acquire an SSL certificate to protect that name, install the certificate on your Remote Desktop Gateway server, and then specify the name here. Since this is a test lab and my server doesn't even have real connectivity to the internet, my wizard recognizes that there is no SSL certificate installed and is instead asking me to define a name that it can use for generating a self-signed SSL certificate. In a production environment, self-signed certificates are a no-no, but one could serve our purposes and allow connectivity within the lab. If you decide to proceed with utilizing a self-signed certificate, be aware that many current browsers are going to block connections to this website. In this event, you have two choices. First, you can hack into the registry for Edge or Chrome and tell it to proceed anyway when accessing sites protected by self-signed certificates (feel free to search RSAKeyUsageForLocalA nchorsEnabled on the internet for details on that), or even better, just get yourself a real certificate!

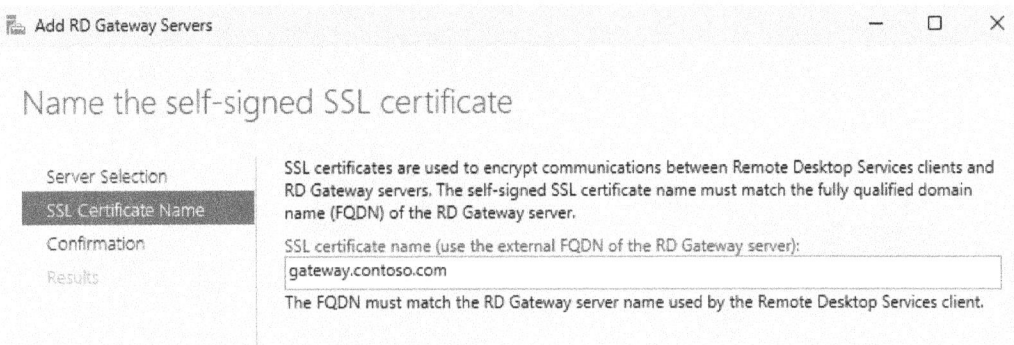

Figure 16.6: RD Gateway requires an SSL certificate to protect its traffic

Next is our mini-wizard for adding Remote Desktop Licensing, and this one is as simple as selecting RDS-MGMT as the home for RD Licensing and letting it install. Installing actual RDS CALs into License Manager is entirely different, but we'll talk a little more about that later in the chapter.

Collection configuration

At this point, all RDS components are installed across our three servers (remember that I am saving RDSH3 for the time being, so that we can add it later into the already-existing collection). RDS-MGMT is carrying the bulk of the responsibility, and our two RDSH servers are patiently waiting in the wings, ready to receive user sessions sent to them by the gateway and broker.

How do we do that?

The only remaining step to get clients connected to this RDS environment is to officially configure our collection, which again is the collection of settings and servers that will make RDS connections possible. Still inside the **Remote Desktop Services** section of Server Manager, find the option in the middle pane called **Collections** and click on it. As you can see, there are currently no collections listed, but if you drop down the **TASKS** menu near the top-right corner of your screen, you can select **Create Session Collection** to get things started.

The first step is simply creating a name for your collection: no explanation needed there, but it is important to note that this name will be visible to users when they log in to Remote Desktop Web Access.

Next, we specify which session host servers (RDSH) are going to be part of this collection. As I mentioned earlier, I am going to initially configure my new collection with two nodes, RDSH1 and RDSH2. Moving those two servers into the **Selected** column means that these two servers are going to be able to receive connections for my collection.

Now, moving on to the **User Groups** screen, this is where things start to get interesting. By default, you will see your domain's *Domain Users* group listed here. If you proceed forward with this default setting, in the end, any user who has an **Active Directory** (**AD**) account in your network will have permission to log in to this RDS collection. Since I want to be a little more selective about who I allow in here, I have removed that group and instead added a new AD security group that I created for exactly this purpose, called **Contoso RDS Users**.

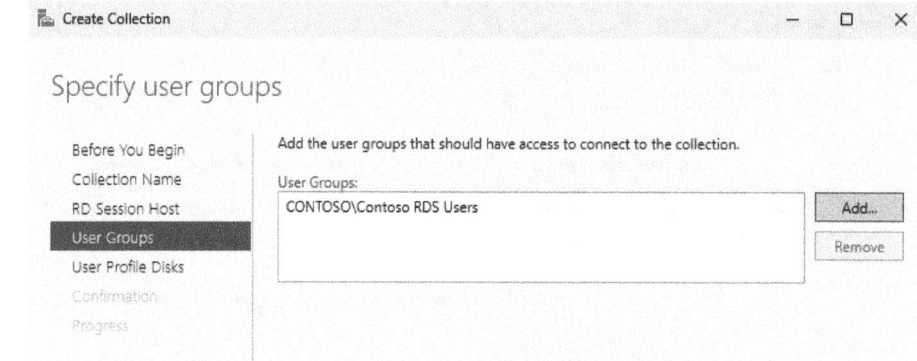

Figure 16.7: Only group members will be allowed to connect

Our next selection screen is called **User Profile Disks**. We will discuss what exactly **user profile disks** (**UPDs**) are later in the chapter, but a summary is that every user who logs in to an RDSH receives a Windows profile, just like on any Windows computer, and for the user's profile to remain consistent between both RDSH servers, it must be stored in a central location, rather than on RDSH1 and RDSH2 directly. I have created a simple file share on my RDS-MGMT server and am going to use that location for the storage of my UPDs. You'll notice an information box near the bottom of this screen that declares that each RDSH server needs to have full control permissions within this share. I have added RDSH1, RDSH2, and RDSH3 (for the future) to have **Full control** NTFS permissions on my new Profiles folder and share to meet this requirement.

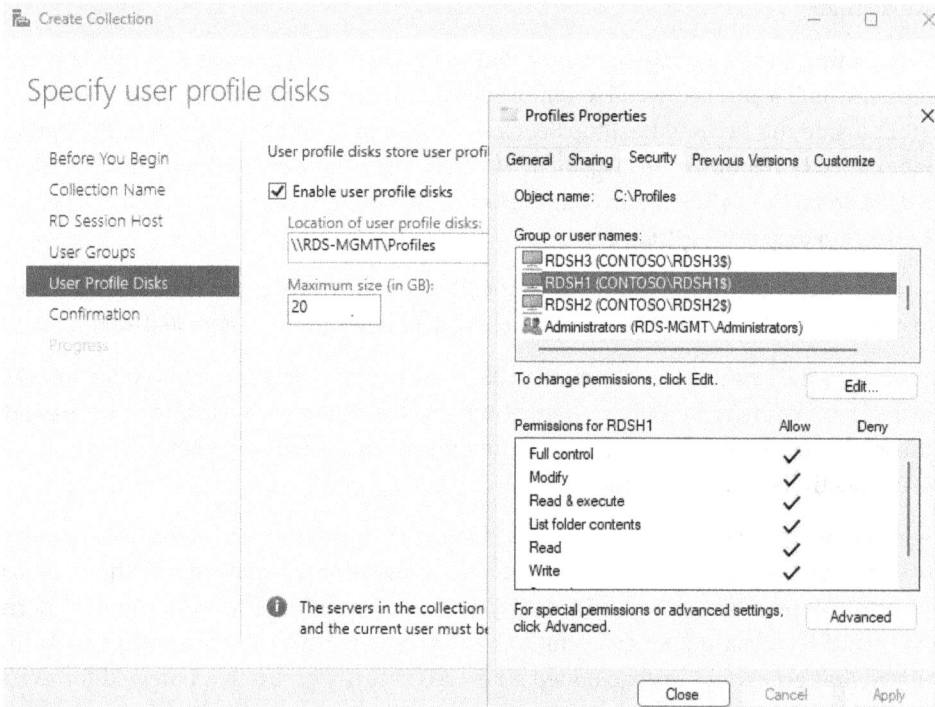

Figure 16.8: Specifying UPDs and file permissions

That's it! Simply use the **Confirmation** screen to verify that everything looks in order, and when you click the **Create** button, you will find your new collection sitting inside Server Manager.

Connecting to it

Contoso RDS (the name of my collection) is now live and able to be connected to. At this point, I could connect to my new collection by using the DNS name of the Connection Broker server, RDS-MGMT. contoso.local. However, I also specified the DNS name gateway.contoso.com in my RD Gateway settings, and that is a cleaner and friendlier name to use for connectivity, whether I am inside or outside of the office. To be able to use this same name both inside and outside the network, I need to create a DNS record with that name and point it at my Gateway/Connection Broker server, in my case, RDS-MGMT. I have created such a record in my internal DNS and confirmed now that gateway.contoso. com resolves to 10.10.10.45, the IP address of RDS-MGMT.

With DNS squared away, I log in to a client computer, launch a web browser, and receive a login prompt when visiting https://gateway.contoso.com/rdweb.

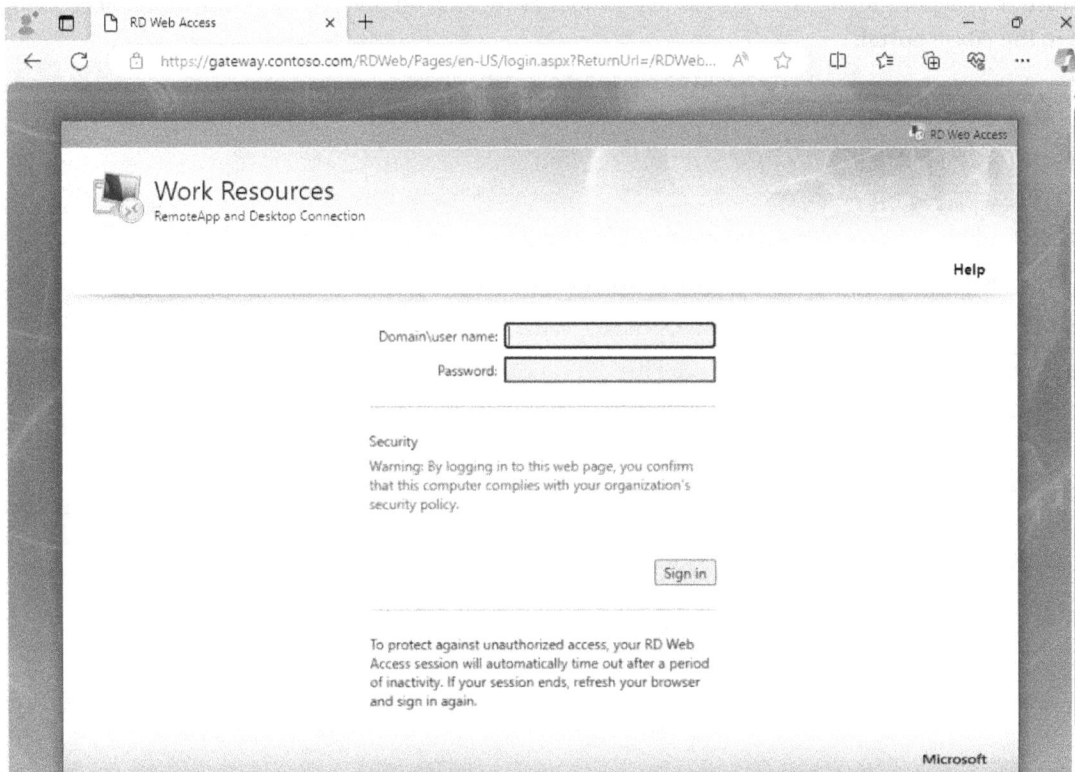

Figure 16.9: RD Web Access is up and running!

Remember that if you haven't done the work of getting an SSL certificate yet for the DNS name you are trying to use here, you may receive some errors from your web browser. Get your certificate, install it on your Remote Desktop Gateway server, and select it inside **RDS Deployment Properties** to resolve this situation.

Accessing this website proves that Remote Desktop Web Access is up and running, but the first time that I logged in to the portal, I had exactly zero applications waiting for me to launch. I'm not going to lie, I was genuinely confused as to why my Contoso RDS connection was not listed in the portal. It took me far too many minutes to realize that when we created this new collection, I had removed the default *Domain Users* group from having access and instead narrowed it down to only my AD group called *Contoso RDS Users*. What I never did was add my own user account to that group, and therefore, I was facing an RD Web Access portal, but with nothing inside to click on.

As soon as I added my user account to the *Contoso RDS Users* group, I logged back in to this rdweb page and found my connection to Contoso RDS waiting for me. This is good verification that when you publish items through RDS, they are only visible and accessible to those users or groups that you have specified per collection. Double-clicking on this connection downloads an RDP connection file into your web browser's standard downloads location. From here, you can launch the connection by clicking on the downloaded RDP file, or you could even visit your Downloads folder and then copy out that RDP file for safekeeping. For example, if a user were to save this RDP file on their desktop, future connections to the farm are as easy as double-clicking on that file; they don't even need to log in to the rdweb portal.

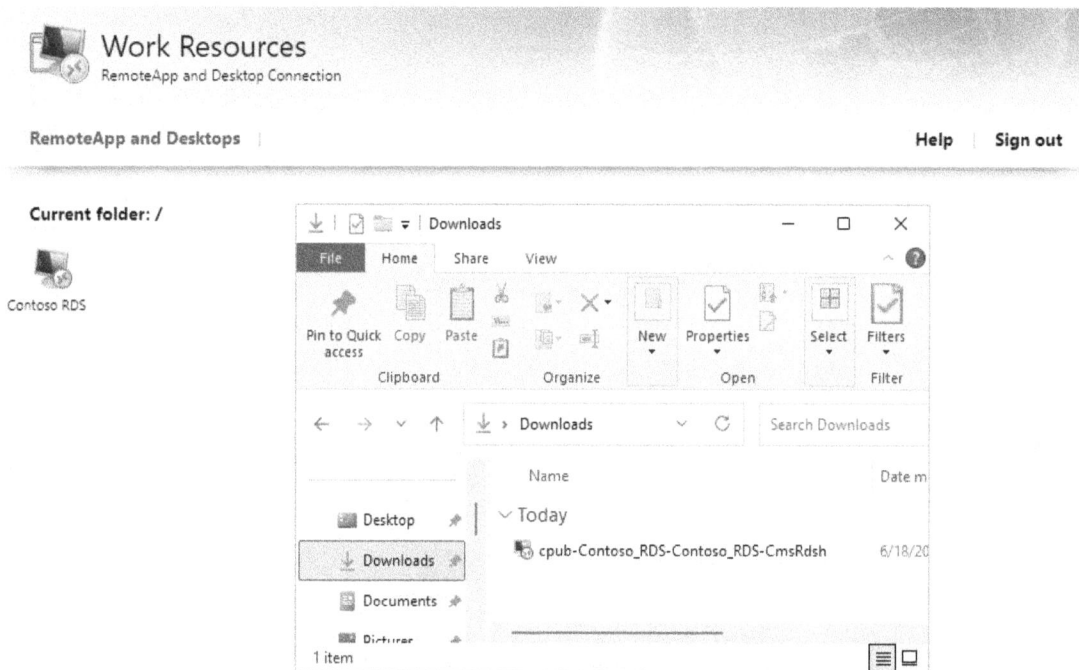

Figure 16.10: RD Web Access now has Contoso RDS available to launch

Whether you launch this RDP connection file from within your web browser, your Downloads folder, or by copying the RDP file to another computer and double-clicking it there, you will be asked to sign in to the RDS collection. Once authenticated, you will be logged in to and looking at a virtual desktop session that is completely hosted on one of your RDSH servers. You can see in the following screenshot that my first session has landed on RDSH1.

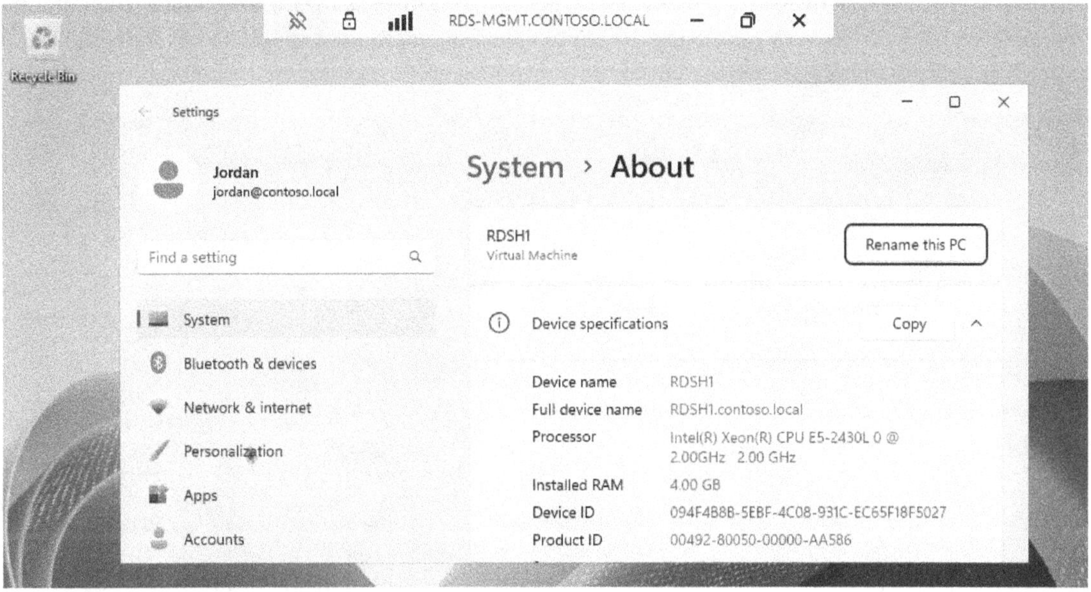

Figure 16.11: Successfully connected to an RDS user session!

Many companies don't even require their users to log in to the rdweb portal, or may even have it disabled altogether. Instead, if you have already acquired these RDP connection files, you could easily distribute them to everyone's desktop via Group Policy.

We did it! We have successfully built RDS servers, created a collection, and connected to it.

Editing deployment and collection properties

If you have ever worked within an RDS environment before, you probably know that there are various options and settings that can be enabled or disabled, and we have not seen many of them in our text so far. Running through the initial configuration wizards will get you an RDS collection up and running, but revisiting configuration screens will provide access to even more. This functionality is defined inside the **Remote Desktop Services** section of Server Manager, within which we have been working so far, but now that we have a fully published collection, we can revisit these screens and find some additional buttons.

Deployment Properties

The higher tier, where you may need to view or change settings, is **Deployment Properties**. Find these properties by navigating to the **Collections** page inside Server Manager, where you can see information about all of the different RDS collections that are established within your deployment (yes, you can have many collections!). Near the top-right corner of the **COLLECTIONS** screen, there is a small **TASKS** drop-down menu, within which you can choose either **Create Session Collection** to add another collection to your deployment or **Edit Deployment Properties**.

Deployment Properties is where you define or change information about your Remote Desktop Gateway, Remote Desktop Licensing server, specific settings about how Remote Desktop Web Access works, and certificates. We will visit the **Certificates** screen when we later discuss RDS maintenance. **Deployment Properties** is the place to visit for settings or configurations that are not specific to an individual RDS collection. Rather, these settings pertain to the entire RDS environment.

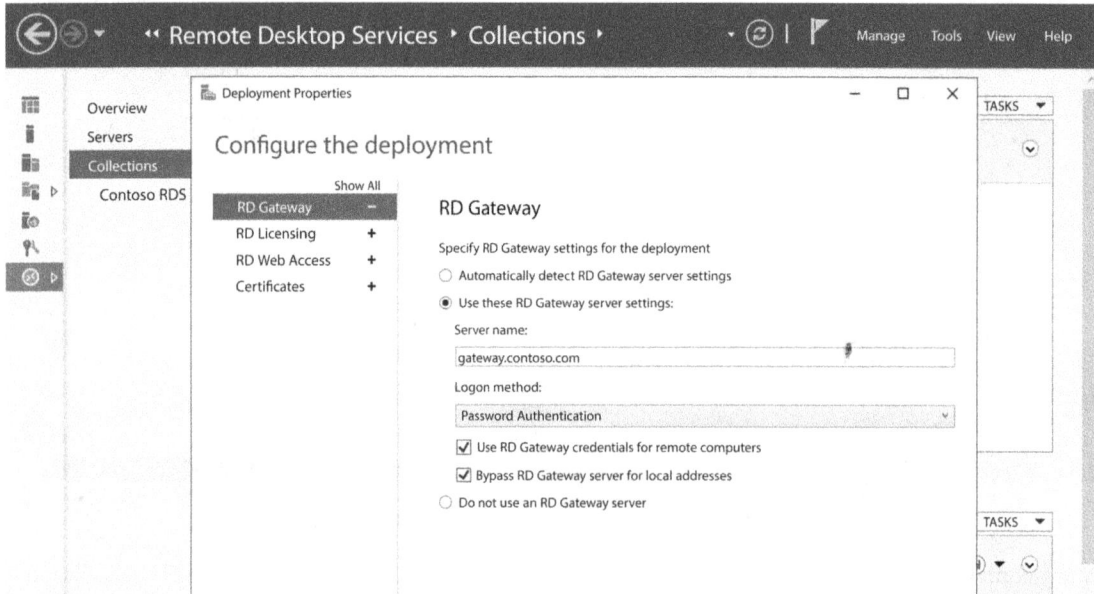

Figure 16.12: RDS Deployment Properties

Collection Properties

In addition to the overarching RDS role properties, you, of course, have options within each and every RDS collection that can also be tweaked. These are generally the most interesting settings to pore over. Still inside Server Manager, as you add new RDS collections, you will notice that each one is listed separately, under the primary **Collections** section. Selecting any collection will display many pieces of information about that collection, such as which RDSH servers are part of the collection and what user sessions are currently active on this collection. You can see in our next screenshot that my user session is still active on RDSH1. Near the top of this screen is a **PROPERTIES** section, with another **TASKS** drop-down menu. This time inside **TASKS**, we have but one item to click—**Edit Properties**.

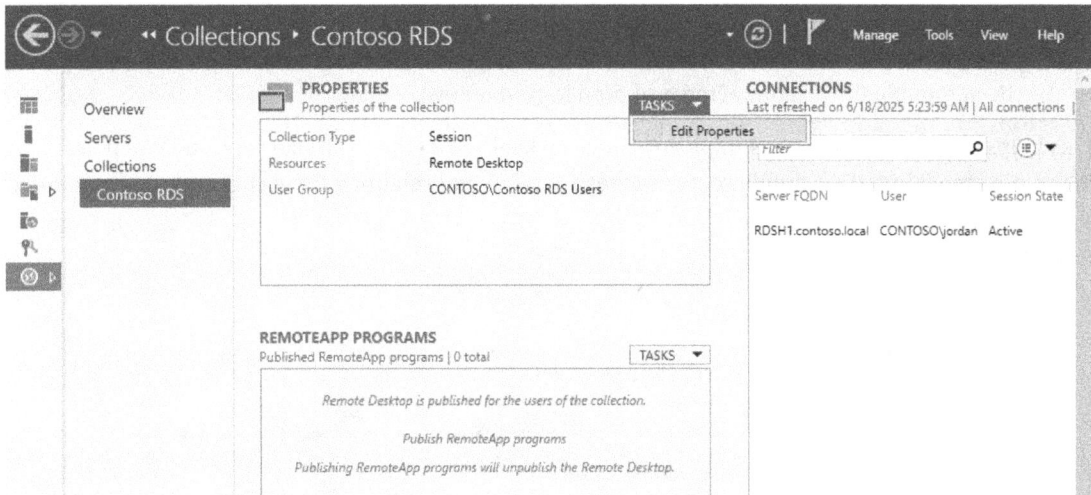

Figure 16.13: Editing properties for an individual RDS collection

Many of the properties here are self-explanatory, such as changing the name of your collection and tweaking general **Security** settings for RDS user connections. **User Groups** is where you can change at any time which users or groups are allowed to access this particular collection. You can even configure detailed **Load Balancing** metrics, which tell the RD Connection Broker how to distribute incoming user sessions across your multiple RDSH servers. There are two primary screens that I want to show in more detail, because these are the places where I find many RDS administrators visiting regularly to make changes.

Session

When users connect to an RDS session, their login is running processes and consuming resources from the RDSH server that they are connected to. When users log out of their sessions, they very rarely do an actual "logoff," which is the only way for those resources to truly be released. Instead, most users click the **X** button near the top of their RDP window, which closes their connection but leaves the virtual session hanging open on the server, along with any resources that the session is consuming. This disconnect behavior is purposeful so that the users can reconnect to RDS later in the day and pick back up where they left off, much like putting a laptop to sleep and waking it up again. However, when you have 25 or 50 or more people who could be logging in to the same RDSH server, that can equate to a lot of resources being consumed unnecessarily, which has a negative impact on those users who are actively logged in to their sessions.

All that to say, it is very common for companies to implement session timeout policies. The **Session** screen is exactly the place to do this. The two most common pieces of information to populate on this screen are as follows:

- **End a disconnected session** means that any user sessions sitting in a disconnected state will be fully logged off, and therefore will release their resources, after X number of minutes or hours. It is very common to set this between 1 and 3 hours.

- Secondly, it is common to see **Idle session limit** configured for something like 6 or 8 hours. By combining these two session limits, you mostly guarantee that everybody's RDS session will be automatically disconnected and then logged off every night.

This helps to keep resource consumption at an even keel across the RDSH servers, and when users log in the next morning, they simply receive a fresh session and relaunch their applications from there.

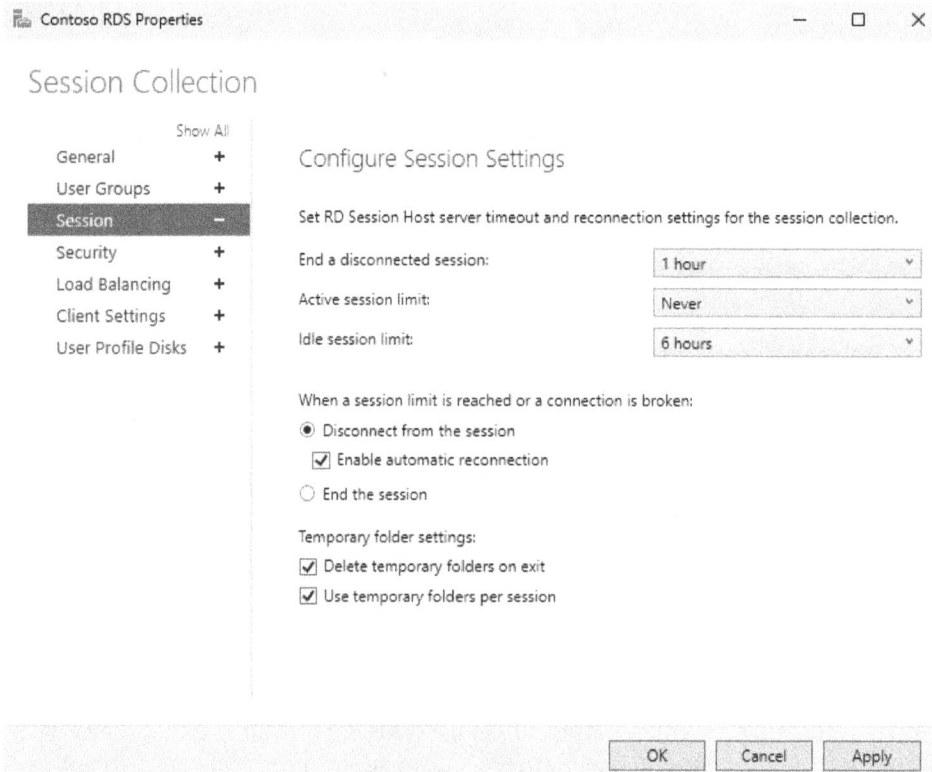

Figure 16.14: RDS session timeout settings

Client Settings

Another common settings screen to visit occasionally is **Client Settings**. When a user connects to an RDS farm, it is possible to pull local resources from their own computer into the RDS session. For example, the workstation's hard drives or printers, or even the clipboard, can be automatically mapped through as connections that are accessible from inside RDS. This way, users can copy text or files between their RDS server session and their local computer, and they can even click **File | Print** inside an RDS session and have the option of printing back to their home printer. These mappings happen within the RDP tunnels, and whether or not those functions are allowed is determined by this **Client Settings** screen. Simply check or uncheck the local resources you want to be accessible from inside user RDS sessions.

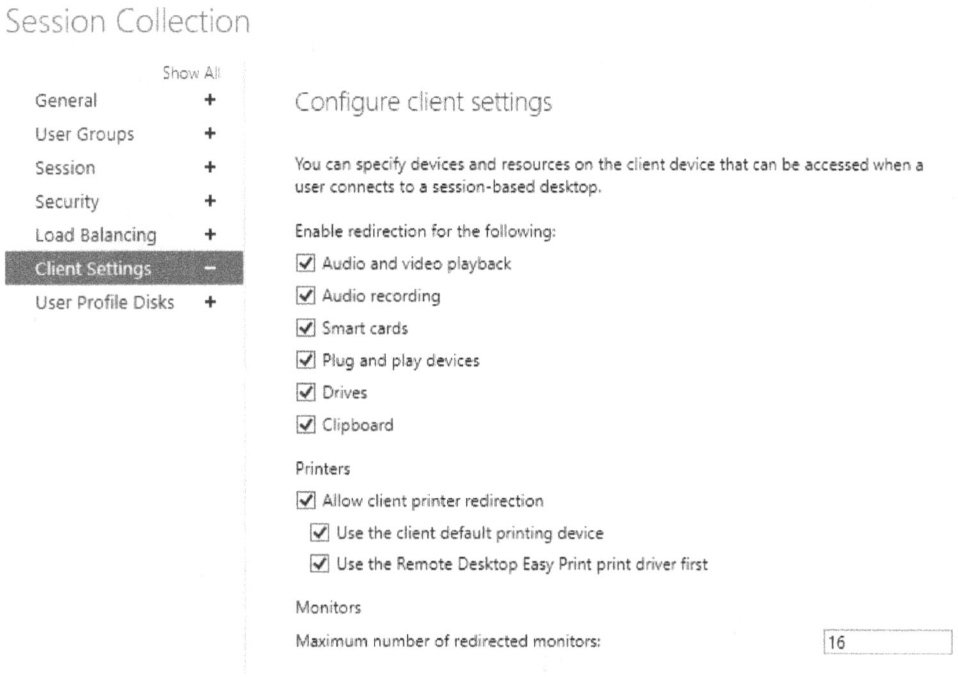

Session Collection

Show All

General	+
User Groups	+
Session	+
Security	+
Load Balancing	+
Client Settings	−
User Profile Disks	+

Configure client settings

You can specify devices and resources on the client device that can be accessed when a user connects to a session-based desktop.

Enable redirection for the following:

- ☑ Audio and video playback
- ☑ Audio recording
- ☑ Smart cards
- ☑ Plug and play devices
- ☑ Drives
- ☑ Clipboard

Printers

- ☑ Allow client printer redirection
  - ☑ Use the client default printing device
  - ☑ Use the Remote Desktop Easy Print print driver first

Monitors

Maximum number of redirected monitors: `16`

Figure 16.15: RDS client settings, configured per collection

Adding RDSH servers to your collection

During the build of our RDS collection, we identified a server to use as Gateway/Licensing/Web Access/Connection Broker, and we added two RDSH servers to the collection. Let's pretend this has been up and running for a while, but we are now starting to outgrow the original design. We scoped these RDSH servers to handle around 25 users each, but our business has continued to grow, and we now have 60 people logging in every day. RDSH1 and RDSH2 are keeping up, but users notice slowness during peak times of the day. The answer to this question is pretty straightforward—we need an RDSH3 server.

I have built another Windows Server 2025 instance, and the only things I have done with it so far are give it an IP address and a hostname and join it to my domain. In a real-world scenario, I would also need to make sure that all my installed applications mirrored those of RDSH1 and RDSH2, so that when we introduce RDSH3 into the farm, users are not lacking access to any apps they might need to launch. But in my test lab, I haven't installed applications on any of my RDSH servers, so that is currently not a consideration for me.

Assuming those pieces are accomplished, the next action we need to perform is adding RDSH into this same Server Manager instance from which I am already administering my farm. This step is not obvious—nothing in the console will tell you to do it, but it makes sense once you think about it. How could this copy of Server Manager reach out and manipulate RDSH3 to bring it into the collection if we do not first add RDSH3 as a managed server inside Server Manager? Thankfully, you already know how to do this, but as a quick reminder, simply head to **Manage** | **Add Servers** and add the name of your new server.

Now that Server Manager knows about RDSH3, I want to head back into the **Remote Desktop Services** section of Server Manager and visit the primary **Overview** tab. This screen shows me high-level information about my whole RDS deployment, and there are some quick links near the top of this screen. One of those links, option 2, says **Add RD Session Host servers**. Click on this link, specify the new RDSH node, and the wizard gets to work configuring that server to be part of your RDS deployment.

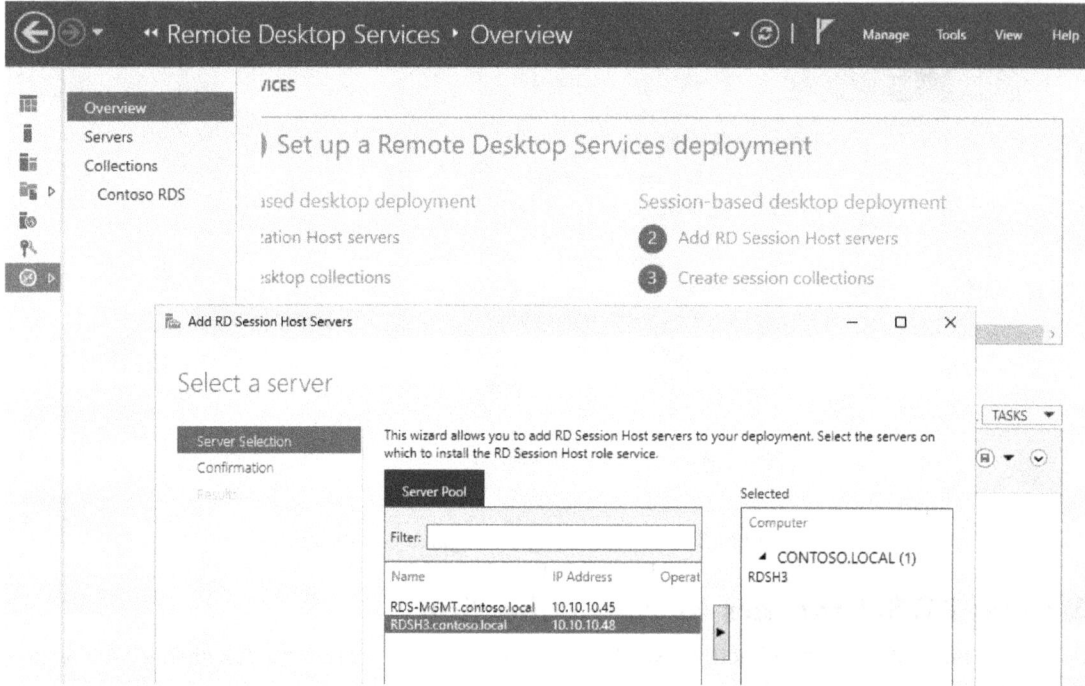

Figure 16.16: Adding RDSH3 to my RDS deployment

But wait, there's more! We are almost to the finish line, but there is one more step to accomplish before user sessions will flow to RDSH3. At this point, Server Manager has reached out to RDSH3 and installed the necessary Remote Desktop components on it, and RDSH3 is now visible inside Server Manager since it is part of our RDS deployment. However, an RDS deployment could contain many different RDS collections, which is the level at which connectivity really happens. So, all we need to do is add RDSH3 to the appropriate RDS collection; in my case, it is my collection called Contoso RDS.

Still inside the **Remote Desktop Services** section of Server Manager, all I have to do is click on my **Contoso RDS** collection and then scroll down to the bottom, where there is a section called **HOST SERVERS**. Here, you will find another one of those **TASKS** drop-down menus, inside which is an **Add RD Session Host Servers** option. While this option is called the exact same thing as the wizard we ran just a minute ago to add RDSH3 to our overall deployment, we need to additionally run through this one to now add RDSH3 to this specific collection.

Collections

Contoso RDS

HOST SERVERS
Last refreshed on 6/18/2025 5:55:11 AM | All servers | 2 total   TASKS ▼

Filter   🔎   (☰) ▼   (🖫) ▼

Server Name	Type		Virtual Desktops	Allow New Connections
				Add RD Session Host Servers
				Remove RD Session Host servers
				Refresh
RDSH1	RD Session Host	N/A		True
RDSH2	RD Session Host	N/A		True

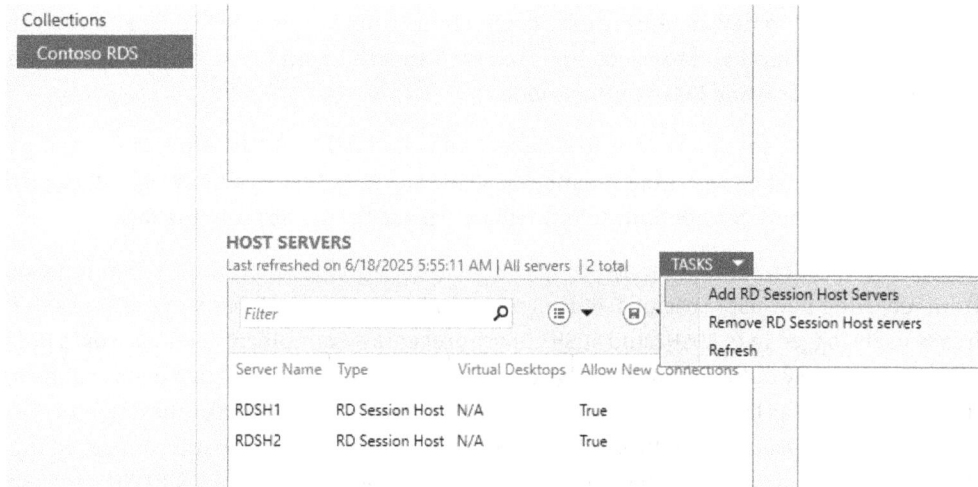

Figure 16.17: RDSH3 is becoming a farm member and servicing user sessions

Now that RDSH3 is part of our deployment and our collection, it will be included in load balancing for this collection, and users' sessions will start to flow to it.

Drain-stopping an RDSH for maintenance

Occasionally, you will need to remove an RDSH node from a collection so that you can perform maintenance on it. Perhaps you need to install a new application or update an application, or otherwise investigate and repair something within Windows on that node. It is a very common task to temporarily remove an RDSH server from a collection and add it back again later. These functions are very quick and simple, and if the last screenshot is still burned into your brain, you are already looking at the right place from which to do so.

Inside the **Remote Desktop Services** section of Server Manager, select the name of your collection and scroll down to the bottom of this screen. Here you will see all of the host servers that are part of your collection; these are the RDSH servers currently servicing user connections. Simply right-click on a node and select the only option, **Do not allow new connections**.

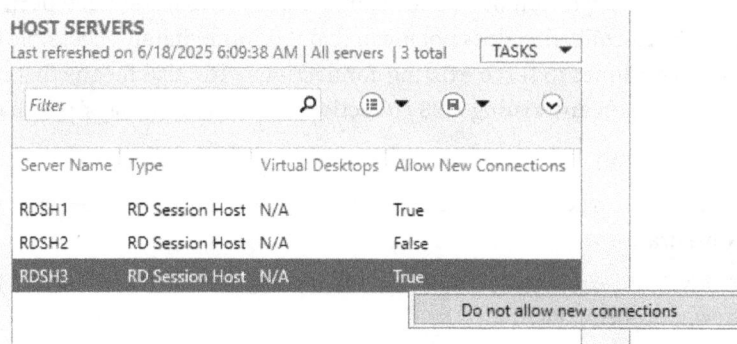

HOST SERVERS
Last refreshed on 6/18/2025 6:09:38 AM | All servers | 3 total   TASKS ▼

Filter   🔎   (☰) ▼   (🖫) ▼   (⌄)

Server Name	Type		Virtual Desktops	Allow New Connections
RDSH1	RD Session Host	N/A		True
RDSH2	RD Session Host	N/A		False
RDSH3	RD Session Host	N/A		True
				Do not allow new connections

Figure 16.18: Temporarily blocking new connections to an RDSH

This will immediately stop new incoming user connections from landing on RDSH3, and you can see in the screenshot that I have already accomplished the same thing on RDSH2, which is indicated by **Allow New Connections** stating **False** for that node.

At this point, all new user sessions to our RDS collection would fall on RDSH1—that one is going to be busy! As soon as I am finished with maintenance on RDSH2 and RDSH3, I can simply right-click on them again and select **Allow new connections** to immediately place them back into the farm.

The heading of this section said "drain-stopping"—what exactly do I mean by that? When you block an RDSH from receiving new user sessions, it does not change anything with existing sessions. If there were already users logged in to RDSH2 and RDSH3 in my preceding example, my actions would not have affected them, and they would remain happily connected to those servers. No *new* connections would flow to these servers, so as those users naturally end their sessions or log off for the day, and then log on again next time, they would be redirected to RDSH1 or any other node that is still configured to allow connections. This is important to understand because you cannot expect to block RDSH servers from receiving connections and immediately get to work on those servers. You will have to either forcibly log users out of those nodes, which would be intrusive and disruptive to them, or remove an RDSH from its collection and then wait, possibly until the next business day, to accomplish your maintenance.

Installing applications on an RDSH

The installation of applications is obviously very important in the RDS world: you are providing users with a virtual desktop session from which you expect them to work, and to work, they will need to be able to launch the applications necessary to do their jobs. That means these applications must be installed on every RDSH server upon which a user session might land. In general, every RDSH server that is part of the same collection should have the same applications installed. This also means the same versions of the same applications are installed, so you can imagine that application updates and maintenance are a little bit trickier on an RDSH than on a normal workstation.

No users logged in

Whenever installing applications on an RDSH server, it is recommended to make sure all users are logged out of that server (other than yourself, of course). This brings us back to drain-stopping those servers and understanding how to remove nodes from a farm for maintenance purposes. Since the removal of an RDSH from its collection does not mean that it is immediately accessible for performing that maintenance, as it continues to serve existing connections, this also means that many times the installation of new software on an existing RDS collection involves many days' worth of work:

- **Day 1:** Drain-stop RDSH1.
- **Day 2:** Users are now logged out of RDSH1; install the application on RDSH1 and put it back into the farm. Now, drain-stop RDSH2.
- **Day 3:** Users are now logged out of RDSH2; install the application on RDSH2 and put it back into the farm. Now, drain-stop RDSH3.
- **Day 4:** Users are now logged out of RDSH3; install the application on RDSH3 and put it back into the farm.

Whew! That is a lot of days for the installation of a single application. Alternatively, you could likely install the application on all three on the same day, at 3:00 a.m., but...really.

...yes, even for updates

The installation-of-software rules apply whether you are installing a new application that has never been on the RDSH server before, or simply installing an update to that application. If there are any users already logged in to the RDSH server and potentially utilizing the application that you are attempting to update, you could run into problems. Or worse yet, your update installer might finish successfully but perhaps not be able to do everything that it needs to do in the background, which could cause you mysterious problems down the road. Better to be safe than sorry: make sure that when you install applications or application updates onto an RDSH server, you are the only user logged in to it.

Install mode

An RDSH server is a multi-user environment with various user profiles and user registry hives scattered throughout the operating system. When applications get installed onto an RDSH, something needs to ensure that the necessary files and regkeys get distributed to the proper locations so that every user account is able to make use of them. Have you ever installed an application that asked you, **Do you want to install this application for only the current user, or for everyone on the system?** On an RDSH server, you would, of course, select **For everyone on the system** and carry on. Thankfully, most applications are RDS-aware, recognize automatically when you are installing them onto an RDSH server, and take the necessary adjustments in the background to ensure the application is installed properly.

But...

Some application installers do not. They have no idea or care in the world where you are installing their app, and if you simply log in to RDSH1 and launch the installer, it *might* work okay for you, but it is just as likely to have all kinds of problems in any other user session. You certainly don't want to reinstall the application inside every user session. This is why, **every time that you install any application onto any RDSH server**, you should first put that RDSH into **install mode**.

Install mode is unique to RDS servers and, if you are going to be working with them, is a command you should memorize right now. It is very simple; before launching your application installer or update installer, open a Command Prompt or PowerShell window and perform the following:

```
change user /install
```

That's it! Your RDS server is now in `install` mode, and this causes Windows to understand that any installers need to be nannied a little bit. If the installer is about to put a file or registry key into a place where it might have issues from other user accounts, Windows will remap those things to more central locations.

When you are finished installing the application, simply place your server back into its standard **execute mode**:

```
change user /execute
```

If ever you are unsure what mode you are currently running in (it's easy to lose track if you are installing multiple things and rebooting in between), you can easily find out what mode your server is currently running by using the following:

```
change user /query
```

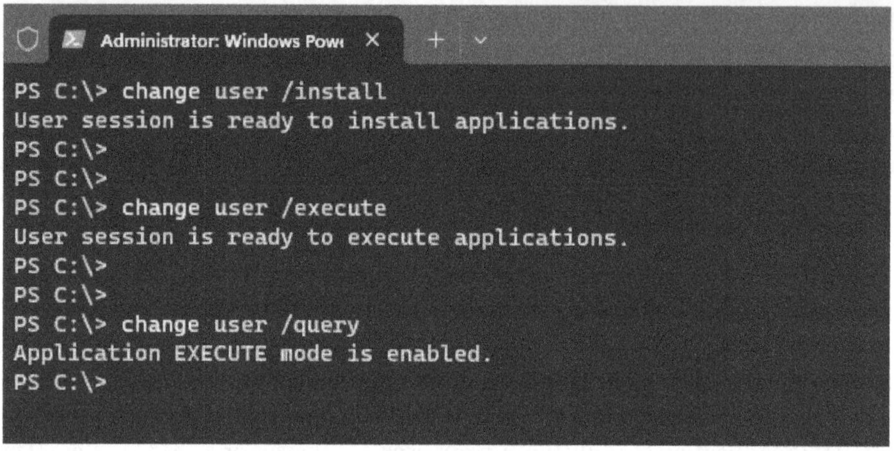

Figure 16.19: Install mode and execute mode

Remember install mode—it helps save you headaches. Also, remember that every RDSH server in the same collection should have the exact same applications installed on it to provide your users with a uniform experience every time they log in.

RDS licensing

Every incoming connection that lands on an RDS server must have a valid CAL. These licenses are available for purchase from any normal avenue through which you purchase your Windows Server licensing, so I cannot tell you the best place to go to get these licenses, only that you need them, and how they work. There are two types of RDS CAL, and we will describe both, but the reality is that almost every RDS farm in the world uses User CALs.

User CALs

User CALs are the normal way to go. As the name implies, every user who is connecting to your RDS farm needs to have a User CAL. These CALs are installed on your Remote Desktop Licensing server, which may co-exist alongside some other RDS roles, and once licenses are installed, the RDSH servers check in with the Remote Desktop License server to ensure there is sufficient licensing to allow the connection to happen.

User CAL limits are not restricted at a technical level. Similar to the way that a lot of Microsoft licensing works, it is essentially an honor system. You could purchase 20 RDS User CALs, or you could purchase 150. Whichever you install on your licensing server, that will green-light RDSH servers to allow users to connect, and from that point, there is no monitoring happening in the licensing system to know whether you have 20 people connected or 300.

Also, as with all other Microsoft licensing, you don't want to cheat that system. Your organization may need to be part of an annual true-up where you would have to define and pay for any discrepancies, or you may be large enough you have a Microsoft licensing rep, or you may work with a service provider and they are not going to put their necks on the line by allowing you to cheat the licensing system and purchase fewer CALs than you have users. Make sure you own enough! It is your responsibility to make sure all users have a valid license.

Device CALs

Device CALs are extremely rare to find in the wild. Again, the name is fairly self-explanatory; in this licensing model, RDS doesn't care at all about how many users are connecting but rather how many unique *computers* are connecting to your RDS farm. Device CALs *are* restricted at a technical level. This type of license would be applicable for a business that has multiple shifts of people who are using the same computers. The general idea is that you would own a Device CAL for every workstation that you own. RDS License Manager keeps track through a temporary certificate of sorts about which computers are connecting, and as long as you have as many CALs as you do computers, you will be fine in this scenario.

The problem is that what I just described is almost never how companies try to use Device CALs. Instead, in the places where I have found them, they are using them simply because they are cheaper, and they are trying to get away with using Device CALs as if they were "concurrent connection CALs"—which they are not.

One key benefit of RDS environments is the ease with which you can provide users access to their virtual desktops from a home computer. Are you really going to purchase Device CALs for every home device each of your users might own?

Whenever a computer connects to an RDS farm that uses Device CALs, the license manager knows about it and records it. That CAL is then dedicated to that particular computer for roughly 8 days. If a particular computer does not reconnect after that timeframe, it generally falls off the licensing map, so to speak, until it connects again. In this sense, you might be able to get away with having fewer Device CALs than devices, but you'll always be rolling the dice. There is also a function to manually revoke CALs, and I have literally watched admins approach these CALs in a mindset that they'll just revoke all of their Device CALs every day. That is not only ridiculous, but License Manager won't let you do that anyway. You are only allowed to manually revoke up to 20% of active RDS CALs at any given time. Not 20% each day—20% of them, period.

The valid use cases for Device CALs are pretty slim. When you are purchasing RDS CALs, it is generally safe to approach that purchase through the assumption that you are going to need User CALs.

Specifying the RD License server

You probably don't remember configuring any RDS licensing settings during our farm deployment, and that is because we never did. New RDS environments enter automatically into a 120-day grace period, where user sessions and connections are allowed without having any licensing whatsoever. Once you have acquired your RDS CALs, you will need to accomplish two things to get them working. Specify the RD License server inside **Deployment Properties** and plug the CALs into the Remote Desktop License Manager.

Go ahead and edit your overall **Deployment Properties** (not **Collection Properties**) and visit the screen called **RD Licensing**. Here, you simply select whether you are using **Per Device** or **Per User** licenses, and make sure that your Remote Desktop License server name is specified. This is all you need to do to tell your entire RDS deployment where the Remote Desktop License server is.

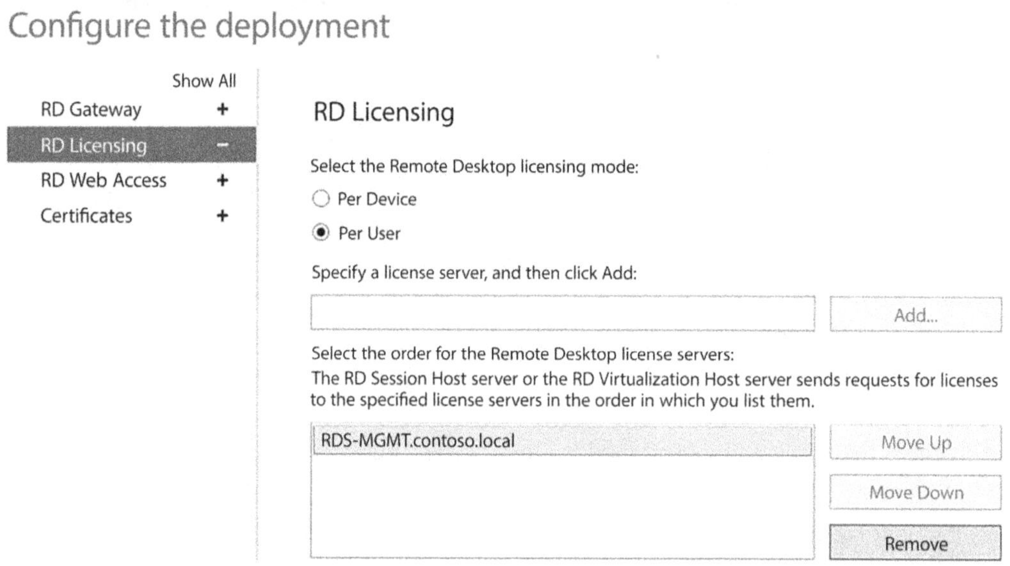

Configure the deployment

Show All		RD Licensing
RD Gateway	+	
RD Licensing	−	Select the Remote Desktop licensing mode:
RD Web Access	+	○ Per Device
Certificates	+	● Per User

Specify a license server, and then click Add:

[   ]   [Add...]

Select the order for the Remote Desktop license servers:
The RD Session Host server or the RD Virtualization Host server sends requests for licenses to the specified license servers in the order in which you list them.

RDS-MGMT.contoso.local	Move Up
	Move Down
	Remove

Figure 16.20: Specifying RDS licensing within Deployment Properties

RD Licensing Manager

Strangely, there is no accommodation inside the standard RDS configuration screens to apply or review RDS licensing. For this task, we must visit the older MMC-based console related to this topic. Once a server has been configured via Server Manager as your RD Licensing server, as RDS-MGMT has been in our test lab, you will find a new folder listed inside **Administrative Tools** called Remote Desktop Services, and within that folder, a management tool called **Remote Desktop Licensing Manager**. Launching **Remote Desktop Licensing Manager** will bring you to the place where you can add new RDS licensing CALs, view existing ones, or even revoke Device CALs if that scenario applies to you.

When building up a fresh RDS environment, you will need to visit this console, right-click on the name of your Remote Desktop licensing server, use the **Activate Server** wizard to paste in the key that you received from Microsoft containing your RDS CALs, and step through the wizard to activate those CALs. This will check in with Microsoft activation servers, and after successful activation, your RDS licensing is ready to roll!

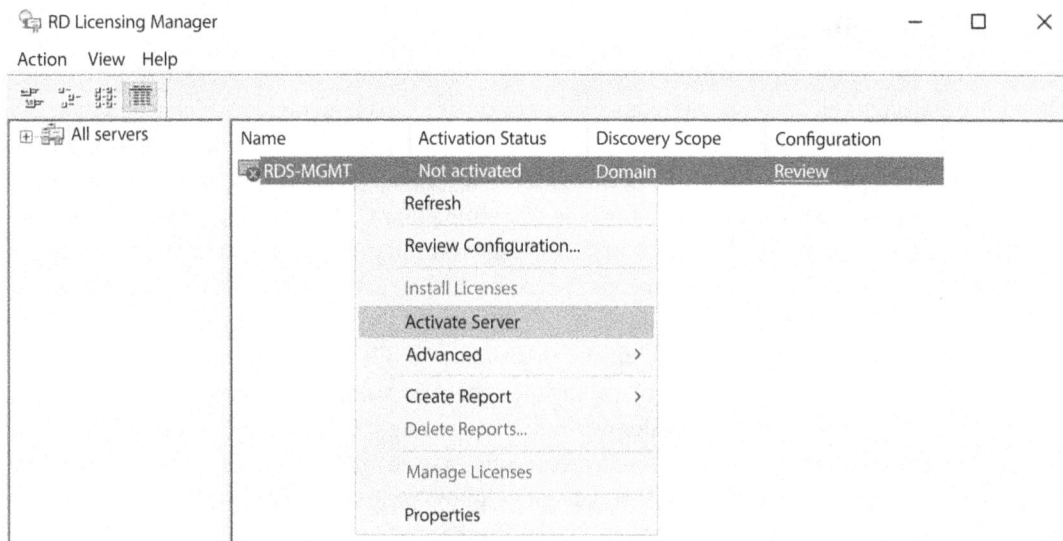

Figure 16.21: Using the older toolset to activate RDS CALs

RDS user profiles

As a generalization, user profiles in the Microsoft Windows world are fairly straightforward. A user account authenticates, usually via AD, and the user is permitted to log in to whatever computer or server they are sitting in front of. If this is the first time this user has logged in to this computer, a new Windows user profile is created on that computer. These user profiles, unless you have done some significant tweaking to your operating systems, all reside inside a folder called C:\Users. Additionally, a new section of the registry is created to contain settings specific to this user account.

Local profiles

When RDS began life, it was known as Terminal Server, and this default user profile behavior of the Windows world was exactly what happened on terminal servers whenever a user would log in. This means that each Terminal Server had its own C:\Users directory, and that directory could contain hundreds of different user profiles, one for every person who ever logged in to the server. This in itself is not an issue, but it was certainly cumbersome for users when, on Monday, they would log in to TS1 and set up all of their files, configuration settings, desktop visualization tweaks, and other preferences, and then on Tuesday morning, they would log in again and wouldn't you know it—they were then logged in to TS2 and all of those tweaks they made yesterday were "gone." They still exist on TS1, and the next time the user logs in and happens to land on TS1, they see everything again, but today is not that day, and today they are now re-tweaking everything on TS2.

Allowing a Terminal Server or RDS environment to run local Windows profiles is problematic and effectively dead as an idea. Let me clarify that: it is effectively dead as an idea *in the RDS world*; Windows desktop computers continue to land user data inside C:\Users as normal behavior.

Roaming profiles

Clearly, some uniformity to user profiles was needed, perhaps empowering users to have a certain collection of settings and for those settings to follow the user around, no matter which RDS server they logged in to. The answer to this question in the 2000s was called roaming profiles. **Roaming profiles** are just like local profiles, except they are stored in a centralized location. Most likely, roaming profiles are all stored on a network file share, maybe something like \\FS1\RoamingProfiles. Microsoft integrated this idea firmly into its ecosystem. When users logged in to a terminal server or RDS server, Active Directory would recognize that this user account had a roaming profile location defined and would also recognize when a user was logging in to a normal desktop versus an RDS. In the event that said user was logging in to an RDS, the user's profile would be redirected to the user profile on that network share, rather than using a local profile. This was a fantastic idea and was the de facto standard for many years. Roaming profiles were such a big thing that Microsoft modified the AD user configuration screens so that if your company was using roaming profiles, when setting up new user accounts, all you needed to do was specify the location of the profile on this tab, and Windows would take care of the rest for you. Now, in the year 2025, this profile option (seen in *Figure 16.22*) still exists.

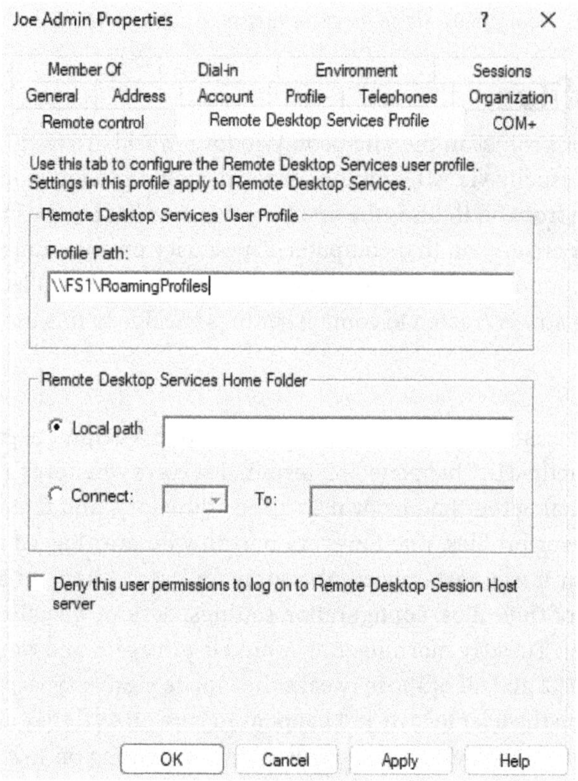

Figure 16.22: Defining roaming profiles via AD

Unfortunately, today, if you ask anyone who has worked in IT for more than 15 years what their thoughts are on roaming profiles, be prepared for a gag reflex. Even though it was a great idea, the reality surrounding roaming profiles is that they were quirky. Network speed and latency had a lot to do with it, but it was common that profiles took a very long time to load when users logged in, or would corrupt themselves, sometimes even resulting in the loss of user data. There are certainly ways to make roaming profiles work, but it is no longer a common practice due to the advent of...

User Profile Disks

We now find ourselves looking at the default profile option of today's Remote Desktop servers. The idea of UPDs is very much like roaming profiles, but rather than a collection of files and folders containing the user profile sitting out there on a network share, the user's profile is contained within its own VHDX file. For anyone who made it through our chapter on Hyper-V, you'll know that this is Microsoft's virtual hard disk file, the same type of file used as a virtual hard drive on a virtual server.

UPDs are stored on a network share, and every user who logs in to your RDS environment gets their own VHDX virtual disk spun up during the login process. Initial login takes a few extra seconds due to the creation of this file, but then the file exists and remains intact so that future logins are faster. While users are logged in to an RDSH server, they are primarily referencing their UPD so that files or settings saved within their profile are saved to that virtual disk, but you'll find that C:\Users on the RDSH server is still populated with what look to be classic Windows user profile folders. This is because the RDSH still needs somewhere locally on the server to interact with, and when a UPD-based user account logs in, certain pieces of information are pulled from their VHDX and stored locally on the RDSH server. It's easy to think about these folders inside C:\Users as being temporary profile locations, just remember that the user's primary profile is that VHDX file, located somewhere on the network. This, of course, enables users to be able to tap into any of the RDSH servers in a collection and have the same profile layout, settings, and files no matter where they are logged in.

Telling your RDS environment to use UPDs is very simple. In fact, we have already done it if you are following along with this test lab creation. Create a network share in a central location where all of the RDSH servers can access it, and make sure that NTFS permissions are such that all of the RDSH computer accounts have full control over that shared folder. This is important because the RDSH servers are going to be creating the new VHDX files as new users log in. Then, inside RDS **Collection Properties** (UPDs are configured per collection, not per deployment), visit the **User Profile Disks** screen and simply check the **Enable user profile disks** box. Specify the network share location that you have created for these VHDX files to reside, and then select whether you want all user settings to be stored in this disk or only select pieces.

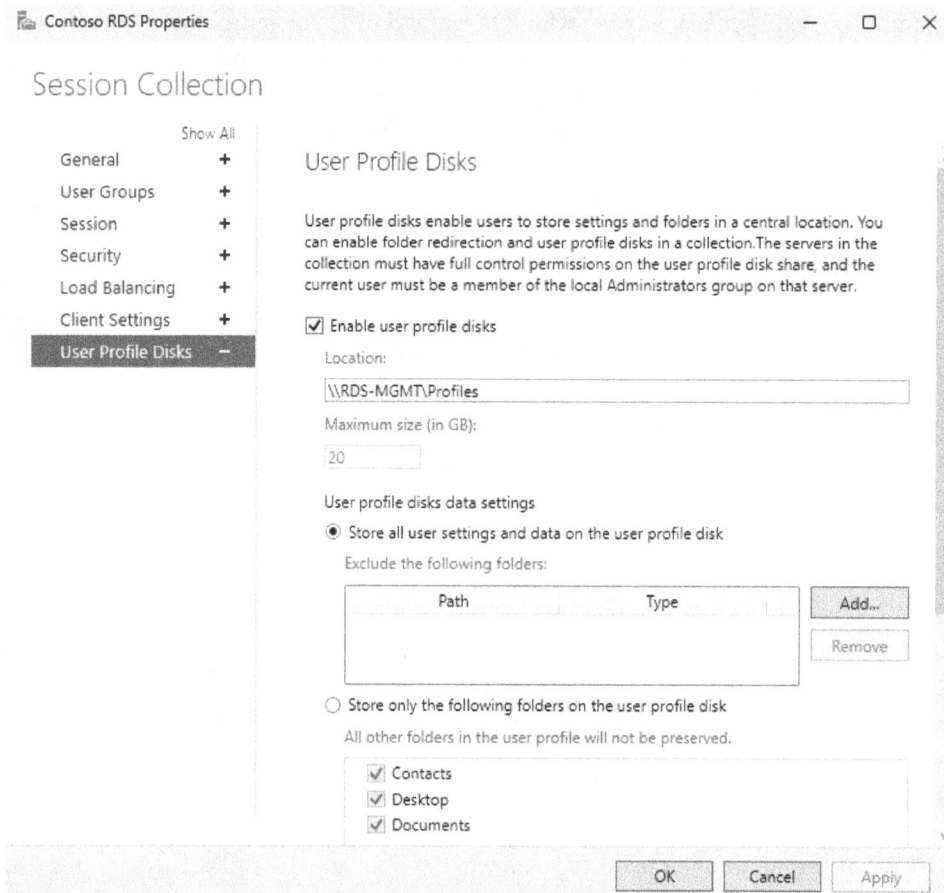

Figure 16.23: Configuring User Profile Disks

UPDs work well and are in use in many RDS deployments across the world today. They do come with some interesting behavior, though; as I mentioned, a temporary C:\Users profile is still created for each user as they log in, and for some reason, it is very common for RDSH servers configured with UPDs to end up littered with multiple copies of this temp profile. Many times, this is the result of something going wrong during user login or logoff. If a temp profile already exists for a user, sometimes during the next login process, rather than reusing that same folder, the RDSH server will decide to create another one. This results in a messy C:\Users folder on the RDSH server, but it generally does not create actual problems for the users, as their data and settings are still ultimately stored inside the VHDX. If you visit C:\Users on your RDSH servers, you may find something similar to the following screenshot. Here, I have logged my administrator account in and out of the RDS farm many times, and this has resulted in multiple temporary profiles for the administrator account.

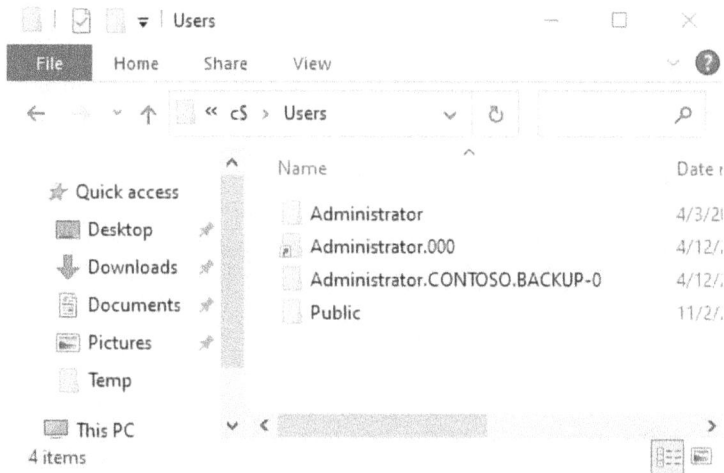

Figure 16.24: Having multiple temp profiles is normal UPD behavior

When this happens, cleanup is fairly simple. These temp accounts are not needed, again, as the real data is inside the VHDX file. So, as long as the user account is not currently logged in to the RDSH server that you are looking into, it is generally safe to simply delete all instances of these temp profiles for that user account. If the user is logged in and actively using one of the temp accounts, then you may want to hold off until a time when they are not logged in to that server.

FSLogix

It is most often appropriate to think about RDS user profile options with a "good, better, best" mindset. Roaming profiles are fine, UPDs are better, and FSLogix profiles are as good as it gets. FSLogix used to be its own company, improving centralized profile capabilities as a third-party add-on, until Microsoft acquired it in 2018. RDS profiles that are managed through FSLogix policies are similar in ideology to UPDs, in that profiles are stored in a central location and make use of VHDX files to keep data. One of the primary reasons to utilize FSLogix profiles instead of classic UPDs is for scenarios where you want users to have a good experience with Microsoft Office applications inside an RDS farm. Office applications don't always play well with UPDs, particularly things such as Outlook OST files. FSLogix accommodates that and makes login times much faster in these scenarios.

Another big reason to move toward FSLogix profiles is if your business is using OneDrive to sync users' documents/desktop/pictures across all their devices. This is now a built-in capability of the OneDrive agent and is very useful for maintaining consistency across multiple computers that users may log in to, and for keeping an online backup of their document data. RDS servers are not entirely OneDrive-friendly: users often have to wait for large sync cycles every time they log in to their RDS session, and in many cases, OneDrive simply fails to work. This is one area where FSLogix does a much better job than UPDs.

FSLogix brings some enhancements to Windows profiles that enable Microsoft Office applications to better interact with RDS servers, and it also includes access control functionality for applications, printers, and a few other items. When you install something like an application or printer on an RDSH server, it is generally true that every user who logs in to the RDSH will have access to it. Application Rule Sets in FSLogix give you the ability to control access to these resources via user rules or group memberships.

Another large advantage FSLogix holds over UPDs is that the FSLogix profile disks (VDHXs) can be used across multiple RDS collections. UPDs can only be bound to one collection.

The configuration hurdle of FSLogix can range from "sort of simple" to "very complex." There are many options and selections to choose from, making it impossible to cover them all here. However, I love walk-throughs, so let's talk over the steps required to get a basic instance of FSLogix profiles up and running in our environment.

Installing the agent on RDSH servers

The core component of FSLogix is an agent that needs to be installed on each of your RDSH servers. Since only RDSH servers interact with user profiles, these are the nodes that need the agent installed. In other words, there is no need to install the FSLogix agent on your RDS Management server, such as my RDS-MGMT server.

The following link takes you to a page where Microsoft keeps the latest version of FSLogix. Simply download it and install it on each RDSH server: https://aka.ms/fslogix-latest.

Updating the agent

Microsoft regularly releases new versions of the FSLogix agent; thankfully, it is easy to put new versions into place. Simply download the newest version of the FSLogix agent, make sure no users are logged in to your RDS farm, and run the new installer on each RDSH server to in-place upgrade them. Typically, this requires a reboot of each RDSH server.

Importing FSLogix settings into Group Policy

Your agent is now installed, but as of this moment, it has no idea what it is supposed to be doing. The configuration of the FSLogix agent rolls out to it via Group Policy. Unfortunately, FSLogix GPO settings are not in Group Policy out of the box, even with Windows Server 2025. In our chapter on Group Policy, you already learned how to download ADMX/ADML files and import them into the Central Store, thereby injecting new settings and configuration options into Group Policy. To successfully use FSLogix, you will do exactly that with the following ADMX/ADML files:

*   FSLOGIX.ADMX
*   FSLOGIX.ADML

Where do we get those files? You already have them! Look inside that ZIP file you downloaded for the FSLogix agent installer, and you will find both of these files, waiting for you to push them into Group Policy's Central Store. Once imported, you can create a new GPO, apply it to your RDSH servers, and configure myriad options:

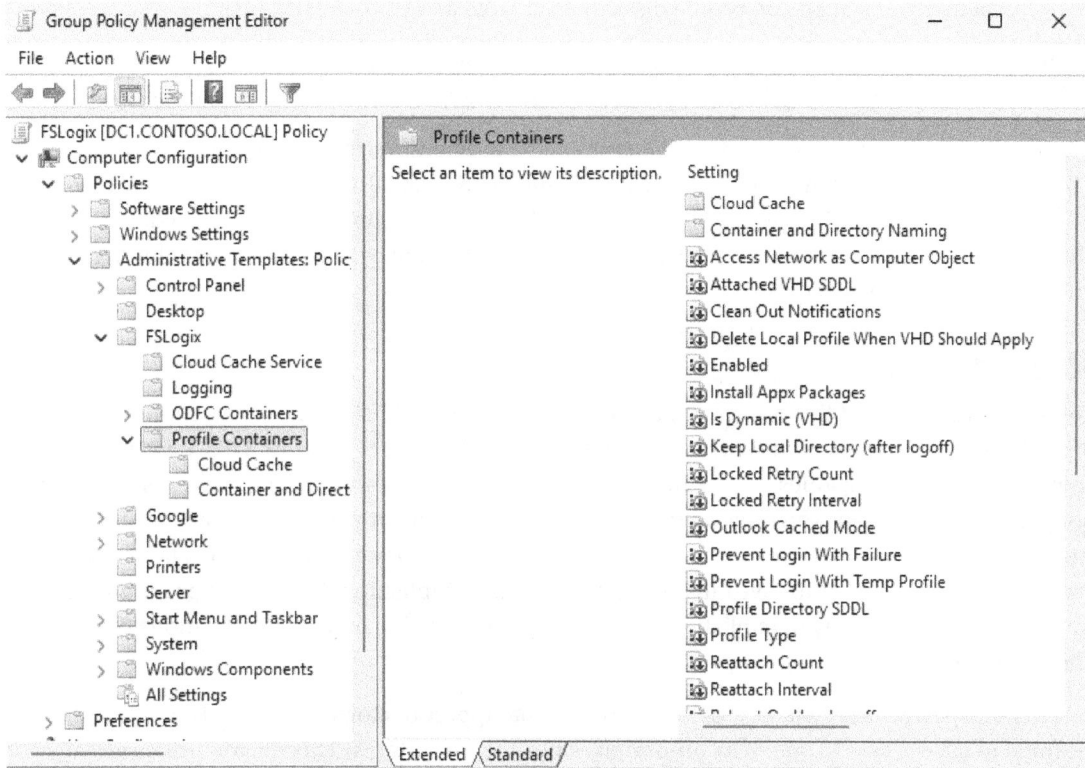

Figure 16.25: FSLogix policy settings inside Group Policy

Let's call out some of the most important options that must be configured to create a successful FSLogix profile solution:

- **Profile Containers > Enabled:** This enables FSLogix profiles in general.
- **Profile Containers > VHD Locations:** Specify your network path for storage of the FSLogix VHDX files. Just like UPDs, you need to create a centralized storage location for the profile disks to reside.
- **Profile Containers > Size in MBs:** Configure size limits for each user profile.
- **Profile Containers > Is Dynamic:** You'll want to set this one! When configured, those VHDX disks will be dynamically expanding and consume only the space users actually need. Without this setting, each VHDX will be created to its full max size.

- **Profile Containers > Delete Local Profile When VHD Should Apply:** This can be helpful when implementing FSLogix profiles where local profiles existed previously, telling the RDSH servers to clean up the old local profiles once new FSLogix profiles are created.

- **Profile Containers > Container and Directory Naming > Volume Type:** Here, you can specify whether you want those profile disks to be created as VHD or VHDX files.

With your GPO now crafted and applying to the RDSH servers (with the FSLogix agent installed), they will immediately begin using FSLogix profiles and storing them in the location you specified!

Microsoft says, as of this writing, that FSLogix can be used on pretty much any currently supported Microsoft operating system, even specifically calling out Server 2012R2. In my experience, however, FSLogix being used for RDS profile storage does not always work properly with the older versions of the operating system. Indeed, I would personally not deploy FSLogix on anything older than Server 2019, based on my own experience.

RemoteApp

You now understand RDS topology and the steps required to publish an RDS collection, upon which virtual sessions can land, and users have access to an entire virtual desktop. This, however, is much more access than companies sometimes want to provide, and it can become overly complicated for some use cases. Perhaps you only want to provide access to one or two applications when users connect; they don't need to have access to an entire desktop where they could potentially launch anything installed on the server, or to save files within their profile. Publishing RemoteApp programs through an RDS collection is a way to publish access to a single application or set of applications from within the Remote Desktop Web Access portal.

Here is one perfect example of a use case for RemoteApp. A doctor's office needs to allow its local hospital to have access to one of its on-premises healthcare systems. This doctor's office already has an RDS farm, and we could simply provide hospital staff with logins and virtual sessions on that RDS farm, but that would have given them access to double-click on any application installed on the RDSH servers. It sounds better if we could restrict hospital staff to only run a single application. The answer? Publish that lone application as a RemoteApp application inside a new RDS collection. These are the bare steps to utilizing RemoteApp:

1. Create an RDS deployment; maybe you already have one.
2. Create a new RDS collection to keep these RemoteApp applications separate from your full virtual sessions. It is possible to host both full desktop sessions and RemoteApp on the same RDS collection and on the same RDSH servers, but Microsoft does not recommend it. Best to keep them separated.
3. It usually makes sense to narrow the scope of this new collection so that only members of a specific group have access. This way, you can easily restrict who has access to launch this application.
4. Install the necessary application on your RDSH servers in the collection.
5. Publish a RemoteApp application inside your RDS collection properties.

6. Instruct your users to log in to the RD Web Access web portal. When they log in, as long as you have made them members of the appropriate group, they will now have an icon to launch this application from inside the web portal. This launches an RDP session in the background, but the only information that passes to the user's computer is the screen of the individual application that is being clicked on. No virtual desktop is ever shown to the user, only the application.

7. When users are finished with the application, they simply click the X button in the top-right corner, and their application closes. To the user, the application behaves as if it were installed on their local computer (even though it never was). In the background, the RDSH servers are spinning up an RDP session for the user and auto-launching that single application. When users click the X button, that session goes into a disconnected state.

Let's publish a quick application or two into an RDS collection so you can see how it really works. I have just finished creating a new collection called `Contoso RemoteApps`. I removed RDSH3 from my existing collection and added it to this new collection. Now, inside **Collection Properties**, I want to visit that section in the middle called **REMOTEAPP PROGRAMS**. Here, simply click the **TASKS** menu or the link right in the middle of this screen that says **Publish RemoteApp Programs**.

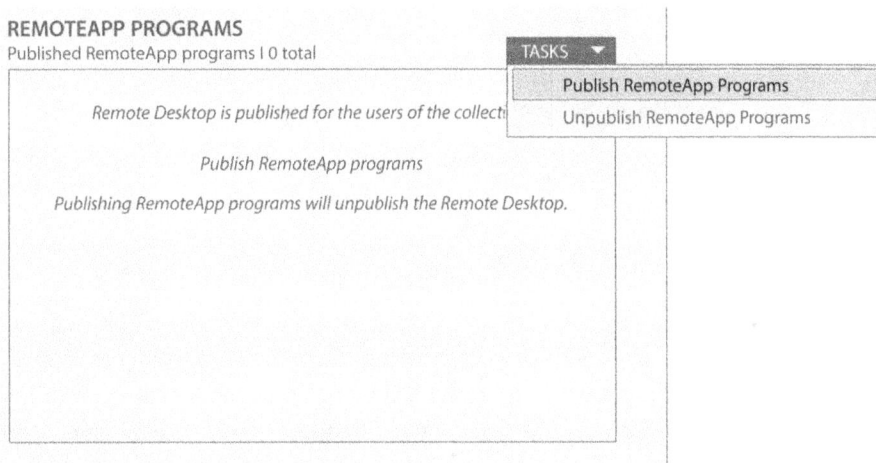

Figure 16.26: Publishing our first RemoteApp application

The coolest thing about RemoteApp applications is how incredibly simple they are to publish. This wizard polls the RDSH servers for a list of installed applications; if you have already installed any apps needing to be published, they will appear in this list. Now, you simply decide which apps need to be published inside this collection, select them, and finish out the wizard! I have not installed any custom applications onto RDSH3, but I have a plethora of options for preinstalled apps. For the sake of example, I will publish **Calculator** and **Notepad**.

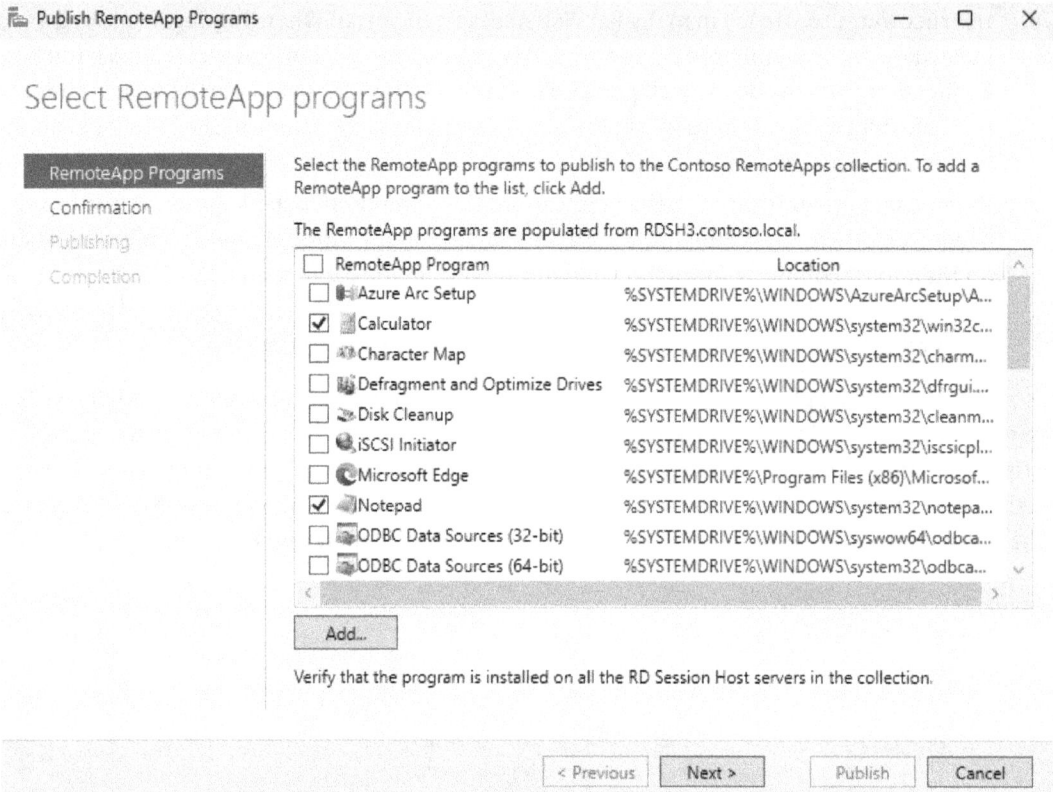

Figure 16.27: Publishing Calculator and Notepad

We are essentially finished. The only thing left to do is log in as a user account and test to make sure that we see and have the ability to launch these applications from the RD Web Access portal. Logging in to the **RD Web Access** portal, you can see in the following screenshot that my two RemoteApp programs are happily waiting for me. You will also notice that I still see my third icon, **Contoso RDS**. This is because the user account that I am testing with is a member of the group to provide me access to this new RDS collection and is still also a member of the group that grants me access to see the other RDS farm that still exists for RDSH1 and RDSH2. I could now click any of these icons and launch whatever level of access I need in order to do my job.

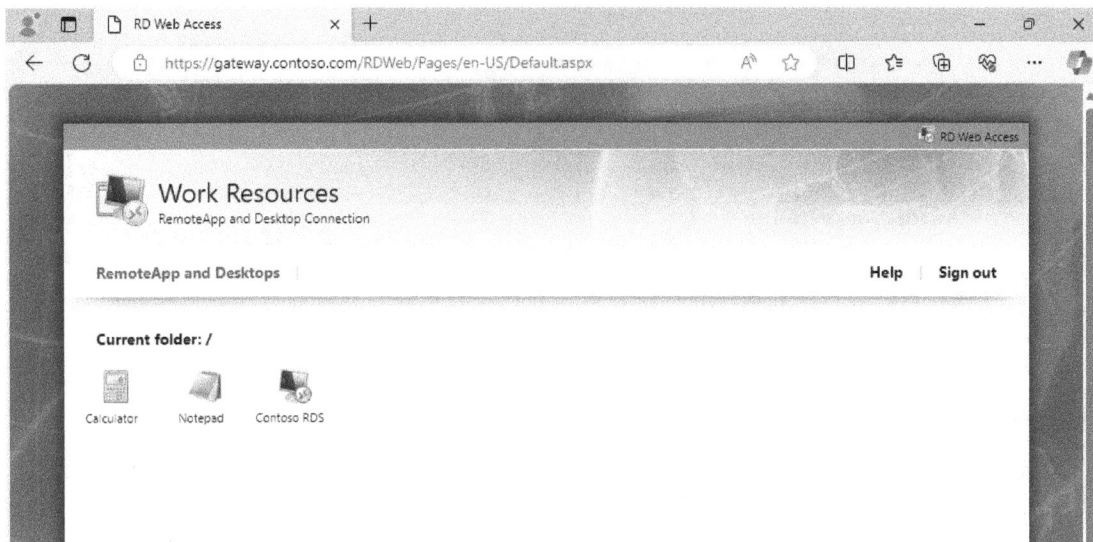

Figure 16.28: We have published RemoteApp programs!

Just like when clicking on the connection to my full Contoso RDS session, clicking on one of these RemoteApp applications results in my web browser downloading an RDP connection file. This RDP file is preconfigured to launch directly into my new RDS collection and auto-launch whatever RemoteApp program I had clicked on. Users may choose to always visit the **RD Web Access** interface and click on their applications from here, knowing that they will be redownloading a new copy of that RDP file every single time. They would then have to click on that downloaded file from inside the browser to launch the connection.

Alternatively, if you wanted to copy out the saved RDP connection file from your Downloads folder, this file could then be copied to a desktop or even distributed to other users, where they could simply double-click on the RDP connection file to launch their RemoteApp program.

I have tried to show all of this in the following screenshot. You can see the open **RD Web Access** page, the Downloads folder where my RDP connection file was downloaded when I clicked on **Notepad**, and the open **Notepad** window. Now, why would you believe me that this instance of Notepad is actually running on RDSH3 and is not simply Notepad installed on my WIN11 machine? If I click **File** > **Save** inside Notepad, I am clearly browsing the folder structure of RDSH3's hard drive. This **Notepad** window that I am interacting with is running completely on RDSH3, through a virtual RDS session.

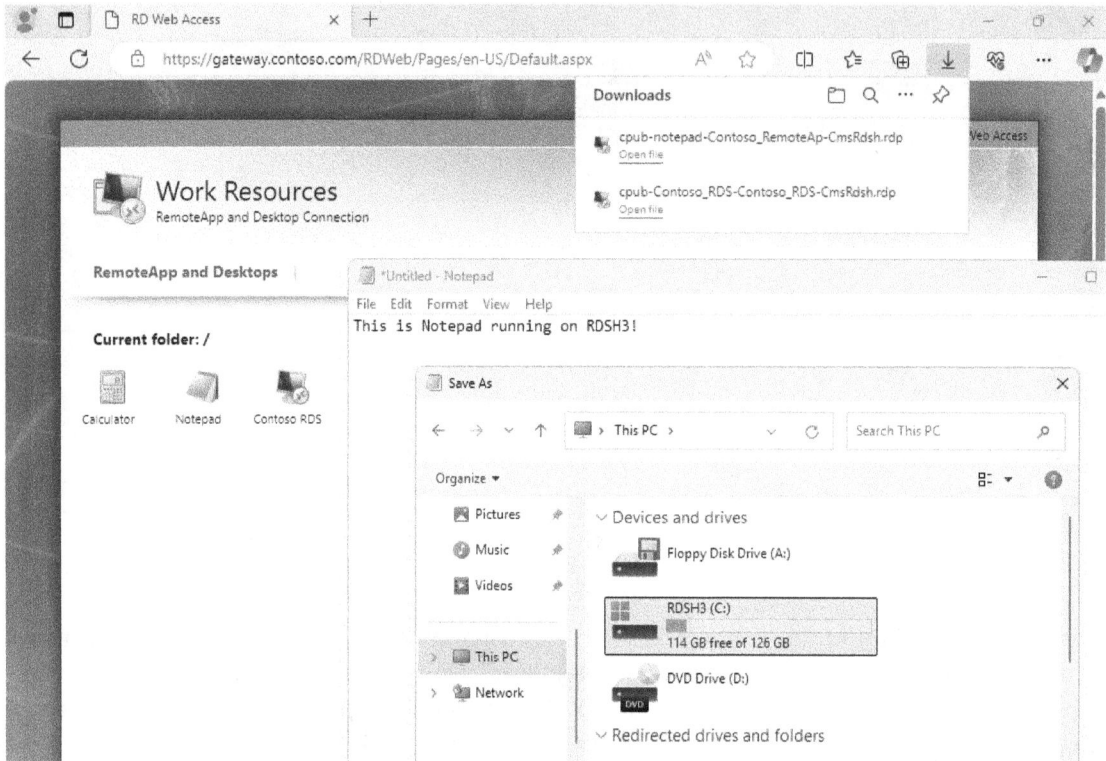

Figure 16.29: Logged into WIN11 at home, but running Notepad on RDSH3

The key benefit of RemoteApp is the restriction of access. This is a simple method to provide many users access to many different applications that are installed on the same set of RDS servers, but at the same time, ensuring that users only have access to the applications you want them to touch.

RDS maintenance considerations

Maintaining and troubleshooting RDS servers can be an art of its own. They are Windows Server instances, yes, but in many ways, you treat them more like workstations, since they are the place where users log in to utilize applications and save documents. However, many different users are logged in to these "workstations" at the same time, which creates complexities we do not normally face on workstations or other types of servers. This final section is a bit of a tips-and-tricks session for some of the common maintenance considerations you will doubtless face during your RDS administration tenure.

Install mode

There is no need to rehash this; we already covered `install` mode in detail earlier in this chapter. But if there is one thing that I find administrators forgetting to do most often when dealing with RDS servers, it is placing them into `install` mode before installing applications, and even more often, forgetting to do so before updating existing applications. Don't forget to always use `install` mode!

Additionally, make sure all users are logged out of your RDSH server when installing or updating applications. Your admin account should be the only account logged in to the entire server when performing these functions.

Server Manager errors related to RDS

Most RDS configuration happens from within Server Manager, and most often, I find administrators turning to the instance of Server Manager on whatever server is their RDS management server. This server probably hosts some or all RDS roles, other than RDSH, of course. In my case, that was my RDS-MGMT server that we referenced so many times throughout this chapter. There is no technical reason that you *must* use that central RDS administration server to perform these tasks—Server Manager is intended to be decentralized and capable of administering servers outside of itself, right? A very common issue that I watch administrators struggle with is when trying to launch Server Manager, with the intention of manipulating an RDS configuration setting, from a different RDS server in the deployment. Let's give it a try together and see what happens.

I am logged directly into RDSH2. This server's duty in life is to host user sessions, but I have never tried running any RDS administration tools on it. Launching Server Manager, since RDSH2 has a Remote Desktop component installed on it, I see the **Remote Desktop Services** option inside Server Manager. When I click on it, however, things *appear* to be very broken...

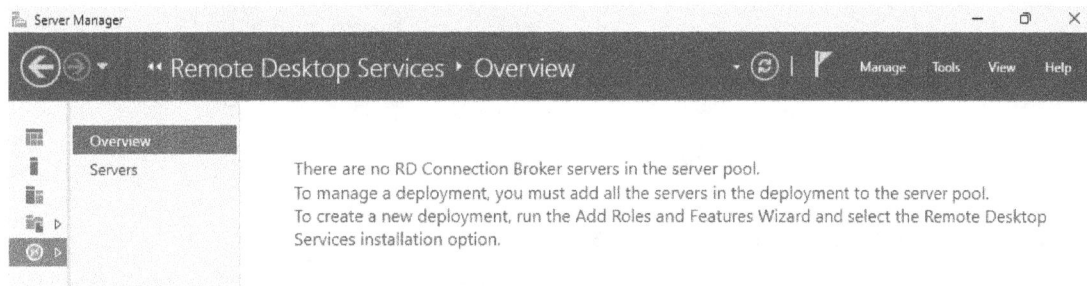

Figure 16.30: Red alert! I think RDS is broken

This is the point where many admins get stuck. They assume that something is really broken or really misconfigured with RDS, and they escalate whatever ticket they are working on. In some cases, they try rebooting this server over and over, to no avail. The hard reality of this error message is that it is telling you, right in your face, how to fix the issue. Most people just miss it. **To manage a deployment, you must add all the servers in the deployment to the server pool**. This is Server Manager telling you (I'm paraphrasing here), "Hey admin, if you want to manage RDS from this window, you're gonna have to add all RDS servers into Server Manager, so that I know how to reach them!"

The only thing you need to do is click **Manage** at the top of Server Manager, then **Add Servers**. From here, you know what to do: add all RDS-related servers into Server Manager so that it is capable of reaching them, and if you refresh the Remote Desktop screen, it will now light up with all of the information and options you expect.

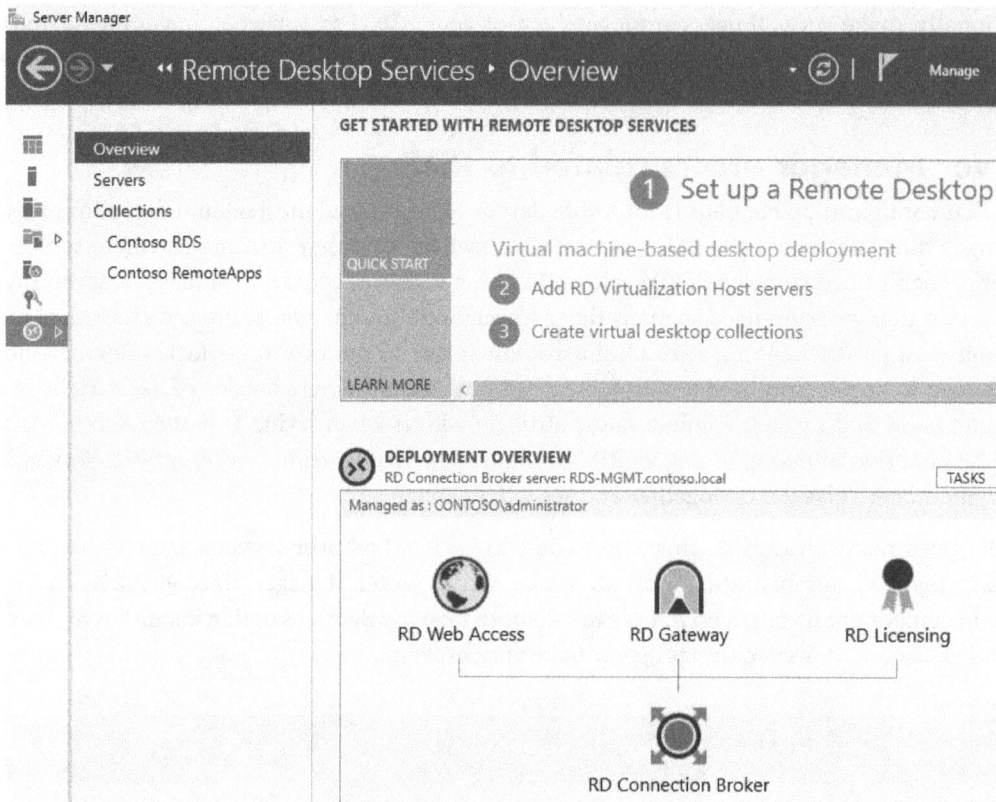

Figure 16.31: Server Manager is happy again

Logging directly into RDSH servers

Most Windows Server instances are very easy to connect to remotely by using the Remote Desktop Connection tool and simply creating an RDP connection to log in to them. RDSH servers, when part of an RDS collection, suddenly get finicky about RDP connections coming into them unless those connections are happening via the farm. I'll show you an example. My RDSH1 and RDSH2 servers are just Windows Server 2025 instances, and I was able to RDP successfully into them before I made them RDS servers inside my collection. Now that they are part of the collection, I can obviously connect to them by using my RDS connectivity file that connects me through the farm, just like my users are going to do.

Connecting this way will land me on either RDSH1 or RDSH2, but I do not get to choose which one. If I were to be connecting to one of these servers for maintenance purposes, I would want to be able to easily hop into one or the other at my choosing.

From my WIN11 client machine, I have simply tried to RDP into RDSH2, using the `mstsc.exe` tool. Here is the result:

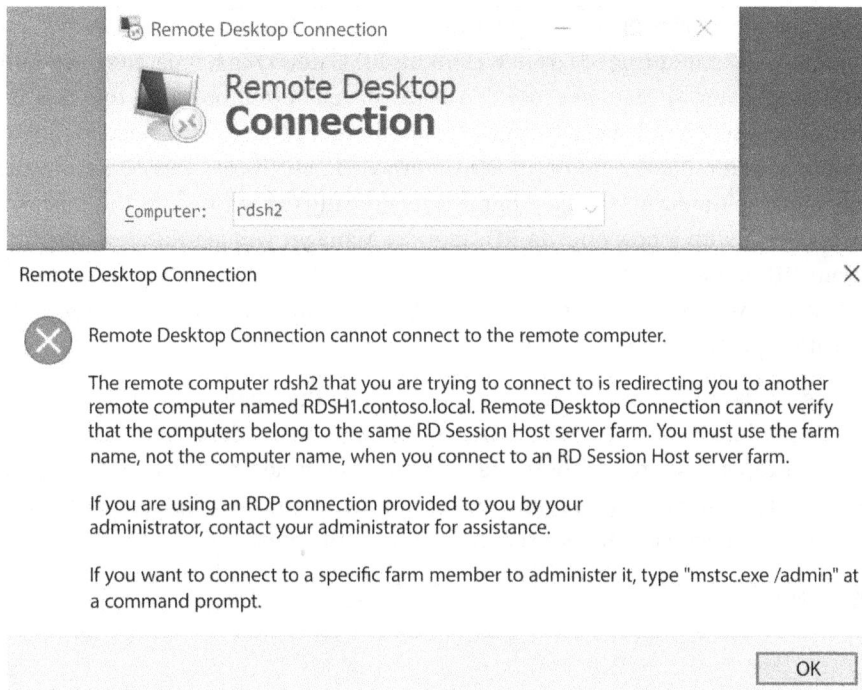

Figure 16.32: I can no longer RDP directly into my RDSH servers

If you have some other form of connectivity tool to connect directly to the console of RDSH2, you could, of course, utilize that to log in directly. Otherwise, if RDSH2 were a VM, as it is in my case, then I could use the Hyper-V console session to log directly into it as well. However, there is a third option staring us right in the face, buried at the bottom of the text in our previous error output:

```
mstsc.exe /admin
```

When you launch mstsc.exe, there are a few optional switches that you can use, which enable special functionality within this tool. These switches enable things like specifying the height and width of the Remote Desktop session, specifying the use of a saved RDP connection file, or even connecting in a way that you can shadow another user's session. For our purposes today, we simply want to be able to log directly into RDSH2, and our switch for doing that is called mstsc.exe /admin. The /admin switch connects you directly to a special session on an RDS, intended for the administration of the machine. In our case with RDSH2, it means that it will allow us to RDP directly into this server, whereas normal mstsc.exe connectivity would not, because of its membership in the farm.

SSL certificate replacements

Assuming that you have been following along throughout this chapter, you know that Remote Desktop Gateway utilizes an SSL certificate, which makes sense because it is permitting connectivity and traffic streams coming inbound to your environment from anywhere in the world. The Remote Desktop Web Access component also makes use of an SSL certificate, because it is a web page running on port 443, and any user's browser would throw a hissy fit if there were not a valid certificate on that website.

SSL certificates need to be renewed every year in most cases. A common mistake that I watch RDS administrators make is that during SSL renewal for an RD Gateway instance, they head directly into the Remote Desktop Gateway Manager tool. We really haven't even looked at this tool through our chapter on RDS, because it is only used for certain functions, and there is no need to touch it in many RDS environments. The replacement of an RD Gateway SSL certificate can be accomplished from inside Remote Desktop Gateway Manager, but it is technically the wrong place to perform this task. Replacing a certificate with a new one via RD Gateway Manager will get the new certificate up and running on your RD Gateway, but only on your RD Gateway. The other components inside RDS that utilize SSL certificates will not be changed or updated, which can then cause you other problems once the old certificate expires.

Avoiding this mistake is an easy matter of changing habits. Rather than grabbing your new certificate and heading directly into Remote Desktop Gateway Manager, visit Server Manager and your overall RDS **Deployment Properties** screen. There are not a lot of common reasons to visit the overarching **Deployment Properties** screen on a regular basis, but SSL certificate replacement is one of them. Inside **Deployment Properties**, there is a screen called **Certificates**.

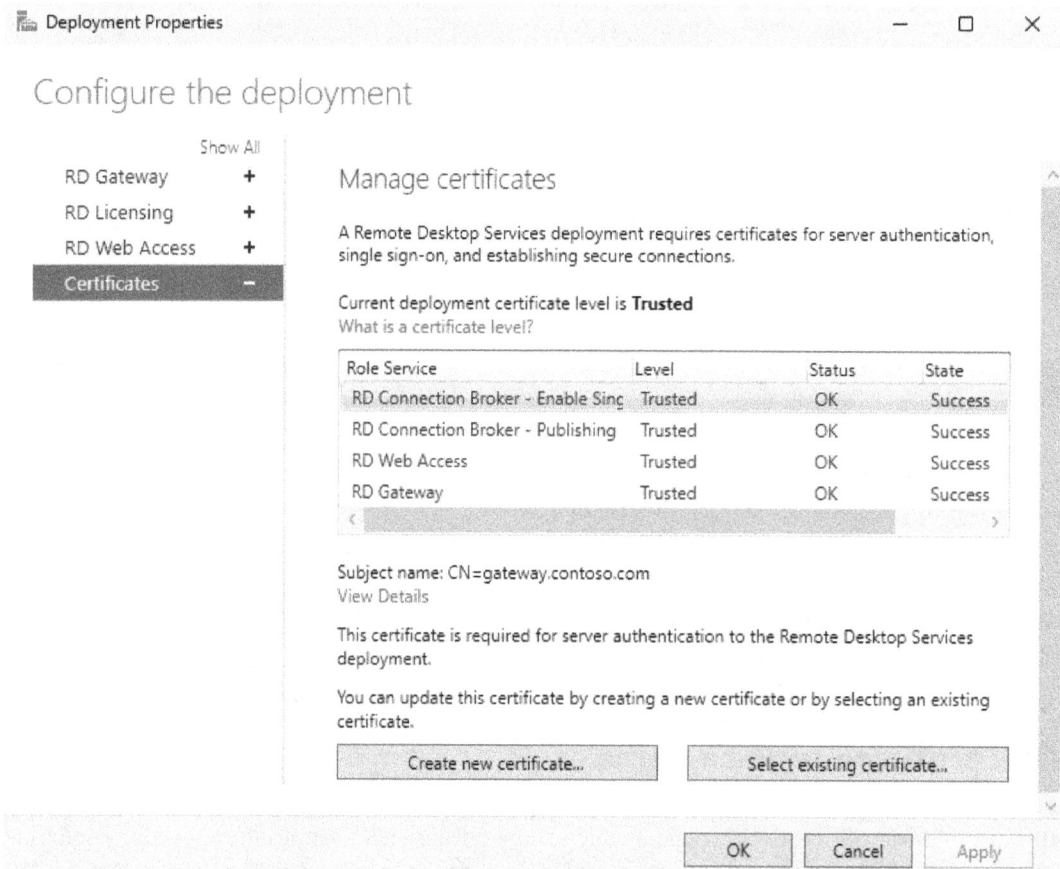

Figure 16.33: Replacing an SSL certificate the right way

This screen is a little confusing, but what it is trying to tell you is that there are four different components in RDS that are making use of a certificate. These are the four entities shown in our previous screenshot. **RD Connection Broker** has two, and then **RD Web Access** and **RD Gateway**, as we already discussed.

When replacing a certificate with a fresh one, you want to change it for all four components on this screen. If you were to swap your Remote Desktop Gateway certificate via Remote Desktop Gateway Manager, you would be only 25% complete with your certificate replacement.

The **Create new certificate…** option is interesting, allowing you to generate a self-signed certificate for the task, but it is most likely not what you want to accomplish. Instead, acquire your new certificate through whatever means you normally would, and in the end, make sure that you have a PFX file that contains both the certificate and the private key. Feel free to go back and visit our chapter on certificates if none of that makes sense. Copy that PFX file to your server where you are administering your RDS deployment, and now utilize the **Select existing certificate…** button to put it into place.

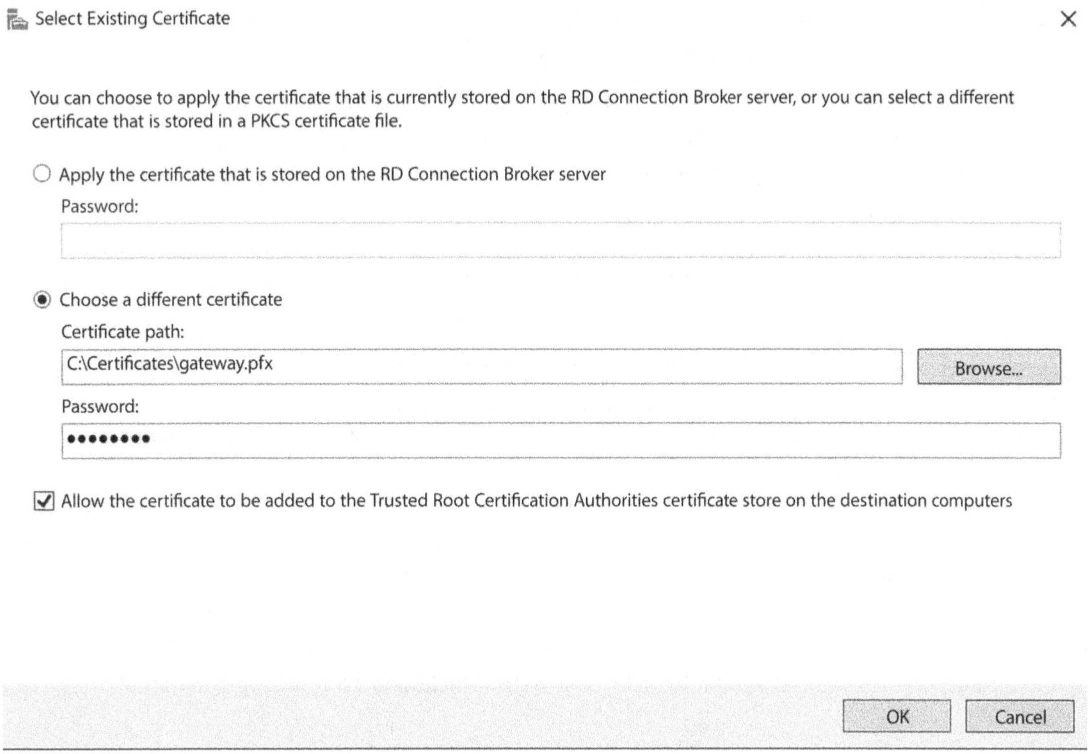

🗁 Select Existing Certificate   ✕

You can choose to apply the certificate that is currently stored on the RD Connection Broker server, or you can select a different certificate that is stored in a PKCS certificate file.

○ Apply the certificate that is stored on the RD Connection Broker server

    Password:

    [   ]

◉ Choose a different certificate

    Certificate path:

    [C:\Certificates\gateway.pfx   ]   [Browse…]

    Password:

    [••••••••   ]

☑ Allow the certificate to be added to the Trusted Root Certification Authorities certificate store on the destination computers

                                                            [OK]   [Cancel]

Figure 16.34: Creating a PFX file and making use of it here

The critical information to understand is that you must repeat this process for each of these four RDS components. Select them individually, walk through the **Select existing certificate…** screen for each of them, and in the end, your entire RDS deployment will now be running on the new certificate.

Cloning RDSH servers

When building our test lab RDS farm, I got off easy because I only needed it for testing and screenshot purposes, and so I simply created four new VMs that were running fresh copies of Windows Server 2025 and configured them as needed. When building a production environment RDS farm, it is almost a guarantee that you are going to be additionally installing numerous applications onto your RDSH servers, so that users can launch these applications once connected. Rather than prepping all RDSH servers from scratch and having to deal with running through application installers on each of them, it will be very tempting to, in some way, image or clone them from each other. Perhaps you create RDSH1 and then install everything you need. This RDSH server is now the perfect example to replicate 3, 4, or 46 more times, and for new RDSH servers, you simply clone the existing one.

If you do this, make sure you sysprep every new one!

We have already covered the topic of sysprep in this book, so I won't rehash it here. If you clone a server and do not sysprep it, you will certainly cause collisions and issues within your network and Active Directory. Sysprepping a server scrubs key pieces of identification information from inside Windows, allowing it to run side by side with its clone.

Depending on how your applications behave, you may or may not be able to get away with clone and sysprep. Some applications plug information into files and the registry that utilize the hostname of a server, which will certainly be changing during the clone process. There is no way I can tell you whether or not you will be able to clone RDSH servers in your environment; it would be a matter of trial and error. But if you do, make sure that sysprep is part of that equation. I know some RDS admins who clone servers all the time and love it, and I know some who have had poor enough experiences that they would never even think about doing it. The decision is yours...

Sidder

At some point in your RDS administration journey, you will find yourself staring at the network share location where all of your UPDs reside and scratching your head. You know that every user session creates a new UPD inside this location, as you specified during the RDS deployment wizard. You already know that each UPD is really a VHDX file that is sitting in this location. What we haven't discussed is that these VHDX files are named in a very non-intuitive way. The names of these files are a long GUID, an identifier for the user account to which they are associated. FSLogix profiles do a better job of plugging the username directly into the name of this file so that you can quickly identify which VHDX belongs to which user, but for classic UPDs, you are looking at a lot of nonsense, like this:

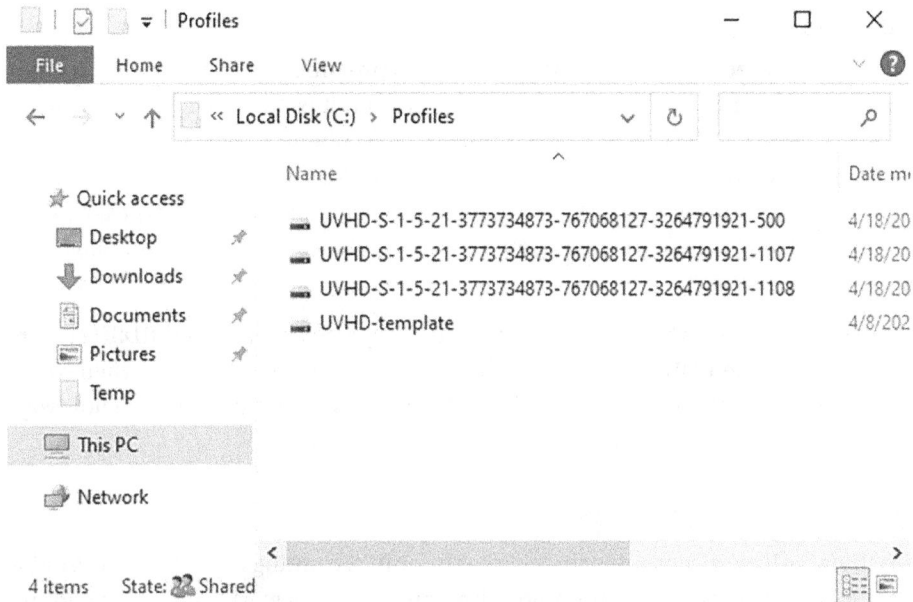

Figure 16.35: A robot must have named these UPDs

Thankfully, there is a free tool available that fills in this knowledge gap! It is called **Sidder**, but since it is not a tool created by Microsoft, I am not going to give you an official download link. It's easily searchable on the internet, but I am disclaiming this one with "use at your own risk."

If you decide to move forward and download Sidder, it is a standalone executable that you can copy to your server where UPDs are stored, and running Sidder displays information to quickly identify which UPD belongs to which user account.

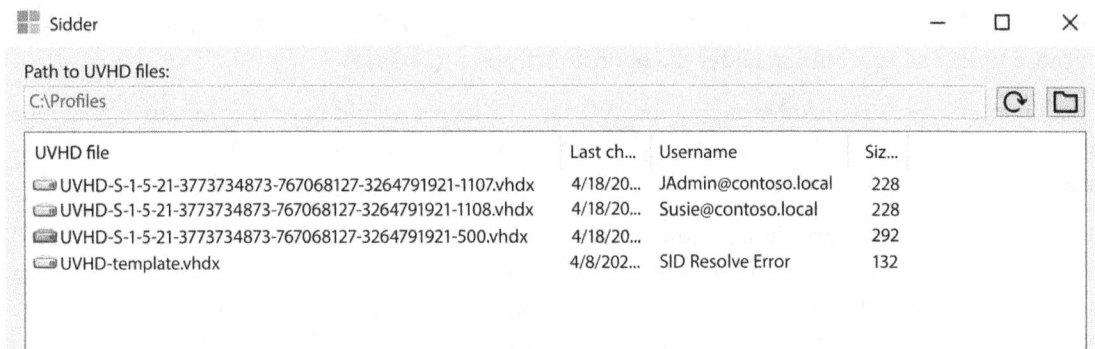

Figure 16.36: Sidder quickly associates usernames with UPDs

GPOs and RDS

GPOs are commonly used to secure or manipulate domain-joined workstations for a company and can be just as easily used to modify RDSH servers. However, it is most likely true that the configurations and settings that you want to push to workstations do not directly apply to your intentions for RDSH servers, and vice versa. It is very common to find all RDSH servers secluded to their own OU inside Active Directory and for that OU to have **Block Inheritance** enabled. It is easy to accidentally break an RDSH server by applying general domain-scope policies to it, so I recommend blocking this inheritance as a best practice.

What this means, of course, is that any GPOs that you do want to apply to your RDSH servers must be intentionally linked to their OU. This is something that is good to keep in mind whenever building a new RDS environment, and also when modifying GPOs in any way. Stay conscious of how your changes may or may not impact your RDS farm users.

Azure Virtual Desktop

So far, everything we have discussed in this chapter is for RDS running in your classic Windows Server environment. RDS servers are typically on-premises, but like many workloads, you could spin up VMs inside a cloud hoster such as Azure, and deploy RDS capabilities there.

However, Microsoft has done one better.

Azure Virtual Desktop (AVD) is essentially "RDS in Azure," with fewer components required than classic RDS. Within AVD, you craft multiple RDSH-like servers where users can log in, and they accomplish these logins from the newer Remote Desktop tool in Windows. Identity and authentication into the AVD sessions are tied into Entra, so you can make use of your M365 identities and MFA requirements natively. All of the AVD servers are obviously hosted in Azure, so you have no requirements for on-premises infrastructure. Another distinct difference between AVD and RDS is that AVD farms do not require the non-RDSH components, such as RD Gateway, RD Web, and RD Licensing, because all of those functions are running under the hood in Azure.

Cost of entry into AVD includes paying for AVD servers, as you would pay for compute and storage space for any Azure-based VM. Additionally, users are only able to connect to AVD instances if they are assigned an M365 license that includes access to AVD, such as Business Premium.

For the most part, if you are already comfortable with the concepts and administration of RDS, you'll make quick work of learning how to navigate AVD. One last significant difference I wanted to point out to you administrators is that RDS servers are always running the Windows Server operating system, but AVDs are not. While Windows Server looks and behaves much like Windows 10 or Windows 11, they are technically different, and that can pose some interesting differences in user experience when users are logging into RDS farms, staring at Windows Server 2022 or Windows Server 2025. A vast difference in the way that AVD operates compared to RDS is that the base operating system for AVD "servers" is actually a special multi-session version of Windows 10 or 11 that allows many user sessions to be logged into it at the same time! Using the consumer version look/feel for this GUI helps users feel a little bit more at home, and helps you sleep at night, a little less worried about application compatibility issues when trying to run end user software on Windows Server operating systems.

Is AVD the new RDS? Sort of. They serve slightly different purposes and in considerably different ways. If you already have infrastructure in Azure and want to explore a centralized compute environment where users with low-powered laptops could remote into virtual sessions hosted in Azure, AVD is the ticket!

Summary

RDS has been around for more than 20 years and is still widely used around the world. It has seen many improvements over the years and continues to be a fantastic way to provide a multi-user virtual platform for your workers, where they don't have to worry about what local computer they are using to perform the work, and you don't have to worry about securing whatever that device looks like. You maintain complete control over the centralized RDS compute environment, providing secure access to the resources that employees need.

In fact, RDS is still so commonly used that it has carried over into one of the most common Azure-based resource pools that I find in the SMB market. AVD, formerly known as Windows Virtual Desktop, is a way to provide users with login from anywhere to Azure-based servers that contain virtual user sessions. The capabilities in AVD are extremely similar to RDS on-premises, with the exception that the base operating system for AVD is generally a multi-user Windows 11 platform, rather than straight-up Windows Server 2025. AVD even makes use of FSLogix profiles to keep user information secure and working properly!

Remote Desktop connections of yesteryear were never a feasible solution for graphically intensive applications, as there could be a lot of lag when dragging high-resolution things across that remote connection, but much has changed in recent history. RDS and AVD are not only great platforms for knowledge worker tasks, but with new protocol efficiencies, GPU sharing technologies, and increased internet connections, it is now possible to run something as intense as SolidWorks from inside a Remote Desktop connection.

Questions

Put your knowledge to the test with the following questions. If you need a hand (or just want to double-check), you'll find all the answers in the *Appendix* section of the book.

1. What RDS component is responsible for distributing user sessions among multiple servers?
2. Are RDS-related certificates defined in RDS collection properties or RDS deployment properties?
3. What is the command you should run to prepare an RDSH server for application installation?
4. What type of RDS **client access licenses** (**CALs**) are most common?
5. True or False? To prepare a fresh Windows Server instance to become an RDSH member of an existing collection, you must first log in to that server and install the Remote Desktop role.
6. What are the four types of RDS user profiles?
7. How can you launch the Remote Desktop Connection tool in a way that allows you to RDP directly into an RDSH server that is already part of a collection?
8. How are FSLogix configurations put into place on RDSH servers?
9. Bonus question: What animals live on an RDS farm?

Join us on Discord

For discussions around the book and to connect with your peers, join us on Discord at `https://packt.link/discordcloud` or scan the QR code below:

17

Troubleshooting

When dreaming of a position in server or system administration, we often think of designing infrastructure, spinning up new servers, implementing fresh technology, and always living on the bleeding edge. The truth can reflect those tasks, but it can just as easily include 3 A.M. wakeup calls to deal with a system being down, poring over event and diagnostic logs, and living on Google and Bing when your acquired knowledge and wisdom just isn't cutting the mustard. Hardware breaks. Software freaks out. Patch installations go sideways. Certificates expire, internet connections fail, and occasionally, you work on an issue from a certain angle all day, only to discover in the end that it was being caused by something entirely different. Working in IT can bring with it great mysteries every single day, which is one of the reasons I love it. This final chapter uncovers some of the tools available in Windows Server 2025 that can assist with troubleshooting, maintenance, and repair:

- Backup and restore
- Task Manager
- Resource Monitor
- Performance Monitor
- Sysinternals tools
- DTrace
- Windows Firewall with Advanced Security
- System Insights
- Remote toolsets
- Event Logs
- MMC and MSC shortcuts
- Feedback Hub

Backup and restore

The need to back up and occasionally restore your servers is, unfortunately, still present in Windows Server 2025. Many dream of a day when servers are 100 percent reliable and stable throughout their lifetimes, unaffected by viruses and rogue software, but today is not that day (that would be a little boring, to be honest).

While there are many third-party tools available on the market that can improve and automate your backup experience when managing many servers, we do have these capabilities baked right into the Server 2025 operating system, and we should all be familiar with how to utilize them. Maintaining good backups should be priority number one for any business and is the most important troubleshooting component that exists. There are a myriad of reasons why you may fail to repair a server that is having a problem, and sometimes, your only two options are to build from scratch or restore from backup. Ransomware attacks are on the increase, and attackers are targeting companies of all sizes. If you have one bad firewall rule in place, it's only a matter of time before they find their way into your network, and before you know it, every single one of your servers will be encrypted and held for ransom. If you don't have a solid backup system and a restoration plan that spells out exactly how you recover from those backups should the need arise, then you had better have a very deep wallet to pay the ransom because that will be your only option.

For clarity, of course, you should never pay the ransom! If you pay, the hackers who locked down your system in the first place will release your files (if they didn't, they would immediately kick themselves out of the ransom business), but they will also build as many backdoors in your network as they possibly can before they do release your data, so that down the road, they can simply reconnect and do it again. Unfortunately, as we have seen recently in the news, failing to keep good backups results in being stuck between a rock and a hard place, where paying the ransom is the only available course of action. Don't let that be *your* story.

Schedule regular backups

Logging in to your servers and launching a manual backup task every day is obviously not feasible for most organizations, as the process of running backups would turn into a full-time job. Thankfully, the Windows Server Backup feature gives us the option to create a backup schedule. This way, we can define what we want to back up, where we want to back it up to, and how often this backup should run. Then, we can sit back, relax, and know that our systems are performing this task on their own.

Before we can do anything with backups, we need to install the appropriate feature in Windows. Using the **Add roles and features** link, go ahead and install the feature called **Windows Server Backup**. Remember that I said *feature*—you won't find Windows Server Backup on the primary **Server Roles** selection screen; you need to move ahead one screen further in the wizard to find **Features**. Once the feature has finished installing, you can launch the **Windows Server Backup** console that is available inside the **Tools** menu of Server Manager. Once inside, click on **Local Backup** in the left-hand-side window; you will see some actions appear on the right-hand side of your screen.

As you can see, there is an option listed here called **Backup Once...** that, as the name implies, performs an ad hoc backup job. While this is a nice feature, there is no way that any server administrator is going to log in to all their servers and do this every day. Instead, clicking on the **Backup Schedule...** action will launch a configuration wizard to create a scheduled, recurring backup job:

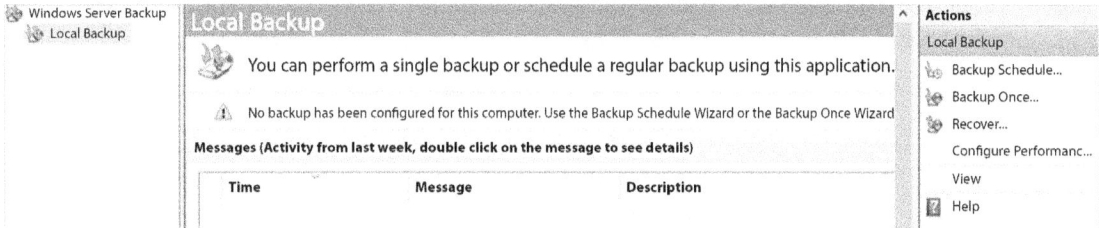

Figure 17.1: The Windows Server Backup console

The first option you will come across is for deciding what it is that you want to back up. The default option is set to **Full server**, which will take a backup of everything in the operating system. If you want to customize the amount of data that is being backed up, you can choose the **Custom** option and proceed from there. Since I have lots of disk space available to me, I am going to stick with the recommended path of creating full server backups.

Next, we get to the real advantage of using the scheduling concept: choosing how often we run our backup. The most common way is to choose a particular time of day and then let the backup run every day at that allotted time. If you have a server whose data is being updated regularly throughout the day and you want to shorten your window of lost information in the event of needing to perform a restore, you can also specify to back up multiple times per day:

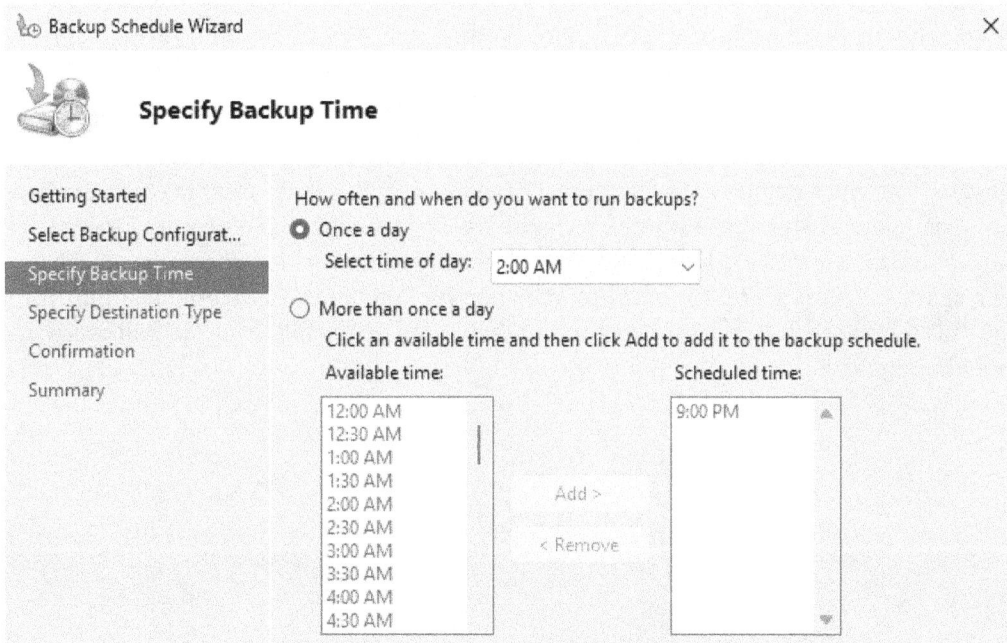

Figure 17.2: Setting a backup schedule

The last screen where we need to make a decision for our scheduled backups is the **Specify Destination Type** screen, where we set the location for our backup files. You can see that there are a couple of different options to store the backup locally on the physical hard disks of the same server where you configure the backups. Storing backup files on a local, dedicated disk or volume can be advantageous because the speed of the backup process will be increased compared to network storage. For servers that you try to back up continually during workdays, this can decrease the resources being used by the backup and increase the number of backups that can be squeezed into a day. Another advantage of using a locally connected disk for backups is that you can create multiple rollback points within your backup schema, keeping multiple days' worth of backup information in case you need to roll back to a particular point in time.

There are also downsides to retaining backups on locally attached storage. One potential showstopper is a ransomware attack. If you have never been part of cleanup efforts following such an attack, you may not realize that ransomware locks down and encrypts all the files it can get its hands on. This almost always means that it encrypts the operating system volume, and any other volume (drive letter) that it can find attached to the system. Additional hard disks and USB drives where you might store backups will almost certainly be pulverized, along with your server, in a ransomware attack.

This brings up another good point—keeping off-site copies of your backups. This is not a chapter about disaster recovery scenarios, but you should absolutely keep copies of your server backups in a second location, whether that be in cloud storage or in another physical building.

I find that most admins prefer to keep all their backup files in a centralized location, and that means choosing the third option on this screen, the one entitled **Back up to a shared network folder**. By choosing this option, we can specify a network location, such as a file server or drive mapping to a NAS, and we can set all our different servers to back up to this same location. That way, we have a central, standardized location where we know that all our backup files are going to be sitting, if we need to pull one out and use it for restoration.

I cannot tell you which option is best, because it depends on how you are planning to utilize backups in your environment. The screen where we choose which destination type we want for our backups includes some good text to read over related to these options, such as the important note that when using a shared network folder for backups, only one backup file can be stored at a time for your server. This is because the process of creating a new backup on the following day will overwrite the previous backup:

Specify Destination Type

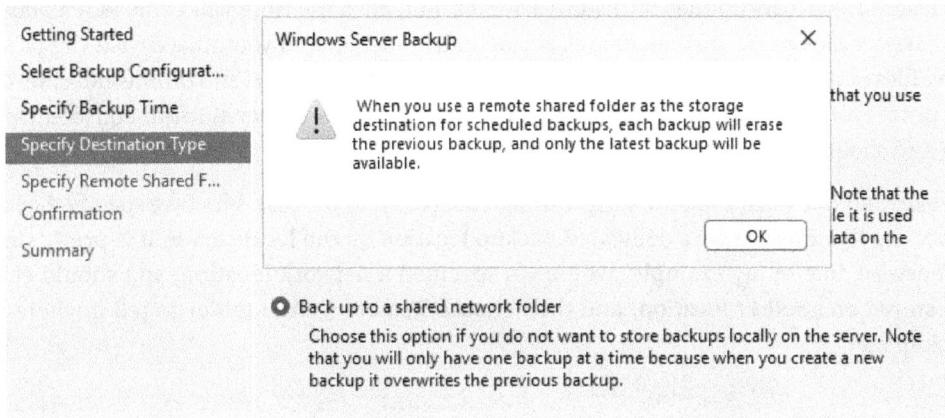

Getting Started

Select Backup Configurat...

Specify Backup Time

Specify Destination Type

Specify Remote Shared F...

Confirmation

Summary

Windows Server Backup   ✕

⚠ When you use a remote shared folder as the storage
   destination for scheduled backups, each backup will erase
   the previous backup, and only the latest backup will be
   available.

                                                    OK

that you use

Note that the
le it is used
ata on the

🔘 Back up to a shared network folder
   Choose this option if you do not want to store backups locally on the server. Note
   that you will only have one backup at a time because when you create a new
   backup it overwrites the previous backup.

Figure 17.3: A warning about backups stored remotely

Once you have chosen a destination for your backups and specified a network share location, if that is the option you have chosen, you are finished in the wizard. Your backup jobs will automatically kick off at the allocated time that you specified during the wizard, and tomorrow, you will see a new backup file for your server. If you are impatient, like me, and want to see the backup job run right now, you can walk through the other action that's available in the **Windows Server Backup** console, called **Backup Once...**, to run a manual backup right away:

Backup Progress

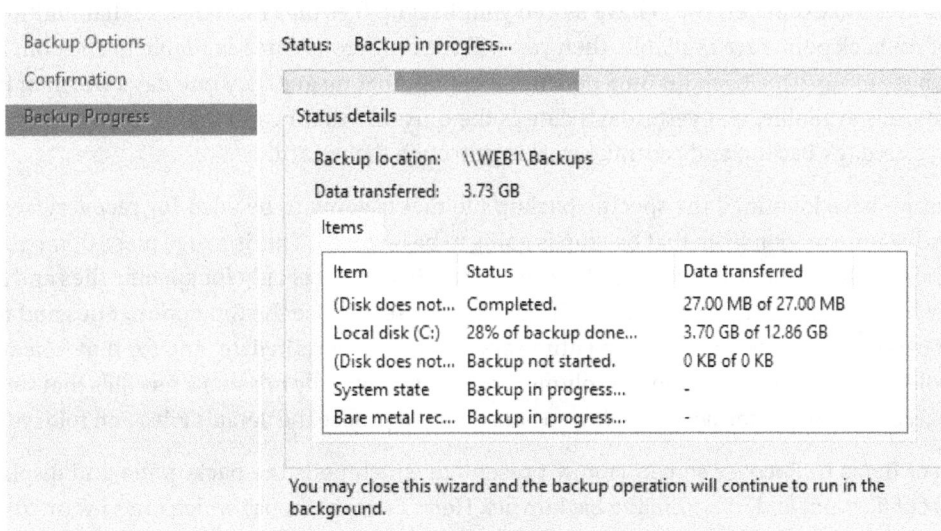

Backup Options

Confirmation

Backup Progress

Status: Backup in progress...

Status details

Backup location: \\WEB1\Backups

Data transferred: 3.73 GB

Items

Item	Status	Data transferred
(Disk does not...	Completed.	27.00 MB of 27.00 MB
Local disk (C:)	28% of backup done...	3.70 GB of 12.86 GB
(Disk does not...	Backup not started.	0 KB of 0 KB
System state	Backup in progress...	-
Bare metal rec...	Backup in progress...	-

You may close this wizard and the backup operation will continue to run in the
background.

Figure 17.4: My first backup is running

Restoring from Windows

Since you are being diligent and keeping good backups of your servers, the hope is that you will never have to utilize those backup files to restore a server. But, alas, the time *will* come when you have a server that goes sideways, or some data is accidentally deleted, and you must revisit the process of restoring files or an entire server in your infrastructure. If your server is still online and running, the restore process is quite easy to invoke from the same **Windows Server Backup** console. Open the console and choose the action that says **Recover...**.

This invokes another wizard that walks us through the recovery process. First, we specify the location of our backup file. If you have a dedicated backup location on the local server, it is pretty simple to find; otherwise, like in my example, where we specified a network location, you should choose **A backup stored on another location**, and then choose **Remote shared folder** to tell it where to find that backup file:

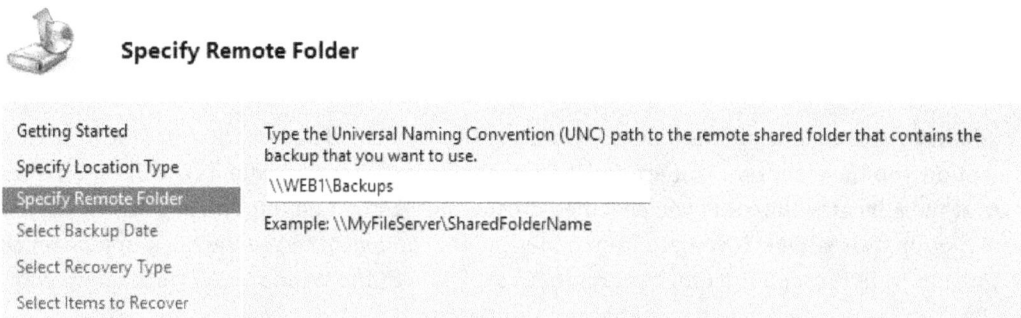

Specify Remote Folder

Getting Started	Type the Universal Naming Convention (UNC) path to the remote shared folder that contains the backup that you want to use.
Specify Location Type	
Specify Remote Folder	\\WEB1\Backups
Select Backup Date	Example: \\MyFileServer\SharedFolderName
Select Recovery Type	
Select Items to Recover	

Figure 17.5: Specifying the location of backup files

Based on your chosen backup location, the wizard will now identify all rollback dates that are available within the backup files. If you have stored your backup files on a local disk so that multiple days' worth of rollback points are available, then you will see numerous dates available to click on. For me, since I chose to store my backups on a network location, that means only one day's worth of backup information is available, and yesterday's date is the only one that I can choose. So, I will choose to restore yesterday's backup and continue working through the wizard.

Now that we have identified the specific backup file that is going to be used for recovery, we get to choose what information from that backup is going to be restored. This is a nice piece of the recovery platform because, often, when we need to restore from backup, it is only for specific files and folders that may have been deleted or corrupted. If that is the case, choose the top option, **Files and folders**. In other cases, you may want to roll the entire server back to a certain date, and for that functionality, you should choose to recover an entire volume. Right now, I am only missing a few files that somehow disappeared between yesterday and today, so I am going to choose the default **Files and folders** option.

The **Select Items to Recover** screen is now presented, which polls the backup file and displays the entire list of files and folders within the backup file. Here, I simply choose which ones I want to restore. This kind of recovery can be critical to your daily management of a file server, where the potential is high for users to accidentally delete information:

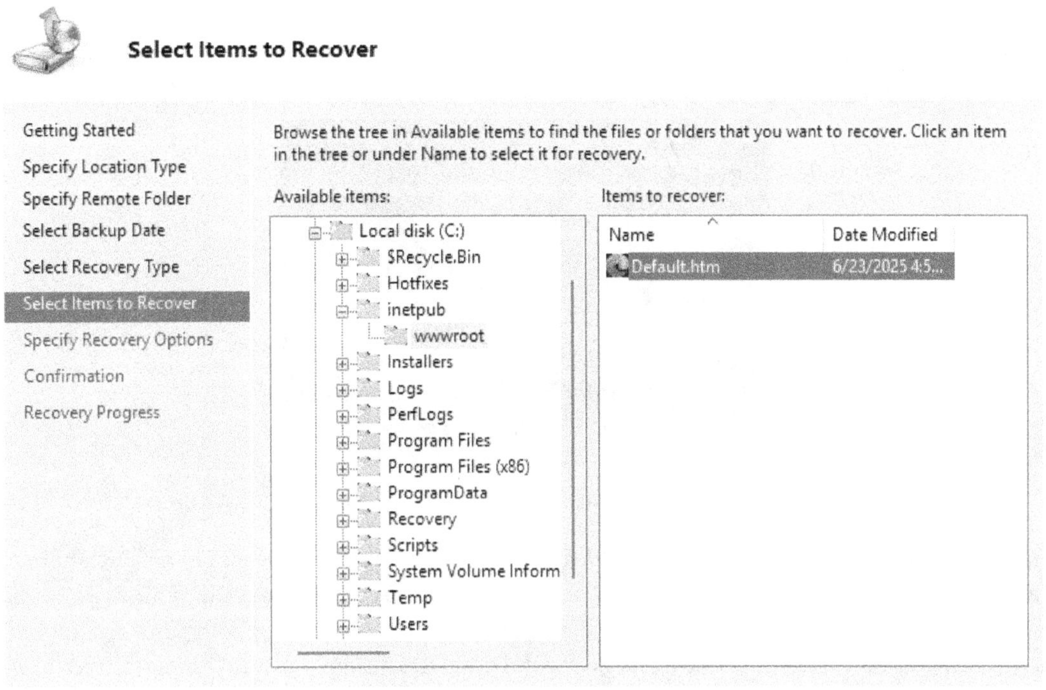

Select Items to Recover

Getting Started
Specify Location Type
Specify Remote Folder
Select Backup Date
Select Recovery Type
Select Items to Recover
Specify Recovery Options
Confirmation
Recovery Progress

Browse the tree in Available items to find the files or folders that you want to recover. Click an item in the tree or under Name to select it for recovery.

Available items:

- Local disk (C:)
  - $Recycle.Bin
  - Hotfixes
  - inetpub
    - wwwroot
  - Installers
  - Logs
  - PerfLogs
  - Program Files
  - Program Files (x86)
  - ProgramData
  - Recovery
  - Scripts
  - System Volume Inform
  - Temp
  - Users

Items to recover:

Name	Date Modified
Default.htm	6/23/2025 4:5...

Figure 17.6: Restoring individual files

All that remains is to specify where you want these recovered files to be restored. You can choose for the recovered files to be placed back in their original location, or if you are running this recovery process on a different machine, you can choose to restore the files to a new location that you can grab them from and then place them manually, wherever they now need to reside.

Restoring from the installer disk

Recovery from the console inside Windows is a nice wizard-driven experience, but what if your server has completely crashed? If you cannot get into Windows on your server, you cannot run the Windows Server Backup console to initiate your recovery process. In this case, we can still utilize our backup file that has been created, but we need to use it in combination with a Windows Server 2025 installation disk, from which we can invoke the recovery process.

It is important to note that this recovery process cannot access locations on the network, and your backup file will have to be stored on a disk attached to your server. You can utilize a USB drive for this purpose during the recovery process if you did not originally set up your backup job to be stored on an existing locally attached disk.

To make things interesting, I'm going to crash my own server. This is the server that we took a backup of a few minutes ago. I accidentally deleted some very important files in my C:\Windows directory. Whoops! Now, this is all I see when I try to boot my server:

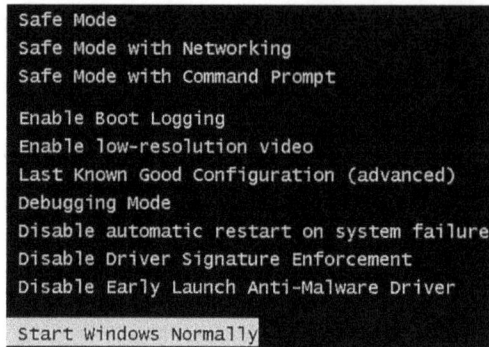

```
Safe Mode
Safe Mode with Networking
Safe Mode with Command Prompt

Enable Boot Logging
Enable low-resolution video
Last Known Good Configuration (advanced)
Debugging Mode
Disable automatic restart on system failure
Disable Driver Signature Enforcement
Disable Early Launch Anti-Malware Driver

Start Windows Normally
```

Figure 17.7: The C:\Windows folder is important – don't delete files from it!

That's not a very friendly screen to see first thing in the morning! Since I seem to be stuck here and unable to boot into Windows, my chances of running the recovery wizard are nil. What to do? Boot to the Windows Server 2025 installer ISO (or DVD or USB stick, if you are dealing with physical hardware)! That is really my only option, but I want to be careful that I don't simply install Windows afresh, as all of my programs and data could be overwritten in that scenario. Rather, once I get to the screen asking me what type of setup I would like to pursue, I want to select **Repair my PC**.

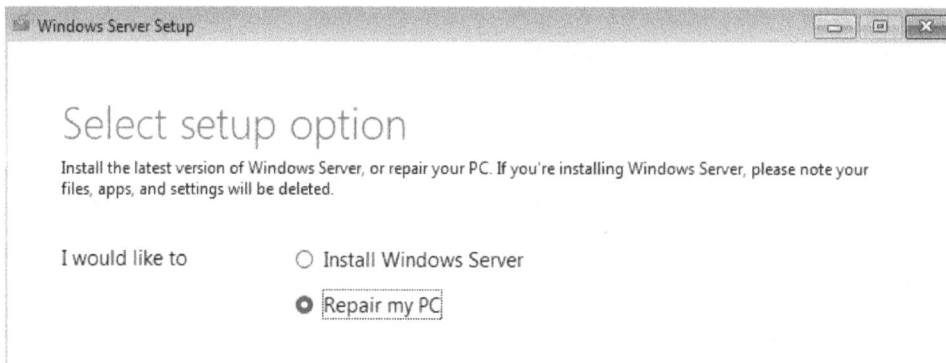

```
Windows Server Setup

Select setup option

Install the latest version of Windows Server, or repair your PC. If you're installing Windows Server, please note your
files, apps, and settings will be deleted.

I would like to        ○  Install Windows Server
                       ●  Repair my PC
```

Figure 17.8: Beginning the Windows recovery process

This will launch you into the more traditional blue background of Windows setup. Once inside, click on **Troubleshoot**, and you'll find a subset of advanced options that can be used to troubleshoot the operating system from this console outside of the OS itself. If you think you can fix whatever the issue is from **Command Prompt**, choose that option, as shown in *Figure 17.9*, and try to fix it yourself.

For our example, I am pretty sure that I significantly damaged the operating system, so I am going to do a full **System Image Recovery** and click on that button:

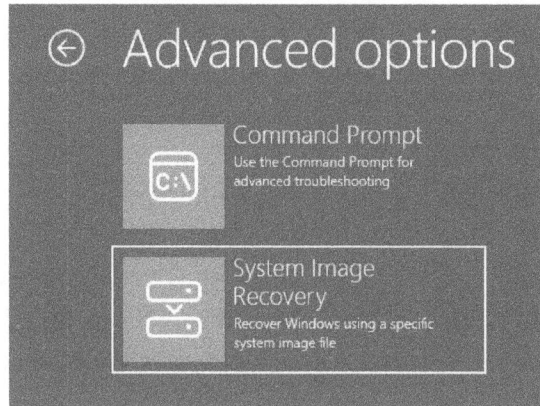

Figure 17.9: Running a System Image Recovery from installation media

As long as you have a hard drive connected that contains a Windows Server Backup file, the wizard will launch and pull in the information about the backup. Since I had originally chosen to store my backup file on a network location, I copied the backup files onto a disk and connected it as a second disk to my server. The wizard automatically recognizes that backup file and displays it on the **Select a system image backup** screen:

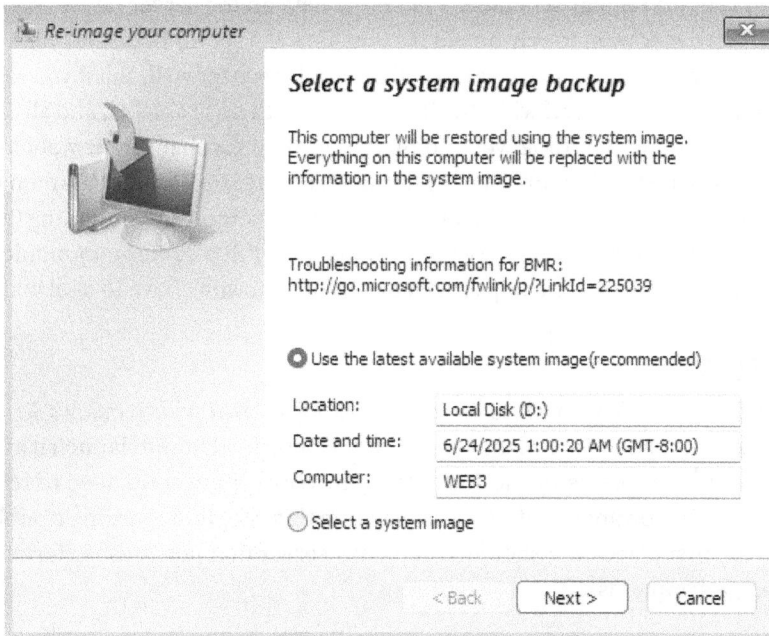

Figure 17.10: The recovery process recognizes backup files on attached storage

Now, by simply clicking on **Next** a few times to progress through the wizard, my backup image restores on my server:

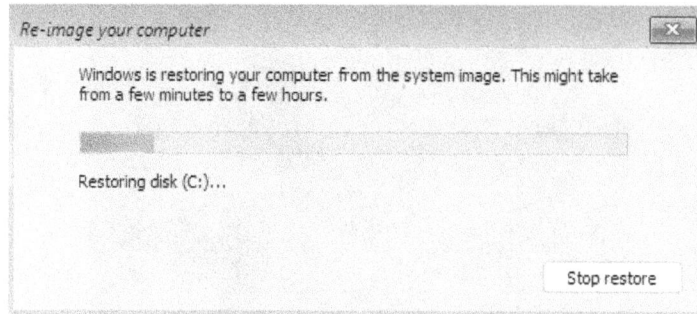

Figure 17.11: Restoring the server via advanced recovery options

Once the restore process has completed, the system reboots and launches itself right back into Windows, where it is fully functional back to the restore point. My test server doesn't have much of anything running on it, so the time that it took to restore was minimal. A production box may take a little longer, but I'd say that 20 minutes from blowing up the server to being fully recovered is a pretty awesome length of time!

Keeping good and recent backup files is critical to your operation's sustainability. I have worked on quite a few systems where the admins took some manual backups after initially configuring their servers, but never set up a regular schedule. Even if the data on the server never changes, if you are part of a domain, you never want to rely on old backup files. If a server fails, and you need to recover it, restoring a backup that is only a few days old will generally recover well. But if you restore an image that is six months old, Windows itself will come back online with no problems, and all of your data will exist. However, in that amount of time, your computer account for that server would most certainly have fallen out of sync with the domain, causing authentication errors against the domain controllers. In some cases, you may even have to do goofy things such as disjoining and rejoining the server to the domain after working through the recovery process, just to get that server communicating with the domain again. If you keep regular backups to restore from, you won't have to deal with those issues.

Task Manager

If you can remember all the way back to *Chapter 1, Getting Started with Windows Server 2025*, you'll know that we already discussed Task Manager. There, we described how to launch it and took a quick look at the different tabs available inside Task Manager. While there is no need to rehash the same information here, it is important to note Task Manager in this chapter regarding troubleshooting, because it is one of the first places you should visit on any server that portrays performance problems or otherwise strange symptoms.

Task Manager gives you a quick glance at the overall CPU and memory utilization on a server, letting you know how taxed the server is. One of the most common tabs to review on any server is **Processes**, which allows you to sort all the running applications and processes by their CPU or memory consumption, which can quickly identify a problematic application that may be hindering the entire server. Once identified, you can easily right-click on any running process and quickly select **End task**, killing that process and freeing up those resources on your server.

When administering RDS servers, you will find yourself often visiting Task Manager to troubleshoot the slowness of one particular session host server. Sometimes, you can identify individual applications that soak up resources in the **Processes** or **Details** tab, while other times, you may want to go even further and review the **Users** tab to see status information about every user who is logged in to that RDSH server. Oftentimes, this is the fastest way to find out how many users are logged in to a particular server, and to quickly identify which user session might be causing grief for the others by consuming an extraordinary amount of server resources:

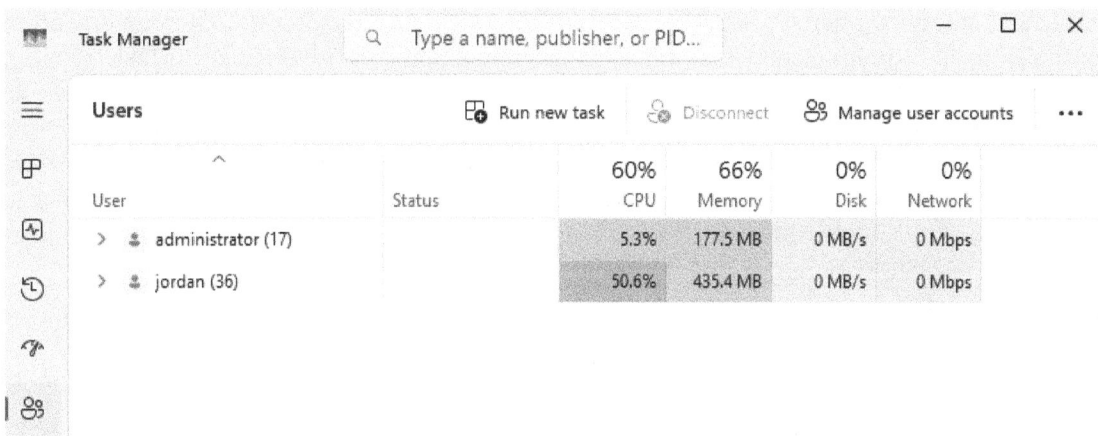

Figure 17.12: The user named Jordan is consuming over 50% of this server's CPU

One of the most common reasons I open **Task Manager** is to visit the **Performance** tab and view system uptime information. While generally more stable than workstation computers, Windows servers do need to be restarted occasionally, and uptime is a good indicator as to whether you should attempt a restart as a first form of troubleshooting. If your server has only been running for two days, you may want to focus your efforts elsewhere and not cause anyone a service interruption by rebooting in the middle of the day. On the other hand, if your server is really crawling and causing slowness, and it has a reported uptime of 120 days, you may want to go ahead and just reboot the thing to see if it resolves the issue.

Another easy way to view system uptime is by typing `systeminfo` into a Command Prompt or Power-Shell window! Taking it one step further, if your server rebooted unexpectedly and you want to find out how long it had been running prior to the restart, visit **System Event Logs** and search for event ID 6013. You'll have to calculate seconds into minutes/hours/days, but this event is logged at noon every day, so you always have an ongoing record of system uptime.

Task Manager's look and feel will be familiar to anyone who has been supporting Windows 11, but if you've been in IT for a few years, you likely remember back to the more square, plain-looking Task Manager of Windows 10 and earlier. Indeed, even Windows Server 2022 is running the old version of the Windows graphical interface; 2025 is the first year bringing these updates into the server world. *Figure 17.12* also depicts a glimpse into one of the nicest features brought to us by this newer instance of Task Manager, a search bar! In these days of data overload, search engines, and AI, the human brain is accustomed to quickly searching out whatever it is you are looking for. Task Manager is finally on track with this idea, giving you powerful options for searching out an individual application or process.

In cases where you find Task Manager to be lacking and want to dig a little bit deeper, go ahead and launch the newer **Resource Monitor**. This can be invoked by using the **Start** menu search function, but if you have Task Manager open anyway, visit the **Performance** tab. Near the top-right, you will find extra menu settings hiding behind an ellipsis. Click on that and launch **Resource Monitor**.

Resource Monitor

Like Task Manager on steroids, Resource Monitor can take system monitoring and troubleshooting even further. It contains plenty of the same information that we just experienced in Task Manager, but lays things out in a different format. CPU, memory, and disk utilization metrics are present, as well as monitoring of your network interfaces. There are various ways to sort the items that utilize resources, quickly identifying the high hitters for CPU and memory, and there are also right-click functions to end or suspend processes. On the **Overview** tab, as shown in *Figure 17.13*, you'll see that I am able to quickly identify the reason for my high CPU utilization—PowerShell is consuming most of the available CPU resources:

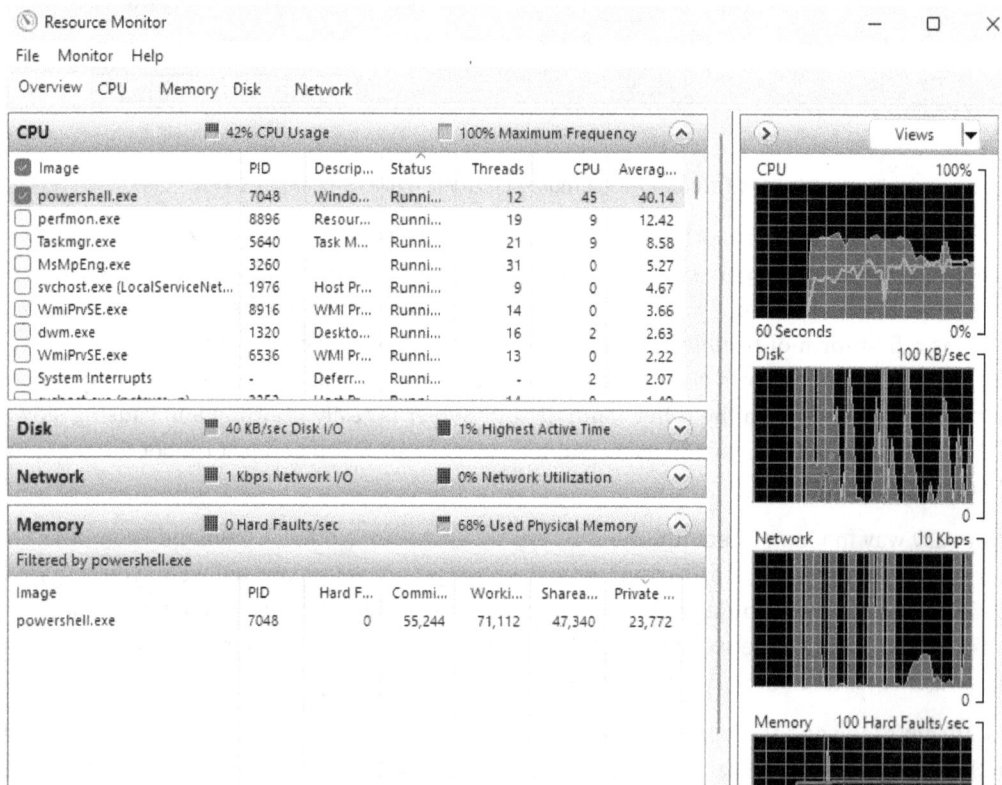

Figure 17.13: Using Resource Monitor to investigate high CPU utilization

Exploring the different tabs in Resource Monitor will show you more detailed information about CPU, memory, and even disk resource consumption. This is particularly cool because you can see disk storage stats and available disk space right alongside metrics, such as **Disk Queue Length**, which is an important indicator to monitor when hard disk performance may be a bottleneck.

The only tab I haven't mentioned yet is **Network**, which is my favorite place to visit in Resource Monitor. A fairly common client/server troubleshooting task is to track down what a particular application may be calling for at a network level, and this can be a difficult thing to ascertain. For example, I have installed an application on a client or server, and this application makes calls to another server to grab information or to interact with it in some way. Let's pretend the application isn't working correctly. First, you do some basic network troubleshooting and verify that the two machines can communicate with each other, by pinging back and forth. This means network traffic is flowing, but the application still won't connect. Your next thought is the firewall—what if the firewall on the receiving server is not allowing the traffic, or perhaps there is even a physical firewall device somewhere in between that is restricting the ports being used by the application? You are unsure of what ports the app may be trying to use, and it's too late in the day to call the software vendor (if one exists).

Resource Monitor to the rescue! Now, if you've been around the block once or twice, you may be thinking, "Couldn't I just install Wireshark and use it to review network traffic leaving my machine?" The answer would be yes, but here we are portraying a similar capability baked right into Windows.

In the **Network** tab of Resource Monitor, you can see the list of applications and **Process IDs (PIDs)** that are currently generating network traffic on this computer or server. Keep in mind that Resource Monitor is available in Windows Server, and it is also available in Windows 10/11! Launch your application, look for the PID, and check the box next to it. Then, drop down the **TCP Connections** section, and if that application utilizes a TCP traffic stream (or attempts to), as most applications do, you will see right here exactly what server name or IP address the application is calling for, and what ports it is using to attempt a connection. The interesting columns here are **Remote Address** and **Remote Port**:

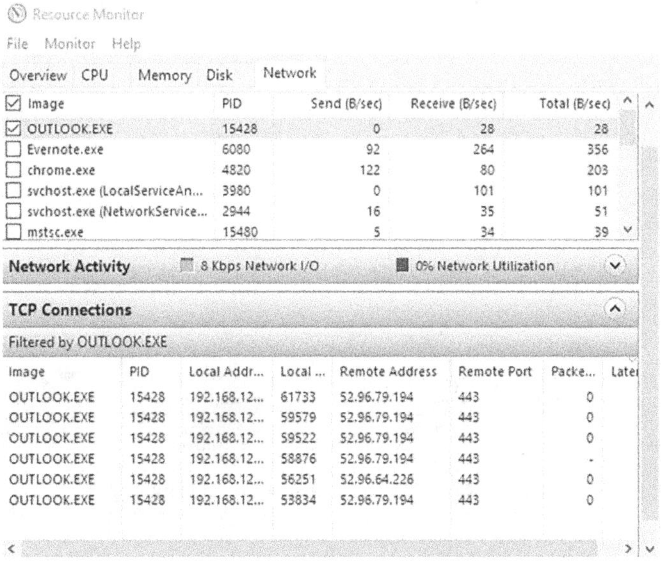

Figure 17.14: Using Resource Monitor for network troubleshooting

It is easy to see that my `Outlook.exe` application reaches out to a couple of different IP addresses, using TCP port 443. If this information were from your own application, you could now use this information to verify that the application is calling for the IP or server that you expect, and that the port being used is accessible, listening, and not being blocked on the receiving server or a firewall in between.

Performance Monitor

Another built-in monitoring tool is called Performance Monitor, commonly referred to as **Perfmon**. Almost every component of Windows Server has predefined performance monitor counters, and Perfmon taps into those counters to display extremely in-depth information about what is happening with those components, but only when you specifically set up reporting to see it. Perfmon does not log anything by default, because to do so would consume plenty of server resources, so this tool is generally only to be used temporarily during troubleshooting or for a specific reason and then disabled again when you are finished.

The easiest way to launch Perfmon is by going to **Start | Run** or opening Command Prompt or Power-Shell, simply typing `Perfmon` and then clicking *Enter*. This launches the interface, and by default, you can see that it has plugged in a counter for % **Processor Time**. You can obviously find CPU percentage information in much easier and better-looking places than Perfmon, so this is displayed simply as a sample of data:

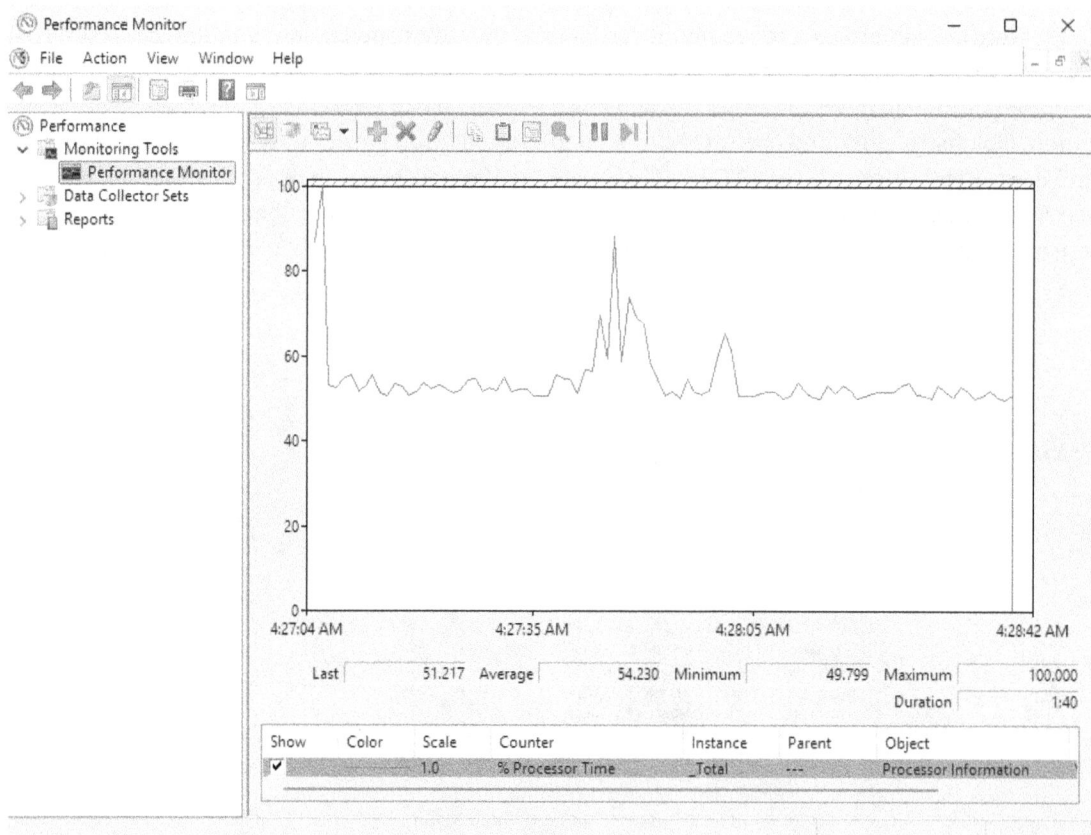

Figure 17.15: Performance Monitor default counter

What is very interesting here is that you can quickly see the **Average**, **Minimum**, and **Maximum** data fields. You will find that these fields exist with most counters, and this is some of the most useful information that I have pulled using Perfmon during real-life troubleshooting scenarios.

Right-click anywhere inside that graph and select **Add Counters....** Here, we can discover the incredible breadth of data counters that are available to monitor with Perfmon:

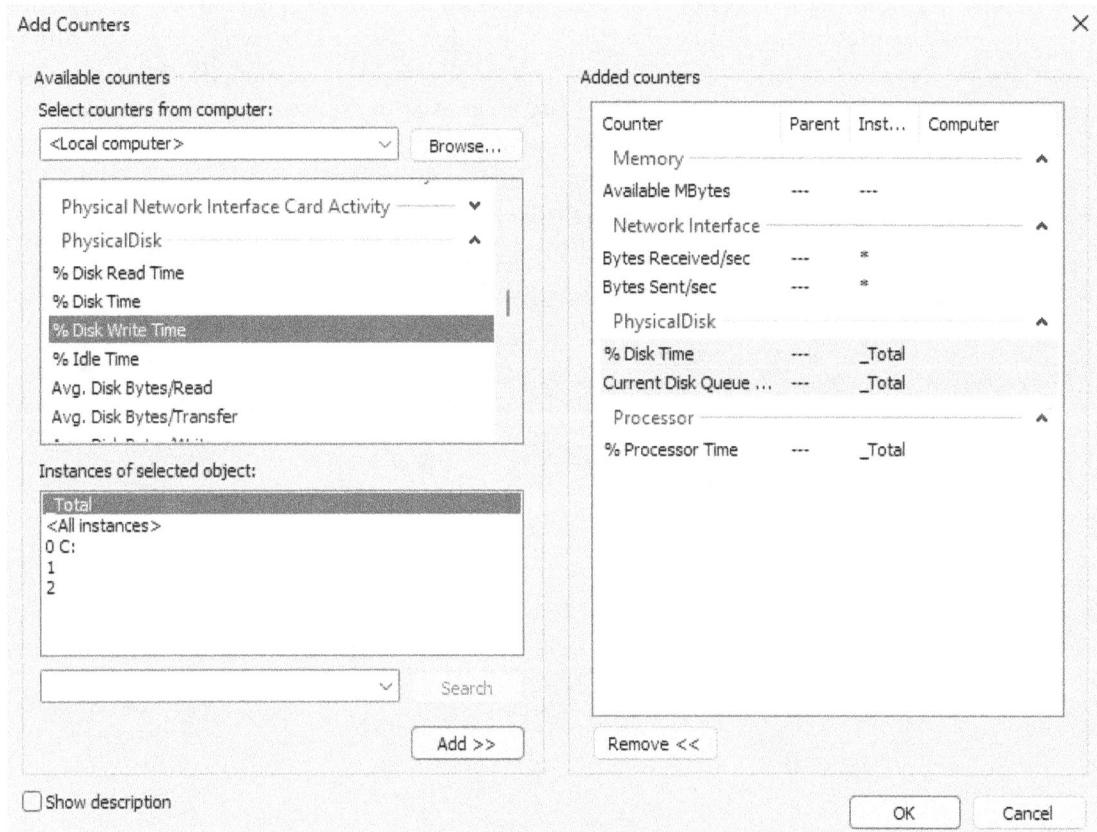

Figure 17.16: Adding counters to Perfmon

There is no way we can cover everything here, so I'll list out a few examples of counters that are useful in most server performance troubleshooting scenarios:

- **Processor > % Processor Time** (this is the one added by default)
- **Memory > Available MBytes**
- **Network Interface > Bytes Received/sec**
- **Network Interface > Bytes Sent/sec** (and these can be further defined per-NIC)
- **PhysicalDisk > % Disk Time**
- **PhysicalDisk > Current Disk Queue Length**

Many counters are role-specific. Things such as **Terminal Services** > **Total Sessions** can give you counters on how many users you have logged in to your RDSH hosts. Or, you can use **Print Queue** > **Total Jobs Printed** when trying to gain an idea of how busy or overworked your print server might be. In a previous job, I often utilized IP-HTTPS, DNS64, and IPsec counters to keep tabs on under-the-hood components within the Microsoft Remote Access technologies.

I have gone ahead and added all the performance-related counters that I specified previously (there are many, many more options available), and the Perfmon data graph has become a mess of multiple colors and overlapping line graphs. While the default graph view is interesting, it's not very easy to follow. Instead, if you drop down the toolbar icon that looks like a little graph, you'll find three options for how to display this data: **Line**, **Histogram bar**, and **Report**. I prefer looking at numbers, but the **Report** view does not display the average-minimum-maximum, and those are really useful. So, you may find yourself utilizing a combination of all three views on a regular basis:

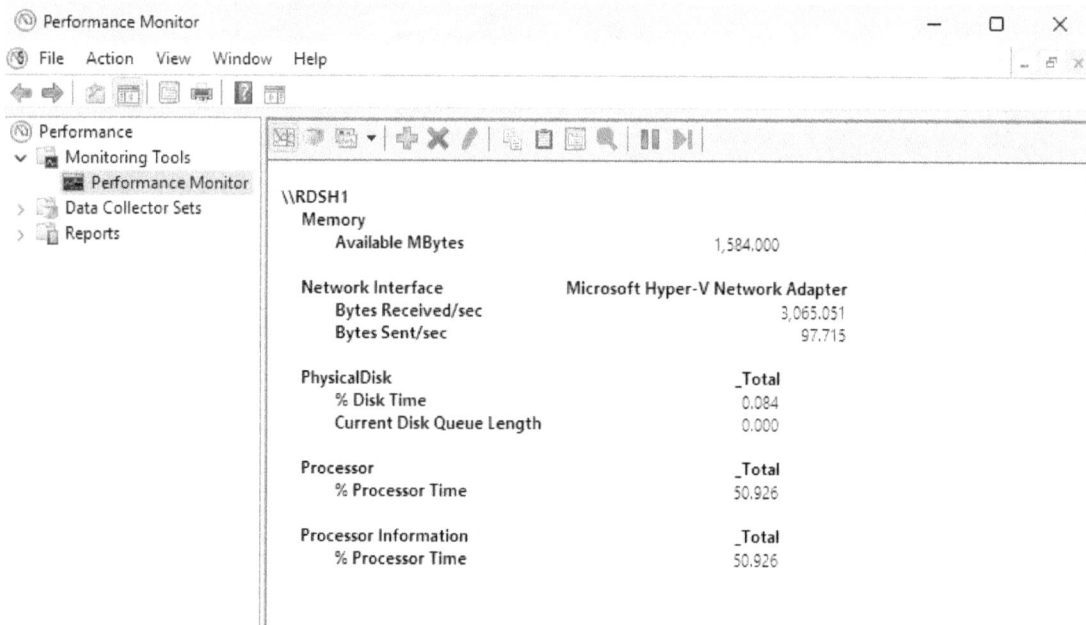

Figure 17.17: Performance metrics in the Report view

This is cool real-time information, but how often do you really dig in and troubleshoot a real-time problem with this much depth? Let's be honest—if you have a server tanking performance during working hours, you are probably going to restart the entire server to get things normalized before using Perfmon for a hardware review. Instead, what I have always found Perfmon to be most useful for is gathering statistics over a period of time. A great example is repeated reports of slowness on a particular server. Perhaps an RDSH or Remote Access server where users interact with it every day. Every few days, you receive support tickets indicating that the system was running slowly or wouldn't allow anyone new to log in. By the time that ticket crosses your desk and you hop into the server, the problem has disappeared, and the server runs happily again.

This is where Perfmon can shine. After defining the performance counters that you are interested in monitoring, you can create your own **Data Collector Set** (which is a collection of counters) and configure it to run on a schedule. Expand **Data Collector Sets,** then right-click on **User Defined** and select **New > Data Collector Set.** Walking through this wizard, you can use some predefined templates to gather common metrics, or you can define your data collector set manually. Pick and choose which performance counters you would like to include and how often the data collector set will log data for each counter (every 15 seconds by default). You can see in *Figure 17.18* that I am working my way through defining a manual list of counters, and I have added some of the classic hardware utilization metrics to my collection list:

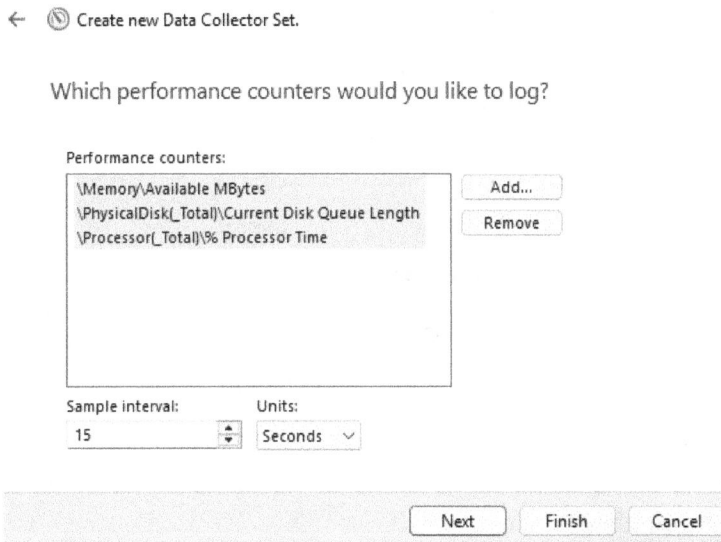

Figure 17.18: Adding performance counters to a data collector set

After defining your counters and specifying a location for this data to be saved, the last screen of the wizard provides the **Run as** option. In many cases, you can leave <**Default**> configured here and your dataset will work just fine, but if any of your counters struggle to gather data, you could alternatively specify a different account here, such as an administrator account. Leave the **Save and close** option selected and click **Finish**. I want to use this option, rather than one of the others that invokes immediate action, so that we can see where it is inside the Perfmon console that our new data collector set is stored.

Back inside the Perfmon console, looking under the **User Defined** folder, you will find the data collector set that you just created. This is our new set of counters, ready to be run at any time. This is a nice way to save common sets of performance counters for easy running and reference later, and if you right-click on this new data collector set and head into **Properties**, you will also find a **Schedule** tab, which allows you to set this data collector up to start at specific times. Then, inside the **Stop Condition** tab, you can define how long you would like these metrics to be gathered. Remember that we set the interval to 15 seconds, so this data collector set will start at the time you specify and will log data from the included counters every 15 seconds for as long as you determine the data collector set should run, with data collection stopping as specified in the **Stop Condition** tab:

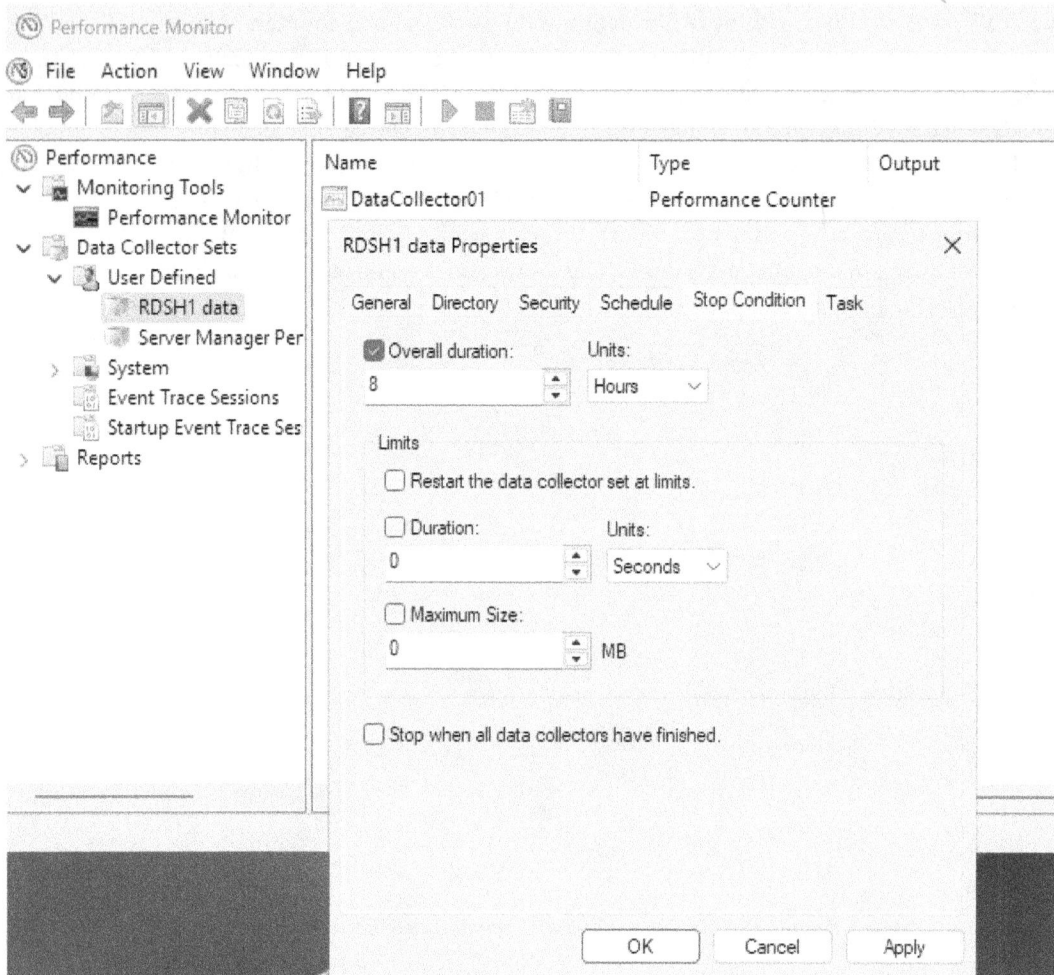

Figure 17.19: Configuring a scheduled runtime for the new data collector set

In the future, if I want to tweak which counters are included in this dataset, I can right-click on DataCollector01, shown in _Figure 17.19_, and visit **Properties** here to add new counters or remove existing ones.

I have allowed the new data collector set to run for a few minutes and gather some data. Now that I'm finished with the defined runtime, how do I find the data that was generated? Still inside the Perfmon console, look just a little further down the tree for **Reports**. Inside **User Defined** reports, you'll find a folder for your new data collector set. Each time that your collector set runs, it will generate a new file here with a date stamp. Clicking on today's file shows me all the data gathered, and I have the same options available to manipulate the data or change how the graph looks as I did in the live data view:

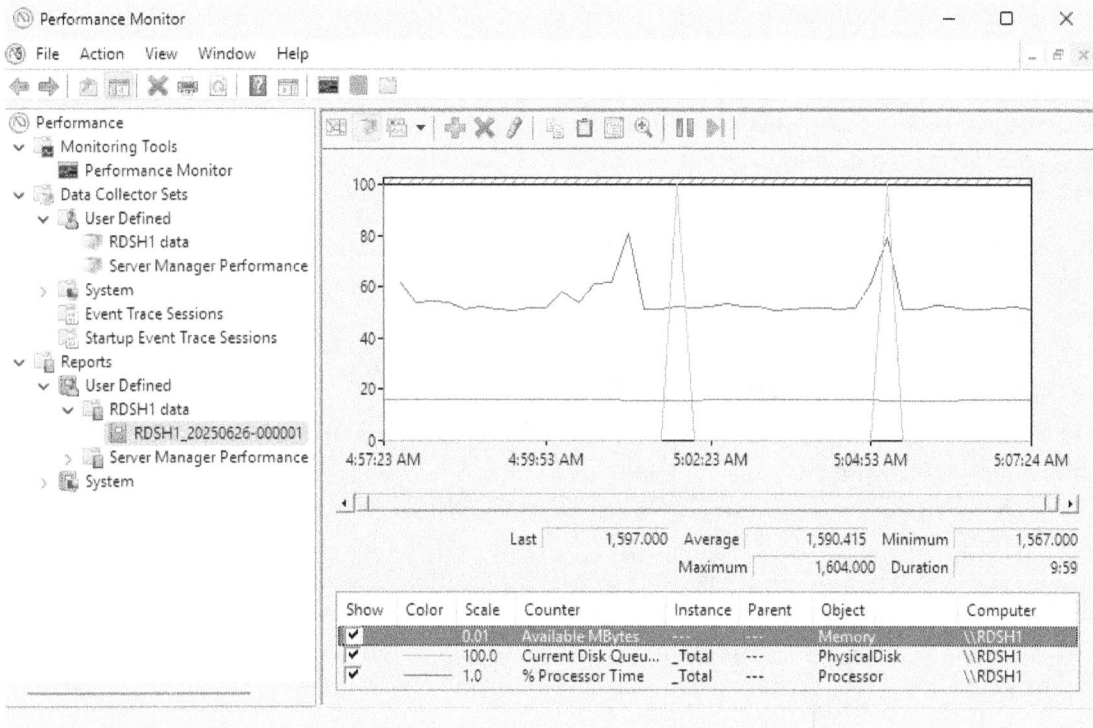

Figure 17.20: Viewing the report following a scheduled data collection run

Scheduled Perfmon datasets can be extremely useful when troubleshooting regularly occurring performance problems on a server. In the example of an RDSH server that we discussed earlier, when tackling reported slowness on that server, you could establish a Perfmon data collector set that takes metrics surrounding hardware utilization. You could include session count metrics to see how many users are logged in at the same time. This Perfmon report could then shed some very interesting and helpful light on the situation; perhaps you simply have too many people connected during the times that hardware is taxed. Or, maybe you find that the server slows down at the top of every hour and then use that information to realize that you have backups running at the top of every hour, which leads you in the direction of problem resolution.

Sysinternals tools

Windows Server has many wonderful tools built right into it, but there's always room to improve.

This seems to be exactly what Mark Russinovich was thinking back in the mid-90s, when he and Bryce Cogswell created Winternals and started crafting apps that could do even more advanced actions and data collection within the Microsoft Windows operating systems than was possible with the native toolset. Fast-forward to today, Winternals has been acquired by Microsoft, the conglomeration of tools that were created under that umbrella are now known as the Microsoft Sysinternals tools, and Mark is now CTO of Azure.

These tools are simple, helpful, and effective. Most of them don't even require an installation. Simply download a standalone executable, copy it over to your server, and run it. When finished, you can delete the executable and easily remove any trace of that application from your server. We already looked at a couple of these tools earlier in the book, TCPView and PsPing. There are many tools available that serve many different purposes; some of them are even written specifically for Nano Server or Linux machines!

In just a minute, we will outline some of these tools for ourselves, but if you're interested in a list of the entire Sysinternals toolset, here is a good link to get started: `https://learn.microsoft.com/en-us/ sysinternals/downloads/`.

Descriptions of popular tools

Here are some of the Sysinternals tools that I have found most helpful to deal with Windows Server tasks and troubleshooting.

TCPView

We already looked closely at TCPView a few chapters ago; this standalone executable is incredibly useful to monitor all active TCP socket connections on a computer or server. It will show you active connections, and immediately display and highlight new connections being made, or stale connections falling away. This is very useful to troubleshoot application networking.

PsPing

PsPing is another Sysinternals tool that we already looked into and executed back in our chapter about networking, but is worth an honorable mention here. Like ping on steroids, PsPing can easily become one of your favorite network probing and testing tools in that you can very easily throw connectivity tests between systems on your network. In addition to normal ICMP requests and acknowledgements (like ping already offers), you can very quickly throw TCP packet testing against specific port numbers on remote systems. This negates the need to run longer and more complex PowerShell cmdlets such as `Test-NetConnection`. In addition to all this, with a little PsPing trickery on both the remote machine as well as your local workstation, it can be used to measure bandwidth throughput between the two devices. I often watch admins download third-party tools for such a feat, measuring total throughput across various segments of their network, unknowing that their Sysinternals toolbox already provides a method to do exactly that.

Disk2vhd

This is a simple tool that makes it incredibly easy to convert a live, running Windows physical server into a VHDX file, making it possible to spin up that VHDX on a Hyper-V server and very quickly convert a physical server into a virtual server. Anybody who has virtualized physical servers before has probably used Disk2vhd, perhaps without realizing it is one of the Sysinternals tools. A major advantage Disk2vhd has over other P2V tools is that you can run it on a server that is online; many of the other tools require you to shut down the server that you are converting.

Autologon

The name really says it all; running this tool and populating the presented fields will cause a computer or server to be configured to automatically bypass the login screen with the provided username and password. While this is not a great idea from a security perspective, some software running on servers insists on the server being logged in for the software to operate properly. In these cases, if that server restarts due to Windows updates or anything else, the server needs to be able to automatically log in during boot, and this tool can accomplish that function. It is also possible to do this directly in the Windows Registry, but the Autologon tool makes it so easy.

Autoruns

There are various places where applications can be configured to automatically launch during the start of Windows. Sometimes it can be a nuisance to figure out where an app is configured like this if you want to stop that behavior from happening. The Autoruns tool quickly shows you a list of these startup items and a lot of detail about each one.

Diskmon

Shortly, we will take a look at Procmon, which provides a pretty comprehensive look into what goes on under the hood of Microsoft Windows, but if you are tracking down an issue and are interested in looking closely into all disk activity that is happening on your system, Diskmon is particularly useful for that. This can be helpful when figuring out why a certain application or application installer is seizing up or failing; it may be attempting to access or write a file or folder, but doesn't have the permissions to do so.

LogonSessions

Task Manager can be a quick go-to to view different user profiles that are logged in to a server, but the LogonSessions tool provides much more detailed information about every session. With this tool, you can see not only user sessions but also system-level sessions that are authenticated and work behind the scenes. As an example, I just ran LogonSessions on my Windows 11 laptop where I am writing this text, and while I am the only user logged in to the machine, there are 10 active logon sessions. Using the -p switch with this tool displays the entire list of processes that are in use with each session, which can also be very useful!

PsExec

Executing applications or processes on remote systems is possible through remote PowerShell connections or third-party software, but Sysinternals brings a free and powerful option to the table. PsExec can be run on a Windows computer to launch programs or enact commands on other remote Windows systems. Most software developers worthy of the title now design their server-side applications to run as Windows services, so that they are active and responsive even if the software is not launched on that server. Alas, not all programmers have this skillset, and there are plenty of nuisance applications in the world that require their server to be logged in, and the piece of software to always be running, or it won't be able to serve up any information. PsExec can be utilized to launch such applications from a remote computer, or it can be used to send troubleshooting commands to a remote system that is struggling so much that you may not be able to log in to it.

To give you an idea of how easy it is to run PsExec, here's an example command that I might run on my laptop to be able to launch an executable on a remote server called WEB1. This example also displays an optional function where you can specify a username and password to be used on the remote system while executing this command:

```
Psexec \\WEB1 "C:\Tools\Application.exe" -u contoso\administrator -p
password123!
```

One very useful switch to keep in your back pocket when working with PsExec is -s. Adding -s to your PsExec command will cause your command to run under the SYSTEM account, which can be useful for commands or executions that require unlimited permissions on the recipient computer.

PsKill

If PsExec is used to launch commands or applications, can we assume PsKill is the opposite? Yes, that is exactly what we have at our fingertips with PsKill. This tool can be used to force applications or processes to close on remote systems. Recent versions of Windows also include a built-in command-line tool called TaskKill that can accomplish similar functionality, but it is less powerful and doesn't easily translate into running against remote systems. PsKill is very easy to reach out to remote servers and stop running processes. As a real-world example, I often work with a company that has **QuickBooks (QB)** and another finance application integrated together. Both components are installed on a server, but users launch QB on their own computers, of course, not directly on the server. The third-party component that taps into QB gets fussy if there are any instances of QBW32.exe running on this server, but QB loves to self-launch QBW32.exe for various reasons. This was causing a lot of grief for the customer, and the only solution from the software vendor was to force QBW32.exe to close in order to fix their software. So, we turned to PsKill. If users ever encounter an error in this application, they simply double-click on a batch file that calls PsKill into action. This batch file sits on their local computers, and when they click on it, PsKill reaches over to the QB server and closes any instances of QBW32.exe that are open. It takes mere milliseconds for this to run, and the user is immediately back in action.

While I truly hope this software vendor can figure out a better long-term solution to this problem, for now, we have a very fast and effective stopgap solution in place to allow these folks to be successful in their work. Here is the sanitized PsKill command we use to accomplish what I just described:

```
C:\Tools\PsKill.exe \\SERVERNAME -u admin -p <password> QBW32.exe
```

PsShutdown

Many of you have probably used Microsoft's built-in `shutdown` command to enact a shutdown or reboot from Command Prompt, but generally from the server where you are currently logged in. As with most Sysinternals tools, PsShutdown works similarly to what is already built into Windows but adds a few extra pieces of functionality, including the ability to easily initiate a shutdown or restart against remote systems. There are many special switches that can be used alongside PsShutdown, enabling things such as hibernating, locking the computer, displaying a message before shutdown or restart, logging a shutdown reason code in the event logs, plus many more options.

Process Monitor (Procmon)

There are lots and lots of Sysinternals tools, and the purpose here is not to cover all of them but to outline some of the common ones, especially those that I personally find useful. Descriptive text about these tools is helpful, but I'm getting bored with typing, and for these last couple of tools, I would rather download and use them than just tell you about them.

Procmon is an evolution and combination of multiple Sysinternals tools that were always extremely helpful in troubleshooting Windows. Old-school Procmon showed you a bunch of information about running processes on a system. That is great, but it doesn't usually tell the full story about what is happening on your computer or server. You could glean a lot more information by combining output from Procmon, Filemon, and Regmon. As their names suggest, Filemon shows detailed information about files being accessed in Windows, and Regmon shows registry information. Filemon and Regmon have now gone by the wayside, as the current flavor of Procmon combines all three of these toolsets into one fantastic troubleshooting interface.

To check this out for yourself, simply download Procmon from the following location and then launch it: `https://learn.microsoft.com/en-us/sysinternals/downloads/procmon`

Immediately after launching, I am presented with an overwhelming amount of information about what is happening on my Windows system.

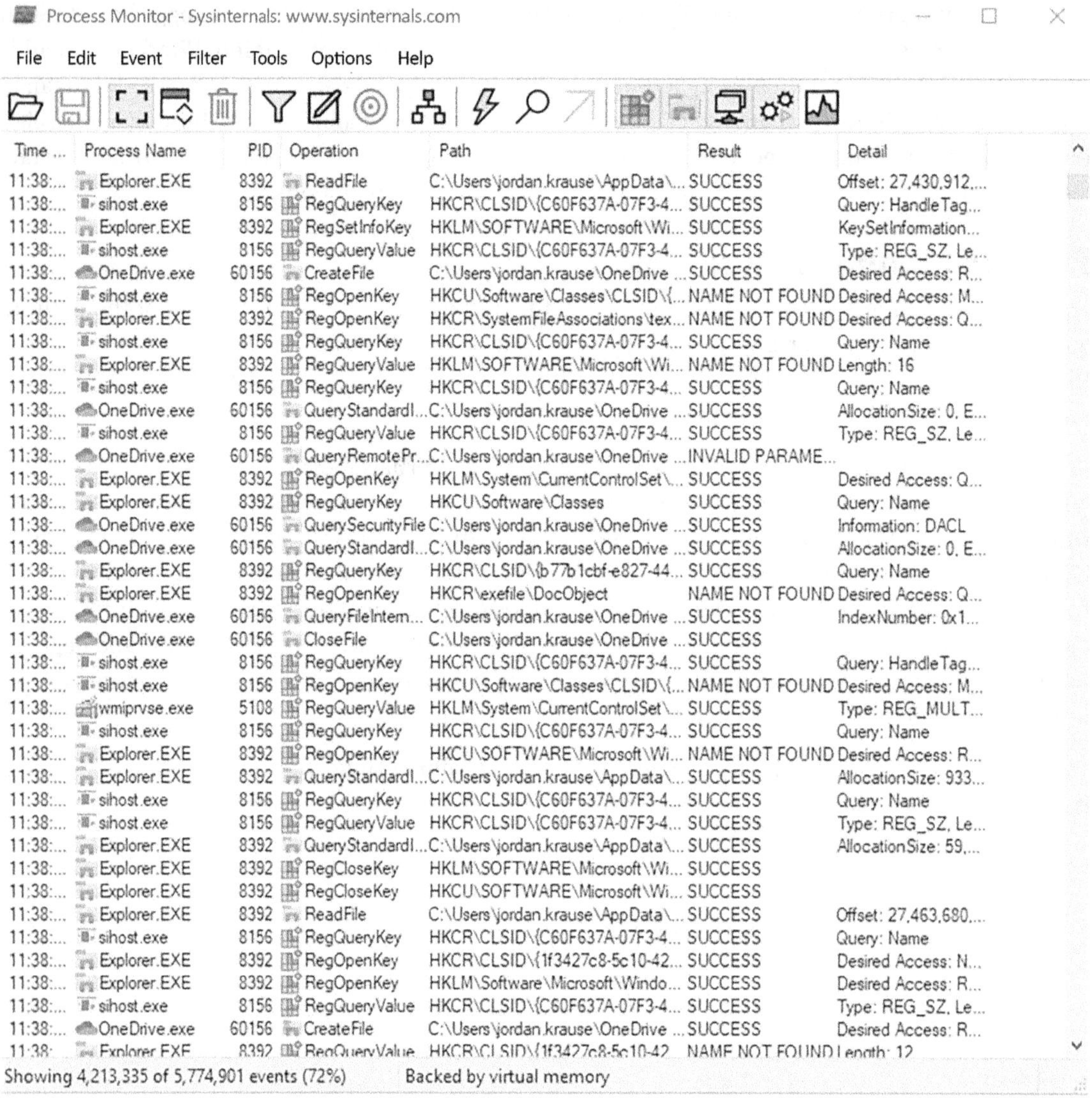

Figure 17.21: There is so much data in Procmon!

Procmon displays detailed information about every process on my computer, including every file that is being interfaced and every registry key being accessed, written, removed, or in any way touched. In the previous screenshot, you can see that File Explorer has hooks into many places, which makes sense because I have various Word and Excel documents open, as well as multiple instances of File Explorer itself. I also have a lot of OneDrive activity, as my Documents and Pictures folders automatically sync to OneDrive, and this means that an application is always at work in the background.

You'll also notice that there are more than 5 million events seen by Procmon, with a percentage next to the number indicating that Procmon has not even finished gathering up the data yet. Since taking the screenshot and typing the previous paragraph, that number has grown to 12 million. Your human brain could never keep up with the activity happening in your operating system, so you will find it most useful to launch Procmon, then immediately perform whatever action is causing you trouble (such as launching an application or running an installer), and then pause the collection of Procmon data. This way, you have a set of static information that hopefully includes information about what is going wrong with whatever function or application you are working on at that moment. Then this output can be filtered to particular processes or locations, to quickly narrow down the issue.

To throw out another real-world example, I have utilized Procmon multiple times to solve mysteries about why software installation packages failed to run without presenting any error codes. This issue is very frustrating; you know that something is going wrong during installation, and it's probably related to some missing prerequisite or permission issue, but where do you even begin to start looking if there is no error presented onscreen, and nothing is logged in Windows event logs?

In this scenario, if you launch Procmon, and then run the problematic installer through until it fails, you can then pause the Procmon output and filter down the data to find the answer you are looking for. Most likely, the installer is attempting to access a particular file or registry location that it doesn't have permission to access, or it is simply not finding what it needs, and the installer then bombs. By narrowing down the scope of the Procmon output to the process name of the installer, you can see anything and everything that the installer does as it progresses.

To pause data collection, simply click the toolbar button called **Capture**. Click it again to restart the data collection. Once paused, use the **Filter** button to narrow in on the data that you want to view. As a test, I launched Procmon, then launched a new instance of Microsoft Edge, and navigated to a couple of websites. If I then pause and filter my Procmon output to only show me information about the msedge.exe process, amazingly, Edge performed 344 tasks within about 10 seconds of use. If Edge had been an application that crashed on me and I wanted to investigate why that was happening, I could scroll through this output or sort for results that did not say **SUCCESS**, and there's a good chance that I could figure out what was going wrong with this quick troubleshooting process.

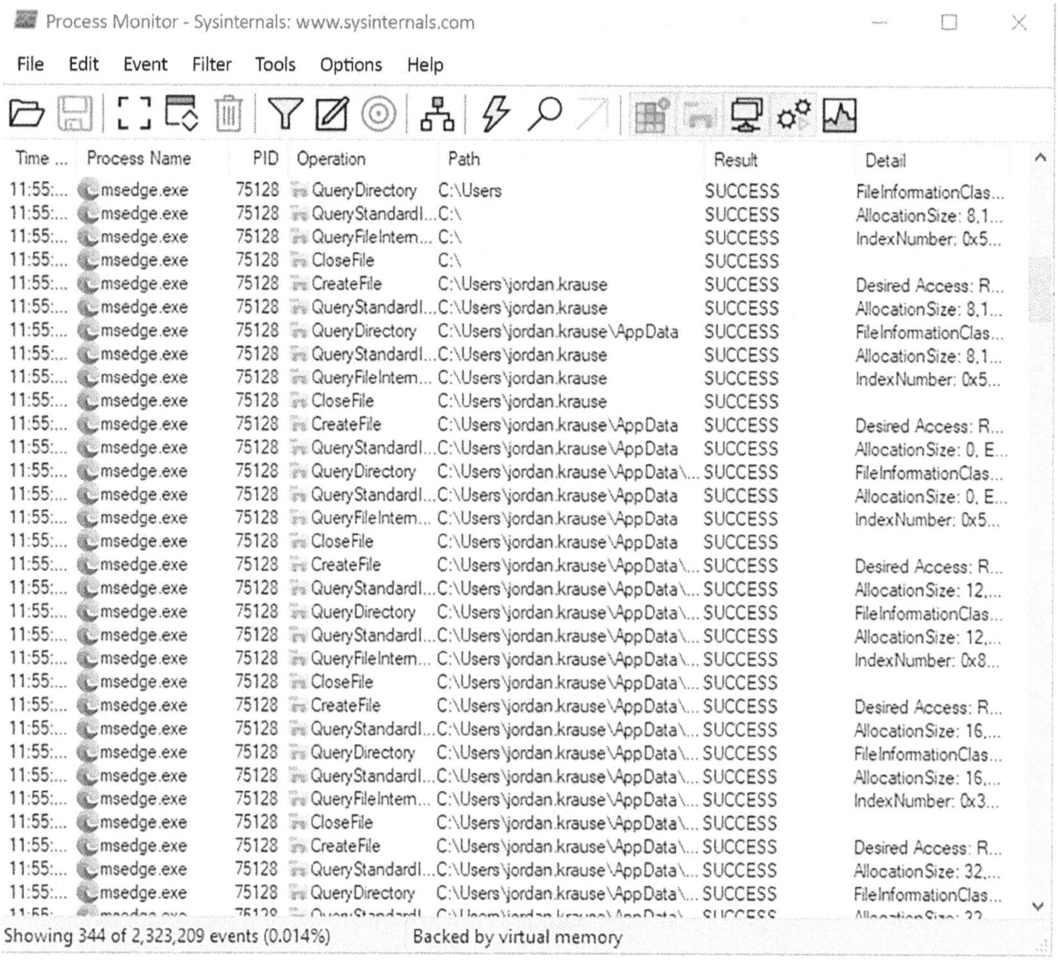

Time ...	Process Name	PID	Operation	Path	Result	Detail
11:55:...	msedge.exe	75128	QueryDirectory	C:\Users	SUCCESS	FileInformationClas...
11:55:...	msedge.exe	75128	QueryStandardI...	C:\	SUCCESS	AllocationSize: 8,1...
11:55:...	msedge.exe	75128	QueryFileIntern...	C:\	SUCCESS	IndexNumber: 0x5...
11:55:...	msedge.exe	75128	CloseFile	C:\	SUCCESS	
11:55:...	msedge.exe	75128	CreateFile	C:\Users\jordan.krause	SUCCESS	Desired Access: R...
11:55:...	msedge.exe	75128	QueryStandardI...	C:\Users\jordan.krause	SUCCESS	AllocationSize: 8,1...
11:55:...	msedge.exe	75128	QueryDirectory	C:\Users\jordan.krause\AppData	SUCCESS	FileInformationClas...
11:55:...	msedge.exe	75128	QueryStandardI...	C:\Users\jordan.krause	SUCCESS	AllocationSize: 8,1...
11:55:...	msedge.exe	75128	QueryFileIntern...	C:\Users\jordan.krause	SUCCESS	IndexNumber: 0x5...
11:55:...	msedge.exe	75128	CloseFile	C:\Users\jordan.krause	SUCCESS	
11:55:...	msedge.exe	75128	CreateFile	C:\Users\jordan.krause\AppData	SUCCESS	Desired Access: R...
11:55:...	msedge.exe	75128	QueryStandardI...	C:\Users\jordan.krause\AppData	SUCCESS	AllocationSize: 0, E...
11:55:...	msedge.exe	75128	QueryDirectory	C:\Users\jordan.krause\AppData\...	SUCCESS	FileInformationClas...
11:55:...	msedge.exe	75128	QueryStandardI...	C:\Users\jordan.krause\AppData	SUCCESS	AllocationSize: 0, E...
11:55:...	msedge.exe	75128	QueryFileIntern...	C:\Users\jordan.krause\AppData	SUCCESS	IndexNumber: 0x5...
11:55:...	msedge.exe	75128	CloseFile	C:\Users\jordan.krause\AppData	SUCCESS	
11:55:...	msedge.exe	75128	CreateFile	C:\Users\jordan.krause\AppData\...	SUCCESS	Desired Access: R...
11:55:...	msedge.exe	75128	QueryStandardI...	C:\Users\jordan.krause\AppData\...	SUCCESS	AllocationSize: 12,...
11:55:...	msedge.exe	75128	QueryDirectory	C:\Users\jordan.krause\AppData\...	SUCCESS	FileInformationClas...
11:55:...	msedge.exe	75128	QueryStandardI...	C:\Users\jordan.krause\AppData\...	SUCCESS	AllocationSize: 12,...
11:55:...	msedge.exe	75128	QueryFileIntern...	C:\Users\jordan.krause\AppData\...	SUCCESS	IndexNumber: 0x8...
11:55:...	msedge.exe	75128	CloseFile	C:\Users\jordan.krause\AppData\...	SUCCESS	
11:55:...	msedge.exe	75128	CreateFile	C:\Users\jordan.krause\AppData\...	SUCCESS	Desired Access: R...
11:55:...	msedge.exe	75128	QueryStandardI...	C:\Users\jordan.krause\AppData\...	SUCCESS	AllocationSize: 16,...
11:55:...	msedge.exe	75128	QueryDirectory	C:\Users\jordan.krause\AppData\...	SUCCESS	FileInformationClas...
11:55:...	msedge.exe	75128	QueryFileIntern...	C:\Users\jordan.krause\AppData\...	SUCCESS	IndexNumber: 0x3...
11:55:...	msedge.exe	75128	CloseFile	C:\Users\jordan.krause\AppData\...	SUCCESS	
11:55:...	msedge.exe	75128	CreateFile	C:\Users\jordan.krause\AppData\...	SUCCESS	Desired Access: R...
11:55:...	msedge.exe	75128	QueryStandardI...	C:\Users\jordan.krause\AppData\...	SUCCESS	AllocationSize: 32,...
11:55:...	msedge.exe	75128	QueryDirectory	C:\Users\jordan.krause\AppData\...	SUCCESS	FileInformationClas...
11:55:...	msedge.exe	75128	QueryStandardI...	C:\Users\jordan.krause\AppData\...	SUCCESS	AllocationSize: 32...

Showing 344 of 2,323,209 events (0.014%)   Backed by virtual memory

Figure 17.22: Data is filtered down to only msedge.exe

AccessEnum

File permissions on company file servers can be very simple or incredibly complicated. Some companies handle this very well and determine file access based on top-level folders and shares. For example, you can create a share called *Accounting* and decide that anybody who is part of an Active Directory group called Accounting will have access to the `Accounting` folder, and everything inside of it. You can also decide that nobody else in the company has access to that entire folder or share, and you will never deviate from this top-level rule. This is easy and works great.

However, the longer your file server has been up and running, the greater the likelihood that you or a previous administrator has fielded unique situations that encroached on that pure and lovely set of NTFS permissions. Perhaps your CEO, who is not a member of the Accounting group, needed to have access to files inside that Accounting share. He's the CEO, so what are you going to do? Say no? I don't think so, and perhaps that interaction now means that an individual user account has also been granted access to the entire Accounting share.

No biggie, right? That's not too difficult to keep track of, but what if that same situation happened 50 times over the next year? And others who needed to have access to information only needed access to *some* of the Accounting information, but not all of it. Your director of HR needed access to some spreadsheets that are inside a subfolder, but they didn't need access to anything else inside Accounting, so you disabled inheritance on the subfolder in order to grant your HR director access only to the subfolder. Brilliant! You have successfully minimized risk by only giving this person access to the specific things that they need, but you have done so at the expense of the future manageability of that subfolder. Now that inheritance has been disabled, that folder will no longer pay attention to higher-level permission changes that you make. Or, perhaps worse, someone may later make additional changes to additional subfolders, and now you have NTFS permission rabbit trails scattered throughout your entire file server.

Any IT administrator who has stepped into an environment that has been running for many years and has been administered by numerous people before them has encountered this scenario. File permissions can be an amazing mess, and you're probably going to be tasked with cleaning it up. I can promise you that the first time a permission change goes wrong and suddenly a shop-floor user has access to sensitive HR documents because your file permissions are all messed up, you will immediately have a very high-priority project on your plate to figure out who has access to what, and how to fix it.

Enter AccessEnum. While this tool isn't going to magically fix all of your file permission problems, it can help with the first task of that project—quickly determining who has access to what files and folders. Download AccessEnum and launch it on your file server, and you will see all of the files and folders on the system, including information about who has read and write access to them. There is no capability native in Windows that displays information in this format; without AccessEnum, you are faced with many mouse clicks to manually gather and lay out this information in your own format. Here, you can see what AccessEnum looks like; I have some shared folders on my file server and ran AccessEnum against the D: volume where they all reside. Very quickly, I can see that most permissions stack up how I would expect them to, but for some reason, JAdmin has read access to my HR share. Suspicious...

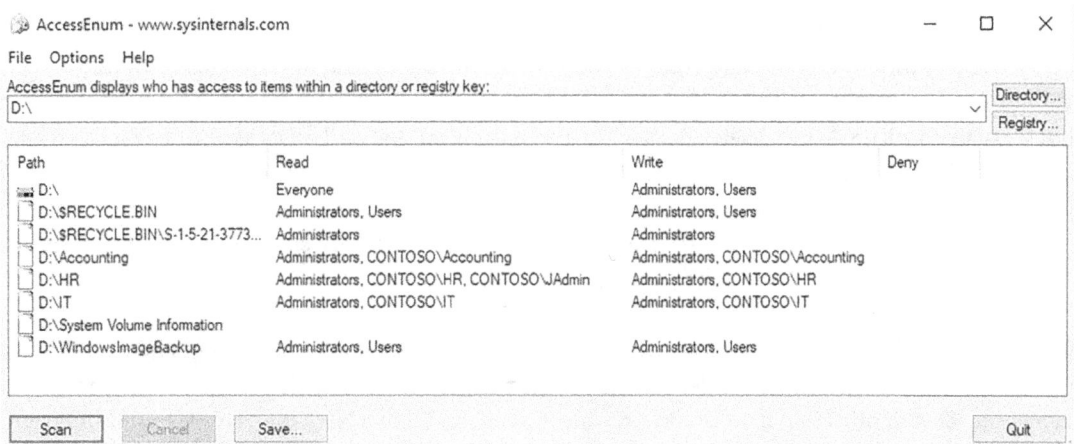

Figure 17.23: Looks like I need to have a conversation with Joe Admin

DTrace

DTrace is not a new toolset, but rather one taken from another world and recently translated into Windows. DTrace (dynamic tracing) was originally developed for the Solaris operating system, and has been used there and even within macOS for a while. The core capability of DTrace is super in-depth monitoring of applications or processes to figure out what files they are touching, how hard they are hitting the CPU, and whether they are leaking any memory. This can be helpful to correct applications going rogue and to discover bottlenecks that applications or processes may introduce at the kernel level.

DTrace can help a software developer to answer questions such as the following...

- *Which of my threads consumes the most CPU time?*
- *Which functions are allocating large blocks of memory?*
- *Are there any threads or services hanging in my application?*
- *What files are being touched by this process?*
- *What function was executing prior to the application crash?*

DTrace requires some special things to be enabled in the operating system to make real use of it, and is purely command-line driven. DTrace commands almost always accompany scripts written to seek out specialized information. To engage with DTrace most likely means that you are a software developer, and so this tool does not directly correlate to the content of this chapter, but I wanted to establish a baseline to ensure you know it exists, if ever you need to dig into something like this.

There are clearly some areas of DTrace that are purely for the developer world, and other areas that sound somewhat useful. For example, *What files are being touched by this process?* As you will probably remember, we have other tools at our disposal, such as Procmon, that can give us this same information in a much friendlier way.

Windows Firewall with Advanced Security

When thinking about Windows Server troubleshooting, the firewall is probably not one of the first things that comes to mind. However, the Windows Firewall with Advanced Security console can be a very friendly tool to identify and resolve issues that crop up related to networking on our servers. So far in this book, you have already been given instructions on some of the most important things that you can do within WFAS. We discussed the three different firewall profiles and the fact that each individual NIC on a server can utilize a different firewall profile. This knowledge really comes into play within a corporate domain environment. When servers run inside your network and can contact a domain controller, their NICs that are connected to that network should always self-assign the Domain firewall profile. This is important because the firewall rules you expect to be in place while that server is inside the network (which is probably at all times) are only in effect when the Domain profile is active. Even if you choose to have Windows Firewall turned off when inside the network, most companies set up those policies so that *only* if the Domain profile is active will the firewall be turned off. This implies that if a different profile gets assigned to a NIC, the Private or Public profile, then the firewall could indeed be engaged and block traffic flow.

If the server is inside the network, why would it ever self-assign the Public or Private profiles? If a domain controller is not available when the server boots, it won't grab the Domain profile. Sometimes it won't grab the Domain profile simply because Windows occasionally goofs when it boots. This scenario is a regular ticket I encounter at work where a server is not communicating properly, and after a little bit of discovery, we find that the NIC for that server reports that it is using the Public or Private profile, even though it is on the same LAN as a DC. The three firewall profiles have potentially very different firewall rules and can even turn the firewall on or off, depending on how each profile is configured.

Another scenario is a server with multiple NICs, which increases the chances that one of those NICs may grab the wrong firewall profile upon boot. A common issue I've had to face with deploying DirectAccess in many enterprise environments is that we would almost always be using two NICs, one on the internal network and one inside a DMZ. While deploying the server, we would expect that the internal NIC would use the Domain profile, but the DMZ NIC would use the Public or Private profile, as you *should never* be able to loop back inside the network and contact a DC from inside a DMZ network, right? You would be amazed at the number of times the installation of our DirectAccess server brought to light major security holes that existed in these enterprise-class DMZ networks. It is a very common thing to see that DMZ External NIC receive a Domain profile classification inside the firewall, which definitively means that the NIC was able to successfully contact a domain controller. It is often difficult to convince network administrators that they have a loop they don't know about, allowing traffic from the DMZ back into the internal network, but the Domain profile doesn't lie...

The moral of the story with this section is not to rehash the WFAS tool that you have already seen and experienced, but to shed a little more light on how it can be used for troubleshooting purposes. If a server has trouble communicating with something, or something has trouble communicating with that server, take five seconds to pop open WF.MSC and verify that the correct firewall profiles are active. If you have booted a domain-joined server and expect it to run the Domain firewall profile but find that it is not, you can visit SERVICES.MSC and restart the **Network Location Awareness** (NLA) service, and that will usually clear up the behavior. Following the service restart, the Domain profile should then be active on the NIC, assuming, of course, that it can successfully contact a domain controller.

System Insights

System Insights is a tool that quickly gathers all the right parts and pieces to help us build a comprehensive story about what is going on with our servers, and to help predict critical points at which servers may run out of resources and need to be upgraded or expanded.

System Insights is all about predictive analytics. It is available on Windows Server 2022 or 2025 (you just need to enable it) and utilizes performance counters to monitor the system and record data. This data is stored on the local server, which is important because it means you do not have to go through a bunch of work and hoops to implement some kind of centralized database to retain the data, nor perform any cloud work to maintain these metrics. The information collected by System Insights is individual per server and is retained on each server for up to a year.

Once System Insights is up and running, you can tap into the data it collects via PowerShell or **Windows Admin Center** (WAC). Let's flip the switch to enable System Insights on my WEB1 server and see what it looks like.

All we need to do on WEB1 is install the Windows feature called… you guessed it… **System Insights**! This can be installed using the **Add Roles and Features** wizard in Server Manager, or by running the following PowerShell command:

```
Add-WindowsFeature System-Insights -IncludeManagementTools
```

Bonus feature! You can even install System Insights by pulling up WAC, selecting a server, and then visiting the System Insights tool on the left-hand side of the screen. Here, you will find a simple **Install** button, which will roll System Insights to the server with one click!

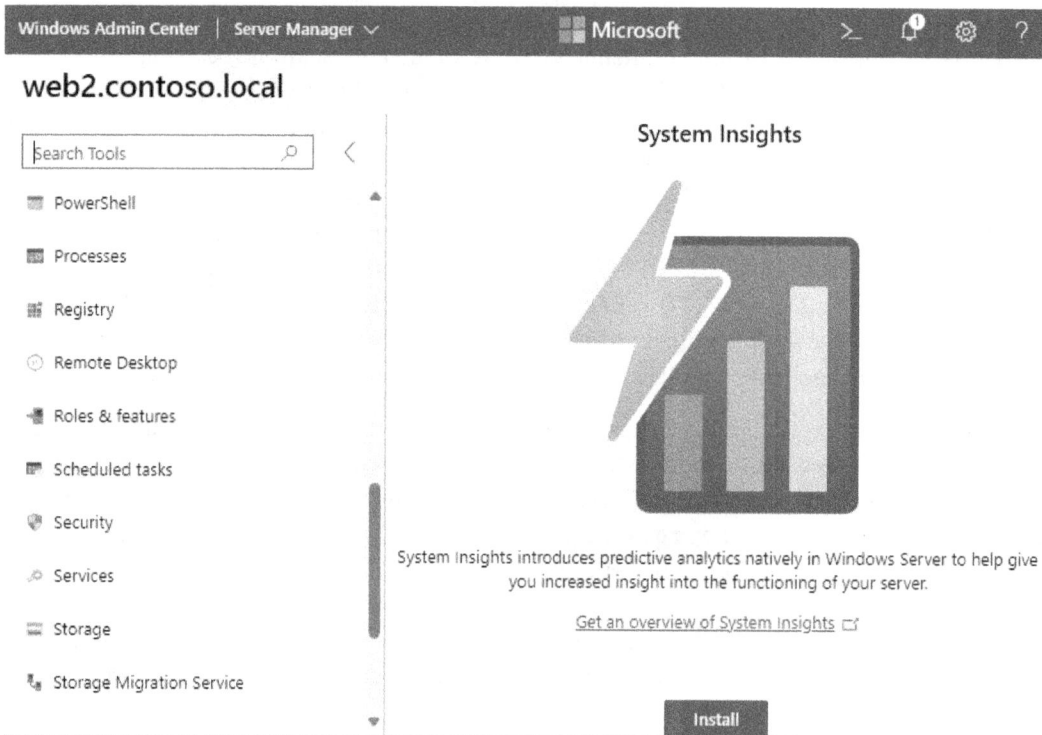

Figure 17.24: Installing System Insights from WAC with a single click

Once the feature is installed, revisit the System Insights screen inside WAC, and you will see four different insight options available. These are the four predictive items that System Insights can help plan and forecast:

- CPU capacity forecasting
- Networking capacity forecasting
- Total storage consumption forecasting
- Volume consumption forecasting

Depending on what stats and hardware you are interested in monitoring, select the appropriate capability and click the **Invoke** button, or select them all just to see what System Insights comes back with. As you can see in *Figure 17.25*, I invoked all four, and currently, they are all reporting green. System

Insights has determined that these components of my WEB1 virtual server are in good shape and are forecast to remain that way:

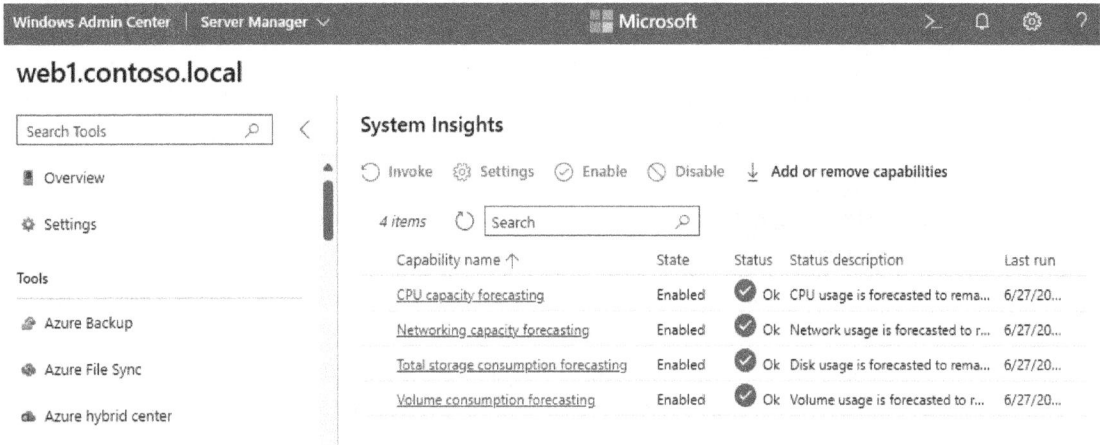

Figure 17.25: System Insights data displayed inside WAC

These predictive analytics can become useful information for preventing issues before they become issues. As you have seen, System Insights is not enabled by default. If you want to make use of this pre-problem information, log in and enable System Insights today!

Remote toolsets

Here is another section where you already have the information you need if you have been working through this book from start to finish, but it never hurts to receive a gentle reminder of taking what you have learned and putting it into practice.

Remote Desktop, Hyper-V console, PowerShell, Sconfig, WAC, **Microsoft Management Console (MMC)**, and Server Manager—these are all different remote-enabled tools, any of which could be used to accomplish similar tasks on your servers. I love training new IT staff on our service desk and working alongside them on tickets, especially in areas where they have limited experience and are hesitant to dive in. Using the Remote Desktop client to RDP into servers is still by far the most common way that administrators log in to their servers to make changes or for any reason, and when you do that all day every day, it is easy to forget about all the other ways that you can interact with those servers. RDP is one of the first things that will quit working when a server is under heavy load or struggling to breathe.

I have watched many an admin attempt to RDP to a server that is having trouble, be unsuccessful at making the RDP connection, and sit for a while at a roadblock, not knowing what to do next. There are so many ways that you can check the status of that server remotely or even reboot it remotely, but these options seem like distant memories when you're on the phone with an angry CEO who wants their stuff to work *right now*.

Incorporate these remote administration tools into your daily workflow. Some are more efficient than others, but continue to utilize them all at various times. That way, when you're in the heat of the moment and facing a difficult situation, muscle memory will take over, and you'll soon become the quickest draw in the West – when tapping into server administration toolsets, anyway.

Event Logs

Any investigatory work on a server is well complemented by Windows event logs. Sometimes you catch a server in the act of misbehaving and can utilize all the tools we have discussed so far to figure out, in real time, what is happening and how to remediate it. Other times, you may have experienced a problem—an unexpected restart of a server is a prime example—and even though things are running smoothly again, you are now tasked with answering that enormous question, "What happened?"

The Windows operating system logs a lot of data, all the time. These logs can answer questions when nothing else in the system can, as they provide a historical roadmap of wins and challenges happening within the OS, visible in static text where patterns emerge and details are given.

The tool that is home to Windows event logs is called **Event Viewer**. Opening Event Viewer can be accomplished in a few ways. You can seek out Event Viewer in the **Start** search function, but there is also a quick link to open Event Viewer when right-clicking on the **Start** button. A third option is to call EVENTVWR.MSC from **Start | Run**, Command Prompt, or PowerShell. When you open this tool, you will see that your most common places to go are inside the folder called Windows Logs. Here, you will find Application, Security, and System event logs. For most log review tasks, these are the three most common sets of logs to visit to seek out information related to diagnosing a problem that occurred:

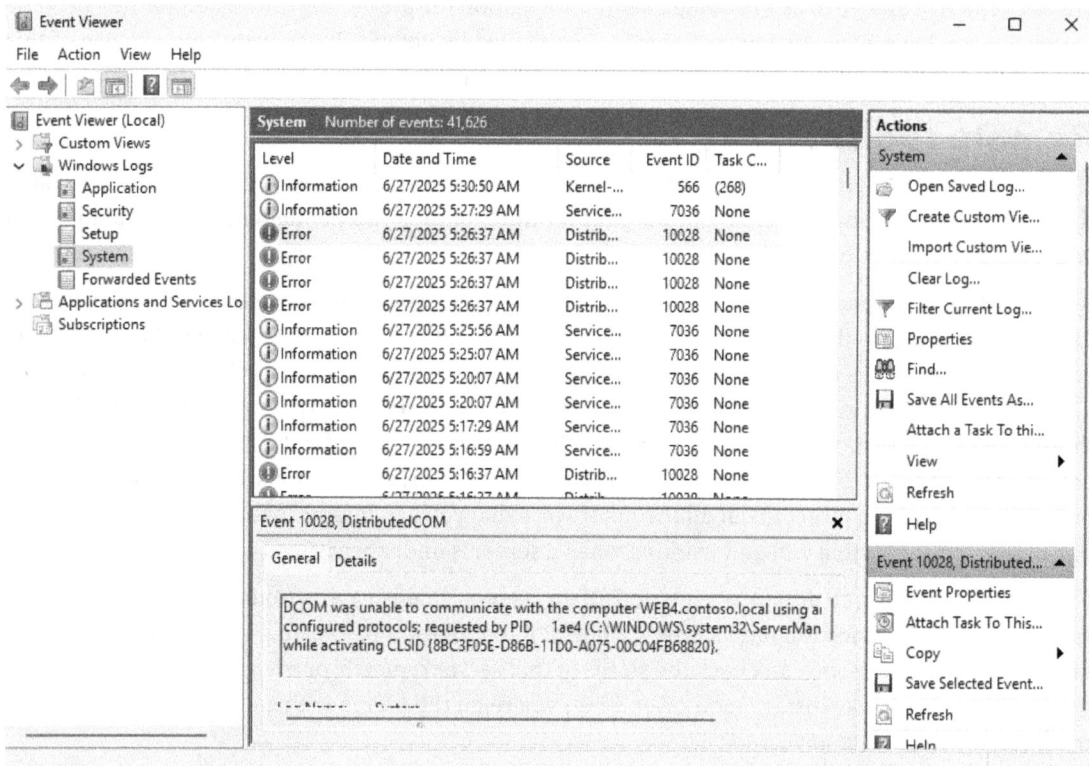

Figure 17.26: Event Viewer

I find myself spending most of my time inside Application and System event logs. As you can tell by the names of these logs, Application logs will contain information about the applications running on the server, while System logs pertain to the system itself. However, there is definitely some crossover, as "applications" in Windows could also relate to roles, and so you will find some information related to the operating system inside the Application event logs. For Security logs, the most common reason that the average server administrator would visit here would be to dig into authentication issues, such as a locked user account. The Security logs are also useful when you're investigating a security breach. Spending any amount of time in the Security logs will quickly overwhelm you because there is a *lot* of information in there, and much of it is ambiguous. Boy, I wish there was a way to filter out some of the noise here...

Filtering event logs

Oh yeah, there *is* a way to filter these logs! I rarely visit event logs *without* filtering in some way, lest I find myself lost in a sea of information for the entire day. While inside any log file, you can right-click on the name of the log (such as Application or System) and choose **Filter Current Log....** There are many ways that filtering can be accomplished here, but one of the most common is to hide away all informational events. If you find yourself reviewing Windows log files just to peruse information events, without a doubt, you have too much time on your hands. I'm kidding, of course, but seriously—when you're looking inside event logs, you are likely looking for the cause of a problem. Informational event logs will rarely be helpful in this scenario. Instead, selecting the following checkboxes will rid your Event Viewer view of all informational logs, focusing instead on warnings and errors that are present:

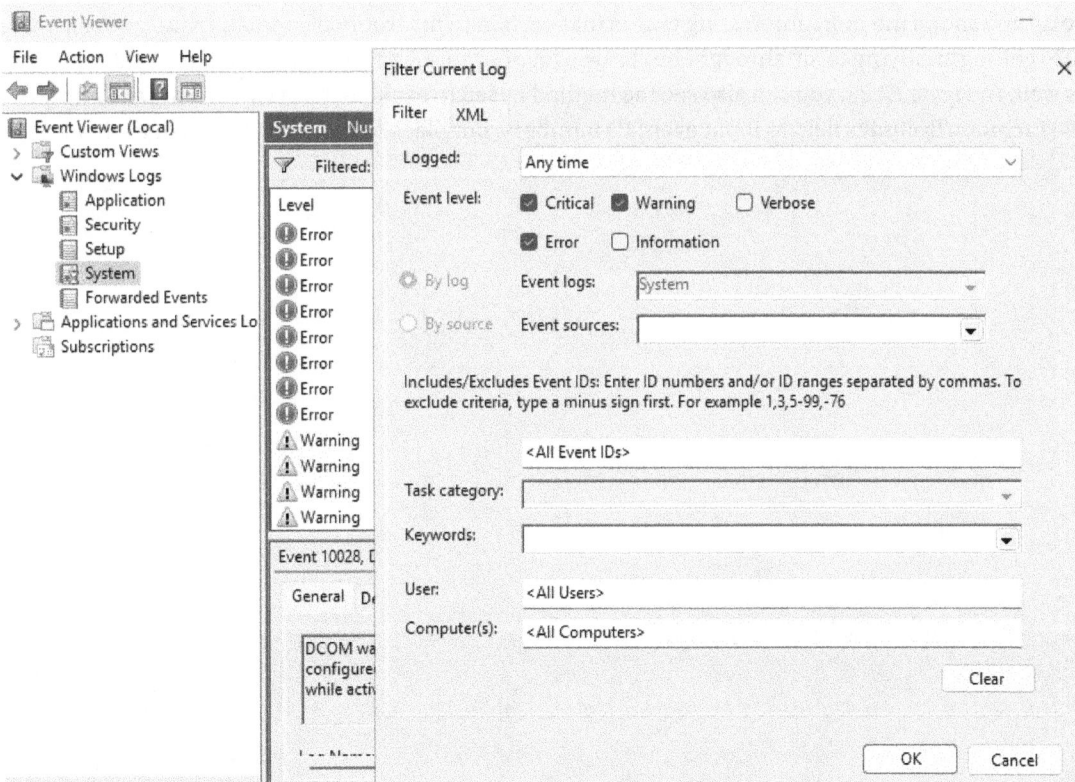

Figure 17.27: Filtering event logs to only display warnings and errors

Once filtered, you can easily scroll through all the errors and warnings listed in this event log and search for clues to help identify whatever issues you are trying to solve. If you identify something interesting, you could note the date and timestamp of that log entry, and then re-include informational events, and search through everything that was being logged during that timeframe. This often helps tell a server's story as it approaches some form of trouble. In many cases, using a combination of `Application` and `System` event logs will give you a well-rounded picture of what happened on the system during that time.

Looking at *Figure 17.27*, you can also see a filter option right in the middle to include or exclude event IDs. Each event type has an identifier number. Once you've latched onto a particular event as being related to a problem that you are troubleshooting, a common question that comes up is, "How often has this issue occurred?" To answer this, you can filter the logs to a particular event ID simply by typing that ID number into this field. Event Viewer will then show you only instances of that event ID. You can comma-separate multiple event IDs to include more information in the log view, while maintaining a view only containing data that you are actually interested in seeing.

An alternative feature that I absolutely love and use all the time is to exclude particular event IDs. As an example, my `System` event log is filled with informational events from Service Control Manager, which is just noise that I generally don't care about. I can see that these events have an event ID number of `7036`. In *Figure 17.28*, I have two instances of Event Viewer side by side—one showing the `System` event log and the other showing the same log but with event 7036 excluded. This really helps cut the noise and shows me more interesting events that pertain to my troubleshooting. In fact, not only was 7036 getting annoying to sift through, but I saw a lot of event ID 81, so I have excluded (hidden) those as well. In *Figure 17.28*, you can also see the method I used to exclude those two event IDs. Simply use the **Includes/Excludes** field to input event ID numbers, but place a minus (-) in front of each number:

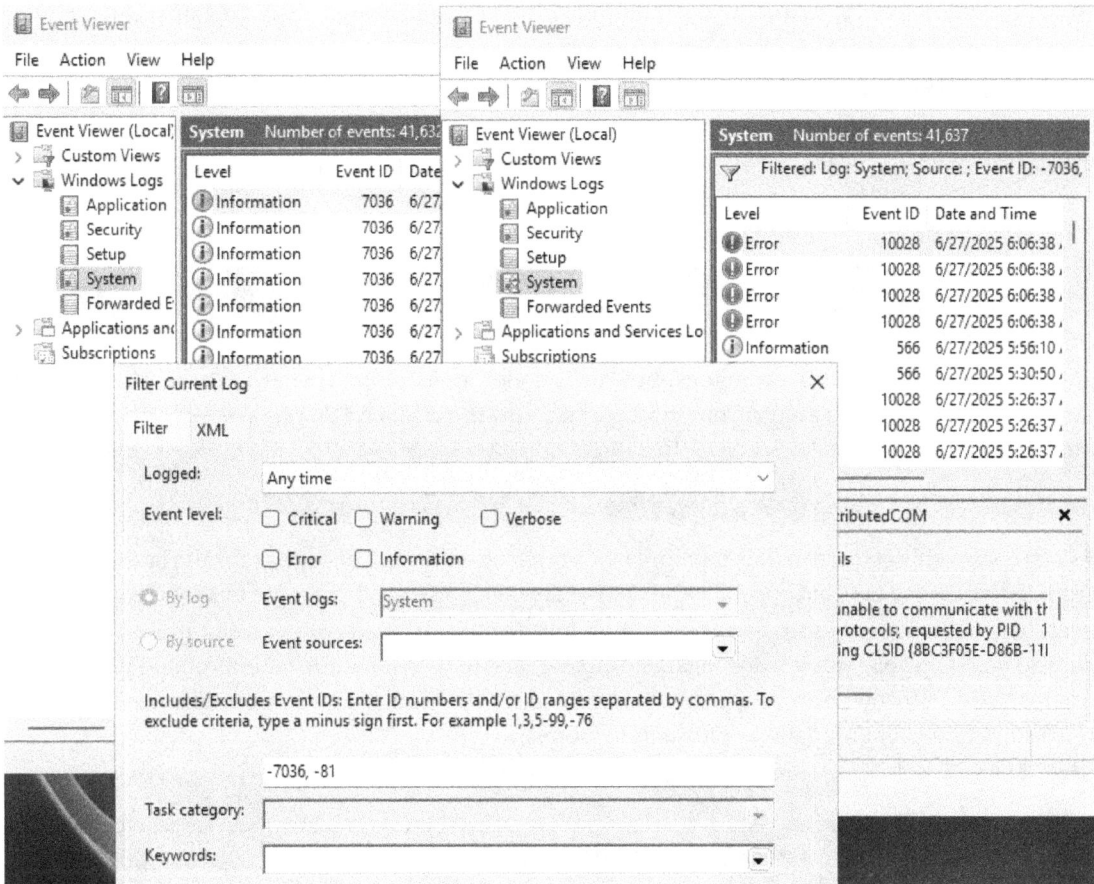

Figure 17.28: Using filters to exclude event IDs 7036 and 81

When you've finished filtering the logs, to get back to the default view, there is no need to reverse all the filtering settings that you have put into place. Simply right-click on the log file and choose **Clear Filter**. This will immediately set that log file back to showing all events.

You'll notice options in the right-click menu to save log files, save filtered log files, and even save filters to views for later use. There is a lot of power available inside event log filtering!

Exporting Windows event logs with PowerShell

While using the Event Viewer console is the most common way to review and parse through log files, sometimes, you may wish for a way to easily export all this data and do some other types of manipulation on it, perhaps through Excel spreadsheets or something similar. To make this happen, we would need a way to export the information in these logs into something such as a CSV file. Is this possible? You bet!

PowerShell can tap into anything inside Windows, including event logs. PowerShell also has a built-in function to export data into a CSV file, so let's combine those two capabilities and build out some commands that will suck Windows event logs out of Windows, directly into a CSV file. Here are some examples:

```
Get-EventLog -LogName Application | Export-CSV C:\Logs\Application_Logs.csv
```

This command exports the entire contents of the `Application` event logs to a CSV file:

```
Get-EventLog -LogName System -Newest 100 | Export-CSV C:\Logs\System_Logs_
Newest.csv
```

Here, we export the `System` event logs, but you'll notice an extra parameter in there. This time, we only grab the newest 100 events from the log and throw them into a CSV file:

```
Get-EventLog -LogName Security -Newest 50 -ComputerName WEB1 | Export-CSV C:\
Logs\WEB1_Security_Logs.csv
```

As our commands get larger, they do more comprehensive things. This one grabs the latest 50 events from the `Security` logs but specifies the `WEB1` server. This is a good example to show that you don't even have to be logged in to the server to pull logs from it. Instead, you can run these PowerShell commands from your workstation, against your servers, pulling log information remotely. You could then take this information and apply it to scheduled scripts, perhaps if you wanted to maintain long-term storage of event log data for particular systems:

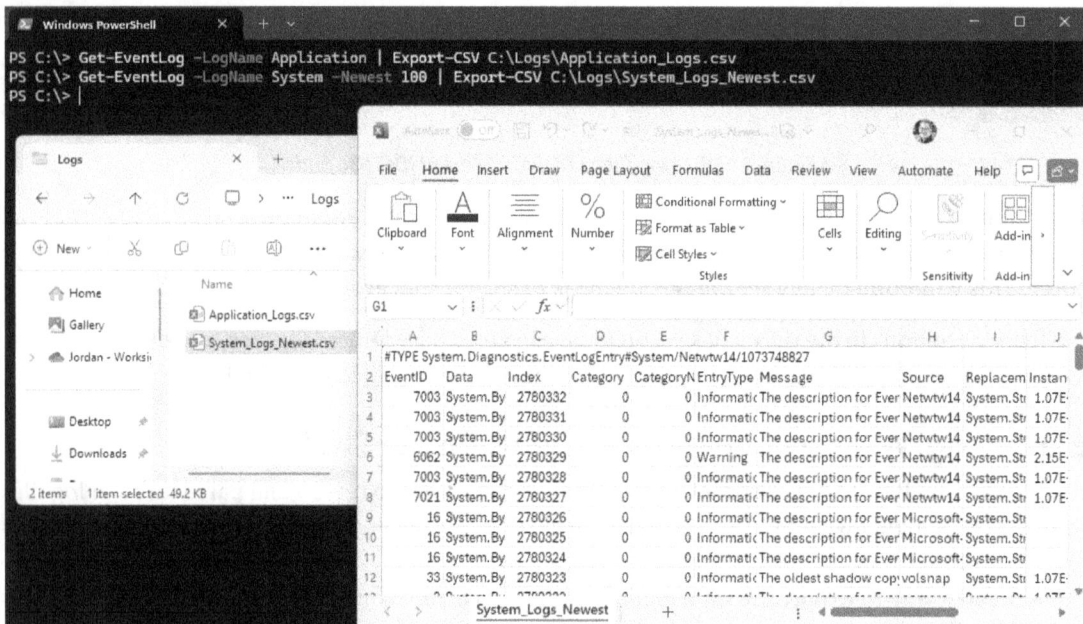

Figure 17.29: Exporting logs to CSV for easy searching and sorting

As you begin working with Windows log files, you will find that Event Viewer does a fantastic job of sorting by log type, and that using event ID inclusions and exclusions will often find you the information that you are looking for. The one thing that is majorly lacking inside Event Viewer is the ability to easily search for text that exists inside events. When clicking on any event, you can see all the descriptive text that is included inside that log event, but there is no good way to search within that text across all of your event logs. This is where exporting to CSV can be especially handy. Throw those commands in PowerShell to export the log, open the CSV file, and use Excel's search functions to find what you are looking for.

Common event IDs

Exploring event logs on a regular basis will start to form patterns in your brain about what types of events to look for, where to find them, and even which event IDs are commonly searched for in daily troubleshooting and investigations. Here is a quick listing of some event ID numbers that I keep locked in memory, as I often search for them:

- **4740 (Security log) – User account locked:** This is the first event to search for when investigating a user account lockout issue. Oftentimes, 4740 will show you a "Source computer name," which steers you toward which device in the network is causing the lockout.

- **4625 (Security log) – Account failed to log on:** I often search for 4625 alongside 4740. While 4740 will hopefully tell you which device to review, 4625 will give a reason as to why the account was locked out – for example, if a bad username or password was given.

- **4767 (Security log) – User account unlocked:** Corresponding logs related to user account lockouts. Check these to find unlock events.

- **4624 (Security log) – Successful logon:** The flipside of 4625, useful for finding true login events.

- **4648 (Security log) – Logon using explicit credentials:** Typically, even more useful than 4624, this narrows in on explicitly authenticated sessions, such as RDP connections.

- **6013 (System log) – System uptime:** Every day at noon, every Windows computer and server logs this event. It shows, in seconds, the amount of time that the system has been up and running. This can be useful to take a historical look at how long a server has been running. For example, you may need to determine how long a server had run prior to an unexpected restart, as this information could be critical to figuring out why a machine locked up or crashed.

- **6008 (System log) – Unexpected shutdown:** Many times, when a server unexpectedly restarts, it's not too concerning. All computers do that occasionally. If, however, you are investigating a server because it has unexpectedly restarted numerous times, you'll want to start searching for patterns about what is happening surrounding each of those unexpected restarts. Event 6008 is the event that is logged, and it will show you the exact timestamp of the unexpected shutdown event. Filtering for 6008 will give you a quick way to see all the instances of the unexpected shutdown. You can then document and dig into the logs surrounding each of those timestamps to gain further information.

While this is simply a short list of common events I search for, I'm sure that, depending on your role in IT, you will add many more event IDs to your own "common event ID" lists.

MMC and MSC shortcuts

You have probably noticed that many of the management consoles we utilize to configure components inside Windows Server 2025 bear a striking resemblance to each other. What happens under the hood with a number of these consoles is that you are shown a snap-in function, a specific set of tools that are snapped into a generic console tool called the MMC. In fact, rather than opening all these management functions from inside Server Manager, for many of them, you could simply type MMC by navigating to **Start | Run** or Command Prompt/PowerShell/Terminal and invoking the generic MMC console. From here, you can click on the **File** menu and choose **Add/Remove Snap-in…**:

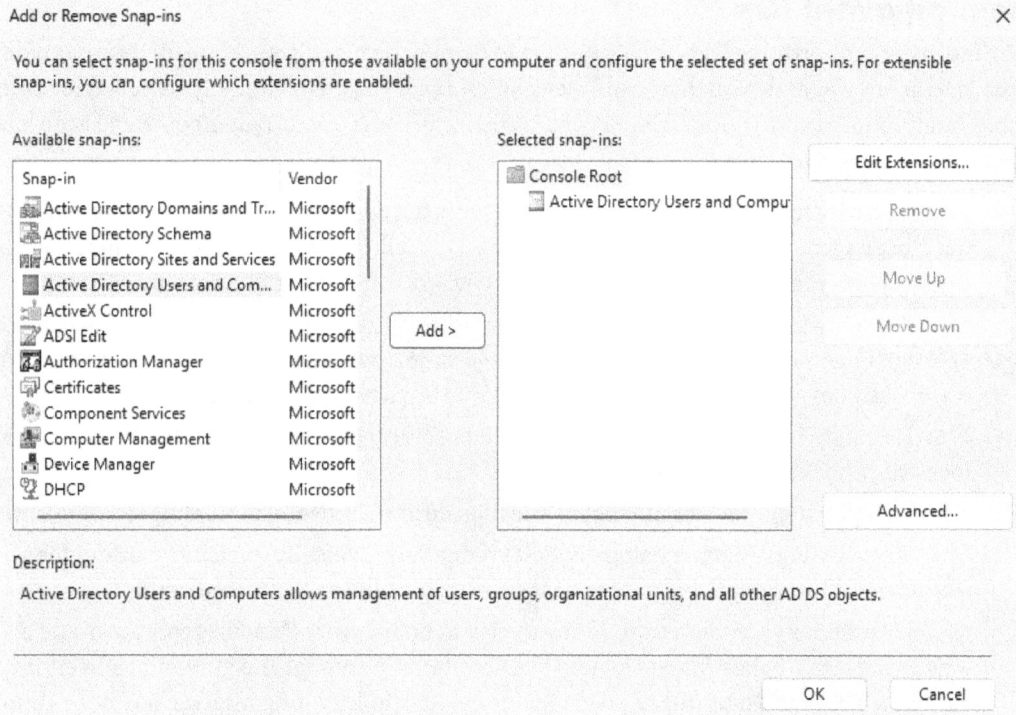

Figure 17.30: Using MMC to snap in management consoles

Choose the management snap-in that you would like to work in, and add it to the console. There are many management functions that can be accessed through the standard MMC console, and even some functions where MMC is the preferred, or perhaps the only, method for interacting with certain components of Windows – for example, when we utilized MMC to review certificates installed on the local computer back in *Chapter 7, Certificates*.

Another interesting way to open many of the management consoles is by using their direct **MSC** tool name. An MSC file is simply a saved configuration of an MMC console session. There are many MSC shortcuts stored in Windows Server 2025 out of the box. If a given management console can be launched by an MSC, all you need to do is type in the name of the MSC by navigating to either **Start | Run**, Command Prompt, or a PowerShell or Terminal window, and it will immediately launch into that particular management console without needing to snap anything in, and without any need to open Server Manager whatsoever. Since I tend to prefer using a keyboard over a mouse, I always have a Terminal window open on each system I'm working with, and I can very quickly use that window to open any of my MSC administrative consoles. Let's show one example, so that you know exactly how to use this functionality, and then I will provide a list of the common MSCs that I find useful on a day-to-day basis.

Open an elevated Terminal or PowerShell window, type WF.MSC, and press *Enter*:

Figure 17.31: Launching a management console via the MSC shortcut

The **Windows Defender Firewall with Advanced Security** window will open and is ready to accept input from you. We didn't have to poke through **Control Panel** or open the regular **Windows Firewall** and then click on the **Advanced Settings** link, which are the common ways to get into this console by using a mouse. By knowing our MSC shortcut name, we were able to take a direct route to open the full WFAS console, which is where I often go to check firewall rules or statuses:

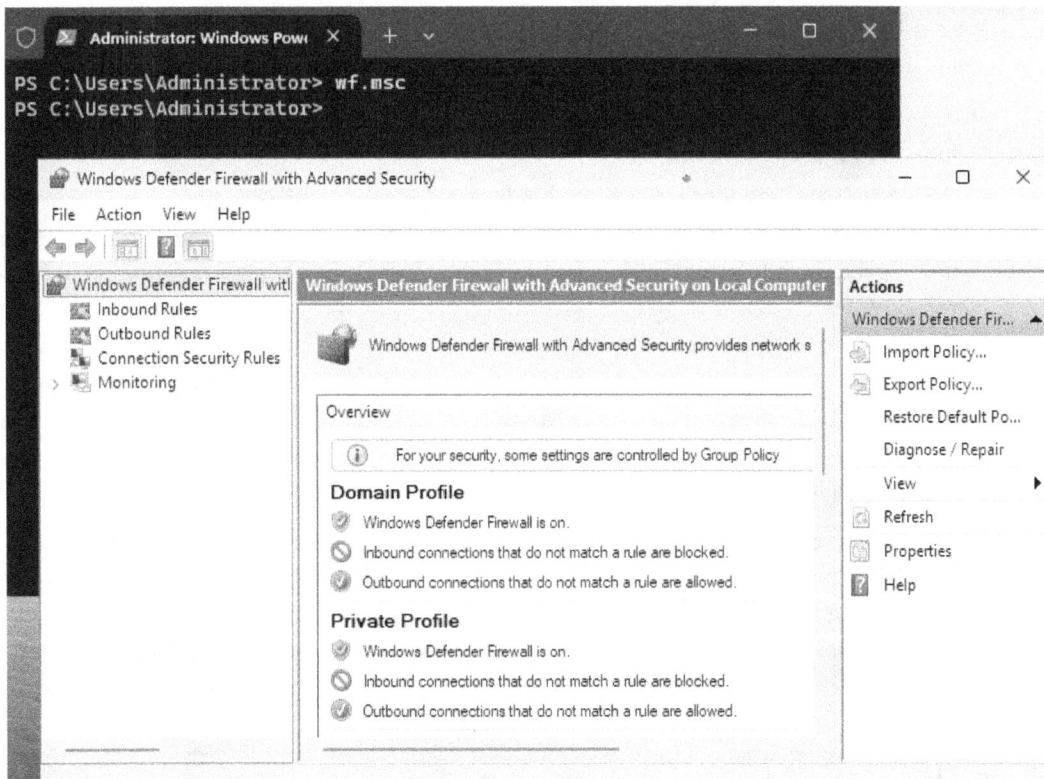

Figure 17.32: The fastest way to access Windows Defender Firewall is via WF.MSC

Now that you've seen how an MSC command works, and again, there are many different places where you can type in the name of an MSC and invoke it, I want to leave you with a list of common MSC consoles that you can use to quickly gain access to many administrative consoles on your servers:

- `DSA.MSC`: Active Directory Users and Computers
- `DSSITE.MSC`: Active Directory Sites and Services
- `DNSMGMT.MSC`: DNS Manager
- `GPEDIT.MSC`: Local Group Policy Editor
- `GPMC.MSC`: Group Policy Management Console
- `CERTSRV.MSC`: Certification Authority Management
- `CERTTMPL.MSC`: Certificate Template Management
- `CERTLM.MSC`: Local Computer Certificates Store
- `CERTMGR.MSC`: Current User Certificates Store
- `COMPMGMT.MSC`: Computer Management
- `DEVMGMT.MSC`: Device Manager
- `DHCPMGMT.MSC`: DHCP Manager
- `DISKMGMT.MSC`: Disk Management
- `DFSMGMT.MSC`: DFS Management
- `EVENTVWR.MSC`: Event Viewer
- `PERFMON.MSC`: Performance Monitor
- `SECPOL.MSC`: Local Security Policy Console
- `FSMGMT.MSC`: Shared Folders
- `WF.MSC`: Windows Defender Firewall with Advanced Security (WFAS)
- `shell:startup`: While not an MSC, this is a shortcut that opens the logged-in user's `Start Menu\Programs\Startup` folder. This is a useful location to visit when looking for a program running on startup that you can't find elsewhere, or when you want to cause an application to start every time this user logs in to the computer.
- `shell:common startup`: Similar to `shell:startup`, but this launches into the `Public User's Startup` folder. Shortcuts added here will auto-launch whenever *any* user logs in to the system.

Feedback Hub

Windows operating systems are built by Microsoft, obviously, but they have always sought input and feedback from the community about what features and options are important. For as long as I can remember, submitting requests or feedback involved being in "the club," some kind of insider track or program where feedback was submitted in a channeled fashion. For the first time in Windows Server land, 2025 brings us an application called Feedback Hub. You can still join the Windows Insider program and have the full inside track on what new things are coming, and even get your hands on preview copies of the newest operating systems. But if you simply want to provide suggestions or report issues within Windows and are not interested in giving them your information to create an account, launching Feedback Hub offers up quick buttons: **Report a problem** and **Suggest a feature**.

Either of these functions invokes a quick four-step wizard asking you to define the problem or feature request, and then submit it to Microsoft.

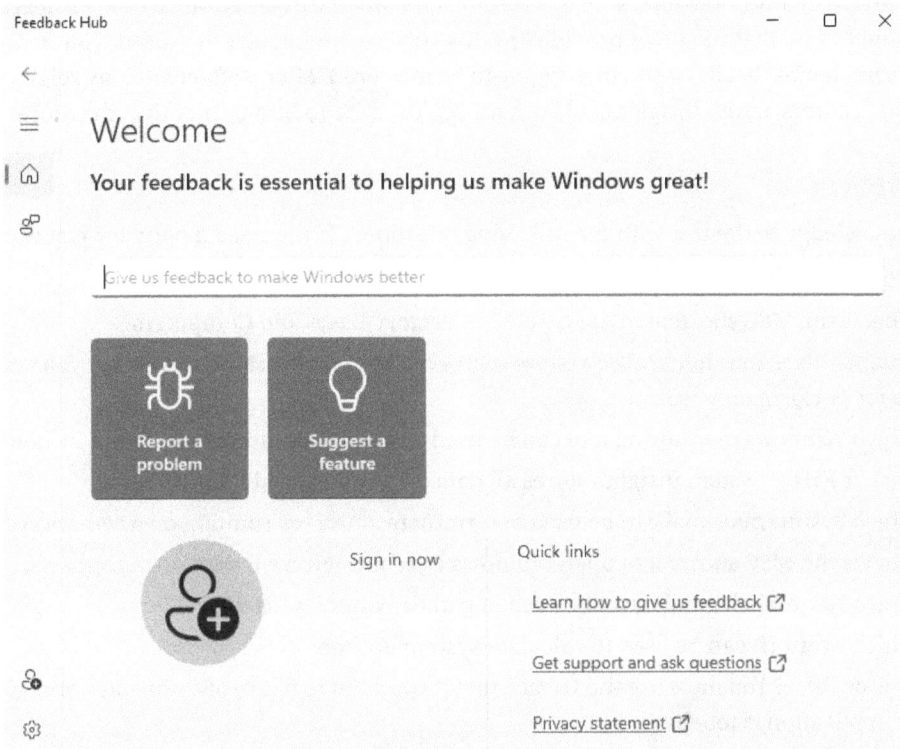

Figure 17.33: Reporting issues via Feedback Hub

There are definite advantages to signing into Feedback Hub with an account. This will enable you to track progress on your submitted issues and compare them against other submission entries. But no matter what, if you encounter something inside Windows that you think could be improved, make sure to let them know about it!

Summary

Designing and building brand-new servers rarely presents challenges, and if they are encountered, those issues are typically low priority, since the new server won't yet affect a production workforce. Normally, you can tear down and set a server back up as many times as you need, before anybody is relying on it. Troubleshooting existing servers, on the other hand, can be very stressful and requires quick, on-the-fly decision-making and recollection of tools and command sets available inside the operating system that can be used to identify issues and resolutions. I will dare to say that most systems administrators are going to spend more time working on reactive server issues than they are going to spend designing new installs. I hope this chapter has given you the ammunition needed to feel more confident in those situations and to become the 'go-to' person in your IT department when it comes to diagnosing server problems and digging deep into problems that arise.

This brings us to the end of our story on Windows Server 2025. While the information provided in these pages should put you on a path to be able to jump into any Windows Server environment and make sense of it, many of the topics we discussed could fill entire books. Much of life is learning how to learn, and I hope that the ideas provided in this volume are enough to prompt you to dig further into the technologies that draw you in, begging to be mastered. Microsoft technology reigns supreme in most data centers across the globe. Make sure you're ready to be a part of the adventure!

Questions

Put your knowledge to the test with the following questions. If you need a hand (or just want to double-check), you'll find all the answers in the *Appendix* section of the book.

1. What is the MSC shortcut to open Active Directory Users and Computers?
2. True or False? You should always store server backups on the same server that you are backing up for performance reasons.
3. Which Windows monitoring tool can be used to graph CPU utilization over a 24-hour period?
4. True or False? System Insights stores all data on a centralized RADIUS server.
5. Which Sysinternals tool can be used to terminate a process running on a remote system?
6. What is the MSC shortcut to open Windows Defender Firewall with Advanced Security?
7. Which PowerShell cmdlet can be used to gather Windows log files?
8. Which Event ID can be used to calculate system uptime?
9. True or False? You must use the DTrace tool if you want to figure out what files or registry keys an application is touching.
10. What is the fastest way to view SSL certificates contained within the Local Computer certificate store on Windows Server?

Unlock this book's exclusive benefits now

UNLOCK NOW

Scan this QR code or go to https://packtpub.com/unlock, then search for this book by name.

Note: Keep your purchase invoice ready before you start.

Appendix: Answers to the End-of-Chapter Questions

Chapter 1: Getting Started with Windows Server 2025

1. In Windows Server 2025, how can you launch an elevated Terminal prompt with two mouse clicks?

   Answer: Right-click on the **Start** button and select **Terminal (Admin)** from the **Quick Admin Tasks** menu.

2. What is the keyboard combination to open the **Quick Admin Tasks** menu?

   Answer: *WinKey + X*

3. What is the name of Microsoft's cloud service offering?

   Answer: Microsoft Azure

4. Which Windows Server release model disappeared with the advent of Windows Server 2022?

   Answer: SAC

5. How many virtual machines can run on top of a Windows Server 2025 Standard host, with default licensing?

   Answer: 2

6. What installation option for Windows Server 2025 does not have a graphical user interface?

   Answer: Server Core

7. Which is the correct verbiage for the latest release of Windows Server 2025: **Long-Term Servicing Branch (LTSB)** or **Long-Term Servicing Channel (LTSC)**?

   Answer: LTSC

8. What is the correct tool from which to change configurations on Windows Server 2025: **Windows Settings** or **Control Panel**?

   Answer: Both, although Windows Settings is the preferred method for most configuration options.

9. What key combination can be used to launch **Task View** without touching your mouse?

   Answer: *WinKey + Tab*

Chapter 2: Installation and Management

1. What is the name of the new web-based, centralized server management tool from Microsoft (fun fact: this toolset was originally known as **Project Honolulu**)?

    Answer: Windows Admin Center (WAC)

2. True or False? Windows Server 2025 needs to be installed on rack-mount server hardware.

    Answer: False. Windows Server 2025 can be installed on physical hardware or as a virtual machine instance.

3. True or False? By choosing the default installation option for Windows Server 2025, you will end up with a user interface that looks quite like Windows 11.

    Answer: False. The default installation option for Server 2025 will land you with a Server Core instance with no graphical interface.

4. What is the PowerShell cmdlet that displays currently installed roles and features in Windows Server 2025?

    Answer: `Get-WindowsFeature | Where Installed`

5. True or False? Server Manager can be used to manage many different servers at the same time.

    Answer: True

6. What is the name of the toolset that can be installed on a Windows 11 computer in order to run Server Manager on that client workstation?

    Answer: Remote Server Administration Tools (RSAT)

7. Which built-in tool is used to prepare the Windows operating systems for imaging or replication?

    Answer: `Sysprep`

8. What is the oldest version of Windows Server that can be in-place upgraded to Windows Server 2025?

    Answer: Windows Server 2012 R2

Chapter 3: Active Directory

1. Inside Active Directory, a container (folder) that holds computer and user accounts is called a(n)...

    Answer: Organizational Unit (OU)

2. What is the term for creating a computer account inside Active Directory prior to that computer being joined to your domain?

    Answer: Prestaging the account

3. Which management tool is used to specify that certain physical locations in your network are bound to particular IP subnets?

    Answer: Active Directory Sites and Services

4. What is the name of a special DC that cannot accept new information, only synchronize from an existing DC?

    Answer: Read-Only Domain Controller (RODC)

5. What tool is needed to create a fine-grained password policy?

    Answer: Active Directory Administrative Center

6. What must be configured inside DNS prior to establishing a forest trust?

    Answer: Conditional forwarder

7. What is the command-line command that shows you all FSMO role holders at once?

    Answer: `netdom query fsmo`

8. True or False? It is faster to manually remove a DC from the domain than it is to follow the Server Manager role removal wizard.

    Answer: True! It is quite a bit faster to simply delete the DC object and then clean up the mess. However, Microsoft's recommendation for a clean DC removal is always to run the role removal via either Server Manager or PowerShell.

9. What identity and authentication service underpins Microsoft 365?

    Answer: Entra ID

Chapter 4: DNS and DHCP

1. What kind of DNS record directs email flow?

    Answer: MX record

2. Which type of DNS record resolves a name to an IPv6 address?

    Answer: AAAA record

3. Which DNS zone type resolves IP addresses backward into hostnames?

    Answer: Reverse lookup zone

4. What DHCP option is often used for VoIP phone provisioning?

   Answer: Option 66

5. Which mode of DHCP failover is often used between branch offices and a primary site?

   Answer: Hot standby mode

6. What is the standard recommendation and default setting for **Maximum Client Lead Time** when configuring load-balanced DHCP failover?

   Answer: One hour

7. Which Windows Server roles can IPAM tap into?

   Answer: Active Directory, DNS, DHCP, and NPS! We didn't talk about NPS in this chapter because we have not yet covered any NPS material, but it is a fourth role that can report data into IPAM.

8. What does the ingenious acronym "DoH" stand for?

   Answer: DNS-over-HTTPS

Chapter 5: Group Policy

1. Are screensaver settings computer or user configuration?

   Answer: User configuration

2. Do domain-level or OU-level links process first?

   Answer: Domain-level links are processed before OU-level links, meaning that OU-level links will overwrite domain-level links when in conflict.

3. What is the special GPO setting that forces user settings to apply to any user on a given computer?

   Answer: Group Policy loopback processing

4. What type of GPO filtering do you configure inside the GPO itself, such as with a mapped network drives policy?

   Answer: Item-level targeting

5. True or False? It is possible for a user to override a Group Policy preference.

   Answer: True

6. What is the default timer between Group Policy background refresh cycles?

   Answer: 90 minutes

7. What kind of GPO filtering could be utilized to assign settings only to laptop computers?

   Answer: WMI filtering

8. If you find a USB stick on the ground labeled "CEO financials," what should you do with it?

   Answer: Burn it, as in literally set it on fire.

9. Bonus question: What is the name of Microsoft's cloud-based technology that provides some of the same functionality as Group Policy, but specifically for Entra-joined computers?

   Answer: Microsoft Intune (sometimes called Endpoint Manager)

Chapter 6: File Management

1. On a shared folder, do permissions under the **Share** tab or the **Security** tab take priority?

   Answer: When a user accesses this folder, **Share** permissions are processed first. If a user is not allowed to traverse this folder based on share permissions, then permissions in the **Security** tab don't even matter.

2. When mapping network drives via GPO, are these settings stored in the **Computer Configuration** or **User Configuration** section of the policy?

   Answer: User Configuration

3. As more companies move into cloud environments, how would you automate the mapping of network drives on your client computers, if those computers are joined to Entra and not part of a local domain?

   Answer: By using an Intune policy

4. If Tom has access to the entire HR directory today, what change could you make to block his access to the HR\Payroll subfolder?

   Answer: You could stop the Payroll folder from inheriting permissions from its parent folder (HR), and then manually configure security permissions on Payroll, blocking Tom's access.

5. What is the minimum number of member servers required to create a hub-and-spoke DFS replication group?

   Answer: A hub-and-spoke DFS replication group requires at least three servers.

6. When creating a DFS namespace, what kind of information is stored inside C:\DFSRoots (assuming you chose the default options when creating the namespace)?

   Answer: The C:\DFSRoots folder stores information about the DFS namespace; most importantly, this is where pointers (shortcuts) are created that DFS uses to send users to their proper file server destinations.

7. Which free FTP client software did we utilize to connect to our FTP server?

   Answer: WinSCP

8. When issuing the SSL certificate used by SMB over QUIC, which two DNS names must be included inside that certificate's DNS names?

    Answer: The SSL certificate must cover the public DNS name used to access files (such as files.contoso.com) as well as the internal DNS name of the file server (fs02.contoso.local).

9. What ports are used by SMB over QUIC when KDC Proxy is enabled?

    Answer: SMB over QUIC uses ports TCP 443 and UDP 443.

Chapter 7: Certificates

1. What is the name of the role inside Windows Server 2025 that allows you to issue certificates from your server?

    Answer: Certification authority

2. What kind of CA server is typically installed first in a domain environment?

    Answer: Enterprise root CA

3. Should you install the certification authority role onto a domain controller?

    Answer: No, this is not a recommended scenario.

4. After creating a new certificate template, what next step needs to be taken before you can issue certificates to your computers or users from that new template?

    Answer: The new certificate template must be published.

5. What is the general name of the GPO setting that forces certificates to be issued without manual intervention by an administrator?

    Answer: Certificate auto-enrollment

6. An SSL certificate will only be able to validate traffic properly if it shares key information with the web server.

    Answer: Private

7. What is the primary piece of information that a public certification authority needs in order to issue you a new SSL certificate (hint: you generate this from your web server)?

    Answer: Certificate signing request (CSR)

8. What kind of file contains both a certificate and a private key?

    Answer: PFX file

9. What is a command-line tool that can be used to manipulate certificates?

    Answer: OpenSSL

Chapter 8: Networking with Windows Server 2025

1. What is the CIDR that represents a subnet mask of 255.255.255.0?

   Answer: /24

2. Why could a corporate subnet of 192.168.1.0/24 cause problems for remote employees?

   Answer: 192.168.1.0/24 is a common IP addressing scheme for home routers. If you use this same subnet designation inside the corporate network, users whose home routers overlap this subnet will have problems routing traffic over their VPN.

3. How many bits in length is an IPv6 address?

   Answer: 128 bits

4. Rewrite the following IPv6 address in condensed form: 2001:ABCD:0001:0002:0000:0000:0000:0001.

   Answer: 2001:ABCD:1:2::1

5. What is the name of the command that is similar to tracert but displays the local NIC that traffic is flowing out of?

   Answer: PATHPING

6. True or False? On a server with multiple NICs, you should input a default gateway address on each of those NICs.

   Answer: False. Doing so will cause routing issues. You should only ever have one default gateway address on a system, no matter how many NICs it has.

7. What is the PowerShell cmdlet that can be used to create new routes on a Windows Server?

   Answer: New-NetRoute

8. Which Windows Server operating systems can be used with the Azure Network Adapter in order to connect them directly to Azure virtual networks?

   Answer: Windows Server 2025, 2022, 2019, 2016, and 2012 R2

9. Which connectivity method between a local datacenter and Azure provides the fastest, most robust, and most reliable connection?

   Answer: Azure ExpressRoute

Chapter 9: Remote Access

1. What two VPN protocols are no longer enabled by default in Windows Server 2025?

   Answer: L2TP and PPTP

2. What does AOVPN stand for?

   Answer: Always On VPN

3. What are the two primary protocols used for connecting AOVPN clients?

   Answer: IKEv2 and SSTP

4. In which version of Windows 10 was AOVPN released?

   Answer: Windows 10 1607

5. In what special instance would an AOVPN client be required to be joined to your domain?

   Answer: When you want to utilize the AOVPN device tunnel

6. Does DirectAccess require your corporate internal network to be running IPv6?

   Answer: No, your internal network can be completely IPv4.

7. What is the name of the internal website that DirectAccess clients check in with to determine when they are inside the corporate network?

   Answer: Network location server (NLS)

8. What ports are used by Teredo and IP-HTTPS?

   Answer: Teredo uses UDP 3544, while IP-HTTPS uses TCP 443.

9. How do you provision DirectAccess configuration settings to the client machines?

   Answer: With Group Policy

10. What role does a Web Application Proxy server hold in a federation environment?

    Answer: WAP can be implemented as an AD FS proxy.

Chapter 10: Hardening and Security

1. What is the name of the antimalware product built into Windows Server 2025?

   Answer: Microsoft Defender Antivirus

2. When a domain-joined computer is sitting inside the corporate LAN, which Microsoft Defender Firewall profile should be active?

   Answer: The domain profile

3. Other than the domain profile, what are the other two possible firewall profiles inside Microsoft Defender Firewall?

   Answer: Public and private

4. When creating a firewall rule to allow IPv4 ping replies, what protocol type must you specify inside your inbound rule?

   Answer: ICMPv4

5. What is the easiest way to push standardized Microsoft Defender Firewall rules to your entire workforce?

   Answer: Group Policy

6. A virtual machine whose virtual hard disk file is encrypted is called a...?

   Answer: Shielded VM

7. True or False? LAPS passwords can be stored only in Active Directory.

   Answer: False. LAPS passwords can be stored in Active Directory or Entra.

8. What is the name of the (deprecated) Microsoft technology that parses domain controller information in order to identify pass-the-hash and pass-the-ticket attacks?

   Answer: Advanced Threat Analytics

9. Which inbound RDP port number is considered safe to open on your external firewall?

   Answer: Trick question—none! Please never do this!

10. What third-party tool can you use to disable TLS 1.0 on Windows Server?

    Answer: IIS Crypto

Chapter 11: Server Core

1. True or False? Server Core is the default installation option for Windows Server 2025.

   Answer: True

2. True or False? You can utilize PowerShell to change a Server 2025 from *Server Core* mode to *Desktop Experience* mode.

   Answer: False. Switching back and forth is not possible in Windows Server 2025.

3. True or False? You can utilize PowerShell to change a Server 2019 from *Server Core* mode to *Desktop Experience* mode.

   Answer: Still false!

4. Bonus points: What is the last version of Windows Server that allowed for on-the-fly changing of a server back and forth between Server Core and Desktop Experience?

   Answer: Server 2012 R2

5. When sitting in front of the console of a freshly booted Windows Server 2025 Server Core instance, what application do you see on the screen?

   Answer: The `Sconfig` utility

6. When sitting in front of the console of a freshly booted Windows Server 2019 Server Core instance, what application do you see on the screen?

   Answer: Command Prompt

7. What cmdlet can be used to view the current networking configuration on a Server Core?

   Answer: `Get-NetIPConfiguration`

8. Which PowerShell cmdlet can be used to configure the hostname of a Server Core?

   Answer: `Rename-Computer`

9. Name some of the management tools that can be used to remotely interface with a Server Core.

   Answer: PowerShell, Server Manager, RSAT, and Windows Admin Center

10. What is the name of the utility built into Server Core that can be launched from the console to provide quick task links for configuring IP addresses, hostnames, and domain membership?

    Answer: `Sconfig.exe`

11. What movie reference did I make at the beginning of this chapter?

    Answer: *Honey, I Shrunk the Kids*

Chapter 12: PowerShell

1. What is the fastest way to get from Command Prompt to PowerShell?

   Answer: Simply type the word `powershell` and press *Enter*.

2. What is the cmdlet that will display all available PowerShell cmdlets?

   Answer: `Get-Command`

3. What PowerShell cmdlet can be used to connect your PowerShell prompt to a remote computer?

   Answer: `Enter-PSSession`

4. What file extension does a PowerShell scripting file have?

   Answer: `.PS1`

5. To which setting is the Default Execution Policy configured on a fresh Windows Server 2025 instance?

   Answer: `RemoteSigned`

6. What key on your keyboard can be used to auto-populate the remainder of a cmdlet or filename when working in a PowerShell prompt?

   Answer: *Tab*

7. Which service must be running on a system before it can be connected to by a remote PowerShell connection?

   Answer: The WinRM service

8. Why do you think Windows Terminal is not installed in Windows Server 2022 by default?

   Answer: Windows Server 2022 is built on Windows 10 code, not Windows 11.

9. What command triggers an update for all applications that WinGet is capable of managing?

   Answer: `Winget upgrade --all`

10. With modules installed, what cmdlet is used to tap PowerShell into Microsoft 365?

   Answer: `Connect-ExchangeOnline`

Chapter 13: Redundancy in Windows Server 2025

1. Which technology is more appropriate for making web server traffic redundant: Network Load Balancing or failover clustering?

   Answer: Network Load Balancing

2. Is website traffic generally stateful or stateless?

   Answer: Stateless

3. In Network Load Balancing, what do the acronyms DIP and VIP stand for?

   Answer: Dedicated IP address and virtual IP address

4. What are the three NLB modes?

   Answer: Unicast, Multicast, and Multicast IGMP

5. In Windows Server 2025, is Network Load Balancing a role or a feature?

   Answer: NLB is a feature.

6. What roles are most often used with failover clustering?

   Answer: Hyper-V and file services

7. What are cluster rolling OS upgrades?

   Answer: Rolling OS upgrades for clustered servers is the ability to upgrade the entire operating system on these servers, one at a time (rolling), without cluster or workload downtime.

8. True or False? Storage Spaces Direct requires the use of SSD hard drives.

   Answer: False. You may use any type of hard drive with S2D.

9. What is the difference between Storage Spaces and Storage Spaces Direct?

   Answer: Storage Spaces combines hard drives on a single server to create a larger storage pool to be used by that server. Storage Spaces Direct combines hard disk space across multiple servers for increased performance, growth, and resiliency.

Chapter 14: Containers

1. There are three base operating systems that can be used for a Windows Server 2022 container. What are they?

   Answer: Nano Server, Server Core, and Windows Server

2. Compared to a Windows Server container, what type of container provides even greater levels of isolation?

   Answer: Hyper-V container

3. True or False? In Windows Server 2016, you could run both Windows and Linux containers on the same Windows Server host platform.

   Answer: False. The ability to run Windows and Linux containers is new as of Windows Server 2019.

4. What is the Docker command to see a list of container images on your local system?

   Answer: `docker images`

5. What is currently the most popular container orchestration software that integrates with Windows Server 2025?

   Answer: Kubernetes

6. True or False? Developers can install Docker on their Windows 10 workstations to start building applications inside containers.

   Answer: True

7. What is a common reason that a developer may need to utilize Server Core containers, rather than Nano Server?

   Answer: Application compatibility and dependencies

8. What service allows you to manage on-premises containers from inside the Azure portal?

   Answer: Azure Kubernetes Service on Azure Local

Chapter 15: Hyper-V

1. What are the three types of virtual switches inside Hyper-V?

   Answer: External, Internal, and Private

2. If you needed to build a VM that boots using UEFI, which generation of VM would you need to create?

   Answer: Generation 2

3. True or False? In Windows Server 2025 Hyper-V, you must shut down a VM in order to change its allocated amount of memory (RAM).

   Answer: False. You can adjust a VM's RAM count on the fly.

4. Must I shut down my VM in order to add a second NIC to it?

   Answer: Yes, the addition of a network adapter is grayed out whenever a VM is running.

5. True or False? The only way to interact with a VM is through the Hyper-V console.

   Answer: False. Once your VM's operating system is installed, you can interact with it through any traditional administration methods, such as RDP.

6. What is the name of the technology inside Hyper-V that allows you to take snapshot images of VMs that can later be restored?

   Answer: Checkpoints

7. When running shielded VMs in your environment, what is the name of the role that handles the attestation of your Hyper-V host servers?

   Answer: Host Guardian Service

8. Which is the most comprehensive attestation method for shielded VMs: host key attestation, TPM trusted attestation, or admin trusted attestation?

   Answer: TPM trusted attestation

9. How many VMs can run on top of a Windows Server 2025 Standard edition host?

   Answer: Two

10. What editions of Windows Server allow me to run an unlimited number of VMs?

    Answer: Windows Server Datacenter edition (2019, 2022, 2025), or that special version of the OS called Hyper-V Server 2019.

Chapter 16: Remote Desktop Services

1. What RDS component is responsible for distributing user sessions among multiple servers?

    Answer: Remote Desktop Connection Broker

2. Are RDS-related certificates defined in RDS collection properties or RDS deployment properties?

    Answer: Certificates are defined at the RDS deployment tier.

3. What is the command you should run to prepare an RDSH server for application installation?

    Answer: `change user /install`

4. What type of RDS **client access licenses (CALs)** are most common?

    Answer: Remote Desktop Per-User CALs

5. True or False? To prepare a fresh Windows Server instance to become an RDSH member of an existing collection, you must first log in to that server and install the Remote Desktop role.

    Answer: False. Server Manager from an existing server can easily reach into this new instance and configure everything that it needs.

6. What are the four types of RDS user profiles?

    Answer: Local profiles, roaming profiles, **User Profile Disks (UPDs)**, and FSLogix profiles.

7. How can you launch the Remote Desktop Connection tool in a way that allows you to RDP directly into an RDSH server that is already part of a collection?

    Answer: `mstsc.exe /admin`

8. How are FSLogix configurations put into place on RDSH servers?

    Answer: Through the installation of an agent, alongside policy settings being pushed through Group Policy

9. Bonus question: What animals live on an RDS farm?

    Answer: Cows, they're always moooving from one session host to another. Wow, tossing a dad joke into a technical book: #LifeGoals.

Chapter 17: Troubleshooting

1. What is the MSC shortcut for opening Active Directory Users and Computers?

    Answer: `DSA.MSC`

2. True or False? You should always store server backups on the same server that you are backing up for performance reasons.

    Answer: This is a trick question that is sort of true, sort of false. While it is true that backups will be most performant when kept on locally attached storage, you should store backups in a separate location in case the server completely dies or is taken by ransomware.

3. Which Windows monitoring tool can be used to graph CPU utilization over a 24-hour period?

   Answer: Performance Monitor

4. True or False? System Insights stores all data on a centralized RADIUS server.

   Answer: False. System Insights stores data on the local server where it is installed.

5. Which Sysinternals tool can be used to terminate a process running on a remote system?

   Answer: `PsKill`

6. What is the MSC shortcut for opening Windows Defender Firewall with Advanced Security?

   Answer: `WF.MSC`

7. Which PowerShell cmdlet can be used to gather Windows log files?

   Answer: `Get-EventLog`

8. Which event ID can be used to calculate system uptime?

   Answer: `6013`

9. True or False? You must use the DTrace tool if you want to figure out what files or registry keys an application is touching.

   Answer: False. While DTrace can show this information, so can the Sysinternals tool Procmon.

10. What is the fastest way to view SSL certificates contained within the Local Computer certificate store on a Windows Server?

    Answer: `CERTLM.MSC`

‹packt›

packtpub.com

Subscribe to our online digital library for full access to over 7,000 books and videos, as well as industry leading tools to help you plan your personal development and advance your career. For more information, please visit our website.

Why subscribe?

- Spend less time learning and more time coding with practical eBooks and Videos from over 4,000 industry professionals
- Improve your learning with Skill Plans built especially for you
- Get a free eBook or video every month
- Fully searchable for easy access to vital information
- Copy and paste, print, and bookmark content

At www.packtpub.com, you can also read a collection of free technical articles, sign up for a range of free newsletters, and receive exclusive discounts and offers on Packt books and eBooks.

Other Books You May Enjoy

If you enjoyed this book, you may be interested in these other books by Packt:

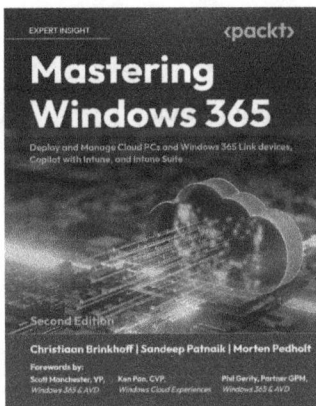

Mastering Windows 365 - Second Edition

Christiaan Brinkhoff, Sandeep Patnaik, Morten Pedholt

ISBN: 978-1-83620-670-5

- Deploy and configure Windows 365 cloud PCs for a seamless cloud experience
- Manage and secure cloud PCs using Microsoft Intune
- Automate workflows with Microsoft Graph to improve efficiency
- Strengthen security with Copilot in Intune and Microsoft security protocols
- Optimize performance, diagnose issues, and troubleshoot cloud environments
- Explore future advancements in cloud computing and Windows 365
- Secure Windows 365 Cloud PC connections using best practices

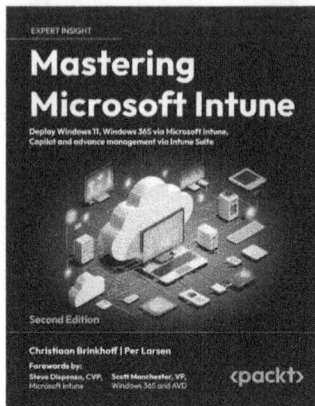

Mastering Microsoft Intune – Second Edition

Christiaan Brinkhoff, Per Larsen

ISBN: 978-1-83546-247-8

- Simplify the deployment of Windows in the cloud with Windows 365 Cloud PCs
- Deliver next-generation security features with Intune Suite
- Simplify Windows Updates with Windows Autopatch
- Configure advanced policy management within Intune
- Discover modern profile management and migration options for physical and Cloud PCs
- Harden security with baseline settings and other security best practices
- Find troubleshooting tips and tricks for Intune, Windows 365 Cloud PCs, and more
- Discover deployment best practices for physical and cloud-managed endpoints

Packt is searching for authors like you

If you're interested in becoming an author for Packt, please visit authors.packt.com and apply today. We have worked with thousands of developers and tech professionals, just like you, to help them share their insight with the global tech community. You can make a general application, apply for a specific hot topic that we are recruiting an author for, or submit your own idea.

Share your thoughts

Now you've finished *Mastering Windows Server 2025, Fifth Edition*, we'd love to hear your thoughts! Scan the QR code below to go straight to the Amazon review page for this book and share your feedback or leave a review on the site that you purchased it from.

https://packt.link/r/1837029911

Your review is important to us and the tech community and will help us make sure we're delivering excellent quality content.

Index